THE NORTON READER
Twelfth Edition

THE NORTON READER
An Anthology of Nonfiction

TWELFTH EDITION

LINDA H. PETERSON, *General Editor*
Yale University

JOHN C. BRERETON
Boston Athenaeum

W·W·NORTON & COMPANY
NEW YORK · LONDON

W. W. Norton & Company has been independent since its founding in 1923, when William Warder Norton and Mary D. Herter Norton first published lectures delivered at the People's Institute, the adult education division of New York City's Cooper Union. The Nortons soon expanded their program beyond the Institute, publishing books by celebrated academics from America and abroad. By mid-century, the two major pillars of Norton's publishing program—trade books and college texts—were firmly established. In the 1950s, the Norton family transferred control of the company to its employees, and today—with a staff of four hundred and a comparable number of trade, college, and professional titles published each year—W. W. Norton & Company stands as the largest and oldest publishing house owned wholly by its employees.

Acknowledgments and copyrights continue on page 1251, which serves as a continuation of the copyright page.

Editor: Marilyn Moller
Associate Editor: Erin Granville
Editorial Assistants: Catherine Spencer and Ana Cooke
Copy Editor: Katharine Ings
Production Manager: Diane O'Connor
Art Director: Rubina Yeh
Book Designer: Martin Lubin Graphic Design
Managing Editor, College: Marian Johnson
Composition: PennSet, Inc.
Manufacturing: Courier Companies

Library of Congress Cataloging-in-Publication Data

The Norton reader : an anthology of nonfiction / Linda H. Peterson, general editor,
  John C. Brereton. — 12th ed.
    p.   cm.
  Includes bibliographical references and index.

ISBN 978-0-393-92948-5 (pbk.)

  1. College readers.   2. Exposition (Rhetoric)—Problems, exercises, etc.   3. English language—Rhetoric—Problems, exercises, etc.   4. Report writing—Problems, exercises, etc.   I. Peterson, Linda H.   II. Brereton, John C.
  PE1122 .N68 2008
  808'.0427—dc22

                                                                    2007038466

W. W. Norton & Company, Inc., 500 Fifth Avenue, New York, N.Y. 10110-0017
www.wwnorton.com

W. W. Norton & Company Ltd., Castle House,
75/76 Wells Street, London W1T 3QT

5   6   7   8   9   0

BRIEF CONTENTS

Contents

HUMAN NATURE 223

CULTURAL CRITIQUE 297

Prose Forms: Op-Eds   403

Education   428

Philosophy and Religion   1139

PREFACE

The Norton Reader brings together a wide selection of essays on a wide range of subjects—from Chang-Rae Lee recalling his return home to cook Korean food for his dying mother to Barbara Tuchman describing the eruption of bubonic plague in medieval Europe to Rita Dove meditating on the Pauline Epistle to the Ephesians and her religious heritage. With 206 selections in the Regular Edition and 123 in the Shorter Edition, *The Norton Reader* offers depth, breadth, and variety for instructors who wish to teach the essay in its many modes and forms—including the seminal experiments of Francis Bacon and John Donne, the modern classics of George Orwell, Virginia Woolf, and E. B. White, and contemporary examples by such diverse writers as Jamaica Kincaid, Terry Tempest Williams, Malcolm Gladwell, and Barry Lopez.

Since its first edition, *The Norton Reader* has upheld a tradition of anthologizing excellent prose. Arthur Eastman, the founding editor, always insisted that essays be selected for their achievement. "Excellence would be their pillar of smoke by day, of fire by night," he wrote in the preface to the eighth edition. With this vision, the original editors of the *Reader* anthologized the classic essays that appeal to modern readers and that we now recognize as comprising the essay canon. Yet the *Reader* has also continued to adapt and renew itself by adding new writers who keep the essay alive (and lively) and whose writing appeals to new generations of student readers.

This new edition blends the new and the old, the innovative and the classic. Features that distinguish the *Reader* include:

- Both canonical and contemporary essays by authors as diverse as Mary Wollstonecraft and Toni Morrison, Henry David Thoreau and Richard Selzer, Martin Luther King Jr. and Patricia Williams.

- Coverage of important themes and influential styles of writing. Sections on education, ethics, language and communication, nature and the environment, history, and religion, among others, introduce students to important academic ideas and ongoing civic debates, while special "Prose Forms" sections focus on journals, Op-Eds, speeches, and other forms that expand the range of the traditional essay. Instructors have the flexibility to use these sections as they choose.

- Pedagogical apparatus to serve the instructors' and students' needs, but not too much to overwhelm the essays themselves. We provide contextual notes to indicate when, where, and why the essay was written; annotations to explain unfamiliar persons, events, and concepts; and study questions for all essays.

- A section called "Authors," located at the end of the volume, gives information about the men and women who wrote the essays, and allows readers to choose whether to find out about the authors before reading their essays or to encounter the authors as unknowns and let them identify themselves within their essays.

Among the new and expanded features in the twelfth edition, we have added materials to offer more guidance for students on critical reading and on writing, to extend the formal range of the essay, and to locate the essay within the larger context of visual culture:

- Fifty new selections, including essays that represent the work of American, Canadian, African, Indian, English, Irish, and Caribbean writers. New voices include Alberto Alvaro Ríos discussing the significance of "green cards," Bill McKibben making a case for single-child families, Lauren Slater meditating on the meaning of love, and Michael Pollan arguing for the greater rights of animals.

- A new, extensive introduction for students that offers advice on critical reading and on writing college essays. The introduction addresses key features of the "Outcomes Statement" of the Council of Writing Program Administrators and highlights rhetorical skills essential to college success.

- A new Genres Index locates readings in major genres, such as memoirs, profiles of people and places, visual and textual analysis, and argument. The Genres Index is designed to help instructors meet crucial goals of the WPA "Outcomes Statement," including teaching students to write in several genres, to identify conventions of format and structure, and to understand how genres shape reading and writing.

- Visual images—photographs, drawings, graphs, and other illustrations—that accompanied the essays are included, with original captions, for more than twenty selections, including a visual essay on the graphic novel, "Understanding Comics." We hope that these images will encourage readers to think about the ways in which the visual and the verbal interact in modern culture, and the ways in which images enrich, highlight, and sometimes challenge the written text.

- Contextual notes provide information about when and where the essay first appeared and, if it began as a talk, when and where it was delivered and to what audience.

- Study questions for all selections, emphasizing both individual response and collaborative effort, encourage students to become active critical readers and writers.

- *A Guide to The Norton Reader*, written by Anne Fernald, Melissa Goldthwaite, and Charles Hood, offers a wealth of suggestions for classroom discussion and writing assignments. A new twenty-five-page section provides invaluable practical classroom support, with suggested in-class activities, tips for planning a writing course (including five sample syllabi), advice for teachers of developmental writing, and more.

ACKNOWLEDGMENTS

Among our many critics, advisors, and friends, the following were of special help in the preparation of the twelfth edition, either by offering advice or by nominating essays to be included in this edition: Alan Ainsworth (Houston Community College), Greg Clark (Brigham Young University), Anne Fernald (Fordham University), Melissa Goldthwaite (St. Joseph's University), Paul Heilker (Virginia Polytechnic Institute and State University), Charles Hood (Antelope Valley Community College), Paul Matsuda (University of New Hampshire), Ira Nadel (University of British Columbia), Peggy Oliver (San Jacinto College South), Kate Ryan (University of Montana), Raul Sanchez (University of Florida), Linda Smith (Midlands Technical College). Our colleague and editor emerita Joan Hartman deserves our deep gratitude for her ongoing contributions to *The Norton Reader*.

The editors would like to express appreciation and thanks to the many teachers who provided reviews: Kathy Albertson (Georgia Southern University), David Anderson (Butler County Community College), Melissa Bader (Riverside Community College, Norco), Kim Ballerini (Nassau Community College), Maryam Barrie (Washtenaw Community College), Barbara Bengels (Hofstra University), Mark E. Bingham (Florida College), Joseph Bizup (Columbia University), Joseph Blaih (Youngstown State University), Monica Bosson (City College of San Francisco), Dawn Brickey (Charleston Southern University), Brock Brower (Dartmouth College), Cheryl Brown (Towson University), Danika M. Brown (University of Texas, Pan American), Sheree Brown (College of Mount St. Joseph), John C. Cabral (L.A. Mission College), David Calonne (Eastern Michigan University), Robert Carlton (Palomar College), William Carney (Texas Tech University), Shannon Carroll (Frank Phillips College), Lynn Casmier-Paz (University of Central Florida), Isaac Cates (Long Island University, C.W. Post Campus), Anthony Collins (Inver Hills Community College), Samuel Collins (Towson University), Keith Comer (Idaho State University), Richard Compean (City College of San Francisco), Sonni Cooper (Sierra College), Imraan Coovadia (Adelphi University), Walter Corbella (Kent State University), Kathleen Crosby (Hofstra University), Jennine Crucet (University of Minnesota), Robert E. Cummings (University of Georgia), Denise Curry (University of Saint Francis), Jill Cutler (Yale University), Laurie Dashnau (Houghton College), Laurie Dawson (Sonoma State University), Jackie DiSalvo (Baruch College), John Dudley (University of South Dakota), Richard Durocher (St. Olaf College), Anne Dvorak (Longview Community College), Olivia Edenfield (Georgia Southern University), Kim Edwards (Monroe County Community College), Jodi Egerton (The University of Texas at Austin), Jeff Ellis (Towson University), Breanne Ertmer (Texas A&M University), Kenneth D. Fisher (Pennsylvania State University, Wilkes-Barre), George Friend

(Millersville University), Kim Gainer (Radford University), Ann D. Garbett (Averett University), Stephen D. Gibson (Utah Valley State), Lisa Giles (Brandeis University), Tim Giles (Georgia Southern University), William Gillard (Farleigh Dickinson University), C. Herbert Gilliland (United States Naval Academy), Donald Gilzinger, Jr. (Suffolk County Community College), Karen Gocsik (Dartmouth College), Hazel Greenberg (San Jacinto College South), Alfred Guy (Yale University), Tami Haaland (Montana State University, Billings), Douglas Haneline (Ferris State University), Shona Harrison (Malaspina University-College), Judy Hart (Frank Phillips College), John Hartner (Community College of Allegheny County, North Campus), William Heath (University of Mary, Hardin-Baylor), Jacob Heller (SUNY College at Old Westbury), Sally Henschel (Midwestern State University), Marc Hewson (University of Ottawa), Suzanne Hill (Towson University), Will Hochman (Southern Connecticut State University), Melanie Hunter (Tulsa Community College), Sherrie Inness (Miami University), Sue Iseman (Ohio Northern University), Emily A. Bernhard Jackson (University of Arkansas), M.W. Jackson (St. Bonaventure University), Joanne Ciske Jacobs (Shenandoah University), Ann Jagoe (North Central Texas College), Allison James (Monterey Peninsula College), Emily Janda (Texas A&M University), Mary Ann Janda (Utica College), Michelle Jarenski (Loyola University), Scott Jarvis (Hofstra University), Trish Jenkins (University of Alaska, Anchorage), Margaret Johnson (Idaho State University), Gabriel Jones (San Diego State University), Stewart Justman (University of Montana), J. Kastely (University of Houston), Elaine M. Kauver (Baruch College), Karen Rae Keck (Texas Tech University), Paul Kellerman (Penn State University), Audrey Kerr (Southern Connecticut State University), Joy Kidwell (Boise State University), Lew Klatt (Calvin College), Michael J. Krozel (Central Connecticut State University), Celena Kusch (Merrimack College), Carol Kushner (Dutchess Community College), Ethna Lay (Hofstra University), Mary Levitt (Massachusetts College of Liberal Arts), Keming Liu (Medgar Evers College), Elise Maglio (Providence College), Julie Maia (West Valley College), David Malone (Union University), Joshua J. Mark (Marist College), Jim Martin (Mount Ida College), Sharan McBride (Houston Community College System), Thomas McConnell (University of South Carolina, Upstate), Margaret McKenzie (Diablo Valley College), Margaret A. McLaughlin (Georgia Southern University), Becky Jo McShane (Weber State University), Carla Mettling (Columbia College), Deborah Miller (University of Georgia), Susan J. Miller (Santa Fe Community College), Melaney Moisan (Chemeketa Community College), Albert S. Moorin (San Diego State University), Michael Moreau (Glendale College), Michael Mulvey (Central Connecticut State University), Joseph Musser (Ohio Wesleyan University), Nancy Nahra (Champlain College), Amy Nawrocki (Sacred Heart University), Vanita Neelakanta (Brandeis University), Beverley Neiderman (Kent State University), Nathan K. Nelson (Ferris State University), Tor Nielsen (Elmira College), Monica Norris (Texas Tech University), Nathan Oates (University of Missouri, Columbia), Peggy Oliver (San Jacinto College South), Corey Palmer (Mesa State College), John G. Parks (Miami University), Robert Piasecki (Norwich University), Phil Poulos (California State University, Los Angeles),

Patricia T. Price (Georgia Southern University), Dale Purvis (Georgia Southern University), Daniela Rugasa (Southern Connecticut State University), Cleatus Rattan (University of Mary, Hardin-Baylor), J. Lisa Ray (Thomas Nelson Community College), Doug Rice (Sacramento State University), Rich Rice (Texas Tech University), Charles Riley (Baruch College), Beth Ritter-Guth (Lehigh Carbon Community College), Aaron Ritzenberg (Yale University), Mark Roberts (California Polytechnic State University, San Luis Obispo), Susan Roberts (Central Connecticut State University), Juliet Rodeman (University of Missouri, Columbia), Kristina Rogers (American River College), Carl Rollyson (Baruch College), Kathy Roosa (San Jacinto College South), Rae Rosenthal (Community College of Baltimore County Essex), Jeff Runyon (University of Northern Colorado), Kara Russell (Central Connecticut State University), Mary A. Sadler (College of Charleston), Shelley Saltzman (Columbia University), Mike Sanders (Kent State University), Diane Scharper (Towson University), Andrew Schonebaum (Barnard College), Kreg Segall (Suffolk County Community College, Grant Campus), Eileen Seifert (DePaul University), M. P. A. Sheaffer (Millersville University of Pennsylvania), Audell Shelburne (University of Mary, Hardin-Baylor), Claude Clayton Smith (Ohio Northern University), Greg Smith (San Jacinto College South), Jeanne Smith (McPherson College), Whitney Womack Smith (Miami University, Hamilton), William Smith (Weatherford College), Margaret Spillane (Yale University), John Staines (Earlham College), Andrew Stambuk (Hofstra University), Katherine Staples (Austin Community College), Carla Steinberg (College of Marin), Rebecca Steinitz (Ohio Wesleyan University), Pamela Stinson (Northern Oklahoma College), Barbara Stuart (Yale University), Yuko Taniguchi (The University of Minnesota), Jonathan Taylor (Ferris State University), Victor H. Thompson (Thomas Nelson Community College), John Trimble (University of Texas), Brenda Tuberville (University of Texas, Tyler), Trevor Tucker (University of Ottawa), Deborah Uman (St. John Fisher College), Nicole B. Wallack (Columbia University), Carmen Walsh (Towson University), John Wang (Queens College), Denise C. White (Kennesaw State University), Patricia Whiting (Carleton University), Audrey Wick (University of Texas, Arlington), Jane E. Wohl (Sheridan College), Mark Wolzenburg (Champlain College), Deborah Workman (Myers University), and Scott D. Yarbrough (Charleston Southern University).

Special thanks goes to Carol Hollar-Zwick for her excellent editorial work on the introduction. At Yale University, we thank Abigail Deutsch for advice on annotations; Paula Resch, Margaret Spillane, Barbara Stuart, and Deborah Tenney for new essay suggestions; and Randi Saloman for her work on the biographical sketches. At Norton, we owe thanks to Katharine Ings for her copyediting; Diane O'Connor and Marian Johnson for their help with production; Nancy Rodwan and Margaret Gorenstein for their able help with permissions; and our editors past and present, Jennifer Bartlett, Carol Hollar-Zwick, Marilyn Moller, Nicole Netherton, and Julia Reidhead, for their new ideas and constant encouragement. A special thanks goes to our newest editor, Erin Granville, and to editorial assistants Catherine Spencer and Ana Cooke—their patience, intelligence, and commitment to the *Reader* have been exemplary.

INTRODUCTION
Reading and Writing with The Norton Reader

Reading with a Writer's Eye

During the coming term your writing instructor will ask you to read a selection of essays in *The Norton Reader*. Whether you read many essays or just a few, we hope that you will enjoy them. Reading essays in a college textbook may seem different from the reading you usually do in magazines, books, or on-line—and reading essays for a college course *is* different, even though you will find some aspects quite familiar. When you read on your own, you choose the topics and the formats, letting your personal interests guide you. When you read in a college writing course, you will discover essays that reflect your own interests, but your instructor will also introduce you to topics you've never before encountered, to forms of writing common in college but new to you, and to levels of difficulty that will prepare you for the reading in future college classes and the writing assigned in them.

In *The Norton Reader* you will find essays that address these various interests, forms, and goals. The 206 pieces collected here originally appeared in many different venues—from a daily newspaper in Baltimore to a beautifully produced book of art photographs, from a speech given publicly by a U.S. president to a collection of private meditations by a famous author. In an anthology like *The Norton Reader*, all of these selections appear in the same format, with the same typeface and layout; all have annotations to explain references and allusions; and all have questions to urge you to think about major issues and themes. In these visible ways, the essays in this collection differ from their originals.

Even so, we hope that the original pleasure, purpose, and power of each essay will come through. To help in the reading process, we provide you with information about the context in which the essay first appeared—including the readers for whom it was intended, the magazine, book, or newspaper in which it was published, and the knowledge that its original readers brought to their reading or listening. (See "Who is the audience?" p. xxi, and "What is the rhetorical context and purpose?" p. xxiv.) We also suggest, in this introduction, some ways of reading essays that will help you to analyze them. (See "What is the genre and its conventions?" p. xxvi.) Finally, we provide strategies for writing your own essays. (See "Writing in College," p. xl.) Among the goals of a college reader like this one are connecting reading and writing, linking the two processes as interactive, and making your reading enrich, inspire, and improve your writing.

Most of the essays in *The Norton Reader* originally appeared in magazines or books written for general readers—educated people but not specialists in the subject. The essays were read by people like you who wanted to know—or know more—about their subjects, who knew about—or were intrigued by—their authors, or who were tempted to launch into unfamiliar subjects because they encountered them in a magazine they ordinarily read. In the world outside the classroom, readers bring their own interests and motives to the essays they read. Although putting essays in a textbook might make them seem a little artificial, we hope to make your reading process more "real" by suggesting strategies that help you understand their contexts, purposes, and ongoing relevance.

When you begin reading an essay that your instructor assigns, ask yourself some or all of the following questions. These questions—about the audience for the essay, the author and his or her purpose in writing the essay, and the genre of the essay—will help you understand the essay, re-create its original context, analyze its meaning, recognize its organization and rhetorical strategies, and imagine how you might use similar strategies for your own writing.

Who is the audience?

An *audience* consists of those to whom the essay is directed—the people who read the article, listen to the speech, or view the text. The question about audience might be posed in related ways: For whom did the author write? What readers does the author hope to reach? What readers did he or she actually reach?

Sometimes that audience is a single reader, as in an entry in a private diary; sometimes the audience is national or international, as in an editorial for a newspaper like the *Washington Post* or the *New York Times*. Often, the audience shares a common interest, as the readers of an environmental magazine might do or the buyers of books of biography or history. To help you understand the original audience for each essay, we provide *contextual notes* at the bottom of the first page of each essay. Contextual notes give information about when and where the essay first appeared and, if it began as a talk, when and where it was delivered and to what audience. If we know, we try to give a sense of what the original audience was like or, at least, what we can gauge from the publishing context.

For example, the contextual note for Scott Russell Sanders's "Looking at Women" (p. 226) tells you that it appeared in the *Georgia Review*, a small-circulation magazine that attracts readers who enjoy fiction, essays, and poetry and who like essays with a literary feel. In contrast, Nicholas Kristof's "Saudis in Bikinis" (p. 340) appeared as an editorial in the *New York Times*, a daily newspaper with a huge national readership, where Kristof has a regular column on the Op-Ed page. Sanders could assume that his audience would like reading personal memoirs and biographical profiles, whereas Kristof knew that he needed to speak to a large, diverse national audience of people holding very different opinions on matters of education, politics, religion, and social questions like gender. Knowing these audiences gives a window into the writers' choices, strategies, and styles. Sanders's essays begins as if it were a story, in an intriguing yet leisurely way:

> On that sizzling July afternoon, the girl who crossed at the stoplight in front of our car looked, as my mother would say, as though she had been poured into her pink shorts.

Kristof, in contrast, gets down to business quickly, since he knows he has only 750 or so words to explain the issue to his readers and convince them of his position. Kristof may begin with an intriguing observation—"On my first evening in Riyadh, I spotted a surreal scene"—but by his fourth sentence, he has reached the issue under consideration:

> Saudi women may be regarded in the West as antique doormats covered in black veils, but the women themselves vigorously reject the stereotype. "It hurts when you hear what people say about us, that we're repressed."

The expectations of the two different audiences explain, in part, the writers' different approaches and styles.

Sometimes contextual notes give information about where the selection was published and how it was received—another way to understand the audience. Maya Angelou's "Graduation" (p. 34) comes from her autobiography, *I Know Why the Caged Bird Sings*, published in 1969; Angelou then continued writing her life story in five sequential volumes, most recently *A Song Flung Up to Heaven* (2002)—a sequence that testifies to her book's success and its appeal to a wide variety of readers. A different example of success with readers appears in the contextual note for David Baltimore's "Limiting Science: A Biologist's Perspective" (p. 957), which gives this information:

> Written by a Nobel Prize-winning scientist and originally published in *Daedalus* (Spring 1978), the professional journal of the American Academy of Arts and Sciences; the Academy re-published the essay in *Daedalus* (Fall 2005).

This note lets you know that the author, a world-class biologist, meant to reach a wide audience of educated men and women and had the clout to argue for the importance of freedom in research. Members of the Academy of Arts and Sciences were his immediate audience, but the author knew that his argument would extend beyond them to politicians and government officials, given his own stature and that of the Academy. The fact that Baltimore's essay was published a second time, twenty-five years later, reveals that the American Academy of Arts and Sciences believes his argument remains timely in today's debate over issues of cloning, genetic engineering, and organ research.

In each contextual note, we try to explain a little about the books, magazines, and newspapers that published these essays—the *New York Times Magazine*, a large-circulation weekly magazine included with the Sunday newspaper, or the *Georgia Review*, a small, but well-respected literary journal published three times a year by the University of Georgia, or *I Know Why the*

Caged Bird Sings, a free-standing book. As editors, we could swamp you with information about publication and authorship, but we prefer to include more essays and keep contextual information focused on the original audience and publication context—that is, on where the essay appeared, who read it, and (if we know) what reaction it received.

Who is the author?

If the audience consists of those who read the essays, the *author* is the term we use for the person who writes them. Essayists, as authors, tend to introduce themselves to their audiences, revealing personal experiences, preferences, and beliefs that bear on the subject at hand and that help explain the essayist's point of view. The essayist's self-presentation—sometimes called *persona*, sometimes *ethos*—is more important than the essayist's actual name. In "We Do Abortions Here: A Nurse's Story" (p. 747), the title gives us an important fact about the author and her perspective: she is a nurse and has seen abortions up close. Knowing this fact is more important than knowing the essayist's name (Sallie Tisdale). In "Who Shot Johnny?" (p. 399), Debra Dickerson introduces herself directly to her readers in the opening paragraph:

> I am unrepentant and vocal about having gained admittance to Harvard through affirmative action; I am a feminist, stoic about my marriage chances as a well-educated, 36-year-old black woman who won't pretend to need help taking care of herself.

Who the author is—where she comes from, what her background is, what her educational and professional experience are—becomes part of Dickerson's story, and it influences her perspective on the random shooting of her nephew, about which she writes.

Not all authors are as direct as Tisdale or Dickerson. In "Insomnia" (p. 274) Edward Thomas doesn't really tell us who he is—other than a man with sleepless nights. But you don't need to know much more than that to appreciate his brief essay; he presents himself as "a sleepless man" rather than as an Englishman or a poet (both of which he was). Nor do you need to know that David Guterson, the author of "Enclosed. Encyclopedic. Endured: The Mall of America" (p. 210), later became famous for the novel *Snow Falling on Cedars*. In his article about the largest mall in America, Guterson presents himself as a reporter, observing what he sees, shaping the information for his readers, and posing questions for himself and them about what the mall means and why it is so popular. His distance and objectivity as a reporter are important aspects of his self-presentation, of who he is as author of this essay.

Because we believe that essayists prefer to introduce themselves and reveal details of personality and experience that they consider most relevant, we do not preface each essay with a biographical note. We think they, as authors, should step forward and we, as editors, should stand back and let them speak. But if you want to learn more about the writer of an essay, you can check the *Authors* section at the end of the book. The entries there provide information about the men and women who wrote the essays. Putting this information at the end of the book gives you a choice. You may already know something about an author and not wish to consult this section. You may wish to find out something about an author before you read his or her writing. Or you may just prefer to encounter the authors on their own terms, letting them identify themselves within the essay. Sometimes knowing who authors are and where their voices come from helps readers grasp what they say—but sometimes it doesn't.

WHAT IS THE RHETORICAL CONTEXT AND PURPOSE?

The *rhetorical context*, sometimes called *rhetorical situation* or *rhetorical occasion*, refers to the context—social, political, biographical, historical—in which writing takes place and becomes public. The term *purpose*, in a writing class, refers to the author's goal—whether to inform, to persuade, to entertain, to analyze, or to do something else through the essay. We could also pose this question as follows: What goals did the writer have in composing and publishing the essay? What effect did the author wish to have on the audience?

For some selections, the rhetorical context is indicated by the *title*. Abraham Lincoln's "Second Inaugural Address" (p. 881) and John F. Kennedy's "Inaugural Address" (p. 883) were presidential speeches made on the formal occasion of their swearing in. An inauguration represents a significant moment in a leader's—and the nation's—life. The speech given on such an occasion requires a statement of the president's goals for the next four years. In addition to the title, you can discover more about the rhetorical context of a president's inaugural speech in the *opening paragraph* because he (so far it's only *he*) will often refer to the historical context early on. Lincoln, for example, refers back to his first inaugural address and the "impending civil war"; then he acknowledges that the war continues and that he prays "this mighty scourge of war may speedily pass away." In the midst of the American civil war, Lincoln knows that he must, as president, address the political conflict that faces the nation, offer hope for its resolution, and set the moral tone for the aftermath. That's his purpose.

Like the presidential speech, many essays establish the rhetorical context in their opening paragraphs. Editorials and Op-Eds begin with a "hook"—an opening reference to the issue at hand or the news report under consideration. You might even say that the editorial writer "creates" the rhetorical context and shows us her purpose straight away. In her Op-Ed "Get a Knife, Get a Dog, but Get Rid of Guns" (p. 405), Molly Ivins begins with "Guns. Everywhere guns"—letting her readers know that she's addressing the hot topic of gun control and establishing her position right up front (she's pro-control). Ivins's main purpose is to persuade others to adopt her position, but another purpose is, through humor, to amuse her readers and laugh the anti-control group out of court. Jo-Ann Pilardi's "The Immigration Problem Is About Us,

Not Them" (p. 406) reveals, in its title, her rhetorical purpose: to re-consider the immigration debate. In her opening paragraphs, Pilardi reminds us of the social and political context:

> The immigration debates always focus on small brown bodies jumping fences and scooting through the brush of our Southwestern states (land that was *Mexico* about 150 years ago). Our self-righteous anger at those brown bodies is fueled by our narrow use of the word "illegal"—a term re-served only for those immigrant workers.

Even if you haven't followed newspaper reports about immigration, you can tell from this opening that the writer is engaging a highly contested American debate about what to do about immigrants who cross the U.S.-Mexico border and enter the United States. Pilardi's purpose is to disrupt the us/them think-ing that hinders fruitful discussion of the issue.

Sometimes we provide information about the rhetorical context in the *contextual note* (described above) or in the *annotations* to each essay (de-scribed below). The contextual note for Martin Luther King Jr.'s "I Have a Dream" explains that the speech was:

> Delivered on the steps of the Lincoln Memorial in Washington, D.C., on August 28, 1963, at one of the largest Civil Rights demonstrations in U.S. history.

The annotations (footnotes marked with small numerals) give further clues. For instance, note 3 on p. 909 tells us:

> George Wallace (1919–1998), Alabama's segregationist governor, used big legal terms such as "interposition" and "nullification" in his unsuccessful attempt to prevent the integration of the University of Alabama.

This annotation explains who Wallace was (a fact that King's audience would have known), but it also reveals that King is answering the arguments of his segregationist opponent, that he is debating and talking back. Use the contex-tual notes and annotations to help re-create the original context. But if you re-ally want to comprehend that rhetorical occasion in 1963, when the Rev. Martin Luther King spoke in Washington, you need to use your imagina-tion. Envision the Lincoln Memorial in the U.S. capital, fill the space with thousands of demonstrators, and wait in anticipation for one of the greatest American orators to begin his speech. Or watch a video of King at youtube.com.

Here is some additional information about *annotations* and how to use them as you read an essay: The annotations are explanatory footnotes—a com-mon feature of a textbook. Commercial magazines and newspapers usually do not include footnotes, whereas academic writing often does. When the origi-nal authors wrote the footnotes themselves, we indicate that in square brack-ets, for example, [Angelou's note] or [Wallace's note]. This tells you that the author wished to cite an expert, add information, or send the reader to another source. In most cases, however, we the editors have written the footnotes to help with difficult words, allusions, and references. We provide information about people, places, works, theories, and other unfamiliar things that the original audience may have known. For example, for Maya Angelou's "Graduation" (p. 34) we give an annotation for Gabriel Prosser and Nat Turner, but not Abraham Lincoln and Christopher Columbus. Angelou's readers, many of them African American, would have known that Prosser and Turner were executed leaders of slave rebellions in the nineteenth century. But because not all readers today know (or remember) this part of American history, we add a footnote.

Here's a final important point: Annotation, while it facilitates the making of meaning in reading, can never take its place. Reading is an active process. Experienced readers take responsibility for that action—reading critically, constructing meaning, interpreting what they read. If our annotations help you read critically, then use them; if they interfere, then just continue reading the main text and skip over them.

WHAT IS THE GENRE AND ITS CONVENTIONS?

Genre is a term used by composition and literature teachers to refer to form—specifically, to forms that have common features and follow certain conventions of style, presentation, and subject matter. Literary genres include the short story and novel, the tragedy and comedy, the lyric and the epic poem. Essay genres include the memoir and the biographical profile, the visual analysis and Op-Ed, the literacy narrative and the parable. For the essay, *genre* partially determines the form's content and organization, but it should never do so in a "cookie-cutter" way.

Conventions are practices or customs commonly used in a genre—like a handshake for a social introduction or a eulogy at a funeral. Genre and convention are linked concepts, the one implying the other. Scientific articles (a genre) begin with a title and an abstract (conventions) and include sections about the methodology and the results (also conventions). Op-Eds, by convention, begin with a "hook"; profiles of persons or places include a physical description of the subject; literacy narratives include a key episode in the acquisition of reading or writing skills. But in reading and writing essays, conventions should not be treated in an automatic, rigid, or insincere way. They should be seen as guidelines, strategies, or special features, not as rules.

As you read an essay, think about its form: what it includes, how the writer presents the subject, what features seem distinctive. If you read a pair or group of essays assigned by your teacher, you might ask yourself whether they represent the same genre or are noticeably different. If they are the same, you will recognize similar features; if they are different, you will notice less overlap.

Below are some common genres included in *The Norton Reader* and some features to watch for as you read:

Narrative genres

Narrative genres tell a story, using vivid details, about people, events, and conflicts or crises. They also reflect on the meaning of the stories, offering the reader an interpretation or explanation of what occurred. Common narrative genres include the autobiographical essay, literacy narrative, historical narrative, and biographical narrative.

Autobiographical essay   The genre of *autobiography* focuses on a significant personal experience in the writer's past and draws out the meaning as the writer tells the story and reflects on the experience. Sometimes an autobiographical essay is called *memoir, personal narrative,* or *mini-autobiography*. Its key features include a dramatic event or episode; vivid details and narration; and an interweaving of narration with reflection on and interpretation of the essayist's experience.

If you are assigned Alice Walker's "Beauty: When the Other Dancer Is the Self" (p. 69) or George Orwell's "Shooting an Elephant" (p. 852), you will immediately spot the dramatic event. For Walker, it is the day a BB pellet strikes her eye and causes "a glob of whitish scar tissue, a hideous cataract." For Orwell, it is the day when he, a young British official in Burma, must shoot an elephant that has gone "must." Walker introduces the drama in two italicized sentences: *"It was great fun being cute. But then, one day, it ended."* In the remainder of the essay she reflects on how the injury affected her sense of self, her identity. Orwell builds up to the dramatic moment more slowly, taking us through the thoughts and events that lead to his pulling the trigger. As he tells his story, Orwell reflects on the motivations of his action and reaches a point of insight:

> And it was at this moment, as I stood there with the rifle in my hands, that I first grasped the hollowness, the futility of the white man's dominion in the East.

These two essayists handle the conventions of their autobiographical essays differently, with different narrative styles and different pacing, but they both focus on a significant event and draw out its significance in the course of the essay.

Literacy narrative   A subcategory of the autobiographical essay, the *literacy narrative* focuses on learning to read or write. Like other narrative genres, it uses personal experience, requires vivid details and a sharp narrative style, and gives a clear indication of the narrative's significance. Teachers frequently assign this genre in composition courses, for reading or writing or both.

If you read Frederick Douglass's "Learning to Read" (p. 428) or Ben Franklin's "Learning to Write" (p. 539), you will encounter two classic versions of the literacy narrative. For Douglass, a slave, reading was a forbidden, illegal activity, so to learn to read he was "compelled to resort to various stratagems," as he phrases it. Douglass's literacy narrative includes rich details about his life as a slave, the strategies he used to acquire literacy, and the essential value that reading held for someone who did not want to remain "*a slave for life.*" For Franklin, a young man trained as a printer, writing became a means to raise himself in his social and professional world, and his narrative explains some of the tactics that allowed him to succeed. As you read Douglass or Franklin, watch for the details they choose to include and the anecdotes they recount as important to their stories. Other literacy narratives in *The Norton Reader* include Eudora Welty's "Clamorous to Learn" (p. 432) and Richard Rodriguez's "Aria" (p. 517), both by modern American writers who tell of their educational experiences with fascinating, sometimes painful details and with serious reflection on the meaning of reading and writing in American culture.

Historical narrative   This genre also relies on narrative—on telling a story— but focuses on the larger social or political patterns that the story reveals. Like other narrative genres, *historical narrative* requires vivid details and an indication of the narrative's significance, but it may incorporate more than a single, dramatic event (though it will often begin by describing one) and offer multiple stories or episodes.

You will find several examples of historical narrative in the "History" section, including Barbara Tuchman's " 'This Is the End of the World': The Black Death" (p. 779) and Philip Gourevitch's "After the Genocide" (p. 839). Both writers know that vivid descriptions and compelling anecdotes are central to good historical narratives. In her opening paragraph, Tuchman shows us—in gory detail—what the "black death" (bubonic plague) looked like:

> The diseased sailors showed strange swellings about the size of an egg or an apple in the armpits and groin. The swellings oozed blood and pus and were followed by spreading boils and black blotches on the skin from internal bleeding.

A gruesome picture, but it captures the reader's attention and fascinates us enough to read on. Gourevitch opens more quietly by setting his historical narrative in eastern Rwanda, but the vivid details of death, murder, and genocide appear very soon:

> At least fifty mostly decomposed cadavers covered the floor, wadded in clothing, their belongings strewn about and smashed. Macheted skulls had rolled here and there.

This description, which continues in almost clinical detail for a long paragraph, sets the context for the history of the Rwandan genocide that Gourevitch will tell. But it does much more: it establishes the significance of the event, justifies the label of mass murder or "genocide," and alerts the reader to the historical and international crisis in Africa. Both essayists continue with many episodes—rather than focus on a single one—because their histories require evidence of widespread events and consequences.

Biographical narrative   The *biographical narrative* is a subcategory of the historical narrative discussed above, and it is related to the *biographical profile* described below. Sometimes writers choose to focus their accounts of historical events on a specific person, perhaps because that person was a "key player," the moving force in the event, or perhaps because that person allows a window into how a large historical event felt to an average citizen.

You will find both techniques—and variations on them—in essays throughout *The Norton Reader*. Walt Whitman tells the story of an American president's assassination in his "Death of Abraham Lincoln" (p. 803). Logically, Whitman focuses his narrative on the president, telling what happened on the day of the assassination but including other biographical details that he recalls from previous sightings of Lincoln and ending with his reflections on the significance of what he calls "a heroic-eminent life." In contrast, the authors of three mini-biographies included under the rubric "World War II: Victims, Villains, Heroes" (p. 831) focus on "little people"—ordinary or average men and women who, in the throes of war, took heroic stances or did heroic deeds that involved great danger. As you read historical and biographical narratives, compare their features and try to notice their conventions: people and places need to be described with accuracy and interest, stories need to be told with clarity and good pace, significance needs to emerge from the narrative, not just be tacked on at the end.

Descriptive genres

Descriptive genres let the reader know how a person, place, or thing looks, sounds, feels, or maybe even smells. But they do more: they give a dominant impression, interpret a person's actions, offer a reflection on the significance of place, or in some other way put the objective details into a larger framework. Descriptive genres in *The Norton Reader* include the profile of a person, profile of a place, and natural history.

Profile of a person   Also called a *biographical sketch* or a *mini-biography*, the *profile of a person* features an individual or a group of people and uses firsthand knowledge, interviews, and/or research to present its subject. Since readers like to read about interesting subjects, it is sometimes assumed that the person must be interesting beforehand. But, really, it's the writer who makes the person interesting by discovering special characteristics or qualities through interviews or observation, by finding an interesting angle from which to present the subject, and by including engaging details, anecdotes, or dialogue to enliven the portrait. These are the special features, or conventions, of the biographical profile.

Profiles can be free-standing essays or parts of books. Tom Wolfe's "Yeager" (p. 148) is a portrait of the astronaut Chuck Yeager and part of a book about the first American astronauts in space, *The Right Stuff*. When you read this essay, you will see that Wolfe does not begin in the usual, boring way with date of birth, place of birth, parents, and education (though those details eventually make it into the profile). Instead, Wolfe lets us *hear* Yeager's voice by imitating its sound and style. Then Wolfe suggests the importance of Yeager's place in American aviation by describing how every American pilot tries to imitate this man with "the right stuff." The profile is chock-full of tales about Yeager's daring, often reckless, escapades—even as it narrates the story of how Yeager made history by breaking the sound barrier.

Profiles about family members can be difficult. Even if an essayist loves his or her parents, not every reader will find someone else's parents distinctive, memorable, or worth reading about. So it takes vivid details, humorous (or chilling) stories, and a bit of distance to succeed in the family profile. Annie Dillard *makes* her mother memorable in "An American Childhood" (p. 132) by recalling idiosyncratic stories and sayings, including the line "Terwilliger bunts one" that amuses and annoys her mother. Scott Russell Sanders, perhaps unfortunately, remembers too many characteristic episodes about his father. His profile, titled "Under the Influence" (p. 121), begins: "My father drank." Both of these writers had ordinary parents, but they make them seem extraordinary by the vividness of their memories, the special angles they take, and the overarching perspective on their parents' character that they bring to the essay.

Profile of a place   Places can also become the focus of a profile, in a subcategory sometimes simply called a *place essay*. The features of this genre involve discovering the special characteristics or qualities of the place, finding an interpretive framework in which to present it, and including engaging details, anecdotes, or dialogue to enliven the essay. Since places can't speak, the essayist must speak for them and say enough about them to make them come alive.

Essayists re-create places in different ways. Margaret Atwood, writing about northern Canada in "True North" (p. 199), begins with a camp song that she—like lots of other Canadians and Americans—remembers from childhood:

> Land of the silver birch,
> Home of the beaver,
> Where still the mighty moose
> Wanders at will.
> Blue lake and rocky shore,
> I will return once more.

Atwood goes on to re-create the northern landscape that she loves so well, that brings "tears to our eyes, not for simple reasons." In contrast, David Guterson begins with hard facts in "The Mall of America" (p. 210):

> 140,000 hot dogs sold each week, 10,000 permanent jobs, 44 escalators and 17 elevators, 12,750 parking spaces, 13,300 short tons of steel, $1 million in cash dispersed weekly from 8 automatic-teller machines.

Guterson's facts give us the immense scale of the mall—details that boggle the imagination, but that speak to some deep-seated American desire for immensity. Both essayists bring their places to life, but in different ways and with different approaches to understanding the meaning of a place.

If a profile includes both person and place, it is what the writer Anne Fadiman calls a "Character in Context" piece. Many times, we learn about a person by seeing him or her in a characteristic space; the place defines the person, the person defines the place. N. Scott Momaday's "The Way to Rainy Mountain" (p. 182) gives us a sacred place of the Kiowas, an old landmark that they called "Rainy Mountain." Yet his profile is also about his grandmother, Abo, whom he associates with the sacred mountain:

> Her forebears came down from the high country in western Montana nearly three centuries ago. They were mountain people, a mysterious tribe of hunters whose language has never been positively classified in any major group.

To understand the significance of Momaday's return to Rainy Mountain, we must understand the mountain's associations with his grandmother. And vice versa: to understand Abo's significance to her grandson, we must understand the meaning of Rainy Mountain to the Kiowa.

Natural history   The term *natural history* can refer generally to any historical writing about nature, but it also designates a genre related to the profile: the life cycle or biography of a plant or animal. (Think of it as profiling not a person but a bear or a dragonfly or a weed like goldenrod.) You will find some of these essays in the "Nature and Environment" section of this book, and you may also encounter them in biology classes. They describe a plant or animal, take it through its life cycle, and sometimes explain its significance or relationship to the human species.

In "The Spider and the Wasp" (p. 636), Alexander Petrunkevitch describes the life cycle of two animals, starting with the tarantula, then moving to its archenemy, the digger wasp of the genus *Pepsis*. His essay raises a puzzling scientific question about "intelligence pitted against instinct—a strange situation in which the victim, though fully able to defend itself, submits unwittingly to its destruction." In "The Work of Honeybees" (p. 629), Allison Wallace, too, gives a natural history—in this case of a mature worker bee she names "Bella." Wallace puzzles not over a scientific question, but a human one: a question about the meaning of work. As she observes the seemingly endless, repetitive work of the honeybees, it leads her to ask about the work humans do:

> *Everything you do will be insignificant, but you must do it anyway.* The question persists: what in the world *for*?

Both versions of natural history—raising scientific questions, raising questions about human actions—appear in *The Norton Reader*. Look for them in David Foster Wallace's "Consider the Lobster" (p. 75), in Henry David Thoreau's "The Battle of the Ants" (p. 776), in Edward Abbey's "The Serpents of Paradise" (p. 623), and even in Aldo Leopold's "Marshland Elegy" (p. 643), which gives a natural history of one of the writer's favorite places.

Analytic genres

Analytic genres carefully and methodically examine a text, an image, a cultural object, or a social trend by breaking it into parts, closely reading its components, and noting how the parts work in relation to the whole. In *The Norton Reader* you will find examples of textual analysis, visual analysis, and cultural analysis.

Textual analysis   Also called *close reading*, *textual analysis* focuses on written words. It examines words and phrases for explicit and implicit meanings; it looks for similes (comparisons using *like* or *as*) and metaphors (comparisons without explicit connectors) to reveal patterns of association and hidden meanings; and it interprets the whole text on the basis of these methodical, individual observations. The *text* may be anything from the Bible or Koran, to poems and novels, to ads, billboards, or official memos.

In "The Epistle of Paul the Apostle to the Ephesians" (p. 1144), Rita Dove analyzes a book from the New Testament. Traditionally, Christians have analyzed the Bible to clarify difficult or obscure passages, to understand the book's message, and to apply it to their lives. Dove recalls her first experience with biblical analysis in a Sunday school class at her church, African Methodist Episcopal:

> I was thirteen when the man who would introduce me to the apostle Paul walked into our senior Sunday-school class. He was tall, dark, and hellishly handsome, severely dressed in a matte-black narrow suit and black shirt from which rose a ring of shocking white, like a slipped halo.

In class, Dove's teacher focuses on words like "grace" and concepts like "mortal sin." But little details in this opening description—"hellishly handsome," "like a slipped halo"—clue us into the fact that Dove, the adult essayist, will do her own textual analysis, not rely on one handed down from a male clergyman. As you read her essay, notice how Dove probes the meaning of words like "human agency" and delves into the implications of textual metaphors, like Paul's "comparing the church to a marriage." For a different take on analysis, consider Gilbert Highet's essay "The Mystery of Zen" (p. 1201), and note how he uses analysis (to understand the concept of *meditation*), yet ultimately rejects analysis as a tool for comprehending Zen's mystery: "The doctrine of Zen," he states, "cannot be analyzed from without: it must be lived."

Visual analysis   Like textual analysis, *visual analysis* looks for explicit and implicit meanings; searches for patterns of association and hidden intentions; and interprets the whole object on the basis of these methodical, individual observations. Instead of a written text, visual analysis focuses on an image, a photograph, a painting, or another visual phenomenon.

Some visual analyses have as their goal the explanation of the image itself. For example, John Updike's "Moving Along" (p. 1087) looks closely at two paintings—one by a sixteenth-century Indian artist, the other by a contemporary American "Funk Artist." Updike devotes a paragraph to each painting, describing what he sees, commenting on the little details, and connecting both works to the theme of "moving along" and the human desire to walk, run, ride, and fly. Other selections use visual analysis as part of a larger argument. An example of this appears in H. Bruce Franklin's "From Realism to Virtual Reality: Images of America's Wars" (p. 810). Franklin writes as a historian; to make his argument about how changes in technology affect our understanding of war, he analyzes a sequence of images from the Civil War through the Iraqi war of the 1990s. As you read this essay, watch how Franklin cites historical descriptions of the photographs, refers to the "dominant metaphor" or "structuring metaphor" of movies and television shows, and points to motifs repeated from image to image.

In *The Norton Reader* you will find essays that combine textual and visual analysis or that use images to trigger both kinds of analysis. (Watch for essays that include photographs, drawings, graphs, and other visual material.) In writing "Strangers" (p. 158), Toni Morrison began by thinking about a book of photographs, interpreting the images, and pondering their significance, but her essay also analyzes the ethical implications of writing narratives, of creating life stories for people she does not know. In other essays, such as N. Scott Momaday's "The Way to Rainy Mountain" (p. 182) and Fred Strebeigh's "The Wheels of Freedom: The Bicycle in China" (p. 344), the authors provide images to accompany their prose: in Momaday's case, his father's drawings; in Strebeigh's, photographs he took during his travels in China at the time of the Tiananmen uprising. These images enrich the primary analyses of the authors by underscoring key points and adding visual evidence to their arguments.

Cultural analysis   This genre, called both *cultural analysis* and *cultural critique*, takes an object, trend, fad, or other phenomenon as the subject of its analysis. It uses the strategies of textual and visual analysis described above, adding personal response and library research, if desirable, to explain and interpret. Examples of this form appear in the section "Cultural Critique."

What kinds of cultural objects and trends do essayists analyze? Almost anything and everything, it seems. The French critic Roland Barthes analyzes toys, concluding that they "*literally* prefigure the world of adult functions" (p. 342). The American writer Fred Strebeigh analyzes the Chinese bicycle (p. 344), interviewing people who rely on them for work and play, giving us a history of their manufacture, reflecting on their names ("Forever," "Flying Pigeon"), and concluding that they represent "the wheels of freedom" to many Chinese people. The African American scholar Henry Louis Gates analyzes hairstyles popular in his youth (p. 323)—how they were created, how movie stars, singers, and black icons popularized them, and why the styles remain so important for him.

Other essayists analyze trends or social practices. Both Jessica Mitford and Thomas Lynch, for example, look at the funeral industry, one from the outside, the other from within. In "Behind the Formaldehyde Curtain" (p. 310), Mitford engages many different strategies in making her analysis—

from "the arrival of the corpse at the mortuary" to the process of embalming to the presentation of the body for open-casket viewing. Her goal is to debunk the "American way of death," as she calls it, and to show how the undertaker has assumed the place formerly held by the clergyman. In "The Bang & Whimper and the Boom" (p. 317), Lynch, a former funeral director whose father was also in the business, analyzes caskets rather than processes. (He calls condoms and caskets the "late-century emblems of sex and death.") Lynch describes the caskets, visually re-creating them for the reader (an important strategy for this genre); he also discusses the language with which the undertaker presents the caskets (a strategy drawn from textual analysis). In other words, in doing cultural analysis, essayists draw on the tactics of textual and visual analysis, and add to them analyses of social practices, including everyday and unusual rituals.

Argumentative genres

Forms of modern argument have their roots in classical Greece and Rome—that is, they go back at least 2,500 years. The Greek philosopher Aristotle held that there were really only two essential parts of an argument: (1) the statement of the case, and (2) the proof of the case. But he conceded that in practice most orators added two other parts: an introduction and a conclusion.

Roman rhetoricians like Quintillian refined and expanded this simple Aristotelian approach to include five or six parts:

(1) *exordium*: the introduction

(2) *narratio*: the statement or exposition of the case under discussion

(3) *divisio*: the outline of the points or steps in the argument

(4) *confirmatio*: the proof of the case (sometimes called *probatio*)

(5) *confutatio*: the refutation of opposing arguments

(6) *peroratio*: the conclusion

Yet Roman rhetoricians also acknowledged that, for any given argument, orators might want to omit parts. (They might, for example, omit *divisio* if the steps of the argument were simple.) And orators would often rearrange the parts of their speeches. They might, for instance, refute an opponent's arguments before advancing their own case.

Unless you participate in a debating society, you—like most modern college students—won't see this formal version of classical argument very often. Yet all Americans study it in civics class when they discuss the "Declaration of Independence" (p. 876) because Thomas Jefferson used the tactics of classical rhetoric as revived in the eighteenth century. Today, we hear its legacy in public speeches and see traces of it in newspaper editorials. The Greek and Roman philosophers weren't so much prescribing a genre as they were describing common argumentative practices. It makes sense that, if you want to argue your case effectively, you need to introduce it, outline the key points, present your evidence, and refute your opponent's position—all the steps they described. You will find these steps in the argumentative genres considered below: Op-Eds and editorials, public speeches and orations, and parables.

Op-Eds and editorials   This genre focuses on issues of public interest and encourages ordinary citizens to contribute their perspectives, opinions, and arguments to the public debate. *Op-Eds* and *editorials* begin with a "hook"—a link to a recent event or news article that grabs readers' attention—as the introduction. Specific features, or conventions, include a forthright statement of position, evidence in support, often a counterargument or rebuttal of the opposition, and sometimes a formal conclusion.

Brent Staples's "Why Colleges Shower Their Students with A's" (p. 410) features most of these conventions. Staples begins by citing the principle of a famous economist, Milton Friedman, to the effect that superior products flourish and shabby ones die out. But Staples refutes this principle when applied to colleges and argues that, in fact, colleges are giving too many A's and thus "stoking grade inflation and devaluing degrees." When you read Staples's Op-Ed, note how he puts forward his evidence, then rebuts a common argument of his opposition:

> The argument that grades are rising because students are better prepared is simply not convincing. The evidence suggests that students and parents are demanding—and getting—what they think of as their money's worth.

Staples wraps up with some proposals to remedy grade inflation and a final stab at parents and students who are "addicted to counterfeit excellence." Although he no doubt wrote from the evidence he had gathered and the conclusion he had independently reached, you will discover that Staples uses five of the six parts of the "formal" classical argument—all but number 3.

Public speeches and orations   Because *speeches* and *orations* derive directly, if also distantly, from the classical tradition of argument, they often show its formal features. Many speechwriters introduce the issue at hand, state their position, offer evidence in support and counterarguments against, and sum up—sometimes with a high rhetorical flourish. These modern tactics are based on the older classical conventions.

William Lloyd Garrison, the nineteenth-century American abolitionist, shows his knowledge of public oratory in "No Compromise with Slavery" (p. 910). His speech begins: "Let me define my positions, and at the same time challenge anyone to show wherein they are untenable." Garrison marshals evidence, uses logic, and appeals to the law of God to make his case and to refute those who advocate slavery. So, too, does Elizabeth Cady Stanton in the "Declaration of Sentiments and Resolutions" (p. 879), presented at the first U.S. women's rights convention and modeled on the American Declaration of Independence. A century later, the Rev. Martin Luther King, one of the great civil rights leaders and orators of modern America, continues the tradition in his "I Have a Dream" speech (p. 907) and in "A Letter from Birmingham Jail" (p. 892). In the first, King argues that America must make good on the Emancipation Proclamation and "open the doors of opportunity to all of God's children"; in the second, he makes the case for civil disobedience, taking his audience through the steps of his thinking and quietly refuting those who disagree. It is no coincidence that these important American speeches and documents use the formal conventions of argument: in so doing, the speakers demonstrate their education, ability, and right to debate the pressing issues of their day.

James van Tholen's "Surprised by Death" (p. 931) is *not* an oration or formal argument; it is a Sunday sermon, preached upon van Tholen's return to the pulpit after months of treatment for cancer. Van Tholen uses techniques from several genres, including autobiographical narrative as he talks about his illness and fear in fighting cancer, and textual analysis as he analyzes the meaning of the Christian concept of *grace* and the Greek word *eti* in Romans 5. Yet van Tholen also makes an argument: that he is right to have hope, "unwavering hope," in God and that his listeners must have this hope, too. His personal experience and his careful study of the Bible become part of the evidence he marshals to state this conclusion.

Parables   A *parable* is a story that illustrates a point, poses or answers a question, or suggests a lesson. A parable can imply an argument—though it does not make that argument directly or simply. The word *parable* means "thrown beside," and there's a sense in which any attempt to interpret a parable too specifically will always just miss the mark: the form is too complex to be reduced to a single meaning or simple moral. It is worth considering the parable as an alternative form of argument—a genre a writer might use when more formal arguments won't quite work. Feminists, for example, have sometimes turned to the parable when they find that masculine logic fails to grasp an issue. Native Americans, including Chief Seattle, have traditionally used the parable to refute the wrong-headed logic of white Americans.

Most religious traditions include parables—such as those told by Jesus or the Zen parables we include just before the section on "Philosophy and Religion." In the Zen parable "Muddy Road" (p. 1131) there's a literal-minded character, Ekido, who lives strictly by the rules, and a more knowing character, Tanzan, who has deeper wisdom. Ekido knows that a monk is supposed to avoid women, so he chastises Tanzan for picking up a "lovely girl in a silk kimono and sash" and carrying her across a muddy intersection. Tanzan responds with a question: "I left the girl there. Are you still carrying her?" Tanzan's question suggests that it's not the literal touching of a woman that matters. What matters is sexual desire. By carrying the image of the girl in his mind and brooding on it, Ekido is harboring desire within his heart, perhaps giving it space to grow. The parable is about the complexities of human desire—but it's hard to argue Tanzan's position without using many more words and perhaps being less effective. The parable—a narrative with a probing final twist—does the trick.

As you read arguments in various sections of *The Norton Reader*—whether in "Ethics" or "Politics," in "Spoken Words" or "Science and Technology"—consider where and why authors use formal techniques (conventions of argument) and where and why they turn to alternative strategies—strategies identified with other genres. In the end, the goal is to make an effective argument, to convince the reader of the validity of your evidence, or urge the listener to take a prescribed course of action.

STRATEGIES FOR CRITICAL READING

The previous pages have focused on reading specific kinds of essays and on strategies for recognizing genres and their conventions. Here we offer some general tips for approaching the reading your instructor assigns this semester.

Preview the essay

Think about the essay's title, read its opening paragraph, skim the topic sentences (usually, the first sentence of each paragraph). Look at the contextual note on the first page, and try to imagine the experience, issue, or debate that motivated the essayist to write. *Previewing* is a technique widely used for college reading, but not all writing teachers encourage it. Some teachers encourage previewing for academic writing, explaining that it helps readers focus on key issues; other teachers discourage previewing, pointing out that a good essay—like a good novel or movie—can be ruined by knowing the ending.

Write in the margin

As you read, note points that seem interesting and important, forecast issues that you think the writer will address, pose questions of your own. Talk back. Most essayists want active readers who think about what the essay says, implies, and urges as a personal response or course of action. Similarly, note points that you don't understand or that you find ambiguous. Puzzling over a sentence or a passage with your classmates can lead to crucial points of debate. Mark your queries and use them to energize class discussion.

Analyze the illustrations

Many of the essays in *The Norton Reader* include illustrations from their original publications. Think about how the essays and the images "speak" to each other. Consider whether the images enrich, highlight, or possibly challenge the essay. Does the image primarily illustrate the essay, or does it emphasize a feature unexplained by the essayist? Does the image enrich and make clearer one aspect of the writing, or does it minimize certain aspects of the subject, perhaps aspects you find important? What do you see in the images that the essayist discusses or explains? What do you see that he or she overlooks or minimizes? Thinking about images can help you clarify the author's argument or reveal points the author may have missed.

Summarize the essay

Write a summary of the essay. Begin by making a list of its key points and identifying the evidence used in support of each; then try to state briefly, in your own words, the "gist" or core of the essay. The goal is to condense the argument and evidence, while remaining faithful to the author's meaning. Your summary will be useful when you discuss the essay in class or write about it in a paper. For some genres, including the scientific report, a summary or *abstract* is included in the essay itself (see p. 976 for an example).

Keep a reading journal

Buy a class notebook or designate a special section of your college notebook for reflections on the essays you read. For each essay, take notes, record your responses, write questions about what puzzles you and what you want to discuss in class. Write down sentences or passages that you like and that you might want to use as models for your own essays. You may also want to list questions that the essayist raises and answers, as well as write down questions that you think the essayist has overlooked.

Use the study questions

Review the questions that follow each essay in *The Norton Reader*, and think about the issues—the subject, the structure, the language—that they pose. We include these questions to help you become an active reader, to focus attention on key issues, and sometimes to make suggestions for *doing* or *writing* something.

- Some questions ask you to locate or mark the essays' structural features, the patterns that undergird and clarify meaning. Narrative, description, exposition, persuasion, and argument follow conventional shapes—or distort them—and your ability to recognize these shapes will improve your comprehension.

- Other questions ask you to paraphrase meanings or extend them—that is, to express the meaning in your own words, to amplify points by providing your own examples, or to reframe points by connecting them with points in other essays.

- Still other questions ask you to notice special features or conventions that contribute to meaning: the author's choice of title, the author's voice (or persona), the author's assumptions about audience (and how the author speaks to the audience), and the author's choice of style and forms of expression.

- At least one question, usually the last, asks you to write. Sometimes we ask you to demonstrate comprehension by writing about something from your experience or reading that extends an essay and enforces its argument. Sometimes, we invite you to express disagreement or dissent by writing about something from your experience or knowledge that qualifies the author's argument or calls it into question. The final question may ask you to compare or contrast two authors' positions—especially when their positions seem opposed. Or we may ask you to adapt one of the essay's rhetorical strategies to a topic of your own choice and to make the essay even more your own by basing it on personal experience.

Re-read the essay

If possible, read the essay a second time before you discuss it in class. If you're short on time, re-read the key passages and paragraphs that you marked in marginal notes. Ask yourself what you see the second time that you didn't register on first reading.

As these tactics suggest, reading need not be only a private activity; it can also become communal and cooperative. Sharing reading journals in class helps to reveal points of ambiguity and to generate debate. Discussion, with the whole class or in smaller groups, can clarify your own and others' interpretation of the essays. What interests and motives does each reader bring to particular essays? Do some interests and motives yield better readings than others? What meanings do readers agree about? What meanings do they disagree about? Can we account for our differences? What are responsive and responsible readings? Are there irresponsible readings, and how do we decide? All these questions—and others—can emerge as private reading moves into the more public arena of the classroom.

Readers write, writers read. Making meaning by writing is the flip side of making it by reading, and we hope to engage you in both processes. But in neither process are meanings passed from hand to hand like nickels, dimes, and quarters. Instead, they are constructed—as a quilt or a house or an institution. We hope that these suggestions for reading will lead you to engaged and fruitful writing.

Writing in College

Much of the writing you will do in a composition course will start with an assignment from your instructor. Perhaps you will be asked to respond to some of the essays in *The Norton Reader*—to expand on something a writer has said, to agree or disagree with a claim a writer has made, or to do some research to extend an author's argument and say something new about it. Or, you may be assigned a particular genre or kind of writing—a literacy narrative, a profile of a person or place, a visual or textual analysis, or an argumentative paper—and asked to use selections in this book as models of these kinds of writing. We have selected the readings because they are full of important ideas you can react to, either by agreeing or disagreeing, and also because the essays represent excellent examples of good writers at their best, models for aspiring writers to follow.

What follows is a brief guide for writing with *The Norton Reader*. We'll look at discovering your purpose, addressing your audience, finding a subject, determining what genre to employ, using rhetorical strategies, and understanding the writing process.

KNOWING YOUR PURPOSE

Your *purpose* is, put simply, the goal for your writing. What do you want to achieve? What points do you want to make? What idea or cause motivates you to write? Anything you can do to sharpen your thinking and infuse your writing with a clear sense of purpose will be to the good: you will find it easier to stay focused and help your readers see your key point and main ideas about your subject.

What are some common purposes writers have? The authors of the essays in *The Norton Reader* had informing, persuading, entertaining, or expressing as some of their purposes. So, too, your writing will have a primary purpose, usually defined in an assignment by words such as "explain," "describe," "analyze," "argue." Each is a signal about the purpose for your writing.

For instance, if an assignment asks you to *analyze* the persuasiveness of Nicholas Kristof's Op-Ed "Saudis in Bikinis" (p. 340), then your purpose is to explain the claims Kristof makes, examine the evidence he uses to support them, discuss points or perspectives he misses, and develop a thesis about the reasons for the essay's persuasiveness. If an assignment asks you to *argue* for or against Kristof's claim about women in Saudi Arabia, then your purpose is to take a side, defending or refuting his claims and using evidence from your own knowledge and from reputable sources to support your argument.

Use these questions to think about your purpose for writing:

- What does the assignment ask you to do? Is the goal to inform readers, entertain them, argue a point, or express an idea or feeling? Beyond a general purpose, what does the assignment require in terms of a specific purpose?

- How does your purpose affect your choice of a subject? What do you know about the subject? How can you find out more about this subject?

- How can you connect to your readers? What will they want or need to know? How do you want them to respond to your writing?

ADDRESSING YOUR AUDIENCE

Just as the authors in *The Norton Reader* aimed their essays at different *audiences*—readers of books, large newspapers, magazines, small journals, and scholarly publications, as well as activists, ordinary citizens, and churchgoers—so you need to imagine your audience as you write. Too wide an audience—"the general public"—and you run the risk of making your essay too diffuse, trying to reach everyone. Too narrow an audience—"my roommate Zach"—and you run the risk of being too specific.

How can you imagine an audience of your own? One way is to look around your writing classroom: that's your immediate audience, the people who are taking the course with you and your instructor. Another way is to think about your home community: your family, your neighbors, and the people of your town or city. Think of your audience as readers like yourself, with some of the same knowledge of the world and some of the same tastes. Consider your audience's range of reference: historical events they have witnessed first-hand, movies and TV shows they know about or have seen, and the books they have read or heard of. Think of them as willing to be convinced by whatever you write, but in need of good evidence.

Inevitably, some writers find that imagining an audience made only of class members seems too restrictive. That's fine; feel free to invoke another audience, say a group of people who share a certain passion, perhaps for a team, a sport, a game, or a type of music or film. (But remember to take into account your instructor, who may need some filling in about the special knowledge you share with your audience.)

Use these questions to guide you in thinking about audience:

- What readers are you hoping to reach with your writing?

- What information can you assume your readers know? What information do you need to explain?

- In what ways will you need to adjust the style of your writing—the language, tone, sentence structure and complexity, and examples—to meet the needs of your audience?

FINDING A SUBJECT

Like the audience and purpose for your writing, the *subject* of your writing—what you write about—will often be assigned by your instructor. Some assignments are very specific, such as this study question following Virginia Woolf's essay "My Father. Leslie Stephen" (p. 137): "Write a sketch about a father, real or fictional, adopting a tone similar to Woolf's in this sketch." In this assignment the subject matter (a father), the genre (a biographical sketch), and even the tone ("similar to Woolf's") are prescribed. You'll have to use Woolf's essay as a model and try to capture her tone as best you can. Other assignments may be more general, such as the following study question on Scott Russell Sanders's profile of his father, "Under the Influence" (p. 121): "Drawing on your memories of a friend or family member, write an essay about some problem that person had and its effect on your life." This broader assignment requires you to determine the person you wish to discuss, the problem you wish to analyze, and the larger effect the person and problem had on your life.

Some assignments give you even more leeway in choosing a subject, leaving you with the inevitable question "What should I write about?" In this case, write about what you know or care about, drawing on knowledge you've already gleaned about a subject from personal experience, your reading, or research. Your knowledge does not have to be totally new, but your perspective on a subject needs to come from you—a real person writing about a subject that matters.

How do you find what you know or care about? One way is to raise questions about an essay you've read:

- What is the author's main point? Do you agree or disagree with the main point?

- Has the author said enough about the subject? What gaps or omissions do you see, if any? Are there sentences or paragraphs that you could expand into an essay of your own?

- Are the author's examples and evidence convincing? If not, why not? Can you provide a more compelling example, additional evidence, or a counter example?

- Does this reading "speak" to anything else you've read in *The Norton Reader*? Can you explain how this reading connects to the other? Do the readings agree or disagree?

- Is this reading true to your own experience? Has anything like this happened to you, or have you ever observed anything like this?

You can also choose a subject by reflecting on your own experience:

- Has someone you know affected your life in some way—by teaching you, by serving as an example (good or bad), or by changing your attitude?

- Is there a place that you can describe to others, telling them what makes it unique or special to you?

- Is there a subject you feel strongly about, something you believe others need to learn about—for example, a program on your campus or in your neighborhood, a controversial item of national significance, or a matter of global importance?

- Have you had an experience that has taught you something valuable, influenced the way you live, or made you think differently about life, school, work, family, or friends? Readers will be interested in the details of the experience, including how it affected you and what you have learned.

DETERMINING GENRE

Like the purpose, audience, and subject of your writing, the *genre* or form of your writing may be prescribed in your instructor's assignment. *The Norton Reader* contains a variety of essay genres:

- **Narrative genres**, which tell stories and include autobiographical essays, literacy narratives, historical narratives, and biographical narratives.
- **Descriptive genres**, which give details about how a person, place, or thing looks, sounds, and feels, often in a larger framework. These include profiles of people and places and essays about nature and natural history.
- **Analytic genres**, which examine texts, images, and cultural objects and trends.
- **Argumentative genres**, which take stands and provide evidence to support them. These include Op-Eds, editorials, public speeches, and parables.

These genres are discussed on pp. xxvii–xxxvii and listed in the Genres Index on pp. 1259–62.

If you're assigned a literacy narrative, for example, your writing will tell a vivid, detailed story about an experience you've had with reading, writing, or schooling. To write a profile of a place, you will need to give a coherent impression of it by gathering and organizing detailed descriptions of how the place looks, smells, or even feels. If you're asked to take a stand on an important issue, you will write in an argumentative genre; if you choose an Op-Ed or editorial, you will need to focus on a central claim, support that claim with solid evidence, consider opposing views, and be brief. Or, if your assignment is a textual analysis of one of the readings in this book, you will need to examine features of the essay—its structure, style, key metaphors and phrases—paying close attention to rhetorical details.

If you have some leeway in choosing the genre in which you will write, consider what genre best fits your purpose, audience, and subject:

- What goal do you have for your writing? What genre is most appropriate for that goal?
- Who will read your writing? What genre will best convey the point of your writing to your readers?
- What are you writing about? What genre is well-suited to your subject?

To gain more understanding of these genres, read plenty of examples, analyze the forms and strategies they use, and then try out a genre on your own. There's no better way to understand how a genre works than to try your hand at writing it.

USING RHETORICAL STRATEGIES

As you plan your essay, you will want to think about the *rhetorical strategies* by which you will present your ideas and evidence to readers. These strategies, sometimes called *rhetorical modes* or *techniques*, help a writer organize evidence, connect facts into a sequence, and provide clusters of information necessary for conveying a purpose or an argument. You might choose to *analyze* the cause of an outcome, *compare* one thing to another, *classify* your facts into categories, *define* a key term, *describe* a person, place, or phenomenon, *explain* how a process works, or *narrate* a pertinent event or experience.

Sometimes, the writing assignment that your instructor gives will determine the strategy: for example, an assignment to compare Jack Hitt's position on binge drinking with Kenneth Bruffee's (see pp. 422–25) will require that you use a compare/contrast strategy. Similarly, a study question in this book might imply a strategy: for example, one of the questions following E. B. White's "Democracy" (p. 891) states, "Using White's technique, write a definition for an abstract term," and thus asks that you think about definition and how that strategy might work in an essay about "generosity" or "love" or "virtue."

Many essays use a mix of strategies. You might want to define a key term in an opening paragraph, narrate a story to make a point in the next paragraph, and analyze cause and effect in yet another. Except for very short pieces, most writers use several rhetorical strategies in an essay, choosing the one they think best fits their material. In "The Tyranny of the Majority" (p. 886), Lani Guinier uses a childhood story in her opening paragraph—an episode in which a girl in her Brownie troop wins a contest by having her mother make her entry. Guinier then follows this example of foul play with a definition of "fair play": "To me fair play means that the rules encourage everyone to play. They should reward those who win, but they must be acceptable to those who lose." Later she compares different ways of conceptualizing democracy, some that take only winners into account, others that allow the views of the minority to be included. The mix of rhetorical strategies keeps the reader involved, shows that the writer is engaged in complex thinking, and creates an effective argument.

Following are some rhetorical strategies that you will encounter in *The Norton Reader* and that you will want to use in your own writing.

Analyzing cause and effect

Focusing on causes helps a writer think about why something happened; focusing on effects helps a writer think about what might or could happen.

Cause is oriented toward the future; effect looks back to the past. But you can use this strategy by working in either direction: from present to future, or from present to the past.

If you were writing about global warming and intending to show its harmful effects, you might lay out your evidence in this sequence:

Cause → leads to → these effects.

If you were writing about binge drinking and trying to identify the reasons for its rise among college students, you might reverse the direction:

Effect ← is the result of ← these causes.

Analyzing a cause (or causes) is a crucial strategy for genres such as cultural critique, Op-Ed, and historical narrative. But you can also use it in an autobiographical essay, where you might analyze the effects of a childhood trauma on your later life, or in a profile of a person, where you might seek the sources (the causes) of the person's adult personality or achievements.

Comparing and contrasting

Comparisons look for similarities between things; contrasts look for differences. In most uses of this rhetorical strategy, you will want to consider both similarities and differences—that is, you will want to compare *and* contrast. That's because most things worth comparing have something in common, even if they also have significant differences. You may end up finding more similarities than differences, or vice versa, but when using this strategy, think about both.

Comparison-contrast may be used for a single paragraph or for an entire essay. It tends to be set up in one of two ways: block or point-by-point. In the block technique, the writer gives all the information about one item and then follows with all the information about the other. Think of it as giving all the A's, then all the B's. Usually, the order of the information is the same for both. In the point-by-point technique, the writer focuses on specific points of comparison, alternating A, B, A, B, A, B, and so on until the main points have been covered.

Comparing and contrasting is an excellent strategy to use in writing a report, making an argument in an Op-Ed, or giving a speech to persuade your audience to take a specific course of action. You can set forth the pros and cons of different programs, political policies, or courses of action, leading up to the recommendation you endorse and believe is the more effective.

Classifying and dividing

Classifying and dividing involves either putting things into groups or dividing up a large block into smaller units. While this strategy might seem better suited to a biology lab than to a writing class, in fact it works well for organizing facts that seem chaotic or for handling big topics that at first glance seem overwhelming. Classifying and dividing allow the writer—and the reader—to get control of a big topic and break it into smaller units of analysis.

How does the essayist Susan Allan Toth discuss ways of "Going to the Movies" (p. 1105)? She classifies movies by the kinds of men who accompany her and who have different tastes in what they like to see. This technique gives the essayist four manageable categories: art films, movies with "a redeeming social conscience," movies that entertain, and romantic oldies that she watches on her own. In other words, Toth is classifying. How does the composer Aaron Copland discuss "How We Listen" (p. 1121)? He divides his essay—and the modes of listening to music—into three "planes" or levels of listening. This basic division helps the writer explain the different goals and experiences that listeners bring to a piece of music. Dividing goals into levels allows the writer to manage a difficult, abstract topic and to lead the reader from the simpler to the more complex level of listening.

You will find that classifying and dividing is helpful in writing all genres of analysis: textual, visual, and cultural. You will also find that it can help in argumentative genres because it enables you, as a writer or speaker, to break down a complex argument into parts or to group pieces of evidence into similar categories.

Defining

Defining involves telling your reader what something means—and what it does not. It involves saying what something is—and what it is not. As a strategy, defining means making sure you—and your readers—understand what you mean by a key term. It may mean re-defining a common term to have a more precise meaning or giving nuance to a term that is commonly used too broadly. Defining and re-defining are great strategies to use in argumentative writing: they help the writer reshape the thinking of the audience and see a concept in a new light.

This rhetorical strategy is not as simple as looking up a word in a dictionary, though often that is a good place to begin. If you look up your key word in a good collegiate dictionary, you may discover that it meant something one hundred years ago that it no longer means, or that it is used in technical writing in a specific sense, or that it has a range of meanings from which you must choose to convey *your* intention. Citing one of these definitions can help in composing your essay. But defining as a rhetorical strategy may also include giving examples or providing descriptions: What does *democracy* feel like to the citizen? (See E. B. White's "Democracy," p. 891.) What does *salvation* look like to the unconverted? (See Langston Hughes's "Salvation," p. 1139.) What is a *postcard* in a literary sense? (See Garrison Keillor's "Postcards," p. 537.) In these versions of defining, the rhetorical strategy overlaps with the next one: describing.

Describing

When writers describe a person, place, or thing, they indicate what it looks like and often how it feels, smells, sounds, or tastes. As a strategy, describing involves showing rather than telling, helping readers see rather than giving them a formal definition, making the subject come alive rather than remaining abstract. When you describe, you want to choose precise verbs, specific nouns, vivid adjectives—unless your subject is dullness itself.

As a writer, you will use description in many kinds of assignments: in profiles of people and places to provide a key to their essence, in visual analysis to reveal the crucial features of a painting or photograph, in cultural critique to highlight the features of the object or phenomenon you will analyze, and in scientific lab reports to give details of an experiment. Almost no essay can be written without at least some description, and many essays rely on this strategy as a fundamental technique. In *The Norton Reader* you will find study questions in almost every section that begin with "Describe": "Describe a 'treasure' someone found and held on to," "Take a flower or tree and write a close-up description of it," "Describe some particular experience that raises a large social question"—these are just a few examples of writing assignments that ask for description.

Explaining a process

With this rhetorical strategy, the writer explains how something is done: from everyday processes like how to write a letter, how to play basketball, or how to make French fries, to unusual or extreme processes like how to embalm a corpse or how to face death. Sometimes, writers use this strategy in historical essays to show how something was done in the past. As these examples suggest, explaining a process can be useful in a range of genres: from a literacy narrative that explains learning to read, to a cultural analysis that treats the funeral industry, to a sermon or philosophical essay that explores the meaning and purpose of death and dying.

To make a process accessible to the reader, you will need to identify the main steps or stages and then explain them in order, one after the other. Sequence matters. In preparing to write a paragraph explaining a process, it might help to list the steps as a flow chart or as a cookbook recipe—and then turn your list into a paragraph (or more) of fully elaborated prose.

Narrating

This final rhetorical strategy—narrating—may be the most fundamental. We tell stories about ourselves, about our families, and about friends and neighbors. We tell stories to make a point, to illustrate an argument, to offer evidence or counter-evidence, and sometimes even to substitute for an argument. As these uses suggest, narrating appears in many genres: from memoirs and biographies, to Op-Eds, formal speeches, and parables. Narrating is basic to essay writing.

As you plan a paragraph or segment of narration, think about sequence: the order in which the events occurred (chronological order) or an order in which the events might be most dramatically presented (reverse chronological order or the present moment with flashback). Often, sequential order is easier for the reader to comprehend, but sometimes beginning *in medias res* (at the present moment *in the middle of things*) and then flashing back to the past creates a more compelling story. Consider incorporating time markers—not only dates, but also sequential phrases: early one evening, later that night, the next morning. And use transitions and transitional words: first, then, meanwhile, later, finally. When you've finished narrating your event or episode, re-read it and ask, What have I left out that the reader needs to know? What might I omit because the reader doesn't need to know it?

STRATEGIES FOR WRITING

If you were to watch a writer at work, you would observe that the task of writing often occurs in stages. Most writers generate ideas, write a draft, revise the draft (sometimes once, often many times), edit (make sentence- or word-level changes), and finally, proofread (check to see that the grammar, spelling, and formatting are correct). Along the way, writers develop a main point for their writing, find examples and evidence to support that point, and integrate the evidence into their work. You would be observing what teachers of writing call the *writing process*, a series of stages that writers use, though some omit a stage, some combine one or more of them, and others follow each one carefully. Your writing will benefit if you understand how the writing process works, and, even more important, how to make the process work for *you*.

Generate ideas

For many people, the hardest part of writing is looking at the blank page or empty screen. What can you say? How can you even get started? Sometimes your task is made easier when your instructor gives you a specific assignment or asks a particular question. In the next pages, we'll follow one student as she develops an essay responding to Brent Staples's "Why Colleges Shower Their Students with A's." Her instructor assigned the following study question (p. 410):

> How broad is Staples's range of examples? Would he need to adjust his position if he considered other colleges? Write an analysis of the situation at your college either to confirm or to contest Staples's argument.

The student knew she had to analyze Staples's range of examples and so began gathering ideas by rereading his essay. She noted that he cites only three colleges by name—the University of Pennsylvania, the University of Phoenix, and Duke University—and decided to do research on her own campus. Her instructor directed her to the Office of Institutional Research, which supplied her with a summary of grade distribution at her college. The summary showed that 30 percent of grades were A's, 45 percent were B's, and 25 percent were C's or below. The evidence her research produced did not seem particularly odd to her; it was about what she expected, and it refuted Staples's claim that "colleges shower their students with A's." Notice this student's process for generating ideas and getting started: she began with the question in *The Norton Reader*, reread the essay, conducted research, and discovered hard evidence that did not support Staples's claim. In fact, she developed a claim of her own, a counterclaim to Staples's.

Sometimes, the assignment your teacher gives or a study question in *The Norton Reader* is more open-ended, such as this one following Nancy Mairs's "On Being a Cripple" (p. 59):

> Mairs deliberately chooses to call herself a "cripple." Select a person or group that deliberately chooses its own name or description and explain the rationale behind the choice.

You can respond to this assignment by examining your own memory for stories you've heard, incidents you've witnessed, or people you've met, or you may need to do some research in order to have enough to say. Use one or more of the following techniques to mine your memory or generate ideas:

- Freewrite for several minutes to discover what you already know and think about a subject.

- Make a list of everything you know about the subject. Group or cluster related ideas.

- Read some articles about the subject. Take notes on what you read.

- Ask questions about the subject, starting with *who, what, when, why,* and *how.*

Different writers develop different ways of finding their material, so experiment with different techniques until you discover one or more that work for you.

Develop a main point or thesis

Most writing in college courses needs a central claim, often called a *thesis*. Most papers contain a thesis statement, often stated in the introduction, that tells readers the main point that will be supported, developed, and extended in the body of the paper.

Sometimes the thesis statement will be an arguable claim supported by evidence, such as Brent Staples's thesis, which falls at the end of the first paragraph of his Op-Ed: "Faced with demanding consumers and stiff competition, colleges have simply issued more and more A's, stoking grade inflation and devaluating degrees." The student who responded to Staples's essay also developed a thesis statement, narrowing a broad initial claim—"Staples is wrong about colleges showering their students with A's"—to a specific, arguable claim—"For most students at Central College, however, Staples is wrong: 70 percent of students on this campus are not being showered with A's." Her thesis statement is good because it is emerges from the research she has carried out on her own campus.

At other times, the main point of your writing won't be stated so plainly. Instead, it will be "in the air," or evident to the reader, but you won't be trying to argue a claim with evidence. If you're writing in a narrative or descriptive genre, for example, you'll have a main point, of course, particularly if you're writing a historical or biographical narrative or creating a profile of a person or place. You will make a claim about the reasons something happened or about the reasons for a person's or place's distinctive characteristics, as Margaret Atwood does in "True North" (p. 199):

> The north is another country. It's also another language. Or languages.

Those three sentences are main point, the guiding principle by which she thinks about the Canadian north.

Gather evidence

What counts as adequate evidence for your claim or thesis? The student whose response to Brent Staples's "Why Colleges Shower Students with A's" was not convinced by the evidence Staples used and found evidence that refuted his claim. Her argument would have been even stronger if she had looked for other sources, such as published survey results and reports of grade distribution at other colleges, to find out whether Staples's claim or her hunch was more accurate.

In other kinds of writing, evidence is drawn more often from personal experience than from secondary sources. In a literacy narrative, for example, the evidence will be in the examples and details of the story you tell about a formative time in your education. In a profile of a person, the evidence will also take the form of examples—the descriptive details about the person's personality, accomplishments, talents, weaknesses, looks, and behavior; anecdotes or stories about the person's life; or testimony from people who've observed the person closely. Evidence is also often drawn directly from reading. In a textual analysis, the evidence will be examples that demonstrate the text's structure, style, and language.

Organize your ideas

How you organize your ideas in a piece of writing depends to a large extent on your genre and purpose. Margaret Atwood organizes "True North" as a journey to the north, inching us there by describing her impressions of a trip, using the historical present tense ("A bunch of us are sitting around the table, at what is now a summer cottage in Georgian Bay"), and pausing occasionally to fill us in on what happens at different times, thus linking her impressions together loosely in her narrative. Similarly, David Guterson organizes "Enclosed, Encyclopedic, Endured: The Mall of America" (p. 210) as an answer to a question:

> Here was a new structure that had cost more than half a billion dollars to erect—what might it tell us about ourselves?

His essay proceeds as a narrative exploration of the Mall itself, over a number of days; he links his observations to stops he makes on his trip through the complex.

For many of the essays you write in college, you will use the familiar format of an introduction, body, and conclusion, with separate paragraphs in the body for each major piece of evidence. The introduction often connects your ideas to what your readers already know and seeks to interest them in what you have to say. For instance, the student writing in response to Brent Staples's Op-Ed began her essay this way:

> The notion of grade inflation has been in the air for the past decade. Critics have complained that today's students are receiving far too many A's and not enough C's, D's, and F's. Things were different in the past, these critics say; grades really meant something back when the critics went to college; today's college students have it far too easy. In his recent Op-Ed piece, Brent Staples struck the familiar theme when he claimed to explain why colleges nowadays "shower" their students with A's. For most students at Central College, however, Staples is wrong: 70 percent of students on this campus are not being showered with A's.

In the body of an essay, you may want to place your most compelling piece of evidence first, or you may want it to come last to tie matters up for the reader. (But don't hide your best bit of evidence by placing it in the middle.) The student who wrote in response to Staples decided to use the body of her essay to present anecdotal evidence from her roommates, informal survey results from classmates about their grades, and finally the results of her research at the Office of Institutional Research. Whatever type of organization you choose, try the ideas out and write a different outline for each type of placement to see which works more successfully.

In the conclusion, you try to wrap things up, finish off your line of reasoning, and send your readers off with a final thought. Brent Staples ends "Why Colleges Shower Their Students with A's" with a predication:

> Addicted to counterfeit excellence, colleges, parents and students are unlikely to give it up. As a consequence, diplomas will become weaker and more ornamental as the years go by.

That's a fine way to conclude. Our student writer, responding to Staples, takes a different approach in her conclusion:

> Those of us who work hard and study at Central College note that we have never been "showered" with A's. We study at a place where high grades re-

main difficult to earn, and our situation makes me wonder whether Staples gathered only the evidence he wanted to find. Had he considered other colleges, he would not have made such a sweeping assertion.

Write multiple drafts

Even the most experienced writers know they can't do everything at once: find or invent material, assess its usefulness, arrange it in paragraphs, and write it out in well-formed sentences. If you try to produce a good essay at one sitting, in a single draft, you are likely to thin out your material, lock yourself into a structure that may not work and that you don't have time to change, and write jumbled paragraphs and clumsy sentences that won't fully convey your meaning or intention. In the end, writing a few drafts—in short periods spaced over more than a day—will produce a better essay, one that is thoughtful and deserving of a respectable grade. Here are some tips for drafting in stages:

- Get started by composing a rough draft or small sections of a draft. Don't feel obliged to start with the introduction and write straight through to the conclusion. If you don't know where to begin, write a section you know you want to include, then move to another. As you compose, you will begin to find out what you mean, what is important to your argument, what is missing, and what needs to be revised. Think of composing a rough draft as a way of discovering what you want to say.

- If you get stuck, try focused freewriting. That is, write all you can in response to a particular point or about a particular idea, not stopping for five minutes. After you're done, read what you've written looking for your thoughts on the subject. Much of what you've written won't be worthwhile, but you may have come up with key notions or put yourself in touch with useful ideas.

- Write a single paragraph for each key piece of evidence you have to support your thesis. Later on you can refine these paragraphs, combining some and breaking up others.

- At any point in this process, print out a clean version of your draft, read it through, and make changes. Add to, subtract from, rearrange, and revise the parts of your essay.

Acknowledge others' words and ideas

Your writing should reflect your own thinking, of course, but you'll often incorporate the ideas and actual words of others. Synthesizing and citing the work of others shows your readers that you have consulted reputable sources and, if you use sources honestly and skillfully, will make readers more open to your argument. It may help you to think of anything you write as part of a dialogue you are having with other writers and scholars; just be sure to credit the other writers and scholars whose words and ideas you borrow, so your readers can follow the dialogue and know who said what.

When you cite information from another source in your writing, you must credit the source. First, give the author credit by acknowledging his or her work in your text. If you cite someone's exact words, put them in quotation marks, or, if you quote more than five lines, indent them without quotation marks. Tell your readers where you got the words by including the author's name in your text and putting the page number of the book or article in parentheses right after the quote. Here is an example of a direct quotation with appropriate citation:

> Staples argues that the rise of part-time instructors is partially responsible for grade inflation: "Writing in the last issue of *Academe*, two part-timers suggest that students routinely corner adjuncts, threatening to complain if they do not turn C's into A's" (411).

If you paraphrase a source, that is, if you use another person's idea but not the exact words, you still need to cite the source of that idea, even though you have expressed it in your own words. Here is an example of a paraphrase:

> Staples dismisses the argument that grades are getting higher because of students' better preparation (411).

At the end of your paper on a separate page, list all the sources you have quoted and paraphrased. Many style guides provide directions for formatting source material. The guide used most frequently in English classes is the *MLA Handbook for Writers of Research Papers*, Seventh Edition (2009), published by the Modern Language Association.

Sometimes writers in a hurry are tempted to absorb others' writing wholesale into their papers. This is *plagiarism*. Plagiarism is unethical because it involves the theft of another writer's words and ideas; in college courses, it is a guarantee of failure when discovered. Avoid plagiarizing at all costs. If you have fallen behind on a writing assignment, tell your instructor. You will often find that he or she will accept a late submission, and even if you are graded down for submitting the paper late, that is better than stealing others' ideas and words.

Revise alone and with peers

Although writers can and often do compose and revise alone, we all need helpful responses, whether from professional editors, classmates, or friends. You, too, will need to become a good reviser, both of your own work and of the work of your peers. It is useful first to internalize another reader for yourself and revise your work on your own, and then to give your draft to an actual reader who can read and comment on it.

All writers need to try out their arguments and ideas before they produce a final draft. Many writing classes encourage that process, teaching students to draft and revise independently but also enabling them to put less-than-final drafts forward for responses from the instructor and fellow students. Examples and arguments that seem clear to the writer may seem forced or exaggerated to another reader. In peer groups, listen to readers who disagree with you, who find your position slanted, overstated, or not fully convincing. Be responsive to their comments, and qualify interpretations or further explain points that they do not understand.

Here are some all-purpose questions that you can use to review a draft on your own or in a peer group. The questions should probably be asked in the order below, since they move from larger elements to smaller ones.

Introduction   Treat the introduction as a promise by asking, "Does this essay keep the promises the introduction makes?" If it doesn't, either the introduction or the essay needs to be revised. Try to determine where the problem lies: Is the introduction off track? Does one or more of the paragraphs wander off the topic? Does the introduction promise an organization that isn't followed?

Content   Next ask yourself, "Does this essay include enough material?" You may feel that some of the essays in *The Norton Reader* are dense and overspecific; your instructor, on the other hand, may find your essays skimpy and underspecific, with too few details and examples. As you read your own work and that of your classmates, look for examples and details that transmit meaning and engage your interest, understanding, and imagination. Check for adequate and persuasive evidence and multiple illustrative examples that clarify main points. If you or your readers think you need more evidence, examples, or information, revise accordingly.

Evidence and source material   Then ask, "Does the essay interpret its material clearly and connect its examples to the main argument?" Your essay, and those you read as a peer reviewer, should specify the meanings of the examples you use; don't expect the examples to speak for themselves. A case in point is the use of quotations. How many are there? How necessary are they? How well are they integrated? What analysis or commentary follows each? Watch for quotations that are simply dropped in, without enough introduction or "placing" so that the reader can understand their significance. Quotations should be well integrated, clearly explaining who is speaking, where the voice is coming from, and what to attend to.

Organization and transitions   Then ask, "Are the main and supporting points of this essay well-organized?" Writing puts readers in possession of material in a temporal order: that is, readers read from start to finish. Sometimes material that appears near the end of an essay might work better near the beginning; sometimes material that appears near the beginning might better be postponed. Pay attention to transitions between and within paragraphs; if they are unclear, the difficulty may lie in the organization of the material.

Tone   Then ask, "Is the tone of the essay appropriate for its purpose and its audience?" Whether the tone is light-hearted, serious, reasoned, funny, enraged, thoughtful, or anything else, it needs to be appropriate to the purpose of the essay and sensitive to the expectations of the audience. Be aware of how formal your writing should be and whether contractions, abbreviations, and slang are acceptable.

Sentences   Then ask, "Which sentences unfold smoothly and which sentences might cause readers to stumble?" If working in a group, ask your classmates to help you rephrase a sentence or write the thought in new words. Remember, you're trying to reach readers just like your peers, so take their questions and reactions seriously.

Learning to be a responsive reader of essays in *The Norton Reader* can teach you to respond helpfully to the essays of peer writers in your composition class—and to improve your own. Large and small elements of the composing process are reciprocal. Learn to work back and forth among wholes and parts, sections and paragraphs, introductions and conclusions. As shape and meaning come together, you can begin to refine smaller elements: sentences, phrases, specific words. You can qualify your assertions, complicate your generalizations, and tease out the implications of your examples.

Edit, proofread, and format the final draft

After you have revised the structure of your writing, you should devote time to pruning for excess, reviewing the words, and correcting errors in grammar, punctuation, and spelling—what experienced writers call editing and proofreading. This work is best done after giving the paper a rest and coming to it afresh. You may be tempted to move directly to the proofreading stage, thus shortchanging the larger, more important revision work described above. So long as the larger elements of an essay need repair, it's too soon to work on the smaller ones, so save the tinkering for last. When you're satisfied with the overall shape of your essay, turn to the work of tightening your writing by eliminating repetition and awkward phrases, correcting grammar, punctuation, and spelling, and putting your work in its final form. Be sure you know what style and format your work should take, be it that of an academic paper with set margins, double-spacing, and a title page, or some other format. Ask your instructor if you are unsure about any of these, and make the necessary changes. Then, like other writers, you will need to stop—not because there isn't more to be done but because you have other things to do.

THE NORTON READER
Twelfth Edition

PERSONAL REPORT

CHANG-RAE LEE *Coming Home Again*

W HEN MY MOTHER began using the electronic pump that fed her liquids and medication, we moved her to the family room. The bedroom she shared with my father was upstairs, and it was impossible to carry the machine up and down all day and night. The pump itself was attached to a metal stand on casters, and she pulled it along wherever she went. From anywhere in the house, you could hear the sound of the wheels clicking out a steady time over the grout lines of the slate-tiled foyer, her main thoroughfare to the bathroom and the kitchen. Sometimes you would hear her halt after only a few steps, to catch her breath or steady her balance, and whatever you were doing was instantly suspended by a pall of silence.

I was usually in the kitchen, preparing lunch or dinner, poised over the butcher block with her favorite chef's knife in my hand and her old yellow apron slung around my neck. I'd be breathless in the sudden quiet, and, having ceased my mincing and chopping, would stare blankly at the brushed sheen of the blade. Eventually, she would clear her throat or call out to say she was fine, then begin to move again, starting her rhythmic *ka-jug*; and only then could I go on with my cooking, the world of our house turning once more, wheeling through the black.

I wasn't cooking for my mother but for the rest of us. When she first moved downstairs she was still eating, though scantily, more just to taste what we were having than from any genuine desire for food. The point was simply to sit together at the kitchen table and array ourselves like a family again. My mother would gently set herself down in her customary chair near the stove. I sat across from her, my father and sister to my left and right, and crammed in the center was all the food I had made—a spicy codfish stew, say, or a casserole of gingery beef, dishes that in my youth she had prepared for us a hundred times.

It had been ten years since we'd all lived together in the house, which at fifteen I had left to attend boarding school in New Hampshire. My mother would sometimes point this out, by speaking of our present time as being "just like before Exeter," which surprised me, given how proud she always was that I was a graduate of the school.

Published in the New Yorker (*October 16, 1995*), *an American magazine of literature and the arts, just after the appearance of Lee's award-winning novel,* Native Speaker (*1995*).

5   My going to such a place was part of my mother's not so secret plan to
change my character, which she worried was becoming too much like hers. I
was clever and able enough, but without outside pressure I was readily given
to sloth and vanity. The famous school—which none of us knew the first thing
about—would prove my mettle. She was right, of course, and while I was there
I would falter more than a few times, academically and otherwise. But I never
thought that my leaving home then would ever be a problem for her, a private
quarrel she would have even as her life waned.

       Now her house was full again. My sister had just resigned from her job in
New York City, and my father, who typically saw his psychiatric patients until
eight or nine in the evening, was appearing in the driveway at four-thirty. I had
been living at home for nearly a year and was in the final push of work on what
would prove a dismal failure of a novel. When I wasn't struggling over my
prose, I kept occupied with the things she usually did—the daily errands, the
grocery shopping, the vacuuming and the cleaning, and, of course, all the
cooking.

       When I was six or seven years old, I used to watch my mother as she pre-
pared our favorite meals. It was one of my daily pleasures. She shooed me
away in the beginning, telling me that the kitchen wasn't my place, and
adding, in her half-proud, half-deprecating way, that her kind of work would
only serve to weaken me. "Go out and play with your friends," she'd snap in
Korean, "or better yet, do your reading and homework." She knew that I had
already done both, and that as the evening approached there was no place to
go save her small and tidy kitchen, from which the clatter of her mixing bowls
and pans would ring through the house.

       I would enter the kitchen quietly and stand beside her, my chin lodging
upon the point of her hip. Peering through the crook of her arm, I beheld the
movements of her hands. For *kalbi*,[1] she would take up a butchered short rib
in her narrow hand, the flinty bone shaped like a section of an airplane wing
and deeply embedded in gristle and flesh, and with the point of her knife cut
so that the bone fell away, though not completely, leaving it connected to the
meat by the barest opaque layer of tendon. Then she methodically butterflied
the flesh, cutting and unfolding, repeating the action until the meat lay out on
her board, glistening and ready for seasoning. She scored it diagonally, then
sifted sugar into the crevices with her pinched fingers, gently rubbing in the
crystals. The sugar would tenderize as well as sweeten the meat. She did this
with each rib, and then set them all aside in a large shallow bowl. She minced
a half-dozen cloves of garlic, a stub of gingerroot, sliced up a few scallions,
and spread it all over the meat. She wiped her hands and took out a bottle of
sesame oil, and, after pausing for a moment, streamed the dark oil in two swift
circles around the bowl. After adding a few splashes of soy sauce, she thrust
her hands in and kneaded the flesh, careful not to dislodge the bones. I asked
her why it mattered that they remain connected. "The meat needs the bone
nearby," she said, "to borrow its richness." She wiped her hands clean of the

1. Korean-style beef ribs.

marinade, except for her little finger, which she would flick with her tongue from time to time, because she knew that the flavor of a good dish developed not at once but in stages.

Whenever I cook, I find myself working just as she would, readying the ingredients—a mash of garlic, a julienne of red peppers, fantails of shrimp—and piling them in little mounds about the cutting surface. My mother never left me any recipes, but this is how I learned to make her food, each dish coming not from a list or a card but from the aromatic spread of a board.

I've always thought it was particularly cruel that the cancer was in her stomach, and that for a long time at the end she couldn't eat. The last meal I made for her was on New Year's Eve, 1990. My sister suggested that instead of a rib roast or a bird, or the usual overflow of Korean food, we make all sorts of finger dishes that our mother might fancy and pick at.

10

We set the meal out on the glass coffee table in the family room. I prepared a tray of smoked-salmon canapés,[2] fried some Korean bean cakes, and made a few other dishes I thought she might enjoy. My sister supervised me, arranging the platters, and then with some pomp carried each dish in to our parents. Finally, I brought out a bottle of champagne in a bucket of ice. My mother had moved to the sofa and was sitting up, surveying the low table. "It looks pretty nice," she said. "I think I'm feeling hungry."

This made us all feel good, especially me, for I couldn't remember the last time she had felt any hunger or had eaten something I cooked. We began to eat. My mother picked up a piece of salmon toast and took a tiny corner in her mouth. She rolled it around for a moment and then pushed it out with the tip of her tongue, letting it fall back onto her plate. She swallowed hard, as if to quell a gag, then glanced up to see if we had noticed. Of course we all had. She attempted a bean cake, some cheese, and then a slice of fruit, but nothing was any use.

She nodded at me anyway, and said, "Oh, it's very good." But I was already feeling lost and I put down my plate abruptly, nearly shattering it on the thick glass. There was an ugly pause before my father asked me in a weary, gentle voice if anything was wrong, and I answered that it was nothing, it was the last night of a long year, and we were together, and I was simply relieved. At midnight, I poured out glasses of champagne, even one for my mother, who took a deep sip. Her manner grew playful and light, and I helped her shuffle to her mattress, and she lay down in the place where in a brief week she was dead.

My mother could whip up most anything, but during our first years of living in this country we ate only Korean foods. At my harangue-like behest, my mother set herself to learning how to cook exotic American dishes. Luckily, a kind neighbor, Mrs. Churchill, a tall, florid young woman with flaxen hair, taught my mother her most trusted recipes. Mrs. Churchill's two young sons, palish, weepy boys with identical crew cuts, always accompanied her, and though I liked them well enough, I would slip away from them after a few minutes, for

2. Appetizers, usually toast, crackers, or bread slices with toppings.

I knew that the real action would be in the kitchen, where their mother was playing guide. Mrs. Churchill hailed from the state of Maine, where the finest Swedish meatballs and tuna casserole and angel food cake in America are made. She readily demonstrated certain techniques—how to layer wet sheets of pasta for a lasagna or whisk up a simple roux,[3] for example. She often brought gift shoeboxes containing curious ingredients like dried oregano, instant yeast, and cream of mushroom soup. The two women, though at ease and jolly with each other, had difficulty communicating, and this was made worse by the often confusing terminology of Western cuisine ("corned beef," "deviled eggs"). Although I was just learning the language myself, I'd gladly play the interlocutor, jumping back and forth between their places at the counter, dipping my fingers into whatever sauce lay about.

15   I was an insistent child, and, being my mother's firstborn, much too prized. My mother could say no to me, and did often enough, but anyone who knew us—particularly my father and sister—could tell how much the denying pained her. And if I was overconscious of her indulgence even then, and suffered the rushing pangs of guilt that she could inflict upon me with the slightest wounded turn of her lip, I was too happily obtuse and venal to let her cease. She reminded me daily that I was her sole son, her reason for living, and that if she were to lose me, in either body or spirit, she wished that God would mercifully smite her, strike her down like a weak branch.

In the traditional fashion, she was the house accountant, the maid, the launderer, the disciplinarian, the driver, the secretary, and, of course, the cook. She was also my first basketball coach. In South Korea, where girls' high school basketball is a popular spectator sport, she had been a star, the point guard for the national high school team that once won the all-Asia championships. I learned this one Saturday during the summer, when I asked my father if he would go down to the schoolyard and shoot some baskets with me. I had just finished the fifth grade, and wanted desperately to make the middle school team the coming fall. He called for my mother and sister to come along. When we arrived, my sister immediately ran off to the swings, and I recall being annoyed that my mother wasn't following her. I dribbled clumsily around the key, on the verge of losing control of the ball, and flung a flat shot that caromed wildly off the rim. The ball bounced to my father, who took a few not so graceful dribbles and made an easy layup. He dribbled out and then drove to the hoop for a layup on the other side. He rebounded his shot and passed the ball to my mother, who had been watching us from the foul line. She turned from the basket and began heading the other way.

"Um-mah,"[4] I cried at her, my exasperation already bubbling over, "the basket's over *here!*"

After a few steps she turned around, and from where the professional three-point line must be now, she effortlessly flipped the ball up in a two-handed set shot, its flight truer and higher than I'd witnessed from any boy or

3. Thickening agent for sauces and soups.
4. Korean for "mommy."

man. The ball arced cleanly into the hoop, stiffly popping the chain-link net. All afternoon, she rained in shot after shot, as my father and I scrambled after her.

When we got home from the playground, my mother showed me the photograph album of her team's championship run. For years I kept it in my room, on the same shelf that housed the scrapbooks I made of basketball stars, with magazine clippings of slick players like Bubbles Hawkins and Pistol Pete and George (the Iceman) Gervin.

It puzzled me how much she considered her own history to be immaterial, 20
and if she never patently diminished herself, she was able to finesse a kind of self-removal by speaking of my father whenever she could. She zealously recounted his excellence as a student in medical school and reminded me, each night before I started my homework, of how hard he drove himself in his work to make a life for us. She said that because of his Asian face and imperfect English, he was "working two times the American doctors." I knew that she was building him up, buttressing him with both genuine admiration and her own brand of anxious braggadocio, and that her overarching concern was that I might fail to see him as she wished me to—in the most dawning light, his pose steadfast and solitary.

In the year before I left for Exeter, I became weary of her oft-repeated accounts of my father's success. I was a teenager, and so ever inclined to be dismissive and bitter toward anything that had to do with family and home. Often enough, my mother was the object of my derision. Suddenly, her life seemed so small to me. She was there, and sometimes, I thought, *always* there, as if she were confined to the four walls of our house. I would even complain about her cooking. Mostly, though, I was getting more and more impatient with the difficulty she encountered in doing everyday things. I was afraid for her. One day, we got into a terrible argument when she asked me to call the bank, to question a discrepancy she had discovered in the monthly statement. I asked her why she couldn't call herself. I was stupid and brutal, and I knew exactly how to wound her.

"Whom do I talk to?" she said. She would mostly speak to me in Korean, and I would answer in English.

"The bank manager, who else?"

"What do I say?"

"Whatever you want to say." 25

"Don't speak to me like that!" she cried.

"It's just that you should be able to do it yourself," I said.

"You know how I feel about this!"

"Well, maybe then you should consider it *practice*," I answered lightly, using the Korean word to make sure she understood.

Her face blanched, and her neck suddenly became rigid, as if I were throt- 30
tling her. She nearly struck me right then, but instead she bit her lip and ran upstairs. I followed her, pleading for forgiveness at her door. But it was the one time in our life that I couldn't convince her, melt her resolve with the blandishments of a spoiled son.

When my mother was feeling strong enough, or was in particularly good spir-its, she would roll her machine into the kitchen and sit at the table and watch me work. She wore pajamas day and night, mostly old pairs of mine.

She said, "I can't tell, what are you making?"

"*Mahn-doo*[5] filling."

"You didn't salt the cabbage and squash."

35   "Was I supposed to?"

"Of course. Look, it's too wet. Now the skins will get soggy before you can fry them."

"What should I do?"

"It's too late. Maybe it'll be OK if you work quickly. Why didn't you ask me?"

"You were finally sleeping."

40   "You should have woken me."

"No way."

She sighed, as deeply as her weary lungs would allow.

"I don't know how you were going to make it without me."

"I don't know, either. I'll remember the salt next time."

45   "You better. And not too much."

We often talked like this, our tone decidedly matter-of-fact, chin up, just this side of being able to bear it. Once, while inspecting a potato fritter batter I was making, she asked me if she had ever done anything that I wished she hadn't done. I thought for a moment, and told her no. In the next breath, she wondered aloud if it was right of her to have let me go to Exeter, to live away from the house while I was so young. She tested the batter's thickness with her finger and called for more flour. Then she asked if, given a choice, I would go to Exeter again.

I wasn't sure what she was getting at, and I told her that I couldn't be cer-tain, but probably yes, I would. She snorted at this and said it was my leaving home that had once so troubled our relationship. "Remember how I had so much difficulty talking to you? Remember?"

She believed back then that I had found her more and more ignorant each time I came home. She said she never blamed me, for this was the way she knew it would be with my wonderful new education. Nothing I could say seemed to quell the notion. But I knew that the problem wasn't simply the *edu-cation*; the first time I saw her again after starting school, barely six weeks later, when she and my father visited me on Parents Day, she had already grown nervous and distant. After the usual campus events, we had gone to the motel where they were staying in a nearby town and sat on the beds in our room. She seemed to sneak looks at me, as though I might discover a horrible new truth if our eyes should meet.

My own secret feeling was that I had missed my parents greatly, my mother especially, and much more than I had anticipated. I couldn't tell them

---

5. Korean dumplings, usually filled with cabbage and meat.

that these first weeks were a mere blur to me, that I felt completely over-whelmed by all the studies and my much brighter friends and the thousand ir-ritating details of living alone, and that I had really learned nothing, save perhaps how to put on a necktie while sprinting to class. I felt as if I had plunged too deep into the world, which, to my great horror, was much larger than I had ever imagined.

I welcomed the lull of the motel room. My father and I had nearly dozed off when my mother jumped up excitedly, murmured how stupid she was, and hurried to the closet by the door. She pulled out our old metal cooler and dragged it between the beds. She lifted the top and began unpacking plastic containers, and I thought she would never stop. One after the other they came out, each with a dish that traveled well—a salted stewed meat, rolls of Korean-style sushi. I opened a container of radish kimchi[6] and suddenly the room bloomed with its odor, and I reveled in the very peculiar sensation (which per-haps only true kimchi lovers know) of simultaneously drooling and gagging as I breathed it all in. For the next few minutes, they watched me eat. I'm not cer-tain that I was even hungry. But after weeks of pork parmigiana and chicken patties and wax beans, I suddenly realized that I had lost all the savor in my life. And it seemed I couldn't get enough of it back. I ate and I ate, so much and so fast that I actually went to the bathroom and vomited. I came out dizzy and sated with the phantom warmth of my binge.

And beneath the face of her worry, I thought, my mother was smiling.

From that day, my mother prepared a certain meal to welcome me home. It was always the same. Even as I rode the school's shuttle bus from Exeter to Lo-gan airport, I could already see the exact arrangement of my mother's table.

I knew that we would eat in the kitchen, the table brimming with plates. There was the *kalbi*, of course, broiled or grilled depending on the season. Leaf lettuce, to wrap the meat with. Bowls of garlicky clam broth with miso and tofu and fresh spinach. Shavings of cod dusted in flour and then dipped in egg wash and fried. Glass noodles with onions and shiitake. Scallion-and-hot-pepper pancakes. Chilled steamed shrimp. Seasoned salads of bean sprouts, spinach, and white radish. Crispy squares of seaweed. Steamed rice with bar-ley and red beans. Homemade kimchi. It was all there—the old flavors I knew, the beautiful salt, the sweet, the excellent taste.

After the meal, my father and I talked about school, but I could never say enough for it to make any sense. My father would often recall his high school principal, who had gone to England to study the methods and traditions of the public schools, and regaled students with stories of the great Eton man. My mother sat with us, paring fruit, not saying a word but taking everything in. When it was time to go to bed, my father said good night first. I usually watched television until the early morning. My mother would sit with me for an hour or two, perhaps until she was accustomed to me again, and only then would she kiss me and head upstairs to sleep.

During the following days, it was always the cooking that started our con-

6. Spicy Korean relish.

versations. She'd hold an inquest over the cold leftovers we ate at lunch, discussing each dish in terms of its balance of flavors or what might have been prepared differently. But mostly I begged her to leave the dishes alone. I wish I had paid more attention. After her death, when my father and I were the only ones left in the house, drifting through the rooms like ghosts, I sometimes tried to make that meal for him. Though it was too much for two, I made each dish anyway, taking as much care as I could. But nothing turned out quite right—not the color, not the smell. At the table, neither of us said much of anything. And we had to eat the food for days.

I remember washing rice in the kitchen one day and my mother's saying in English, from her usual seat, "I made a big mistake."

"About Exeter?"

"Yes. I made a big mistake. You should be with us for that time. I should never let you go there."

"So why did you?" I said.

"Because I didn't know I was going to die."

I let her words pass. For the first time in her life, she was letting herself speak her full mind, so what else could I do?

"But you know what?" she spoke up. "It was better for you. If you stayed home, you would not like me so much now."

I suggested that maybe I would like her even more.

She shook her head. "Impossible."

Sometimes I still think about what she said, about having made a mistake. I would have left home for college, that was never in doubt, but those years I was away at boarding school grew more precious to her as her illness progressed. After many months of exhaustion and pain and the haze of the drugs, I thought that her mind was beginning to fade, for more and more it seemed that she was seeing me again as her fifteen-year-old boy, the one she had dropped off in New Hampshire on a cloudy September afternoon.

I remember the first person I met, another new student, named Zack, who walked to the welcome picnic with me. I had planned to eat with my parents—my mother had brought a coolerful of food even that first day—but I learned of the cookout and told her that I should probably go. I wanted to go, of course. I was excited, and no doubt fearful and nervous, and I must have thought I was only thinking ahead. She agreed wholeheartedly, saying I certainly should. I walked them to the car, and perhaps I hugged them, before saying goodbye. One day, after she died, my father told me what happened on the long drive home to Syracuse.

He was driving the car, looking straight ahead. Traffic was light on the Massachusetts Turnpike, and the sky was nearly dark. They had driven for more than two hours and had not yet spoken a word. He then heard a strange sound from her, a kind of muffled chewing noise, as if something inside her were grinding its way out.

"So, what's the matter?" he said, trying to keep an edge to his voice.

She looked at him with her ashen face and she burst into tears. He began to cry himself, and pulled the car over onto the narrow shoulder of the turn-

pike, where they stayed for the next half hour or so, the blank-faced cars droning by them in the cold, onrushing night.

Every once in a while, when I think of her, I'm driving alone somewhere   70
on the highway. In the twilight, I see their car off to the side, a blue Olds
coupe with a landau top, and as I pass them by I look back in the mirror and I
see them again, the two figures huddling together in the front seat. Are they
sleeping? Or kissing? Are they all right?

QUESTIONS

1. Chang-Rae Lee begins his essay *in medias res*—in the middle of things. How does
his choice create drama, sympathy, and significance for the personal experience that he
narrates?

2. Because Lee begins his account at a late stage of his mother's illness, he often
flashes back to earlier points in their relationship. Mark the flashbacks in the text and
explain the purpose of each.

3. Details of food and cooking appear throughout the essay—for example, in paragraphs 8–9, 11–13, and 32–34. Besides giving us a flavor of Korean food, what function
do these details serve?

4. Lee titles his essay "Coming Home Again," whereas Joan Didion titles hers "On Going Home" (see the next essay in "Personal Report"). What different connotations do
"coming home" and "going home" suggest? How do these differences emerge in the personal accounts of each writer?

5. Write a personal essay about "coming home" or "going home."

JOAN DIDION   *On Going Home*

I
AM HOME for my daughter's first birthday. By
"home" I do not mean the house in Los Angeles
where my husband and I and the baby live, but the
place where my family is, in the Central Valley of
California. It is a vital although troublesome distinction. My husband likes my family but is uneasy in
their house, because once there I fall into their ways, which are difficult,
oblique, deliberately inarticulate, not my husband's ways. We live in dusty
houses ("D-U-S-T," he once wrote with his finger on surfaces all over the house,
but no one noticed it) filled with mementos quite without value to him (what
could the Canton dessert plates mean to him? how could he have known about

From Slouching towards Bethlehem *(1966), Didion's first volume of nonfiction, which includes both autobiographical essays and articles analyzing American culture of the 1960s.*

the assay scales, why should he care if he did know?), and we appear to talk exclusively about people we know who have been committed to mental hospitals, about people we know who have been booked on drunk-driving charges, and about property, particularly about property, land, price per acre and C-2 zoning and assessments and freeway access. My brother does not understand my husband's inability to perceive the advantage in the rather common real-estate transaction known as "sale-leaseback," and my husband in turn does not understand why so many of the people he hears about in my father's house have recently been committed to mental hospitals or booked on drunk-driving charges. Nor does he understand that when we talk about sale-leasebacks and right-of-way condemnations we are talking in code about the things we like best, the yellow fields and the cottonwoods and the rivers rising and falling and the mountain roads closing when the heavy snow comes in. We miss each other's points, have another drink and regard the fire. My brother refers to my husband, in his presence, as "Joan's husband." Marriage is the classic betrayal.

Or perhaps it is not any more. Sometimes I think that those of us who are now in our thirties were born into the last generation to carry the burden of "home," to find in family life the source of all tension and drama. I had by all objective accounts a "normal" and a "happy" family situation, and yet I was almost thirty years old before I could talk to my family on the telephone without crying after I had hung up. We did not fight. Nothing was wrong. And yet some nameless anxiety colored the emotional charges between me and the place that I came from. The question of whether or not you could go home again was a very real part of the sentimental and largely literary baggage with which we left home in the fifties; I suspect that it is irrelevant to the children born of the fragmentation after World War II. A few weeks ago in a San Francisco bar I saw a pretty young girl on crystal[1] take off her clothes and dance for the cash prize in an "amateur-topless" contest. There was no particular sense of moment about this, none of the effect of romantic degradation, of "dark journey," for which my generation strived so assiduously. What sense could that girl possibly make of, say, *Long Day's Journey into Night*?[2] Who is beside the point?

That I am trapped in this particular irrelevancy is never more apparent to me than when I am home. Paralyzed by the neurotic lassitude engendered by meeting one's past at every turn, around every corner, inside every cupboard, I go aimlessly from room to room. I decide to meet it head-on and clean out a drawer, and I spread the contents on the bed. A bathing suit I wore the summer I was seventeen. A letter of rejection from *The Nation,* an aerial photograph of the site for a shopping center my father did not build in 1954. Three teacups hand-painted with cabbage roses and signed "E.M.," my grandmother's initials. There is no final solution for letters of rejection from *The Nation* and teacups hand-painted in 1900. Nor is there any answer to snapshots of one's grandfather as a young man on skis, surveying around Donner Pass in the year 1910. I smooth out the snapshot and look into his face, and do and do not see my own.

1. A methamphetamine.
2. Tragedy by playwright Eugene O'Neill (1888–1952), based on the shame and deception that haunted his own family.

I close the drawer, and have another cup of coffee with my mother. We get along very well, veterans of a guerrilla war we never understood.

Days pass. I see no one. I come to dread my husband's evening call, not only because he is full of news of what by now seems to me our remote life in Los Angeles, people he has seen, letters which require attention, but because he asks what I have been doing, suggests uneasily that I get out, drive to San Francisco or Berkeley. Instead I drive across the river to a family graveyard. It has been vandalized since my last visit and the monuments are broken, over-turned in the dry grass. Because I once saw a rattlesnake in the grass I stay in the car and listen to a country-and-Western station. Later I drive with my fa-ther to a ranch he has in the foothills. The man who runs his cattle on it asks us to the roundup, a week from Sunday, and although I know that I will be in Los Angeles I say, in the oblique way my family talks, that I will come. Once home I mention the broken monuments in the graveyard. My mother shrugs.

I go to visit my great-aunts. A few of them think now that I am my cousin, or their daughter who died young. We recall an anecdote about a relative last seen in 1948, and they ask if I still like living in New York City. I have lived in Los Angeles for three years, but I say that I do. The baby is offered a hore-hound drop, and I am slipped a dollar bill "to buy a treat." Questions trail off, answers are abandoned, the baby plays with the dust motes in a shaft of after-noon sun.   5

It is time for the baby's birthday party: a white cake, strawberry-marsh-mallow ice cream, a bottle of champagne saved from another party. In the evening, after she has gone to sleep, I kneel beside the crib and touch her face, where it is pressed against the slats, with mine. She is an open and trust-ing child, unprepared for and unaccustomed to the ambushes of family life, and perhaps it is just as well that I can offer her little of that life. I would like to give her more. I would like to promise her that she will grow up with a sense of her cousins and of rivers and of her great-grandmother's teacups, would like to pledge her a picnic on a river with fried chicken and her hair uncombed, would like to give her *home* for her birthday, but we live differently now and I can promise her nothing like that. I give her a xylophone and a sundress from Madeira, and promise to tell her a funny story.

QUESTIONS

1. Didion speaks of herself at home as "paralyzed by the neurotic lassitude engendered by meeting one's past at every turn" (paragraph 3). What about the essay helps explain these feelings?

2. What does Didion mean by "the ambushes of family life" (paragraph 6)? (Besides "ambushes" note Didion's other highly charged language: e.g., "betrayal" in paragraph 1 and "guerrilla war" in paragraph 3.)

3. In paragraph 6 Didion says she would like to give her daughter "*home* for her birth-day, but we live differently now." In an essay, explain whether or not you think parents today can give their children "home." Include examples.

ANDREA BARRETT   *A Hole in the Wall*

J ULY AND AUGUST. After living in the same house for fifteen years, my husband and I moved from Rochester—upstate New York, a small city surrounded by farms—to Brooklyn. Our plan was to live for a year in the city, during which Barry would take a leave from his university teaching job, concentrating instead on his photography, and I'd hold a fellowship at the New York Public Library. Although Barry was excited and optimistic, I was mostly nervous: I'd written all my books in the same little room and feared my work might not weather the transplant.

Hopefully, foolishly, we'd signed a lease in May for a space behind a big hole in the wall of an industrial building in Williamsburg. Windows had filled the hole by the time we arrived on a hot July day; a floor had been laid, wallboard was up, appliances stood in the kitchen. But the appliances weren't connected, and neither was the gas; there was no hot water and no way to cook; no screens, no key for the door, no way to get mail; no phone lines or radiators or shelves or closet poles; no lights in the bathroom nor stair rails nor a thousand other things. An apologetic trickle of electricity flowed through an orange extension cord strung from a neighboring building: not enough to power an air-conditioner. Each time we entered or left we picked our way over rubble, unlocked a padlock, unwrapped a heavy chain binding the wire fence that caged us off from the street. At the stroke of eight each morning the polyglot crew arrived and began working loudly everywhere at once. We showered at the public pool and ate in the local bars, moaning and groaning all the while. At first it was funny, and then it wasn't.

Later it was funny again. Our first four weeks in Brooklyn were preposterous, ridiculous, a cosmic joke. In the muddy back courtyard three piglets appeared, wallowing and oinking and gaining weight until the night they were carried away, each one shrieking, to become someone's festival meal. By the end of that month—after the pigs and after the heat wave, which I spent largely immersed in a tub of cold water; after the bouts with no electricity at all and the weeks of jack-hammering; after the arrival of the giant spinning truck that submerged the pigs' former home (a garden-in-the-making, we'd believed) beneath a sea of red concrete—we were dining out on our disaster stories, our first-month-in-the-city tales. We joked that we'd moved to a third-world country: it was like Bosnia, like Beirut. What did we know? New York is a pit, I said cheerfully. I could say that because it wasn't true, because I had no idea what I was saying, because the worst was over.

• •

Published in The American Scholar *(Autumn 2002), a general-interest magazine published by the Phi Beta Kappa Society.*

By the end of August we had a home: we could shower, hang up our clothes, cook dinner, phone our friends. Most of the workmen were gone most of the time. I was starting to notice that, although our neighborhood was untidy and loud, I was interested in everything around me. My neighbors were people new to me, who'd come here from much farther than Rochester. Some were Polish immigrants, most of them elderly; they moved, talking under their breath, through a sea of recent young colonizers: artists, photographers, writers, and filmmakers. Construction sites all over the neighborhood brought in crews of workmen—Russian, Ecuadoran, Mexican, and Polish—until five or six languages rose from the morning streets. Our dog, an ill-bred, ill-behaved, somewhat scruffy pound-mutt disliked in Rochester, where the owners of poodles and borzois and Yorkshire terriers would cross the park to avoid her, here found herself a model of daintiness among a pack of pit bulls, Dobermans, Rottweilers, Great Danes, and peculiar crosses.

The subway, I discovered, would take me safely anywhere, at almost any hour: what freedom! And there was music, too—on the L train platform, and also at the Union Square station I passed through each day, someone was always playing: bass and saxophone, solo accordion, a pair of percussionists, one on trap set and the other on white plastic buckets and big glass bottles. Both underground and above I was surrounded by faces: so much emotion, so much expression, so many different countenances registering so many different things. In Rochester everything had been hidden. Here much was played out in public, before my eyes—and to my surprise, I liked this. There might be, I was learning to think (during those ten or eleven days of real life, during what felt like a kind of flowering) some reason to put up with the expense and inconvenience of living here. 5

Tuesday. What kind of a city was this, where a plane—no, two planes—could crash into a building? I think I thought that: truly, everything that happened that day is muddled. I saw the second one hit, while I was walking home from the dogsitter's. The pilot had fallen asleep, the air-traffic system was down, someone had made an awful and clumsy mistake and something I couldn't imagine had happened: a hijacking never crossed my mind, I was to naïve to think that thought. But in a city where it sometimes seemed that nothing worked—in Brooklyn, I had told my family, everything is broken—a mistake of even this magnitude seemed possible.

It was my upstairs neighbor, leaning out the window and shouting down to me—I must have run to our building—who first used the word "they": some "they" had attacked the second tower. But who were "they"? Nothing he said made sense. My husband, now framed in our front window, looked similarly puzzled; I ran upstairs and we turned on the TV. Somewhere during those minutes we also first heard the words *terrorist* and *hijacking*. We looked out the window again. Then at the TV. Then we ran up to the roof.

In our part of Williamsburg, the East River is only a block and a half away and the buildings are low, a mixture of warehouses, three-and four-story tenements, and industrial buildings. Nothing impedes the view of the jagged wall of stone and metal across the river, so near it seems one can touch it. The other tenants—two young Brits, a photographer and a filmmaker; a ballet dancer from Mexico and her musician boyfriend; the older French photographer who'd called down to me—were already up on the roof, staring at what had always dominated the sky. Smoke rose from the towers; flames began to shoot from the sides; by then we were crying. The builder and a friend appeared, also some neighbors from next door, while the Brits, who had cell phones, called their families in London to say they were alive. All over the world, I realized, this must be on TV; in Florida, my mother would be terrified. I ran downstairs to call her.

When I returned, what I saw was impossible. Someone tried to explain it to me—the south tower had collapsed while I was gone—but I couldn't hear it; I turned again and again to the sight and each time covered my eyes and turned away. Where had the tower gone? Soon the builder said, in a low sad voice, "Shit. There goes the other one," and when I opened my eyes I saw the second tower unmaking itself, the sides curling away from the middle like skin peeling off a banana, the smoke spewing upward until everything was gone.

• •

10   Why talk about the rest of that morning, the rest of that day? All of us were glued alternately to the desecrated skyline and the television, watching the same images again and again, each minute more deeply aware of the people who'd been inside those towers and what had happened to them. The trains closed down, the city closed down. No one knew what to do or say. At two that afternoon the L train opened; Barry took his camera and went into Manhattan, working his way farther and farther downtown—so far that he was uncomfortably close to building #7 when it came down. When he returned that evening to fetch more film, he convinced me to go back in with him. I should see this, he said: the way so much of daily life was still being lived; the tremendous social momentum that keeps us moving through the forms of life even after the heart has stopped. I would, he said, find the people and the sight of what still stood consoling. While I didn't believe that, I knew that if I didn't go into Manhattan soon, I would never go there again. I'd put the dog and cat in the car and start driving and never stop—as if I could drive away from this, or that it would matter, now, where I lived.

• •

Below Houston, then below Canal: closed streets, tired cops, an endless line of trucks and bulldozers and cranes and flatbed trailers mounded with lights and generators, machines whose names I don't know parked end to end with their engines running and their headlights on, a procession that stretched for miles and seemed to pulse with longing to get going, to do something, to move toward their grim tasks, prevented from that by the fires burning at what was already being termed Ground Zero. But also, among the tired firemen trudging toward the nearest open subway station, at West Fourth, between the young police cadets and the Port Authority workers and the volunteer nurses and EMTs, we saw people walking dogs, pushing babies in strollers, sitting in bars and talking earnestly over supper and drinks. People on bikes. People holding hands. People unable not to do what they had always done, in the neighborhoods where they made their homes; people moving about, people living.

Where North Moore intersects with West Street, volunteers had gathered. Meaning to see what we could do, we joined the crowd. Cots and stretchers filled a courtyard rimmed with face masks, bottled water, food, all sorts of supplies. No one walked or crawled or was carried from the rubble and there was nothing for the rest of us to do. We could see the fire burning, still. The smoke was lashing through the crowd, the trucks still waited helplessly. So did we.

Wednesday, Thursday, Friday. We watch the TV, we read the papers, we watch the TV, we read the papers. We talk to people on the streets and in bars and cafés. At dusk we stand on abandoned lots at the riverside along with everyone else. We used to walk the dog here at night, in the silent but pleasant company of others who, like us, had picked their way through the broken grass and the holes in the fence, around the garbage and over the rocks, to get a taste of the breeze blowing up the river and a sight of the city, so close. Now there are hundreds of people here, faces glimpsed before at windows or on the subway platform or in the park. In silent ranks we watch the sun set over the smoking hole. The first night the cloud of smoke blew east, over Brooklyn Heights, and we could hardly smell it. But the wind has shifted since then, and, as the sun sets, the smoke drapes Manhattan like a scarf and slides across the water into our nostrils.

It rains on Thursday night, after bolts of lightning first strike so close by that sparks fly and our next-door neighbor's television and amplifier are fried: a steady, unrelenting rain pushed toward us by a strong wind blowing up the river. Before I think to close the front windows (which face the bridge, and used to face the towers), the rain pours through the screens, all over the sill and down the wall to the floor. I wipe up what I can. The next morning I head for the sill with a rag, having learned during my first city rainstorm that each drop coming through the screens leaves behind a dot of the filth it has carried from the air. Now the entire sill is dark gray, six linear feet of grime. What I dab comes up like ash and as I back away, the rag still in my hand, I realize that's what it is: ash of buildings, ash of planes. Ash of people.

Everything in the apartment is gritty, I now see. Table, floor, pillows and sheets; after that I can't stand to touch anything, and I can't sleep. Neither can Barry, who has processed his photos and is now obsessively editing them. He can't stop looking, and neither can I. We ought to stop looking, we ought to stop thinking like this, we ought to get in the car and go someplace, anyplace; we ought to do something to take care of everyone hurt, but we can't. We try to give blood and we can't do that either: for the moment every place is full. On the TV, banners run across the screen saying no more volunteers are needed, please don't come to these places to help, stop stop stop.

15

• •

The dog paces nervously, trying to understand why we're acting so strangely. If a dog can think, we think she thinks this: Why can't I run at the river now; who are all these people? Why do they have candles in their hands? The smells in the wind make her nervous, too, along with our frantic comings and goings and the way that we're perpetually staring at glowing screens. The TV (we still can't stop watching). The screen at which Barry edits the digital versions of his photographs (he can't stop that either). The computers on which we try to retrieve and answer scores of e-mail messages, everyone either of us has ever known asking: Are you all right? Are you all right?

We are, we write back. Knowing we aren't, exactly; and also that we've been extraordinarily lucky. We write and write and write and write, and the more we say the worse we feel until finally we decide we shouldn't say anything at all.

• •

What, then, are we supposed to say to all those people who ask, "Don't you want to go back to Rochester? Are you going back? You must want to go back." I *did* think of going, sometime after the first minutes, during the first hour; I was stopped not by courage or a sense of shared community but by the physical impossibility of leaving. The dog, the cat, two people, the car; I imagined us crammed with all the rest of Brooklyn onto the BQE,[1] that narrow, broken-down, torn-up excuse for a highway. A sea of vehicles trying, like red blood corpuscles in a wounded capillary, to squeeze their way through the construction bottlenecks and across the bridges to the thruway: who was I kidding? No one was getting out of here, I thought despairingly on that first day; if something else was going to happen, then it would just have to happen.

Now the roads are working again, some of them, some of the time. But now leaving seems impossible for other reasons, which I can feel but can't articulate, even to myself.

• •

20   On Thursday, when I go into my office nervously—the library remains open, like the museums; much is made of getting back to "normal life," of "not giving in to them" (whoever they are)—we all try to pretend we're working. No one is very convincing; less so after someone notices that people are stampeding down 42nd Street, in front of our windows, and that the street is now closed off. Uneasy minutes pass, during which we hear too many sirens and see too many police cars and too many running people, before learning that Grand Central and the Condé Nast building have been evacuated because of bomb threats.

President Bush is scheduled to visit Ground Zero on Friday. Traffic will be blocked, the trains will stop, security will be crazy everywhere: is going in

---

1. Brooklyn–Queens Expressway.

worth it? I ponder staying home, feel like a coward, and solve the problem by waking Friday morning with an enormous migraine that I blame, in my bleary and delirious state, on the ash we are breathing: what is on my sills is also in my sinuses. Whatever the cause, I am sick. Certainly it's not my fault, then, that I don't go into Manhattan?

That evening, when I can see enough to walk, I return to the edge of the river with Barry, the dog, and a great many neighbors: the now-usual gathering, we stand and stare at the hole. Tonight we're joined by military transport helicopters flying low overhead, scanning us with their headlamps, and by fighter jets—four of them: F-16s, someone tells me—zooming back and forth in pairs, looping around the island. Since Tuesday the sky has been silent and empty, except for other ominous jets with their distinctive sound. These four extend their ellipses across the river and over us. Each time they pass us, I start to cry. Barry reminds me gently that they must be patrolling because of the president's visit; that they're American jets and won't attack us; that a war hasn't started, that *the* war hasn't started. A friend tells me I should welcome the sound: it means we are being protected.

Saturday. For twenty-four hours, what seems most relevant to me are the New York City newspapers from July 30 and 31, 1916, reporting the last huge explosion in New York: the munitions storage site at Black Tom Island, near Jersey City and the Statue of Liberty. For months I'd been meaning to look at these papers, as research for a novel I hoped to write. Now the stories seem to have an entirely different, and urgent, point. All day I hide in the library, reading microfilm, obsessed with this and determined to share it with others. How analogous, I think. German sabotage was blamed; a wave of anti-German hate crimes followed; the United States was not yet in the war, but this would be one of the factors swaying public opinion toward participation. I print out sheaves of pages.

Later, this will seem crazy. Reading through those fuzzy copies, I'll notice that although thousands of people were shaken up, windows were broken not only in Jersey City but all across lower Manhattan and Brooklyn, businesses were damaged and warehouses burned, and two hundred people were initially reported dead, only a few people really died. Property damage, not mass slaughter. The pages are meaningless.

Sunday, Monday. The jets continue, the helicopters continue; these start to seem almost normal. Months ago I accepted an invitation to visit a school a few hours north of the city and talk to the students about reading and writing. As the school has decided to go on with the planned event (miraculously, not a single student has lost a relative, and everyone is eager, the headmaster says, to "return to normal"), I gingerly board a train on Sunday afternoon. A few seats down from me, a firefighter who's clearly been working for days—his face is drawn, his clothes are filthy, his hat is covered with ash, or worse—falls asleep before we leave the station. Across from him a man in his fifties thumbs through a news magazine, a special edition devoted entirely to September 11. When I look at him next he is weeping silently as he stares at whatever photo

25

occupies the last page. Meanwhile the woman next to me, who clutches a bag labeled "Baby Gap," keeps looking over my shoulder. (Of course I'm still reading about the events, and staring at the photographs: why can't I stop this?) When I offer her part of my paper she accepts and then confides that she can't stop this either, indeed has been reading my pages surreptitiously. Russian-born, a recent immigrant, she lives in the suburbs and has a baby who, when the planes came, was staying with her father near Coney Island. Everyone is all right—but oh, she says. How terrified I was!

As we talk, the landscape beyond the window changes. Trees, lush green grass. Flowers, hedges, marshes, birds—it looks like paradise. White houses. How starved I have been, I realize, for a glimpse of nature. For a few moments I am madly homesick.

And yet—although I stay in a guest room in a lovely house; although I walk across glistening fields that smell like hay, and gaze at old and beautiful trees; although the school's faculty members are immensely kind and the students are smart and attentive, as Monday passes I feel steadily odder, more disoriented, more unhappy. People here have seen the events on TV, rather than with their own eyes. They haven't smelled them or touched them or felt them. It's not their fault, they're not hard-hearted, they don't suffer from a failure of the imagination—it's simply that they are removed, and that their lives (of course!) are going on.

Don't I want them to go on? Don't I want the students studying, and necking in the corners, and worrying about their boy- and girlfriends, and if they have the right clothes and how volleyball practice will go and what will happen at the dance?

I do, and I also don't. I want to shriek at them and am horrified at my desire to shriek at them. I understand how unfair I am being. But all I can think about, by the end of the day, is how much I want to go home.

• •

30   By "home," I mean Brooklyn.

• •

I can't sleep, I can't work, I can't think. I can't afford to live here, nor can I do without the life and friends I left behind in Rochester. And so how, exactly, have I come to think of this place as home? When I walk the block and a half to the river now I see, instead of the giant towers that once filled the skyline, a hole that continues to smoke. Everything that fell into that hole, and everyone still living their lives around it, is what keeps me here and makes me feel that I can't bear to leave.

Later. If this were fiction, I would have stopped with the line above, on that note of muted adaptation. But the truth is this: the second week is harder than the first, and the third seems harder still. One night the first thing Barry tells me when I arrive home is that our car has been broken into and the CD player stolen. Without thinking, I ask, "Did they smash the windows?"

"No," he says.

"Then how did they get in?"

"I don't know. The doors are all locked, I checked."   35

We stare at each other, puzzled, until I remember that we have never *had* a CD player. When I point this out to Barry, he says, "But there's a big empty hole in the dash."

"That's always been there," I say carefully.

A long, silent minute later, he says, "I don't know. It just seemed like something was missing."

• •

We are, all of us, daily more exhausted and more distressed, battered not just by the constant grief and the new difficulties of daily life, but by the stories spreading through the city like a virus. In another context we might dismiss these as urban legends. Now there's no way of knowing whether they're true or false, unbearable fact or manifestation of what we most dread. They spread at the river shore, at the dog park, at dinner parties and hospitals, delineating the circles of damage and trauma: the friend who finds out, after days of ignorance, that an acquaintance was on one of the fatal planes. The young relative whose first day in New York includes a meeting with a friend who retrieved his car from Battery Park City and found the windshield spattered with blood and parts. The fellow dog owner whose journalist friend, walking through rubble near Ground Zero, saw a gun and holster on the ground and—thoughtfully, kindly, wanting no one else to be damaged—bent to pick it up and so, inadvertently, held for a second the fragment of torso it still enclosed. The medical students who, another acquaintance says, have volunteered at the morgue to help sort through and label the heaps of remains and whose lives are being reshaped by this experience.

Everyone has a story, or knows a story; they spread like shards of shrapnel,   40 hacking parts off the people who hear them. Yet we can't, despite that, keep from repeating them; only repetition seems to make the wounds bearable. At a lunch delayed, and then finally held, all any of us can talk about are the events of the past weeks. Where we were when it happened and what we first knew; who knows the person to whom this or that happened; who lived, who died, who saw what unspeakable thing: the stories, the stories, the stories. On the table, which is in a lovely room filled with congenial people, in a nice restaurant on a pretty day, a long wooden tray filled with rows of green apples sits glowing, demanding to be recognized as beautiful and worthy. All of us look at it, all of us are for a moment consoled and refreshed. A minute later, all of us are bent close to each other again, urgently telling more stories. This is home now, I realize once more. This is where I live. This is not going to get easier.

QUESTIONS

1. Barrett ends her essay with "This is not going to get easier." Do you think that in the years that have passed things might have become "easier" for her? Could writing this piece have been part of the process of making things "easier"?

2. What do you think transformed Barrett into a New Yorker? Can you point to specific details in her essay?

3. Write about how you react when Barrett speaks of her neighborhood's having become international and multicultural (paragraph 4). Is it anything like neighborhoods you have lived in or know? Can you imagine yourself living in such a neighborhood? What might attract you or repel you about such a neighborhood?

4. What is there about humans who insist on transforming their experience into stories, as Barrett emphasizes in her concluding paragraph? Do you find yourself similarly telling stories?

LARS EIGHNER   *On Dumpster Diving*

Long before I began Dumpster diving I was impressed with Dumpsters, enough so that I wrote the Merriam-Webster[1] research service to discover what I could about the word *Dumpster*. I learned from them that it is a proprietary word belonging to the Dempster Dumpster company. Since then I have dutifully capitalized the word, although it was lowercased in almost all the citations Merriam-Webster photocopied for me. Dempster's word is too apt. I have never heard these things called anything but Dumpsters. I do not know anyone who knows the generic name for these objects. From time to time I have heard a wino or hobo give some corrupted credit to the original and call them Dipsy Dumpsters.

I began Dumpster diving about a year before I became homeless.

I prefer the word *scavenging* and use the word *scrounging* when I mean to be obscure. I have heard people, evidently meaning to be polite, use the word *foraging*, but I prefer to reserve that word for gathering nuts and berries and such, which I do also according to the season and the opportunity. *Dumpster diving* seems to me to be a little too cute and, in my case, inaccurate because I lack the athletic ability to lower myself into the Dumpsters as the true divers do, much to their increased profit.

I like the frankness of the word *scavenging*, which I can hardly think of without picturing a big black snail on an aquarium wall. I live from the refuse of others. I am a scavenger. I think it a sound and honorable niche, although

From Travels with Lizbeth *(1993), an account of Eighner's life as a homeless person.*

1. A large publisher of dictionaries.

if I could I would naturally prefer to live the comfortable consumer life, perhaps—and only perhaps—as a slightly less wasteful consumer, owing to what I
have learned as a scavenger.

While Lizbeth[2] and I were still living in the shack on Avenue B as my sav-   5
ings ran out, I put almost all my sporadic income into rent. The necessities of
daily life I began to extract from Dumpsters. Yes, we ate from them. Except for
jeans, all my clothes came from Dumpsters. Boom boxes, candles, bedding,
toilet paper, a virgin male love doll, medicine, books, a typewriter, dishes, furnishings, and change, sometimes amounting to many dollars—I acquired
many things from the Dumpsters.

I have learned much as a scavenger. I mean to put some of what I have
learned down here, beginning with the practical art of Dumpster diving and
proceeding to the abstract.

What is safe to eat?
After all, the finding of objects is becoming something of an urban art.
Even respectable employed people will sometimes find something tempting
sticking out of a Dumpster or standing beside one. Quite a number of people,
not all of them of the bohemian type, are willing to brag that they found this or
that piece in the trash. But eating from Dumpsters is what separates the dilet-
tanti from the professionals. Eating safely from the Dumpsters involves three
principles: using the senses and common sense to evaluate the condition of the
found materials, knowing the Dumpsters of a given area and checking them
regularly, and seeking always to answer the question, "Why was this discarded?"

Perhaps everyone who has a kitchen and a regular supply of groceries has,
at one time or another, made a sandwich and eaten half of it before discovering mold on the bread or got a mouthful of milk before realizing the milk had
turned. Nothing of the sort is likely to happen to a Dumpster diver because he
is constantly reminded that most food is discarded for a reason. Yet a lot of
perfectly good food can be found in Dumpsters.

Canned goods, for example, turn up fairly often in the Dumpsters I fre-   10
quent. All except the most phobic people would be willing to eat from a can,
even if it came from a Dumpster. Canned goods are among the safest of foods
to be found in Dumpsters but are not utterly foolproof.

Although very rare with modern canning methods, botulism is a possibility. Most other forms of food poisoning seldom do lasting harm to a healthy
person, but botulism is almost certainly fatal and often the first symptom is
death. Except for carbonated beverages, all canned goods should contain a
slight vacuum and suck air when first punctured. Bulging, rusty, and dented
cans and cans that spew when punctured should be avoided, especially when
the contents are not very acidic or syrupy.

Heat can break down the botulin, but this requires much more cooking
than most people do to canned goods. To the extent that botulism occurs at
all, of course, it can occur in cans on pantry shelves as well as in cans from

2. The author's dog.

Dumpsters. Need I say that home-canned goods are simply too risky to be recommended.

From time to time one of my companions, aware of the source of my provisions, will ask, "Do you think these crackers are really safe to eat?" For some reason it is most often the crackers they ask about.

This question has always made me angry. Of course I would not offer my companion anything I had doubts about. But more than that, I wonder why he cannot evaluate the condition of the crackers for himself. I have no special knowledge and I have been wrong before. Since he knows where the food comes from, it seems to me he ought to assume some of the responsibility for deciding what he will put in his mouth. For myself I have few qualms about dry foods such as crackers, cookies, cereal, chips, and pasta if they are free of visible contaminates and still dry and crisp. Most often such things are found in the original packaging, which is not so much a positive sign as it is the absence of a negative one.

15   Raw fruits and vegetables with intact skins seem perfectly safe to me, excluding of course the obviously rotten. Many are discarded for minor imperfections that can be pared away. Leafy vegetables, grapes, cauliflower, broccoli, and similar things may be contaminated by liquids and may be impractical to wash.

Candy, especially hard candy, is usually safe if it has not drawn ants. Chocolate is often discarded only because it has become discolored as the cocoa butter de-emulsified. Candying, after all, is one method of food preservation because pathogens do not like very sugary substances.

All of these foods might be found in any Dumpster and can be evaluated with some confidence largely on the basis of appearance. Beyond these are foods that cannot be correctly evaluated without additional information.

I began scavenging by pulling pizzas out of the Dumpster behind a pizza delivery shop. In general, prepared food requires caution, but in this case I knew when the shop closed and went to the Dumpster as soon as the last of the help left.

Such shops often get prank orders; both the orders and the products made to fill them are called *bogus*. Because help seldom stays long at these places, pizzas are often made with the wrong topping, refused on delivery for being cold, or baked incorrectly. The products to be discarded are boxed up because inventory is kept by counting boxes: A boxed pizza can be written off; an unboxed pizza does not exist.

20   I never placed a bogus order to increase the supply of pizzas and I believe no one else was scavenging in this Dumpster. But the people in the shop became suspicious and began to retain their garbage in the shop overnight. While it lasted I had a steady supply of fresh, sometimes warm pizza. Because I knew the Dumpster I knew the source of the pizza, and because I visited the Dumpster regularly I knew what was fresh and what was yesterday's.

The area I frequent is inhabited by many affluent college students. I am not here by chance; the Dumpsters in this area are very rich. Students throw out many good things, including food. In particular they tend to throw everything out when they move at the end of a semester, before and after breaks, and around midterm, when many of them despair of college. So I find it advantageous to keep an eye on the academic calendar.

Students throw food away around breaks because they do not know whether it has spoiled or will spoil before they return. A typical discard is a half jar of peanut butter. In fact, nonorganic peanut butter does not require refrigeration and is unlikely to spoil in any reasonable time. The student does not know that, and since it is Daddy's money, the student decides not to take a chance. Opened containers require caution and some attention to the question, "Why was this discarded?" But in the case of discards from student apartments, the answer may be that the item was thrown out through carelessness, ignorance, or wastefulness. This can sometimes be deduced when the item is found with many others, including some that are obviously perfectly good.

Some students, and others, approach defrosting a freezer by chucking out the whole lot. Not only do the circumstances of such a find tell the story, but also the mass of frozen goods stays cold for a long time and items may be found still frozen or freshly thawed.

Yogurt, cheese, and sour cream are items that are often thrown out while they are still good. Occasionally I find a cheese with a spot of mold, which of course I just pare off, and because it is obvious why such a cheese was discarded, I treat it with less suspicion than an apparently perfect cheese found in similar circumstances. Yogurt is often discarded, still sealed, only because the expiration date on the carton had passed. This is one of my favorite finds because yogurt will keep for several days, even in warm weather.

Students throw out canned goods and staples at the end of semesters and when they give up college at midterm. Drugs, pornography, spirits, and the like are often discarded when parents are expected—Dad's Day, for example. And spirits also turn up after big party weekends, presumably discarded by the newly reformed. Wine and spirits, of course, keep perfectly well even once opened, but the same cannot be said of beer.

My test for carbonated soft drinks is whether they still fizz vigorously. Many juices or other beverages are too acidic or too syrupy to cause much concern, provided they are not visibly contaminated. I have discovered nasty molds in vegetable juices, even when the product was found under its original seal; I recommend that such products be decanted slowly into a clear glass. Liquids always require some care. One hot day I found a large jug of Pat O'Brien's Hurricane mix. The jug had been opened but was still ice cold. I drank three large glasses before it became apparent to me that someone had added the rum to the mix, and not a little rum. I never tasted the rum, and by the time I began to feel the effects I had already ingested a very large quantity of the beverage. Some divers would have considered this a boon, but being suddenly intoxicated in a public place in the early afternoon is not my idea of a good time.

I have heard of people maliciously contaminating discarded food and even handouts, but mostly I have heard of this from people with vivid imaginations who have had no experience with the Dumpsters themselves. Just before the

25

pizza shop stopped discarding its garbage at night, jalapeños began showing up on most of the thrown-out pizzas. If indeed this was meant to discourage me, it was a wasted effort because I am a native Texan.

For myself, I avoid game, poultry, pork, and egg-based foods, whether I find them raw or cooked. I seldom have the means to cook what I find, but when I do I avail myself of plentiful supplies of beef, which is often in very good condition. I suppose fish becomes disagreeable before it becomes dangerous. Lizbeth is happy to have any such thing that is past its prime and, in fact, does not recognize fish as food until it is quite strong.

Home leftovers, as opposed to surpluses from restaurants, are very often bad. Evidently, especially among students, there is a common type of personality that carefully wraps up even the smallest leftover and shoves it into the back of the refrigerator for six months or so before discarding it. Characteristic of this type are the reused jars and margarine tubs to which the remains are committed. I avoid ethnic foods I am unfamiliar with. If I do not know what it is supposed to look like when it is good, I cannot be certain I will be able to tell if it is bad.

30   No matter how careful I am I still get dysentery at least once a month, oftener in warm weather. I do not want to paint too romantic a picture. Dumpster diving has serious drawbacks as a way of life.

I learned to scavenge gradually, on my own. Since then I have initiated several companions into the trade. I have learned that there is a predictable series of stages a person goes through in learning to scavenge.

At first the new scavenger is filled with disgust and self-loathing. He is ashamed of being seen and may lurk around, trying to duck behind things, or he may try to dive at night. (In fact, most people instinctively look away from a scavenger. By skulking around, the novice calls attention to himself and arouses suspicion. Diving at night is ineffective and needlessly messy.)

Every grain of rice seems to be a maggot. Everything seems to stink. He can wipe the egg yolk off the found can, but he cannot erase from his mind the stigma of eating garbage.

That stage passes with experience. The scavenger finds a pair of running shoes that fit and look and smell brand-new. He finds a pocket calculator in perfect working order. He finds pristine ice cream, still frozen, more than he can eat or keep. He begins to understand: People throw away perfectly good stuff, a lot of perfectly good stuff.

35   At this stage, Dumpster shyness begins to dissipate. The diver, after all, has the last laugh. He is finding all manner of good things that are his for the taking. Those who disparage his profession are the fools, not he.

He may begin to hang on to some perfectly good things for which he has neither a use nor a market. Then he begins to take note of the things that are not perfectly good but are nearly so. He mates a Walkman with broken earphones and one that is missing a battery cover. He picks up things that he can repair.

At this stage he may become lost and never recover. Dumpsters are full of things of some potential value to someone and also of things that never have much intrinsic value but are interesting. All the Dumpster divers I have known come to the point of trying to acquire everything they touch. Why not take it, they reason, since it is all free? This is, of course, hopeless. Most divers come to realize that they must restrict themselves to items of relatively immediate utility. But in some cases the diver simply cannot control himself. I have met several of these pack-rat types. Their ideas of the values of various pieces of junk verge on the psychotic. Every bit of glass may be a diamond, they think, and all that glisters, gold.

I tend to gain weight when I am scavenging. Partly this is because I always find far more pizza and doughnuts than water-packed tuna, nonfat yogurt, and fresh vegetables. Also I have not developed much faith in the reliability of Dumpsters as a food source, although it has been proven to me many times. I tend to eat as if I have no idea where my next meal is coming from. But mostly I just hate to see food go to waste and so I eat much more than I should. Something like this drives the obsession to collect junk.

As for collecting objects, I usually restrict myself to collecting one kind of small object at a time, such as pocket calculators, sunglasses, or campaign buttons. To live on the street I must anticipate my needs to a certain extent: I must pick up and save warm bedding I find in August because it will not be found in Dumpsters in November. As I have no access to health care, I often hoard essential drugs, such as antibiotics and antihistamines. (This course can be recommended only to those with some grounding in pharmacology. Antibiotics, for example, even when indicated are worse than useless if taken in insufficient amounts.) But even if I had a home with extensive storage space, I could not save everything that might be valuable in some contingency.

I have proprietary feelings about my Dumpsters. As I have mentioned, it is 40 no accident that I scavenge from ones where good finds are common. But my limited experience with Dumpsters in other areas suggests to me that even in poorer areas, Dumpsters, if attended with sufficient diligence, can be made to yield a livelihood. The rich students discard perfectly good kiwifruit; poorer people discard perfectly good apples. Slacks and Polo shirts are found in the one place; jeans and T-shirts in the other. The population of competitors rather than the affluence of the dumpers most affects the feasibility of survival by scavenging. The large number of competitors is what puts me off the idea of trying to scavenge in places like Los Angeles.

Curiously, I do not mind my direct competition, other scavengers, so much as I hate the can scroungers.

People scrounge cans because they have to have a little cash. I have tried scrounging cans with an able-bodied companion. Afoot a can scrounger simply cannot make more than a few dollars a day. One can extract the necessities of life from the Dumpsters directly with far less effort than would be required to accumulate the equivalent value in cans. (These observations may not hold in places with container redemption laws.)

Can scroungers, then, are people who must have small amounts of cash. These are drug addicts and winos, mostly the latter because the amounts of cash are so small. Spirits and drugs do, like all other commodities, turn up in Dumpsters and the scavenger will from time to time have a half bottle of a rather good wine with his dinner. But the wino cannot survive on these occasional finds; he must have his daily dose to stave off the DTs. All the cans he can carry will buy about three bottles of Wild Irish Rose.

I do not begrudge them the cans, but can scroungers tend to tear up the Dumpsters, mixing the contents and littering the area. They become so specialized that they can see only cans. They earn my contempt by passing up change, canned goods, and readily hockable items.

45   There are precious few courtesies among scavengers. But it is common practice to set aside surplus items: pairs of shoes, clothing, canned goods, and such. A true scavenger hates to see good stuff go to waste, and what he cannot use he leaves in good condition in plain sight.

Can scroungers lay waste to everything in their path and will stir one of a pair of good shoes to the bottom of a Dumpster, to be lost or ruined in the muck. Can scroungers will even go through individual garbage cans, something I have never seen a scavenger do.

Individual garbage cans are set out on the public easement only on garbage days. On other days going through them requires trespassing close to a dwelling. Going through individual garbage cans without scattering litter is almost impossible. Litter is likely to reduce the public's tolerance of scavenging. Individual cans are simply not as productive as Dumpsters; people in houses and duplexes do not move so often and for some reason do not tend to discard as much useful material. Moreover, the time required to go through one garbage can that serves one household is not much less than the time required to go through a Dumpster that contains the refuse of twenty apartments.

But my strongest reservation about going through individual garbage cans is that this seems to me a very personal kind of invasion to which I would object if I were a householder. Although many things in Dumpsters are obviously meant never to come to light, a Dumpster is somehow less personal.

I avoid trying to draw conclusions about the people who dump in the Dumpsters I frequent. I think it would be unethical to do so, although I know many people will find the idea of scavenger ethics too funny for words.

50   Dumpsters contain bank statements, correspondence, and other documents, just as anyone might expect. But there are also less obvious sources of information. Pill bottles, for example. The labels bear the name of the patient, the name of the doctor, and the name of the drug. AIDS drugs and antipsychotic medicines, to name but two groups, are specific and are seldom prescribed for any other disorders. The plastic compacts for birth-control pills usually have complete label information.

Despite all of this sensitive information, I have had only one apartment resident object to my going through the Dumpster. In that case it turned out the resident was a university athlete who was taking bets and who was afraid I would turn up his wager slips.

Occasionally a find tells a story. I once found a small paper bag containing some unused condoms, several partial tubes of flavored sexual lubricants, a partially used compact of birth-control pills, and the torn pieces of a picture of a young man. Clearly she was through with him and planning to give up sex altogether.

Dumpster things are often sad—abandoned teddy bears, shredded wedding books, despaired-of sales kits. I find many pets lying in state in Dumpsters. Although I hope to get off the streets so that Lizbeth can have a long and comfortable old age, I know this hope is not very realistic. So I suppose when her time comes she too will go into a Dumpster. I will have no better place for her. And after all, it is fitting, since for most of her life her livelihood has come from the Dumpster. When she finds something I think is safe that has been spilled from a Dumpster, I let her have it. She already knows the route around the best ones. I like to think that if she survives me she will have a chance of evading the dog catcher and of finding her sustenance on the route.

Silly vanities also come to rest in the Dumpsters. I am a rather accomplished needleworker. I get a lot of material from the Dumpsters. Evidently sorority girls, hoping to impress someone, perhaps themselves, with their mastery of a womanly art, buy a lot of embroider-by-number kits, work a few stitches horribly, and eventually discard the whole mess. I pull out their stitches, turn the canvas over, and work an original design. Do not think I refrain from chuckling as I make gifts from these kits.

I find diaries and journals. I have often thought of compiling a book of literary found objects. And perhaps I will one day. But what I find is hopelessly commonplace and bad without being, even unconsciously, camp. College students also discard their papers. I am horrified to discover the kind of paper that now merits an A in an undergraduate course. I am grateful, however, for the number of good books and magazines the students throw out.   55

In the area I know best I have never discovered vermin in the Dumpsters, but there are two kinds of kitty surprise. One is alley cats whom I meet as they leap, claws first, out of Dumpsters. This is especially thrilling when I have Lizbeth in tow. The other kind of kitty surprise is a plastic garbage bag filled with some ponderous, amorphous mass. This always proves to be used cat litter.

City bees harvest doughnut glaze and this makes the Dumpster at the doughnut shop more interesting. My faith in the instinctive wisdom of animals is always shaken whenever I see Lizbeth attempt to catch a bee in her mouth, which she does whenever bees are present. Evidently some birds find Dumpsters profitable, for birdie surprise is almost as common as kitty surprise of the first kind. In hunting season all kinds of small game turn up in Dumpsters, some of it, sadly, not entirely dead. Curiously, summer and winter, maggots are uncommon.

The worst of the living and near-living hazards of the Dumpsters are the fire ants. The food they claim is not much of a loss, but they are vicious and aggressive. It is very easy to brush against some surface of the Dumpster and pick up half a dozen or more fire ants, usually in some sensitive area such as the underarm. One advantage of bringing Lizbeth along as I make Dumpster rounds is that, for obvious reasons, she is very alert to ground-based fire ants.

When Lizbeth recognizes a fire-ant infestation around our feet, she does the Dance of the Zillion Fire Ants. I have learned not to ignore this warning from Lizbeth, whether I perceive the tiny ants or not, but to remove ourselves at Lizbeth's first pas de bourée. All the more so because the ants are the worst in the summer months when I wear flip-flops if I have them. (Perhaps someone will misunderstand this. Lizbeth does the Dance of the Zillion Fire Ants when she recognizes more fire ants than she cares to eat, not when she is being bitten. Since I have learned to react promptly, she does not get bitten at all. It is the isolated patrol of fire ants that falls in Lizbeth's range that deserves pity. She finds them quite tasty.)

By far the best way to go through a Dumpster is to lower yourself into it. Most of the good stuff tends to settle at the bottom because it is usually weightier than the rubbish. My more athletic companions have often demonstrated to me that they can extract much good material from a Dumpster I have already been over.

60   To those psychologically or physically unprepared to enter a Dumpster, I recommend a stout stick, preferably with some barb or hook at one end. The hook can be used to grab plastic garbage bags. When I find canned goods or other objects loose at the bottom of a Dumpster, I lower a bag into it, roll the desired object into the bag, and then hoist the bag out—a procedure more easily described than executed. Much Dumpster diving is a matter of experience for which nothing will do except practice.

Dumpster diving is outdoor work, often surprisingly pleasant. It is not entirely predictable; things of interest turn up every day and some days there are finds of great value. I am always very pleased when I can turn up exactly the thing I most wanted to find. Yet in spite of the element of chance, scavenging more than most other pursuits tends to yield returns in some proportion to the effort and intelligence brought to bear. It is very sweet to turn up a few dollars in change from a Dumpster that has just been gone over by a wino.

The land is now covered with cities. The cities are full of Dumpsters. If a member of the canine race is ever able to know what it is doing, then Lizbeth knows that when we go around to the Dumpsters, we are hunting. I think of scavenging as a modern form of self-reliance. In any event, after having survived nearly ten years of government service, where everything is geared to the lowest common denominator, I find it refreshing to have work that rewards initiative and effort. Certainly I would be happy to have a sinecure again, but I am no longer heartbroken that I left one.

I find from the experience of scavenging two rather deep lessons. The first is to take what you can use and let the rest go by. I have come to think that there is no value in the abstract. A thing I cannot use or make useful, perhaps by trading, has no value however rare or fine it may be. I mean useful in a broad sense—some art I would find useful and some otherwise.

I was shocked to realize that some things are not worth acquiring, but now I think it is so. Some material things are white elephants that eat up the possessor's substance. The second lesson is the transience of material being. This has not quite converted me to a dualist, but it has made some headway in that direction. I do not suppose that ideas are immortal, but certainly mental things are longer lived than other material things.

Once I was the sort of person who invests objects with sentimental value.   65
Now I no longer have those objects, but I have the sentiments yet.

Many times in our travels I have lost everything but the clothes I was wearing and Lizbeth. The things I find in Dumpsters, the love letters and rag dolls of so many lives, remind me of this lesson. Now I hardly pick up a thing without envisioning the time I will cast it aside. This I think is a healthy state of mind. Almost everything I have now has already been cast out at least once, proving that what I own is valueless to someone.

Anyway, I find my desire to grab for the gaudy bauble has been largely sated. I think this is an attitude I share with the very wealthy—we both know there is plenty more where what we have came from. Between us are the rat-race millions who nightly scavenge the cable channels looking for they know not what.

I am sorry for them.

QUESTIONS

1. How does Eighner organize his essay? What does such an organization imply?

2. Eighner's simple, understated tone suggests that anyone can adapt to Dumpster diving with a little practice. Why do you think he uses such a tone?

3. Write about someone who does what Eighner deplores in his closing paragraphs, "invests objects with sentimental value." Let your description reveal whether or not you agree with Eighner.

WALLACE STEGNER   *The Dump Ground*

THE TOWN DUMP of Whitemud, Saskatchewan, could only have been a few years old when I knew it, for the village was born in 1913 and I left there in 1919. But I remember the dump better than I remember most things in that town, better than I remember most of the people. I spent more time with it, for one thing; it has more poetry and excitement in it than people did.

It lay in the southeast corner of town, in a section that was always full of

From Wolf Willow: A History, a Story, and a Memory of the Last Plains Frontier *(1962),* *a combination of memoir, history, and fiction about the Great Plains and Stegner's boyhood* *in Saskatchewan, Canada. Often called the "Dean of Western American Writing," Stegner* *wrote about and defended the American West in the face of neglect and environmental* *degradation.*

adventure for me. Just there the Whitemud River left the hills, bent a little south, and started its long traverse across the prairie and international boundary to join the Milk. For all I knew, it might have been on its way to join the Alph:[1] simply, before my eyes, it disappeared into strangeness and wonder.

Also, where it passed below the dumpground, it ran through willowed bottoms that were a favorite campsite for passing teamsters, gypsies, sometimes Indians. The very straw scattered around those camps, the ashes of those strangers' campfires, the manure of their teams and saddle horses, were hot with adventurous possibilities.

It was as an extension, a living suburb, as it were, of the dumpground that we most valued those camps. We scoured them for artifacts of their migrant tenants as if they had been archaeological sites full of the secrets of ancient civilizations. I remember toting around for weeks the broken cheek strap of a bridle. Somehow or other its buckle looked as if it had been fashioned in a far place, a place where they were accustomed to flatten the tongues of buckles for reasons that could only be exciting, and where they made a habit of plating the metal with some valuable alloy, probably silver. In places where the silver was worn away the buckle underneath shone dull yellow: probably gold.

5   It seemed that excitement liked that end of town better than our end. Once old Mrs. Gustafson, deeply religious and a little raddled in the head, went over there with a buckboard full of trash, and as she was driving home along the river she looked and saw a spent catfish, washed in from Cypress Lake or some other part of the watershed, floating on the yellow water. He was two feet long, his whiskers hung down, his fins and tail were limp. He was a kind of fish that no one had seen in the Whitemud in the three or four years of the town's life, and a kind that none of us children had ever seen anywhere. Mrs. Gustafson had never seen one like him either; she perceived at once that he was the devil, and she whipped up the team and reported him at Hoffman's elevator.

We could hear her screeching as we legged it for the river to see for ourselves. Sure enough, there he was. He looked very tired, and he made no great effort to get away as we pushed out a half-sunken rowboat from below the flume, submerged it under him, and brought him ashore. When he died three days later we experimentally fed him to two half-wild cats, but they seemed to suffer no ill effects.

Upstream from the draw that held the dump, the irrigation flume crossed the river. It always seemed to me giddily high when I hung my chin over its plank edge and looked down, but it probably walked no more than twenty feet above the water on its spidery legs. Ordinarily in summer it carried about six or eight inches of smooth water, and under the glassy hurrying of the little boxed stream the planks were coated with deep sun-warmed moss as slick as frogs' eggs. A boy could sit in the flume with the water walling up against his back, and grab a cross brace above him, and pull, shooting himself sledlike ahead until he could reach the next brace for another pull and another slide, and so on across the river in four scoots.

---

1. The imaginary, mysterious river of Samuel Taylor Coleridge's poem "Kubla Khan."

After ten minutes in the flume he would come out wearing a dozen or more limber black leeches, and could sit in the green shade where darning needles flashed blue, and dragonflies hummed and darted and stopped, and skaters dimpled slack and eddy with their delicate transitory footprints, and there stretch the leeches out one by one while their sucking ends clung and clung, until at last, stretched far out, they let go with a tiny wet *puk* and snapped together like rubber bands. The smell of the river and the flume and the clay cutbanks and the bars of that part of the river was the smell of wolf willow.

But nothing in that end of town was as good as the dumpground that scattered along a little runoff coulee[2] dipping down toward the river from the south bench. Through a historical process that went back, probably, to the roots of community sanitation and distaste for eyesores, but that in law dated from the Unincorporated Towns Ordinance of the territorial government, passed in 1888, the dump was one of the very first community enterprises, almost our town's first institution.

More than that, it contained relics of every individual who had ever lived   10
there, and of every phase of the town's history. The bedsprings on which the town's first child was begotten might be there; the skeleton of a boy's pet colt; two or three volumes of Shakespeare bought in haste and error from a peddler, later loaned in carelessness, soaked with water and chemicals in a house fire, and finally thrown out to flap their stained eloquence in the prairie wind.

Broken dishes, rusty tinware, spoons that had been used to mix paint; once a box of percussion caps, sign and symbol of the carelessness that most of those people felt about all matters of personal or public safety. We put them on the railroad tracks and were anonymously denounced in the *Enterprise*. There were also old iron, old brass, for which we hunted assiduously, by night conning junkmen's catalogues and the pages of the *Enterprise* to find how much wartime value there might be in the geared insides of clocks or in a pound of tea lead[3] carefully wrapped in a ball whose weight astonished and delighted us. Sometimes the unimaginable outside world reached in and laid a finger on us. I recall that, aged no more than seven, I wrote a St. Louis junk house asking if they preferred their tea lead and tinfoil wrapped in balls, or whether they would rather have it pressed flat in sheets, and I got back a typewritten letter in a window envelope instructing me that they would be happy to have it in any way that was convenient for me. They added that they valued my business and were mine very truly. Dazed, I carried that windowed grandeur around in my pocket until I wore it out, and for months I saved the letter as a souvenir of the wondering time when something strange and distinguished had singled me out.

We hunted old bottles in the dump, bottles caked with dirt and filth, half buried, full of cobwebs, and we washed them out at the horse trough by the elevator, putting in a handful of shot along with the water to knock the dirt loose; and when we had shaken them until our arms were tired, we hauled

---

2. A gully.

3. An alloy used for lining the chests in which tea was stored and transported.

them off in somebody's coaster wagon and turned them in at Bill Anderson's
pool hall, where the smell of lemon pop was so sweet on the dark pool-hall air
that I am sometimes awakened by it in the night, even yet.

Smashed wheels of wagons and buggies, tangles of rusty barbed wire, the
collapsed perambulator that the French wife of one of the town's doctors had
once pushed proudly up the planked sidewalks and along the ditchbank paths.
A welter of foul-smelling feathers and coyote-scattered carrion which was all
that remained of somebody's dream of a chicken ranch. The chickens had all
got some mysterious pip at the same time, and died as one, and the dream lay
out there with the rest of the town's history to rustle to the empty sky on the
border of the hills.

There was melted glass in curious forms, and the half-melted office safe
left from the burning of Bill Day's Hotel. On very lucky days we might find a
piece of the lead casing that had enclosed the wires of the town's first telephone system. The casing was just the right size for rings, and so soft that it
could be whittled with a jackknife. It was a material that might have made
artists of us. If we had been Indians of fifty years before, that bright soft metal
would have enlisted our maximum patience and craft and come out as ring
and metal and amulet inscribed with the symbols of our observed world. Perhaps there were too many ready-made alternatives in the local drug, hardware,
and general stores; perhaps our feeble artistic response was a measure of the
insufficiency of the challenge we felt. In any case I do not remember that we
did any more with the metal than to shape it into crude seal rings with our initials or pierced hearts carved in them; and these, though they served a purpose
in juvenile courtship, stopped something short of art.

15   The dump held very little wood, for in that country anything burnable got
burned. But it had plenty of old iron, furniture, papers, mattresses that were
the delight of field mice, and jugs and demijohns that were sometimes their
bane, for they crawled into the necks and drowned in the rain water or redeye
that was inside.

If the history of our town was not exactly written, it was at least hinted, in
the dump. I think I had a pretty sound notion even at eight or nine of how significant was that first institution of our forming Canadian civilization. For
rummaging through its foul purlieus I had several times been surprised and
shocked to find relics of my own life tossed out there to rot or blow away.

The volumes of Shakespeare belonged to a set that my father had bought
before I was born. It had been carried through successive moves from town to
town in the Dakotas, and from Dakota to Seattle, and from Seattle to Bellingham, and Bellingham to Redmond, and from Redmond back to Iowa, and
from there to Saskatchewan. Then, stained in a stranger's house fire, these
volumes had suffered from a house-cleaning impulse and been thrown away
for me to stumble upon in the dump. One of the Cratchet girls had borrowed
them, a hatchet-faced, thin, eager, transplanted Cockney girl with a frenzy, almost a hysteria, for reading. And yet somehow, through her hands, they found
the dump, to become a symbol of how much was lost, how much thrown
aside, how much carelessly or of necessity given up, in the making of a new

country. We had so few books that I was familiar with them all, had handled them, looked at their pictures, perhaps even read them. They were the lares and penates, part of the skimpy impedimenta of household gods we had brought with us into Latium.[4] Finding those three thrown away was a little like finding my own name on a gravestone.

And yet not the blow that something else was, something that impressed me even more with the dump's close reflection of the town's intimate life. The colt whose picked skeleton lay out there was mine. He had been incurably crippled when dogs chased our mare, Daisy, the morning after she foaled. I had labored for months to make him well; had fed him by hand, curried him, exercised him, adjusted the iron braces that I had talked my father into having made. And I had not known that he would have to be destroyed. One weekend I turned him over to the foreman of one of the ranches, presumably so that he could be cared for. A few days later I found his skinned body, with the braces still on his crippled front legs, lying on the dump.

Not even that, I think, cured me of going there, though our parents all forbade us on pain of cholera or worse to do so. The place fascinated us, as it should have. For this was the kitchen midden of all the civilization we knew; it gave us the most tantalizing glimpses into our lives as well as into those of the neighbors. It gave us an aesthetic distance from which to know ourselves.

The dump was our poetry and our history. We took it home with us by the   20
wagonload, bringing back into town the things the town had used and thrown away. Some little part of what we gathered, mainly bottles, we managed to bring back to usefulness, but most of our gleanings we left lying around barn or attic or cellar until in some renewed fury of spring cleanup our families carted them off to the dump again, to be rescued and briefly treasured by some other boy with schemes for making them useful. Occasionally something we really valued with a passion was snatched from us in horror and returned at once. That happened to the mounted head of a white mountain goat, some-body's trophy from old times and the far Rocky Mountains, that I brought home one day in transports of delight. My mother took one look and discovered that his beard was full of moths.

I remember that goat; I regret him yet. Poetry is seldom useful, but always memorable. I think I learned more from the town dump than I learned from school: more about people, more about how life is lived, not elsewhere but here, not in other times but now. If I were a sociologist anxious to study in detail the life of any community, I would go very early to its refuse piles. For a community may be as well judged by what it throws away—what it has to throw away and what it chooses to—as by any other evidence. For whole civilizations we have sometimes no more of the poetry and little more of the history than this.

---

4. In Virgil's *Aeneid,* the Trojans who escaped the fall of Troy carried their household gods (*lares* and *penates*) as they wandered the Mediterranean, finally settling in Latium, the region around Rome.

QUESTIONS

1. Through what details does Stegner portray the dump as a record of his childhood? How is it also a record of the town's history? Is it also a record of the North American West? In what sense?

2. How seriously do you take Stegner's claim (paragraph 21) that "I learned more from the town dump than I learned from school"? He has been making allusions to Coleridge and Virgil; what kind of learning is he thinking of?

3. Describe a "treasure" someone found and held on to.

MAYA ANGELOU   *Graduation*

THE CHILDREN IN STAMPS[1] trembled visibly with anticipation. Some adults were excited too, but to be certain the whole young population had come down with graduation epidemic. Large classes were graduating from both the grammar school and the high school. Even those who were years removed from their own day of glorious release were anxious to help with preparations as a kind of dry run. The junior students who were moving into the vacating classes' chairs were tradition-bound to show their talents for leadership and management. They strutted through the school and around the campus exerting pressure on the lower grades. Their authority was so new that occasionally if they pressed a little too hard it had to be overlooked. After all, next term was coming, and it never hurt a sixth grader to have a play sister in the eighth grade, or a tenth-year student to be able to call a twelfth grader Bubba. So all was endured in a spirit of shared understanding. But the graduating classes themselves were the nobility. Like travelers with exotic destinations on their minds, the graduates were remarkably forgetful. They came to school without their books or tablets or even pencils. Volunteers fell over themselves to secure replacements for the missing equipment. When accepted, the willing workers might or might not be thanked, and it was of no importance to the pregraduation rites. Even teachers were respectful of the now quiet and aging seniors, and tended to speak to them, if not as equals, as beings only slightly lower than themselves. After tests were returned and grades given, the student body, which acted like an extended family, knew who did well, who excelled, and what piteous ones had failed.

From I Know Why the Caged Bird Sings *(1970), the first volume of Angelou's autobiography of growing up in a segregated southern town. After its popular success, Angelou continued her life story in five sequential volumes, ending with* A Song Flung Up to Heaven *(2002), an account of the turbulent years of the civil rights movement and the assassinations of Malcolm X and Martin Luther King Jr.*

1. A town in Arkansas.

Unlike the white high school, Lafayette County Training School distinguished itself by having neither lawn, nor hedges, nor tennis court, nor climbing ivy. Its two buildings (main classrooms, the grade school and home economics) were set on a dirt hill with no fence to limit either its boundaries or those of bordering farms. There was a large expanse to the left of the school which was used alternately as a baseball diamond or basketball court. Rusty hoops on swaying poles represented the permanent recreational equipment, although bats and balls could be borrowed from the P.E. teacher if the borrower was qualified and if the diamond wasn't occupied.

Over this rocky area relieved by a few shady tall persimmon trees the graduating class walked. The girls often held hands and no longer bothered to speak to the lower students. There was a sadness about them, as if this old world was not their home and they were bound for higher ground. The boys, on the other hand, had become more friendly, more outgoing. A decided change from the closed attitude they projected while studying for finals. Now they seemed not ready to give up the old school, the familiar paths and classrooms. Only a small percentage would be continuing on to college—one of the South's A & M (agricultural and mechanical) schools, which trained Negro youths to be carpenters, farmers, handymen, masons, maids, cooks and baby nurses. Their future rode heavily on their shoulders, and blinded them to the collective joy that had pervaded the lives of the boys and girls in the grammar school graduating class.

Parents who could afford it had ordered new shoes and readymade clothes for themselves from Sears and Roebuck or Montgomery Ward. They also engaged the best seamstresses to make the floating graduating dresses and to cut down secondhand pants which would be pressed to a military slickness for the important event.

Oh, it was important, all right. Whitefolks would attend the ceremony, and two or three would speak of God and home, and the Southern way of life, and Mrs. Parsons, the principal's wife, would play the graduation march while the lower-grade graduates paraded down the aisles and took their seats below the platform. The high school seniors would wait in empty classrooms to make their dramatic entrance.

In the Store I was the person of the moment. The birthday girl. The center. Bailey[2] had graduated the year before, although to do so he had had to forfeit all pleasures to make up for his time lost in Baton Rouge.

My class was wearing butter-yellow piqué dresses, and Momma launched out on mine. She smocked the yoke into tiny crisscrossing puckers, then shirred the rest of the bodice. Her dark fingers ducked in and out of the lemony cloth as she embroidered raised daisies around the hem. Before she considered herself finished she had added a crocheted cuff on the puff sleeves, and a pointy crocheted collar.

I was going to be lovely. A walking model of all the various styles of fine

2. The author's brother.

hand sewing and it didn't worry me that I was only twelve years old and merely graduating from the eighth grade. Besides, many teachers in Arkansas Negro schools had only that diploma and were licensed to impart wisdom.

The days had become longer and more noticeable. The faded beige of former times had been replaced with strong and sure colors. I began to see my classmates' clothes, their skin tones, and the dust that waved off pussy willows. Clouds that lazed across the sky were objects of great concern to me. Their shiftier shapes might have held a message that in my new happiness and with a little bit of time I'd soon decipher. During that period I looked at the arch of heaven so religiously my neck kept a steady ache. I had taken to smiling more often, and my jaws hurt from the unaccustomed activity. Between the two physical sore spots, I suppose I could have been uncomfortable, but that was not the case. As a member of the winning team (the graduating class of 1940) I had outdistanced unpleasant sensations by miles. I was headed for the freedom of open fields.

10   Youth and social approval allied themselves with me and we trammeled memories of slights and insults. The wind of our swift passage remodeled my features. Lost tears were pounded to mud and then to dust. Years of withdrawal were brushed aside and left behind, as hanging ropes of parasitic moss.

My work alone had awarded me a top place and I was going to be one of the first called in the graduating ceremonies. On the classroom blackboard, as well as on the bulletin board in the auditorium, there were blue stars and white stars and red stars. No absences, no tardinesses, and my academic work was among the best of the year. I could say the preamble to the Constitution even faster than Bailey. We timed ourselves often: "We the people of the United States in order to form a more perfect union . . ." I had memorized the Presidents of the United States from Washington to Roosevelt in chronological as well as alphabetical order.

My hair pleased me too. Gradually the black mass had lengthened and thickened, so that it kept at last to its braided pattern, and I didn't have to yank my scalp off when I tried to comb it.

Louise and I had rehearsed the exercises until we tired out ourselves. Henry Reed was class valedictorian. He was a small, very black boy with hooded eyes, a long, broad nose and an oddly shaped head. I had admired him for years because each term he and I vied for the best grades in our class. Most often he bested me, but instead of being disappointed I was pleased that we shared top places between us. Like many Southern Black children, he lived with his grandmother, who was as strict as Momma and as kind as she knew how to be. He was courteous, respectful and soft-spoken to elders, but on the playground he chose to play the roughest games. I admired him. Anyone, I reckoned, sufficiently afraid or sufficiently dull could be polite. But to be able to operate at a top level with both adults and children was admirable.

His valedictory speech was entitled "To Be or Not to Be." The rigid tenth-grade teacher had helped him write it. He'd been working on the dramatic stresses for months.

15   The weeks until graduation were filled with heady activities. A group of

small children were to be presented in a play about buttercups and daisies and bunny rabbits. They could be heard throughout the building practicing their hops and their little songs that sounded like silver bells. The older girls (non-graduates, of course) were assigned the task of making refreshments for the night's festivities. A tangy scent of ginger, cinnamon, nutmeg and chocolate wafted around the home economics building as the budding cooks made samples for themselves and their teachers.

In every corner of the workshop, axes and saws split fresh timber as the woodshop boys made sets and stage scenery. Only the graduates were left out of the general bustle. We were free to sit in the library at the back of the building or look in quite detachedly, naturally, on the measures being taken for our event.

Even the minister preached on graduation the Sunday before. His subject was, "Let your light so shine that men will see your good works and praise your Father, Who is in Heaven." Although the sermon was purported to be addressed to us, he used the occasion to speak to backsliders, gamblers and general ne'er-do-wells. But since he had called our names at the beginning of the service we were mollified.

Among Negroes the tradition was to give presents to children going only from one grade to another. How much more important this was when the person was graduating at the top of the class. Uncle Willie and Momma had sent away for a Mickey Mouse watch like Bailey's. Louise gave me four embroidered handkerchiefs. (I gave her crocheted doilies.) Mrs. Sneed, the minister's wife, made me an undershirt to wear for graduation, and nearly every customer gave me a nickel or maybe even a dime with the instruction "Keep on moving to higher ground," or some such encouragement.

Amazingly the great day finally dawned and I was out of bed before I knew it. I threw open the back door to see it more clearly, but Momma said, "Sister, come away from that door and put your robe on."

I hoped the memory of that morning would never leave me. Sunlight was itself young, and the day had none of the insistence maturity would bring it in a few hours. In my robe and barefoot in the backyard, under cover of going to see about my new beans, I gave myself up to the gentle warmth and thanked God that no matter what evil I had done in my life He had allowed me to live to see this day. Somewhere in my fatalism I had expected to die, accidentally, and never have the chance to walk up the stairs in the auditorium and gracefully receive my hard-earned diploma. Out of God's merciful bosom I had won reprieve.

Bailey came out in his robe and gave me a box wrapped in Christmas paper. He said he had saved his money for months to pay for it. It felt like a box of chocolates, but I knew Bailey wouldn't save money to buy candy when we had all we could want under our noses.

He was as proud of the gift as I. It was a soft-leather-bound copy of a collection of poems by Edgar Allan Poe, or, as Bailey and I called him, "Eap." I turned to "Annabel Lee" and we walked up and down the garden rows, the cool dirt between our toes, reciting the beautifully sad lines.

20

Momma made a Sunday breakfast although it was only Friday. After we finished the blessing, I opened my eyes to find the watch on my plate. It was a dream of a day. Everything went smoothly and to my credit, I didn't have to be reminded or scolded for anything. Near evening I was too jittery to attend to chores, so Bailey volunteered to do all before his bath.

Days before, we had made a sign for the Store, and as we turned out the lights Momma hung the cardboard over the doorknob. It read clearly: CLOSED. GRADUATION.

25   My dress fitted perfectly and everyone said that I looked like a sunbeam in it. On the hill, going toward the school, Bailey walked behind with Uncle Willie, who muttered, "Go on, Ju." He wanted him to walk ahead with us because it embarrassed him to have to walk so slowly. Bailey said he'd let the ladies walk together, and the men would bring up the rear. We all laughed, nicely.

Little children dashed by out of the dark like fireflies. Their crepe-paper dresses and butterfly wings were not made for running and we heard more than one rip, dryly, and the regretful "uh uh" that followed.

The school blazed without gaiety. The windows seemed cold and unfriendly from the lower hill. A sense of ill-fated timing crept over me, and if Momma hadn't reached for my hand I would have drifted back to Bailey and Uncle Willie, and possibly beyond. She made a few slow jokes about my feet getting cold, and tugged me along to the now-strange building.

Around the front steps, assurance came back. There were my fellow "greats," the graduating class. Hair brushed back, legs oiled, new dresses and pressed pleats, fresh pocket handkerchiefs and little handbags, all homesewn. Oh, we were up to snuff, all right. I joined my comrades and didn't even see my family go in to find seats in the crowded auditorium.

The school band struck up a march and all classes filed in as had been rehearsed. We stood in front of our seats, as assigned, and on a signal from the choir director, we sat. No sooner had this been accomplished than the band started to play the national anthem. We rose again and sang the song, after which we recited the pledge of allegiance. We remained standing for a brief minute before the choir director and the principal signaled to us, rather desperately I thought, to take our seats. The command was so unusual that our carefully rehearsed and smooth-running machine was thrown off. For a full minute we fumbled for our chairs and bumped into each other awkwardly. Habits change or solidify under pressure, so in our state of nervous tension we had been ready to follow our usual assembly pattern: the American national anthem, then the pledge of allegiance, then the song every Black person I knew called the Negro National Anthem. All done in the same key, with the same passion and most often standing on the same foot.

30   Finding my seat at last, I was overcome with a presentiment of worse things to come. Something unrehearsed, unplanned, was going to happen, and we were going to be made to look bad. I distinctly remember being explicit in the choice of pronoun. It was "we," the graduating class, the unit, that concerned me then.

The principal welcomed "parents and friends" and asked the Baptist minister to lead us in prayer. His invocation was brief and punchy, and for a second I thought we were getting on the high road to right action. When the principal came back to the dais, however, his voice had changed. Sounds always affected me profoundly and the principal's voice was one of my favorites. During assembly it melted and lowed weakly into the audience. It had not been in my plan to listen to him, but my curiosity was piqued and I straightened up to give him my attention.

He was talking about Booker T. Washington, our "late great leader," who said we can be as close as the fingers on the hand, etc. . . . Then he said a few vague things about friendship and the friendship of kindly people to those less fortunate than themselves. With that his voice nearly faded, thin, away. Like a river diminishing to a stream and then to a trickle. But he cleared his throat and said, "Our speaker tonight, who is also our friend, came from Texarkana to deliver the commencement address, but due to the irregularity of the train schedule, he's going to, as they say, 'speak and run.' " He said that we understood and wanted the man to know that we were most grateful for the time he was able to give us and then something about how we were willing always to adjust to another's program, and without more ado—"I give you Mr. Edward Donleavy."

Not one but two white men came through the door off-stage. The shorter one walked to the speaker's platform, and the tall one moved to the center seat and sat down. But that was our principal's seat, and already occupied. The dislodged gentleman bounced around for a long breath or two before the Baptist minister gave him his chair, then with more dignity than the situation deserved, the minister walked off the stage.

Donleavy looked at the audience once (on reflection, I'm sure that he wanted only to reassure himself that we were really there), adjusted his glasses and began to read from a sheaf of papers.

He was glad "to be here and to see the work going on just as it was in the other schools."

At the first "Amen" from the audience I willed the offender to immediate death by choking on the word. But Amens and Yes, sirs began to fall around the room like rain through a ragged umbrella.

He told us of the wonderful changes we children in Stamps had in store. The Central School (naturally, the white school was Central) had already been granted improvements that would be in use in the fall. A well-known artist was coming from Little Rock to teach art to them. They were going to have the newest microscopes and chemistry equipment for their laboratory. Mr. Donleavy didn't leave us long in the dark over who made these improvements available to Central High. Nor were we to be ignored in the general betterment scheme he had in mind.

He said that he had pointed out to people at a very high level that one of the first-line football tacklers at Arkansas Agricultural and Mechanical College had graduated from good old Lafayette County Training School. Here fewer Amens were heard. Those few that did break through lay dully in the air with the heaviness of habit.

He went on to praise us. He went on to say how he had bragged that "one

35

of the best basketball players at Fisk sank his first ball right here at Lafayette County Training School."

40   The white kids were going to have a chance to become Galileos and Madame Curies and Edisons and Gauguins, and our boys (the girls weren't even in on it) would try to be Jesse Owenses and Joe Louises.

Owens and the Brown Bomber were great heroes in our world, but what school official in the white-goddom of Little Rock had the right to decide that those two men must be our only heroes? Who decided that for Henry Reed to become a scientist he had to work like George Washington Carver, as a boot-black, to buy a lousy microscope? Bailey was obviously always going to be too small to be an athlete, so which concrete angel glued to what country seat had decided that if my brother wanted to become a lawyer he had to first pay penance for his skin by picking cotton and hoeing corn and studying corre-spondence books at night for twenty years?

The man's dead words fell like bricks around the auditorium and too many settled in my belly. Constrained by hard-learned manners I couldn't look behind me, but to my left and right the proud graduating class of 1940 had dropped their heads. Every girl in my row had found something new to do with her handkerchief. Some folded the tiny squares into love knots, some into triangles, but most were wadding them, then pressing them flat on their yellow laps.

On the dais, the ancient tragedy was being replayed. Professor Parsons sat, a sculptor's reject, rigid. His large, heavy body seemed devoid of will or willingness, and his eyes said he was no longer with us. The other teachers ex-amined the flag (which was draped stage right) or their notes, or the windows which opened on our now-famous playing diamond.

Graduation, the hush-hush magic time of frills and gifts and congratula-tions and diplomas, was finished for me before my name was called. The ac-complishment was nothing. The meticulous maps, drawn in three colors of ink, learning and spelling decasyllabic words, memorizing the whole of *The Rape of Lucrece*[3]—it was for nothing. Donleavy had exposed us.

45   We were maids and farmers, handymen and washerwomen, and anything higher that we aspired to was farcical and presumptuous.

Then I wished that Gabriel Prosser and Nat Turner[4] had killed all white-folks in their beds and that Abraham Lincoln had been assassinated before the signing of the Emancipation Proclamation, and that Harriet Tubman[5] had been killed by that blow on her head and Christopher Columbus had drowned in the *Santa Maria*.

It was awful to be a Negro and have no control over my life. It was brutal

---

3. A 1,855-line narrative poem by Shakespeare, which recounts the story of the daugh-ter of a Roman prefect. When she was defiled, she stabbed herself in the presence of her father and her husband.

4. Gabriel Prosser (c. 1776–1800) and Nat Turner (1800–1831), executed leaders of slave rebellions in Virginia.

5. Black abolitionist (c. 1820–1913), known for her work as a "conductor" on the Un-derground Railroad.

to be young and already trained to sit quietly and listen to charges brought against my color with no chance of defense. We should all be dead. I thought I should like to see us all dead, one on top of the other. A pyramid of flesh with the whitefolks on the bottom, as the broad base, then the Indians with their silly tomahawks and teepees and wigwams and treaties, the Negroes with their mops and recipes and cotton sacks and spirituals sticking out of their mouths. The Dutch children should all stumble in their wooden shoes and break their necks. The French should choke to death on the Louisiana Purchase (1803) while silkworms ate all the Chinese with their stupid pigtails. As a species, we were an abomination. All of us.

Donleavy was running for election, and assured our parents that if he won we could count on having the only colored paved playing field in that part of Arkansas. Also—he never looked up to acknowledge the grunts of acceptance—also, we were bound to get some new equipment for the home economics building and the workshop.

He finished, and since there was no need to give any more than the most perfunctory thank-you's, he nodded to the men on the stage, and the tall white man who was never introduced joined him at the door. They left with the attitude that now they were off to something really important. (The graduation ceremonies at Lafayette County Training School had been a mere preliminary.)

The ugliness they left was palpable. An uninvited guest who wouldn't leave. The choir was summoned and sang a modern arrangement of "Onward, Christian Soldiers," with new words pertaining to graduates seeking their place in the world. But it didn't work. Elouise, the daughter of the Baptist minister, recited "Invictus,"[6] and I could have cried at the impertinence of "I am the master of my fate, I am the captain of my soul." 50

My name had lost its ring of familiarity and I had to be nudged to go and receive my diploma. All my preparations had fled. I neither marched up to the stage like a conquering Amazon, nor did I look in the audience for Bailey's nod of approval. Marguerite Johnson, I heard the name again, my honors were read, there were noises in the audience of appreciation, and I took my place on the stage as rehearsed.

I thought about colors I hated: ecru, puce, lavender, beige and black.

There was shuffling and rustling around me, then Henry Reed was giving his valedictory address, "To Be or Not to Be." Hadn't he heard the white-folks? We couldn't *be,* so the question was a waste of time. Henry's voice came out clear and strong. I feared to look at him. Hadn't he got the message? There was no "nobler in the mind" for Negroes because the world didn't think we had minds, and they let us know it. "Outrageous fortune"? Now, that was a joke. When the ceremony was over I had to tell Henry Reed some things. That is, if I still cared. Not "rub," Henry, "erase." "Ah, there's the erase." Us.

Henry had been a good student in elocution. His voice rose on tides of promise and fell on waves of warnings. The English teacher had helped him to

6. An inspirational poem by William Ernest Henley (1849–1903), once very popular for occasions such as this one.

create a sermon winging through Hamlet's soliloquy. To be a man, a doer, a
builder, a leader, or to be a tool, an unfunny joke, a crusher of funky toadstools.
I marveled that Henry could go through with the speech as if we had a choice.

55   I had been listening and silently rebutting each sentence with my eyes
closed; then there was a hush, which in an audience warns that something unplanned is happening. I looked up and saw Henry Reed, the conservative, the
proper, the A student, turn his back to the audience and turn to us (the proud
graduating class of 1940) and sing, nearly speaking,

> "Lift ev'ry voice and sing
> Till earth and heaven ring
> Ring with the harmonies of Liberty . . ."

It was the poem written by James Weldon Johnson. It was the music composed
by J. Rosamond Johnson. It was the Negro national anthem. Out of habit we
were singing it.

Our mothers and fathers stood in the dark hall and joined the hymn of encouragement. A kindergarten teacher led the small children onto the stage and
the buttercups and daisies and bunny rabbits marked time and tried to follow:

> "Stony the road we trod
> Bitter the chastening rod
> Felt in the days when hope, unborn, had died.
> Yet with a steady beat
> Have not our weary feet
> Come to the place for which our fathers sighed?"

Each child I knew had learned that song with his ABC's and along with
"Jesus Loves Me This I Know." But I personally had never heard it before.
Never heard the words, despite the thousands of times I had sung them. Never
thought they had anything to do with me.

On the other hand, the words of Patrick Henry had made such an impression on me that I had been able to stretch myself tall and trembling and say, "I
know not what course others may take, but as for me, give me liberty or give
me death."

And now I heard, really for the first time:

> "We have come over a way that with tears
>   has been watered,
> We have come, treading our path through
>   the blood of the slaughtered."

60   While echoes of the song shivered in the air, Henry Reed bowed his head,
said "Thank you," and returned to his place in the line. The tears that slipped
down many faces were not wiped away in shame.

We were on top again. As always, again. We survived. The depths had
been icy and dark, but now a bright sun spoke to our souls. I was no longer

simply a member of the proud graduating class of 1940; I was a proud member of the wonderful, beautiful Negro race.

Oh, Black known and unknown poets, how often have your auctioned pains sustained us? Who will compute the lonely nights made less lonely by your songs, or the empty pots made less tragic by your tales?

If we were a people much given to revealing secrets, we might raise monuments and sacrifice to the memories of our poets, but slavery cured us of that weakness. It may be enough, however, to have it said that we survive in exact relationship to the dedication of our poets (include preachers, musicians and blues singers).

QUESTIONS

1. Presumably, all of Angelou's readers would have witnessed a graduation ceremony and brought their memories to her essay. How does she fulfill the reader's expectations for what graduation includes? How does she surprise us with details we don't expect?

2. In paragraph 43 Angelou writes that "the ancient tragedy was being replayed." What does she mean? How does her essay help to resist the tragic script?

3. Write a personal essay about an event you anticipated hopefully but that did not fulfill your expectations, incorporating an explanation of your disappointment into your account, as Angelou does.

ZORA NEALE HURSTON *How It Feels to Be Colored Me*

I AM COLORED but I offer nothing in the way of extenuating circumstances except the fact that I am the only Negro in the United States whose grandfather on the mother's side was not an Indian chief.

I remember the very day that I became colored. Up to my thirteenth year I lived in the little Negro town of Eatonville, Florida. It is exclusively a colored town. The only white people I knew passed through the town going to or coming from Orlando. The native whites rode dusty horses, the Northern tourists chugged down the sandy village road in automobiles. The town knew the Southerners and never stopped cane chewing[1] when they passed. But the Northerners were some-

Originally published in the World Tomorrow *in May 1928, just as Hurston was graduating from Barnard College; collected and reprinted in* I Love Myself When I Am Laughing . . . and Then Again When I Am Looking Mean and Impressive *(1973), a volume of Hurston's writings edited by the African American writer Alice Walker.*

1. Chewing sugar cane.

thing else again. They were peered at cautiously from behind curtains by the timid. The more venturesome would come out on the porch to watch them go past and got just as much pleasure out of the tourists as the tourists got out of the village.

The front porch might seem a daring place for the rest of the town, but it was a gallery seat for me. My favorite place was atop the gate-post. Proscenium box for a born first-nighter. Not only did I enjoy the show, but I didn't mind the actors knowing that I liked it. I usually spoke to them in passing. I'd wave at them and when they returned my salute, I would say something like this: "Howdy-do-well-I-thank-you-where-you-goin'?" Usually automobile or the horse paused at this, and after a queer exchange of compliments, I would probably "go a piece of the way" with them, as we say in farthest Florida. If one of my family happened to come to the front in time to see me, of course negotiations would be rudely broken off. But even so, it is clear that I was the first "welcome-to-our-state" Floridian, and I hope the Miami Chamber of Commerce will please take notice.

During this period, white people differed from colored to me only in that they rode through town and never lived there. They liked to hear me "speak pieces" and sing and wanted to see me dance the parse-me-la, and gave me generously of their small silver for doing these things, which seemed strange to me for I wanted to do them so much that I needed bribing to stop. Only they didn't know it. The colored people gave no dimes. They deplored any joyful tendencies in me, but I was their Zora nevertheless. I belonged to them, to the nearby hotels, to the county—everybody's Zora.

5   But changes came in the family when I was thirteen, and I was sent to school in Jacksonville. I left Eatonville, the town of the oleanders,[2] as Zora. When I disembarked from the river-boat at Jacksonville, she was no more. It seemed that I had suffered a sea change. I was not Zora of Orange County any more, I was now a little colored girl. I found it out in certain ways. In my heart as well as in the mirror, I became a fast brown—warranted not to rub nor run.

But I am not tragically colored. There is no great sorrow dammed up in my soul, nor lurking behind my eyes. I do not mind at all. I do not belong to the sobbing school of Negrohood who hold that nature somehow has given them a lowdown dirty deal and whose feelings are all hurt about it. Even in the helter-skelter skirmish that is my life, I have seen that the world is to the strong regardless of a little pigmentation more or less. No, I do not weep at the world—I am too busy sharpening my oyster knife.[3]

Someone is always at my elbow reminding me that I am the granddaughter of slaves. It fails to register depression with me. Slavery is sixty years in the past. The operation was successful and the patient is doing well, thank

2. Fragrant tropical flowers, common in the South.
3. Cf. the popular expression "The world is my oyster."

you. The terrible struggle[4] that made me an American out of a potential slave
said "On the line!" The Reconstruction said "Get set!"; and the generation before said "Go!" I am off to a flying start and I must not halt in the stretch to
look behind and weep. Slavery is the price I paid for civilization, and the
choice was not with me. It is a bully adventure and worth all that I have paid
through my ancestors for it. No one on earth ever had a greater chance for
glory. The world to be won and nothing to be lost. It is thrilling to think—to
know that for any act of mine, I shall get twice as much praise or twice as
much blame. It is quite exciting to hold the center of the national stage, with
the spectators not knowing whether to laugh or to weep.

The position of my white neighbor is much more difficult. No brown
specter pulls up a chair beside me when I sit down to eat. No dark ghost
thrusts its leg against mine in bed. The game of keeping what one has is never
so exciting as the game of getting.

I do not always feel colored. Even now I often achieve the unconscious
Zora of Eatonville before the Hegira.[5] I feel most colored when I am thrown
against a sharp white background.

For instance at Barnard. "Beside the waters of the Hudson"[6] I feel my   10
race. Among the thousand white persons, I am a dark rock surged upon, and
overswept, but through it all, I remain myself. When covered by the waters, I
am; and the ebb but reveals me again.

Sometimes it is the other way around. A white person is set down in our midst,
but the contrast is just as sharp for me. For instance, when I sit in the drafty
basement that is The New World Cabaret with a white person, my color
comes. We enter chatting about any little nothing that we have in common
and are seated by the jazz waiters. In the abrupt way that jazz orchestras have,
this one plunges into a number. It loses no time in circumlocutions, but gets
right down to business. It constricts the thorax and splits the heart with its
tempo and narcotic harmonies. This orchestra grows rambunctious, rears on
its hind legs and attacks the tonal veil with primitive fury, rending it, clawing it
until it breaks through to the jungle beyond. I follow those heathen—follow
them exultingly. I dance wildly inside myself; I yell within, I whoop; I shake my
assegai[7] above my head, I hurl it true to the mark yeeeeooww! I am in the jungle and living in the jungle way. My face is painted red and yellow and my body
is painted blue. My pulse is throbbing like a war drum. I want to slaughter
something—give pain, give death to what, I do not know. But the piece ends.
The men of the orchestra wipe their lips and rest their fingers. I creep back

4. The Civil War. The Reconstruction was the period immediately following the war; one
of its better effects was that northern educators came South to teach newly freed slaves.

5. A journey undertaken away from a dangerous situation into a more highly desirable
one (literally, the flight of Muhammad from Mecca in 622 C.E.).

6. Barnard is an American women's college in New York City, near the Hudson River;
cf. the psalmist's "by the waters of Babylon."

7. South African hunting spear.

slowly to the veneer we call civilization with the last tone and find the white friend sitting motionless in his seat, smoking calmly.

"Good music they have here," he remarks, drumming the table with his fingertips.

Music. The great blobs of purple and red emotion have not touched him. He has only heard what I felt. He is far away and I see him but dimly across the ocean and the continent that have fallen between us. He is so pale with his whiteness then and I am *so* colored.

At certain times I have no race, I am *me*. When I set my hat at a certain angle and saunter down Seventh Avenue, Harlem City, feeling as snooty as the lions in front of the Forty-Second Street Library, for instance. So far as my feelings are concerned, Peggy Hopkins Joyce on the Boule Mich[8] with her gorgeous raiment, stately carriage, knees knocking together in a most aristocratic manner, has nothing on me. The cosmic Zora emerges. I belong to no race nor time. I am the eternal feminine with its string of beads.

15   I have no separate feeling about being an American citizen and colored. I am merely a fragment of the Great Soul that surges within the boundaries. My country, right or wrong.

Sometimes, I feel discriminated against, but it does not make me angry. It merely astonishes me. How *can* any deny themselves the pleasure of my company? It's beyond me.

But in the main, I feel like a brown bag of miscellany propped against a wall. Against a wall in company with other bags, white, red and yellow. Pour out the contents, and there is discovered a jumble of small things priceless and worthless. A first-water diamond, an empty spool, bits of broken glass, lengths of string, a key to a door long since crumbled away, a rusty knife-blade, old shoes saved for a road that never was and never will be, a nail bent under the weight of things too heavy for any nail, a dried flower or two still a little fragrant. In your hand is the brown bag. On the ground before you is the jumble it held—so much like the jumble in the bags, could they be emptied, that all might be dumped in a single heap and the bags refilled without altering the content of any greatly. A bit of colored glass more or less would not matter. Perhaps that is how the Great Stuffer of Bags filled them in the first place— who knows?

8. Peggy Hopkins Joyce, American beauty and fashion-setter of the twenties; the Boule Mich, the Boulevard Saint-Michel, a fashionable Parisian street.

QUESTIONS

1. From the beginning Hurston startles us: "I remember the very day that I became colored." Why does Hurston insist that one *becomes* colored? What happened on that day to make her so?

2. Each section of Hurston's essay explores a different possible identity, some based on

skin color, others emphasizing history, culture, or gender. What does Hurston accomplish by such an approach?

3. The final paragraph introduces a key metaphor: "like a brown bag of miscellany propped against a wall." How does Hurston develop this metaphor? What does she mean by it?

4. Like other writers in "Personal Report," including Bruno Bettelheim in "A Victim" and Nancy Mairs in "On Being a Cripple," Hurston chooses a label, "colored me," to explore questions of personal identity. Compare Hurston's use of "colored" with either Bettelheim's use of "victim" or Mairs's use of "cripple."

ALBERTO ALVARO RÍOS *Green Cards*

ALL COLORS EXIST to satisfy the longing for blue.

There's a folk saying in Spanish, *el que quiera azul que le cueste*. One must pay for what one wants; it's a variation of the older Spanish proverb, "Take what you want and pay for it, says God." But the phrase means, more literally, *he who wants blue, let it cost him.*

A green card is what you get if you are a citizen of another country but you find yourself in, or cross over to, the United States. The card is a first step toward applying for citizenship. My wife, who was born in Mexico, had one. My mother, who was born in England, had one. My father, who was born in Mexico, didn't have one. But that's another story, involving some curious papers and shady explanations. My mother-in-law, after more than forty years here, still has one. She's never been quite sure what to do next. But she's learned well that you don't raise your hand to ask the Immigration Service anything. They notice you then. Everybody knows that.

They notice you, and then they do something. And they're everywhere, maybe. So you don't speak loudly, you don't ask questions, you don't make trouble. Run away when you have to. Don't sign anything. Get a job only where everybody else is getting one, where it's safe.

There were all kinds of stories. The one my mother-in-law lived with the longest was how, her sister in Guaymas told her, they had heard that when you become a citizen of the United States, you have to spit on the flag of Mexico. And they would all shake their heads in a *no*.

My mother, when she became a citizen, recalls a curious moment. After the ceremony, the high-school band came in to the courtroom and, because she was special—which is to say, in this border town with Mexico, she was not Mexican—they played the British national anthem. Someone thought it was a good

5

First appeared in the Spring 1995 issue of Indiana Review, *a small-circulation quarterly magazine; included in Ríos's memoir,* Capirotada: A Nogales Memoir *(1999).*

idea. At that moment, though, she says she felt a little funny. She never forgot.

None of this is easy, and nobody knows what will happen when you come, and everybody is not treated the same. And things do happen. I think, finally, they were right.

Crossing over from Mexico, for example, was more than just being there and then being here. It was a change in how one walked, and a change in color. Over there, the ground moved one way, coiled and trailed and offered itself. Here was not there, and the coiling and trailing and offering were to the left and to the right, but never the same. To this, the legs and the body had to adjust. It was not the same ground.

And in Mexico, the color was green. Here, it is blue. And that Latin-American green is not the green of here, in the way that this blue is not the same blue in Mexico. The eyes, like the legs, have to learn over.

10   It is more than the music and the food and the clothing. It is the walk, and the color. And smell—not of food, but of things. And if one walked this other walk, and smells were new so the nose had to accommodate itself, one then began to look different. The body and the mirror made their changes.

I remember something from the middle of all this, from the middle of color and the middle of the century. During the '50s, I remember driving through town and seeing pickup trucks full of men dressed in white. They were *braceros*, the workers imported specifically from Mexico for a brief time, sometimes only a day, just to work. After work, either at the end of the day or the end of the growing season, they had to go back to Mexico. What that meant was taking the pickup truck to the border and dropping them all off.

Arizona was the last state to hold out against minimum wage, championing the *laissez-faire* system of government oversight; in this case, let the growers pay what the workers will accept and don't get in the way. And these workers worked for almost nothing. It seemed, for a while, like a good idea to the growers and to the government, whose program this was.

As a kid, I remember only all these men dressed in white. It was a color that meant they didn't belong anywhere.

Crossing over from Mexico to the United States is not a small thing, but not large either. This is an incorrect vocabulary. To cross over was big, but that part was easy. The big is like that. It was the small that was difficult.

15   To cross the border was made up of these smaller things, then. It was lived as these more difficult-to-explain changes in color, more like that, more something of the body than one might suspect. It was the different way of walking because the ground was new, in all things. A different way of walking or a different way of hiding. More surprise, or more dullness, dullness or quiet. Something.

It is a movement from green, but who would know it? How to explain it? This is what I've heard all my life. It is a movement like the planet's, a movement that is there absolute, but who can feel it? A movement from green, from green to what is next.

For my family, crossing over was crossing over from green, not from Mexico. Green from before, but sorted out, from all the moments of green in a life, sorted and lifted out and then assembled together, into a big green, into green only. Fresh from the inhuman jungles of Chiapas and farther still, somewhere middle on the Western-hemisphere map, into the green day, into the green night, into the in-between—the light and the dark greens, the green that is brown and the green that is white—but green, and inside green, green incarnate, from the back and from the front, from the shoulders and the feet, green from yesterday and green from before yesterday, all of it ocean-like, all of it water, all of it moving as claws and tendrils and tongues, as eyes, as webs, and as base and rough flight, so that to navigate upon it one needed to ride above it to move through it, and even then to be careful and to look around. One needed to paddle and to chart, the paddle as a half-weapon and a half-tool, remembering never to dangle foolishly—for the one moment green takes—an arm into it.

From green utterly and in whispers, green eyes and green tongue, green taste and green sound; green from tea; but then from coffee; from bitter, but then from sweet; green from garden, and a little then from bean and root and tuber, but then from sky and from air and from light.

But at light, and in dream, sound and strong, four-square and, yet, in that moment of pellucid strength, in that moment also inexplicably tinged with rue, there it is that green wavers and is for a moment inconstant, is for a moment green that is hollowed, or absent; is, for a moment, blue. There is the pivotal point, the narrows in this repeating hourglass of colors, in this life. There for a second, but there absolutely: green shifts to blue, and it is done.

It is Blue. Only and just blue. It is the log sawed and in its moment of breaking. It is the yawn pushed fully and then fully engaged. It is a blue. Blue and not green. Only blue. Only blue and the memory of green. Not a desire yet—green is too close—but a memory. 20

So much was the green.

On the far other side of green was a yellow, somewhere out there, somewhere only in imagination perhaps, yellow and red and some other colors on the other side of memory. Yellow, then the green, but now blue. It was the end at last, or the beginning. It was not the middle. But it was the discovery of the middle.

In this way, the green stayed, the way the Virgin Mary was painted, and in the shades of the hillside houses. It stayed in the Chinese teas, in the *yerba buena*,[1] how that green was a cure for things, and in the afternoons, in talk. Green stayed, and had a place in my family, but always as a memory. It stayed as a sadness for something.

It stayed as what used to be.

1. A species of mint used for medicinal purposes.

QUESTIONS

1. What do you think Ríos means when he says that Mexico is green and the United States is blue (paragraph 9)?

2. What is Ríos's attitude toward immigration, both legal and illegal?

3. Even though Ríos lives in the United States, he has elements of green left, as he says in the next-to-last paragraph. Do those elements serve as an argument against his blue–green dichotomy?

4. Characterize some thing or some person you know well in terms of colors, as Ríos does, especially in paragraph 17.

RICHARD SELZER *The Knife*

O NE HOLDS THE KNIFE as one holds the bow of a cello or a tulip—by the stem. Not palmed nor gripped nor grasped, but lightly, with the tips of the fingers. The knife is not for pressing. It is for drawing across the field of skin. Like a slender fish, it waits, at the ready, then, go! It darts, followed by a fine wake of red. The flesh parts, falling away to yellow globules of fat. Even now, after so many times, I still marvel at its power—cold, gleaming, silent. More, I am still struck with a kind of dread that it is I in whose hand the blade travels, that my hand is its vehicle, that yet again this terrible steel-bellied thing and I have conspired for a most unnatural purpose, the laying open of the body of a human being.

A stillness settles in my heart and is carried to my hand. It is the quietude of resolve layered over fear. And it is this resolve that lowers us, my knife and me, deeper and deeper into the person beneath. It is an entry into the body that is nothing like a caress; still, it is among the gentlest of acts. Then stroke and stroke again, and we are joined by other instruments, hemostats and forceps, until the wound blooms with strange flowers whose looped handles fall to the sides in steely array.

There is sound, the tight click of clamps fixing teeth into severed blood vessels, the snuffle and gargle of the suction machine clearing the field of blood for the next stroke, the litany of monosyllables with which one prays his way down and in; *clamp, sponge, suture, tie, cut*. And there is color. The green of the cloth, the white of the sponges, the red and yellow of the body. Beneath the fat lies the fascia, the tough fibrous sheet encasing the muscles. It must be sliced and the red beef of the muscles separated. Now there are retractors to hold apart the wound. Hands move together, part, weave. We are fully engaged, like children absorbed in a game or the craftsmen of some place like Damascus.

Deeper still. The peritoneum, pink and gleaming and membranous, bulges into the wound. It is grasped with forceps, and opened. For the first time we

Published in Selzer's first collection of autobiographical essays, Mortal Lessons: Notes on the Art of Surgery *(1976).*

can see into the cavity of the abdomen. Such a primitive place. One expects to find drawings of buffalo on the walls. The sense of trespassing is keener now, heightened by the world's light illuminating the organs, their secret colors revealed—maroon and salmon and yellow. The vista is sweetly vulnerable at this moment, a kind of welcoming. An arc of the liver shines high and on the right, like a dark sun. It laps over the pink sweep of the stomach, from whose lower border the gauzy omentum is draped, and through which veil one sees, sinuous, slow as just-fed snakes, the indolent coils of the intestine.

You turn aside to wash your gloves. It is a ritual cleansing. One enters this temple doubly washed. Here is man as microcosm, representing in all his parts the earth, perhaps the universe.

I must confess that the priestliness of my profession has ever been impressed on me. In the beginning there are vows, taken with all solemnity. Then there is the endless harsh novitiate of training, much fatigue, much sacrifice. At last one emerges as celebrant, standing close to the truth lying curtained in the Ark of the body. Not surplice and cassock but mask and gown are your regalia. You hold no chalice, but a knife. There is no wine, no wafer. There are only the facts of blood and flesh.

And if the surgeon is like a poet, then the scars you have made on countless bodies are like verses into the fashioning of which you have poured your soul. I think that if years later I were to see the trace from an old incision of mine, I should know it at once, as one recognizes his pet expressions.

But mostly you are a traveler in a dangerous country, advancing into the moist and jungly cleft your hands have made. Eyes and ears are shuttered from the land you left behind; mind empties itself of all other thought. You are the root of groping fingers. It is a fine hour for the fingers, their sense of touch so enhanced. The blind must know this feeling. Oh, there is risk everywhere. One goes lightly. The spleen. No! No! Do not touch the spleen that lurks below the left leaf of the diaphragm, a manta ray in a coral cave, its bloody tongue protruding. One poke and it might rupture, exploding with sudden hemorrhage. The filmy omentum must not be torn, the intestine scraped or denuded. The hand finds the liver, palms it, fingers running along its sharp lower edge, admiring. Here are the twin mounds of the kidneys, the apron of the omentum hanging in front of the intestinal coils. One lifts it aside and the fingers dip among the loops, searching, mapping territory, establishing boundaries. Deeper still, and the womb is touched, then held like a small muscular bottle—the womb and its earlike appendages, the ovaries. How they do nestle in the cup of a man's hand, their power all dormant. They are frailty itself.

There is a hush in the room. Speech stops. The hands of the others, assistants and nurses, are still. Only the voice of the patient's respiration remains. It is the rhythm of a quiet sea, the sound of waiting. Then you speak, slowly, the terse entries of a Himalayan climber reporting back.

"The stomach is okay. Greater curvature clean. No sign of ulcer. Pylorus,[1]

---

1. The opening from the stomach to the duodenum, which is the first part of the small intestine.

duodenum fine. Now comes the gall-bladder. No stones. Right kidney, left, all right. Liver . . . uh-oh."

Your speech lowers to a whisper, falters, stops for a long, long moment, then picks up again at the end of a sigh that comes through your mask like a last exhalation.

"Three big hard ones in the left lobe, one on the right. Metastatic deposits. Bad, bad. Where's the primary? Got to be coming from somewhere."

The arm shifts direction and the fingers drop lower and lower into the pelvis—the body impaled now upon the arm of the surgeon to the hilt of the elbow.

"Here it is."

15   The voice goes flat, all business now.

"Tumor in the sigmoid colon, wrapped all around it, pretty tight. We'll take out a sleeve of the bowel. No colostomy. Not that, anyway. But, God, there's a lot of it down there. Here, you take a feel."

You step back from the table, and lean into a sterile basin of water, resting on stiff arms, while the others locate the cancer.

When I was a small boy, I was taken by my father, a general practitioner in Troy, New York, to St. Mary's Hospital, to wait while he made his rounds. The solarium where I sat was all sunlight and large plants. It smelled of soap and starch and clean linen. In the spring, clouds of lilac billowed from the vases; and in the fall, chrysanthemums crowded the magazine tables. At one end of the great high-ceilinged, glass-walled room was a huge cage where colored finches streaked and sang. Even from the first, I sensed the nearness of that other place, the Operating Room, knew that somewhere on these premises was that secret dreadful enclosure where *surgery* was at that moment happening. I sat among the cut flowers, half drunk on the scent, listening to the robes of the nuns brush the walls of the corridor, and felt the awful presence of *surgery*.

Oh, the pageantry! I longed to go there. I feared to go there. I imagined surgeons bent like storks over the body of the patient, a circle of red painted across the abdomen. Silence and dignity and awe enveloped them, these surgeons; it was the bubble in which they bent and straightened. Ah, it was a place I would never see, a place from whose walls the hung and suffering Christ turned his affliction to highest purpose. It is thirty years since I yearned for that old Surgery. And now I merely break the beam of an electric eye, and double doors swing open to let me enter, and as I enter, always, I feel the surging of a force that I feel in no other place. It is as though I am suddenly stronger and larger, heroic. Yes, that's it!

20   The operating room is called a theatre. One walks onto a set where the cupboards hold tanks of oxygen and other gases. The cabinets store steel cutlery of unimagined versatility, and the refrigerators are filled with bags of blood. Bodies are stroked and penetrated here, but no love is made. Nor is it ever allowed to grow dark, but must always gleam with a grotesque brightness. For the special congress into which patient and surgeon enter, the one must have his senses deadened, the other his sensibilities restrained. One lies

naked, blind, offering; the other stands masked and gloved. One yields; the other does his will.

I said no love is made here, but love happens. I have stood aside with low-ered gaze while a priest, wearing the purple scarf of office, administers Last Rites to the man I shall operate upon. I try not to listen to those terrible last questions, the answers, but hear, with scorching clarity, the words that formal-ize the expectation of death. For a moment my resolve falters before the resig-nation, the *attentiveness*, of the other two. I am like an executioner who hears the cleric comforting the prisoner. For the moment I am excluded from the centrality of the event, a mere technician standing by. But it is only for the moment.

The priest leaves, and we are ready. Let it begin.

Later, I am repairing the strangulated hernia of an old man. Because of his age and frailty, I am using local anesthesia. He is awake. His name is Abe Kaufman, and he is a Russian Jew. A nurse sits by his head, murmuring to him. She wipes his forehead. I know her very well. Her name is Alexandria, and she is the daughter of Ukrainian peasants. She has a flat steppe of a face and slanting eyes. Nurse and patient are speaking of blintzes, borscht, piroshki—Russian food that they both love. I listen, and think that it may have been her grandfather who raided the shtetl where the old man lived long ago, and in his high boots and his blouse and his fury this grandfather pulled Abe by his side curls to the ground and stomped his face and kicked his groin. Per-haps it was that ancient kick that caused the hernia I am fixing. I listen to them whispering behind the screen at the head of the table. I listen with breath held before the prism of history.

"Tovarich," she says, her head bent close to his.

He smiles up at her, and forgets that his body is being laid open.   25

"You are an angel," the old man says.

One can count on absurdity. There, in the midst of our solemnities, appears, small and black and crawling, an insect: The Ant of the Absurd. The belly is open; one has seen and felt the catastrophe within. It seems the patient is al-ready vaporizing into angelhood in the heat escaping therefrom. One could warm one's hands in that fever. All at once that ant is there, emerging from be-neath one of the sterile towels that border the operating field. For a moment one does not really see it, or else denies the sight, so impossible it is, marching precisely, heading briskly toward the open wound.

Drawn from its linen lair, where it snuggled in the steam of the great ster-ilizer, and survived, it comes. Closer and closer, it hurries toward the incision. Ant, art thou in the grip of some fatal *ivresse*?[2] Wouldst hurtle over these scar-let cliffs into the very boil of the guts? Art mad for the reek we handle? Or in some secret act of formication engaged?

The alarm is sounded. An ant! An ant! And we are unnerved. Our fear of defilement is near to frenzy. It is not the mere physical contamination that we

2. French for "drunkenness."

loathe. It is the evil of the interloper, that he scurries across our holy place, and filthies our altar. He *is* disease—that for whose destruction we have gathered. Powerless to destroy the sickness before us, we turn to its incarnation with a vengeance, and pluck it from the lip of the incision in the nick of time. Who would have thought an ant could move so fast?

30   Between thumb and forefinger, the intruder is crushed. It dies as quietly as it lived. Ah, but now there is death in the room. It is a perversion of our purpose. Albert Schweitzer[3] would have spared it, scooped it tenderly into his hand, and lowered it to the ground.

The corpselet is flicked into the specimen basin. The gloves are changed. New towels and sheets are placed where it walked. We are pleased to have done something, if only a small killing. The operation resumes, and we draw upon ourselves once more the sleeves of office and rank. Is our reverence for life in question?

In the room the instruments lie on trays and tables. They are arranged precisely by the scrub nurse, in an order that never changes, so that you can reach blindly for a forceps or hemostat without looking away from the operating field. The instruments lie *thus!* Even at the beginning, when all is clean and tidy and no blood has been spilled, it is the scalpel that dominates. It has a figure the others do not have, the retractors and the scissors. The scalpel is all grace and line, a fierceness. It grins. It is like a cat—to be respected, deferred to, but which returns no amiability. To hold it above a belly is to know the knife's force—as though were you to give it slightest rein, it would pursue an intent of its own, driving into the flesh, a wild energy.

In a story by Borges,[4] a deadly knife fight between two rivals is depicted. It is not, however, the men who are fighting. It is the knives themselves that are settling their own old score. The men who hold the knives are mere adjuncts to the weapons. The unguarded knife is like the unbridled war-horse that not only carries its helpless rider to his death, but tramples all beneath its hooves. The hand of the surgeon must tame this savage thing. He is a rider reining to capture a pace.

So close is the joining of knife and surgeon that they are like the Centaur—the knife, below, all equine energy, the surgeon, above, with his delicate art. One holds the knife back as much as advances it to purpose. One is master of the scissors. One is partner, sometimes rival, to the knife. In a moment it is like the long red fingernail of the Dragon Lady. Thus does the surgeon curb in order to create, restraining the scalpel, governing it shrewdly, setting the action of the operation into a pattern, giving it form and purpose.

35   It is the nature of creatures to live within a tight cuirass that is both their constriction and their protection. The carapace of the turtle is his fortress and retreat, yet keeps him writhing on his back in the sand. So is the surgeon ren-

3. French doctor and philosopher (1875–1965) noted for his humanitarian work in Africa.
4. Jorge Luis Borges (1899–1986), Argentinean writer of poems and short stories that have a fantastical quality.

dered impotent by his own empathy and compassion. The surgeon cannot weep. When he cuts the flesh, his own must not bleed. Here it is all work. Like an asthmatic hungering for air, longing to take just one deep breath, the surgeon struggles not to feel. It is suffocating to press the feeling out. It would be easier to weep or mourn—for you know that the lovely precise world of proportion contains, just beneath, *there*, all disaster, all disorder. In a surgical operation, a risk may flash into reality: the patient dies . . . of *complication*. The patient knows this too, in a more direct and personal way, and he is afraid.

And what of that *other*, the patient, you, who are brought to the operating room on a stretcher, having been washed and purged and dressed in a white gown? Fluid drips from a bottle into your arm, diluting you, leaching your body of its personal brine. As you wait in the corridor, you hear from behind the closed door the angry clang of steel upon steel, as though a battle were being waged. There is the odor of antiseptic and ether, and masked women hurry up and down the halls, in and out of rooms. There is the watery sound of strange machinery, the tinny beeping that is the transmitted heartbeat of yet another *human being*. And all the while the dreadful knowledge that soon you will be taken, laid beneath great lamps that will reveal the secret linings of your body. In the very act of lying down, you have made a declaration of surrender. One lies down gladly for sleep or for love. But to give over one's body and will for surgery, to *lie down* for it, is a yielding of more than we can bear.

Soon a man will stand over you, gowned and hooded. In time the man will take up a knife and crack open your flesh like a ripe melon. Fingers will rummage among your viscera. Parts of you will be cut out. Blood will run free. Your blood. All the night before you have turned with the presentiment of death upon you. You have attended your funeral, wept with your mourners. You think, "I should never have had surgery in the springtime." It is too cruel. Or on a Thursday. It is an unlucky day.

Now it is time. You are wheeled in and moved to the table. An injection is given. "Let yourself go," I say. "It's a pleasant sensation," I say. "Give in," I say.

Let go? Give in? When you know that you are being tricked into the hereafter, that you will end when consciousness ends? As the monstrous silence of anesthesia falls discourteously across your brain, you watch your soul drift off.

Later, in the recovery room, you awaken and gaze through the thickness of drugs at the world returning, and you guess, at first dimly, then surely, that you have not died. In pain and nausea you will know the exultation of death averted, of life restored.

40

What is it, then, this thing, the knife, whose shape is virtually the same as it was three thousand years ago, but now with its head grown detachable? Before steel, it was bronze. Before bronze, stone—then back into unremembered time. Did man invent it or did the knife precede him here, hidden under ages of vegetation and hoofprints, lying in wait to be discovered, picked up, used?

The scalpel is in two parts, the handle and the blade. Joined, it is six inches from tip to tip. At one end of the handle is a narrow notched prong upon which the blade is slid, then snapped into place. Without the blade, the handle has a blind, decapitated look. It is helpless as a trussed maniac. But slide on the blade, click it home, and the knife springs instantly to life. It is headed now, edgy, leaping to mount the fingers for the gallop to its feast.

Now is the moment from which you have turned aside, from which you have averted your gaze, yet toward which you have been hastened. Now the scalpel sings along the flesh again, its brute run unimpeded by germs or other frictions. It is a slick slide home, a barracuda spurt, a rip of embedded talon. One listens, and almost hears the whine—nasal, high, delivered through that gleaming metallic snout. The flesh splits with its own kind of moan. It is like the penetration of rape.

The breasts of women are cut off, arms and legs sliced to the bone to make ready for the saw, eyes freed from sockets, intestines lopped. The hand of the surgeon rebels. Tension boils through his pores, like sweat. The flesh of the patient retaliates with hemorrhage, and the blood chases the knife wherever it is withdrawn.

45   Within the belly a tumor squats, toadish, fungoid. A gray mother and her brood. The only thing it does not do is croak. It too is hacked from its bed as the carnivore knife lips the blood, turning in it in a kind of ecstasy of plenty, a gluttony after the long fast. It is just for this that the knife was created, tempered, heated, its violence beaten into paper-thin force.

At last a little thread is passed into the wound and tied. The monstrous booming fury is stilled by a tiny thread. The tempest is silenced. The operation is over. On the table, the knife lies spent, on its side, the bloody meal smeardried upon its flanks. The knife rests.

And waits.

QUESTIONS

1. This essay seems very revealing, but of what? What does Selzer want us to know? (He doesn't seem to reason with us or to persuade us of anything by means of well-reasoned argument.)

2. At one point, Selzer switches from straight exposition to second-person address, employing "you" (paragraph 36). What impact does this switch have on you as reader? What rationale can you give for this switch?

3. Selzer assumes his readers know about surgery from personal experience. Is this a correct assumption? Imagine how a person who has never had surgery might respond. Write about the impact Selzer's essay has upon you from your own perspective of someone familiar or unfamiliar with surgery.

BRUNO BETTELHEIM   *A Victim*

M ANY STUDENTS of discrimination are aware that the victim often reacts in ways as undesirable as the action of the aggressor. Less attention is paid to this because it is easier to excuse a defendant than an offender, and because they assume that once the aggression stops the victim's reactions will stop too. But I doubt if this is of real service to the persecuted. His main interest is that the persecution cease. But that is less apt to happen if he lacks a real understanding of the phenomenon of persecution, in which victim and persecutor are inseparably interlocked.

Let me illustrate with the following example: in the winter of 1938 a Polish Jew murdered the German attaché in Paris, vom Rath. The Gestapo used the event to step up anti-Semitic actions, and in the camp new hardships were inflicted on Jewish prisoners. One of these was an order barring them from the medical clinic unless the need for treatment had originated in a work accident.

Nearly all prisoners suffered from frostbite which often led to gangrene and then amputation. Whether or not a Jewish prisoner was admitted to the clinic to prevent such a fate depended on the whim of an SS private. On reaching the clinic entrance, the prisoner explained the nature of his ailment to the SS man, who then decided if he should get treatment or not.

I too suffered from frostbite. At first I was discouraged from trying to get medical care by the fate of Jewish prisoners whose attempts had ended up in no treatment, only abuse. Finally things got worse and I was afraid that waiting longer would mean amputation. So I decided to make the effort.

When I got to the clinic, there were many prisoners lined up as usual, a score of them Jews suffering from severe frostbite. The main topic of discussion was one's chances of being admitted to the clinic. Most Jews had planned their procedure in detail. Some thought it best to stress their service in the German army during World War I: wounds received or decorations won. Others planned to stress the severity of their frostbite. A few decided it was best to tell some "tall story," such as that an SS officer had ordered them to report at the clinic.

Most of them seemed convinced that the SS man on duty would not see through their schemes. Eventually they asked me about my plans. Having no definite ones, I said I would go by the way the SS man dealt with other Jewish prisoners who had frostbite like me, and proceed accordingly. I doubted how

From The Informed Heart: Autonomy in a Mass Age *(1960), a book combining an account of Bettelheim's experience in German concentration camps during World War II and a critique of European Jews for going "like sheep to the slaughter." This book and its predecessor,* Individual and Mass Behavior in Extreme Situations *(1943), a psychological study of inmate behavior in concentration camps, have generated much controversy over the accuracy of Bettelheim's facts, observations, and analysis.*

57

wise it was to follow a preconceived plan, because it was hard to anticipate the reactions of a person you didn't know.

The prisoners reacted as they had at other times when I had voiced similar ideas on how to deal with the SS. They insisted that one SS man was like another, all equally vicious and stupid. As usual, any frustration was immediately discharged against the person who caused it, or was nearest at hand. So in abusive terms they accused me of not wanting to share my plan with them, or of intending to use one of theirs; it angered them that I was ready to meet the enemy unprepared.

No Jewish prisoner ahead of me in the line was admitted to the clinic. The more a prisoner pleaded, the more annoyed and violent the SS became. Expressions of pain amused him; stories of previous services rendered to Germany outraged him. He proudly remarked that *he* could not be taken in by Jews, that fortunately the time had passed when Jews could reach their goal by lamentations.

When my turn came he asked me in a screeching voice if I knew that work accidents were the only reason for admitting Jews to the clinic, and if I came because of such an accident. I replied that I knew the rules, but that I couldn't work unless my hands were freed of the dead flesh. Since prisoners were not allowed to have knives, I asked to have the dead flesh cut away. I tried to be matter-of-fact, avoiding pleading, deference, or arrogance. He replied: "If that's all you want, I'll tear the flesh off myself." And he started to pull at the festering skin. Because it did not come off as easily as he may have expected, or for some other reason, he waved me into the clinic.

10   Inside, he gave me a malevolent look and pushed me into the treatment room. There he told the prisoner orderly to attend to the wound. While this was being done, the guard watched me closely for signs of pain but I was able to suppress them. As soon as the cutting was over, I started to leave. He showed surprise and asked why I didn't wait for further treatment. I said I had gotten the service I asked for, at which he told the orderly to make an exception and treat my hand. After I had left the room, he called me back and gave me a card entitling me to further treatment, and admittance to the clinic without inspection at the entrance.

* * *

Because my behavior did not correspond to what he expected of Jewish prisoners on the basis of his projection, he could not use his prepared defenses against being touched by the prisoner's plight. Since I did not act as the dangerous Jew was expected to, I did not activate the anxieties that went with his stereotype. Still he did not altogether trust me, so he continued to watch while I received treatment.

Throughout these dealings, the SS felt uneasy with me, though he did not unload on me the annoyance his uneasiness aroused. Perhaps he watched me closely because he expected that sooner or later I would slip up and behave the way his projected image of the Jew was expected to act. This would have meant that his delusional creation had become real.

QUESTIONS

1. In paragraphs 6–7, Bettelheim refers to the Jews standing in line with him generally as "they." He uses phrases such as "they asked," "they insisted," "they accused me," and "it angered them." What is the effect of this grouping together of all prisoners (except himself) in the line?

2. In the final two paragraphs, Bettelheim offers an explanation for why he received medical treatment when others in line did not. Do you agree with his explanation? Why or why not? If not, provide another plausible explanation for why Bettelheim was treated differently.

3. Bettelheim tells his story in order to illustrate his point about victims reacting to persecutors "in ways as undesirable as the action of the aggressor" (paragraph 1). Does his story effectively illustrate his overall point? Why or why not? Write a brief analysis in which you explain your judgment.

NANCY MAIRS   *On Being a Cripple*

> To escape is nothing. Not to escape is nothing.
> — LOUISE BOGAN

THE OTHER DAY I was thinking of writing an essay on being a cripple. I was thinking hard in one of the stalls of the women's room in my office building, as I was shoving my shirt into my jeans and tugging up my zipper. Preoccupied, I flushed, picked up my book bag, took my cane down from the hook, and unlatched the door. So many movements unbalanced me, and as I pulled the door open I fell over backward, landing fully clothed on the toilet seat with my legs splayed in front of me: the old beetle-on-its-back routine. Saturday afternoon, the building deserted, I was free to laugh aloud as I wriggled back to my feet, my voice bouncing off the yellowish tiles from all directions. Had anyone been there with me, I'd have been still and faint and hot with chagrin. I decided that it was high time to write the essay.

First, the matter of semantics. I am a cripple. I choose this word to name me. I choose from among several possibilities, the most common of which are "handicapped" and "disabled." I made the choice a number of years ago, without thinking, unaware of my motives for doing so. Even now, I'm not sure what those motives are, but I recognize that they are complex and not entirely flattering. People—crippled or not—wince at the word "cripple," as they do not at "handicapped" or "disabled." Perhaps I want them to wince. I want

From Plaintext *(1986), a collection of personal essays, many about Mairs's life with multiple sclerosis.*

them to see me as a tough customer, one to whom the fates/gods/viruses have not been kind, but who can face the brutal truth of her existence squarely. As a cripple, I swagger.

But, to be fair to myself, a certain amount of honesty underlies my choice. "Cripple" seems to me a clean word, straightforward and precise. It has an honorable history, having made its first appearance in the Lindisfarne Gospel[1] in the tenth century. As a lover of words, I like the accuracy with which it describes my condition: I have lost the full use of my limbs. "Disabled," by contrast, suggests any incapacity, physical or mental. And I certainly don't like "handicapped," which implies that I have deliberately been put at a disadvantage, by whom I can't imagine (my God is not a Handicapper General), in order to equalize chances in the great race of life. These words seem to me to be moving away from my condition, to be widening the gap between word and reality. Most remote is the recently coined euphemism "differently abled," which partakes of the same semantic hopefulness that transformed countries from "undeveloped" to "underdeveloped," then to "less developed," and finally to "developing" nations. People have continued to starve in those countries during the shift. Some realities do not obey the dictates of language.

Mine is one of them. Whatever you call me, I remain crippled. But I don't care what you call me, so long as it isn't "differently abled," which strikes me as pure verbal garbage designed, by its ability to describe anyone, to describe no one. I subscribe to George Orwell's thesis that "the slovenliness of our language makes it easier for us to have foolish thoughts."[2] And I refuse to participate in the degeneration of the language to the extent that I deny that I have lost anything in the course of this calamitous disease; I refuse to pretend that the only differences between you and me are the various ordinary ones that distinguish any one person from another. But call me "disabled" or "handicapped" if you like. I have long since grown accustomed to them; and if they are vague, at least they hint at the truth. Moreover, I use them myself. Society is no readier to accept crippledness than to accept death, war, sex, sweat, or wrinkles. I would never refer to another person as a cripple. It is the word I use to name only myself.

5   I haven't always been crippled, a fact for which I am soundly grateful. To be whole of limb is, I know from experience, infinitely more pleasant and useful than to be crippled; and if that knowledge leaves one open to bitterness at my loss, the physical soundness I once enjoyed (though I did not enjoy it half enough) is well worth the occasional stab of regret. Though never any good at sports, I was a normally active child and young adult. I climbed trees, played hopscotch, jumped rope, skated, swam, rode my bicycle, sailed. I despised team sports, spending some of the wretchedest afternoons of my life, sweaty and hu-

1. Illustrated manuscript of the four gospels of the New Testament done by Irish monks; English commentaries were added in the tenth century.
2. A quotation from "Politics and the English Language" (included in the section "Language and Communication") by Orwell (1903–1950), British essayist and novelist, famous for his political commentaries.

miliated, behind a field-hockey stick and under a basketball hoop. I tramped alone for miles along the bridle paths that webbed the woods behind the house I grew up in. I swayed through countless dim hours in the arms of one man or another under the scattered shot of light from mirrored balls, and gyrated through countless more as Tab Hunter and Johnny Mathis[3] gave way to the Rolling Stones, Creedence Clearwater Revival, Cream. I walked down the aisle. I pushed baby carriages, changed tires in the rain, marched for peace.

When I was twenty-eight I started to trip and drop things. What at first seemed my natural clumsiness soon became too pronounced to shrug off. I consulted a neurologist, who told me that I had a brain tumor. A battery of tests, increasingly disagreeable, revealed no tumor. About a year and a half later I developed a blurred spot in one eye. I had, at last, the episodes "disseminated in space and time" requisite for a diagnosis: multiple sclerosis. I have never been sorry for the doctor's initial misdiagnosis, however. For almost a week, until the negative results of the tests were in, I thought that I was going to die right away. Every day for the past nearly ten years, then, has been a kind of gift. I accept all gifts.

Multiple sclerosis is a chronic degenerative disease of the central nervous system, in which the myelin that sheathes the nerves is somehow eaten away and scar tissue forms in its place, interrupting the nerves' signals. During its course, which is unpredictable and uncontrollable, one may lose vision, hearing, speech, the ability to walk, control of bladder and/or bowels, strength in any or all extremities, sensitivity to touch, vibration, and/or pain, potency, coordination of movements—the list of possibilities is lengthy and, yes, horrifying. One may also lose one's sense of humor. That's the easiest to lose and the hardest to survive without.

In the past ten years, I have sustained some of these losses. Characteristic of MS are sudden attacks, called exacerbations, followed by remissions, and these I have not had. Instead, my disease has been slowly progressive. My left leg is now so weak that I walk with the aid of a brace and a cane; and for distances I use an Amigo, a variation on the electric wheelchair that looks rather like an electrified kiddie car. I no longer have much use of my left hand. Now my right side is weakening as well. I still have the blurred spot in my right eye. Overall, though, I've been lucky so far. My world has, of necessity, been circumscribed by my losses, but the terrain left me has been ample enough for me to continue many of the activities that absorb me: writing, teaching, raising children and cats and plants and snakes, reading, speaking publicly about MS and depression, even playing bridge with people patient and honorable enough to let me scatter cards every which way without sneaking a peek.

Lest I begin to sound like Pollyanna, however, let me say that I don't like having MS. I hate it. My life holds realities—harsh ones, some of them—that no right-minded human being ought to accept without grumbling. One of

---

3. Tab Hunter (b. 1931), American actor and singer popular in the 1960s; Johnny Mathis (b. 1935), American singer popular in the 1950s and 1960s and well known for his love ballads.

them is fatigue. I know of no one with MS who does not complain of bone-weariness; in a disease that presents an astonishing variety of symptoms, fatigue seems to be a common factor. I wake up in the morning feeling the way most people do at the end of a bad day, and I take it from there. As a result, I spend a lot of time *in extremis*[4] and, impatient with limitation, I tend to ignore my fatigue until my body breaks down in some way and forces rest. Then I miss picnics, dinner parties, poetry readings, the brief visits of old friends from out of town. The offspring of a puritanical tradition of exceptional venerability, I cannot view these lapses without shame. My life often seems a series of small failures to do as I ought.

10   I lead, on the whole, an ordinary life, probably rather like the one I would have led had I not had MS. I am lucky that my predilections were already solitary, sedentary, and bookish—unlike the world-famous French cellist I have read about, or the young woman I talked with one long afternoon who wanted only to be a jockey. I had just begun graduate school when I found out something was wrong with me, and I have remained, interminably, a graduate student. Perhaps I would not have if I'd thought I had the stamina to return to a full-time job as a technical editor; but I've enjoyed my studies.

In addition to studying, I teach writing courses. I also teach medical students how to give neurological examinations. I pick up freelance editing jobs here and there. I have raised a foster son and sent him into the world, where he has made me two grandbabies, and I am still escorting my daughter and son through adolescence. I go to Mass every Saturday. I am a superb, if messy, cook. I am also an enthusiastic laundress, capable of sorting a hamper full of clothes into five subtly differentiated piles, but a terrible housekeeper. I can do italic writing and, in an emergency, bathe an oil-soaked cat. I play a fiendish game of Scrabble. When I have the time and the money, I like to sit on my front steps with my husband, drinking Amaretto and smoking a cigar, as we imagine our counterparts in Leningrad and make sure that the sun gets down once more behind the sharp childish scrawl of the Tucson Mountains.

This lively plenty has its bleak complement, of course, in all the things I can no longer do. I will never run again, except in dreams, and one day I may have to write that I will never walk again. I like to go camping, but I can't follow George and the children along the trails that wander out of a campsite through the desert or into the mountains. In fact, even on the level I've learned never to check the weather or try to hold a coherent conversation: I need all my attention for my wayward feet. Of late, I have begun to catch myself wondering how people can propel themselves without canes. With only one usable hand, I have to select my clothing with care not so much for style as for ease of ingress and egress, and even so, dressing can be laborious. I can no longer do fine stitchery, pick up babies, play the piano, braid my hair. I am immobilized by acute attacks of depression, which may or may not be physiologically related to MS but are certainly its logical concomitant.

These two elements, the plenty and the privation, are never pure, nor are

4. Latin for "in the last straits"—here it means "at the limits of endurance."

the delight and wretchedness that accompany them. Almost every pickle that I get into as a result of my weakness and clumsiness—and I get into plenty—is funny as well as maddening and sometimes painful. I recall one May afternoon when a friend and I were going out for a drink after finishing up at school. As we were climbing into opposite sides of my car, chatting, I tripped and fell, flat and hard, onto the asphalt parking lot, my abrupt departure interrupting him in mid-sentence. "Where'd you go?" he called as he came around the back of the car to find me hauling myself up by the door frame. "Are you all right?" Yes, I told him, I was fine, just a bit rattly, and we drove off to find a shady patio and some beer. When I got home an hour or so later, my daughter greeted me with "What have you done to yourself?" I looked down. One elbow of my white turtleneck with the green froggies, one knee of my white trousers, one white kneesock were blood-soaked. We peeled off the clothes and inspected the damage, which was nasty enough but not alarming. That part wasn't funny: The abrasions took a long time to heal, and one got a little infected. Even so, when I think of my friend talking earnestly, suddenly, to the hot thin air while I dropped from his view as though through a trap door, I find the image as silly as something from a Marx Brothers movie.

I may find it easier than other cripples to amuse myself because I live propped by the acceptance and the assistance and, sometimes, the amusement of those around me. Grocery clerks tear my checks out of my checkbook for me, and sales clerks find chairs to put into dressing rooms when I want to try on clothes. The people I work with make sure I teach at times when I am least likely to be fatigued, in places I can get to, with the materials I need. My students, with one anonymous exception (in an end-of-the-semester evaluation), have been unperturbed by my disability. Some even like it. One was immensely cheered by the information that I paint my own fingernails; she decided, she told me, that if I could go to such trouble over fine details, she could keep on writing essays. I suppose I became some sort of bright-fingered muse. She wrote good essays, too.

The most important struts in the framework of my existence, of course, are my husband and children. Dismayingly few marriages survive the MS test, and why should they? Most twenty-two- and nineteen-year-olds, like George and me, can vow in clear conscience, after a childhood of chicken pox and summer colds, to keep one another in sickness and in health so long as they both shall live. Not many are equipped for catastrophe: the dismay, the depression, the extra work, the boredom that a degenerative disease can insinuate into a relationship. And our society, with its emphasis on fun and its association of fun with physical performance, offers little encouragement for a whole spouse to stay with a crippled partner. Children experience similar stresses when faced with a crippled parent, and they are more helpless, since parents and children can't usually get divorced. They hate, of course, to be different from their peers, and the child whose mother is tacking down the aisle of a school auditorium packed with proud parents like a Cape Cod dinghy in a stiff breeze jolly well stands out in a crowd. Deprived of legal divorce, the child can at least deny the mother's disability, even her existence, forgetting to tell her

15

about recitals and PTA meetings, refusing to accompany her to stores or church or the movies, never inviting friends to the house. Many do.

But I've been limping along for ten years now, and so far George and the children are still at my left elbow, holding tight. Anne and Matthew vacuum floors and dust furniture and haul trash and rake up dog droppings and button my cuffs and bake lasagna and Toll House cookies with just enough grumbling so I know that they don't have brain fever. And far from hiding me, they're forever dragging me by racks of fancy clothes or through teeming school corridors, or welcoming gaggles of friends while I'm wandering through the house in Anne's filmy pink babydoll pajamas. George generally calls before he brings someone home, but he does just as many dumb thankless chores as the children. And they all yell at me, laugh at some of my jokes, write me funny letters when we're apart—in short, treat me as an ordinary human being for whom they have some use. I think they like me. Unless they're faking. . . .

Faking. There's the rub. Tugging at the fringes of my consciousness always is the terror that people are kind to me only because I'm a cripple. My mother almost shattered me once, with that instinct mothers have—blind, I think, in this case, but unerring nonetheless—for striking blows along the fault-lines of their children's hearts, by telling me, in an attack on my selfishness, "We all have to make allowances for you, of course, because of the way you are." From the distance of a couple of years, I have to admit that I haven't any idea just what she meant, and I'm not sure that she knew either. She was awfully angry. But at the time, as the words thudded home, I felt my worst fear, suddenly realized. I could bear being called selfish: I am. But I couldn't bear the corroboration that those around me were doing in fact what I'd always suspected them of doing, professing fondness while silently putting up with me because of the way I am. A cripple. I've been a little cracked ever since.

Along with this fear that people are secretly accepting shoddy goods comes a relentless pressure to please—to prove myself worth the burdens I impose, I guess, or to build a substantial account of goodwill against which I may write drafts in times of need. Part of the pressure arises from social expectations. In our society, anyone who deviates from the norm had better find some way to compensate. Like fat people, who are expected to be jolly, cripples must bear their lot meekly and cheerfully. A grumpy cripple isn't playing by the rules. And much of the pressure is self-generated. Early on I vowed that, if I had to have MS, by God I was going to do it well. This is a class act, ladies and gentlemen. No tears, no recriminations, no faintheartedness.

One way and another, then, I wind up feeling like Tiny Tim,[5] peering over the edge of the table at the Christmas goose, waving my crutch, piping down God's blessing on us all. Only sometimes I don't want to play Tiny Tim. I'd rather be Caliban,[6] a most scurvy monster. Fortunately, at home no one much cares whether I'm a good cripple or a bad cripple as long as I make vichyssoise

5. A crippled, frail young boy saved by Scrooge's eventual generosity in Charles Dickens's novel *A Christmas Carol.*

6. The monstrous son of the witch Sycorax in Shakespeare's play *The Tempest.*

with fair regularity. One evening several years ago, Anne was reading at the dining-room table while I cooked dinner. As I opened a can of tomatoes, the can slipped in my left hand and juice spattered me and the counter with bloody spots. Fatigued and infuriated, I bellowed, "I'm so sick of being crippled!" Anne glanced at me over the top of her book. "There now," she said, "do you feel better?" "Yes," I said, "yes, I do." She went back to her reading. I felt better. That's about all the attention my scurviness ever gets.

Because I hate being crippled, I sometimes hate myself for being a cripple. Over the years I have come to expect—even accept—attacks of violent self-loathing. Luckily, in general our society no longer connects deformity and disease directly with evil (though a charismatic once told me that I have MS because a devil is in me) and so I'm allowed to move largely at will, even among small children. But I'm not sure that this revision of attitude has been particularly helpful. Physical imperfection, even freed of moral disapprobation, still defies and violates the ideal, especially for women, whose confinement in their bodies as objects of desire is far from over. Each age, of course, has its ideal, and I doubt that ours is any better or worse than any other. Today's ideal woman, who lives on the glossy pages of dozens of magazines, seems to be between the ages of eighteen and twenty-five; her hair has body, her teeth flash white, her breath smells minty, her underarms are dry; she has a career but is still a fabulous cook, especially of meals that take less than twenty minutes to prepare; she does not ordinarily appear to have a husband or children; she is trim and deeply tanned; she jogs, swims, plays tennis, rides a bicycle, sails, but does not bowl; she travels widely, even to out-of-the-way places like Finland and Samoa, always in the company of the ideal man, who possesses a nearly identical set of characteristics. There are a few exceptions. Though usually white and often blonde, she may be black, Hispanic, Asian, or Native American, so long as she is unusually sleek. She may be old, provided she is selling a laxative or is Lauren Bacall. If she is selling a detergent, she may be married and have a flock of strikingly messy children. But she is never a cripple.

Like many women I know, I have always had an uneasy relationship with my body. I was not a popular child, largely, I think now, because I was peculiar: intelligent, intense, moody, shy, given to unexpected actions and inexplicable notions and emotions. But as I entered adolescence, I believed myself unpopular because I was homely: my breasts too flat, my mouth too wide, my hips too narrow, my clothing never quite right in fit or style. I was not, in fact, particularly ugly, old photographs inform me, though I was well off the ideal; but I carried this sense of self-alienation with me into adulthood, where it regenerated in response to the depredations of MS. Even with my brace I walk with a limp so pronounced that, seeing myself on the videotape of a television program on the disabled, I couldn't believe that anything but an inchworm could make progress humping along like that. My shoulders droop and my pelvis thrusts forward as I try to balance myself upright, throwing my frame into a bony S. As a result of contractures, one shoulder is higher than the other and I carry one arm bent in front of me, the fingers curled into a claw. My left arm

20

and leg have wasted into pipe-stems, and I try always to keep them covered. When I think about how my body must look to others, especially to men, to whom I have been trained to display myself, I feel ludicrous, even loathsome.

At my age, however, I don't spend much time thinking about my appearance. The burning egocentricity of adolescence, which assures one that all the world is looking all the time, has passed, thank God, and I'm generally too caught up in what I'm doing to step back, as I used to, and watch myself as though upon a stage. I'm also too old to believe in the accuracy of self-image. I know that I'm not a hideous crone, that in fact, when I'm rested, well dressed, and well made up, I look fine. The self-loathing I feel is neither physically nor intellectually substantial. What I hate is not me but a disease.

I am not a disease.

And a disease is not—at least not singlehandedly—going to determine who I am, though at first it seemed to be going to. Adjusting to a chronic incurable illness, I have moved through a process similar to that outlined by Elisabeth Kübler-Ross in *On Death and Dying*. The major difference—and it is far more significant than most people recognize—is that I can't be sure of the outcome, as the terminally ill cancer patient can. Research studies indicate that, with proper medical care, I may achieve a "normal" life span. And in our society, with its vision of death as the ultimate evil, worse even than decrepitude, the response to such news is, "Oh well, at least you're not going to *die*." Are there worse things than dying? I think that there may be.

25   I think of two women I know, both with MS, both enough older than I to have served me as models. One took to her bed several years ago and has been there ever since. Although she can sit in a high-backed wheelchair, because she is incontinent she refuses to go out at all, even though incontinence pants, which are readily available at any pharmacy, could protect her from embarrassment. Instead, she stays at home and insists that her husband, a small quiet man, a retired civil servant, stay there with her except for a quick weekly foray to the supermarket. The other woman, whose illness was diagnosed when she was eighteen, a nursing student engaged to a young doctor, finished her training, married her doctor, accompanied him to Germany when he was in the service, bore three sons and a daughter, now grown and gone. When she can, she travels with her husband; she plays bridge, embroiders, swims regularly; she works, like me, as a symptomatic-patient instructor of medical students in neurology. Guess which woman I hope to be.

At the beginning, I thought about having MS almost incessantly. And because of the unpredictable course of the disease, my thoughts were always terrified. Each night I'd get into bed wondering whether I'd get out again the next morning, whether I'd be able to see, to speak, to hold a pen between my fingers. Knowing that the day might come when I'd be physically incapable of killing myself, I thought perhaps I ought to do so right away, while I still had the strength. Gradually I came to understand that the Nancy who might one day lie inert under a bedsheet, arms and legs paralyzed, unable to feed or bathe herself, unable to reach out for a gun, a bottle of pills, was not the Nancy I was at present, and that I could not presume to make decisions for that future Nancy, who might well not want in the least to die. Now the only provision I've made for the future Nancy is that when the time comes—and it is likely to come in the form of pneumonia, friend to the weak and the old—I am not to be treated with machines and medications. If she is unable to communicate by then, I hope she will be satisfied with these terms.

Thinking all the time about having MS grew tiresome and intrusive, especially in the large and tragic mode in which I was accustomed to considering my plight. Months and even years went by without catastrophe (at least without one related to MS), and really I was awfully busy, what with George and children and snakes and students and poems, and I hadn't the time, let alone the inclination, to devote myself to being a disease. Too, the richer my life became, the funnier it seemed, as though there were some connection between largesse and laughter, and so my tragic stance began to waver until, even with the aid of a brace and a cane, I couldn't hold it for very long at a time.

After several years I was satisfied with my adjustment. I had suffered my grief and fury and terror, I thought, but now I was at ease with my lot. Then one summer day I set out with George and the children across the desert for a vacation in California. Part way to Yuma I became aware that my right leg felt funny. "I think I've had an exacerbation," I told George. "What shall we do?" he asked. "I think we'd better get the hell to California," I said, "because I don't know whether I'll ever make it again." So we went on to San Diego and then to Orange, up the Pacific Coast Highway to Santa Cruz, across to Yosemite, down to Sequoia and Joshua Tree, and so back over the desert to home. It was a fine two-week trip, filled with friends and fair weather, and I wouldn't have missed it for the world, though I did in fact make it back to California two years later. Nor would there have been any point in missing it, since in MS, once the symptoms have appeared, the neurological damage has been done, and there's no way to predict or prevent that damage.

The incident spoiled my self-satisfaction, however. It renewed my grief and fury and terror, and I learned that one never finishes adjusting to MS. I don't know now why I thought one would. One does not, after all, finish adjusting to life, and MS is simply a fact of my life—not my favorite fact, of course—but as ordinary as my nose and my tropical fish and my yellow Mazda station wagon. It may at any time get worse, but no amount of worry or anticipation can prepare me for a new loss. My life is a lesson in losses. I learn one at a time.

And I had best be patient in the learning, since I'll have to do it like it or ³⁰ not. As any rock fan knows, you can't always get what you want. Particularly when you have MS. You can't, for example, get cured. In recent years researchers and the organizations that fund research have started to pay MS some attention even though it isn't fatal; perhaps they have begun to see that life is something other than a quantitative phenomenon, that one may be very much alive for a very long time in a life that isn't worth living. The researchers have made some progress toward understanding the mechanism of the disease: It may well be an autoimmune reaction triggered by a slowacting virus. But they are nowhere near its prevention, control, or cure. And most of us want to

be cured. Some, unable to accept incurability, grasp at one treatment after another, no matter how bizarre: megavitamin therapy, gluten-free diet, injections
of cobra venom, hypothermal suits, lymphocytopharesis, hyperbaric chambers.
Many treatments are probably harmless enough, but none are curative.

The absence of a cure often makes MS patients bitter toward their doctors. Doctors are, after all, the priests of modern society, the new shamans,
whose business is to heal, and many an MS patient roves from one to another,
searching for the "good" doctor who will make him well. Doctors too think of
themselves as healers, and for this reason many have trouble dealing with MS
patients, whose disease in its intransigence defeats their aims and mocks their
skills. Too few doctors, it is true, treat their patients as whole human beings,
but the reverse is also true. I have always tried to be gentle with my doctors,
who often have more at stake in terms of ego than I do. I may be frustrated,
maddened, depressed by the incurability of my disease, but I am not diminished by it, and they are. When I push myself up from my seat in the waiting
room and stumble toward them, I incarnate the limitation of their powers. The
least I can do is refuse to press on their tenderest spots.

This gentleness is part of the reason that I'm not sorry to be a cripple. I
didn't have it before. Perhaps I'd have developed it anyway—how could I know
such a thing?—and I wish I had more of it, but I'm glad of what I have. It has
opened and enriched my life enormously, this sense that my frailty and need
must be mirrored in others, that in searching for and shaping a stable core in
a life wrenched by change and loss, change and loss, I must recognize the
same process, under individual conditions, in the lives around me. I do not
deprecate such knowledge, however I've come by it.

All the same, if a cure were found, would I take it? In a minute. I may be a
cripple, but I'm only occasionally a loony and never a saint. Anyway, in my
brand of theology God doesn't give bonus points for a limp. I'd take a cure; I
just don't need one. A friend who also has MS startled me once by asking, "Do
you ever say to yourself, 'Why me, Lord?'" "No, Michael, I don't," I told him,
"because whenever I try, the only response I can think of is 'Why not?'" If I
could make a cosmic deal, who would I put in my place? What in my life would
I give up in exchange for sound limbs and a thrilling rush of energy? No one.
Nothing. I might as well do the job myself. Now that I'm getting the hang of it.

QUESTIONS

1. How does Mairs organize her essay? What connects the different parts to each
other?

2. What stereotypes of "disabled" people does Mairs expect us to believe in? How does
she set out to counter them?

3. Mairs deliberately chooses to call herself a "cripple." Select a person or group that
deliberately chooses its own name or description and explain the rationale behind the
choice.

ALICE WALKER   *Beauty: When the Other Dancer Is the Self*

I

T IS A BRIGHT summer day in 1947. My father, a fat, funny man with beautiful eyes and a subversive wit, is trying to decide which of his eight children he will take with him to the county fair. My mother, of course, will not go. She is knocked out from getting most of us ready: I hold my neck stiff against the pressure of her knuckles as she hastily completes the braiding and then beribboning of my hair.

My father is the driver for the rich old white lady up the road. Her name is Miss Mey. She owns all the land for miles around, as well as the house in which we live. All I remember about her is that she once offered to pay my mother thirty-five cents for cleaning her house, raking up piles of her magnolia leaves, and washing her family's clothes, and that my mother—she of no money, eight children, and a chronic earache—refused it. But I do not think of this in 1947. I am two and a half years old. I want to go everywhere my daddy goes. I am excited at the prospect of riding in a car. Someone has told me fairs are fun. That there is room in the car for only three of us doesn't faze me at all. Whirling happily in my starchy frock, showing off my biscuit-polished patent-leather shoes and lavender socks, tossing my head in a way that makes my ribbons bounce, I stand, hands on hips, before my father. "Take me, Daddy," I say with assurance; "I'm the prettiest!"

Later, it does not surprise me to find myself in Miss Mey's shiny black car, sharing the back seat with the other lucky ones. Does not surprise me that I thoroughly enjoy the fair. At home that night I tell the unlucky ones all I can remember about the merry-go-round, the man who eats live chickens, and the teddy bears, until they say: that's enough, baby Alice. Shut up now, and go to sleep.

It is Easter Sunday, 1950. I am dressed in a green, flocked, scalloped-hem dress (handmade by my adoring sister, Ruth) that has its own smooth satin petticoat and tiny hot-pink roses tucked into each scallop. My shoes, new T-strap patent leather, again highly biscuit-polished. I am six years old and have learned one of the longest Easter speeches to be heard that day, totally unlike the speech I said when I was two: "Easter lilies/pure and white/blossom in/the morning light." When I rise to give my speech I do so on a great wave of love and pride and expectation. People in the church stop rustling their new crinolines. They seem to hold their breath. I can tell they admire my dress, but it is my spirit, bordering on sassiness (womanishness), they secretly applaud.

From In Search of Our Mother's Gardens: Womanist Prose *(1983), a collection of essays meditating on African American and feminist sources of inspiration, published the year after Walker's highly successful novel* The Color Purple.

"That girl's a little *mess*," they whisper to each other, pleased.

Naturally I say my speech without stammer or pause, unlike those who stutter, stammer, or, worst of all, forget. This is before the word "beautiful" exists in people's vocabulary, but "Oh, isn't she the *cutest* thing!" frequently floats my way. "And got so much sense!" they gratefully add . . . for which thoughtful addition I thank them to this day.

It was great fun being cute. But then, one day, it ended.

I am eight years old and a tomboy. I have a cowboy hat, cowboy boots, checkered shirt and pants, all red. My playmates are my brothers, two and four years older than I. Their colors are black and green, the only difference in the way we are dressed. On Saturday nights we all go to the picture show, even my mother; Westerns are her favorite kind of movie. Back home, "on the ranch," we pretend we are Tom Mix, Hopalong Cassidy, Lash LaRue (we've even named one of our dogs Lash LaRue); we chase each other for hours rustling cattle, being outlaws, delivering damsels from distress. Then my parents decide to buy my brothers guns. These are not "real" guns. They shoot "BBs," copper pellets my brothers say will kill birds. Because I am a girl, I do not get a gun. Instantly I am relegated to the position of Indian. Now there appears a great distance between us. They shoot and shoot at everything with their new guns. I try to keep up with my bow and arrows.

One day while I am standing on top of our makeshift "garage"—pieces of tin nailed across some poles—holding my bow and arrow and looking out toward the fields, I feel an incredible blow in my right eye. I look down just in time to see my brother lower his gun.

10   Both brothers rush to my side. My eye stings, and I cover it with my hand. "If you tell," they say, "we will get a whipping. You don't want that to happen, do you?" I do not. "Here is a piece of wire," says the older brother, picking it up from the roof; "say you stepped on one end of it and the other flew up and hit you." The pain is beginning to start. "Yes," I say, "Yes, I will say that is what happened." If I do not say this is what happened, I know my brothers will find ways to make me wish I had. But now I will say anything that gets me to my mother.

Confronted by our parents we stick to the lie agreed upon. They place me on a bench on the porch and I close my left eye while they examine the right. There is a tree growing from underneath the porch that climbs past the railing to the roof. It is the last thing my right eye sees. I watch as its trunk, its branches, and then its leaves are blotted out by the rising blood.

I am in shock. First there is intense fever, which my father tries to break using lily leaves bound around my head. Then there are chills: my mother tries to get me to eat soup. Eventually, I do not know how, my parents learn what has happened. A week after the "accident" they take me to see a doctor. "Why did you wait so long to come?" he asks, looking into my eye and shaking his head. "Eyes are sympathetic," he says. "If one is blind, the other will likely become blind too."

This comment of the doctor's terrifies me. But it is really how I look that bothers me most. Where the BB pellet struck there is a glob of whitish scar tissue, a hideous cataract, on my eye. Now when I stare at people—a favorite pastime, up to now—they will stare back. Not at the "cute" little girl, but at her scar. For six years I do not stare at anyone, because I do not raise my head.

Years later, in the throes of a mid-life crisis, I ask my mother and sister whether I changed after the "accident." "No," they say, puzzled. "What do you mean?"

What do I mean?   15

I am eight, and, for the first time, doing poorly in school, where I have been something of a whiz since I was four. We have just moved to the place where the "accident" occurred. We do not know any of the people around us because this is a different county. The only time I see the friends I knew is when we go back to our old church. The new school is the former state penitentiary. It is a large stone building, cold and drafty, crammed to overflowing with boisterous, ill-disciplined children. On the third floor there is a huge circular imprint of some partition that has been torn out.

"What used to be here?" I ask a sullen girl next to me on our way past it to lunch.

"The electric chair," says she.

At night I have nightmares about the electric chair, and about all the people reputedly "fried" in it. I am afraid of the school, where all the students seem to be budding criminals.

"What's the matter with your eye?" they ask, critically.   20

When I don't answer (I cannot decide whether it was an "accident" or not), they shove me, insist on a fight.

My brother, the one who created the story about the wire, comes to my rescue. But then brags so much about "protecting" me, I become sick.

After months of torture at the school, my parents decide to send me back to our old community, to my old school. I live with my grandparents and the teacher they board. But there is no room for Phoebe, my cat. By the time my grandparents decide there *is* room, and I ask for my cat, she cannot be found. Miss Yarborough, the boarding teacher, takes me under her wing, and begins to teach me to play the piano. But soon she marries an African—a "prince," she says—and is whisked away to his continent.

At my old school there is at least one teacher who loves me. She is the teacher who "knew me before I was born" and bought my first baby clothes. It is she who makes life bearable. It is her presence that finally helps me turn on the one child at the school who continually calls me "one-eyed bitch." One day I simply grab him by his coat and beat him until I am satisfied. It is my teacher who tells me my mother is ill.

My mother is lying in bed in the middle of the day, something I have never   25
seen. She is in too much pain to speak. She has an abscess in her ear. I stand looking down on her, knowing that if she dies, I cannot live. She is being treated with warm oils and hot bricks held against her cheek. Finally a doctor

comes. But I must go back to my grandparents' house. The weeks pass but I am hardly aware of it. All I know is that my mother might die, my father is not so jolly, my brothers still have their guns, and I am the one sent away from home.

"You did not change," they say.

Did I imagine the anguish of never looking up?

I am twelve. When relatives come to visit I hide in my room. My cousin Brenda, just my age, whose father works in the post office and whose mother is a nurse, comes to find me. "Hello," she says. And then she asks, looking at my recent school picture, which I did not want taken, and on which the "glob," as I think of it, is clearly visible, "You still can't see out of that eye?"

"No," I say, and flop back on the bed over my book.

30   That night, as I do almost every night, I abuse my eye. I rant and rave at it, in front of the mirror. I plead with it to clear up before morning. I tell it I hate and despise it. I do not pray for sight. I pray for beauty.

"You did not change," they say.

I am fourteen and baby-sitting for my brother Bill, who lives in Boston. He is my favorite brother and there is a strong bond between us. Understanding my feelings of shame and ugliness he and his wife take me to a local hospital, where the "glob" is removed by a doctor named O. Henry. There is still a small bluish crater where the scar tissue was, but the ugly white stuff is gone. Almost immediately I become a different person from the girl who does not raise her head. Or so I think. Now that I've raised my head I win the boyfriend of my dreams. Now that I've raised my head I have plenty of friends. Now that I've raised my head classwork comes from my lips as faultlessly as Easter speeches did, and I leave high school as valedictorian, most popular student, and *queen,* hardly believing my luck. Ironically, the girl who was voted most beautiful in our class (and was) was later shot twice through the chest by a male companion, using a "real" gun, while she was pregnant. But that's another story in itself. Or is it?

"You did not change," they say.

It is now thirty years since the "accident." A beautiful journalist comes to visit and to interview me. She is going to write a cover story for her magazine that focuses on my latest book. "Decide how you want to look on the cover," she says. "Glamorous, or whatever."

35   Never mind "glamorous," it is the "whatever" that I hear. Suddenly all I can think of is whether I will get enough sleep the night before the photography session: if I don't, my eye will be tired and wander, as blind eyes will.

At night in bed with my lover I think up reasons why I should not appear on the cover of a magazine. "My meanest critics will say I've sold out," I say. "My family will now realize I write scandalous books."

"But what's the real reason you don't want to do this?" he asks.

"Because in all probability," I say in a rush, "my eye won't be straight."

"It will be straight enough," he says. Then, "Besides, I thought you'd made your peace with that."

And I suddenly remember that I have. 40

I remember:

I am talking to my brother Jimmy, asking if he remembers anything unusual about the day I was shot. He does not know I consider that day the last time my father, with his sweet home remedy of cool lily leaves, chose me, and that I suffered and raged inside because of this. "Well," he says, "all I remember is standing by the side of the highway with Daddy, trying to flag down a car. A white man stopped, but when Daddy said he needed somebody to take his little girl to the doctor, he drove off."

I remember:

I am in the desert for the first time. I fall totally in love with it. I am so overwhelmed by its beauty, I confront for the first time, consciously, the meaning of the doctor's words years ago: "Eyes are sympathetic. If one is blind, the other will likely become blind too." I realize I have dashed about the world madly, looking at this, looking at that, storing up images against the fading of the light. *But I might have missed seeing the desert!* The shock of that possibility—and gratitude for over twenty-five years of sight—sends me literally to my knees. Poem after poem comes—which is perhaps how poets pray.

On Sight

I am so thankful I have seen
The Desert
And the creatures in the desert
And the desert Itself.

The desert has its own moon
Which I have seen
With my own eye.
There is no flag on it.

Trees of the desert have arms
All of which are always up
That is because the moon is up
The sun is up

Also the sky
The stars
Clouds
None with flags.

If there were flags, I doubt
the trees would point.
Would you?

45   *But mostly, I remember this:*
            I am twenty-seven, and my baby daughter is almost three. Since her birth
       I have worried about her discovery that her mother's eyes are different from
       other people's. Will she be embarrassed? I think. What will she say? Every day
       she watches a television program called "Big Blue Marble." It begins with a
       picture of the earth as it appears from the moon. It is bluish, a little battered-
       looking, but full of light, with whitish clouds swirling around it. Every time I
       see it I weep with love, as if it is a picture of Grandma's house. One day when
       I am putting Rebecca down for her nap, she suddenly focuses on my eye.
       Something inside me cringes, gets ready to try to protect myself. All children
       are cruel about physical differences, I know from experience, and that they
       don't always mean to be is another matter. I assume Rebecca will be the same.
            But no-o-o-o. She studies my face intently as we stand, her inside and me
       outside her crib. She even holds my face maternally between her dimpled lit-
       tle hands. Then, looking every bit as serious and lawyerlike as her father, she
       says, as if it may just possibly have slipped my attention: "Mommy, there's a
       world in your eye." (As in, "Don't be alarmed, or do anything crazy.") And then,
       gently, but with great interest: "Mommy, where did you *get* that world in your
       eye?"
            For the most part, the pain left then. (So what, if my brothers grew up to
       buy even more powerful pellet guns for their sons and to carry real guns them-
       selves. So what, if a young "Morehouse man"[1] once nearly fell off the steps of
       Trevor Arnett Library because he thought my eyes were blue.) Crying and
       laughing I ran to the bathroom, while Rebecca mumbled and sang herself off
       to sleep. Yes indeed, I realized, looking into the mirror. There *was* a world in
       my eye. And I saw that it was possible to love it: that in fact, for all it had
       taught me of shame and anger and inner vision, I *did* love it. Even to see it
       drifting out of orbit in boredom, or rolling up out of fatigue, not to mention
       floating back at attention in excitement (bearing witness, a friend has called
       it), deeply suitable to my personality, and even characteristic of me.
            That night I dream I am dancing to Stevie Wonder's[2] song "Always" (the
       name of the song is really "As," but I hear it as "Always"). As I dance, whirling
       and joyous, happier than I've ever been in my life, another bright-faced dancer
       joins me. We dance and kiss each other and hold each other through the
       night. The other dancer has obviously come through all right, as I have done.
       She is beautiful, whole and free. And she is also me.

1. A student at Morehouse College in Atlanta, Georgia.
2. African American singer, songwriter, and music producer (b. 1950).

QUESTIONS

1. Throughout her essay Walker refers to the "accident." Why does she put the word in
quotation marks? Has Walker made her peace with the "accident" and its consequences?

2. Walker writes her essay by selecting particular moments in her life. What does each moment show? How do these moments relate to Walker's theme?

3. What is the effect of ending the essay by recounting a dream? How does the dream relate to the essay's title?

4. Write an essay comparing and contrasting Walker's essay and Mairs's "On Being a Cripple." Consider especially their responses to injury or illness and their attitudes toward those subjects.

DAVID FOSTER WALLACE *Consider the Lobster*

THE ENORMOUS, pungent, and extremely well marketed Maine Lobster Festival is held every late July in the state's midcoast region, meaning the western side of Penobscot Bay, the nerve stem of Maine's lobster industry. What's called the midcoast runs from Owl's Head and Thomaston in the south to Belfast in the north. * * * The region's two main communities are Camden, with its very old money and yachty harbor and five-star restaurants and phenomenal B&Bs, and Rockland, a serious old fishing town that hosts the Festival every summer in historic Harbor Park, right along the water.[1]

Tourism and lobster are the midcoast region's two main industries, and they're both warm-weather enterprises, and the Maine Lobster Festival represents less an intersection of the industries than a deliberate collision, joyful and lucrative and loud. * * * Festival highlights: concerts by Lee Ann Womack and Orleans, annual Maine Sea Goddess beauty pageant, Saturday's big parade, Sunday's William G. Atwood Memorial Crate Race, annual Amateur Cooking Competition, carnival rides and midway attractions and food booths, and the MLF's Main Eating Tent, where something over 25,000 pounds of fresh-caught Maine lobster is consumed after preparation in the World's Largest Lobster Cooker near the grounds' north entrance. Also available are lobster rolls, lobster turnovers, lobster sauté, Down East lobster salad, lobster bisque, lobster ravioli, and deep-fried lobster dumplings. Lobster Thermidor is obtainable at a sit-down restaurant called The Black Pearl on Harbor Park's northwest wharf. A large all-pine booth sponsored by the Maine Lobster Promotion Council has free pamphlets with recipes, eating tips, and Lobster Fun Facts. The winner of Friday's Amateur Cooking Competition prepares Saffron Lobster Ramekins, the recipe for which is available for public downloading at www.mainelobsterfesti-

First published in Gourmet *(August 2004), a magazine for food lovers; later included in* Wallace's collection Consider the Lobster, *and Other Essays (2005).*

1. There's a comprehensive native apothegm: "Camden by the sea, Rockland by the smell" [Wallace's note].

val.com. There are lobster T-shirts and lobster bobblehead dolls and inflatable lobster pool toys and clamp-on lobster hats with big scarlet claws that wobble on springs. Your assigned correspondent saw it all, accompanied by one girl-friend and both his own parents—one of which parents was actually born and raised in Maine, albeit in the extreme northern inland part, which is potato country and a world away from the touristic midcoast.[2]

For practical purposes, everyone knows what a lobster is. As usual, though, there's much more to know than most of us care about—it's all a matter of what your interests are. Taxonomically speaking, a lobster is a marine crus-tacean of the family Homaridae, characterized by five pairs of jointed legs, the first pair terminating in large pincerish claws used for subduing prey. Like many other species of benthic[3] carnivore, lobsters are both hunters and scav-engers. They have stalked eyes, gills on their legs, and antennae. There are dozens of different kinds worldwide, of which the relevant species here is the Maine lobster, *Homarus americanus*. The name "lobster" comes from the Old English *loppestre*, which is thought to be a corrupt form of the Latin word for locust combined with the Old English *loppe*, which meant spider.

Moreover, a crustacean is an aquatic arthropod of the class Crustacea, which comprises crabs, shrimp, barnacles, lobsters, and freshwater crayfish. All this is right there in the encyclopedia. And an arthropod is an invertebrate member of the phylum Arthropoda, which phylum covers insects, spiders, crustaceans, and centipedes/millipedes, all of whose main commonality, be-sides the absence of a centralized brain-spine assembly, is a chitinous[4] exo-skeleton composed of segments, to which appendages are articulated in pairs.

The point is that lobsters are basically giant sea-insects.[5] Like most arthropods, they date from the Jurassic period, biologically so much older than mammalia that they might as well be from another planet. And they are—particularly in their natural brown-green state, brandishing their claws like weapons and with thick antennae awhip—not nice to look at. And it's true that they are garbagemen of the sea, eaters of dead stuff,[6] although they'll also eat some live shellfish, certain kinds of injured fish, and some-times each other.

But they are themselves good eating. Or so we think now. Up until some-time in the 1800s, though, lobster was literally low-class food, eaten only by the poor and institutionalized. Even in the harsh penal environment of early America, some colonies had laws against feeding lobsters to inmates more

2. N.B. All personally connected parties have made it clear from the start that they do not want to be talked about in this article. [Wallace's note].

3. Related to the bottom of a body of water.

4. A tough, protective semitransparent substance, related to cellulose.

5. Midcoasters' native term for a lobster is, in fact, "bug," as in "Come around on Sun-day and we'll cook up some bugs" [Wallace's note].

6. Factoid: Lobster traps are usually baited with dead herring [Wallace's note].

than once a week because it was thought to be cruel and unusual, like making people eat rats. One reason for their low status was how plentiful lobsters were in old New England. "Unbelievable abundance" is how one source describes the situation, including accounts of Plymouth pilgrims wading out and capturing all they wanted by hand, and of early Boston's seashore being littered with lobsters after hard storms—these latter were treated as a smelly nuisance and ground up for fertilizer. There is also the fact that premodern lobster was often cooked dead and then preserved, usually packed in salt or crude hermetic containers. Maine's earliest lobster industry was based around a dozen such seaside canneries in the 1840s, from which lobster was shipped as far away as California, in demand only because it was cheap and high in protein, basically chewable fuel.

Now, of course, lobster is posh, a delicacy, only a step or two down from caviar. The meat is richer and more substantial than most fish, its taste subtle compared to the marine-gaminess of mussels and clams. In the U.S. pop-food imagination, lobster is now the seafood analog to steak, with which it's so often twinned as Surf 'n' Turf on the really expensive part of the chain steak house menu.

In fact, one obvious project of the MLF, and of its omnipresently sponsorial Maine Lobster Promotion Council, is to counter the idea that lobster is unusually luxe or rich or unhealthy or expensive, suitable only for effete palates or the occasional blow-the-diet treat. It is emphasized over and over in presentations and pamphlets at the Festival that Maine lobster meat has fewer calories, less cholesterol, and less saturated fat than chicken.[7] And in the Main Eating Tent, you can get a "quarter" (industry shorthand for a 1¼-pound lobster), a 4-ounce cup of melted butter, a bag of chips, and a soft roll w/ butter-pat for around $12.00, which is only slightly more expensive than supper at McDonald's.

                                        *   *   *

Lobster is essentially a summer food. This is because we now prefer our lobsters fresh, which means they have to be recently caught, which for both tactical and economic reasons takes place at depths of less than 25 fathoms. Lobsters tend to be hungriest and most active (i.e., most trappable) at summer water temperatures of 45–50°F. In the autumn, some Maine lobsters migrate out into deeper water, either for warmth or to avoid the heavy waves that pound New England's coast all winter. Some burrow into the bottom. They might hibernate; nobody's sure. Summer is also lobsters' molting season—specifically early- to mid-July. Chitinous arthropods grow by molting, rather the way people have to buy bigger clothes as they age and gain weight. Since lobsters can live to be over 100, they can also get to be quite large, as in 20 pounds or more—though truly senior lobsters are rare now, because New En-

---

7. Of course, the common practice of dipping the lobster meat in melted butter torpedoes all these happy fat-specs, which none of the Council's promotional stuff ever mentions, any more than potato-industry PR talks about sour cream and bacon bits [Wallace's note].

gland's waters are so heavily trapped.[8] Anyway, hence the culinary distinction between hard- and soft-shell lobsters, the latter sometimes a.k.a. shedders. A soft-shell lobster is one that has recently molted. In midcoast restaurants, the summer menu often offers both kinds, with shedders being slightly cheaper even though they're easier to dismantle and the meat is allegedly sweeter. The reason for the discount is that a molting lobster uses a layer of seawater for insulation while its new shell is hardening, so there's slightly less actual meat when you crack open a shedder, plus a redolent gout of water that gets all over everything and can sometimes jet out lemonlike and catch a tablemate right in the eye. If it's winter or you're buying lobster someplace far from New England, on the other hand, you can almost bet that the lobster is a hard-shell, which for obvious reasons travel better.

10   As an à la carte entrée, lobster can be baked, broiled, steamed, grilled, sautéed, stir-fried, or microwaved. The most common method, though, is boiling. If you're someone who enjoys having lobster at home, this is probably the way you do it, since boiling is so easy. You need a large kettle w/cover, which you fill about half full with water (the standard advice is that you want 2.5 quarts of water per lobster). Seawater is optimal, or you can add two tbsp salt per quart from the tap. It also helps to know how much your lobsters weigh. You get the water boiling, put in the lobsters one at a time, cover the kettle, and bring it back up to a boil. Then you bank the heat and let the kettle simmer—ten minutes for the first pound of lobster, then three minutes for each pound after that. (This is assuming you've got hard-shell lobsters, which, again, if you don't live between Boston and Halifax, is probably what you've got. For shedders, you're supposed to subtract three minutes from the total.) The reason the kettle's lobsters turn scarlet is that boiling somehow suppresses every pigment in their chitin but one. If you want an easy test of whether the lobsters are done, you try pulling on one of their antennae—if it comes out of the head with minimal effort, you're ready to eat.

A detail so obvious that most recipes don't even bother to mention it is that each lobster is supposed to be alive when you put it in the kettle. This is part of lobster's modern appeal: It's the freshest food there is. There's no decomposition between harvesting and eating. And not only do lobsters require no cleaning or dressing or plucking (though the mechanics of actually eating them are a different matter), but they're relatively easy for vendors to keep alive. They come up alive in the traps, are placed in containers of seawater, and can, so long as the water's aerated and the animals' claws are pegged or banded to keep them from tearing one another up under the stresses of captivity,[9] survive right up until they're boiled. Most of us have been in supermarkets

---

8. Datum: in a good year, the U.S. industry produces around 80 million pounds of lobster, and Maine accounts for more than half of that total [Wallace's note].

9. N.B. Similar reasoning underlies the practice of what's termed "debeaking" broiler chickens and brood hens in modern factory farms. Maximum commercial efficiency requires that enormous poultry populations be confined in unnaturally close quarters, under which conditions many birds go crazy and peck one another to death. As a purely

or restaurants that feature tanks of live lobster, from which you can pick out your supper while it watches you point. And part of the overall spectacle of the Maine Lobster Festival is that you can see actual lobstermen's vessels docking at the wharves along the northeast grounds and unloading freshly caught product, which is transferred by hand or cart 100 yards to the great clear tanks stacked up around the Festival's cooker—which is, as mentioned, billed as the World's Largest Lobster Cooker and can process over 100 lobsters at a time for the Main Eating Tent.

So then here is a question that's all but unavoidable at the World's Largest Lobster Cooker, and may arise in kitchens across the U.S.: Is it all right to boil a sentient creature alive just for our gustatory pleasure? A related set of concerns: Is the previous question irksomely PC or sentimental? What does "all right" even mean in this context? Is it all just a matter of individual choice?

As you may or may not know, a certain well-known group called People for the Ethical Treatment of Animals thinks that the morality of lobster-boiling is not just a matter of individual conscience. In fact, one of the very first things we hear about the MLF . . . well, to set the scene: We're coming in by cab from the almost indescribably odd and rustic Knox County Airport[10] very late on the night before the Festival opens, sharing the cab with a wealthy political consultant who lives on Vinalhaven Island in the bay half the year (he's headed for the island ferry in Rockland). The consultant and cabdriver are responding to informal journalistic probes about how people who live in the midcoast region actually view the MLF, as in is the Festival just a big-dollar tourist thing or is it something local residents look forward to attending, take genuine civic pride in, etc. The cabdriver—who's in his seventies, one of apparently a whole platoon of retirees the cab company puts on to help with the summer rush, and wears a U.S.-flag lapel pin, and drives in what can only be called a very deliberate way—assures us that locals do endorse and enjoy the MLF, although he himself hasn't gone in years, and now come to think of it no one he and his wife know has, either. However, the demilocal consultant's been to recent Festivals a couple times (one gets the impression it was at his wife's behest), of which his most vivid impression was that "you have to line up for an ungodly long time to get your lobsters, and meanwhile there are all these ex–flower children coming up and down along the line handing out pamphlets that say the lobsters die in terrible pain and you shouldn't eat them."

And it turns out that the post-hippies of the consultant's recollection were

---

observational side-note, be apprised that debeaking is usually an automated process and that the chickens receive no anesthetic. It's not clear to me whether most *Gourmet* readers know about debeaking, or about related practices like dehorning cattle in commercial feedlots, cropping swine's tails in factory hog farms to keep psychotically bored neighbors from chewing them off, and so forth. It so happens that your assigned correspondent knew almost nothing about standard meat-industry operations before starting work on this article [Wallace's note].

10. The terminal used to be somebody's house, for example, and the lost-luggage-reporting room was clearly once a pantry [Wallacer's note].

activists from PETA. There were no PETA people in obvious view at the 2003 MLF,[11] but they've been conspicuous at many of the recent Festivals. Since at least the mid-1990s, articles in everything from *The Camden Herald* to *The New York Times* have described PETA urging boycotts of the MLF, often deploying celebrity spokespeople like Mary Tyler Moore for open letters and ads saying stuff like "Lobsters are extraordinarily sensitive" and "To me, eating a lobster is out of the question." More concrete is the oral testimony of Dick, our florid and extremely gregarious rental-car guy, to the effect that PETA's been around so much in recent years that a kind of brittlely tolerant homeostasis now obtains between the activists and the Festival's locals, e.g.: "We had some incidents a couple years ago. One lady took most of her clothes off and painted herself like a lobster, almost got herself arrested. But for the most part they're let alone. [Rapid series of small ambiguous laughs, which with Dick happens a lot.] They do their thing and we do our thing."

15   This whole interchange takes place on Route 1, 30 July, during a four-mile, 50-minute ride from the airport[12] to the dealership to sign car-rental papers. Several irreproducible segues down the road from the PETA anecdotes, Dick—whose son-in-law happens to be a professional lobsterman and one of the Main Eating Tent's regular suppliers—articulates what he and his family feel is the crucial mitigating factor in the whole morality-of-boiling-lobsters-alive issue: "There's a part of the brain in people and animals that lets us feel pain, and lobsters' brains don't have this part."

Besides the fact that it's incorrect in about 11 different ways, the main reason Dick's statement is interesting is that its thesis is more or less echoed

11. It turned out that Mr. William R. Rivas-Rivas, a high-ranking PETA official out of the group's Virginia headquarters, was indeed there this year, albeit solo, working the Festival's main and side entrances on Saturday, August 2, handing out pamphlets and adhesive stickers emblazoned with "Being Boiled Hurts," which is the tagline in most of PETA's published material about lobster. I learned that he'd been there only later, when speaking with Mr. Rivas-Rivas on the phone. I'm not sure how we missed seeing him *in situ* at the Festival, and I can't see much to do except apologize for the oversight—although it's also true that Saturday was the day of the big MLF parade through Rockland, which basic journalistic responsibility seemed to require going to (and which, with all due respect, meant that Saturday was maybe not the best day for PETA to work the Harbor Park grounds, especially if it was going to be just one person for one day, since a lot of diehard MLF partisans were off-site watching the parade (which, again with no offense intended, was in truth kind of cheesy and boring, consisting mostly of slow homemade floats and various midcoast people waving at one another, and with an extremely annoying man dressed as Blackbeard ranging up and down the length of the crowd saying "Arrr" over and over and brandishing a plastic sword at people, etc.; plus it rained)) [Wallace's note].

12. The short version regarding why we were back at the airport after already arriving the previous night involves lost luggage and a miscommunication about where and what the local National Car Rental franchise was—Dick came out personally to the airport and got us, out of no evident motive but kindness. (He also talked nonstop the entire way, with a very distinctive speaking style that can be described only as manically laconic; the truth is that I now know more about this man than I do about some members of my own family) [Wallace's note].

by the Festival's own pronouncement on lobsters and pain, which is part of a Test Your Lobster IQ quiz that appears in the 2003 MLF program courtesy of the Maine Lobster Promotion Council: "The nervous system of a lobster is very simple, and is in fact most similar to the nervous system of the grasshopper. It is decentralized with no brain. There is no cerebral cortex, which in humans is the area of the brain that gives the experience of pain."

Though it sounds more sophisticated, a lot of the neurology in this latter claim is still either false or fuzzy. The human cerebral cortex is the brain-part that deals with higher faculties like reason, metaphysical self-awareness, language, etc. Pain reception is known to be part of a much older and more primitive system of nociceptors and prostaglandins that are managed by the brain stem and thalamus.[13] On the other hand, it is true that the cerebral cortex is involved in what's variously called suffering, distress, or the emotional experience of pain—i.e., experiencing painful stimuli as unpleasant, very unpleasant, unbearable, and so on.

Before we go any further, let's acknowledge that the questions of whether and how different kinds of animals feel pain, and of whether and why it might be justifiable to inflict pain on them in order to eat them, turn out to be extremely complex and difficult. And comparative neuroanatomy is only part of the problem. Since pain is a totally subjective mental experience, we do not have direct access to anyone or anything's pain but our own; and even just the principles by which we can infer that others experience pain and have a legitimate interest in not feeling pain involve hard-core philosophy—metaphysics, epistemology, value theory, ethics. The fact that even the most highly evolved nonhuman mammals can't use language to communicate with us about their subjective mental experience is only the first layer of additional complication in trying to extend our reasoning about pain and morality to animals. And everything gets progressively more abstract and convoluted as we move farther and farther out from the higher-type mammals into cattle and swine and dogs and cats and rodents, and then birds and fish, and finally invertebrates like lobsters.

The more important point here, though, is that the whole animal-cruelty-and-eating issue is not just complex, it's also uncomfortable. It is, at any rate, uncomfortable for me, and for just about everyone I know who enjoys a variety of foods and yet does not want to see herself as cruel or unfeeling. As far as I can tell, my own main way of dealing with this conflict has been to avoid thinking about the whole unpleasant thing. I should add that it appears to me unlikely that many readers of GOURMET wish to think hard about it, either, or to be queried about the morality of their eating habits in the pages of a culinary monthly. Since, however, the assigned subject of this article is what it was

13. To elaborate by way of example: The common experience of accidentally touching a hot stove and taking your hand back before you're even aware that anything's going on is explained by the fact that many of the processes by which we detect and avoid painful stimuli do not involve the cortex. In the case of the hand and stove, the brain is bypassed altogether; all the important neurochemical action takes place in the spine [Wallace's note].

like to attend the 2003 MLF, and thus to spend several days in the midst of a
great mass of Americans all eating lobster, and thus to be more or less impelled to think hard about lobster and the experience of buying and eating lobster, it turns out that there is no honest way to avoid certain moral questions.

20   There are several reasons for this. For one thing, it's not just that lobsters
get boiled alive, it's that you do it yourself—or at least it's done specifically for
you, on-site.[14] As mentioned, the World's Largest Lobster Cooker, which is
highlighted as an attraction in the Festival's program, is right out there on the
MLF's north grounds for everyone to see. Try to imagine a Nebraska Beef Festival[15] at which part of the festivities is watching trucks pull up and the live
cattle get driven down the ramp and slaughtered right there on the World's
Largest Killing Floor or something—there's no way.

The intimacy of the whole thing is maximized at home, which of course is
where most lobster gets prepared and eaten (although note already the semi-
conscious euphemism "prepared," which in the case of lobsters really means
killing them right there in our kitchens). The basic scenario is that we come in
from the store and make our little preparations like getting the kettle filled and
boiling, and then we lift the lobsters out of the bag or whatever retail container they came home in . . . whereupon some uncomfortable things start to
happen. However stuporous the lobster is from the trip home, for instance, it
tends to come alarmingly to life when placed in boiling water. If you're tilting
it from a container into the steaming kettle, the lobster will sometimes try to
cling to the container's sides or even to hook its claws over the kettle's rim like
a person trying to keep from going over the edge of a roof. And worse is when
the lobster's fully immersed. Even if you cover the kettle and turn away, you
can usually hear the cover rattling and clanking as the lobster tries to push it
off. Or the creature's claws scraping the sides of the kettle as it thrashes

---

14. Morality-wise, let's concede that this cuts both ways. Lobster-eating is at least not
abetted by the system of corporate factory farms that produces most beef, pork, and
chicken. Because, if nothing else, of the way they're marketed and packaged for sale, we
eat these latter meats without having to consider that they were once conscious, sentient
creatures to whom horrible things were done. (N.B. PETA distributes a certain video—
the title of which is being omitted as part of the elaborate editorial compromise by which
this note appears at all—in which you can see just about everything meat-related you
don't want to see or think about. (N.B. 2. Not that PETA's any sort of font of unspoken
truth. Like many partisans in complex moral disputes, the PETA people are fanatics, and
a lot of their rhetoric seems simplistic and self-righteous. Personally, though, I have to
say that I found this unnamed video both credible and deeply upsetting.)) [Wallace's
note].

15. Is it significant that "lobster," "fish," and "chicken" are our culture's words for the
animal and the meat, whereas most mammals seem to require euphemisms like "beef"
and "pork" that help us separate the meat we eat from the living creature the meat once
was? Is this evidence that some kind of deep unease about eating higher animals is en-
demic enough to show up in the English usage, but that the unease diminishes as we
move out of the mammalian order? (And is "lamb"/"lamb" the counterexample that
sinks the whole theory, or are there special, biblico-historical reasons for that equivalence?) [Wallace's note].

around. The lobster, in other words, behaves very much as you or I would behave if we were plunged into boiling water (with the obvious exception of
screaming).[16] A blunter way to say this is that the lobster acts as if it's in terrible pain, causing some cooks to leave the kitchen altogether and to take one of
those little light-weight plastic oven timers with them into another room and
wait until the whole process is over.

There happen to be two main criteria that most ethicists agree on for determining whether a living creature has the capacity to suffer and so has genuine interests that it may or may not be our moral duty to consider.[17] One is
how much of the neurological hardware required for pain-experience the animal comes equipped with—nociceptors, prostaglandins, neuronal opioid receptors, etc. The other criterion is whether the animal demonstrates behavior
associated with pain. And it takes a lot of intellectual gymnastics and behaviorist hairsplitting not to see struggling, thrashing, and lid-clattering as just such
pain-behavior. According to marine zoologists, it usually takes lobsters between 35 and 45 seconds to die in boiling water. (No source I could find
talked about how long it takes them to die in superheated steam; one rather
hopes it's faster.)

There are, of course, other fairly common ways to kill your lobster on-site
and so achieve maximum freshness. Some cooks' practice is to drive a sharp
heavy knife point-first into a spot just above the midpoint between the lobster's
eyestalks (more or less where the Third Eye is in human foreheads). This is alleged either to kill the lobster instantly or to render it insensate—and is said at
least to eliminate the cowardice involved in throwing a creature into boiling
water and then fleeing the room. As far as I can tell from talking to proponents
of the knife-in-the-head method, the idea is that it's more violent but ultimately more merciful, plus that a willingness to exert personal agency and accept responsibility for stabbing the lobster's head honors the lobster somehow
and entitles one to eat it. (There's often a vague sort of Native American spiri-
tuality-of-the-hunt flavor to pro-knife arguments.) But the problem with the
knife method is basic biology: Lobsters' nervous systems operate off not one

16. There's a relevant populist myth about the high-pitched whistling sound that sometimes issues from a pot of boiling lobster. The sound is really vented steam from the
layer of seawater between the lobster's flesh and its carapace (this is why shedders whistle more than hard-shells), but the pop version has it that the sound is the lobster's rab-
bitlike death scream. Lobsters communicate via pheromones in their urine and don't
have anything close to the vocal equipment for screaming, but the myth's very persistent—which might, once again, point to a low-level cultural unease about boiling the
thing [Wallace's note].

17. "Interests" basically means strong and legitimate preferences, which obviously require some degree of consciousness, responsiveness to stimuli, etc. See, for instance,
the utilitarian philosopher Peter Singer, whose 1974 *Animal Liberation* is more or less
the bible of the modern animal-rights movement: "It would be nonsense to say that it
was not in the interests of a stone to be kicked along the road by a schoolboy. A stone
does not have interests because it cannot suffer. Nothing that we can do to it could possibly make any difference to its welfare. A mouse, on the other hand, does have an interest in not being kicked along the road, because it will suffer if it is" [Wallace's note].

but several ganglia, a.k.a. nerve bundles, which are sort of wired in series and distributed all along the lobster's underside, from stem to stern. And disabling only the frontal ganglion does not normally result in quick death or unconsciousness. Another alternative is to put the lobster in cold salt water and then very slowly bring it up to a full boil. Cooks who advocate this method are going mostly on the analogy to a frog, which can supposedly be kept from jumping out of a boiling pot by heating the water incrementally. In order to save a lot of research-summarizing, I'll simply assure you that the analogy between frogs and lobsters turns out not to hold.

Ultimately, the only certain virtues of the home-lobotomy and slow-heating methods are comparative, because there are even worse/crueler ways people prepare lobster. Time-thrifty cooks sometimes microwave them alive (usually after poking several extra vent holes in the carapace, which is a precaution most shellfish-microwavers learn about the hard way). Live dismemberment, on the other hand, is big in Europe: Some chefs cut the lobster in half before cooking; others like to tear off the claws and tail and toss only these parts in the pot.

25   And there's more unhappy news respecting suffering-criterion number one. Lobsters don't have much in the way of eyesight or hearing, but they do have an exquisite tactile sense, one facilitated by hundreds of thousands of tiny hairs that protrude through their carapace. "Thus," in the words of T. M. Prudden's industry classic *About Lobster*, "it is that although encased in what seems a solid, impenetrable armor, the lobster can receive stimuli and impressions from without as readily as if it possessed a soft and delicate skin." And lobsters do have nociceptors,[18] as well as invertebrate versions of the prostaglandins and major neurotransmitters via which our own brains register pain.

Lobsters do not, on the other hand, appear to have the equipment for making or absorbing natural opioids like endorphins and enkephalins, which are what more advanced nervous systems use to try to handle intense pain. From this fact, though, one could conclude either that lobsters are maybe even *more* vulnerable to pain, since they lack mammalian nervous systems' built-in analgesia, or, instead, that the absence of natural opioids implies an absence of the really intense pain-sensations that natural opioids are designed to mitigate. I for one can detect a marked upswing in mood as I contemplate this latter possibility: It could be that their lack of endorphin/enkephalin hardware means that lobsters' raw subjective experience of pain is so radically different from mammals' that it may not even deserve the term *pain*. Perhaps lobsters are more like those frontal-lobotomy patients one reads about who report experiencing pain in a totally different way than you and I. These patients evidently do feel physical pain, neurologically speaking, but don't dislike it—though neither do they like it; it's more that they feel it but don't feel anything

18. This is the neurological term for special pain receptors that are (according to Jane A. Smith and Kenneth M. Boyd's *Lives in the Balance*) "sensitive to potentially damaging extremes of temperature, to mechanical forces, and to chemical substances which are released when body tissues are damaged" [Wallace's note].

about it—the point being that the pain is not distressing to them or something they want to get away from. Maybe lobsters, who are also without frontal lobes, are detached from the neurological-registration-of-injury-or-hazard we call pain in just the same way. There is, after all, a difference between (1) pain as a purely neurological event, and (2) actual suffering, which seems crucially to involve an emotional component, an awareness of pain as unpleasant, as something to fear/dislike/want to avoid.

Still, after all the abstract intellection, there remain the facts of the frantically clanking lid, the pathetic clinging to the edge of the pot. Standing at the stove, it is hard to deny in any meaningful way that this is a living creature experiencing pain and wishing to avoid/escape the painful experience. To my lay mind, the lobster's behavior in the kettle appears to be the expression of a *preference*; and it may well be that an ability to form preferences is the decisive criterion for real suffering.[19] The logic of this (preference → suffering) relation may be easiest to see in the negative case. If you cut certain kinds of worms in half, the halves will often keep crawling around and going about their vermiform business as if nothing had happened. When we assert, based on their post-op behavior, that these worms appear not to be suffering, what we're really saying is that there's no sign that the worms know anything bad has happened or would *prefer* not to have gotten cut in half.

Lobsters, however, are known to exhibit preferences. Experiments have shown that they can detect changes of only a degree or two in water temperature; one reason for their complex migratory cycles (which can often cover 100-plus miles a year) is to pursue the temperatures they like best.[20] And, as

19. "Preference" is maybe roughly synonymous with "interest," but it is a better term for our purposes because it's less abstractly philosophical—"preference" seems more personal, and it's the whole idea of a living creature's personal experience that's at issue [Wallace's note].

20. Of course, the most common sort of counterargument here would begin by objecting that "like best" is really just a metaphor, and a misleadingly anthropomorphic one at that. The counterarguer would posit that the lobster seeks to maintain a certain optimal ambient temperature out of nothing but unconscious instinct (with a similar explanation for the low-light affinities about to be mentioned in the main text). The thrust of such a counterargument will be that the lobster's thrashings and clankings in the kettle express not unpreferred pain but involuntary reflexes, like your leg shooting out when the doctor hits your knee. Be advised that there are professional scientists, including many researchers who use animals in experiments, who hold to the view that nonhuman creatures have no real feelings at all, only "behaviors." Be further advised that this view has a long history that goes all the way back to Descartes, although its modern support comes mostly from behaviorist psychology.

To these what-look-like-pain-are-really-only-reflexes counterarguments, however, there happen to be all sorts of scientific and pro-animal-rights counter-counterarguments. And then further attempted rebuttals and redirects, and so on. Suffice to say that both the scientific and the philosophical arguments on either side of the animal-suffering issue are involved, abstruse, technical, often informed by self-interest or ideology, and in the end so totally inconclusive that as a practical matter, in the kitchen or restaurant, it all still seems to come down to individual conscience, going with (no pun) your gut [Wallace's note].

mentioned, they're bottom-dwellers and do not like bright light: If a tank of food lobsters is out in the sunlight or a store's fluorescence, the lobsters will always congregate in whatever part is darkest. Fairly solitary in the ocean, they also clearly dislike the crowding that's part of their captivity in tanks, since (as also mentioned) one reason why lobsters' claws are banded on capture is to keep them from attacking one another under the stress of close-quarter storage.

In any event, at the Festival, standing by the bubbling tanks outside the World's Largest Lobster Cooker, watching the fresh-caught lobsters pile over one another, wave their hobbled claws impotently, huddle in the rear corners, or scrabble frantically back from the glass as you approach, it is difficult not to sense that they're unhappy, or frightened, even if it's some rudimentary version of these feelings . . . and, again, why does rudimentariness even enter into it? Why is a primitive, inarticulate form of suffering less urgent or un-comfortable for the person who's helping to inflict it by paying for the food it results in? I'm not trying to give you a PETA-like screed here—at least I don't think so. I'm trying, rather, to work out and articulate some of the troubling questions that arise amid all the laughter and saltation and community pride of the Maine Lobster Festival. The truth is that if you, the Festival attendee, permit yourself to think that lobsters can suffer and would rather not, the MLF can begin to take on aspects of something like a Roman circus or me-dieval torture-fest.

30   Does that comparison seem a bit much? If so, exactly why? Or what about this one: Is it not possible that future generations will regard our own present agribusiness and eating practices in much the same way we now view Nero's entertainments or Aztec sacrifices? My own immediate reaction is that such a comparison is hysterical, extreme—and yet the reason it seems ex-treme to me appears to be that I believe animals are less morally important than human beings;[21] and when it comes to defending such a belief, even to myself, I have to acknowledge that (a) I have an obvious selfish interest in this belief, since I like to eat certain kinds of animals and want to be able to keep doing it, and (b) I have not succeeded in working out any sort of per-sonal ethical system in which the belief is truly defensible instead of just self-ishly convenient.

Given this article's venue and my own lack of culinary sophistication, I'm curious about whether the reader can identify with any of these reactions and acknowledgments and discomforts. I am also concerned not to come off as shrill or preachy when what I really am is confused. Given the (possible) moral status and (very possible) physical suffering of the animals involved, what eth-

---

21. Meaning a *lot* less important, apparently, since the moral comparison here is not the value of one human's life vs. the value of one animal's life, but rather the value of one animal's life vs. the value of one human's taste for a particular kind of protein. Even the most diehard carniphile will acknowledge that it's possible to live and eat well with-out consuming animals [Wallace's note].

ical convictions do gourmets evolve that allow them not just to eat but to savor and enjoy flesh-based viands (since of course refined *enjoyment*, rather than just ingestion, is the whole point of gastronomy)? And for those gourmets who'll have no truck with convictions or rationales and who regard stuff like the previous paragraph as just so much pointless navel-gazing, what makes it feel okay, inside, to dismiss the whole issue out of hand? That is, is their refusal to think about any of this the product of actual thought, or is it just that they don't want to think about it? Do they ever think about their reluctance to think about it? After all, isn't being extra aware and attentive and thoughtful about one's food and its overall context part of what distinguishes a real gourmet? Or is all the gourmet's extra attention and sensibility just supposed to be aesthetic, gustatory?

These last couple queries, though, while sincere, obviously involve much larger and more abstract questions about the connections (if any) between aesthetics and morality, and these questions lead straightaway into such deep and treacherous waters that it's probably best to stop the public discussion right here. There are limits to what even interested persons can ask of each other.

QUESTIONS

1. Wallace finally admits to being "confused" (paragraph 31) about the morality of eating lobsters. After reading his essay, what are your feelings? Are they changed from what they were before you read his essay?

2. Comment on Wallace's footnotes, which sometimes add information but at other times seem to carry on another argument on the bottom of the page. Why do you think he includes both kinds?

3. Do you share any of Wallace's ambivalence about being a tourist? When does such ambivalence bother you most, if ever?

4. Why do you think *Gourmet* published Wallace's essay?

5. Write about some festival you have attended, trying for Wallace's mode of outsider observation.

LOREN EISELEY   *The Brown Wasps*

THERE IS A CORNER in the waiting room of one of the great Eastern stations where women never sit. It is always in the shadow and overhung by rows of lockers. It is, however, always frequented—not so much by genuine travelers as by the dying. It is here that a certain element of the abandoned poor seeks a refuge out of the weather, clinging for a few hours longer to the city that has fathered them. In a precisely similar manner I have seen, on a sunny day in midwinter, a few old brown wasps creep slowly over an abandoned wasp nest in a thicket. Numbed and forgetful and frost-blackened, the hum of the spring hive still resounded faintly in their sodden tissues. Then the temperature would fall and they would drop away into the white oblivion of the snow. Here in the station it is in no way different save that the city is busy in its snows. But the old ones cling to their seats as though these were symbolic and could not be given up. Now and then they sleep, their gray old heads resting with painful awkwardness on the backs of the benches.

Also they are not at rest. For an hour they may sleep in the gasping exhaustion of the ill-nourished and aged who have to walk in the night. Then a policeman comes by on his round and nudges them upright.

"You can't sleep here," he growls.

A strange ritual then begins. An old man is difficult to waken. After a muttered conversation the policeman presses a coin into his hand and passes fiercely along the benches prodding and gesturing toward the door. In his wake, like birds rising and settling behind the passage of a farmer through a cornfield, the men totter up, move a few paces and subside once more upon the benches.

5   One man, after a slight, apologetic lurch, does not move at all. Tubercularly thin, he sleeps on steadily. The policeman does not look back. To him, too, this has become a ritual. He will not have to notice it again officially for another hour.

Once in a while one of the sleepers will not awake. Like the brown wasps, he will have had his wish to die in the great droning center of the hive rather than in some lonely room. It is not so bad here with the shuffle of footsteps and the knowledge that there are others who share the bad luck of the world. There are also the whistles and the sounds of everyone, everyone in the world, starting on journeys. Amidst so many journeys somebody is bound to come out all right. Somebody.

Maybe it was on a like thought that the brown wasps fell away from the old paper nest in the thicket. You hold till the last, even if it is only to a public seat in a railroad station. You want your place in the hive more than you want a room or a place where the aged can be eased gently out of the way. It is the place that matters, the place at the heart of things. It is life that you

From The Night Country *(1971), a book of natural history.*

want, that bruises your gray old head with the hard chairs; a man has a right
to his place.

But sometimes the place is lost in the years behind us. Or sometimes it is
a thing of air, a kind of vaporous distortion above a heap of rubble. We cling to
a time and place because without them man is lost, not only man but life. This
is why the voices, real or unreal, which speak from the floating trumpets at
spiritualist seances are so unnerving. They are voices out of nowhere whose
only reality lies in their ability to stir the memory of a living person with some
fragment of the past. Before the medium's cabinet both the dead and the living revolve endlessly about an episode, a place, an event that has already been
engulfed by time.

This feeling runs deep in life; it brings stray cats running over endless
miles, and birds homing from the ends of the earth. It is as though all living
creatures, and particularly the more intelligent, can survive only by fixing or
transforming a bit of time into space or by securing a bit of space with its objects immortalized and made permanent in time. For example, I once saw, on
a flower pot in my own living room, the efforts of a field mouse to build a remembered field. I have lived to see this episode repeated in a thousand guises,
and since I have spent a large portion of my life in the shade of a nonexistent
tree, I think I am entitled to speak for the field mouse.

One day as I cut across the field which at that time extended on one side   10
of our suburban shopping center, I found a giant slug feeding from a runnel of
pink ice cream in an abandoned Dixie cup. I could see his eyes telescope and
protrude in a kind of dim, uncertain ecstasy as his dark body bunched and
elongated in the curve of the cup. Then, as I stood there at the edge of the
concrete, contemplating the slug, I began to realize it was like standing on a
shore where a different type of life creeps up and fumbles tentatively among
the rocks and sea wrack. It knows its place and will only creep so far until
something changes. Little by little as I stood there I began to see more of this
shore that surrounds the place of man. I looked with sudden care and attention at things I had been running over thoughtlessly for years. I even waded
out a short way into the grass and the wild-rose thickets to see more. A huge
black-belted bee went droning by and there were some indistinct scurryings in
the underbrush.

Then I came to a sign which informed me that this field was to be the site
of a new Wanamaker suburban store. Thousands of obscure lives were about
to perish, the spores of puffballs would go smoking off to new fields, and the
bodies of little white-footed mice would be crunched under the inexorable
wheels of the bulldozers. Life disappears or modifies its appearances so fast
that everything takes on an aspect of illusion—a momentary fizzing and boiling with smoke rings, like pouring dissident chemicals into a retort. Here man
was advancing, but in a few years his plaster and bricks would be disappearing once more into the insatiable maw of the clover. Being of an archaeological cast of mind, I thought of this fact with an obscure sense of
satisfaction and waded back through the rose thickets to the concrete parking
lot. As I did so, a mouse scurried ahead of me, frightened of my steps if not of

that ominous Wanamaker sign. I saw him vanish in the general direction of my apartment house, his little body quivering with fear in the great open sun on the blazing concrete. Blinded and confused, he was running straight away from his field. In another week scores would follow him.

I forgot the episode then and went home to the quiet of my living room. It was not until a week later, letting myself into the apartment, that I realized I had a visitor. I am fond of plants and had several ferns standing on the floor in pots to avoid the noon glare by the south window.

As I snapped on the light and glanced carelessly around the room, I saw a little heap of earth on the carpet and a scrabble of pebbles that had been kicked merrily over the edge of one of the flower pots. To my astonishment I discovered a full-fledged burrow delving downward among the fern roots. I waited silently. The creature who had made the burrow did not appear. I remembered the wild field then, and the flight of the mice. No house mouse, no *Mus domesticus*,[1] had kicked up this little heap of earth or sought refuge under a fern root in a flower pot. I thought of the desperate little creature I had seen fleeing from the wild-rose thicket. Through intricacies of pipes and attics, he, or one of his fellows, had climbed to this high green solitary room. I could visualize what had occurred. He had an image in his head, a world of seed pods and quiet, of green sheltering leaves in the dim light among the weed stems. It was the only world he knew and it was gone.

Somehow in his flight he had found his way to this room with drawn shades where no one would come till nightfall. And here he had smelled green leaves and run quickly up the flower pot to dabble his paws in common earth. He had even struggled half the afternoon to carry his burrow deeper and had failed. I examined the hole, but no whiskered twitching face appeared. He was gone. I gathered up the earth and refilled the burrow. I did not expect to find traces of him again.

15   Yet for three nights thereafter I came home to the darkened room and my ferns to find the dirt kicked gaily about the rug and the burrow reopened, though I was never able to catch the field mouse within it. I dropped a little food about the mouth of the burrow, but it was never touched. I looked under beds or sat reading with one ear cocked for rustlings in the ferns. It was all in vain; I never saw him. Probably he ended in a trap in some other tenant's room.

But before he disappeared I had come to look hopefully for his evening burrow. About my ferns there had begun to linger the insubstantial vapor of an autumn field, the distilled essence, as it were, of a mouse brain in exile from its home. It was a small dream, like our dreams, carried a long and weary journey along pipes and through spider webs, past holes over which loomed the shadows of waiting cats, and finally, desperately, into this room where he had played in the shuttered daylight for an hour among the green ferns on the floor. Every day these invisible dreams pass us on the street, or rise from beneath our feet, or look out upon us from beneath a bush.

Some years ago the old elevated railway in Philadelphia was torn down

1. The Latin genus and species of the house mouse.

and replaced by a subway system. This ancient El with its barnlike stations containing nut-vending machines and scattered food scraps had, for generations, been the favorite feeding ground of flocks of pigeons, generally one flock to a station along the route of the El. Hundreds of pigeons were dependent upon the system. They flapped in and out of its stanchions and steel work or gathered in watchful little audiences about the feet of anyone who rattled the peanut-vending machines. They even watched people who jingled change in their hands, and prospected for food under the feet of the crowds who gathered between trains. Probably very few among the waiting people who tossed a crumb to an eager pigeon realized that this El was like a food-bearing river, and that the life which haunted its banks was dependent upon the running of the trains with their human freight.

I saw the river stop.

The time came when the underground tubes were ready; the traffic was transferred to a realm unreachable by pigeons. It was like a great river subsiding suddenly into desert sands. For a day, for two days, pigeons continued to circle over the El or stand close to the red vending machines. They were patient birds, and surely this great river which had flowed through the lives of unnumbered generations was merely suffering from some momentary drought.

They listened for the familiar vibrations that had always heralded an approaching train; they flapped hopefully about the head of an occasional workman walking along the steel runways. They passed from one empty station to another, all the while growing hungrier. Finally they flew away. [20]

I thought I had seen the last of them about the El, but there was a revival and it provided a curious instance of the memory of living things for a way of life or a locality that has long been cherished. Some weeks after the El was abandoned workmen began to tear it down. I went to work every morning by one particular station, and the time came when the demolition crews reached this spot. Acetylene torches showered passersby with sparks, pneumatic drills hammered at the base of the structure, and a blind man who, like the pigeons, had clung with his cup to a stairway leading to the change booth, was forced to give up his place.

It was then, strangely, momentarily, one morning that I witnessed the return of a little band of the familiar pigeons. I even recognized one or two members of the flock that had lived around this particular station before they were dispersed into the streets. They flew bravely in and out among the sparks and the hammers and the shouting workmen. They had returned—and they had returned because the hubbub of the wreckers had convinced them that the river was about to flow once more. For several hours they flapped in and out through the empty windows, nodding their heads and watching the fall of girders with attentive little eyes. By the following morning the station was reduced to some burned-off stanchions in the street. My bird friends had gone. It was plain, however, that they retained a memory for an insubstantial structure now compounded of air and time. Even the blind man clung to it. Someone had provided him with a chair, and he sat at the same corner staring sightlessly at an invisible stairway where, so far as he was concerned, the crowds were still ascending to the trains.

I have said my life has been passed in the shade of a nonexistent tree, so that such sights do not offend me. Prematurely I am one of the brown wasps and I often sit with them in the great droning hive of the station, dreaming sometimes of a certain tree. It was planted sixty years ago by a boy with a bucket and a toy spade in a little Nebraska town. That boy was myself. It was a cottonwood sapling and the boy remembered it because of some words spoken by his father and because everyone died or moved away who was supposed to wait and grow old under its shade. The boy was passed from hand to hand, but the tree for some intangible reason had taken root in his mind. It was under its branches that he sheltered; it was from this tree that his memories, which are my memories, led away into the world.

After sixty years the mood of the brown wasps grows heavier upon one. During a long inward struggle I thought it would do me good to go and look upon that actual tree. I found a rational excuse in which to clothe this madness. I purchased a ticket and at the end of two thousand miles I walked another mile to an address that was still the same. The house had not been altered.

25   I came close to the white picket fence and reluctantly, with great effort, looked down the long vista of the yard. There was nothing there to see. For sixty years that cottonwood had been growing in my mind. Season by season its seeds had been floating farther on the hot prairie winds. We had planted it lovingly there, my father and I, because he had a great hunger for soil and live things growing, and because none of these things had long been ours to protect. We had planted the little sapling and watered it faithfully, and I remembered that I had run out with my small bucket to drench its roots the day we moved away. And all the years since it had been growing in my mind, a huge tree that somehow stood for my father and the love I bore him. I took a grasp on the picket fence and forced myself to look again.

A boy with the hard bird eye of youth pedaled a tricycle slowly up beside me.

"What'cha lookin' at?" he asked curiously.

"A tree," I said.

"What for?" he said.

30   "It isn't there," I said, to myself mostly, and began to walk away at a pace just slow enough not to seem to be running.

"What isn't there?" the boy asked. I didn't answer. It was obvious I was attached by a thread to a thing that had never been there, or certainly not for long. Something that had to be held in the air, or sustained in the mind, because it was part of my orientation in the universe and I could not survive without it. There was more than an animal's attachment to a place. There was something else, the attachment of the spirit to a grouping of events in time; it was part of our mortality.

So I had come home at last, driven by a memory in the brain as surely as the field mouse who had delved long ago into my flower pot or the pigeons flying forever amidst the rattle of nut-vending machines. These, the burrow under the greenery in my living room and the red-bellied bowls of peanuts now hovering in midair in the minds of pigeons, were all part of an elusive world that existed nowhere and yet everywhere. I looked once at the real world about me while the persistent boy pedaled at my heels.

It was without meaning, though my feet took a remembered path. In sixty years the house and street had rotted out of my mind. But the tree, the tree that no longer was, that had perished in its first season, bloomed on in my individual mind, unblemished as my father's words. "We'll plant a tree here, son, and we're not going to move any more. And when you're an old, old man you can sit under it and think how we planted it here, you and me, together."

I began to outpace the boy on the tricycle.

"Do you live here, Mister?" he shouted after me suspiciously. I took a firm grasp on airy nothing—to be precise, on the bole of a great tree. "I do," I said. I spoke for myself, one field mouse, and several pigeons. We were all out of touch but somehow permanent. It was the world that had changed.

35

QUESTIONS

1. Eiseley writes of old men in train stations, brown wasps, a field mouse, pigeons near the El, and his own return to his boyhood home in Nebraska. What do these all have in common? State what you believe to be the essay's theme.

2. Some psychologists study animal behavior in order to learn about human behavior, but others write about animals in a very different fashion. Do you think that Eiseley's way of relating the behavior of animals to human behavior makes sense? Why or why not?

3. From close observation of an animal's behavior, write two brief descriptions, one using animal–human comparisons and one simply sticking to what you see.

E. B. WHITE   *Once More to the Lake*

ONE SUMMER, ALONG ABOUT 1904, my father rented a camp on a lake in Maine and took us all there for the month of August. We all got ringworm from some kittens and had to rub Pond's Extract on our arms and legs night and morning, and my father rolled over in a canoe with all his clothes on; but outside of that the vacation was a success and from then on none of us ever thought there was any place in the world like that lake in Maine. We returned

Originally appeared in "One Man's Meat," White's column for Harper's Magazine *(October 1941); later included in* One Man's Meat *(1942), a collection of his columns about life on a Maine saltwater farm, and then in* Essays of E. B. White *(1977).*

summer after summer—always on August 1st for one month. I have since become a salt-water man, but sometimes in summer there are days when the restlessness of the tides and the fearful cold of the sea water and the incessant wind which blows across the afternoon and into the evening make me wish for the placidity of a lake in the woods. A few weeks ago this feeling got so strong I bought myself a couple of bass hooks and a spinner and returned to the lake where we used to go, for a week's fishing and to revisit old haunts.

I took along my son, who had never had any fresh water up his nose and who had seen lily pads only from train windows. On the journey over to the lake I began to wonder what it would be like. I wondered how time would have marred this unique, this holy spot—the coves and streams, the hills that the sun set behind, the camps and the paths behind the camps. I was sure the tarred road would have found it out and I wondered in what other ways it would be desolated. It is strange how much you can remember about places like that once you allow your mind to return into the grooves which lead back. You remember one thing, and that suddenly reminds you of another thing. I guess I remembered clearest of all the early mornings, when the lake was cool and motionless, remembered how the bedroom smelled of the lumber it was made of and of the wet woods whose scent entered through the screen. The partitions in the camp were thin and did not extend clear to the top of the rooms, and as I was always the first up I would dress softly so as not to wake the others, and sneak out into the sweet outdoors and start out in the canoe, keeping close along the shore in the long shadows of the pines. I remembered being very careful never to rub my paddle against the gunwale for fear of disturbing the stillness of the cathedral.

The lake had never been what you would call a wild lake. There were cottages sprinkled around the shores, and it was in farming country although the shores of the lake were quite heavily wooded. Some of the cottages were owned by nearby farmers, and you would live at the shore and eat your meals at the farmhouse. That's what our family did. But although it wasn't wild, it was a fairly large and undisturbed lake and there were places in it which, to a child at least, seemed infinitely remote and primeval.

I was right about the tar: it led to within half a mile of the shore. But when I got back there, with my boy, and we settled into a camp near a farmhouse and into the kind of summertime I had known, I could tell that it was going to be pretty much the same as it had been before—I knew it, lying in bed the first morning, smelling the bedroom, and hearing the boy sneak quietly out and go off along the shore in a boat. I began to sustain the illusion that he was I, and therefore, by simple transposition, that I was my father. This sensation persisted, kept cropping up all the time we were there. It was not an entirely new feeling, but in this setting it grew much stronger. I seemed to be living a dual existence. I would be in the middle of some simple act, I would be picking up a bait box or laying down a table fork, or I would be saying something, and suddenly it would be not I but my father who was saying the words or making the gesture. It gave me a creepy sensation.

5   We went fishing the first morning. I felt the same damp moss covering

the worms in the bait can, and saw the dragonfly alight on the tip of my rod as it hovered a few inches from the surface of the water. It was the arrival of this fly that convinced me beyond any doubt that everything was as it always had been, that the years were a mirage and there had been no years. The small waves were the same, chucking the rowboat under the chin as we fished at anchor, and the boat was the same boat, the same color green and the ribs broken in the same places, and under the floor-boards the same fresh-water leavings and débris—the dead helgrammite,[1] the wisps of moss, the rusty discarded fishhook, the dried blood from yesterday's catch. We stared silently at the tips of our rods, at the dragonflies that came and went. I lowered the tip of mine into the water, tentatively, pensively dislodging the fly, which darted two feet away, poised, darted two feet back, and came to rest again a little farther up the rod. There had been no years between the ducking of this dragonfly and the other one—the one that was part of memory. I looked at the boy, who was silently watching his fly, and it was my hands that held his rod, my eyes watching. I felt dizzy and didn't know which rod I was at the end of.

We caught two bass, hauling them in briskly as though they were mackerel, pulling them over the side of the boat in a businesslike manner without any landing net, and stunning them with a blow on the back of the head. When we got back for a swim before lunch, the lake was exactly where we had left it, the same number of inches from the dock, and there was only the merest suggestion of a breeze. This seemed an utterly enchanted sea, this lake you could leave to its own devices for a few hours and come back to, and find that it had not stirred, this constant and trustworthy body of water. In the shallows, the dark, water-soaked sticks and twigs, smooth and old, were undulating in clusters on the bottom against the clean ribbed sand, and the track of the mussel was plain. A school of minnows swam by, each minnow with its small individual shadow, doubling the attendance, so clear and sharp in the sunlight. Some of the other campers were in swimming, along the shore, one of them with a cake of soap, and the water felt thin and clear and unsubstantial. Over the years there had been this person with the cake of soap, this cultist, and here he was. There had been no years.

Up to the farmhouse to dinner through the teeming, dusty field, the road under our sneakers was only a two-track road. The middle track was missing, the one with the marks of the hooves and the splotches of dried, flaky manure. There had always been three tracks to choose from in choosing which track to walk in; now the choice was narrowed down to two. For a moment I missed terribly the middle alternative. But the way led past the tennis court, and something about the way it lay there in the sun reassured me; the tape had loosened along the backline, the alleys were green with plantains and other weeds, and the net (installed in June and removed in September) sagged in the dry noon, and the whole place steamed with midday heat and hunger and emptiness. There was a choice of pie for dessert, and one was blueberry and one was apple, and the waitresses were the same country girls, there having

1. The larvae of the dobsonfly (usually spelled "hellgrammite").

been no passage of time, only the illusion of it as in a dropped curtain—the waitresses were still fifteen; their hair had been washed, that was the only difference—they had been to the movies and seen the pretty girls with the clean hair.

Summertime, oh summertime, pattern of life indelible, the fade-proof lake, the woods unshatterable, the pasture with the sweetfern and the juniper forever and ever, summer without end; this was the background, and the life along the shore was the design, the cottagers with their innocent and tranquil design, their tiny docks with the flagpole and the American flag floating against the white clouds in the blue sky, the little paths over the roots of the trees leading from camp to camp and the paths leading back to the outhouses and the can of lime for sprinkling, and at the souvenir counters at the store the miniature birch-bark canoes and the post cards that showed things looking a little better than they looked. This was the American family at play, escaping the city heat, wondering whether the newcomers in the camp at the head of the cove were "common" or "nice," wondering whether it was true that the people who drove up for Sunday dinner at the farmhouse were turned away because there wasn't enough chicken.

It seemed to me, as I kept remembering all this, that those times and those summers had been infinitely precious and worth saving. There had been jollity and peace and goodness. The arriving (at the beginning of August) had been so big a business in itself, at the railway station the farm wagon drawn up, the first smell of the pine-laden air, the first glimpse of the smiling farmer, and the great importance of the trunks and your father's enormous authority in such matters, and the feel of the wagon under you for the long ten-mile haul, and at the top of the last long hill catching the first view of the lake after eleven months of not seeing this cherished body of water. The shouts and cries of the other campers when they saw you, and the trunks to be unpacked, to give up their rich burden. (Arriving was less exciting nowadays, when you sneaked up in your car and parked it under a tree near the camp and took out the bags and in five minutes it was all over, no fuss, no loud wonderful fuss about trunks.)

10   Peace and goodness and jollity. The only thing that was wrong now, really, was the sound of the place, an unfamiliar nervous sound of the outboard motors. This was the note that jarred, the one thing that would sometimes break the illusion and set the years moving. In those other summertimes all motors were inboard; and when they were at a little distance, the noise they made was a sedative, an ingredient of summer sleep. They were one-cylinder and two-cylinder engines, and some were make-and-break and some were jump-spark,[2] but they all made a sleepy sound across the lake. The one-lungers throbbed and fluttered, and the twin-cylinder ones purred and purred, and that was a quiet sound too. But now the campers all had outboards. In the daytime, in the hot mornings, these motors made a petulant, irritable sound; at night, in the still evening when the afterglow lit the water, they whined about one's ears

2. Methods of ignition timing.

like mosquitoes. My boy loved our rented outboard, and his great desire was to achieve singlehanded mastery over it, and authority, and he soon learned the trick of choking it a little (but not too much), and the adjustment of the needle valve. Watching him I would remember the things you could do with the old one-cylinder engine with the heavy flywheel, how you could have it eating out of your hand if you got really close to it spiritually. Motor boats in those days didn't have clutches, and you would make a landing by shutting off the motor at the proper time and coasting in with a dead rudder. But there was a way of reversing them, if you learned the trick, by cutting the switch and putting it on again exactly on the final dying revolution of the flywheel, so that it would kick back against compression and begin reversing. Approaching a dock in a strong following breeze, it was difficult to slow up sufficiently by the ordinary coasting method, and if a boy felt he had complete mastery over his motor, he was tempted to keep it running beyond its time and then reverse it a few feet from the dock. It took a cool nerve, because if you threw the switch a twentieth of a second too soon you would catch the flywheel when it still had speed enough to go up past center, and the boat would leap ahead, charging bull-fashion at the dock.

We had a good week at the camp. The bass were biting well and the sun shone endlessly, day after day. We would be tired at night and lie down in the accumulated heat of the little bedrooms after the long hot day and the breeze would stir almost imperceptibly outside and the smell of the swamp drift in through the rusty screens. Sleep would come easily and in the morning the red squirrel would be on the roof, tapping out his gay routine. I kept remembering everything, lying in bed in the mornings—the small steamboat that had a long rounded stern like the lip of a Ubangi, and how quietly she ran on the moonlight sails, when the older boys played their mandolins and the girls sang and we ate doughnuts dipped in sugar, and how sweet the music was on the water in the shining night, and what it had felt like to think about girls then. After breakfast we would go up to the store and the things were in the same place— the minnows in a bottle, the plugs and spinners disarranged and pawed over by the youngsters from the boys' camp, the fig newtons and the Beeman's gum. Outside, the road was tarred and cars stood in front of the store. Inside, all was just as it had always been, except there was more Coca-Cola and not so much Moxie and root beer and birch beer and sarsaparilla. We would walk out with a bottle of pop apiece and sometimes the pop would backfire up our noses and hurt. We explored the streams, quietly, where the turtles slid off the sunny logs and dug their way into the soft bottom; and we lay on the town wharf and fed worms to the tame bass. Everywhere we went I had trouble making out which was I, the one walking at my side, the one walking in my pants.

One afternoon while we were there at that lake a thunderstorm came up. It was like the revival of an old melodrama that I had seen long ago with childish awe. The second-act climax of the drama of the electrical disturbance over a lake in America had not changed in any important respect. This was the big scene, still the big scene. The whole thing was so familiar, the first

feeling of oppression and heat and a general air around camp of not wanting
to go very far away. In midafternoon (it was all the same) a curious darkening
of the sky, and a lull in everything that had made life tick; and then the way
the boats suddenly swung the other way at their moorings with the coming of
a breeze out of the new quarter, and the premonitory rumble. Then the kettle
drum, then the snare, then the bass drum and cymbals, then crackling light
against the dark, and the gods grinning and licking their chops in the hills. Afterward the calm, the rain steadily rustling in the calm lake, the return of light
and hope and spirits, and the campers running out in joy and relief to go
swimming in the rain, their bright cries perpetuating the deathless joke about
how they were getting simply drenched, and the children screaming with delight at the new sensation of bathing in the rain, and the joke about getting
drenched linking the generations in a strong indestructible chain. And the co-
median who waded in carrying an umbrella.

When the others went swimming my son said he was going in too. He
pulled his dripping trunks from the line where they had hung all through the
shower, and wrung them out. Languidly, and with no thought of going in, I
watched him, his hard little body, skinny and bare, saw him wince slightly as
he pulled up around his vitals the small, soggy, icy garment. As he buckled the
swollen belt suddenly my groin felt the chill of death.

QUESTIONS

1. What has guided White in his selection of the details he gives about the trip? Why,
for example, does he talk about the road, the dragonfly, the boat's motor?

2. White speaks of the lake as a "holy spot." What about it was holy?

3. White's last sentence often surprises first-time readers. Go back through the essay
and pick out sections or words or phrases that seem to prepare for the ending.

4. Write about revisiting a place that has a special meaning for you.

PROSE FORMS:
JOURNALS

Occasionally we catch ourselves having said something aloud, obviously with no concern to be heard, even by ourselves. And all of us have overheard, perhaps while walking, a solitary person muttering or laughing softly or exclaiming abruptly. Something floats up from the world within, forces itself to be expressed, takes no real account of the time or the place, and certainly intends no conscious communication.

With more self-consciousness, and yet without a specific audience, we sometimes speak out at something from the world outside. A sharp play at the ball game, the twist of a political speech, an old photograph—something from the outer world impresses the mind, stimulates it, focuses its memories and values, interests and needs. Thus stimulated, we may wish to share an experience with another, to inform or amuse that person, to rouse him or her to action, or to persuade someone to a certain belief. Often, though, we may want most to talk to ourselves, to give a shape in words to thoughts and feelings for the sake of a private dialogue. Communication to another may be an ultimate desire, but the immediate motive is to articulate the experience for ourselves.

Articulating and shaping experience in language for one's own sake often means keeping a journal. Literally a daybook, the journal enables the writer to record something about the experiences of a day that was especially memorable or impressive. The journal entry may be merely a few words to call to mind a thing done, a person seen, a meal enjoyed with friends. It may be concerned at length with a political crisis in the community or a personal crisis in the home. It may even be used, as by pious people in the past, to keep a record of our conduct and conscience, a reckoning of moral and spiritual accounts. In its most public aspect, the idea of a journal calls to mind the newspaper or a record of proceedings like the U.S. Congressional Record *and the Canadian* Hansard.

To keep a journal is to hold on to experiences through writing. But to get it down on paper begins another adventure. The journalist has to focus on what he or she has experienced, and to be able to say what, in fact, the experience is and what it means. What of it is new? What of it is remarkable because of associations in the memory it stirs up? Is this like anything I—or others—have experienced before? Is it a good or a bad thing to have happened? And why, specifically? The questions multiply, and as the journalist seeks to answer them, he or she begins to know what is being contemplated. As we try to find the words that best represent this discovery, the experience becomes even more clear in its shape and meaning. We can imagine Emerson going to the ballet, being absorbed in the spectacle, thinking casually of associations the dancer and the movements suggest. When he writes about the experience in his journal, a good many questions, judgments, and speculations get tied up with the spectacle, and it is this complex of event and his relation to it that becomes the experience he records. The simple facts of time, place, people, and actions set in motion responses, ideas, and feelings that give those facts their real meaning.

Once this consciousness of events is formulated in words, the journalist has it, not only in the sense of understanding what has been seen, felt, or thought, but also in the sense of having it there to contemplate long after the event itself. When we read a carefully kept journal covering a long period and varied experiences, we have the pleasure of a small world re-created for us in the consciousness of one who experienced it. Even more, we feel the continuity, the wholeness, of the writer. Something of the same feeling was there for the person who kept the journal: a world of events preserved in the form of their experienced reality and with it the persistent self in the midst of that world. That world and that self are always accessible on the page and ultimately, therefore, usably real.

Beyond the value of the journal as record, there is the instructive value of the habit of mind and hand that journal keeping can assure. We begin to attend more carefully to what happens to and around us. We learn the resources of language as a means of representing what we see and gain skill in doing justice to experience and to our own consciousness. The journal represents a discipline. It brings together an individual and a complex environment in a relation that teaches the individual something of himself or herself, something of the world, and something of the meaning of their relation. There is scarcely a moment in life when we are not poised for the lesson. And so we commit ourselves to language. To have put our experience into words is to have begun marking out the limits and potential of its meaning. In the journal that meaning is developed and clarified to ourselves primarily. When the development and clarification are intended for another reader, the method of the journal redirects itself to become that of the essay.

JOAN DIDION: *On Keeping a Notebook*

"'That woman Estelle,'" the note reads, "'is partly the reason why George Sharp and I are separated today.' *Dirty crepe-de-Chine wrapper, hotel bar, Wilmington RR, 9:45 a.m. August Monday morning.*"

Since the note is in my notebook, it presumably has some meaning to me. I study it for a long while. At first I have only the most general notion of what I was doing on an August Monday morning in the bar of the hotel across from the Pennsylvania Railroad station in Wilmington, Delaware (waiting for a train? missing one? 1960? 1961? why Wilmington?), but I do remember being there. The woman in the dirty crepe-de-Chine wrapper had come down from her room for a beer, and the bartender had heard before the reason why George Sharp and she were separated today. "Sure," he said, and went on mopping the floor. "You told me." At the other end of the bar is a girl. She is

From Slouching towards Bethlehem *(1966), Didion's first volume of nonfiction, which includes both autobiographical essays and articles analyzing American culture of the 1960s.*

talking, pointedly, not to the man beside her but to a cat lying in the triangle
of sunlight cast through the open door. She is wearing a plaid silk dress from
Peck & Peck, and the hem is coming down.

Here is what it is: the girl has been on the Eastern Shore, and now she is
going back to the city, leaving the man beside her, and all she can see ahead are
the viscous summer sidewalks and the 3 a.m. long-distance calls that will make
her lie awake and then sleep drugged through all the steaming mornings left in
August (1960? 1961?). Because she must go directly from the train to lunch in
New York, she wishes that she had a safety pin for the hem of the plaid silk
dress, and she also wishes that she could forget about the hem and the lunch
and stay in the cool bar that smells of disinfectant and malt and make friends
with the woman in the crepe-de-Chine wrapper. She is afflicted by a little self-
pity, and she wants to compare Estelles. That is what that was all about.

Why did I write it down? In order to remember, of course, but exactly
what was it I wanted to remember? How much of it actually happened? Did
any of it? Why do I keep a notebook at all? It is easy to deceive oneself on all
those scores. The impulse to write things down is a peculiarly compulsive one,
inexplicable to those who do not share it, useful only accidentally, only secondarily, in the way that any compulsion tries to justify itself. I suppose that it
begins or does not begin in the cradle. Although I have felt compelled to write
things down since I was five years old, I doubt that my daughter ever will, for
she is a singularly blessed and accepting child, delighted with life exactly as
life presents itself to her, unafraid to go to sleep and unafraid to wake up.
Keepers of private notebooks are a different breed altogether, lonely and resistant rearrangers of things, anxious malcontents, children afflicted apparently
at birth with some presentiment of loss.

My first notebook was a Big Five tablet, given to me by my mother with the   5
sensible suggestion that I stop whining and learn to amuse myself by writing
down my thoughts. She returned the tablet to me a few years ago; the first entry is an account of a woman who believed herself to be freezing to death in the
Arctic night, only to find, when day broke, that she had stumbled onto the Sahara Desert, where she would die of the heat before lunch. I have no idea what
turn of a five-year-old's mind could have prompted so insistently "ironic" and
exotic a story, but it does reveal a certain predilection for the extreme which has
dogged me into adult life; perhaps if I were analytically inclined I would find it
a truer story than any I might have told about Donald Johnson's birthday party
or the day my cousin Brenda put Kitty Litter in the aquarium.

So the point of my keeping a notebook has never been, nor is it now, to have
an accurate factual record of what I have been doing or thinking. That would
be a different impulse entirely, an instinct for reality which I sometimes envy
but do not possess. At no point have I ever been able successfully to keep a diary; my approach to daily life ranges from the grossly negligent to the merely
absent, and on those few occasions when I have tried dutifully to record a
day's events, boredom has so overcome me that the results are mysterious at
best. What is this business about "shopping, typing piece, dinner with E,

depressed"? Shopping for what? Typing what piece? Who is E? Was this "E"
depressed, or was I depressed? Who cares?

In fact I have abandoned altogether that kind of pointless entry; instead I
tell what some would call lies. "That's simply not true," the members of my
family frequently tell me when they come up against my memory of a shared
event. "The party was *not* for you, the spider was *not* a black widow, *it wasn't
that way at all.*" Very likely they are right, for not only have I always had trouble
distinguishing between what happened and what merely might have happened,
but I remain unconvinced that the distinction, for my purposes, matters. The
cracked crab that I recall having for lunch the day my father came home from
Detroit in 1945 must certainly be embroidery, worked into the day's pattern to
lend verisimilitude; I was ten years old and would not now remember the
cracked crab. The day's events did not turn on cracked crab. And yet it is precisely that fictitious crab that makes me see the afternoon all over again, a
home movie run all too often, the father bearing gifts, the child weeping, an exercise in family love and guilt. Or that is what it was to me. Similarly, perhaps
it never did snow that August in Vermont; perhaps there never were flurries in
the night wind, and maybe no one else felt the ground hardening and summer
already dead even as we pretended to bask in it, but that was how it felt to me,
and it might as well have snowed, could have snowed, did snow.

How it felt to me: that is getting closer to the truth about a notebook. I
sometimes delude myself about why I keep a notebook, imagine that some
thrifty virtue derives from preserving everything observed. See enough and
write it down, I tell myself, and then some morning when the world seems
drained of wonder, some day when I am only going through the motions of doing what I am supposed to do, which is write—on that bankrupt morning I will
simply open my notebook and there it will all be, a forgotten account with accumulated interest, paid passage back to the world out there: dialogue overheard in hotels and elevators and at the hat-check counter in Pavillon (one
middle-aged man shows his hat check to another and says, "That's my old football number"); impressions of Bettina Aptheker and Benjamin Sonnenberg
and Teddy ("Mr. Acapulco") Stauffer; careful *aperçus*[1] about tennis bums and
failed fashion models and Greek shipping heiresses, one of whom taught me a
significant lesson (a lesson I could have learned from F. Scott Fitzgerald, but
perhaps we all must meet the very rich for ourselves) by asking, when I arrived
to interview her in her orchid-filled sitting room on the second day of a paralyzing New York blizzard, whether it was snowing outside.

I imagine, in other words, that the notebook is about other people. But of
course it is not. I have no real business with what one stranger said to another
at the hat-check counter in Pavillon; in fact I suspect that the line "That's my
old football number" touched not my own imagination at all, but merely some
memory of something once read, probably "The Eighty-Yard Run."[2] Nor is my
concern with a woman in a dirty crepe-de-Chine wrapper in a Wilmington bar.

1. Perceptions, insights (French).
2. Short story by Irwin Shaw (1914–1984).

My stake is always, of course, in the unmentioned girl in the plaid silk dress. *Remember what it was to be me:* that is always the point.

It is a difficult point to admit. We are brought up in the ethic that others, any others, all others, are by definition more interesting than ourselves; taught to be diffident, just this side of self-effacing. ("You're the least important person in the room and don't forget it," Jessica Mitford's[3] governess would hiss in her ear on the advent of any social occasion; I copied that into my notebook because it is only recently that I have been able to enter a room without hearing some such phrase in my inner ear.) Only the very young and the very old may recount their dreams at breakfast, dwell upon self, interrupt with memories of beach picnics and favorite Liberty lawn dresses and the rainbow trout in a creek near Colorado Springs. The rest of us are expected, rightly, to affect absorption in other people's favorite dresses, other people's trout.

And so we do. But our notebooks give us away, for however dutifully we record what we see around us, the common denominator of all we see is always, transparently, shamelessly, the implacable "I." We are not talking here about the kind of notebook that is patently for public consumption, a structural conceit for binding together a series of graceful *pensées*;[4] we are talking about something private, about bits of the mind's string too short to use, an indiscriminate and erratic assemblage with meaning only for its maker.

And sometimes even the maker has difficulty with the meaning. There does not seem to be, for example, any point in my knowing for the rest of my life that, during 1964, 720 tons of soot fell on every square mile of New York City, yet there it is in my notebook, labeled "FACT." Nor do I really need to remember that Ambrose Bierce liked to spell Leland Stanford's[5] name "£eland $tanford" or that "smart women almost always wear black in Cuba," a fashion hint without much potential for practical application. And does not the relevance of these notes seem marginal at best?:

> In the basement museum of the Inyo County Courthouse in Independence, California, sign pinned to a mandarin coat: "This MANDARIN COAT was often worn by Mrs. Minnie S. Brooks when giving lectures on her TEAPOT COLLECTION."
> Redhead getting out of car in front of Beverly Wilshire Hotel, chinchilla stole, Vuitton bags with tags reading:
>
> MRS LOU FOX
> HOTEL SAHARA
> VEGAS

3. British essayist and social critic (1917–1996).

4. Thoughts, meditations (French).

5. Bierce (1842–1914), American journalist and fiction writer, known for such ironic writing as *The Devil's Dictionary* (see p. 601); Stanford (1824–1893), railroad magnate, governor of California, and founder of Stanford University.

Well, perhaps not entirely marginal. As a matter of fact, Mrs. Minnie S. Brooks and her MANDARIN COAT pull me back into my own childhood, for although I never knew Mrs. Brooks and did not visit Inyo County until I was thirty, I grew up in just such a world, in houses cluttered with Indian relics and bits of gold ore and ambergris and the souvenirs my Aunt Mercy Farnsworth brought back from the Orient. It is a long way from that world to Mrs. Lou Fox's world, where we all live now, and is it not just as well to remember that? Might not Mrs. Minnie S. Brooks help me to remember what I am? Might not Mrs. Lou Fox help me to remember what I am not?

But sometimes the point is harder to discern. What exactly did I have in mind when I noted down that it cost the father of someone I know $650 a month to light the place on the Hudson in which he lived before the Crash?[6] What use was I planning to make of this line by Jimmy Hoffa:[7] "I may have my faults, but being wrong ain't one of them"? And although I think it interesting to know where the girls who travel with the Syndicate have their hair done when they find themselves on the West Coast, will I ever make suitable use of it? Might I not be better off just passing it on to John O'Hara?[8] What is a recipe for sauerkraut doing in my notebook? What kind of magpie keeps this notebook? *"He was born the night the Titanic went down."* That seems a nice enough line, and I even recall who said it, but is it not really a better line in life than it could ever be in fiction?

15   But of course that is exactly it: not that I should ever use the line, but that I should remember the woman who said it and the afternoon I heard it. We were on her terrace by the sea, and we were finishing the wine left from lunch, trying to get what sun there was, a California winter sun. The woman whose husband was born the night the *Titanic* went down wanted to rent her house, wanted to go back to her children in Paris. I remember wishing that I could afford the house, which cost $1,000 a month. "Someday you will," she said lazily. "Someday it all comes." There in the sun on her terrace it seemed easy to believe in someday, but later I had a low-grade afternoon hangover and ran over a black snake on the way to the supermarket and was flooded with inexplicable fear when I heard the checkout clerk explaining to the man ahead of me why she was finally divorcing her husband. "He left me no choice," she said over and over as she punched the register. "He has a little seven-month-old baby by her, he left me no choice." I would like to believe that my dread then was for the human condition, but of course it was for me, because I wanted a baby and did not then have one and because I wanted to own the house that cost $1,000 a month to rent and because I had a hangover.

It all comes back. Perhaps it is difficult to see the value in having one's self back in that kind of mood, but I do see it; I think we are well advised to

6. The stockmarket crash of 1929.
7. Head of the Teamsters' Union who disappeared in 1975 and was presumed dead (b. 1913).
8. American novelist (1905–1970).

keep on nodding terms with the people we used to be whether we find them attractive company or not. Otherwise they turn up unannounced and surprise us, come hammering on the mind's door at 4 a.m. of a bad night and demand to know who deserted them, who betrayed them, who is going to make amends. We forget all too soon the things we thought we could never forget. We forget the loves and the betrayals alike, forget what we whispered and what we screamed, forget who we were. I have already lost touch with a couple of people I used to be; one of them, a seventeen-year-old, presents little threat, although it would be of some interest to me to know again what it feels like to sit on a river levee drinking vodka-and-orange-juice and listening to Les Paul and Mary Ford[9] and their echoes sing "How High the Moon" on the car radio. (You see I still have the scenes, but I no longer perceive myself among those present, no longer could even improvise the dialogue.) The other one, a twenty-three-year-old, bothers me more. She was always a good deal of trouble, and I suspect she will reappear when I least want to see her, skirts too long, shy to the point of aggravation, always the injured party, full of recriminations and little hurts and stories I do not want to hear again, at once saddening me and angering me with her vulnerability and ignorance, an apparition all the more insistent for being so long banished.

It is a good idea, then, to keep in touch, and I suppose that keeping in touch is what notebooks are all about. And we are all on our own when it comes to keeping those lines open to ourselves: your notebook will never help me, nor mine you. "So what's new in the whiskey business?" What could that possibly mean to you? To me it means a blonde in a Pucci bathing suit sitting with a couple of fat men by the pool at the Beverly Hills Hotel. Another man approaches, and they all regard one another in silence for a while. "So what's new in the whiskey business?" one of the fat men finally says by way of welcome, and the blonde stands up, arches one foot and dips it in the pool, looking all the while at the cabaña where Baby Pignatari[10] is talking on the telephone. That is all there is to that, except that several years later I saw the blonde coming out of Saks Fifth Avenue in New York with her California complexion and a voluminous mink coat. In the harsh wind that day she looked old and irrevocably tired to me, and even the skins in the mink coat were not worked the way they were doing them that year, not the way she would have wanted them done, and there is the point of the story. For a while after that I did not like to look in the mirror, and my eyes would skim the newspapers and pick out only the deaths, the cancer victims, the premature coronaries, the suicides, and I stopped riding the Lexington Avenue IRT[11] because I noticed for the first time that all the strangers I had seen for years—the man with the seeing-eye dog, the spinster who read the classified pages every day, the fat girl who always got off with me at Grand Central—looked older than they once had.

9. Husband-and-wife musical team of the 1940s and 1950s.

10. Brazilian playboy (1916–1977).

11. A New York City subway line; one of its stops is the Grand Central railway terminal.

It all comes back. Even that recipe for sauerkraut: even that brings it back. I was on Fire Island when I first made that sauerkraut, and it was raining, and we drank a lot of bourbon and ate the sauerkraut and went to bed at ten, and I listened to the rain and the Atlantic and felt safe. I made the sauerkraut again last night and it did not make me feel any safer, but that is, as they say, another story.

QUESTIONS

1. What distinction does Didion make between a diary and a notebook? What uses does a notebook have for Didion?

2. Didion says she uses her notebook to "tell what some would call lies" (paragraph 7). Why does she do this? Would some people call these things truths? Why?

3. Didion says, "*How it felt to me:* that is getting closer to the truth about a notebook." What writing strategies does she use to convey "how it felt"?

4. Try keeping a notebook for a week, jotting down the sort of things that Didion does. At the end of the week, take one or two of your entries and expand on them, as Didion does with the entries on Mrs. Minnie S. Brooks and Mrs. Lou Fox.

RALPH WALDO EMERSON: from *Journals*

I like to have a man's knowledge comprehend more than one class of topics, one row of shelves. I like a man who likes to see a fine barn as well as a good tragedy. [1828]

The Religion that is afraid of science dishonors God and commits suicide. [1831]

The things taught in colleges and schools are not an education, but the means of education. [1831]

Don't tell me to get ready to die. I know not what shall be. The only preparation I can make is by fulfilling my present duties. This is the everlasting life. [1832]

From The Journals of Ralph Waldo Emerson, *begun in 1819, when he was a college sophomore, and continued throughout his life. The journals, which reached one hundred volumes by 1839, were mined for public essays during Emerson's lifetime, but only after his death were his journals and notebooks published, in ten book-length volumes between 1909 and 1914.*

My aunt [Mary Moody Emerson] had an eye that went through and through   5
you like a needle. "She was endowed," she said, "with the fatal gift of penetration." She disgusted everybody because she knew them too well. [1832]

I am sure of this, that by going much alone a man will get more of a noble
courage in thought and word than from all the wisdom that is in books. [1833]

I fretted the other night at the hotel at the stranger who broke into my chamber after midnight, claiming to share it. But after his lamp had smoked the
chamber full and I had turned round to the wall in despair, the man blew out
his lamp, knelt down at his bedside, and made in low whisper a long earnest
prayer. Then was the relation entirely changed between us. I fretted no more,
but respected and liked him. [1835]

I believe I shall some time cease to be an individual, that the eternal tendency
of the soul is to become Universal, to animate the last extremities of organization. [1837]

It is very hard to be simple enough to be good. [1837]

A man must have aunts and cousins, must buy carrots and turnips, must have   10
barn and woodshed, must go to market and to the blacksmith's shop, must
saunter and sleep and be inferior and silly. [1838]

How sad a spectacle, so frequent nowadays, to see a young man after ten years
of college education come out, ready for his voyage of life—and to see that the
entire ship is made of rotten timber, of rotten, honeycombed, traditional timber without so much as an inch of new plank in the hull. [1839]

A sleeping child gives me the impression of a traveler in a very far country.
[1840]

In reading these letters of M.M.E.[1] I acknowledge (with surprise that I could
ever forget it) the debt of myself and my brothers to that old religion which, in
those years, still dwelt like a Sabbath peace in the country population of New
England, which taught privation, self-denial, and sorrow. A man was born, not
for prosperity, but to suffer for the benefit of others, like the noble rock-maple
tree which all around the villages bleeds for the service of man.[2] Not praise, not
men's acceptance of our doing, but the Spirit's holy errand through us, absorbed the thought. How dignified is this! how all that is called talents and
worth in Paris and in Washington dwindles before it! [1841]

---

1. Mary Moody Emerson (1774–1863), Emerson's aunt, his father's sister.
2. The sap of the rock or sugar maple is collected and made into maple syrup.

All writing is by the grace of God. People do not deserve to have good writing, they are so pleased with bad. In these sentences that you show me, I can find no beauty, for I see death in every clause and every word. There is a fossil or a mummy character which pervades this book. The best sepulchers, the vastest catacombs, Thebes and Cairo, Pyramids, are sepulchers to me. I like gardens and nurseries. Give me initiative, spermatic, prophesying, man-making words. [1841]

15 When summer opens, I see how fast it matures, and fear it will be short; but after the heats of July and August, I am reconciled, like one who has had his swing, to the cool of autumn. So will it be with the coming of death. [1846]

In England every man you meet is some man's son; in America, he may be some man's father. [1848]

Every poem must be made up of lines that are poems. [1848]

Love is necessary to righting the estate of woman in this world. Otherwise nature itself seems to be in conspiracy against her dignity and welfare; for the cultivated, high-thoughted, beauty-loving, saintly woman finds herself unconsciously desired for her sex, and even enhancing the appetite of her savage pursuers by these fine ornaments she has piously laid on herself. She finds with indignation that she is herself a snare, and was made such. I do not wonder at her occasional protest, violent protest against nature, in fleeing to nunneries, and taking black veils. Love rights all this deep wrong. [1848]

Natural Aristocracy. It is a vulgar error to suppose that a gentleman must be ready to fight. The utmost that can be demanded of the gentleman is that he be incapable of a lie. There is a man who has good sense, is well informed, well-read, obliging, cultivated, capable, and has an absolute devotion to truth. He always means what he says, and says what he means, however courteously. You may spit upon him—nothing could induce him to spit upon you—no praises, and no possessions, no compulsion of public opinion. You may kick him—he will think it the kick of a brute—but he is not a brute, and will not kick you in return. But neither your knife and pistol, nor your gifts and courting will ever make the smallest impression on his vote or word; for he is the truth's man, and will speak and act the truth until he dies. [1849]

20 Love is temporary and ends with marriage. Marriage is the perfection which love aimed at, ignorant of what it sought. Marriage is a good known only to the parties—a relation of perfect understanding, aid, contentment, possession of themselves and of the world—which dwarfs love to green fruit. [1850]

I found when I had finished my new lecture that it was a very good house, only the architect had unfortunately omitted the stairs. [1851]

This filthy enactment [The Fugitive Slave Law][3] was made in the nineteenth century, by people who could read and write. I will not obey it, by God. [1851]

Henry [Thoreau] is military. He seemed stubborn and implacable; always manly and wise, but rarely sweet. One would say that, as Webster[4] could never speak without an antagonist, so Henry does not feel himself except in opposition. He wants a fallacy to expose, a blunder to pillory, requires a little sense of victory, a roll of the drums, to call his powers into full exercise. [1853]

Shall we judge the country by the majority or by the minority? Certainly, by the minority. The mass are animal, in state of pupilage, and nearer the chimpanzee. [1854]

All the thoughts of a turtle are turtle. [1854]

Resources or feats. I like people who can do things. When Edward and I struggled in vain to drag our big calf into the barn, the Irish girl put her finger into the calf's mouth, and led her in directly. [1862]

George Francis Train said in a public speech in New York, "Slavery is a divine institution." "So is hell," exclaimed an old man in the crowd. [1862]

You complain that the Negroes are a base class. Who makes and keeps the Jew or the Negro base, who but you, who exclude them from the rights which others enjoy? [1867]

3. A law enacted in 1850 to compel the arrest of runaway slaves and their return to their owners.
4. Daniel Webster (1782–1852), American statesman and orator, known for his advocacy of nationalism, as opposed to state sovereignty.

Henry David Thoreau: from *Journal*

As the least drop of wine tinges the whole goblet, so the least particle of truth colors our whole life. It is never isolated, or simply added as treasure to our stock. When any real progress is made, we unlearn and learn anew what we thought we knew before. [1837]

Not by constraint or severity shall you have access to true wisdom, but by abandonment, and childlike mirthfulness. If you would know aught, be gay before it. [1840]

From The Journal of Henry David Thoreau, *kept from 1837, when Thoreau was twenty years old, until his death in 1861; first published in 1906 and reissued with additional volumes in 1984.*

It is the man determines what is said, not the words. If a mean person uses a wise maxim, I bethink me how it can be interpreted so as to commend itself to his meanness; but if a wise man makes a commonplace remark, I consider what wider construction it will admit. [1840]

Nothing goes by luck in composition. It allows of no tricks. The best you can write will be the best you are. Every sentence is the result of a long probation. The author's character is read from title-page to end. Of this he never corrects the proofs. We read it as the essential character of a handwriting without regard to the flourishes. And so of the rest of our actions; it runs as straight as a ruled line through them all, no matter how many curvets about it. Our whole life is taxed for the least thing well done: it is its net result. How we eat, drink, sleep, and use our desultory hours, now in these indifferent days, with no eye to observe and no occasion [to] excite us, determines our authority and capacity for the time to come. [1841]

5   What does education often do? It makes a straight-cut ditch of a free, meandering brook. [1850]

All perception of truth is the detection of an analogy; we reason from our hands to our head. [1851]

To set down such choice experiences that my own writings may inspire me and at last I may make wholes of parts. Certainly it is a distinct profession to rescue from oblivion and to fix the sentiments and thoughts which visit all men more or less generally, that the contemplation of the unfinished picture may suggest its harmonious completion. Associate reverently and as much as you can with your loftiest thoughts. Each thought that is welcomed and recorded is a nest egg, by the side of which more will be laid. Thoughts accidentally thrown together become a frame in which more may be developed and exhibited. Perhaps this is the main value of a habit of writing, of keeping a journal—that so we remember our best hours and stimulate ourselves. My thoughts are my company. They have a certain individuality and separate existence, aye, personality. Having by chance recorded a few disconnected thoughts and then brought them into juxtaposition, they suggest a whole new field in which it was possible to labor and to think. Thought begat thought. [1852]

There is no such thing as pure *objective* observation. Your observation, to be interesting, *i.e.* to be significant, must be *subjective*. The sum of what the writer of whatever class has to report is simply some human experience, whether he be poet or philosopher or man of science. The man of most science is the man most alive, whose life is the greatest event. Senses that take cognizance of outward things merely are of no avail. It matters not where or how far you travel—the farther commonly the worse—but how much alive you are. If it is possible to conceive of an event outside to humanity, it is not of the slightest significance, though it were the explosion of a planet. Every important worker will report what life there is in him. It makes no odds into what seeming deserts the poet is born. Though all his neighbors pronounce it a Sahara, it will be a paradise to him; for the desert which we see is the result of the barrenness of our experience. No mere willful activity whatever, whether in writing verses or collecting statistics, will produce true poetry or science. If you are really a sick man, it is indeed to be regretted, for you cannot accomplish so much as if you were well. All that a man has to say or do that can possibly concern mankind, is in some shape or other to tell the story of his love—to sing, and, if he is fortunate and keeps alive, he will be forever in love. This alone is to be alive to the extremities. It is a pity that this divine creature should ever suffer from cold feet; a still greater pity that the coldness so often reaches to his heart. I look over the report of the doings of a scientific association and am surprised that there is so little life to be reported; I am put off with a parcel of dry technical terms. Anything living is easily and naturally expressed in popular language. I cannot help suspecting that the life of these learned professors has been almost as inhuman and wooden as a rain-gauge or self-registering magnetic machine. They communicate no fact which rises to the temperature of bloodheat. It doesn't all amount to one rhyme. [1854]

It is pardonable when we spurn the proprieties, even the sanctities, making them stepping-stones to something higher. [1858]

There is always some accident in the best things, whether thoughts or expressions or deeds. The memorable thought, the happy expression, the admirable deed are only partly ours. The thought came to us because we were in a fit mood; also we were unconscious and did not know that we had said or done a good thing. We must walk consciously only part way toward our goal, and then leap in the dark to our success. What we do best or most perfectly is what we have most thoroughly learned by the longest practice, and at length it falls from us without our notice, as a leaf from a tree. It is the *last* time we shall do it—our unconscious leavings. [1859]

The expression "a *liberal* education" originally meant one worthy of freemen. Such is education simply in a true and broad sense. But education ordinarily so called—the learning of trades and professions which is designed to enable men to earn their living, or to fit them for a particular station in life—is *servile*. [1859]

QUESTIONS FOR EMERSON AND THOREAU

1. Emerson frequently uses similes and metaphors in his journal—for example, "My aunt had an eye that went through and through you like a needle" (1832) or "A sleeping child gives me the impression of a traveler in a very far country" (1840). Unpack these and other metaphors you find in his journals, and discuss what they add to his thoughts.

2. Thoreau writes that "Nothing goes by luck in composition. . . . The best you can write will be the best you are." In what sense are his journal entries examples of this belief?

3. Both Thoreau and Emerson write journal entries on the subject of education, both using metaphorical language. Compare their beliefs on education, in part by comparing the metaphors they use.

4. Choose one journal entry from either Emerson or Thoreau and write an essay by expanding, amplifying, or showing exceptions to it.

WALT WHITMAN: *Abraham Lincoln*

August 12th.—I see the President almost every day, as I happen to live where he passes to or from his lodgings out of town. He never sleeps at the White House during the hot season, but has quarters at a healthy location some three miles north of the city, the Soldiers' home, a United States military establishment. I saw him this morning about 8½ coming in to business, riding on Vermont avenue, near L street. He always has a company of twenty-five or thirty cavalry, with sabres drawn and held upright over their shoulders. They say this guard was against his personal wish, but he let his counselors have their way. The party makes no great show in uniform or horses. Mr. Lincoln on the saddle generally rides a good-sized, easy-going gray horse, is dress'd in plain black, somewhat rusty and dusty, wears a black stiff hat, and looks about as ordinary in attire, &c., as the commonest man. A lieutenant, with yellow straps, rides at his left, and following behind, two by two, come the cavalry men, in their yellow-striped jackets. They are generally going at a slow trot, as that is the pace set them by the one they wait upon. The sabres and accoutrements clank, and the entirely unornamental *cortège* as it trots towards Lafayette square arouses no sensation, only some curious stranger stops and gazes. I see very plainly ABRAHAM LINCOLN's dark brown face, with the deep-cut lines, the eyes, always to me with a deep latent sadness in the expression. We have got so that we exchange bows, and very cordial ones. Sometimes the President goes and comes in an open barouche. The cavalry always accompany him, with drawn sabres. Often I notice as he goes out evenings—and sometimes in the morning, when he returns early—he turns off and halts at the large and handsome residence of the Secretary of War, on K street, and holds conference there. If in his barouche, I can see from my window he does not alight, but sits in his vehicle, and Mr. Stanton comes out to attend him. Sometimes one of his sons, a boy of ten or twelve, accompanies him, riding at his right on a pony. Earlier in the summer I occasionally saw the President and his wife, toward the latter part of the afternoon, out in a barouche, on a pleasure ride through the city. Mrs. Lincoln was dress'd in complete black, with a

From Specimen Days *(1882), an autobiographical collection that Whitman described as "the most wayward, spontaneous, fragmentary book ever printed."*

long crape veil. The equipage is of the plainest kind, only two horses, and they nothing extra. They pass'd me once very close, and I saw the President in the face fully, as they were moving slowly, and his look, though abstracted, happen'd to be directed steadily in my eye. He bow'd and smiled, but far beneath his smile I noticed well the expression I have alluded to. None of the artists or pictures has caught the deep, though subtle and indirect expression of this man's face. There is something else there. One of the great portrait painters of two or three centuries ago is needed.

THE INAUGURATION

March 4.—The President very quietly rode down to the capitol in his own carriage, by himself, on a sharp trot, about noon, either because he wish'd to be on hand to sign bills, or to get rid of marching in line with the absurd procession, the muslin temple of liberty, and pasteboard monitor. I saw him on his return, at three o'clock, after the performance was over. He was in his plain two-horse barouche, and look'd very much worn and tired; the lines, indeed, of vast responsibilities, intricate questions, and demands of life and death, cut deeper than ever upon his dark brown face; yet all the old goodness, tenderness, sadness, and canny shrewdness, underneath the furrows. (I never see that man without feeling that he is one to become personally attach'd to, for his combination of purest, heartiest tenderness, and native western form of manliness.) By his side sat his little boy, of ten years. There were no soldiers, only a lot of civilians on horseback, with huge yellow scarfs over their shoulders, riding around the carriage. (At the inauguration four years ago, he rode down and back again surrounded by a dense mass of arm'd cavalrymen eight deep, with drawn sabres; and there were sharpshooters station'd at every corner on the route.) I ought to make mention of the closing levee[1] of Saturday night last. Never before was such a compact jam in front of the White House—all the grounds fill'd, and away out to the spacious sidewalks. I was there, as I took a notion to go—was in the rush inside with the crowd—surged along the passage-ways, the blue and other rooms, and through the great east room. Crowds of country people, some very funny. Fine music from the Marine band, off in a side place. I saw Mr. Lincoln, drest all in black, with white kid gloves and a claw-hammer coat, receiving, as in duty bound, shaking hands, looking very disconsolate, and as if he would give anything to be somewhere else.

DEATH OF PRESIDENT LINCOLN

April 16, '65.—I find in my notes of the time, this passage on the death of Abraham Lincoln: He leaves for America's history and biography, so far, not only its most dramatic reminiscence—he leaves, in my opinion, the greatest, best, most characteristic, artistic, moral personality. Not but that he had faults, and show'd them in the Presidency; but honesty, goodness, shrewdness,

1. An occasion of state for the receiving of visits, ceremonial greetings, and interviews.

conscience, and (a new virtue, unknown to other lands, and hardly yet really
known here, but the foundation and tie of all, as the future will grandly develop,) UNIONISM, in its truest and amplest sense, form'd the hard-pan of his
character. These he seal'd with his life. The tragic splendor of his death, purging, illuminating all, throws round his form, his head, an aureole that will remain and will grow brighter through time, while history lives, and love of
country lasts. By many has this Union been help'd; but if one name, one man,
must be pick'd out, he, most of all, is the conservator of it, to the future. He
was assassinated—but the Union is not assassinated—*çaira!*[2] One falls, and
another falls. The soldier drops, sinks like a wave—but the ranks of the ocean
eternally press on. Death does its work, obliterates a hundred, a thousand—
President, general, captain, private—but the Nation is immortal.

No Good Portrait of Lincoln

Probably the reader has seen physiognomies (often old farmers, sea-
captains, and such) that, behind their homeliness, or even ugliness, held
superior points so subtle, yet so palpable, making the real life of their faces
almost as impossible to depict as a wild perfume or fruit-taste, or a passionate
tone of the living voice—and such was Lincoln's face, the peculiar color, the
lines of it, the eyes, mouth, expression. Of technical beauty it had nothing—
but to the eye of a great artist it furnished a rare study, a feast and fascination.
The current portraits are all failures—most of them caricatures.

2. It goes on; it succeeds.

Questions

1. The first entries in Whitman's journal record his personal observances of Abraham
Lincoln. Which details best give a sense of the president? Why?

2. The last entries in Whitman's journal give an assessment of Lincoln's character. How
are these entries different from the first ones?

3. If you have an opportunity to observe a public figure up close, write a journal entry
like the first of Whitman's, perhaps followed by an entry that reflects on the person's
character.

RACHEL CARSON: from *Field Notebooks*

Saturday

    Hiked north on beach. Very windy, a quick shower or two, much froth. Saw
a little one-legged sanderling hopping along hunting food. Without my glasses I
couldn't be sure whether the injured leg was cut off or drawn up under the

These transcriptions from Carson's notebooks were collected in Lost Woods: The Discovered Writings of Rachel Carson *(1998).*

body, but it was completely useless. Still he ran and probed, not venturing as near the surf as they usually do. When I came near he wheeled out over the water, his sharp "pit, pil" quickly lost in the sound of the waves. I thought of the long miles of travel ahead of him and wondered how long he would last. As I came back down the beach I saw him again still hopping along bravely.

A very few ghost crabs were out, but scuttled back quickly into their holes. I sat down on a box to wait for one to come out, feeling like a cat watching a mouse hole, but soon it began to rain and I moved on.

Saw tracks of a shore bird—probably a sanderling, and followed them a little, then they turned toward the water and were soon obliterated by the sea. How much it washes away, and makes as though it had never been. Time itself is like the sea, containing all that came before us, sooner or later sweeping us away on its flood and washing over and obliterating the traces of our presence, as the sea this morning erased the footprints of the bird.

On the way back I met the little one-legged sanderling again, the one I had seen Saturday afternoon. Remembering how the legs of the normal ones twinkle as they dash up and down the beach, it was amazing to see how fast this little fellow got about just hopping, hopping on his good right leg. This time I could see that his left leg is only a short stump less than an inch long. I wondered if some animal, maybe a fox, had caught it in the Arctic, or whether it had gotten into a trap. Their way of feeding being what it is, one would say he would have been eliminated before this as "unfit"—yet he must be even tougher than his two-legged comrades. That last word is a misnomer, he had no companions—either time I saw him—just hunting alone, he would hop, hop, hop, toward the surf; probing and jabbing busily with opened bill, turn and hop away from the advancing foam. Only twice did I see him have to take to his wings to escape a wetting. It made my heart ache to think how tired his little leg must be, but his whole manner suggested a cheerfulness of spirit and a gameness which must mean that the God of fallen sparrows has not forgotten him.

Little Dog

The next day, out on these same flats in early morning for low tide, I saw *Callianassa* scooting around in pools left in depressions—thanks to the help of a little dog. I first saw him away out on the flats apparently by himself, and I thought he was chasing birds. There were the usual willets and a snowy egret and they'd get up and move on when he approached. But he was interested in the shallow pools of water and would wade in and go trotting around, his stumpy tail wagging constantly. I first wondered if he was noticing the little glittering reflections that were dancing all over the bottom, for the breeze kept little ripples stirring and the sun was very bright. When I came back down the beach later, he was still out, trotting around in the same pool. Everyone had gone in; the tide had turned, and I was worried for fear he might be cut off— he was very far out—get bewildered about where the shore was, and drown. So

I decided to go out after him. He just wouldn't be distracted, but went on trotting in circles. Then I saw the darting of the little, almost transparent forms of
shrimp and knew what was attracting him. In the end I had to pick him up and
carry him a little distance; then he scampered ahead to another pool and resumed his shrimp hunting, but since that was near the upper beach I didn't
worry. [. . .]

There are a fair number of *Diapatra* tubes [plumed worms] out on these flats.
In some of the depressions (winding ones almost like creek beds) that seem always to have water even when tide is out—you see many tracks winding back
and forth. When you can see where one ends (and sometimes there will be
movement evident) you dig down and find a live moon snail moving along.

I think *Callianassa* holes differ in appearance according to the kind of bottom:
where it is sandy you get the little excreted pellets looking like chocolate, and
scattered closely around mouth of hole but not much mounded up. Where it
is muddy, you seem to get elevated chimneys. The mud is sort of coiled, as
though squeezed out of pastry tube with fancy fillips. [. . .] Some are flattened—others go up to a peak. On digging, I could get canal going down into
sand, but could never get shrimp.

While digging, found empty *Cystoidean* tube.

Out here, I also watched sand dollars burying themselves in sand. You see a
broad track, explore end of it carefully with fingers and find dollar. If you dig
one out, it will immediately start to disappear into the sand—there is a considerable current stirred up all around edge, and body starts to dip under at forward edge. It takes it only a couple of minutes to disappear under sand again.

Dunes

10   What peculiar brand of magic is inherent in that combination of sand and
sky and water it is hard to say. It is bleak and stark. But somehow it is not forbidding. Its bleakness is part of its quiet, calm strength.
        The dune land is a place of overwhelming silence, or so it seems at first.
But soon you realize that what you take for silence is an absence of human
created sound. For the dunes have a voice of their own, which you may hear if
you will but sit down and listen to it. It is compounded of many natural sounds
which are never heard in the roar of a city or even in the stir of a small town.
A soft, confused, hollow rustling fills the air. In part it is the sound of surf on
the beach half a mile away—a wide sand valley and another ridge of sand hills
between us—the deep thunder of the surf reduced to a sigh by the intervening
distance. In part it is the confused whisperings of the wind, which seems to be
never wholly still there, but always to be exploring the contours of the land it
made, roaming down into the valleys and leaping in little, unexpected gusts
over the crests of the sand hills. And there are the smaller voices, the voices of
the sand and the dune grass. The soft swish of the grass as it dips and bends

in the wind to trace its idle arcs and circles in the sand at its feet. Arcs, especially on the southeast side of the grass, mean unsettled weather, so they say; whole circles foretell fair weather because they show the wind to be blowing alternately from different quarters. I cannot say as to that; but the scribblings of the dune grass always enchant me, though I cannot read their meaning.

I knew the history of that land, and there, under the wind and beside the surf that had carved it, I recalled the story—

I stood where a new land was being built out of the sea, and I came away deeply moved. Although our intelligence forbids the idea, I believe our deeply rooted attitude toward the creation of the earth and the evolution of living things is a feeling that it all took place in a time infinitely remote. Now I understood. Here, as if for the benefit of my puny human understanding, the processes of creation—of earth building—had been speeded up so that I could trace the change within the life of my own contemporaries. The changes that were going on before my eyes were part and parcel of the same processes that brought the first dry land emerging out of the ancient and primitive ocean; or that led the first living creatures step by step out of the sea into the perilous new world of earth.

Water and wind and sand were the builders, and only the gulls and I were there to witness this act of creation.

Strange thoughts come to a man or woman who stands alone in that bleak and   15 barren world. It is a world stripped of the gracious softness of the trees, the concealing mercies of abundant vegetation, the refreshment of a quiet lake, the beguilement of shade. It is a world stripped to the naked elements of life. And it is, after all, so newly born of the sea that it could hardly be otherwise. And then there is the voice of the sand itself—the quick sharp sibilance of a gust of sand blown over a dune crest by a sudden shift of the breeze, the all but silent sound of the never ending, restless shifting of the individual grains, one over another.

I am not sure that I can recommend the dunes as a tonic for all souls, nor for all moods. But I can say that anyone who will go alone into the dune lands for a day, or even for an hour, will never forget what he has seen and felt there.

QUESTIONS

1. What fascinates Carson the most about the one-legged sanderling (paragraphs 1–3)?

2. These are journal entries, composed on the spot or shortly afterwards. Yet do they seem unfinished and tentative, or fully fashioned? What gives them their quality?

3. Write about what kind of observer Carson is. Think about what she sees when she looks at nature.

4. Describe what gets left out of Carson's accounts of what she sees. What doesn't she include?

COLBY BUZZELL: *Killing Time in Iraq*

BRUTAL ATTACK ON A COUNTERMORTAR MISSION

It was at night, the moon was gone, and the visibility was almost zero. Had my night vision goggles on. We set our gun position down on this hill, me and Pfc. Pointz. I laid down in the prone position and scanned my sector. I was only on the ground for like thirty seconds when I started feeling a tingling sensation all down my back and up my arms. I was like, What the f*** is that?? I had my NODs on and I looked down on the ground, and at first it looked like the TV screen when the cable goes out, you know like millions of bees in a snowstorm, but once I took a closer look I realized that I was lying down on a huge pile of literally thousands and thousands of ants. I looked at my arms and there were hundreds of ants crawling all over me, in fact I could hear them crawling on me. The ants here are not like the itty-bitty house ants back home, the ones in Iraq are f***ing huge, like as big as the ones at Fort Benning. I freaked out, they were all over me, crawling all up and down my back, up my arms, on my face, everywhere. I jumped up, threw my helmet off, tore my vest off as fast as I could, swearing and cussing every profanity in the f***ing book, slapping and hitting myself all over trying to get them off of me as fast as I could. Every now and then I could feel one of them biting into me and I'd grit my teeth in pain. I yelled at my assistant gunner to help me out and start slapping them off me as well.

Pfc. Pointz and Spc. Cummings both found all of this very comical. I tore my top off, my T-shirt, they were down my pants as well now. That wasn't too pleasant a feeling.

Lesson: Don't be a f***ing idiot like me, and always look before you lie down anywhere, especially in this country.

On the way back to the FOB, our shocks and hydraulics completely went tits up and the vehicle was bouncing up and down like an East L.A. low-rider Impala the whole way. It was sort of fun for like the first couple minutes, but then after a while I started feeling seasick, and I almost barfed up my beef enchilada MRE. (That wasn't a racist joke, I seriously ate a beef enchilada MRE prior to this.)

Posted by CBFTW[1] at 8:11 a.m., July 26, 2004

CAR BOMB

5   Last night a car bomb was discovered along a busy freeway here in Mosul. My platoon was placed on QRF while 3rd Platoon rolled out to secure the area and blow the thing up.

Car bombs are starting to become a very popular thing here in Mosul. The car bombs in Iraq are not like the car bombs you see in the movies, where they just blow up and the car just catches on fire. The psychopaths who are mak-

Taken from Buzzell's blog, composed while he was serving in Iraq and collected in his book My War: Killing Time in Iraq *(2005).*

1. This is the name of Buzzell's blog.

ing these things have got the art of car bomb making down to a f***ing science, where they can produce the highest amount of casualties and damage humanly possible. It's mind blowing the amount of damage one single car bomb can do.

When they go off there will literally be nothing left of the VBIED, there'll be a huge hole in the street where the car once was. The explosions create these huge mushroom clouds of dust that can be seen miles away and the cars that were around it will all be thrown on their backs, and windows in buildings blocks away will be shattered from the concussion of the blast.

> We like the cars, the cars that go boom.
> —Some rap song in the eighties

Posted by CBFTW[1] on July 18, 2004

ANOTHER DAMN CAR BOMB

At 0330 last night I woke up to a very loud explosion. At first I thought it was another bad dream, but my roommate also heard it and woke up and said, "Hey, did you hear that?!" Yeah, I told him. We stayed up for a couple minutes silently after that, wondering what the hell was that, and then we both went back to sleep. We later found out that it was an IED.

This morning we all went to breakfast and when we returned I took my weekly dose of anti-malaria medication and went to my room. Shortly after that, Sgt. L banged on my door and said that our platoon just got placed on QRF (Quick Reaction Force) and to stand by and be ready to go at any minute, today might be another 24th of June (that was the day of the Mohammed Al Noory Mosque/Sheikh Fatih police attack). The main gate to the airfield to our FOB just got hit by a vehicle-borne IED (car bomb) and there's mass casualties.

The vehicle-borne IED was a Toyota pickup with a female driver.   10

The airfield here also got mortared several times today.

Posted by CBFTW at 8:11 p.m., July 26, 2004

AND ANOTHER DAMN CAR BOMB

I'm getting pretty good at guessing just from the noise an explosion makes if it was a mortar impact, vehicle-borne IED, or a controlled detonation. This morning I went to breakfast at the chow hall. Had the usual—eggs, sausage, side of bacon. And as I was leaving the chow hall with my morning dose of coffee in my hand, I heard a loud explosion off in the distance and observed a huge cloud of dust. I thought to myself, damn, that was probably a car bomb.

Guess what? It was.

Posted by CBFTW at 9:53 a.m., August 2, 2004

"MASSEM?"

Today my squad had gate guard duty.

My platoon had a countermortar observation post up on OP Abrams to at-   15

tend during the afternoon. My squad on the other hand lucked out and had
gate guard duty. When the guys exited our gate they all cursed at us and flipped
us off as they drove by. We all just waved and smiled at them. Suckers. They
were just jealous that they didn't have gate guard, instead of an OP. I don't
blame them, anything is better than an OP. We have a lot of Iraqis working on
our FOB, building shit and doing stuff. We had an Iraqi come up to us in the
heat of the afternoon with two large bags of ice. With a smile he said that he
wanted to help us, because we were helping them. That was very cool of him.

Pfc. Evans and I ripped open one of the bags of ice and started cooling
ourselves off with it, rubbing our foreheads with it and stuff. Pfc. Evans then
looked over at me and said, "Damn, that was the nicest thing I've heard from
an Iraqi the whole time I've been here."

Later on in the afternoon, another Iraqi contractor came up to our gate
and kept on saying, "Massem? Massem?"

What the hell is "Massem"?

After a couple minutes of trying to figure out what the hell "Massem" was,
we finally realized that he was asking us if we had a *Maxim* magazine.

20   Every Stryker pretty much has a *Maxim* inside of it, it's like required reading or something here in the Stryker Brigade. The ceilings of some of the
Strykers are actually covered in pinup girls from *Maxim*. So we lent him the
latest issue, and he just sat there turning the pages with an ear-to-ear smile,
wide-eyed and saying, "Good! Good!" every time there was a photo of some girl
in skimpy underwear looking all sexy. After flipping through the *Maxim*, he
handed it back to us, thanked us, and walked off.

Happy.

Posted by CBFTW at 4:01 p.m., July 20, 2004

QUESTIONS

1. Does Buzzell write the way you'd expect a soldier to write? What signs of his profession appear in his writing? What elements surprise you?

2. What seems to be Buzzell's attitude toward warfare? Toward Iraqis? Toward his fellow soldiers?

3. Begin and maintain a journal or blog about your own daily actions, and then compare
what you write with Buzzell's blog. What is different? What is the same?

PEOPLE, PLACES

SCOTT RUSSELL SANDERS *Under the Influence*

M Y FATHER DRANK. He drank as a gut-punched boxer gasps for breath, as a starving dog gobbles food—compulsively, secretly, in pain and trembling. I use the past tense not because he ever quit drinking but because he quit living. That is how the story ends for my father, age sixty-four, heart bursting, body cooling and forsaken on the linoleum of my brother's trailer. The story continues for my brother, my sister, my mother, and me, and will continue so long as memory holds.

In the perennial present of memory, I slip into the garage or barn to see my father tipping back the flat green bottles of wine, the brown cylinders of whiskey, the cans of beer disguised in paper bags. His Adam's apple bobs, the liquid gurgles, he wipes the sandy-haired back of a hand over his lips, and then, his bloodshot gaze bumping into me, he stashes the bottle or can inside his jacket, under the workbench, between two bales of hay, and we both pretend the moment has not occurred.

"What's up, buddy?" he says, thick-tongued and edgy.

"Sky's up," I answer, playing along.

"And don't forget prices," he grumbles. "Prices are always up. And taxes." 5

In memory, his white 1951 Pontiac with the stripes down the hood and the Indian head on the snout jounces to a stop in the driveway; or it is the 1956 Ford station wagon, or the 1963 Rambler shaped like a toad, or the sleek 1969 Bonneville that will do 120 miles per hour on straightaways; or it is the robin's-egg blue pickup, new in 1980, battered in 1981, the year of his death. He climbs out, grinning dangerously, unsteady on his legs, and we children interrupt our game of catch, our building of snow forts, our picking of plums, to watch in silence as he weaves past into the house, where he slumps into his overstuffed chair and falls asleep. Shaking her head, our mother stubs out the cigarette he has left smoldering in the ashtray. All evening, until our bedtimes, we tiptoe past him, as past a snoring dragon. Then we curl in our fearful sheets, listening. Eventually he wakes with a grunt, Mother slings accusations at him, he snarls back, she yells, he growls, their voices clashing.

Originally published in Harper's Magazine (*November 1989*), *a monthly dedicated to discussing American politics, literature, and culture.*

Before long, she retreats to their bedroom, sobbing—not from the blows of fists, for he never strikes her, but from the force of words.

Left alone, our father prowls the house, thumping into furniture, rummaging in the kitchen, slamming doors, turning the pages of the newspaper with a savage crackle, muttering back at the late-night drivel from television. The roof might fly off, the walls might buckle from the pressure of his rage. Whatever my brother and sister and mother may be thinking on their own rumpled pillows, I lie there hating him, loving him, fearing him, knowing I have failed him. I tell myself he drinks to ease an ache that gnaws at his belly, an ache I must have caused by disappointing him somehow, a murderous ache I should be able to relieve by doing all my chores, earning A's in school, winning baseball games, fixing the broken washer and the burst pipes, bringing in money to fill his empty wallet. He would not hide the green bottles in his tool box, would not sneak off to the barn with a lump under his coat, would not fall asleep in the daylight, would not roar and fume, would not drink himself to death, if only I were perfect.

I am forty-two as I write these words, and I know full well now that my father was an alcoholic, a man consumed by disease rather than by disappointment. What had seemed to me a private grief is in fact a public scourge. In the United States alone some ten or fifteen million people share his ailment, and behind the doors they slam in fury or disgrace, countless other children tremble. I comfort myself with such knowledge, holding it against the throb of memory like an ice pack against a bruise. There are keener sources of grief: poverty, racism, rape, war. I do not wish to compete for a trophy in suffering. I am only trying to understand the corrosive mixture of helplessness, responsibility, and shame that I learned to feel as the son of an alcoholic. I realize now that I did not cause my father's illness, nor could I have cured it. Yet for all this grown-up knowledge, I am still ten years old, my own son's age, and as that boy I struggle in guilt and confusion to save my father from pain.

Consider a few of our synonyms for *drunk*: tipsy, tight, pickled, soused, and plowed; stoned and stewed, lubricated and inebriated, juiced and sluiced; three sheets to the wind, in your cups, out of your mind, under the table; lit up, tanked up, wiped out; besotted, blotto, bombed, and buzzed; plastered, polluted, putrified; loaded or looped, boozy, woozy, fuddled, or smashed; crocked and shit-faced, corked and pissed, snockered and sloshed.

10   It is a mostly humorous lexicon, as the lore that deals with drunks—in jokes and cartoons, in plays, films, and television skits—is largely comic. Aunt Matilda nips elderberry wine from the sideboard and burps politely during supper. Uncle Fred slouches to the table glassy-eyed, wearing a lamp shade for a hat and murmuring, "Candy is dandy but liquor is quicker." Inspired by cocktails, Mrs. Somebody recounts the events of her day in a fuzzy dialect, while Mr. Somebody nibbles her ear and croons a bawdy song. On the sofa with Boyfriend, Daughter giggles, licking gin from her lips, and loosens the bows in her hair. Junior knocks back some brews with his chums at the Leopard Lounge and stumbles home to the wrong house, wonders foggily why he

cannot locate his pajamas, and crawls naked into bed with the ugliest girl in school. The family dog slurps from a neglected martini and wobbles to the nursery, where he vomits in Baby's shoe.

It is all great fun. But if in the audience you notice a few laughing faces turn grim when the drunk lurches on stage, don't be surprised, for these are the children of alcoholics. Over the grinning mask of Dionysus,[1] the leering mask of Bacchus,[2] these children cannot help seeing the bloated features of their own parents. Instead of laughing, they wince, they mourn. Instead of celebrating the drunk as one freed from constraints, they pity him as one enslaved. They refuse to believe *in vino veritas*,[3] having seen their befuddled parents skid away from truth toward folly and oblivion. And so these children bite their lips until the lush staggers into the wings.

My father, when drunk, was neither funny nor honest; he was pathetic, frightening, deceitful. There seemed to be a leak in him somewhere, and he poured in booze to keep from draining dry. Like a torture victim who refuses to squeal, he would never admit that he had touched a drop, not even in his last year, when he seemed to be dissolving in alcohol before our very eyes. I never knew him to lie about anything, ever, except about this one ruinous fact. Drowsy, clumsy, unable to fix a bicycle tire, throw a baseball, balance a grocery sack, or walk across the room, he was stripped of his true self by drink. In a matter of minutes, the contents of a bottle could transform a brave man into a coward, a buddy into a bully, a gifted athlete and skilled carpenter and shrewd businessman into a bumbler. No dictionary of synonyms for *drunk* would soften the anguish of watching our prince turn into a frog.

Father's drinking became the family secret. While growing up, we children never breathed a word of it beyond the four walls of our house. To this day, my brother and sister rarely mention it, and then only when I press them. I did not confess the ugly, bewildering fact to my wife until his wavering walk and slurred speech forced me to. Recently, on the seventh anniversary of my father's death, I asked my mother if she ever spoke of his drinking to friends. "No, no, never," she replied hastily. "I couldn't bear for anyone to know."

The secret bores under the skin, gets in the blood, into the bone, and stays there. Long after you have supposedly been cured of malaria, the fever can flare up, the tremors can shake you. So it is with the fevers of shame. You swallow the bitter quinine[4] of knowledge, and you learn to feel pity and compassion toward the drinker. Yet the shame lingers in your marrow, and, because of the shame, anger.

For a long stretch of my childhood we lived on a military reservation in Ohio,   15
an arsenal where bombs were stored underground in bunkers, vintage air-

1. Greek god of wine and intoxication.
2. Roman god of wine and intoxication.
3. "In wine is truth."
4. Drug from the bark of the South American cinchona tree, used to treat malaria.

planes burst into flames, and unstable artillery shells boomed nightly at the
dump. We had the feeling, as children, that we played in a mine field, where a
heedless footfall could trigger an explosion. When Father was drinking, the
house, too, became a mine field. The least bump could set off either parent.

The more he drank, the more obsessed Mother became with stopping
him. She hunted for bottles, counted the cash in his wallet, sniffed at his
breath. Without meaning to snoop, we children blundered left and right into
damning evidence. On afternoons when he came home from work sober, we
flung ourselves at him for hugs, and felt against our ribs the telltale lump in
his coat. In the barn we tumbled on the hay and heard beneath our sneakers
the crunch of buried glass. We tugged open a drawer in his workbench, looking for screwdrivers or crescent wrenches, and spied a gleaming six-pack
among the tools. Playing tag, we darted around the house just in time to see
him sway on the rear stoop and heave a finished bottle into the woods. In his
good night kiss we smelled the cloying sweetness of Clorets, the mints he
chewed to camouflage his dragon's breath.

I can summon up that kiss right now by recalling Theodore Roethke's[5]
lines about his own father in "My Papa's Waltz":

> The whiskey on your breath
> Could make a small boy dizzy;
> But I hung on like death:
> Such waltzing was not easy.

Such waltzing was hard, terribly hard, for with a boy's scrawny arms I was trying to hold my tipsy father upright.

For years, the chief source of those incriminating bottles and cans was a
grimy store a mile from us, a cinder block place called Sly's, with two gas
pumps outside and a moth-eaten dog asleep in the window. A strip of fly-
paper, speckled the year round with black bodies, coiled in the doorway. Inside, on rusty metal shelves or in wheezing coolers, you could find pop and
Popsicles, cigarettes, potato chips, canned soup, raunchy postcards, fishing
gear, Twinkies, wine, and beer. When Father drove anywhere on errands,
Mother would send us kids along as guards, warning us not to let him out of
our sight. And so with one or more of us on board, Father would cruise up to
Sly's, pump a dollar's worth of gas or plump the tires with air, and then, telling
us to wait in the car, he would head for that fly-spangled doorway.

20   Dutiful and panicky, we cried, "Let us go in with you!"

"No," he answered. "I'll be back in two shakes."

"Please!"

"No!" he roared. "Don't you budge, or I'll jerk a knot in your tails!"

So we stayed put, kicking the seats, while he ducked inside. Often, when
he had parked the car at a careless angle, we gazed in through the window and
saw Mr. Sly fetching down from a shelf behind the cash register two green

---

5. American poet (1908–1963) whose father also drank too much.

pints of Gallo wine. Father swigged one of them right there at the counter, stuffed the other in his pocket, and then out he came, a bulge in his coat, a flustered look on his red face.

Because the Mom and Pop who ran the dump were neighbors of ours, living just down the tar-blistered road, I hated them all the more for poisoning my father. I wanted to sneak in their store and smash the bottles and set fire to the place. I also hated the Gallo brothers, Ernest and Julio, whose jovial faces shone from the labels of their wine, labels I would find, torn and curled, when I burned the trash. I noted the Gallo brothers' address, in California, and I studied the road atlas to see how far that was from Ohio, because I meant to go out there and tell Ernest and Julio what they were doing to my father, and then, if they showed no mercy, I would kill them.

25

While growing up on the back roads and in the country schools and cramped Methodist churches of Ohio and Tennessee, I never heard the word *alcoholism*, never happened across it in books or magazines. In the nearby towns, there were no addiction treatment programs, no community mental health centers, no Alcoholics Anonymous chapters, no therapists. Left alone with our grievous secret, we had no way of understanding Father's drinking except as an act of will, a deliberate folly or cruelty, a moral weakness, a sin. He drank because he chose to, pure and simple. Why our father, so playful and competent and kind when sober, would choose to ruin himself and punish his family, we could not fathom.

Our neighborhood was high on the Bible, and the Bible was hard on drunkards. "Woe to those who are heroes at drinking wine, and valiant men in mixing strong drink," wrote Isaiah. "The priest and the prophet reel with strong drink, they are confused with wine, they err in vision, they stumble in giving judgment. For all tables are full of vomit, no place is without filthiness." We children had seen those fouled tables at the local truck stop where the notorious boozers hung out, our father occasionally among them. "Wine and new wine take away the understanding," declared the prophet Hosea. We had also seen evidence of that in our father, who could multiply seven-digit numbers in his head when sober, but when drunk could not help us with fourth-grade math. Proverbs warned: "Do not look at wine when it is red, when it sparkles in the cup and goes down smoothly. At the last it bites like a serpent, and stings like an adder. Your eyes will see strange things, and your mind utter perverse things." Woe, woe.

Dismayingly often, these biblical drunkards stirred up trouble for their own kids. Noah made fresh wine after the flood, drank too much of it, fell asleep without any clothes on, and was glimpsed in the buff by his son Ham, whom Noah promptly cursed. In one passage—it was so shocking we had to read it under our blankets with flashlights—the patriarch Lot fell down drunk and slept with his daughters. The sins of the fathers set their children's teeth on edge.

Our ministers were fond of quoting St. Paul's pronouncement that drunkards would not inherit the kingdom of God. These grave preachers assured us that the wine referred to during the Last Supper was in fact grape juice. Bible and sermons and hymns combined to give us the impression that Moses should have brought down from the mountain another stone tablet, bearing the Eleventh Commandment: Thou shalt not drink.

30   The scariest and most illuminating Bible story apropos of drunkards was the one about the lunatic and the swine. Matthew, Mark, and Luke each told a version of the tale. We knew it by heart: When Jesus climbed out of his boat one day, this lunatic came charging up from the graveyard, stark naked and filthy, frothing at the mouth, so violent that he broke the strongest chains. Nobody would go near him. Night and day for years this madman had been wailing among the tombs and bruising himself with stones. Jesus took one look at him and said, "Come out of the man, you unclean spirits!" for he could see that the lunatic was possessed by demons. Meanwhile, some hogs were conveniently rooting nearby. "If we have to come out," begged the demons, "at least let us go into those swine." Jesus agreed. The unclean spirits entered the hogs, and the hogs rushed straight off a cliff and plunged into a lake. Hearing the story in Sunday school, my friends thought mainly of the pigs. (How big a splash did they make? Who paid for the lost pork?) But I thought of the redeemed lunatic, who bathed himself and put on clothes and calmly sat at the feet of Jesus, restored—so the Bible said—to "his right mind."

When drunk, our father was clearly in his wrong mind. He became a stranger, as fearful to us as any graveyard lunatic, not quite frothing at the mouth but fierce enough, quick-tempered, explosive; or else he grew maudlin and weepy, which frightened us nearly as much. In my boyhood despair, I reasoned that maybe he wasn't to blame for turning into an ogre. Maybe, like the lunatic, he was possessed by demons. I found support for my theory when I heard liquor referred to as "spirits," when the newspapers reported that somebody had been arrested for "driving under the influence," and when church ladies railed against that "demon drink."

If my father was indeed possessed, who would exorcise him? If he was a sinner, who would save him? If he was ill, who would cure him? If he suffered, who would ease his pain? Not ministers or doctors, for we could not bring ourselves to confide in them; not the neighbors, for we pretended they had never seen him drunk; not Mother, who fussed and pleaded but could not budge him; not my brother and sister, who were only kids. That left me. It did not matter that I, too, was only a child, and a bewildered one at that. I could not excuse myself.

On first reading a description of delirium tremens—in a book on alcoholism I smuggled from the library—I thought immediately of the frothing lunatic and the frenzied swine. When I read stories or watched films about grisly metamorphoses—Dr. Jekyll becoming Mr. Hyde,[6] the mild husband changing into a werewolf, the kindly neighbor taken over by a brutal alien —I could not help seeing my own father's mutation from sober to drunk. Even today, knowing

6. London physician and his evil alter ego, in Robert Louis Stevenson's novel.

better, I am attracted by the demonic theory of drink, for when I recall my father's transformation, the emergence of his ugly second self, I find it easy to believe in possession by unclean spirits. We never knew which version of Father would come home from work, the true or the tainted, nor could we guess how far down the slope toward cruelty he would slide.

How far a man *could* slide we gauged by observing our back-road neighbors—the out-of-work miners who had dragged their families to our corner of Ohio from the desolate hollows of Appalachia, the tight-fisted farmers, the surly mechanics, the balked and broken men. There was, for example, whiskey-soaked Mr. Jenkins, who beat his wife and kids so hard we could hear their screams from the road. There was Mr. Lavo the wino, who fell asleep smoking time and again, until one night his disgusted wife bundled up the children and went outside and left him in his easy chair to burn; he awoke on his own, staggered out coughing into the yard, and pounded her flat while the children looked on and the shack turned to ash. There was the truck driver, Mr. Sampson, who tripped over his son's tricycle one night while drunk and got so mad that he jumped into his semi and drove away, shifting through the dozen gears, and never came back. We saw the bruised children of these fathers clump onto our school bus, we saw the abandoned children huddle in the pews at church, we saw the stunned and battered mothers begging for help at our doors.

Our own father never beat us, and I don't think he ever beat Mother, but he threatened often. The Old Testament Yahweh was not more terrible in his wrath. Eyes blazing, voice booming, Father would pull out his belt and swear to give us a whipping, but he never followed through, never needed to, because we could imagine it so vividly. He shoved us, pawed us with the back of his hand, as an irked bear might smack a cub, not to injure, just to clear a space. I can see him grabbing Mother by the hair as she cowers on a chair during a nightly quarrel. He twists her neck back until she gapes up at him, and then he lifts over her skull a glass quart bottle of milk, the milk running down his forearm; and he yells at her, "Say just one more word, one goddamn word, and I'll shut you up!" I fear she will prick him with her sharp tongue, but she is terrified into silence, and so am I, and the leaking bottle quivers in the air, and milk slithers through the red hair of my father's uplifted arm, and the entire scene is there to this moment, the head jerked back, the club raised.

When the drink made him weepy, Father would pack a bag and kiss each of us children on the head, and announce from the front door that he was moving out. "Where to?" we demanded, fearful each time that he would leave for good, as Mr. Sampson had roared away for good in his diesel truck. "Someplace where I won't get hounded every minute," Father would answer, his jaw quivering. He stabbed a look at Mother, who might say, "Don't run into the ditch before you get there," or, "Good riddance," and then he would slink away. Mother watched him go with arms crossed over her chest, her face closed like the lid on a box of snakes. We children bawled. Where could he go? To the truck stop, that den of iniquity? To one of those dark, ratty flophouses in town? Would he wind up sleeping under a railroad bridge or on a park

35

bench or in a cardboard box, mummied in rags, like the bums we had seen on our trips to Cleveland and Chicago? We bawled and bawled, wondering if he would ever come back.

He always did come back, a day or a week later, but each time there was a sliver less of him.

In Kafka's[7] *The Metamorphosis,* which opens famously with Gregor Samsa waking up from uneasy dreams to find himself transformed into an insect, Gregor's family keep reassuring themselves that things will be just fine again, "When he comes back to us." Each time alcohol transformed our father, we held out the same hope, that he would really and truly come back to us, our authentic father, the tender and playful and competent man, and then all things would be fine. We had grounds for such hope. After his weepy departures and chapfallen returns, he would sometimes go weeks, even months without drinking. Those were glad times. Joy banged inside my ribs. Every day without the furtive glint of bottles, every meal without a fight, every bedtime without sobs encouraged us to believe that such bliss might go on forever.

Mother was fooled by just such a hope all during the forty-odd years she knew this Greeley Ray Sanders. Soon after she met him in a Chicago delicatessen on the eve of World War II and fell for his butter-melting Mississippi drawl and his wavy red hair, she learned that he drank heavily. But then so did a lot of men. She would soon coax or scold him into breaking the nasty habit. She would point out to him how ugly and foolish it was, this bleary drinking, and then he would quit. He refused to quit during their engagement, however, still refused during the first years of marriage, refused until my sister came along. The shock of fatherhood sobered him, and he remained sober through my birth at the end of the war and right on through until we moved in 1951 to the Ohio arsenal, that paradise of bombs. Like all places that make a business of death, the arsenal had more than its share of alcoholics and drug addicts and other varieties of escape artists. There I turned six and started school and woke into a child's flickering awareness, just in time to see my father begin sneaking swigs in the garage.

40   He sobered up again for most of a year at the height of the Korean War, to celebrate the birth of my brother. But aside from that dry spell, his only breaks from drinking before I graduated from high school were just long enough to raise and then dash our hopes. Then during the fall of my senior year—the time of the Cuban missile crisis, when it seemed that the nightly explosions at the munitions dump and the nightly rages in our household might spread to engulf the globe—Father collapsed. His liver, kidneys, and heart all conked out. The doctors saved him, but only by a hair. He stayed in the hospital for weeks, going through a withdrawal so terrible that Mother would not let us visit him. If he wanted to kill himself, the doctors solemnly warned him, all he had to do was hit the bottle again. One binge would finish him.

7. Franz Kafka (1883–1924), Prague-born novelist and short-story writer whose works raise puzzling moral, spiritual, and political dilemmas.

Father must have believed them, for he stayed dry the next fifteen years. It was an answer to prayer, Mother said, it was a miracle. I believe it was a reflex of fear, which he sustained over the years through courage and pride. He knew a man could die from drink, for his brother Roscoe had. We children never laid eyes on doomed Uncle Roscoe, but in the stories Mother told us he became a fairy-tale figure, like a boy who took the wrong turning in the woods and was gobbled up by the wolf.

The fifteen-year dry spell came to an end with Father's retirement in the spring of 1978. Like many men, he gave up his identity along with his job. One day he was a boss at the factory, with a brass plate on his door and a reputation to uphold; the next day he was a nobody at home. He and Mother were leaving Ontario, the last of the many places to which his job had carried them, and they were moving to a new house in Mississippi, his childhood stomping grounds. As a boy in Mississippi, Father sold Coca-Cola during dances while the moonshiners peddled their brew in the parking lot; as a young blade, he fought in bars and in the ring, seeking a state Golden Gloves championship; he gambled at poker, hunted pheasants, raced motorcycles and cars, played semiprofessional baseball, and, along with all his buddies—in the Black Cat Saloon, behind the cotton gin, in the woods—he drank. It was a perilous youth to dream of recovering.

After his final day of work, Mother drove on ahead with a car full of begonias and violets, while Father stayed behind to oversee the packing. When the van was loaded, the sweaty movers broke open a six-pack and offered him a beer.

"Let's drink to retirement!" they crowed. "Let's drink to freedom! to fishing! hunting! loafing! Let's drink to a guy who's going home!"

At least I imagine some such words, for that is all I can do, imagine, and I see Father's hand trembling in midair as he thinks about the fifteen sober years and about the doctors' warning, and he tells himself *God damnit, I am a free man,* and *Why can't a free man drink one beer after a lifetime of hard work?* and I see his arm reaching, his fingers closing, the can tilting to his lips. I even supply a label for the beer, a swaggering brand that promises on television to deliver the essence of life. I watch the amber liquid pour down his throat, the alcohol steal into his blood, the key turn in his brain.

45

Soon after my parents moved back to Father's treacherous stomping ground, my wife and I visited them in Mississippi with our five-year-old daughter. Mother had been too distraught to warn me about the return of the demons. So when I climbed out of the car that bright July morning and saw my father napping in the hammock, I felt uneasy, for in all his sober years I had never known him to sleep in daylight. Then he lurched upright, blinked his bloodshot eyes, and greeted us in a syrupy voice. I was hurled back helpless into childhood.

"What's the matter with Papaw?" our daughter asked.

"Nothing," I said. "Nothing!"

Like a child again, I pretended not to see him in his stupor, and behind my phony smile I grieved. On that visit and on the few that remained before his death, once again I found bottles in the workbench, bottles in the woods. Again his hands shook too much for him to run a saw, to make his precious miniature furniture, to drive straight down back roads. Again he wound up in the ditch, in the hospital, in jail, in treatment centers. Again he shouted and wept. Again he lied. "I never touched a drop," he swore. "Your mother's making it up."

50   I no longer fancied I could reason with the men whose names I found on the bottles—Jim Beam, Jack Daniels—nor did I hope to save my father by burning down a store. I was able now to press the cold statistics about alcoholism against the ache of memory: ten million victims, fifteen million, twenty. And yet, in spite of my age, I reacted in the same blind way as I had in childhood, ignoring biology, forgetting numbers, vainly seeking to erase through my efforts whatever drove him to drink. I worked on their place twelve and sixteen hours a day, in the swelter of Mississippi summers, digging ditches, running electrical wires, planting trees, mowing grass, building sheds, as though what nagged at him was some list of chores, as though by taking his worries on my shoulders I could redeem him. I was flung back into boyhood, acting as though my father would not drink himself to death if only I were perfect.

I failed of perfection; he succeeded in dying. To the end, he considered himself not sick but sinful. "Do you want to kill yourself?" I asked him. "Why not?" he answered. "Why the hell not? What's there to save?" To the end, he would not speak about his feelings, would not or could not give a name to the beast that was devouring him.

In silence, he went rushing off the cliff. Unlike the biblical swine, however, he left behind a few of the demons to haunt his children. Life with him and the loss of him twisted us into shapes that will be familiar to other sons and daughters of alcoholics. My brother became a rebel, my sister retreated into shyness, I played the stalwart and dutiful son who would hold the family together. If my father was unstable, I would be a rock. If he squandered money on drink, I would pinch every penny. If he wept when drunk—and only when drunk—I would not let myself weep at all. If he roared at the Little League umpire for calling my pitches balls, I would throw nothing but strikes. Watching him flounder and rage, I came to dread the loss of control. I would go through life without making anyone mad. I vowed never to put in my mouth or veins any chemical that would banish my everyday self. I would never make a scene, never lash out at the ones I loved, never hurt a soul. Through hard work, relentless work, I would achieve something dazzling—in the classroom, on the basketball floor, in the science lab, in the pages of books—and my achievement would distract the world's eyes from his humiliation. I would become a worthy sacrifice, and the smoke of my burning would please God.

It is far easier to recognize these twists in my character than to undo them. Work has become an addiction for me, as drink was an addiction for my father. Knowing this, my daughter gave me a placard for the wall: WORK-AHOLIC. The labor is endless and futile, for I can no more redeem myself through work than I could redeem my father. I still panic in the face of other people's anger, because his drunken temper was so terrible. I shrink from causing sadness or disappointment even to strangers, as though I were still concealing the family shame. I still notice every twitch of emotion in the faces around me, having learned as a child to read the weather in faces, and I blame myself for their least pang of unhappiness or anger. In certain moods I blame myself for everything. Guilt burns like acid in my veins.

I am moved to write these pages now because my own son, at the age of ten, is taking on himself the griefs of the world, and in particular the griefs of his father. He tells me that when I am gripped by sadness he feels responsible; he feels there must be something he can do to spring me from depression, to fix my life. And that crushing sense of responsibility is exactly what I felt at the age of ten in the face of my father's drinking. My son wonders if I, too, am possessed. I write, therefore, to drag into the light what eats at me—the fear, the guilt, the shame—so that my own children may be spared.

   I still shy away from nightclubs, from bars, from parties where the solvent 55
is alcohol. My friends puzzle over this, but it is no more peculiar than for a man to shy away from the lions' den after seeing his father torn apart. I took my own first drink at the age of twenty-one, half a glass of burgundy. I knew the odds of my becoming an alcoholic were four times higher than for the sons of nonalcoholic fathers. So I sipped warily.

   I still do—once a week, perhaps, a glass of wine, a can of beer, nothing stronger, nothing more. I listen for the turning of a key in my brain.

QUESTIONS

1. Sanders frequently punctuates his memories of his father with information from other sources—dictionaries, medical encyclopedias, poems and short stories, the Bible. What function do these sources perform? How do they enlarge and enrich Sanders's essay?

2. Why does Sanders include the final three paragraphs (53–55)? What effect do they create that would be lost without them?

3. Drawing on your memories of a friend or family member, write an essay about some problem that person had and its effect on your life.

ANNIE DILLARD   from *An American Childhood*

O NE SUNDAY AFTERNOON Mother wandered through our kitchen, where Father was making a sandwich and listening to the ball game. The Pirates were playing the New York Giants at Forbes Field. In those days, the Giants had a utility infielder named Wayne Terwilliger. Just as Mother passed through, the radio announcer cried—with undue drama—"Terwilliger bunts one!"

"Terwilliger bunts one?" Mother cried back, stopped short. She turned. "Is that English?"

"The player's name is Terwilliger," Father said. "He bunted."

"That's marvelous," Mother said. " 'Terwilliger bunts one.' No wonder you listen to baseball. 'Terwilliger bunts one.' "

5   For the next seven or eight years, Mother made this surprising string of syllables her own. Testing a microphone, she repeated, "Terwilliger bunts one"; testing a pen or a typewriter, she wrote it. If, as happened surprisingly often in the course of various improvised gags, she pretended to whisper something else in my ear, she actually whispered, "Terwilliger bunts one." Whenever someone used a French phrase, or a Latin one, she answered solemnly, "Terwilliger bunts one." If Mother had had, like Andrew Carnegie, the opportunity to cook up a motto for a coat of arms, hers would have read simply and tellingly, "Terwilliger bunts one." (Carnegie's was "Death to Privilege.")

She served us with other words and phrases. On a Florida trip, she repeated tremulously, "That . . . is a royal poinciana." I don't remember the tree; I remember the thrill in her voice. She pronounced it carefully, and spelled it. She also liked to say "portulaca."

The drama of the words "Tamiami Trail" stirred her, we learned on the same Florida trip. People built Tampa on one coast, and they built Miami on another. Then—the height of visionary ambition and folly—they piled a slow, tremendous road through the terrible Everglades to connect them. To build the road, men stood sunk in muck to their armpits. They fought off cottonmouth moccasins and six-foot alligators. They slept in boats, wet. They blasted muck with dynamite, cut jungle with machetes; they laid logs, dragged drilling machines, hauled dredges, heaped limestone. The road took fourteen years to build up by the shovelful, a Panama Canal in reverse, and cost hundreds of lives from tropical, mosquito-carried diseases. Then, capping it all, some genius thought of the word Tamiami: they called the road from Tampa to Miami, this very road under our spinning wheels, the Tamiami Trail. Some called it Alligator Alley. Anyone could drive over this road without a thought.

Hearing this, moved, I thought all the suffering of road building was worth it (it wasn't my suffering), now that we had this new thing to hang these new words on—Alligator Alley for those who liked things cute, and, for con-

From An American Childhood, *Dillard's 1987 memoir of growing up in Pittsburgh.*

132

noisseurs like Mother, for lovers of the human drama in all its boldness and terror, the Tamiami Trail.

Back home, Mother cut clips from reels of talk, as it were, and played them back at leisure. She noticed that many Pittsburghers confuse "leave" and "let." One kind relative brightened our morning by mentioning why she'd brought her son to visit: "He wanted to come with me, so I left him." Mother filled in Amy and me on locutions we missed. "I can't do it on Friday," her pretty sister told a crowded dinner party, "because Friday's the day I lay in the stores."

(All unconsciously, though, we ourselves used some pure Pittsburghisms.   10
We said "tele pole," pronounced "telly pole," for that splintery sidewalk post I loved to climb. We said "slippy"—the sidewalks are "slippy." We said, "That's all the farther I could go." And we said, as Pittsburghers do say, "This glass needs washed," or "The dog needs walked"—a usage our father eschewed; he knew it was not standard English, nor even comprehensible English, but he never let on.)

"Spell 'poinsettia,' " Mother would throw out at me, smiling with pleasure. "Spell 'sherbet.' " The idea was not to make us whizzes, but, quite the contrary, to remind us—and I, especially, needed reminding—that we didn't know it all just yet.

"There's a deer standing in the front hall," she told me one quiet evening in the country.

"Really?"

"No. I just wanted to tell you something once without your saying, 'I know.' "

Supermarkets in the middle 1950s began luring, or bothering, customers by   15
giving out Top Value Stamps or Green Stamps. When, shopping with Mother, we got to the head of the checkout line, the checker, always a young man, asked, "Save stamps?"

"No," Mother replied genially, week after week, "I build model airplanes." I believe she originated this line. It took me years to determine where the joke lay.

Anyone who met her verbal challenges she adored. She had surgery on one of her eyes. On the operating table, just before she conked out, she appealed feelingly to the surgeon, saying, as she had been planning to say for weeks, "Will I be able to play the piano?" "Not on me," the surgeon said. "You won't pull that old one on me."

It was, indeed, an old one. The surgeon was supposed to answer, "Yes, my dear, brave woman, you will be able to play the piano after this operation," to which Mother intended to reply, "Oh, good, I've always wanted to play the piano." This pat scenario bored her; she loved having it interrupted. It must have galled her that usually her acquaintances were so predictably unalert; it must have galled her that, for the length of her life, she could surprise everyone so continually, so easily, when she had been the same all along. At any rate, she loved anyone who, as she put it, saw it coming, and called her on it.

She regarded the instructions on bureaucratic forms as straight lines. "Do you advocate the overthrow of the United States government by force or violence?" After some thought she wrote, "Force." She regarded children, even babies, as straight men. When Molly learned to crawl, Mother delighted in buying her gowns with drawstrings at the bottom, like Swee'pea's,[1] because, as she explained energetically, you could easily step on the drawstring without the baby's noticing, so that she crawled and crawled and crawled and never got anywhere except into a small ball at the gown's top.

20   When we children were young, she mothered us tenderly and dependably; as we got older, she resumed her career of anarchism. She collared us into her gags. If she answered the phone on a wrong number, she told the caller, "Just a minute," and dragged the receiver to Amy or me, saying, "Here, take this, your name is Cecile," or, worse, just, "It's for you." You had to think on your feet. But did you want to perform well as Cecile, or did you want to take pity on the wretched caller?

During a family trip to the Highland Park Zoo, Mother and I were alone for a minute. She approached a young couple holding hands on a bench by the seals, and addressed the young man in dripping tones: "Where have you been? Still got those baby-blue eyes; always did slay me. And this"—a swift nod at the dumbstruck young woman, who had removed her hand from the man's— "must be the one you were telling me about. She's not so bad, really, as you used to make out. But listen, you know how I miss you, you know where to reach me, same old place. And there's Ann over there—see how she's grown? See the blue eyes?"

And off she sashayed, taking me firmly by the hand, and leading us around briskly past the monkey house and away. She cocked an ear back, and both of us heard the desperate man begin, in a high-pitched wail, "I swear, I never saw her before in my life. . . ."

On a long, sloping beach by the ocean, she lay stretched out sunning with Father and friends, until the conversation gradually grew tedious, when without forethought she gave a little push with her heel and rolled away. People were stunned. She rolled deadpan and apparently effortlessly, arms and legs extended and tidy, down the beach to the distant water's edge, where she lay at ease just as she had been, but half in the surf, and well out of earshot.

She dearly loved to fluster people by throwing out a game's rules at whim—when she was getting bored, losing in a dull sort of way, and when everybody else was taking it too seriously. If you turned your back, she moved the checkers around on the board. When you got them all straightened out, she denied she'd touched them; the next time you turned your back, she lined them up on the rug or hid them under your chair. In a betting rummy game called Michigan, she routinely played out of turn, or called out a card she didn't hold, or counted backward, simply to amuse herself by causing an uproar and watching the rest of us do double takes and have fits. (Much later, when serious suitors came to call, Mother subjected them to this fast card

---

1. The infant in the comic strip "Popeye" by Elzie Crisler Segar.

game as a trial by ordeal; she used it as an intelligence test and a measure of spirit. If the poor man could stay a round without breaking down or running out, he got to marry one of us, if he still wanted to.)

She excelled at bridge, playing fast and boldly, but when the stakes were low   25
and the hands dull, she bid slams for the devilment of it, or raised her opponents' suit to bug them, or showed her hand, or tossed her cards in a handful behind her back in a characteristic swift motion accompanied by a vibrantly innocent look. It drove our stolid father crazy. The hand was over before it began, and the guests were appalled. How do you score it, who deals now, what do you do with a crazy person who is having so much fun? Or they were down seven, and the guests were appalled. "Pam!" "Dammit, Pam!" He groaned. What ails such people? What on earth possesses them? He rubbed his face.

She was an unstoppable force; she never let go. When we moved across town, she persuaded the U.S. Post Office to let her keep her old address— forever—because she'd had stationery printed. I don't know how she did it. Every new post office worker, over decades, needed to learn that although the Doaks' mail is addressed to here, it is delivered to there.

Mother's energy and intelligence suited her for a greater role in a larger arena—mayor of New York, say—than the one she had. She followed American politics closely; she had been known to vote for Democrats. She saw how things should be run, but she had nothing to run but our household. Even there, small minds bugged her; she was smarter than the people who designed the things she had to use all day for the length of her life.

"Look," she said. "Whoever designed this corkscrew never used one. Why would anyone sell it without trying it out?" So she invented a better one. She showed me a drawing of it. The spirit of American enterprise never faded in Mother. If capitalizing and tooling up had been as interesting as theorizing and thinking up, she would have fired up a new factory every week, and chaired several hundred corporations.

"It grieves me," she would say, "it grieves my heart," that the company that made one superior product packaged it poorly, or took the wrong tack in its advertising. She knew, as she held the thing mournfully in her two hands, that she'd never find another. She was right. We children wholly sympathized, and so did Father; what could she do, what could anyone do, about it? She was Samson in chains.[2] She paced.

She didn't like the taste of stamps so she didn't lick stamps; she licked the   30
corner of the envelope instead. She glued sandpaper to the sides of kitchen drawers, and under kitchen cabinets, so she always had a handy place to strike a match. She designed, and hounded workmen to build against all norms, doubly wide kitchen counters and elevated bathroom sinks. To splint a finger, she stuck it in a lightweight cigar tube. Conversely, to protect a pack of cigarettes, she carried it in a Band-Aid box. She drew plans for an over-the-finger toothbrush for babies, an oven rack that slid up and down, and—the family

2. The Israelite champion against the Philistines, to whom he was betrayed by Delilah (see Judges 14–16).

favorite—Lendalarm. Lendalarm was a beeper you attached to books (or tools) you loaned friends. After ten days, the beeper sounded. Only the rightful owner could silence it.

She repeatedly reminded us of P. T. Barnum's dictum: You could sell anything to anybody if you marketed it right. The adman who thought of making Americans believe they needed underarm deodorant was a visionary. So, too, was the hero who made a success of a new product, Ivory soap. The executives were horrified, Mother told me, that a cake of this stuff floated. Soap wasn't supposed to float. Anyone would be able to tell it was mostly whipped-up air. Then some inspired adman made a leap: Advertise that it floats. Flaunt it. The rest is history.

She respected the rare few who broke through to new ways. "Look," she'd say, "here's an intelligent apron." She called upon us to admire intelligent control knobs and intelligent pan handles, intelligent andirons and picture frames and knife sharpeners. She questioned everything, every pair of scissors, every knitting needle, gardening glove, tape dispenser. Hers was a restless mental vigor that just about ignited the dumb household objects with its force.

Torpid conformity was a kind of sin; it was stupidity itself, the mighty stream against which Mother would never cease to struggle. If you held no minority opinions, or if you failed to risk total ostracism for them daily, the world would be a better place without you.

Always I heard Mother's emotional voice asking Amy and me the same few questions: Is that your own idea? Or somebody else's? *"Giant* is a good movie," I pronounced to the family at dinner. "Oh, really?" Mother warmed to these occasions. She all but rolled up her sleeves. She knew I hadn't seen it. "Is that your considered opinion?"

35   She herself held many unpopular, even fantastic, positions. She was scathingly sarcastic about the McCarthy hearings[3] while they took place, right on our living-room television; she frantically opposed Father's wait-and-see calm. "We don't know enough about it," he said. "I do," she said. "I know all I need to know."

She asserted, against all opposition, that people who lived in trailer parks were not bad but simply poor, and had as much right to settle on beautiful land, such as rural Ligonier, Pennsylvania, as did the oldest of families in the finest of hidden houses. Therefore, the people who owned trailer parks, and sought zoning changes to permit trailer parks, needed our help. Her profound belief that the country-club pool sweeper was a person, and that the department-store saleslady, the bus driver, telephone operator, and housepainter were people, and even in groups the steelworkers who carried pickets and the Christmas shoppers

3. The televised hearings in 1954 (the Army accused Wisconsin senator Joseph R. McCarthy [1908–1957] of improperly seeking preferential treatment for a former colleague then in the service; Senator McCarthy, widely known as a Communist-hunter, accused the Army of covering up certain espionage action) led to the senator's loss of public favor and contributed to his "condemnation" by the Senate in December 1954.

who clogged intersections were people—this was a conviction common enough in democratic Pittsburgh, but not altogether common among our friends' parents, or even, perhaps, among our parents' friends.

Opposition emboldened Mother, and she would take on anybody on any issue—the chairman of the board, at a cocktail party, on the current strike; she would fly at him in a flurry of passion, as a songbird selflessly attacks a big hawk.

"Eisenhower's going to win," I announced after school. She lowered her magazine and looked me in the eyes: "How do you know?" I was doomed. It was fatal to say, "Everyone says so." We all knew well what happened. "Do you consult this Everyone before you make your decisions? What if Everyone decided to round up all the Jews?" Mother knew there was no danger of cowing me. She simply tried to keep us all awake. And in fact it was always clear to Amy and me, and to Molly when she grew old enough to listen, that if our classmates came to cruelty, just as much as if the neighborhood or the nation came to madness, we were expected to take, and would be each separately capable of taking, a stand.

QUESTIONS

1. Dillard piles up examples in this excerpt, barely creating transitions between them. What do the many examples add up to? Is there an overall point she wishes to make about her mother? Try to state it in your own words.

2. When this piece was originally published in Dillard's *An American Childhood*, the chapter had no title. If you could title this piece, what would that title be? Why?

3. Do some free-writing about one of your own parents (or someone important in your life when you were a child). Like Dillard, use as many specific examples as possible to communicate that person's character and personality.

VIRGINIA WOOLF   *My Father: Leslie Stephen*

BY THE TIME that his children were growing up, the great days of my father's life were over. His feats on the river and on the mountains had been won before they were born. Relics of them were to be found lying about the house—the silver cup on the study mantelpiece; the rusty alpenstocks that leaned against the bookcase in the corner; and to the end of his days he would speak of great climbers and explorers with a peculiar mixture of admiration

This affectionate portrait of a person famous in his own right appeared first as an essay in the London Times *(November 28, 1932) and was later reprinted in one of Woolf's many collections,* The Captain's Death Bed and Other Essays *(1950).*

and envy. But his own years of activity were over, and my father had to content himself with pottering about the Swiss valleys or taking a stroll across the Cornish moors.

That to potter and to stroll meant more on his lips than on other people's is becoming obvious now that some of his friends have given their own version of those expeditions. He would start off after breakfast alone, or with one companion. Shortly after dinner he would return. If the walk had been successful, he would have out his great map and commemorate a new short cut in red ink. And he was quite capable, it appears, of striding all day across the moors without speaking more than a word or two to his companion. By that time, too, he had written the *History of English Thought in the Eighteenth Century,* which is said by some to be his masterpiece; and the *Science of Ethics*—the book which interested him most; and *The Playground of Europe,* in which is to be found "The Sunset on Mont Blanc"—in his opinion the best thing he ever wrote. He still wrote daily and methodically, though never for long at a time.

In London he wrote in the large room with three long windows at the top of the house. He wrote lying almost recumbent in a low rocking chair which he tipped to and fro as he wrote, like a cradle, and as he wrote he smoked a short clay pipe, and he scattered books round him in a circle. The thud of a book dropped on the floor could be heard in the room beneath. And often as he mounted the stairs to his study with his firm, regular tread he would burst, not into song, for he was entirely unmusical, but into a strange rhythmical chant, for verse of all kinds, both "utter trash," as he called it, and the most sublime words of Milton and Wordsworth, stuck in his memory, and the act of walking or climbing seemed to inspire him to recite whichever it was that came uppermost or suited his mood.

But it was his dexterity with his fingers that delighted his children before they could potter along the lanes at his heels or read his books. He would twist a sheet of paper beneath a pair of scissors and out would drop an elephant, a stag, or a monkey, with trunks, horns, and tails delicately and exactly formed. Or, taking a pencil, he would draw beast after beast—an art that he practiced almost unconsciously as he read, so that the flyleaves of his books swarm with owls and donkeys as if to illustrate the "Oh, you ass!" or "Conceited dunce" that he was wont to scribble impatiently in the margin. Such brief comments, in which one may find the germ of the more temperate statements of his essays, recall some of the characteristics of his talk. He could be very silent, as his friends have testified. But his remarks, made suddenly in a low voice between the puffs of his pipe, were extremely effective. Sometimes with one word—but his one word was accompanied by a gesture of the hand—he would dispose of the tissue of exaggerations which his own sobriety seemed to provoke. "There are 40,000,000 unmarried women in London alone!" Lady Ritchie once informed him. "Oh, Annie, Annie!" my father exclaimed in tones of horrified but affectionate rebuke. But Lady Ritchie, as if she enjoyed being rebuked, would pile it up even higher next time she came.

5   The stories he told to amuse his children of adventures in the Alps—but accidents only happened, he would explain, if you were so foolish as to disobey

your guides—or of those long walks, after one of which, from Cambridge to London on a hot day, "I drank, I am sorry to say, rather more than was good for me," were told very briefly, but with a curious power to impress the scene. The things that he did not say were always there in the background. So, too, though he seldom told anecdotes, and his memory for facts was bad, when he described a person—and he had known many people, both famous and obscure—he would convey exactly what he thought of him in two or three words. And what he thought might be the opposite of what other people thought. He had a way of upsetting established reputations and disregarding conventional values that could be disconcerting, and sometimes perhaps wounding, though no one was more respectful of any feeling that seemed to him genuine. But when, suddenly opening his bright blue eyes and rousing himself from what had seemed complete abstraction, he gave his opinion, it was difficult to disregard it. It was a habit, especially when deafness made him unaware that this opinion could be heard, that had its inconveniences.

"I am the most easily bored of men," he wrote, truthfully as usual; and when, as was inevitable in a large family, some visitor threatened to stay not merely for tea but also for dinner, my father would express his anguish at first by twisting and untwisting a certain lock of hair. Then he would burst out, half to himself, half to the powers above, but quite audibly, "Why can't he go? Why can't he go?" Yet such is the charm of simplicity—and did he not say, also truthfully, that "bores are the salt of the earth"?—that the bores seldom went, or, if they did, forgave him and came again.

Too much, perhaps, has been said of his silence; too much stress has been laid upon his reserve. He loved clear thinking; he hated sentimentality and gush; but this by no means meant that he was cold and unemotional, perpetually critical and condemnatory in daily life. On the contrary, it was his power of feeling strongly and of expressing his feeling with vigor that made him sometimes so alarming as a companion. A lady, for instance, complained of the wet summer that was spoiling her tour in Cornwall. But to my father, though he never called himself a democrat, the rain meant that the corn was being laid; some poor man was being ruined; and the energy with which he expressed his sympathy—not with the lady—left her discomfited. He had something of the same respect for farmers and fishermen that he had for climbers and explorers. So, too, he talked little of patriotism, but during the South African War—and all wars were hateful to him—he lay awake thinking that he heard the guns on the battlefield. Again, neither his reason nor his cold common sense helped to convince him that a child could be late for dinner without having been maimed or killed in an accident. And not all his mathematics together with a bank balance which he insisted must be ample in the extreme could persuade him, when it came to signing a check, that the whole family was not "shooting Niagara to ruin,"[1] as he put it. The pictures that he would draw of old age and the bankruptcy court, of ruined men of letters who have to support large families in small houses at Wimbledon (he owned a very small

1. The reference is to going over Niagara Falls in a boat.

house at Wimbledon), might have convinced those who complain of his understatements that hyperbole was well within his reach had he chosen.

Yet the unreasonable mood was superficial, as the rapidity with which it vanished would prove. The checkbook was shut; Wimbledon and the workhouse were forgotten. Some thought of a humorous kind made him chuckle. Taking his hat and his stick, calling for his dog and his daughter, he would stride off into Kensington Gardens, where he had walked as a little boy, where his brother Fitzjames and he had made beautiful bows to young Queen Victoria and she had swept them a curtsy; and so, round the Serpentine, to Hyde Park Corner, where he had once saluted the great Duke himself; and so home. He was not then in the least "alarming"; he was very simple, very confiding; and his silence, though one might last unbroken from the Round Pond to the Marble Arch, was curiously full of meaning, as if he were thinking half aloud, about poetry and philosophy and people he had known.

He himself was the most abstemious of men. He smoked a pipe perpetually, but never a cigar. He wore his clothes until they were too shabby to be tolerable; and he held old-fashioned and rather puritanical views as to the vice of luxury and the sin of idleness. The relations between parents and children today have a freedom that would have been impossible with my father. He expected a certain standard of behavior, even of ceremony, in family life. Yet if freedom means the right to think one's own thoughts and to follow one's own pursuits, then no one respected and indeed insisted upon freedom more completely than he did. His sons, with the exception of the Army and Navy, should follow whatever professions they chose; his daughters, though he cared little enough for the higher education of women, should have the same liberty. If at one moment he rebuked a daughter sharply for smoking a cigarette—smoking was not in his opinion a nice habit in the other sex—she had only to ask him if she might become a painter, and he assured her that so long as she took her work seriously he would give her all the help he could. He had no special love for painting; but he kept his word. Freedom of that sort was worth thousands of cigarettes.

10   It was the same with the perhaps more difficult problem of literature. Even today there may be parents who would doubt the wisdom of allowing a girl of fifteen the free run of a large and quite unexpurgated library. But my father allowed it. There were certain facts—very briefly, very shyly he referred to them. Yet "Read what you like," he said, and all his books, "mangy and worthless," as he called them, but certainly they were many and various, were to be had without asking. To read what one liked because one liked it, never to pretend to admire what one did not—that was his only lesson in the art of reading. To write in the fewest possible words, as clearly as possible, exactly what one meant—that was his only lesson in the art of writing. All the rest must be learned for oneself. Yet a child must have been childish in the extreme not to feel that such was the teaching of a man of great learning and wide experience, though he would never impose his own views or parade his own knowledge. For, as his tailor remarked when he saw my father walk past his shop up Bond Street, "There goes a gentleman that wears good clothes without knowing it."

In those last years, grown solitary and very deaf, he would sometimes call himself a failure as a writer; he had been "jack of all trades, and master of none." But whether he failed or succeeded as a writer, it is permissible to believe that he left a distinct impression of himself on the minds of his friends. Meredith[2] saw him as "Phoebus Apollo turned fasting friar" in his earlier days; Thomas Hardy, years later, looked at the "spare and desolate figure" of the Schreckhorn[3] and thought of

> him,
> Who scaled its horn with ventured life and limb,
> Drawn on by vague imaginings, maybe,
> Of semblance to his personality
> In its quaint glooms, keen lights, and rugged trim.

But the praise he would have valued most, for though he was an agnostic nobody believed more profoundly in the worth of human relationships, was Meredith's tribute after his death: "He was the one man to my knowledge worthy to have married your mother." And Lowell,[4] when he called him "L.S., the most lovable of men," has best described the quality that makes him, after all these years, unforgettable.

2. George Meredith (1828–1909), English novelist and poet.
3. One of the peaks in the Swiss Alps; the quotation comes from "The Schreechorn," a poem by Hardy (1840–1928) with the subtitle "with Thoughts of Leslie Stephen, June 1897."
4. James Russell Lowell (1819–1891), American poet, essayist, and editor.

QUESTIONS

1. Would you like to have been Leslie Stephen's son or daughter? Why or why not?

2. Giving praise can be a difficult rhetorical and social undertaking. How does Woolf avoid the pitfalls or try to?

3. In some of her other work, Woolf shows a deep and sensitive concern for women's experience and awareness. Do you find a feminist awareness here? In what way?

4. Write a sketch about a father, real or fictional, adopting a tone similar to Woolf's in this sketch.

THOMAS JEFFERSON *George Washington*

I THINK I KNEW General Washington intimately and thoroughly; and were I called on to delineate his character, it should be in terms like these.

His mind was great and powerful, without being of the very first order; his penetration strong, though not so acute as that of a Newton, Bacon, or Locke; and as far as he saw, no judgment was ever sounder. It was slow in operation, being little aided by invention or imagination, but sure in conclusion. Hence the common remark of his officers, of the advantage he derived from councils of war, where hearing all suggestions, he selected whatever was best; and certainly no general ever planned his battles more judiciously. But if deranged during the course of the action, if any member of his plan was dislocated by sudden circumstances, he was slow in readjustment. The consequence was, that he often failed in the field, and rarely against an enemy in station, as at Boston and York. He was incapable of fear, meeting personal dangers with the calmest unconcern. Perhaps the strongest feature in his character was prudence, never acting until every circumstance, every consideration, was maturely weighed; refraining if he saw a doubt, but, when once decided, going through with his purpose, whatever obstacles opposed. His integrity was most pure, his justice the most inflexible I have ever known, no motives of interest or consanguinity, of friendship or hatred, being able to bias his decision. He was, indeed, in every sense of the words, a wise, a good, and a great man. His temper was naturally irritable and high toned; but reflection and resolution had obtained a firm and habitual ascendency over it. If ever, however, it broke its bonds, he was most tremendous in his wrath. In his expenses he was honorable, but exact; liberal in contributions to whatever promised utility; but frowning and unyielding on all visionary projects, and all unworthy calls on his charity. His heart was not warm in its affections; but he exactly calculated every man's value, and gave him a solid esteem proportioned to it. His person, you know, was fine, his stature exactly what one would wish, his deportment easy, erect and noble; the best horseman of his age, and the most graceful figure that could be seen on horseback. Although in the circle of his friends, where he might be unreserved with safety, he took a free share in conversation, his colloquial talents were not above mediocrity, possessing neither copiousness of ideas, nor fluency of words. In public, when called on for a sudden opinion, he was unready, short and embarrassed. Yet he wrote readily, rather diffusely, in an easy and correct style. This he had acquired by conversation with the world, for his education was merely reading, writing and common arithmetic, to which he added surveying at a later day. His time was employed

When Washington was president, the much younger Thomas Jefferson observed him closely, both as a politician and as a human being. This description appeared in an 1814 letter to a Doctor Jones, who was writing a history and wanted to know about Washington's role in the Federalist–Republican controversy.

in action chiefly, reading little, and that only in agriculture and English history. His correspondence became necessarily extensive, and, with journalizing his agricultural proceedings, occupied most of his leisure hours within doors. On the whole, his character was, in its mass, perfect, in nothing bad, in few points indifferent; and it may truly be said, that never did nature and fortune combine more perfectly to make a man great, and to place him in the same constellation with whatever worthies have merited from man an everlasting remembrance. For his was the singular destiny and merit, of leading the armies of his country successfully through an arduous war, for the establishment of its independence; of conducting its councils through the birth of a government, new in its forms and principles, until it had settled down into a quiet and orderly train; and of scrupulously obeying the laws through the whole of his career, civil and military, of which the history of the world furnishes no other example.

* * *

I am satisfied, the great body of republicans think of him as I do. We were, indeed, dissatisfied with him on his ratification of the British treaty. But this was short lived. We knew his honesty, the wiles with which he was encompassed, and that age had already begun to relax the firmness of his purposes; and I am convinced he is more deeply seated in the love and gratitude of the republicans, than in the Pharisaical homage of the federal monarchists.[1] For he was no monarchist from preference of his judgment. The soundness of that gave him correct views of the rights of man, and his severe justice devoted him to them. He has often declared to me that he considered our new Constitution as an experiment on the practicability of republican government, and with what dose of liberty man could be trusted for his own good; that he was determined the experiment should have a fair trial, and would lose the last drop of his blood in support of it. And these declarations he repeated to me the oftener and more pointedly, because he knew my suspicions of Colonel Hamilton's views,[2] and probably had heard from him the same declarations which I had, to wit, "that the British constitution, with its unequal representation, corruption and other existing abuses, was the most perfect government which had ever been established on earth, and that a reformation of those abuses would make it an impracticable government." I do believe that General Washington had not a firm confidence in the durability of our government. He was naturally distrustful of men, and inclined to gloomy apprehensions; and I was ever persuaded that a belief that we must at length end in something like a British constitution, had some weight in his adoption of the ceremonies of levees,[3]

1. Jefferson here compares those who sought to make the new United States a kingdom, with Washington as king, to the biblical Pharisees, a sect of ancient Israel often considered haughty and hypocritical.

2. Alexander Hamilton (1755–1804) advocated a strong central federal government, led by the "wealthy, good, and wise." His views were opposed by the relatively more democratic views of Jefferson.

3. Morning receptions held by a head of state to enable him to attend to public affairs while rising and dressing. The form was characteristic of European monarchs.

birthdays, pompous meetings with Congress, and other forms of the same character, calculated to prepare us gradually for a change which he believed possible, and to let it come on with as little shock as might be to the public mind.

These are my opinions of General Washington which I would vouch at the judgment seat of God, having been formed on an acquaintance of thirty years. I served with him in the Virginia legislature from 1769 to the Revolutionary war, and again, a short time in Congress, until he left us to take command of the army. During the war and after it we corresponded occasionally, and in the four years of my continuance in the office of Secretary of State, our intercourse was daily, confidential and cordial. After I retired from that office, great and malignant pains were taken by our federal monarchists, and not entirely without effect, to make him view me as a theorist, holding French principles of government,[4] which would lead infallibly to licentiousness and anarchy. And to this he listened the more easily, from my known disapprobation of the British treaty. I never saw him afterwards, or these malignant insinuations should have been dissipated before his just judgment, as mists before the sun. I felt on his death, with my countrymen, that "verily a great man hath fallen this day in Israel."

4. Radical political views advanced by extreme democrats in the course of the French Revolution.

QUESTIONS

1. What, in Jefferson's view, are Washington's outstanding virtues? What are Washington's greatest defects? From what he writes about Washington, can you infer those qualities of character that Jefferson most admires?

2. Do we learn anything from Jefferson's portrait about what Washington looked like? About his family life? About his hobbies? About his religion? If not, are these important omissions in the characterization of a person in public life?

3. Write in the manner of Jefferson a characterization of an important figure in public life today. Consider whether this manner enables you to present what you think is essential truth and whether the attempt brings to light any special problems concerning either the task itself or public life today.

NATHANIEL HAWTHORNE *Abraham Lincoln*

O F COURSE, there was one other personage, in the class of statesmen, whom I should have been truly mortified to leave Washington without seeing; since (temporarily, at least, and by force of circumstances) he was the man of men. But a private grief had built up a barrier about him, impeding the customary free intercourse of Americans with their chief magistrate; so that I might have come away without a glimpse of his very remarkable physiognomy, save for a semi-official opportunity of which I was glad to take advantage. The fact is, we were invited to annex ourselves, as supernumeraries, to a deputation that was about to wait upon the President, from a Massachusetts whip factory, with a present of a splendid whip.

Our immediate party consisted only of four or five (including Major Ben Perley Poore,[1] with his note-book and pencil), but we were joined by several other persons, who seemed to have been lounging about the precincts of the White House, under the spacious porch, or within the hall, and who swarmed in with us to take the chances of a presentation. Nine o'clock had been appointed as the time for receiving the deputation, and we were punctual to the moment; but not so the President, who sent us word that he was eating his breakfast, and would come as soon as he could. His appetite, we were glad to think, must have been a pretty fair one; for we waited about half an hour in one of the antechambers, and then were ushered into a reception-room, in one corner of which sat the Secretaries of War and of the Treasury, expecting, like ourselves, the termination of the Presidential breakfast. During this interval there were several new additions to our group, one or two of whom were in a working-garb, so that we formed a very mis-cellaneous collection of people, mostly unknown to each other, and without any common sponsor, but all with an equal right to look our head servant in the face.

By and by there was a little stir on the staircase and in the passageway,[2]

Published in the Atlantic Monthly *in 1862, during the second year of Lincoln's presidency; as the campaign biographer of his friend and college classmate Franklin Pierce, Hawthorne had experience in describing a person at the highest reaches of American politics.*

1. American journalist and biographer.
2. The balance of this paragraph and the following four paragraphs were omitted from the article as originally published, and the following note was appended to explain the omission, which had been indicated by a line of points:

"We are compelled to omit two or three pages, in which the author describes the interview, and gives his idea of the personal appearance and deportment of the President. The sketch appears to have been written in a benign spirit, and perhaps conveys a not inaccurate impression of its august subject; but it lacks *reverence*, and it pains us to see a gentleman of ripe age, and who has spent years under the corrective influence of foreign institutions, falling into the characteristic and most ominous fault of Young America."

and in lounged a tall, loose-jointed figure, of an exaggerated Yankee port and demeanor, whom (as being about the homeliest man I ever saw, yet by no means repulsive or disagreeable) it was impossible not to recognize as Uncle Abe.

Unquestionably, Western man though he be, and Kentuckian by birth, President Lincoln is the essential representative of all Yankees, and the veritable specimen, physically, of what the world seems determined to regard as our characteristic qualities. It is the strangest and yet the fittest thing in the jumble of human vicissitudes, that he, out of so many millions, unlooked for, unselected by any intelligible process that could be based upon his genuine qualities, unknown to those who chose him, and unsuspected of what endowments may adapt him for his tremendous responsibility, should have found the way open for him to fling his lank personality into the chair of state—where, I presume, it was his first impulse to throw his legs on the council-table, and tell the Cabinet Ministers a story. There is no describing his lengthy awkwardness, nor the uncouthness of his movement; and yet it seemed as if I had been in the habit of seeing him daily, and had shaken hands with him a thousand times in some village street; so true was he to the aspect of the pattern American, though with a certain extravagance which, possibly, I exaggerated still further by the delighted eagerness with which I took it in. If put to guess his calling and livelihood, I should have taken him for a country school-master as soon as anything else. He was dressed in a rusty black frock coat and pantaloons, unbrushed, and worn so faithfully that the suit had adapted itself to the curves and angularities of his figure, and had grown to be an outer skin of the man. His hair was black, still unmixed with gray, stiff, somewhat bushy, and had apparently been acquainted with neither brush nor comb that morning, after the disarrangement of the pillow; and as to a nightcap, Uncle Abe probably knows nothing of such effeminacies. His complexion is dark and sallow, betokening, I fear, a insalubrious atmosphere around the White House; he has thick black eyebrows and an impending brow; his nose is large, and the lines about his mouth are very strongly defined.

5   The whole physiognomy is as coarse a one as you would meet anywhere in the length and breadth of the States; but, withal, it is redeemed, illuminated, softened, and brightened by a kindly though serious look out of his eyes, and an expression of homely sagacity, that seems weighted with rich results of village experience. A great deal of native sense; no bookish cultivation, no refinement; honest at heart, and thoroughly so, and yet, in some sort, sly—at least, endowed with a sort of tact and wisdom that are akin to craft, and would impel him, I think, to take an antagonist in flank, rather than to make a bull-run at him right in front. But, on the whole, I like this sallow, queer, sagacious visage, with the homely human sympathies that warmed it; and, for my small share in the matter, would as lief have Uncle Abe for a ruler as any man whom it would have been practicable to put in his place.

Immediately on his entrance the President accosted our member of Congress, who had us in charge, and, with a comical twist of his face, made some jocular remark about the length of his breakfast. He then greeted us all round, not waiting for an introduction, but shaking and squeezing everybody's hand with the utmost cordiality, whether the individual's name was announced to him or not. His manner towards us was wholly without pretence, but yet had a kind of natural dignity, quite sufficient to keep the forwardest of us from clapping him on the shoulder and asking him for a story. A mutual acquaintance being established, our leader took the whip out of its case, and began to read the address of presentation. The whip was an exceedingly long one, its handle wrought in ivory (by some artist in the Massachusetts State Prison, I believe), and ornamented with a medallion of the President, and other equally beautiful devices; and along its whole length there was a succession of golden bands and ferrules. The address was shorter than the whip, but equally well made, consisting chiefly of an explanatory description of these artistic designs, and closing with a hint that the gift was a suggestive and emblematic one, and that the President would recognize the use to which such an instrument should be put.

This suggestion gave Uncle Abe rather a delicate task in his reply, because, slight as the matter seemed, it apparently called for some declaration, or intimation, or faint foreshadowing of policy in reference to the conduct of the war, and the final treatment of the Rebels. But the President's Yankee aptness and not-to-be-caughtness stood him in good stead, and he jerked or wiggled himself out of the dilemma with an uncouth dexterity that was entirely in character; although, without his gesticulation of eye and mouth—and especially the flourish of the whip, with which he imagined himself touching up a pair of fat horses—I doubt whether his words would be worth recording, even if I could remember them. The gist of the reply was, that he accepted the whip as an emblem of peace, not punishment; and, this great affair over, we retired out of the presence in high good humor, only regretting that we could not have seen the President sit down and fold up his legs (which is said to be a most extraordinary spectacle), or have heard him tell one of those delectable stories for which he is so celebrated. A good many of them are afloat upon the common talk of Washington, and are certainly the aptest, pithiest, and funniest little things imaginable; though, to be sure, they smack of the frontier freedom, and would not always bear repetition in a drawing-room, or on the immaculate page of the *Atlantic*.[3]

Good Heavens! what liberties have I been taking with one of the potentates of the earth, and the man on whose conduct more important consequences depend than on that of any other historical personage of the century! But with whom is an American citizen entitled to take a liberty, if not with his own chief magistrate? However, lest the above allusions to President Lincoln's little peculiarities (already well known to the country and to the world) should be misinterpreted, I deem it proper to say a word or two in regard to him, of unfeigned respect and measurable confidence. He is evidently a man of keen faculties, and, what is still more to the purpose, of powerful character. As to his integrity, the people have that intuition of it which is never deceived. Before he actually entered upon his great office, and for a considerable time af-

---

3. The article as originally published picks up here.

terwards, there is no reason to suppose that he adequately estimated the gigantic task about to be imposed on him, or, at least, had any distinct idea how it was to be managed; and I presume there may have been more than one veteran politician who proposed to himself to take the power out of President Lincoln's hands into his own, leaving our honest friend only the public responsibility for the good or ill success of the career. The extremely imperfect development of his statesmanly qualities, at that period, may have justified such designs. But the President is teachable by events, and has now spent a year in a very arduous course of education; he has a flexible mind, capable of much expansion, and convertible towards far loftier studies and activities than those of his early life; and if he came to Washington a backwoods humorist, he has already transformed himself into as good a statesman (to speak moderately) as his prime minister.[4]

4. Presumably the secretary of state, William H. Seward.

QUESTIONS

1. In his final paragraph Hawthorne seeks to prevent misunderstanding by stressing his respect for and confidence in Lincoln. Is there anything in the paragraph that runs counter to that expression? To what effect?

2. In the footnote to the third paragraph the editor of the *Atlantic Monthly* explains his omission of the following four paragraphs. On the evidence of this statement, what sort of person does the editor seem to be? Is there anything in the omitted paragraphs that would tend to justify his decision as editor? Is the full description superior to the last paragraph printed alone? Explain.

3. What is the basic pattern of the opening sentence of the fifth paragraph? Find other examples of this pattern. What is their total impact on Hawthorne's description?

4. Write a paragraph of description of someone you know, using the same pattern that you discovered in the previous question.

TOM WOLFE   *Yeager*

ANYONE WHO TRAVELS very much on airlines in the United States soon gets to know the voice of *the airline pilot . . . coming* over the intercom . . . with a particular drawl, a particular folksiness, a particular down-home calmness that is so exaggerated it begins to parody itself (nevertheless!—it's reassuring) . . . the voice that tells you, as

From The Right Stuff, *Wolfe's 1979 account of the first astronauts, which was made into a 1983 movie.*

the airliner is caught in thunderheads and goes bolting up and down a thousand feet at a single gulp, to check your seat belts because "it might get a little choppy" . . . the voice that tells you (on a flight from Phoenix preparing for its final approach into Kennedy Airport, New York, just after dawn): "Now, folks, uh . . . this is the captain . . . ummmm . . . We've got a little ol' red light up here on the control panel that's tryin' to tell us that the *land*in' gears're not . . . uh . . . *lock*in' into position when we lower 'em . . . Now . . . I don't believe that little ol' red light knows what it's *talk*in' about—I believe it's that little ol' red light that iddn' workin' right" . . . faint chuckle, long pause, as if to say, *I'm not even sure all this is really worth going into—still, it may amuse you* . . . "*But* . . . I guess to play it by the rules, we oughta *humor* that little ol' light . . . so we're gonna take her down to about, oh, two or three hundred feet over the runway at Kennedy, and the folks down there on the ground are gonna see if they caint give us a *vis*ual inspection of those ol' landin' gears"— with which he is obviously on intimate ol'-buddy terms, as with every other working part of this mighty ship—"and if I'm right . . . they're gonna tell us everything is copa*cet*ic all the way aroun' an' we'll jes take her on in" . . . and, after a couple of low passes over the field, the voice returns: "Well, folks, those folks down there on the ground—it must be too early for 'em or somethin'—I 'spect they still got the *sleep*ers in their eyes . . . 'cause they say they caint tell if those ol' landin' gears are all the way down or not . . . But, you know, up here in the cockpit we're convinced they're all the way down, so we're jes gonna take her on in . . . And oh" . . . (*I almost forgot*) . . . "while we take a little swing out over the ocean an' empty some of that surplus fuel we're not gonna be needin' anymore—that's what you might be seein' comin' out of the wings—our lovely little ladies . . . if they'll be so kind . . . they're gonna go up and down the aisles and show you how we do what we call 'assumin' the position' " . . . another faint chuckle (*We do this so often, and it's so much fun, we even have a funny little name for it*) . . . and the stewardesses, a bit grimmer, by the looks of them, than *that voice,* start telling the passengers to take their glasses off and take the ballpoint pens and other sharp objects out of their pockets, and they show them *the position,* with the head lowered . . . while down on the field at Kennedy the little yellow emergency trucks start roaring across the field—and even though in your pounding heart and your sweating palms and your broiling brainpan you *know* this is a critical moment in your life, you still can't quite bring yourself to be*lieve* it, because if it were . . . how could *the captain,* the man who knows the actual situation most intimately . . . how could he keep on drawlin' and chucklin' and driftin' and lollygaggin' in that particular voice of his—

Well!—who doesn't know that voice! And who can forget it!—even after he is proved right and the emergency is over.

That particular voice may sound vaguely Southern or Southwestern, but it is specifically Appalachian in origin. It originated in the mountains of West Virginia, in the coal country, in Lincoln County, so far up in the hollows that, as the saying went, "they had to pipe in daylight." In the late 1940's and early 1950's this up-hollow voice drifted down from on high, from over the high desert of California, down, down, down, from the upper reaches of the Brotherhood into all phases of American aviation. It was amazing. It was *Pygmalion*[1] in reverse. Military pilots and then, soon, airline pilots, pilots from Maine and Massachusetts and the Dakotas and Oregon and everywhere else, began to talk in that poker-hollow West Virginia drawl, or as close to it as they could bend their native accents. It was the drawl of the most righteous of all the possessors of the right stuff: Chuck Yeager.

Yeager had started out as the equivalent, in the Second World War, of the legendary Frank Luke of the 27th Aero Squadron in the First. Which is to say, he was the boondocker, the boy from the back country, with only a high-school education, no credentials, no cachet or polish of any sort, who took off the feed-store overalls and put on a uniform and climbed into an airplane and lit up the skies over Europe.

Yeager grew up in Hamlin, West Virginia, a town on the Mud River not far from Nitro, Hurricane Whirlwind, Salt Rock, Mud, Sod, Crum, Leet, Dollie, Ruth, and Alum Creek. His father was a gas driller (drilling for natural gas in the coalfields), his older brother was a gas driller, and he would have been a gas driller had he not enlisted in the Army Air Force in 1941 at the age of eighteen. In 1943, at twenty, he became a flight officer, i.e., a non-com who was allowed to fly, and went to England to fly fighter planes over France and Germany. Even in the tumult of the war Yeager was somewhat puzzling to a lot of other pilots. He was a short, wiry, but muscular little guy with dark curly hair and a tough-looking face that seemed (to strangers) to be saying: "You best not be lookin' me in the eye, you peckerwood, or I'll put four more holes in your nose." But that wasn't what was puzzling. What was puzzling was the way Yeager talked. He seemed to talk with some older forms of English elocution, syntax, and conjugation that had been preserved up-hollow in the Appalachians. There were people up there who never said they disapproved of anything, they said: "I don't hold with it." In the present tense they were willing to *help* out, like anyone else; but in the past tense they only *holped*. "H'it weren't nothin' I hold with, but I holped him out with it, anyways."

In his first eight missions, at the age of twenty, Yeager shot down two German fighters. On his ninth he was shot down over German-occupied French territory, suffering flak wounds; he bailed out, was picked up by the French underground, which smuggled him across the Pyrenees into Spain disguised as a peasant. In Spain he was jailed briefly, then released, whereupon he made it back to England and returned to combat during the Allied invasion of France. On October 12, 1944, Yeager took on and shot down five German fighter planes in succession. On November 6, flying a propeller-driven P-51 Mustang, he shot down one of the new jet fighters the Germans had developed, the Messerschmitt-262, and damaged two more, and on November 20 he shot down four FW-190s. It was a true Frank Luke–style display of warrior

1. An allusion to the play by Bernard Shaw (1856–1950), in which a teacher of phonetics attempts to transform a Cockney flower girl into an elegant lady by means of transforming her speech.

fury and personal prowess. By the end of the war he had thirteen and a half kills. He was twenty-two years old.

In 1946 and 1947 Yeager was trained as a test pilot at Wright Field in Dayton. He amazed his instructors with his ability at stunt-team flying, not to mention the unofficial business of hassling. That plus his up-hollow drawl had everybody saying, "He's a natural-born stick 'n' rudder man." Nevertheless, there was something extraordinary about it when a man so young, with so little experience in flight test, was selected to go to Muroc Field in California for the XS-1 project.

Muroc was up in the high elevations of the Mojave Desert. It looked like some fossil landscape that had long since been left behind by the rest of terrestrial evolution. It was full of huge dry lake beds, the biggest being Rogers Lake. Other than sagebrush the only vegetation was Joshua trees, twisted freaks of the plant world that looked like a cross between cactus and Japanese bonsai. They had a dark petrified green color and horribly crippled branches. At dusk the Joshua trees stood out in silhouette on the fossil wasteland like some arthritic nightmare. In the summer the temperature went up to 110 degrees as a matter of course, and the dry lake beds were covered in sand, and there would be windstorms and sandstorms right out of a Foreign Legion movie. At night it would drop to near freezing, and in December it would start raining, and the dry lakes would fill up with a few inches of water, and some sort of putrid prehistoric shrimps would work their way up from out of the ooze, and sea gulls would come flying in a hundred miles or more from the ocean, over the mountains, to gobble up these squirming little throwbacks. A person had to see it to believe it: flocks of sea gulls wheeling around in the air out in the middle of the high desert in the dead of winter and grazing on antediluvian crustaceans in the primordial ooze.

When the wind blew the few inches of water back and forth across the lake beds, they became absolutely smooth and level. And when the water evaporated in the spring, and the sun baked the ground hard, the lake beds became the greatest natural landing fields ever discovered, and also the biggest, with miles of room for error. That was highly desirable, given the nature of the enterprise at Muroc.

Besides the wind, sand, tumbleweed, and Joshua trees, there was nothing at Muroc except for two quonset-style hangars, side by side, a couple of gasoline pumps, a single concrete runway, a few tarpaper shacks, and some tents. The officers stayed in the shacks marked "barracks," and lesser souls stayed in the tents and froze all night and fried all day. Every road into the property had a guardhouse on it manned by soldiers. The enterprise the Army had undertaken in this godforsaken place was the development of supersonic jet and rocket planes.

10

At the end of the war the Army had discovered that the Germans not only had the world's first jet fighter but also a rocket plane that had gone 596 miles an hour in tests. Just after the war a British jet, the Gloster Meteor, jumped the official world speed record from 469 to 606 in a single day. The next great plateau would be Mach 1, the speed of sound, and the Army Air Force considered it crucial to achieve it first.

The speed of sound, Mach 1, was known (thanks to the work of the physicist Ernst Mach) to vary at different altitudes, temperatures, and wind speeds. On a calm 60-degree day at sea level it was about 760 miles an hour, while at 40,000 feet, where the temperature would be at least sixty below, it was about 660 miles an hour. Evil and baffling things happened in the transonic zone, which began at about .7 Mach. Wind tunnels choked out at such velocities. Pilots who approached the speed of sound in dives reported that the controls would lock or "freeze" or even alter their normal functions. Pilots had crashed and died because they couldn't budge the stick. Just last year Geoffrey de Havilland, son of the famous British aircraft designer and builder, had tried to take one of his father's DH 108s to Mach 1. The ship started buffeting and then disintegrated, and he was killed. This led engineers to speculate that the shock waves became so severe and unpredictable at Mach 1, no aircraft could survive them. They started talking about "the sonic wall" and "the sound barrier."

So this was the task that a handful of pilots, engineers, and mechanics had at Muroc. The place was utterly primitive, nothing but bare bones, bleached tarpaulins, and corrugated tin rippling in the heat with caloric waves; and for an ambitious young pilot it was perfect. Muroc seemed like an outpost on the dome of the world, open only to a righteous few, closed off to the rest of humanity, including even the Army Air Force brass of command control, which was at Wright Field. The commanding officer at Muroc was only a colonel, and his superiors at Wright did not relish junkets to the Muroc rat shacks in the first place. But to pilots this prehistoric throwback of an airfield became . . . shrimp heaven! the rat-shack plains of Olympus!

Low Rent Septic Tank Perfection . . . yes; and not excluding those traditional essentials for the blissful hot young pilot: Flying & Drinking and Drinking & Driving.

15   Just beyond the base, to the southwest, there was a rickety windblown 1930's-style establishment called Pancho's Fly Inn, owned, run, and bartended by a woman named Pancho Barnes. Pancho Barnes wore tight white sweaters and tight pants, after the mode of Barbara Stanwyck in *Double Indemnity*.[2] She was only forty-one when Yeager arrived at Muroc, but her face was so weather-beaten, had so many hard miles on it, that she looked older, especially to the young pilots at the base. She also shocked the pants off them with her vulcanized tongue. Everybody she didn't like was an old bastard or a sonofabitch. People she liked were old bastards and sonsabitches, too. "I tol' 'at ol' bastard to get 'is ass on over here and I'd g'im a drink." But Pancho Barnes was anything but Low Rent. She was the granddaughter of the man who designed the old Mount Lowe cable-car system, Thaddeus S. C. Lowe. Her maiden name was Florence Leontine Lowe. She was brought up in San Marino, which ad-

---

2. A 1944 film featuring a femme fatale housewife (played by Stanwyck) and a likable insurance salesman (played by Fred MacMurray) who concoct a cold-blooded scheme to murder her husband for purposes of lustful desire and financial gain; because the murder doesn't pass for an accident, their scheme ultimately fails.

joined Pasadena and was one of Los Angeles' wealthiest suburbs, and her first husband—she was married four times—was the pastor of the Pasadena Episcopal Church, the Rev. C. Rankin Barnes. Mrs. Barnes seemed to have few of the conventional community interests of a Pasadena matron. In the late 1920's, by boat and plane, she ran guns for Mexican revolutionaries and picked up the nickname Pancho. In 1930 she broke Amelia Earhart's[3] airspeed record for women. Then she barnstormed around the country as the featured performer of "Pancho Barnes's Mystery Circus of the Air." She always greeted her public in jodhpurs and riding boots, a flight jacket, a white scarf, and a white sweater that showed off her terrific Barbara Stanwyck chest. Pancho's desert Fly Inn had an airstrip, a swimming pool, a dude ranch corral, plenty of acreage for horseback riding, a big old guest house for the lodgers, and a connecting building that was the bar and restaurant. In the barroom the floors, the tables, the chairs, the walls, the beams, the bar were of the sort known as extremely weatherbeaten, and the screen doors kept banging. Nobody putting together such a place for a movie about flying in the old days would ever dare make it as dilapidated and generally go-to-hell as it actually was. Behind the bar were many pictures of airplanes and pilots, lavishly autographed and inscribed, badly framed and crookedly hung. There was an old piano that had been dried out and cracked to the point of hopeless desiccation. On a good night a huddle of drunken aviators could be heard trying to bang, slosh, and navigate their way through old Cole Porter[4] tunes. On average nights the tunes were not that good to start with. When the screen door banged and a man walked through the door into the saloon, every eye in the place checked him out. If he wasn't known as somebody who had something to do with flying at Muroc, he would be eyed like some lame goddamned mouseshit sheepherder from Shane.[5]

The plane the Air Force wanted to break the sound barrier with was called the X-1 at the outset and later on simply the X-1. The Bell Aircraft Corporation had built it under an Army contract. The core of the ship was a rocket of the type first developed by a young Navy inventor, Robert Truax, during the war. The fuselage was shaped like a 50-caliber bullet—an object that was known to go supersonic smoothly. Military pilots seldom drew major test assignments; they went to highly paid civilians working for the aircraft corporations. The prime pilot for the X-1 was a man whom Bell regarded as the best of the breed. This man looked like a movie star. He looked like a pilot from out of Hell's Angels.[6] And on top of everything else there was his name: Slick Goodlin.

3. Pioneering aviator (1897–1937) who disappeared while attempting a world flight in 1937.

4. American composer of popular music (1891–1964), including Broadway show tunes.

5. A 1953 classic Western set in Jackson Hole, Wyoming, about an impressionable young boy, Joey Starrett, who idolizes a mysterious golden-haired gunslinger (Shane).

6. A 1930 movie about World War I aviation.

The idea in testing the X-1 was to nurse it carefully into the transonic zone, up to seven-tenths, eight-tenths, nine-tenths the speed of sound (.7 Mach, .8 Mach, .9 Mach) before attempting the speed of sound itself, Mach 1, even though Bell and the Army already knew the X-1 had the rocket power to go to Mach 1 and beyond, if there *was* any *beyond*. The consensus of aviators and engineers, after Geoffrey de Havilland's death, was that the speed of sound was an absolute, like the firmness of the earth. The sound barrier was a farm you could buy in the sky. So Slick Goodlin began to probe the transonic zone in the X-1, going up to .8 Mach. Every time he came down he'd have a riveting tale to tell. The buffeting, it was so fierce—and the listeners, their imaginations aflame, could practically see poor Geoffrey de Havilland disintegrating in midair. And the goddamned aerodynamics—and the listeners got a picture of a man in ballroom pumps skidding across a sheet of ice, pursued by bears. A controversy arose over just how much bonus Slick Goodlin should receive for assaulting the dread Mach 1 itself. Bonuses for contract test pilots were not unusual; but the figure of $150,000 was now bruited about. The Army balked, and Yeager got the job. He took it for $283 a month, or $3,396 a year; which is to say, his regular Army captain's pay.

The only trouble they had with Yeager was in holding him back. On his first powered flight in the X-1 he immediately executed an unauthorized zero-g roll with a full load of rocket fuel, then stood the ship on its tail and went up to .85 Mach in a vertical climb, also unauthorized. On subsequent flights, at speeds between .85 Mach and .9 Mach, Yeager ran into most known airfoil problems—loss of elevator, aileron, and rudder control, heavy trim pressures, Dutch rolls, pitching and buffeting, the lot—yet was convinced, after edging over .9 Mach, that this would all get better, not worse, as you reached Mach 1. The attempt to push beyond Mach 1—"breaking the sound barrier"—was set for October 14, 1947. Not being an engineer, Yeager didn't believe the "barrier" existed.

October 14 was a Tuesday. On Sunday evening, October 12, Chuck Yeager dropped in at Pancho's, along with his wife. She was a brunette named Glennis, whom he had met in California while he was in training, and she was such a number, so striking, he had the inscription "Glamorous Glennis" written on the nose of his P-51 in Europe and, just a few weeks back, on the X-1 itself. Yeager didn't go to Pancho's and knock back a few because two days later the big test was coming up. Nor did he knock back a few because it was the weekend. No, he knocked back a few because night had come and he was a pilot at Muroc. In keeping with the military tradition of Flying & Drinking, that was what you did, for no other reason than that the sun had gone down. You went to Pancho's and knocked back a few and listened to the screen doors banging and to other aviators torturing the piano and the nation's repertoire of Familiar Favorites and to lonesome mouseturd strangers wandering in through the banging doors and to Pancho classifying the whole bunch of them as old bastards and miserable peckerwoods. That was what you did if you were a pilot at Muroc and the sun went down.

20   So about eleven Yeager got the idea that it would be a hell of a kick if he

and Glennis saddled up a couple of Pancho's dude-ranch horses and went for a romp, a little rat race, in the moonlight. This was in keeping with the military tradition of Flying & Drinking and Drinking & Driving, except that this was prehistoric Muroc and you rode horses. So Yeager and his wife set off on a little proficiency run at full gallop through the desert in the moonlight amid the arthritic silhouettes of the Joshua trees. Then they start racing back to the corral, with Yeager in the lead and heading for the gateway. Given the prevailing conditions, it being nighttime, at Pancho's, and his head being filled with a black sandstorm of many badly bawled songs and vulcanized oaths, he sees too late that the gate has been closed. Like many a hard-driving midnight pilot before him, he does not realize that he is not equally gifted in the control of all forms of locomotion. He and the horse hit the gate, and he goes flying off and lands on his right side. His side hurts like hell.

The next day, Monday, his side still hurts like hell. It hurts every time he moves. It hurts every time he breathes deep. It hurts every time he moves his right arm. He knows that if he goes to a doctor at Muroc or says anything to anybody even remotely connected with his superiors, he will be scrubbed from the flight on Tuesday. They might even go so far as to put some other miserable peckerwood in his place. So he gets on his motorcycle, an old junker that Pancho had given him, and rides over to see a doctor in the town of Rosamond, near where he lives. Every time the goddamned motorcycle hits a pebble in the road, his side hurts like a sonofabitch. The doctor in Rosamond informs him he has two broken ribs and he tapes them up and tells him that if he'll just keep his right arm immobilized for a couple of weeks and avoid any physical exertion or sudden movements, he should be all right.

Yeager gets up before daybreak on Tuesday morning—which is supposed to be the day he tries to break the sound barrier—and his ribs still hurt like a sonofabitch. He gets his wife to drive him over to the field, and he has to keep his right arm pinned down to his side to keep his ribs from hurting so much. At dawn, on the day of a flight, you could hear the X-1 screaming long before you got there. The fuel for the X-1 was alcohol and liquid oxygen, oxygen converted from a gas to a liquid by lowering its temperature to 297 degrees below zero. And when the lox, as it was called, rolled out of the hoses and into the belly of the X-1, it started boiling off and the X-1 started steaming and screaming like a teakettle. There's quite a crowd on hand, by Muroc standards . . . perhaps nine or ten souls. They're still fueling the X-1 with the lox, and the beast is wailing.

The X-1 looked like a fat orange swallow with white markings. But it was really just a length of pipe with four rocket chambers in it. It had a tiny cockpit and a needle nose, two little straight blades (only three and a half inches thick at the thickest part) for wings, and a tail assembly set up high to avoid the "sonic wash" from the wings. Even though his side was throbbing and his right arm felt practically useless, Yeager figured he could grit his teeth and get through the flight—except for one specific move he had to make. In the rocket launches, the X-1, which held only two and a half minutes' worth of fuel, was carried up to twenty-six thousand feet underneath a B-29. At seven thousand feet, Yeager was to climb down a ladder from the bomb bay of the B-29 to the open doorway of the X-1, hook up to the oxygen system and the radio microphone and earphones, and put his crash helmet on and prepare for the launch, which would come at twenty-five thousand feet. This helmet was a homemade number. There had never been any such thing as a crash helmet before, except in stunt flying. Throughout the war pilots had used the old skin-tight leather helmet-and-goggles. But the X-1 had a way of throwing the pilot around so violently that there was danger of getting knocked out against the walls of the cockpit. So Yeager had bought a big leather football helmet—there were no plastic ones at the time—and he butchered it with a hunting knife until he carved the right kind of holes in it, so that it would fit down over his regular flying helmet and the earphones and the oxygen rig. Anyway, then his flight engineer, Jack Ridley, would climb down the ladder, out in the breeze, and shove into place the cockpit door, which had to be lowered out of the belly of the B-29 on a chain. Then Yeager had to push a handle to lock the door airtight. Since the X-1's cockpit was minute, you had to push the handle with your right hand. It took quite a shove. There was no way you could move into position to get enough leverage with your left hand.

Out in the hangar Yeager makes a few test shoves on the sly, and the pain is so incredible he realizes that there is no way a man with two broken ribs is going to get the door closed. It is time to confide in somebody, and the logical man is Jack Ridley. Ridley is not only the flight engineer but a pilot himself and a good old boy from Oklahoma to boot. He will understand about Flying & Drinking and Drinking & Driving through the goddamned Joshua trees. So Yeager takes Ridley off to the side in the tin hangar and says: Jack, I got me a little ol' problem here. Over at Pancho's the other night I sorta . . . dinged my goddamned ribs. Ridley says, Whattya mean . . . *dinged?* Yeager says, Well, I guess you might say I damned near like to . . . *broke* a coupla the sonsabitches. Whereupon Yeager sketches out the problem he foresees.

25   Not for nothing is Ridley the engineer on this project. He has an inspiration. He tells a janitor named Sam to cut him about nine inches off a broom handle. When nobody's looking, he slips the broomstick into the cockpit of the X-1 and gives Yeager a little advice and counsel.

So with that added bit of supersonic flight gear Yeager went aloft.

At seven thousand feet he climbed down the ladder into the X-1's cockpit, clipped on his hoses and lines, and managed to pull the pumpkin football helmet over his head. Then Ridley came down the ladder and lowered the door into place. As Ridley had instructed, Yeager now took the nine inches of broomstick and slipped it between the handle and the door. This gave him just enough mechanical advantage to reach over with his left hand and whang the thing shut. So he whanged the door shut with Ridley's broomstick and was ready to fly.

At 26,000 feet the B-29 went into a shallow dive, then pulled up and released Yeager and the X-1 as if it were a bomb. Like a bomb it dropped and shot forward (at the speed of the mother ship) at the same time. Yeager had been launched straight into the sun. It seemed to be no more than six feet in front of him, filling up the sky and blinding him. But he managed to get his bearings and set off the four rocket chambers one after the other. He then experienced something that became known as the ultimate sensation in flying: "booming and zooming." The surge of the rockets was so tremendous, forced him back into his seat so violently, he could hardly move his hands forward the few inches necessary to reach the controls. The X-1 seemed to shoot straight up in an absolutely perpendicular trajectory, as if determined to snap the hold of gravity via the most direct route possible. In fact, he was only climbing at the 45-degree angle called for in the flight plan. At about .87 Mach the buffeting started.

On the ground the engineers could no longer see Yeager. They could only hear . . . that poker-hollow West Virginia drawl.

"Had a mild buffet there . . . jes the usual instability . . ."   30

Jes the usual instability?

Then the X-1 reached the speed of .96 Mach, and that incredible caint-hardlyin' aw-shuckin' drawl said:

"Say, Ridley . . . make a note here, will ya?" (*if you ain't got nothin' better to do*) ". . . elevator effectiveness *regained.*"

Just as Yeager had predicted, as the X-1 approached Mach 1, the stability improved. Yeager had his eyes pinned on the machometer. The needle reached .96, fluctuated, and went off the scale.

And on the ground they heard . . . that voice: 35

"Say, Ridley . . . make another note, will ya?" (*if you ain't too bored yet*) ". . . there's somethin' wrong with this ol' machometer . . ." (faint chuckle) ". . . it's gone kinda screwy on me . . ."

And in that moment, on the ground, they heard a boom rock over the desert floor—just as the physicist Theodore von Kármán had predicted many years before.

Then they heard Ridley back in the B-29: "If it is, Chuck, we'll fix it. Personally I think you're seeing things."

Then they heard Yeager's poker-hollow drawl again:

"Well, I guess I am, Jack . . . And I'm still goin' upstairs like a bat."   40

The X-1 had gone through "the sonic wall" without so much as a bump. As the speed topped out at Mach 1.05, Yeager had the sensation of shooting straight through the top of the sky. The sky turned a deep purple and all at once the stars and the moon came out—and the sun shone at the same time. He had reached a layer of the upper atmosphere where the air was too thin to contain reflecting dust particles. He was simply looking out into space. As the X-1 nosed over at the top of the climb, Yeager now had seven minutes of . . . Pilot Heaven . . . ahead of him. He was going faster than any man in history, and it was almost silent up here, since he had exhausted his rocket fuel, and he was so high in such a vast space that there was no sensation of motion. He was master of the sky. His was a king's solitude, unique and inviolate, above the dome of the world. It would take him seven minutes to glide back down and land at Muroc. He spent the time doing victory rolls and wing-over-wing aerobatics while Rogers Lake and the High Sierras spun around below.

QUESTIONS

1. Before recounting Yeager's personal history or the story of breaking the sound barrier, Wolfe begins with the voice of an airline pilot. Why does he begin this way? What connection does the first paragraph have with the rest of the essay?

2. Wolfe interweaves Yeager's personal history with a more public, official history of the space program. Make a flowchart or diagram to show how this interweaving works.

3. Write an essay that interweaves some part of your personal history with some larger, public story.

TONI MORRISON   *Strangers*

I AM IN THIS river place—newly mine—walking in the yard when I see a woman sitting on the seawall at the edge of a neighbor's garden. A homemade fishing pole arcs into the water some twenty feet from her hand. A feeling of welcome washes over me. I walk toward her, right up to the fence that separates my place from the neighbor's, and notice with pleasure the clothes she wears: men's shoes, a man's hat, a well-worn colorless sweater over a long black dress. The woman turns her head and greets me with an easy smile and a "How you doing?" She tells me her name (Mother Something) and we talk for some time—fifteen minutes or so—about fish recipes and weather and children. When I ask her if she lives there, she answers no. She lives in a nearby village, but the owner of the house lets her come to this spot any time she wants to fish, and she comes every week, sometimes several days in a row when the perch or catfish are running and even if they aren't because she likes eel, too, and they are always there. She is witty and full of the wisdom that older women always seem to have a lock on. When we part, it is with an understanding that she will be there the next day or very soon after and we will visit again. I imagine more conversations with her. I will invite her into my house for coffee, for tales, for laughter. She reminds me of someone, something. I imagine a friendship, casual, effortless, delightful.

She is not there the next day. She is not there the following days, either. And I look for her every morning. The summer passes, and I have not seen her at all. Finally, I approach the neighbor to ask about her and am bewildered to learn that the neighbor does not know who or what I am talking about. No old woman fished from her wall—ever—and none had permission to do so. I decide that the fisherwoman fibbed about the permission and took advantage of the neighbor's frequent absences to poach. The fact of the neighbor's presence is

Morrison wrote this essay to introduce a book of photographs by Robert Bergman, A Kind of Rapture *(1998).*

proof that the fisherwoman would not be there. During the months following, I ask lots of people if they know Mother Something. No one, not even people who have lived in nearby villages for seventy years, has ever heard of her.

I feel cheated, puzzled, but also amused, and wonder off and on if I have dreamed her. In any case, I tell myself, it was an encounter of no value other than anecdotal. Still. Little by little, annoyance then bitterness takes the place of my original bewilderment. A certain view from my windows is now devoid of her, reminding me every morning of her deceit and my disappointment. What was she doing in that neighborhood, anyway? She didn't drive, had to walk four miles if indeed she lived where she said she did. How could she be missed on the road in that hat, those awful shoes? I try to understand the intensity of my chagrin, and why I am missing a woman I spoke to for fifteen minutes. I get nowhere except for the stingy explanation that she had come into my space (next to it, anyway—at the property line, at the edge, just at the fence, where the most interesting things always happen), and had implied promises of female camaraderie, of opportunities for me to be generous, of protection and protecting. Now she is gone, taking with her my good opinion of myself, which, of course, is unforgivable.

Isn't that the kind of thing that we fear strangers will do? Disturb. Betray. Prove they are not like us. That is why it is so hard to know what to do with them. The love that prophets have urged us to offer the stranger is the same love that Jean-Paul Sartre[1] could reveal as the very mendacity of Hell. The

---

1. French existentialist philosopher (1905–1980). The line in Sartre's 1944 play *No Exit* is usually translated as "Hell is other people."

signal line of "No Exit," "*L'enfer, c'est les autres*," raises the possibility that "other people" are responsible for turning a personal world into a public hell. In the admonition of a prophet and the sly warning of an artist, strangers as well as the beloved are understood to tempt our gaze, to slide away or to stake claims. Religious prophets caution against the slide, the looking away; Sartre warns against love as possession.

5   The resources available to us for benign access to each other, for vaulting the mere blue air that separates us, are few but powerful: language, image, and experience, which may involve both, one, or neither of the first two. Language (saying, listening, reading) can encourage, even mandate, surrender, the breach of distances among us, whether they are continental or on the same pillow, whether they are distances of culture or the distinctions and indistinctions of age or gender, whether they are the consequences of social invention or biology. Image increasingly rules the realm of shaping, sometimes becoming, often contaminating, knowledge. Provoking language or eclipsing it, an image can determine not only what we know and feel but also what we believe is worth knowing about what we feel.

These two godlings, language and image, feed and form experience. My instant embrace of an outrageously dressed fisherwoman was due in part to an image on which my representation of her was based. I immediately sentimentalized and appropriated her. I owned her or wanted to (and I suspect she glimpsed it). I had forgotten the power of embedded images and stylish language to seduce, reveal, control. Forgot, too, their capacity to help us pursue the human project—which is to remain human and to block the dehumanization of others.

But something unforeseen has entered into this admittedly oversimplified menu of our resources. Far from our original expectations of increased intimacy and broader knowledge, routine media presentations deploy images and language that narrow our view of what humans look like (or ought to look like) and what in fact we are like. Succumbing to the perversions of media can blur vision, resisting them can do the same. I was clearly and aggressively resisting such influences in my encounter with the fisherwoman. Art as well as the market can be complicit in the sequestering of form from formula, of nature from artifice, of humanity from commodity. Art gesturing toward representation has, in some exalted quarters, become literally beneath contempt. The concept of what it is to be human has altered, and the word *truth* needs quotation marks around it so that its absence (its elusiveness) is stronger than its presence.

Why would we want to know a stranger when it is easier to estrange another? Why would we want to close the distance when we can close the gate? Appeals in arts and religion for comity in the Common Wealth are faint.

It took some time for me to understand my unreasonable claims on that fisherwoman. To understand that I was longing for and missing some aspect of myself, and that there are no strangers. There are only versions of ourselves, many of which we have not embraced, most of which we wish to protect ourselves from. For the stranger is not foreign, she is random, not alien but remembered; and it is the randomness of the encounter with our already known—although unacknowledged—selves that summons a ripple of alarm. That makes us reject the figure and the emotions it provokes—especially when these emotions are profound. It is also what makes us want to own, govern, administrate the Other. To romance her, if we can, back into our own mirrors. In either instance (of alarm or false reverence), we deny her personhood, the specific individuality we insist upon for ourselves.

Robert Bergman's radiant portraits of strangers provoked this meditation.   10
Occasionally, there arises an event or a moment that one knows immediately will forever mark a place in the history of artistic endeavor. Bergman's portraits represent such a moment, such an event. In all its burnished majesty his gallery refuses us unearned solace, and one by one by one the photographs unveil *us*, asserting a beauty, a kind of rapture, that is as close as can be to a master template of the singularity, the community, the unextinguishable sacredness of the human race.

QUESTIONS

1. In his book, *A Kind of Rapture*, Robert Bergman included people he encountered on the streets of America. Why does Morrison not dwell on that fact?

2. In the opening paragraphs (1–3) Morrison relates a story about a woman she sees fishing near her property; later in the essay she expresses regret, even guilt, that her story "sentimentalized and appropriated" the woman (paragraphs 6–7). What does Morrison mean by this self-criticism? Do you agree that it may be ethically wrong to create stories about the strangers we see?

3. What do you see in these photographs? More than Morrison does? Different things? Can you read these images the way Updike reads paintings in "Little Lightnings" (p. 1085) and "Moving Along" (p. 1087)?

EAVAN BOLAND   *The Woman, the Place, the Poet*

T HERE IS A DUALITY TO PLACE. There is the place which existed before you came to it, closed in the secrets and complexities of history; and there is the place you experience in the present. This essay is about such a duality as I discovered it in two locations. I begin with Dundrum, a suburb south of Dublin, where I have lived for eighteen of my forty-five years—longer, in fact, than in any other single environment. The second is an altogether darker, grimmer region, a hundred miles southwest. Both of them prove to me there is the place that happened and the place that happens to you. That there are moments—in work, in perception, in experience—when they are hard to disentangle from one another. And that, at such times, the inward adventure can become so enmeshed with the outward continuum that we live not in one or the other but at the point of intersection.

I suspect this piece is about just such an intersection. It is, of course, a particular version of particular locales. But there may well be a more general truth disguised in it: that what we call place is really only that detail of it which we understand to be ourselves. "That's my Middle West," writes Fitzgerald in *The Great Gatsby*,[1] "not the wheat or the prairies or the lost Swede towns but the thrilling returning trains of my youth and the streetlamps and sleigh bells in the frosty dark and the shadows of holly wreaths thrown by lighted windows on the snow. I am part of that."

Questions of place were far from my mind that first winter, the second of our marriage, when we moved out here. We unpacked our books, put up our shelves, and looked doubtfully at the raw floors and white walls of a new house. From the upstairs window we saw little to console us. Dundrum at this time, in the early seventies, was already starting to wander out toward the foothills of the Dublin mountains. On those winter nights, in the first weeks of January, we learned to look for the lamps on the hills after dark, yellow and welcome as nocturnal crocuses.

For all that, we were disoriented. I, at least, was thoroughly urban. The Dublin I had known until then was a sympathetic prospect of stone and water and wet dusks over Stephen's Green,[2] a convivial town of coffee and endlessly renewable talk. I knew nothing of the city of contingencies. Now here it was, visible and oppressive and still at a distance from the love I would come to feel for it.

First published in the Georgia Review *(Spring/Summer 1990), a literary magazine known for the high quality of its poetry, stories, essays, and art; later incorporated into Boland's prose memoir,* Object Lessons: The Life of the Woman and the Poet in Our Time *(1995).*

1. F. Scott Fitzgerald (1898–1940), American novelist best known for *The Great Gatsby* (1925).
2. Officially St. Stephen's Green, this public park lies at the center of Dublin, Ireland.

The road outside our window was only half laid, but the house next door   5
and the houses opposite were finished. There was good progress about
halfway down our road. Walls were up, roofs were on, gardens were rotovated
and, in some cases, even seeded. After about seven houses, however, it
gave out into mud and rubble. In a cold dusk it all seemed incomplete and
improbable.

Now, on a summer morning, when the whitebeams are so thick they almost obscure the mimicking greens and grays of the mountains, I look back to
that time and consider its revelations. That first spring, however, I thought of
little else but practicalities. Ovens and telephones became images and emblems of the real world. The house was cold. We had no curtains. At night, the
lights on the hills furnished the upper rooms with a motif of adventure and estrangement. In the morning, the hills marched in, close or distant, promising
rain or the dry breezes of a March day.

Now, also, I find myself wishing I had had less sense of locale and more of
local history. It was all too easy then to allow a day to come down to the detail
of a fabric or the weight of a chicken. If I had looked about me with a wider
sense of curiosity I would have noticed more. To start with, I would have seen
a past as well as a present. I was oblivious, for instance, to the fact that Dundrum had its roots in Anglo-Norman times, when the castle had first been
built to ward off the Wicklow[3] clans. Its destiny as a residential center had
been settled centuries later, when the Harcourt Street railway line was
opened: with its assistance, the distance between Dundrum and the city center became a mere sixteen minutes.

All was changing by the time we arrived. Indeed, the arrival of young
couples like ourselves was a signal of that change. But enough distinction
remained to give a sense of the grace and equilibrium of the place it had
been. Granted, the farriers[4] at the corner of the village had been gone some
twenty years. But the cobbler remained. Further down, the experiment of
a mink farm had failed and a shopping center was in the process of replacing it. Above all, the location remained: the wonderful poise of the village at
the edge of theatrical, wooded cliffs and under the incline of the Dublin
mountains.

Occasionally I would be aware of the contradictions and poignance of our
new home. But in the main I missed the fact that the shops, the increasing
traffic, the lights on the hills, and we ourselves were not isolated pieces of information. They and we were part of a pattern—one that was being repeated
throughout Ireland in those years. Before our eyes, and because of them, a village was turning into a suburb.

My account of the other place begins with a journey. If this were a poem,   10
that journey would become a descent. I packed the car one summer night—a
camera, biscuits—and set out at dawn. I left the suburb folded in light, the

3. Irish county south of Dublin and bordering the Irish Sea.
4. Specialists in the care of horses' hooves.

whitebeams already taking on a grayish glitter, a dog barking somewhere.

It was a necessary departure. Like so many Irish, I knew too little about my family. Ancestor-worship is not sanctioned by the Irish past. Whatever I knew about previous generations was a matter of rumor and accidental memory; conversations overheard and reluctant answerings. Now—in something of the spirit in which the puzzled citizens of an older culture traveled to their oracles—I was setting out for a place of origin: the answers might be ambiguous, but there was a relief in the interrogation.

I drove southwest. The Irish roads offer no ornament. Fifty years ago, all but the most direct of them would have been witnessed only by locals going at the place of the herd. The average road between small towns is bordered by fern-choked ditches and, in summer, by weedy altitudes of cow parsley.

It was summer now. And now, for a brief moment, those roadsides were colored. I was used to blond splashes of coltsfoot[5] and, further west, to the pageant of hawthorn. What kept taking my eye was something different: a shrubby, low plant with blue flowers. It was unsettling. I had seen that shade of blue before in the lips of old people—the terrible blush of shallow breathing. Now it occurred at every turn; it became the color of the journey. Later I would find out that the name of the plant was *Cyanotis*.

By midmorning I was turning left at the rock of Cashel, the old stone fort of the kings of Munster.[6] Its towers and sharp rock facings still look out over the fertile plain of Tipperary.[7] Ten miles up the road and I had reached Clonmel. I asked an elderly man for directions. He pointed me to the Old Western road on the far side of the town. Then he lifted his hand higher to the peak of the Comeragh mountains[8] which reared up at the end of the street. You could get a grouse up there, he assured me.

15   I had lived in cities all my life. I made a distinction between a city one loved and a city one submitted to. I had not loved London, for instance, where I had spent the greater part of my childhood. The iron and gutted stone of its postwar prospect had seemed to me merely hostile. I was not won over by its parks, nor the scarlet truculence of its buses which carried me forward and backward from school in the early fifties. I learned quickly, by inference at school and reference at home, that the Irish were unwelcome in London. I absorbed enough of that information to regard everything—even the jittery gleam from the breastplates of the Horseguards[9] as they rode through the city—with a sort of churlish inattention. All I knew, all I needed to know, was that none of this was mine.

5. A yellow flower used in herbal medicine to suppress cough.
6. The southernmost of the Irish provinces.
7. A county in southwest Ireland.
8. A mountain range in County Waterford, in the south of Ireland.
9. English cavalry housed in Horse Guards Parade, near the entrance to Buckingham Palace.

New York was a different matter. The noise and speed of it persuaded me to try again. I was just twelve when I went there. I liked putting on skates in winter and shorts in summer. I had never known extremes, whether of dress or season, before—and, on the edge of puberty, I responded to their drama.

Then there was Dublin. By the time I came to know it, those other cities had prepared me to relish a place which had something of the theater of a city, and all of the intimacy of a town. These were the early sixties. There were still coffee bars set into the basements of Georgian houses, where a turf fire burned from four o'clock in the afternoon and you could get brown scones with your coffee.

None of it prepared me for a suburb. There is, after all, a necessity about cities. By the time you come to them, there is something finished and inevitable about their architecture, even about their grime. You accept both.

A suburb is altogether more fragile and transitory. To start with, it is composed of lives in a state of process. The public calendar defines a city, when banks are shut and shops are opened. But the private one shapes a suburb; it waxes and wanes on christenings, weddings, birthdays. One year it can seem the whole road is full of bicycles, roller skates, jumble sales. Garages will be wide open, with children selling comics and out-of-date raisin buns. There will be shouting and calling far into the summer night. Almost as soon, it seems, the same road will be quiet. The bicycles will be gone. The shouting and laughing will be replaced by one or two dogs barking in back gardens. Curtains will be drawn till late morning and doors will stay closed.

Clonmel is the county town of Tipperary. Its name comes from the Irish—*Cluain meala,* meadow of honey. This is a storied part of Ireland. The Danes[10] visited it in the eighth century. Cromwell[11] fixed his batteries here on rising ground to the north of the town and received one of the worst reverses of his Irish campaign.

In the first decades of the nineteenth century Clonmel prospered. Travelers praised its regular streets, its well-built houses "the greater part of which are rough cast, and are either cream-coloured or white, save here and there one of neat appearance, whose front is often curiously ornamented with blue slates." The rows of thatched cabins had been cleared from the outskirts of the town. Corn stores were hoarded by the river; the quays were embanked with limestone ashlar.[12] "Mr. Banfield," simpers one contemporary account, "has added much to the appearance of the town by the erection of a row of very genteel houses."

20

10. Vikings began to land in Ireland in the eighth century, settling there after much initial violence.

11. Oliver Cromwell (1599–1658), English military leader and politician who, during his stint as "Lord Protector" of Britain, staged a campaign to conquer Ireland in 1649–50.

12. Stonework, typically composed of large rectangular blocks with polished faces.

It was a garrison town with two militia regiments of the Tipperary Artillery quartered there. Sometime after the Crimean War[13] my great-grandfather took up a position on this headquarters staff as a sergeant major. He could read and write, that much is certain. Otherwise, he could not have kept accounts or made a note of provisions. And he was something of a dandy. "He had a head of thick nut-brown hair the colour of your own," wrote my grandfather to his son. "My mother used to tell us how, on parade days when his toilet was of special care, he used to curse the waves in his hair that prevented him getting it to lie as he wanted."

A peacock, a soldier, a literate Irishman in a dark century. But I had not come to find him. I turned out past the town center and took the Old Western road. After a hundred yards or so it takes a broad, bluish turn—those shrubs again—and becomes a gradual hill. To the right there is a sudden crest with a straggle of buildings.

I walked up the hill. It was steep, the path winding and edged by trees. They had a dark, inappropriate presence. I would not have recognized cypress or yew, but these I thought deserved their legend. The higher I went, the more the valley—the old meadow of honey—scrolled beneath me.

25   The buildings were grim. One ran the length of the hill, an institutional ramble of granite and drainpipes. Below it, further down, was a smaller building. Over to one side was a separate house, and further down again, at road level, a small church and a deserted school.

I needed to see all this. Sometime in 1874, with a growing family to maintain, my great-grandfather cast around for a secure position. He took the only one vacant—"the only one," as my grandfather put it, "to which a Catholic could hope for appointment." Sometime in the autumn of that year, with the approval of the Board of Guardians, he became master of that most dreaded Irish institution—the workhouse.

More than a hundred years later, it was hard enough to distinguish, from that scatter of granite, which building was which. The largest one now served as the local hospital. I went inside. Two women, one elderly, both dressed as nurses, came over. The older one was sweet-faced and vague. The younger one was definite. Yes, this had been the poorhouse—she gave it its folk name—this building overlooking the hill.

Poetic license is an age-old concept. Traditionally, poets have been free to invoke place as a territory between invention and creation. I myself might once have proposed place as an act of imagination or an article of faith. But here, on a blue summer morning, I could feel it to be what it has been for so many: brute, choiceless fact.

We yield to our present but we choose our past. In a defeated country like Ireland we choose it over and over again, relentlessly, obsessively. Standing there

13. A war (1853–56) in the region of the Black Sea between Russia and a confederacy comprising England, France, and the Ottoman Empire.

looking back at the bleak length of the building, I refused to imagine him—my ancestor, with his shock of nut-brown hair. In truth I was ashamed of his adroit compliance, the skillful opportunism by which he had ensured our family's survival.

Instead, I imagined a woman. A woman like myself, with two small children, who must have come to this place as I came to the suburb. She would have come here in her twenties or thirties, but whereas my arrival in the suburb marked a homecoming, hers in the workhouse would have initiated a final, and almost certainly fatal, homelessness. At an age when I was observing the healings of place, she would have been a scholar of its violations.

There were several reasons why she might have been there. The most obvious—unmarried motherhood—remains the most likely. But she could as easily have been a survivor of an eviction—hundreds of them, complete with bailiff and battering ram, took place in Ireland every year of that century. British cartoons and a few old photographs tell the story: wretched homemade tables strewn on the road, the cabin door barred, the windows boarded up. She may even have married a soldier—Clonmel, after all, was a garrison town. Hadn't my own great-grandfather fallen for the stagy glitter of the uniforms? Didn't his wife fear that her children might do the same?

Whatever my woman's reasons for being there, her sufferings would have been terrible. When I looked up the hill I could see how the main length of the building ended in a kitchen garden. There was a small house with blunt gables and an outhouse. Was this where my great-grandfather lived? Where he stabled his pony, collected his ration, sheltered his children in the security of his position as overseer of other people's tragedies? At least, by these visible survivals, I could guess at his existence. There was no trace of hers.

The Clonmel workhouse—or, to give it its more respectable title, the Clonmel Union—was founded in 1838. In that year, and against all informed advice, the English Poor Law of 1834[14] was extended to Ireland. Until then this building had served as a catchall: asylum, orphanage, geriatric ward. The Survey of Clonmel, for instance, published in 1813, clothes its account of it in the chilly language of nineteenth-century altruism:

> A very extensive House Of Industry was finished two years ago in the west end of the town, both at the public expense of the county and by private subscription. It is a common receptacle for all descriptions of mals fortunes, serving at the same time as a place of confinement for vagrants and lunatics, as well as an asylum for the poor and helpless.

In 1838, when the Poor Law was introduced, Ireland stood at the edge of her greatest ordeal: the famine. In the next few years the workhouses would fill to overflowing with the children of emigrants, the orphans of typhus, the debris of a preventable tragedy.

---

14. An act intended to reform the system of outdoor parish relief and instead put the poor and indigent in workhouses.

35   Most of the buildings which accommodated them were themselves casualties of bad planning and hasty decision making. The walls and ceilings were
not plastered. Limestone was burned on the site and then used as a crude
whitewash. Maintenance was scanty. Contemporary accounts tell of sparrows
nesting in the downpipes and water leaking through the mortar. Subsistence
was deliberately harsh. The diet consisted of oatmeal and bread; milk at times,
but by no means always or in every workhouse. In many, the children got gruel
instead. In the 1860's a radical improvement consisted in putting ox-heads in
the soup: three ox-heads for each hundred inmates. There were small, carefully planned degradations to go with the larger ones. Children, for instance,
were refused footwear whatever the weather—the Guardians believed it unwise to get them accustomed to shoes.

By the 1870's, when my great-grandfather became master of the Clonmel
Union, there were some improvements. But of what interest are historical
modifications to the person—to this woman—for whom suffering is fresh, first
time, without memory or hope? She would have felt no hope at 6:00 A.M.
when she rose; no hope at 9:00 P.M. when she finished a day of carefully
scheduled monotony.

Yet she also would have seen the coming and going of the seasons. She
also, like me, must have seen them in her children's faces. The meadow would
have glittered beneath her on fine days; on wet ones the Comeraghs would have
loomed in heathery colors. She may not, however, have seen them for long. Statistics argue persuasively that, more than likely, she would have died—still of
childbearing age—in the fever hospital a hundred yards down the hill. Clonmel
was low-lying. The River Suir ran behind its streets with an ornamental slug-
gishness, and drainage was poor. Every few years typhus swept through the
town. Its first victims must have been the inmates of the workhouse. It would
have been my great-grandfather's decision where to bury them. He would have
consulted the Board of Guardians. There were rules for such things.

II

And where does poetry come in? Here, as in so many other instances, it enters
at the point where myth touches history. Let me explain. At one level, I could
have said that there were summer dusks and clear, vacant winter mornings
when I was certain the suburb nurtured my poetry. I might have found it hard
to say how or why. In every season the neighborhood gathered around me and
filled my immediate distance. At times it could be a shelter; it was never a
cloister. Everywhere you looked there were reminders—a child's bicycle
thrown sideways on the grass, a single roller skate, a tree in its first April of
blossom—that lives were not lived here in any sort of static pageant; they
thrived, waned, changed, began, and ended here.

Inevitably, this sense of growth could not remain just at the edge of
things. Apart from anything else, time was passing. Roads were laid. Houses
were finished. The builders moved out. Summers came and went and trees began to define the road. Garden walls were put up, and soon enough the voices

calling over them on long evenings, the bicycle thrown on its side, and the single roller skate, belonged to my children. Somewhat to my surprise, I had done what most human beings have done. I had found a world and I had populated it. In so doing, my imagination had been radically stirred and redirected. It was not, of course, a simple process. In poetry, let alone in life, it never is. It would be wrong, even now, to say that my poetry expressed the suburb. The more accurate version is that my poetry allowed me to experience it.

Yet there remained a sense of unease, as if some part of me could not assent   40
to the reassurance of patterning. On bright days, for no apparent reason, my mind would swerve. Then I could sense, below the levels of my own conscious perception, something different: as if I could still remember—indeed had never forgotten—that place is never so powerful as when it is suffered in silence.

At what point does an actual, exact landscape—those details which are recurrent and predictable—begin to blur and soften? Sometimes on a summer evening, walking between my house and a neighbor's, past the whitebeam trees and the bicycles left glinting in the dusk, I could imagine that I myself was a surreal and changing outline; that there was something almost profound in these reliable shadows; that such lives as mine and my neighbors' were mythic not because of their strangeness but because of their powerful ordinariness. When I reached a point in the road where I could see the children at the end of it, milling around and shrieking in the consciousness that they would have to come in soon, I would stand there with my hand held sickle shaped above my eyes. Almost always I was just trying to remember which cotton T-shirts my children were wearing so I could pick them out in the summer twilight and go and scoop them up and bring them in. But just occasionally, standing there and breathing in the heavy musks of rose beds and buddleias, I would feel an older and less temporary connection to the moment. Then I would feel all the sweet, unliterate melancholy of women who must have stood as I did, throughout continents and centuries, feeling the timelessness of that particular instant and the cruel time underneath its surface. They must have measured their children, as I did, against the seasons; they too must have looked at the hedges and rowan trees, their height and the color of their berries, as an index of the coming loss.

Is it true, as Patrick Kavanagh[15] says in his beautiful poem "Epic," that "gods make their own importance"? Is the origin, in other words, so restless in the outcome that the parish, the homestead, the place is a powerful source as well as a practical location? On those summer evenings, if my thoughts had not been full of details and children, I could have wondered where myth begins. Is it in the fears for harvest and the need for rain? Are its roots in the desire to make the strange familiar, to domesticate the thunder and give a shape to the frost? Or does it have, as Kavanagh argues, a more local and ritual source? Is there something about the repeated action—about lifting a child, clearing a dish, watching the seasons return to a tree and depart from a vista—

15. Irish poet (1904–1967).

which reveals a deeper meaning to existence and heals some of the worst abrasions of time?

Not suddenly, then, but definitely and gradually, a place I lived became a country of the mind. Perhaps anywhere I had grown used to, raised my children in, written my poetry about, would have become this. But a suburb by its very nature—by its hand-to-mouth compromises between town and country—was particularly well suited to the transformation. Looking out my window at familiar things, I could realize that there had always been something compromised in my own relation to places. They had never been permanent, therefore I had never developed a permanent perception about them.

Now here at last was permanence—an illusory permanence, of course, but enough stability to make me realize that the deepest sustenances are not in the new or surprising. And with that realization came the surrender of any prospect of loving new things, a prospect so vital when I was younger. Instead, many of the things I now did—from the casual gesture of looking out a window to the writing of poems—became an act of possessing the old things in a new way. I watched for the return of the magpies every February to their nest in the poplars just beyond my garden. I took an almost concert-hall pleasure, in an August twilight, in listening to the sound of my neighbor's garden shears as she cut and pruned and made things ready for another season.

None of this was purely instinctive; none of it involved an intellectual suppression or simplification. I had a clearer and clearer sense, as time went on, of the meaning of all this to me as a poet. I knew what repetitions meant in poetry. I understood those values in language and restraint. When Coleridge[16] wrote, in the *Biographia Literaria*, of metrical units as "at first the offspring of passion and then the adopted children of power," I felt I understood a concept of linguistic patterning that both lulled the mind and facilitated the meaning.

Now here, in front of me every day, were repetitions which had almost exactly the same effect. The crocuses under the rowan tree, the same child wheeled down to the shops at the same time every day, a car that returned home with the same dinge on its bumper every night, and the lamps which sprang into symmetries across our hills at dusk in November. What were all these if not—as language and music in poetry are—a sequence and repetition that allowed the deeper meanings to emerge: a sense of belonging, of nourishment, of a life revealed, and not restrained, by ritual and patterning?

Now let me rewrite that scenario, darken the evening and harden the detail. The road is no longer paved; there are no streetlamps. My own outline is no longer surreal. It is the harsh shape of that woman, that client of my ancestor. My lips now are as blue as hers—the shallow blue of those shrubs. I have no house, no room in which I write, no books. My children are not healthy and noisy. They are the fractions of my own grief clinging at my skirt, their expressions scarred with hunger and doubt. Instead of bright cotton and denim

16. Samuel Taylor Coleridge (1772–1834), English Romantic poet who co-published *Lyrical Ballads* (1798) with William Wordsworth; his *Biographia* appeared in 1817.

clothes they wear fustian[17] and the hated flannel. And they, like me, are ripe for the fevers that come in off the marshes and stagnate in the water of the town.

Of course this is impossible. The most awkward memory is known to be a figment, not a ghost. Yet even as a figment this woman was important. She cast her shadow across the suburb. She made me doubt the pastoral renewals of day-to-day life. And whenever I tried to find the quick meanings of my day in the deeper ones of the past, she interposed a fierce presence in case the transaction should be too comfortable, too lyric.

It would be wrong to say her presence changed my idea of poetry, but it changed my idea of place. Then again, it would also be true to say that my most optimistic view of place had never excluded her. Familiar, compound ghosts such as hers—paragons of dispossession—haunt the Irish present. She is a part of all our histories. The cadences I learned in that suburb, those melodies of renewal, had their roots in her silence—which involved a hard, unglamorous suffering. And I imagined the woman's pain often, imagined the mute hatred with which she must have looked at my great-grandfather as he descended from his trap, unharnessed his pony.

In thinking about her at all I was exercising a peculiar, perhaps even dangerous, freedom inherent in the shifting outlines of a defeated history. Such a history is full of silences. Hers is only one of them. And those silences, in turn, are the quicksand on which any stable or expressive view of place will forever after be built. The more I thought of her, the more it seemed to me that a sense of place can happen at the very borders of myth and history. In myth there are the healing repetitions, the technology of propitiation. In history there is the consciousness of violent and random event. In the zone between them something happens. Ideas of belonging take on the fluidity of sleep. Here is a nose, an eye, a mouth, but they may belong to different people. And here, on the edge of dream, is a place in which I locate myself as a poet: not exactly the suburb, not entirely the hill colored with blue shrubs, but somewhere composed of both.

I could put it another way: A suburb is all about futures. Trees grow; a small car becomes a bigger one to accommodate new arrivals. Then again, there is little enough history, almost no appeal to memory. The children learn the names of the sweet shop and the bike repair shop. They talk about the sixty-foot tree in the grounds of an old castle. The fact that the castle is a Norman keep and may cover Norman remains is of no interest.

A workhouse, on the other hand, is—to adapt Yeats's[18] phrase—the fiery shorthand of a history. Fever, eviction, the statistics of poverty—it infers them all. The immediate past of a nation sleeps in its cots and eats its coarse rations. What a workhouse lacks is a future.

What I have tried to write about here is neither the metaphorical nor the emblematic but something which may, in fact, be the common source of both.

17. Sturdy, often rough woven cloth.
18. William Butler Yeats (1865–1939), Irish poet. Boland paraphrases a letter that Yeats wrote in early December 1889 to Father Matthew Russell.

There is a quality about the minute changes, the gradations of a hedge, the small growth of a small boy, that makes a potent image out of an ordinary day in a suburb. Nothing I have described here can catch the simple force of looking out my window on one of those mornings at the end of winter, when a few, small burgundy rags would be on the wild cherry tree, but otherwise everything was bare and possessed a muted sort of expectancy. The hills would have the staring blues that signaled rain. A car would pass by. A neighbor's dog would bark, then be silent. Maybe the daffodils, which had been closed the week before, would now be open after an afternoon of that quick, buttery sunshine that is the best part of an Irish spring.

But all of this constitutes the present tense, and the present tense is surely instructed by the past. Women poets—Anna Akhmatova and Adrienne Rich[19] come immediately to mind—are key witnesses to the fact that myth is instructed by history, although the tradition is full of poets who argue the opposite with force and eloquence. In my case, to paraphrase the myth, I gradually came to know at what price my seasons and my suburb had been bought. My underworld was a hundred miles southwest, but there too the bargains had been harsh, the outcome a terrible compromise. The woman I imagined—if the statistics are anything to go by—must have lost her children in that underworld, just as I came to possess mine through the seasons of my neighborhood. These reflections have been about how that past, those images and her compromised life, came to find me in the midst of my incomparably easier one. And how I wanted to be found.

19. Akhmatova (1889–1966), Russian poet; Rich (b. 1929), American poet.

QUESTIONS

1. Boland's title names two persons: the woman and the poet. Do these two nouns indicate the same person or different ones? What aspects of the essay link the two? What aspects separate them?

2. In the first section of her essay, beginning with paragraph 10, Boland tells of her trip to Clonmel, an Irish town in the county of Tipperary. Why does she drive to that town? What does she learn on her visit? How does her knowledge alter the way she understands her life in the suburb of Dundrum where she lives?

3. At various points, Boland includes details about the history of places she has lived or visited—especially Dublin, Dundrum, and Clonmel. Locate those points and think about why she chooses the details, and how those details ultimately lead her to think broadly about the "idea of place" in the final paragraphs (41–52) of the essay.

4. Write an essay in which you connect the past history of a place with the present. You might visit a historic site in the place you now live and learn about its history, or you might visit a place important in your family history and gather details about your family's life there. Among your goals should be conveying to the reader some history of the place you have chosen, as well as some links between the past and the present.

JAMAICA KINCAID *Sowers and Reapers*

WHY MUST PEOPLE INSIST that the garden is a place of rest and repose, a place to forget the cares of the world, a place in which to distance yourself from the painful responsibility that comes with being a human being?

The day after I spoke to a group of people at the Garden Conservancy's tenth-anniversary celebration, in Charleston, South Carolina, an American man named Frank Cabot, the chairman and founder of the organization and a very rich man, who has spent some of his money creating a spectacular garden in the surprisingly hospitable climate of eastern Canada, told me that he was sorry I had been invited, that he was utterly offended by what I had said and the occasion I had used to say it, for I had done something unforgivable—I had introduced race and politics into the garden.

There were three of us on a panel, and our topic was "My Favorite Garden." One of the speakers said that his favorite was Hidcote Manor, in England, created by an American Anglophile named Lawrence Johnston. (A very nice climbing yellow rose, which is sometimes available through the Wayside Gardens catalogue, is named after him.) There are at least a thousand gardens in every corner of the world, but especially in England, that should come before Hidcote as a choice for favorite garden. The garden of the filmmaker Derek Jarman, who succumbed to AIDS in 1994, is a particularly good example. Dramatically set in the shadow of a nuclear-power station in Dungeness, Kent, surrounding a one-story house that has been painted black, this garden, when I saw it, was abloom with poppies in brilliant shades and with *Crambe maritima* (sea kale) and pathways lined with pebbles, the kind found at the seashore, and all sorts of worn-down objects that looked as if they were the remains of a long-ago shipwreck just found. When you see it for the first time, it so defies what you expect that this thought really will occur to you: Now, what is a garden? And, at the same time, you will be filled with pleasure and inspiration.

Another man spoke of a garden he was designing in Chicago which would include a re-creation of a quadripartite garden made by prisoners in Auschwitz. (This way of organizing a garden is quite common, and it has a history that begins with Genesis 2:10—"A river issues from Eden to water the garden, and it then divides and becomes four branches.") The garden in Auschwitz was created over many years and by many people, all of whom were facing death, and it gave me a sharp pang to realize that, while waiting to be brutally murdered, some people had made a garden.

I had prepared a talk in which I was going to say that my favorite garden   5

First published in the New Yorker *(January 22, 2001), a magazine of literature and the arts. Kincaid is perhaps best known as a novelist, but as a staff writer for the* New Yorker *she has produced many essays like this one examining her own experiences.*

is the Garden of Eden, because every time I see a garden that I love it becomes my favorite garden until I see another garden that I love and completely forget the garden that so dominated my affections a short time before; and also because this garden, Eden, is described in the fewest words I have ever seen used to describe a garden, and yet how unforgettable and vivid the description remains: "And from the ground the Lord God caused to grow every tree that was pleasing to the sight and good for food, with the tree of life in the middle of the garden, and the tree of knowledge of good and bad."

But after that man spoke of the Holocaust garden, a nice speech on Eden was no longer possible.

I heard myself telling my audience that I had been surprised to see, on the way into my hotel, in the little park across the way, a statue of John Caldwell Calhoun,[1] that inventor of the rhetoric of states' rights and the evil encoded in it, who was elected Vice-President of the United States twice. I remarked on how hard it must be for the black citizens of Charleston to pass each day by the statue of a man who hated them, cast in a heroic pose. And then I wondered if anyone in the audience had seen the Holocaust memorial right next to the statue of John Caldwell Calhoun: a strange cryptlike, criblike structure, another commemoration of some of the people who were murdered by the Germans. Then I said that John Caldwell Calhoun was not altogether so far removed from Adolf Hitler; that these two men seem to be more in the same universe than not.

It was all this and more that I said that made Frank Cabot angry at me, but not long after his outburst I joined a group of attendees to the conference who were going off to tour and have dinner at Middleton Place, the famous plantation. Middleton is a popular destination for Americans who are interested in gardens, garden history, or a whiff of the sweet stench that makes up so much of American history. It is, on the one hand, a series of beautiful rooms in the garden sense: there is a part for roses only, there is a part for azaleas, there is a part for camellias, and so on and so on. The most spectacular part of the garden is a grassy terrace made by human hands, and on the slope of the terrace are small and perfectly regular risings, so that when seen from below they look like stiff pleats in a skirt that has just been disturbed by a faint breeze. At the foot of the terrace are two small lakes that have been fashioned to look like a butterfly stilled by chloroform. It is all very beautiful, even slightly awesome; and then there is the awfulness, for those gardens and that terrace and those lakes were made by slaves. The water from the river adjacent to the plantation was channelled to flood the rice fields, and this was done by slaves, who had brought their rice-cultivation skills with them from Africa. For, as far as I know, there are no rice fields in England, Scotland, Ireland, or Wales. I was feeling quite sad about all this when I came upon a big rubble of

1. Calhoun (1782–1850), senator from South Carolina, U.S. vice president 1825–32, and ardent segregationist and theoretician of States' Rights, the doctrine of limited federal power and individual states' choice in such matters as slavery.

bricks. It was all that remained of the main house on the plantation in the wake of the strategy, conceived by that ingenious pyromaniac and great general from the North, William Tecumseh Sherman,[2] which had helped to bring the traitorous South to its knees. As I walked toward a tent to have a dinner of black-eyed peas and rice, ribs and chicken and sweet potatoes, a dinner that I think of as the cuisine of black people from the American South, and where I would hear the Lester Lanin[3] orchestra accompany a white man imitating the voice of Louis Armstrong as he sang songs made famous by Louis Armstrong, I ran into Mr. Frank Cabot, and I kept from him a fact that I happen to know: Arthur Middleton, of Middleton plantation, was one of the signers of the Declaration of Independence.

Nowhere is the relationship between the world and the garden better documented than in Thomas Jefferson's "Garden and Farm Books," an obsessively detailed account of his domestic life. People like to say that Jefferson is an enigma, that he was a man of contradictions, as if those things could not be said of just about anybody. But you have only to read anything he wrote, and you will find the true man, Thomas Jefferson, who is always so unwittingly transparent, always most revealing when confident that he has covered his tracks. He tried to write an autobiography, but he stopped before he had written a hundred pages. In it he states that he was born, that his father's name was Peter, that he wrote the Declaration of Independence, that he went to France and witnessed the French Revolution. The whole thing reads as if it were composed by one of the many marble busts of him which decorate the vestibules of government buildings. The Jefferson to be found in the autobiography is the unwittingly transparent Jefferson. The Jefferson who is confident that he has covered his tracks is to be found in the "Garden and Farm Books." The first entry in the "Garden" book is so beautiful, and so simple a statement: "1766. Shadwell. Mar. 30. Purple hyacinth begins to bloom." It goes on: "Apr. 6. Narcissus and Puckoon open. [Apr.] 13. Puckoon flowers fallen. [Apr.] 16. a bluish colored, funnel-formed flower in low-grounds in bloom." (This must have been *Mertensia virginica*.) The entries continue in this way for years, until 1824: the peas are sown, the asparagus planted, the fruit trees planted, the vegetables reaped. Each entry reads as if it were a single line removed from a poem: something should come before, and something should come after. And what should come before and after is to be found in the "Farm" book, and it comes in the form of a list of names: Ursula, George, Jupiter, Davy, Minerva, Caesar, and Jamy; and the Hemings, Beverly, Betty, Peter, John, and Sally. (Why is it that people who readily agree that Jefferson owned Sally Hemings cannot believe that he slept with her?)[4] It is they who

2. Union Civil War general (1820–1891) famous for his scorched-earth policy designed to destroy the South's means of production.

3. Orchestra leader (1911–2004) associated with upper-class social events.

4. Sally Hemings (1773–1835) was Jefferson's slave and was rumored to be the mother of his child; recent DNA testing has confirmed a genetic link.

sowed the peas, dug the trenches, and filled them with manure. It is they who planted and harvested the corn. And when Jefferson makes this entry in his "Garden" book, on April 8, 1794—"our first dish of Asparagus"—it is they who have made it possible for him to enjoy asparagus. None of these names appear in the "Garden" book; the garden is free of their presence, but they turn up in the "Farm" book, and in painful, but valuable-to-know, detail. Little Beverly Hemings, Jefferson's son by Sally, must have been a very small boy the year that he was allotted one and a half yards of wool. One year, John Hemings, Sally's uncle, received, along with Sally's mother, seven yards of linen, five yards of blue wool, and a pair of shoes. On and on it goes: the garden emerging from the farm, the garden unable to exist without the farm, the garden kept apart from the farm, race and politics kept out of the garden.

10   But, you know, the garden Jefferson made at Monticello is not really very good. You don't see it and think, Now, there is something I would like to do. It is not beautiful in the way that the garden George Washington's slaves made at Mount Vernon is beautiful. (I owe this new appreciation of Mount Vernon to Mac Griswold and her excellent book "Washington's Gardens at Mount Vernon: Landscape of the Inner Man.") There is hardly anything featured in the garden at Monticello that makes you want to rush home, subdue a few people, and re-create it. And the reason might be that Jefferson was less interested in the garden than in the marvellous things grown there. Each year, I order packets of something he grew, *Dolichos lablab*, purple hyacinth beans, something no garden should be without. What is beautiful about Monticello is the views, whether you are looking out from the house or looking at it from far away. Jefferson did not so much make a garden as a landscape. The explanation for this may be very simple: his father was a surveyor. This might also explain why he is responsible for some of the great vistas we know—the American West.

Not long after I returned from Charleston, a small amount of money that I had not expected came my way. In my ongoing conversation with my garden, I had for a very long time wanted to build a wall to add to its shape and character. So I immediately called Ron Pembroke, the maker of the most excellent landscapes in the area where I live. My house is situated on a little rise, a knoll, and I find the way it looks from many angles in the general landscape to be very pleasing, and so I had firmly in mind just the kind of wall I wanted. But Ron Pembroke, after walking me up and down and back and forth with a measuring tape in his hand, and taking me in his truck to see the other walls he had built, convinced me that my design was really quite ugly and that his was beautiful and superior.

And so began the building of two hundred-foot-long walls, one above the other, separated by a terrace eight feet wide. One day, four men arrived in the yard, and they were accompanied by big pieces of machinery, including, of course, an earthmover. The men began to rearrange the slope that fell away from the house, and by the end of the day my nice house looked as if it were the only thing left standing after a particularly disastrous natural event. The construction of the walls went on. Day after day, four men, whose names were Jared Clawson, Dan, Tony, and John, came and dug trenches and pounded stakes into the ground after they had looked through a surveyor's instrument many times. One day, truckloads of coarsely pummelled gray stone were deposited in the driveway and carefully laid at the bottom of the trenches. Another day, truckloads of a beautiful gray, blue, yellowish, and glistening stone were delivered and left on the lawn. This stone came from a quarry in Goshen, Massachusetts, Ron Pembroke told me. It is the stone he prefers to use when he builds walls, and it is more expensive than other kinds of stone, but it does display his work to best advantage. My two walls, he said, would most likely require a hundred tons of stone.

The walls started to take shape, at first almost mysteriously. The four men began by placing stones atop one another, in a staggered arrangement, so that always one stone was resting on top of two. In the beginning, each stone they picked up seemed to be just the perfect one needed. But then things began to get more difficult. Sometimes a stone would be carried to the wall with great effort and, after being pounded into place, it would not look quite right to Tony and Dan and John and Jared Clawson.

And did I say that all this was being done in the autumn? I do not know if that is the ideal time to build a wall, but I was so happy to see my walls being made that I became very possessive of the time spent on them and wanted the four men to be building only my walls. I didn't begrudge them lunchtime or time taken to smoke a cigarette, but why did they have to stop working when the day was at an end, and why did the day have to come to an end, for that matter? How I loved to watch those men work, especially the man named Jared Clawson. It was he who built the stairs that made it possible to walk from the lower wall to the eight-foot-wide terrace, and then up to the level ground of a patio, which was made flush with the top of the upper wall. And the stairs were difficult to make, or so it seemed to me, for it took Jared Clawson ten days to make them.

One day, it was finished. The walls were built, and they looked fantastic.   15
My friend Paige had given me twelve bottles of champagne, a present for my twentieth wedding anniversary. I loved the taste of this champagne so much that I gave a bottle to each of the men who had helped build my walls. How glad was my spirit when, at the end of all this, Ron Pembroke presented me with a bill, and I in turn gave him a check for the complete amount, and there was nothing between us but complete respect and admiration and no feeling of the injustice of it all, no disgust directed toward me and my nice house, beautifully set off by those dramatic walls, for he had his own house and his own wall and his own spouse and his own anniversary.

At the foot of the lower wall, I have planted five hundred daffodils, ranging in shade from bright yellow to creamy white. In the terrace separating the lower and the upper walls, I have planted two hundred *Tulipa* 'Mrs. J.T. Scheepers,' which is perhaps my favorite tulip in the world. In the four beds on either side of the patio, I have planted two hundred *Tulipa* 'Blue Diamond,' a hundred *Tulipa* 'Angélique,' and only fifty of *Tulipa* 'Black Hero' because they were so expensive. Towering above these hundreds of bulbs, I planted the magnolias 'Woodsman' and 'Elizabeth' and 'Miss Honeybee'; and then *Magnolia zenii* and *Magnolia denudata*. At the beginning of the woodland, which I can see from a certain angle if I am standing on the upper wall, I planted a hundred *Fritillaria meleagris* and fifty each of *Galanthus elwesii* and *Galanthus nivalis*.

Ron Pembroke refilled the trenches with a rich topsoil, a mixture of composted organic material and riverbank soil, but I did not see one earthworm wriggling around in it, and this made me worry, for I have such a reverence for earthworms, whose presence signifies that the soil is good. Their anxious, iridescent, wriggly form, when confronted with broad daylight, is very reassuring. We may be made from dust (the dust of the garden, I presume), but it is not to dust that we immediately return; first, we join the worms.

The garden is not a place to lose your cares; the garden is not a place of rest and repose. Even God did not find it so.

QUESTIONS

1. According to Kincaid, Frank Cabot, chairman of the Garden Conservancy, said she did the "unforgivable—I had introduced race and politics into the garden" (paragraph 2). Can you imagine how race and politics could ever have been left out? What might have led some garden people to ignore or suppress them?

2. The essay has two parts: the Charleston speech and the garden building project. What is the relationship between the two? Why does Kincaid spend so much time on her admiration for the workers?

3. Write an essay describing how you took on a task and completed it successfully. Or write about how someone you know did a good job on a difficult assignment. Go into the kind of detail Kincaid does about her wall.

JUDITH ORTIZ COFER *More Room*

M Y GRANDMOTHER'S HOUSE is like a chambered nautilus; it has many rooms, yet it is not a mansion. Its proportions are small and its design simple. It is a house that has grown organically, according to the needs of its inhabitants. To all of us in the family it is known as *la casa de Mamá.*[1] It is the place of our origin; the stage for our memories and dreams of Island life.

I remember how in my childhood it sat on stilts; this was before it had a downstairs. It rested on its perch like a great blue bird, not a flying sort of bird, more like a nesting hen, but with spread wings. Grandfather had built it soon after their marriage. He was a painter and housebuilder by trade, a poet and meditative man by nature. As each of their eight children were born, new rooms were added. After a few years, the paint did not exactly match, nor the materials, so that there was a chronology to it, like the rings of a tree, and Mamá could tell you the history of each room in her *casa,* and thus the genealogy of the family along with it.

Her room is the heart of the house. Though I have seen it recently, and both woman and room have diminished in size, changed by the new perspective of my eyes, now capable of looking over countertops and tall beds, it is not this picture I carry in my memory of Mamá's *casa.* Instead, I see her room as a queen's chamber where a small woman loomed large, a throne-room with a massive four-poster bed in its center which stood taller than a child's head. It was on this bed where her own children had been born that the smallest grandchildren were allowed to take naps in the afternoons; here too was where Mamá secluded herself to dispense private advice to her daughters, sitting on the edge of the bed, looking down at whoever sat on the rocker where generations of babies had been sung to sleep. To me she looked like a wise empress right out of the fairy tales I was addicted to reading.

Though the room was dominated by the mahogany four-posters, it also contained all of Mamá's symbols of power. On her dresser instead of cosmetics there were jars filled with herbs: *yerba buena, yerba mala,*[2] the making of purgatives and teas to which we were all subjected during childhood crises. She had a steaming cup for anyone who could not, or would not, get up to face life on any given day. If the acrid aftertaste of her cures for malingering did not get you out of bed, then it was time to call *el doctor.*

And there was the monstrous chifforobe she kept locked with a little   5
golden key she did not hide. This was a test of her dominion over us; though my cousins and I wanted a look inside that massive wardrobe more than any-

From Cofer's 1990 book, Silent Dancing: A Partial Reminiscence of a Puerto Rican Childhood, *which won the 1991 PEN/Martha Albrand Special Citation for Nonfiction.*

1. Mama's house.
2. Good herbs, bad herbs.

thing, we never reached for that little key lying on top of her Bible on the dresser. This was also where she placed her earrings and rosary at night. God's word was her security system. This chifforobe was the place where I imagined she kept jewels, satin slippers, and elegant sequined, silk gowns of heart-breaking fineness. I lusted after those imaginary costumes. I had heard that Mamá had been a great beauty in her youth, and the belle of many balls. My cousins had other ideas as to what she kept in that wooden vault: its secret could be money (Mamá did not hand cash to strangers, banks were out of the question, so there were stories that her mattress was stuffed with dollar bills, and that she buried coins in jars in her garden under rosebushes, or kept them in her inviolate chifforobe); there might be that legendary gun salvaged from the Spanish-American conflict over the Island. We went wild over suspected treasures that we made up simply because children have to fill locked trunks with something wonderful.

On the wall above the bed hung a heavy silver crucifix. Christ's agonized head hung directly over Mamá's pillow. I avoided looking at this weapon suspended over where her head would lay; and on the rare occasions when I was allowed to sleep on that bed, I scooted down to the safe middle of the mattress, where her body's impression took me in like a mother's lap. Having taken care of the obligatory religious decoration with a crucifix, Mamá covered the other walls with objects sent to her over the years by her children in the States. *Los Nueva Yores*[3] were represented by, among other things, a postcard of Niagara Falls from her son Hernán, postmarked, Buffalo, N.Y. In a conspicuous gold frame hung a large color photograph of her daughter Nena, her husband and their five children at the entrance to Disneyland in California. From us she had gotten a black lace fan. Father had brought it to her from a tour of duty with the Navy in Europe (on Sundays she would remove it from its hook on the wall to fan herself at Sunday mass). Each year more items were added as the family grew and dispersed, and every object in the room had a story attached to it, a *cuento*[4] which Mamá would bestow on anyone who received the privilege of a day alone with her. It was almost worth pretending to be sick, though the bitter herb purgatives of the body were a big price to pay for the spirit revivals of her story-telling.

Mamá slept alone on her large bed, except for the times when a sick grandchild warranted the privilege, or when a heartbroken daughter came home in need of more than herbal teas. In the family there is a story about how this came to be.

When one of the daughters, my mother or one of her sisters, tells the *cuento* of how Mamá came to own her nights, it is usually preceded by the qualifications that Papá's exile from his wife's room was not a result of animosity between the couple, but that the act had been Mamá's famous bloodless coup for her personal freedom. Papá was the benevolent dictator of her body and her life who had had to be banished from her bed so that Mamá could

3. The New Yorkers.
4. Tale.

better serve her family. Before the telling, we had to agree that the old man was not to blame. We all recognized that in the family Papá was as an *alma de Dios,*[5] a saintly, soft-spoken presence whose main pleasures in life, such as writing poetry and reading the Spanish large-type editions of *Reader's Digest,* always took place outside the vortex of Mamá's crowded realm. It was not his fault, after all, that every year or so he planted a babyseed in Mamá's fertile body, keeping her from leading the active life she needed and desired. He loved her and the babies. Papá composed odes and lyrics to celebrate births and anniversaries and hired musicians to accompany him in singing them to his family and friends at extravagant pig-roasts he threw yearly. Mamá and the oldest girls worked for days preparing the food. Papá sat for hours in his painter's shed, also his study and library, composing the songs. At these celebrations he was also known to give long speeches in praise of God, his fecund wife, and his beloved island. As a middle child, my mother remembers these occasions as a time when the women sat in the kitchen and lamented their burdens, while the men feasted out in the patio, their rum-thickened voice rising in song and praise for each other, *compañeros* all.[6]

It was after the birth of her eighth child, after she had lost three at birth or in infancy, that Mamá made her decision. They say that Mamá had had a special way of letting her husband know that they were expecting, one that had begun when, at the beginning of their marriage, he had built her a house too confining for her taste. So, when she discovered her first pregnancy, she supposedly drew plans for another room, which he dutifully executed. Every time a child was due, she would demand, *more space, more space.* Papá acceded to her wishes, child after child, since he had learned early that Mamá's renowned temper was a thing that grew like a monster along with a new belly. In this way Mamá got the house that she wanted, but with each child she lost in heart and energy. She had knowledge of her body and perceived that if she had any more children, her dreams and her plans would have to be permanently forgotten, because she would be a chronically ill woman, like Flora with her twelve children: asthma, no teeth, in bed more than on her feet.

And so, after my youngest uncle was born, she asked Papá to build a large   10
room at the back of the house. He did so in joyful anticipation. Mamá had asked him special things this time: shelves on the walls, a private entrance. He thought that she meant this room to be a nursery where several children could sleep. He thought it was a wonderful idea. He painted it his favorite color, sky blue, and made large windows looking out over a green hill and the church spires beyond. But nothing happened. Mamá's belly did not grow, yet she seemed in a frenzy of activity over the house. Finally, an anxious Papá approached his wife to tell her that the new room was finished and ready to be occupied. And Mamá, they say, replied: "Good, it's for *you.*"

And so it was that Mamá discovered the only means of birth control available to a Catholic woman of her time: sacrifice. She gave up the comfort of

5. Literally, "soul of God." A thoroughly good person.
6. Companions.

Papá's sexual love for something she deemed greater: the right to own and control her body, so that she might live to meet her grandchildren—me among them—so that she could give more of herself to the ones already there, so that she could be more than a channel for other lives, so that even now that time has robbed her of the elasticity of her body and of her amazing reservoir of energy, she still emanates the kind of joy that can only be achieved by living according to the dictates of one's own heart.

QUESTIONS

1. At the end of the essay, Cofer explains in fairly direct terms why her grandmother wanted "more room." Why do you think she uses narration as the primary mode in the rest of the essay? What does she gain by first narrating, then explaining?

2. Cofer uses many similes and metaphors—for example, in paragraph 1 she says that her grandmother's house was "like a chambered nautilus" and in paragraph 5 that her grandmother's Bible was "her security system." Discuss the use of one or two such comparisons that you find particularly effective.

3. What are the possible meanings of the title?

4. Write about a favorite or mysterious place you remember from childhood.

N. SCOTT MOMADAY *The Way to Rainy Mountain*

A SINGLE KNOLL RISES out of the plain in Oklahoma, north and west of the Wichita Range. For my people, the Kiowas, it is an old landmark, and they gave it the name Rainy Mountain. The hardest weather in the world is there. Winter brings blizzards, hot tornadic winds arise in the spring, and in summer the prairie is an anvil's edge. The grass turns brittle and brown, and it cracks beneath your feet. There are green belts along the rivers and creeks, linear groves of hickory and pecan, willow and witch hazel. At a distance in July or August the steaming foliage seems almost to writhe in fire. Great green and yellow grasshoppers are everywhere in the tall grass, popping up like corn to sting the flesh, and tortoises crawl about on the red earth, going nowhere in the plenty of time. Loneliness is an aspect of the land. All things in the plain are isolate; there is no confusion of objects in the eye, but *one* hill or *one* tree or *one* man. To look upon that landscape in the early morning, with the sun at your back, is to lose the sense of proportion. Your imagination comes to life,

First published in 1967 in the Reporter, *a now defunct small-circulation American magazine; reprinted in* The Way to Rainy Mountain, *Momaday's 1969 book about the West. The illustrations were drawn by the author's father, Al Momaday.*

and this, you think, is where Creation was begun.

I returned to Rainy Mountain in July. My grandmother had died in the spring, and I wanted to be at her grave. She had lived to be very old and at last infirm. Her only living daughter was with her when she died, and I was told that in death her face was that of a child.

I like to think of her as a child. When she was born, the Kiowas were living the last great moment of their history. For more than a hundred years they had controlled the open range from the Smoky Hill River to the Red, from the headwaters of the Canadian to the fork of the Arkansas and Cimarron. In alliance with the Comanches, they had ruled the whole of the southern Plains. War was their sacred business, and they were among the finest horsemen the world has ever known. But warfare for the Kiowas was preeminently a matter of disposition rather than of survival, and they never understood the grim, unrelenting advance of the U.S. Cavalry. When at last, divided and ill-provisioned, they were driven onto the Staked Plains in the cold rains of autumn, they fell into panic. In Palo Duro Canyon they abandoned their crucial stores to pillage and had nothing then but their lives. In order to save themselves, they surrendered to the soldiers at Fort Sill and were imprisoned in the old stone corral that now stands as a military museum. My grandmother was spared the humiliation of those high gray walls by eight or ten years, but she must have known from birth the affliction of defeat, the dark brooding of old warriors.

Her name was Aho, and she belonged to the last culture to evolve in North America. Her forebears came down from the high country in western Montana nearly three centuries ago. They were a mountain people, a mysterious tribe of hunters whose language has never been positively classified in any major group. In the late seventeenth century they began a long migration to the south and east. It was a journey toward the dawn, and it led to a golden age. Along the way the Kiowas were befriended by the Crows, who gave them the culture and religion of the Plains. They acquired horses, and their ancient nomadic spirit was suddenly free of the ground. They acquired Tai-me, the sacred Sun Dance doll, from that moment the object and symbol of their worship, and so shared in the divinity of the sun. Not least, they acquired the sense of destiny, therefore courage and pride. When they entered upon the southern Plains they had been transformed. No longer were they slaves to the simple necessity of survival; they were a lordly and dangerous society of fighters and thieves, hunters and priests of the sun. According to their origin

myth, they entered the world through a hollow log. From one point of view, their migration was the fruit of an old prophecy, for indeed they emerged from a sunless world.

5   Although my grandmother lived out her long life in the shadow of Rainy Mountain, the immense landscape of the continental interior lay like memory in her blood. She could tell of the Crows, whom she had never seen, and of the Black Hills, where she had never been. I wanted to see in reality what she had seen more perfectly in the mind's eye, and traveled fifteen hundred miles to begin my pilgrimage.

Yellowstone, it seemed to me, was the top of the world, a region of deep lakes and dark timber, canyons and waterfalls. But, beautiful as it is, one might have the sense of confinement there. The skyline in all directions is close at hand, the high wall of the woods and deep cleavages of shade. There is a perfect freedom in the mountains, but it belongs to the eagle and the elk, the badger and the bear. The Kiowas reckoned their stature by the distance they could see, and they were bent and blind in the wilderness.

Descending eastward, the highland meadows are a stairway to the plain. In July the inland slope of the Rockies is luxuriant with flax and buckwheat, stonecrop and larkspur. The earth unfolds and the limit of the land recedes.

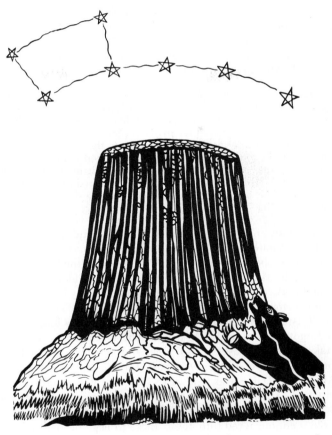

Clusters of trees, and animals grazing far in the distance, cause the vision to reach away and wonder to build upon the mind. The sun follows a longer course in the day, and the sky is immense beyond all comparison. The great billowing clouds that sail upon it are the shadows that move upon the grain like water, dividing light. Farther down, in the land of the Crows and Black-feet, the plain is yellow. Sweet clover takes hold of the hills and bends upon it-self to cover and seal the soil. There the Kiowas paused on their way; they had come to the place where they must change their lives. The sun is at home on the plains. Precisely there does it have the certain character of a god. When the Kiowas came to the land of the Crows, they could see the dark lees of the hills at dawn across the Bighorn River, the profusion of light on the grain shelves, the oldest deity ranging after the solstices. Not yet would they veer southward to the caldron of the land that lay below; they must wean their blood from the northern winter and hold the mountains a while longer in their view. They bore Tai-me in procession to the east.

A dark mist lay over the Black Hills, and the land was like iron. At the top of a ridge I caught sight of Devil's Tower upthrust against the gray sky as if in the birth of time the core of the earth had broken through its crust and the motion of the world was begun. There are things in nature that engender an awful quiet in the heart of man; Devil's Tower is one of them. Two centuries ago, because they could not do otherwise, the Kiowas made a legend at the base of the rock. My grandmother said:

> Eight children were there at play, seven sisters and their brother. Suddenly the boy was struck dumb; he trembled and began to run upon his hands and feet. His fingers became claws, and his body was covered with fur. Directly there was a bear where the boy had been. The sisters were terrified; they ran, and the bear after them. They came to the stump of a great tree, and the tree spoke to them. It bade them climb upon it, and as they did so it began to rise into the air. The bear came to kill them, but they were just beyond its reach. It reared against the tree and scored the bark all around with its claws. The seven sisters were borne into the sky, and they became the stars of the Big Dipper.

From that moment, and so long as the legend lives, the Kiowas have kinsmen in the night sky. Whatever they were in the mountains, they could be no more. However tenuous their well-being, however much they had suffered and would suffer again, they had found a way out of the wilderness.

My grandmother had a reverence for the sun, a holy regard that now is all but gone out of mankind. There was a wariness in her, and an ancient awe. She was a Christian in her later years, but she had come a long way about, and she never forgot her birthright. As a child she had been to the Sun Dances; she had taken part in those annual rites, and by them she had learned the restoration of her people in the presence of Tai-me. She was about seven when the last Kiowa Sun Dance was held in 1887 on the Washita River above Rainy Mountain Creek. The buffalo were gone. In order to consummate the ancient sacrifice—to impale the head of a buffalo bull upon the medicine tree—a delegation of old men journeyed into Texas, there to beg and barter for an animal from the Goodnight herd. She was ten when the Kiowas came together for the last time as a living Sun Dance culture. They could find no buffalo; they had to hang an old hide from the sacred tree. Before the dance could begin, a company of soldiers rode out from Fort Sill under orders to disperse the tribe. Forbidden without cause the essential act of their faith, having seen the wild herds slaughtered and left to rot upon the ground, the Kiowas backed away forever from the medicine tree. That was July 20, 1890, at the great bend of the Washita. My grandmother was there. Without bitterness, and for as long as she lived, she bore a vision of deicide.

10   Now that I can have her only in memory, I see my grandmother in the several postures that were peculiar to her: standing at the wood stove on a winter morning and turning meat in a great iron skillet; sitting at the south window, bent above her beadwork, and afterwards, when her vision failed, looking down for a long time into the fold of her hands; going out upon a cane, very slowly as she did when the weight of age came upon her; praying. I remember her most often at prayer. She made long, rambling prayers out of suffering and hope, having seen many things. I was never sure that I had the right to hear,

so exclusive were they of all mere custom and company. The last time I saw her she prayed standing by the side of her bed at night, naked to the waist, the light of a kerosene lamp moving upon her dark skin. Her long, black hair, always drawn and braided in the day, lay upon her shoulders and against her breasts like a shawl. I do not speak Kiowa, and I never understood her prayers, but there was something inherently sad in the sound, some merest hesitation upon the syllables of sorrow. She began in a high and descending pitch, exhausting her breath to silence; then again and again—and always the same intensity of effort, of something that is, and is not, like urgency in the human voice. Transported so in the dancing light among the shadows of her room, she seemed beyond the reach of time. But that was illusion; I think I knew then that I should not see her again.

Houses are like sentinels in the plain, old keepers of the weather watch. There, in a very little while, wood takes on the appearance of great age. All colors wear soon away in the wind and rain, and then the wood is burned gray and the grain appears and the nails turn red with rust. The windowpanes are black and opaque; you imagine there is nothing within, and indeed there are many ghosts, bones given up to the land. They stand here and there against the sky, and you approach them for a longer time than you expect. They belong in the distance; it is their domain.

Once there was a lot of sound in my grandmother's house, a lot of coming and going, feasting and talk. The summers there were full of excitement and reunion. The Kiowas are a summer people; they abide the cold and keep to themselves, but when the season turns and the land becomes warm and vital they cannot hold still; an old love of going returns upon them. The aged visitors who came to my grandmother's house when I was a child were made of lean and leather, and they bore themselves upright. They wore great black hats and bright ample shirts that shook in the wind. They rubbed fat upon their hair and wound their braids with strips of colored cloth. Some of them painted their faces and carried the scars of old and cherished enmities. They were an old council of warlords, come to remind and be reminded of who they were. Their wives and daughters served them well. The women might indulge themselves; gossip was at once the mark and compensation of their servitude. They made loud and elaborate talk among themselves, full of jest and gesture, fright and false alarm. They went abroad in fringed and flowered shawls, bright beadwork and German silver. They were at home in the kitchen, and they prepared meals that were banquets.

There were frequent prayer meetings, and great nocturnal feasts. When I was a child I played with my cousins outside, where the lamplight fell upon the ground and the singing of the old people rose up around us and carried away into the darkness. There were a lot of good things to eat, a lot of laughter and surprise. And afterwards, when the quiet returned, I lay down with my grandmother and could hear the frogs away by the river and feel the motion of the air.

Now there is a funeral silence in the rooms, the endless wake of some final word. The walls have closed in upon my grandmother's house. When I returned to it in mourning, I saw for the first time in my life how small it was. It was late at night, and there was a white moon, nearly full. I sat for a long time on the stone steps by the kitchen door. From there I could see out across the land; I could see the long row of trees by the creek, the low light upon the rolling plains, and the stars of the Big Dipper. Once I looked at the moon and caught sight of a strange thing. A cricket had perched upon the handrail, only a few inches away from me. My line of vision was such that the creature filled the moon like a fossil. It had gone there, I thought, to live and die, for there, of all places, was its small definition made whole and eternal. A warm wind rose up and purled like the longing within me.

15   The next morning I awoke at dawn and went out on the dirt road to Rainy Mountain. It was already hot, and the grasshoppers began to fill the air. Still, it was early in the morning, and the birds sang out of the shadows. The long yellow grass on the mountain shone in the bright light, and a scissortail hied above the land. There, where it ought to be, at the end of a long and legendary way, was my grandmother's grave. Here and there on the dark stones were ancestral names. Looking back once, I saw the mountain and came away.

Questions

1. Throughout this essay, Momaday uses similes (comparisons with "like" or "as") and metaphors (comparisons without specific connectors). Which comparisons were most helpful in aiding your understanding? Which comparison was most surprising?

2. Momaday connects personal and cultural history to a particular place. Find another essay, either in "People, Places" or "Nature and the Environment," that makes similar connections. Write a comparison of the two essays.

3. In paragraph 10, Momaday describes the roles that women played in his grandmother's Kiowa culture. Consider the roles women played in your grandmother's generation and culture; perhaps ask your mother or grandmother about their experiences. To what extent have those roles remained the same or changed in your generation? Write an account based on your conversations with older family members and your own personal knowledge.

BARRY LOPEZ *The American Geographies*

IT HAS BECOME commonplace to observe that Americans know little of the geography of their country, that they are innocent of it as a landscape of rivers, mountains, and towns. They do not know, supposedly, the location of the Delaware Water Gap, the Olympic Mountains, or the Piedmont Plateau;[1] and, the indictment continues, they have little conception of the way the individual components of this landscape are imperiled, from a human perspective, by modern farming practices or industrial pollution.

I do not know how true this is, but it is easy to believe that it is truer than most of us would wish. A recent Gallup Organization and National Geographic Society survey found Americans woefully ignorant of world geography. Three out of four couldn't locate the Persian Gulf.[2] The implication was that we knew no more about our own homeland, and that this ignorance undermined the integrity of our political processes and the efficiency of our business enterprises.

As Americans, we profess a sincere and fierce love for the American landscape, for our rolling prairies, free-flowing rivers, and "purple mountains' majesty"; but it is hard to imagine, actually, where this particular landscape is. It is not just that a nostalgic landscape has passed away—Mark Twain's Mississippi[3] is now dammed from Illinois to Louisiana and the prairies have all been sold and fenced. It is that it's always been a romantic's landscape. In the attenuated form in which it is presented on television today, in magazine articles and in calendar photographs, the essential wildness of the American landscape is reduced to attractive scenery. We look out on a familiar, memorized landscape that portends adventure and promises enrichment. There are no distracting people in it and few artifacts of human life. The animals are all beautiful, diligent, one might even say well behaved. Nature's unruliness, the power of rivers and skies to intimidate, and any evidence of disastrous human land management practices are all but invisible. It is, in short, a magnificent garden, a colonial vision of paradise imposed on a real place that is, at best, only selectively known.

First published in Orion *(Autumn 1989), a magazine begun in 1982 "to reconnect human culture with the natural world, blending scientific thinking with the arts, engaging the heart and mind, and striving to make clear what we all have in common"; later included in* About This Life: Journeys on the Threshold of Memory *(1998) and* Vintage Lopez *(2004).*

1. Delaware Water Gap: section of the Appalachian Mountains where the Delaware River divides New Jersey from Pennsylvania; Olympic Mountains: a mountain range in western Washington State; Piedmont Plateau: a relatively flat region in the eastern United States, running from New Jersey in the north to Alabama in the south.

2. Body of water separating Persia (present-day Iran) from the Arabian peninsula (Saudi Arabia).

3. American author Mark Twain, born Samuel L. Clemens (1835–1910), wrote frequently about the Mississippi River.

The real American landscape is a face of almost incomprehensible depth and complexity. If one were to sit for a few days, for example, among the ponderosa pine[4] forests and black lava fields of the Cascade Mountains in western Oregon, inhaling the pines' sweet balm on an evening breeze from some point on the barren rock, and then were to step off to the Olympic Peninsula in Washington, to those rain forests with sphagnum moss floors soft as fleece underfoot and Douglas firs too big around for five people to hug, and then head south to walk the ephemeral creeks and sun-blistered playas[5] of the Mojave Desert in southern California, one would be reeling under the sensations. The contrast is not only one of plants and soils, a different array, say, of brilliantly colored beetles. The shock to the senses comes from a different shape to the silence, a difference in the very quality of light, in the weight of the air. And this relatively short journey down the West Coast would still leave the traveler with all that lay to the east to explore—the anomalous sand hills of Nebraska, the heat and frog voices of Okefenokee Swamp, the fetch of Chesapeake Bay, the hardwood copses and black bears of the Ozark Mountains.[6]

5   No one of these places, of course, can be entirely fathomed, biologically or aesthetically. They are mysteries upon which we impose names. Enchantments. We tick the names off glibly but lovingly. We mean no disrespect. Our genuine desire, though we may be skeptical about the time it would take and uncertain of its practical value to us, is to actually know these places. As deeply ingrained in the American psyche as the desire to conquer and control the land is the desire to sojourn in it, to sail up and down Pamlico Sound,[7] to paddle a canoe through Minnesota's boundary waters, to walk on the desert of the Great Salt Lake,[8] to camp in the stony hardwood valleys of Vermont.

To do this well, to really come to an understanding of a specific American geography, requires not only time but a kind of local expertise, an intimacy with place few of us ever develop. There is no way around the former requirement: if you want to know you must take the time. It is not in books. A specific geographical understanding, however, can be sought out and borrowed. It resides with men and women more or less sworn to a place, who abide there, who have a feel for the soil and history, for the turn of leaves and night sounds. Often they are glad to take the outlander in tow.

These local geniuses[9] of American landscape, in my experience, are people in whom geography thrives. They are the antithesis of geographical ignorance. Rarely known outside their own communities, they often seem, at the

4. A species of tall pine tree found in western North America.

5. A dry lakebed; from the Spanish *playa*, meaning "beach."

6. Okefenokee Swamp: a shallow wetland dividing Florida and Georgia; Chesapeake Bay: an estuary off the coasts of Virginia and Maryland; Ozark Mountains: a mountain range covering parts of Missouri, Oklahoma, Kansas, and Arkansas.

7. A wetland in North Carolina.

8. Largest lake in the Western Hemisphere, located in Utah.

9. The spirit of a place, often a guardian spirit.

first encounter, unremarkable and anonymous. They may not be able to recall the name of a particular wildflower—or they may have given it a name known only to them. They might have forgotten the precise circumstances of a local historical event. Or they can't say for certain when the last of the Canada geese passed through in the fall, or can't differentiate between two kinds of trout in the same creek. Like all of us, they have fallen prey to the fallacies of memory and are burdened with ignorance; but they are nearly flawless in the respect they bear these places they love. Their knowledge is intimate rather than encyclopedic, human but not necessarily scholarly. It rings with the concrete details of experience.

America, I believe, teems with such people. The paradox here, between a faulty grasp of geographical knowledge for which Americans are indicted and the intimate, apparently contradictory familiarity of a group of largely anonymous people, is not solely a matter of confused scale. (The local landscape is easier to know than a national landscape—and many local geographers, of course, are relatively ignorant of a national geography.)

And it is not simply ironic. The paradox is dark. To be succinct: the politics and advertising that seek a national audience must project a national geography; to be broadly useful that geography must, inevitably, be generalized and it is often romantic. It is therefore frequently misleading and imprecise. The same holds true with the entertainment industry, but here the problem might be clearer. The same films, magazines, and television features that honor an imaginary American landscape also tout the worth of the anonymous men and women who interpret it. Their affinity for the land is lauded, their local allegiance admired. But the rigor of their local geographies, taken as a whole, contradicts a patriotic, national vision of unspoiled, untroubled land. These men and women are ultimately forgotten, along with the details of the landscapes they speak for, in the face of more pressing national matters. It is the chilling nature of modern society to find an ignorance of geography, local or national, as excusable as an ignorance of hand tools; and to find the commitment of people to their home places only momentarily entertaining. And finally naïve.

If one were to pass time among Basawara people in the Kalahari Desert,[10] or with Tikuna on the upper Amazon, or with Pitjantjatjara Aborigines in Australia,[11] the most salient impression they might leave is of an absolutely stunning knowledge of their local geography—geology, hydrology, biology, and weather. In short, the extensive particulars of their intercourse with it.

In forty thousand years of human history, it has only been in the last few hundred years or so that a people could afford to ignore their local geographies as completely as we do and still survive. Technological innovations from refrigerated trucks to artificial fertilizers, from sophisticated cost accounting to

10. Large, dry region in southern Africa, home to the Basawara people.

11. The native people of Brazil, and a group originating in the central Australian desert, respectively.

mass air transportation, have utterly changed concepts of season, distance, soil productivity, and the real cost of drawing sustenance from the land. It is now possible for a resident of Kansas City to bite into a fresh mango in the dead of winter; for someone in San Francisco to travel to Atlanta in a few hours with no worry of how formidable might be crossings of the Great Basin Desert[12] or the Mississippi River; for an absentee farmer to gain a tax advantage from a farm that leaches poisons into its water table and on which crops are left to rot. The Pitjantjatjara might shake their heads in bewilderment and bemusement, not because they are primitive or ignorant people, not because they have no sense of irony or are incapable of marveling, but because they have not (many would say not yet) realized a world in which such manipulation of the land—surmounting the imperatives of distance it imposes, for example, or turning the large-scale destruction of forests and arable land into wealth—is desirable or plausible.

In the years I have traveled through America, in cars and on horseback, on foot and by raft, I have repeatedly been brought to a sudden state of awe by some gracile[13] or savage movement of animal, some odd wrapping of a tree's foliage by the wind, an unimpeded run of dew-laden prairie stretching to a horizon flat as a coin where a pin-dot sun pales the dawn sky pink. I know these things are beyond intellection, that they are the vivid edges of a world that includes but also transcends the human world. In memory, when I dwell on these things, I know that in a truly national literature there should be odes to the Triassic reds of the Colorado Plateau,[14] to the sharp and ghostly light of the Florida Keys,[15] to the aeolian soils of southern Minnesota and the Palouse in Washington,[16] though the modern mind abjures the literary potential of such subjects. (If the sand and floodwater farmers of Arizona and New Mexico were to take the black loams of Louisiana in their hands they would be flabbergasted, and that is the beginning of literature.) I know there should be eloquent evocations of the cobbled beaches of Maine, the plutonic walls of the Sierra Nevada, the orange canyons of the Kaibab Plateau.[17] I have no doubt, in fact, that there are. They are as numerous and diverse as the eyes and fingers that ponder the country—it is that only a handful of them are known. The great majority are to be found in drawers and boxes, in the letters and private

12. Large, dry region in the western United States, bordered by the Sierra Nevada Mountains to the west, the Rocky Mountains to the east, the Columbia Plateau to the north, and the Mojave and Sonoran deserts to the south.

13. Gracefully thin.

14. Triassic: originating from the Triassic Period, which occurred between 230 and 190 million years ago; Colorado Plateau: a flat region in the southwestern United States that stretches over parts of Arizona, Utah, New Mexico, and Colorado, and includes the Grand Canyon.

15. Approximately 1,700 islands lying off the southern coast of Florida.

16. A region in parts of Idaho and Washington that includes prairie, woods, and rivers.

17. A sequence moving from the rocky beaches of the Northeast, to a mountain range that runs north-south in California, to a flat region in Arizona that includes the Grand Canyon.

journals of millions of workaday people who have regarded their encounters with the land as an engagement bordering on the spiritual, as being fundamentally linked to their state of health.

One cannot acknowledge the extent and the history of this kind of testimony without being forced to the realization that something strange, if not dangerous, is afoot. Year by year, the number of people with firsthand experience in the land dwindles. Rural populations continue to shift to the cities. The family farm is in a state of demise, and government and industry continue to apply pressure on the native peoples of North America to sever their ties with the land. In the wake of this loss of personal and local knowledge, the knowledge from which a real geography is derived, the knowledge on which a country must ultimately stand, has come something hard to define but I think sinister and unsettling—the packaging and marketing of land as a form of entertainment. An incipient industry, capitalizing on the nostalgia Americans feel for the imagined virgin landscapes of their ancestors, and on a desire for adventure, now offers people a convenient though sometimes incomplete or even spurious geography as an inducement to purchase a unique experience. But the line between authentic experience and a superficial exposure to the elements of experience is blurred. And the real landscape, in all its complexity, is distorted even further in the public imagination. No longer innately mysterious and dignified, a ground from which experience grows, it becomes a curiously generic backdrop on which experience is imposed.

In theme parks the profound, subtle, and protracted experience of running a river is reduced to a loud, quick, safe equivalence, a pleasant distraction. People only able to venture into the countryside on annual vacations are, increasingly, schooled in the belief that wild land will, and should, provide thrills and exceptional scenery on a timely basis. If it does not, something is wrong, either with the land itself or possibly with the company outfitting the trip.

People in America, then, face a convoluted situation. The land itself, vast and differentiated, defies the notion of a national geography. If applied at all it must be applied lightly, and it must grow out of the concrete detail of local geographies. Yet Americans are daily presented with, and have become accustomed to talking about, a homogenized national geography, one that seems to operate independently of the land, a collection of objects rather than a continuous bolt of fabric. It appears in advertisements, as a background in movies, and in patriotic calendars. The suggestion is that there *can* be a national geography because the constituent parts are interchangeable and can be treated as commodities. In day-to-day affairs, in other words, one place serves as well as another to convey one's point. On reflection, this is an appalling condescension and a terrible imprecision, the very antithesis of knowledge. The idea that either the Green River in Utah or the Salmon River in Idaho will do, or that the valleys of Kentucky and West Virginia are virtually interchangeable, is not just misleading. For people still dependent on the soil for their sustenance, or for people whose memories tie them to those places, it betrays a numbing casualness, a utilitarian, expedient, and commercial frame of mind. It heralds a society in which it is no longer necessary for human beings to know where

15

they live, except as those places are described and fixed by numbers. The truly difficult and lifelong task of discovering where one lives is finally disdained.

If a society forgets or no longer cares where it lives, then anyone with the political power and the will to do so can manipulate the landscape to conform to certain social ideals or nostalgic visions. People may hardly notice that anything has happened, or assume that whatever happens—a mountain stripped of timber and eroding into its creeks—is for the common good. The more superficial a society's knowledge of the real dimensions of the land it occupies becomes, the more vulnerable the land is to exploitation, to manipulation for short-term gain. The land, virtually powerless before political and commercial entities, finds itself finally with no defenders. It finds itself bereft of intimates with indispensable, concrete knowledge. (Oddly, or perhaps not oddly, while American society continues to value local knowledge as a quaint part of its heritage, it continues to cut such people off from any real political power. This is as true for small farmers and illiterate cowboys as it is for American Indians, native Hawaiians, and Eskimos.)

The intense pressure of imagery in America, and the manipulation of images necessary to a society with specific goals, means the land will inevitably be treated like a commodity; and voices that tend to contradict the proffered image will, one way or another, be silenced or discredited by those in power. This is not new to America; the promulgation in America of a false or imposed geography has been the case from the beginning. All local geographies, as they were defined by hundreds of separate, independent native traditions, were denied in the beginning in favor of an imported and unifying vision of America's natural history. The country, the landscape itself, was eventually defined according to dictates of Progress like Manifest Destiny,[18] and laws like the Homestead Act[19] which reflected a poor understanding of the physical lay of the land.

When I was growing up in southern California, I formed the rudiments of a local geography—eucalyptus trees, February rains, desert cottontails. I lost much of it when my family moved to New York City, a move typical of the modern, peripatetic style of American life, responding to the exigencies of divorce and employment. As a boy I felt a hunger to know the American landscape that was extreme; when I was finally able to travel on my own, I did so. Eventually I visited most of the United States, living for brief periods of time in Arizona, Indiana, Alabama, Georgia, Wyoming, New Jersey, and Montana before settling years ago in western Oregon.

The astonishing level of my ignorance confronted me everywhere I went. I knew early on that the country could not be held together in a few phrases, that its geography was magnificent and incomprehensible, that a man or

18. A doctrine that originates in the nineteenth century and refers to the American belief in the necessity of westward expansion.

19. A law of 1862 that granted 160 acres to settlers of the American West who promised to build, live on, and improve their "homesteads" for at least five years; it provided an important incentive for westward expansion.

woman could devote a lifetime to its elucidation and still feel in the end that he or she had but sailed many thousands of miles over the surface of the ocean. So I came into the habit of traversing landscapes I wanted to know with local tutors and reading what had previously been written about, and in, those places. I came to value exceedingly novels and essays and works of non-fiction that connected human enterprise to real and specific places, and I grew to be mildly distrustful of work that occurred in no particular place, work so cerebral and detached as to be refutable only in an argument of ideas.

These sojourns in various corners of the country infused me, somewhat to my surprise on thinking about it, with a great sense of hope. Whatever despair I had come to feel at a waning sense of the real land and the emergence of false geographies—elements of the land being manipulated, for example, to create erroneous but useful patterns in advertising—was dispelled by the depth of a single person's local knowledge, by the serenity that seemed to come with that intelligence. Any harm that might be done by people who cared nothing for the land, to whom it was not innately worthy but only something ultimately for sale, I thought, would one day have to meet this kind of integrity, people with the same dignity and transcendence as the land they occupied. So when I traveled, when I rolled my sleeping bag out on the shores of the Beaufort Sea or in the high pastures of the Absaroka Range in Wyoming, or at the bottom of the Grand Canyon,[20] I absorbed those particular testaments to life, the indigenous color and songbird song, the smell of sun-bleached rock, damp earth, and wild honey, with some crude appreciation of the singular magnificence of each of those places. And the reassurance I felt expanded in the knowledge that there were, and would likely always be, people speaking out whenever they felt the dignity of the earth imperiled in these places.

The promulgation of false geographies, which threaten the fundamental notion of what it means to live somewhere, is a current with a stable and perhaps growing countercurrent. People living in New York City are familiar with the stone basements, the cratonic geology, of that island and have a feeling for birds migrating through in the fall, their sequence and number. They do not find the city alien but human, its attenuated natural history merely different from that of rural Georgia or Wisconsin. I find the countermeasure, too, among Eskimos who cannot read but who might engage you for days on the subtleties of sea-ice topography. And among men and women who, though they have followed in the footsteps of their parents, have come to the conclusion that they cannot farm or fish or log in the way their ancestors did; the finite boundaries to this sort of wealth have appeared in their lifetime. Or among young men and women who have taken several decades of book-learned agronomy, zoology, silviculture[21] and horticulture, ecology, ethnobotany, and fluvial geomorphology and turned it into a new kind of local

20. A sequence that moves from the Arctic Ocean north of Alaska, to a mountain range straddling the boundary of Montana and Wyoming, to the famous gorge in Arizona, formed by the eroding action of the Colorado River.

21. The science of sustainably influencing forest growth to meet the needs of humans.

knowledge, who have taken up residence in a place and sought, both because of and in spite of their education, to develop a deep intimacy with it. Or they have gone to work, idealistically, for the National Park Service or the fish and wildlife services or for a private institution like the Nature Conservancy. They are people to whom the land is more than politics or economics. These are people for whom the land is alive. It feeds them, directly, and that is how and why they learn its geography.

In the end, then, if you begin among the blue crabs of Chesapeake Bay and wander for several years, down through the Smoky Mountains[22] and back to the bluegrass hills, along the drainages of the Ohio and into the hill country of Missouri, where in summer a chorus of cicadas might drown out human conversation, then up the Missouri itself,[23] reading on the way the entries of Meriwether Lewis and William Clark[24] and musing on the demise of the plains grizzly and the sturgeon, cross west into the drainage of the Platte[25] and spend the evenings with Gene Weltfish's *The Lost Universe*, her book about the Pawnee[26] who once thrived there, then drop south to Palo Duro Canyon and the irrigated farms of the Llano Estacado in Texas, turn west across the Sangre de Cristo,[27] southernmost of the Rocky Mountain ranges, and move north and west up onto the slickrock mesas of Utah, those browns and oranges, the ocherous hues reverberating in the deep canyons, then go north, swinging west to the insular ranges that sit like battleships in the pelagic space of Nevada, camp at the steaming edge of sulphur springs in the Black Rock Desert,[28] where alkaline pans are glazed with a ferocious light, a heat to melt iron, then cross the northern Sierra Nevada, waist-deep in summer snow in the passes, to descend to the valley of the Sacramento, and rise through groves of elephantine redwoods in the Coast Range, to arrive at Cape Mendocino,[29] before Balboa's Pacific,[30] cormorants and gulls, gray whales headed north for Unimak

---

22. Range in the southern section of the Appalachian Mountains that marks the border between North Carolina and Tennessee.

23. Missouri River, which flows between Montana and Missouri.

24. Lewis (1774–1809) and Clark (1770–1838), American explorers who journeyed west of the original thirteen states to survey the land bought in the Louisiana Purchase.

25. Tributary of the Missouri River that runs through Nebraska and drains smaller rivers in Colorado and Wyoming.

26. Native Americans who lived in Nebraska.

27. Palo Duro: the second-largest canyon in the United States, located in the Texas panhandle; Llana Estacado: Spanish for "stakes plains" and referring to a large, flat region in parts of New Mexico and Texas; Sangre de Christo: Spanish for "Blood of Christ," a region in the southernmost part of the Rocky Mountains, located in Colorado.

28. A flat, dry region in Nevada.

29. The mountains along the Pacific coast of the United States, ending at the westernmost point of the north California coast.

30. Vasco Nuñez de Balboa (1475–1519), a Spanish explorer, was the first known European to see the Pacific Ocean.

Pass in the Aleutians,[31] the winds crashing down on you, facing the ocean over the blue ocean that gives the scene its true vastness, making this crossing, having been so often astonished at the line and the color of the land, the ingenious lives of its plants and animals, the varieties of its darknesses, the intensity of the stars overhead, you would be ashamed to discover, then, in yourself, any capacity to focus on ravages in the land that left you unsettled. You would have seen so much, breathtaking, startling, and outsize, that you might not be able for a long time to break the spell, the sense, especially finishing your journey in the West, that the land had not been as rearranged or quite as compromised as you had first imagined.

After you had slept some nights on the beach, however, with that finite line of the ocean before you and the land stretching out behind you, the wind first battering then cradling you, you would be compelled by memory, obligated by your own involvement, to speak of what left you troubled. To find the rivers dammed and shrunken, the soil washed away, the land fenced, a tracery of pipes and wires and roads laid down everywhere, blocking and channeling the movement of water and animals, cutting the eye off repeatedly and confining it—you had expected this. It troubles you no more than your despair over the ruthlessness, the insensitivity, the impetuousness of modern life. What underlies this obvious change, however, is a less noticeable pattern of disruption: acidic lakes, skies empty of birds, fouled beaches, the poisonous slags of industry, the sun burning like a molten coin in ruined air.

It is a tenet of certain ideologies that man is responsible for all that is ugly, that everything nature creates is beautiful. Nature's darkness goes partly unreported, of course, and human brilliance is often perversely ignored. What is true is that man has a power, literally beyond his comprehension, to destroy. The lethality of some of what he manufactures, the incompetence with which he stores it or seeks to dispose of it, the cavalier way in which he employs in his daily living substances that threaten his health, the leniency of the courts in these matters (as though products as well as people enjoyed the protection of the Fifth Amendment),[32] and the treatment of open land, rivers, and the atmosphere as if, in some medieval way, they could still be regarded as disposal sinks of infinite capacity, would make you wonder, standing face to in the wind at Cape Mendocino, if we weren't bent on an errand of madness.

The geographies of North America, the myriad small landscapes that   25
make up the national fabric, are threatened—by ignorance of what makes them unique, by utilitarian attitudes, by failure to include them in the moral universe, and by brutal disregard. A testament of minor voices can clear away an ignorance of any place, can inform us of its special qualities; but no voice, by merely telling a story, can cause the poisonous wastes that saturate some parts of the land to decompose, to evaporate. This responsibility falls ulti-

---

31. A pass in the largest and easternmost of the Aleutian Islands, which are located off the coast of southwestern Alaska.

32. Amendment of the United States Constitution (in the Bill of Rights) that guarantees due process, the right to remain silent, and protection against double jeopardy.

mately to the national community, a vague and fragile entity to be sure, but one that, in America, can be ferocious in exerting its will.

Geography, the formal way in which we grapple with this areal mystery, is finally knowledge that calls up something in the land we recognize and respond to. It gives us a sense of place and a sense of community. Both are indispensable to a state of well-being, an individual's and a country's.

One afternoon on the Siuslaw River in the Coast Range of Oregon, in January, I hooked a steelhead, a sea-run trout, that told me, through the muscles of my hands and arms and shoulders, something of the nature of the thing I was calling "the Siuslaw River." Years ago I had stood under a pecan tree in Upson County, Georgia, idly eating the nuts, when slowly it occurred to me that these nuts would taste different from pecans growing somewhere up in South Carolina. I didn't need a sharp sense of taste to know this, only to pay attention at a level no one had ever told me was necessary. One November dawn, long before the sun rose, I began a vigil at the Dumont Dunes in the Mojave Desert in California, which I kept until a few minutes after the sun broke the horizon. During that time I named to myself the colors by which the sky changed and by which the sand itself flowed like a rising tide through grays and silvers and blues into yellows, pinks, washed duns, and fallow beiges.

It is through the power of observation, the gifts of eye and ear, of tongue and nose and finger, that a place first rises up in our mind; afterward it is memory that carries the place, that allows it to grow in depth and complexity. For as long as our records go back, we have held these two things dear, landscape and memory. Each infuses us with a different kind of life. The one feeds us, figuratively and literally. The other protects us from lies and tyranny. To keep landscapes intact and the memory of them, our history in them, alive, seems as imperative a task in modern time as finding the extent to which individual expression can be accommodated before it threatens to destroy the fabric of society.

If I were to now visit another country, I would ask my local companion, before I saw any museum or library, any factory or fabled town, to walk me in the country of his or her youth, to tell me the names of things and how, traditionally, they have been fitted together in a community. I would ask for the stories, the voice of memory over the land. I would ask to taste the wild nuts and fruits, to see their fishing lures, their bouquets, their fences. I would ask about the history of storms there, the age of the trees, the winter color of the hills. Only then would I ask to see the museums. I would want first the sense of a real place, to know that I was not inhabiting an idea. I would want to know the lay of the land first, the real geography, and take some measure of the love of it in my companion before I stood before the paintings or read works of scholarship. I would want to have something real and remembered against which I might hope to measure their truth.

Questions

1. Lopez begins with a "commonplace": "that Americans know little of the geography of their country" (paragraph 1). How does he counter that common view with his concepts of "local expertise" (paragraphs 6–9) and "local geographies" (paragraph 15)? How does the title of his essay—with the last word in the plural—suggest the direction his argument will take?

2. Throughout the essay Lopez writes about the distortions that the concept of a "national geography" imposes on the "real landscape" (paragraph 15). What examples of distortion does Lopez give? How do his personal examples of experiencing the landscape represent an alternative?

3. The final section of the essay begins with a long catalogue of places in America—from the Chesapeake Bay to the Unimak Pass in the Aleutian Islands. What purpose does this catalogue serve? How does it both sum up the preceding parts of the essay and prepare for the conclusion?

4. "If you want to know [a place] you must take the time"—Lopez explains in paragraph 6. Spend time in a "local geography," observe what is there, and write an essay about the place.

Margaret Atwood *True North*

> Land of the silver birch,
> Home of the beaver,
> Where still the mighty moose
> Wanders at will,
> Blue lake and rocky shore,
> I will return once more;
> Boom-diddy-boom-boom
> Boom-diddy-boom-boom
> Boo-OO-oo-oo-oom.
> —Archaic Song

WE SANG THIS ONCE, squatting around the papier-mâché Magic Mushroom in the Brownie pack, while pretending to be wolves in Cub Scouts, or while watching our marshmallows turn to melted Styrofoam on the ends of our sticks at some well-run, fairly safe summer camp in the wilds of Muskoka, Haliburton, or Algonquin Park. Then we grew up and found it corny. By that time we were into

Atwood wrote this piece for Saturday Night *(January 1987), Canada's oldest general circulation magazine, published from 1887 to 2001.*

Jean-Paul Sartre[1] and the lure of the nauseous. Finally, having reached the age of nostalgia, we rediscovered it on a cassette in The Children's Book Store, in a haunting version that invested it with all the emotional resonance we once thought it possessed, and bought it, under the pretense of giving our children a little ethnic musical background.

It brought tears to our eyes, not for simple reasons. Whales get to us that way too, and whooping cranes, and other things hovering on the verge of extinction but still maintaining a tenuous foothold in the world of the actual. The beavers are doing all right—we know this because they just decimated our poplars—but the mighty moose is having a slimmer time of it. As for the blueness of the lakes, we worry about it: too blue and you've got acid rain.

Will we return once more, or will we go to Portugal instead? It depends, we have to admit, partly on the exchange rate, and this makes us feel disloyal. I am, rather quixotically, in Alabama, teaching, even more quixotically, a course in Canadian literature. Right now we're considering Marian Engel's novel *Bear.* Since everything in Canada, outside Toronto, begins with geography, I've unfolded a large map of Ontario and traced the heroine's route north; I've located the mythical house of the book somewhere on the actual shore of Georgian Bay, northern edge. I've superimposed a same-scale map of Alabama on this scheme, to give the students an idea of the distances. In the north, space is larger than you think, because the points of reference are farther apart.

"Are there any words you came across that puzzled you?" I ask.

Blackfly comes up. A large black fly is proposed. I explain blackflies, their smallness, their multitude, their evil habits. It gives me a certain kick to do this: I'm competing with the local water moccasins.

Mackinaw. A raincoat? Not quite. *Loon. Tamarack. Reindeer moss. Portage. Moose. Wendigo.*

"Why does she make Lucy the old Indian woman talk so funny?" they ask. Lucy, I point out, is not merely Indian but a *French-speaking* Indian. This, to them, is a weird concept.

The north is another country. It's also another language. Or languages.

Where is the north, exactly? It's not only a place but a direction, and as such its location is relative: to the Mexicans, the United States is the north, to Americans Toronto is, even though it's on roughly the same latitude as Boston.

Wherever it is for us, there's a lot of it. You stand in Windsor and imagine a line going north, all the way to the pole. The same line going south would end up in South America. That's the sort of map we grew up with, at the front of the classroom in Mercator projection, which made it look even bigger than it was, all that pink stretching on forever, with a few cities sprinkled along the bottom edge. It's not only geographical space, it's space related to body image. When we face south, as we often do, our conscious mind may be directed down there, towards crowds, bright lights, some Hollywood version of fame and fortune, but

---

1. French existentialist philosopher, novelist, playwright, essayist, literary critic, and political activist (1905–1980). One of his novels was entitled *Nausea.*

the north is at the back of our minds, always. There's something, not someone, looking over our shoulders; there's a chill at the nape of the neck.

The north focuses our anxieties. Turning to face north, face the north, we enter our own unconscious. Always, in retrospect, the journey north has the quality of dream.

Where does the north begin?

Every province, every city, has its own road north. From Toronto you go up the 400. Where you cross the border, from here to there, is a matter of opinion. Is it the Severn River, where the Shield granite appears suddenly out of the earth? Is it the sign announcing that you're halfway between the equator and the North Pole? Is it the first gift shop shaped like a wigwam, the first town—there are several—that proclaims itself The Gateway to the North?

As we proceed, the farms become fewer, rockier, more desperate-looking, the trees change their ratios, coniferous moving in on deciduous. More lakes appear, their shorelines scraggier. Our eyes narrow and we look at the clouds: the weather is important again.

One of us used to spend summers in a cottage in Muskoka, before the road   15
went in, when you took the train, when there were big cruise ships there, and matronly motor launches, and tea dances at the hotels, and men in white flannels on the lawns, which there may still be. This was not just a cottage but a Muskoka cottage, with boathouse and maid's quarters. Rich people went north in the summers then, away from cities and crowds; that was before the cure for polio, which has made a difference. In this sort of north, they tried to duplicate the south, or perhaps some dream of country life in England. In the living room there were armchairs, glass-fronted bookcases, family photos in silver frames, stuffed birds under glass bells. The north, as I said, is relative.

For me, the north used to be completely in force by the Trout Creek planing mill. Those stacks of fresh-cut lumber were the true gateway to the north, and north of that was North Bay, which used to be, to be blunt, a bit of an armpit. It was beef-sandwich-on-white-bread-with-gravy-and-canned-peas country. But no more. North Bay now has shopping malls, and baskets of flowers hanging from lampposts above paving-stone sidewalks, downtown. It has a Granite Club. It has the new, swish, carpeted buildings of Laurentian University. It has gourmet restaurants. And in the airport, where southbound DC-9s dock side by side with northbound Twin Otters, there's a book rack in the coffee shop that features Graham Greene and Kierkegaard,[2] hardly standard airport fare.

The south is moving north.

---

2. Greene (1904–1991), English novelist; Søren Kierkegaard (1813–1855), Danish clergyman and philosopher who criticized Christianity and set the stage for modern existentialism.

We bypass North Bay, which now has a bypass, creeping southerliness, and do not go, this time, to the Dionne Quints Museum, where five little silhouettes in black play forever beside an old log cabin, complete with the basket where they were packed in cotton wool, the oven where they were warmed, the five prams, the five Communion dresses.

Beyond North Bay there is a brief flurry of eccentricity—lawns populated with whole flocks of wooden-goose windmills—and then we go for miles and miles past nothing but trees, meeting nothing but the occasional truck loaded with lumber. This area didn't used to be called anything. Now it's the Near North Travel Area. You can see signs telling you that. Near what, we wonder uneasily? We don't want to be near. We want to be far.

At last we see the Ottawa River, which is the border. There's a dam across it, two dams, and an island between them. If there were a customs house it would be here. A sign faces us saying *Bienvenue;* out the back window there's one saying *Welcome.* This was my first lesson in points of view.

And there, across the border in Québec, in Témiscaming, is an image straight from my childhood: a huge mountain made of sawdust. I always wanted to slide down this sawdust mountain until I finally did, and discovered it was not like sand, dry and slippery, but damp and sticky and hard to get out of your clothes. This was my first lesson in the nature of illusion.

Continue past the sawdust mountain, past the baseball diamond, up the hill, and you're in the centre of town, which is remarkable for at least three things: a blocks-long public rock garden, still flourishing after more than forty-five years; a pair of statues, one a fountain, that look as if they've come straight from Europe, which I think they did; and the excellent, amazingly low-priced hamburgers you can get at the Boulevard Restaurant, where the décor, featuring last year's cardboard Santa Claus and a stuffed twenty-three-pound pike, is decidedly northern. Ask the owner about the pike and he'll tell you about one twice as big, forty-five pounds in fact, that a fellow showed him strapped to the tailgate of his van, and that long, too.

You can have this conversation in either French or English: Témiscaming is a border town and a northern one, and the distinctions made here are as likely to be north-south as French-English. Up in these parts you'll hear as much grumbling, or more, about Québec City as you will about Ottawa, which is, after all, closer. Spit in the river and it gets to Ottawa, eh?

For the north, Témiscaming is old, settled, tidy, even a little prosperous looking. But it's had its crises. Témiscaming is the resource economy personified. Not long ago it was a company town, and when the company shut down the mill, which would have shut down the town too, the workers took the unprecedented step of trying to buy it. With some help they succeeded, and the result was Tembec, still going strong. But Témiscaming is still a one-industry town, like many northern towns, and its existence is thus precarious.

Not so long ago, logging was a different sort of business. The men went into the woods in winter, across the ice, using horse-drawn sledges, and set up camp. (You still come across these logging camps now and then in your travels through the lakes, abandoned, already looking as ancient as Roman aqueducts; more ancient, since there's been no upkeep.) They'd cut selectively, tree by tree, using axes and saws and the skills that were necessary to avoid being squashed or hacked. They'd skid the trees to the ice; in the spring, after the ice went out, there would be a run down the nearest fast river to the nearest sawmill.

Now it's done with bulldozers and trucks, and the result is too often a blitzed shambles; cut everything, leave a wreck of dead and, incidentally, easily flammable branches behind. Time is money. Don't touch the shoreline though, we need that for tourists. In some places, the forest is merely a scrim along the water. In behind it's been hollowed out.

Those who look on the positive side say it's good for the blueberries.

Sometimes we went the other way, across to Sudbury, the trees getting smaller and smaller and finally disappearing as you approached. Sudbury was another magic place of my childhood. It was like interplanetary travel, which we liked to imagine, which was still just imagination in those days. With its heaps of slag and its barren shoulders of stone, it looked like the moon. Back then, we tell the children, before there were washer-dryers and you used something called a wringer washer and hung the sheets out on something called a clothesline, when there weren't even coloured sheets but all sheets were white, when Rinso white and its happy little washday song were an item, and Whiter than White was a catch phrase and female status really did have something to do with your laundry, Sudbury was a housewife's nightmare. We knew people there; the windowsills in their houses were always grey.

Now the trees are beginning to come back because they built higher smokestacks. But where is all that stuff going now?

The Acid Rain Dinner, in Toronto's Sheraton Centre, in 1985. The first of these fund-raising events was fairly small. But the movement has grown, and this dinner is huge. The leaders of all three provincial parties are here. So is the minister of the environment from the federal government. So are several labour leaders, and several high-ranking capitalists, and representatives of numerous northerly chambers of commerce, summer residents' associations, tourist-camp runners, outfitters. Wishy washy urban professionals who say "frankly" a lot bend elbows with huntin', shootin', fishin', and cussin' burnt necks who wouldn't be caught dead saying "frankly." This is not a good place to be overheard saying that actually acid rain isn't such a bad thing because it gets rid of all that brown scum and leeches in the lake, or who cares because you can water-ski anyway. Teddy Kennedy, looking like a bulky sweater, is the guest speaker. Everyone wears a little gold pin in the shape of a rain drop. It looks like a tear.

Why has acid rain become the collective Canadian nightmare? Why is it— as a good cause—bigger than baby-seal bashing? The reasons aren't just economic, although there are lots of those, as the fishing-camp people and foresters will tell you. It's more than that, and cognate with the outrage aroused by the uninvited voyage of the American icebreaker *Polar Sea* through the Northwest Passage, where almost none of us ever goes. It's territorial, partly; partly a felt violation of some area in us that we hardly ever think about unless it's invaded or tampered with. It's the neighbours throwing guck into our yard. It's our childhood dying.

On location, in summer and far from the glass and brass of the Sheraton Centre, we nervously check our lakes. Leeches still in place? Have the cray-fish, among the first to go, gone yet? (We think in terms of "yet.") Are the loons reproducing, have you seen any young? Any minnows? How about the lichen on the rocks? These inventories have now become routine, and that is why we're willing to fork out a hundred dollars a plate to support our acid-rain lob-byists in Washington. A summer without loons is unthinkable, but how do you tell that to people who don't know it because they've never had any to begin with?

We're driving through Glencoe, in the Highlands of Scotland. It's imposing, as a landscape: bleak, large, bald, apparently empty. We can see why the Scots took so well to Canada. Yet we know that the glens and crags round about are crawling with at least a thousand campers, rock climbers, and other seekers after nature; we also know that, at one end of this glen, the Campbells butchered the MacDonalds in the seventeenth century, thus pro-pelling both of them into memorable history. Go walking here and you'll find things human: outlines of stone fences now overgrown, shards of abandoned crofts.

In Europe, every scrap of land has been claimed, owned, re-owned, fought over, captured, bled on. The roads are the only no-man's-land. In northern Canada, the roads are civilization, owned by the collective human *we*. Off the road is *other*. Try walking in it, and you'll soon find out why all the early traffic here was by water. "Impenetrable wilderness" is not just verbal.

35   And suppose you get off the road. Suppose you get lost. Getting lost, else-where and closer to town, is not knowing exactly where you are. You can al-ways ask, even in a foreign country. In the north, getting lost is not knowing how to get out.

You can get lost on a lake, of course, but getting lost in the forest is worse. It's tangly in there, and dim, and one tree does begin to look remarkably like another. The leaves and needles blot up sound, and you begin to feel watched: not by anyone, not by an animal even, or anything you can put a name to, just watched. You begin to feel judged. It's as if something is keeping an eye on you just to see what you will do.

What will you do? Which side of the tree does moss grow on, and here, where there are ferns and the earth is damp, or where it's dry as tinder, it seems that moss grows everywhere, or does not grow at all. Snippets of Boy Scout lore or truisms learned at summer camp come back to you, but scram-bled. You tell yourself not to panic: you can always live off the land.

Easier said than done, you'd soon find. The Canadian Shield is a relatively foodless area, which is why even the Indians tended to pass through it, did not form large settlements except where there was arable land, and remained limited in numbers. This is not the Mekong delta.[3] If you had a gun you could shoot something, maybe, a red squirrel perhaps; but if you're lost you probably don't have a gun, or a fishing rod either. You could eat blueberries, or cattail stems, or crayfish, or other delicacies dimly remembered from stories about people who got lost in the woods and were found later in good health although somewhat thinner. You could cook some reindeer moss, if you had matches.

Thus you pass on to fantasies about how to start a fire with a magnifying glass—you don't have one—or by rubbing two bits of stick together, a feat at which you suspect you would prove remarkably inept.

The fact is that not very many of us know how to survive in the north. Rumour has it that only one German prisoner of war ever made it out, although many made it out of the actual prisoner-of-war camps. The best piece of northern survival advice is: *Don't get lost.*

40

One way of looking at a landscape is to consider the typical ways of dying in it. Given the worst, what's the worst it could do? Will it be delirium from drinking salty water on the high seas, shrivelling in the desert, snakebite in the jungle, tidal waves on a Pacific isle, volcanic fumes? In the north, there are several hazards. Although you're probably a lot safer there than you are on the highway at rush hour, given the odds, you still have to be a little wary.

Like most lessons of this sort, those about the north are taught by precept and example, but also, more enjoyably, by cautionary nasty tale. There is death by blackfly, the one about the fellow who didn't have his shirt cuffs tight enough in the spring and undressed at night only to find he was running with blood, the ones about the lost travellers who bloated up from too many bites and who, when found, were twice the size, unrecognizable, and dead. There is death from starvation, death by animal, death by forest fire; there is death from something called "exposure," which used to confuse me when I heard about men who exposed themselves: why would they intentionally do anything that fatal? There's death by thunderstorm, not to be sneered at: on the open lake, in one of the excessive northern midsummer thunderstorms, a canoe or a bush plane is a vulnerable target. The north is full of Struwelpeter-like[4] stories about people who didn't do as they were told and got struck by lightning. Above all, there are death by freezing and death by drowning. Your body's heat-loss rate in the water is twenty times that in air, and northern lakes are cold. Even in a life jacket, even holding on to the tipped canoe, you're at risk. Every summer the numbers pile up.

Every culture has its exemplary dead people, its hagiography of landscape martyrs, those unfortunates who, by their bad ends, seem to sum up in one grisly episode what may be lurking behind the next rock for all of us, all of us who enter the territory they once claimed as theirs. I'd say that two of the top

3. A vast plain in southeast Vietnam where the Mekong River empties into the South China Sea.
4. Like a person with long, thick, unkempt hair, from a character in a children's book by Heinrich Hoffman (1809–1894).

northern landscape martyrs are Tom Thomson, the painter who was found mysteriously drowned near his overturned canoe with no provable cause in sight, and the Mad Trapper of Rat River, also mysterious, who became so thoroughly bushed that he killed a Mountie and shot two others during an amazing wintertime chase before being finally mowed down. In our retelling of these stories, mystery is a key element. So, strangely enough, is a presumed oneness with the landscape in question. The Mad Trapper knew his landscape so well he survived in it for weeks, living off the land and his own bootlaces, eluding capture. One of the hidden motifs in these stories is a warning: maybe it's not so good to get *too* close to Nature.

I remember a documentary on Tom Thomson that ended, rather ominously, with the statement that the north had taken him to herself. This was, of course, pathetic fallacy[5] gone to seed, but it was also a comment on our distrust of the natural world, a distrust that remains despite our protests, our studies in the ethics of ecology, our elevation of "the environment" to a numinous noun, our save-the-tree campaigns. The question is, would the trees save us, given the chance? Would the water, would the birds, would the rocks? In the north, we have our doubts.

45   A bunch of us are sitting around the table, at what is now a summer cottage in Georgian Bay. Once it was a house, built by a local man for his family, which finally totalled eleven children, after they'd outgrown this particular house and moved on to another. The original Findlay wood-burning cook stove is still in the house, but so also are some electric lights and a propane cooker, which have come since the end of the old days. In the old days, this man somehow managed to scrape a living from the land: a little of this, a little of that, some fishing here, some lumbering there, some hunting in the fall. That was back when you shot to eat. "Scrape" is an appropriate word: there's not much here between the topsoil and the rock.

We sit around the table and eat, fish among other things, caught by the children. Someone mentions the clams: there are still a lot of them, but who knows what's in them any more? Mercury, lead, things like that. We pick at the fish. Someone tells me not to drink the tap water. I already have. "What will happen?" I ask. "Probably nothing," they reply. "Probably nothing" is a relatively recent phrase around here. In the old days, you ate what looked edible.

We are talking about the old days, as people often do once they're outside the cities. When exactly did the old days end? Because we know they did. The old days ended when the youngest of us was ten, fifteen, or twenty; the old days ended when the oldest of us was five, or twelve, or thirty. Plastic-hulled superboats are not old days, but ten-horse-power outboard motors, circa 1945, are. There's an icebox in the back porch, unused now, a simple utilitarian model from Eaton's, ice chamber in the top section, metal shelves in the bottom one. We all go and admire it. "I remember iceboxes," I say, and indeed I can dimly remember them, I must have been five. What bits of our daily

5. The attribution of human emotions to inanimate objects, often the landscape.

junk—our toasters, our pocket computers—will soon become obsolete and therefore poignant? Who will stand around, peering at them and admiring their design and the work that went into them, as we do with this icebox? "So this was a *toilet seat*," we think, rehearsing the future. "Ah! A *light bulb*," the ancient syllables thick in our mouths.

The kids have decided some time ago that all this chat is boring, and have asked if they can go swimming off the dock. They can, though they have to watch it, as this is a narrow place and speedboats tend to swoosh through, not always slowing down. Waste of gas, in the old days. Nobody then went anywhere just for pleasure, it was the war and gas was rationed.

"Oh, *that* old days," says someone.

There goes a speedboat now, towing a man strapped in a kneeling position   50
to some kind of board, looking as if he's had a terrible accident, or is about to have one. This must be some newfangled variety of water-skiing.

"Remember Klim?" I say. The children come through, trailing towels. "What's Klim?" one asks, caught by the space-age sound of the word.

"Klim was 'milk' spelled backwards," I say. "It was powdered milk."

"Yuk," they say.

"Not the same as now," I say. "It was whole milk, not skim; it wasn't instant. You had to beat it with an eggbeater." And even then some of it wouldn't dissolve. One of the treats of childhood was the little nodules of pure dry Klim that floated on top of your milk.

"There was also Pream," says someone. How revolutionary it seemed.   55

The children go down to take their chances in the risky motorized water. Maybe, much later, they will remember us sitting around the table, eating fish they themselves had caught, back when you could still (what? Catch a fish? See a tree? What desolations lie in store, beyond the plasticized hulls and the knee-skiers?). By then we will be the old days, for them. Almost we are already.

A different part of the north. We're sitting around the table, by lamplight—it's still the old days here, no electricity—talking about bad hunters. Bad hunters, bad fishers, everyone has a story. You come upon a campsite, way in the back of beyond, no roads into the lake, they must have come in by float plane, and there it is, garbage all over the place, beer cans, blobs of human poop flagged by melting toilet paper, and twenty-two fine pickerel left rotting on a rock. Business executives who get themselves flown in during hunting season with their high-powered rifles, shoot a buck, cut off the head, fill their quota, see another one with a bigger spread of antlers, drop the first head, cut off the second. The woods are littered with discarded heads, and who cares about the bodies?

New way to shoot polar bear: you have the natives on the ground finding them for you, then they radio the location in to the base camp, the base camp phones New York, fellow gets on the plane, gets himself flown in, they've got the rifle and the clothing all ready for him, fly him to the bear, he pulls the trigger from the plane, doesn't even get out of the g.d. *plane,* they fly him back, cut off the head, skin it, send the lot down to New York.

These are the horror stories of the north, one brand. They've replaced the ones in which you got pounced upon by a wolverine or had your arm chewed off by a she-bear with cubs or got chased into the lake by a moose in rut, or even the ones in which your dog got porcupine quills or rolled in poison ivy and gave it to you. In the new stories, the enemies and the victims of old have done a switch. Nature is no longer implacable, dangerous, ready to jump you; it is on the run, pursued by a number of unfair bullies with the latest technology.

60   One of the key nouns in these stories is "float plane." These outrages, this banditry, would not be possible without them, for the bad hunters are notoriously weak-muscled and are deemed incapable of portaging a canoe, much less paddling one. Among their other badnesses, they are sissies. Another key motif is money. What money buys these days, among other things, is the privilege of no-risk slaughter.

As for us, the ones telling the stories, tsk-tsking by lamplight, we are the good hunters, or so we think. We've given up saying we only kill to eat; Kraft dinner and freeze-dried food have put paid to that one. Really there's no excuse for us. However, we do have some virtues left. We can still cast a fly. We don't cut off heads and hang them stuffed on the wall. We would never buy an ocelot coat. We paddle our own canoes.

We're sitting on the dock at night, shivering despite our sweaters, in mid-August, watching the sky. There are a few shooting stars, as there always are at this time in August, as the earth passes through the Perseids. We pride ourselves on knowing a few things like that, about the sky; we find the Dipper, the North Star, Cassiopeia's Chair, and talk about consulting a star chart, which we know we won't actually do. But this is the only place you can really *see* the stars, we tell each other. Cities are hopeless.

Suddenly, an odd light appears, going very fast. It spirals around like a newly dead firecracker, and then bursts, leaving a cloud of luminous dust, caught perhaps in the light from the sun, still up there somewhere. What could this be? Several days later, we hear that it was part of an extinct Soviet satellite, or that's what they say. That's what they would say, wouldn't they? It strikes us that we don't really know very much about the night sky at all any more. There's all kinds of junk up there: spy planes, old satellites, tin cans, man-made matter gone out of control. It also strikes us that we are totally dependent for knowledge of these things on a few people who don't tell us very much.

Once, we thought that if the balloon ever went up we'd head for the bush and hide out up there, living—we naively supposed—off the land. Now we know that if the two superpowers begin hurling things at each other through the sky, they're likely to do it across the Arctic, with big bangs and fallout all over the north. The wind blows everywhere. Survival gear and knowing which moss you can eat is not going to be a large help. The north is no longer a refuge.

65   Driving back towards Toronto from the Near North, a small reprise runs through my head:

Land of the septic tank,
Home of the speedboat,
Where still the four-wheel-drive
Wanders at will,
Blue lake and tacky shore,
I will return once more:
Vroom-diddy-vroom-vroom
Vroom-diddy-vroom-vroom
Vroo-OO-oo-oom.

Somehow, just as the drive north inspires saga and tragedy, the drive south inspires parody. And here it comes: the gift shops shaped like teepees, the maple-syrup emporiums that get themselves up like olde-tyme sugaring-off huts; and, farther south, the restaurants that pretend to offer wholesome farm fare, the stores that pretend to be general stores, selling quilts, soap shaped like hearts, high-priced fancy conserves done up in frilly cloth caps, the way Grandma (whoever she might be) was fondly supposed to have made them.

And then come the housing developments, acres of prime farmland turning overnight into Quality All-Brick Family Homes; and then come the Industrial Parks; and there, in full anti-bloom, is the city itself, looming like a mirage or a chemical warfare zone on the horizon. A browny-grey scuzz hovers above it, and we think, as we always do when facing re-entry, we're going into *that*? We're going to breathe *that*?

But we go forward, as we always do, into what is now to us the unknown. And once inside, we breathe the air, not much bad happens to us, we hardly notice. It's as if we've never been anywhere else. But that's what we think, too, when we're in the north.

QUESTIONS

1. What context does Atwood set for the opening section? How does her need to explain to American Southerners in a college classroom help her communicate with the readers of this essay?

2. Beginning in paragraph 18, Atwood reenacts a journey to the "north." What does this journey, re-created for the reader, help her achieve?

3. Why does Atwood include a section about "typical ways of dying" in a northern landscape? What qualities about northern Canada can she present through this unusual approach?

4. Write an essay about a geographical region that appeals to you but that may be unknown or unappealing to others. Using techniques learned from Atwood or other writers in this section, try to communicate the region's appeal as you write.

DAVID GUTERSON *Enclosed. Encyclopedic. Endured:*
The Mall of America

L AST APRIL, on a visit to the new Mall of America near
Minneapolis, I carried with me the public-relations press
kit provided for the benefit of reporters. It included an
assortment of "fun facts" about the mall: 140,000 hot
dogs sold each week, 10,000 permanent jobs, 44
escalators and 17 elevators, 12,750 parking
places, 13,300 short tons of steel, $1 million in cash disbursed weekly from 8
automatic-teller machines. Opened in the summer of 1992, the mall was built
on the 78-acre site of the former Metropolitan Stadium, a five-minute drive
from the Minneapolis–St. Paul International Airport. With 4.2 million square
feet of floor space—including twenty-two times the retail footage of the average American shopping center—the Mall of America was "the largest fully enclosed combination retail and family
entertainment complex in the United
States."

Eleven thousand articles, the press
kit warned me, had already been written on the mall. Four hundred trees had
been planted in its gardens, $625 mil-
lion had been spent to build it, 350
stores had been leased. Three thousand
bus tours were anticipated each year
along with a half-million Canadian visitors and 200,000 Japanese tourists.
Sales were projected at $650 million for
1993 and at $1 billion for 1996. Donny
and Marie Osmond had visited the
mall, as had Janet Jackson and Sally
Jesse Raphael, Arnold Schwarzenegger,
and the 1994 Winter Olympic Committee. The mall was five times larger than
Red Square and twenty times larger
than St. Peter's Basilica; it incorporated
2.3 miles of hallways and almost twice as much steel as the Eiffel Tower. It
was also home to the nation's largest indoor theme park, a place called Knott's
Camp Snoopy.

On the night I arrived, a Saturday, the mall was spotlit dramatically in the
manner of a Las Vegas casino. It resembled, from the outside, a castle or fort,
the Emerald City or Never-Never Land, impossibly large and vaguely unreal,

Published in Harper's Magazine *(August 1993), a monthly magazine that often prints critical accounts of American cultural phenomena.*

an unbroken, windowless multi-storied edifice the size of an airport terminal. Surrounded by parking lots and new freeway ramps, monolithic and imposing in the manner of a walled city, it loomed brightly against the Minnesota night sky with the disturbing magnetism of a mirage.

I knew already that the Mall of America had been imagined by its creators not merely as a marketplace but as a national tourist attraction, an immense zone of entertainments. Such a conceit raised provocative questions, for our architecture testifies to our view of ourselves and to the condition of our souls. Large buildings stand as markers in the lives of nations and in the stream of a people's history. Thus I could only ask myself: Here was a new structure that had cost more than half a billion dollars to erect—what might it tell us about ourselves? If the Mall of America was part of America, what was that going to mean?

I passed through one of the mall's enormous entranceways and took myself inside. Although from a distance the Mall of America had appeared menacing— exuding the ambience of a monstrous hallucination—within it turned out to be simply a shopping mall, certainly more vast than other malls but in tone and aspect, design and feel, not readily distinguishable from them. Its nuances were instantly familiar as the generic features of the American shopping mall at the tail end of the twentieth century: polished stone, polished tile, shiny chrome and brass, terrazzo floors, gazebos. From third-floor vistas, across vaulted spaces, the Mall of America felt endlessly textured—glass-enclosed elevators, neon-tube lighting, bridges, balconies, gas lamps, vaulted skylights— and densely crowded with hordes of people circumambulating in an endless promenade. Yet despite the mall's expansiveness, it elicited claustrophobia, sensory deprivation, and an unnerving disorientation. Everywhere I went I spied other pilgrims who had found, like me, that the straight way was lost and that the YOU ARE HERE landmarks on the map kiosks referred to nothing in particular.

Getting lost, feeling lost, being lost—these states of mind are intentional features of the mall's psychological terrain. There are, one notices, no clocks or windows, nothing to distract the shopper's psyche from the alternate reality the mall conjures. Here we are free to wander endlessly and to furtively watch our fellow wanderers, thousands upon thousands of milling strangers who have come with the intent of losing themselves in the mall's grand, stimulating design. For a few hours we share some common ground—a fantasy of infinite commodities and comforts—and then we drift apart forever. The mall exploits our acquisitive instincts without honoring our communal requirements, our eternal desire for discourse and intimacy, needs that until the twentieth century were traditionally met in our marketplaces but that are not met at all in giant shopping malls.

On this evening a few thousand young people had descended on the mall in pursuit of alcohol and entertainment. They had come to Gators, Hooters, and Knuckleheads, Puzzles, Fat Tuesday, and Ltl Ditty's. At Players, a sports bar,

5

the woman beside me introduced herself as "the pregnant wife of an Iowa pig farmer" and explained that she had driven five hours with friends to "do the mall party scene together." She left and was replaced by Kathleen from Minnetonka, who claimed to have "a real shopping thing—I can't go a week without buying new clothes. I'm not fulfilled until I buy something."

Later a woman named Laura arrived, with whom Kathleen was acquainted. "I *am* the mall," she announced ecstatically upon discovering I was a reporter. "I'd move in here if I could bring my dog," she added. "This place is heaven, it's a *mecca.*"

"We egg each other on," explained Kathleen, calmly puffing on a cigarette. "It's like, sort of, an addiction."

10   "You want the truth?" Laura asked. "I'm constantly suffering from megamall withdrawal. I come here all the time."

Kathleen: "It's a sickness. It's like cocaine or something; it's a drug."

Laura: "Kathleen's got this thing about buying, but I just need to *be* here. If I buy something it's an added bonus."

Kathleen: "She buys stuff all the time; don't listen."

Laura: "Seriously, I feel sorry for other malls. They're so small and *boring.*"

15   Kathleen seemed to think about this: "Richdale Mall," she blurted finally. She rolled her eyes and gestured with her cigarette. "Oh, my God, Laura. Why did we even *go* there?"

There is, of course, nothing naturally abhorrent in the human impulse to dwell in marketplaces or the urge to buy, sell, and trade. Rural Americans traditionally looked forward to the excitement and sensuality of market day; Native Americans traveled long distances to barter and trade at sprawling, festive encampments. In Persian bazaars and in the ancient Greek agoras the very soul of the community was preserved and could be seen, felt, heard, and smelled as it might be nowhere else. All over the planet the humblest of people have always gone to market with hope in their hearts and in expectation of something beyond mere goods—seeking a place where humanity is temporarily in ascendance, a palette for the senses, one another.

But the illicit possibilities of the marketplace also have long been acknowledged. The Persian bazaar was closed at sundown; the Greek agora was off-limits to those who had been charged with certain crimes. One myth of the Old West we still carry with us is that market day presupposes danger; the faithful were advised to make purchases quickly and repair without delay to the farm, lest their attraction to the pleasures of the marketplace erode their purity of spirit.

In our collective discourse the shopping mall appears with the tract house, the freeway, and the backyard barbecue as a product of the American postwar years, a testament to contemporary necessities and desires and an invention not only peculiarly American but peculiarly of our own era too. Yet the mall's varied and far-flung predecessors—the covered bazaars of the Middle East, the stately arcades of Victorian England, Italy's vaulted and skylit gallerias, Asia's monsoon-protected urban markets—all suggest that the rituals of indoor shopping, although in their nuances not often like our own, are nevertheless broadly known. The late twentieth-century American contribution has been to transform the enclosed bazaar into an economic institution that is vastly profitable yet socially enervated, one that redefines in fundamental ways the human relationship to the marketplace. At the Mall of America—an extreme example—we discover ourselves thoroughly lost among strangers in a marketplace intentionally designed to serve no community needs.

In the strict sense the Mall of America is not a marketplace at all—the soul of a community expressed as a *place*—but rather a tourist attraction. Its promoters have peddled it to the world at large as something more profound than a local marketplace and as a destination with deep implications. "I believe we can make Mall of America stand for all of America," asserted the mall's general manager, John Wheeler, in a promotional video entitled *There's a Place for Fun in Your Life*. "I believe there's a shopper in all of us," added the director of marketing, Maureen Hooley. The mall has memorialized its opening-day proceedings by producing a celebratory videotape: Ray Charles singing "America the Beautiful," a laser show followed by fireworks, "The Star-Spangled Banner" and "The Stars and Stripes Forever," the Gatlin Brothers, and Peter Graves. "Mall of America . . . ," its narrator intoned. "The name alone conjures up images of greatness, of a retail complex so magnificent it could only happen in America."

Indeed, on the day the mall opened, Miss America visited. The mall's logo—a red, white, and blue star bisected by a red, white, and blue ribbon—decorated everything from the mall itself to coffee mugs and the flanks of buses. The idea, director of tourism Colleen Hayes told me, was to position America's largest mall as an institution on the scale of Disneyland or the Grand Canyon, a place simultaneously iconic and totemic, a revered symbol of the United States and a mecca to which the faithful would flock in pursuit of all things purchasable.

20

On Sunday I wandered the hallways of the pleasure dome with the sensation that I had entered an M. C. Escher drawing—there was no such thing as up or down, and the escalators all ran backward. A 1993 Ford Probe GT was displayed as if popping out of a giant packing box; a full-size home, complete with artificial lawn, had been built in the mall's rotunda. At the Michael Ricker Pewter Gallery I came across a miniature tableau of a pewter dog peeing on a pewter man's leg; at Hologram Land I pondered 3-D hallucinations of the Medusa and Marilyn Monroe. I passed a kiosk called The Sportsman's Wife; I stood beside a life-size statue of the Hamm's Bear, carved out of pine and available for $1,395 at a store called Minnesot-ah!

At Pueblo Spirit I examined a "dream catcher"—a small hoop made from deer sinew and willow twigs and designed to be hung over its owner's bed as a tactic for filtering bad dreams. For a while I sat in front of Glamour Shots and watched while women were groomed and brushed for photo sessions yielding high-fashion self-portraits at $34.95 each. There was no stopping, no slowing down. I passed Mug Me, Queen for a Day, and Barnyard Buddies, and stood in the Brookstone store examining a catalogue: a gopher "eliminator" for $40 (it's a vibrating, anodized-aluminum stake), a "no-stoop" shoehorn for $10, a nose-hair trimmer for $18. At the arcade inside Knott's Camp Snoopy I watched while teenagers played Guardians of the 'Hood, Total Carnage, Final Fight, and Varth Operation Thunderstorm; a small crowd of them had gathered around a lean, cool character who stood calmly shooting video cowpokes in a game called Mad Dog McCree. Left thumb on his silver belt buckle, biceps pulsing, he banged away without remorse while dozens of his enemies crumpled and died in alleyways and dusty streets.

At Amazing Pictures a teenage boy had his photograph taken as a bodybuilder—his face smoothly grafted onto a rippling body—then proceeded to purchase this pleasing image on a poster, a sweatshirt, and a coffee mug. At Painted Tipi there was wild rice for sale, hand-harvested from Leech Lake, Minnesota. At Animalia I came across a polyresin figurine of a turtle retailing for $3,200. At Bloomingdale's I pondered a denim shirt with its sleeves ripped away, the sort of thing available at used-clothing stores (the "grunge look," a Bloomingdale's employee explained), on sale for $125. Finally, at a gift shop in Knott's Camp Snoopy, I came across a game called Electronic Mall Madness, put out by Milton Bradley. On the box, three twelve-year-old girls with good features happily vied to beat one another to the game-board mall's best sales.

At last I achieved an enforced self-arrest, anchoring myself against a bench while the mall tilted on its axis. Two pubescent girls in retainers and braces sat beside me sipping coffees topped with whipped cream and chocolate sprinkles, their shopping bags gathered tightly around their legs, their eyes fixed on the passing crowds. They came, they said, from Shakopee—"It's nowhere," one of them explained. The megamall, she added, was "a buzz at first, but now it seems pretty normal. 'Cept my parents are like Twenty Questions every time I want to come here. 'Specially since the shooting."

On a Sunday night, she elaborated, three people had been wounded when shots were fired in a dispute over a San Jose Sharks jacket. "In the *mall*," her friend reminded me. "Right here at megamall. A shooting."

"It's like nowhere's safe," the first added.

The sipped their coffees and explicated for me the plot of a film they saw as relevant, a horror movie called *Dawn of the Dead*, which they had each viewed a half-dozen times. In the film, they explained, apocalypse had come, and the survivors had repaired to a shopping mall as the most likely place to make their last stand in a poisoned, impossible world. And this would have been perfectly all right, they insisted, except that the place had also attracted hordes of the infamous living dead—sentient corpses who had not relinquished their attraction to indoor shopping.

I moved on and contemplated a computerized cash register in the infant's section of the Nordstrom store: "The Answer Is Yes!!!" its monitor reminded clerks. "Customer Service Is Our Number One Priority!" Then back at Bloomingdale's I contemplated a bank of televisions playing incessantly an advertisement for Egoïste, a men's cologne from Chanel. In the ad a woman on a wrought-iron balcony tossed her black hair about and screamed long and passionately; then there were many women screaming passionately, too, and throwing balcony shutters open and closed, and this was all followed by a bottle of the cologne displayed where I could get a good look at it. The brief, strange drama repeated itself until I could no longer stand it.

America's first fully enclosed shopping center—Southdale Center, in Edina, Minnesota—is a ten-minute drive from the Mall of America and thirty-six years its senior. (It is no coincidence that the Twin Cities area is such a prominent player in mall history: Minnesota is subject to the sort of severe weather that makes climate-controlled shopping seductive.) Opened in 1956, Southdale spawned an era of fervid mall construction and generated a vast new industry. Shopping centers proliferated so rapidly that by the end of 1992, says the National Research Bureau, there were nearly 39,000 of them operating everywhere across the country. But while malls recorded a much-ballyhooed success in the America of the 1970s and early 1980s, they gradually became

25

less profitable to run as the exhausted and overwhelmed American worker in-evitably lost interest in leisure shopping. Pressed for time and short on money, shoppers turned to factory outlet centers, catalogue purchasing, and "category killers" (specialty stores such as Home Depot and Price Club) at the expense of shopping malls. The industry, unnerved, reinvented itself, relying on smaller and more convenient local centers—especially the familiar neighborhood strip mall—and building far fewer large regional malls in an effort to stay afloat through troubled times. With the advent of cable television's Home Shopping Network and the proliferation of specialty catalogue retailers (whose access to computerized market research has made them, in the Nineties, powerful com-petitors), the mall industry reeled yet further. According to the International Council of Shopping Centers, new mall construction in 1992 was a third of what it had been in 1989, and the value of mall-construction contracts dropped 60 percent in the same three-year period.

Anticipating a future in which millions of Americans will prefer to shop in the security of their living rooms—conveniently accessing online retail compa-nies as a form of quiet evening entertainment—the mall industry, after less than forty years, experienced a full-blown mid-life crisis. It was necessary for the industry to re-invent itself once more, this time with greater attentiveness to the qualities that would allow it to endure relentless change. Anxiety-ridden and sapped of vitality, mall builders fell back on an ancient truth, one capable of sustaining them through troubled seasons: they discovered what humanity had always understood, that shopping and frivolity go hand in hand and are inherently symbiotic. *If you build it fun, they will come.*

30   The new bread-and-circuses approach to mall building was first ventured in 1985 by the four Ghermezian brothers—Raphael, Nader, Bahman, and Es-kandar—builders of Canada's $750 million West Edmonton Mall, which in-cluded a water slide, an artificial lake, a miniature-golf course, a hockey rink, and forty-seven rides in an amusement park known as Fantasyland. The com-plex quickly generated sales revenues at twice the rate per square foot of retail space that could be squeezed from a conventional outlet mall, mostly by devel-oping its own shopping synergy: people came for a variety of reasons and to do a variety of things. West Edmonton's carnival atmosphere, it gradually emerged, lubricated pocketbooks and inspired the sort of impulse buying on which malls everywhere thrive. To put the matter another way, it was time for a shopping-and-pleasure palace to be attempted in the United States.

After selling the Mall of America concept to Minnesotans in 1985, the Ghermezians joined forces with their American counterparts—Mel and Herb Simon of Indianapolis, owners of the NBA's Indiana Pacers and the nation's second-largest developers of shopping malls. The idea, in the beginning, was to outdo West Edmonton by building a mall far larger and more expensive—something visionary, a wonder of the world—and to include such attractions as fashionable hotels, an elaborate tour de force aquarium, and a monorail to the Minneapolis–St. Paul airport. Eventually the project was downscaled sub-stantially: a million square feet of floor space was eliminated, the construction budget was cut, and the aquarium and hotels were never built (reserved, said marketing director Maureen Hooley, for "phase two" of the mall's development). Japan's Mitsubishi Bank, Mitsui Trust, and Chuo Trust together put up a reported $400 million to finance the cost of construction, and Teachers Insurance and Annuity Association (the majority owner of the Mall of America) came through with another $225 million. At a total bill of $625 million, the mall was ultimately a less ambitious project than its forebear up north on the Canadian plains, and neither as large nor as gaudy. Reflecting the economy's downturn, the parent companies of three of the mall's anchor tenants—Sears, Macy's, and Bloomingdale's—were battling serious financial trouble and needed substantial transfusions from mall developers to have their stores ready by opening day.

The mall expects to spend millions on marketing itself during its initial year of operation and has lined up the usual corporate sponsors—Ford, Pepsi, US West—in an effort to build powerful alliances. Its public-relations representatives travel to towns such as Rapid City, South Dakota, and Sioux City, Iowa, in order to drum up interest within the Farm Belt. Northwest Airlines, another corporate sponsor, offers package deals from London and Tokyo and fare adjustments for those willing to come from Bismarck, North Dakota; Cedar Rapids, Iowa; and Kalamazoo or Grand Rapids, Michigan. Calling itself a "premier tourism destination," the mall draws from a primary tourist market that incorporates the eleven Midwest states (and two Canadian provinces) lying within a day's drive of its parking lots. It also estimates that in its first six months of operation, 5.3 million out of 16 million visitors came from beyond the Twin Cities metropolitan area.

The mall has forecast a much-doubted figure of 46 million annual visits by 1996—four times the number of annual visits to Disneyland, for example, and twelve times the visits to the Grand Canyon. The number, Maureen Hooley explained, seems far less absurd when one takes into account that mall pilgrims make far more repeat visits—as many as eighty in a single year—than visitors to theme parks such as Disneyland. Relentless advertising and shrewd promotion, abetted by the work of journalists like myself, assure the mall that visitors will come in droves—at least for the time being. The national media have comported themselves as if the new mall were a place of light and promise, full of hope and possibility. Meanwhile the Twin Cities' media have been shameless: on opening night Minneapolis's WCCO-TV aired a one-hour mall special, hosted by local news anchors Don Shelby and Colleen Needles, and the St. Paul Pioneer Press (which was named an "official" sponsor of the opening) dedicated both a phone line and a weekly column to answering esoteric mall questions. Not to be outdone, the Minneapolis Star Tribune developed a special graphic to draw readers to mall stories and printed a vast Sunday supplement before opening day under the heading A WHOLE NEW MALLGAME. By the following Wednesday all perspective was in eclipse: the local press reported that at 9:05 A.M., the mall's Victoria's Secret outlet had recorded its first sale, a pair of blue/green silk men's boxer shorts; that mall developers Mel and Herb Simon ate black-bean soup for lunch at 12:30 P.M.; that Kimberly Levis, four years old, constructed a rectangular column nineteen bricks high at the mall's Lego Imagination Center; and that mall officials had retained a plumber on standby in case difficulties arose with the mall's toilets.

From all of this coverage—and from the words you now read—the mall gains status as a phenomenon worthy of our time and consideration: place as celebrity. The media encourage us to visit our megamall in the obligatory fashion we flock to *Jurassic Park*—because it is there, all glitter and glow, a piece of the terrain, a season's diversion, an assumption on the cultural landscape. All of us will want to be in on the conversation and, despite ourselves, we will go.

35   Lost in the fun house I shopped till I dropped, but the scale of the mall eventually overwhelmed me and I was unable to make a purchase. Finally I met Chuck Brand on a bench in Knott's Camp Snoopy; he was seventy-two and, in his personal assessment of it, had lost at least 25 percent of his mind. "It's fun being a doozy," he confessed to me. "The security cops got me figured and keep their distance. I don't get hassled for hanging out, not shopping. Because the deal is, when you're seventy-two, man, you're just about all done shopping."

After forty-seven years of selling houses in Minneapolis, Chuck comes to the mall every day. He carries a business card with his picture on it, his company name and phone number deleted and replaced by his pager code. His wife drops him at the mall at 10:00 A.M. each morning and picks him up again at six; in between he sits and watches. "I can't sit home and do nothing," he insisted. When I stood to go he assured me he understood: I was young and had things I had to do. "Listen," he added, "thanks for talking to me, man. I've been sitting in this mall for four months now and nobody ever said nothing."

The next day I descended into the mall's enormous basement, where its business offices are located. "I'm sorry to have to bring this up," my prearranged mall guide, Michelle Biesiada, greeted me. "But you were seen talking to one of our housekeepers—one of the people who empty the garbage? —and really, you aren't supposed to do that."

Later we sat in the mall's security center, a subterranean computerized command post where two uniformed officers manned a bank of television screens. The Mall of America, it emerged, employed 109 surveillance cameras to monitor the various activities of its guests, and had plans to add yet more. There were cameras in the food courts and parking lots, in the hallways and in Knott's Camp Snoopy. From where we sat, it was possible to monitor thirty-six locations simultaneously; it was also possible, with the use of a zoom feature, to narrow in on an object as small as a hand, a license plate, or a wallet.

While we sat in the darkness of the security room, enjoying the voyeuristic pleasures it allowed (I, for one, felt a giddy sense of power), a security guard noted something of interest occurring in one of the parking lots. The guard engaged a camera's zoom feature, and soon we were given to understand that a couple of bored shoppers were enjoying themselves by fornicating in the front seat of a parked car. An officer was dispatched to knock on their door and discreetly suggest that they move themselves along; the Mall of America was no place for this. "If they want to have sex they'll have to go elsewhere," a security officer told me. "We don't have anything against sex, per se, but we don't want it happening in our parking lots."

I left soon afterward for a tour of the mall's basement, a place of perpetual concrete corridors and home to a much-touted recyclery. Declaring itself "the most environmentally conscious shopping center in the industry," the Mall of America claims to recycle up to 80 percent of its considerable refuse and points to its "state-of-the-art" recycling system as a symbol of its dedication to Mother Earth. Yet Rick Doering of Browning-Ferris Industries—the company contracted to manage the mall's 700 tons of monthly garbage— described the on-site facility as primarily a public-relations gambit that actually recycles only a third of the mall's tenant waste and little of what is discarded by its thousands of visitors; furthermore, he admitted, the venture is unprofitable to Browning-Ferris, which would find it far cheaper to recycle the mall's refuse somewhere other than in its basement.

A third-floor "RecycleNOW Center," located next to Macy's and featuring educational exhibits, is designed to enhance the mall's self-styled image as a national recycling leader. Yet while the mall's developers gave Macy's $35 million to cover most of its "build-out" expenses (the cost of transforming the mall's basic structure into finished, customer-ready floor space), Browning-Ferris got nothing in build-out costs and operates the center at a total loss, paying rent equivalent to that paid by the mall's retailers. As a result, the company has had to look for ways to keep its costs to a minimum, and the mall's garbage is now sorted by developmentally disabled adults working a conveyor belt in the basement. Doering and I stood watching them as they picked at a stream of paper and plastic bottles; when I asked about their pay, he flinched and grimaced, then deflected me toward another supervisor, who said that wages were based on daily productivity. Did this mean that they made less than minimum wage? I inquired. The answer was yes.

Upstairs once again, I hoped for relief from the basement's oppressive, concrete gloom, but the mall felt densely crowded and with panicked urgency I made an effort to leave. I ended up instead at Knott's Camp Snoopy —the seven-acre theme park at the center of the complex—a place intended to alleviate claustrophobia by "bringing the outdoors indoors." Its interior landscape, the press kit claims, "was inspired by Minnesota's natural habitat— forests, meadows, river banks, and marshes . . ." And "everything you see, feel, smell and hear adds to the illusion that it's summertime, seventy degrees and you're outside enjoying the awesome splendor of the Minnesota woods."

Creators of this illusion had much to contend with, including sixteen carnival-style midway rides, such as the Pepsi Ripsaw, the Screaming Yellow Eagle, Paul Bunyan's Log Chute by Brawny, Tumbler, Truckin', and Huff 'n' Puff; fifteen places for visitors to eat, such as Funnel Cakes, Stick Dogs and Campfire Burgers, Taters, Pizza Oven, and Wilderness Barbecue; seven shops with names like Snoopy's Boutique, Joe Cool's Hot Shop, and Camp Snoopy Toys; and such assorted attractions as Pan for Gold, Hunter's Paradise Shooting Gallery, the Snoopy Fountain, and the video arcade that includes the game Mad Dog McCree.

40

As if all this were not enough to cast a serious pall over the Minnesota woods illusion, the theme park's designers had to contend with the fact that they could use few plants native to Minnesota. At a constant temperature of seventy degrees, the mall lends itself almost exclusively to tropical varieties— orange jasmine, black olive, oleander, hibiscus—and not at all to the conifers of Minnesota, which require a cold dormancy period. Deferring ineluctably to this troubling reality, Knott's Camp Snoopy brought in 526 tons of plants— tropical rhododendrons, willow figs, buddhist pines, azaleas—from such places as Florida, Georgia, and Mississippi.

45   Anne Pryor, a Camp Snoopy marketing representative, explained to me that these plants were cared for via something called "integrated pest management," which meant the use of predators such as ladybugs instead of pesticides. Yet every member of the landscape staff I spoke to described a campaign of late-night pesticide spraying as a means of controlling the theme park's enemies—mealybugs, aphids, and spider mites. Two said they had argued for integrated pest management as a more environmentally sound method of controlling insects but that to date it had not been tried.

Even granting that Camp Snoopy is what it claims to be—an authentic version of Minnesota's north woods tended by environmentally correct means—the question remains whether it makes sense to place a forest in the middle of the country's largest shopping complex. Isn't it true that if people want woods, they are better off not going to a mall?

On Valentine's Day last February—cashing in on the promotional scheme of a local radio station—ninety-two couples were married en masse in a ceremony at the Mall of America. They rode the roller coaster and the Screaming Yellow Eagle and were photographed beside a frolicking Snoopy, who wore an immaculate tuxedo. "As we stand here together at the Mall of America," presiding district judge Richard Spicer declared, "we are reminded that there is a place for fun in your life and you have found it in each other." Six months earlier, the Reverend Leith Anderson of the Wooddale Church in Eden Prairie conducted services in the mall's rotunda. Six thousand people had congregated by 10:00 A.M., and Reverend Anderson delivered a sermon entitled "The Unknown God of the Mall." Characterizing the mall as a "direct descendant" of the ancient Greek agoras, the reverend pointed out that, like the Greeks before us, we Americans have many gods. Afterward, of course, the flock went shopping, much to the chagrin of Reverend Delton Krueger, president of the Mall Area Religious Council, who told the *Minneapolis Star Tribune* that as a site for church services, the mall may trivialize religion. "A good many people in the churches," said Krueger, "feel a lot of the trouble in the world is because of materialism."

But a good many people in the mall business today apparently think the trouble lies elsewhere. They are moving forward aggressively on the premise that the dawning era of electronic shopping does not preclude the building of shopping-and-pleasure palaces all around the globe. Japanese developers, in a joint venture with the Ghermezians known as International Malls Incorporated, are planning a $400 million Mall of Japan, with an ice rink, a water park, a fantasy-theme hotel, three breweries, waterfalls, and a sports center. We might shortly predict, too, a Mall of Europe, a Mall of New England, a Mall of California, and perhaps even a Mall of the World. The concept of shopping in a frivolous atmosphere, concocted to loosen consumers' wallets, is poised to proliferate globally. We will soon see monster malls everywhere, rooted in the soil of every nation and offering a preposterous, impossible variety of commodities and entertainments.

The new malls will be planets unto themselves, closed off from this world in the manner of space stations or of science fiction's underground cities. Like the Mall of America and West Edmonton Mall—prototypes for a new generation of shopping centers—they will project a separate and distinct reality in which an "outdoor café" is not outdoors, a "bubbling brook" is a concrete watercourse, and a "serpentine street" is a hallway. Safe, surreal, and outside of time and space, they will offer the mind a potent dreamscape from which there is no present waking. This carefully controlled fantasy—now operable in Minnesota—is so powerful as to inspire psychological addiction or to elicit in visitors a catatonic obsession with the mall's various hallucinations. The new malls will be theatrical, high-tech illusions capable of attracting enormous crowds from distant points and foreign ports. Their psychology has not yet been tried pervasively on the scale of the Mall of America, nor has it been perfected. But in time our marketplaces, all over the world, will be in essential ways interchangeable, so thoroughly divorced from the communities in which they sit that they will appear to rest like permanently docked spaceships against the landscape, windowless and turned in upon their own affairs. The affluent will travel as tourists to each, visiting the holy sites and taking photographs in the catacombs of far-flung temples.

Just as Victorian England is acutely revealed beneath the grandiose domes of its overwrought train stations, so is contemporary America well understood from the upper vistas of its shopping malls, places without either windows or clocks where the temperature is forever seventy degrees. It is facile to believe, from this vantage point, that the endless circumambulations of tens of thousands of strangers—all loaded down with the detritus of commerce—resemble anything akin to community. The shopping mall is not, as the architecture critic Witold Rybczynski has concluded, "poised to become a real urban place" with "a variety of commercial and noncommercial functions." On the contrary, it is poised to multiply around the world as an institution offering only a desolate substitute for the rich, communal lifeblood of the traditional marketplace, which will not survive its onslaught.

Standing on the Mall of America's roof, where I had ventured to inspect its massive ventilation units, I finally achieved a full sense of its vastness, of how it overwhelmed the surrounding terrain—the last sheep farm in sight, the Mississippi River incidental in the distance. Then I peered through the skylights down into Camp Snoopy, where throngs of my fellow citizens caroused happily in the vast entrails of the beast.

50

QUESTIONS

1. In this article, Guterson often uses lists. Why do you think he does so? What effect do the long lists have on readers?

2. At various points in the article, the Mall of America is compared to Mecca, heaven, or a church, and those who shop and seek entertainment there are referred to as "pilgrims." In other places, the mall is referred to as "an addiction" or a drug. Which metaphor do you find more persuasive? Why?

3. Guterson claims that "our architecture testifies to our view of ourselves and to the condition of our souls" (paragraph 4). Write an article about a building you frequently go to (for example, the building in which your classroom is housed; a church, mosque, or synagogue; your dorm; or your parents' home). What does the architecture of that building say about those who frequent it? How does the architecture influence behavior or beliefs?

HUMAN NATURE

PAUL THEROUX *Being a Man*

THERE IS A PATHETIC sentence in the chapter "Fetishism" in Dr. Norman Cameron's book *Personality Development and Psychopathology*. It goes, "Fetishists are nearly always men; and their commonest fetish is a woman's shoe." I cannot read that sentence without thinking that it is just one more awful thing about being a man—and perhaps it is an important thing to know about us.

I have always disliked being a man. The whole idea of manhood in America is pitiful, in my opinion. This version of masculinity is a little like having to wear an ill-fitting coat for one's entire life (by contrast, I imagine femininity to be an oppressive sense of nakedness). Even the expression "Be a man!" strikes me as insulting and abusive. It means: Be stupid, be unfeeling, obedient, soldierly and stop thinking. Man means "manly"—how can one think about men without considering the terrible ambition of manliness? And yet it is part of every man's life. It is a hideous and crippling lie; it not only insists on difference and connives at superiority, it is also by its very nature destructive—emotionally damaging and socially harmful.

The youth who is subverted, as most are, into believing in the masculine ideal is effectively separated from women and he spends the rest of his life finding women a riddle and a nuisance. Of course, there is a female version of this male affliction. It begins with mothers encouraging little girls to say (to other adults) "Do you like my new dress?" In a sense, little girls are traditionally urged to please adults with a kind of coquettishness, while boys are enjoined to behave like monkeys toward each other. The nine-year-old coquette proceeds to become womanish in a subtle power game in which she learns to be sexually indispensable, socially decorative and always alert to a man's sense of inadequacy.

Femininity—being lady-like—implies needing a man as witness and seducer; but masculinity celebrates the exclusive company of men. That is why it is so grotesque; and that is also why there is no manliness without inadequacy—because it denies men the natural friendship of women.

It is very hard to imagine any concept of manliness that does not belittle

5

From Theroux's collection of essays Sunrise with Seamonsters *(1985).*

women, and it begins very early. At an age when I wanted to meet girls—let's say the treacherous years of thirteen to sixteen—I was told to take up a sport, get more fresh air, join the Boy Scouts, and I was urged not to read so much. It was the 1950s and if you asked too many questions about sex you were sent to camp—boy's camp, of course: the nightmare. Nothing is more unnatural or prison-like than a boy's camp, but if it were not for them we would have no Elks' Lodges, no pool rooms, no boxing matches, no Marines.

And perhaps no sports as we know them. Everyone is aware of how few in number are the athletes who behave like gentlemen. Just as high school basketball teaches you how to be a poor loser, the manly attitude toward sports seems to be little more than a recipe for creating bad marriages, social misfits, moral degenerates, sadists, latent rapists and just plain louts. I regard high school sports as a drug far worse than marijuana, and it is the reason that the average tennis champion, say, is a pathetic oaf.

Any objective study would find the quest for manliness essentially right-wing, puritanical, cowardly, neurotic and fueled largely by a fear of women. It is also certainly philistine. There is no book-hater like a Little League coach. But indeed all the creative arts are obnoxious to the manly ideal, because at their best the arts are pursued by uncompetitive and essentially solitary people. It makes it very hard for a creative youngster, for any boy who expresses the desire to be alone seems to be saying that there is something wrong with him.

It ought to be clear by now that I have something of an objection to the way we turn boys into men. It does not surprise me that when the President of the United States has his customary weekend off he dresses like a cowboy—it is both a measure of his insecurity and his willingness to please. In many ways, American culture does little more for a man than prepare him for modeling clothes in the L. L. Bean catalog. I take this as a personal insult because for many years I found it impossible to admit to myself that I wanted to be a writer. It was my guilty secret, because being a writer was incompatible with being a man.

There are people who might deny this, but that is because the American writer, typically, has been so at pains to prove his manliness that we have come to see literariness and manliness as mingled qualities. But first there was a fear that writing was not a manly profession—indeed, not a profession at all. (The paradox in American letters is that it has always been easier for a woman to write and for a man to be published.) Growing up, I had thought of sports as wasteful and humiliating, and the idea of manliness was a bore. My wanting to become a writer was not a flight from that oppressive roleplaying, but I quickly saw that it was at odds with it. Everything in stereotyped manliness goes against the life of the mind. The Hemingway personality is too tedious to go into here, and in any case his exertions are well known, but certainly it was not until this aberrant behavior was examined by feminists in the 1960s that any male writer dared question the pugnacity in Hemingway's fiction. All the bullfighting and arm wrestling and elephant shooting diminished Hemingway as a writer, but it is consistent with a prevailing attitude in American writing: one cannot be a male writer without first proving that one is a man.

It is normal in America for a man to be dismissive or even somewhat   10
apologetic about being a writer. Various factors make it easier. There is a
heartiness about journalism that makes it acceptable—journalism is the man-
liest form of American writing and, therefore, the profession the most
independent-minded women seek (yes, it is an illusion, but that is my
point). Fiction-writing is equated with a kind of dispirited failure and is only
manly when it produces wealth—money is masculinity. So is drinking. Being a
drunkard is another assertion, if misplaced, of manliness. The American male
writer is traditionally proud of his heavy drinking. But we are also a very
literal-minded people. A man proves his manhood in America in old-
fashioned ways. He kills lions, like Hemingway; or he hunts ducks, like
Nathanael West; or he makes pronouncements like, "A man should carry
enough knife to defend himself with," as James Jones once said to a *Life* inter-
viewer. Or he says he can drink you under the table. But even tiny drunken
William Faulkner loved to mount a horse and go fox hunting, and Jack Ker-
ouac roistered up and down Manhattan in a lumberjack shirt (and spent every
night of *The Subterraneans* with his mother in Queens). And we are familiar
with the lengths to which Norman Mailer is prepared, in his endearing way, to
prove that he is just as much a monster as the next man.[1]

When the novelist John Irving was revealed as a wrestler, people took him to
be a very serious writer; and even a bubble reputation like Erich (*Love Story*) Se-
gal's was enhanced by the news that he ran the marathon in a respectable time.
How surprised we would be if Joyce Carol Oates were revealed as a sumo
wrestler or Joan Didion active in pumping iron. "Lives in New York City with her
three children" is the typical woman writer's biographical note, for just as the
male writer must prove he has achieved a sort of muscular manhood, the woman
writer—or rather her publicists—must prove her motherhood.

There would be no point in saying any of this if it were not generally accepted that to be a man is somehow—even now in feminist-influenced America—a privilege. It is on the contrary an unmerciful and punishing burden.
Being a man is bad enough; being manly is appalling (in this sense, women's
lib has done much more for men than for women). It is the sinister silliness of
men's fashions, and a clubby attitude in the arts. It is the subversion of good
students. It is the so-called Dress Code of the Ritz-Carlton Hotel in Boston,
and it is the institutionalized cheating in college sports. It is the most primitive
insecurity.

And this is also why men often object to feminism but are afraid to explain why: of course women have a justified grievance, but most men believe—
and with reason—that their lives are just as bad.

---

1. The writers named in this paragraph and the next are twentieth-century Americans
whose personal lives may be seen as conforming (or not conforming, in the cases of
Oates and Didion) to stereotypical ideas of masculinity.

QUESTIONS

1. In this essay, Theroux makes many negative statements about being a man—or worse, being manly. Do you agree with his assessment of what it means to be a man or to be "manly"? Why or why not?

2. In paragraph 2, Theroux uses similes to describe his feelings about masculinity and femininity, claiming that "masculinity is . . . like having to wear an ill-fitting coat for one's entire life" and imagining "femininity to be an oppressive sense of nakedness." Write two similes, one describing your sense of what it is to be masculine, the other describing your sense of what it is to be feminine. How do your similes supplement, or differ from, Theroux's?

3. In paragraph 6, Theroux says he regards "high school sports as a drug far worse than marijuana." Consider his attitude toward sports throughout the essay. How does his sense of sports compare to yours? Explain the differences and similarities in a brief essay.

SCOTT RUSSELL SANDERS *Looking at Women*

ON THAT SIZZLING July afternoon, the girl who crossed at the stoplight in front of our car looked, as my mother would say, as though she had been poured into her pink shorts. The girl's matching pink halter bared her stomach and clung to her nubbin breasts, leaving little to the imagination, as my mother would also say. Until that moment, it had never made any difference to me how much or little a girl's clothing revealed, for my imagination had been entirely devoted to other mysteries. I was eleven. The girl was about fourteen, the age of my buddy Norman who lounged in the back seat with me. Staring after her, Norman elbowed me in the ribs and murmured, "Check out that chassis."

His mother glared around from the driver's seat. "Hush your mouth."

"I was talking about that sweet Chevy," said Norman, pointing out a souped-up jalopy at the curb.

"I know what you were talking about," his mother snapped.

No doubt she did know, since mothers could read minds, but at first I did not have a clue. Chassis? I knew what it meant for a car, an airplane, a radio, or even a cannon to have a chassis. But could a girl have one as well? I glanced after the retreating figure, and suddenly noticed with a sympathetic twitching in my belly the way her long raven ponytail swayed in rhythm to her walk and the way her fanny jostled in those pink shorts. In July's dazzle of sun, her swinging legs and arms beamed at me a semaphore I could almost read.

First published in the Georgia Review (Spring 1989); later reprinted in Sanders's essay collection Secrets of the Universe (1991).

As the light turned green and our car pulled away, Norman's mother cast one more scowl at her son in the rearview mirror, saying, "Just think how it makes her feel to have you two boys gawking at her."

How? I wondered.

"Makes her feel like hot stuff," said Norman, owner of a bold mouth.

"If you don't get your mind out of the gutter, you're going to wind up in the state reformatory," said his mother.

Norman gave a snort. I sank into the seat, and tried to figure out what power had sprung from that sashaying girl to zap me in the belly.   10

Only after much puzzling did it dawn on me that I must finally have drifted into the force-field of sex, as a space traveler who has lived all his years in free fall might rocket for the first time within gravitational reach of a star. Even as a bashful eleven-year-old I knew the word *sex*, of course, and I could paste that name across my image of the tantalizing girl. But a label for a mystery no more explains a mystery than the word *gravity* explains gravity. As I grew a beard and my taste shifted from girls to women, I acquired a more cagey language for speaking of desire, I picked up disarming theories. First by hearsay and then by experiment, I learned the delicious details of making babies. I came to appreciate the urgency for propagation that litters the road with maple seeds and drives salmon up waterfalls and yokes the newest crop of boys to the newest crop of girls. Books in their killjoy wisdom taught me that all the valentines and violins, the waltzes and glances, the long fever and ache of romance, were merely embellishments on biology's instructions that we multiply our kind. And yet, the fraction of desire that actually leads to procreation is so vanishingly small as to seem irrelevant. In his lifetime a man sways to a million longings, only a few of which, or perhaps none at all, ever lead to the fathering of children. Now, thirty years away from that July afternoon, firmly married, twice a father, I am still humming from the power unleashed by the girl in pink shorts, still wondering how it made her feel to have two boys gawk at her, still puzzling over how to dwell in the force-field of desire.

How should a man look at women? It is a peculiarly and perhaps neurotically human question. Billy goats do not fret over how they should look at nanny goats. They look or don't look, as seasons and hormones dictate, and feel what they feel without benefit of theory. There is more billy goat in most men than we care to admit. None of us, however, is pure goat. To live utterly as an animal would make the business of sex far tidier but also drearier. If we tried, like Rousseau,[1] to peel off the layers of civilization and imagine our way back to some pristine man and woman who have not yet been corrupted by hand-me-down notions of sexuality, my hunch is that we would find, in our speculative state of nature, that men regarded women with appalling simplicity. In any case, unlike goats, we dwell in history. What attracts our eyes and rouses our

1. Jean-Jacques Rousseau (1712–1778), Swiss-born French philosopher, author, political theorist, and composer. His closeness to nature, individualism, rebellion against the established social and political order, and glorification of the emotions made him the father of French romanticism.

blood is only partly instinctual. Other forces contend in us as well: the voices of books and religions, the images of art and film and advertising, the entire chorus of culture. Norman's telling me to relish the sight of females and his mother's telling me to keep my eyes to myself are only two of the many voices quarreling in my head.

If there were a rule book for sex, it would be longer than the one for baseball (that byzantine sport), more intricate and obscure than tax instructions from the Internal Revenue Service. What I present here are a few images and reflections that cling, for me, to this one item in such a compendium of rules: How should a man look at women?

Well before I was to see any women naked in the flesh, I saw a bevy of them naked in photographs, hung in a gallery around the bed of my freshman roommate at college. A *Playboy* subscriber, he would pluck the centerfold from its staples each month and tape another airbrushed lovely to the wall. The gallery was in place when I moved in, and for an instant before I realized what I was looking at, all that expanse of skin reminded me of a meat locker back in Newton Falls, Ohio. I never quite shook that first impression, even after I had inspected the pinups at my leisure on subsequent days. Every curve of buttock and breast was news to me, an innocent kid from the Puritan back roads. Today you would be hard pressed to find a college freshman as ignorant as I was of female anatomy, if only because teenagers now routinely watch movies at home that would have been shown, during my teen years, exclusively on the fly-speckled screens of honky-tonk cinemas or in the basement of the Kinsey Institute.[2] I studied those alien shapes on the wall with a curiosity that was not wholly sexual, a curiosity tinged with the wonder that astronomers must have felt when they pored over the early photographs of the far side of the moon.

15   The paper women seemed to gaze back at me, enticing or mocking, yet even in my adolescent dither I was troubled by the phony stare, for I knew this was no true exchange of looks. Those mascaraed eyes were not fixed on me but on a camera. What the models felt as they posed I could only guess—perhaps the boredom of any numbskull job, perhaps the weight of dollar bills, perhaps the sweltering lights of fame, perhaps a tingle of the power that launched a thousand ships.

Whatever their motives, these women had chosen to put themselves on display. For the instant of the photograph, they had become their bodies, as a prizefighter does in the moment of landing a punch, as a weightlifter does in the moment of hoisting a barbell, as a ballerina does in the whirl of a pirouette, as we all do in the crisis of making love or dying. Men, ogling such photographs, are supposed to feel that where so much surface is revealed there can be no depths. Yet I never doubted that behind the makeup and the plump curves and the two dimensions of the image there was an inwardness, a feel-

2. Indiana University's Institute for Sex Research, directed, beginning in 1942, by American biologist Alfred Charles Kinsey (1894–1956).

ing self as mysterious as my own. In fact, during moments when I should have been studying French or thermodynamics, I would glance at my roommate's wall and invent mythical lives for those goddesses. The lives I made up were adolescent ones, to be sure; but so was mine. Without that saving aura of inwardness, these women in the glossy photographs would have become merely another category of objects for sale, alongside the sports cars and stereo systems and liquors advertised in the same pages. If not extinguished, however, their humanity was severely reduced. And if by simplifying themselves they had lost some human essence, then by gaping at them I had shared in the theft.

What did that gaping take from me? How did it affect my way of seeing other women, those who would never dream of lying nude on a fake tiger rug before the million-faceted eye of a camera? The bodies in the photographs were implausibly smooth and slick and inflated, like balloon caricatures that might be floated overhead in a parade. Free of sweat and scars and imperfections, sensual without being fertile, tempting yet impregnable, they were Platonic ideals of the female form, divorced from time and the fluster of living, excused from the perplexities of mind. No actual woman could rival their insipid perfection.

The swains who gathered to admire my roommate's gallery discussed the pinups in the same tones and in much the same language as the farmers back home in Ohio used for assessing cows. The relevant parts of male or female bodies are quickly named—and, the *Kamasutra* and Marquis de Sade[3] notwithstanding, the number of ways in which those parts can be stimulated or conjoined is touchingly small—so these studly conversations were more tedious than chitchat about the weather. I would lie on my bunk pondering calculus or Aeschylus and unwillingly hear the same few nouns and fewer verbs issuing from one mouth after another, and I would feel smugly superior. Here I was, improving my mind, while theirs wallowed in the notorious gutter. Eventually the swains would depart, leaving me in peace, and from the intellectual heights of my bunk I would glance across at those photographs—and yield to the gravity of lust. Idiot flesh! How stupid that a counterfeit stare and artful curves, printed in millions of copies on glossy paper, could arouse me. But there it was, not the first proof of my body's automatism and not the last.

Nothing in men is more machinelike than the flipping of sexual switches. I have never been able to read with a straight face the claims made by D. H. Lawrence[4] and lesser pundits that the penis is a god, a lurking dragon. It more nearly resembles a railroad crossing signal, which stirs into life at intervals to

3. The *Kamasutra*, detailed account (fourth-to-seventh centuries C.E.) of the art and technique of Indian erotics by the sage Vātsyāyana; Marquis de Sade (1740–1814), French author whose works, because of their pornographic and blasphemous subject matter, led to his repeated imprisonment and have been suppressed by the French courts as recently as 1957.
4. David Herbert Lawrence (1885–1930), English novelist and author of *Lady Chatterley's Lover* (1928).

announce, "Here comes a train." Or, if the penis must be likened to an animal, let it be an ill-trained circus dog, sitting up and playing dead and heeling whenever it takes a notion, oblivious of the trainer's commands. Meanwhile, heart, lungs, blood vessels, pupils, and eyelids all assert their independence like the members of a rebellious troupe. Reason stands helpless at the center of the ring, cracking its whip.

20   While he was president, Jimmy Carter raised a brouhaha by confessing in a *Playboy* interview, of all shady places, that he occasionally felt lust in his heart for women. What man hasn't, aside from those who feel lust in their hearts for other men? The commentators flung their stones anyway. Naughty, naughty, they chirped. Wicked Jimmy. Perhaps Mr. Carter could derive some consolation from psychologist Allen Wheelis, who blames male appetite on biology: "We have been selected for desiring. Nothing could have convinced us by argument that it would be worthwhile to chase endlessly and insatiably after women, but something has transformed us from within, a plasmid has invaded our DNA, has twisted our nature so that now this is exactly what we *want* to do." Certainly, by Darwinian logic, those males who were most avid in their pursuit of females were also the most likely to pass on their genes. Consoling it may be, yet it is finally no solution to blame biology. "I am extremely sexual in my desires: I carry them everywhere and at all times," William Carlos Williams[5] tells us on the opening page of his autobiography. "I think that from that arises the drive which empowers us all. Given that drive, a man does with it what his mind directs. In the manner in which he directs that power lies his secret." Whatever the contents of my DNA, however potent the influence of my ancestors, I still must direct that rebellious power. I still must live with the consequences of my looking and my longing.

Aloof on their blankets like goddesses on clouds, the pinups did not belong to my funky world. I was invisible to them, and they were immune to my gaze. Not so the women who passed me on the street, sat near me in classes, shared a table with me in the cafeteria: it was risky to stare at them. They could gaze back, and sometimes did, with looks both puzzling and exciting. It only complicated matters for me to realize that so many of these strangers had taken precautions that men should notice them. The girl in matching pink halter and shorts who set me humming in my eleventh year might only have wanted to keep cool in the sizzle of July. But these alluring college femmes had deeper designs. Perfume, eye shadow, uplift bras (about which I learned in the Sears catalog), curled hair, stockings, jewelry, lipstick, lace—what were these if not hooks thrown out into male waters?

          I recall being mystified in particular by spike heels. They looked painful to me, and dangerous. Danger may have been the point, since the spikes would have made good weapons—they were affectionately known, after all, as stilettos. Or danger may have been the point in another sense, because a woman teetering along on such heels is tipsy, vulnerable, broadcasting her need for

5. American poet and physician (1883–1963).

support. And who better than a man to prop her up, some guy who clomps around in brogans wide enough for the cornerstones of flying buttresses? (For years after college, I felt certain that spike heels had been forever banned, like bustles and foot-binding, but lately they have come back in fashion, and once more one encounters women teetering along on knife points.)

Back in those days of my awakening to women, I was also baffled by lingerie. I do not mean underwear, the proletariat of clothing, and I do not mean foundation garments, pale and sensible. I mean what the woman who lives in the house behind ours—owner of a shop called "Bare Essentials"—refers to as "intimate apparel." Those two words announce that her merchandise is both sexy and expensive. These flimsy items cost more per ounce than truffles, more than frankincense and myrrh. They are put-ons whose only purpose is in being taken off. I have a friend who used to attend the men's-only nights at Bare Essentials, during which he would invariably buy a slinky outfit or two, by way of proving his serious purpose, outfits that wound up in the attic because his wife would not be caught dead in them. Most of the customers at the shop are women, however, as the models are women, and the owner is a woman. What should one make of that? During my college days I knew about intimate apparel only by rumor, not being that intimate with anyone who would have tricked herself out in such finery, but I could see the spike heels and other female trappings everywhere I turned. Why, I wondered then and wonder still, do so many women decorate themselves like dolls? And does that mean they wish to be viewed as dolls?

On this question as on many others, Simone de Beauvoir has clarified matters for me, writing in *The Second Sex*:[6] "The 'feminine' woman in making herself prey tries to reduce man, also, to her carnal passivity; she occupies herself in catching him in her trap, in enchaining him by means of the desires she arouses in him in submissively making herself a thing." Those women who transform themselves into dolls, in other words, do so because that is the most potent identity available to them. "It must be admitted," Beauvoir concedes, "that the males find in woman more complicity than the oppressor usually finds in the oppressed. And in bad faith they take authorization from this to declare that she has *desired* the destiny they have imposed on her."

Complicity, oppressor, bad faith: such terms yank us into a moral realm unknown to goats. While I am saddled with enough male guilt to believe three-quarters of Beauvoir's claim, I still doubt that men are so entirely to blame for the turning of women into sexual dolls. I believe human history is more collaborative than her argument would suggest. It seems unlikely to me that one-half the species could have "imposed" a destiny on the other half, unless that other half were far more craven than the females I have known. Some women have expressed their own skepticism on this point. Thus Joan Didion: "That

25

6. De Beauvoir, French novelist and essayist (1908–1986) who served as one of the most articulate exponents of existentialism; *Le Deuxième Sexe* (1949; translated as *The Second Sex*, 1953), a thorough analysis of women's status in society, became a classic of feminist literature.

many women are victims of condescension and exploitation and sex-role stereotyping was scarcely news, but neither was it news that other women are not: nobody forces women to buy the package." Beauvoir herself recognized that many members of her sex refuse to buy the "feminine" package: "The emancipated woman, on the contrary, wants to be active, a taker, and refuses the passivity man means to impose on her."

Since my college years, back in the murky 1960s, emancipated women have been discouraging their unemancipated sisters from making spectacles of themselves. Don't paint your face like a clown's or drape your body like a mannequin's, they say. Don't bounce on the sidelines in skimpy outfits, screaming your fool head off, while men compete in the limelight for victories. Don't present yourself to the world as a fluff pastry, delicate and edible. Don't waddle across the stage in a bathing suit in hopes of being named Miss This or That.

A great many women still ignore the exhortations. Wherever a crown for beauty is to be handed out, many still line up to stake their claims. Recently, Miss Indiana Persimmon Festival was quoted in our newspaper about the burdens of possessing the sort of looks that snag men's eyes. "Most of the time I enjoy having guys stare at me," she said, "but every once in a while it makes me feel like a piece of meat." The news photograph showed a cheerleader's perky face, heavily made-up, with starched hair teased into a blond cumulus. She put me in mind not of meat but of a plastic figurine, something you might buy from a booth outside a shrine. Nobody should ever be seen as meat, mere juicy stuff to satisfy an appetite. Better to appear as a plastic figurine, which is not meant for eating, and which is a gesture, however crude, toward art. Joyce[7] described the aesthetic response as a contemplation of form without the impulse to action. Perhaps that is what Miss Indiana Persimmon Festival wishes to inspire in those who look at her, perhaps that is what many women who paint and primp themselves desire: to withdraw from the touch of hands and dwell in the eye alone, to achieve the status of art.

By turning herself (or allowing herself to be turned into) a work of art, does a woman truly escape men's proprietary stare? Not often, says the British critic John Berger. Summarizing the treatment of women in Western painting, he concludes that—with a few notable exceptions, such as works by Rubens and Rembrandt—the woman on canvas is a passive object displayed for the pleasure of the male viewer, especially for the owner of the painting, who is, by extension, owner of the woman herself. Berger concludes: "Men look at women. Women watch themselves being looked at. This determines not only most relations between men and women but also the relation of women to themselves. The surveyor of woman in herself is male: the surveyed female. Thus she turns herself into an object—and most particularly an object of vision: a sight."

That sweeping claim, like the one quoted earlier from Beauvoir, also seems to me about three-quarters truth and one-quarter exaggeration. I know

7. James Joyce (1882–1941), Irish novelist.

men who outdo the peacock for show, and I know women who are so fully possessed of themselves that they do not give a hang whether anybody notices
them or not. The flamboyant gentlemen portrayed by Van Dyck are no less
aware of being *seen* than are the languid ladies portrayed by Ingres.[8] With or
without clothes, both gentlemen and ladies may conceive of themselves as objects of vision, targets of envy or admiration or desire. Where they differ is in
their potential for action: the men are caught in the midst of a decisive gesture
or on the verge of making one; the women wait like fuel for someone else to
strike a match.

I am not sure the abstract nudes favored in modern art are much of an advance over the inert and voluptuous ones of the old school. Think of two famous examples: Duchamp's *Nude Descending a Staircase* (1912), where the
faceless woman has blurred into a waterfall of jagged shards, or Picasso's *Les
Demoiselles d'Avignon* (1907), where the five angular damsels have been hammered as flat as cookie sheets and fitted with African masks. Neither painting
invites us to behold a woman, but instead to behold what Picasso or Duchamp
can make of one.

The naked women in Rubens, far from being passive, are gleefully active,
exuberant, their sumptuous pink bodies like rainclouds or plump nebulae.
"His nudes are the first ones that ever made me feel happy about my own
body," a woman friend told me in one of the Rubens galleries of the Prado
Museum. I do not imagine any pinup or store-window mannequin or bathing-
suited Miss Whatsit could have made her feel that way. The naked women in
Rembrandt, emerging from the bath or rising from bed, are so private, so cherished in the painter's gaze, that we as viewers see them not as sexual play-
things but as loved persons. A man would do well to emulate that gaze.

I have never thought of myself as a sight. How much that has to do with being
male and how much with having grown up on the back roads where money
was scarce and eyes were few, I cannot say. As a boy, apart from combing my
hair when I was compelled to and regretting the patches on my jeans (only the
poor wore patches), I took no trouble over my appearance. It never occurred to
me that anybody outside my family, least of all a girl, would look at me twice.
As a young man, when young women did occasionally glance my way, without
any prospect of appearing handsome I tried at least to avoid appearing odd. A
standard haircut and the cheapest versions of the standard clothes were camouflage enough. Now as a middle-aged man I have achieved once more that
boyhood condition of invisibility, with less hair to comb and fewer patches to
humble me.

Many women clearly pass through the world aspiring to invisibility. Many
others just as clearly aspire to be conspicuous. Women need not make spectacles of themselves in order to draw the attention of men. Indeed, for my taste,
the less paint and fewer bangles the better. I am as helpless in the presence of

30

8. Anthony Van Dyck (1599–1641), Flemish painter who settled in England in 1632;
Jean-Auguste-Dominique Ingres (1780–1867), French painter.

subtle lures as a male moth catching a whiff of pheromones. I am a sucker for hair ribbons, a scarf at the throat, toes leaking from sandals, teeth bared in a smile. By contrast, I have always been more amused than attracted by the enameled exhibitionists whom our biblical mothers would identify as brazen hussies or painted Jezebels or, in the extreme cases, as whores of Babylon.

To encounter female exhibitionists in their full glory and variety, you need to go to a city. I never encountered ogling as a full-blown sport until I visited Rome, where bands of Italian men joined with gusto in appraising the charms of every passing female, and the passing females vied with one another in demonstrating their charms. In our own cities the most notorious bands of oglers tend to be construction gangs or street crews, men who spend much of their day leaning on the handles of shovels or pausing between bursts of riveting guns, their eyes tracing the curves of passersby. The first time my wife and kids and I drove into Boston we followed the signs to Chinatown, only to discover that Chinatown's miserably congested main street was undergoing repairs. That street also proved to be the city's home for X-rated cinemas and girlie shows and skin shops. LIVE SEX ACTS ON STAGE. PEEP SHOWS. PRIVATE BOOTHS. Caught in a traffic jam, we spent an hour listening to jackhammers and wolf whistles as we crept through the few blocks of pleasure palaces, my son and daughter with their noses hanging out the windows, my wife and I steaming. Lighted marquees peppered by burnt-out bulbs announced the titles of sleazy flicks; life-size posters of naked women flanked the doorways of clubs: leggy strippers in miniskirts, the originals for some of the posters, smoked on the curb between numbers.

35   After we had finally emerged from the zone of eros, eight-year-old Jesse inquired, "What was *that* place all about?"

"Sex for sale," my wife Ruth explained.

That might carry us some way toward a definition of pornography: making flesh into a commodity, flaunting it like any other merchandise, divorcing bodies from selves. By this reckoning, there is a pornographic dimension to much advertising, where a charge of sex is added to products ranging from cars to shaving cream. In fact, the calculated imagery of advertising may be more harmful than the blatant imagery of the pleasure palaces, that frank raunchiness which Kate Millett refers to as the "truthful explicitness of pornography." One can leave the X-rated zone of the city, but one cannot escape the sticky reach of commerce, which summons girls to the high calling of cosmetic glamor, fashion, and sexual display, while it summons boys to the panting chase.

You can recognize pornography, according to D. H. Lawrence, "by the insult it offers, invariably, to sex, and to the human spirit." He should know, Millett argues in *Sexual Politics,* for in her view Lawrence himself was a purveyor of patriarchal and often sadistic pornography. I think she is correct about the worst of Lawrence, and that she identifies a misogynist streak in his work; but she ignores his career-long struggle to achieve a more public, tolerant vision of sexuality as an exchange between equals. Besides, his novels and stories all bear within themselves their own critiques. George Steiner reminds us that "the list of writers who have had the genius to enlarge our actual compass of sexual awareness, who have given the erotic play of the mind a novel focus, an area of recognition previously unknown or fallow, is very small." Lawrence belongs on that brief list. The chief insult to the human spirit is to deny it, to claim that we are merely conglomerations of molecules, to pretend that we exist purely as bundles of appetites or as food for the appetites of others.

Men commit that insult toward women out of ignorance, but also out of dread. Allen Wheelis again: "Men gather in pornographic shows, not to stimulate desire, as they may think, but to diminish fear. It is the nature of the show to reduce the woman, discard her individuality, her soul, make her into an object, thereby enabling the man to handle her with greater safety, to use her as a toy. . . . As women move increasingly toward equality, the felt danger to men increases, leading to an increase in pornography and, since there are some men whose fears cannot even so be stilled, to an increase also in violence against women."

Make her into an object: all the hurtful ways for men to look at women are variations on this betrayal. "Thus she turns herself into an object," writes Berger. A woman's ultimate degradation is in "submissively making herself a thing," writes Beauvoir. To be turned into an object—whether by the brush of a painter or the lens of a photographer or the eye of a voyeur, whether by hunger or poverty or enslavement, by mugging or rape, bullets or bombs, by hatred, racism, car crashes, fires, or falls—is for each of us the deepest dread; and to reduce another person to an object is the primal wrong.

40

Caught in the vortex of desire, we have to struggle to recall the wholeness of persons, including ourselves. Beauvoir speaks of the temptation we all occasionally feel to give up the struggle for a self and lapse into the inertia of an object: "Along with the ethical urge of each individual to affirm his subjective existence, there is also the temptation to forgo liberty and become a thing." A woman in particular, given so much encouragement to lapse into thinghood, "is often very well pleased with her role as the *Other*."

Yet one need not forgo liberty and become a thing, without a center or a self, in order to become the Other. In our mutual strangeness, men and women can be doorways one for another, openings into the creative mystery that we share by virtue of our existence in the flesh. "To be sensual," James Baldwin writes, "is to respect and rejoice in the force of life, of life itself, and to be *present* in all that one does, from the effort of loving to the breaking of bread." The effort of loving is reciprocal, not only in act but in desire, an *I* addressing a *Thou*, a meeting in that vivid presence. The distance a man stares across at a woman, or a woman at a man, is a gulf in the soul, out of which a voice cries, *Leap, leap*. One day all men may cease to look on themselves as prototypically human and on women as lesser miracles; women may cease to feel themselves the targets for desire; men and women both may come to realize that we are all mere flickerings in the universal fire; and then none of us, male or female, need give up humanity in order to become the *Other*.

Ever since I gawked at the girl in pink shorts, I have dwelt knowingly in the force-field of sex. Knowingly or not, it is where we all dwell. Like the masses of planets and stars, our bodies curve the space around us. We radiate signals constantly, radio sources that never go off the air. We cannot help being centers of attraction and repulsion for one another. That is not all we are by a long shot, nor all we are capable of feeling, and yet, even after our much-needed revolution in sexual consciousness, the power of eros will still turn our heads and hearts. In a world without beauty pageants, there will still be beauty, however its definition may have changed. As long as men have eyes, they will gaze with yearning and confusion at women.

When I return to the street with the ancient legacy of longing coiled in my DNA, and the residues from a thousand generations of patriarchs silting my brain, I encounter women whose presence strikes me like a slap of wind in the face. I must prepare a gaze that is worthy of their splendor.

QUESTIONS

1. Several sections of this essay are grounded in specific episodes from Sanders's life. Identify the episodes and explain how he uses them.

2. The five sections of this essay are separated by typographical space rather than connected by prose transitions. Determine the content of each section and explain its relation to the content of the section that precedes it. Describe Sanders's strategies of organization and development.

3. In paragraph 12 Sanders asks: "How should a man look at women?" What is his answer? Where does he provide it?

4. Write an essay in which you answer, in your own terms, Sanders's question, "How should a man look at women?"

ANDREW SULLIVAN   *What Is a Homosexual?*

GAY ADOLESCENTS are offered what every heterosexual teenager longs for: to be invisible in the girls' locker room. But you are invisible in the boys' locker room, your desire as unavoidable as its object. In that moment, you learn the first homosexual lesson: that your survival depends upon self-concealment. I remember specifically coming back to high school after a long summer when I was fifteen and getting changed in the locker room for the first time again with a guy I had long had a crush on. But since the vacation, he

From Sullivan's 1995 book, Virtually Normal: An Argument about Homosexuality.

had developed enormously: suddenly he had hair on his chest, his body had grown and strengthened, he was—clearly—no longer a boy. In front of me, he took off his shirt, and unknowingly, slowly, erotically stripped. I became literally breathless, overcome by the proximity of my desire. The gay teenager learns in that kind of event a form of control and sublimation, of deception and self-contempt, that never leaves his consciousness. He learns that that which would most give him meaning is most likely to destroy him in the eyes of others; that the condition of his friendships is the subjugation of himself.

In the development of any human being, these are powerful emotions. They form a person. The homosexual learns to make distinctions between his sexual desire and his emotional longings—not because he is particularly prone to objectification of the flesh, but because he needs to survive as a social and sexual being. The society separates these two entities, and for a long time the homosexual has no option but to keep them separate. He learns certain rules; and, as with a child learning grammar, they are hard, later on in life, to unlearn.

It's possible, I think, that whatever society teaches or doesn't teach about homosexuality, this fact will always be the case. No homosexual child, surrounded overwhelmingly by heterosexuals, will feel at home in his sexual and emotional world, even in the most tolerant of cultures. And every homosexual child will learn the rituals of deceit, impersonation, and appearance. Anyone who believes political, social, or even cultural revolution will change this fundamentally is denying reality. This isolation will always hold. It is definitional of homosexual development. And children are particularly cruel. At the age of eleven, no one wants to be the odd one out; and in the arena of dating and hormones, the exclusion is inevitably a traumatic one.

It's also likely to be forlorn. Most people are liable to meet emotional rejection by sheer force of circumstance; but for a homosexual, the odds are simply far, far higher. My own experience suggests that somewhere between two and five percent of the population have involuntarily strong emotional and sexual attractions to the same sex. Which means that the pool of possible partners *starts* at one in twenty to one in fifty. It's no wonder, perhaps, that male homosexual culture has developed an ethic more of anonymous or promiscuous sex than of committed relationships. It's as if the hard lessons of adolescence lower permanently—by the sheer dint of the odds—the aspiration for anything more.

Did I know what I was? Somewhere, maybe. But it was much easier to know what I wasn't. I wasn't going to be able to enter into the world of dating girls; I wasn't going to be able to feel fully comfortable among the heterosexual climate of the male teenager. So I decided, consciously or subconsciously, to construct a trajectory of my life that would remove me from their company; give me an excuse, provide a dignified way out. In Anglo-Saxon culture, the wonk has such an option: he's too nerdy or intellectual to be absorbed by girls. And there is something masculine and respected in the discipline of the arts and especially the sciences. You can gain respect and still be different.

So I threw myself into my schoolwork, into (more dubiously) plays, into

5

creative writing, into science fiction. Other homosexuals I have subsequently met pursued other strategies: some paradoxically threw themselves into sports, outjocking the jocks, gaining ever greater proximity, seeking respect, while knowing all the time that they were doomed to rejection. Others withdrew into isolation and despair. Others still, sensing their difference, flaunted it. At my high school, an older boy insisted on wearing full makeup to class; and he was accepted in a patronizing kind of way, his brazen otherness putting others at ease. They knew where they were with him; and he felt at least comfortable with their stable contempt. The rest of us who lived in a netherworld of sexual insecurity were not so lucky.

Most by then had a far more acute sense of appearances than those who did not need to hide anything; and our sense of irony, and of aesthetics, assumed a precociously arch form, and drew us subtly together. Looking back, I realize that many of my best friends in my teen years were probably homosexual; and that somewhere in our coded, embarrassed dialogue we admitted it. Many of us also embraced those ideologies that seemed most alien to what we feared we might be: of the sports jock, of the altar boy, of the young conservative. They were the ultimate disguises. And our recognition of ourselves in the other only confirmed our desire to keep it quiet.

I should add that many young lesbians and homosexuals seem to have had a much easier time of it. For many, the question of sexual identity was not a critical factor in their life choices or vocation, or even a factor at all. Perhaps because of a less repressive upbringing or because of some natural ease in the world, they affected a simple comfort with their fate, and a desire to embrace it. These people alarmed me: their very ease was the sternest rebuke to my own anxiety, because it rendered it irrelevant. But later in life, I came to marvel at the naturalness of their self-confidence, in the face of such concerted communal pressure, and to envy it. I had the more common self-dramatizing urge of the tortured homosexual, trapped between feeling wicked and feeling ridiculous. It's shameful to admit it, but I was more traumatized by the latter than by the former: my pride was more formidable a force than my guilt.

When people ask the simple question, *What is a homosexual?* I can only answer with stories like these. I could go on, but too many stories have already been told. Ask any lesbian or homosexual, and they will often provide a similar account. I was once asked at a conservative think tank what evidence I had that homosexuality was far more of an orientation than a choice, and I was forced to reply quite simply: my life. It's true that I have met a handful of lesbians and gay men over the years who have honestly told me that they genuinely had a choice in the matter (and a few heterosexuals who claim they too chose their orientation). I believe them; but they are the exception and not the rule. As homosexual lives go, my own was somewhat banal and typical.

10   This is not, of course, the end of the matter. Human experience begins with such facts, it doesn't end with them. There's a lamentable tendency to try to find some definitive solution to permanent human predicaments—in a string of DNA, in a conclusive psychological survey, in an analysis of hypo-

thalami, in a verse of the Bible—in order to cut the argument short. Or to insist on the emotional veracity of a certain experience and expect it to trump any other argument on the table. But none of these things can replace the political and moral argument about how a society should deal with the presence of homosexuals in its midst. I relate my experience here not to impress or to shock or to gain sympathy, but merely to convey what the homosexual experience is actually like. You cannot discuss something until you know roughly what it is. * * *

In a society more and more aware of its manifold cultures and subcultures, we have been educated to be familiar and comfortable with what has been called "diversity": the diversity of perspective, culture, meaning. And this diversity is usually associated with what are described as cultural constructs: race, gender, sexuality, and so on. But as the obsession with diversity intensifies, the possibility of real difference alarms and terrifies all the more. The notion of collective characteristics—of attributes more associated with blacks than with whites, with Asians than with Latinos, with gay men than with straight men, with men than with women—has become anathema. They are marginalized as "stereotypes." The acceptance of diversity has come to mean the acceptance of the essential sameness of all types of people, and the danger of generalizing among them at all. In fact, it has become virtually a definition of "racist" to make any substantive generalizations about a particular ethnicity, and a definition of "homophobic" to make any generalizations about homosexuals.

What follows, then, is likely to be understood as "homophobic." But I think it's true that certain necessary features of homosexual life lead to certain unavoidable features of homosexual character. This is not to say that they define any random homosexual: they do not. As with any group or way of life, there are many, many exceptions. Nor is it to say that they define the homosexual life: it should be clear by now that I believe that the needs and feelings of homosexual children and adolescents are largely interchangeable with those of their heterosexual peers. But there are certain generalizations that can be made about adult homosexuals and lesbians that have the ring of truth.

Of course, in a culture where homosexuals remain hidden and wrapped in self-contempt, in which their emotional development is often stunted and late, in which the closet protects all sorts of self-destructive behavior that a more open society would not, it is still very hard to tell what is inherent in a homosexual life that makes it different, and what is simply imposed upon it. Nevertheless, it seems to me that even in the most tolerant societies, some of the differences that I have just described would inhere.

The experience of growing up profoundly different in emotional and psychological makeup inevitably alters a person's self-perception, tends to make him or her more wary and distant, more attuned to appearance and its foibles, more self-conscious and perhaps more reflective. The presence of homosexuals in the arts, in literature, in architecture, in design, in fashion could be understood, as some have, as a simple response to oppression. Homosexuals have created safe professions within which to hide and protect each other. But

why these professions? Maybe it's also that these are professions of appearance. Many homosexual children, feeling distant from their peers, become experts at trying to figure out how to disguise their inner feelings, to "pass." They
notice the signs and signals of social interaction, because they do not come instinctively. They develop skills early on that help them notice the inflections of
a voice, the quirks of a particular movement, and the ways in which meaning
can be conveyed in code. They have an ear for irony and for double meanings.
Sometimes, by virtue of having to suppress their natural emotions, they find
formal outlets to express themselves: music, theater, art. And so their lives become set on a trajectory which reinforces these trends.

15   As a child, I remember, as I suppressed the natural emotions of an adolescent, how I naturally turned in on myself—writing, painting, and participating
in amateur drama. Or I devised fantasies of future exploits—war leader, parlia-
mentarian, famous actor—that could absorb those emotions that were being
diverted from meeting other boys and developing natural emotional relationships with them. And I developed mannerisms, small ways in which I could express myself, tiny revolts of personal space—a speech affectation, a ridiculous
piece of clothing—that were, in retrospect, attempts to communicate something in code which could not be communicated in language. In this homosexual archness there was, of course, much pain. And it came as no surprise that
once I had become more open about my homosexuality, these mannerisms declined. Once I found the strength to be myself, I had no need to act myself. So
my clothes became progressively more regular and slovenly; I lost interest in
drama; my writing moved from fiction to journalism; my speech actually became less affected.

This, of course, is not a universal homosexual experience. Many homosexuals never become more open, and the skills required to survive the closet remain skills by which to earn a living. And many homosexuals, even once they
no longer need those skills, retain them. My point is simply that the
universal experience of self-conscious difference in childhood and adolescence—common, but not exclusive, to homosexuals—develops identifiable
skills. They are the skills of mimesis; and one of the goods that homosexuals
bring to society is undoubtedly a more highly developed sense of form, of style.
Even in the most open of societies, I think, this will continue to be the case. It
is not something genetically homosexual; it is something environmentally homosexual. And it begins young.

QUESTIONS

1. Throughout this essay Sullivan distinguishes between the "human experience" of all
adolescents and experiences particular to or common among "homosexuals." Make a list
of each. Were there features that you would have listed in the opposite column? What
features did you expect Sullivan to mention that he did not?

2. Sullivan notes that it is currently unfashionable to think in terms of "stereotypes" of

any group, whether based on race, gender, sexuality, or some other classification (paragraph 11). Even so, he has set himself the task of answering the question "What is a homosexual?" How does he define this key term without resorting to stereotypes?

3. Although Sullivan does not advance a political agenda or a set of social reforms, his essay implies actions that would be beneficial to homosexuals and, more generally, to American society. What are these?

4. Write an essay that attempts to define the characteristics of a particular group, using a variation of Sullivan's title, "What Is a ——?"

ANNA QUINDLEN   *Between the Sexes, a Great Divide*

PERHAPS WE ALL have the same memory of the first boy-girl party we attended. The floors were waxed, the music loud, the air thick with the smell of cologne. The boys stood on one side of the room and the girls on the other, each affecting a nonchalance belied by the shuffling male loafers and the occasional high birdlike sound of a female giggle.

Eventually, one of the taller, better-looking boys, perhaps dogged by two slightly shorter, squeakier acolytes, would make the big move across the chasm to ask the cutest girl to dance. Eventually, one of the girls would brave the divide to start a conversation on the other side. We would immediately develop a certain opinion of that girl, so that for the rest of our school years together, pajama parties would fairly crackle when she was not there.

None of us would consciously know it then, but what we were seeing, that great empty space in the center of the floor as fearful as a trapdoor, was the great division between the sexes. It was wonderful to think of the time when it would no longer be there, when the school gym would be a great meeting ground in which we would mingle freely, girl and boy, boy and girl, person to person, all alike. And maybe that's going to happen sometime in my lifetime, but I can't say I know when.

I've thought about this for some time, because I've written some loving things about men, and some nasty things too, and I meant them all. And I've always been a feminist, and I've been one of the boys as well, and I've given both sides a pretty good shot. I've spent a lot of time telling myself that men and women are fundamentally alike, mainly in the service of arguing that women should not only be permitted but be welcomed into a variety of positions and roles that only men occupied.

And then something happens, a little thing usually, and all I can see is   5

Quindlen wrote a twice-weekly Op-Ed column for the New York Times *from 1981 to 1994. This essay appeared in the "Hers" column of the* Times *on March 24, 1988.*

that great shiny space in the middle of the dance floor where no one ever meets. "I swear to God we are a different species," one of my friends said on the telephone recently. I can't remember whether the occasion was a fight with her husband, a scene at work or a contretemps with a mutual male friend of ours. No matter. She's said it before and she'll say it again, just like all my other friends have said it to me, and I to them. Men are the other.

We are the other, too, of course. That's why we want to believe so badly that there are no others at all, because over the course of human history being other has meant being symbols of divinity, evil, carnal degeneration, perfect love, fertility and death, to name a few. And anybody who has ever been a symbol knows that it's about as relaxing as sitting on a piece of Louis XV furniture. It is also true that over the course of history, we have been subordinate to others, symbols of weakness, dependency and emotions run amok.

Yet isn't it odd that I feel that the prejudice is somehow easier to deal with than the simple difference? Prejudice is evil and can be fought, while difference simply is. I live with three males, one husband and two sons, and occasionally I realize with great clarity that they are gazing across a divide at me, not because of big differences among us, but because of small ones.

The amaryllis bulb haunts me. "Why did you put an onion in a pot in the bathroom?" my elder son asked several months ago. I explained that it was not an onion but an amaryllis bulb and that soon it would grow into fabulous flowers. "What is that thing in the bathroom?" his father said later the same day. Impatiently I explained again. A look flashed between them, and then the littlest boy, too. Mom. Weird. Women.

Once I would have felt anger flame inside me at that. But I've done the same so many times now. On the telephone a friend and I will be commiserating about the failure of our husbands to listen when we talk, or their inexorable linear thinking, or their total blindness to the use and necessity of things like amaryllis bulbs. One of us will sigh, and the other will know what the sigh means. Husband. Strange. Men. Is it any wonder that our relationships are so often riddled with misunderstandings and disappointments?

10   In the children you can see the beginnings, even though we raise them in households in which mothers do things fathers once did, and vice versa. Children try to nail down the world, and themselves, early on and in a very primitive and real way. I remember a stage with my elder son in which, going through the supermarket or walking down the street, he would pin me down on each person walking by, and on such disparate cultural influences as Vanna White and Captain Kangaroo, by demanding that I tell him which genitalia category they fell in. Very soon, he got the idea: us and them, him and her. It was all very well to say that all people are the same inside (even if I had believed it) but he thought the outside was very important, too, and it helped him classify the world.

I must never forget, I suppose, that even in the gym, with all that space between us, we still managed to pick partners and dance. It's the dance that's important, not the difference. (I shouldn't leave out who leads and who follows. But I speak to that from a strange perspective, since any man who has ever danced with me can attest to the fact that I have never learned to follow.)

I have just met the dance downstairs. My elder son has one of his best friends over, and he does not care that she is a girl, and she does not care that he is a boy. But she is complaining that he is chasing her with the plastic spider and making her scream, and he is grinning maniacally because that is just exactly the response he is looking for, and they are both having a great time. Two children, raised in egalitarian households in the 1980s. Between them the floor already stretches, an ocean to cross before they can dance uneasily in one another's arms.

QUESTIONS

1. Mark the places in this essay where Quindlen, after describing "the first boy-girl party we attended" (paragraph 1), returns to it. How does she turn an event into a symbol of male–female differences?

2. Consider Quindlen's statement, "I've spent a lot of time telling myself that men and women are fundamentally alike, mainly in the service of arguing that women should not only be permitted but be welcomed into a variety of positions and roles that only men occupied" (paragraph 4). Does her admission that they are not fundamentally alike mean that women should not be welcomed into male positions and roles? Why?

3. As Quindlen, in this essay, casts men as the Other, so Scott Russell Sanders, in "Looking at Women" (p. 226), casts women as the Other. How do they present and try to decipher what they do not fully know or understand?

4. Write an essay in which you turn an event into a symbol.

LAUREN SLATER   *Love*

MY HUSBAND AND I got married at eight in the morning. It was winter, freezing, the trees encased in ice and a few lone blackbirds balancing on telephone wires. We were in our early 30s, considered ourselves hip and cynical, the types who decried the institution of marriage even as we sought its status. During our wedding brunch we put out a big suggestion box and asked people to slip us advice on how to avoid divorce; we thought it was a funny,

Published in National Geographic *(February 2006), a magazine founded as a vehicle for the "diffusion of geographical knowledge" and traditionally associated with travel and nature writing; recently the magazine has expanded to include articles of general human interest, while maintaining its commitment to issues of nature and the environment.*

clear-eyed, grounded sort of thing to do, although the suggestions were mostly foolish: Screw the toothpaste cap on tight. After the guests left, the house got quiet. There were flowers everywhere: puckered red roses and fragile ferns. "What can we do that's really romantic?" I asked my newly wed one. Benjamin suggested we take a bath. I didn't want a bath. He suggested a lunch of chilled white wine and salmon. I was sick of salmon.

What can we do that's really romantic? The wedding was over, the silence seemed suffocating, and I felt the familiar disappointment after a longed-for event has come and gone. We were married. Hip, hip, hooray. I decided to take a walk. I went into the center of town, pressed my nose against a bakery window, watched the man with flour on his hands, the dough as soft as skin, pushed and pulled and shaped at last into stars. I milled about in an antique store. At last I came to our town's tattoo parlor. Now I am not a tattoo type person, but for some reason, on that cold silent Sunday, I decided to walk in. "Can I help you?" a woman asked.

"Is there a kind of tattoo I can get that won't be permanent?" I asked.

"Henna[1] tattoos," she said.

5   She explained that they lasted for six weeks, were used at Indian weddings, were stark and beautiful and all brown. She showed me pictures of Indian women with jewels in their noses, their arms scrolled and laced with the henna markings. Indeed they were beautiful, sharing none of the gaudy comic strip quality of the tattoos we see in the United States. These henna tattoos spoke of intricacy, of the webwork between two people, of ties that bind and how difficult it is to find their beginnings and their ends. And because I had just gotten married, and because I was feeling a post wedding letdown, and because I wanted something really romantic to sail me through the night, I decided to get one.

"Where?" she asked.

"Here," I said. I laid my hands over my breasts and belly.

She raised her eyebrows. "Sure," she said.

I am a modest person. But I took off my shirt, lay on the table, heard her in the back room mixing powders and paints. She came to me carrying a small black-bellied pot inside of which was a rich red mush, slightly glittering. She adorned me. She gave me vines and flowers. She turned my body into a stake supporting whole new gardens of growth, and then, low around my hips, she painted a delicate chain-linked chastity belt. An hour later, the paint dry, I put my clothes back on, went home to find my newly wed one. This, I knew, was my gift to him, the kind of present you offer only once in your lifetime. I let him undress me.

10   "Wow," he said, standing back.

I blushed, and we began.

We are no longer beginning, my husband and I. This does not surprise me. Even back then, wearing the decor of desire, the serpentining tattoos, I knew

---

1. A reddish dye derived from a shrub of the same name.

they would fade, their red-clay color bleaching out until they were gone. On my wedding day I didn't care.

I do now. Eight years later, pale as a pillowcase, here I sit, with all the extra pounds and baggage time brings. And the questions have only grown more insistent. Does passion necessarily diminish over time? How reliable is romantic love, really, as a means of choosing one's mate? Can a marriage be good when Eros[2] is replaced with friendship, or even economic partnership, two people bound by bank accounts?

Let me be clear: I still love my husband. There is no man I desire more. But it's hard to sustain romance in the crumb-filled quotidian that has become our lives. The ties that bind have been frayed by money and mortgages and children, those little imps who somehow manage to tighten the knot while weakening its actual fibers. Benjamin and I have no time for chilled white wine and salmon. The baths in our house always include Big Bird.

If this all sounds miserable, it isn't. My marriage is like a piece of comfortable clothing; even the arguments have a feel of fuzziness to them, something so familiar it can only be called home. And yet . . .

In the Western world we have for centuries concocted poems and stories and plays about the cycles of love, the way it morphs and changes over time, the way passion grabs us by our flung-back throats and then leaves us for something saner. If *Dracula*—the frail woman, the sensuality of submission—reflects how we understand the passion of early romance, the *Flintstones* reflects our experiences of long-term love:[3] All is gravel and somewhat silly, the song so familiar you can't stop singing it, and when you do, the emptiness is almost unbearable.

We have relied on stories to explain the complexities of love, tales of jealous gods and arrows. Now, however, these stories—so much a part of every civilization—may be changing as science steps in to explain what we have always felt to be myth, to be magic. For the first time, new research has begun to illuminate where love lies in the brain, the particulars of its chemical components.

Anthropologist Helen Fisher may be the closest we've ever come to having a doyenne of desire. At 60 she exudes a sexy confidence, with corn-colored hair, soft as floss, and a willowy build. A professor at Rutgers University, she lives in New York City, her book-lined apartment near Central Park, with its green trees fluffed out in the summer season, its paths crowded with couples holding hands.

Fisher has devoted much of her career to studying the biochemical pathways of love in all its manifestations: lust, romance, attachment, the way they wax and wane. One leg casually crossed over the other, ice clinking in her

15

2. Greek for romantic or sexual love.
3. *Dracula*: novel by Bram Stoker (1847–1912), published in 1897; it features a bloodsucking vampire by the same name and a beloved woman who wastes away. *Flintstones*: an animated television series dating from the 1960s, featuring the hi-jinks of a Stone Age family.

glass, she speaks with appealing frankness, discussing the ups and downs of love the way most people talk about real estate. "A woman unconsciously uses orgasms as a way of deciding whether or not a man is good for her. If he's impatient and rough, and she doesn't have the orgasm, she may instinctively feel he's less likely to be a good husband and father. Scientists think the fickle female orgasm may have evolved to help women distinguish Mr. Right from Mr. Wrong."

20   One of Fisher's central pursuits in the past decade has been looking at love, quite literally, with the aid of an MRI[4] machine. Fisher and her colleagues Arthur Aron and Lucy Brown recruited subjects who had been "madly in love" for an average of seven months. Once inside the MRI machine, subjects were shown two photographs, one neutral, the other of their loved one.

What Fisher saw fascinated her. When each subject looked at his or her loved one, the parts of the brain linked to reward and pleasure—the ventral tegmental area and the caudate nucleus—lit up. What excited Fisher most was not so much finding a location, an address, for love as tracing its specific chemical pathways. Love lights up the caudate nucleus because it is home to a dense spread of receptors for a neurotransmitter called dopamine, which Fisher came to think of as part of our own endogenous love potion. In the right proportions, dopamine creates intense energy, exhilaration, focused attention, and motivation to win rewards. It is why, when you are newly in love, you can stay up all night, watch the sun rise, run a race, ski fast down a slope ordinarily too steep for your skill. Love makes you bold, makes you bright, makes you run real risks, which you sometimes survive, and sometimes you don't.

I first fell in love when I was only 12, with a teacher. His name was Mr. McArthur, and he wore open-toed sandals and sported a beard. I had never had a male teacher before, and I thought it terribly exotic. Mr. McArthur did things no other teacher dared to do. He explained to us the physics of farting. He demonstrated how to make an egg explode. He smoked cigarettes at recess, leaning languidly against the side of the school building, the ash growing longer and longer until he casually tapped it off with his finger.

What unique constellation of needs led me to love a man who made an egg explode is interesting, perhaps, but not as interesting, for me, as my memory of love's sheer physical facts. I had never felt anything like it before. I could not get Mr. McArthur out of my mind. I was anxious; I gnawed at the lining of my cheek until I tasted the tang of blood. School became at once terrifying and exhilarating. Would I see him in the hallway? In the cafeteria? I hoped. But when my wishes were granted, and I got a glimpse of my man, it satisfied nothing; it only inflamed me all the more. Had he looked at me? Why had he not looked at me? When would I see him again? At home I looked him up in the phone book; I rang him, this in a time before caller ID. He answered.

"Hello?" Pain in my heart, ripped down the middle. Hang up.

---

4. Magnetic Resonance Imaging, a medical technique that reveals the insides of an organism.

Call back. "Hello?" I never said a thing. 25

Once I called him at night, late, and from the way he answered the phone it was clear, even to a prepubescent like me, that he was with a woman. His voice fuzzy, the tinkle of her laughter in the background. I didn't get out of bed for a whole day.

Sound familiar? Maybe you were 30 when it happened to you, or 8 or 80 or 25. Maybe you lived in Kathmandu or Kentucky; age and geography are irrelevant. Donatella Marazziti is a professor of psychiatry at the University of Pisa in Italy who has studied the biochemistry of lovesickness. Having been in love twice herself and felt its awful power, Marazziti became interested in exploring the similarities between love and obsessive-compulsive disorder.

She and her colleagues measured serotonin levels in the blood of 24 subjects who had fallen in love within the past six months and obsessed about this love object for at least four hours every day. Serotonin is, perhaps, our star neurotransmitter,[5] altered by our star psychiatric medications: Prozac and Zoloft and Paxil, among others. Researchers have long hypothesized that people with obsessive-compulsive disorder (OCD) have a serotonin "imbalance." Drugs like Prozac seem to alleviate OCD by increasing the amount of this neurotransmitter available at the juncture between neurons.[6]

Marazziti compared the lovers' serotonin levels with those of a group of people suffering from OCD and another group who were free from both passion and mental illness. Levels of serotonin in both the obsessives' blood and the lovers' blood were 40 percent lower than those in her normal subjects. Translation: Love and obsessive-compulsive disorder could have a similar chemical profile. Translation: Love and mental illness may be difficult to tell apart. Translation: Don't be a fool. Stay away.

Of course that's a mandate none of us can follow. We do fall in love, 30 sometimes over and over again, subjecting ourselves, each time, to a very sick state of mind. There is hope, however, for those caught in the grip of runaway passion—Prozac. There's nothing like that bicolored bullet for damping down the sex drive and making you feel "blah" about the buffet. Helen Fisher believes that the ingestion of drugs like Prozac jeopardizes one's ability to fall in love—and stay in love. By dulling the keen edge of love and its associated libido, relationships go stale. Says Fisher, "I know of one couple on the edge of divorce. The wife was on an anti-depressant. Then she went off it, started having orgasms once more, felt the renewal of sexual attraction for her husband, and they're now in love all over again."

Psychoanalysts have concocted countless theories about why we fall in love with whom we do. Freud[7] would have said your choice is influenced by the unrequited wish to bed your mother, if you're a boy, or your father, if

5. Chemicals that, when released into the juncture between nerve cells, enable the cells to communicate with each other.

6. A type of cell in the nervous system.

7. Sigmund Freud (1856–1939), Austrian neurologist and father of psychoanalysis.

you're a girl. Jung[8] believed that passion is driven by some kind of collective unconscious. Today psychiatrists such as Thomas Lewis from the University of California at San Francisco's School of Medicine hypothesize that romantic love is rooted in our earliest infantile experiences with intimacy, how we felt at the breast, our mother's face, these things of pure unconflicted comfort that get engraved in our brain and that we ceaselessly try to recapture as adults. According to this theory we love whom we love not so much because of the future we hope to build but because of the past we hope to reclaim. Love is reactive, not proactive, it arches us backward, which may be why a certain person just "feels right." Or "feels familiar." He or she is familiar. He or she has a certain look or smell or sound or touch that activates buried memories.

When I first met my husband, I believed this psychological theory was more or less correct. My husband has red hair and a soft voice. A chemist, he is whimsical and odd. One day before we married he dunked a rose in liquid nitrogen so it froze, whereupon he flung it against the wall, spectacularly shattering it. That's when I fell in love with him. My father, too, has red hair, a soft voice, and many eccentricities. He was prone to bursting into song, prompted by something we never saw.

However, it turns out my theories about why I came to love my husband may be just so much hogwash. Evolutionary psychology has said good riddance to Freud and the Oedipal complex[9] and all that other transcendent stuff and hello to simple survival skills. It hypothesizes that we tend to see as attractive, and thereby choose as mates, people who look healthy. And health, say these evolutionary psychologists, is manifested in a woman with a 70 percent waist-to-hip ratio and men with rugged features that suggest a strong supply of testosterone in their blood. Waist-to-hip ratio is important for the successful birth of a baby, and studies have shown this precise ratio signifies higher fertility. As for the rugged look, well, a man with a good dose of testosterone probably also has a strong immune system and so is more likely to give his partner healthy children.

Perhaps our choice of mates is a simple matter of following our noses. Claus Wedekind of the University of Lausanne in Switzerland did an interesting experiment with sweaty T-shirts. He asked 49 women to smell T-shirts previously worn by unidentified men with a variety of the genotypes that influence both body odor and immune systems. He then asked the women to rate which T-shirts smelled the best, which the worst. What Wedekind found was that women preferred the scent of a T-shirt worn by a man whose genotype was most different from hers, a genotype that, perhaps, is linked to an immune system that possesses something hers does not. In this way she increases the chance that her offspring will be robust.

8. Carl Jung (1865–1961), Swiss psychologist, father of "analytical psychology" and originator of such concepts as the "collective unconscious," "archetype," and "extrovert–introvert."

9. A concept developed by Sigmund Freud positing that boys unconsciously desire sexual relationships with their mothers and wish for their fathers' deaths.

It all seems too good to be true, that we are so hardwired and yet unconscious of the wiring. Because no one to my knowledge has ever said, "I married him because of his B.O." No. We say, "I married him (or her) because he's intelligent, she's beautiful, he's witty, she's compassionate." But we may just be as deluded about love as we are when we're *in* love. If it all comes down to a sniff test, then dogs definitely have the edge when it comes to choosing mates.

Why doesn't passionate love last? How is it possible to see a person as beautiful on Monday, and 364 days later, on another Monday, to see that beauty as bland? Surely the object of your affection could not have changed that much. She still has the same shaped eyes. Her voice has always had that husky sound, but now it grates on you—she sounds like she needs an antibiotic. Or maybe you're the one who needs an antibiotic, because the partner you once loved and cherished and saw as though saturated with starlight now feels more like a low-level infection, tiring you, sapping all your strength.

Studies around the world confirm that, indeed, passion usually ends. Its conclusion is as common as its initial flare. No wonder some cultures think selecting a life-long mate based on something so fleeting is folly. Helen Fisher has suggested that relationships frequently break up after four years because that's about how long it takes to raise a child through infancy. Passion, that wild, prismatic insane feeling, turns out to be practical after all. We not only need to copulate; we also need enough passion to start breeding, and then feelings of attachment take over as the partners bond to raise a helpless human infant. Once a baby is no longer nursing, the child can be left with sister, aunts, friends. Each parent is now free to meet another mate and have more children.

Biologically speaking, the reasons romantic love fades may be found in the way our brains respond to the surge and pulse of dopamine that accompanies passion and makes us fly. Cocaine users describe the phenomenon of tolerance: The brain adapts to the excessive input of the drug. Perhaps the neurons become desensitized and need more and more to produce the high—to put out pixie dust, metaphorically speaking.

Maybe it's a good thing that romance fizzles. Would we have railroads, bridges, planes, faxes, vaccines, and television if we were all always besotted? In place of the ever evolving technology that has marked human culture from its earliest tool use, we would have instead only bonbons, bouquets, and birth control. More seriously, if the chemically altered state induced by romantic love is akin to a mental illness or a drug-induced euphoria, exposing yourself for too long could result in psychological damage. A good sex life can be as strong as Gorilla Glue,[10] but who wants that stuff on your skin?

Once upon a time, in India, a boy and a girl fell in love without their parents' permission. They were from different castes, their relationship radical and unsanctioned. Picture it: the sparkling sari, the boy in white linen, the clandes-

40

10. An extremely strong household glue.

tine meetings on tiled terraces with a fat, white moon floating overhead. Who could deny these lovers their pleasure, or condemn the force of their attraction?

Their parents could. In one recent incident a boy and girl from different castes were hanged at the hands of their parents as hundreds of villagers watched. A couple who eloped were stripped and beaten. Yet another couple committed suicide after their parents forbade them to marry.

Anthropologists used to think that romance was a Western construct, a bourgeois by-product of the Middle Ages. Romance was for the sophisticated, took place in cafés, with coffees and Cabernets, or on silk sheets, or in rooms with a flickering fire. It was assumed that non-Westerners, with their broad familial and social obligations, were spread too thin for particular passions. How could a collectivist culture celebrate or in any way sanction the obsession with one individual that defines new love? Could a lice-ridden peasant really feel passion?

Easily, as it turns out. Scientists now believe that romance is panhuman, embedded in our brains since Pleistocene times. In a study of 166 cultures, anthropologists William Jankowiak and Edward Fischer observed evidence of passionate love in 147 of them. In another study men and women from Europe, Japan, and the Philippines were asked to fill out a survey to measure their experiences of passionate love. All three groups professed feeling passion with the same searing intensity.

But though romantic love may be universal, its cultural expression is not. To the Fulbe tribe of northern Cameroon, poise matters more than passion. Men who spend too much time with their wives are taunted, and those who are weak-kneed are thought to have fallen under a dangerous spell. Love may be inevitable, but for the Fulbe its manifestations are shameful, equated with sickness and social impairment.

45   In India romantic love has traditionally been seen as dangerous, a threat to a well-crafted caste system in which marriages are arranged as a means of preserving lineage and bloodlines. Thus the gruesome tales, the warnings embedded in fables about what happens when one's wayward impulses take over.

Today love marriages appear to be on the rise in India, often in defiance of parents' wishes. The triumph of romantic love is celebrated in Bollywood films. Yet most Indians still believe arranged marriages are more likely to succeed than love marriages. In one survey of Indian college students, 76 percent said they'd marry someone with all the right qualities even if they weren't in love with the person (compared with only 14 percent of Americans). Marriage is considered too important a step to leave to chance.

Renu Dinakaran is a striking 45-year-old woman who lives in Bangalore, India. When I meet her, she is dressed in Western-style clothes—black leggings and a T-shirt. Renu lives in a well-appointed apartment in this thronging city, where cows sleep on the highways as tiny cars whiz around them, plumes of black smoke rising from their sooty pipes.

Renu was born into a traditional Indian family where an arranged marriage was expected. She was not an arranged kind of person, though, emerging from her earliest days as a fierce tennis player, too sweaty for saris, and smarter than many of the men around her. Nevertheless at the age of 17 she was married off to a first cousin, a man she barely knew, a man she wanted to learn to love, but couldn't. Renu considers many arranged marriages to be acts of "state-sanctioned rape."

Renu hoped to fall in love with her husband, but the more years that passed, the less love she felt, until, at the end, she was shrunken, bitter, hiding behind the curtains of her in-laws' bungalow, looking with longing at the couple on the balcony across from theirs. "It was so obvious to me that couple had married for love, and I envied them. I really did. It hurt me so much to see how they stood together, how they went shopping for bread and eggs."

Exhausted from being forced into confinement, from being swaddled in 50 saris that made it difficult to move, from resisting the pressure to eat off her husband's plate, Renu did what traditional Indian culture forbids one to do. She left. By this time she had had two children. She took them with her. In her mind was an old movie she'd seen on TV, a movie so strange and enticing to her, so utterly confounding and comforting at the same time, that she couldn't get it out of her head. It was 1986. The movie was *Love Story*.

"Before I saw movies like *Love Story*, I didn't realize the power that love can have," she says.

Renu was lucky in the end. In Mumbai she met a man named Anil, and it was then, for the first time, that she felt passion. "When I first met Anil, it was like nothing I'd ever experienced. He was the first man I ever had an orgasm with. I was high, just high, all the time. And I knew it wouldn't last, couldn't last, and so that infused it with a sweet sense of longing, almost as though we were watching the end approach while we were also discovering each other."

When Renu speaks of the end, she does not, to be sure, mean the end of her relationship with Anil; she means the end of a certain stage. The two are still happily married, companionable, loving if not "in love," with a playful black dachshund they bought together. Their relationship, once so full of fire, now seems to simmer along at an even temperature, enough to keep them well fed and warm. They are grateful.

"Would I want all that passion back?" Renu asks. "Sometimes, yes. But to tell you the truth, it was exhausting."

From a physiological point of view, this couple has moved from the 55 dopamine-drenched state of romantic love to the relative quiet of an oxytocin-induced attachment. Oxytocin is a hormone that promotes a feeling of connection, bonding. It is released when we hug our long-term spouses, or our children. It is released when a mother nurses her infant. Prairie voles, animals with high levels of oxytocin, mate for life. When scientists block oxytocin receptors in these rodents, the animals don't form monogamous bonds and tend to roam. Some researchers speculate that autism, a disorder marked by a profound inability to forge and maintain social connections, is linked to an oxytocin deficiency. Scientists have been experimenting by treating autistic people with oxytocin, which in some cases has helped alleviate their symptoms.

In long-term relationships that work—like Renu and Anil's—oxytocin is believed to be abundant in both partners. In long-term relationships that never get off the ground, like Renu and her first husband's, or that crumble once the high is gone, chances are the couple has not found a way to stimulate or sustain oxytocin production.

"But there are things you can do to help it along," says Helen Fisher. "Massage. Make love. These things trigger oxytocin and thus make you feel much closer to your partner."

Well, I suppose that's good advice, but it's based on the assumption that you still want to have sex with that boring windbag of a husband. Should you fake-it-till-you-make-it?

"Yes," says Fisher. "Assuming a fairly healthy relationship, if you have enough orgasms with your partner, you may become attached to him or her. You will stimulate oxytocin."

60   This may be true. But it sounds unpleasant. It's exactly what your mother always said about vegetables: "Keep eating your peas. They are an acquired taste. Eventually, you will come to like them."

But I have never been a peas person.

It's 90 degrees on the day my husband and I depart, from Boston for New York City, to attend a kissing school. With two kids, two cats, two dogs, a lopsided house, and a questionable school system, we may know how to kiss, but in the rough and tumble of our harried lives we have indeed forgotten how to *kiss*.

The sky is paved with clouds, the air as sticky as jam in our hands and on our necks. The Kissing School, run by Cherie Byrd, a therapist from Seattle, is being held on the 12th floor of a run-down building in Manhattan. Inside, the room is whitewashed; a tiled table holds bottles of banana and apricot nectar, a pot of green tea, breath mints, and Chapstick. The other Kissing School students—sometimes they come from as far away as Vietnam and Nigeria—are sprawled happily on the bare floor, pillows and blankets beneath them. The class will be seven hours long.

Byrd starts us off with foot rubs. "In order to be a good kisser," she says, "you need to learn how to do the foreplay before the kissing." Foreplay involves rubbing my husband's smelly feet, but that is not as bad as when he has to rub mine. Right before we left the house, I accidentally stepped on a diaper the dog had gotten into, and although I washed, I now wonder how well.

65   "Inhale," Byrd says, and shows us how to draw in air.

"Exhale," she says, and then she jabs my husband in the back. "Don't focus on the toes so much," she says. "Move on to the calf."

Byrd tells us other things about the art of kissing. She describes the movement of energy through various chakras,[11] the manifestation of emotion in the lips; she describes the importance of embracing all your senses, how to make eye contact as a prelude, how to whisper just the right way. Many hours go by. My cell phone rings. It's our babysitter. Our one-year-old has a high fever. We

---

11. In several Asian cultures, the center of spiritual and/or physical energy residing in the body.

must cut the long lesson short. We rush out. Later on, at home, I tell my friends what we learned at Kissing School: We don't have time to kiss.

A perfectly typical marriage. Love in the Western world.

Luckily I've learned of other options for restarting love. Arthur Aron, a psychologist at Stony Brook University in New York, conducted an experiment that illuminates some of the mechanisms by which people become and stay attracted. He recruited a group of men and women and put opposite sex pairs in rooms together, instructing each pair to perform a series of tasks, which included telling each other personal details about themselves. He then asked each couple to stare into each other's eyes for two minutes. After this encounter, Aron found most of the couples, previously strangers to each other, reported feelings of attraction. In fact, one couple went on to marry.

Fisher says this exercise works wonders for some couples. Aron and Fisher also suggest doing novel things together, because novelty triggers dopamine in the brain, which can stimulate feelings of attraction. In other words, if your heart flutters in his presence, you might decide it's not because you're anxious but because you love him. Carrying this a step further, Aron and others have found that even if you just jog in place and then meet someone, you're more likely to think they're attractive. So first dates that involve a nerve-racking activity, like riding a roller coaster, are more likely to lead to second and third dates. That's a strategy worthy of posting on Match.com. Play some squash. And in times of stress—natural disasters, blackouts, predators on the prowl— lock up tight and hold your partner.

In Somerville, Massachusetts, where I live with my husband, our predators are primarily mosquitoes. That needn't stop us from trying to enter the windows of each other's soul. When I propose this to Benjamin, he raises an eyebrow.

"Why don't we just go out for Cambodian food?" he says.

"Because that's not how the experiment happened."

As a scientist, my husband is always up for an experiment. But our lives are so busy that, in order to do this, we have to make a plan. We will meet next Wednesday at lunchtime and try the experiment in our car.

On the Tuesday night before our rendezvous, I have to make an unplanned trip to New York. My husband is more than happy to forget our date. I, however, am not. That night, from my hotel room, I call him.

"We can do it on the phone," I say.

"What am I supposed to stare into?" he asks. "The keypad?"

"There's a picture of me hanging in the hall. Look at that for two minutes. I'll look at a picture I have of you in my wallet."

"Come on," he says.

"Be a sport," I say. "It's better than nothing."

Maybe not. Two minutes seems like a long time to stare at someone's picture with a receiver pressed to your ear. My husband sneezes, and I try to imagine his picture sneezing right along with him, and this makes me laugh.

Another 15 seconds pass, slowly, each second stretched to its limit so I can almost hear time, feel time, its taffy-like texture, the pop it makes when

70

75

80

it's done. Pop pop pop. I stare and stare at my husband's picture. It doesn't produce any sense of startling intimacy, and I feel defeated.

Still, I keep on. I can hear him breathing on the other end. The photograph before me was taken a year or so ago, cut to fit my wallet, his strawberry blond hair pulled back in a ponytail. I have never really studied it before. And I realize that in this picture my husband is not looking straight back at me, but his pale blue eyes are cast sideways, off to the left, looking at something I can't see. I touch his eyes. I peer close, and then still closer, at his averted face. Is there something sad in his expression, something sad in the way he gazes off?

I look toward the side of the photo, to find what it is he's looking at, and then I see it: a tiny turtle coming toward him. Now I remember how he caught it after the camera snapped, how he held it gently in his hands, showed it to our kids, stroked its shell, his forefinger moving over the scaly dome, how he held the animal out toward me, a love offering. I took it, and together we sent it back to the sea.

QUESTIONS

1. "Love" might be called a "definition essay": it takes on a large concept and expands and enriches our understanding of it. What aspects of love that Slater describes did you recognize from experience? What new aspects or facts did you learn by reading this essay?

2. Slater draws on many experts in writing about love—on scientists, psychologists, historians, and so on. Find three or four places where she quotes these experts, and explain why she does so.

3. Even with Slater's frequent use of expert witnesses, we learn a lot about her own experiences in love. What does she reveal? What is the relationship between her personal experience and the information provided by experts?

4. Choose a concept that, like love, can become the title of a "definition essay": for example, human emotions (hate, anger, hope, doubt, happiness) or human states (friendship, childhood, marriage, divorce, death). As you think about the concept, look to the research and analysis of experts. Write an essay that interweaves your own experience with experts' testimony.

E. S. MADURO   *Excuse Me While I Explode:*
My Mother, Myself, My Anger

Y PARENTS MET and started dating on the same day, at the age of thirteen. Forty-five years later, my father still glows when he tells the story of seeing my mother on her first day at his school, and how he offered to walk her home that very afternoon. They dated throughout high school, went to the same college, and got married the day before their graduation, at age twenty-one— three years younger than I am today. After college my father went to graduate school and eventually became a history professor; my mother worked as a schoolteacher for a while; they bought a cheap house in the countryside and started a family. Presto, the American Dream.

When my older sister was born, my mother stopped working out of the house and became the mom I know her as. The mom who maintained a spotless house and a balanced checkbook and found the time to praise and nurture two growing children, all while having dinner ready and waiting, on the table, every night by 6:30. The mom who put off a career until her mid-forties so she would be available to her family—which she still is—though that is not to say she didn't work. My mother's job included, but was never limited to, pickling cucumbers, making jam, doing laundry for four people, changing diapers, teaching two children to read, doing all the grocery shopping for a family, cooking three meals a day (making sure a vegetable was included at dinner), cleaning the house, doing art projects, building snowmen, feeding a dog, driving to the doctor's office, picking kids up from piano lessons, going to parent-teacher conferences, sewing hems in school uniforms, ironing men's button-down shirts . . . and so on. I think there are few résumés out there that could top my mother's were she ever to think it worthy of writing—which she never would.

As a young child—naturally, I suppose—I don't really remember being aware that my mother existed between the time I left for school in the morning and the time she arrived at the bus stop to meet me coming home. Laundry and dusting and shopping were far outside my elementary-school-age mind, and if chores were done when I got home, it certainly didn't catch my attention. As I grew older, however, my awareness of our household began to change. My mother went back to school and, at age forty-five, became a special ed teacher. After that, she often came home exhausted at 5:30 and began making dinner. Saturdays and Sundays she woke up early to rush all over, cleaning, cooking, shopping, organizing the calendar. Monday mornings she'd

Included in a collection titled The Bitch in the House: 26 Women Tell the Truth about Sex, Solitude, Work, Motherhood, and Marriage *(2002), edited by Cathi Hanauer. The collection was intended to explore the causes of the domestic anger experienced by women in contemporary society.*

be up at 4:30 to write a report that had been neglected over the weekend, then she'd make me breakfast before school and zip off to work. Gradually, I began to notice that she never seemed to have a moment to herself. Simultaneously, I realized that my father, who took care of all the "manly" household chores—chopping wood, killing mice—still had time for a well-respected career and a whole slew of regular hobbies. The setup began to seem drastically unfair to me. Free time, to my high school mind, was an absolute necessity, and I was witness to the fact that my mother seemed to be getting none of it.

This is not to say that I suddenly dropped to my knees before my mother, realized the saint that she was, and thanked her. Instead, I became disappointed in her and—to my current shame and regret—ridiculed her for being so undemanding about her own needs and so willing to dedicate herself to maintaining the house and serving us. I became angry at both of my parents: at my father that his chores (take apart and reassemble the kitchen sink, work in the garden, snow-blow the driveway) seemed interesting and challenging and were always impressive to friends and relatives, while my mother's endless chores seemed layered in routine and monotony. Both my parents had careers now, but it still fell to my mother to do every trivial and mindless thing that needed to be done, and I was frustrated with her for never seeming to mind this or to demand more help from my father.

5   I spent hours as a teenager talking to her (rarely listening) about why she was so accepting of her role in our family. I would recount the way my father would stride into the house after work and she would politely have dinner waiting for him; the way there was an unspoken sentiment in our house that his career was more important than hers. "Why don't you divorce him and find a husband who will offer to clean up the kitchen after dinner and let you sit down for once?" I would yell; or, "How come his job takes precedence over everything else while yours has to fit around all the other things you do and have always done?" Somehow, my mother was always able to shrug me off—to reply that she was fine, that someday I would understand. But I wasn't at all sure that I would, or that she was. What's more, I believed myself to be a feminist, and I vowed never to fall into the same trap of domestic boredom and servitude that I saw my mother as being fully entrenched in; never to settle for a life that was, as I saw it, lacking independence, authority, and respect.

I met my own boyfriend, Paul, during my senior year of college. He was absolutely the furthest thing possible from my father, which was exactly what I was looking for at the time. Though I love my father passionately, I was certain that the man of my life would know how to cook dinner and clean the house, would offer to do the dishes, would fold the laundry without being asked. My goal was to avoid the domestic life that my mother had found for herself; the first step was to have a liberal, open-minded boyfriend. I found one with dreadlocks, a nose ring, and a passion for that most nonacademic of subjects, music—just the opposite of my traditional and overly intellectual father.

On our first date, Paul offered to cook me dinner, and when it was over he did all the dishes. When I'd stop by his house (which he shared with three other male friends), I would marvel at the way he seemed to take care of cleaning up the kitchen, the way he would look disapprovingly at his house-mates' dirty underwear on the bathroom floor. His books were neatly arranged on a shelf in his bedroom, his clothes were well folded in drawers, and he even had a laundry bag with his name on it. I was hooked. This man seemed to know how to do all the things my own father couldn't or wouldn't ever do. After a few months of dating, I called a friend from home one night and talked at length about how this guy seemed so perfect; how he was so respon-sible, so thoughtful; how I just couldn't imagine him ever expecting me to take care of all the housework, the child care, the dinners, were we ever to get married.

My mother and I had long conversations about how she had gone from her father to her husband without ever spending a segment of her life inde-pendently. She commented often about how lucky I was, and how glad she was for me, that I was part of a generation that got to make educated decisions about how their lives would go. "You have choices," she'd say. "Be thankful that you're so aware of the qualities that are important to you in a husband, before you run off to get married. When I was your age, girls didn't even real-ize what they were getting into when they got married. It was just the thing to do." Once, during one of these conversations, I asked her if she'd do it over again differently if she could. In one of her most open and honest moments with me, she said, "Yes. Definitely." Though I realize now that her answer had to do with more than just household responsibilities, at the time I felt so lucky knowing that I would never repeat her domestic lot, that I would not go from my father's home to my husband's. I felt proud that I would create a home with my husband based on shared responsibility and input; proud that I was, in fact, already on the road to doing it.

Then I visited Paul's family.

Paul and I were upstairs watching a movie when his mother called us down to dinner. The table was set, the food was ready, and we sat down. In a few mo-ments Paul's father arrived and instantly complained that his favorite hot sauce was not on the table. His mother leapt up to get it. Dinner was over in about eight minutes, and almost as if by a feat of magic, everyone was gone from the kitchen before I had even put down my fork. Paul was on the piano, improvis-ing a song to play for me; his father was upstairs reading the paper. Paul's mother and I spent the next twenty minutes cleaning up, loading the dish-washer, and putting the food away. A mother of two sons, she immediately loved me and has been fond of me ever since. She was delighted with Paul's choice.

I, on the other hand, suddenly felt my first twinge of anger and resent-ment toward Paul. *Surely he can't realize I'm still in the kitchen, washing his plate,* I thought. But I knew he did. And it was as if, in a matter of minutes, his personality had a whole new side I hadn't noticed before. This man, who had been so different from my father, was immediately just like him, all because of what he didn't do or even notice. And I believe, looking back on that evening, that had I not already been so filled with a kind of rage at the ease with which

10

so many men seemed able to overlook the daily tasks that women did for them, I would not even have really minded doing dishes with Paul's mother. Certainly, I would not have suddenly decided to be on the lookout for this trend in him—would not have begun the awful, silent process of tallying up and storing away and keeping tabs on what he helped out with and what he did not.

Now it is almost three years later, and the same boyfriend is lying in our bed, in our apartment, trying to recover from a winter flu. I glance at him while writing these words, and seeing his peaceful breaths rise and fall under our soft down comforter, I feel total affection for him. He is delightful—considerate, attentive, and kind—and I feel lucky to share my life with him. I look the other way, however, into our kitchen, and upon seeing a pile of dirty dishes in the sink, I fall back into a silent conversation that has been going on in my head since we happily, if blindly, moved in together last fall.

It begins something like this: "Does it just not occur to him that I worked all day and might like to come home to a place where I don't immediately have to start cleaning in order to feel some sense of peace with where I am? Am I the only one who cares that our house is a mess?" And then the list of things he hasn't done, or has done wrong, comes flooding, pouring, rushing into my mind. I count the number of times I stopped at the grocery store on my way home this week and compare it with the number of times he has voluntarily done the same. I replay the scene from last weekend, when we were expecting friends to come for dinner, and he showed up at 5:30 after a full day of cross-country skiing with a friend and claimed to have "forgotten" that we were responsible for making a meal for four.

Or I think about the numerous times that I have come into the house, exhausted, at 7:00 after a full day of work and a meeting after school, and found him searching for music on the Internet instead of preparing a dinner for us both. On those days, I have silently walked into the kitchen and begun chopping vegetables or boiling water for spaghetti, and with every slice of my knife, every pot that I pulled from the cupboard, I grow angrier and angrier, until I could not even stand his presence in the same room. He might walk in and say something as innocent as "What can I do to help?" or even "Why don't you sit down and let me make dinner?" and I would absolutely explode with fury, shooting back at him, "Well, I'm starving and exhausted and I don't really feel like waiting around for you to finish your f***ing Internet search so that I can eat something before nine o'clock!"

15   On such occasions I will be angry for thirty minutes, or maybe until I have eaten something. I will ruminate on the place of the woman in today's "modern" society. I will cook and clean, and all the while think about how I am falling into the same trap of housework that my own mother fell into. As I scrub the kitchen sink, I will hear her voice saying, "You have choices," and I will scowl at the concept of a choice. I will decide that my modern, liberal, open-minded boyfriend, having been raised by a mother who did everything in the home (in addition to having a job), will never notice or care if his girlfriend or wife takes over those same domestic responsibilities. He is capable of doing

all of them, but if they get done for him, my thoughts go, he might never even realize that they needed doing in the first place.

But then slowly, as I finish picking up the dirty clothes from the floor, I will think about his day, will remember that he works long hours, too—and that he loves music, that finding new albums to record off our computer is a way for him to relax, to wind down. It will occur to me that maybe he was waiting for me to come home so that we could eat together; that he didn't know I would be arriving so late; that he was sincere, rather than just trying to avoid a fight, when he offered to cook for me. Perhaps I will remember that he had a meeting after school, too, and had probably arrived home only fifteen minutes before I did. Gradually, my anger will start to wane, and in its place will come guilt and confusion and sadness. I will imagine my own mother, coming in from a long day—or, worse, having never even left the work of the house—and wanting nothing more than to sit down and read the paper; and in a million years, her husband would never have offered to make her dinner, as my boyfriend has just done for me. The question in my mind then becomes, Why didn't I let him? Why, when he was standing right there, ready and willing, did I ignore the chance to pour myself a glass of wine and sit on the couch for twenty minutes while he prepared a meal for me? Why, instead, did I become so angry so fast?

The answer, sadly, surprisingly, self-defeatingly, is that I want to be angry. Or at least, I *choose* to be angry over the long list of alternate emotions waiting in line: guilt, sadness, the exhaustion of trying to change things, to figure it all out. I feel angry at the confusion of adoring my mother, of thinking she is a phenomenal woman who raised her children with grace and style, of thinking I would give anything to be like her . . . and at the same time, looking down on her for all the things she quietly accepted, and knowing that I want to be nothing like that. I feel angry at the confusion of wanting my own relationship to be balanced, to share all responsibilities equally, yet at the same time, wanting things done my way—with the tidiness and timeliness that I have inherited from my parents. I feel frustrated by the guilt that accompanies asking Paul to take the initiative to run the dishwasher, to do the laundry without shrinking my sweaters, to buy groceries that are healthy . . . to ask for what my mother never would have, to be what she would have considered a "nag." In wanting my home to be as well organized as my mother kept hers, I feel as though I must choose between doing everything myself and constantly asking Paul to do more.

I already know how to manage a household, not because I asked someone to teach me, but because I watched my mother and learned while I spent countless hours by her side (or on her hip) all those Saturdays when she worked from 7:00 A.M. to bedtime to keep our house running. I never asked for this knowledge. I never wanted the internal clock that tells me enough time has gone by that we really should change our sheets; never requested the awareness of how long it takes to make lasagna and thus the willingness to give up an afternoon so that dinner will be ready when the guests arrive. I never asked for anyone to teach me how to wash my silk shirts by hand. But, of course, as almost all girls do, I learned, and now I'm stuck with it. And no matter how much I sometimes wish I wasn't the one in my relationship who knows all this, I admit that I also sometimes feel proud of knowing it all, and proud that I do it all well.

Last weekend, Paul and I agreed to house-sit and baby-sit for neighbors of ours with four children. Almost immediately, I found myself taking over everything, rather than showing Paul how to do it. Though he asked me several times to show him how to run the fancy washing machine, I never did teach him. Instead, I did all the laundry myself, making the trip down the basement steps three or four times a day, furious that he was watching a movie with the kids while I was doing chores. When Keith, the six-year-old, needed breakfast, rather than mentioning it to Paul or asking him for help, I simply made pancakes for everyone, then fumed as we all ate them together. When Paul asked me what was the best way to clean a cast-iron skillet, I responded harshly to just leave it and I would take care of it myself. The weekend was a seemingly endless stream of moments when I angrily "did it myself" instead of showing him how. Every dish that he didn't notice I had picked up for him, every morsel of food he ate that I had cooked, every stair I descended that led to the clothes dryer, was another tick in my mental log of things to resent him for.

20   I returned home from the weekend of baby-sitting exhausted physically, mentally, and emotionally, commenting again and again how glad I was that we don't have kids or pets or even our own washing machine. But as my anger waned, I realized I was feeling something else, too: a sense of power and pride in knowing that I had been the supermom for the weekend. I was the one who had kept everything under control. It was I who'd made sure that the kids were picked up on time, took showers each night, ate a vegetable at dinner. I felt as though I could have done the whole thing myself. The package was complete: anger and pride.

So there it is. In trying to find a man as different as possible from my own father, in trying to avoid the life of an overworked housewife that I see my mother as having occupied for more than thirty years now, in choosing a boyfriend partly for his willingness and readiness to share the "woman's work," I am freely walking closer and closer to everything I had wanted to escape, enraged with every step I take. Somehow, some part of this cycle seems unavoidable, unchangeable. Paul will read what I've written here and ask me, so earnestly, "What can we do to solve this problem?" and already I know that I will shrug him off. "It's just me," I'll respond, "this is something I need to deal with."

Rather than trying to impart to him some of the domestic knowledge and sense of responsibility that I have, I will, I fear, go on being angry that he wasn't given it to begin with; angry that, unlike me, he was not closely observing, for his future, his own mother during the many hours she spent taking care of everyone in the family, and therefore now doesn't have the voice in his head telling him he *should* be constantly aware of tasks that need to be done, of meeting everyone else's needs before his own. And yet, side by side with this anger, will be the pride, the satisfaction of knowing that someday I could be an excellent mother, always available to my children and maintaining a well-kept home, all with a kid by my side or on my hip—like my own mother. I will, I fear, go on doing as much as I can, caught between pride and anger, furious at my exhaustion and Paul's inadequacy. Almost as if to entitle my anger, to justify or even fuel a frustration that's already there, I will—for now, at least—refuse any help from anyone, then bask in the fury of having too much to do and no time for myself. Recently, I have been thinking back to the years I spent as a kid living at home with my parents. Only now, when I have an apartment of my own and am responsible for my own meals and dishes and laundry and everything else, am I beginning to gain a more complete understanding of what my mother was doing between five or six or seven in the morning and bedtime. Owning a home, raising a family, maintaining sanity in a house— these are not small jobs, and my mother accomplished them all expertly, even after she added a career to the list. Though I wish she could have been more relaxed, that she and my father could have shared the chores in the house more equally, I'm beginning to understand why she didn't leave him. I'm beginning to see that she didn't just lie down and accept everything from the start, but that her role, her tasks, her *dissatisfaction*, came gradually, over a period of years. And along with whatever anger she felt beneath her cool exterior, there must have been, too, a tremendous sense of pride that came with knowing she was such an integral part of our family.

Whether I will follow her steps and have a family of my own I don't yet know. I do know that as I write these words and glance at my still-sleeping companion, I feel an odd mixture of frustration and love. Together we have a wonderful, open, trusting relationship, but sometimes I wonder if the hostility already in me, and my need to be angry at someone or something, could eventually destroy our bond. I suppose only time will tell. Unlike my mother, I don't have to go from my father's house to my husband's. And perhaps it's simply this time and space to think about the future and to love and live with and learn from whomever I please—time and space and freedom my mother never had—that she referred to when she said I have choices. At twenty-four, living in this day and age, I still have years to figure things out; to try to learn how to feel pride and even power without running myself ragged; to be with a man without being angry for the rest of my life. I hope I can.

QUESTIONS

1. The roles of women in marriage—and the differences between mothers' and daughters' expectations—is a topic of great debate, a "hot button" issue. What critique of her mother's role in the family does Maduro offer? What differences does Maduro see (or wish to see) between herself and her mother? What does she suggest prevents her from being entirely different from her mother and achieving her own goals in a male-female relationship?

2. The title comes from a phrase used in ordinary conversation. What does that choice tell the reader about the approach that Maduro will take to family structure and gener-

ational differences? If you have read Lauren Slater's "Love," compare the authors' techniques and suggest the values of each.

3. The subtitle of Maduro's essay includes three parts: mother, myself, anger. What connection is there between anger and the first two?

4. How are you like your father or mother? How do you hope to be different? Write a personal essay that uses description, comparison, contrast, and analysis to present your views.

AMY CUNNINGHAM   *Why Women Smile*

AFTER SMILING BRILLIANTLY for nearly four decades, I now find myself trying to quit. Or, at the very least, seeking to lower the wattage a bit.

Not everyone I know is keen on this. My smile has gleamed like a cheap plastic night-light so long and so reliably that certain friends and relatives worry that my mood will darken the moment my smile dims. "Gee," one says, "I associate you with your smile. It's the essence of you. I should think you'd want to smile more!" But the people who love me best agree that my smile—which springs forth no matter where I am or how I feel—hasn't been serving me well. Said my husband recently, "Your smiling face and unthreatening demeanor make people like you in a fuzzy way, but that doesn't seem to be what you're after these days."

Smiles are not the small and innocuous things they appear to be: Too many of us smile in lieu of showing what's really on our minds. Indeed, the success of the women's movement might be measured by the sincerity—and lack of it—in our smiles. Despite all the work we American women have done to get and maintain full legal control of our bodies, not to mention our destinies, we still don't seem to be fully in charge of a couple of small muscle groups in our faces.

We smile so often and so promiscuously—when we're angry, when we're tense, when we're with children, when we're being photographed, when we're interviewing for a job, when we're meeting candidates to employ—that the Smiling Woman has become a peculiarly American archetype. This isn't entirely a bad thing, of course. A smile lightens the load, diffuses unpleasantness, redistributes nervous tension. Women doctors smile more than their male counterparts, studies show, and are better liked by their patients.

5   Oscar Wilde's[1] old saw that "a woman's face is her work of fiction" is often quoted to remind us that what's on the surface may have little connection to

Many of Cunningham's writings have appeared in wide-circulation magazines aimed at women, like this 1993 essay from Lear's Magazine, *a periodical no longer published.*

1. Irish-born Victorian dramatist (1854–1900).

what we're feeling. What is it in our culture that keeps our smiles on automatic pilot? The behavior seems to be an equal blend of nature and nurture. Research has demonstrated that since females often mature earlier than males and are less irritable, girls smile more than boys from the very beginning. But by adolescence, the differences in the smiling rates of boys and girls are so robust that it's clear the culture has done more than its share of the dirty work. Just think of the mothers who painstakingly embroidered the words ENTER SMILING on little samplers, and then hung their handiwork on doors by golden chains. Translation: "Your real emotions aren't welcome here."

Clearly, our instincts are another factor. Our smiles have their roots in the greetings of monkeys, who pull their lips up and back to show their fear of attack, as well as their reluctance to vie for a position of dominance. And like the opossum caught in the light by the clattering garbage cans, we, too, flash toothy grimaces when we make major mistakes. By declaring ourselves nonthreatening, our smiles provide an extremely versatile means of protection.

Our earliest baby smiles are involuntary reflexes having only the vaguest connection to contentment or comfort. In short, we're genetically wired to pull on our parents' heartstrings. As Desmond Morris explains in *Babywatching*, this is our way of attaching ourselves to our caretakers, as truly as baby chimps clench their mothers' fur. Even as babies we're capable of projecting onto others (in this case, our parents) the feelings we know we need to get back in return.

Bona fide social smiles occur at two-and-a-half to three months of age, usually a few weeks after we first start gazing with intense interest into the faces of our parents. By the time we are six months old, we are smiling and laughing regularly in reaction to tickling, feedings, blown raspberries, hugs, and peekaboo games. Even babies who are born blind intuitively know how to react to pleasurable changes with a smile, though their first smiles start later than those of sighted children.

Psychologists and psychiatrists have noted that babies also smile and laugh with relief when they realize that something they thought might be dangerous is not dangerous after all. Kids begin to invite their parents to indulge them with "scary" approach-avoidance games; they love to be chased or tossed up into the air. (It's interesting to note that as adults, we go through the same gosh-that's-shocking-and-dangerous-but-it's-okay-to-laugh-and-smile cycles when we listen to raunchy stand-up comics.)

From the wilds of New Guinea to the sidewalks of New York, smiles are associated with joy, relief, and amusement. But smiles are by no means limited to the expression of positive emotions: People of many different cultures smile when they are frightened, embarrassed, angry, or miserable. In Japan, for instance, a smile is often used to hide pain or sorrow.

10

Psychologist Paul Ekman, the head of the University of California's Human Interaction Lab in San Francisco, has identified 18 distinct types of smiles, including those that show misery, compliance, fear, and contempt. The smile of true merriment, which Dr. Ekman calls the Duchenne Smile, after the 19th century French doctor who first studied it, is characterized by heightened circulation, a feeling of exhilaration, and the employment of two major facial muscles: the zygomaticus major of the lower face, and the orbicularis oculi, which crinkles the skin around the eyes. But since the average American woman's smile often has less to do with her actual state of happiness than it does with the social pressure to smile no matter what, her baseline social smile isn't apt to be a felt expression that engages the eyes like this. Ekman insists that if people learned to read smiles, they could see the sadness, misery, or pain lurking there, plain as day.

Evidently, a woman's happy, willing deference is something the world wants visibly demonstrated. Woe to the waitress, the personal assistant or receptionist, the flight attendant, or any other woman in the line of public service whose smile is not offered up to the boss or client as proof that there are no storm clouds—no kids to support, no sleep that's been missed—rolling into the sunny workplace landscape. Women are expected to smile no matter where they line up on the social, cultural, or economic ladder: College professors are criticized for not smiling, political spouses are pilloried for being too serious, and women's roles in films have historically been smiling ones. It's little wonder that men on the street still call out, "Hey, baby, smile! Life's not *that* bad, is it?" to women passing by, lost in thought.

A friend remembers being pulled aside by a teacher after class and asked, "What is wrong, dear? You sat there for the whole hour looking so sad!" "All I could figure," my friend says now, "is that I wasn't smiling. And the fact that *she* felt sorry for me for looking normal made me feel horrible."

Ironically, the social laws that govern our smiles have completely reversed themselves over the last 2,000 years. Women weren't always expected to seem animated and responsive; in fact, immoderate laughter was once considered one of the more conspicuous vices a woman could have, and mirth was downright sinful. Women were kept apart, in some cultures even veiled, so that they couldn't perpetuate Eve's seductive, evil work. The only smile deemed appropriate on a privileged woman's face was the serene, inward smile of the Virgin Mary at Christ's birth, and even that expression was best directed exclusively at young children. Cackling laughter and wicked glee were the kinds of sounds heard only in hell.

15   What we know of women's facial expressions in other centuries comes mostly from religious writings, codes of etiquette, and portrait paintings. In 15th century Italy, it was customary for artists to paint lovely, blank-faced women in profile. A viewer could stare endlessly at such a woman, but she could not gaze back. By the Renaissance, male artists were taking some pleasure in depicting women with a semblance of complexity, Leonardo da Vinci's Mona Lisa, with her veiled enigmatic smile, being the most famous example.

The Golden Age of the Dutch Republic marks a fascinating period for studying women's facial expressions. While we might expect the drunken young whores of Amsterdam to smile devilishly (unbridled sexuality and lasciviousness were *supposed* to addle the brain), it's the faces of the Dutch women from fine families that surprise us. Considered socially more free, these women demonstrate a fuller range of facial expressions than their European sisters. Frans Hals's 1622 portrait of Stephanus Geraerdt and Isabella Coymans, a married couple, is remarkable not just for the full, friendly smiles on each face, but for the frank and mutual pleasure the couple take in each other.

In the 1800s, sprightly, pretty women began appearing in advertisements for everything from beverages to those newfangled Kodak Land cameras. Women's faces were no longer impassive, and their willingness to bestow status, to offer, proffer, and yield, was most definitely promoted by their smiling images. The culture appeared to have turned the smile, originally a bond shared between intimates, into a socially required display that sold capitalist ideology as well as kitchen appliances. And female viewers soon began to emulate these highly idealized pictures. Many longed to be more like her, that perpetually smiling female. She seemed so beautiful. So content. So whole.

By the middle of the 19th century, the bulk of America's smile burden was falling primarily to women and African-American slaves, providing a very portable means of protection, a way of saying, "I'm harmless. I won't assert myself here." It reassured those in power to see signs of gratitude and contentment in the faces of subordinates. As long ago as 1963, adman David Ogilvy declared the image of a woman smiling approvingly at a product clichéd, but we've yet to get the message. Cheerful Americans still appear in ads today, smiling somewhat less disingenuously than they smiled during the middle of the century, but smiling broadly nonetheless.

Other countries have been somewhat reluctant to import our "Don't worry, be happy" American smiles. When McDonald's opened in Moscow not long ago and when EuroDisney debuted in France last year, the Americans involved in both business ventures complained that they couldn't get the natives they'd employed to smile worth a damn.

Europeans visiting the United States for the first time are often surprised   20
at just how often Americans smile. But when you look at our history, the relentless good humor (or, at any rate, the pretense of it) falls into perspective. The American wilderness was developed on the assumption that this country had a shortage of people in relation to its possibilities. In countries with a more rigid class structure or caste system, fewer people are as captivated by the idea of quickly winning friends and influencing people. Here in the States, however, every stranger is a potential associate. Our smiles bring new people on board. The American smile is a democratic version of a curtsy or doffed hat, since, in this land of free equals, we're not especially formal about the ways we greet social superiors.

The civil rights movement never addressed the smile burden by name, but activists worked on their own to set new facial norms. African-American males stopped smiling on the streets in the 1960s, happily aware of the unsettling effect this action had on the white population. The image of the simpleminded, smiling, white-toothed black was rejected as blatantly racist, and it gradually retreated into the distance. However, like the women of Sparta and the wives of samurai, who were expected to look happy upon learning their sons or husbands had died in battle, contemporary American women have yet to unilaterally declare their faces their own property.

For instance, imagine a woman at a morning business meeting being asked if she could make a spontaneous and concise summation of a complicated project she's been struggling to get under control for months. She might draw the end of her mouth back and clench her teeth—*Eek!*—in a protective response, a polite, restrained expression of her surprise, not unlike the expression of a conscientious young schoolgirl being told to get out paper and pencil for a pop quiz. At the same time, the woman might be feeling resentful of the supervisor who sprang the request, but she fears taking that person on. So she holds back a comment. The whole performance resolves in a weird grin collapsing into a nervous smile that conveys discomfort and unpreparedness. A pointed remark by way of explanation or self-defense might've worked better for her—but her mouth was otherwise engaged.

We'd do well to realize just how much our smiles misrepresent us, and swear off for good the self-deprecating grins and ritual displays of deference. Real smiles have beneficial physiological effects, according to Paul Ekman. False ones do nothing for us at all.

"Smiles are as important as sound bites on television," insists producer and media coach Heidi Berenson, who has worked with many of Washington's most famous faces. "And women have always been better at understanding this than men. But the smile I'm talking about is not a cutesy smile. It's an authoritative smile. A genuine smile. Properly timed, it's tremendously powerful."

25   To limit a woman to one expression is like editing down an orchestra to one instrument. And the search for more authentic means of expression isn't easy in a culture in which women are still expected to be magnanimous smilers, helpmates in crisis, and curators of everybody else's morale. But change is already floating in the high winds. We see a boon in assertive female comedians who are proving that women can *dish out* smiles, not just wear them. Actress Demi Moore has stated that she doesn't like to take smiling roles. Nike is running ads that show unsmiling women athletes sweating, reaching, pushing themselves. These women aren't overly concerned with issues of rapport; they're not being "nice" girls—they're working out.

If a woman's smile were truly her own, to be smiled or not, according to how the *woman* felt, rather than according to what someone else needed, she would smile more spontaneously, without ulterior, hidden motives. As Rainer Maria Rilke wrote in *The Journal of My Other Self*, "Her smile was not meant to be seen by anyone and served its whole purpose in being smiled."

That smile is my long-term aim. In the meantime, I hope to stabilize on the smile continuum somewhere between the eliciting grin of Farrah Fawcett and the haughty smirk of Jeane Kirkpatrick.[2]

2. Fawcett (b. 1947), television star and pinup girl of the 1970s, famous for her feathered hair; Kirkpatrick (1926–2006), American educator and diplomat and U.S. ambassador to the United Nations under Ronald Reagan, 1981–85.

Questions

1. Were you or some people you know urged to smile or to smile more? How was the advice given? What do you think was the motive?

2. Collect some observational data on the way men and women interact with strangers and see if you can confirm any part of Cunningham's essay.

3. Several years after Cunningham wrote "Why Women Smile," she discovered new research on smiling (see "All Smiles Now," below). This research has made her change her view on women's smiles. Write a brief account of what these changes are and what new evidence they reflect.

4. Do you think that Paul Ekman's research on Buddhist monks fully applies to American women and their smiles? What issues remain? Write about the issues in an essay that draws on your own experience and observation.

Friday, December 29, 2006[3]
All Smiles Now

I once wrote an essay called "Why Women Smile" for the women's magazine *Lear's*. More than fifteen years later, I'm still receiving checks from academic presses planning to re-run the article because, apparently, it "teaches well" in first-year college writing classes. . . .

But here's the quandary: I now know that a whole chunk of my article is incorrect. . . . For my research at the time, I interviewed a noted psychologist and facial expression expert Paul Ekman. I remember that when the piece was published, Ekman didn't seem so thrilled with it. He didn't write me back. I now know that's because he had been trying to tell me that he was conceiving of the human smile in a new way and that the feminists who thought women should smile less weren't approaching smiles from the right perspective. But I couldn't hear him. Ekman then was just a short time from researching Tibetan monks and the Dalai Lama's smiling meditations. He was on his way to substantiating that smiles—even fake plastered-on smiles—can indeed lift our moods and keep us happier. So actually, smiling women have had the right idea all along.

But I was so attached to the notion that feminine niceness was some kind of pathology that I couldn't hear what Ekman was telling me. Indeed, I couldn't imagine that if you smiled while seated quietly in meditation, you would spread the energy of cheer throughout the world and rise up feeling better. I couldn't conceive of the topic spiritually.

Since then, Ekman has published his findings. And my melancholy little prose piece (which my mother always hated anyway) is out there like the Energizer Bunny banging its drum. So until I can make this wrong a right, do me a favor: Smile freely and broadly. Get happy.

---

3. Posted on Cunningham's blog (on Beliefnet.com) on this date.

GLORIA STEINEM   *The Good News Is: These Are Not the Best Years of Your Life*

I F YOU HAD ASKED ME a decade or more ago, I certainly would have said the campus was the first place to look for the feminist or any other revolution. I also would have assumed that student-age women, like student-age men, were much more likely to be activist and open to change than their parents. After all, campus revolts have a long and well-publicized tradition, from the students of medieval France, whose "heresy" was suggesting that the university be separate from the church, through the anticolonial student riots of British India; from students who led the cultural revolution of the People's Republic of China, to campus demonstrations against the Shah of Iran. Even in this country, with far less tradition of student activism, the populist movement to end the war in Vietnam was symbolized by campus protests and mistrust of anyone over thirty.

It has taken me many years of traveling as a feminist speaker and organizer to understand that I was wrong about women; at least, about women acting on their own behalf. In activism, as in so many other things, I had been educated to assume that men's cultural pattern was the natural or the only one. If student years were the peak time of rebellion and openness to change for men, then the same must be true for women. In fact, a decade of listening to every kind of women's group—from brown-bag lunchtime lectures organized by office workers to all-night rap sessions at campus women's centers; from housewives' self-help groups to campus rallies—has convinced me that the reverse is more often true. Women may be the one group that grows more radical with age. Though some students are big exceptions to this rule, women in general don't begin to challenge the politics of our own lives until later.

Looking back, I realize that this pattern has been true for my life, too. My college years were full of uncertainties and the personal conservatism that comes from trying to win approval and fit into the proper grown-up and womanly role whether that means finding a well-to-do man to be supported by or a male radical to support. Nonetheless, I went right on assuming that brave exploring youth and cowardly conservative old age were the norms for everybody, and that I must be just an isolated and guilty accident. Though every generalization based on female culture has many exceptions, and should never be used as a crutch or excuse, I think we might be less hard on ourselves and each other as students, feel better about our potential for change as we grow older—and educate reporters who announce feminism's demise because its red-hot center is not on campus—if we figured out that for most of us as women, the traditional college period is an unrealistic and cautious time. Consider a few of the reasons.

First published in Ms. *(September 1979), a feminist magazine begun in 1971 during the women's movement and aimed at "exploring the truths and complexities of women's lives and patriarchal oppression." Steinem was a founding editor.*

As students, women are probably treated with more equality than we ever will be again. For one thing, we're consumers. The school is only too glad to get the tuitions we pay, or that our families or government grants pay on our behalf. With population rates declining because of women's increased power over childbearing, that money is even more vital to a school's existence. Yet more than most consumers, we're too transient to have much power as a group. If our families are paying our tuition, we may have even less power.

As young women, whether students or not, we're still in the stage most valued by male-dominant cultures: We have our full potential as workers, wives, sex partners, and childbearers.   5

That means we haven't yet experienced the life events that are most radicalizing for women: entering the paid-labor force and discovering how women are treated there; marrying and finding out that it is not yet an equal partnership; having children and discovering who is responsible for them and who is not; and aging, still a greater penalty for women than for men.

Furthermore, new ambitions nourished by the rebirth of feminism may make young women feel and behave a little like a classical immigrant group. We are determined to prove ourselves, to achieve academic excellence, and to prepare for interesting and successful careers. More noses are kept to more grindstones in an effort to demonstrate newfound abilities, and perhaps to allay suspicions that women still have to have more and better credentials than men. This doesn't leave much time for activism. Indeed, we may not yet know that it is necessary.

In addition, the very progress into previously all-male careers that may be revolutionary for women is seen as conservative and conformist by outside critics. Assuming male radicalism to be the measure of change, they interpret any concern with careers as evidence of "campus conservatism." In fact, "dropping out" may be a departure for men, but "dropping in" is a new thing for women. Progress lies in the direction we have not been.

Like most groups of the newly arrived or awakened, our faith in education and paper degrees also has yet to be shaken. For instance, the percentage of women enrolled in colleges and universities has been increasing at the same time that the percentage of men has been decreasing. Among students entering college in 1978, women *outnumbered* men for the first time. This hope of excelling at the existing game is probably reinforced by the greater cultural pressure on females to be "good girls" and observe somebody else's rules.

Though we may know intellectually that we need to have new games with new rules, we probably haven't quite absorbed such facts as the high unemployment rate among female Ph.D.s; the lower average salary among women college graduates of all races than among counterpart males who graduated from high school or less; the middle-management ceiling against which even those eagerly hired new business-school graduates seem to bump their heads after five or ten years; and the barrier-breaking women in nontraditional fields who become the first fired when recession hits. Sadly enough, we may have to personally experience some of these reality checks before we accept the idea   10 that lawsuits, activism, and group pressure will have to accompany our individual excellence and crisp new degrees.

Then there is the female guilt trip, student edition. If we're not sailing along as planned, it must be *our* fault. If our mothers didn't "do anything" with their educations, it must have been *their* fault. If we can't study as hard as we think we must (because women still have to be better prepared than men), and have a substantial personal and sexual life at the same time (because women are supposed to care more about relationships than men do), then we feel inadequate, as if each of us were individually at fault for a problem that is actually culture-wide.

I've yet to be on a campus where most women weren't worrying about some aspect of combining marriage, children, and a career. I've yet to find one where many men were worrying about the same thing. Yet women will go right on suffering from the double-role problem and terminal guilt until men are encouraged, pressured, or otherwise forced, individually and collectively, to integrate themselves into the "women's work" of raising children and homemaking. Until then, and until there are changed job patterns to allow equal parenthood, children will go right on growing up with the belief that only women can be loving and nurturing, and only men can be intellectual or active outside the home. Each half of the world will go on limiting the full range of its human talent.

Finally, there is the intimate political training that hits women in the teens and early twenties: the countless ways we are still brainwashed into assuming that women are dependent on men for our basic identities, both in our work and our personal lives, much more than vice versa. After all, if we're going to enter a marriage system that's still legally designed for a person and a half, submit to an economy in which women still average about fifty-nine cents on the dollar earned by men, and work mainly as support staff and assistants, or *co*-directors and *vice*-presidents at best, then we have to be convinced that we are not whole people on our own.

In order to make sure that we will see ourselves as half-people, and thus be addicted to getting our identity from serving others, society tries hard to convert us as young women into "man junkies"; that is, into people who are addicted to regular shots of male-approval and presence, both professionally and personally. We need a man standing next to us, actually and figuratively, whether it's at work, on Saturday night, or throughout life. (If only men realized how little it matters *which* man is standing there, they would understand that this addiction depersonalizes them, too.) Given the danger to a male-dominant system if young women stop internalizing this political message of derived identity, it's no wonder that those who try to kick the addiction—and, worse yet, to help other women do the same—are likely to be regarded as odd or dangerous by everyone from parents to peers.

15   With all that pressure combined with little experience, it's no wonder that younger women are often less able to support each other. Even young women who espouse feminist goals as individuals may refrain from identifying themselves as "feminist": it's okay to want equal pay for yourself (just one small re-

form) but it's not okay to want equal pay for women as a group (an economic revolution). Some retreat into individualized career obsessions as a way of avoiding this dangerous discovery of shared experience with women as a group. Others retreat into the safe middle ground of "I'm not a feminist but . . ." Still others become politically active, but only on issues that are taken seriously by their male counterparts.

The same lesson about the personal conservatism of younger women is taught by the history of feminism. If I hadn't been conned into believing the masculine stereotype of youth as the "natural" time for freedom and rebellion, a time of "sowing wild oats" that actually is made possible by the assurance of power and security later on, I could have figured out the female pattern of activism by looking at women's movements of the past.

In this country, for instance, the nineteenth-century wave of feminism was started by older women who had been through the radicalizing experience of getting married and becoming the legal chattel of their husbands (or the equally radicalizing experience of *not* getting married and being treated as spinsters). Most of them had also worked in the antislavery movement and learned from the political parallels between race and sex. In other countries, that wave was also led by women who were past the point of maximum pressure toward marriageability and conservatism.

Looking at the first decade of this second wave, it's clear that the early feminist activist and consciousness-raising groups of the 1960s were organized by women who had experienced the civil rights movement, or homemakers who had discovered that raising kids and cooking didn't occupy all their talents. While most campuses of the late sixties were still circulating the names of illegal abortionists privately (after all, abortion could damage our marriage value), slightly older women were holding press conferences and speak-outs about the reality of abortions (including their own, even though that often meant confessing to an illegal act) and demanding reform or repeal of anti-choice laws. Though rape had been a quiet epidemic on campus for generations, younger women victims were still understandably fearful of speaking up, and campuses encouraged silence in order to retain their reputation for safety with tuition-paying parents. It took many off-campus speak-outs, demonstrations against laws of evidence and police procedures, and testimonies in state legislatures before most student groups began to make demands on campus and local cops for greater rape protection. In fact, "date rape"—the common campus phenomenon of a young woman being raped by someone she knows, perhaps even by several students in a fraternity house—is just now being exposed. Marital rape, a more difficult legal issue, was taken up several years ago. As for battered women and the attendant exposé of husbands and lovers as more statistically dangerous than unknown muggers in the street, that issue still seems to be thought of as a largely noncampus concern, yet at many of the colleges and universities where I've spoken, there has been at least one case within current student memory of a young woman beaten or murdered by a jealous lover.

This cultural pattern of youthful conservatism makes the growing number

of older women going back to school very important. They are life examples
and pragmatic activists who radicalize women young enough to be their
daughters. Now that the median female undergraduate age in this country is
twenty-seven because so many older women have returned, the campus is becoming a major place for cross-generational connections.

20   None of this should denigrate the courageous efforts of young women, especially women on campus, and the many changes they've pioneered. On the
contrary, they should be seen as even more remarkable for surviving the conservative pressures, recognizing societal problems they haven't yet fully experienced, and organizing successfully in the midst of a transient student
population. Every women's history course, rape hot line, or campus newspaper
that is finally covering *all* the news; every feminist professor whose job has
been created or tenure saved by student pressure, or male administrator whose
consciousness has been permanently changed; every counselor who's stopped
guiding women one way and men another; every lawsuit that's been fueled by
student energies against unequal athletic funds or graduate school requirements: all those accomplishments are even more impressive when seen against
the backdrop of the female pattern of activism.

Finally, it would help to remember that a feminist revolution rarely resembles a masculine-style one—just as a young woman's most radical act toward
her mother (that is, connecting as women in order to help each other get some
power) doesn't look much like a young man's most radical act toward his father (that is, breaking the father-son connection in order to separate identities
or take over existing power).

It's those father-son conflicts at a generational, national level that have often provided the conventional definition of revolution; yet they've gone on for
centuries without basically changing the role of the female half of the world.
They have also failed to reduce the level of violence in society, since both fathers and sons have included some degree of aggressiveness and superiority to
women in their definition of masculinity, thus preserving the anthropological
model of dominance.

Furthermore, what current leaders and theoreticians define as revolution
is usually little more than taking over the army and the radio stations. Women
have much more in mind than that. We have to uproot the sexual caste system
that is the most pervasive power structure in society, and that means transforming the patriarchal values of those who run the institutions, whether they
are politically the "right" or the "left," the fathers or the sons. This cultural
part of the change goes very deep, and is often seen as too intimate, and perhaps too threatening, to be considered as either serious or possible. Only conflicts among men are "serious." Only a takeover of existing institutions is
"possible."

That's why the definition of "political," on campus as elsewhere, tends to
be limited to who's running for president, who's demonstrating against corporate investments in South Africa, or which is the "moral" side of some conventional revolution, preferably one that is thousands of miles away.

25   As important as such activities are, they are also the most comfortable

ones when we're young. They provide a sense of virtue without much disruption in the power structure of our daily lives. Even when the most consistent energies on campus are actually concentrated around feminist issues, they may be treated as apolitical and invisible. Asked "What's happening on campus?" a student may reply, "The antinuke movement," even though that resulted in one demonstration of two hours, while student antirape squads have been patrolling the campus every night for two years and women's studies have begun to transform the very textbooks we read.

No wonder reporters and sociologists looking for revolution on campus often miss the depth of feminist change and activity that is really there. Women students themselves may dismiss it as not political and not serious. Certainly, it rarely comes in the masculine sixties style of bombing buildings or burning draft cards. In fact, it goes much deeper than protesting a temporary symptom—say, the draft—and challenges the right of one group to dominate another, which is the disease itself.

Young women have a big task of resisting pressures and challenging definitions. Their increasing success is a miracle of foresight and courage that should make us all proud. But they should know that they, too, may grow more radical with age.

One day, an army of gray-haired women may quietly take over the earth.

QUESTIONS

1. Trace Steinem's use of pronouns (I, we, they) throughout this piece. Why does she use "we" to refer to college-aged women in some places and "they" in other places? What is the effect of her choice of pronouns?

2. In "Being a Man," Paul Theroux bristles against what seems to be expected of men, rejecting current definitions of masculinity. Steinem, in paragraph 22 of her essay, seems to imply that men have control over definitions of masculinity, arguing that "both fathers and sons have included some degree of aggressiveness and superiority to women in their definition of masculinity." Where do you think definitions of masculinity and femininity come from? Who can change them?

3. Steinem's article was originally published in 1979. Are her observations of college-age women applicable to women on your campus today? Write a brief essay discussing the differences and similarities between the young women she describes and the young women on your campus.

EDWARD THOMAS *Insomnia*

NIGHT AFTER NIGHT deliberately we take upon ourselves the utmost possible weakness, because it is the offering most acceptable to sleep. Our thick coverings give us warmth without need of motion. The night air we moderate into a harmless rustling or stroking coolness; or, if it be an obstreperous air, we may shut it out altogether, and with it all sounds. We choose to be alone, and in darkness. We make ourselves so weak, so easy, so content with nothing, that scarce anything but personal danger, and that immediate and certain, could stir us. Thus cunningly we oppose the utmost possible weakness to the assault of sleep.

Sometimes I have a lighted candle and a book at my bedside, but seldom for more than five minutes. The light and the effort of reading, though I may have gone early to bed, are too much for my instinctive weakness, this religious malingering. I find that I desire to enter without gradation into perfect helplessness, and I exercise a quiet resolution against the strains even of memory. For once I have lain down, safe, warm, and unanxious, nothing I can remember is worthy for more than a moment to interrupt. In this weakness there is a kind of power. Still and relaxed, as it were lacking bones and muscles entirely, I lie in a composed eagerness for sleep. And most often sleep will stoop and swallow me up, and I have no more dream or trouble than a grain swallowed by a bird.

But the mighty weakness that so allures sleep is turned to a powerless strength during the night. I wake before dawn, and then, much as I desire sleep, I cannot have it. I am now the prey of anything but sleep, anything real or unreal that comes to sight, touch, or hearing, or straight to the brain. It seems that all night I have heard the poplars shivering across the street in the strong lamplight, with a high singing note like a flame instead of a noise of showers; it seems that this shivering and this light will continue for ever, and for ever shall I lie restless under their afflictions. I strive, but no longer with unconscious power, to sink into the weakness that commands or deserves sleep. Any memory now can discompose me; any face, any word, any event, out of the past has to be entertained for a minute or an hour, according to its will, not mine. Those poplar leaves in the bright street are mightier than I or sleep. In vain I seek the posture and simulate the gesture of an already favoured victim. I am too weak. I am too strong, yet I cannot rise and darken the room or go out and contemn[1] sleep. It is a blessed thing if I am strong enough at last to wear myself out to sleep.

Published in The Last Sheaf *(1928), a collection of essays about nature and the author's experiences with birds, animals, and wild places. The collection was assembled after Thomas's death in World War I.*

1. View with contempt.

The other night I awoke just as the robin was beginning to sing outside in the dark garden. Beyond him the wind made a moan in the little fir-copse as of a forest in a space magically enclosed and silent, and in the intervals of his song silence fell about him like a cloak which the wind could not penetrate. As well as I knew the triple cry farther off for the crow of the first cock, I knew this for the robin's song, pausing but unbroken, though it was unlike any song of robin I had heard in daylight, standing or walking among trees. Outside, in the dark hush, to me lying prostrate, patient, unmoving, the song was absolutely monotonous, absolutely expressionless, a chain of little thin notes linked mechanically in a rhythm identical at each repetition. This was not the voluntary personal utterance of a winged sprite that I used to know, but a note touched on the instrument of night by a player unknown to me, save that it was he who delighted in the moaning fir-trees and in my silence. Nothing intelligible to me was expressed by it; since he, the player, alone knew, I call it expressionless.

When the light began to arrive, the song in the enclosed hush, and the sound of the trees beyond it, remained the same. I remained awake, silently and as stilly as possible, cringing for sleep. I was an unwilling note on the instrument; yet I do not know that the robin was less unwilling. I strove to escape out of that harmony of bird, wind, and man. But as fast as I made my mind a faintly heaving, shapeless, grey blank, some form or colour appeared; memory or anticipation was at work. 5

Gradually I found myself trying to understand this dawn harmony. I vowed to remember it and ponder it in the light of day. To make sure of remembering I tried putting it into rhyme. I was resolved not to omit the date; and so much so that the first line had to be "The seventh of September," nor could I escape from this necessity. Then September was to be rhymed with. The word "ember" occurred and stayed; no other would respond to all my calling. The third and fourth lines, it seemed, were bound to be something like—

> The sere[2] and the ember
> Of the year and of me.

This gave me no satisfaction, but I was under a very strong compulsion. I could do no more; not a line would add itself to the wretched three; nor did they cease to return again and again to my head. It was fortunate for me as a man, if not as an unborn poet, that I could not forget the lines; for by continual helpless repetition of them I rose yet once more to the weakness that sleep demanded. Gradually I became conscious of nothing but the moan of trees, the monotonous expressionless robin's song, the slightly aching body to which I was, by ties more and more slender, attached. I felt, I knew, I did not think that there would always be an unknown player, always wind and trees, always a robin singing, always a listener listening in the stark dawn: and I knew also

---

2. Withered, dry; the lines echo an earlier poem, "A Forsaken Garden," by Algernon Charles Swinburne (1837–1909): "The sun burns sere and the rain dishevels / One gaunt bleak blossom of scentless breath."

that if I were the listener I should not always lie thus in a safe warm bed thinking myself alive. . . . And so I fell asleep again on the seventh of September.

QUESTIONS

1. This essay begins with the pleasures of night and sleep, and then asks a seemingly
simple question: Why, given the pleasures of sleep, do we wake up in the middle of the
night? What answers does Thomas suggest?

2. What pleasures does Thomas find in insomnia? How does the essay turn from the
"afflictions" of insomnia (paragraph 3) to its pleasures (paragraphs 4–6)?

3. Write about a state of mind or experience of the body in which you turn from its difficulties or frustrations to its pleasures.

ELISABETH KÜBLER-ROSS *On the Fear of Death*

> Let me not pray to be sheltered from
> dangers but to be fearless in facing them.
> Let me not beg for the stilling of
> my pain but for the heart to conquer it.
> Let me not look for allies in life's
> battlefield but to my own strength.
> Let me not crave in anxious fear to
> be saved but hope for the patience to
> win my freedom.
> Grant me that I may not be a
> coward, feeling your mercy in my
> success alone; but let me find the grasp
> of your hand in my failure.
>
> —RABINDRANATH TAGORE,
> *Fruit-Gathering*

EPIDEMICS HAVE TAKEN a great toll of lives in past
generations. Death in infancy and early childhood
was frequent and there were few families who
didn't lose a member of the family at an early age.
Medicine has changed greatly in the last decades.
Widespread vaccinations have practically eradi-
cated many illnesses, at least in western Europe and the United States. The
use of chemotherapy, especially the antibiotics, has contributed to an ever de-

---

A chapter from Kübler-Ross's celebrated 1969 book, On Death and Dying, *which traces
the "stages of grief"—denial, anger, bargaining, depression, and acceptance—through
which a dying person passes when told of a terminal illness.*

creasing number of fatalities in infectious diseases. Better child care and education has effected a low morbidity and mortality among children. The many diseases that have taken an impressive toll among the young and middle-aged have been conquered. The number of old people is on the rise, and with this fact come the number of people with malignancies and chronic diseases associated more with old age.

Pediatricians have less work with acute and life-threatening situations as they have an ever increasing number of patients with psychosomatic disturbances and adjustment and behavior problems. Physicians have more people in their waiting rooms with emotional problems than they have ever had before, but they also have more elderly patients who not only try to live with their decreased physical abilities and limitations but who also face loneliness and isolation with all its pains and anguish. The majority of these people are not seen by a psychiatrist. Their needs have to be elicited and gratified by other professional people, for instance, chaplains and social workers. It is for them that I am trying to outline the changes that have taken place in the last few decades, changes that are ultimately responsible for the increased fear of death, the rising number of emotional problems, and the greater need for understanding of and coping with the problems of death and dying.

When we look back in time and study old cultures and people, we are impressed that death has always been distasteful to man and will probably always be. From a psychiatrist's point of view this is very understandable and can perhaps best be explained by our basic knowledge that, in our unconscious, death is never possible in regard to ourselves. It is inconceivable for our unconscious to imagine an actual ending of our own life here on earth, and if this life of ours has to end, the ending is always attributed to a malicious intervention from the outside by someone else. In simple terms, in our unconscious mind we can only be killed; it is inconceivable to die of a natural cause or of old age. Therefore death in itself is associated with a bad act, a frightening happening, something that in itself calls for retribution and punishment.

One is wise to remember these fundamental facts as they are essential in understanding some of the most important, otherwise unintelligible communications of our patients.

The second fact that we have to comprehend is that in our unconscious mind we cannot distinguish between a wish and a deed. We are all aware of some of our illogical dreams in which two completely opposite statements can exist side by side—very acceptable in our dreams but unthinkable and illogical in our wakening state. Just as our unconscious mind cannot differentiate between the wish to kill somebody in anger and the act of having done so, the young child is unable to make this distinction. The child who angrily wishes his mother to drop dead for not having gratified his needs will be traumatized greatly by the actual death of his mother—even if this event is not linked closely in time with his destructive wishes. He will always take part or the whole blame for the loss of his mother. He will always say to himself—rarely to others—"I did it, I am responsible, I was bad, therefore Mommy left me." It is

5

well to remember that the child will react in the same manner if he loses a parent by divorce, separation, or desertion. Death is often seen by a child as an impermanent thing and has therefore little distinction from a divorce in which he may have an opportunity to see a parent again.

Many a parent will remember remarks of their children such as, "I will bury my doggy now and next spring when the flowers come up again, he will get up." Maybe it was the same wish that motivated the ancient Egyptians to supply their dead with food and goods to keep them happy and the old American Indians to bury their relatives with their belongings.

When we grow older and begin to realize that our omnipotence is really not so omnipotent, that our strongest wishes are not powerful enough to make the impossible possible, the fear that we have contributed to the death of a loved one diminishes—and with it the guilt. The fear remains diminished, however, only so long as it is not challenged too strongly. Its vestiges can be seen daily in hospital corridors and in people associated with the bereaved.

A husband and wife may have been fighting for years, but when the partner dies, the survivor will pull his hair, whine and cry louder and beat his chest in regret, fear and anguish, and will hence fear his own death more than before, still believing in the law of talion—an eye for an eye, a tooth for a tooth—"I am responsible for her death, I will have to die a pitiful death in retribution."

Maybe this knowledge will help us understand many of the old customs and rituals which have lasted over the centuries and whose purpose is to diminish the anger of the gods or the people as the case may be, thus decreasing the anticipated punishment. I am thinking of the ashes, the torn clothes, the veil, the *Klage Weiber*[1] of the old days—they are all means to ask you to take pity on them, the mourners, and are expressions of sorrow, grief, and shame. If someone grieves, beats his chest, tears his hair, or refuses to eat, it is an attempt at self-punishment to avoid or reduce the anticipated punishment for the blame that he takes on the death of a loved one.

10   This grief, shame, and guilt are not very far removed from feelings of anger and rage. The process of grief always includes some qualities of anger. Since none of us likes to admit anger at a deceased person, these emotions are often disguised or repressed and prolong the period of grief or show up in other ways. It is well to remember that it is not up to us to judge such feelings as bad or shameful but to understand their true meaning and origin as something very human. In order to illustrate this I will again use the example of the child—and the child in us. The five-year-old who loses his mother is both blaming himself for her disappearance and being angry at her for having deserted him and for no longer gratifying his needs. The dead person then turns into something the child loves and wants very much but also hates with equal intensity for this severe deprivation.

The ancient Hebrews regarded the body of a dead person as some-

1. Wailing wives.

thing unclean and not to be touched. The early American Indians talked about the evil spirits and shot arrows in the air to drive the spirits away. Many other cultures have rituals to take care of the "bad" dead person, and they all originate in this feeling of anger which still exists in all of us, though we dislike admitting it. The tradition of the tombstone may originate in this wish to keep the bad spirits deep down in the ground, and the pebbles that many mourners put on the grave are left-over symbols of the same wish. Though we call the firing of guns at military funerals a last salute, it is the same symbolic ritual as the Indian used when he shot his spears and arrows into the skies.

I give these examples to emphasize that man has not basically changed. Death is still a fearful, frightening happening, and the fear of death is a universal fear even if we think we have mastered it on many levels.

What has changed is our way of coping and dealing with death and dying and our dying patients.

Having been raised in a country in Europe where science is not so advanced, where modern techniques have just started to find their way into medicine, and where people still live as they did in this country half a century ago, I may have had an opportunity to study a part of the evolution of mankind in a shorter period.

I remember as a child the death of a farmer. He fell from a tree and was not expected to live. He asked simply to die at home, a wish that was granted without questioning. He called his daughters into the bedroom and spoke with each one of them alone for a few moments. He arranged his affairs quietly, though he was in great pain, and distributed his belongings and his land, none of which was to be split until his wife should follow him in death. He also asked each of his children to share in the work, duties, and tasks that he had carried on until the time of the accident. He asked his friends to visit him once more, to bid good-bye to them. Although I was a small child at the time, he did not exclude me or my siblings. We were allowed to share in the preparations of the family just as we were permitted to grieve with them until he died. When he did die, he was left at home, in his own beloved home which he had built, and among his friends and neighbors who went to take a last look at him where he lay in the midst of flowers in the place he had lived in and loved so much. In that country today there is still no make-believe slumber room, no embalming, no false makeup to pretend sleep. Only the signs of very disfiguring illnesses are covered up with bandages and only infectious cases are removed from the home prior to the burial.

Why do I describe such "old-fashioned" customs? I think they are an indication of our acceptance of a fatal outcome, and they help the dying patient as well as his family to accept the loss of a loved one. If a patient is allowed to terminate his life in the familiar and beloved environment, it requires less adjustment for him. His own family knows him well enough to replace a sedative with a glass of his favorite wine; or the smell of a home-cooked soup may give him the appetite to sip a few spoons of fluid which, I think, is still more enjoyable than an infusion. I will not minimize the need for sedatives and infusions and realize full well from my own experience as a country doctor that they are

15

sometimes life-saving and often unavoidable. But I also know that patience and familiar people and foods could replace many a bottle of intravenous fluids given for the simple reason that it fulfills the physiological need without involving too many people and/or individual nursing care.

The fact that children are allowed to stay at home where a fatality has stricken and are included in the talk, discussions, and fears gives them the feeling that they are not alone in the grief and gives them the comfort of shared responsibility and shared mourning. It prepares them gradually and helps them view death as part of life, an experience which may help them grow and mature.

This is in great contrast to a society in which death is viewed as taboo, discussion of it is regarded as morbid, and children are excluded with the presumption and pretext that it would be "too much" for them. They are then sent off to relatives, often accompanied with some unconvincing lies of "Mother has gone on a long trip" or other unbelievable stories. The child senses that something is wrong, and his distrust in adults will only multiply if other relatives add new variations of the story, avoid his questions or suspicions, shower him with gifts as a meager substitute for a loss he is not permitted to deal with. Sooner or later the child will become aware of the changed family situation and, depending on the age and personality of the child, will have an unresolved grief and regard this incident as a frightening, mysterious, in any case very traumatic experience with untrustworthy grownups, which he has no way to cope with.

It is equally unwise to tell a little child who lost her brother that God loved little boys so much that he took little Johnny to heaven. When this little girl grew up to be a woman she never solved her anger at God, which resulted in a psychotic depression when she lost her own little son three decades later.

20   We would think that our great emancipation, our knowledge of science and of man, has given us better ways and means to prepare ourselves and our families for this inevitable happening. Instead the days are gone when a man was allowed to die in peace and dignity in his own home.

The more we are making advancements in science, the more we seem to fear and deny the reality of death. How is this possible?

We use euphemisms, we make the dead look as if they were asleep, we ship the children off to protect them from the anxiety and turmoil around the house if the patient is fortunate enough to die at home, we don't allow children to visit their dying parents in the hospitals, we have long and controversial discussions about whether patients should be told the truth—a question that rarely arises when the dying person is tended by the family physician who has known him from delivery to death and who knows the weaknesses and strengths of each member of the family.

I think there are many reasons for this flight away from facing death calmly. One of the most important facts is that dying nowadays is more gruesome in many ways, namely, more lonely, mechanical, and dehumanized; at times it is even difficult to determine technically when the time of death has occurred.

Dying becomes lonely and impersonal because the patient is often taken out of his familiar environment and rushed to an emergency room. Whoever has been very sick and has required rest and comfort especially may recall his experience of being put on a stretcher and enduring the noise of the ambulance siren and hectic rush until the hospital gates open. Only those who have lived through this may appreciate the discomfort and cold necessity of such transportation which is only the beginning of a long order—hard to endure when you are well, difficult to express in words when noise, light, pumps, and voices are all too much to put up with. It may well be that we might consider more the patient under the sheets and blankets and perhaps stop our well-meant efficiency and rush in order to hold the patient's hand, to smile, or to listen to a question. I include the trip to the hospital as the first episode in dying, as it is for many. I am putting it exaggeratedly in contrast to the sick man who is left at home—not to say that lives should not be saved if they can be saved by a hospitalization but to keep the focus on the patient's experience, his needs and his reactions.

When a patient is severely ill, he is often treated like a person with no right to an opinion. It is often someone else who makes the decision if and when and where a patient should be hospitalized. It would take so little to remember that the sick person too has feelings, has wishes and opinions, and has—most important of all—the right to be heard.

Well, our presumed patient has now reached the emergency room. He will be surrounded by busy nurses, orderlies, interns, residents, a lab technician perhaps who will take some blood, an electrocardiogram technician who takes the cardiogram. He may be moved to X-ray and he will overhear opinions of his condition and discussions and questions to members of the family. He slowly but surely is beginning to be treated like a thing. He is no longer a person. Decisions are made often without his opinion. If he tries to rebel he will be sedated and after hours of waiting and wondering whether he has the strength, he will be wheeled into the operating room or intensive treatment unit and become an object of great concern and great financial investment.

He may cry for rest, peace, and dignity, but he will get infusions, transfusions, a heart machine, or tracheotomy if necessary. He may want one single person to stop for one single minute so that he can ask one single question—but he will get a dozen people around the clock, all busily preoccupied with his heart rate, pulse, electrocardiogram or pulmonary functions, his secretions or excretions but not with him as a human being. He may wish to fight it all but it is going to be a useless fight since all this is done in the fight for his life, and if they can save his life they can consider the person afterwards. Those who consider the person first may lose precious time to save his life! At least this seems to be the rationale or justification behind all this—or is it? Is the reason for this increasingly mechanical, depersonalized approach our own defensiveness? Is this approach our own way to cope with and repress the anxieties that a terminally or critically ill patient evokes in us? Is our concentration on equipment, on blood pressure our desperate attempt to deny the impending death which is so frightening and discomforting to us that we displace all our knowledge onto machines, since they are less close to us than the suffering face of another human being which would remind us once more of our lack of omnipotence, our own limits and failures, and last but not least perhaps our own mortality?

Maybe the question has to be raised: Are we becoming less human or more human? * * * [I]t is clear that whatever the answer may be, the patient is suffering more—not physically, perhaps, but emotionally. And his needs have not changed over the centuries, only our ability to gratify them.

QUESTIONS

1. In this essay Kübler-Ross incorporates various kinds of evidence: experience, observation, and reading. Mark the various kinds and describe how she integrates them into her text.

2. Kübler-Ross attends to the needs of the living and the rights of the dying. Describe where and how she attends to each and how she presents the conflicts, actual and potential, between them.

3. In paragraphs 24–27 Kübler-Ross describes the experience of the trip by ambulance, the emergency room, and the hospital from a patient's point of view. What does this shift in point of view contribute to the essay?

4. Imagine a situation in which a child or children are not isolated from death. What might be the consequences? Using this situation and its possible consequences, write an essay in which you agree or disagree with Kübler-Ross's views.

MARY ROACH   *How to Know If You're Dead*

A PATIENT ON THE WAY to surgery travels at twice the speed of a patient on the way to the morgue. Gurneys that ferry the living through hospital corridors move forward in an aura of purpose and push, flanked by caregivers with long strides and set faces, steadying IVs, pumping ambu bags,[1] barreling into double doors. A gurney with a cadaver commands no urgency. It is wheeled by a single person, calmly and with little notice, like a shopping cart.

For this reason, I thought I would be able to tell when the dead woman

A chapter from Stiff: The Curious Life of Human Cadavers *(2003). The book addresses the questions: What happens to our bodies when we die? When our bodies shut down, what comes next?*

1. A manual resuscitator that helps provide patients with artificial ventilation.

was wheeled past. I have been standing around at the nurses' station on one of the surgery floors of the University of California at San Francisco Medical Center, watching gurneys go by and waiting for Von Peterson, public affairs manager of the California Transplant Donor Network, and a cadaver I will call H. "There's your patient," says the charge nurse. A commotion of turquoise legs passes with unexpected forward-leaning urgency.

H is unique in that she is both a dead person *and* a patient on the way to surgery. She is what's known as a "beating-heart cadaver," alive and well everywhere but her brain. Up until artificial respiration was developed, there was no such entity; without a functioning brain, a body will not breathe on its own. But hook it up to a respirator and its heart will beat, and the rest of its organs will, for a matter of days, continue to thrive.

H doesn't look or smell or feel dead. If you leaned in close over the gurney, you could see her pulse beating in the arteries of her neck. If you touched her arm, you would find it warm and resilient, like your own. This is perhaps why the nurses and doctors refer to H as a patient, and why she makes her entrance to the OR[2] at the customary presurgery clip.

Since brain death is the legal definition of death in this country, H the person is certifiably dead. But H the organs and tissues is very much alive. These two seemingly contradictory facts afford her an opportunity most corpses do not have: that of extending the lives of two or three dying strangers. Over the next four hours, H will surrender her liver, kidneys, and heart. One at a time, surgeons will come and go, taking an organ and returning in haste to their stricken patients. Until recently, the process was known among transplant professionals as an "organ harvest," which had a joyous, celebratory ring to it, perhaps a little too joyous, as it has been of late replaced by the more businesslike "organ recovery."

In H's case, one surgeon will be traveling from Utah to recover her heart, and another, the one recovering both the liver and the kidneys, will be taking them two floors down. UCSF is a major transplant center, and organs removed here often remain in house. More typically, a transplant patient's surgeon will travel from UCSF to a small town somewhere to retrieve the organ—often from an accident victim, someone young with strong, healthy organs, whose brain took an unexpected hit. The doctor does this because typically there is no doctor in that small town with experience in organ recovery. Contrary to rumors about surgically trained thugs cutting people open in hotel rooms and stealing their kidneys, organ recovery is tricky work. If you want to be sure it's done right, you get on a plane and go do it yourself.

Today's abdominal recovery surgeon is named Andy Posselt. He is holding an electric cauterizing[3] wand, which looks like a cheap bank pen on a cord but functions like a scalpel. The wand both cuts and burns, so that as the incision is made, any vessels that are severed are simultaneously melted shut. The result is that there is a good deal less bleeding and a good deal more smoke and

___

2. Operating room.
3. Burning a part of the human body, with the goal of removing or sealing it.

smell. It's not a bad smell, but simply a seared-meat sort of smell. I want to ask Dr. Posselt whether he likes it, but I can't bring myself to, so instead I ask whether he thinks it's bad that I like the smell, which I don't really, or maybe just a little. He replies that it is neither bad nor good, just morbid.

I have never before seen major surgery, only its scars. From the length of them, I had imagined surgeons doing their business, taking things out and putting them in, through an opening maybe eight or nine inches long, like a woman poking around for her glasses at the bottom of her purse. Dr. Posselt begins just above H's pubic hair and proceeds a good two feet north, to the base of her neck. He's unzipping her like a parka. Her sternum is sawed lengthwise so that her rib cage can be parted, and a large retractor is installed to pull the two sides of the incision apart so that it is now as wide as it is long. To see her this way, held open like a Gladstone bag,[4] forces a view of the human torso for what it basically is: a large, sturdy container for guts.

On the inside, H looks very much alive. You can see the pulse of her heartbeat in her liver and all the way down her aorta. She bleeds where she is cut and her organs are plump and slippery-looking. The electronic beat of the heart monitor reinforces the impression that this is a living, breathing, thriving person. It is strange, almost impossible, really, to think of her as a corpse. When I tried to explain beating-heart cadavers to my step-daughter Phoebe yesterday, it didn't make sense to her. But if their heart is beating, aren't they still a person? she wanted to know. In the end she decided they were "a kind of person you could play tricks on but they wouldn't know." Which, I think, is a pretty good way of summing up most donated cadavers. The things that happen to the dead in labs and ORs are like gossip passed behind one's back. They are not felt or known and so they cause no pain.

10   The contradictions and counterintuitions of the beating-heart cadaver can exact an emotional toll on the intensive care unit (ICU) staff, who must, in the days preceding the harvest, not only think of patients like H as living beings, but treat and care for them that way as well. The cadaver must be monitored around the clock and "life-saving" interventions undertaken on its behalf. Since the brain can no longer regulate blood pressure or the levels of hormones and their release into the bloodstream, these things must be done by ICU staff, in order to keep the organs from degrading. Observed a group of Case Western Reserve University School of Medicine physicians in a *New England Journal of Medicine* article entitled "Psychosocial and Ethical Implications of Organ Retrieval": "Intensive care unit personnel may feel confused about having to perform cardiopulmonary resuscitation on a patient who has been declared dead, whereas a 'do not resuscitate' order has been written for a living patient in the next bed."

The confusion people feel over beating-heart cadavers reflects centuries of confusion over how, exactly, to define death, to pinpoint the precise moment

---

4. A type of bag, named for British prime minister William Ewart Gladstone (1809–1898), that has two hinged compartments.

when the spirit—the soul, the chi,[5] whatever you wish to call it—has ceased to exist and all that remains is a corpse. Before brain activity could be measured, the stopping of the heart had long been considered the defining moment. In point of fact, the brain survives for six to ten minutes after the heart has stopped pumping blood to it, but this is splitting hairs, and the definition works quite well for the most part. The problem, for centuries, was that doctors couldn't tell for sure whether the heart had ceased to beat or whether they were merely having trouble hearing it. The stethoscope wasn't invented until the mid-1800s, and the early models amounted to little more than a sort of medical ear trumpet. In cases where the heartbeat and pulse are especially faint—drownings, stroke, certain types of narcotic poisoning—even the most scrupulous physician had difficulty telling, and patients ran the risk of being dispatched to the undertaker before they'd actually expired.

To allay patients' considerable fears of live burial, as well as their own insecurities, eighteenth- and nineteenth-century physicians devised a diverting roster of methods for verifying death. Welsh physician and medical historian Jan Bondeson collected dozens of them for his witty and admirably researched book *Buried Alive.* The techniques seemed to fall into two categories: those that purported to rouse the unconscious patient with unspeakable pain, and those that threw in a measure of humiliation. The soles of the feet were sliced with razors, and needles jammed beneath toenails. Ears were assaulted with bugle fanfares and "hideous Shrieks and excessive Noises." One French clergyman recommended thrusting a red-hot poker up what Bondeson genteelly refers to as "the rear passage." A French physician invented a set of nipple pincers specifically for the purpose of reanimation. Another invented a bagpipelike contraption for administering tobacco enemas, which he demonstrated enthusiastically on cadavers in the morgues of Paris. The seventeenth-century anatomist Jacob Winslow[6] entreated his colleagues to pour boiling Spanish wax on patients' foreheads and warm urine into their mouths. One Swedish tract on the matter suggested that a crawling insect be put into the corpse's ear. For simplicity and originality, though, nothing quite matches the thrusting of "a sharp pencil" up the presumed cadaver's nose.

In some cases, it is unclear who was the more humiliated, patient or doctor. French physician Jean Baptiste Vincent Laborde wrote at great length of his technique of rhythmic tongue-pulling, which was to be carried out for no less than three hours following the suspected death. (He later invented a hand-cranked tongue-pulling machine, which made the task less unpleasant though only marginally less tedious.) Another French physician instructed doctors to stick one of the patient's fingers in their ear, to listen for the buzzing sound produced by involuntary muscle movement.

Not all that surprisingly, none of these techniques gained wide acceptance, and most doctors felt that putrefaction was the only reliable way to ver-

5. A concept in Chinese culture that means, approximately, "life force."
6. Dutch anatomist (1669–1760).

ify that someone was dead. This meant that corpses had to sit around the house or the doctor's office for two or three days until the telltale signs and smells could be detected, a prospect perhaps even less appealing than giving them enemas. And so it was that special buildings, called waiting mortuaries, were built for the purpose of warehousing the moldering dead. These were huge, ornate halls, common in Germany in the 1800s. Some had separate halls for male and female cadavers, as though, even in death, men couldn't be trusted to comport themselves respectably in the presence of a lady. Others were segregated by class, with the well-to-do deceased paying extra to rot in luxury surroundings. Attendants were employed to keep watch for signs of life, which they did via a system of strings linking the fingers of corpses to a bell[7] or, in one case, the bellows of a large organ, so that any motion on the part of the deceased would alert the attendant, who was posted, owing to the considerable stench, in a separate room. As years passed and not a single resident was saved, the establishments began to close, and by 1940, the waiting mortuary had gone the way of the nipple pincer and the tongue puller.

* * *

15   With improvements in stethoscopes and gains in medical knowledge, physicians began to trust themselves to be able to tell when a heart had stopped, and medical science came to agree that this was the best way to determine whether a patient had checked out for good or was merely down the hall getting ice. Placing the heart center stage in our definition of death served to give it, by proxy, a starring role in our definition of life and the soul, or spirit or self. It has long had this anyway, as evidenced by a hundred thousand love songs and sonnets and I ♥ bumper stickers. The concept of the beating-heart cadaver, grounded in a belief that the self resides in the brain and the brain alone, delivered a philosophical curveball. The notion of the heart as fuel pump took some getting used to.

The seat-of-the-soul debate has been ongoing some four thousand years. It started out not as a heart-versus-brain debate, but as heart-versus-liver. The ancient Egyptians were the original heart guys. They believed that the ka resided in the heart. Ka was the essence of the person: spirit, intelligence, feelings and passions, humor, grudges, annoying television theme songs, all the things that make a person a person and not a nematode. The heart was the only organ left inside a mummified corpse, for a man needed his ka in the afterlife. The brain he clearly did not need: cadaver brains were scrambled and pulled out in globs, through the nostrils, by way of a hooked bronze needle. Then they were thrown away. (The liver, stomach, intestines, and lungs were taken out of the body, but kept: They were stored in earthen jars inside the

---

7. I read on a Web site somewhere that this was the origin of the saying "Saved by the bell." In fact, by one reckoning, not a single corpse of the million-plus sent to waiting mortuaries over a twenty-year period awakened. If the bell alerted the attendant, which it often did, it was due to the corpse's shifting and collapsing as it decomposed. This was the origin of the saying "Driven to seek new employment by the bell," which you don't hear much anymore and probably never did, because I made it up [Roach's note].

tomb, on the assumption, I guess, that it is better to overpack than to leave something behind, particularly when packing for the afterlife.)

The Babylonians were the original liver guys, believing the organ to be the source of human emotion and spirit. The Mesopotamians played both sides of the argument, assigning emotion to the liver and intellect to the heart. These guys clearly marched to the beat of a freethinking drummer, for they assigned a further portion of the soul (cunning) to the stomach. Similar freethinkers throughout history have included Descartes,[8] who wrote that the soul could be found in the walnut-sized pineal gland, and the Alexandrian anatomist Strato,[9] who decided it lived "behind the eyebrows."

With the rise of classical Greece, the soul debate evolved into the more familiar heart-versus-brain, the liver having been demoted to an accessory role.[10] Though Pythagoras and Aristotle[11] viewed the heart as the seat of the soul—the source of "vital force" necessary to live and grow—they believed there to be a secondary, "rational" soul, or mind, located in the brain. Plato[12] agreed that both the heart and the brain were soul terrain, but assigned primacy to the brain. Hippocrates,[13] for his part, seemed confused (or perhaps it's me). He noted the effects of a crushed brain upon speech and intelligence, yet referred to it as a mucus-secreting gland, and wrote elsewhere that intelligence and "heat," which he said controlled the soul, were located in the heart.

The early anatomists weren't able to shed much light on the issue, as the soul wasn't something you could see or set your scalpel to. Lacking any scientific means of pinning down the soul, the first anatomists settled on generative primacy: What shows up first in the embryo must be most important and therefore most likely to hold the soul. The trouble with this particular avenue of learning, known as ensoulment, was that early first-trimester human embryos were difficult to come by. Classical scholars of ensoulment, Aristotle among them, attempted to get around the problem by examining the larger, more easily obtained poultry embryo. To quote Vivian Nutton, author of "The Anatomy of the Soul in Early Renaissance Medicine" in *The Human Embryo*, "Analogies drawn from the inspection of hen's eggs foundered on the objection that man was not a chicken."

According to Nutton, the man who came closest to actually examining a   20

8. René Descartes (1596–1650), French philosopher and mathematician.

9. Strato, short for Erasistratus (fl. 3rd century B.C.E.), placed the soul in the forefront of the brain.

10. We are fortunate that this is so, for we would otherwise have been faced with Céline Dion singing "My Liver Belongs to You" and movie houses playing *The Liver Is a Lonely Hunter*. Every Spanish love song that contains the word *corazón*, which is all of them, would contain the somewhat less lilting *higado*, and bumper stickers would proclaim, "I [liver symbol] my Pekingese" [Roach's note].

11. Pythagoras (582–507 B.C.E.) and Aristotle (384–322 B.C.E.), Greek philosophers.

12. Greek philosopher (428/7–347 B.C.E.).

13. Greek physician (460–377 B.C.E.), known today as the father of medicine.

human embryo was an anatomist named Realdo Colombo,[14] who, at the behest of the Renaissance philosopher Girolamo Pontano,[15] dissected a one-month-old fetus. Colombo returned from his lab—which in all likelihood was not equipped with a microscope, as the device had barely been invented—bearing the fascinating if flat-out wrong news that the liver formed before the heart.

Living amid our culture's heart-centric rhetoric, the valentines and the pop song lyrics, it is hard to imagine assigning spiritual or emotional sovereignty to the liver. Part of the reason for its exalted status among the early anatomists was that they erroneously believed it to be the origin of all the body's blood vessels. (William Harvey's[16] discovery of the circulatory system dealt the liver-as-seat-of-the-soul theory a final fatal blow; Harvey, you will not be surprised to hear, believed that the soul was carried in the blood.) I think it was something else too. The human liver is a boss-looking organ. It's glossy, aerodynamic, Olympian. It looks like sculpture, not guts. I've been marveling at H's liver, currently being prepped for its upcoming journey. The organs around it are amorphous and unappealing. Stomachs are flappy, indistinct; intestines, chaotic and soupy. Kidneys skulk under bundles of fat. But the liver gleams. It looks engineered and carefully wrought. Its flanks have a subtle curve, like the horizon seen from space. If I were an ancient Babylonian, I guess I might think God splashed down here too.

Dr. Posselt is isolating the vessels and connectors on the liver and kidneys, prepping them for the organs' removal. The heart will go first—hearts remain viable only four to six hours; kidneys, by contrast, can be held in cold storage eighteen or even twenty-four hours—but the heart recovery surgeon hasn't arrived. He's flying in from Utah.

Minutes later a nurse puts her head through the OR doors. "Utah's in the building." People who work in ORs talk to each other in the truncated, slang-heavy manner of pilots and flight control types. The schedule on the OR wall lists today's procedure—the removal of four vital organs in preparation for death-defying transplantation into three desperate human beings—as "Recovery abdm (liv/kid x2) ♥." A few minutes ago, someone made reference to "the panky," meaning "the pancreas."

"Utah's changing."

Utah is a gentle-looking man of perhaps fifty, with graying hair and a thin, tanned face. He has finished changing and a nurse is snapping on his gloves. He looks calm, competent, even a little bored. (This just slays me. The man is about to cut a beating heart out of a human chest.) The heart has been hidden until now behind the pericardium, a thick protective sac which Dr. Posselt now cuts away.

There is her heart. I've never seen one beating. I had no idea they moved

14. Matteo Realdo Colombo (c. 1516–1559), professor of anatomy and surgeon at the University of Padua; Pontano (fl. 1597), Italian philosopher.
15. I'd never heard of him either [Roach's note].
16. British doctor (1578–1657).

so much. You put your hand on your heart and you picture something pulsing slightly but basically still, like a hand on a desktop tapping Morse code. This thing is going wild in there. It's a mixing-machine part, a stoat squirming in its burrow, an alien life form that's just won a Pontiac on *The Price Is Right*. If you were looking for the home of the human body's animating spirit, I could imagine believing it to be here, for the simple reason that it is the human body's most animated organ.

Utah places clamps on the arteries of H's heart, stanching the flow of blood in preparation for the cuts. You can tell by the vital signs monitor that something monumental is happening to her body. The ECG[17] has quit drawing barbed wire and begun to look like a toddler's Etch-a-Sketch scrawls. A quick geyser of blood splashes Utah's glasses, then subsides. If H weren't dead, she'd be dying now.

This is the moment, reported the Case Western Reserve group who interviewed transplant professionals, when OR staff have been known to report sensing a "presence" or "spirit" in the room. I try to raise the mental aerial and keep myself open to the vibes. Of course I have no idea how to do this. When I was six, I tried as hard as I could to will my brother's GI Joe to walk across the room to him. This is how these extrasensory deals go with me: Nothing comes of it, and then I feel stupid for trying.

Here is the deeply unnerving thing: The heart, cut from the chest, keeps beating on its own. Did Poe[18] know this when he wrote "The Tell-Tale Heart"? So animated are these freestanding hearts that surgeons have been known to drop them. "We wash them off and they do just fine," replied New York heart transplant surgeon Mehmet Oz when I asked him about it. I imagined the heart slipping across the linoleum, the looks exchanged, the rush to retrieve it and clean it off, like a bratwurst that's rolled off the plate in a restaurant kitchen. I ask about these things, I think, because of a need to make human what otherwise verges on the godlike: taking live organs from bodies and making them live in another body. I also asked whether the surgeons ever set aside the old, damaged hearts of transplant recipients for them to keep. Surprisingly (to me, anyway), only a few express an interest in seeing or keeping their hearts.

Oz told me that a human heart removed from its blood supply can continue beating for as long as a minute or two, until the cells begin to starve from lack of oxygen. It was phenomena like this that threw eighteenth-century medical philosophers into a tizzy: If the soul was in the brain and not the heart, as many believed at that time, how could the heart keep beating outside the body, cut off from the soul?

* * *

The modern medical community is on the whole quite unequivocal about the brain being the seat of the soul, the chief commander of life and death. It is similarly unequivocal about the fact that people like H are, despite the

30

17. Short for electrocardiogram, an imaging of the electrical voltage of the heart.
18. Edgar Allan Poe (1809–1849), American poet and short story writer.

hoochy-koochy going on behind their sternums, dead. We now know that the heart keeps beating on its own not because the soul is in there, but because it contains its own bioelectric power source, independent of the brain. As soon as H's heart is installed in someone else's chest and that person's blood begins to run through it, it will start beating anew—with no signals from the recipient's brain.

The legal community took a little longer than the physicians to come around to the concept of brain death. It was 1968 when the *Journal of the American Medical Association* published a paper by the Ad Hoc Committee of the Harvard Medical School to Examine the Definition of Brain Death advocating that irreversible coma be the new criterion for death, and clearing the ethical footpath for organ transplantation. It wasn't until 1974 that the law began to catch up. What forced the issue was a bizarre murder trial in Oakland, California.

The killer, Andrew Lyons, shot a man in the head in September 1973 and left him brain-dead. When Lyons's attorneys found out that the victim's family had donated his heart for transplantation, they tried to use this in Lyons's defense: If the heart was still beating at the time of surgery, they maintained, then how could it be that Lyons had killed him the day before? They tried to convince the jury that, technically speaking, Andrew Lyons hadn't murdered the man, the organ recovery surgeon had. According to Stanford University heart transplant pioneer Norman Shumway, who testified in the case, the judge would have none of it. He informed the jury that the accepted criteria for death were those set forth by the Harvard committee, and that that should inform their decision. (Photographs of the victim's brains "oozing from his skull," to quote the *San Francisco Chronicle*, probably didn't help Lyons's case.) In the end, Lyons was convicted of murder. Based on the outcome of the case, California passed legislation making brain death the legal definition of death. Other states quickly followed suit.

Andrew Lyons's defense attorney wasn't the first person to cry murder when a transplant surgeon removed a heart from a brain-dead patient. In the earliest days of heart transplants, Shumway, the first U.S. surgeon to carry out the procedure, was continually harangued by the coroner in Santa Clara County, where he practiced. The coroner didn't accept the brain-death concept of death and threatened that if Shumway went ahead with his plans to remove a beating heart from a brain-dead person and use it to save another person's life, he would initiate murder charges. Though the coroner had no legal ground to stand on and Shumway went ahead anyway, the press gave it a vigorous chew. New York heart transplant surgeon Mehmet Oz recalls the Brooklyn district attorney around that time making the same threat. "He said he'd indict and arrest any heart transplant surgeon who went into his borough and harvested an organ."

35   The worry, explained Oz, was that someday someone who wasn't actually brain-dead was going to have his heart cut out. There exist certain rare medical conditions that can look, to the untrained or negligent eye, a lot like brain death, and the legal types didn't trust the medical types to get it right. To a

very, very small degree, they had reason to worry. Take, for example, the condition known as "locked-in state." In one form of the disease, the nerves, from eyeballs to toes, suddenly and rather swiftly drop out of commission, with the result that the body is completely paralyzed, while the mind remains normal. The patient can hear what's being said but has no way of communicating that he's still in there, and that no, it's definitely not okay to give his organs away for transplant. In severe cases, even the muscles that contract to change the size of the pupils no longer function. This is bad news, for a common test of brain death is to shine a light in the patient's eyes to check for the reflexive contraction of the pupils. Typically, victims of locked-in state recover fully, provided no one has mistakenly wheeled them off to the OR to take out their heart.

Like the specter of live burial that plagued the French and German citizenry in the 1800s, the fear of live organ harvesting is almost completely without foundation. A simple EEG[19] will prevent misdiagnosis of the locked-in state and conditions like it.

On a rational level, most people are comfortable with the concept of brain death and organ donation. But on an emotional level, they may have a harder time accepting it, particularly when they are being asked to accept it by a transplant counselor who would like them to okay the removal of a family member's beating heart. Fifty-four percent of families asked refuse consent. "They can't deal with the fear, however irrational, that the true end of their loved one will come when the heart is removed," says Oz. That they, in effect, will have killed him.

Even heart transplant surgeons sometimes have trouble accepting the notion that the heart is nothing more than a pump. When I asked Oz where he thought the soul resided, he said, "I'll confide in you that I don't think it's all in the brain. I have to believe that in many ways the core of our existence *is* in our heart." Does that mean he thinks the brain-dead patient isn't dead? "There's no question that the heart without a brain is of no value. But life and death is not a binary system." It's a continuum. It makes sense, for many reasons, to draw the legal line at brain death, but that doesn't mean it's really a line. "In between life and death is a state of near-death, or pseudo-life. And most people don't want what's in between."

If the heart of a brain-dead heart donor does contain something loftier than tissue and blood, some vestige of the spirit, then one could imagine that this vestige might travel along with the heart and set up housekeeping in the person who receives it. Oz once got a letter from a transplant patient who, shortly after receiving his new heart, began to experience what he could only imagine was some sort of contact with the consciousness of its previous owner. The patient, Michael "Med-O" Whitson, gave permission to quote the letter:

19. Short for electroencephalogram, an image representing the electric signals coursing through the brain.

I write all this with respect for the possibility that rather than some kind of contact with the consciousness of my donor's heart, these are merely hallucinations from the medications or my own projections. I know this is a very slippery slope. . . .

What came to me in the first contact . . . was the horror of dying. The utter suddenness, shock, and surprise of it all. . . . The feeling of being ripped off and the dread of dying before your time. . . . This and two other incidents are by far the most terrifying experiences I have ever had. . . .

What came to me on the second occasion was my donor's experience of having his heart being cut out of his chest and transplanted. There was a profound sense of violation by a mysterious, omnipotent outside force. . . .

. . . The third episode was quite different than the previous two. This time the consciousness of my donor's heart was in the present tense. . . . He was struggling to figure out where he was, even what he was. . . . It was as if none of your senses worked. . . . An extremely frightening awareness of total dislocation. . . . As if you are reaching with your hands to grasp something . . . but every time you reach forward your fingers end up only clutching thin air.

40   Of course, one man named Med-O does not a scientific inquiry make. A step in that direction is a study carried out in 1991 by a team of Viennese surgeons and psychiatrists. They interviewed forty-seven heart transplant patients about whether they had noticed any changes in their personality that they thought were due to the influence of the new heart and its former owner. Forty-four of the forty-seven said no, although the authors, in the Viennese psychoanalytic tradition, took pains to point out that many of these people responded to the question with hostility or jokes, which, in Freudian theory, would indicate some level of denial about the issue.

The experiences of the three patients who answered yes were decidedly more prosaic than were Whitson's. The first was a forty-five-year-old man who had received the heart of a seventeen-year-old boy and told the researchers, "I love to put on earphones and play loud music, something I never did before. A different car, a good stereo—those are my dreams now." The other two were less specific. One said simply that the person who had owned his heart had been a calm person and that these feelings of calm had been "passed on" to him; another felt that he was living two people's lives, replying to questions with "we" instead of "I," but offered no details about the newly acquired personality or what sort of music he enjoyed.

For juicy details, we must turn to Paul Pearsall, the author of a book called *The Heart's Code* (and another called *Super Marital Sex* and one called *Superimmunity*). Pearsall interviewed 140 heart transplant patients and presented quotes from five of them as evidence for the heart's "cellular memory" and its influence on recipients of donated hearts. There was the woman who got the heart of a gay robber who was shot in the back, and suddenly began dressing in a more feminine manner and getting "shooting pains" in her back. There was another rendition of the middle-aged man with a teenage male heart who now feels compelled to "crank up the stereo and play loud rock-and-roll music"—which I had quickly come to see as the urban myth of heart transplantation. My out-and-out favorite was the woman who got a prostitute's heart and suddenly began renting X-rated videos, demanding sex with her husband every night, and performing strip teases for him. Of course, if the woman knew that her new heart had come from a prostitute, this might have caused the changes in her behavior. Pearsall doesn't mention whether the woman knew of her donor's occupation (or, for that matter, whether he'd sent her a copy of *Super Marital Sex* before the interview).

Pearsall is not a doctor, or not, at least, one of the medical variety. He is a doctor of the variety that gets a Ph.D. and attaches it to his name on self-help book covers. I found his testimonials iffy as evidence of any sort of "cellular" memory, based as they are on crude and sometimes absurd stereotypes: that women become prostitutes because they want to have sex all day long, that gay men—gay robbers, no less—like to dress in feminine clothing. But bear in mind that I am, to quote item 13 of Pearsall's Heart Energy Amplitude Test, "cynical and distrusting of others' motives."

Mehmet Oz, the transplant surgeon I spoke with, also got curious about the phenomenon of heart transplant patients' claiming to experience memories belonging to their donors. "There was this one fellow," he told me, "who said, 'I know who gave me this heart.' He gave me a detailed description of a young black woman who died in a car accident. 'I see myself in the mirror with blood on my face and I taste French fries in my mouth. I see that I'm black and I was in this accident.' It spooked me," says Oz, "and so I went back and checked. The donor was an elderly white male." Did he have other patients who claimed to experience their donor's memories or to know something specific about their donor's life? He did. "They're all wrong."

After I spoke to Oz, I tracked down three more articles on the psychological consequences of having someone else's heart stitched into your chest. Fully half of all transplant patients, I found out, develop postoperative psychological problems of some sort. Rausch and Kneen described a man utterly terrified by the prospect of the transplant surgery, fearing that in giving up his heart he would lose his soul. Another paper presented the case of a patient who became convinced that he had been given a hen's heart. No mention was made of why he might have come to believe this or whether he had been exposed to the writings of Robert Whytt,[20] which actually might have provided some solace, pointing out, as they do, that a chicken heart can be made to beat on for several hours in the event of decapitation—always a plus.

The worry that one will take on traits of the heart donor is quite common, particularly when patients have received, or think that they have, a heart from a donor of a different gender or sexual orientation. According to a paper by James Tabler and Robert Frierson, recipients often wonder whether the donor "was promiscuous or oversexed, homosexual or bisexual, excessively masculine or feminine or afflicted with some sort of sexual dysfunction." They spoke to a man who fantasized that his donor had had a sexual "reputation" and said he had no choice but to live up to it. Rausch and Kneen describe a forty-two-year-

45

20. British doctor and medical professor (1714–1766).

old firefighter who worried that his new heart, which had belonged to a woman, would make him less masculine and that his firehouse buddies would no longer accept him. (A male heart, Oz says, is in fact slightly different from a female heart. A heart surgeon can tell one from the other by looking at the ECG, because the intervals are slightly different. When you put a female heart into a man, it will continue to beat like a female heart. And vice versa.)

From reading a paper by Kraft, it would seem that when men believe their new hearts came from another man, they often believe this man to have been a stud and that some measure of this studliness has somehow been imparted to them. Nurses on transplant wards often remark that male transplant patients show a renewed interest in sex. One reported that a patient asked her to wear "something other than that shapeless scrub so he could see her breasts." A post-op who had been impotent for seven years before the operation was found holding his penis and demonstrating an erection. Another nurse spoke of a man who left the fly of his pajamas unfastened to show her his penis. Conclude Tabler and Frierson, "This irrational but common belief that the recipient will somehow develop characteristics of the donor is generally transitory but may alter sexual patterns . . . ." Let us hope that the man with the chicken heart was blessed with a patient and open-minded spouse.

The harvesting of H is winding down. The last organs to be taken, the kidneys, are being brought up and separated from the depths of her open torso. Her thorax and abdomen are filled with crushed ice, turned red from blood. "Cherry Sno-Kone," I write in my notepad. It's been almost four hours now, and H has begun to look more like a conventional cadaver, her skin dried and dulled at the edges of the incision.

The kidneys are placed in a blue plastic bowl with ice and perfusion fluid.[21] A relief surgeon arrives for the final step of the recovery, cutting off pieces of veins and arteries to be included, like spare sweater buttons, along with the organs, in case the ones attached to them are too short to work with. A half hour later, the relief surgeon steps aside and the resident comes over to sew H up.

50   As he talks to Dr. Posselt about the stitching, the resident strokes the bank of fat along H's incision with his gloved hand, then pats it twice, as though comforting her. When he turns back to his work, I ask him if it feels different to be working on a dead patient.

"Oh, yes," he answers. "I mean, I would never use this kind of stitch." He has begun stitching more widely spaced, comparatively crude loops, rather than the tight, hidden stitches used on the living.

I rephrase the question: Does it feel odd to perform surgery on someone who isn't alive?

His answer is surprising. "The patient *was* alive." I suppose surgeons are used to thinking about patients—particularly ones they've never met—as no more than what they see of them: open plots of organs. And as far as that goes, I guess you could say H *was* alive. Because of the cloths covering all but her

---

21. Liquid pumped into organs, usually by way of blood vessels.

opened torso, the young man never saw her face, didn't know if she was male or female.

While the resident sews, a nurse picks stray danglies of skin and fat off the operating table with a pair of tongs and drops them inside the body cavity, as though H were a handy waste basket. The nurse explains that this is done intentionally: "Anything not donated stays with her." The jigsaw puzzle put back in its box.

The incision is complete, and a nurse washes H off and covers her with a blanket for the trip to the morgue. Out of habit or respect, he chooses a fresh one. The transplant coordinator, Von, and the nurse lift H onto a gurney. Von wheels H into an elevator and down a hallway to the morgue. The workers are behind a set of swinging doors, in a back room. "Can we leave this here?" Von shouts. H has become a "this." We are instructed to wheel the gurney into the cooler, where it joins five others. H appears no different from the corpses already here.[22]

But H *is* different. She has made three sick people well. She has brought them extra time on earth. To be able, as a dead person, to make a gift of this magnitude is phenomenal. Most people don't manage this sort of thing while they're alive. Cadavers like H are the dead's heroes.

It is astounding to me, and achingly sad, that with eighty thousand people on the waiting list for donated hearts and livers and kidneys, with sixteen a day dying there on that list, that more than half of the people in the position H's family was in will say no, will choose to burn those organs or let them rot. We abide the surgeon's scalpel to save our own lives, our loved ones' lives, but not to save a stranger's life. H has no heart, but heartless is the last thing you'd call her.

22. Unless H's family is planning a naked open-casket service, no one at her funeral will be able to tell she's had organs removed. Only with tissue harvesting, which often includes leg and arm bones, does the body take on a slightly altered profile, and in this case PVC piping or dowels are inserted to normalize the form and make life easier for mortuary staff and others who need to move the otherwise somewhat noodle-ized body [Roach's note]. PVC: short for polyvinyl chloride, a material now commonly used in plumbing parts.

QUESTIONS

1. The title of Roach's book—*Stiff*—and the title of this excerpt—"How to Know If You're Dead"—suggest that the author has a sense of humor. Where does Roach use humor? Why? How does humor allow Roach to raise questions about death that serious or solemn approaches might not allow?

2. In the second section of this essay, Roach introduces historical anecdotes that focus on the desire to define death and "pinpoint the precise moment when the spirit . . . has ceased to exist" (paragraph 11). What is at stake in this attempt? What role does belief in the "spirit" or "soul" play in understanding death? Why is the moment of "death" so difficult to know?

3. In addition to engaging in historical research, Roach interviews living scientists, doctors, and patients to explore her subject. Locate three or four of these interviews, and explain what they add to our understanding of human life and death.

4. Read either Elisabeth Kübler-Ross's "On the Fear of Death" (in "Human Nature") or Jessica Mitford's "Behind the Formaldehyde Curtain" (in "Cultural Critique"), and compare Roach's treatment of the body and death with either of theirs. What concerns do they share? What different focuses and concerns emerge from your comparison?

CULTURAL CRITIQUE

ANTHONY BURGESS *Is America Falling Apart?*

I AM BACK IN BRACCIANO, a castellated town about 13 miles north of Rome, after a year in New Jersey. I find the Italian Government still unstable, gasoline more expensive than anywhere in the world, butchers and bank clerks and tobacconists (which also means saltsellers) ready to go on strike at the drop of a *cappello*,[1] neo-Fascists at their dirty work, the hammer and sickle painted on the rumps of public statues, a thousand-lire note (officially worth about $1.63) shrunk to the slightness of a dollar bill.

Nevertheless, it's delightful to be back. People are underpaid but they go through an act of liking their work, the open markets are luscious with esculent color, the community is more important than the state, the human condition is humorously accepted. The *tramontana*[2] blows viciously today, and there's no central heating to turn on, but it will be pleasant when the wind drops. The two television channels are inadequate, but next Wednesday's rerun of an old Western, with Gary Cooper coming into a saloon saying "*Ciao, ragazzi,*"[3] is something to look forward to. Manifold consumption isn't important here. The quality of life has nothing to do with the quantity of brand names. What matters is talk, family, cheap wine in the open air, the wresting of minimal sweetness out of the long-known bitterness of living. I was spoiled in New Jersey. The Italian for *spoiled* is *viziato*, cognate with *vitiated*, which has to do with vice.

Spoiled? Well, yes. I never had to shiver by a fire that wouldn't draw, or go without canned kraut juice or wild rice. America made me develop new appetites in order to make proper use of the supermarket. A character in Evelyn Waugh's *Put Out More Flags* said that the difference between prewar and postwar life[4] was that, prewar, if one thing went wrong the day was ruined; postwar,

Written during 1970–71, when Burgess, an English novelist then famous for A Clockwork Orange, *was a visiting professor at Princeton University; published in the* New York Times *(November 7, 1971).*

1. Hat.
2. North wind.
3. "Howdy, boys."
4. Waugh published *Put Out More Flags* in 1942. "Prewar" refers to conditions before World War II.

if one thing went right the day would be made. America is a prewar country, psychologically unprepared for one thing to go wrong. Now everything seems to be going wrong. Hence the neurosis, despair, the Kafka feeling that the whole marvelous fabric of American life is coming apart at the seams. Italy is used to everything going wrong. This is what the human condition is about.

Let me stay for a while on this subject of consumption. American individualism, on the face of it an admirable philosophy, wishes to manifest itself in independence of the community. You don't share things in common; you have your own things. A family's strength is signalized by its possessions. Herein lies a paradox. For the desire for possessions must eventually mean dependence on possessions. Freedom is slavery. Once let the acquisitive instinct burgeon (enough flour for the winter, not just for the week), and there are ruggedly individual forces only too ready to make it come to full and monstrous blossom. New appetites are invented; what to the European are bizarre luxuries become, to the American, plain necessities.

5   During my year's stay in New Jersey I let my appetites flower into full Americanism except for one thing. I did not possess an automobile. This self-elected deprivation was a way into the nastier side of the consumer society. Where private ownership prevails, public amenities decay or are prevented from coming into being. The wretched run-down rail services of America are something I try, vainly, to forget. The nightmare of filth, outside and in, that enfolds the trip from Springfield, Mass., to Grand Central Station would not be accepted in backward Europe. But far worse is the nightmare of travel in and around Los Angeles, where public transport does not exist and people are literally choking to death in their exhaust fumes. This is part of the price of the metaphysic of individual ownership.

But if the car owner can ignore the lack of public transport, he can hardly ignore the decay of services in general. His car needs mechanics, and mechanics grow more expensive and less efficient. The gadgets in the home are cheaper to replace than repair. The more efficiently self-contained the home, primary fortress of independence, seems to be, the more dependent it is on the great impersonal corporations, as well as a diminishing army of servitors. Skills at the lowest level have to be wooed slavishly and exorbitantly rewarded. Plumbers will not come. Nor, at the higher level, will doctors. And doctors and dentists, in a nation committed to maiming itself with sugar and cholesterol, know their scarcity value and behave accordingly.

Americans are at last realizing that the acquisition of goods is not the whole of life. Consumption, on one level, is turning insipid, especially as the quality of the artifacts themselves seems to be deteriorating. Planned obsolescence is not conducive to pride in workmanship. On another level, consumption is turning sour. There is a growing guilt about the masses of discarded junk—rusting automobiles and refrigerators and washing machines and dehumidifiers—that it is uneconomical to recycle. Indestructible plastic hasn't even the grace to undergo chemical change. America, the world's biggest consumer, is the world's biggest polluter. Awareness of this is a kind of redemptive grace, but it doesn't appreciably lead to repentance and a revolution in consumer habits. Citizens of Los Angeles are horrified by that daily pall of golden smog, but they don't noticeably clamor for a decrease in the number of owner-vehicles. There is no worse neurosis than that which derives from a consciousness of guilt and an inability to reform.

America is anachronistic in so many ways, and not least in its clinging to a belief—now known to be unviable—in the capacity of the individual citizen to do everything for himself. Americans are admirable in their distrust of the corporate state—they have fought both Fascism and Communism—but they forget that there is a use for everything, even the loathesome bureaucratic machine. America needs a measure of socialization, as Britain needed it. Things—especially those we need most—don't always pay their way, and it is here that the state must enter, dismissing the profit element. Part of the present American neurosis, again, springs from awareness of this but inability to do anything about practical implementation. Perhaps only a country full of bombed cities feels capable of this kind of social revolution.

It would be supererogatory for me to list those areas in which thoughtful Americans feel that collapse is coming. It is enough for me to concentrate on what, during my New Jersey stay, impinged on my own life. Education, for instance, since I have a 6-year-old son to be brought up. America has always despised its teachers and, as a consequence, it has been granted the teachers it deserves. The quality of first-grade education that my son received, in a New Jersey town noted for the excellence of its public schools, could not, I suppose, be faulted on the level of dogged conscientiousness. The principal had read all the right pedagogic books, and was ready to quote these in the footnotes to his circular exhortations to parents. The teachers worked rigidly from the approved rigidly programed primers, ensuring that school textbook publication remains the big business it is.

But there seemed to be no spark; no daring, no madness, no readiness to engage the individual child's mind as anything other than raw material for statistical reductions. The fear of being unorthodox is rooted in the American teacher's soul: you can be fired for treading the path of experimental enterprise. In England, teachers cannot be fired, except for raping girl students and getting boy students drunk. In consequence, there is the kind of security that breeds eccentric genius, the capacity for firing mad enthusiasms.

10

I know that American technical genius, and most of all the moon landings, seems to give the lie to too summary a condemnation of the educational system, but there is more to education than the segmental equipping of the mind. There is that transmission of the value of the past as a force still miraculously fertile and moving—mostly absent from American education at all levels.

Of course, America was built on a rejection of the past. Even the basic Christianity which was brought to the continent in 1620 was of a novel and bizarre kind that would have nothing to do with the great rank river of belief that produced Dante and Michelangelo. America as a nation has never been able to settle to a common belief more sophisticated than the dangerous naiveté of the Declaration of Independence. "Life, liberty and the pursuit of happiness," indeed. And now America, filling in the vacuum left by the liquefied British Empire, has the task of telling the rest of the world that there's something better than Communism. The something better can only be money-making and consumption for its own sake. In the name of this ghastly creed the jungles must be defoliated.[5]

No wonder the guilt of the thoughtful Americans I met in Princeton and New York and, indeed, all over the Union tended to express itself as an extravagant masochism, a desire for flagellation. Americans want to take on all the blame they can find, gluttons for punishment. "What do Europeans really think of us?" is a common question at parties. The expected answer is: "They think you're a load of decadent, gross-lipped, potbellied, callous, overbearing neoimperialists." Then the head can be bowed and the chest smitten: *"Nostra culpa, nostra maxima culpa. . . ."*[6] But the fact is that such an answer, however much desired, would not be an honest one. Europeans think more highly of Americans now than they ever did. Let me try to explain why.

When Europe, after millennia of war, rapine, slavery, famine, intolerance, had sunk to the level of a sewer, America became the golden dream, the Eden where innocence could be recovered. Original sin was the monopoly of that dirty continent over there; in America man could glow in an aura of natural goodness, driven along his shining path by divine reason. The Declaration of Independence itself is a monument to reason. Progress was possible, and the wrongs committed against the Indians, the wildlife, the land itself, could be explained away in terms of the rational control of environment necessary for the building of a New Jerusalem.[7] Right and wrong made up the moral dichotomy; evil—that great eternal inextirpable entity—had no place in America.

15   At last, with the Vietnam war and especially the Mylai horror,[8] Americans are beginning to realize that they are subject to original sin as much as Europeans are. Some things—the massive crime figures, for instance—can now be explained only in terms of absolute evil. Europe, which has long known about evil and learned to live with it (*live* is *evil* spelled backwards), is now grimly pleased to find that America is becoming like Europe. America is no longer Europe's daughter nor her rich stepmother: she is Europe's sister. The agony that America is undergoing is not to be associated with breakdown so much as with the parturition of self-knowledge.

5. That is, in order to deny the enemy protective cover—a part of American strategy during the Vietnam War.

6. "Through our fault, through our most grievous fault," a modification of *Mea culpa, mea maxima culpa* ("Through my fault . . ."), part of the act of confession in the Roman Catholic Church.

7. The holy city described by John in Revelation 21, here a figurative expression for a perfected society.

8. A massacre by American troops of more than three hundred Vietnamese civilians in the village of My Lai.

It has been assumed by many that the youth of America has been in the vanguard of the discovery of both the disease and the cure. The various copping-out movements, however, from the Beats on, have committed the gross error of assuming that original sin rested with their elders, their rulers, and that they themselves could manifest their essential innocence by building little neo-Edens. The drug culture could confirm that the paradisal vision was available to all who sought it. But instant ecstasy has to be purchased, like any other commodity, and, in economic terms, that passive life of pure being involves parasitism. Practically all of the crime I encountered in New York—directly or through report—was a preying of the opium-eaters on the working community. There has to be a snake in paradise. You can't escape the heritage of human evil by building communes, usually on an agronomic ignorance that, intended to be a rejection of inherited knowledge, that suspect property of the elders, does violence to life. The American young are well-meaning but misguided, and must not themselves be taken as guides.

The guides, as always, lie among the writers and artists. And Americans ought to note that, however things may seem to be falling apart, arts and the humane scholarship are flourishing here, as they are not, for instance, in England. I'm not suggesting that Bellow, Mailer, Roth[9] and the rest have the task of finding a solution to the American mess, but they can at least clarify its nature and show how it relates to the human condition in general. Literature, that most directly human of the arts, often reacts magnificently to an ambience of unease or apparent breakdown. The Elizabethans,[10] to whose era we look back as to an irrecoverable Golden Age, were far more conscious than modern Americans of the chaos and corruption and incompetence of the state. Shakespeare's period was one of poverty, unemployment, ghastly inflation, violence in the streets. Twenty-six years after his death there was a bloody civil war, followed by a dictatorship of religious fanatics, followed by a calm respite in which the seeds of a revolution were sown. England survived. America will survive.

I'm not suggesting that Americans sit back and wait for a transient period of mistrust and despair to resolve itself, like a disease, through the unconscious healing forces which lie deep in organic nature. Man, as Thornton Wilder showed in *The Skin of Our Teeth*,[11] always comes through—though sometimes only just. Americans living here and now have a right to an improvement in the quality of their lives, and they themselves, not the remote governors, must do something about it. It is not right that men and women should fear to go on the streets at night, and that they should sometimes fear the police as much as the criminals, both of whom sometimes look like mirror images of each other. I have had too much evidence, in my year in New Jersey, of the police behaving like the "Fascist pigs" of the revolutionary press. There

9. Saul Bellow (1915–2005), Norman Mailer (b. 1923), and Philip Roth (b. 1933)—all American writers.
10. The British during the reign of Elizabeth I, 1558–1603.
11. Pulitzer Prize–winning comedy, written in 1942 by Thornton Wilder (1897–1975).

are too many guns about, and the disarming of the police should be a natural aspect of the disarming of the entire citizenry.

American politics, at both the state and the Federal levels, is too much concerned with the protection of large fortunes, America being the only example in history of a genuine timocracy.[12] The wealth qualification for the aspiring politician is taken for granted; a governmental system dedicated to the promotion of personal wealth in a few selected areas will never act for the public good. The time has come, nevertheless, for citizens to demand, from their government, a measure of socialization—the provision of amenities for the many, of which adequate state pensions and sickness benefits, as well as nationalized transport, should be priorities.

20   As for those remoter solutions to the American nightmare—only an aspect, after all, of the human nightmare—an Englishman must be diffident about suggesting that America made her biggest mistake in becoming America—meaning a revolutionary republic based on a romantic view of human nature. To reject a limited monarchy in favor of an absolute one (which is, after all, what the American Presidency is) argues a trust in the disinterestedness of an elected ruler which is, of course, no more than a reflection of belief in the innate goodness of man—so long as he happens to be American man. The American Constitution is out of date. Republics tend to corruption. Canada and Australia have their own problems, but they are happier countries than America.

This *Angst*[13] about America coming apart at the seams, which apparently is shared by nearly 50 per cent of the entire American population, is something to rejoice about. A sense of sin is always admirable, though it must not be allowed to become neurotic. If electric systems break down and gadgets disintegrate, it doesn't matter much. There is always wine to be drunk by candlelight, uniced. If America's position as a world power collapses, and the Union dissolves into independent states, there is still the life of the family or the individual to be lived. England has survived her own dissolution as an imperial power, and Englishmen seem to be happy enough. But I ask the reader to note that I, an Englishman, no longer live in England, and I can't spend more than six months at a stretch in Italy—or any other European country, for that matter. I come to America as to a country more stimulating than depressing. The future of mankind is being worked out there on a scale typically American—vast, dramatic, almost apocalyptical. I brave the brutality and the guilt in order to be in on the scene. I shall be back.

12. A state in which power depends on wealth.
13. Anxiety.

QUESTIONS

1. This essay appeared in 1971. What might Burgess leave out, add, or modify if he were to write it today?

2. Burgess says that in his son's school there was "no readiness to engage the individual child's mind as anything other than raw material for statistical reductions" (paragraph 10). Precisely what is he referring to? Does your own experience support or counter Burgess's claim?

3. Visitors like Burgess can sometimes see things natives miss; they can also overlook the obvious. Write a response to Burgess, pointing out where he is on target and what he has missed.

ADAM GOODHEART *9.11.01: The Skyscraper and the Airplane*

> And as the smart ship grew
> In stature, grace, and hue,
> In shadowy silent distance grew the Iceberg too.
>
> —THOMAS HARDY,[1]
> "The Convergence of the Twain"

BEFORE THE FIRE, before the ash, before the bodies tumbling solitary through space, one thin skin of metal and glass met another. Miles apart only moments before, then feet, and then, in an almost inconceivable instant, only a fraction of an inch. Try to imagine them there, suspended: two man-made behemoths joined in a fatal kiss.

Fatal, fated: perhaps even long foreseen. The skyscraper and the airplane were born side by side, and ever since then have occupied adjacent rooms in our collective unconscious. To call September 11th a nightmare is to be clinically precise about it, for like all true nightmares, it was grafted together out of preexisting elements, fragments of our waking lives and our imaginations.

Nearly a century ago, just five years after the first scrawny aircraft left the ground at Kitty Hawk, a widely circulated illustration by a Manhattan publisher named Moses King—"King's Dream of New York," he titled it—showed a fantasy cityscape in which biplanes buzzed among the downtown office towers and a vast dirigible brushed the uppermost cupola. In that same year, 1908, E. M. Forster[2] wrote a short story envisioning a world of the future

Originally published in the American Scholar *(Winter 2002), a journal of the Phi Beta Kappa Honor Society that "strives to preserve the essay."*

1. Hardy (1840–1928), English novelist and poet, whose poem "The Convergence of the Twain" meditates on the sinking of the *Titanic*, the largest and most luxurious ocean liner of the day.
2. English novelist (1879–1970).

where humans lived in huge structures composed of tiny, airless chambers, each one "like the cell of a bee," leaving them to travel in airships that criss-crossed the globe (though the earth had become so drably uniform, he observed, that "what was the good of going to Pekin when it was just like Shrewsbury?"). In the last paragraph of the story, "The Machine Stops," Forster imagined this world coming to an end: "The whole city was broken like a honeycomb. An air-ship . . . crashed downwards, exploding as it went, rending gallery after gallery with its wings of steel."

Skyscraper and airplane: fragile containers for even-more-fragile flesh and blood. Each an artificial shell of our own manufacture—or not quite of our own manufacture, since, strictly speaking, very few of us, as individuals, have any direct involvement in their creation. Each a capsule of recycled air, with windows sealed shut against the blue. Each an innovation that, in Forsterian terms, has made Pekin more and more like Shrewsbury. Each a honeycomb that traps us side by side with strangers. Each a rig that suspends us far above the ground, half-willing aerialists, and then whispers: *Trust me*. Each a machine that teaches us, in similar ways, how to be modern.

5   What keeps it up? What, that is to say, keeps *us* up? Perhaps one person in a thousand really knows, understanding coolly why it is that the contraption doesn't plummet back to earth under our weight. For the rest of us, the precise functioning of wing and girder, the mathematical intricacies of gravitational thrust and counterthrust, remain lifelong mysteries. Our animal selves, quite sensibly, would rather stick close to solid ground. But this is where we must steel ourselves to be something more than animals. We must summon up the will to trust—not so much in the metal armature beneath us as in the faceless experts who designed and built it, in the corporations that own and maintain it, in the armature of civilization and science. No wonder we sometimes get dizzy.

The cultural critic Marshall Berman,[3] in selecting a title for his 1982 treatise on the experience of modernity, borrowed a newly resonant phrase from Karl Marx:[4] *All That Is Solid Melts Into Air*. "To be modern," he wrote, "is to find ourselves in an environment that promises us adventure, power, joy, growth, transformation of ourselves and the world—and, at the same time, that threatens to destroy everything we have, everything we know, everything we are." It is to ride atop a skyscraper, to soar in an airplane. And both threatened us with such destruction, not just on that machine-bright morning in September, but long before.

Both sprang from the late nineteenth century, and from the American Middle West (Louis Sullivan's Chicago, the Wright Brothers' Ohio)[5]—a place where earth and sky were blank canvases waiting to be filled with movement and form. Yet both had deeper roots as well. In England in the 1780s, the

3. Writer and political theorist (b. 1940).

4. Author of *Das Kapital* and famous originator of communist theory (1818–1883).

5. Sullivan (1856–1924), American architect; Wright brothers, inventors of the airplane.

decade in which the Montgolfiers took to the air in their balloons, and the young Wordsworth and Coleridge sharpened their pens at grammar school, the Duke of Bedford owned an exceptionally large racehorse that one of his grooms named Skyscraper—the first recorded appearance of the word. (The mare finished first at the Epson Derby in 1789.) In the years that followed, *skyscraper* was used to describe the uppermost sail on a ship's rigging (1794), a high hat or bonnet (1800), or simply a very tall person (1857). After crossing the Atlantic, it was used by American sportswriters as early as the 1860s to describe a towering fly ball. Like so many of the next century's most important words (*computer, rocket, network*), *skyscraper* jostled around indecisively for a while, hesitating between one meaning and another before settling into its ultimate niche. However they used the word, people were clearly grasping toward the sky, toward something up there that they could almost brush with their fingertips—and that they were determined to reach by one contrivance or another.

When the earliest buildings to be called skyscrapers appeared, in the 1870s and 1880s, they sprang into shape so suddenly as to seem born in a single piece. The pioneering architects of Chicago, one recent historian has written, "learned almost everything of importance that would be known a century later about how to build skyscrapers." Yet the skyscraper was not, as it seems to us now, a single unified invention, but rather many inventions knit into one.

First and foremost, of course, was the ability to produce cheap, high-quality structural steel—the first truly revolutionary architectural innovation since the Romans invented the arch and the dome two millennia before. One nineteenth-century engineer couched this development in almost Darwinian terms: For the first time, he explained, tall buildings were designed as vertebrates instead of crustaceans. For the first time, their loads and stresses could be carried not by massive carapaces of masonry but by a web of slender struts and braces whose strength lay in its interconnectedness: a prototypical modern form, destined to be replicated in everything from computer chips to international airline routes. Louis Sullivan might have boasted of his buildings' pure functionalism, but in fact the skyscraper's exterior was merely its skin, its only function (besides shelter from the elements) to provide a kind of movie screen onto which the architect could project any embellishment he chose: rich Gothic traceries, Art Deco's silvery sheen, or, eventually, the stern theatrics of high modernism.

Still, if architects had had only steel to work with, the interiors of their skyscrapers would have just been little more than dark and dreary warrens. Office towers of ten and twenty stories required, for their basic functioning, a whole list of innovations that are now taken for granted, but that were still brand new in the second half of the nineteenth century: electric lights and central heating, passenger elevators and fire escapes, telephones and flush toilets. As fate had it, all of these appeared on the American scene at approximately the same time. And all of them, moreover, required a wholly new type of city to support them: one with reliable, centrally managed electric and gas companies, sewer systems, water mains, fire departments, elevator inspectors,

10

telephone operators, trash collectors. Did the modern city give birth to the skyscraper, or vice versa? The answer, probably, is a bit of both.

Of all these varied accoutrements, none was more critical to the skyscraper's development than the passenger elevator. At New York's Crystal Palace exposition in 1854, a Yonkers mechanic named Elisha Graves Otis would periodically ascend high above the crowds on an open platform of wrought iron. As the machine creaked up to its zenith, the inventor gestured to an assistant, who cut through the hoisting rope with a hatchet. The spectators gasped in horror—but instead of plummeting to the ground, the elevator merely settled back into its ratcheted safety lock. "All safe, gentlemen, all safe," Otis announced.

Otis's words would become the constant refrain of the dawning era. In the nineteenth century, for the first time in human history, millions of ordinary people would be required to entrust their lives, on a daily basis, to technologies whose inner workings remained a mystery. They were a generation of pioneers, the men and women of New York and Chicago, no less than the settlers of the Great Plains. The odd thing, in retrospect, is how easily they seem to have taken the changes in stride. When the architect Bradford Gilbert,[6] in 1888, topped off his Tower Building at eleven stories, many New York pedestrians avoided that block of Broadway, certain that the structure would topple in the first stiff breeze. But Gilbert, in an Otis-like show of confidence, moved his own office onto the uppermost floor; the building withstood a hurricane soon after, and before long was taken for granted. Barely two decades later, when the Metropolitan Life Building reached a record fifty stories, the only question was who would try for sixty. (It would be the retailing magnate Frank Woolworth, who began planning his skyscraper a few weeks after the Metropolitan tower opened.)

Even more remarkable, the mythology of the skyscraper was born fullfledged with the building itself. Here is the earliest recorded appearance of the word in its contemporary sense, from an 1883 issue of *American Architect and Building News*: "This form of sky-scraper gives that peculiar refined, independent, self-contained, daring, bold, heaven-reaching, erratic, piratic, Quixotic, American thought." (Those were the days when even trade journals waxed Whitmanesque.)[7]

A century earlier, Thomas Jefferson, proclaiming American exceptionalism in his *Notes on Virginia*, cited the extraordinary size of native bears and elk, caverns and waterfalls. (He even vigorously defended American Indians against a French naturalist's insinuation that their "organs of generation" were smaller than average.) But the skyscraper rendered all of Jefferson's examples irrelevant. Here was the final proof of America's towering stature, in a tower raised not by God but by its citizens.

6. American architect (1853–1911) who built some of the first skyscrapers, including the Tower Building (1889) in New York City, now demolished.
7. Referring to Walt Whitman (1819–1892), American poet known for his romantic, democratic, all-embracing *Leaves of Grass*.

Before long, the race to scrape the sky lifted off the ground. And like the sky-   15
scraper's, the airplane's infancy was shortlived, its full maturity quick to arrive:
Orville Wright would live to see the era of inflight movies. Strut and brace, spar
and rib formed the bones of the plane as they did of the skyscraper, stiffening
an outer shell designed to cut through hostile wind. And the airplane, too,
would become a sort of capsule of human amenities, but to an even greater degree: a mobile life-support system, no less than a spaceship would be.

And yet, after nearly a century aloft, we have never learned to occupy
planes as comfortably as we do skyscrapers. Antoine de Saint-Exupéry,[8] in the
1930s, predicted that within a generation or two, the airplane would come to
seem a perfectly commonplace thing, "an object as natural as a pebble polished by the waves." Instead, it still seems the very epitome of what is artificial
and mechanical. Stepping aboard one, even the most habitual of flyers must
exercise a small act of conscious will. The passenger never forgets that he is
wagering his life on the journey, even if he knows that the odds in this type of
roulette are relatively good.

Air travel is a unique experience in modern life, the sociologist Mark
Gottdiener[9] recently wrote, "because, deep down inside us, it is a 'near death'
experience. It is the most common way individuals surrender control and voluntarily place themselves in harm's way in contemporary society. If they drive,
they are also at risk, but they remain in control behind the wheel." Strapped
into our seats, waiting on the runway, staring out the window at the stained
frailty of the wing, we toy with fantasies of annihilation. We look at our fellow
travelers and wonder what it would be like to face death alongside these
strangers. A terribly intimate, terribly modern way to go: so close to one another in these well-lit rows, so far from family and home.

In a seminar for phobic flyers offered by American Airlines, participants
spend ten consecutive hours being lectured by pilots, flight attendants, mechanics, and psychologists, who repeat this phrase like a mantra: "Airplanes
do not drop, dive, plummet, or fall." In doing so, they merely voice the silent
chant of every airborne congregation. For flying requires an act of almost religious faith, the surrender of oneself, in absolute trust, to the wisdom and
benevolent expertise of corporations, pilots, governments, engineers—the
whole apparatus of modernity. In this setting, the smallest acts take on ritual
significance: the pantomimed instructions of flight attendants, the dimming
of lights, the serving of food. Airline meals, tiny and perfectly formed, are like
the Japanese tea ceremony, in which gesture is more important than nourishment. In giving us food, the airline offers us a promise of sustenance; in eating, we accept. All of us know one or two stiff-necked dissenters who refuse
to fly at all, and they irritate us more than their mild neurosis would warrant,

8. French poet and aviator (1900–1944), best known for *The Little Prince* (1943).

9. Professor of sociology at the State University of New York–Buffalo, author of *The
Social Production of Urban Space* (1985), and editor of *The City and the Sign: Introduction to Urban Semiotics* (1986).

as if they had renounced their citizenship in the commonwealth of flight.

If the skyscraper, with its crudely phallic thrust, is male, the airplane is female. Entering, we pass into a place that promises—if rarely quite delivering—all the amenities of the womb: shelter, nourishment, warmth, dimness, sleep. The earliest flight attendants, in the 1920s, were men, but airlines quickly discovered that passengers preferred to be cared for by women, and before long they were openly competing with one another to provide the most beautiful and provocatively clad stewardesses. Erotic currents move among the passengers as well. Skyscrapers place us alongside strangers and demand that we work; airplanes seat us side by side and whisper idle fantasies of sex. This is the double face of modern alienation: the limitless pain of loneliness, the limitless promise of random encounters. Proximity, anonymity: the world of skyscrapers and airplanes is one in which terrorists stalk freely among their prey.

20   The architect of the World Trade Center, Minoru Yamasaki,[10] was afraid of heights. He once wrote that in a world of perfect freedom, he'd have created nothing but one-story buildings overlooking fields of flowers. He designed the Trade Center with narrow windows framed by vertical columns like prison bars, close enough together that he could steady himself against them when looking out. Instead of one-story buildings overlooking fields of flowers, he built gargantuan monoliths overlooking a windswept plaza. Their scale was brutal, unsoftened by the slightest hint of stylishness. Only at a great distance did they impress, jutting like a double bowsprit from the prow of Manhattan, from the prow of America itself. Or, if you preferred, like a pair of middle fingers, raised against the hostile vastness of the Atlantic Ocean.

But to take in this view you had to stand far away: in Hoboken, or Hamburg, or Kabul. (Or to observe the towers through a lens. Like so many twentieth-century creations, they seemed designed to be seen not in person but on film, as though the cinematic eye were the only one that mattered.) Standing at the base of the towers and looking up, the human observer had the sense mostly not of their height, but of their immense weight. They were two mountains of trapped kinetic energy, perpetually poised at the brink of release. The irony of architecture, all architecture, is that we create structures to shelter ourselves, yet in building them, we set ourselves at risk. The surest way to stay safe from fires, earthquakes, and bombs is never to go indoors. The surest way not to fall is to stay on the ground.

In *Anna Karenina*,[11] Levin is terrified by the birth of his first child, for he realizes that he has brought into the world a new means for him to be hurt beyond all previous imagining. Tolstoy recognized that every act of creation has its shadow double, a coequal act of destruction. When Yamasaki created buildings on an unprecedented scale, he also created the potential for disaster on an unprecedented scale, a nightmare knit into every cubic inch of glass and

10. Founder of the Michigan-based architectural firm that built the World Trade Center in 1973.

11. Novel (1875–77) by Russian author Leo Tolstoy (1828–1910).

steel. (The man who would eventually engineer their destruction understood this: he came from a family of builders.) They fascinated us, as airplanes do, because part of us always imagined them falling. It is the same part of us that loves our children because we can imagine them dying.

And when the towers did fall, we watched with the horror of witnesses to a death half foreseen, in dreams and shadowy portents. They buckled, released their long-held burden, and wearily sank to earth.

The authors of the catastrophe—who can doubt it?—created something terrible and permanent: an image that will stand for as long as any tower. In a thousand years, anyone who knows anything at all about us, the ancient Modern Americans, will probably know about the skyscraper and the airplane, and about the bright September morning that welded them together.

Eight days after the collapse, I stood on lower Broadway near where the skycrapers had been. The destruction was all strangely contained behind chain-link fences and squads of stolid cops: all the familiar markers of a Situation Under Control. The mounded ruins poured out a thick column of white smoke, its innards glowing sickly yellow under the slanting rays of late-afternoon sun. It looked exactly as if the crater of a volcano had somehow opened up among the downtown office buildings, and now was being probed and monitored by businesslike teams of geologists and seismologists, lest it erupt again without warning, I was reminded of being atop Mount Etna,[12] and peering alongside other tourists into the gassy abyss of the caldera, looking fruitlessly for some deep-buried source of smoke and heat. Above everything, above the place where the towers had stood, a helicopter whirred, miraculously suspended, riding on a column of newly liberated air.

25

12. Still-active volcano in Sicily.

QUESTIONS

1. After the destruction of the World Trade Center towers on September 11, 2001, many writers attempted to analyze and comprehend the event. What is Goodheart's approach? As you (re)read the essay, mark sentences that articulate or summarize his key points.

2. Goodheart chooses an epigraph from Thomas Hardy's poem "The Convergence of the Twain," originally subtitled "Lines on the Loss of the Titanic," to introduce his analysis. To what extent is the tragedy of the *Titanic* like or unlike the tragedy of September 11?

3. Throughout his analysis Goodheart quotes other writers, thinkers, and inventors. Choose one quotation that you think is particularly effective and explain why.

4. Goodheart's essay is, in a sense, an analysis of a visual image from September 11; he calls it "an image that will stand for as long as any tower" (paragraph 24). Choose another image from that day or the aftermath and, like Goodheart, write an essay in which you analyze its meaning and significance.

JESSICA MITFORD   *Behind the Formaldehyde Curtain*

THE DRAMA BEGINS to unfold with the arrival of the corpse at the mortuary.

Alas, poor Yorick![1] How surprised he would be to see how his counterpart of today is whisked off to a funeral parlor and is in short order sprayed, sliced, pierced, pickled, trussed, trimmed, creamed, waxed, painted, rouged and neatly dressed—transformed from a common corpse into a Beautiful Memory Picture. This process is known in the trade as embalming and restorative art, and is so universally employed in the United States and Canada that the funeral director does it routinely, without consulting corpse or kin. He regards as eccentric those few who are hardy enough to suggest that it might be dispensed with. Yet no law requires embalming, no religious doctrine commends it, nor is it dictated by considerations of health, sanitation, or even of personal daintiness. In no part of the world but in Northern America is it widely used. The purpose of embalming is to make the corpse presentable for viewing in a suitably costly container; and here too the funeral director routinely, without first consulting the family, prepares the body for public display.

Is all this legal? The processes to which a dead body may be subjected are after all to some extent circumscribed by law. In most states, for instance, the signature of next of kin must be obtained before an autopsy may be performed, before the deceased may be cremated, before the body may be turned over to a medical school for research purposes; or such provision must be made in the decedent's will. In the case of embalming, no such permission is required nor is it ever sought. A textbook, *The Principles and Practices of Embalming*, comments on this: "There is some question regarding the legality of much that is done within the preparation room." The author points out that it would be most unusual for a responsible member of a bereaved family to instruct the mortician, in so many words, to "embalm" the body of a deceased relative. The very term "embalming" is so seldom used that the mortician must rely upon custom in the matter. The author concludes that unless the family specifies otherwise, the act of entrusting the body to the care of a funeral establishment carries with it an implied permission to go ahead and embalm.

Embalming is indeed a most extraordinary procedure, and one must wonder at the docility of Americans who each year pay hundreds of millions of dollars for its perpetuation, blissfully ignorant of what it is all about, what is done, how it is done. Not one in ten thousand has any idea of what actually

From The American Way of Death *(1963), an exposé of the funeral industry, which was revised and updated by Mitford just before her death in 1996 as* The American Way of Death Revisited *(1998).*

1. Hamlet says this (V.i.184) upon seeing the skull of the court clown he had known as a child.

takes place. Books on the subject are extremely hard to come by. They are not to be found in most libraries or bookshops.

In an era when huge television audiences watch surgical operations in the comfort of their living rooms, when, thanks to the animated cartoon, the geography of the digestive system has become familiar territory even to the nursery school set, in a land where the satisfaction of curiosity about almost all matters is a national pastime, the secrecy surrounding embalming can, surely, hardly be attributed to the inherent gruesomeness of the subject. Custom in this regard has within this century suffered a complete reversal. In the early days of American embalming, when it was performed in the home of the deceased, it was almost mandatory for some relative to stay by the embalmer's side and witness the procedure. Today, family members who might wish to be in attendance would certainly be dissuaded by the funeral director. All others, except apprentices, are excluded by law from the preparation room.

A close look at what does actually take place may explain in large measure the undertaker's intractable reticence concerning a procedure that has become his major *raison d'être*.[2] Is it possible he fears that public information about embalming might lead patrons to wonder if they really want this service? If the funeral men are loath to discuss the subject outside the trade, the reader may, understandably, be equally loath to go on reading at this point. For those who have the stomach for it, let us part the formaldehyde curtain. . . .

The body is first laid out in the undertaker's morgue—or rather, Mr. Jones is reposing in the preparation room—to be readied to bid the world farewell.

The preparation room in any of the better funeral establishments has the tiled and sterile look of a surgery, and indeed the embalmer-restorative artist who does his chores there is beginning to adopt the term "dermasurgeon" (appropriately corrupted by some mortician-writers as "demi-surgeon") to describe his calling. His equipment, consisting of scalpels, scissors, augers, forceps, clamps, needles, pumps, tubes, bowls and basins, is crudely imitative of the surgeon's, as is his technique, acquired in a nine- or twelve-month post-high-school course in an embalming school. He is supplied by an advanced chemical industry with a bewildering array of fluids, sprays, pastes, oils, powders, creams, to fix or soften tissue, shrink or distend it as needed, dry it here, restore the moisture there. There are cosmetics, waxes and paints to fill and cover features, even plaster of Paris to replace entire limbs. There are ingenious aids to prop and stabilize the cadaver: a Vari-Pose Head Rest, the Edwards Arm and Hand Positioner, the Repose Block (to support the shoulders during the embalming), and the Throop Foot Positioner, which resembles an old-fashioned stocks.

Mr. John H. Eckels, president of the Eckels College of Mortuary Science, thus describes the first part of the embalming procedure: "In the hands of a skilled practitioner, this work may be done in a comparatively short time and without mutilating the body other than by slight incision—so slight that it scarcely would cause serious inconvenience if made upon a living per-

2. Reason for being.

son. It is necessary to remove the blood, and doing this not only helps in the disinfecting, but removes the principal cause of disfigurements due to discoloration."

10   Another textbook discusses the all-important time element: "The earlier this is done, the better, for every hour that elapses between death and embalming will add to the problems and complications encountered. . . ." Just how soon should one get going on the embalming? The author tells us, "On the basis of such scanty information made available to this profession through its rudimentary and haphazard system of technical research, we must conclude that the best results are to be obtained if the subject is embalmed before life is completely extinct—that is, before cellular death has occurred. In the average case, this would mean within an hour after somatic death." For those who feel that there is something a little rudimentary, not to say haphazard, about this advice, a comforting thought is offered by another writer. Speaking of fears entertained in early days of premature burial, he points out, "One of the effects of embalming by chemical injection, however, has been to dispel fears of live burial." How true; once the blood is removed, chances of live burial are indeed remote.

To return to Mr. Jones, the blood is drained out through the veins and replaced by embalming fluid pumped in through the arteries. As noted in *The Principles and Practices of Embalming,* "every operator has a favorite injection and drainage point—a fact which becomes a handicap only if he fails or refuses to forsake his favorites when conditions demand it." Typical favorites are the carotid artery, femoral artery, jugular vein, subclavian vein. There are various choices of embalming fluid. If Flextone is used, it will produce a "mild, flexible rigidity. The skin retains a velvety softness, the tissues are rubbery and pliable. Ideal for women and children." It may be blended with B. and G. Products Company's Lyf-Lyk tint, which is guaranteed to reproduce "nature's own skin texture . . . the velvety appearance of living tissue." Suntone comes in three separate tints: Suntan; Special Cosmetic Tint, a pink shade "especially indicated for young female subjects"; and Regular Cosmetic Tint, moderately pink.

About three to six gallons of a dyed and perfumed solution of formaldehyde, glycerin, borax, phenol, alcohol and water is soon circulating through Mr. Jones, whose mouth has been sewn together with a "needle directed upward between the upper lip and gum and brought out through the left nostril," with the corners raised slightly "for a more pleasant expression." If he should be bucktoothed, his teeth are cleaned with Bon Ami and coated with colorless nail polish. His eyes, meanwhile, are closed with flesh-tinted eye caps and eye cement.

The next step is to have at Mr. Jones with a thing called a trocar. This is a long, hollow needle attached to a tube. It is jabbed into the abdomen, poked around the entrails and chest cavity, the contents of which are pumped out and replaced with "cavity fluid." This done, and the hole in the abdomen sewn up, Mr. Jones's face is heavily creamed (to protect the skin from burns which may be caused by leakage of the chemicals), and he is covered with a sheet and left unmolested for a while. But not for long—there is more, much more, in store for him. He has been embalmed, but not yet restored, and the best time to start the restorative work is eight to ten hours after embalming, when the tissues have become firm and dry.

The object of all this attention to the corpse, it must be remembered, is to make it presentable for viewing in an attitude of healthy repose. "Our customs require the presentation of our dead in the semblance of normality . . . unmarred by the ravages of illness, disease or mutilation," says Mr. J. Sheridan Mayer in his *Restorative Art.* This is rather a large order since few people die in the full bloom of health, unravaged by illness and unmarked by some disfigurement. The funeral industry is equal to the challenge: "In some cases the gruesome appearance of a mutilated or disease-ridden subject may be quite discouraging. The task of restoration may seem impossible and shake the confidence of the embalmer. This is the time for intestinal fortitude and determination. Once the formative work is begun and affected tissues are cleaned or removed, all doubts of success vanish. It is surprising and gratifying to discover the results which may be obtained."

The embalmer, having allowed an appropriate interval to elapse, returns   15
to the attack, but now he brings into play the skill and equipment of sculptor and cosmetician. Is a hand missing? Casting one in plaster of Paris is a simple matter. "For replacement purposes, only a cast of the back of the hand is necessary; this is within the ability of the average operator and is quite adequate." If a lip or two, a nose or an ear should be missing, the embalmer has at hand a variety of restorative waxes with which to model replacements. Pores and skin texture are simulated by stippling with a little brush, and over this cosmetics are laid on. Head off? Decapitation cases are rather routinely handled. Ragged edges are trimmed, and head joined to torso with a series of splints, wires and sutures. It is a good idea to have a little something at the neck—a scarf or a high collar—when time for viewing comes. Swollen mouth? Cut out tissue as needed from inside the lips. If too much is removed, the surface contour can easily be restored by padding with cotton. Swollen necks and cheeks are reduced by removing tissue through vertical incisions made down each side of the neck. "When the deceased is casketed, the pillow will hide the suture incisions . . . as an extra precaution against leakage, the suture may be painted with liquid sealer."

The opposite condition is more likely to present itself—that of emaciation. His hypodermic syringe now loaded with massage cream, the embalmer seeks out and fills the hollowed and sunken areas by injection. In this procedure the backs of the hands and fingers and the under-chin area should not be neglected.

Positioning the lips is a problem that recurrently challenges the ingenuity of the embalmer. Closed too tightly, they tend to give a stern, even disapproving expression. Ideally, embalmers feel, the lips should give the impression of being ever so slightly parted, the upper lip protruding slightly for a more youthful appearance. This takes some engineering, however, as the lips tend to drift apart. Lip drift can sometimes be remedied by pushing one or two straight pins through the inner margin of the lower lip and then inserting them between the two front upper teeth. If Mr. Jones happens to have no teeth, the pins can just as easily be anchored in his Armstrong Face Former and Denture Replacer. Another method to maintain lip closure is to dislocate the lower jaw, which is then held in its new position by a wire run through holes which have been drilled through the upper and lower jaws at the midline. As the French are fond of saying, *il faut souffrir pour être belle*.[3]

If Mr. Jones has died of jaundice, the embalming fluid will very likely turn him green. Does this deter the embalmer? Not if he has intestinal fortitude. Masking pastes and cosmetics are heavily laid on, burial garments and casket interiors are color-correlated with particular care, and Jones is displayed beneath rose-colored lights. Friends will say "How *well* he looks." Death by carbon monoxide, on the other hand, can be rather a good thing from the embalmer's viewpoint: "One advantage is the fact that this type of discoloration is an exaggerated form of a natural pink coloration." This is nice because the healthy glow is already present and needs but little attention.

The patching and filling completed, Mr. Jones is now shaved, washed and dressed. Cream-based cosmetic, available in pink, flesh, suntan, brunette and blond, is applied to his hands and face, his hair is shampooed and combed (and, in the case of Mrs. Jones, set), his hands manicured. For the horny-handed son of toil special care must be taken; cream should be applied to remove ingrained grime, and the nails cleaned. "If he were not in the habit of having them manicured in life, trimming and shaping is advised for better appearance—never questioned by kin."

20   Jones is now ready for casketing (this is the present participle of the verb "to casket"). In this operation his right shoulder should be depressed slightly "to turn the body a bit to the right and soften the appearance of lying flat on the back." Positioning the hands is a matter of importance, and special rubber positioning blocks may be used. The hands should be cupped slightly for a more lifelike, relaxed appearance. Proper placement of the body requires a delicate sense of balance. It should lie as high as possible in the casket, yet not so high that the lid, when lowered, will hit the nose. On the other hand, we are cautioned, placing the body too low "creates the impression that the body is in a box."

Jones is next wheeled into the appointed slumber room where a few last touches may be added—his favorite pipe placed in his hand or, if he was a great reader, a book propped into position. (In the case of little Master Jones a Teddy bear may be clutched.) Here he will hold open house for a few days, visiting hours 10 A.M. to 9 P.M.

All now being in readiness, the funeral director calls a staff conference to make sure that each assistant knows his precise duties. Mr. Wilber Kriege writes: "This makes your staff feel that they are a part of the team, with a definite assignment that must be properly carried out if the whole plan is to succeed. You never heard of a football coach who failed to talk to his entire team

---

3. It is necessary to suffer to be beautiful.

before they go on the field. They have drilled on the plays they are to execute for hours and days, and yet the successful coach knows the importance of making even the bench-warming third-string substitute feel that he is important if the game is to be won." The winning of *this* game is predicated upon glass-smooth handling of the logistics. The funeral director has notified the pallbearers whose names were furnished by the family, has arranged for the presence of clergyman, organist, and soloist, has provided transportation for everybody, has organized and listed the flowers sent by friends. In *Psychology of Funeral Service* Mr. Edward A. Martin points out: "He may not always do as much as the family thinks he is doing, but it is his helpful guidance that they appreciate in knowing they are proceeding as they should. . . . The important thing is how well his services can be used to make the family believe they are giving unlimited expression to their own sentiment."

The religious service may be held in a church or in the chapel of the funeral home; the funeral director vastly prefers the latter arrangement, for not only is it more convenient for him but it affords him the opportunity to show off his beautiful facilities to the gathered mourners. After the clergyman has had his say, the mourners queue up to file past the casket for a last look at the deceased. The family is *never* asked whether they want an open-casket ceremony; in the absence of their instruction to the contrary, this is taken for granted. Consequently well over 90 per cent of all American funerals feature the open casket—a custom unknown in other parts of the world. Foreigners are astonished by it. An English woman living in San Francisco described her reaction in a letter to the writer:

> I myself have attended only one funeral here—that of an elderly fellow worker of mine. After the service I could not understand why everyone was walking towards the coffin (sorry, I mean casket), but thought I had better follow the crowd. It shook me rigid to get there and find the casket open and poor old Oscar lying there in his brown tweed suit, wearing a suntan makeup and just the wrong shade of lipstick. If I had not been extremely fond of the old boy, I have a horrible feeling that I might have giggled. Then and there I decided that I could never face another American funeral—even dead.

The casket (which has been resting throughout the service on a Classic Beauty Ultra Metal Casket Bier) is now transferred by a hydraulically operated device called Porto-Lift to a balloon-tired, Glide Easy casket carriage which will wheel it to yet another conveyance, the Cadillac Funeral Coach. This may be lavender, cream, light green—anything but black. Interiors, of course, are color-correlated, "for the man who cannot stop short of perfection."

At graveside, the casket is lowered into the earth. This office, once the prerogative of friends of the deceased, is now performed by a patented mechanical lowering device. A "Lifetime Green" artificial grass mat is at the ready to conceal the sere earth, and overhead, to conceal the sky, is a portable Steril Chapel Tent ("resists the intense heat and humidity of summer and the terrific storms of winter . . . available in Silver Grey, Rose or Evergreen"). Now is the

25

time for the ritual scattering of earth over the coffin, as the solemn words "earth to earth, ashes to ashes, dust to dust" are pronounced by the offi-ciating cleric. This can today be accomplished "with a mere flick of the wrist with the Gordon Leak-Proof Earth Dispenser. No grasping of a hand-ful of dirt, no soiled fingers. Simple, dignified, beautiful, reverent! The modern way!" The Gordon Earth Dispenser (at $5) is of nickel-plated brass construc-tion. It is not only "attractive to the eye and long wearing"; it is also "one of the 'tools' for building better public relations" if presented as "an appropriate non-commercial gift" to the clergyman. It is shaped something like a salt-shaker.

Untouched by human hand, the coffin and the earth are now united.

It is in the function of directing the participants through this maze of gad-getry that the funeral director has assigned to himself his relatively new role of "grief therapist." He has relieved the family of every detail, he has revamped the corpse to look like a living doll, he has arranged for it to nap for a few days in a slumber room, he has put on a well-oiled performance in which the con-cept of *death* has played no part whatsoever—unless it was inconsiderately mentioned by the clergyman who conducted the religious service. He has done everything in his power to make the funeral a real pleasure for everybody con-cerned. He and his team have given their all to score an upset victory over death.

QUESTIONS

1. Mitford's description might be called a "process essay"—that is, it describes the process by which a corpse becomes a "Beautiful Memory Picture." What are the stages of the process? Mark them in the margins of the essay, and think about how Mitford treats each one.

2. Mitford objects to the American funeral industry and its manipulation of death, yet she never directly says so. How do we as readers know her attitude? Cite words, phrases, or sentences that reveal her position.

3. Describe a process that you object to, letting your choice of words reveal your atti-tude.

THOMAS LYNCH   *The Bang & Whimper*
and the Boom

M Y SON AND I were moving caskets—an oak with Celtic crosses on the corners, a cherry with a finish like our dining room table, a cardboard box with a reinforced bottom—each could be buried, each could be burned, each could be blown into space or set adrift. The baby boomers who are buying now do better with a broad selection. I was talking to my son about "protection"—about condoms and careful choices and coming of age. He'd been out too late the night before.

Caskets and condoms serve well as late-century emblems of sex and death, how it is we come and go, the corruptible body's effort to put on incorruption. Practically speaking, one size fits all, but existentially they border on the voids between human being and human ceasing to be.

But my son had heard all of this before. The X his generation is named for marks the spot where pleasure and peril intersect, and he and his siblings are experts in these cautionary tales. In a display room full of caskets and cremation urns, he wants to talk about his future.

He says he wants to be a funeral director. He wonders if I'd ever sell to one of the huge conglomerates. They're buying up firms like ours across the globe: Frank E. Campbell in Manhattan; Kenyon in London, who used to bury the royals; most everything in Paris; and, closer to home, here in Michigan, they bought out our nearest competition last year. Cash and stock options for his brick and mortar, rolling stock, receivables and the name on the sign. They are banking on the boomer years, the next twenty or thirty, when the death rate will top the ten-per-thousand mark and the number of deaths in the United States will increase by one million every year. The talk inside the trade is that they raise the prices, cut services, centralize the management, push pre-need and after-care sales-ops and pay the shareholders handsomely. Less for more, voice mail and corporate cover, a good rating on the stock exchange—they have become the mortuary version of the American Way.

"The only problem is they buy your name. It's all you really have." I tell my son. The name on the sign—ours says LYNCH & SONS—is the one they call in the middle of the night when there is trouble. It's the one that makes you accountable to the community you live in, the people you live with. It's who can be trusted if the job is done well and who is to blame if ever it's not. We can build new buildings, buy new cars, do a brisk traffic in caskets and cremation urns and vaults and markers, but any damage to the name is permanent. It is the one asset we can't replace and dare not sell. It's an elderly form of consumer protection.

5

From Bodies in Motion and at Rest *(2000), one of several books that Lynch has written about his experiences as a Michigan funeral director.*

My father taught me about protection. It was the late sixties, early seventies. The planet was perilous and changing. I think he wanted me to "be prepared."

He taught me by role playing. It was all the rage. We'd go into the casket selection room at the funeral home. He'd be the undertaker—no stretch for him. I'd be the bereaved client with the dead mother—pure theater for me. My mother was going strong back then, full of life, still surrounded by my toddling younger siblings. I was floundering between colleges and careers, not quite certain about my "future," interested mostly in Irish poetry and Italian women. I had been to West Clare and to the Continent, back and forth a couple of times, learning to speak with a brogue and to woo dark beauties in the dialects of Venice and the Dolomites.

I worked at the funeral home to finance my travel and indecision. It was a job then, not a living, not a life. I was paid by the hour. I caught the phones at night, slept in the apartment on the second floor, kept my passport handy, my bag packed. I never knew if I was coming or going.

My father's insistence that I learn caskets seemed, in the parlance of my generation, "weird," "bizarre," "far out, man!" A child of those boom years at the confluence of industry and technology, mine was a mind-set of gleaming new products and possibilities. The retail end of the mortuary trade was boring by contrast, a downer indeed—an underworld of macabre and morbid curiosities about which I was anything but curious. What possible interest would a young boomer have in Elgin Permaseals and Wilbert Monticello burial vaults and the adjustable beds of Batesville Monogard casket? The only adjustable bed I'd any interest in was the one I was sharing, more or less à la carte, with Elena Pascuzzi in the back of her van, Tuesdays and Saturdays—my evenings off. Elena, a bookish woman with admirable bone structure, had read Simone de Beauvoir and Germaine Greer, *The Feminine Mystique* and the voluptuously titled *Our Bodies, Ourselves*. She was a lapsed Catholic, a born-again and braless communicant of the Good News that, thanks to the Mamas and the Papas and the Pill, she would exercise, at will, her right as a woman to initiate sex and enjoy sex out loud and to its fullest and to treat men as equals and sexual objects. This, of course, was fine with me and fine I reckon with the other happy objects of her affections, however fleeting, with whom she field-tested these notions those nights of the week that I was stuck at work. So to have my father rub my nose so deeply in the fact of death at a time when the Facts of Life seemed like so much fun no doubt damaged me in ways I'm only lately recovering the memory of. Surely, some twitch or addiction can be traced to it. Certainly I am permanently scarred. Hadn't Kennedy and Vietnam and the threat of Nuclear Holocaust been sufficient lessons in mortality? Hadn't we boomers bummers enough? For crissakes, where was Oprah when we needed her?

10   "The first one you show them is very important—it establishes the midrange, the average—you know, not the most expensive and not the least."

I'd already learned never to say "cheap."

My father would stop at the first casket, and eighteen-gauge steel number called the Praying Hands because of the appliqué in the cap panel. He'd lift the velvet overlay to expose the rubber gasket on the edge and, looking earnestly in my eyes, he'd begin.

"The most important difference between one casket and another has to do with its *protective qualities*. Most of the metal caskets in this room are what we call *sealed* caskets, because of this gum-rubber gasket that runs around the perimeter of the casket shell and *seals against air and moisture*."

Properly impressed with the technical splendor of a casket with a gasket but perplexed at the notion of safety when it came to corpses, I'd get into character readily.

"Who cares," I'd say, acting the doubtful Thomas, "about a *sealed* casket?   15
Who needs it? Anyway, isn't she dead?"

He'd show me the crank used to close the casket, insert it in the end and seal the lid shut with a few turns, then hand me the "key." The key to my poor dead mother's casket!

"Of course, it's not for *her*. It won't get her into heaven or keep her out. I suppose it has to do with peace of mind."

During the decades of the cold war, peace of mind sold many things: mouthwash, contraceptives, defense budgets.

"To some families *protection* is *very important*." He would pause. "To others it means *nothing at all*."

This declarative, according to my tutor, encouraged the customer to con-   20
sider which kind of family he or she was a part of—one for whom things were *very important* or one for whom things meant *nothing at all*.

"Here, for example"—he'd cross the aisle to a carved-top mahogany—"is a fine hardwood casket, a bit more *dear*, but not a *sealed* casket in the way the metal caskets are. Many families appreciate wooden caskets for their *warmth* and *beauty* and *natural qualities*. Still, the costliest of woods will not last as long as the least expensive metal."

I'd consider the price card on the big mahogany—three times the price of the eighteen-gauge—and say something like "Thanks, but no thanks. Mom would come back to haunt me if I spent that much." Even, then, my generation, famously oblivious to "costs," had learned to blame our parents, dead or alive, for any shortage of largesse.

My father, backing through the casket selection from unit to unit, would nod empathetically and move to another metal casket that shone like a new penny.

"This is thirty-two-ounce solid copper, a *permanent* metal. Unlike steel, which might rust or corrode, copper and bronze *oxidize* with age—that green you see on old rooftops, statues, caves, troughs . . . it gets *stronger and stronger*. These *precious metals* are the best *value* in *protective caskets*."

I would consider the copper. My father stood his ground. The room was   25
thick with anticipation. *Stronger, precious, values . . . Mom?*

The notions of protection and permanence were organizing principles of my parents' generation. Children of economic collapse and citizens of a planet constantly at war, they were schooled against waste and letting down their guard. Thus, diapers, life insurance, personal-hygiene products, all offered different forms of "protection." There was this general low-grade anxiety over "exposure" and liabilities. Well-engineered tampons, strident regulatory agencies, movie ratings, underarm deodorants, each offered a line of defense against some contagion, embarrassment or invader. That diamonds were forever was some comfort in the face of the ever-present threats to marriage and family. A piece of the rock, a tune from the past that was built to last, seatbelts, Tupperware, sealed caskets and nuclear submarines—to some people these were very important; to others, they meant nothing at all. We were all "right."

When I wouldn't opt for the copper or mahogany or praying hands, my father would eventually stand aside and, with a wave of his arm like a philharmonic conductor, open the rest of the options to me. I'd wander through the showroom, pausing over the carefully worded descriptions and price cards. *Tufted velvet, hand-hammered bronze deposit, $1775.00, solid cherry, stainless steel, cedar, doeskin, 20-gauge nonsealer.* I wanted to see them all, every one, and maybe some catalogs. Were there other colors available? I wondered. I couldn't quite make a decision, it seemed.

In the rosy light of the casket room, at twenty-one, my thoughts would sometimes drift from my choice of caskets to the inventory of my other options. Should I return to school and finish my education? Should I marry Elena Pascuzzi? Should I return to Ireland? Italy? The former Yugoslavia, where I'd met, the month before, a woman who made love in Serbo-Croatian? Should I go into teaching, undertaking, politics or show biz? Nuclear physics or the ministry? Pizza for lunch or Coney Islands? Smoking or non-smoking, cash or charge, acoustic or electric, coffee or tea? Should I get to California on a Harley or on psychedelics? Zen or vegetarian or Christianity?

The abundance of choices made choosing difficult.

30   "Which one?" My father's voice would yank me from my reveries.

"I don't know," I would tell him. "They're all so lovely."

Thus was I instructed in the sale of caskets. And over the years, I have sold my share to friends and family and perfect strangers. Of course, we don't push protection and permanence anymore. Forever isn't all it was cracked up to be in diamonds or in caskets. Divorce and cremation have taken their toll.

Indeed, the generation in the market now for mortuary wares is redefining death in much the same way that three decades back we redefined sex and gender. I think we thought that we invented it all.

Disabused of the connection between copulation and conception, we boomers didn't need to be told twice that if we couldn't be with the one we loved (Honey) we ought to love the one we were with. To such tunes, dancing came naturally. Pleasure could be a destination point. Unlike our parents, for whom sex held, quite frequently, bouncing-baby consequences and who, consequently, consigned it to their most intimate and deliberate vocabulary, sex for us was a flexible lexicon. Spontaneous, serendipitous, no strings attached. With some partners, it could be very important. With others, it could mean nothing at all.

Love was "free." 35

Funerals, I am here to tell you, aren't. And though we are masters at reinvention, and though the fashions of love and grief might change, love and grief remain—the dance and the piper, the tax we pay on our heart's attachments.

If my father sold caskets on protection and permanence, I offer choices, options, New Age alternatives. Where he occupied a world of black and white, ritual and tradition, moral certainty, our rights and wrongs are relative; we roll our own orthodoxies, in Polaroid and Technicolor. His generation buried the dead and burned their garbage; we do landfills and crematoria. He peddled copper and concrete and granite memorials. We do combustible, eco-friendly, video, virtual, cyber-obsequies—a little something for the ashes? He sold velvet and satin and crepe interiors. We sell denim and linen and warm-fuzzies.

But these are fashions, always in flux, fickle as the market-place, priced at whatever the traffic will bear. Bookstores are giving shelves formerly filled with *The Joy of Sex* to *The Meaning of Death*. Titles multiply on bereavement and hospice care and "end-of-life issues." TV and talk radio and tabloids follow suit. We boomers in our forties and early fifties are discovering mortality, burying and burning our mothers and fathers, hustling to reinvent the wheels that got our parents and their parents through age and sickness and sadness and loss in case, just in case, it could happen to us. Faced with the deaths of the ones we love, we are stuck between the will to do everything, anything and nothing at all.

And the generation-old arguments over our right to choose are giving way to contentions over our so-called right to die. Aborting and *kevorking* share the same vocabulary—for each there's a coat hanger and a back alley and an old van; bishops and politicos and true believers. The quacks who want to clone us and do us in sound much the same.

Back at the funeral home the hot topics—forgive me—are cremation and 40 designer funerals. My parents' generation, in their seventies now, are buying motor homes and time-shares in casino towns, trading in their piece of the rock for a piece of the action, taking a walk on the wild side of slot machines and casual sex, beginning to behave like their children used to: scattered, mobile, portable, still crazy after all these years. They do not want to be a burden to their children. They do not want to be "grounded" to the graves they bought, pre-need, back in the old days when people stayed put. Their ashes are FedExed and parcel-posted and UPSed around the hemisphere day and night in little packages, roughly the weight of a bowling ball, roughly the shape of that first starter home, roughly the size of a coffee can squared. Not nearly the full, life-sized burden of a casket, not nearly the bother or expense. Less for them is less. For us it's more. They get sent back from Vegas and Phoenix, Florida and the Carolinas, to old homes in the cold North and Rust Belt states.

Still, their sons and daughters, in receipt of these tiny reminders, are beginning to wonder. *Is that all there is?* Is it enough to get out our cell phones and our gold cards and have our dead elders disappeared with no more pause than it takes to order up sushi to go? Can we distance ourselves entirely from the physical realities of death and still expect to enjoy the physical wonders of life?

If the old become young again, maybe the young are coming of age.

Always the demographic bullies on the block, now that we boomers are grieving and dying, grief and death are all the rage. The market is bullish on ritual and metaphor, for acting out our hurts the way our ancients did. Whether we burn or bury our dead or blast them into space is less important than what we do before we dispose of them. More and more we care for our own dying. More and more we are making up new liturgies to say good-bye. More and more we seem willing to engage fully in the process of leave-taking. We rise early to watch the TV obsequies of princesses, and modern saints. We read the obits every day. We eulogize, elegize and memorialize with vigor. The trade is brisk in wakes and funerals. We sell copper and combustibles, bronze and biodegradables, eco-friendly and economy models. We do urns that look like golf bags and go to cemeteries with names like golf courses. You can buy a casket off the Internet, or buy plans for a self-built coffin table or one that doubles as a bookshelf or an armoire until you "need" it. There's a kind of push for "do-it-yourself" funerals, as if grief were ever anything but. Cremated remains can be cast into bookends or paper weights or duck decoys. They can be recycled as memorial kitty litter, sprinkled on our rose bushes, mixed with our oil paints to add texture to fresh masterpieces. We have, as Batesville Casket Company calls its latest marketing approach, "Options." And as the demographic aneurysm gets nearer to bursting in two or three decades, the marketplace is readying for another boom. Soon every off-ramp on every interstate across the continent will have a Best Buy, Builders Square, Burger King, Barnes & Noble and Casket Express. The expanding choices in mortuary wares make it seem as if we really have choices about mortality.

The facts of life and death remain the same. We live and die, we love and grieve, we breed and disappear. And between these existential gravities, we search for meaning, save our memories, leave a record for those who will remember us.

45   I remember my father. I remember being his son. I hear my father's caution in the way I caution my son now—and his sister and his brothers—about life's changes and dangers, about drugs and drink and being "sexually active." We talk about making responsible choices, safe sex, committed relationships, condoms and consequences: permanence and protection come round again.

One of these days I'll have to teach them caskets.

QUESTIONS

1. How would you describe Lynch's tone in this essay? What are the most striking characteristics of his writing that create this tone?

2. Compare this essay to one of two classics: "Once More to the Lake" (p. 93) for its intergenerational topic or "Behind the Formaldehyde Curtain" (p. 310) for its similar sub-

ject matter. In what ways is Lynch's essay similar? In what ways different? Does it strike you as more modern, and if so, how?

3. Why do you think fashions in funerals change? Write a brief essay presenting your views.

HENRY LOUIS GATES JR. *In the Kitchen*

W E ALWAYS HAD a gas stove in the kitchen, in our house in Piedmont, West Virginia, where I grew up. Never electric, though using electric became fashionable in Piedmont in the sixties, like using Crest toothpaste rather than Colgate, or watching Huntley and Brinkley rather than Walter Cronkite.[1] But not us: gas, Colgate, and good ole Walter Cronkite, come what may. We used gas partly out of loyalty to Big Mom, Mama's Mama, because she was mostly blind and still loved to cook, and could feel her way more easily with gas than with electric. But the most important thing about our gas-equipped kitchen was that Mama used to do hair there. The "hot comb" was a fine-toothed iron instrument with a long wooden handle and a pair of iron curlers that opened and closed like scissors. Mama would put it in the gas fire until it glowed. You could smell those prongs heating up.

I liked that smell. Not the smell so much, I guess, as what the smell meant for the shape of my day. There was an intimate warmth in the women's tones as they talked with my Mama, doing their hair. I knew what the women had been through to get their hair ready to be "done," because I would watch Mama do it to herself. How that kink could be transformed through grease and fire into that magnificent head of wavy hair was a miracle to me, and still is.

Mama would wash her hair over the sink, a towel wrapped around her shoulders, wearing just her slip and her white bra. (We had no shower—just a galvanized tub that we stored in the kitchen—until we moved down Rat Tail Road into Doc Wolverton's house, in 1954.) After she dried it, she would grease her scalp thoroughly with blue Bergamot hair grease, which came in a short, fat jar with a picture of a beautiful colored lady on it. It's important to grease your scalp real good, my Mama would explain, to keep from burning yourself. Of course, her hair would return to its natural kink almost as soon as the hot water and shampoo hit it. To me, it was another miracle how hair so

Originally published in the New Yorker *(April 18, 1994), a magazine distinguished for its fiction, essays, and reviews, in advance of the publication of Gates's memoir,* Colored People *(1994).*

1. Newscasters of the 1960s: Chet Huntley and David Brinkley were on NBC; Walter Cronkite was on CBS.

"straight" would so quickly become kinky again the second it even approached some water.

My Mama had only a few "clients" whose heads she "did"—did, I think, because she enjoyed it, rather than for the few pennies it brought in. They would sit on one of our red plastic kitchen chairs, the kind with the shiny metal legs, and brace themselves for the process. Mama would stroke that red-hot iron—which by this time had been in the gas fire for half an hour or more—slowly but firmly through their hair, from scalp to strand's end. It made a scorching, crinkly sound, the hot iron did, as it burned its way through kink, leaving in its wake straight strands of hair, standing long and tall but drooping over at the ends, their shape like the top of a heavy willow tree. Slowly, steadily, Mama's hands would transform a round mound of Odetta[2] kink into a darkened swamp of everglades. The Bergamot made the hair shiny; the heat of the hot iron gave it a brownish-red cast. Once all the hair was as straight as God allows kink to get, Mama would take the wellheated curling iron and twirl the straightened strands into more or less loosely wrapped curls. She claimed that she owed her skill as a hairdresser to the strength in her wrists, and as she worked her little finger would poke out, the way it did when she sipped tea. Mama was a southpaw, and wrote upside down and backward to produce the cleanest, roundest letters you've ever seen.

5   The "kitchen" she would all but remove from sight with a handheld pair of shears, bought just for this purpose. Now, the kitchen was the room in which we were sitting—the room where Mama did hair and washed clothes, and where we all took a bath in that galvanized tub. But the word has another meaning, and the kitchen that I'm speaking of is the very kinky bit of hair at the back of your head, where your neck meets your shirt collar. If there was ever a part of our African past that resisted assimilation, it was the kitchen. No matter how hot the iron, no matter how powerful the chemical, no matter how stringent the mashed-potatoes-and-lye formula of a man's "process," neither God nor woman nor Sammy Davis, Jr.,[3] could straighten the kitchen. The kitchen was permanent, irredeemable, irresistible kink. Unassimilably African. No matter what you did, no matter how hard you tried, you couldn't de-kink a person's kitchen. So you trimmed it off as best you could.

When hair had begun to "turn," as they'd say—to return to its natural kinky glory—it was the kitchen that turned first (the kitchen around the back, and nappy edges at the temples). When the kitchen started creeping up the back of the neck, it was time to get your hair done again.

Sometimes, after dark, a man would come to have his hair done. It was Mr. Charlie Carroll. He was very light-complected and had a ruddy nose—it made me think of Edmund Gwenn, who played Kris Kringle in "Miracle on 34th

2. Singer (b. 1930) of blues and spirituals in the 1950s and a leading figure in the American folk revival of the 1960s; she wore a large Afro hairdo.
3. African American singer, dancer, and entertainer (1925–1990) with notably "processed" hair.

Street." At first, Mama did him after my brother, Rocky, and I had gone to sleep. It was only later that we found out that he had come to our house so Mama could iron his hair—not with a hot comb or a curling iron but with our very own Proctor-Silex steam iron. For some reason I never understood, Mr. Charlie would conceal his Frederick Douglass–like mane[4] under a big white Stetson hat. I never saw him take it off except when he came to our house, at night, to have his hair pressed. (Later, Daddy would tell us about Mr. Charlie's most prized piece of knowledge, something that the man would only confide after his hair had been pressed, as a token of intimacy. "Not many people know this," he'd say, in a tone of circumspection, "but George Washington was Abraham Lincoln's daddy." Nodding solemnly, he'd add the clincher: "A white man told me." Though he was in dead earnest, this became a humorous refrain around our house—"a white man told me"—which we used to punctuate especially preposterous assertions.)

My mother examined my daughters' kitchens whenever we went home to visit, in the early eighties. It became a game between us. I had told her not to do it, because I didn't like the politics it suggested—the notion of "good" and "bad" hair. "Good" hair was "straight," "bad" hair kinky. Even in the late sixties, at the height of Black Power, almost nobody could bring themselves to say "bad" for good and "good" for bad. People still said that hair like white people's hair was "good," even if they encapsulated it in a disclaimer, like "what we used to call 'good.'"

Maggie would be seated in her high chair, throwing food this way and that, and Mama would be cooing about how cute it all was, how I used to do just like Maggie was doing, and wondering whether her flinging her food with her left hand meant that she was going to be left-handed like Mama. When my daughter was just about covered with Chef Boyardee Spaghetti-O's, Mama would seize the opportunity: wiping her clean, she would tilt Maggie's head to one side and reach down the back of her neck. Sometimes Mama would even rub a curl between her fingers, just to make sure that her bifocals had not deceived her. Then she'd sigh with satisfaction and relief: No kink . . . yet. Mama! I'd shout, pretending to be angry. Every once in a while, if no one was looking, I'd peek, too.

I say "yet" because most black babies are born with soft, silken hair. But   10
after a few months it begins to turn, as inevitably as do the seasons or the leaves on a tree. People once thought baby oil would stop it. They were wrong.

Everybody I knew as a child wanted to have good hair. You could be as ugly as homemade sin dipped in misery and still be thought attractive if you had good hair. "Jesus moss," the girls at Camp Lee, Virginia, had called Daddy's naturally "good" hair during the war. I know that he played that thick head of hair for all it was worth, too.

My own hair was "not a bad grade," as barbers would tell me when they cut it for the first time. It was like a doctor reporting the results of the first full

4. Douglass (1817–1895) was an escaped slave turned abolitionist; photographs show him with a lionlike mane of hair.

physical he has given you. Like "You're in good shape" or "Blood pressure's kind of high—better cut down on salt."

I spent most of my childhood and adolescence messing with my hair. I definitely wanted straight hair. Like Pop's. When I was about three, I tried to stick a wad of Bazooka bubble gum to that straight hair of his. I suppose what fixed that memory for me is the spanking I got for doing so: he turned me upside down, holding me by my feet, the better to paddle my behind. Little *nigger*, he had shouted, walloping away. I started to laugh about it two days later, when my behind stopped hurting.

When black people say "straight," of course, they don't usually mean literally straight—they're not describing hair like, say, Peggy Lipton's (she was the white girl on "The Mod Squad"), or like Mary's of Peter, Paul & Mary[5] fame; black people call that "stringy" hair. No, "straight" just means not kinky, no matter what contours the curl may take. I would have done *anything* to have straight hair—and I used to try everything, short of getting a process.[6]

15   Of the wide variety of techniques and methods I came to master in the challenging prestidigitation of the follicle, almost all had two things in common: a heavy grease and the application of pressure. It's not an accident that some of the biggest black-owned companies in the fifties and sixties made hair products. And I tried them all, in search of that certain silken touch, the one that would leave neither the hand nor the pillow sullied by grease.

I always wondered what Frederick Douglass put on *his* hair, or what Phillis Wheatley[7] put on hers. Or why Wheatley has that rag on her head in the little engraving in the frontispiece of her book. One thing is for sure: you can bet that when Phillis Wheatley went to England and saw the Countess of Huntingdon she did not stop by the Queen's coiffeur on her way there. So many black people still get their hair straightened that it's a wonder we don't have a national holiday for Madame C. J. Walker, the woman who invented the process of straightening kinky hair. Call it Jheri-Kurled or call it "relaxed," it's still fried hair.

I used all the greases, from sea-blue Bergamot and creamy vanilla Duke (in its clear jar with the orange-white-and-green label) to the godfather of grease, the formidable Murray's. Now, Murray's was some *serious* grease. Whereas Bergamot was like oily jello, and Duke was viscous and sickly sweet, Murray's was light brown and *hard*. Hard as lard and twice as greasy, Daddy used to say. Murray's came in an orange can with a press-on top. It was so hard that some people would put a match to the can, just to soften the stuff and make it more manageable. Then, in the late sixties, when Afros came into style, I used Afro Sheen. From Murray's to Duke to Afro Sheen: that was my progression in black consciousness.

---

5. Folksinging group famous in the 1960s for "Puff the Magic Dragon" and a version of Bob Dylan's "Blowing in the Wind."

6. Hair-straightening treatment that used chemicals for smoothing out kinks.

7. African American poet and slave (1753–1784) and America's first published black writer. She was taken to England to meet royalty.

We used to put hot towels or washrags over our Murray-coated heads, in order to melt the wax into the scalp and the follicles. Unfortunately, the wax also had the habit of running down your neck, ears, and forehead. Not to mention your pillowcase. Another problem was that if you put two palmfuls of Murray's on your head your hair turned white. (Duke did the same thing.) The challenge was to get rid of that white color. Because if you got rid of the white stuff you had a magnificent head of wavy hair. That was the beauty of it: Murray's was so hard that it froze your hair into the wavy style you brushed it into. It looked really good if you wore a part. A lot of guys had parts *cut* into their hair by a barber, either with the clippers or with a straight-edge razor. Especially if you had kinky hair—then you'd generally wear a short razor cut, or what we called a Quo Vadis.

We tried to be as innovative as possible. Everyone knew about using a stocking cap, because your father or your uncle wore one whenever something really big was about to happen, whether sacred or secular: a funeral or a dance, a wedding or a trip in which you confronted official white people. Any time you were trying to look really sharp, you wore a stocking cap in preparation. And if the event was really a big one, you made a new cap. You asked your mother for a pair of her hose, and cut it with scissors about six inches or so from the open end—the end with the elastic that goes up to the top of the thigh. Then you knotted the cut end, and it became a beehive-shaped hat, with an elastic band that you pulled down low on your forehead and down around your neck in the back. To work well, the cap had to fit tightly and snugly, like a press. And it had to fit that tightly because it *was* a press: it pressed your hair with the force of the hose's elastic. If you greased your hair down real good, and left the stocking cap on long enough, voilà: you got a head of pressed-against-the-scalp waves. (You also got a ring around your forehead when you woke up, but it went away.) And then you could enjoy your concrete do. Swore we were bad, too, with all that grease and those flat heads. My brother and I would brush it out a bit in the mornings, so that it looked—well, "natural." Grown men still wear stocking caps—especially older men, who generally keep their stocking caps in their top drawers, along with their cufflinks and their see-through silk socks, their "Maverick" ties, their silk handkerchiefs, and whatever else they prize the most.

A Murrayed-down stocking cap was the respectable version of the process, which, by contrast, was most definitely not a cool thing to have unless you were an entertainer by trade. Zeke and Keith and Poochie and a few other stars of the high-school basketball team all used to get a process once or twice a year. It was expensive, and you had to go somewhere like Pittsburgh or D.C. or Uniontown—somewhere where there were enough colored people to support a trade. The guys would disappear, then reappear a day or two later, strutting like peacocks, their hair burned slightly red from the lye base. They'd also wear "rags"—cloths or handkerchiefs—around their heads when they slept or played basketball. Do-rags, they were called. But the result was straight hair, with just a hint of wave. No curl. Do-it-yourselfers took their chances at home with a concoction of mashed potatoes and lye.

20

The most famous process of all, however, outside of the process Malcolm X describes in his "Autobiography," and maybe the process of Sammy Davis, Jr., was Nat King Cole's[8] process. Nat King Cole had patent-leather hair. That man's got the finest process money can buy, or so Daddy said the night we saw Cole's TV show on NBC. It was November 5, 1956. I remember the date because everyone came to our house to watch it and to celebrate one of Daddy's buddies' birthdays. Yeah, Uncle Joe chimed in, they can do shit to his hair that the average Negro can't even *think* about—secret shit.

Nat King Cole was *clean.* I've had an ongoing argument with a Nigerian friend about Nat King Cole for twenty years now. Not about whether he could sing—any fool knows that he could—but about whether or not he was a hand-kerchief head for wearing that patent-leather process.

Sammy Davis, Jr.'s process was the one I detested. It didn't look good on him. Worse still, he liked to have a fried strand dangling down the middle of his forehead, so he could shake it out from the crown when he sang. But Nat King Cole's hair was a thing unto itself, a beautifully sculpted work of art that he and he alone had the right to wear. The only difference between a process and a stocking cap, really, was taste; but Nat King Cole, unlike, say, Michael Jackson, looked *good* in his. His head looked like Valentino's[9] head in the twenties, and some say it was Valentino the process was imitating. But Nat King Cole wore a process because it suited his face, his demeanor, his name, his style. He was as clean as he wanted to be.

I had forgotten all about that patent-leather look until one day in 1971, when I was sitting in an Arab restaurant on the island of Zanzibar surrounded by men in fezzes and white caftans, trying to learn how to eat curried goat and rice with the fingers of my right hand and feeling two million miles from home. All of a sudden, an old transistor radio sitting on top of a china cupboard stopped blaring out its Swahili music and started playing "Fly Me to the Moon," by Nat King Cole. The restaurant's din was not affected at all, but in my mind's eye I saw it: the King's magnificent sleek black tiara. I managed, barely, to blink back the tears.

8. Singer and jazz pianist (1919–1965).
9. Film star (1895–1926) known for, among other things, his slicked-back hair.

QUESTIONS

1. "Kitchen" has two meanings in Gates's essay; write a brief summary of the essay explaining the significance of both uses of "kitchen."

2. Why do you think Gates uses so many allusions to celebrities (mostly from the 1950s and 1960s) and brand-name products? Note his preferences and progression. What is the significance of the allusions and brand names?

3. Write an essay in which you use memories from childhood—including sensory details, popular allusions, and brand-name products—to describe some element of your culture or identity.

MALCOLM GLADWELL *Java Man*

THE ORIGINAL COCA-COLA was a late-nineteenth-century concoction known as Pemberton's French Wine Coca, a mixture of alcohol, the caffeine-rich kola nut, and coca, the raw ingredient of cocaine. In the face of social pressure, first the wine and then the coca were removed, leaving the more banal modern beverage in its place: carbonated, caffeinated sugar water with less kick to it than a cup of coffee. But is that the way we think of Coke? Not at all. In the nineteen-thirties, a commercial artist named Haddon Sundblom had the bright idea of posing a portly retired friend of his in a red Santa Claus suit with a Coke in his hand, and plastering the image on billboards and advertisements across the country. Coke, magically, was reborn as caffeine for children, caffeine without any of the weighty adult connotations of coffee and tea. It was—as the ads with Sundblom's Santa put it—"the pause that refreshes." It added life. It could teach the world to sing.

One of the things that have always made drugs so powerful is their cultural adaptability, their way of acquiring meanings beyond their pharmacology. We think of marijuana, for example, as a drug of lethargy, of disaffection. But in Colombia, the historian David T. Courtwright points out in "Forces of Habit," "peasants boast that cannabis helps them to *quita el cansancio* or reduce fatigue; increase their *fuerza* and *ánimo*, force and spirit; and become *incansable*, tireless." In Germany right after the Second World War, cigarettes briefly and suddenly became the equivalent of crack cocaine. "Up to a point, the majority of the habitual smokers preferred to do without food even under extreme conditions of nutrition rather than to forgo tobacco," according to one account of the period. "Many housewives . . . bartered fat and sugar for cigarettes." Even a drug as demonized as opium has been seen in a more favorable light. In the eighteen-thirties, Franklin Delano Roosevelt's grandfather Warren Delano II made the family fortune exporting the drug to China, and Delano was able to sugar-coat his activities so plausibly that no one ever accused his grandson of being the scion of a drug lord. And yet, as Bennett Alan Weinberg and Bonnie K. Bealer remind us in their marvellous book "The World of Caffeine," there is no drug quite as effortlessly adaptable as caffeine, the Zelig of chemical stimulants.

At one moment, in one form, it is the drug of choice of café intellectuals and artists; in another, of housewives; in another, of Zen monks; and, in yet another, of children enthralled by a fat man who slides down chimneys. King Gustav III, who ruled Sweden in the latter half of the eighteenth century, was so convinced of the particular perils of coffee over all other forms of caffeine that he devised an elaborate experiment. A convicted murderer was sentenced to drink cup after cup of coffee until he died, with another murderer

First published in the New Yorker *(July 30, 2001), an American magazine of literature, culture, and the arts, for which Gladwell has been a regular writer since 1996.*

sentenced to a lifetime of tea drinking, as a control. (Unfortunately, the two doctors in charge of the study died before anyone else did; then Gustav was murdered; and finally the tea drinker died, at eighty-three, of old age—leaving the original murderer alone with his espresso, and leaving coffee's supposed toxicity in some doubt.) Later, the various forms of caffeine began to be divided up along sociological lines. Wolfgang Schivelbusch, in his book "Tastes of Paradise," argues that, in the eighteenth century, coffee symbolized the rising middle classes, whereas its great caffeinated rival in those years—cocoa, or, as it was known at the time, chocolate—was the drink of the aristocracy. "Goethe, who used art as a means to lift himself out of his middle class background into the aristocracy, and who as a member of a courtly society maintained a sense of aristocratic calm even in the midst of immense productivity, made a cult of chocolate, and avoided coffee," Schivelbusch writes. "Balzac, who despite his sentimental allegiance to the monarchy, lived and labored for the literary marketplace and for it alone, became one of the most excessive coffee-drinkers in history. Here we see two fundamentally different working styles and means of stimulation—fundamentally different psychologies and physiologies." Today, of course, the chief cultural distinction is between coffee and tea, which, according to a list drawn up by Weinberg and Bealer, have come to represent almost entirely opposite sensibilities:

Coffee Aspect	Tea Aspect
Male	Female
Boisterous	Decorous
Indulgence	Temperance
Hardheaded	Romantic
Topology	Geometry
Heidegger	Carnap
Beethoven	Mozart
Libertarian	Statist
Promiscuous	Pure

That the American Revolution began with the symbolic rejection of tea in Boston Harbor, in other words, makes perfect sense. Real revolutionaries would naturally prefer coffee. By contrast, the freedom fighters of Canada, a hundred years later, were most definitely tea drinkers. And where was Canada's autonomy won? Not on the blood-soaked fields of Lexington and Concord but in the genteel drawing rooms of Westminster, over a nice cup of Darjeeling and small, triangular cucumber sandwiches.

5   All this is a bit puzzling. We don't fetishize the difference between salmon eaters and tuna eaters, or people who like their eggs sunny-side up and those who like them scrambled. So why invest so much importance in the way people prefer their caffeine? A cup of coffee has somewhere between a hundred and two hundred and fifty milligrams; black tea brewed for four minutes has between forty and a hundred milligrams. But the disparity disappears if you consider that many tea drinkers drink from a pot, and have more than one cup. Caffeine is caffeine. "The more it is pondered," Weinberg and Bealer

write, "the more paradoxical this duality within the culture of caffeine appears. After all, both coffee and tea are aromatic infusions of vegetable matter, served hot or cold in similar quantities; both are often mixed with cream or sugar; both are universally available in virtually any grocery or restaurant in civilized society; and both contain the identical psychoactive alkaloid stimulant, caffeine."

It would seem to make more sense to draw distinctions based on the way caffeine is metabolized rather than on the way it is served. Caffeine, whether it is in coffee or tea or a soft drink, moves easily from the stomach and intestines into the bloodstream, and from there to the organs, and before long has penetrated almost every cell of the body. This is the reason that caffeine is such a wonderful stimulant. Most substances can't cross the blood-brain barrier, which is the body's defensive mechanism, preventing viruses or toxins from entering the central nervous system. Caffeine does so easily. Within an hour or so, it reaches its peak concentration in the brain, and there it does a number of things—principally, blocking the action of adenosine, the neuromodulator that makes you sleepy, lowers your blood pressure, and slows down your heartbeat. Then, as quickly as it builds up in your brain and tissues, caffeine is gone—which is why it's so safe. (Caffeine in ordinary quantities has never been conclusively linked to serious illness.)

But how quickly it washes away differs dramatically from person to person. A two-hundred-pound man who drinks a cup of coffee with a hundred milligrams of caffeine will have a maximum caffeine concentration of one milligram per kilogram of body weight. A hundred-pound woman having the same cup of coffee will reach a caffeine concentration of two milligrams per kilogram of body weight, or twice as high. In addition, when women are on the Pill, the rate at which they clear caffeine from their bodies slows considerably. (Some of the side effects experienced by women on the Pill may in fact be caffeine jitters caused by their sudden inability to tolerate as much coffee as they could before.) Pregnancy reduces a woman's ability to process caffeine still further. The half-life of caffeine in an adult is roughly three and a half hours. In a pregnant woman, it's eighteen hours. (Even a four-month-old child processes caffeine more efficiently.) An average man and woman sitting down for a cup of coffee are thus not pharmaceutical equals: in effect, the woman is under the influence of a vastly more powerful drug. Given these differences, you'd think that, instead of contrasting the caffeine cultures of tea and coffee, we'd contrast the caffeine cultures of men and women.

But we don't, and with good reason. To parse caffeine along gender lines does not do justice to its capacity to insinuate itself into every aspect of our lives, not merely to influence culture but even to create it. Take coffee's reputation as the "thinker's" drink. This dates from eighteenth-century Europe, where coffeehouses played a major role in the egalitarian, inclusionary spirit that was then sweeping the continent. They sprang up first in London, so alarming Charles II that in 1676 he tried to ban them. It didn't work. By 1700, there were hundreds of coffeehouses in London, their subversive spirit best captured by a couplet from a comedy of the period: "In a coffeehouse just now among the rabble I bluntly asked, which is the treason table." The movement then spread to Paris, and by the end of the eighteenth century coffeehouses numbered in the hundreds—most famously; the Café de la Régence, near the Palais Royal, which counted among its customers Robespierre, Napoleon, Voltaire, Victor Hugo, Théophile Gautier, Rousseau, and the Duke of Richelieu. Previously, when men had gathered together to talk in public places, they had done so in bars, which drew from specific socioeconomic niches and, because of the alcohol they served, created a specific kind of talk. The new coffeehouses, by contrast, drew from many different classes and trades, and they served a stimulant, not a depressant. "It is not extravagant to claim that it was in these gathering spots that the art of conversation became the basis of a new literary style and that a new ideal of general education in letters was born," Weinberg and Bealer write.

It is worth nothing, as well, that in the original coffeehouses nearly everyone smoked, and nicotine also has a distinctive physiological effect. It moderates mood and extends attention, and, more important, it doubles the rate of caffeine metabolism: it allows you to drink twice as much coffee as you could otherwise. In other words, the original coffeehouse was a place where men of all types could sit all day; the tobacco they smoked made it possible to drink coffee all day; and the coffee they drank inspired them to talk all day. Out of this came the Enlightenment. (The next time we so perfectly married pharmacology and place, we got Joan Baez.)

10   In time, caffeine moved from the café to the home. In America, coffee triumphed because of the country's proximity to the new Caribbean and Latin American coffee plantations, and the fact that throughout the nineteenth century duties were negligible. Beginning in the eighteen-twenties, Courtwright tells us, Brazil "unleashed a flood of slave-produced coffee. American per capita consumption, three pounds per year in 1830, rose to eight pounds by 1859."

What this flood of caffeine did, according to Weinberg and Bealer, was to abet the process of industrialization—to help "large numbers of people to coordinate their work schedules by giving them the energy to start work at a given time and continue it as long as necessary." Until the eighteenth century, it must be remembered, many Westerners drank beer almost continuously, even beginning their day with something called "beer soup." (Bealer and Weinberg helpfully provide the following eighteenth-century German recipe: "Heat the beer in a saucepan; in a separate small pot beat a couple of eggs. Add a chunk of butter to the hot beer. Stir in some cool beer to cool it, then pour over the eggs. Add a bit of salt, and finally mix all the ingredients together, whisking it well to keep it from curdling.") Now they began each day with a strong cup of coffee. One way to explain the industrial revolution is as the inevitable consequence of a world where people suddenly preferred being jittery to being drunk. In the modern world, there was no other way to keep up. That's what Edison meant when he said that genius was ninety-nine per cent perspiration and one per cent inspiration. In the old paradigm, working with your mind had been associated with leisure. It was only the poor who worked hard. (The quintessential preindustrial narrative of inspiration belonged to Archimedes, who made his discovery, let's not forget, while taking a bath.) But Edison was saying that the old class distinctions no longer held true—that in the industrialized world there was as much toil associated with the life of the mind as there had once been with the travails of the body.

In the twentieth century, the professions transformed themselves accordingly: medicine turned the residency process into an ordeal of sleeplessness, the legal profession borrowed a page from the manufacturing floor and made its practitioners fill out time cards like union men. Intellectual heroics became a matter of endurance. "The pace of computation was hectic," James Gleick writes of the Manhattan Project in "Genius," his biography of the physicist Richard Feynman. "Feynman's day began at 8:30 and ended fifteen hours later. Sometimes he could not leave the computing center at all. He worked through for thirty-one hours once and the next day found that an error minutes after he went to bed had stalled the whole team. The routine allowed just a few breaks." Did Feynman's achievements reflect a greater natural talent than his less productive forebears had? Or did he just drink a lot more coffee? Paul Hoffman, in "The Man Who Loved Only Numbers," writes of the legendary twentieth-century mathematician Paul Erdös that "he put in nineteen-hour days, keeping himself fortified with 10 to 20 milligrams of Benzedrine or Ritalin, strong espresso and caffeine tablets. 'A mathematician,' Erdös was fond of saying, 'is a machine for turning coffee into theorems.' " Once, a friend bet Erdös five hundred dollars that he could not quit amphetamines for a month. Erdös took the bet and won, but, during his time of abstinence, he found himself incapable of doing any serious work. "You've set mathematics back a month," he told his friend when he collected, and immediately returned to his pills.

Erdös's unadulterated self was less real and less familiar to him than his adulterated self, and that is a condition that holds, more or less, for the rest of society as well. Part of what it means to be human in the modern age is that we have come to construct our emotional and cognitive states not merely from the inside out—with thought and intention—but from the outside in, with chemical additives. The modern personality is, in this sense, a synthetic creation: skillfully regulated and medicated and dosed with caffeine so that we can always be awake and alert and focussed when we need to be. On a bet, no doubt, we could walk away from caffeine if we had to. But what would be the point? The lawyers wouldn't make their billable hours. The young doctors would fall behind in their training. The physicists might still be stuck out in the New Mexico desert. We'd set the world back a month.

That the modern personality is synthetic is, of course, a disquieting notion. When we talk of synthetic personality—or of constructing new selves through chemical means—we think of hard drugs, not caffeine. Timothy Leary used to make such claims about LSD, and the reason his revolution never took flight was that most of us found the concept of tuning in, turning on, and dropping out to be a bit creepy. Here was this shaman, this visionary—and yet, if his consciousness was so great, why was he so intent on altering it? More important, what exactly were we supposed to be tuning in to? We were given hints, with psychedelic colors and deep readings of "Lucy in the Sky with Diamonds," but that was never enough. If we are to re-create ourselves, we would like to know what we will become.

15   Caffeine is the best and most useful of our drugs because in every one of its forms it can answer that question precisely. It is a stimulant that blocks the action of adenosine, and comes in a multitude of guises, each with a ready-made story attached, a mixture of history and superstition and whimsy which infuses the daily ritual of adenosine blocking with meaning and purpose. Put caffeine in a red can and it becomes refreshing fun. Brew it in a teapot and it becomes romantic and decorous. Extract it from little brown beans and, magically, it is hardheaded and potent. "There was a little known Russian émigré, Trotsky by name, who during World War I was in the habit of playing chess in Vienna's Café Central every evening," Bealer and Weinberg write, in one of the book's many fascinating café yarns:

> A typical Russian refugee, who talked too much but seemed utterly harmless, indeed, a pathetic figure in the eyes of the Viennese. One day in 1917 an official of the Austrian Foreign Ministry rushed into the minister's room, panting and excited, and told his chief, "Your excellency . . . Your excellency . . . Revolution has broken out in Russia." The minister, less excitable and less credulous than his official, rejected such a wild claim and retorted calmly, "Go away . . . Russia is not a land where revolutions break out. Besides, who on earth would make a revolution in Russia? Perhaps Herr Trotsky from the Café Central?"

The minister should have known better. Give a man enough coffee and he's capable of anything.

QUESTIONS

1. How serious do you think Gladwell is when he says that we're all drugged on caffeine? How can you tell?

2. Gladwell creates a binary between coffee and tea. Describe another binary between two closely similar forms—such as seashore vs. mountains; Coke vs. Pepsi; skis vs. snowboards; rap vs. metal. How do binaries work? What limitations do you see in the binary you created or in Gladwell's?

3. Write a description of some of the rituals that you or someone you know indulges in with coffee or tea.

SONIA SHAH   *Tight Jeans and Chania Chorris*

I HAD ALREADY BEEN away at college for a few years when my little sister unleashed her budding sexuality onto my unsuspecting suburban Indian family. When I came home to Connecticut from Oberlin on breaks, I would find her furtively posing for the mirror. At dinner, she sat opposite the window, and her eyes darted from the conversation to her reflection, trying to catch a "candid" glimpse of herself. She wore tight, tight stirrup pants and off-the-shoulder blouses and dark lipstick. In the beginning, my parents and I were merely chagrined.

I had just gathered enough resolve, egged on by my feminist boyfriend of the time, to stop shaving my legs and armpits. It felt good, but in a shaky kind of way, like if anyone asked me why I did it I might just get enraged and teary and not be able to explain. That was usually how I got when I tried to explain my new "college ideas" to my parents. I remember confessing to my mother, shyly but slightly self-righteously, that I had applied for a job at a women's newspaper. "You want to work with just women?" she asked. "That's not right. You shouldn't separate yourself from half of humanity. Men and women together, boys and girls together, that's how it should be. I'd get bored with just one or the other," she went on. Defeated, but secretly condemning her for her lack of consciousness, I didn't say more.

I was having even less luck testing out my new ideas on Dad. He seemed to think my insistence on using gender-neutral language, for instance, was a symptom of weak logic. We actually got into some fights over it. He'd argue that I was losing the forest for the trees: "What, we're supposed to say 'snow-person' instead of 'snowman'? How does that help anything?" I'd get flustered and high-strung.

So at the time when my sister started parading and preening about the house, I wasn't feeling too secure as a feminist in the family setting. It seemed I could rant against MTV images of disembodied women, discuss the efficacy of affirmative action for women and debate the philosophy of Simone de Beauvoir[1] only with my friends at college. But I knew, from the building tension in the house and my sister's growing narcissism and self-objectification, that a feminist intervention was necessary; my class-privileged, sheltered life had actually provided me with a situation in which I needed to *act*.

What to do? I worried, privately, that she was exploiting herself and set-   5
ting herself up for the kinds of exploitation and abuse I had suffered at the hands of the white boys of our local public high school when I sexualized my dress and manner in high school. I wanted them to notice me, and they did—

Included in Listen Up: Voices from the Next Feminist Generation *(1995), a collection of essays by young women writers, edited by Barbara Findlen.*

1. French existentialist, social essayist, and feminist (1908–1986).

when they couldn't get the attention of any of the pretty girls from "nice" (that is, white) families. And then they wanted action, fast. And if they didn't get it, they got mad. They spread ugly rumors, harassed me, orchestrated humiliating pranks.

I had just gotten over all that, purging it as a time of insecurity and naiveté in a sexist, racist high school, when my sister seemed to be starting it all over again. Only she was getting better results: Boys were calling her on the phone; when I picked her up from the mall with her friends, she was surrounded by adoring white boys (their brothers had called me names); she was charming, lovely, flirtatious, everyone wanted to be near her.

So I was a little jealous, hating myself for feeling jealous, and trying to use the blunt tools of my college-learned feminism to understand why and what to do. My friends advised me. "She's objectifying herself. If she sets herself up as a sexualized Other, she will never centralize herself, she'll never be truly Subject," they said. "Tell her to throw away her tight jeans!"

One morning, we were both combing our hair in front of the big bathroom mirror. She was done up in typical regalia: scant, restrictive clothes with straps and belts and chains. "Aren't you kind of uncomfortable in that?" I asked. "Nooooo," she cooed, "why should I be?" "Well, don't you wish that boys would like you even if you didn't wear things like that?" I couldn't help feeling like I was coming off as jealous or something. "They would," she said resolutely, as if I were crazy for thinking things could be otherwise. "Sonia, you wear your clothes because you like them and you like how you look in them— not just because they are comfortable," she shot at me. "So don't give me this thing like you don't care how you look." She paused. "I like these clothes for me."

Fair enough, I guessed.

10   She's not going to throw away the tight jeans.

Vaguely displeased with the results of my intervention, but quelled, I turned my attention elsewhere.

A year passed. I graduated from college and moved to Boston. The challenges presented me were overwhelming; home and family life seemed dreamily effortless in contrast. So I was disturbed when my mother confided in me that she was having trouble with my sister.

"She doesn't listen, she's stubborn, she's wayward, she talks on the phone all the time, she always wants to go out, she's boy-crazy!" Pause. "I bet she's having sex," she whispered.

It was brave for my mother to say this last thing. She seemed a little scared when she said it, almost as if it was profane to even think this, but what could she do? My mother grew up in a small town in southern India, the smartest girl in the family, the one they all saved for to send to medical school. But not everyone in her family was so supported. My mother's oldest sister was abruptly taken out of school at the age of fourteen for writing a scandalous secret love letter to a local boy. Afterwards, she slit her wrists. This situation was never spoken of again. She never went back to school. She stayed in the kitchen with my grandmother and got married young, to a sensible and kind man of limited possibilities. Her sisters and brothers all live in a big world, speak many languages, are upwardly mobile. This oldest aunt stays at home all day in a dusty, exploited village and prays. She seems much older than she is.

In contrast, my mother emigrated to New York City when she was twenty-five years old, shortly after graduating from medical school and marrying my father by arrangement. He settled here first, and she followed six months later, arriving in a wintry JFK airport in her thickest sari, a woolen shawl and chappals. On her first day, while my dad was at work, she took two trains and a bus to Macy's and rode the escalators up and down, up and down, for hours, enthralled by the glitter and lights. She hadn't been on an escalator before, nor had she heard the delicate rhythmic ticking of a car's turn indicator, both of which signified the great advances and ingenuity of the New World to her. Now, perhaps, with her daughter at the brink of one of women's oldest tragedies, U.S. society did not seem so rich.

I didn't know whether my sister was having sex or not, but beyond the fact that I didn't like how she chose to express her sexuality (still those tight jeans!), I thought she should be supported if she were having sex. It's her sexuality, and any attempt on our part to rein it in would be disingenuous and oppressive, I reasoned. Sure, she's young, but with the proper guidance and support, she can gain from the wisdom of others. Knowing my mother's attitude—that is, absolute terror that her daughter may be having sex before marriage—I knew my sister would be getting no guidance from her.

Intervention Number Two. I invited her up to Boston, and we talked about it. I told her she shouldn't do anything she doesn't want to do, she should practice safe sex, she should know what she does and does not want, and in general tried to instill a healthy mistrust of the boy's so-called expertise. She seemed prepared.

I don't know how it went with the boy, but soon afterwards, in a flurry of family disgruntlement, my sister was sent on a three-month visit to India with our extended family. Exile.

She came back changed. More introspective, less self-conscious. She had brought back presents. When I came home, my parents prodded her excitedly to show me the new *chania chorri* she had bought in India. Chania chorris are sets of midriff-baring blouses and long full skirts worn under saris. Young girls get colorful brocaded ones to wear without the sari. She put it on. It was beautiful: all covered up in the front, regal, royal looking. When she turned around, I saw that it was backless, with just two little bows holding the front part on.

I was shocked at this taboo display of flesh in full parental view. Apparently unlike my sister, I remembered my dad's stern command to us not to wear nightgowns around the house. I remembered her having to conceal her tiny outfits with big flannel shirts.

But my parents loved the backless chania chorri. Both Mom and Dad oohed and ahhed, telling her to turn around again, to wear it to an upcoming festival. She pirouetted about flirtatiously. They beamed and clapped.

I was dumbfounded, the family friction over my sister's sexuality suddenly and miraculously dissipated. Gone! No problem! Feeling suckered and resentful of my obvious misunderstanding, I gave up: We lived in different families, she and I.

It was years before I felt I finally understood the rollercoaster conflict over my sister's budding sexuality. By flaunting her tight jeans and red lipstick outfits and by insistently making boys her first priority, she was demanding parental approval for her sexuality, obviously, as many young people do. But for us, Indian daughters isolated from India, parental approval means cultural approval. And my sister picked the wrong culture. She wore "Western" sexiness and asked her parents to say: sexy is okay, Western is okay.

Like me, she had to deal with her sexuality in the context of both white patriarchy and Indian patriarchy. When she played to white patriarchy, my parents didn't like it. They were scared of its possibilities, that she would lose her "Indian" female self, which is obedient, never talks back and doesn't have sex before marriage. I was scared too, of the possibility of violence. But when she played to Indian patriarchy, when she played the Indian coquette, all covered up but safely naughty on the side, like one of Krishna's cow-girls,[2] they felt safe again. And so did she.

25   Though it didn't make sense in my cultural setting, I had tried to force my intellectualized, white feminist ideas on my family. Tell my father to use gender-neutral language! This is a man for whom English is a second, less evocative language. Tell my mother to give my sister condoms for safe sex! This is a woman who knows firsthand the tragedy that can occur when patriarchal systems are challenged. Tell my sister not to wear tight jeans and to stop shaving! She'll just revert to revealing saris, and that's no better.

I was analyzing the situation on white feminism's terms, which don't recognize cultural duality. So I thought my sister was buying into sexist myths about beauty and female sexuality, when she was seeking an appropriate cultural expression of her sexuality in a society that doesn't recognize anything outside the monoculture of "Americanism." Telling her to throw away her tight jeans was never the answer. The answer was to establish that an Indian American feminist girl doesn't have to choose between American patriarchy and Indian patriarchy. She also doesn't have to lose her culture, whatever it may be.

I could have shown her how Asian American feminists incorporate feminism into their Asian lives and their American lives, and thus create new spaces for action. That far from needing approval from the cultural guardians (either white boys or parents in this case), we can subvert both. If instead of criticizing her for wearing tight jeans I had perhaps encouraged her to wear a chorri with them, knowing what I know now, she would have been amenable, maybe even interested in doing so. And doing so at once marks her as outside of the cultural arena controlled by white patriarchy and the one

---

2. Krishna, the playful eighth incarnation of Vishnu, one of the three gods in the Hindu trinity, played a prank on a group of bathing women by stealing these "cow-girls' " clothing and forcing them to emerge naked from the water to retrieve their garments.

controlled by Indian patriarchy. It is uniquely hers. And it gives her so much more: the ability to envision new realities.

As I realized that I couldn't simply graft white feminist ideas onto my life, things started to work out better. I explained to my dad about how feminism was also about spiritual liberation, about subverting both the internal and external cages that keep women down. I explained to my mom about how sexual experimentation, in the context of a supporting, loving environment, is useful in preparing kids for the responsibilities of adult relationships and families. A simple concern for the spirit and for the family is vitally important to them and to me; reinterpreting feminist ideas in this context lets the ideas actually get heard.

Qᴜᴇsᴛɪᴏɴs

1. The two phrases of the title—tight jeans and chania chorris—refer to two objects of clothing, one from American culture, the other from Indian. In Shah's analysis, how do these two objects represent a split in her sister's cultural identity? Do they also represent a split in her sister's sexual identity?

2. Shah incorporates her parents' biographies into her account. What relationship does she assume between their personal histories and their present-day actions? Can—or should—writers always assume such a relationship between a person's past and present?

3. At the end of her essay Shah wonders if she should have encouraged her younger sister to wear a chorri with her tight jeans. Do you think this combination would have resolved the problem of her dual cultural identity?

4. If you have read Henry Louis Gates Jr.'s essay "In the Kitchen" (p. 323), compare the ways the two writers respond to and resolve the question of dual cultural identities—Indian and American, black and white.

5. Recall a family conflict that involved cultural (or ethnic, religious, sexual, or political) difference. Write about that conflict, both analyzing the cause of the difference and imagining how it might have been resolved.

NICHOLAS D. KRISTOF *Saudis in Bikinis*

RIYADH, SAUDI ARABIA—On my first evening in Riyadh, I spotted a surreal scene: three giggly black ghosts, possibly young women enveloped in black cloaks called abayas, clustered around a display in a shopping mall, enthusiastically fingering a blouse so sheer and low-cut that my wife would never be caught dead in it. Afterward, I delicately asked a Saudi woman to explicate the scene.

"What do you think the 'black ghosts' wear underneath their abayas?" she replied archly.

Saudi women may be regarded in the West as antique doormats covered in black veils, but the women themselves vigorously reject that stereotype. "It hurts when you hear what people say about us, that we're repressed," Monira Abdulaziz, an assistant professor, said reproachfully.

"I cover up my body and my face, and I'm happy that I'm a religious girl obeying God's rules," a dietician named Lana scolded me after I wrote a typically snide reference to repressed Saudi women. "I can swim and do sports and go to restaurants and wear what I want, but not in front of men. Why should I show my legs and breasts to men? Is that really freedom?"

In Riyadh, several Saudi women offered the same scathing critique, effectively arguing that Saudi women are the free ones—free from sexual harassment, free from pornography, free from seeing their bodies used to market cars and colas. It is Western women, they say, who have been manipulated into becoming the toys of men.

Saudi Arabia is a bizarre place. It has McDonald's restaurants that look just like those at home except that there is one line for men and one for women. *Al Riyadh* newspaper has women journalists, but they're kept in their own room; when a male editor must edit a woman's copy, he does it by phone. Saudi women wear bikinis—but only in home swimming pools or in all-women pools. They claim all this reflects not repression but a culture they cherish.

"You can't go to an Indian woman and say, 'Why are you wearing a sari?' " fumed Hend al-Khuthaila, a university professor who was the first female university dean in Saudi Arabia. "You can't go up to a Western woman and say, 'Why are you wearing a short dress?' Well, this is our abaya. This is part of my culture. It's part of my tradition. It never bothered me."

Maha Muneef, a female pediatrician, emphasized that Saudi Arabia is progressing, albeit more slowly than many women would like. "My mother didn't go to any school at all, because then there were no girls' schools at all," she said. "My older sister, who is 20 years older than me, she went up to the sixth grade and then quit, because the feeling was that a girl only needs to

Published on October 25, 2002, in the New York Times, *where Kristof has written a twice-weekly Op-Ed column since 2001.*

learn to read and write. Then I went to college and medical school on scholarship to the States. My daughter, maybe she'll be president, or an astronaut."

Another doctor, Hanan Balkhy, seemed ambivalent. "I don't think women here have equal opportunities," she acknowledged. "There are meetings I can't go to. There are buildings I can't go into. But you have to look at the context of development. Discrimination will take time to overcome."

Dr. Balkhy emphasized that Saudi women want to solve their problems   10
themselves. These days in particular, she said, even liberal Saudis feel on the defensive and are reluctant to discuss their concerns for fear that foreigners will seize upon the problems to discredit their country.

All this created an awkward series of interviews. I kept asking women how they felt about being repressed, and they kept answering indignantly that they aren't repressed.

So what should we make of this? Is it paternalistic of us in the West to try to liberate women who insist that they're happy as they are?

No, I think we're on firm ground.

If most Saudi women want to wear a tent, if they don't want to drive, then that's fine. But why not give them the choice? Why ban women drivers and why empower the religious police, the mutawwa, to scold those loose hussies who choose to show a patch of hair?

If Saudi Arabians choose to kill their economic development and sacrifice   15
international respect by clinging to the 15th century, if the women prefer to remain second-class citizens, then I suppose that's their choice. But if anyone chooses to behave so foolishly, is it any surprise that outsiders point and jeer?

QUESTIONS

1. Kristof believes that Saudi Arabia's strict rules for women—no driving, no public mixing of the sexes, no revealing clothing—are "foolish." What do you think? And what do you think of the Saudi Arabian women who defend such practices?

2. How should one country behave toward another that has starkly different standards of morality (e.g., capital punishment, polygamy, repression of women)? Think about the evidence you might give in support of your view.

3. Describe a time when you got into an argument or dispute over standards of behavior with someone you disagreed with. What triggered it? How did it get resolved? What happened?

ROLAND BARTHES *Toys*

RENCH TOYS: One could not find a better illustration of the fact that the adult Frenchman sees the child as another self. All the toys one commonly sees are essentially a microcosm of the adult world; they are all reduced copies of human objects, as if in the eyes of the public the child was, all told, nothing but a smaller man, a homunculus to whom must be supplied objects of his own size.

Invented forms are very rare: a few sets of blocks, which appeal to the spirit of do-it-yourself, are the only ones which offer dynamic forms. As for the others, French toys *always mean something*, and this something is always entirely socialized, constituted by the myths or the techniques of modern adult life: the army, broadcasting, the post office, medicine (miniature instrument-cases, operating theaters for dolls), school, hair styling (driers for permanent-waving), the air force (parachutists), transport (trains, Citroëns, Vedettes, Vespas,[1] petrol stations), science (Martian toys).

The fact that French toys *literally* prefigure the world of adult functions obviously cannot but prepare the child to accept them all, by constituting for him, even before he can think about it, the alibi of a Nature which has at all times created soldiers, postmen and Vespas. Toys here reveal the list of all the things the adult does not find unusual: war, bureaucracy, ugliness, Martians, etc. It is not so much, in fact, the imitation which is a sign of an abdication, as its literalness. French toys are like a Jivaro[2] head, in which one recognizes, shrunken to the size of an apple, the wrinkles and hair of an adult. There exist, for instance, dolls which urinate; they have an esophagus, one gives them a bottle, they wet their nappies; soon, no doubt, milk will turn to water in their stomachs. This is meant to prepare the little girl for the causality of housekeeping, to "condition" her to her future role as mother. However, faced with this world of faithful and complicated objects, the child can only identify himself as owner, as user, never as creator; he does not invent the world, he uses it: There are, prepared for him, actions without adventure, without wonder, without joy. He is turned into a little stay-at-home householder who does not even have to invent the mainsprings of adult causality; they are supplied to him ready-made: He has only to help himself, he is never allowed to discover anything from start to finish. The merest set of blocks, provided it is not too refined, implies a very different learning of the world: Then, the child does not in any way create meaningful objects, it matters little to him whether they have an adult name; the actions he performs are not those of a user but those

From Mythologies *(1957), a collection of brief essays on French culture that originally appeared as general-circulation newspaper pieces; selected and translated for American readers by Annette Lavers in* Mythologies *(1972).*

1. French automobiles, French motor boats, Italian motor scooters.
2. South American Indian head-hunting tribe.

of a demiurge. He creates forms which walk, which roll, he creates life, not property: Objects now act by themselves, they are no longer an inert and complicated material in the palm of his hand. But such toys are rather rare: French toys are usually based on imitation, they are meant to produce children who are users, not creators.

The bourgeois status of toys can be recognized not only in their forms, which are all functional, but also in their substances. Current toys are made of a graceless material, the product of chemistry, not of nature. Many are now molded from complicated mixtures; the plastic material of which they are made has an appearance at once gross and hygienic, it destroys all the pleasure, the sweetness, the humanity of touch. A sign which fills one with consternation is the gradual disappearance of wood, in spite of its being an ideal material because of its firmness and its softness, and the natural warmth of its touch. Wood removes, from all the forms which it supports, the wounding quality of angles which are too sharp, the chemical coldness of metal. When the child handles it and knocks it, it neither vibrates nor grates, it has a sound at once muffled and sharp. It is a familiar and poetic substance, which does not sever the child from close contact with the tree, the table, the floor. Wood does not wound or break down; it does not shatter, it wears out, it can last a long time, live with the child, alter little by little the relations between the object and the hand. If it dies, it is in dwindling, not in swelling out like those mechanical toys which disappear behind the hernia of a broken spring. Wood makes essential objects, objects for all time. Yet there hardly remain any of these wooden toys from the Vosges, these fretwork farms with their animals, which were only possible, it is true, in the days of the craftsman. Henceforth, toys are chemical in substance and color; their very material introduces one to a coenaesthesis[3] of use, not pleasure. These toys die in fact very quickly, and once dead, they have no posthumous life for the child.

3. General awareness of the body and its condition.

QUESTIONS

1. What parts of Barthes's critique of French toys could also be applied to American toys? Think of specific toys that you might use as evidence in class discussion.

2. Consider the use of punctuation in this essay. What is the effect of the frequent use of colons and the frequent use of commas to separate independent clauses? (Barthes originally wrote this piece in French, and Annette Lavers translated it into English. To what extent might translation affect punctuation choices?)

3. Write a two-page essay that begins with your own version of the following sentence: "American toys: One could not find a better illustration of the fact that the adult American sees the child as . . ."

4. Write an analysis of a toy you remember from childhood. What meaning can you find in that toy? As Barthes does, note its shape, function, purpose, materials, and so forth.

FRED STREBEIGH   *The Wheels of Freedom:*
Bicycles in China

"**H**ELLO." She appeared at my right shoulder, her face inches from mine. We were cycling together, though I had never seen her before. We rode side by side through the city of Beijing, and around us streamed thousands of bicycles with red banners flying. Beijing was in revolt. And as we rode together we broke the law.

I had gone to China with an odd goal: to learn a bit about what the bicycle means to people who live in a country with only a few thousand privately owned cars but some 220 million cycles—vastly more than any other nation. And I had arrived at an odd time.

My first day in China was also the first day of what became known as the Beijing Spring of 1989. As I awoke, students and citizens by the hundreds of thousands were flowing from all over Beijing to Tiananmen Square, the vast plaza at the city's heart, creating the largest spontaneous demonstration in the history of China and perhaps the world. They came on foot and by bus and subway, of course, but mostly they came by bicycle, calling for freedom. (I could see why bicycles are forbidden in the capital of North Korea, China's more repressive neighbor. Its government reportedly fears that bikes give people too much independence.)

Within hours of my arrival in Beijing, bicycles became more crucial than ever. Buses stopped. Subways shut. Taxis struck. But on flowed the bikes of Beijing. Bicyclists carried messages from university to university. Tricyclists rushed round delivering food to demonstrators. Families and schoolmates and couples and commuters smiled and waved as they rode, in twos and threes and throngs.

5   On my own bicycle, hesitant at first and then lost in the cycling masses, I roamed freely. Daily I rode to Tiananmen Square, with its mood of carnival, its students from all regions, and its uncountable cycles. Bicycles and tricycles became flag holders and tent supporters. They became tea dispensers and cold-drink stands. They became photographers' perches, families' viewing platforms, old men's reading chairs, and children's racing toys.

On my bicycle I also strayed far from Tiananmen, to the quiet corners of the city. Everywhere the bicycle set the rhythm of life. Martial artists rode to practice with swords strapped to their bikes. Women in jet-black business suits pedalled their daughters to school. Boys fished beside parked bicycles at placid

Sent to China on a magazine assignment to analyze the cultural role of the bicycle, Strebeigh found himself immersed in a political uprising in Beijing, its capital. The essay was first published in Bicycling Magazine *(April 1991) and then adapted for* China Update *(Winter 1991), a magazine published by the Yale–China Association. The latter version is reprinted here.*

344

lakes. Bakers in white toques headed for work on transport tricycles. Pedalling beside them at their slow pace, I felt at ease and oddly at home. I felt as I had years ago in my small hometown, where automobiles never clogged the streets and where the bicycle offered a mix of peace and freedom.

Riding among the bicycles of Beijing, I began to recognize dozens of China's famous brands: Golden Lion and Mountain River, Plum Flower and Chrysanthemum, Red Flag and Red Cotton, Flying Arrival and Flying Pigeon, Pheasant and Phoenix and Forever. Long and stately bicycles, recalling decades past, they possessed the rake and sheer and grace that today I associ-

Afternoon rush hour in Chengdu.

ate less with cycling than with yachting. I felt as if I were cruising, on the wake of clippers like *Red Jacket* or *Flying Cloud,* in a regatta of tall ships.

Then the Chinese government declared martial law. It forbade citizens to attend the student demonstrations and forbade foreigners, like me, to visit Tiananmen or talk to students. It sent its army in a first push into the city, but citizens peacefully blocked its way. My Chinese hosts (I had been invited to lecture at a couple of universities) warned me to obey the government, and I said I would try.

In the second day under martial law, as I was riding down one of Beijing's leafy boulevards, suddenly a young woman appeared at my shoulder. She said "hello," and we were cycling together.

10   I had been rolling at Beijing speed, eight miles an hour—in synch with commuters, demonstrators, and vegetable haulers. To catch me she had accelerated, maybe to eight-and-a-half miles an hour.

"What," she wanted to know, did I "think about the students?" She wore tinted glasses, a shy smile in a radiant face, a lab coat—she was a science student, and by law we were forbidden to talk.

"I think what they are doing is very brave," I said, "and very scary." And so we became two petty criminals, riding handlebar-to-handlebar.

We floated together and others floated past. But they travelled fractions of a pedal-turn faster or fractions slower, and we were left alone in talk, our handlebars occasionally nudging each other, in the bizarre intimacy of Beijing cycling. I worried aloud about the Chinese army—now half a mile to our west, still blocked but still pressing towards us. She praised George Washington. We would not have talked so freely in a restaurant or hotel, I realized; police could have demanded our names. But here we were just two bicycles lost in the mass—the most private place in Beijing.

Ahead of us appeared Tiananmen Square, where some of her classmates had been starving themselves in protest and others had been singing "We Shall Overcome." Within moments, she drifted south and I north. Soon I was at the American embassy. They warned me against talking to students.

15   To stay in Beijing, I decided, was to endanger anyone I met. And so I resolved to travel out from the capital and return later, in order to talk about bicycles in a time of greater calm and, I hoped, greater freedom.

One of the people I most wanted to meet outside Beijing was a student in Sichuan Province named Fang Hui. The year before, she had become the first woman to ride a bicycle from Chengdu, the capital of Sichuan in central China, to Lhasa, the capital of Tibet—bumping for thirteen hundred miles over one of China's worst roads, a sawtooth of rock tracks and mountain passes which reach altitudes above 15,000 feet. In recognition, China honored her as one of the nation's "Ten Brave Young People."

I didn't care much about Fang Hui's honors. I cared more about her motivations, her goals. I guess I expected her to be a hot but somewhat dull athlete, the sort who wins Chinese honors by excelling in volleyball. When we met at her university in Chengdu, where she is a graduate student in English, she surprised me.

As we pedalled through the streets of Chengdu, I asked Fang Hui if she had always been a cyclist. Not really, she said. Before her trip she had not owned a bicycle. The day before departing for Tibet she bought an old, single-speed Arched Eyebrow for 75 yuan ($15). She then taught herself to ride, over a thousand miles of mountains.

I asked how she chose Tibet. She said she had answered a poster advertisement. I was shocked. So, apparently, were the five men, mostly teachers from a local school, who had planned the trip and posted invitations for fellow travellers. Only Fang Hui accepted.

The men doubted she could reach Tibet, perhaps because she looked like a pudgy schoolgirl. Uphill she always rode more slowly than they, falling miles behind. Downhill, because her old bike had wretched brakes, she squeezed its levers with all her strength as the Arched Eyebrow hurtled down pitted roads. "I went very fast," she said. "I felt as if I would become light." At the end of each day of clinging to her brake levers, her hands were so cramped she could not open them.

Eventually, the men admitted that her strength egged them on. "If even a girl can do this," they said, "how shameful for a man to give up."

Fang Hui had not really worried about giving up on the journey, she told me. But, earlier, she had worried about giving up on life. "Before," she said, "yesterday, today, tomorrow were all alike—so dull. What I most wanted was to meet something unexpected."

Not just the road's pain but also its loneliness changed Fang Hui. At remote outposts she would meet soldiers, mere isolated boys, who would write love letters that followed her up the Lhasa road, carried by lone truck drivers. In yet remoter terrain she would ride half a day, she recalled, and "not see a single man. So when I heard a dog bark, it would arouse a tender feeling—a reminder of the human world. When I came back, people all said I had changed. Now I can find something new in every day." And now at night, she added with glee, "sometimes I dream I am riding very fast downhill."

As I rode through Chengdu, sometimes talking with Fang Hui or with other university students and teachers, I began to see that the bicycle offered an escape not just *from* everyday life. It also offered escape within everyday life.

One day as Fang Hui and I rode through a crush of cyclists, a young couple passed us riding two bicycles side-by-side. They rode pedal-to-pedal and almost arm-in-arm. At first the girl rode with her left hand on the boy's right, controlling his hand and handlebar, steering them both. Then he moved his hand to round the small of her back. They reminded me of partners in a waltz.

The boy lowered his hand to the girl's bicycle seat and leaned to her, and as they rode they whispered. In the often-dehumanizing crush of urban China, two bicycles had made space for romance. Fang Hui said that young "lovers" often ride so utterly together, so alone in their world.

Providing such measures of human dignity, one professor told me, was one of the bicycle's gifts to China—and particularly to people like his parents, who were "peasants" (the term in China for all people who work the land).

Here in the center of China's richest farmlands, he said, I could watch the bicycle making life less hard. Flower farmers with hollyhocks and asters tied to their bicycles arrived in Chengdu at dawn, flicked down their kickstands on side streets, and began to sell. Farmers' sons strapped saws and other carpenters' tools to their bicycles, rode into the city, and waited at curbside for customers to hire them to build beds or bureaus. In Sichuan's booming "free markets" (free, that is, of government control), geese came to town on the backs of farmers' tricycles, were sold to families for domestic egg laying, and then departed with their wings still flapping, strapped to the buyers' handlebars. Everywhere, cycles kept life rolling.

The professor told me that peasants in his parents' remote village always refer to the bicycle, appreciatively, as the "foreign horse." The government opposes the name, he said, but it helps explain the history of the bicycle in China. The first bicycle arrived in 1886, carrying Thomas Stevens, a young San Franciscan who was completing the first cycling journey around the world. With its huge front wheel and small rear one, his penny-farthing[1] cycle must have looked very foreign but, unlike a good horse, not very practical.

The first practical bicycle to reach China came in 1891, again transporting a round-the-world cyclist. By the early twentieth century, the foreign horse had won the fascination of China's last emperor, the young Puyi, who rode one around his palace, Beijing's "Forbidden City."

30   Slowly cycling trickled down from the throne toward the masses. By the 1940s China's bicycle factories were producing a vehicle like today's most common model, a virtual twin of England's stately Raleigh Tourist.

In the years before the Chinese revolution of 1949, the professor told me, almost everyone called the bicycle "foreign horse," because "foreign" suggested both "modern" and "admirable." Since peasants carried most goods on their backs, they particularly admired the bicycle. Every peasant longed to shift his burden to the back of a foreign horse—a longing frustrated by high price and short supply.

Then came the revolution of 1949. Hoping to "raise the people's dignity," the professor continued, the young government made two decisions. Happily,

---

1. Referring to wheels of unequal size: pennies were big, farthings small.

in an effort to give wheels to an impoverished population, it encouraged bicycle production, which began doubling and redoubling. But sadly, because the old name suggested blind worship of foreign things, the government banned the lyrical phrase "foreign horse" (which, pronounced *yang ma* in Chinese, resounds like a ringing gong). The government imposed, instead, the unpoetic "self-running cart" (*zi xing che* in Chinese, which sounds like a dental problem).

Not surprisingly, the cycle's foreign resonance remains. Peasants in remote villages still pedal "foreign horses." And many Chinese factories, seeking a touch of class, still adorn their bicycles with prominent English names: "Forever" or "Light Roadster" or, on the most celebrated of foreign horses, "Flying Pigeon—The All-Steel Bicycle." (When George Bush[2] made his first presidential visit to China, his welcoming gift from the nation was a pair of Flying Pigeons.)

A regional branch of the Flying Pigeon Bicycle Factory lies an hour's ride from the center of Chengdu, and one day I was given a tour of its old-style assembly line by Jiang Guoji, the factory's present director—the first ever elected by its workers. He spoke with the ease of a manager whose workers trust his judgment and whose society trusts his product.

Since Jiang Guoji's factory sits in the middle of China's best farmland, he and his co-workers decided to specialize in what Jiang called the "ZA-62" or "Reinforced Flying Pigeon." This bike, which I came to think of as the "Peasant Pigeon," comes with massive tubing, a formidable rack, a second set of

35

2. George H. W. Bush (b. 1924), president of the United States from 1989 to 1993.

forks to hold the front wheels, and—probably unique among Chinese bicycles—a three-year warranty. It contains 68 pounds of steel which, together with some leather and rubber, brings its total weight above 72 pounds—three times that of my average American bike.

Jiang Guoji's factory has raised production steadily, along with all Chinese cycle factories, creating an unprecedented problem. The year before my visit, Chinese bicycle production reached 42 million cycles—dwarfing any other nation's output and, more significantly, overtaking Chinese demand for the first time in history. For years, bicycles had been rationed, and families had longed to own a good one. Now "if a person has money, he can buy," Jiang told me, with a mix of pride and regret—because prices have begun dropping and "bicycle factories have real competition."

In response, Jiang said, he was trying to spur international demand for Peasant Pigeons. Looking for good "propaganda," two years earlier he donated "Peasant Pigeons" to five local riders who wanted to go around the world. Alas, one had been run down by a truck in Pakistan. But the other four were riding on, circling the globe back towards his factory. He expected his 72-pound Pigeons home within a year, still under warranty. (He added that, despite transport costs and import duties, he would gladly sell Peasant Pigeons wholesale in America for less than a dollar a pound.)

All Chinese bicycles—whether sturdy Flying Pigeons or sad Arched Eyebrows—must survive long after their warranties have expired. To help them along, repairmen have set up roadside stands in every city. Entering the business proves simple. A would-be repairman chooses a site, asks the city to license it to him, and lays down his tools. He then puts up his advertisement—a circle of overlapping innertubes, colored black and deep pink, perhaps hung on a tree limb.

Some Chinese portray repairmen in a style that outdoes American caricatures of car mechanics. Most of my Chinese acquaintances knew one repairman they relied on and dozens they distrusted. One university professor insisted that underemployed repairmen scatter tacks to puncture passing tires and inflate profits.

40   Another professor invited me to meet her revered neighborhood repairman. Since he worked incessantly and had little time for chatter, she devised a ruse to buy time for asking questions: we would take him her Flying Arrival, which had a useless rear brake.

We found him at the back gate of her university beneath a circle of innertubes. When my friend arrived, the repairman put aside a Phoenix he was polishing and greeted her as a long-term client. She presented the brake problem. He took a quick look, produced two sets of pliers, loosened a nut, tightened a cable, tensioned a spring and, after 30 seconds of work, handed the bike back to her—fixed. He refused payment. The job was too small. He resumed polishing the Phoenix.

Though her ruse had failed, the professor pressed forward: How did he become a repairman? Three years ago when he was twenty-seven, he told us, he stopped working his family's farm because the land was small and the fam-

A bike repairman's job may be the freest in China. All that's needed is a street corner and a few tools.

ily had more than enough laborers—including his wife, their three children, his two sisters and two brothers, and their aging parents. He still lives on the farm but commutes three miles to the city on his Forever. He works seven days a week, from 9 A.M. to 8 P.M., except when it rains.

He likes bike repair because it "makes *money,*" he said, emphasizing the word as if it were a novelty. Back on the farm, where he hopes never to work again, he "just produced *crops,*" which sold for "not-so-much money."

When we asked him how much he made in a month, he told us 800 yuan ($216). The professor gasped. To me she said, quietly, "That's five university professors!" Still, she seemed to believe him. She pointed out to me that he had paid the government's penalty for having three children. The penalty in recent years has run as high as 2,000 yuan ($540), she said, too much for most professors—but not for an industrious bike fixer.

As I talked to more repairmen, I saw that their job may be the freest in China. A hard worker needed only a street corner and a few tools. Before his eyes bikes would inevitably break down and, if he was skilled, clients would multiply. Bicycle repair seemed to offer an extension of what the bike itself offered and what so many Chinese sought: modest dignity, new choices, ample freedom.

The farm country outside Chengdu, contrary to the complaints of one peasant-turned-repairman, generates much of the new agricultural wealth enjoyed by the Chinese people. In early June, by train and by bicycle, I travelled to the southern mountains that rim this rich agricultural bowl within Sichuan province. There I was the guest at another university, tucked in verdant hills.

During my stay, one teacher lent me an old "Peasant Pigeon"—one well past its warranty. I rode it daily over farm tracks of rut and rock that would

45

have jolted the nuts off my light American bike. The big Pigeon just bobbed along, high and easy.

One midday while I was exploring narrow paths through emerald-colored rice paddies, two girls whizzed past me, riding double on a black Forever. Both wore red uniforms and one carried an abacus—students dashing home for lunch.

With me was a professor who was fluent not only in English but also the quite-obscure local dialect. She suggested we follow the students so I could meet a "peasant family."

50   We travelled through flooded paddies, past water buffaloes, up to a newly built home that stretched around a cement courtyard, and found the older of the two girls talking with her mother next to their vegetable garden. The professor introduced us. Their mother, Mrs. Fang, invited us for tea and introduced her daughters: Liya, third-grader and bicycle passenger, and Jianmei, sixth-grader and bicyclist. Because Jianmei's Forever still had protective wrapping paper on its top bar, as if it had just come from the store, I asked if it was new.

Jianmei, who was gulping down rice in preparation for her afternoon at school, said proudly that she won it just last year. Her mother explained that the family offers their daughters prizes for each year that they sustain grades of 90% or better. In autumn each daughter names a prize she wants, and then for the rest of the school year she tries to win it. In third grade Jianmei won a set of nice clothes; in fourth grade, a golden wristwatch; in fifth grade, the Forever. (I said to the professor, in English, "Are you sure we're talking to *peasants*?")

Mrs. Fang then led us through her tiled kitchen to a room that held, along with awards won by Jianmei for track and basketball, another full-sized bicycle—a cherry-red "Cuckoo," also still wrapped to protect its paint. It was Jianmei's earlier bike. I was astonished; ten years ago here, the professor had told me, only one family in ten could afford even a single bicycle.

Jianmei explained that she wanted the Forever because it was strong and smooth enough to carry her little sister. With it, she rides not just to school but up to the university, off to a nearby temple, even to a town 22 miles away to see the world's largest carved Buddha.

As we walked away from the Fang household—so imbued with work and reward and independence—I said to the professor: "Don't you wish you grew up in a place like that?" A bit later I thought to myself: "I *did* grow up in a place like that." Riding off to school, studying hard, cycling ten and twenty miles on a whim—this was like being back in sixth grade in my small hometown.

55   On the same day I talked with the Fang family, stories of the Beijing massacre—of hundreds or perhaps thousands of citizens killed by army troops and tanks—were reaching our remote region. Soon travellers arrived with tales of killing in other provincial cities. Students began to flee our rural campus, fearing the army would next descend on them. I returned to Chengdu.

There, I tried to continue the work I had planned—looking for the city's used bicycle market, avoiding the army troops who had arrived to quell out-

These bicycles were more than crushed machines. They represented crushed dignity, humanity, and freedom.

bursts, gathering statistics on bicycle ownership. But I could not concentrate. My mind was on Beijing. Finally I decided to return, to what just days before had been the world's most exuberant city.

Again I rode its leafy boulevards, but no excited voice at my shoulder asked what I thought of the students. No banners waved. No people smiled. All faces seemed as if carved, years ago, in soft stone—at once fixed and badly weathered.

Each evening, Beijing television proudly showed the now-barren Tiananmen Square, cleared of all students and, for that matter, all life. Understandably, the TV cameras did not show what people in Beijing had seen: citizens trying to stop tanks by shoving bicycles at them, flatbed tricycles turned into ambulances for slaughtered children. Less understandably, the cameras often began their pan across the square with an image of a pile of crumpled bicycles.

That odd image haunted me for months, long after I had left China. Only slowly did I realize that the government had chosen that scene precisely. The government cameras wanted to show more than a few crushed machines. They wanted to show crushed dignity, crushed humanity, crushed freedom—so much that the bicycle means in China.

And finally I realized that of course the old men who cling to power in China would want to show off the crumpled bicycles of the young men and women who had called for freedom. How terrifying it must have been, to those old men, to see millions of young people cycling towards them—so independent, so alive, so free—all those wheels turning and turning beyond the control of fear or fiat. Of course those old men would want to crush the cycles of the young. For they would know too well that history itself runs in cycles—sometimes foreign horses, sometimes self-running carts, always wheels of change.

60

How sad: Four decades earlier these same old men, seeking to "raise the people's dignity," had set rolling the cycles of modern China. And then, in a few days of a Beijing spring, they sought to crush, all at once, cycles and dignity and change together. They might as easily have sought to stop the circling, round the sun, of earth's revolution. For as each spring comes round, the old fade and the young quicken. And every day throughout China, the wheels of freedom roll.

QUESTIONS

1. Strebeigh's magazine assignment was to depict and analyze the role of bicycles in modern-day China. What important roles does the bicycle play? Which do you think are most important—to Strebeigh? to the Chinese people he interviewed?

2. The article is titled "The Wheels of Freedom." Why? What relationship between bicycles and freedom does the essay suggest?

3. Write about an important product or artifact in American culture, analyzing its significance to its users and, if relevant, to yourself.

JOHN McMURTRY   *Kill 'Em! Crush 'Em! Eat 'Em Raw!*

A FEW MONTHS AGO my neck got a hard crick in it. I couldn't turn my head; to look left or right I'd have to turn my whole body. But I'd had cricks in my neck since I started playing grade-school football and hockey, so I just ignored it. Then I began to notice that when I reached for any sort of large book (which I do pretty often as a philosophy teacher at the University of Guelph) I had trouble lifting it with one hand. I was losing the strength in my left arm, and I had such a steady pain in my back I often had to stretch out on the floor of the room I was in to relieve the pressure.

A few weeks later I mentioned to my brother, an orthopedic surgeon, that I'd lost the power in my arm since my neck began to hurt. Twenty-four hours later I was in a Toronto hospital not sure whether I might end up with a wasted upper limb. Apparently the steady pounding I had received playing college and professional football in the late Fifties and early Sixties had driven my head into my backbone so that the discs had crumpled together at the neck—"acute herniation"—and had cut the nerves to my left arm like a pinched telephone wire (without nerve stimulation, of course, the muscles atrophy, leaving the arm crippled). So I spent my Christmas holidays in the hospital in heavy traction

Originally published in Maclean's *(October 1971), one of Canada's most prominent weekly magazines.*

and much of the next three months with my neck in a brace. Today most of the pain has gone, and I've recovered most of the strength in my arm. But from time to time I still have to don the brace, and surgery remains a possibility.

Not much of this will surprise anyone who knows football. It is a sport in which body wreckage is one of the leading conventions. A few days after I went into hospital for that crick in my neck, another brother, an outstanding football player in college, was undergoing spinal surgery in the same hospital two floors above me. In his case it was a lower, more massive herniation, which every now and again buckled him so that he was unable to lift himself off his back for days at a time. By the time he entered the hospital for surgery he had already spent several months in bed. The operation was successful, but, as in all such cases, it will take him a year to recover fully.

These aren't isolated experiences. Just about anybody who has ever played football for any length of time, in high school, college or one of the professional leagues, has suffered for it later physically.

Indeed, it is arguable that body shattering is the very *point* of football, as   5
killing and maiming are of war. (In the United States, for example, the game results in 15 to 20 deaths a year and about 50,000 major operations on knees alone.) To grasp some of the more conspicuous similarities between football and war, it is instructive to listen to the imperatives most frequently issued to the players by their coaches, teammates and fans. "Hurt 'em!" "Level 'em!" "Kill 'em!" "Take 'em apart!" Or watch for the plays that are most enthusiastically applauded by the fans. Where someone is "smeared," "knocked silly," "creamed," "nailed," "broken in two," or even "crucified." (One of my coaches when I played corner linebacker with the Calgary Stampeders in 1961 elaborated, often very inventively, on this language of destruction: admonishing us to "unjoin" the opponent, "make 'im remember you" and "stomp 'im like a bug.") Just as in hockey, where a fight will bring fans to their feet more often than a skillful play, so in football the mouth waters most of all for the really crippling block or tackle. For the kill. Thus the good teams are "hungry," the best players are "mean," and "casualties" are as much a part of the game as they are of a war.

The family resemblance between football and war is, indeed, striking. Their languages are similar: "field general," "long bomb," "blitz," "take a shot," "front line," "pursuit," "good hit," "the draft" and so on. Their principles and practices are alike: mass hysteria, the art of intimidation, absolute command and total obedience, territorial aggression, censorship, inflated insignia and propaganda, blackboard maneuvers and strategies, drills, uniforms, formations, marching bands and training camps. And the virtues they celebrate are almost identical: hyper-aggressiveness, coolness under fire and suicidal bravery. All this has been implicitly recognized by such jock-loving Americans as media stars General Patton and President Nixon, who have talked about war as a football game. Patton wanted to make his Second World War tank men look like football players. And Nixon, as we know, was fond of comparing attacks on Vietnam to football plays and drawing coachly diagrams on a blackboard for TV war fans.

One difference between war and football, though, is that there is little or no protest against football. Perhaps the most extraordinary thing about the game is that the systematic infliction of injuries excites in people not concern, as would be the case if they were sustained at, say, a rock festival, but a collective rejoicing and euphoria. Players and fans alike revel in the spectacle of a combatant felled into semiconsciousness, "blindsided," "clotheslined" or "decapitated." I can remember, in fact, being chided by a coach in pro ball for not "getting my hat" injuriously into a player who was already lying helpless on the ground. (On another occasion, after the Stampeders had traded the celebrated Joe Kapp to BC, we were playing the Lions in Vancouver and Kapp was forced on one play to run with the ball. He was coming "down the chute," his bad knee wobbling uncertainly, so I simply dropped on him like a blanket. After I returned to the bench I was reproved for not exploiting the opportunity to unhinge his bad knee.)

After every game, of course, the papers are full of reports on the day's injuries, a sort of post-battle "body count," and the respective teams go to work with doctors and trainers, tape, whirlpool baths, cortisone and morphine to patch and deaden the wounds before the next game. Then the whole drama is reenacted—injured athletes held together by adhesive, braces and drugs—and the days following it are filled with even more feverish activity to put on the show yet again at the end of the next week. (I remember being so taped up in college that I earned the nickname "mummy.") The team that survives this merry-go-round spectacle of skilled masochism with the fewest incapacitating injuries usually wins. It is a sort of victory by ordeal: "We hurt them more than they hurt us."

My own initiation into this brutal circus was typical. I loved the game from the moment I could run with a ball. Played shoeless on a green open field with no one keeping score and in a spirit of reckless abandon and laughter, it's a very different sport. Almost no one gets hurt and it's rugged, open and exciting (it still is for me). But then, like everything else, it starts to be regulated and institutionalized by adult authorities. And the fun is over.

10   So it was as I began the long march through organized football. Now there was a coach and elders to make it clear by their behavior that beating other people was the only thing to celebrate and that trying to shake someone up every play was the only thing to be really proud of. Now there were severe rule enforcers, audiences, formally recorded victors and losers, and heavy equipment to permit crippling bodily moves and collisions (according to one American survey, more than 80% of all football injuries occur to fully equipped players). And now there was the official "given" that the only way to keep playing was to wear suffocating armor, to play to defeat, to follow orders silently and to renounce spontaneity for joyless drill. The game had been, in short, ruined. But because I loved to play and play skillfully, I stayed. And progressively and inexorably, as I moved through high school, college and pro leagues, my body was dismantled. Piece by piece.

I started off with torn ligaments in my knee at 13. Then, as the organization and the competition increased, the injuries came faster and harder. Broken nose (three times), broken jaw (fractured in the first half and dismissed as a "bad wisdom tooth," so I played with it for the rest of the game), ripped knee ligaments again. Torn ligaments in one ankle and a fracture in the other (which I remember feeling relieved about because it meant I could honorably stop drill-blocking a 270-pound defensive end). Repeated rib fractures and cartilage tears (usually carried, again, through the remainder of the game). More dislocations of the left shoulder than I can remember (the last one I played with because, as the Calgary Stampeder doctor said, it "couldn't be damaged any more"). Occasional broken or dislocated fingers and toes. Chronically hurt lower back (I still can't lift with it or change a tire without worrying about folding). Separated right shoulder (as with many other injuries, like badly bruised hips and legs, needled with morphine for the games). And so on. The last pro game I played—against Winnipeg Blue Bombers in the Western finals in 1961—I had a recently dislocated left shoulder, a more recently wrenched right shoulder and a chronic pain center in one leg. I was so tied up with soreness I couldn't drive my car to the airport. But it never occurred to me or anyone else that I miss a play as a corner linebacker.

By the end of my football career, I had learned that physical injury— giving it and taking it—is the real currency of the sport. And that in the final analysis the "winner" is the man who can hit to kill even if only half his limbs are working. In brief, a warrior game with a warrior ethos into which (like almost everyone else I played with) my original boyish enthusiasm had been relentlessly taunted and conditioned.

In thinking back on how all this happened, though, I can pick out no villains. As with the social system as a whole, the game has a life of its own. Everyone grows up inside it, accepts it and fulfills its dictates as obediently as helots. Far from ever questioning the principles of the activity, people simply concentrate on executing these principles more aggressively than anybody around them. The result is a group of people who, as the leagues become of a higher and higher class, are progressively insensitive to the possibility that things could be otherwise. Thus, in football, anyone who might question the wisdom or enjoyment of putting on heavy equipment on a hot day and running full speed at someone else with the intention of knocking him senseless would be regarded simply as not really a devoted athlete and probably "chicken." The choice is made straightforward. Either you, too, do your very utmost to efficiently smash and be smashed, or you admit incompetence or cowardice and quit. Since neither of these admissions is very pleasant, people generally keep any doubts they have to themselves and carry on.

Of course, it would be a mistake to suppose that there is more blind acceptance of brutal practices in organized football than elsewhere. On the contrary, a recent Harvard study has approvingly argued that football's characteristics of "impersonal acceptance of inflicted injury," an overriding "organization goal," the "ability to turn oneself on and off" and being, above all, "out to win" are of "inestimable value" to big corporations. Clearly, our sort of football is no sicker than the rest of our society. Even its organized destruction of physical well-being is not anomalous. A very large part of our wealth, work and time is, after all, spent in systematically destroying and harming human life. Manufacturing, selling and using weapons that tear opponents to pieces. Making ever bigger and faster predator-named cars with which to kill and injure one another by the million every year. And devoting our very lives to outgunning one another for power in an ever more destructive rat race. Yet all these practices are accepted without question by most people, even zealously defended and honored. Competitive, organized injuring is integral to our way of life, and football is simply one of the more intelligible mirrors of the whole process: a sort of colorful morality play showing us how exciting and rewarding it is to Smash Thy Neighbor.

15   Now it is fashionable to rationalize our collaboration in all this by arguing that, well, man *likes* to fight and injure his fellows and such games as football should be encouraged to discharge this original-sin urge into less harmful channels than, say, war. Public-show football, this line goes, plays the same sort of cathartic role as Aristotle said stage tragedy does: without real blood (or not much), it releases players and audience from unhealthy feelings stored up inside them.

As an ex-player in the seasonal coast-to-coast drama, I see little to recommend such a view. What organized football did to me was make me *suppress* my natural urges and re-express them in an alienating, vicious form. Spontaneous desires for free bodily exuberance and fraternization with competitors were shamed and forced under ("If it ain't hurtin' it ain't helpin' ") and in their place were demanded armored mechanical moves and cool hatred of all opposition. Endless authoritarian drill and dressing-room harangues (ever wonder why competing teams can't prepare for a game in the same dressing room?) were the kinds of mechanisms employed to reconstruct joyful energies into mean and alien shapes. I am quite certain that everyone else around me was being similarly forced into this heavily equipped military precision and angry antagonism, because there was always a mutinous attitude about full-dress practices, and everybody (the pros included) had to concentrate incredibly hard for days to whip themselves into just one hour's hostility a week against another club. The players never speak of these things, of course, because everyone is so anxious to appear tough.

The claim that men like seriously to battle one another to some sort of finish is a myth. It only endures because it wears one of the oldest and most propagandized of masks—the romantic combatant. I sometimes wonder whether the violence all around us doesn't depend for its survival on the existence and preservation of this tough-guy disguise.

As for the effect of organized football on the spectator, the fan is not released from supposed feelings of violent aggression by watching his athletic heroes perform it so much as encouraged in the view that people-smashing is an admirable mode of self-expression. The most savage attackers, after all, are, by general agreement, the most efficient and worthy players of all (the biggest applause I ever received as a football player occurred when I ran over people or slammed them so hard they couldn't get up). Such circumstances can hardly be said to lessen the spectators' martial tendencies. Indeed it seems likely that the whole show just further develops and titillates the North American addiction for violent self-assertion. . . . Perhaps, as well, it helps explain why the greater the zeal of U.S. political leaders as football fans (Johnson, Nixon, Agnew), the more enthusiastic the commitment to hard-line politics. At any rate there seems to be a strong correlation between people who relish tough football and people who relish intimidating and beating the hell out of commies, hippies, protest marchers and other opposition groups.

Watching well-advertised strong men knock other people round, make them hurt, is in the end like other tastes. It does not weaken with feeding and variation in form. It grows.

I got out of football in 1962. I had asked to be traded after Calgary had of-   20
fered me a $25-a-week-plus-commissions off-season job as a clothing-store salesman. ("Dear Mr. Finks:" I wrote. [Jim Finks was then the Stampeders' general manager.] "Somehow I do not think the dialectical subtleties of Hegel, Marx and Plato would be suitably oriented amidst the environmental stimuli of jockey shorts and herringbone suits. I hope you make a profitable sale or trade of my contract to the East.") So the Stampeders traded me to Montreal. In a preseason intersquad game with the Alouettes I ripped the cartilages in my ribs on the hardest block I'd ever thrown. I had trouble breathing and I had to shuffle-walk with my torso on a tilt. The doctor in the local hospital said three weeks rest, the coach said scrimmage in two days. Three days later I was back home reading philosophy.

QUESTIONS

1. What similarities does McMurtry see between football and war? How persuasive do you find the linkage?

2. Is McMurtry's essay mainly about his personal experiences in football, or is it about some larger point, with his experiences used as examples?

3. Draw connections between "real life" and some kind of game or play familiar to you. Does this illuminate any social arrangements or help you to see them in a new light? How far can one generalize?

MARK GREIF   *Against Exercise*

ERE "IN THE PENAL COLONY" to be written today, Kafka could only be speaking of an exercise machine. Instead of the sentence to be tattooed on its victims, the machine would inscribe lines of numbers. So many calories, so many miles, so many watts, so many laps.

Modern exercise makes you acknowledge the machine operating inside yourself. Nothing can make you believe we harbor nostalgia for factory work but a modern gym. The lever of the die press no longer commands us at work. But with the gym we import vestiges of the leftover equipment of industry into our leisure. We leave the office, and put the conveyor belt under our feet, and run as if chased by devils. We willingly submit our legs to the mangle, and put our stiffening arms to the press.

It is crucial that the machines are simple. The inclined planes; pins, levers, pulleys, locks, winches, racks, and belts of the Nautilus and aerobic machines put earlier stages of technical progress at our disposal in miniature. The elements are visible and intelligible for our use but not dangerous to us. Displaced, neutralized, they are traces of a necessity that no longer need be met with forethought or ingenuity. A farmer once used a pulley, cable, and bar to lift his roofbeam; you now use the same means to work your lats.

Today, when we assume our brains are computers, the image of a machine-man, whether Descartes's or La Mettrie's,[1] has an old and venerable quality, like a yellowed poster on the infirmary wall. Blood pressure is hydraulics, strength is mechanics, nutrition is combustion, limbs are levers, joints are ball-in-socket. The exercise world does not make any notable conceptual declaration that we are mechanical men and women. We already were that, at least as far as our science is concerned. Rather it expresses a will, on the part of each and every individual, to discover and regulate the machinelike processes in his own body.

5   And we go to this hard labor with no immediate reward but our freedom to do it. Precisely this kind of freedom may be enough. Exercise machines offer you the superior mastery of subjecting your body to experimentation. We hide our reasons for undertaking this labor, and thoughtlessly substitute a new necessity. No one asks whether we want to drag our lives across a threshold into the kingdom of exercise.

Published in the inaugural issue of n + 1 *(Fall 2004), an avant-garde print journal of politics, literature, and culture that Greif founded with three other young editors.*

1. René Descartes (1596–1650), French philosopher who viewed humans as complex organic machines; Julien Offray de La Mettrie (1709–1751), French physician, philosopher, and author of *L'Homme machine (Machine Man)*, which provided simple mechanistic explanations for much human behavior.

Exercise is no choice. It comes to us as an emissary from the realm of biological processes. It falls under the jurisdiction of the obligations of life itself, which only the self-destructive neglect. Our controversial future is supposed to depend on engineered genes, brain scans, neuroscience, laser beams. About those things we have loud, public, sterile debates, while the real historic changes are accomplished on a gym's vinyl mats, to the sound of a flywheel and a ratcheted inclined plane.

In the gym you witness people engaging in a basic biological process of self-regulation. All of its related activities reside in the private realm. A question, then, is why exercise doesn't stay private. It could have belonged at home with other processes it resembles: eating, sleeping, defecating, cleaning, grooming, and masturbating.

Exerciser, what do you see in the mirrored gym wall? You make the faces associated with pain, with tears, with orgasm, with the sort of exertion that would call others to your immediate aid. But you do not hide your face. You groan as if pressing on your bowels. You repeat grim labors as if mopping the floor. You huff and you shout and strain. You appear in tight yet shapeless Lycra costumes. These garments reveal the shape of the genitals and the mashed and bandaged breasts to others' eyes, without acknowledging the lure of sex.

Though we get our word "gymnasium" from the Greeks, our modern gym is not in their spirit. Athletics in the ancient institution were public and agonistic. They consisted of the training of boys for public contests. The gymnasium was closest to what we know as a boxing gym, with the difference that it was also the place adult men gathered to admire the most beautiful boys and, in the Greek fashion, sexually mentor them. It was the preeminent place to promote the systematic education of the young, and for adults to carry on casual debates among themselves, modeling the intellectual sociability, separated from overt politics, that is the origin of Western philosophy. Socrates spent most of his time in gymnasia. Aristotle began his philosophical school in the covered walkway of a gymnasium.

The Socratic and Peripatetic methods could find little support in a modern gym. What we moderns do there belongs to mute privacy. The Greeks put their genuinely private acts into a location, an *oikos*, the household. To the household belonged all the acts that sustained bare biological life. That included the labor of keeping up a habitation and a body, growing food and eating it, bearing children and feeding them. Hannah Arendt[2] interpreted this strong Greek distinction of the household from the public sphere as a symbol of a general truth, that it is necessary to keep the acts that sustain naked life away from others' observation. A hidden sphere, free from scrutiny, provides

10

2. German-American political philosopher (1906–1975) who wrote *The Origins of Totalitarianism* (1951), *The Human Condition* (1958), and *Eichmann in Jerusalem: A Report on the Banality of Evil* (1963); for a selection from the last, see the "History" section.

the foundation for a public person—someone sure enough in his privacy to take the drastic risks of public life, to think, to speak against others' wills, to choose, with utter independence. In privacy, alone with one's family, the dominating necessity and speechless appetites could be gratified in the nonthought and ache of staying alive.

Our gym is better named a "health club," except that it is no club for equal meetings of members. It is the atomized space in which one does formerly private things, before others' eyes, with the lonely solitude of a body acting as if it were still in private. One tries out these contortions to undo and remake a private self; and if the watching others aren't entitled to approve, some imagined aggregate "other" does. Modern gym exercise moves biology into the nonsocial company of strangers. You are supposed to coexist but not look closely, wipe down the metal of handlebars and rubber of mats as if you had not left a trace. As in the elevator, you are expected to face forward.

It is like a punishment for our liberation. The most onerous forms of necessity, the struggle for food, against disease, always by means of hard labor, have been overcome. It might have been naive to think the new human freedom would push us toward a society of public pursuits, like Periclean Athens, or of simple delight in what exists, as in Eden. But the true payoff of a society that chooses to make private freedoms and private leisures its main substance has been much more unexpected. This payoff is a set of forms of bodily self-regulation that drag the last vestiges of biological life into the light as a social attraction.

The only truly essential pieces of equipment in modern exercise are numbers. Whether at the gym or on the running path, rudimentary calculation is the fundamental technology. As the weights that one lifts are counted, so are distances run, time exercised, heart rates elevated.

A simple negative test of whether an activity is modern exercise is to ask whether it could be done meaningfully without counting or measuring it. (In sports, numbers are used differently; there, scores are a way of recording competition in a social encounter.) Forms of exercise that do away with mechanical equipment, as running does, cannot do away with this.

15   In exercise one gets a sense of one's body as a collection of numbers representing capabilities. The other location where an individual's numbers attain such talismanic status is the doctor's office. There is a certain seamlessness between all the places where exercise is done and the sites where people are tested for illnesses, undergo repairs, and die. In the doctor's office, the blood lab, and the hospital, you are at the mercy of counting experts. A lab technician in a white coat takes a sample of blood. A nurse tightens a cuff on your arm, links you to an EKG, takes the basic measurements of your height and weight—never to your satisfaction. She rewards you with the obvious numbers for blood pressure, body fat ratio, height, and weight. The clipboard with your numbers is passed. At last the doctor takes his seat, a mechanic who wears the white robe of an angel and is as arrogant as a boss. In specialist language, exacerbating your dread and expectation, you may learn your numbers for cho-

lesterol (two types), your white cells, your iron, immunities, urinalysis, and so forth. He hardly needs to remind you that these numbers correlate with your chances of survival.

How do we acquire the courage to exist as a set of numbers? Turning to the gym or the track, you gain the anxious freedom to count yourself. What a relief it can be. Here are numbers you can change. You make the exercises into trials you perform upon matter within reach, the exterior armor of your fat and muscle. You are assured these numbers, too, and not only the black marks in the doctor's files, will correspond to how long you have to live. With willpower and sufficient discipline, that is, the straitening of yourself to a rule, you will be changed.

The gym resembles a voluntary hospital. Its staff members are also its patients. Some machines put you in a traction you can escape, while others undo the imprisonment of a respirator, cueing you to pump your lungs yourself and tracking your heart rate on a display. Aided even by a love that can develop for your pains, this self-testing becomes second nature.

The curious compilation of numbers that you are becomes an aspect of your freedom, sometimes the most important, even more preoccupying than your thoughts or dreams. You discover what high numbers you can become, and how immortal. For you, high roller, will live forever. You are eternally maintained.

The justification for the total scope of the responsibility to exercise is health. A further extension of the counting faculty of exercise gives a precise economic character to health. It determines the anticipated numbers for the days and hours of one's life.

Today we really can preserve ourselves for a much longer time. The means   20
of preservation are reliable and cheap. The haste to live one's mortal life diminishes. The temptation toward perpetual preservation grows. We preserve the living corpse in an optimal state, not that we may do something with it, but for its own good feelings of eternal fitness, confidence, and safety. We hoard our capital to earn interest, and subsist each day on crusts of bread. But no one will inherit our good health after we've gone. The hours of life-maintenance vanish with the person.

The person who does not exercise, in our current conception, is a slow suicide. He fails to take responsibility for his life. He doesn't labor strenuously to forestall his death. Therefore we begin to think he causes it.

It may be a comfort to remember when one of your parents' acquaintances dies that he did not eat well or failed to take up running. The nonexerciser is lumped with other unfortunates whom we socially discount. Their lives are worth a percentage of our own, through their own neglect. Their value is compromised by the failure to assure the fullest term of possible physical existence. The nonexerciser joins all the unfit: the slow, the elderly, the poor, and the hopeless. "Don't you want to *live*?" we say. No answer of theirs could satisfy us.

Conceive of a society in which it was believed that the senses could be used up. Eyesight worsened the more vivid sights you saw. Hearing worsened the more intense sounds you heard. It would be inevitable that such a conception would bleed into people's whole pattern of life, changing the way they spent their days. Would they use up their powers on the most saturated colors, listening to the most intoxicating sounds? Or might its members refuse to move, eyes shut, ears covered, nursing the remaining reserves of sensation? We, too, believe our daily lives are not being lived but eaten up by age. And we spend our time desperately. From the desperate materialist gratifications of a hedonistic society, commanding immediate comfort and happiness, we recoil to the desperate economics of health, and chase a longer span of happinesses deferred, and comforts delayed, by disposing of the better portion of our lives in life preservation.

Exercise does make you, as a statistical person, part of different aggregate categories that die with less frequency at successive ages. It furnishes a gain in odds. This is the main public rationale for those billions of man- and woman-hours in the gym. The truth, however, is also that being healthy makes you feel radically different. For a segment of its most ardent practitioners, exercise in its contemporary form is largely a quest for certain states of feeling. A more familiar phenomenon than the young person who is unhappy physically from never exercising is the young exerciser who suffers from missing one or two days of exercise. The most common phenomenon may be the individual who judges, in his own mind if not out loud, the total healthiness of his state at each moment based on what he ate, what he drank, how much he exercised, when, with what feelings as he was doing it, and with what relation to the new recommendation or warning he just heard on the news hour's health report. One feels healthier even when the body doesn't feel discernably different. Or the body does begin to feel different—lighter, stronger, more efficient, less toxic—in ways that exceed the possible consequences of the exercises performed. This may be a more important psychic "medicalization of human life" than anything a doctor can do with his tests.

25   The less respectable but even more powerful justification for day-to-day exercise is thinness. It involves the disciplining of a depraved will rather than the righteous responsibility to maintain the health of the body-machine and its fund of capital.

Women strip their bodies of layers of fat to reveal a shape without its normal excess of flesh. Despite the new emphasis on female athleticism, the task of the woman exerciser remains one of emaciation. Men thin themselves too, but more importantly bloat particular muscles, swelling the major clusters in the biceps, chest, and thighs. They awaken an incipient musculature that no work or normal activity could bring out in toto. Theirs is a task of expansion and discovery. Women's emaciation is a source for feminine eye-rolling and rueful nicknames: the "social x-ray," the actress as skin and bones. Men's proud expansion and discovery of six muscles of the lower abdomen, reminiscent of an insect's segmented exoskeleton, likewise become a byword and a joke: the "six-pack," bringing exercise together with the masculinity of drinking.

Unlike the health model, which seems to make a continuous gain on mortality, thinness and muscle expansion operate in a cruel economy of acceler-ated loss. Mortality began when the first man and woman left the Garden. Everyone has to die, but no one has to shape a physique, and once body alter-ing begins, it is more implacable than death. Every exerciser knows that the body's propensity to put on weight is the physical expression of a moral fall. Every exerciser knows that the tendency of the body to become soft when it is comfortable or at rest, instead of staying perpetually hard, is a failure of disci-pline. This is the taste of our new Tree of Knowledge. In our era of abun-dance, we find that nutrition makes one fat rather than well fed, pleasures make one flabby rather than content, and only anorexics have the willpower to stop eating and die.

Exercise means something other than health to a young person who con-ceives sexual desirability as the truth about herself most worth defending. And youth is becoming permanent in the demand that adults keep up an outward show of juvenile sexuality. The body becomes the location of sexiness, rather than clothes or wit or charisma. This is less true for society—which values personality still—than for the exerciser herself, who imagines an audience that doesn't exist. Saddest of all is the belief that an improved body will bestow bliss on the unloved.

The shock troops of modern exercise are women just past the college years. Only recently the beneficiary of a sexually mature body, and among our cul-ture's few possessors by native right of the reduced body type we prefer—which we daily prefer more openly, more vehemently—the girl of twenty-two is a par-adoxical figure as an exemplar of exercise. She is not yet among the discounted. But she knows her destiny. She starts immediately to get ahead in the race to preserve a form that must never exceed the barest minimum of flesh. A refresh-ing honesty can exist among exercisers who are not yet caught up in the doc-trine of health. The rising incidence of smoking among young women, which worries public-health advocates, is coincident with the rising incidence of gym exercise, which doesn't. While the cigarette suppresses appetite (rebelliously), the StairMaster attacks calories (obediently). Each can become intensely, erot-ically pleasurable, and neither is really meant for health or longevity.

The doctrine of thinness introduces a radical fantasy of exercise down to 30 the bone. It admits the dream of a body unencumbered by any excess of cor-poreality. Thanatos enters through the door opened by Eros, and exercise flirts with a will to annihilate the unattractive body rather than to preserve its longevity. Without an accompanying ideology of health, thinness would in fact liquidate all restraints, generating a death's-head vision of exercise. Health cu-riously returns as the only brake on a practice that otherwise would become a kind of naked aggression against the body.

With health in place, the aggression is more likely to be carried on psychi-cally. It pools, then starts an undercurrent of hatred for this corrupt human form that continually undoes the labor you invest in it. One hundred twenty pounds of one's own flesh starts to seem like the Sisyphean boulder. Yet the bitterness of watching your body undo your work is restrained by a curious compensation that Sisyphus did not know. If the hated body is the scene of a battle, a certain pleasure still emerges from the unending struggle, and in a hedonistic order divided against its own soft luxuries, at least *this* pleasure, if no other, can be made to go on forever.

An enigma of exercise is the proselytizing urge that comes with it. Exercisers are always eager for everyone else to share their experience. Why must others exercise if one person does?

No one who plays baseball or hockey demands that everyone else play the sport. Sports are social. Their victories become visible in the temporary public arrangements of a game. Perhaps accomplishments recognized by others in the act of their occurrence can be left alone. The gym-goer, on the other hand, is a solitary evangelist. He is continually knocking on your door to get you to recognize the power that will not give him peace. You, too, must exercise. Even as he worries for your salvation, nevertheless he has the gleam of someone who is ahead of you already, one chosen by God.

Running is most insidious because of its way of taking proselytizing out of the gym. It is a direct invasion of public space. It lays the counting, the pacing, the controlled frenzy, the familiar undergarment-outergarments and skeletal look, on top of the ordinary practice of an outdoor walk. One thing that can be said for a gym is that an implied contract links everyone who works out in its mirrored and pungent hangar. All consent to undertake separate exertions and hide any mutual regard, as in a well-ordered masturbatorium. The gym is in this sense more polite than the narrow riverside, street, or nature path, wherever runners take over shared places for themselves. With his speed and narcissistic intensity the runner corrupts the space of walking, thinking, talking, and everyday contact. He jostles the idler out of his reverie. He races between pedestrians in conversation. The runner can oppose sociability and solitude by publicly sweating on them.

35   No doubt the unsharability of exercise stimulates an unusual kind of loneliness.

When exercise does become truly shared and mutually visible, as in the aerobics that come close to dance, or the hardcore body-building that is always erotic and fraternal, it nears sport or art and starts to reverse itself. When exercise is done in a private home, or in untenanted landscapes, or without formal method, apparatus, or counting, it recovers certain eccentric freedoms of private techniques of the self.

However, the pure category of modern exercise is concerned with neither the creative process of reproduction (as in activities-in-common) nor the pure discoveries of solitude (as in private eccentricity). It pursues an idea of replication. Replication in exercise recreates the shape and capabilities of others in the material of your own body, without new invention and without exchange with others or crossing over of material between selves.

It is a puzzling question, in fact, whether "you" and "your body" are the same in exercise. If on the one hand exercise seems strongly to identify exercisers with their bodies, by putting them to shared labor, on the other hand it seems to estrange them from the bodies they must care for and manage.

Where does "fitness" actually reside? It seems to be deep inside you; yet that inside has risen to a changeable surface. And this surface is no longer one you can take off, as you did a costume in earlier methods of improving your allure. Fashion historians point out that women freed themselves from corsets worn externally, only to make an internal corset, as they toned the muscles of the abdomen and chest, and dieted and exercised to burn away permanently the well-fed body that whalebone stays temporarily restrained. Though the exerciser acts on his *self*, this self becomes ever more identified with the visible surface. Though he works on *his* body, replication makes it ever more, so to speak, *anybody*.

Does this critique imply a hatred of the body? On the contrary. The ethos of gym exercise annihilates the margin of safety that humans have when they relate to their own bodies. Men and women seem more ashamed of their own actual bodies in the present environment of biological exposure than in a pre-gym past. An era of exercise has brought more obsession and self-hatred rather than less.

A feminist worry becomes important. It is certainly possible to make people used to displaying to others' eyes the biological processes of transformation. And this has been, at times, the aim of feminists, who intended to attack a patriarchy that vilified the natural body or that made biological processes a source of shame and inferiority. But the forms of exposure that have recently arisen are not in line with feminist liberation of the unconditioned body.

40

Patriarchy made biology a negative spectacle, a filth that had to be hidden. The ethos of exercise makes it a positive spectacle, a competitive fascination that must be revealed. The rhetoric of "loving the body" can thus be misused. With the extension of the cliché that one should "not be ashamed" of the body, people are less able to defend themselves against the prospect that their actual bodies, and biological processes, may be manifest at every moment, in new states of disciplining neither public nor private. It becomes a retrogression, a moral failing, in these people to wish to defend against exposure, or to withdraw their health, bodies, arousal, and self-regulation from the social scene, as if privacy of this kind were mere prudery or repression.

Once subjected to this socialization of biological processes, the body suffers a new humiliation no longer rooted in the distinctions between the revealed and the hidden, the natural and the shameful, the sexual ideal and the physical actuality, but in the deeper crime of merely *existing* as the unregulated, the unshaped, the unsexy, the "unfit."

Our practices are turning us inside out. Our hidden flesh becomes our public front. The private medical truth of bodily health becomes our psychic self-regard. Action in public before strangers and acquaintances has disappeared from the lived experience of the citizen and been replaced by *exercise* in public, as speech gives way to biological spectacle.

Your exercise confers superiority in two contests, one of longevity and the other of sex. Facing mortality, the gym-goer believes himself an agent of health—whereas he makes himself a more perfect patient. Facing the sexual struggle, the gym-goer labors to attain a positive advantage, which spurs an ever-receding horizon of further competition.

45   The technical capabilities of gym exercise in fact drive social ideals and demands. The exerciser conforms, in our era's most virulent practice of conformism. But exercise itself pushes medicine and sexual allure toward further extremes. The feedback does not stabilize the system but radicalizes it, year by year. Only in a gym culture does overweight become the "second leading cause of death" (as the news recently reported) rather than a correlation, a relative measure, which positively covaries with the heart attacks, the cancers, the organ failures, and final illnesses that were formerly our killers. Only in a gym culture do physical traits that were formerly considered repellent become marks of sexual superiority. (We are hot now for the annihilation by exercise and dieting of once voluptuous feminine flesh, watching it be starved away in natural form and selectively replaced with breast implants, collagen injections, buttock lifts. We've learned to be aroused by the ripped, vein-popping muscles that make Incredible Hulks of men who actually push papers.) Because health and sex are the places we demand our truth today, newly minted ideals must be promulgated as discoveries of medical science or revelations of permanent, "evolutionary" human desires.

The consequences are not only the flooding of consciousness with a numbered and regulated body or the distraction from living that comes with endless life-maintenance, but the liquidation of the last untouched spheres of privacy, such that biological life itself becomes a spectacle.

"You are condemned. You are condemned. You are condemned." This is the chant the machines make with their grinding rhythm inside the roar of the gym floor. Once upon a time, the authority of health, and the display of our bodies and biological processes, seemed benign, even liberating. We were going to overcome illness, we were going to exorcise the prudish Victorians. But our arrows were turned from their targets, and some of them punctured our privacy.

The thinness we strive for becomes spiritual. This is not the future we wanted. That prickling beneath the exerciser's skin as he steps off the treadmill is only his new self, his reduced existence, scratching the truth of who he is now, from the inside out.

QUESTIONS

1. Were you surprised by the arguments Greif uses against exercise? List some arguments he has left out. Why do you think he has omitted these arguments?

2. Describe some other contemporary obsessions that could be treated in a similarly contrarian essay entitled "Against _____." What techniques might you adapt from Greif for your essay?

3. Write an essay called "For Exercise," arguing against Greif's piece.

BETTY ROLLIN   *Motherhood: Who Needs It?*

MOTHERHOOD IS in trouble, and it ought to be. A rude question is long overdue: Who needs it? The answer used to be (1) society and (2) women. But now, with the impending horrors of overpopulation, society desperately *doesn't* need it. And women don't need it either. Thanks to the Motherhood Myth—the idea that having babies is something that all normal women instinctively want and need and will enjoy doing—they just *think* they do.

The notion that the maternal wish and the activity of mothering are instinctive or biologically predestined is baloney. Try asking most sociologists, psychologists, psychoanalysts, biologists—many of whom are mothers—about motherhood being instinctive: it's like asking department store presidents if their Santa Clauses are real. "Motherhood—instinctive?" shouts distinguished sociologist/author Dr. Jessie Bernard. "Biological destiny? Forget biology! If it were biology, people would die from not doing it."

"Women don't need to be mothers any more than they need spaghetti," says Dr. Richard Rabkin, a New York psychiatrist. "But if you're in a world where everyone is eating spaghetti, thinking they need it and want it, you will think so too. Romance has really contaminated science. So-called instincts have to do with stimulation. They are not things that well up inside of you."

"When a woman says with feeling that she craved her baby from within, she is putting into biological language what is psychological," says University of Michigan psychoanalyst and motherhood-researcher Dr. Frederick Wyatt. "There are no instincts," says Dr. William Goode, president-elect of the American Sociological Association. "There are reflexes, like eye-blinking, and drives, like sex. There is no innate drive for children. Otherwise, the enormous cultural pressures that there are to reproduce wouldn't exist. There are no cultural pressures to sell you on getting your hand out of the fire."

There are, to be sure, biologists and others who go on about biological destiny, that is, the innate or instinctive goal of motherhood. (At the turn of the century, even good old capitalism was explained by a theorist as "the *instinct* of acquisitiveness.") And many psychoanalysts will hold the Freudian view that women feel so rotten about not having a penis that they are necessarily propelled into the child-wish to replace the missing organ. Psychoanalysts also make much of the psychological need to repeat what one's parent of the same sex has done. Since every woman has a mother, it is considered normal to wish to imitate one's mother by being a mother.

There is, surely, a wish to pass on love if one has received it, but to insist women must pass it on in the same way is like insisting that every man whose father is a gardener has to be a gardener. One dissenting psychoanalyst says, simply, "There is a wish to comply with one's biology, yes, but we needn't and

5

Originally published in Look *(September 22, 1970), a popular general-interest magazine that ceased publication in 1971.*

sometimes we shouldn't." (Interestingly, the woman who has been the greatest contributor to child therapy and who has probably given more to children than anyone alive is Dr. Anna Freud, Freud's magnificent daughter, who is not a mother.)

Anyway, what an expert cast of hundreds is telling us is, simply, that biological *possibility* and desire are not the same as biological *need*. Women have childbearing equipment. To choose not to use the equipment is no more blocking what is instinctive than it is for a man who, muscles or no, chooses not to be a weight lifter.

So much for the wish. What about the "instinctive" *activity* of mothering? One animal study shows that when a young member of a species is put in a cage, say, with an older member of the same species, the latter will act in a protective, "maternal" way. But that goes for both males and females who have been "mothered" themselves. And studies indicate that a human baby will also respond to whoever is around playing mother—even if it's father. Margaret Mead and many others frequently point out that mothering can be a fine occupation, if you want it, for either sex. Another experiment with monkeys who were brought up without mothers found them lacking in maternal behavior toward their own offspring. A similar study showed that monkeys brought up without other monkeys of the opposite sex had no interest in mating—all of which suggests that both mothering and mating behavior are learned, not instinctual. And, to turn the cart (or the baby carriage) around, baby ducks who lovingly follow their mothers seemed, in the mother's absence, to just as lovingly follow wooden ducks or even vacuum cleaners.

If motherhood isn't instinctive, when and why, then, was the Motherhood Myth born? Until recently, the entire question of maternal motivation was academic. Sex, like it or not, meant babies. Not that there haven't always been a lot of interesting contraceptive tries. But until the creation of the diaphragm in the 1880's, the birth of babies was largely unavoidable. And, generally speaking, nobody really seemed to mind. For one thing, people tend to be sort of good sports about what seems to be inevitable. For another, in the past, the population needed beefing up. Mortality rates were high, and agricultural cultures, particularly, have always needed children to help out. So because it "just happened" and because it was needed, motherhood was assumed to be innate.

10   Originally, it was the word of God that got the ball rolling with "Be fruitful and multiply," a practical suggestion, since the only people around then were Adam and Eve. But in no time, supermoralists like St. Augustine changed the tone of the message: "Intercourse, even with one's legitimate wife, is unlawful and wicked where the conception of the offspring is prevented," he, we assume, thundered. And the Roman Catholic position was thus cemented. So then and now, procreation took on a curious value among people who viewed (and view) the pleasures of sex as sinful. One could partake in the sinful pleasure, but feel vindicated by the ensuing birth. Motherhood cleaned up sex. Also, it cleaned up women, who have always been considered somewhat evil, because of Eve's transgression (". . . but the woman was deceived and be-

came a transgressor. Yet woman will be saved through bearing children . . . ," I Timothy, 2:14–15), and somewhat dirty because of menstruation.

And so, based on need, inevitability, and pragmatic fantasy—the Myth *worked*, from society's point of view—the Myth grew like corn in Kansas. And society reinforced it with both laws and propaganda—laws that made woman a chattel, denied her education and personal mobility, and madonna propaganda that she was beautiful and wonderful doing it and it was all beautiful and wonderful to do. (One rarely sees a madonna washing dishes.)

In fact, the Myth persisted—breaking some kind of record for long-lasting fallacies—until something like yesterday. For as the truth about the Myth trickled in—as women's rights increased, as women gradually got the message that it was certainly possible for them to do most things that men did, that they live longer, that their brains were not tinier—then, finally, when the really big news rolled in, that they could *choose* whether or not to be mothers—what happened? The Motherhood Myth soared higher than ever. As Betty Friedan made oh-so-clear in *The Feminine Mystique*,[1] the '40's and '50's produced a group of ladies who not only had babies as if they were going out of style (maybe they were) but, as never before, they turned motherhood into a cult. First, they wallowed in the aesthetics of it all—natural childbirth and nursing became maternal musts. Like heavy-bellied ostriches, they grounded their heads in the sands of motherhood, only coming up for air to say how utterly happy and fulfilled they were. But, as Mrs. Friedan says only too plainly, they weren't. The Myth galloped on, moreover, long after making babies had turned from practical asset to liability for both individual parents *and* society. With the average cost of a middle-class child figured conservatively at $30,000 (not including college), any parent knows that the only people who benefit economically from children are manufacturers of consumer goods. Hence all those gooey motherhood commercials. And the Myth gathered momentum long after sheer numbers, while not yet extinguishing us, have made us intensely uncomfortable. Almost all of our societal problems, from minor discomforts like traffic to major ones like hunger, the population people keep reminding us, have to do with there being too many people. And who suffers most? The kids who have been so mindlessly brought into the world, that's who. They are the ones who have to cope with all of the difficult and dehumanizing conditions brought on by overpopulation. They are the ones who have to cope with the psychological nausea of feeling unneeded by society. That's not the only reason for drugs, but, surely, it's a leading contender.

Unfortunately, the population curbers are tripped up by a romantic, stubborn, ideological hurdle. How can birth-control programs really be effective as long as the concept of glorious motherhood remains unchanged? (Even poor

---

1. Friedan began writing *The Feminine Mystique* (1963) after she sent a questionnaire to women in her 1942 Smith College class and discovered that many of them felt a general dissatisfaction with their lives. Friedan defined this "mystique"—"the problem that has no name"—as the worthlessness women feel in roles that make them dependent financially, intellectually, and emotionally on their husbands.

old Planned Parenthood has to euphemize—why not Planned Unparenthood?) Particularly among the poor, motherhood is one of the few inherently positive institutions that are accessible. As Berkeley demographer Judith Blake points out, "Poverty-oriented birth control programs do not make sense as a welfare measure . . . as long as existing pronatalist policies . . . encourage mating, pregnancy, and the care, support, and rearing of children." Or, she might have added, as long as the less-than-idyllic childrearing part of motherhood remains "in small print."

Sure, motherhood gets dumped on sometimes: Philip Wylie's Momism[2] got going in the '40's and Philip Roth's *Portnoy's Complaint* did its best to turn rancid the chicken-soup concept of Jewish motherhood. But these are viewed as the sour cries of a black humorist here, a malcontent there. Everyone shudders, laughs, but it's like the mouse and the elephant joke. Still, the Myth persists. Last April, a Brooklyn woman was indicted on charges of manslaughter and negligent homicide—eleven children died in a fire in a building she owned and criminally neglected—"But," sputtered her lawyer, "my client, Mrs. Breslow, is a mother, a grandmother, and a great-grandmother!"

15   Most remarkably, the Motherhood Myth persists in the face of the most overwhelming maternal unhappiness and incompetence. If reproduction were merely superfluous and expensive, if the experience were as rich and rewarding as the cliché would have us believe, if it were a predominantly joyous trip for everyone riding—mother, father, child—then the going everybody-should-have-two-children plan would suffice. Certainly, there are a lot of joyous mothers, and their children and (sometimes, not necessarily) their hubands reflect their joy. But a lot of evidence suggests that for more women than anyone wants to admit, motherhood can be miserable. ("If it weren't," says one psychiatrist wryly, "the world wouldn't be in the mess it's in.")

There is a remarkable statistical finding from a recent study of Dr. Bernard's, comparing the mental illness and unhappiness of married mothers and single women. The latter group, it turned out, was both markedly less sick and overtly more happy. Of course, it's not easy to measure slippery attitudes like happiness. "Many women have achieved a kind of reconciliation—a conformity," says Dr. Bernard,

> that they interpret as happiness. Since feminine happiness is supposed to lie in devoting one's life to one's husband and children, they do that; so *ipso facto*, they assume they are happy. And for many women, untrained for independence and "processed" for motherhood, they find their state far preferable to the alternatives, which don't really exist.

Also, unhappy mothers are often loath to admit it. For one thing, if in society's view not to be a mother is to be a freak, not to be a *blissful* mother is to be a witch. Besides, unlike a disappointing marriage, disappointing motherhood cannot be terminated by divorce. Of course, none of that stops such a woman from expressing her dissatisfaction in a variety of ways. Again, it is not

---

2. Wylie's *A Generation of Vipers* (1942) blamed many of the ills of American society on dominating mothers.

only she who suffers but her husband and children as well. Enter the harridan housewife, the carping shrew. The realities of motherhood can turn women into terrible people. And, judging from the 50,000 cases of child abuse in the U.S. each year, some are worse than terrible.

In some cases, the unpleasing realities of motherhood begin even before the beginning. In *Her Infinite Variety*, Morton Hunt describes young married women pregnant for the first time as "very likely to be frightened and depressed, masking these feelings in order not to be considered contemptible. The arrival of pregnancy interrupts a pleasant dream of motherhood and awakens them to the realization that they have too little money, or not enough space, or unresolved marital problems. . . ."

The following are random quotes from interviews with some mothers in Ann Arbor, Mich., who described themselves as reasonably happy. They all had positive things to say about their children, although when asked about the best moment of their day, they *all* confessed it was when the children were in bed. Here is the rest:

> Suddenly I had to devote myself to the child totally. I was under the illusion that the baby was going to fit into my life, and I found that I had to switch my life and my schedule to fit *him*. You think, "I'm in love, I'll get married, and we'll have a baby." First there's two, then three, it's simple and romantic. You don't even think about the work. . . .
>
> You never get away from the responsibility. Even when you leave the children with a sitter, you are not out from under the pressure of the responsibility. . . .
>
> I hate ironing their pants and doing their underwear, and they never put their clothes in the laundry basket. . . . As they get older, they make less demands on our time because they're in school, but the demands are greater in forming their values. . . . Best moment of the day is when all the children are in bed. . . . The worst time of the day is 4 P.M., when you have to get dinner started, the kids are tired, hungry and crabby—everybody wants to talk to you about *their* day . . . your day is only half over.
>
> Once a mother, the responsibility and concern for my children became so encompassing. . . . It took a great deal of will to keep up other parts of my personality. . . . To me, motherhood gets harder as they get older because you have less control. . . . In an abstract sense, I'd have several. . . . In the non-abstract, I would not have any. . . .
>
> I had anticipated that the baby would sleep and eat, sleep and eat. Instead, the experience was overwhelming. I really had not thought particularly about what motherhood would mean in a realistic sense. I want to do *other* things, like to become involved in things that are worthwhile—I don't mean women's clubs—but I don't have the physical energy to go out in the evenings. I feel like I'm missing something . . . the experience of being somewhere with people and having them talking about something—something that's going on in the world.

Every grownup person expects to pay a price for his pleasures, but seldom is the price as vast as the one endured "however happily" by most mothers. We have mentioned the literal cost factor. But what does that mean? For middle-class American women, it means a life style with severe and usually unimagined

20

limitations; i.e., life in the suburbs, because who can afford three bedrooms in the city? And what do suburbs mean? For women, suburbs mean other women and children and leftover peanut-butter sandwiches and car pools and seldom-seen husbands. Even the Feminine Mystiqueniks—the housewives who finally admitted that their lives behind brooms (OK, electric brooms) were driving them crazy—were loath to trace their predicament to their children. But it is simply a fact that a childless married woman has no child-work and little housework. She can live in a city, or, if she still chooses the suburbs or the country, she can leave on the commuter train with her husband if she wants to. Even the most ardent job-seeking mother will find little in the way of great op-portunities in Scarsdale.[3] Besides, by the time she wakes up, she usually lacks both the preparation for the outside world and the self-confidence to get it. You will say there are plenty of city-dwelling working mothers. But most of those women do additional-funds-for-the-family kind of work, not the interesting ca-reer kind that takes plugging during child-bearing years.

Nor is it a bed of petunias for the mother who does make it professionally. Says writer critic Marya Mannes:

> If the creative woman has children, she must pay for this indulgence with a long burden of guilt, for her life will be split three ways between them and her husband and her work. . . . No woman with any heart can compose a paragraph when her child is in trouble. . . . The creative woman has no wife to protect her from intrusion. A man at his desk in a room with closed door is a man at work. A woman at a desk in any room is available.

Speaking of jobs, do remember that mothering, salary or not, is a job. Even those who can afford nurses to handle the nitty-gritty still need to put out emotionally. "Well-cared-for" neurotic rich kids are not exactly unknown in our society. One of the more absurd aspects of the Myth is the underlying as-sumption that, since most women are biologically equipped to bear children, they are psychologically, mentally, emotionally, and technically equipped (or interested) to rear them. Never mind happiness. To assume that such an exact-ing, consuming, and important task is something almost all women are equipped to do is far more dangerous and ridiculous than assuming that every-one with vocal chords should seek a career in the opera.

A major expectation of the Myth is that children make a not-so-hot marriage hotter, or a hot marriage, hotter still. Yet almost every available study indicates that childless marriages are far happier. One of the biggest, of 850 couples, was conducted by Dr. Harold Feldman of Cornell University, who states his finding in no uncertain terms: "Those couples with children had a significantly lower level of marital satisfaction than did those without chil-dren." Some of the reasons are obvious. Even the most adorable children make for additional demands, complications, and hardships in the lives of even the most loving parents. If a woman feels disappointed and trapped in her mother role, it is bound to affect her marriage in any number of ways: she may take

3. A wealthy suburb of New York City.

out her frustrations directly on her husband, or she may count on him too heavily for what she feels she is missing in her daily life.

". . . You begin to grow away from your husband," says one of the Michigan ladies. "He's working on his career and you're working on your family. But you both must gear your lives to the children. You do things the children enjoy, more than things you might enjoy." More subtle and possibly more serious is what motherhood may do to a woman's sexuality. Often when the stork flies in, sexuality flies out. Both in the emotional minds of some women *and* in the minds of their husbands, when a woman becomes a mother, she stops being a woman. It's not only that motherhood may destroy her physical attractiveness, but its madonna concept may destroy her *feelings* of sexuality.

And what of the payoff? Usually, even the most self-sacrificing of maternal self-sacrificers expects a little something back. Gratified parents are not unknown to the Western world, but there are probably at least just as many who feel, to put it crudely, shortchanged. The experiment mentioned earlier—where the baby ducks followed vacuum cleaners instead of their mothers—indicates that what passes for love from baby to mother is merely a rudimentary kind of object attachment. Without necessarily feeling like a Hoover, a lot of women become disheartened because babies and children are not only not interesting to talk to (not everyone thrills at the wonders of da-da-ma-ma talk) but they are generally not empathetic, considerate people. Even the nicest children are not capable of empathy, surely a major ingredient of love, until they are much older. Sometimes they're never capable of it. Dr. Wyatt says that often, in later years particularly, when most of the "returns" are in, it is the "good mother" who suffers most of all. It is then she must face a reality: The child—the appendage with her genes—is not an appendage, but a separate person. What's more, he or she may be a separate person who doesn't even like her—or whom she doesn't really like.

So if the music is lousy, how come everyone's dancing? Because the motherhood minuet is taught freely from birth, and whether or not she has rhythm or likes the music, every woman is expected to do it. Indeed, she *wants* to do it. Little girls start learning what to want—and what to be—when they are still in their cribs. Dr. Miriam Keiffer, a young social psychologist at Bensalem, the Experimental College of Fordham University, points to studies showing that

> at six months of age, mothers are already treating their baby girls and boys quite differently. For instance, mothers have been found to touch, comfort, and talk to their females more. If these differences can be found at such an early stage, it's not surprising that the end product is as different as it is. What is surprising is that men and women are, in so many ways, similar.

Some people point to the way little girls play with dolls as proof of their innate motherliness. But remember, little girls are *given* dolls. When Margaret Mead[4]

4. American anthropologist (1901–1978) whose groundbreaking research in *Coming of Age in Samoa* (1928) demonstrated that individual development is shaped by cultural demands and expectations and that the stage of adolescence, especially sexual development, will be more or less problematic depending on the culture.

presented some dolls to New Guinea children, it was the boys, not the girls, who wanted to play with them, which they did by crooning lullabies and rocking them in the most maternal fashion.

By the time they reach adolescence, most girls, unconsciously or not, have learned enough about role definition to qualify for a master's degree. In general, the lesson has been that no matter what kind of career thoughts one may entertain, one must, first and foremost, be a wife and mother. A girl's mother is usually her first teacher. As Dr. Goode says, "A woman is not only taught by society to have a child; she is taught to have a child who will have a child." A woman who has hung her life on the Motherhood Myth will almost always reinforce her young married daughter's early training by pushing for grandchildren. Prospective grandmothers are not the only ones. Husbands, too, can be effective sellers. After all, they have the Fatherhood Myth to cope with. A married man is *supposed* to have children. Often, particularly among Latins, children are a sign of potency. They help him assure the world—and himself—that he is the big man he is supposed to be. Plus, children give him both immortality (whatever that means) and possibly the chance to become more in his lifetime through the accomplishments of his children, particularly his son. (Sometimes it's important, however, for the son to do better, but not *too* much better.)

Friends, too, can be counted on as myth-pushers. Naturally one wants to do what one's friends do. One study, by the way, found a correlation between a woman's fertility and that of her three closest friends. The negative sell comes into play here, too. We have seen what the concept of non-mother means (cold, selfish, unwomanly, abnormal). In practice, particularly in the suburbs, it can mean, simply, exclusion—both from child-centered activities (that is, most activities) and child-centered conversations (that is, most conversations). It can also mean being the butt of a lot of unfunny jokes. ("Whaddya waiting for? An immaculate conception? Ha ha.") Worst of all, it can mean being an object of pity.

In case she's escaped all those pressures (that is, if she was brought up in a cave), a young married woman often wants a baby just so that she'll (1) have something to do (motherhood is better than clerk/typist, which is often the only kind of job she can get, since little more has been expected of her and, besides, her boss also expects her to leave and be a mother); (2) have something to hug and possess, to be needed by and have power over; and (3) have something to *be*—e.g., a baby's mother. Motherhood affords an instant identity. First, through wifehood, you are somebody's wife; then you are somebody's mother. Both give not only identity and activity, but status and stardom of a kind. During pregnancy, a woman can look forward to the kind of attention and pampering she may not ever have gotten or may never otherwise get. Some women consider birth the biggest accomplishment of their lives, which may be interpreted as saying not much for the rest of their lives. As Dr. Goode says, "It's like the gambler who may know the roulette wheel is crooked, but it's the only game in town." Also, with motherhood, the feeling of accomplishment is immediate. It is really much faster and easier to make a baby than paint a painting, or write a book, or get to the point of accomplishment in a job. It is also easier in a way to shift focus from self-development to child development—particularly since, for women, self-development is considered selfish. Even unwed mothers may achieve a feeling of this kind. (As we have seen, little thought is given to the aftermath.) And, again, since so many women are underdeveloped as people, they feel that, besides children, they have little else to give—to themselves, their husbands, to their world.

You may ask why then, when the realities do start pouring in, does a   30
woman want to have a second, third, even fourth child? OK, (1) just because reality is pouring in doesn't mean she wants to *face* it. A new baby can help bring back some of the old illusions. Says psychoanalyst Dr. Natalie Shainess, "She may view each successive child as a knight in armor that will rescue her from being a 'bad unhappy mother.' " (2) Next on the horror list of having no children, is having one. It suffices to say that only children are not only OK, they even have a high rate of exceptionality. (3) Both parents usually want at least one child of each sex. The husband, for reasons discussed earlier, proba-bly wants a son. (4) The more children one has, the more of an excuse one has not to develop in any other way.

What's the point? A world without children? Of course not. Nothing could be worse or more unlikely. No matter what anyone says in *Look* or anywhere else, motherhood isn't about to go out like a blown bulb, and who says it should? Only the Myth must go out, and now it seems to be dimming.

The younger-generation females who have been reared on the Myth have not rejected it totally, but at least they recognize it can be more loving to chil-dren not to have them. And at least they speak of adopting children instead of bearing them. Moreover, since the new nonbreeders are "less hung-up" on ownership, they seem to recognize that if you dig loving children, you don't necessarily have to own one. The end of the Motherhood Myth might make available more loving women (and men!) for those children who already exist.

When motherhood is no longer culturally compulsory, there will, certainly, be less of it. Women are now beginning to think and do more about develop-ment of self, of their individual resources. Far from being selfish, such devel-opment is probably our only hope. That means more alternatives for women. And more alternatives mean more selective, better, happier, motherhood—and childhood and husbandhood (or manhood) and peoplehood. It is not a ques-tion of whether or not children are sweet and marvelous to have and rear; the question is, even if that's so, whether or not one wants to pay the price for it. It doesn't make sense any more to pretend that women need babies, when what they really need is themselves. If God were still speaking to us in a voice we could hear, even He would probably say, "Be fruitful. Don't multiply."

QUESTIONS

1. Why does Rollin use the term "myth" to describe what she believes is the common attitude toward motherhood?

2. Arguing against motherhood is likely to cause problems in persuading an audience. How does Rollin go about dealing with those problems?

3. Rollin allows that "nothing could be worse or more unlikely" than "a world without children" (paragraph 31). Does this contradict her previous argument?

4. Choose a common "myth" in contemporary society and argue against it.

BILL MCKIBBEN   *The Case for Single-Child Families*

THE BUILDING was nondescript; four stories of modern concrete just down the street from Ottawa's Civic Hospital. The receptionist greeted me politely, told me the doctor was running a little late. And so I sat on the couch next to the old and dog-eared magazines and read one more time the list of questions Dr. Phil McGuire wanted his vasectomy patients to answer before he performed The Procedure:

"What would you and your partner feel if you were told tomorrow that she was pregnant? Joy? Despair? Resignation? What about in five years?

"Would you want the chance to have children with another partner if your current relationship ended through separation or death?

"Would you want to have the chance to have more children if one or more of your children died?

"Would more children be in your picture now if your financial circumstances improved significantly?"

5   These are tougher questions than you usually get asked in a doctor's office. If you have heart disease, you have to choose *what* to do; it's rare to have to choose, until the very end, whether you want to do *anything at all*. But I could have gotten up and left, no harm done. I have one child. I'd decided to have no more. But this seemed so final.

Then Dr. McGuire came in, wearing khakis, old Nikes, an earring, a plaid shirt. So far that day, he said, he'd done nine vasectomies, pruned branches of nine family trees. He was calm, gentle—sweet. "I had a couple this morning who'd had one child when they were in their 30s, spent the next ten years trying to have another, and failed. Now they were in their early 40s and just couldn't conceive of conceiving again, so they wanted some insurance." He'd had a police officer, and a guy who builds Web pages, and several couples in their early 30s, each with two kids.

And he'd talked with all of them. "I try to protect people if I don't think they're ready," he said. "I'm a general practitioner and I've seen so many

Published on May 13, 1998, in The Christian Century, *a Protestant magazine with a stated mission to nurture faith and examine issues of politics, culture, and theology. This essay was included in* Maybe One: A Personal and Environmental Argument for Single-Child Families *(1998), a book that extends McKibben's work as a well-known environmental writer, most famous for* The End of the Earth *(1989).*

women come in who are unexpectedly pregnant, and completely delighted about it." But when people have made up their minds, he's ready to help—he's done 1,100 vasectomies, more and more each year. "Someday I hope to have a clinic just devoted to vasectomies—a fish tank and all the hunting and fishing and outdoors magazines," he said.

I'd come to him because Ottawa is not far from my home, because I could afford him (he charged just over $200, less than most American operations), and because I could tell from his Web site (www.ottawa-vas.com) that he thought pretty deeply about the whole issue. He had a sense of humor (his toll-free number is 1-800-LASTKID), but he also had a sense of purpose. "Sometimes I turn people down," he said. "But it's so much safer than having a woman get a tubal ligation, which is a big operation inside a major body cavity with general anaesthesia."

So I sat on the table and pulled my pants down around my ankles. He   10
swabbed my scrotum with iodine ("The iodine needs to be a little warm—the last thing we want is any shrinkage before we start") and then injected a slug of anaesthetic into each side of my testicles. Yes, it was a needle down there, but no, it didn't hurt much—by chance I'd spent the previous afternoon in the dentist's chair, and this was much less painful. (And no flossing!) He cut a small hole in my scrotum, and with a forceps pulled out the vas deferens, the tube that carried sperm to my penis. Then he cauterized it and put it back inside, repeating the procedure on the other side. I could feel a little tugging, nothing more. The wound was so small it didn't require stitches, or even a Band-Aid. For a few days, he said, my groin would be a little sore. After that it would take 20 ejaculations or so to drain the last of the sperm already in my system. And that would be that. In evolutionary terms, I'd be out of business.

It's easy for me to explain why I was lying on the table at the Ottawa Vasectomy Clinic: all I need is a string of statistics. In one recent study, condoms broke 4.8 percent of the time that they were used. Sixty percent of all pregnancies in the U.S. are unintended—60 percent. That doesn't mean all those children are unwanted; half just come when their parents weren't planning on it. But half end in abortion. In fact, six in ten women having abortions did so because their contraceptives failed; among typical couples, 18 percent using diaphragms and 12 percent using condoms managed to get pregnant. And no one's doing much to improve the situation—a nation that spends $600 million developing new cosmetics and fragrances each year has exactly one pharmaceutical company still conducting research on improved methods of birth control. So if I was serious about stopping at one child, this was where I belonged. For my wife, Sue, getting sterilized would have meant a real operation, real risk; for me it meant a bag of ice on my lap as I drove home. It all added up.

Not that we'd come to our decision to have one child easily. Although my work on environmental issues keeps bringing population questions front and center, I have avoided the issue of population for years. I know that by 2050 there will be almost 50 percent more Americans (and nearly 100 percent more human beings) than there are now. I know that in the last ten or 20 or 30 years, our impact has grown so much that we're changing even those places we don't inhabit—changing the way the weather works, changing the plants and animals that live at the poles and deep in the jungle.

I am convinced, too, that simplifying lifestyles alone, although crucial, will not do enough to reduce our impact in the next 50 years. Americans' lifestyles are just so "big." During the next decade India and China will each add to the planet about ten times as many people as the U.S., but the stress on the natural world by those new Americans may exceed that from the new Indians and Chinese combined. My five-year-old daughter has already used more stuff and added more waste to the environment than many of the world's residents do in a lifetime.

When Sue and I faced the issue of how many children to have, these abstract issues of population became personal and practical. What about Sophie? Would being an only child damage her spirit and mind? I explored the myths surrounding "the only child," and the clichés about one child being spoiled and overly dependent. Although these questions are emotionally charged and complex, every bit of research in recent decades shows that only kids do just fine—that they achieve as much and are as well adjusted as children with siblings. So that wasn't the hitch.

15   Along with doing all the research, however, I had to confront the deeply ingrained sense in many of us that there's something inherently *selfish* about not being willing to have children. It's not as strong as the sense of selfishness that can attach itself to abortion, but it's there nonetheless, and particularly strong, I think, in people of faith. It's the relic of our long theological wrestle with the issue of birth control. And it is not easily dismissed. Condoms may not be sinful, but selfishness must be, if anything is. The children of small families are no more selfish than any other kids—but are the parents?

In a consumer society, where we've been drilled relentlessly in selfishness, it's a peril to take seriously. In her book *Beyond Motherhood,* Jeanne Safer interviews dozens of men and women who have decided against children. I have no wish to judge them, for it's often an honorable decision, and people should not bear children if they feel they can't cope with them. On the other hand, I have no wish to *become* them. They are selfish, and proudly; one New York literary agent describes herself as "an advocate of selfishness." Safer says she herself felt her biological clock ticking, but heard other clocks as well:

> My practice is just starting to take off—I'll lose all the momentum if I cut back to part-time. That summer I thought, it'll have to wait until after we get back from Bali and I'm no longer taking medication to prevent malaria. And what about the trip to Turkey we want to take next summer.

She was, she said, "particularly aware that children would change my marriage drastically. . . . Parenthood, I believed, would certainly spell the end of our nightly candlelit sandalwood-scented bubble baths complete with silly bath toys, where we played like children in a deliciously adult incarnation." Not only that, "I realized that having a child of my own would force me to spend a great deal of time doing things I'd disliked; I'd never been crazy about children's birthday parties when I'd attended them years earlier, and a trip to the circus is my idea of purgatory."

Safer found many like-minded folk. Sandra Singer, for instance, a photographer who moonlights as a belly dancer to "guarantee her allure" and who insists that "I've seen too many women who have children lose their sexuality as well as their identity. They let their bodies go, and they complain about their husband's sexual advances. I complain about the lack."

Safer reconciles herself to her decision not to have kids, and celebrates by giving her own belly-dancing performance. "Working through feelings about motherhood had unleashed hidden reserves of creativity and femininity, and I emerged liberated, energized and strong," she reports. In fact one night she dreams of a cantaloupe growing on a vine in her parents' garden in the middle of winter: "The cantaloupe was myself, the fruit of my parents' loins, which, though barren in the biological sense, was ripening out of season."

It's wrong to ridicule such attitudes, at least in a culture that still assigns the work of raising kids mostly to women and allows men to continue their careers at full tilt. Sometimes people have to rescue themselves; in Toni Morrisons novel *Sula*, the heroine won't marry or bear children in order to preserve her "Me-ness." When her grandmother wants her to have babies to "settle" her, Sula says, "I don't want to make somebody else. I want to make myself." Often it's women from very poor backgrounds who decide to remain childless, realizing that it's their best hope for upward mobility against strong odds; in a 1985 study of poor Southern high school students, the 16 percent who wanted no children were the ones with the loftiest ambitions, the ambitions that in other contexts we want such children to have. 20

But it's also possible to understand the concern of popes and rabbis and just ordinary folk that, for some people, the decision to have no children or a small family represents a decision to indulge yourself without a thought for anyone else, a decision to take sandalwood-scented candlelit baths without the danger that there might be stray Legos left in the tub to poke you in the backside.

Theologian Gilbert Meilaender quotes one young man who says, "When you have children, the focus changes from the couple to the kids. Suddenly everything is done for them. Well, I'm 27, I've used up a good portion of my life already. Why should I want to sacrifice for someone who's still got his whole life ahead of him?" Such an attitude is, among other things, environmentally problematic; even if this fellow has no kids, thereby sparing the planet some burden, he seems unlikely to do much else to ensure its future— he's the same guy who's going to be voting against gas taxes and demanding the right to drive his Suburban into the overheated sunset.

John Ryan, an American Catholic theologian of the first half of the 20th century, made this argument most powerfully. A man of impeccable progressive credentials, Ryan was known as "the Right Reverend New Dealer" for his unwavering support of the Roosevelt administration. But this same John Ryan also wanted everyone who married to have many children, not simply as proof that they weren't using birth control but because he thought that raising large families makes people better human beings.

Ryan argued that supporting large families demands "forms of discipline necessary for the successful life," a life "accomplished only at the cost of continuous and considerable sacrifice, of compelling ourselves to do without the immediate and pleasant goods for the sake of remote and permanent goods." One of eleven children himself, Ryan thought that most people practicing birth control would be doing it from a "decadent" frame of mind; that bachelors were not building the kind of character necessary to contribute to the common good of society. Not only that, those with few children might become too wealthy, which was as dangerous as being too poor. In the words of ethicist John Berkman, "He was appealing to hard work, and building character, and he thought that was best achieved for most people in the context of having a large family."

25   This pragmatic argument comes straight from the American sense of purpose. And it is by no means a negligible or stupid argument: successfully raising a large brood of well-adjusted children is a great accomplishment, one that cannot help but change and deepen the parents. You emerge different people when you spend your life focusing, as good parents must, on *someone else's* well-being. If maturity is the realization that you are not at the center of the world, then the most time-honored way to become mature is to be a parent many times over, and a good one. Not just because parenting is tough, but also because it's so *joyful*, because it shows you that real transcendent pleasure comes from putting someone else first. It teaches you how dull self-absorption can be.

Such lessons don't always take, of course. As essayist Katha Pollitt points out, the tendency to ascribe "particular virtues—compassion, patience, common sense, nonviolence—to mothers" is an overdone, and in some ways oppressive, cliché; telling yourself that toilet training a string of two-year-olds is good for your soul may keep you away from other worlds. And in a country where incredible numbers of fathers walk away from their kids, you could argue that fatherhood seems to barely dent the culture's pervasive selfishness. And yet when I think of my circle of friends and acquaintances, the single most common route to maturity has been through raising children, often lots of them.

The problem, of course, is that now we live in an era—maybe only a brief one, maybe only for a few generations—when parenting a bunch of kids clashes with the good of the planet. So is there a different way to achieve some of that maturity, with no children or only a single child to change your life? It's not that one kid won't alter most things in your life; he or she will. But Ryan was right—it's not the total commitment that comes with a large brood. Your career or a calling continues, however hobbled you may sometimes be. Alice Walker, in a pithy essay titled "*One* Child of One's Own," called her single daughter a "meaningful digression," and that's right in many ways; if she had borne five children, she probably wouldn't have been writing many books. But those books represent a serious attempt at maturity in another way, and perhaps that's a clue. We need to find ways to be adults, grownups, *people who focus on others*, without being parents of large families.

In the weeks leading up to the 1994 Cairo Conference on population, the pope led the fight against many of the provisions in the draft documents for that conclave. Though I disagreed with some of his stands, I found much of his language powerful and intriguing. The Catholic Church, he said, does not support "an ideology of fertility at all costs," but instead an ethic in which the decision "whether or not to have a child" is not "motivated by selfish or carelessness, but by a prudent, conscious generosity that weighs the possibilities and circumstances." True, he added that such an ethic "gives priority to the welfare of the unborn child," but several weeks later, arguing that radical individualism and "a sexuality apart from ethical references" was inhuman, he called for a "culture of responsible procreation."

In those words, and the words of many others, I think we can see the outline of an ethic that avoids self-indulgence yet does not deny the physical facts of a planet with 6 billion people who may soon nearly double their numbers— a planet that grows hotter, stormier and less stable by the day, a planet where huge swaths of God's creation are being wiped out by the one species told to tend this particular garden. I don't pretend it is an ethic that can be embraced by the Vatican, or the Hasidim; but I do think it is an ethic that might undergrid a more sustainable world.

The beginning of Genesis contains the fateful command, repeated elsewhere in the Hebrew Bible, to "be fruitful and multiply, and fill the earth." That this was the first commandment gave it special priority. And it was biological, too, a command that echoed what our genes already shouted.

But there is something else unique about it—it is the first commandment 30 we have fulfilled. There's barely a habitable spot on the planet without a human being; in our lifetimes we've filled every inch of the planet with our presence. Everywhere the temperature climbs, the ultraviolet penetrates more deeply. In furthest Alaska, always our national metaphor for emptiness, the permafrost now melts at a rapid pace, trees move on to the tundra, insects infest forests in record numbers, and salmon turn back down streams because the water's gotten too warm to spawn. "There's been a permanent and significant climate regime shift," says an Alaskan scientist. "There has been nothing like this in the record." There's not a creature anywhere on earth whose blood doesn't show the presence of our chemicals, not an ocean that isn't higher because of us. For better and for worse, we are everywhere. We can check this commandment off the list.

And we can check it off for happier reasons as well. There's no denying that we've done great environmental damage, but it's also true that we've spread wondrous and diverse cultures, full of love and song, across the wide earth. We should add a holiday to the calendar of every church to celebrate this achievement.

But when you check something off a list, you don't just throw the list away. You look further down the list, see what comes next. And the list, of course, is long. The Gospels, the Torah, the Koran and a thousand other texts sacred and profane give us plenty of other goals toward which to divert some of the energy we've traditionally used in raising large families, goals on which we've barely begun. Feed the hungry, clothe the naked, comfort the oppressed; love your neighbor as yourself; heal the earth. We live on a planet where 3 billion people don't have clean water, where species die by the score each day, where kids grow up without fathers, where violence overwhelms us, where people judge each other by the color of their skin, where a hypersexualized culture poisons the adolescence of girls, where old people and young people need each other's support. And the energy freed by having smaller families may be some of the energy needed to take on these next challenges. To really take them on, not just to announce that they're important, or to send a check, or to read an article, but to make them central to our lives.

I have one child; she is the light of my life; she makes me care far more about the future than I used to. And I have one child; so even after my work I have some time, money and energy left to do other things. I get to work on Adirondack conservation issues and assist those who are fighting global warming; I've helped my wife start a new school in our town; I can teach Sunday school and help run a nationwide effort to decommercialize Christmas and sit on the board of the local college. (And I belly dance too, though in my case it's hiking, cross-country skiing, mountain biking.) If I had three kids, I would still do those things, but less of them; either that, or my work would come at their expense. As it is, once in a while I'm stretched too thin and don't see Sophie for a day, and that reminds me to slow down, to find the real center of my life. But I want to get further down that list.

35   So the pope strikes me as largely right in his reasoning if not his conclusions. Radical individualism is inhuman. Living as if you were the most important thing on earth is, literally, blasphemy; recreational sex may not bother me, but recreational life does. Our decisions should be motivated "not by selfishness or carelessness, but by a prudent conscious generosity." It's just that at the end of the twentieth century, on this planet, the signs of the times point me in the direction of the kinds of caring, the ways of maturing, that come with small, not large, families.

The church should not find that argument so foreign. Priests are celibate at least in part because it allows them to make Christ their bride, to devote all their energies to the other tasks set before us on this earth. And the wisdom of that argument is proved daily in a million places around the globe where committed priests and nuns take on the hardest and dirtiest challenges the earth has to offer. If we now have plenty of people to guarantee our survival as a race, and if lots more people may make that survival harder, then it's time to follow the lead of those clerics a little—not to embrace celibacy necessarily, but to love your child to pieces, and with whatever you have left to start working your way down the list.

And the same logic should make it clear, of course, that all sorts of other kinds of people—childless gay people, infertile people, people who do not feel called to parenthood—can become every bit as mature (or immature) as a parent of six, as long as they can find some substitute discipline for repeatedly placing someone or something else at the center of their lives.

Sometimes those disciplines are quiet and private, sometimes public. In

Allan Gurganus's novel *Plays Well with Others*, his main character describes taking care of one friend after another as they succumbed to AIDS—describes the almost hydraulic outpouring of love it took to tend them. "My own loved ones were not brought into the world by me, but only, in my company, let out of it," he writes. His own obituary, he knows, will show that he left "no immediate survivors." "And yet I feel I've earned a family too." More so, of course, than many parents.

When she began studying the differences between pro-choice and pro-life advocates in the abortion dispute, Kristin Luker noticed something interesting. It was true that they differed over the morality of terminating pregnancy, but those differences were the product of other, more fundamental splits in their view of the world. They felt differently about God, about the role of women and, most interestingly, they felt very differently about the nature of planning.

Pro-choice activists, she observed, were almost obsessed with planning for   40
their children, trying to give them "maximum parental guidance and every possible advantage," while parents active in the antiabortion movement "tend to be *laissez-faire* individualists in their attitude" toward child-rearing. "Pro-life people," she wrote, "believe that one becomes a parent by *being* a parent; parenthood is for them a 'natural' rather than a social role. The values implied by the in-vogue term 'parenting' (as in parenting classes) are alien to them." One woman she interviewed said, "I think people are foolish to worry about things in the future. The future takes care of itself." Too much planning, including too much family planning, means "playing God."

One of my favorite magazines comes from a small Ohio town. Called *Plain*, it is edited (and its type hand-set) by "conservative" Quakers, which is to say a group of men and women who live more or less in the fashion of Old Order Amish. The magazine recently reprinted a dinner conversation about the subject of family planning. The participants, each of them the parent of four children, were discussing their unease with contraception, and in terms very reminiscent of Luker's study:

> Miriam: It breeds the mentality that "I want what I want, when I want."
>
> Scott: It leads back to self-seeking, which eventually knows no bounds.
>
> Marvin: Actually, it leads to a bottom-line refusal to accept God's will for our lives.
>
> Scott: I think that one of the things Mary Ann and I have learned along the way, and which has further separated us from the mainstream culture, is the realization that we can always make room for one more. Because the room to be made is in our hearts.

That way of seeing the world attracts me—there is in its spontaneity and confidence something of real beauty. It offers a kind of freedom. Not the freedom of unlimited options that we've come to idolize, but a freedom from constant worrying and fretting. Sometimes I hate the calculator instinct in me, the part of me that constantly weighs benefits and risks, the part that keeps me safe and solvent at the expense of experience. There is something incredibly attractive about the mystery of the next child, and the next; I'd love to meet them. I'd love to leave it to God, or to chance, or to biology, or to destiny, or to the wind. Part of me thinks that those conservative Quakers, those pro-lifers, are unequivocally right.

The trouble is, there are now other ways to play God in this world, and *not* planning is one of them.

This was not always the case. In the Book of Job, God appears as a taunting voice from the whirlwind: "Where were you when I laid the foundations of the earth?" God asks Job. "Who shut up the sea with doors . . . and said here shall thy proud waves be stayed? . . . Who has cleft a channel for the torrents of rain, and a way for the thunderbolt?" Job has no way to reply, and no need; the earth is infinitely bigger than he; how absurd he would look standing at the edge of the sea and trying to whistle up the waves. God—the world—was huge, and we were tiny. Creation dwarfed us.

But now there are so many of us, and we have done such a poor job of planning for our numbers, that for the first time we can answer God back. We can say: we set the boundaries of the ocean. If we keep heating the planet at our current pace, the seas will rise two feet in the next century. Every one foot will bring the water 90 feet further inland across the typical American beach, drowning wetland and marsh. It's our lack of planning that changes the rainfall, that means more severe storms and worse flooding. It's not an "act of God." It's an act of us.

45   We no longer have the luxury of not planning; we're simply too big. We dominate the earth. When people first headed west across the plains, they didn't need a zoning board; now Californians try to channel and control growth lest they choke on it. In a crowded world, not planning has as many consequences as planning. This is a special time, and that turns everything on its head.

QUESTIONS

1. McKibben ends his essay by stating: "This is a special time, and that turns everything on its head." How does he demonstrate that this is "a special time"? Do you agree with him? In what sense does his argument depend on this being "a special time"?

2. McKibben tells of how his five-year-old daughter Sophie "has already used more stuff and added more waste to the environment than many of the world's residents do in a lifetime." Make an inventory of how much "stuff" you use in an average week, and then discuss whether your inventory proves McKibben's point.

3. Write an essay arguing that people who decide not to have children are or are not selfish.

JAMES BALDWIN   *Stranger in the Village*

FROM ALL AVAILABLE evidence no black man had ever set foot in this tiny Swiss village before I came. I was told before arriving that I would probably be a "sight" for the village; I took this to mean that people of my complexion were rarely seen in Switzerland, and also that city people are always something of a "sight" outside of the city. It did not occur to me—possibly because I am an American—that there could be people anywhere who had never seen a Negro.

It is a fact that cannot be explained on the basis of the inaccessibility of the village. The village is very high, but it is only four hours from Milan and three hours from Lausanne. It is true that it is virtually unknown. Few people making plans for a holiday would elect to come here. On the other hand, the villagers are able, presumably, to come and go as they please—which they do: to another town at the foot of the mountain, with a population of approximately five thousand, the nearest place to see a movie or go to the bank. In the village there is no movie house, no bank, no library, no theater; very few radios, one jeep, one station wagon; and at the moment, one typewriter, mine, an invention which the woman next door to me here had never seen. There are about six hundred people living here, all Catholic—I conclude this from the fact that the Catholic church is open all year round, whereas the Protestant chapel, set off on a hill a little removed from the village, is open only in the summertime when the tourists arrive. There are four or five hotels, all closed now, and four or five *bistros*, of which, however, only two do any business during the winter. These two do not do a great deal, for life in the village seems to end around nine or ten o'clock. There are a few stores, butcher, baker, *épicerie*,[1] a hardware store, and a money-changer—who cannot change travelers' checks, but must send them down to the bank, an operation which takes two or three days. There is something called the *Ballet Haus,* closed in the winter and used for God knows what, certainly not ballet, during the summer. There seems to be only one schoolhouse in the village, and this for the quite young children; I suppose this to mean that their older brothers and sisters at some point descend from these mountains in order to complete their education—possibly, again, to the town just below. The landscape is absolutely forbidding, mountains towering on all four sides, ice and snow as far as the eye can reach. In this white wilderness, men and women and children move all day, carrying washing, wood, buckets of milk or water, sometimes skiing on Sunday afternoons. All week long boys and young men are to be seen shoveling snow off the rooftops, or dragging wood down from the forest in sleds.

Written in 1953 and included in Notes of a Native Son *(1955), an autobiographical collection that describes and analyzes the experience of being black in America and Europe.*

1. A grocery shop.

The village's only real attraction, which explains the tourist season, is the hot spring water. A disquietingly high proportion of these tourists are cripples, or semi-cripples, who come year after year—from other parts of Switzerland, usually—to take the waters. This lends the village, at the height of the season, a rather terrifying air of sanctity, as though it were a lesser Lourdes. There is often something beautiful, there is always something awful, in the spectacle of a person who has lost one of his faculties, a faculty he never questioned until it was gone, and who struggles to recover it. Yet people remain people, on crutches or indeed on deathbeds; and wherever I passed, the first summer I was here, among the native villagers or among the lame, a wind passed with me—of astonishment, curiosity, amusement, and outrage. That first summer I stayed two weeks and never intended to return. But I did return in the winter, to work; the village offers, obviously, no distractions whatever and has the further advantage of being extremely cheap. Now it is winter again, a year later, and I am here again. Everyone in the village knows my name, though they scarcely ever use it, knows that I come from America—though, this, apparently, they will never really believe: black men come from Africa—and everyone knows that I am the friend of the son of a woman who was born here, and that I am staying in their chalet. But I remain as much a stranger today as I was the first day I arrived, and the children shout *Neger! Neger!* as I walk along the streets.

It must be admitted that in the beginning I was far too shocked to have any real reaction. In so far as I reacted at all, I reacted by trying to be pleasant—it being a great part of the American Negro's education (long before he goes to school) that he must make people "like" him. This smile-and-the-world-smiles-with-you routine worked about as well in this situation as it had in the situation for which it was designed, which is to say that it did not work at all. No one, after all, can be liked whose human weight and complexity cannot be, or has not been, admitted. My smile was simply another unheard-of phenomenon which allowed them to see my teeth—they did not, really, see my smile and I began to think that, should I take to snarling, no one would notice any difference. All of the physical characteristics of the Negro which had caused me, in America, a very different and almost forgotten pain were nothing less than miraculous—or infernal—in the eyes of the village people. Some thought my hair was the color of tar, that it had the texture of wire, or the texture of cotton. It was jocularly suggested that I might let it all grow long and make myself a winter coat. If I sat in the sun for more than five minutes some daring creature was certain to come along and gingerly put his fingers on my hair, as though he were afraid of an electric shock, or put his hand on my hand, astonished that the color did not rub off. In all of this, in which it must be conceded there was the charm of genuine wonder and in which there were certainly no element of intentional unkindness, there was yet no suggestion that I was human: I was simply a living wonder.

5   I knew that they did not mean to be unkind, and I know it now; it is necessary, nevertheless, for me to repeat this to myself each time that I walk out of the chalet. The children who shout *Neger!* have no way of knowing the

echoes this sound raises in me. They are brimming with good humor and the more daring swell with pride when I stop to speak with them. Just the same, there are days when I cannot pause and smile, when I have no heart to play with them; when, indeed, I mutter sourly to myself, exactly as I muttered on the streets of a city these children have never seen, when I was no bigger than these children are now: *Your* mother *was a nigger.* Joyce is right about history being a nightmare[2]—but it may be the nightmare from which no one *can* awaken. People are trapped in history and history is trapped in them.

There is a custom in the village—I am told it is repeated in many villages—of "buying" African natives for the purpose of converting them to Christianity. There stands in the church all year round a small box with a slot for money, decorated with a black figurine, and into this box the villagers drop their francs. During the *carnaval* which precedes Lent, two village children have their faces blackened—out of which bloodless darkness their blue eyes shine like ice—and fantastic horsehair wigs are placed on their blond heads; thus disguised, they solicit among the villagers for money for the missionaries in Africa. Between the box in the church and the blackened children, the village "bought" last year six or eight African natives. This was reported to me with pride by the wife of one of the *bistro* owners and I was careful to express astonishment and pleasure at the solicitude shown by the village for the souls of black folks. The *bistro* owner's wife beamed with a pleasure far more genuine than my own and seemed to feel that I might now breathe more easily concerning the souls of at least six of my kinsmen.

I tried not to think of these so lately baptized kinsmen, of the price paid for them, or the peculiar price they themselves would pay, and said nothing about my father, who having taken his own conversion too literally never, at bottom, forgave the white world (which he described as heathen) for having saddled him with a Christ in whom, to judge at least from their treatment of him, they themselves no longer believed. I thought of white men arriving for the first time in an African village, strangers there, as I am a stranger here, and tried to imagine the astounded populace touching their hair and marveling at the color of their skin. But there is a great difference between being the first white man to be seen by Africans and being the first black man to be seen by whites. The white man takes the astonishment as tribute, for he arrives to conquer and to convert the natives, whose inferiority in relation to himself is not even to be questioned; whereas I, without a thought of conquest, find myself among a people whose culture controls me, has even, in a sense, created me, people who have cost me more in anguish and rage than they will ever know, who yet do not even know of my existence. The astonishment with which I might have greeted them, should they have stumbled into my African village a few hundred years ago, might have rejoiced their hearts. But the astonishment with which they greet me today can only poison mine.

And this is so despite everything I may do to feel differently, despite my

2. James Joyce (1882–1941), Irish novelist; Stephen Daedalus, in Joyce's novel *Ulysses*, says, "History is a nightmare from which I am trying to escape."

friendly conversations with the *bistro* owner's wife, despite their three-year-old son who has at last become my friend, despite the *saluts* and *bonsoirs*[3] which I exchange with people as I walk, despite the fact that I know that no individual can be taken to task for what history is doing, or has done. I say that the culture of these people controls me—but they can scarcely be held responsible for European culture. America comes out of Europe, but these people have never seen America, nor have most of them seen more of Europe than the hamlet at the foot of their mountain. Yet they move with an authority which I shall never have; and they regard me, quite rightly, not only as a stranger in their village but as a suspect latecomer, bearing no credentials, to everything they have—however unconsciously—inherited.

For this village, even were it incomparably more remote and incredibly more primitive, is the West, the West onto which I have been so strangely grafted. These people cannot be, from the point of view of power, strangers anywhere in the world; they have made the modern world, in effect, even if they do not know it. The most illiterate among them is related, in a way that I am not, to Dante, Shakespeare, Michelangelo, Aeschylus, Da Vinci, Rembrandt, and Racine; the cathedral at Chartres says something to them which it cannot say to me, as indeed would New York's Empire State Building, should anyone here ever see it. Out of their hymns and dances come Beethoven and Bach. Go back a few centuries and they are in their full glory—but I am in Africa, watching the conquerors arrive.

10   The rage of the disesteemed is personally fruitless, but it is also absolutely inevitable; this rage, so generally discounted, so little understood even among the people whose daily bread it is, is one of the things that makes history. Rage can only with difficulty, and never entirely, be brought under the domination of the intelligence and is therefore not susceptible to any arguments whatever. This is a fact which ordinary representatives of the *Herren volk*,[4] having never felt this rage and being unable to imagine, quite fail to understand. Also, rage cannot be hidden, it can only be dissembled. This dissembling deludes the thoughtless, and strengthens rage and adds, to rage, contempt. There are, no doubt, as many ways of coping with the resulting complex of tensions as there are black men in the world, but no black man can hope ever to be entirely liberated from this internal warfare—rage, dissembling, and contempt having inevitably accompanied his first realization of the power of white men. What is crucial here is that, since white men represent in the black man's world so heavy a weight, white men have for black men a reality which is far from being reciprocal; and hence all black men have toward all white men an attitude which is designed, really, either to rob the white man of the jewel of his naïveté, or else to make it cost him dear.

The black man insists, by whatever means he finds at his disposal, that the white man cease to regard him as an exotic rarity and recognize him as a human being. This is a very charged and difficult moment, for there is a great

3. "Hellos" and "good evenings."
4. Master race.

deal of will power involved in the white man's naïveté. Most people are not naturally reflective any more than they are naturally malicious, and the white man prefers to keep the black man at a certain human remove because it is easier for him thus to preserve his simplicity and avoid being called to account for crimes committed by his forefathers, or his neighbors. He is inescapably aware, nevertheless, that he is in a better position in the world than black men are, nor can he quite put to death the suspicion that he is hated by black men therefore. He does not wish to be hated, neither does he wish to change places, and at this point in his uneasiness he can scarcely avoid having re-course to those legends which white men have created about black men, the most usual effect of which is that the white man finds himself enmeshed, so to speak, in his own language which describes hell, as well as the attributes which lead one to hell, as being as black as night.

Every legend, moreover, contains its residuum of truth, and the root func-tion of language is to control the universe by describing it. It is of quite con-siderable significance that black men remain, in the imagination, and in overwhelming numbers in fact, beyond the disciplines of salvation; and this de-spite the fact that the West has been "buying" African natives for centuries. There is, I should hazard, an instantaneous necessity to be divorced from this so visibly unsaved stranger, in whose heart, moreover, one cannot guess what dreams of vengeance are being nourished; and, at the same time, there are few things on earth more attractive than the idea of the unspeakable liberty which is allowed the unredeemed. When, beneath the black mask, a human being begins to make himself felt one cannot escape a certain awful wonder as to what kind of human being it is. What one's imagination makes of other people is dictated, of course, by the laws of one's own personality and it is one of the ironies of black-white relations that, by means of what the white man imagines the black man to be, the black man is enabled to know who the white man is.

I have said, for example, that I am as much a stranger in this village to-day as I was the first summer I arrived, but this is not quite true. The villagers wonder less about the texture of my hair than they did then, and wonder rather more about me. And the fact that their wonder now exists on another level is reflected in their attitudes and in their eyes. There are the children who make those delightful, hilarious, sometimes astonishingly grave over-tures of friendship in the unpredictable fashion of children; other children, having been taught that the devil is a black man, scream in genuine anguish as I approach. Some of the older women never pass without a friendly greet-ing, never pass, indeed, if it seems that they will be able to engage me in con-versation; other women look down or look away or rather contemptuously smirk. Some of the men drink with me and suggest that I learn how to ski— partly, I gather, because they cannot imagine what I would look like on skis— and want to know if I am married, and ask questions about my *métier*. But some of the men have accused *le sale nègre*[5]—behind my back—of stealing wood and there is already in the eyes of some of them that peculiar, intent,

5. The dirty Negro.

paranoiac malevolence which one sometimes surprises in the eyes of American white men when, out walking with their Sunday girl, they see a Negro male approach.

There is a dreadful abyss between the streets of this village and the streets of the city in which I was born, between the children who shout *Neger!* today and those who shouted *Nigger!* yesterday—the abyss is experience, the American experience. The syllable hurled behind me today expresses, above all, wonder: I am a stranger here. But I am not a stranger in America and the same syllable riding on the American air expresses the war my presence has occasioned in the American soul.

15   For this village brings home to me this fact: that there was a day, and not really a very distant day, when Americans were scarcely Americans at all but discontented Europeans, facing a great unconquered continent and strolling, say, into a marketplace and seeing black men for the first time. The shock this spectacle afforded is suggested, surely, by the promptness with which they decided that these black men were not really men but cattle. It is true that the necessity on the part of the settlers of the New World of reconciling their moral assumptions with the fact—and the necessity—of slavery enhanced immensely the charm of this idea, and it is also true that this idea expresses, with a truly American bluntness, the attitude which to varying extents all masters have had toward all slaves.

But between all former slaves and slave-owners and the drama which begins for Americans over three hundred years ago at Jamestown, there are at least two differences to be observed. The American Negro slave could not suppose, for one thing, as slaves in past epochs had supposed and often done, that he would ever be able to wrest the power from his master's hands. This was a supposition which the modern era, which was to bring about such vast changes in the aims and dimensions of power, put to death; it only begins, in unprecedented fashion, and with dreadful implications, to be resurrected today. But even had this supposition persisted with undiminished force, the American Negro slave could not have used it to lend his condition dignity, for the reason that this supposition rests on another: that the slave in exile yet remains related to his past, has some means—if only in memory—of revering and sustaining the forms of his former life, is able, in short, to maintain his identity.

This was not the case with the American Negro slave. He is unique among the black men of the world in that his past was taken from him, almost literally, at one blow. One wonders what on earth the first slave found to say to the first dark child he bore. I am told that there are Haitians able to trace their ancestry back to African kings, but any American Negro wishing to go back so far will find his journey through time abruptly arrested by the signature on the bill of sale which served as the entrance paper for his ancestor. At the time—to say nothing of the circumstances—of the enslavement of the captive black man who was to become the American Negro, there was not the remotest possibility that he would ever take power from his master's hands. There was no reason to suppose that his situation would ever change, nor was there, shortly, anything to indicate that his situation had ever been different. It was his necessity, in the words of E. Franklin Frazier,[6] to find a "motive for living under American culture or die." The identity of the American Negro comes out of this extreme situation, and the evolution of this identity was a source of the most intolerable anxiety in the minds and the lives of his masters.

For the history of the American Negro is unique also in this: that the question of his humanity, and of his rights therefore as a human being, became a burning one for several generations of Americans, so burning a question that it ultimately became one of those used to divide the nation. It is out of this argument that the venom of the epithet *Nigger!* is derived. It is an argument which Europe has never had, and hence Europe quite sincerely fails to understand how or why the argument arose in the first place, why its effects are frequently disastrous and always so unpredictable, why it refuses until today to be entirely settled. Europe's black possessions remained—and do remain—in Europe's colonies, at which remove they represented no threat whatever to European identity. If they posed any problem at all for the European conscience it was a problem which remained comfortingly abstract: in effect, the black man, as a *man* did not exist for Europe. But in America, even as a slave, he was an inescapable part of the general social fabric and no American could escape having an attitude toward him. Americans attempt until today to make an abstraction of the Negro, but the very nature of these abstractions reveals the tremendous effects the presence of the Negro has had on the American character.

When one considers the history of the Negro in America it is of the greatest importance to recognize that the moral beliefs of a person, or a people, are never really as tenuous as life—which is not moral—very often causes them to appear; these create for them a frame of reference and a necessary hope, the hope being that when life has done its worst they will be enabled to rise above themselves and to triumph over life. Life would scarcely be bearable if this hope did not exist. Again, even when the worst has been said, to betray a belief is not by any means to have put oneself beyond its power; the betrayal of a belief is not the same thing as ceasing to believe. If this were not so there would be no moral standards in the world at all. Yet one must also recognize that morality is based on ideas and that all ideas are dangerous—dangerous because ideas can only lead to action and where the action leads no man can say. And dangerous in this respect: that confronted with the impossibility of remaining faithful to one's beliefs, and the equal impossibility of becoming free of them, one can be driven to the most inhuman excesses. The ideas on which American beliefs are based are not, though Americans often seem to think so, ideas which originated in America. They came out of Europe. And the establishment of democracy on the American continent was scarcely as radical a break with the past as was the necessity, which Americans faced, of broadening this concept to include black men.

This was, literally, a hard necessity. It was impossible, for one thing, for Americans to abandon their beliefs, not only because these beliefs alone seemed able to justify the sacrifices they had endured and the blood that they

6. African American sociologist (1894–1962).

20

had spilled, but also because these beliefs afforded them their only bulwark against a moral chaos as absolute as the physical chaos of the continent it was their destiny to conquer. But in the situation in which Americans found themselves, these beliefs threatened an idea which, whether or not one likes to think so, is the very warp and woof of the heritage of the West, the idea of white supremacy.

Americans have made themselves notorious by the shrillness and the brutality with which they have insisted on this idea, but they did not invent it; and it has escaped the world's notice that those very excesses of which Americans have been guilty imply a certain, unprecedented uneasiness over the idea's life and power, if not, indeed, the idea's validity. The idea of white supremacy rests simply on the fact that white men are the creators of civilization (the present civilization, which is the only one that matters; all previous civilizations are simply "contributions" to our own) and are therefore civilization's guardians and defenders. Thus it was impossible for Americans to accept the black man as one of themselves, for to do so was to jeopardize their status as white men. But not so to accept him was to deny his human reality, his human weight and complexity, and the strain of denying the overwhelmingly undeniable forced Americans into rationalizations so fantastic that they approached the pathological.

At the root of the American Negro problem is the necessity of the American white man to find a way of living with the Negro in order to be able to live with himself. And the history of this problem can be reduced to the means used by Americans—lynch law and law, segregation and legal acceptance, terrorization and concession—either to come to terms with this necessity, or to find a way around it, or (most usually) to find a way of doing both these things at once. The resulting spectacle, at once foolish and dreadful, led someone to make the quite accurate observation that "the Negro-in-America is a form of insanity which overtakes white men."

In this long battle, a battle by no means finished, the unforeseeable effects of which will be felt by many future generations, the white man's motive was the protection of his identity; the black man was motivated by the need to establish an identity. And despite the terrorization which the Negro in America endured and endures sporadically until today, despite the cruel and totally inescapable ambivalence of his status in his country, the battle for his identity has long ago been won. He is not a visitor to the West, but a citizen there, an American; as American as the Americans who despise him, the Americans who fear him, the Americans who love him—the Americans who became less than themselves, or rose to be greater than themselves by virtue of the fact that the challenge he represented was inescapable. He is perhaps the only black man in the world whose relationship to white men is more terrible, more subtle, and more meaningful than the relationship of bitter possessed to uncertain possessors. His survival depended, and his development depends, on his ability to turn his peculiar status in the Western world to his own advantage and, it may be, to the very great advantage of that world. It remains for him to fashion out of his experience that which will give him sustenance, and a voice.

The cathedral at Chartres, I have said, says something to the people of this village which it cannot say to me; but it is important to understand that this cathedral says something to me which it cannot say to them. Perhaps they are struck by the power of the spires, the glory of the windows; but they have known God, after all, longer than I have known him, and in a different way, and I am terrified by the slippery bottomless well to be found in the crypt, down which heretics were hurled to death, and by the obscene, inescapable gargoyles jutting out of the stone and seeming to say that God and the devil can never be divorced. I doubt that the villagers think of the devil when they face a cathedral because they have never been identified with the devil. But I must accept the status which myth, if nothing else, gives me in the West before I can hope to change the myth.

Yet, if the American Negro has arrived at his identity by virtue of the absoluteness of his estrangement from his past, American white men still nourish the illusion that there is some means of recovering the European innocence, of returning to a state in which black men do not exist. This is one of the greatest errors Americans can make. The identity they fought so hard to protect has, by virtue of that battle, undergone a change: Americans are as unlike any other white people in the world as it is possible to be. I do not think, for example, that it is too much to suggest that the American vision of the world—which allows so little reality, generally speaking, for any of the darker forces in human life, which tends until today to paint moral issues in glaring black and white—owes a great deal to the battle waged by Americans to maintain between themselves and black men a human separation which could not be bridged. It is only now beginning to be borne in on us—very faintly, it must be admitted, very slowly, and very much against our will—that this vision of the world is dangerously inaccurate, and perfectly useless. For it protects our moral high-mindedness at the terrible expense of weakening our grasp of reality. People who shut their eyes to reality simply invite their own destruction, and anyone who insists on remaining in a state of innocence long after that innocence is dead turns himself into a monster.

The time has come to realize that the interracial drama acted out on the American continent has not only created a new black man, it has created a new white man, too. No road whatever will lead Americans back to the simplicity of this European village where white men still have the luxury of looking on me as a stranger. I am not, really, a stranger any longer for any American alive. One of the things that distinguishes Americans from other people is that no other people has ever been so deeply involved in the lives of black men, and vice versa. This fact faced, with all its implications, it can be seen that the history of the American Negro problem is not merely shameful, it is also something of an achievement. For even when the worst has been said, it must also be added that the perpetual challenge posed by this problem was always, somehow, perpetually met. It is precisely this black-white experience which may prove of indispensable value to us in the world we face today. This world is white no longer, and it will never be white again.

25

1. Baldwin begins with the narration of his experience in a Swiss village. At what point do you become aware that he has a larger point? What purpose does he make his experience serve?

2. Baldwin relates the white man's language and legends about black men to the "laws" of the white man's personality. What conviction about the source and the nature of language does this reveal?

3. Describe some particular experience that raises a large social question or shows the working of large social forces. Does Baldwin offer any help in the problem of connecting the particular and the general?

BRENT STAPLES   *Black Men and Public Space*

My FIRST VICTIM was a woman—white, well dressed, probably in her early twenties. I came upon her late one evening on a deserted street in Hyde Park, a relatively affluent neighborhood in an otherwise mean, impoverished section of Chicago. As I swung onto the avenue behind her, there seemed to be a discreet, uninflammatory distance between us. Not so. She cast back a worried glance. To her, the youngish black man—a broad six feet two inches with a beard and billowing hair, both hands shoved into the pockets of a bulky military jacket—seemed menacingly close. After a few more quick glimpses, she picked up her pace and was soon running in earnest. Within seconds she disappeared into a cross street.

That was more than a decade ago, I was twenty-two years old, a graduate student newly arrived at the University of Chicago. It was in the echo of that terrified woman's footfalls that I first began to know the unwieldy inheritance I'd come into—the ability to alter public space in ugly ways. It was clear that she thought herself the quarry of a mugger, a rapist, or worse. Suffering a bout of insomnia, however, I was stalking sleep, not defenseless wayfarers. As a softy who is scarcely able to take a knife to a raw chicken—let alone hold one to a person's throat—I was surprised, embarrassed, and dismayed all at once. Her flight made me feel like an accomplice in tyranny. It also made it clear that I was indistinguishable from the muggers who occasionally seeped into the area

Originally appeared in Harper's Magazine *(December 1986), an American monthly that continues its mission to "explore the issues and ideas in politics, science, and the arts that drive our national conversation." The essay was later incorporated into* Parallel Time: Growing Up in Black and White *(1994), an award-winning memoir of Staples's formative years in Chester, Pennsylvania, that chronicles his escape from poverty and crime and his brother's violent destruction.*

from the surrounding ghetto. That first encounter, and those that followed, signified that a vast, unnerving gulf lay between nighttime pedestrians—particularly women—and me. And I soon gathered that being perceived as dangerous is a hazard in itself. I only needed to turn a corner into a dicey situation, or crowd some frightened, armed person in a foyer somewhere, or make an errant move after being pulled over by a policeman. Where fear and weapons meet—and they often do in urban America—there is always the possibility of death.

In that first year, my first away from my hometown, I was to become thoroughly familiar with the language of fear. At dark, shadowy intersections, I could cross in front of a car stopped at a traffic light and elicit the *thunk, thunk, thunk, thunk* of the driver—black, white, male, or female—hammering down the door locks. On less traveled streets after dark, I grew accustomed to but never comfortable with people crossing to the other side of the street rather than pass me. Then there were the standard unpleasantries with policemen, doormen, bouncers, cabdrivers, and others whose business it is to screen out troublesome individuals *before* there is any nastiness.

I moved to New York nearly two years ago and I have remained an avid night walker. In central Manhattan, the near-constant crowd cover minimizes tense one-on-one street encounters. Elsewhere—in SoHo, for example, where sidewalks are narrow and tightly spaced buildings shut out the sky—things can get very taut indeed.

After dark, on the warrenlike streets of Brooklyn where I live, I often see women who fear the worst from me. They seem to have set their faces on neutral, and with their purse straps strung across their chests bandolier-style, they forge ahead as though bracing themselves against being tackled. I understand, of course, that the danger they perceive is not a hallucination. Women are particularly vulnerable to street violence, and young black males are drastically overrepresented among the perpetrators of that violence. Yet these truths are no solace against the kind of alienation that comes of being ever the suspect, a fearsome entity with whom pedestrians avoid making eye contact.

It is not altogether clear to me how I reached the ripe old age of twenty-two without being conscious of the lethality nighttime pedestrians attributed to me. Perhaps it was because in Chester, Pennsylvania, the small, angry industrial town where I came of age in the 1960s, I was scarcely noticeable against a backdrop of gang warfare, street knifings, and murders. I grew up one of the good boys, had perhaps a half-dozen fistfights. In retrospect, my shyness of combat has clear sources.

As a boy, I saw countless tough guys locked away; I have since buried several, too. They were babies, really—a teenage cousin, a brother of twenty-two, a childhood friend in his mid-twenties—all gone down in episodes of bravado played out in the streets. I came to doubt the virtues of intimidation early on. I chose, perhaps unconsciously, to remain a shadow—timid, but a survivor.

The fearsomeness mistakenly attributed to me in public places often has a perilous flavor. The most frightening of these confusions occurred in the late 1970s and early 1980s, when I worked as a journalist in Chicago. One day, rushing into the office of a magazine I was writing for with a deadline story in hand, I was mistaken for a burglar. The office manager called security and, with an ad hoc[1] posse, pursued me through the labyrinthine halls, nearly to my editor's door. I had no way of proving who I was. I could only move briskly toward the company of someone who knew me.

Another time I was on assignment for a local paper and killing time before an interview. I entered a jewelry store on the city's affluent Near North Side. The proprietor excused herself and returned with an enormous red Doberman pinscher straining at the end of a leash. She stood, the dog extended toward me, silent to my questions, her eyes bulging nearly out of her head. I took a cursory look around, nodded, and bade her good night.

10   Relatively speaking, however, I never fared as badly as another black male journalist. He went to nearby Waukegan, Illinois, a couple of summers ago to work on a story about a murderer who was born there. Mistaking the reporter for the killer, police officers hauled him from his car at gunpoint and but for his press credentials would probably have tried to book him. Such episodes are not uncommon. Black men trade tales like this all the time.

Over the years, I learned to smother the rage I felt at so often being taken for a criminal. Not to do so would surely have led to madness. I now take precautions to make myself less threatening. I move about with care, particularly late in the evening. I give a wide berth to nervous people on subway platforms during the wee hours, particularly when I have exchanged business clothes for jeans. If I happen to be entering a building behind some people who appear skittish, I may walk by, letting them clear the lobby before I return, so as not to seem to be following them. I have been calm and extremely congenial on those rare occasions when I've been pulled over by the police.

And on late-evening constitutionals I employ what has proved to be an excellent tension-reducing measure: I whistle melodies from Beethoven and Vivaldi and the more popular classical composers. Even steely New Yorkers hunching toward nighttime destinations seem to relax, and occasionally they even join in the tune. Virtually everybody seems to sense that a mugger wouldn't be warbling bright, sunny selections from Vivaldi's *Four Seasons*.[2] It is my equivalent of the cowbell that hikers wear when they know they are in bear country.

1. For a particular purpose; improvised.
2. Work by composer Antonio Vivaldi (1678–1741), celebrating the seasons.

QUESTIONS

1. Staples writes of situations rightly perceived as threatening and of situations misperceived as threatening. Give specific instances of each and tell how they are related.

2. Staples's essay contains a mixture of rage and humor. Does this mix distract from or contribute to the seriousness of the matter?

3. Write of a situation in which someone was wrongly perceived as threatening.

DEBRA DICKERSON *Who Shot Johnny?*

G IVEN MY LEVEL of political awareness, it was inevitable that I would come to view the everyday
events of my life through the prism of politics and
the national discourse. I read *The Washington
Post, The New Republic, The New Yorker, Harper's,
The Atlantic Monthly, The Nation, National Review,*
Black Enterprise and *Essence* and wrote a weekly column for the *Harvard Law
School Record* during my three years just ended there. I do this because I
know that those of us who are not well-fed white guys in suits must not yield
the debate to them, however well-intentioned or well-informed they may be.
Accordingly, I am unrepentant and vocal about having gained admittance to
Harvard through affirmative action; I am a feminist, stoic about my marriage
chances as a well-educated, 36-year-old black woman who won't pretend to
need help taking care of herself. My strength flags, though, in the face of the
latest role assigned to my family in the national drama. On July 27, 1995, my
16-year-old nephew was shot and paralyzed.

Talking with friends in front of his home, Johnny saw a car he thought he
recognized. He waved boisterously—his trademark—throwing both arms in
the air in a full-bodied, hip-hop Y. When he got no response, he and his
friends sauntered down the walk to join a group loitering in front of an apartment building. The car followed. The driver got out, brandished a revolver and
fired into the air. Everyone scattered. Then he took aim and shot my running
nephew in the back.

Johnny never lost consciousness. He lay in the road, trying to understand
what had happened to him, why he couldn't get up. Emotionlessly, he told the
story again and again on demand, remaining apologetically firm against all demands to divulge the missing details that would make sense of the shooting
but obviously cast him in a bad light. Being black, male and shot, he must, apparently, be gang- or drug-involved. Probably both. Witnesses corroborate his
version of events.

Nearly six months have passed since that phone call in the night and my
nightmarish, headlong drive from Boston to Charlotte. After twenty hours behind the wheel, I arrived haggard enough to reduce my mother to fresh tears
and to find my nephew reassuring well-wishers with an eerie sangfroid.[1]

I take the day shift in his hospital room; his mother and grandmother, a
clerk and cafeteria worker, respectively, alternate nights there on a cot. They
don their uniforms the next day, gaunt after hours spent listening to Johnny
moan in his sleep. How often must his subconscious replay those events

5

Published in the New Republic *(January 1, 1996), an American journal of politics and the
arts. The essay was selected for* Best American Essays *(1997), a yearly series that reprints
distinguished nonfiction from national and regional American magazines.*

1. Cold blood (French). Composure; self-assurance in the face of difficulty.

and curse its host for saying hello without permission, for being carefree and young while a would-be murderer hefted the weight of his uselessness and failure like Jacob Marley's chains?[2] How often must he watch himself lying stubbornly immobile on the pavement of his nightmares while the sound of running feet syncopate his attacker's taunts?

I spend these days beating him at gin rummy and Scrabble, holding a basin while he coughs up phlegm and crying in the corridor while he catheterizes himself. There are children here much worse off than he. I should be grateful. The doctors can't, or won't, say whether he'll walk again.

I am at once repulsed and fascinated by the bullet, which remains lodged in his spine (having done all the damage it can do, the doctors say). The wound is undramatic—small, neat and perfectly centered—an impossibly pink pit surrounded by an otherwise undisturbed expanse of mahogany. Johnny has asked me several times to describe it but politely declines to look in the mirror I hold for him.

Here on the pediatric rehab ward, Johnny speaks little, never cries, never complains, works diligently to become independent. He does whatever he is told; if two hours remain until the next pain pill, he waits quietly. Eyes blood-shot, hands gripping the bed rails. During the week of his intravenous feeding when he was tormented by the primal need to masticate, he never asked for food. He just listened while we counted down the days for him and planned his favorite meals. Now required to dress himself unassisted, he does so without de-mur, rolling himself back and forth valiantly on the bed and shivering after-wards, exhausted. He "ma'am"s and "sir"s everyone politely. Before his "accident," a simple request to take out the trash could provoke a firestorm of teenage attitude. We, the women who have raised him, have changed as well; we've finally come to appreciate those boxer-baring, oversized pants we used to hate—it would be much more difficult to fit properly sized pants over his diaper.

He spends a lot of time tethered to rap music still loud enough to break my concentration as I read my many magazines. I hear him try to soundlessly mouth the obligatory "mothafuckers" overlaying the funereal dirge of the music tracks. I do not normally tolerate disrespectful music in my or my mother's presence, but if it distracts him now . . .

10   "Johnny," I ask later, "do you still like gangster rap?" During the long pause I hear him think loudly, *I'm paralyzed Auntie, not stupid.* "I mostly just listen to hip hop," he says evasively into his *Sports Illustrated.*

Miserable though it is, time passes quickly here. We always seem to be jerking awake in our chairs just in time for the next pill, his every-other-night bowel program, the doctor's rounds. Harvard feels a galaxy away—the world revolves around Family Members Living With Spinal Cord Injury class, Johnny's urine output and strategizing with my sister to find affordable, accessible housing. There is always another long-distance uncle in need of an update, another

---

2. The ghost of Marley, in chains, visits Ebenezer Scrooge in Dickens's *A Christmas Carol.*

church member wanting to pray with us or Johnny's little brother in need of some attention.

We Dickerson women are so constant a presence the ward nurses and cleaning staff call us by name and join us for cafeteria meals and cigarette breaks. At Johnny's birthday pizza party, they crack jokes and make fun of each other's husbands (there are no men here). I pass slices around and try not to think, "17 with a bullet."

Oddly, we feel little curiosity or specific anger toward the man who shot him. We have to remind ourselves to check in with the police. Even so, it feels pro forma, like sending in those $2 rebate forms that come with new panty-hose: you know your request will fall into a deep, dark hole somewhere but, still, it's your duty to try. We push for an arrest because we owe it to Johnny and to ourselves as citizens. We don't think about it otherwise—our low expectations are too ingrained. A Harvard aunt notwithstanding, for people like Johnny, Marvin Gaye[3] was right that only three things are sure: taxes, death and trouble. At least it wasn't the second.

We rarely wonder about or discuss the brother who shot him because we already know everything about him. When the call came, my first thought was the same one I'd had when I'd heard about Rosa Parks's beating:[4] a brother did it. A non-job-having, middle-of-the-day malt-liquor-drinking, crotch-clutching, loud-talking brother with many neglected children born of many forgotten women. He lives in his mother's basement with furniture rented at an astronomical interest rate, the exact amount of which he does not know. He has a car phone, an $80 monthly cable bill and every possible phone feature but no savings. He steals Social Security numbers from unsuspecting relatives and assumes their identities to acquire large TV sets for which he will never pay. On the slim chance that he is brought to justice, he will have a colorful criminal history and no coherent explanation to offer for this act. His family will raucously defend him and cry cover-up. Some liberal lawyer just like me will help him plea bargain his way to yet another short stay in a prison pesthouse that will serve only to add another layer to the brother's sociopathology and formless, mindless nihilism. We know him. We've known and feared him all our lives.

As a teenager, he called, "Hey, baby, gimme somma that boodie!" at us from car windows. Indignant at our lack of response, he followed up with, "Fuck you, then, 'ho!" He called me a "white-boy lovin' nigger bitch oreo" for being in the gifted program and loving it. At 27, he got my 17-year-old sister pregnant with Johnny and lost interest without ever informing her that he was married. He snatched my widowed mother's purse as she waited in pre-dawn darkness for the bus to work and then broke into our house while she soldered on an assembly line. He chased all the small entrepreneurs from our neighbor-

15

---

3. African American soul singer (1939–1984) who was shot to death in an altercation with his father.
4. The elderly Rosa Parks, the 1950s civil rights pioneer, was the victim of a beating in the 1990s.

hood with his violent thievery, and put bars on our windows. He kept us from sitting on our own front porch after dark and laid the foundation for our periodic bouts of self-hating anger and racial embarrassment. He made our neighborhood a ghetto. He is the poster fool behind the maddening community knowledge that there are still some black mothers who raise their daughters but merely love their sons. He and his cancerous carbon copies eclipse the vast majority of us who are not sociopaths and render us invisible. He is the Siamese twin who has died but cannot be separated from his living, vibrant sibling; which of us must attract more notice? We despise and disown this anomalous loser but, for many, he *is* black America. We know him, we know that he is outside the fold, and we know that he will only get worse. What we didn't know is that, because of him, my little sister would one day be the latest hysterical black mother wailing over a fallen child on TV.

Alone, lying in the road bleeding and paralyzed but hideously conscious, Johnny had lain helpless as he watched his would-be murderer come to stand over him and offer this prophecy: "Betch'ou won't be doin' nomo' wavin', motha'fucker."

Fuck you, asshole. He's fine from the waist up. You just can't do anything right, can you?

QUESTIONS

1. Why did the *New Republic* include the first paragraph? Do you think the essay would be more or less effective if it began simply with the sentence "On July 27, 1995, my 16-year-old nephew was shot and paralyzed"?

2. Dickerson feels—and expresses—anger throughout this essay. How? Against what or whom?

3. Why does Dickerson use the term "brother" in the final paragraphs? How does this composite characterization work? How does it answer the question "Who shot Johnny?"

PROSE FORMS:
OP-EDS

*S*harp *disagreements over public policy, over what the government or a group or individual citizens should do, once took place almost entirely orally, in law courts and parliaments, in the Greek or Roman forum, or on famous occasions such as the Lincoln-Douglas debates. When newspapers and magazines grew popular in the 1700s, they helped carry these arguments into print. The Federalist Papers, by Alexander Hamilton, James Madison, and John Jay, were public policy arguments carried out in the pages of periodicals. Today we still have our political debates at election time, but they are very far removed from Lincoln and Douglas's. The quick-paced format dictated by TV—short opening and closing statements plus brief questions from a panel of reporters—does not lend itself to thoughtful explorations or even to sharply argued attacks of any complexity. It's hard to argue a complicated point in sound bites, so most public policy arguments now appear in print.*

Open any newspaper and, in addition to the news, you'll find a diversity of argument and individual opinion. Personal opinion appears in columns, critical opinion appears in reviews. Additionally, newspapers traditionally reserve a special place, the editorial page, for the owners' official stance on matters of politics, culture, and current events. On the editorial page the paper's owners endorse particular political candidates and take stands on current public controversies. The editorial page stands apart from the news sections; it's a place for discussion, commentary, and the expression of opinion. Often on or near the editorial page appear many of the paper's columnists. There too appears the letters section, a place for the paper's many constituents to sound off or to criticize articles and editorials they disagree with.

In the 1970s, in an effort to reach out more to readers, many newspapers expanded the space given to editorials and expressions of opinion. The term used for this section, "Op-Ed," emerged when the New York Times *appointed one of its most thoughtful editors, Charlotte Curtis, to oversee an enlargement of its editorial page. She doubled the size of the editorial content of the paper, reserving the page opposite the editorials (thus the name Op-Ed) for opinion, commissioning opinion pieces from a whole range of writers, and encouraging readers to write their own arguments.*

Nowadays, almost every paper has followed suit. Most have an editorial page devoted to the official opinion of the paper's owners or their deputies and often to letters from readers. Then, usually opposite the editorial page, is a page devoted to 500- to 800-word essays by professional columnists. Maureen Dowd, George Will, and William F. Buckley Jr., are some prominent current examples; most are "syndicated," that is, their work is bought and reprinted by many papers. On the Op-Ed page is space for similar essays by members of the general public, mostly people with strong ideas about public policy.

Although this section of The Norton Reader *takes its name from a newspaper innovation of the 1970s, it also includes many magazine pieces that argue for or against a point of view. Weekly or biweekly journals such as the* Nation, *the* National Review, *and the* New Republic *have small circulations but great influence, since they are read by policy makers. Such magazines have a long tradition of providing sharply argued essays and reviews on politics, current events, and the arts. And because they offer writers more space for their articles, they often attract more extended or more subtle treatments than a newspaper column can provide.*

Op-Ed essays and columns have some clear ground rules. Length is strictly limited: 500 to 800 words is usual in newspapers; magazine articles can be considerably longer. Styles range from the sharply argued, without a great deal of respect for the opponents, to mild, neutral-sounding inquiries into the logic of the issue. Tone ranges from thoughtful to smart-alecky; name-calling is permitted only discreetly; strongly argued pieces predominate, with nuances of argument tending to get lost in the shorter pieces. These pieces are timely; whether written for a newspaper or a magazine, all open with a hook, a clear reference to the issue at hand.

It is tempting to connect Op-Eds to high school and college debates, which feature starkly opposed viewpoints on an important issue. But many Op-Eds are often a good deal more complex. They are not at all like most school or college debate contests, which have only two possible sides to an issue, pro and con. Sometimes, for instance, the issue is not whether to allow or ban guns but which kinds of guns to regulate and how much regulation is reasonable. That's a more subtle issue, though people can get just as heated over it. Issues are usually not presented as starkly in print; in fact, one reason one writes such an essay is to lay out the issues or to show people what the real issues truly are. (We'll see writers do this in three essays on the issue of binge drinking.)

Furthermore, unlike debaters, who each have an equal chance of being the winner, given an impartial audience simply judging the performance (on logical as well as technical grounds), Op-Ed writers often do not realistically expect to emerge winners. Thoughtful writers know that their pieces will never change everyone's mind (that would take a miracle). Instead, they are often content to force their readers to face unpleasant truths or think in ways they might not have wanted to. Then, too, sometimes it's just important for "the other side" to be heard, to give its best arguments, not to be left out, to show the flag. Sometimes writers don't care about a victory; they would be content to shape the public debate, to point out what the key issues really are.

Molly Ivins: *Get a Knife, Get a Dog, but Get Rid of Guns*

Guns. Everywhere guns.

Let me start this discussion by pointing out that I am not antigun. I'm proknife. Consider the merits of the knife.

In the first place, you have to catch up with someone in order to stab him. A general substitution of knives for guns would promote physical fitness. We'd turn into a whole nation of great runners. Plus, knives don't ricochet. And people are seldom killed while cleaning their knives.

As a civil libertarian, I, of course, support the Second Amendment. And I believe it means exactly what it says:

A well-regulated militia being necessary to the security of a free state, the 5 *right of the people to keep and bear arms shall not be infringed.* Fourteen-year-old boys are not part of a well-regulated militia. Members of wacky religious cults are not part of a well-regulated militia. Permitting unregulated citizens to have guns is destroying the security of this free state.

I am intrigued by the arguments of those who claim to follow the judicial doctrine of original intent. How do they know it was the dearest wish of Thomas Jefferson's heart that teenage drug dealers should cruise the cities of this nation perforating their fellow citizens with assault rifles? Channeling?

There is more hooey spread about the Second Amendment. It says quite clearly that guns are for those who form part of a well-regulated militia, that is, the armed forces, including the National Guard. The reasons for keeping them away from everyone else get clearer by the day.

The comparison most often used is that of the automobile, another lethal object that is regularly used to wreak great carnage. Obviously, this society is full of people who haven't enough common sense to use an automobile properly. But we haven't outlawed cars yet.

We do, however, license them and their owners, restrict their use to presumably sane and sober adults, and keep track of who sells them to whom. At a minimum, we should do the same with guns.

In truth, there is no rational argument for guns in this society. This is no 10 longer a frontier nation in which people hunt their own food. It is a crowded, overwhelmingly urban country in which letting people have access to guns is a continuing disaster. Those who want guns—whether for target shooting, hunting, or potting rattlesnakes (get a hoe)—should be subject to the same restrictions placed on gun owners in England, a nation in which liberty has survived nicely without an armed populace.

The argument that "guns don't kill people" is patent nonsense. Anyone who has ever worked in a cop shop knows how many family arguments end in murder because there was a gun in the house. Did the gun kill someone? No.

Written for Ivins's regular column in the Fort Worth Star-Telegram *and collected in* Nothin' but Good Times Ahead *(1993). Ivins (1944–2007) was famous for her outspoken style, as suggested in the title of her book* Molly Ivins Can't Say That, Can She? *(1991).*

But if there had been no gun, no one would have died. At least not without a good foot race first. Guns do kill. Unlike cars, that is all they do.

Michael Crichton makes an interesting argument about technology in his thriller *Jurassic Park*.[1] He points out that power without discipline is making this society into a wreckage. By the time someone who studies the martial arts becomes a master—literally able to kill with bare hands—that person has also undergone years of training and discipline. But any fool can pick up a gun and kill with it.

"A well-regulated militia" surely implies both long training and long discipline. That is the least, the very least, that should be required of those who are permitted to have guns, because a gun is literally the power to kill. For years I used to enjoy taunting my gun-nut friends about their psychosexual hang-ups—always in a spirit of good cheer, you understand. But letting the noisy minority in the NRA[2] force us to allow this carnage to continue is just plain insane.

I do think gun nuts have a power hang-up. I don't know what is missing in their psyches that they need to feel they have the power to kill. But no sane society would allow this to continue.

15   Ban the damn things. Ban them all.

You want protection? Get a dog.

1. The 1990 novel Jurassic Park, made into a movie in 1994.
2. National Rifle Association.

QUESTIONS

1. What do you think of Ivins's examination of the Constitution? What kind of evidence would convince you even more? Why doesn't Ivins provide more evidence?

2. Characterize Ivins's language. What words, phrases, or structures seem typical of her style?

3. Examine the analogy between guns and cars. How does it hold up? Where does it break down?

JO-ANN PILARDI: *Immigration Problem Is About Us, Not Them*

The immigration debates always focus on small brown bodies jumping fences and scooting through the brush of our Southwestern states (land that was Mexico about 150 years ago).

Our self-righteous anger at those brown bodies is fueled by our narrow

Published as an Op-Ed in the Baltimore Sun *on June 7, 2006. Like many Op-Eds, this piece was not written by a professional journalist on the staff of the newspaper, but contributed by one of its readers, a professor of philosophy and women's studies at a nearby university.*

use of the word "illegal"—a term reserved only for those immigrant workers. Yet aren't there other "illegals" hiding in the American underbrush, and isn't it time to add to the American immigration lexicon a new term?

But where are those other "illegals"—the illegal employers of the illegal workers? Let's call them "illegal native employers." These INEs run the gamut from executives of hotel chains to presidents of agribusiness corporations in California, from nanny-employing parents to restaurant owners, from contractors to employment agencies. And let's not forget the INEs who own huge chicken-processing plants.

Where are the TV news videotapes of those illegals? Let's film them as they leave their homes and arrive at their corporate headquarters, their law offices, their retail establishments, their hotels, their construction sites. Do we dare humiliate them with our cameras—and call them felons?

I'd like to see the Minutemen set up a chapter far from the Arizona border   5
and patrol Wall Street, binoculars in hand, to set their sights on those "illegals"—brokers selling stocks for INE companies.

Let's build fences outside the INE businesses, to separate and stigmatize them. Maybe the National Guard should patrol those fences. Not to worry, though, because President Bush assures us the troops will not be "militarized." (The word is still out, though, on whether there will be bullets in their guns.)

No doubt, these suggestions make us squirm. Maybe that's because many of these "illegals" are us, or our friends or relatives. If 12 million undocumented workers are employed here, thousands of employers must be signing their paychecks.

If 12 million undocumented workers toil in this country as construction workers, gardeners, housekeepers, nannies, agricultural workers, food processors, then thousands of business owners, homeowners, politicians and government officials condone or welcome their work—and look the other way at their illegal status.

Many of our political leaders talk a hard line about "immigration reform" even though they know our country is mired in its demand for the immigrant work force. We use and exploit the labor of these millions every day. In doing so, we also weaken the wages, benefits and organizing power of all our workers.

The Senate voted 62-36 to approve its version of an immigration bill, with   10
most GOP senators opposing it. A battle with the more conservative House over its more vicious bill begins shortly. Evidently, the Senate version includes most of the so-called Ag Jobs bill, which has languished for years under the Bush administration and which has been supported in the past by the United Farm Workers.

Immigrants in the United States for two to five years would be put into a "temporary-worker" program; those here longer would be eligible for citizenship after an 11-year probationary period, with other criteria also to be met.

Conservatives describe the bill as "amnesty" for undocumented workers. So, once again, virtually all of the media attention centers on the workers, not the employers.

This is not the first time, nor will it be the last, that workers have come across the southern border in great numbers to make a living and to contribute to the U.S. economy. We need to create a fair immigration program for those who want to stay, not one that separates them by creating a national caste system of "guest workers." Europeans have learned the hard way that guest-worker programs lead to further national divisions and to virulent racism.

But whatever we do, we should stop thinking the problem is just about "securing our borders"—from them. The immigration problem is fundamentally a demand for cheap labor—for a supply to fill our demand.

15   Noting the problems that arose from Germany's guest-worker program, which imported masses of Turkish and southern European workers, the writer Max Frisch[1] observed, "Labor was called, but it was people who came." This—the moral, economic and political problem—is not the immigrants' problem; it's ours. I hope we have the courage to solve it humanely.

1. Swiss novelist (1911–1991) who often wrote about questions of personal identity.

QUESTIONS

1. What do you think the reaction would be if people did as Pilardi says and started hounding employers, the ones she terms INE?

2. Who benefits from illegal immigration? Who loses?

3. What does Pilardi have against the idea of "guest workers"? Why doesn't she think that solution would work? What do you think?

ANNA QUINDLEN: *In a Peaceful Frame of Mind*

It was the part about reading that got to me. By the time Joan and Chester Nimitz Jr. had decided to die together, their laundry list of physical losses was nearly as long as their rich and fruitful lives. Chester Nimitz, 86, a retired admiral and CEO and the son of the Pacific fleet commander in World War II, was suffering from congestive heart failure, constant back pain and stomach problems so severe that he'd lost 30 pounds. His wife, 89, who had gone to dental school in her native England but stayed at home to raise their three daughters, kept breaking bones because of osteoporosis and needed round-the-clock care. Once she went blind, she could no longer read.

Audio books or no audio books, the very notion of becoming incapable of seeing words on the page gave me a bad case of the shudders, and suggested that the distinction between a life worth living and one worth leaving is probably different for each of us.

Some may fear grinding pain unresponsive to medication. For others it would be the constant losses of physical degeneration or the end of independence, an existence supervised by caregivers. For Joan and Chester Nimitz,

First appeared in Quindlen's Newsweek *column on February 4, 2002.*

who until a few years ago lived a life full of gardening and golfing and reading, it was all of those. "Do not dial 911 in the event we are discovered unconscious but still alive," read a note left behind in their apartment at a retirement facility. It ended, "We wish our friends and relatives to know we are leaving their company in a peaceful frame of mind."

The greatest advance in health care in our lifetime has not been transplants or new pharmaceuticals. It has been the rise of the informed consumer. Beginning with the natural-childbirth movements and breast-cancer activism of the 1970s, inspired by AIDS patients who refused to take no for an answer, Americans have increasingly demanded more information and more control. People who once took orders from their physicians are now willing only to take advice. They look for information on Web sites, in newspapers and magazines, and in conversations with friends, so that cocktail parties sometimes sound more like hospital waiting rooms than social events.

Why would anyone expect people who have become knowledgeable about cholesterol and PSAs, chemotherapy and MRIs, to suddenly cede control at the end of life? Some medical professionals decried the decision the Nimitzes made, insisting that progress in pain management and advances in modern medicine made such draconian action unnecessary. Perhaps they have never been at the bedside of a dying person being tortured by continuing invasive treatment despite the fact that all hope of recovery is long gone. The truth is that modern medicine, which too often does things because they are possible, not because they are useful, has helped make some of this inevitable.

That is apparent in poll figures that show that two out of every three Americans support the right to euthanasia. It was apparent when the people of Oregon twice approved a statute supporting physician-assisted suicide in the form of a prescription for barbiturates for properly screened terminally ill patients. When that law went into effect in 1997, opponents predicted a bloodbath, vans of the depressed converging on the state in a mass suicide binge. Of course it didn't happen. In three years 70 people ended their lives after doctors determined they were already near death. But there are still those so-called right-to-life groups fighting the statute, and they've found a friend in John Ashcroft.[1] In the midst of all the other business of his office, the attorney general took time to try to subvert the will of the people by announcing that Oregon doctors would lose their prescription rights if they "participate in an assisted suicide."

His opponents were skeptical when Ashcroft said in the opening statement at his confirmation hearing, "I well understand that the role of attorney general is to enforce the law as it is, not as I would have it." Their skepticism was well founded. Ashcroft, a proponent of states' rights, even did a bit of jurisdiction shopping to attack the Oregon law from his federal perch. The editor of *Human Events*, a conservative weekly, said on radio that this was entirely proper: "It is the job of the federal government to go in and protect the life of the

1. The conservative attorney general—and thus the nation's chief law enforcement officer—during George W. Bush's first term as president.

person whose life is being taken, even if that person wants to commit suicide."

How unspeakably paternalistic and condescending! How contrary to the American ethos of self-determination and the right to be left alone. Should the Feds have sent marshals in to wrest pills away from the retired admiral and his well-read and tough-minded wife, united in their desire not to become shadows of their former selves? Chester Nimitz Jr., a man who had become accustomed in the service of his country to taking charge, left a meticulously organized file for his daughters labeled "WHEN CWN DIES." He ended his life sooner rather than later because he was afraid if he died first of heart disease his wife would not be strong enough to take pills on her own. "That's the one last thing I have to do for your mother," he told one of his daughters. Since the Nimitzes's deaths their daughters have received many letters, filled with rage and grief, from other grown children detailing the indignities their parents suffered during the dying process.

Maybe you believe you could live with the pain, or the immobility, or the incontinence, or the fear, or the loss of literacy. Maybe you wouldn't mind the tubes or the injections or the medications keeping you alive even if you were only days from death, even if you were turned into a medical marionette. But those who can't bear those conditions should be able to use any means to avoid spending their last days or months or even years in a situation they find humiliating and degrading. Some doctors have determined that life ends with something called brain death; perhaps there are those who conclude that it ought to end with life death, the depletion and disappearance of those things that have defined them and given them solace and pleasure. Then, as Chester and Joan Nimitz wrote, "consciously, rationally, deliberately," lights out.

QUESTIONS

1. Quindlen's Op-Ed is a partisan piece, and so we shouldn't expect her to argue for both sides of the issue. What are the other perspectives Quindlen leaves out?

2. How does Quindlen personalize the issue? Point to places in her writing that "make the political personal, and the personal political."

3. Quindlen writes of "life death" in her final paragraph. What would constitute "life death" for you? Write about it in a brief essay.

BRENT STAPLES: *Why Colleges Shower Their Students with A's*

The economist Milton Friedman taught that superior products flourished and shabby ones died out when consumers voted emphatically with their dollars. But the truth of the marketplace is that shabby products can do just fine if they sustain the veneer of quality while slipping downhill, as has much of higher education. Faced with demanding consumers and stiff competition,

Published on the Op-Ed page of the New York Times *(March 8, 1998).*

colleges have simply issued more and more A's, stoking grade inflation and de-valuing degrees.

Grade inflation is in full gallop at every level, from struggling community institutions to the elites of the Ivy League. In some cases, campuswide aver-ages have crept up from a C just 10 years ago to B-plus today.

Some departments shower students with A's to fill poorly attended courses that might otherwise be canceled. Individual professors inflate grades after consumer-conscious administrators hound them into it. Professors at every level inflate to escape negative evaluations by students, whose opinions now figure in tenure and promotion decisions.

The most vulnerable teachers are the part-timers who have no job security and who now teach more than half of all college courses. Writing in the last is-sue of the journal *Academe,* two part-timers suggest that students routinely corner adjuncts, threatening to complain if they do not turn C's into A's. An Ivy League professor said recently that if tenure disappeared, universities would be "free to sell diplomas outright."

The consumer appetite for less rigorous education is nowhere more evi-dent than in the University of Phoenix, a profit-making school that shuns traditional scholarship and offers a curriculum so superficial that critics compare it to a drive-through restaurant. Two hundred colleges have closed since a businessman dreamed up Phoenix 20 years ago. Meanwhile, the uni-versity has expanded to 60 sites spread around the country, and more than 40,000 students, making it the country's largest private university.   5

Phoenix competes directly with the big state universities and lesser-known small colleges, all of which fear a student drain. But the elite schools fear each other and their customers, the students, who are becoming increasingly restive about the cost of a first-tier diploma, which now exceeds $120,000. Faced with the prospect of crushing debt, students are treating grades as a matter of life and death—occasionally even suing to have grades revised upward.

Twenty years ago students grumbled, then lived with the grades they were given. Today, colleges of every stature permit them to appeal low grades through deans or permanent boards of inquiry. In *The Chronicle of Higher Ed-ucation,* Prof. Paul Korshin of the University of Pennsylvania recently de-scribed his grievance panel as the "rhinoplasty committee," because it does "cosmetic surgery" on up to 500 transcripts a year.

The argument that grades are rising because students are better prepared is simply not convincing. The evidence suggests that students and parents are demanding—and getting—what they think of as their money's worth.

One way to stanch inflation is to change the way the grade point average is calculated. Under most formulas, all courses are given equal weight, so math, science and less-challenging courses have equal impact on the averages. This arrangement rewards students who gravitate to courses where high marks are generously given and punishes those who seek out math and science courses, where far fewer students get the top grade.

Valen Johnson, a Duke University statistics professor, came under heavy fire from both students and faculty when he proposed recalculating the   10 grade point average to give rigorously graded courses greater weight. The student government beat back the plan with the help of teachers in the humanities, who worried that students might abandon them for other courses that they currently avoided. Other universities have expressed interest in adopting the Johnson plan, but want their names kept secret to avoid a backlash.

Addicted to counterfeit excellence, colleges, parents and students are unlikely to give it up. As a consequence, diplomas will become weaker and more ornamental as the years go by.

QUESTIONS

1. What is the grade situation on your campus? Have you been showered with A's recently? Have you noticed professors inflating grades?

2. Staples writes, "An Ivy League professor said recently that if tenure disappeared, universities would be 'free to sell diplomas outright' " (paragraph 4). Analyze this statement. What are its implications? Why does the professor think tenured faculty serve as protection against the "selling" of diplomas? What level of confidence does this professor have in the administration?

3. A Duke University statistics professor proposed "recalculating the grade point average to give rigorously graded courses greater weight" (paragraph 10). He was opposed by humanities professors. What might have been the source of their opposition? What do you think is meant by "rigorously graded"? What is the situation on your campus: do math profs grade more "rigorously" than English profs? Who are the hardest graders?

4. How broad is Staples's range of examples? Would he need to adjust his position if he considered other colleges? Write an analysis of the situation at your college either to confirm or to contest Staples's argument.

DAVID BROOKS: *The Gender Gap at School*

There are three gender-segregated sections in any airport: the restrooms, the security pat-down area and the bookstore. In the men's sections of the bookstore, there are books describing masterly men conquering evil. In the women's sections there are novels about well, I guess feelings and stuff.

The same separation occurs in the home. Researchers in Britain asked 400 accomplished women and 500 accomplished men to name their favorite novels. The men preferred novels written by men, often revolving around loneliness and alienation. Camus's *The Stranger*, Salinger's *Catcher in the Rye* and Vonnegut's *Slaughterhouse-Five* topped the male list.

The women leaned toward books written by women. The women's books described relationships and are a lot better than the books the men chose. The

Published on June 11, 2006, in the New York Times, *where Brooks writes a regular Op-Ed column.*

top six women's books were *Jane Eyre*, *Wuthering Heights*, *The Handmaid's Tale*, *Middlemarch*, *Pride and Prejudice* and *Beloved*.

There are a couple of reasons why the two lists might diverge so starkly. It could be men are insensitive dolts who don't appreciate subtle human connections and good literature. Or, it could be that the part of the brain where men experience negative emotion, the amygdala[1], is not well connected to the part of the brain where verbal processing happens, whereas the part of the brain where women experience negative emotion, the cerebral cortex,[2] is well connected. It could be that women are better at processing emotion through words.

Over the past two decades, there has been a steady accumulation of evidence that male and female brains work differently. Women use both sides of their brain more symmetrically than men. Men and women hear and smell differently (women are much more sensitive). Boys and girls process colors differently (young girls enjoy an array of red, green and orange crayons whereas young boys generally stick to black, gray and blue). Men and women experience risk differently (men enjoy it more). 5

It could be, in short, that biological factors influence reading tastes, even after accounting for culture. Women who have congenital adrenal hyperplasia[3], which leads to high male hormone secretions, are more likely to choose violent stories than other women.

This wouldn't be a problem if we all understood these biological factors and if teachers devised different curriculums to instill an equal love of reading in both boys and girls.

The problem is that even after the recent flurry of attention about why boys are falling behind, there is still intense social pressure not to talk about biological differences between boys and girls (ask Larry Summers)[4]. There is still resistance, especially in the educational world, to the findings of brain researchers. Despite some innovations here and there, in most classrooms boys and girls are taught the same books in the same ways.

Young boys are compelled to sit still in schools that have sacrificed recess for test prep. Many are told in a thousand subtle ways they are not really good students. They are sent home with these new-wave young adult problem novels, which all seem to be about introspectively morose young women whose parents are either suicidal drug addicts or fatally ill manic depressives.

It shouldn't be any surprise that according to a National Endowment for the Arts study, the percentage of young men who read has plummeted over the past 14 years. Reading rates are falling three times as fast among young men 10

1. The portion of the brain that controls emotions and memory.
2. The part of the brain that controls awareness, language, and consciousness.
3. A genetic defect of the adrenal glands. A person with adrenal hyperplasia cannot produce several vital hormones known as corticosteroids, which are significant in sex identification.
4. President of Harvard, 2001–06, who resigned after making controversial remarks about women's biological fitness to pursue careers in science.

as among young women. Nor should it be a surprise that men are drifting away from occupations that involve reading and school. Men now make up a smaller share of teachers than at any time in the past 40 years.

Dr. Leonard Sax,[5] whose book *Why Gender Matters* is a lucid guide to male and female brain differences, emphasizes that men and women can excel at any subject. They just have to be taught in different ways. Sax is a big believer in single-sex schools, which he says allow kids to open up and break free from gender stereotypes. But for most kids it would be a start if they were assigned books they might actually care about. For boys, that probably means more Hemingway, Tolstoy, Homer and Twain.

During the 1970's, it was believed that gender is a social construct and that gender differences could be eliminated via consciousness-raising. But it turns out gender is not a social construct. Consciousness-raising doesn't turn boys into sensitively poetic pacifists. It just turns many of them into high school and college dropouts who hate reading.

5. A Maryland family physician and psychologist who wrote *Why Gender Matters* and *Boys Adrift: What's Really Behind the Growing Epidemic of Unmotivated Boys?*

QUESTIONS

1. Does your experience bear out Brooks's claim that boys and girls read differently? Use some examples from people you know.

2. Examine the evidence that Brooks marshals for his claim that girls' and boys' brains are different. Do you think Brooks produces enough evidence to support his claim? Do you know of evidence that he omits?

3. Do a brief survey of favorite books of males and females, and see if it bears out Brooks's claim. Write up your findings in a brief report or counterargument.

JENNIFER BRITZ: *The Dean's Daughter Gets Thin Envelope*

A few days ago I watched my daughter Madalyn open a thin envelope from one of the five colleges to which she had applied. "Why?" was what she was obviously asking herself as she handed me the letter saying she was wait-listed.

Why, indeed? She had taken the toughest courses in her high school and had done well, sat through several Saturday mornings taking SAT's and the like, participated in the requisite number of extracurricular activities, written a heartfelt and well-phrased essay and even taken the extra step of touring the campus.

Written by an admissions officer at Kenyon College, and originally published with the title "To All the Girls I've Rejected" in the New York Times *(March 23, 2006); this Op-Ed was reprinted under different titles in many other U.S. newspapers during the college admissions season.*

She had not, however, been named a National Merit finalist, dug a well for a village in Africa or climbed to the top of Mount Ranier. She is a smart, well-meaning, hard-working teenage girl, but in this day and age of swollen applicant pools that are decidedly female, that wasn't enough. The fat acceptance envelope is simply more elusive for today's accomplished young women.

I know this well. At my own college these days, we have three applicants for every one we can admit. Just three years ago, it was two to one. Though Kenyon was a men's college until 1969, more than 55 percent of our applicants are female, a proportion that is steadily increasing. My staff and I carefully read these young women's essays about their passion for poetry, their desire to discover vaccines and their conviction that they can make the world a better place.

I was once one of those girls applying to college, but that was 30 years   5
ago, when applying to college was only a tad more difficult than signing up for a membership at the Y. Today, it's a complicated and prolonged dance that begins early, and for young women, there is little margin for error: A grade of C in Algebra II/Trig? Off to the waitlist you go.

Rest assured that admissions officers are not cavalier in making their decisions. Last week, the 10 officers at my college sat around a table, 12 hours every day, deliberating the applications of hundreds of talented young men and women. While gulping down coffee and poring over statistics, we heard about a young woman from Kentucky we were not yet ready to admit outright. She was the leader/president/editor/captain/lead actress in every activity in her school. She had taken six advanced placement courses and had been selected for a prestigious state leadership program. In her free time, this whirlwind of achievement had accumulated more than 300 hours of community service in four different organizations.

Few of us sitting around the table were as talented and as directed at age 17 as this young woman. Unfortunately, her test scores and grade point average placed her in the middle of our pool. We had to have a debate before we decided to swallow the middling scores and write "admit" next to her name.

Had she been a male applicant, there would have been little, if any, hesitation to admit. The reality is that because young men are rarer, they're more valued applicants. Today, two-thirds of colleges and universities report that they get more female than male applicants, and more than 56 percent of undergraduates nationwide are women. Demographers predict that by 2009, only 42 percent of all baccalaureate degrees awarded in the United States will be given to men.

We have told today's young women that the world is their oyster; the problem is, so many of them believed us that the standards for admission to today's most selective colleges are stiffer for women than men.

How's that for an unintended consequence of the women's liberation   10
movement?

The elephant that looms large in the middle of the room is the importance of gender balance. Should it trump the qualifications of talented young female applicants? At those colleges that have reached what the experts call a "tipping point," where 60 percent or more of their enrolled students are female, you'll hear a hint of desperation in the voices of admissions officers.

Beyond the availability of dance partners for the winter formal, gender balance matters in ways both large and small on a residential college campus. Once you become decidedly female in enrollment, fewer males and, as it turns out, fewer females find your campus attractive.

What are the consequences of young men discovering that even if they do less, they have more options? And what messages are we sending young women that they must, nearly 25 years after the defeat of the Equal Rights Amendment, be even more accomplished than men to gain admission to the nation's top colleges? These are questions that admissions officers like me grapple with.

In the meantime, I'm sending out wait list and rejection letters for nearly 3,000 students. Unfortunately, a majority of them will be female, young women just like my daughter. I will linger over letters, remembering individual students I've met, essays I loved, accomplishments I've admired. I know all too well that parents will ache when their talented daughters read the letters and will feel a bolt of anger at the college admissions officers who didn't recognize how special their daughters are.

15   Yes, of course, these talented young women will all find fine places to attend college—Maddie has four acceptance letters in hand—but it doesn't dilute the disappointment they will feel when they receive a rejection or waitlist offer.

I admire the brilliant successes of our daughters. To parents and the students getting thin envelopes, I apologize for the demographic realities.

QUESTIONS

1. Britz wrote this Op-Ed while serving as an admissions officer and while her own daughter was applying to college. Does the fact that Britz's daughter received four acceptances from colleges change your attitude toward the author's case?

2. In the course of her commentary Britz marshals statistics. What function do they serve? How does she balance—or reflect on—statistics with anecdotes, memories, and probing questions?

3. Compare Britz's essay with Brooks's "The Gender Gap at School" (p. 412) and decide whether colleges should have different standards for judging male and female candidates.

4. In paragraph 11, Britz poses a question: "Should it [gender balance] trump the qualifications of talented young female applicants?" Write an opinion piece in which you address this question, using facts and statistics as well as personal experience and anecdotes.

T he three Op-Ed pieces that follow all deal with binge drinking by contemporary college students. Drinking too much is not, of course, a recent phenomenon. We know from diaries, letters, and memoirs that many young people in the eighteenth and nineteenth centuries drank too much, whether after work in a pub or tavern, during their school days in a university room, or when out for an occasional night on the town. We also know that overdrinking in those centuries was railed against (in moral treatises), lamented (in sermons and lectures), and satirized (as in William Hogarth's famous print depicting a drunken "Idle Apprentice" or in George Cruikshank's "Gin Lane").

Why, then, has binge drinking—a recently defined term—become a matter for such serious concern in the public press and in educational journals and newsletters? You may want to propose answers in class discussion, but surely one cause lies in the research of medical scientists at the Harvard School of Public Health who, in the early 1990s, identified and studied the problem, then published their findings in scholarly journals, including the prestigious Journal of the American Medical Association (JAMA).

We have included one example of this medical research in the section "Science and Technology": the article "Health and Behavioral Consequences of Binge Drinking in College: A National Survey of Students at 140 Campuses" (p. 976). For this Op-Ed section, however, we have chosen the scientists' expression of personal concern, written for the educational journal the Chronicle of Higher Education, which devotes its final page to opinion pieces submitted by members of the academic community. Also included in this section are two very different responses to the research, one from the New York Times Magazine, another from the Chronicle of Higher Education, both drawing on personal experience but reaching quite different conclusions.

The debate over binge drinking is still ongoing today. Consult the Harvard School of Public Health Web site (www.hsph.harvard.edu/cas) for the latest research—or look in your own local newspaper or alumni magazine for the latest exchange.

HENRY WECHSLER, CHARLES DEUTSCH, AND GEORGE DOWDALL:

Too Many Colleges Are Still in Denial about Alcohol Abuse

Colleges have a serious problem with alcohol abuse among students, and it's not getting any better. In 1989, a survey by the Carnegie Foundation

Written for the Chronicle of Higher Education (April 14, 1995) and based on the research of the authors in the Harvard School of Public Health. For a recent overview of the extensive findings of these scientists and the implications of their research for college campuses, see the book, coauthored by Wechsler and Bernice Wuethrich, Dying to Drink: Confronting Binge Drinking on College Campuses (2002); for a scientific version of the research, see Wechsler et al., "Health and Behavioral Consequences of Binge Drinking in College," included in "Science and Technology," p. 976.

for the Advancement of Teaching found that college presidents viewed alcohol abuse as their top campus-life problem. The recent national surveys of college students' drinking that we conducted for Harvard University's School of Public Health documented that alcohol abuse is still rife. Perhaps the second-largest problem in campus life is that many colleges are still in denial, just as many family members who live with alcohol abusers are.

To be sure, on some campuses officials are making great efforts to reduce alcohol abuse. At others, however, they seem oblivious to the magnitude and effects of the abuse. Those in denial act as if they believe that this deep-seated American problem can be changed by someone, able and dedicated, working part time in a basement office at the student-health service.

Alcohol abuse is a common, not a marginal, activity at most colleges, and we only fool ourselves if we expect marginal efforts to reduce it. If we really want to deal with the problem, administrators, faculty members, students, and parents must first gain a better understanding of how excessive drinking is affecting the academic and social climate of their institutions. Second, they must believe there are promising, practical strategies they can adopt that will improve the situation. Finally, they must be prepared to contend with the skepticism and resistance bound to be aroused by actions designed to curb the abuse.

We should stress that our concern is with students' alcohol *abuse*—the drinking of amounts large enough to create problems for the drinker or for others around him or her. The crux of the problem is the *behavior* of the drinker, not the quantity of alcohol consumed. When people do dangerous or obnoxious things when they drink, that's alcohol abuse. Unfortunately, behavior that anywhere else would be classified as alcohol abuse now is not only acceptable but actually the norm on many campuses, in spite of excessive drinking's documented role in automobile crashes, violence, suicide, and high-risk sexual behavior.

5   Certainly, excessive drinking is not a new problem, on campus or in the society the campus reflects. A local sheriff still leads Harvard University's graduation procession, a tradition that began in Colonial days, not for a ceremonial purpose but to control drunk and rowdy celebrants. Generations of college alumni have wistfully recalled the boozy high jinks of their student days, filtering out memories of illness, insane risk, unwanted consequences, and friends who never made it out of the hole they had dug for themselves.

Some alumni no doubt think their children and grandchildren deserve the same "good times." The problem is that, because of lethal sexually transmitted diseases, the easy availability of weapons, and roads filled with high-speed automobiles, the consequences of alcohol abuse are much more deadly today.

Binge drinking—defined as the heavy, episodic use of alcohol—has persisted on campuses despite both a general decrease in alcohol consumption among Americans and an increase in the number of abstainers. Some people (including the author of a recent front-page article in *The New York Times*) have assumed that the latter two trends have translated into more-moderate drinking on the campuses. Nothing could be further from the truth.

Our recent research, which received support from the Robert Wood Johnson Foundation, was the only large-scale study to date of the extent and consequences of binge drinking at a representative sample of American colleges and universities. Our detailed findings from surveys of 17,592 students at 140 randomly selected four-year colleges were published in the December 7, 1994, issue of the *Journal of the American Medical Association.*

For men, our study used the generally accepted criterion for binge drinking: the consumption of five or more drinks in a row at least once in the previous two weeks. We reduced the number of drinks to four in a row for women, to take into account our findings that for the average college woman four drinks produce the same level of alcohol-related problems as do five drinks for the average college man.

Our study found that 44 per cent of all students in the sample were binge 10 drinkers—50 per cent of the men and 39 per cent of the women. Although our 1993 study was the only one to survey a representative sample of colleges, the findings were very similar to those of two other national surveys conducted at about the same time. A study done in 1993 by the Institute for Social Research of the University of Michigan found that 40 per cent of the college students surveyed were binge drinkers. And a similar study, conducted from 1990 to 1992 by the Core Institute at Southern Illinois University, also put the figure at 40 per cent. Had our study used a five-drink standard for women, as the other two studies did, 41 per cent of the students surveyed would have been classified as binge drinkers. The agreement among these three independent national studies is remarkable.

Certainly, not all students who have ever binged have an alcohol problem, but colleges with large numbers of binge drinkers *do.* The proportion of binge drinkers among students varied considerably among the 140 colleges in our study—from as low as 1 per cent to as high as 70 per cent. At 44 colleges, more than half of the students responding to the survey were binge drinkers. This variation contradicts the belief that among college students we will find a fairly constant and intractable proportion who will drink to excess. It suggests, instead, that colleges create or perpetuate their own drinking cultures through their selection of students, traditions, policies, and other practices.

Not surprisingly, our study shows a strong relationship between the frequency of binge drinking and alcohol-related problems. Nineteen per cent of all students qualify as frequent binge drinkers—those who binge more than once a week. They were found to be from seven to ten times as likely as non-binge drinkers to fail to use protection when having sex, to engage in unplanned sexual activity, to get into trouble with campus police, to damage property, or to suffer an injury. Half of the frequent binge drinkers reported experiencing five or more *different* alcohol-related problems. Yet very few of those students considered themselves to have an alcohol problem or even to be heavy drinkers.

Our findings break new ground in exploring the extent to which alcohol-related behavior obstructs the possibility of "building communities of civility and respect on campuses," to borrow the title of this year's annual convention of the American Council on Education. On campuses where more than half of the students were binge drinkers, the vast majority of the non-binge drinkers who lived on campus—fully 87 per cent—reported experiencing one or more problems as a result of others' binge drinking. They were the victims of what we call "second-hand binge effects." Such students were up to three times as likely as students on campuses where 35 per cent or fewer of students binge to report being pushed, hit, or assaulted, experiencing an unwanted sexual advance, or otherwise being bothered by the alcohol-related behavior of other students.

Colleges cannot claim to create a supportive learning environment when they tolerate such behavior. To fulfill their missions, colleges will have to reduce alcohol abuse markedly. How can this be done? Each college has its own level of binge drinking, traditions, and circumstances and thus must craft its own response to the problem. Still, our findings suggest strategies that could be effective.

15   Administrators must first decide where to focus their energies. They should realize that about 85 per cent of all college students drink (although they do not all binge) and that alcohol is easily available to students regardless of age. Thus programs at many colleges that seek to reduce drinking among all students are doomed to failure. Other programs try to inform binge drinkers about ways to avoid harmful consequences—for example, by designating a non-drinking friend to drive. But in a social system rife with alcohol abuse, whether a family or a campus, the least effective intervention point is the abuser.

Prevention cannot depend solely on the individual alcohol abuser's recognition of the problem and his or her willingness to accept help, nor can it depend on the cooperation of student organizations that are heavily involved in alcohol abuse. In fact, our study found that more than 80 per cent of the students residing in fraternities or sororities were binge drinkers. If a college or university really aspires to be a community of civility and respect, the principal goal of its prevention efforts must be to help students who are adversely affected by the binge drinking of others to assert their rights. These students deserve to learn that college life need not include cleaning up after a vomiting roommate; being awakened at 3 A.M. several nights a week by revelers; or being physically, verbally, or sexually assaulted.

Students, faculty and staff members, administrators, and trustees should establish and enforce explicit rules about what kinds of behavior will not be tolerated. And since binge drinking is a highly social activity, colleges must offer better ways to help students make friends, find romance, and keep busy. We found that the students who spent the most time studying, performing community service, or working were the least likely to be binge drinkers.

Furthermore, because half of the students who binge in college were binge drinkers in high school, colleges should use the admission process to influence the drinking culture on campus. They can do this by making clear in their promotional material and through the information that recruiters provide to high-school teachers and counselors that they will protect the right of all students to an educational environment free from alcohol abuse and abusive behavior.

College officials also need to work more closely with city officials and with local businesses that sell alcohol to eliminate the sales to minors and to discourage "half-price beer nights" and other practices that encourage drunkenness. For their part, athletics directors can have enormous influence on the drinking culture of a campus if they can be pressed to use it constructively with their athletes. Finally, residence-hall advisers and academic counselors can play a key role in preventing alcohol abuse by intervening quickly in incidents of public drunkenness that violate codes of conduct. But they need much better training and support from the administration than most of them now receive.

Before these or other constructive steps can be taken, campus authorities must stop denying the extent of the problem. Denial includes failing to recognize the impact and extensiveness of campus alcohol abuse and acting as if easy stratagems will produce change. 20

We recommend a weekend tour, beginning on Thursday night. As the night progresses, observe the campus and the clubs on its outskirts. Drop in on the health services, the fraternity houses, and the dorms in the early morning hours. Take a late-night ride with a security guard. Check out class attendance on Friday.

On Saturday, repeat the process. And later station yourself outside sorority houses and residence halls on Sunday morning and witness "the walk of shame"—a phrase students use to describe women's returning from a night's unplanned, and often unprotected, sex. Ask students to describe drinking behavior. Above all, fight the temptation to think of the alcohol abuse you see as merely the problem of "troubled" individuals. When the faces change but the numbers don't, something much more powerful and institutional is happening.

Don't expect change to be easy. Opponents of significant change will cite longstanding traditions, the need not to scare students away in a highly competitive marketplace, the damage to the institution's image of publicly acknowledging an alcohol problem, the real or imagined vulnerability of the institution to legal action, the displeasure of local merchants who depend on student drinking, and opposition from campus newspapers that depend on advertisements from those businesses.

But if you want change, acknowledge the existence of alcohol abuse and the challenge it poses to the college's mission. Commit resources from all parts of the institution, with visible support from the president, to coordinated, long-term actions. Make your intentions clear, not just in speeches but also in the budget. And expect change to be gradual. Remember, not so long ago we resigned ourselves to smoke-filled offices and thought little could be done to stop drunk driving.

QUESTIONS

1. This article, written for college administrators, is a heavily revised version of a scientific study (see the authors' research article in "Science and Technology," p. 976). Note the changes you see between the original study and this version. Are they changes in style? In audience? In format? In details? Which changes matter most to the overall impact of the essays?

2. What does the term "in denial" mean? Where does it come from? Do authorities on your campus act as if they were "in denial" about alcohol abuse?

3. Take the "weekend tour" the authors recommend on your own campus or a campus you know. Write up your results as a newspaper article.

JACK HITT: *The Battle of the Binge*

Back in the 70's—my college time—an English professor I barely knew named Ted Stirling spotted me on the quad and invited me to a small, informal reading after supper. Maybe he felt sorry for me. I had marooned myself in the French ghetto of *la littérature comparative*, and had further exiled myself in the cul-de-sac between Latin and Spanish. So I went that night to sit on stuffed sofas beneath scowling bishops in gilt frames and to discuss Wallace Stevens's poem "Thirteen Ways of Looking at a Blackbird." Afterward, Stirling bought the students a pitcher of beer at the pub, and we strained to act intelligently and comfortably while drinking with an elder. ("Stevens an insurance agent! Surely you jest, Professor. Why, that would make poets the unacknowledged underwriters of the world, wouldn't you agree?")

I started thinking about how I learned to drink at college—I went to Sewanee, in Tennessee—when I read about a recent Harvard study that found that 43 percent, nearly half, of all college students today "binge drink," defined as regularly pounding down four or five stiff ones in a row in order to get blasted. The pandemic is so severe that 113 college presidents united a few weeks ago to publicly admit that a generation is in peril. They have also rolled out a public-service ad, which employs that brand of sarcasm Madison Avenue thinks young people find amusing. "Binge Beer," it says. "Who says falling off a balcony is such a bad thing?" See, you're supposed to realize that falling off a balcony is, in fact, a bad thing.

Other educational tactics include dry rock concerts, abstinent fraternities, "mock 'tail" parties, a Web site of course (www.nasulgc.org/bingedrink) and a new CD-ROM called "Alcohol 101" and featuring a "virtual party" that segues into an anatomical lecture about how quickly the bloodstream absorbs alcohol. Look out, Myst.

What no one seems to have noticed is that the rise in binging has oc-

Published in the New York Times Magazine *(October 24, 1999) in the section titled "The Way We Live Now."*

curred at the very same time that the legal drinking age has been raised everywhere to 21. If you're 18 to 21, it's the 1920's again and a mini-Prohibition is in full swing. As a result, moderate drinking has almost vanished among students and, more tellingly, from school-sponsored events. How anachronistic it feels to describe what used to be routine college functions, like a Dizzy Gillespie concert or a Robert Penn Warren reading, followed by a reception, with drinks and hors d'oeuvres, at which students were expected to at least pretend to be cool about it, i.e., practice drinking. I frequently received dinner invitations from faculty members like Tom Spaccarelli, a Spanish professor who served up tapas while uncorking a Rioja for a few students. We handled the long stems of our wineglasses as confidently as a colt its legs.

And there was always another occasion. Sewanee had dozens of those   5 inane college societies like Green Ribbon, a group whose invitation to membership I haughtily trashed after Professor Paschall, my sponsor, explained that the point was nothing more than "getting dressed up and having cocktails with some alumni."

But I began to see the point about 10 years after graduation when I returned to Sewanee to give a little talk. Afterward, I took some students to the pub where they sheepishly ordered cider. At first, I thought this new college life—clean and sober—was a good idea. Then my nephew, a junior there at that time, explained the typical partygoer's schedule: drive off campus or hide in the woods (often alone), guzzle a pint of bourbon, eat a box of breath mints and then stumble into the dry sorority party serenely blotto. My nephew knew two students who had died—falling off a cliff, blood poisoning—and five others who had been paralyzed or seriously injured in car accidents because of binging. For a college with roughly 1,300 students, this constitutes a statistical massacre.

We drank wildly in the 70's, too. The Phi's had their seasonal Screaming Bull blowout. Kegs were easy to find on weekends. I have drunk tequila only once in my life, and this being a family newspaper, my account of that evening can proceed no further. I was a member of the Sewanee Temperance League, whose annual outdoor party pledged to "rid the world of alcohol by consuming it all ourselves." But all those events were crowded social occasions, almost always with professors and their spouses in attendance—not prowling alone in the woods with a pint. After college, when you got a job, Screaming Bull opportunities quickly tapered off; the working world was different yet, in time, quite familiar, like an evening with Ted Stirling or a dinner at Tom Spaccarelli's.

This year, Ohio University's zero-tolerance program has proudly outlawed *empty* beer cans in the dorm. Nearly 7 percent of the entire 16,000-student enrollment last year was disciplined for alcohol abuse, often handed over as criminals to the Athens Municipal Court. Despite all the tough bluster, the binge rate among students there hasn't budged from an astounding 60 percent.

For college students, booze has been subsumed into the Manichaean battle of our drug war. It's either Prohibition or cave into the hippies' legalization schemes. And it seems fairly unreversible. Legislatures raised the drinking minimum in reaction to the raw emotion deployed by Mothers Against Drunk Driving. Then colleges were bullied by insurance companies that threatened to jack up liability rates if administrators didn't take aggressive action. The old days of looking the other way, when the police used to pick up toasted students and quietly drive them to their dorms, seems like collaboration in today's harsh light.

10   There probably is a way out of this, but it is going to require some larger cultural changes that will make us see the irony, even cruelty, of infantilizing certain young adults. The very people who have urged this situation into existence are too often the people who vent about the increasing lack of "responsibility" in our society (demanding, for example, that juvenile offenders be treated in court as adults). But for middle-class kids in college, they make responsibility an ever-receding ideal, never quite grasped in the pampered ease of an extended adolescence.

In the early 70's, the big political fight among college students was for the right to vote. The argument held that kids who were considered old enough to die for their country and order a drink in a bar should be able to choose their political leaders. It is back to two out of three again. But booze is not like the vote, which can be ignored to no one's immediate peril. Rather, alcohol consumption, like table manners or sexual behavior, is a socialized phenomenon, which if not taught, yields up a kind of wild child. By denying the obvious pleasure of drinking and not teaching it by example, is anyone really surprised that we've loosed upon the world a generation of feral drunks?

QUESTIONS

1. The research by Wechsler and his colleagues at the Harvard School of Public Health has provoked a national debate about the drinking habits of college students. To what extent does Jack Hitt engage the scientific research? To what extent does he agree with the public opinions expressed by Wechsler and his colleagues about actions that should be taken to stop binge drinking?

2. Is Hitt's Op-Ed focused more on the problem of binge drinking or on its solution? Does Hitt propose a solution?

3. Enter the public debate by writing your own Op-Ed on this topic, perhaps for your college or hometown newspaper. Consider your personal experience or other evidence you can add to public knowledge, and use it, as well as existing research, to make your argument.

KENNETH A. BRUFFEE: *Binge Drinking as a Substitute for a "Community of Learning"*

The Harvard School of Public Health found in 1993 that binge drinking is widespread on American college campuses, particularly among members of fraternities and sororities. The school's most recent report documents the disturbing fact that binge drinking has not declined in the five years since that first study. Even though the proportion of students who declare themselves teetotalers is slightly larger, the effects of binge drinking continue to be widespread and severe. They range from poor grades to destruction of property, assault, drunk driving, and death (*The Chronicle*, September 18, 1998).

To stem the tide of binge drinking, colleges have tried closing fraternities and sororities, punishing heavy drinkers, enlisting the help of liquor-store owners, and banning alcohol on their campuses. So far, those efforts have largely failed. One reason may be that missing from most of them, and from most research on the subject, is an understanding of why first-year students join fraternities and sororities in the first place.

I know why I joined one, many more years ago than I care to mention. I arrived on that gracious, learned, sophisticated campus to find myself among people—professors, administrators, upperclassmen (yes, all were men in those days)—who were committed (it seemed to me) to making me feel just how green, scared, lonely, and small-town I was. They all seemed vexed that I wasn't already what they hoped I would become. Administrators told me how much I had to learn and how hard I had to work to learn it. Professors told me how little they valued what I already knew, and how trivial and misleading would be anything that I learned from anyone but themselves. I was an intrusive rube. I didn't belong.

Most of my fellow freshmen seemed committed to making me feel like a rube, too. Today I think I know why, though I certainly did not know it then. They were trying as hard as I was to conceal from everyone, including themselves, that they, too, were green, scared, lonely, and small-town.

I joined a fraternity because I wanted, desperately, to belong.   5

Fraternity members were the only people on the campus who seemed to know what it meant to feel like a rube, who knew the depth and overwhelming intensity of an 18-year-old's need to belong. They knew how to marshal and exploit that need, because they'd been there themselves not long before. Fraternities seemed to be the only place on the campus with a ready supply of friends for freshmen.

There were certainly no friends to be had where I thought I would achieve my most consequential goals as a college student—in my classes. I made no friends there until my last year in college, and then only by chance. Even today, most college students make few friends through their classes until late in their college careers, if at all.

From the back page of the Chronicle of Higher Education (*February 9, 1999*), *which publishes opinion pieces by faculty members, students, and academic administrators.*

That's one reason college students become binge drinkers.

Such a claim may sound like some kind of bad joke, so I hasten to explain.

10 Most of the talk about binge drinking, the research into it, and the administrative attempts to curb it assume a sharp distinction between the "academic" and the "social" connections of college students with their peers. Students also make that distinction. If you ask a cross section of college students about their friends, some may say they occasionally talk with a few of them about their course work and (if they admit at all to such eccentricities) their intellectual and aesthetic interests. With the rest of their friends, they'll say, such topics seldom come up.

It's peculiar, when you think about it, that most American colleges do not help entering students make friends through their course work. Presumably, one goal of liberal education is to enrich life with the kind of conversation that comes with substantive friendship. And when colleges actively provide students with the opportunity to make friends through their classes, they eagerly grasp the chance.

A study of 183 students who entered Brooklyn College in the fall of 1987 and took courses that were organized into "learning communities"—in which the same group of students was registered for three courses together—showed that 73 per cent agreed with the statement that the experience "helps students make new friends more easily." The retention rate of the students studied was 73 per cent, compared with the college's normal average of 59 per cent.

Many students who do make it to their junior and senior years are likely to concede (if only in private) that most of their friendships then tend to merge social interests with academic and aesthetic interests—from pursuing genetic research to listening to Mozart concertos. By then, their sense of belonging is rooted in the academic major they have chosen and in the new interests they have developed in elective courses.

Of course, some freshmen arrive on the campus in the company of old high-school friends. But those students, too—most of them similarly green, scared, lonely 18-year-olds—feel the pressing need to belong to the new world they have entered. And they, too, are willing to belong on any terms, even terms that require them to continue to keep their curiosity and thought deeply buried.

15 Those are the terms of membership that fraternities and sororities offer. In return, these social clubs provide companionship that is predictable, reliable, aesthetically unimaginative, and intellectually unchallenging. So-called "wild parties" and the binge drinking that fuels them are misguided attempts to breathe life into stultifying conventionality.

In contrast, many traditional college classrooms—organized around lectures and class discussions—offer surprise, change, and intellectual stimulation. But their structure emphasizes individual mastery, self-sufficiency, and exclusion of outside distractions. While encouraging individual achievement, such courses often foster little substantive social interaction among students.

Colleges can do a great deal more than they generally do to make classrooms a source of social engagement around substantive issues. One approach is collaborative learning and related ways of organizing course work into learning communities, team projects, and peer tutoring.

Research can guide colleges in such efforts. We need to know whether collaborative learning actually does help students bring to the surface suppressed curiosity and thought, and, if so, how. Most of all, we need to know whether collaborative learning—especially, but not exclusively, during the first year of college—can give students opportunities to make friends in settings that are not merely social, vapid encounters, and, as a result, reduce the social desperation that drives students to binge drinking.

Granted, research is unlikely to show that collaborative learning is a universal solution to social problems at colleges. Research certainly will not demonstrate that collaborative learning alone can empty out fraternity and sorority houses.

But I am confident that research will show that collaborative learning can give entering college students a chance to experience a refreshingly new kind of social intimacy with their peers. It could help American colleges chip away at the problem of binge drinking, by helping to generate social cohesion, civil discourse, and, yes, even friendship among young people who arrive on campuses green, scared, lonely, and small-town.   20

QUESTIONS

1. The research by Wechsler and his colleagues at the Harvard School of Public Health has provoked a national debate about the drinking habits of college students. To what extent does Kenneth Bruffee engage the scientific research? To what extent does he agree with the public opinions expressed by Wechsler and his colleagues about actions that should be taken to stop binge drinking?

2. Is Bruffee's Op-Ed focused more on the causes of binge drinking or on its solution? Does Bruffee propose a solution? How is a "community of learning" a solution?

3. Enter the public debate by writing your own Op-Ed on this topic, perhaps for your college or hometown newspaper. Consider your personal experience or other evidence you can add to public knowledge, and use it, as well as existing research, to make your argument.

QUESTIONS ON OP-EDS

1. What characteristics do the Op-Ed pieces in this section have in common? Consider technique, argument, and attitude.

2. Examine the four column-length Op-Ed pieces: those by Ivins, Staples, Quindlen, and Britz. What features do they have in common? What kind of arguments do they tend to make? How would you characterize their language? From your reading of these four, discuss the range available to the writer of a newspaper Op-Ed column.

3. Look for three essays in other sections of *The Norton Reader* that also fit into the category "Op-Ed." Do they have features similar to or different from those you identified in question 2?

EDUCATION

FREDERICK DOUGLASS *Learning to Read*

I LIVED IN Master Hugh's family about seven years.[1] During this time, I succeeded in learning to read and write. In accomplishing this, I was compelled to resort to various stratagems. I had no regular teacher. My mistress, who had kindly commenced to instruct me, had, in compliance with the advice and direction of her husband, not only ceased to instruct, but had set her face against my being instructed by any one else. It is due, however, to my mistress to say of her, that she did not adopt this course of treatment immediately. She at first lacked the depravity indispensable to shutting me up in mental darkness. It was at least necessary for her to have some training in the exercise of irresponsible power, to make her equal to the task of treating me as though I were a brute.

My mistress was, as I have said, a kind and tender-hearted woman; and in the simplicity of her soul she commenced, when I first went to live with her, to treat me as she supposed one human being ought to treat another. In entering upon the duties of a slaveholder, she did not seem to perceive that I sustained to her the relation of a mere chattel, and that for her to treat me as a human being was not only wrong, but dangerously so. Slavery proved as injurious to her as it did to me. When I went there, she was a pious, warm, and tender-hearted woman. There was no sorrow or suffering for which she had not a tear. She had bread for the hungry, clothes for the naked, and comfort for every mourner that came within her reach. Slavery soon proved its ability to divest her of these heavenly qualities. Under its influence, the tender heart became stone, and the lamblike disposition gave way to one of tigerlike fierceness. The first step in her downward course was in her ceasing to instruct me. She now commenced to practise her husband's precepts. She finally became even more violent in her opposition than her husband himself. She was not satisfied with simply doing as well as he had commanded; she seemed anxious to do better. Nothing seemed to make her more angry than to see me with a newspaper. She seemed to think that here lay the danger. I have had her rush at me with a face made all up of fury, and snatch from me a newspaper, in a manner that fully revealed her apprehension. She was an apt woman; and a lit-

---

From Douglass's autobiography, Narrative of the Life of Frederick Douglass, An American Slave, Written by Himself *(1845), a landmark of African American literature.*

1. In Baltimore, Maryland.

tle experience soon demonstrated, to her satisfaction, that education and slavery were incompatible with each other.

From this time I was most narrowly watched. If I was in a separate room any considerable length of time, I was sure to be suspected of having a book, and was at once called to give an account of myself. All this, however, was too late. The first step had been taken. Mistress, in teaching me the alphabet, had given me the *inch*, and no precaution could prevent me from taking the *ell*.[2]

The plan which I adopted, and the one by which I was most successful, was that of making friends of all the little white boys whom I met in the street. As many of these as I could, I converted into teachers. With their kindly aid, obtained at different times and in different places, I finally succeeded in learning to read. When I was sent of errands, I always took my book with me, and by going one part of my errand quickly, I found time to get a lesson before my return. I used also to carry bread with me, enough of which was always in the house, and to which I was always welcome; for I was much better off in this regard than many of the poor white children in our neighborhood. This bread I used to bestow upon the hungry little urchins, who, in return, would give me that more valuable bread of knowledge. I am strongly tempted to give the names of two or three of those little boys, as a testimonial of the gratitude and affection I bear them; but prudence forbids;—not that it would injure me, but it might embarrass them; for it is almost an unpardonable offence to teach slaves to read in this Christian country. It is enough to say of the dear little fellows, that they lived on Philpot Street, very near Durgin and Bailey's ship-yard. I used to talk this matter of slavery over with them. I would sometimes say to them, I wished I could be as free as they would be when they got to be men. "You will be free as soon as you are twenty-one, *but I am a slave for life!* Have not I as good a right to be free as you have?" These words used to trouble them; they would express for me the liveliest sympathy, and console me with the hope that something would occur by which I might be free.

I was now about twelve years old, and the thought of being *a slave for life* 5 began to bear heavily upon my heart. Just about this time, I got hold of a book entitled "The Columbian Orator."[3] Every opportunity I got, I used to read this book. Among much of other interesting matter, I found in it a dialogue between a master and his slave. The slave was represented as having run away from his master three times. The dialogue represented the conversation which took place between them, when the slave was retaken the third time. In this dialogue, the whole argument in behalf of slavery was brought forward by the master, all of which was disposed of by the slave. The slave was made to say some very smart as well as impressive things in reply to his master—things which had the desired though unexpected effect; for the conversation resulted in the voluntary emancipation of the slave on the part of the master.

In the same book, I met with one of Sheridan's mighty speeches on and in

2. Once a unit of measurement equal to forty-five inches; the saying is proverbial.
3. A popular collection of poems, dialogues, plays, and speeches.

behalf of Catholic emancipation.[4] These were choice documents to me. I read them over and over again with unabated interest. They gave tongue to interesting thoughts of my own soul, which had frequently flashed through my mind, and died away for want of utterance. The moral which I gained from the dialogue was the power of truth over the conscience of even a slaveholder. What I got from Sheridan was a bold denunciation of slavery, and a powerful vindication of human rights. The reading of these documents enabled me to utter my thoughts, and to meet the arguments brought forward to sustain slavery; but while they relieved me of one difficulty, they brought on another even more painful than the one of which I was relieved. The more I read, the more I was led to abhor and detest my enslavers. I could regard them in no other light than a band of successful robbers, who had left their homes, and gone to Africa, and stolen us from our homes, and in a strange land reduced us to slavery. I loathed them as being the meanest as well as the most wicked of men. As I read and contemplated the subject, behold! that very discontentment which Master Hugh had predicted would follow my learning to read had already come, to torment and sting my soul to unutterable anguish. As I writhed under it, I would at times feel that learning to read had been a curse rather than a blessing. It had given me a view of my wretched condition, without the remedy. It opened my eyes to the horrible pit, but to no ladder upon which to get out. In moments of agony, I envied my fellow-slaves for their stupidity. I have often wished myself a beast. I preferred the condition of the meanest reptile to my own. Any thing, no matter what, to get rid of thinking! It was this everlasting thinking of my condition that tormented me. There was no getting rid of it. It was pressed upon me by every object within sight or hearing, animate or inanimate. The silver trump of freedom had roused my soul to eternal wakefulness. Freedom now appeared, to disappear no more forever. It was heard in every sound, and seen in every thing. It was ever present to torment me with a sense of my wretched condition. I saw nothing without seeing it, I heard nothing without hearing it, and felt nothing without feeling it. It looked from every star, it smiled in every calm, breathed in every wind, and moved in every storm.

I often found myself regretting my own existence, and wishing myself dead; and but for the hope of being free, I have no doubt but that I should have killed myself, or done something for which I should have been killed. While in this state of mind, I was eager to hear any one speak of slavery. I was a ready listener. Every little while, I could hear something about the abolitionists. It was some time before I found what the word meant. It was always used in such connections as to make it an interesting word to me. If a slave ran away and succeeded in getting clear, or if a slave killed his master, set fire to a barn, or did any thing very wrong in the mind of a slaveholder, it was spoken of as the fruit of *abolition*. Hearing the word in this connection very often, I

4. Richard Brinsley Sheridan (1751–1815), Irish dramatist and political leader. The speech, arguing for the abolition of laws denying Roman Catholics in Great Britain and Ireland civil and political liberties, was actually made by the Irish patriot Arthur O'Connor.

set about learning what it meant. The dictionary afforded me little or no help. I found it was "the act of abolishing"; but then I did not know what was to be abolished. Here I was perplexed. I did not dare to ask any one about its meaning, for I was satisfied that it was something they wanted me to know very little about. After a patient waiting, I got one of our city papers, containing an account of the number of petitions from the north, praying for the abolition of slavery in the District of Columbia, and of the slave trade between the States. From this time I understood the words *abolition* and *abolitionist*, and always drew near when that word was spoken, expecting to hear something of importance to myself and fellow-slaves. The light broke in upon me by degrees. I went one day down on the wharf of Mr. Waters; and seeing two Irishmen unloading a scow of stone, I went, unasked, and helped them. When we had finished, one of them came to me and asked me if I were a slave. I told him I was. He asked, "Are ye a slave for life?" I told him that I was. The good Irishman seemed to be deeply affected by the statement. He said to the other that it was a pity so fine a little fellow as myself should be a slave for life. He said it was a shame to hold me. They both advised me to run away to the north; that I should find friends there, and that I should be free. I pretended not to be interested in what they said, and treated them as if I did not understand them; for I feared they might be treacherous. White men have been known to encourage slaves to escape, and then, to get the reward, catch them and return them to their masters. I was afraid that these seemingly good men might use me so; but I nevertheless remembered their advice, and from that time I resolved to run away. I looked forward to a time at which it would be safe for me to escape. I was too young to think of doing so immediately; besides, I wished to learn how to write, as I might have occasion to write my own pass. I consoled myself with the hope that I should one day find a good chance. Meanwhile, I would learn to write.

The idea as to how I might learn to write was suggested to me by being in Durgin and Bailey's ship-yard, and frequently seeing the ship carpenters, after hewing, and getting a piece of timber ready for use, write on the timber the name of that part of the ship for which it was intended. When a piece of timber was intended for the larboard side, it would be marked thus—"L." When a piece was for the starboard side, it would be marked thus—"S." A piece for the larboard side forward, would be marked thus—"L. F." When a piece was for starboard side forward, it would be marked thus—"S. F." For larboard aft, it would be marked thus— "L. A." For starboard aft, it would be marked thus— "S. A." I soon learned the names of these letters, and for what they were intended when placed upon a piece of timber in the shipyard. I immediately commenced copying them, and in a short time was able to make the four letters named. After that, when I met with any boy who I knew could write, I would tell him I could write as well as he. The next word would be, "I don't believe you. Let me see you try it." I would then make the letters which I had been so fortunate as to learn, and ask him to beat that. In this way I got a good many lessons in writing, which it is quite possible I should never have gotten in any other way. During this time, my copy-book was the board fence, brick wall, and pavement; my pen and ink was a lump of chalk. With these, I learned mainly how to write. I then commenced and continued copying the Italics in Webster's Spelling Book,[5] until I could make them all without looking on the book. By this time, my little Master Thomas had gone to school, and learned how to write, and had written over a number of copy-books. These had been brought home, and shown to some of our near neighbors, and then laid aside. My mistress used to go to class meeting at the Wilk Street meetinghouse every Monday afternoon, and leave me to take care of the house. When left thus, I used to spend the time in writing in the spaces left in Master Thomas's copy-book, copying what he had written. I continued to do this until I could write a hand very similar to that of Master Thomas. Thus, after a long, tedious effort for years, I finally succeeded in learning how to write.

5. *The American Spelling Book* (1783) by Noah Webster (1758–1843), American lexicographer.

QUESTIONS

1. Douglass's story might today be called a "literacy narrative"—an account of how someone gains the skills of reading and writing. What are the key features of this narrative? What obstacles did Douglass face? How did he overcome them?

2. Many literacy narratives include an enabling figure, someone who helps the young learner along his or her way. Is there such a figure in Douglass's narrative? Why or why not?

3. At the end of this narrative Douglass mentions that he wrote "in the spaces left in Master Thomas's copy-book, copying what he had written" (paragraph 8). To what extent is imitation (copying) part of learning? To what extent does this narrative show originality?

4. Write your own literacy narrative—an account of how you learned to read and write.

EUDORA WELTY *Clamorous to Learn*

ROM THE FIRST I was clamorous to learn—I wanted to know and begged to be told not so much what, or how, or why, or where, as when. How soon?

Pear tree by the garden gate,
How much longer must I wait?

Originally delivered as part of a lecture series at Harvard University in 1983, then published in Welty's memoir, One Writer's Beginnings *(1985).*

This rhyme from one of my nursery books was the one that spoke for me. But I lived not at all unhappily in this craving, for my wild curiosity was in large part suspense, which carries its own secret pleasure. And so one of the godmothers of fiction was already bending over me.

When I was five years old, I knew the alphabet, I'd been vaccinated (for smallpox), and I could read. So my mother walked across the street to Jefferson Davis Grammar School[1] and asked the principal if she would allow me to enter the first grade after Christmas.

"Oh, all right," said Miss Duling. "Probably the best thing you could do with her."

Miss Duling, a lifelong subscriber to perfection, was a figure of authority, the most whole-souled I have ever come to know. She was a dedicated schoolteacher who denied herself all she might have done or whatever other way she might have lived (this possibility was the last that could have occurred to us, her subjects in school). I believe she came of well-off people, well-educated, in Kentucky, and certainly old photographs show she was a beautiful, high-spirited-looking young lady—and came down to Jackson to its new grammar school that was going begging for a principal. She must have earned next to nothing; Mississippi then as now was the nation's lowest-ranking state economically, and our legislature has always shown a painfully loud reluctance to give money to public education. That challenge *brought* her.

In the long run she came into touch, as teacher or principal, with three generations of Jacksonians. My parents had not, but everybody else's parents had gone to school to her. She'd taught most of our leaders somewhere along the line. When she wanted something done—some civic oversight corrected, some injustice made right overnight, or even a tree spared that the fool telephone people were about to cut down—she telephoned the mayor, or the chief of police, or the president of the power company, or the head doctor at the hospital, or the judge in charge of a case, or whoever, and calling them by their first names, *told* them. It is impossible to imagine her meeting with anything less than compliance. The ringing of her brass bell from their days at Davis School would still be in their ears. She also proposed a spelling match between the fourth grade at Davis School and the Mississippi Legislature, who went through with it; and that told the Legislature.

Her standards were very high and of course inflexible, her authority was total; why *wouldn't* this carry with it a brass bell that could be heard ringing for a block in all directions? That bell belonged to the figure of Miss Duling as though it grew directly out of her right arm, as wings grew out of an angel or a tail out of the devil. When we entered, marching, into her school, by strictest teaching, surveillance, and order we learned grammar, arithmetic, spelling, reading, writing, and geography; and she, not the teachers, I believe, wrote out the examinations: need I tell you, they were "hard."

She's not the only teacher who has influenced me, but Miss Duling, in

1. Named after the president of the Confederate States of America (1861–65) and located in Jackson, Mississippi.

some fictional shape or form, has stridden into a larger part of my work than I'd realized until now. She emerges in my perhaps inordinate number of schoolteacher characters. I loved those characters in the writing. But I did not, in life, love Miss Duling. I was afraid of her high-arched bony nose, her eyebrows lifted in half-circles above her hooded, brilliant eyes, and of the Kentucky R's in her speech, and the long steps she took in her hightop shoes. I did nothing but fear her bearing-down authority, and did not connect this (as of course we were meant to) with our own need or desire to learn, perhaps because I already had this wish, and did not need to be driven.

She was impervious to lies or foolish excuses or the insufferable plea of not knowing any better. She wasn't going to have any frills, either, at Davis School. When a new governor moved into the mansion, he sent his daughter to Davis School; her name was Lady Rachel Conner. Miss Duling at once called the governor to the telephone and told him, "She'll be plain Rachel here."

Miss Duling dressed as plainly as a Pilgrim on a Thanksgiving poster we made in the schoolroom, in a longish black-and-white checked gingham dress, a bright thick wool sweater the red of a railroad lantern—she'd knitted it herself—black stockings and her narrow elegant feet in black hightop shoes with heels you could hear coming, rhythmical as a parade drum down the hall. Her silky black curly hair was drawn back out of curl, fastened by high combs, and knotted behind. She carried her spectacles on a gold chain hung around her neck. Her gaze was in general sweeping, then suddenly at the point of concentration upon you. With a swing of her bell that took her whole right arm and shoulder, she rang it, militant and impartial, from the head of the front steps of Davis School when it was time for us all to line up, girls on one side, boys on the other. We were to march past her into the school building, while the fourth-grader she nabbed played time on the piano, mostly to a tune we could have skipped to, but we didn't skip into Davis School.

10   Little recess (open-air exercises) and big recess (lunch-boxes from home opened and eaten on the grass, on the girls' side and the boys' side of the yard) and dismissal were also regulated by Miss Duling's bell. The bell was also used to catch us off guard with fire drill.

It was examinations that drove my wits away, as all emergencies do. Being expected to measure up was paralyzing. I failed to make 100 on my spelling exam because I missed one word and that word was "uncle." Mother, as I knew she would, took it personally. "You couldn't spell *uncle*? When you've got those five perfectly splendid uncles in West Virginia? What would *they* say to that?"

It was never that Mother wanted me to beat my classmates in grades; what she wanted was for me to have my answers right. It was unclouded perfection I was up against.

My father was much more tolerant of possible error. He only said, as he steeply and impeccably sharpened my pencils on examination morning, "Now just keep remembering: the examinations were made out for the *average* student to pass. That's the majority. And if the majority can pass, think how much better *you* can do."

I looked to my mother, who had her own opinions about the majority. My father wished to treat it with respect, she didn't. I'd been born left-handed, but the habit was broken when I entered the first grade in Davis School. My father had insisted. He pointed out that everything in life had been made for the convenience of right-handed people, because they were the majority, and he often used "what the majority wants" as a criterion for what was for the best. My mother said she could not promise him, could not promise him at all, that I wouldn't stutter as a consequence. Mother had been born left-handed too; her family consisted of five left-handed brothers, a left-handed mother, and a father who could write with both hands at the same time, also backwards and forwards and upside down, different words with each hand. She had been broken of it when she was young, and she said she used to stutter.

"But you still stutter," I'd remind her, only to hear her say loftily, "You should have heard me when I was your age." 15

In my childhood days, a great deal of stock was put, in general, in the value of doing well in school. Both daily newspapers in Jackson saw the honor roll as news and published the lists, and the grades, of all the honor students. The city fathers gave the children who made the honor roll free season tickets to the baseball games down at the grandstand. We all attended and all worshiped some player on the Jackson Senators: I offered up my 100's in arithmetic and spelling, reading and writing, attendance and, yes, deportment—I must have been a prig!—to Red McDermott, the third baseman. And our happiness matched that of knowing Miss Duling was on her summer vacation, far, far away in Kentucky.

Every school week, visiting teachers came on their days for special lessons. On Mondays, the singing teacher blew into the room fresh from the early outdoors, singing in her high soprano "How do you do?" to do-mi-sol-do,[2] and we responded in chorus from our desks, "I'm ve-ry well" to do-sol-mi-do. Miss Johnson taught us rounds—"Row row row your boat gently down the stream"—and "Little Sir Echo," with half the room singing the words and the other half being the echo, a competition. She was from the North, and she was the one who wanted us all to stop the Christmas carols and see snow. The snow falling that morning outside the window was the first most of us had ever seen, and Miss Johnson threw up the window and held out wide her own black cape and caught flakes on it and ran, as fast as she could go, up and down the aisles to show us the real thing before it melted.

Thursday was Miss Eyrich and Miss Eyrich was Thursday. She came to give us physical training. She wasted no time on nonsense. Without greeting, we were marched straight outside and summarily divided into teams (no choosing sides), put on the mark, and ordered to get set for a relay race. Miss Eyrich cracked out "Go!" Dread rose in my throat. My head swam. Here was my turn, nearly upon me. (Wait, have I been touched—was that slap the

2. Syllables indicating the first, third, fifth, and eighth tones of the scale.

touch? Go on! Do I go on without our passing a word? What word? Now am I racing too fast to turn around? Now I'm nearly home, but where is the hand waiting for mine to touch? Am I too late? Have I lost the whole race for our side?) I lost the relay race for our side before I started, through living ahead of myself, dreading to make my start, feeling too late prematurely, and standing transfixed by emergency, trying to think of a password. Thursdays still can make me hear Miss Eyrich's voice. "On your mark—get set—GO!"

Very composedly and very slowly, the art teacher, who visited each room on Fridays, paced the aisle and looked down over your shoulder at what you were drawing for her. This was Miss Ascher. Coming from behind you, her deep, resonant voice reached you without being a word at all, but a sort of purr. It was much the sound given out by our family doctor when he read the thermometer and found you were running a slight fever: "Um-hm. Um-hm." Both alike, they let you go right ahead with it.

20   The school toilets were in the boys' and girls' respective basements. After Miss Duling had rung to dismiss school, a friend and I were making our plans for Saturday from adjoining cubicles. "Can you come spend the day with me?" I called out, and she called back, "I might could."

"Who—said—MIGHT—COULD?" It sounded like "Fe Fi Fo Fum!"

We both were petrified, for we knew whose deep measured words those were that came from just outside our doors. That was the voice of Mrs. McWillie, who taught the other fourth grade across the hall from ours. She was not even our teacher, but a very heavy, stern lady who dressed entirely in widow's weeds with a pleated black shirtwaist with a high net collar and velvet ribbon, and a black skirt to her ankles, with black circles under her eyes and a mournful, Presbyterian expression. We children took her to be a hundred years old. We held still.

"You might as well tell me," continued Mrs. McWillie. "I'm going to plant myself right here and wait till you come out. Then I'll see who it was I heard saying 'MIGHT-COULD.' "

If Elizabeth wouldn't go out, of course I wouldn't either. We knew her to be a teacher who would not flinch from standing there in the basement all after-noon, perhaps even all day Saturday. So we surrendered and came out. I prig-gishly hoped Elizabeth would clear it up which child it was—it wasn't me.

25   "So it's you." She regarded us as a brace, made no distinction: whoever didn't say it was guilty by association. "If I ever catch you down here one more time saying 'MIGHT-COULD,' I'm going to carry it to Miss Duling. You'll be kept in every day for a week! I hope you're both sufficiently ashamed of yourselves?" Saying "might-could" was bad, but saying it in the basement made bad grammar a sin. I knew Presbyterians believed that you could go to Hell.

Mrs. McWillie never scared us into grammar, of course. It was my first-year Latin teacher in high school who made me discover I'd fallen in love with it. It took Latin to thrust me into bona fide alliance with words in their true meaning. Learning Latin (once I was free of Caesar) fed my love for words upon words, words in continuation and modification, and the beautiful, sober, accretion of a sentence. I could see the achieved sentence finally standing there, as real, intact, and built to stay as the Mississippi State Capitol at the top of my street, where I could walk through it on my way to school and hear underfoot the echo of its marble floor, and over me the bell of its rotunda.

On winter's rainy days, the schoolrooms would grow so dark that sometimes you couldn't see the figures on the blackboard. At that point, Mrs. McWillie, that stern fourth-grade teacher, would let her children close their books, and she would move, broad in widow's weeds like darkness itself, to the window and by what light there was she would stand and read aloud "The King of the Golden River."[3] But I was excluded—in the other fourth grade, across the hall. Miss Louella Varnado, my teacher, didn't copy Mrs. McWillie; we had a spelling match: you could spell in the dark. I did not then suspect that there was any other way I could learn the story of "The King of the Golden River" than to have been assigned in the beginning to Mrs. McWillie's cowering fourth grade, then wait for her to treat you to it on the rainy day of her choice. I only now realize how much the treat depended, too, on there not having been money enough to put electric lights in Davis School. John Ruskin had to come in through courtesy of darkness. When in time I found the story in a book and read it to myself, it didn't seem to live up to my longings for a story with that name; as indeed, how could it?

3. A fantasy for children by the English author John Ruskin (1819–1900).

QUESTIONS

1. Like Frederick Douglass's narrative (see previous essay), Welty's essay might be called a "literacy narrative"—an account of how someone gains the skills of reading and writing. What are the key features of this narrative?

2. If you have read Douglass's narrative, compare the similarities and differences. Might both learners have been described as "clamorous to learn"?

3. Write your own literacy narrative—an account of how you learned to read and write.

DAVID CHANOFF   *Education Is My Mother and My Father*

I
N EARLY AUGUST OF 2001, 80 young men walked into the milking shed at the University of New Hampshire's Dairy Management Program and were utterly perplexed. Most were tall, many well over six feet. Their skin was jet black—almost blue in the summer sun. All were slender, and many seemed unnaturally gaunt, as if they had been semistarved for a long time. But their faces glowed with a mixture of happiness, expectation, and, most of all, curiosity. Each of these young men was an expert on cattle, although it had been many years since any of them had so much as touched a bull, a cow, or a calf.

The men had come to New Hampshire as guests of the university's highly regarded animal science faculty. Pete Erickson, one of the professors and a dairy nutrition specialist, had heard that in nearby Boston an unusual group of African refugees was in the process of being resettled. Newspapers and television programs were calling them the "Lost Boys of Sudan." They were youngsters who had been orphaned in childhood by the Sudanese civil war and who had trekked by themselves across East Africa. They had fled from their homes as children, some as young as four or five, others nine or ten. As many as 20,000—nobody really knew the numbers—started out. At first they found refuge in Ethiopia; then when revolution came to Addis Ababa,[1] they were driven from their camps with great loss of life before eventually finding their way to the United Nations safe haven in Kenya's Kakuma refugee camp. Six thousand or so had been living there since 1992; some were girls, but most were boys (hence "The Lost Boys"). Approximately 3,500 were later admitted to the United States. Most were Dinkas, from South Sudan's largest tribe, but there were also Acholi, Shilluk, Nuer and others.[2] About 170 of them were bound for Boston; the 80 young men at the university milking shed were the first arrivals. As East African cattle herders whose childhoods had been spent learning about and caring for cattle, they had come to be introduced to the university's dairy herd. Erickson had invited them. He and his colleagues were knowledgeable about the African cattle cultures and were as eager to meet the Sudanese as the Sudanese were to see the cows.

The young men stepped through the anti-hoof-and-mouth disinfectant foot tray, entered the shed, and stopped cold. Well-fed, contented cows stared at them with liquid bovine eyes, Holsteins and Brown Swiss rather than the

Written by an adviser to the Sudanese Education Fund and published in the American Scholar *(September 2005), the magazine of the Phi Beta Kappa Society.*

1. The capital of Ethiopia.
2. The Dinkas, Acholi, Shilluk, and Nuer are all East African tribes.

Crossing the Sudan border into Kenya to reach the Kakuma refugee camp.

native Sudanese Ankole,[3] but intimately familiar anyway. The Sudanese stared back at the cows, instinctively drawn to these creatures who in the boys' still vivid childhood memories had been the objects of their care, the subjects of their songs, their dances, their hopes and aspirations. But as they registered what was actually happening in the milking parlor, attraction turned to confusion. All around the cows was a maze of stainless steel pipes, electronic control panels, and flexible black tubing clamped in some incomprehensible fashion to the teats of each cow's swollen udder.

Until coming to the United States, the young Sudanese men had never ridden in a car, switched on an electric light, watched a television, or used a flush toilet. As children they had lived in conical grass houses and followed their cattle. As refugees they had slept in mud huts, subsisting on a daily bowl of corn porridge. And now here they were, in Durham, New Hampshire, trying to comprehend a computerized milking operation with pulsating vacuums, sterile tanks, and high-tech cooling systems. For one long bewildering moment in that milking shed, the ancient and the modern stood face to face.

Today, more than four years later, some of those same Sudanese are students at the University of New Hampshire, not in dairy management but in mathematics, economics, and business administration. Other Boston-area Sudanese are enrolled at the University of Massachusetts, Brandeis, Dartmouth, Boston College, Boston University, and other schools. Around the country, in Phoenix, Grand Rapids, Burlington, and the other Lost Boy resettlement communities, former tribal herd boys are completing GEDs, finishing up associate

5

3. Holsteins and Brown Swiss: breeds of dairy cattle raised in the United States; Ankole: a breed of cattle native to Africa.

degrees at two-year colleges, progressing toward bachelor degrees at four-year schools, and contemplating their prospects for graduate studies. This is the story of how a historically unique group of young Africans, their minds formed and conditioned by the age-old patterns of life on the Upper Nile savanna, are transforming themselves and being transformed in 21st-century America.

Understanding the immensity of this transformation requires an act of imagination—an effort to slide inside the minds of the children the Lost Boys used to be and to see the world as they saw it before the eruption of violence that sent them into panicked flight across the East African desert. "At the age of five or six," said Mangok Mach, a senior business administration major at New Hampshire, "you are taken to the cattle camp to learn how to care for cattle, calves at first. What you know is that cattle are what provide everything for you. They are the one source of life." Mangok and his Dinka contemporaries learned to graze the calves away from the cows so that the calves wouldn't suckle and consume all the milk, leaving none for the people. Looking after their herds, the children carried small spears, clubs, and bows and arrows. Lions and hyenas abounded near the camps, and practicing weapons skills was an essential part of growing up Dinka.

During the five or six hours a day that the boys were out, their thoughts were mainly about the calves, but they played too—wrestling (the traditional Dinka sport) and composing and singing songs praising themselves, their fathers, their clans, songs about cattle and manly courage, about warrior prowess and the dignity of the people. Looking into their future they saw themselves as young initiated warriors. Further along they would marry; only through marriage would a boy come into full manhood. They expected to become fathers, with their own herds, then elders, basking in the respect of their community. That was how it had been for their fathers and their fathers' fathers, as far back as the clan had memory, and that was how it would be for them. Life in Dinka land was an endlessly repeated cycle, with variations, of course—one might be a better singer, one a more skilled herdsman, one a stronger fighter—but life's essential outline was always and forever one and the same.

For the Dinka children, space, like time, was bounded. Their community's land, its spread-out villages and dry-season pasturelands, had been given to the people by the ancestors. And one had no thoughts of ever leaving. Travel and exploration might have long pedigrees in other cultures, but not among the Dinka. "There's a Dinka word: *kok*," explained David Gai, a University of Massachusetts senior. "It's used about someone who has left the area. It's very negative. Someone might leave who has done something wrong in the community, something shameful, and feels he doesn't belong anymore. Instead of committing suicide, he'd rather go away. People do not leave out of curiosity. They enjoy living among themselves and are not interested in elsewhere."

The universe for the Dinka children and their Nilotic[4] cousins was a closed entity with clear boundaries defining their land, the course of their lives, and the people among whom they would live. They were closest to their

4. Originating from or near the Nile River in Africa.

parents and age mates, but the entire community was small. Everyone knew everyone and everyone's lineages as well as their own, sometimes down to the twenty-first generation. They understood there was a world beyond, but exactly who might be living there was a mystery Maduk Chol, a student at Bunker Hill Community College, remembers asking his father. "Where the sun goes down, do we have people there? Or where the sun comes up? My father said 'Yes,' but I thought maybe they would be people like our clan. 'You can get people over there,' my father said. 'But it takes a long time.'"

Into this closed universe in the dry season of 1987 a lightning bolt of destruction suddenly crashed, as if thrown from the hand of some malevolent god. It shattered villages, clans, and tribes, and it destroyed, among so much else, the comfortable mental world of thousands of children who fled in its wake.

10

Sudan's civil war between the Arab North and the rebelling black South, in which perhaps two million mostly southerners have died, started in 1963 and has flared and subsided intermittently ever since. * * * In 1987 it flared. Northern army and Arab militia forces struck through wide swaths of South Sudan, leaving a devastated and depopulated countryside behind them. With many adults dead or abducted and villages in flames, children and young people abandoned the cattle camps and fled in whichever direction seemed most likely to afford safety. A huge column of youngsters, including Mangok Mach, David Gai, Maduk Chol, and their friends, headed east toward the Ethiopian border.

For some the trek lasted a matter of weeks; for others it took up to three months. With no shoes, no food or water other than what they could find along the way, and no protection, death came in many forms: militia attacks, animal predation, infection, starvation, thirst. "The U.N. did not reach us in time," recalled Jacob Mabil, another New Hampshire student. "We spent days without food, feeding on trees, sick and starved. If you got sick, there was no one to help you." But across the Ethiopian border the United Nations was waiting, together with other aid organizations and a number of Sudanese who had arrived earlier. There the children were divided into *kois*, groups of a hundred, and they set about cutting wood and grasses to make shelters. Most had no idea what had happened. They were children suddenly separated from parents and communities, who had suffered unexpected brutality and hardship and who now found themselves in an alien place with many thousands of other equally confused and traumatized children, many of whom (amazingly to them) could not even understand each other's speech.

With a cruel abruptness, their lives were changed. For most, thinking mainly about how to get food and shelter and wondering when they could start going back, it took time for the truth to hit home. But some, such as David Gai, recognized it immediately. "I ran with others. And the next morning when the sun rose we found ourselves in an open area, just flat, not a single tree. I couldn't even see the end. It came to my mind that something dangerous was happening, that my life was going to be changed completely."

In Ethiopia the children set about building huts to live in. Some were also detailed by U.N. workers to construct makeshift classrooms. Although none of the young refugees could have articulated it, the boundaries of their traditional life and its mindset had already burst. The war had thrust them out of what they had always considered their only possible home. It had thrown them together with vast numbers of strangers, clan with clan, tribe with tribe. Now another mental barrier was about to be breached. With the construction of classrooms and a small number of teachers on hand, school was getting ready to start.

15   Before the deluge, few Dinka children thought much about schooling, and if they did, it was usually with a sense of the shame and stigma of it. Western education was not unknown in South Sudan. English missionaries had established boarding schools earlier in the century, but only Christianized families and townsfolk had sent their children, along with a few cadets from the families of paramount chiefs who understood the advantage of having some Western knowledge at their disposal. A family with too few cows to enable all its sons to marry would also consider sending one or more of its children away. For the rest, school was a place to deposit children too lazy, recalcitrant, or incompetent to be trusted with the family cattle. Sending a child to school meant branding him with the shame of his father's disrespect or his poverty.

But now the adult caretakers overseeing the children were telling them to go to school—only a selected few at first because of the lack of classrooms and teachers, but later more and more. Jacob Mabil was among the first. "I wasn't thinking about going to school," he said. "I was thinking that if I had a chance I would go back and die with my father. But our caretaker told me to go to class. And when I got there the teachers brought cookies. We ate them and we said, Oh, this is good. I have to come everyday. They did that for a week. We learned the ABCs, and I thought that was good. So that's how I started school."

While the first students were in class, the others were doing hard work: cutting wood, building houses, preparing food. Jealousy reared its head. Then there was the curiosity factor. The schoolboys would come home, and everyone would want to know what they had learned. "We learned this," they'd say, and trace an A in the dirt with a stick. Before long everyone else was trying to trace the same A.

Education soon began to seem like a mission. At home, work meant herding. Here, with no cows, there was still at least one thing that had obvious meaning: schoolwork. At home there were older brothers and fathers to look to. "Here," Maduk Chol said, "we had no models except our teachers. Or we might see a doctor. A plane lands at the airstrip and the pilot comes out. He's a human being, and we thought, Why not us?" "I became a thinker when I left home," Mangok Mach remembered. "Things were so strange, and I had to find my own way. Most of us had never thought about the future because we never knew about it. But now you had to think about how you would live. We could see that the lives of people who went to school were changed. We got the idea that when you were educated you could help yourself and your community. You could be a different person."

In 1991 the Sudanese children's encampment in Ethiopia was destroyed. A revolution had taken place in Addis Ababa, and the regime that had been

Moses Ajou (standing) and John Akok at the University of New Hampshire's Dimond Library.

friendly toward the Sudanese rebels and had permitted the resettlement was overthrown by one that wanted to mend fences with Sudan's Arab government. In the violence that accompanied the end of the old regime, forces were dispatched to get rid of the Lost Boys who constituted a potential recruiting ground for the rebels.

For most of the boys, the first hint of trouble was the rattle of small arms and the thud of high explosives. Four years earlier they had suddenly found themselves on the run. Now they were running for their lives again, this time back toward Sudan. At the swollen, crocodile-infested Gilo River the thousands of fleeing youngsters stopped; but as their pursuers closed in, the boys flung themselves into the water. Many perished. From the far bank, those who survived watched their friends die in the river.

After more than a year on the run, the remnants of the Lost Boys crossed into Kenya and were admitted to a United Nations safe haven for refugees at Kakuma.[5] There school started up again, this time sponsored by the Kenyan Department of Education. As the boys progressed from grade to grade, the transformation that had begun in Ethiopia accelerated. It was as if the initial shock of leaving home had, in Mangok's words, "opened up our minds." In Kenya the new mental landscape began to take a clearer shape. In Ethiopia they had been traumatized children who wanted more than anything to go home. Few now had any illusions about going back; South Sudan was a charnel house.[6] They began to see schooling as their one lifeline to the future.

Kakuma camp is a sprawling refugee metropolis of 80,000 people, complete with a United Nations refugee agency infrastructure, a hospital, schools, clinics, food distribution center, and other support mechanisms. Next to Kakuma camp is the town of Kakuma, a fly-bitten backwater by any standards except those of the boys. For them, it seemed a showcase of wonders: cars, trucks, houses, running water, flooring. They visited their teachers' homes and got a quick look at some of the trappings of contemporary life. At the same

5. A town in northwest Kenya that has offered a refugee camp since 1992.
6. A place to put the bones that one might find while digging graves.

20

time they saw in the desperately poor local tribes something very similar to their own past.

"Kakuma was the turning point," Mangok said. "When we came to Kenya, we saw the huge difference between the educated and the noneducated. We saw the hierarchy. Those people who had degrees were the uppermost, and those with high school diplomas were in second place. And we saw the Turkana, the local people, who had their cattle and nothing else. We saw the huge gap, and we understood the real meaning of education in terms of living."

From within the Lost Boy community, a saying had spontaneously generated itself: *Pioc yen e kee ama ku awa* (Education is my mother and my father). It was an altogether remarkable paradigm transfer. In their traditional childhood, everything had depended on parents: their mothers to give them love, sustenance, and early training; their fathers to give them skills, wisdom, and the cattle they would need to make their own lives as adults, conduits of the ancestral bloodlines that connected them to their historical communities of clan and sub-tribe. In all these ways, as orphans their identities had been stripped from them. And there in Kakuma, after all the running and dying and exposure to people and things they had never imagined, they grasped that there was one way to reconstruct themselves, through education.

25   In 1998, after the Lost Boys had spent six years in Kakuma, the U.S. State Department identified them as a group deserving resettlement in America. Two years later, the processing was done, and they began to arrive. A few, like Mangok Mach and David Gai, had finished high school and become teachers themselves—the only real professional opportunity available in Kakuma. Others were as much as three or four years away from their diplomas.

Landing in places like Boston, Philadelphia, and Kansas City, they felt as if the earth had moved. "The flight itself," one boy wrote to a friend, "was a mystery to us who were not familiar with its fluctuating situation and giddy behaviors. Even here in Philadelphia now everything is strange. Very strange!" At every turn, like the young men standing in the milking shed in Durham, they were confronted with the unimaginable. They responded at first with wonder and sometimes, desperation.

Educational assessments performed shortly after their arrival tended to be woeful. High school graduates often tested at the fifth- or sixth-grade level, and those who had been in ninth or tenth grades might test at second or third. Part of the reason was the depth of their disorientation, another the inadequacy of refugee camp schools. "It was confusing," David Gai said. "The school I had gone to was so remote, I didn't know if I would be competent."

But as they started figuring out their new surroundings, their drive for education reasserted itself. In the United States, unlike Kakuma, they saw a galaxy of possibilities. They could, it became evident, make at least a minimal living even without more schooling. For some that seemed enough. For others, even as they worked second-and third-shift entry-level jobs, their eyes were fixed on how Americans lived and what they did to get there. "A higher education," thought Jacob Mabil, "a Ph.D. I could do that!"

But even as this determination worked in them, what they discovered when they picked up their studies was often daunting. English fluency was the first problem. English was the language of the camp schools, and many were versed in the traditional Bible English. But outside of school they had spoken only Dinka or other tribal languages. To Americans their language often seemed oddly elegant yet fractured and barely comprehensible. "It is a fundamental fact and majestic," one newly arrived Lost Boy wrote to friends about his well-being, "to hold up my pen beyond my reasoning capacity to call all my compliments hoping that you are under normal residential area because the pen holder is also kicking well under an umbrella of Almighty God."

More problematic for those interested in college was their utter lack of   30
awareness about world civilization outside of East Africa. Plato, Aristotle, Alexander the Great, Galileo, Michelangelo, Marx, and Freud[7] were not recognized names. In an effort to address the knowledge gap, one volunteer professor set up a pre-college seminar for those who were beginning to take courses in community colleges and were looking forward to studying full-time. "It turned out to be the most interesting teaching experience in my life," he said. "You talk about the most significant watersheds in human history—pastoralism to settled life, oral culture to literacy, animism or pantheism to monotheism. They had never thought about these things critically, or even at all. But they had a remarkable receptivity. They came out of traditional Dinka life, preliterate, pastoral, animist. They became literate, settled; they were baptized into Christianity."

But the biggest hurdle was accommodating themselves to the American way of learning. Educators in Africa generally tend to emphasize memorization rather than critical thinking. People coming from oral cultures typically have quicker, more expansive memories than do those from literate cultures, where books serve as easily accessible, artificial memories. Consequently, in traditional societies rote learning is often the most logical and appropriate route to knowledge. According to Joseph Lugalla, a Tanzanian anthropology professor at the University of New Hampshire, "All over Africa, schools have few resources. Education is underfunded, and so important facilities like books and visual aids are just not available." Of course that is especially true in the camps. Jacob Mabil remembers it well. "When we went to school there," he explained, "10 people might share one book. If you share that book, you might have it for only one day, so you have to memorize everything. You won't see that book again until you have to read the next chapter."

According to Lugalla, the lack of teaching aids in African classrooms—books especially, but also computers, VCRs, films, TVs, transparencies, photo-

---

7. Plato (c. 427–347 B.C.E.), ancient Greek philosopher, believed to have taught Aristotle (c. 384–322 B.C.E.), also an ancient Greek philosopher and teacher; Alexander the Great (356–323 B.C.E.), Macedonian king who conquered most of the known world; Galileo Galilei (1464–1642), Italian astronomer; Michelangelo Buonarroti, (1475–1564), Italian artist; Karl Marx (1818–1883), German social thinker; Sigmund Freud (1856–1939), Austrian neurologist and father of psychoanalysis.

graphs—means that there is no shorthand way to convey information. Teachers must spend most of their time talking just to get across facts. In that environment there isn't much room for the synthesizing and interpreting that characterizes American education. The premium is on acquiring information, not using it. As a result, African students who come to the United States often have little experience with the kind of critical thinking American professors expect.

"It goes beyond that," Lugalla said. "With no lab equipment, no materials to work with, no chemicals for chemistry, no specimens or microscopes for biology students end up acquiring theoretical, abstract knowledge, but they have no way of subjecting theoretical knowledge to practical experience, no way of testing theories."

"When we learned things in the camp," said University of Massachusetts senior David Gai, "often they were about things we had no experience of, that we could not even picture. Carpets, for example. We were told about them and how to clean them. But we had no idea what they were. So we just memorized. The mind got used to picturing things we didn't know. We learned about carpets, wooden floors, electricity. It was as if the teachers were talking about angels in heaven."

35   The Lost Boy students who succeed in college, and most do, are those who manage to reorient their learning psychology, shifting from memorization to critical thinking. "Teaching them to think [along Western lines] has to be done incrementally," explained Vivian Zamel, an English professor at the University of Massachusetts who has designed curricula for immigrant students and teaches the Sudanese. Zamel's programs emphasize reading biographies and autobiographies, which stimulate students to write and think about their own lives and to reflect on others' experiences in relation to their own. The emphasis is not on what students learn but rather on what they think about what they learn. "It's not just saying what the author is saying," Zamel explained, "but why do you think he is saying it, and how does that compare to author X. We get them into questioning instead of regurgitation. You do that slowly and repeatedly, building it up. And they get used to it. It becomes a habit of mind."

Zamel's focus on what might be called metacognition[8] has helped the Sudanese in her programs turn themselves from memorizers into critical thinkers. But even those who don't have the advantage of Zamel's tutelage are usually able to make the transition. Paradoxically perhaps, their former traditional lives, still so present in their memories, give them a springboard. They live, after all, in two worlds. Intellectually and emotionally they are connected not just with their childhoods, as we all are, but with childhoods lived in a time millennially older than our own, kept vivid, even photographic, by the intensifying power of trauma. And because they live these simultaneous lives, the business of analysis and comparison, of synthesis and interpretation, is for them daily fare.

---

8. The process of thinking about thought.

In terms of academic learning, their history gives the Lost Boys a uniquely powerful perspective, at least in many of the humanities and social sciences. Students of history, for example, need to make an imaginative leap; they have to immerse themselves in the data of lives lived in different times and places in order to understand a period in its own terms rather than through contemporary eyes. Studying literature demands a similar imaginative projection. But for the Lost Boys, living in one world and understanding another in its own terms is second nature. It is who they are.

To the extent that their courses deal with pre-modern-era subjects or with the transition from pre-modern to modern, they have an additional advantage. A popular textbook in comparative politics, for example, begins with an exposition on the Enlightenment origins of the social sciences. A Lost Boy taking this course has no trouble grasping pre-Enlightenment modes of thinking. In significant ways his traditional life was similarly bounded. Another Lost Boy studying macroeconomics easily follows the history and meaning of money and modern monetary instruments; he knows what the world was like before money was invented. Talk about the closed world giving way to a new universe in the Renaissance—they have been there. The meaning of religion—they have thought deeply about it. The Exodus—they have made one. The Holocaust—they have survived their own.

The professors interviewed for this article all point to another characteristic that is helping the Lost Boys navigate the academic jungle: their sheer obsessive determination. "For these youngsters," one University of New Hampshire professor said, "being in college is a 24-hour-a-day job. It's 2:00 in the morning, and they're still at it. Usually college kids take breaks; it's party time, it's social time. These guys don't."

"They are such committed students," Vivian Zamel said. "They don't rest easy. Most American students, if they don't get Descartes[9] or something else, think, okay, I'll take care of it tomorrow. They can just go on to the next thing. The Sudanese are very disturbed by not knowing. Knowing how much they don't know disturbs them." What also strikes Zamel, Lugalla, and others is how compelling new knowledge is to the Lost Boys. Behind this phenomenon, so remarkable to almost all their teachers, is a psychological reality born of their history.

For the Lost Boys, learning has become over the years a survival mechanism, not only an internalized value but a driving force. They, who were born into the most insular and static of cultures, have evolved into a community of sojourners, and as such they have acquired the sojourner's two most essential pieces of baggage. They understand, first, that knowledge is a portable commodity, to be gathered like gold at each stop along the way for use at the next. They have learned too that intelligence itself is the most dynamic of human characteristics. "The mind," an eminent educator once quipped, "is like a parachute. When you need it, it has to open." For the Lost Boys of Sudan, that piece of wisdom began to reveal itself 18 years ago when the bombs first

40

9. René Descartes (1596–1650), French scientist, philosopher, and mathematician.

started falling. For those who have watched their progress here, they are the most vivid of witnesses to the inner workings of man's adaptive nature.

Almost universally, their professors mention one more thing about the Lost Boys; they have a profound effect on their college communities and fellow students. "You feel a special bond to these students," Zamel said. "What has happened to them seeps into the things they do." Given what they have experienced, the death of families and friends, the long years of violence and deprivation, they might have been expected to have become aggressive and hard-shelled, violent in their own lives. Yet the opposite seems to be true. "They are open, positive, optimistic," as one of their teachers put it. "Given that they grew up without any real adult guidance, it reaffirms something about what you hope human beings really are. It's like *Lord of the Flies* in reverse."[10]

10. A 1954 novel by William Golding (1911–1993) that features the devolving self-government of a group of young boys.

QUESTIONS

1. Usually, we think of human parents as "mothers" and "fathers." Why does David Chanoff suggest in his title—and later in his essay—that education has become the surrogate parent of the "Lost Boys of Sudan"? In what sense(s) does education represent parenting?

2. In the first section (paragraphs 1–9) and later in the essay (paragraphs 25–31) Chanoff contrasts a Dinka child's education in Sudan with the education that Sudanese boys experience in America. What are the contrasts? Why does Chanoff describe them in two different sections of his essay? Of what importance are the contrasts to Chanoff's argument?

3. The *American Scholar*, the magazine in which this essay appeared, is read by many secondary and college teachers. In what ways does Chanoff address this audience? Does his essay have things to say about education generally?

4. Write an essay about a person or group who needed to make a great adjustment between traditional home life and the educational experience in college. Consider interviewing someone at your college or an older member of your family, or, if relevant, analyze your own adjustment to higher education.

JOHN HOLT

How Teachers Make Children Hate Reading

W HEN I WAS TEACHING English at the Colorado Rocky Mountain School, I used to ask my students the kinds of questions that English teachers usually ask about reading assignments—questions designed to bring out the points that *I* had decided *they* should know. They, on their part, would try to get me to give them hints and clues as to what I wanted. It was a game of wits. I never gave my students an opportunity to say what they really thought about a book.

I gave vocabulary drills and quizzes too. I told my students that every time they came upon a word in their book they did not understand, they were to look it up in the dictionary. I even devised special kinds of vocabulary tests, allowing them to use their books to see how the words were used. But looking back, I realize that these tests, along with many of my methods, were foolish.

My sister was the first person who made me question my conventional ideas about teaching English. She had a son in the seventh grade in a fairly good public school. His teacher had asked the class to read Cooper's *The Deerslayer*.[1] The choice was bad enough in itself; whether looking at man or nature, Cooper was superficial, inaccurate and sentimental, and his writing is ponderous and ornate. But to make matters worse, this teacher had decided to give the book the microscope and x-ray treatment. He made the students look up and memorize not only the definitions but the derivations of every big word that came along—and there were plenty. Every chapter was followed by close questioning and testing to make sure the students "understood" everything.

Being then, as I said, conventional, I began to defend the teacher, who was a good friend of mine, against my sister's criticisms. The argument soon grew hot. What was wrong with making sure that children understood everything they read? My sister answered that until this year her boy had always loved reading, and had read a lot on his own; now he had stopped. (He was not really to start again for many years.)

Still I persisted. If children didn't look up the words they didn't know, how would they ever learn them? My sister said, "Don't be silly! When you were little you had a huge vocabulary, and were always reading very grown-up books. When did you ever look up a word in a dictionary?"

She had me. I don't know that we had a dictionary at home; if we did, I didn't use it. I don't use one today. In my life I doubt that I have looked up as many as fifty words, perhaps not even half that.

Since then I have talked about this with a number of teachers. More than

5

From The Under-Achieving School *(1967), Holt's third book-length critique of American education.*

1. James Fenimore Cooper (1789–1851), American novelist; *The Deerslayer* was published in 1841.

once I have said, "According to tests, educated and literate people like you have a vocabulary of about twenty-five thousand words. How many of these did you learn by looking them up in a dictionary?" They usually are startled. Few claim to have looked up even as many as a thousand. How did they learn the rest?

They learned them just as they learned to talk—by meeting words over and over again, in different contexts, until they saw how they fitted.

Unfortunately, we English teachers are easily hung up on this matter of understanding. Why should children understand everything they read? Why should anyone? Does anyone? I don't, and I never did. I was always reading books that teachers would have said were "too hard" for me, books full of words I didn't know. That's how I got to be a good reader. When about ten, I read all the D'Artagnan stories[2] and loved them. It didn't trouble me in the least that I didn't know why France was at war with England or who was quarreling with whom in the French court or why the Musketeers should always be at odds with Cardinal Richelieu's men. I didn't even know who the Cardinal was, except that he was a dangerous and powerful man that my friends had to watch out for. This was all I needed to know.

10   Having said this, I will now say that I think a big, unabridged dictionary is a fine thing to have in any home or classroom. No book is more fun to browse around in—*if* you're not made to. Children, depending on their age, will find many pleasant and interesting things to do with a big dictionary. They can look up funny-sounding words, which they like, or words that nobody else in the class has ever heard of, which they like, or long words, which they like, or forbidden words, which they like best of all. At a certain age, and particularly with a little encouragement from parents or teachers, they may become very interested in where words came from and when they came into the language and how their meanings have changed over the years. But exploring for the fun of it is very different from looking up words out of your reading because you're going to get into trouble with your teacher if you don't.

While teaching fifth grade two years or so after the argument with my sister, I began to think again about reading. The children in my class were supposed to fill out a card—just the title and author and a one-sentence summary—for every book they read. I was not running a competition to see which child could read the most books, a competition that almost always leads to cheating. I just wanted to know what the children were reading. After a while it became clear that many of these very bright kids, from highly literate and even literary backgrounds, read very few books and deeply disliked reading. Why should this be?

At this time I was coming to realize, as I described in my book *How Chil-*

---

2. Alexandre Dumas (1802–1870), called Dumas *père* to distinguish him from his son Alexandre, called Dumas *fils*, wrote *The Three Musketeers* (1844), a historical novel set in seventeenth-century France. D'Artagnan, the hero of the novel, meets three friends, already musketeers (soldiers who carry muskets), and joins them in fighting cardinals, dodging assassins, and seeking romance.

dren Fail, that for most children school was a place of danger, and their main business in school was staying out of danger as much as possible. I now began to see also that books were among the most dangerous things in school.

From the very beginning of school we make books and reading a constant source of possible failure and public humiliation. When children are little we make them read aloud, before the teacher and other children, so that we can be sure they "know" all the words they are reading. This means that when they don't know a word, they are going to make a mistake, right in front of everyone. Instantly they are made to realize that they have done something wrong. Perhaps some of the other children will begin to wave their hands and say, "Ooooh! O-o-o-oh!" Perhaps they will just giggle, or nudge each other, or make a face. Perhaps the teacher will say, "Are you sure?" or ask someone else what he thinks. Or perhaps, if the teacher is kindly, she will just smile a sweet, sad smile—often one of the most painful punishments a child can suffer in school. In any case, the child who has made the mistake knows he has made it, and feels foolish, stupid, and ashamed, just as any of us would in his shoes.

Before long many children associate books and reading with mistakes, real or feared, and penalties and humiliation. This may not seem sensible, but it is natural. Mark Twain once said that a cat that sat on a hot stove lid would never sit on one again—but it would never sit on a cold one either. As true of children as of cats. If they, so to speak, sit on a hot book a few times, if books cause them humiliation and pain, they are likely to decide that the safest thing to do is to leave all books alone.

After having taught fifth-grade classes for four years I felt quite sure of this theory. In my next class were many children who had had great trouble with schoolwork, particularly reading. I decided to try at all costs to rid them of their fear and dislike of books, and to get them to read oftener and more adventurously.

One day soon after school had started, I said to them, "Now I'm going to say something about reading that you have probably never heard a teacher say before. I would like you to read a lot of books this year, but I want you to read them only for pleasure. I am not going to ask you questions to find out whether you understand the books or not. If you understand enough of a book to enjoy it and want to go on reading it, that's enough for me. Also I'm not going to ask you what words mean.

"Finally," I said, "I don't want you to feel that just because you start a book, you have to finish it. Give an author thirty or forty pages or so to get his story going. Then if you don't like the characters and don't care what happens to them, close the book, put it away, and get another. I don't care whether the books are easy or hard, short or long, as long as you enjoy them. Furthermore I'm putting all this in a letter to your parents, so they won't feel they have to quiz and heckle you about books at home."

The children sat stunned and silent. Was this a teacher talking? One girl, who had just come to us from a school where she had had a very hard time, and who proved to be one of the most interesting, lively, and intelligent children I have ever known, looked at me steadily for a long time after I had fin-

15

ished. Then, still looking at me, she said slowly and solemnly, "Mr. Holt, do you really mean that?" I said just as solemnly, "I mean every word of it."

Apparently she decided to believe me. The first book she read was Dr. Seuss's *How the Grinch Stole Christmas,* not a hard book even for most third graders. For a while she read a number of books on this level. Perhaps she was clearing up some confusion about reading that her teachers, in their hurry to get her up to "grade level," had never given her enough time to clear up. After she had been in the class six weeks or so and we had become good friends, I very tentatively suggested that, since she was a skillful rider and loved horses, she might like to read *National Velvet.*[3] I made my sell as soft as possible, saying only that it was about a girl who loved and rode horses, and that if she didn't like it, she could put it back. She tried it, and though she must have found it quite a bit harder than what she had been reading, finished it and liked it very much.

20   During the spring she really astonished me, however. One day, in one of our many free periods, she was reading at her desk. From a glimpse of the illustrations I thought I knew what the book was. I said to myself, "It can't be," and went to take a closer look. Sure enough, she was reading *Moby Dick,* in the edition with woodcuts by Rockwell Kent. When I came close to her desk she looked up. I said, "Are you really reading that?" She said she was. I said, "Do you like it?" She said, "Oh, yes, it's neat!" I said, "Don't you find parts of it rather heavy going?" She answered, "Oh, sure, but I just skip over those parts and go on to the next good part."

This is exactly what reading should be and in school so seldom is—an exciting, joyous adventure. Find something, dive into it, take the good parts, skip the bad parts, get what you can out of it, go on to something else. How different is our mean-spirited, picky insistence that every child get every last little scrap of "understanding" that can be dug out of a book.

For teachers who really enjoy doing it, and will do it with gusto, reading aloud is a very good idea. I have found that not just fifth graders but even ninth and eleventh graders enjoy it. Jack London's "To Build a Fire" is a good read-aloud story. So are ghost stories, and "August Heat," by W. F. Harvey, and "The Monkey's Paw," by W. W. Jacobs, are among the best. Shirley Jackson's "The Lottery" is sure-fire, and will raise all kinds of questions for discussion and argument.[4] Because of a TV program they had seen and that excited them, I once started reading my fifth graders William Golding's *Lord of the Flies,*[5] thinking to read only a few chapters, but they made me read it to the end.

In my early fifth-grade classes the children usually were of high IQ, came from literate backgrounds and were generally felt to be succeeding in school. Yet it was astonishingly hard for most of those children to express themselves in speech or in writing. I have known a number of five-year-olds who were

3. Enid Bagnold (1889–1981), British author, published *National Velvet* in 1935.
4. London (1876–1916) and Jackson (1919–1965) are American novelists; Harvey (1885–1937) and Jacobs (1863–1943) are British novelists.
5. British novelist (1911–1993), published *Lord of the Flies* in 1954.

considerably more articulate than most of the fifth graders I have known in school. Asked to speak, my fifth graders were covered with embarrassment; many refused altogether. Asked to write, they would sit for minutes on end, staring at the paper. It was hard for most of them to get down a half page of writing, even on what seemed to be interesting topics or topics they chose themselves.

In desperation I hit on a device that I named the Composition Derby. I divided the class into teams, and told them that when I said, "Go," they were to start writing something. It could be about anything they wanted, but it had to be about something—they couldn't just write "dog dog dog dog" on the paper. It could be true stories, descriptions of people or places or events, wishes, made-up stories, dreams—anything they liked. Spelling didn't count, so they didn't have to worry about it. When I said, "Stop," they were to stop and count up the words they had written. The team that wrote the most words would win the derby.

It was a success in many ways and for many reasons. The first surprise 25 was that the two children who consistently wrote the most words were two of the least successful students in the class. They were bright, but they had always had a very hard time in school. Both were very bad spellers, and worrying about this had slowed down their writing without improving their spelling. When they were free of this worry and could let themselves go, they found hidden and unsuspected talents.

One of the two, a very driven and anxious little boy, used to write long adventures, or misadventures, in which I was the central character—"The Day Mr. Holt Went to Jail," "The Day Mr. Holt Fell Into the Hole," "The Day Mr. Holt Got Run Over," and so on. These were very funny, and the class enjoyed hearing me read them aloud. One day I asked the class to write a derby on a topic I would give them. They groaned; they liked picking their own. "Wait till you hear it," I said. "It's 'The Day the School Burned Down.'"

With a shout of approval and joy they went to work, and wrote furiously for 20 minutes or more, laughing and chuckling as they wrote. The papers were all much alike; in them the children danced around the burning building, throwing in books and driving me and the other teachers back in when we tried to escape.

In our first derby the class wrote an average of about ten words a minute; after a few months their average was over 20. Some of the slower writers tripled their output. Even the slowest, one of whom was the best student in the class, were writing 15 words a minute. More important, almost all the children enjoyed the derbies and wrote interesting things.

Some time later I learned that Professor S. I. Hayakawa, teaching freshman English, had invented a better technique. Every day in class he asked his students to write without stopping for about half an hour. They could write on whatever topic or topics they chose, but the important thing was not to stop. If they ran dry, they were to copy their last sentence over and over again until new ideas came. Usually they came before the sentence had been copied once. I use this idea in my own classes, and call this kind of paper a Non-Stop.

Sometimes I ask students to write a Non-Stop on an assigned topic, more often on anything they choose. Once in a while I ask them to count up how many words they have written, though I rarely ask them to tell me; it is for their own information. Sometimes these papers are to be handed in; often they are what I call private papers, for the students' eyes alone.

30   The private paper has proved very useful. In the first place, in any English class—certainly any large English class—if the amount the students write is limited by what the teacher can find time to correct, or even to read, the students will not write nearly enough. The only remedy is to have them write a great deal that the teacher does not read. In the second place, students writing for themselves will write about many things that they would never write on a paper to be handed in, once they have learned (sometimes it takes a while) that the teacher means what he says about the papers' being private. This is important, not just because it enables them to get things off their chest, but also because they are most likely to write well, and to pay attention to how they write, when they are writing about something important to them.

Some English teachers, when they first hear about private papers, object that students do not benefit from writing papers unless the papers are corrected. I disagree for several reasons. First, most students, particularly poor students, do not read the corrections on their papers; it is boring, even painful. Second, even when they do read these corrections, they do not get much help from them, do not build the teacher's suggestions into their writing. This is true even when they really believe the teacher knows what he is talking about.

Third, and most important, we learn to write by writing, not by reading other people's ideas about writing. What most students need above all else is practice in writing, and particularly in writing about things that matter to them, so that they will begin to feel the satisfaction that comes from getting important thoughts down in words and will care about stating these thoughts forcefully and clearly.

Teachers of English—or, as some schools say (ugh!), Language Arts— spend a lot of time and effort on spelling. Most of it is wasted; it does little good, and often more harm than good. We should ask ourselves, "How do good spellers spell? What do they do when they are not sure which spelling of a word is right?" I have asked this of a number of good spellers. Their answer never varies. They do not rush for a dictionary or rack their brains trying to remember some rules. They write down the word both ways, or several ways, look at them and pick the one that looks best. Usually they are right.

Good spellers know what words look like and even, in their writing muscles, feel like. They have a good set of word images in their minds, and are willing to trust these images. The things we do to "teach" spelling to children do little to develop these skills or talents, and much to destroy them or prevent them from developing.

35   The first and worst thing we do is to make children anxious about spelling. We treat a misspelled word like a crime and penalize the misspeller severely; many teachers talk of making children develop a "spelling conscience," and fail otherwise excellent papers because of a few spelling mis-

takes. This is self-defeating. When we are anxious, we don't perceive clearly or remember what we once perceived. Everyone knows how hard it is to recall even simple things when under emotional pressure; the harder we rack our brains, the less easy it is to find what we are looking for. If we are anxious enough, we will not trust the messages that memory sends us. Many children spell badly because although their first hunches about how to spell a word may be correct, they are afraid to trust them. I have often seen on children's papers a word correctly spelled, then crossed out and misspelled.

There are some tricks that might help children get sharper word images. Some teachers may be using them. One is the trick of air writing; that is, of "writing" a word in the air with a finger and "seeing" the image so formed. I did this quite a bit with fifth graders, using either the air or the top of a desk, on which their fingers left no mark. Many of them were tremendously excited by this. I can still hear them saying, "There's nothing there, but I can see it!" It seemed like black magic. I remember that when I was little I loved to write in the air. It was effortless, voluptuous, satisfying, and it was fun to see the word appear in the air. I used to write "Money Money Money," not so much because I didn't have any as because I liked the way it felt, particularly that *y* at the end, with its swooping tail.

Another thing to help sharpen children's image-making machinery is taking very quick looks at words—or other things. The conventional machine for doing this is the tachistoscope. But these are expensive, so expensive that most children can have few chances to use them, if any at all. With some three-by-five and four-by-eight file cards you can get the same effect. On the little cards you put the words or the pictures that the child is going to look at. You hold the larger card over the card to be read, uncover it for a split second with a quick wrist motion, then cover it up again. Thus you have a tachistoscope that costs one cent and that any child can work by himself.

Once when substituting in a first-grade class, I thought that the children, who were just beginning to read and write, might enjoy some of the kind of free, nonstop writing that my fifth graders had. One day about 40 minutes before lunch, I asked them all to take pencil and paper and start writing about anything they wanted to. They seemed to like the idea, but right away one child said anxiously, "Suppose we can't spell a word."

"Don't worry about it," I said. "Just spell it the best way you can."

A heavy silence settled on the room. All I could see were still pencils and anxious faces. This was clearly not the right approach. So I said, "All right, I'll tell you what we'll do. Any time you want to know how to spell a word, tell me and I'll write it on the board."

They breathed a sigh of relief and went to work. Soon requests for words were coming fast; as soon as I wrote one, someone asked me another. By lunchtime, when most of the children were still busily writing, the board was full. What was interesting was that most of the words they had asked for were much longer and more complicated than anything in their reading books or workbooks. Freed from worry about spelling, they were willing to use the most difficult and interesting words that they knew.

40

The words were still on the board when we began school next day. Before I began to erase them, I said to the children, "Listen, everyone. I have to erase these words, but before I do, just out of curiosity, I'd like to see if you remember some of them."

The result was surprising. I had expected that the child who had asked for and used a word might remember it, but I did not think many others would. But many of the children still knew many of the words. How had they learned them? I suppose each time I wrote a word on the board a number of children had looked up, relaxed yet curious, just to see what the word looked like, and these images and the sound of my voice saying the word had stuck in their minds until the next day. This, it seems to me, is how children may best learn to write and spell.

What can a parent do if a school, or a teacher, is spoiling the language for a child by teaching it in some tired way? First, try to get them to change, or at least let them know that you are eager for change. Talk to other parents; push some of these ideas in the PTA; talk to the English department at the school; talk to the child's own teacher. Many teachers and schools want to know what the parents want.

45   If the school or teacher cannot be persuaded, then what? Perhaps all you can do is try not to let your child become too bored or discouraged or worried by what is happening in school. Help him meet the school's demands, foolish though they may seem, and try to provide more interesting alternatives at home—plenty of books and conversation, and a serious and respectful audience when a child wants to talk. Nothing that ever happened to me in English classes at school was as helpful to me as the long conversations I used to have every summer with my uncle, who made me feel that the difference in our ages was not important and that he was really interested in what I had to say.

At the end of her freshman year in college a girl I know wrote home to her mother, "Hooray! Hooray! Just think—I never have to take English any more!" But this girl had always been an excellent English student, had always loved books, writing, ideas. It seems unnecessary and foolish and wrong that English teachers should so often take what should be the most flexible, exciting, and creative of all school courses and make it into something that most children can hardly wait to see the last of. Let's hope that we can and soon will begin to do much better.

QUESTIONS

1. Mark the anecdotes that Holt uses and describe how he orders them in time and by theme. Consider the advantages and disadvantages of his organizing this essay to reflect his own learning.

2. "[F]or most children," Holt observes, "school was a place of danger, and their main business in school was staying out of danger as much as possible" (paragraph 12). Locate instances in which he makes this point explicit and instances in which he implies it.

3. Holt's "Composition Derby" and Hayakawa's "Non-Stop" are now usually called free writing. Have your teachers used free writing? In what grades? From your own experience, how much has the teaching of writing changed since 1967, when Holt wrote this essay?

4. Holt begins this essay by describing the "game of wits" played by teachers and students alike: teachers ask students what teachers want students to know and students ask teachers for clues about what teachers want (paragraph 1). Do you recognize this game? Do you remember learning to play it? Do you think you play it well? Do you like playing it? Write an essay that answers these questions. Be sure to include anecdotes from your own experience.

BENJAMIN R. BARBER *America Skips School*

O N SEPTEMBER 8, the day most of the nation's children were scheduled to return to school, the Department of Education Statistics issued a report, commissioned by Congress, on adult literacy and numeracy in the United States. The results? More than 90 million adult Americans lacked simple literacy. Fewer than 20 percent of those surveyed could compare two metaphors in a poem; not 4 percent could calculate the cost of carpeting at a given price for a room of a given size, using a calculator. As the DOE report was being issued, as if to echo its findings, two of the nation's largest school systems had delayed their openings: in New York, to remove asbestos from aging buildings; in Chicago, because of a battle over the budget.

Inspired by the report and the delays, pundits once again began chanting the familiar litany of the education crisis. We've heard it all many times before: 130,000 children bring guns along with their pencils and books to school each morning; juvenile arrests for murder increased by 85 percent from 1987 to 1991; more than 3,000 youngsters will drop out today and every day for the rest of the school year, until about 600,000 are lost by June—in many urban schools, perhaps half the enrollment. A lot of the dropouts will end up in prison, which is a surer bet for young black males than college: one in four will pass through the correctional system, and at least two out of three of those will be dropouts.

In quiet counterpoint to those staggering facts is another set of statistics: teachers make less than accountants, architects, doctors, lawyers, engineers, judges, health professionals, auditors, and surveyors. They can earn higher

Originally published in Harper's Magazine *(November 1993), a long-standing American periodical devoted to social, political, and literary issues; later included in Barber's book,* A Passion for Democracy *(1999), with the subtitle "Why We Talk So Much about Education and Do So Little."*

salaries teaching in Berlin, Tokyo, Ottawa, or Amsterdam than in New York or Chicago. American children are in school only about 180 days a year, as against 240 days or more for children in Europe or Japan. The richest school districts (school financing is local, not federal) spend twice as much per student as poorer ones do. The poorer ones seem almost beyond help: children with venereal disease or AIDS (2.5 million adolescents annually contract a sexually transmitted disease), gangs in the schoolyard, drugs in the classroom, children doing babies instead of homework, playground firefights featuring Uzis and Glocks.

Clearly, the social contract that obliges adults to pay taxes so that children can be educated is in imminent danger of collapse. Yet for all the astonishing statistics, more astonishing still is that no one seems to be listening. The education crisis is kind of like violence on television: the worse it gets the more inert we become, and the more of it we require to rekindle our attention. We've had a "crisis" every dozen years or so at least since the launch of *Sputnik*, in 1957, when American schools were accused of falling behind the world standard in science education. Just ten years ago, the National Commission on Excellence in Education warned that America's pedagogical inattention was putting America "at risk."[1] What the commission called "a rising tide of mediocrity" was imperiling "our very future as a Nation and a people." What was happening to education was an "act of war."

5   Since then, countless reports have been issued decrying the condition of our educational system, the DOE report being only the most recent. They have come from every side, Republican as well as Democrat, from the private sector as well as the public. Yet for all the talk, little happens. At times, the schools look more like they are being dismantled than rebuilt. How can this be? If Americans over a broad political spectrum regard education as vital, why has nothing been done?

I have spent thirty years as a scholar examining the nature of democracy, and even more as a citizen optimistically celebrating its possibilities, but today I am increasingly persuaded that the reason for the country's inaction is that Americans do not really care about education—the country has grown comfortable with the game of "let's pretend we care."

As America's educational system crumbles, the pundits, instead of looking for solutions, search busily for scapegoats. Some assail the teachers—those "Profscam" pedagogues trained in the licentious Sixties who, as aging hippies, are supposedly still subverting the schools—for producing a dire illiteracy. Others turn on the kids themselves, so that at the same moment as we are transferring our responsibilities to the shoulders of the next generation, we are blaming them for our own generation's most conspicuous failures. Allan Bloom[2] was typical of the many recent critics who have condemned the young

---

1. William Bennett's *A Nation at Risk* was published in 1984.

2. Bloom's *The Closing of the American Mind* was published in 1987, the same year as the other books mentioned in this paragraph.

as vapid, lazy, selfish, complacent, self-seeking, materialistic, small-minded, apathetic, greedy, and, of course, illiterate. E. D. Hirsch in his *Cultural Literacy* and Diane Ravitch and Chester E. Finn Jr. in their *What Do Our Seventeen-Year-Olds Know?* have lambasted the schools, the teachers, and the children for betraying the adult generation from which they were to inherit, the critics seemed confident, a precious cultural legacy.

How this captious literature reeks of hypocrisy! How sanctimonious all the hand-wringing over still another "education crisis" seems. Are we ourselves really so literate? Are our kids stupid or smart for ignoring what we preach and copying what we practice? The young, with their keen noses for hypocrisy, are in fact adept readers—but not of books. They are society-smart rather than school-smart, and what they read so acutely are the social signals emanating from the world in which they will have to make a living. Their teachers in that world, the nation's true pedagogues, are television, advertising, movies, politics, and the celebrity domains they define. We prattle about deficient schools and the gullible youngsters they turn out, so vulnerable to the siren song of drugs, but think nothing of letting the advertisers into the classroom to fashion what an *Advertising Age* essay calls "brand and product loyalties through classroom-centered, peer-powered lifestyle patterning."

Our kids spend 900 hours a year in school (the ones who go to school) and from 1,200 to 1,800 hours a year in front of the television set. From which are they likely to learn more? Critics such as Hirsch and Ravitch want to find out what our seventeen-year-olds know, but it's really pretty simple: they know exactly what our forty-seven-year-olds know and teach them by example—on television, in the boardroom, around Washington, on Madison Avenue, in Hollywood. The very first lesson smart kids learn is that it is much more important to heed what society teaches implicitly by its deeds and reward structures than what school teaches explicitly in its lesson plans and civic sermons. Here is a test for adults that may help reveal what the kids see when they look at our world.

REAL-WORLD CULTURAL LITERACY

1. According to television, having fun in America means
   a) going blond
   b) drinking Pepsi
   c) playing Nintendo
   d) wearing Air Jordans
   e) reading Mark Twain

2. A good way to prepare for a high-income career and to acquire status in our society is to
   a) win a slam-dunk contest
   b) take over a company and sell off its assets
   c) start a successful rock band
   d) earn a professional degree
   e) become a kindergarten teacher

3. Book publishers are financially rewarded today for publishing
    a) mega-cookbooks
    b) mega–cat books
    c) megabooks by Michael Crichton
    d) megabooks by John Grisham
    e) mini-books by Voltaire

4. A major California bank that advertised "no previous credit history re-
    quired" in inviting Berkeley students to apply for Visa cards nonethe-
    less turned down one group of applicants because
    a) their parents had poor credit histories
    b) they had never held jobs
    c) they had outstanding student loans
    d) they were "humanities majors"

5. Colleges and universities are financially rewarded today for
    a) supporting bowl-quality football teams
    b) forging research relationships with large corporations
    c) sustaining professional programs in law and business
    d) stroking wealthy alumni
    e) fostering outstanding philosophy departments

6. Familiarity with *Henry IV, Part II* is likely to be of vital importance in
    a) planning a corporate takeover
    b) evaluating budget cuts in the Department of Education
    c) initiating a medical-malpractice lawsuit
    d) writing an impressive job résumé
    e) taking a test on what our seventeen-year-olds know

7. To help the young learn that "history is a living thing," Scholastic, Inc.,
    a publisher of school magazines and paperbacks, recently distributed
    to 40,000 junior and senior high-school classrooms
    a) a complimentary video of the award-winning series *The Civil War*
    b) free copies of Plato's *Dialogues*
    c) an abridgment of Alexis de Tocqueville's *Democracy in America*
    d) a wall-size Periodic Table of the Elements
    e) gratis copies of Billy Joel's hit single "We Didn't Start the Fire"
       (which recounts history via a vaguely chronological list of warbled
       celebrity names)

10   My sample of forty-seven-year-olds scored very well on the test. Not surprisingly, so did their seventeen-year-old children. (For each question, either
the last entry is correct or all responses are correct *except* the last one.) The
results of the test reveal again the deep hypocrisy that runs through our
lamentations about education. The illiteracy of the young turns out to be our
own reflected back to us with embarrassing force. We honor ambition, we reward greed, we celebrate materialism, we worship acquisitiveness, we cherish
success, and we commercialize the classroom—and then we bark at the young

about the gentle arts of the spirit. We recommend history to the kids but rarely consult it ourselves. We make a fuss about ethics but are satisfied to see it taught as an "add-on," as in "ethics in medicine" or "ethics in business"—as if Sunday morning in church could compensate for uninterrupted sinning from Monday to Saturday.

The children are onto this game. They know that if we really valued schooling, we'd pay teachers what we pay stockbrokers; if we valued books, we'd spend a little something on the libraries so that adults could read, too; if we valued citizenship, we'd give national service and civic education more than pilot status; if we valued children, we wouldn't let them be abused, manipulated, impoverished, and killed in their beds by gang-war cross fire and stray bullets. Schools can and should lead, but when they confront a society that in every instance tells a story exactly opposite to the one they are supposed to be teaching, their job becomes impossible. When the society undoes each workday what the school tries to do each school day, schooling can't make much of a difference.

Inner-city children are not the only ones who are learning the wrong lessons. TV sends the same messages to everyone, and the success of Donald Trump, Pete Rose, Henry Kravis, or George Steinbrenner makes them potent role models, whatever their values. Teen dropouts are not blind; teen drug sellers are not deaf; teen college students who avoid the humanities in favor of pre-business or pre-law are not stupid. Being apt pupils of reality, they learn their lessons well. If they see a man with a rubber arm and an empty head who can throw a ball at 95 miles per hour pulling down millions of dollars a year while a dedicated primary-school teacher is getting crumbs, they will avoid careers in teaching even if they can't make the major leagues. If they observe their government spending up to $35,000 a year to keep a young black behind bars but a fraction of that to keep him in school, they will write off school (and probably write off blacks as well).

Our children's illiteracy is merely our own, which they assume with commendable prowess. They know what we have taught them all too well: there is nothing in Homer or Virginia Woolf, in Shakespeare or Toni Morrison, that will advantage them in climbing to the top of the American heap. Academic credentials may still count, but schooling in and of itself is for losers. Bookworms. Nerds. Inner-city rappers and fraternity-house wise guys are in full agreement about that. The point is to start pulling down the big bucks. Some kids just go into business earlier than others. Dropping out is the national pastime, if by dropping out we mean giving up the precious things of the mind and the spirit in which America shows so little interest and for which it offers so little payback. While the professors argue about whether to teach the ancient history of a putatively white Athens or the ancient history of a putatively black Egypt[3] the kids are watching televised political campaigns driven by mindless image-mongering and inflammatory polemics that ignore history altogether. Why, then, are we so surprised when our students dismiss the debate

3. The debate began with the publication of Martin Bernal's *Black Athena* in 1987.

over the origins of civilization, whether Eurocentric or Afrocentric, and concentrate on cash-and-carry careers? Isn't the choice a tribute not to their ignorance but to their adaptive intelligence? Although we can hardly be proud of ourselves for what we are teaching them, we should at least be proud of them for how well they've learned our lessons.

Not all Americans have stopped caring about the schools, however. In the final irony of the educational endgame, cynical entrepreneurs like Chris Whittle are insinuating television into the classroom itself, bribing impoverished school boards by offering free TV sets on which they can show advertising for children—sold to sponsors at premium rates. Whittle, the mergers and acquisitions mogul of education, is trying to get rich off the poverty of public schools and the fears of parents. Can he really believe advertising in the schools enhances education? Or is he helping to corrupt public schools in ways that will make parents even more anxious to use vouchers for private schools—which might one day be run by Whittle's latest entrepreneurial venture, the Edison Project.[4]

15   According to Lifetime Learning Systems, an educational-software company, "kids spend 40 percent of each day . . . where traditional advertising can't reach them." Not to worry, says Lifetime Learning in an *Advertising Age* promo: "Now, you can enter the classroom through custom-made learning materials created with your specific marketing objectives in mind. Communicate with young spenders directly and, through them, their teachers and families as well." If we redefine young learners as "young spenders," are the young really to be blamed for acting like mindless consumers? Can they become young spenders and still become young critical thinkers, let alone informed citizens? If we are willing to give TV cartoons the government's imprimatur as "educational television" (as we did a few years ago, until the FCC changed its mind), can we blame kids for educating themselves on television trash?

Everyone can agree that we should educate our children to be something more than young spenders molded by "lifestyle patterning." But what should the goals of the classroom be? In recent years it has been fashionable to define the educational crisis in terms of global competition and minimal competence, as if schools were no more than vocational institutions. Although it has talked sensibly about education, the Clinton Administration has leaned toward this approach, under the tutelage of Secretary of Labor Robert Reich.[5]

The classroom, however, should not be merely a trade school. The fundamental task of education in a democracy is what Tocqueville[6] once called the apprenticeship of liberty: learning to be free. I wonder whether Americans still believe liberty has to be learned and that its skills are worth learning. Or have

4. A private corporation founded in 1991 to run public schools for profit.
5. Clinton's first secretary of labor.
6. Alexis de Tocqueville (1805–1859), French author and statesman, best known for his study of American political and social institutions, *Democracy in America* (1835–40).

they been deluded by two centuries of rhetoric into thinking that freedom is "natural" and can be taken for granted?

The claim that all men are born free, upon which America was founded, is at best a promising fiction. In real life, as every parent knows, children are born fragile, born needy, born ignorant, born unformed, born weak, born foolish, born dependent—born in chains. We acquire our freedom over time, if at all. Embedded in families, clans, communities, and nations, we must learn to be free. We may be natural consumers and born narcissists, but citizens have to be made. Liberal-arts education actually means education in the arts of liberty; the "servile arts" were the trades learned by unfree men in the Middle Ages, the vocational education of their day. Perhaps this is why Thomas Jefferson preferred to memorialize his founding of the University of Virginia on his tombstone rather than his two terms as president; it is certainly why he viewed his Bill for the More General Diffusion of Knowledge in Virginia as a centerpiece of his career (although it failed passage as legislation—times were perhaps not so different). John Adams, too, boasted regularly about Massachusetts's high literacy rates and publicly funded education.

Jefferson and Adams both understood that the Bill of Rights offered little protection in a nation without informed citizens. Once educated, however, a people was safe from even the subtlest tyrannies. Jefferson's democratic proclivities rested on his conviction that education could turn a people into a safe refuge—indeed "the only safe depository" for the ultimate powers of society. "Cherish therefore the spirit of our people," he wrote to Edward Carrington in 1787, "and keep alive their attention. Do not be severe upon their errors, but reclaim them by enlightening them. If once they become inattentive to public affairs, you and I and Congress and Assemblies, judges and governors shall all become wolves."

The logic of democracy begins with public education, proceeds to informed citizenship, and comes to fruition in the securing of rights and liberties. We have been nominally democratic for so long that we presume it is our natural condition rather than the product of persistent effort and tenacious responsibility. We have decoupled rights from civic responsibilities and severed citizenship from education on the false assumption that citizens just happen. We have forgotten that the "public" in public schools means not just paid for by the public but procreative of the very idea of a public. Public schools are how a public—a citizenry—is forged and how young, selfish individuals turn into conscientious, community-minded citizens.

20

Among the several literacies that have attracted the anxious attention of commentators, civic literacy has been the least visible. Yet this is the fundamental literacy by which we live in a civil society. It encompasses the competence to participate in democratic communities, the ability to think critically and act with deliberation in a pluralistic world, and the empathy to identify sufficiently with others to live with them despite conflicts of interest and differences in character. At the most elementary level, what our children suffer from most, whether they're hurling racial epithets from fraternity porches or shooting one another down in schoolyards, is the absence of civility. Security guards and metal detectors are poor surrogates for civility, and they make our schools look increasingly like prisons (though they may be less safe than prisons). Jefferson thought schools would produce free men: we prove him right by putting dropouts in jail.

Civility is a work of the imagination, for it is through the imagination that we render others sufficiently like ourselves for them to become subjects of tolerance and respect, if not always affection. Democracy is anything but a "natural" form of association. It is an extraordinary and rare contrivance of cultivated imagination. Give the uneducated the right to participate in making collective decisions, and what results is not democracy but, at best, mob rule: the government of private prejudice once known as the tyranny of opinion. For Jefferson, the difference between the democratic temperance he admired in agrarian America and the rule of the rabble he condemned when viewing the social unrest of Europe's teeming cities was quite simply education. Madison had hoped to "filter" out popular passion through the device of representation. Jefferson saw in education a filter that could be installed within each individual, giving to each the capacity to rule prudently. Education creates a ruling aristocracy constrained by temperance and wisdom; when that education is public and universal, it is an aristocracy to which all can belong. At its best, the American dream of a free and equal society governed by judicious citizens has been this dream of an aristocracy of everyone.

To dream this dream of freedom is easy, but to secure it is difficult as well as expensive. Notwithstanding their lamentations, Americans do not appear ready to pay the price. There is no magic bullet for education. But I no longer can accept that the problem lies in the lack of consensus about remedies—in a dearth of solutions. There is no shortage of debate over how to repair our educational infrastructure. National standards or more local control? Vouchers or better public schools? More parental involvement or more teacher autonomy? A greater federal presence (only 5 or 6 percent of the nation's education budget is federally funded) or fairer local school taxes? More multicultural diversity or more emphasis on what Americans share in common? These are honest disputes. But I am convinced that the problem is simpler and more fundamental. Twenty years ago, writer and activist Frances Moore Lappé[7] captured the essence of the world food crisis when she argued that starvation was caused not by a scarcity of food but by a global scarcity in democracy. The education crisis has the same genealogy. It stems from a dearth of democracy, an absence of democratic will, and a consequent refusal to take our children, our schools, and our future seriously.

Most educators, even while they quarrel among themselves, will agree that a genuine commitment to any one of a number of different solutions could help enormously. Most agree that although money can't by itself solve problems, without money few problems can be solved. Money also can't win

7. American (b. 1944), author of *Diet for a Small Planet* and cofounder of the Institute for Food and Development Policy.

wars or put men in space, but it is the crucial facilitator. It is also how America has traditionally announced, We are serious about this!

If we were serious, we would raise teachers' salaries to levels that would   25
attract the best young professionals in our society: starting lawyers get from $70,000 to $80,000—why don't starting kindergarten teachers get the same? Is their role in vouchsafing our future less significant? And although there is evidence suggesting than an increase in general educational expenditures doesn't translate automatically into better schools, there is also evidence that an increase aimed specifically at instructional services does. Can we really take in earnest the chattering devotion to excellence of a country so wedded in practice to mediocrity, a nation so ready to relegate teachers—conservators of our common future—to the professional backwaters?

If we were serious, we would upgrade physical facilities so that every school met the minimum standards of our better suburban institutions. Good buildings do not equal good education, but can any education at all take place in leaky, broken-down habitats of the kind described by Jonathan Kozol in his *Savage Inequalities*?[8] If money is not a critical factor, why are our most successful suburban school districts funded at nearly twice the level of our inner-city schools? Being even at the starting line cannot guarantee that the runners will win or even finish the race, but not being even pretty much assures failure. We would rectify the balance not by penalizing wealthier communities but by bringing poorer communities up to standard, perhaps, by finding other sources of funding for our schools besides property taxes.

If we were serious, we'd extend the school year by a month or two so that learning could take place throughout the year. We'd reduce class size (which means more teachers) and nurture more cooperative learning so that kids could become actively responsible for their own education and that of their classmates. Perhaps most important, we'd raise standards and make teachers and students responsible for them. There are two ways to breed success: to lower standards so that everybody "passes" in a way that loses all meaning in the real world; and to raise standards and then meet them, so that school success translates into success beyond the classroom. From Confucian China to Imperial England, great nations have built their success in the world upon an education of excellence. The challenge in a democracy is to find a way to maintain excellence while extending educational opportunity to everyone.

Finally, if we were serious, parents, teachers, and students would be the real players while administrators, politicians, and experts would be secondary, at best advisers whose chief skill ought to be knowing when and how to facilitate the work of teachers and then get out of the way. If the Democrats can clean up federal government bureaucracy (the Gore plan), perhaps we can do the same for educational bureaucracy. In New York up to half of the city's teachers occupy jobs outside the classroom. No other enterprise is run that way: Half the soldiers at company headquarters? Half the cops at station-house desks? Half the working force in the assistant manager's office? Once

8. Published in 1991.

the teachers are back in the classroom, they will need to be given more autonomy, more professional responsibility for the success or failure of their students. And parents will have to be drawn in not just because they have rights
or because they are politically potent but because they have responsibilities
and their children are unlikely to learn without parental engagement. How to
define the parental role in the classroom would become serious business for
educators.

Some Americans will say this is unrealistic. Times are tough, money's
short, and the public is fed up with almost all of its public institutions: the
schools are just one more frustrating disappointment. With all the goodwill in
the world, it is still hard to know how schools can cure the ills that stem from
the failure of so many other institutions. Saying we want education to come
first won't put it first.

30   America, however, has historically been able to accomplish what it sets its
mind to. When we wish it and will it, what we wish and will has happened.
Our successes are willed; our failures seem to happen when will is absent.
There are, of course, those who benefit from the bankruptcy of public education and the failure of democracy. But their blame is no greater than our own:
in a world where doing nothing has such dire consequences, complacency has
become a greater sin than malevolence.

In wartime, whenever we have known why we were fighting and believed
in the cause, we have prevailed. Because we believe in profits, we are consummate salespersons and efficacious entrepreneurs. Because we love sports, ours
are the dream teams. Why can't a Chicago junior high school be as good as the
Chicago Bulls? Because we cherish individuality and mobility, we have created
a magnificent (if costly) car culture and the world's largest automotive consumer market. Even as our lower schools are among the worst in the Western
world, our graduate institutions are among the very best—because professional training in medicine, law, and technology is vital to our ambitions and
because corporate America backs up state and federal priorities in this crucial
domain. Look at the things we do well and observe how very well we do them:
those are the things that as a nation we have willed.

Then observe what we do badly and ask yourself, Is it because the challenge is too great? Or is it because, finally, we aren't really serious? Would we
will an end to the carnage and do whatever it took—more cops, state militias,
federal marshals, the Marines?—if the dying children were white and middle
class? Or is it a disdain for the young—white, brown, and black—that inures
us to the pain? Why are we so sensitive to the retirees whose future (however
foreshortened) we are quick to guarantee—don't worry, no reduced cost-of-
living allowances, no taxes on social security except for the well-off—and so
callous to the young? Have you noticed how health care is on every politician's
agenda and education on no one's?

To me, the conclusion is inescapable: we are not serious. We have given
up on the public schools because we have given up on the kids; and we have
given up on the kids because we have given up on the future—perhaps because it looks too multicolored or too dim or too hard. "Liberty," said Jean-
Jacques Rousseau,[9] is a food easy to eat but hard to digest." America is

suffering from a bad case of indigestion. Finally, in giving up on the future, we have given up on democracy. Certainly there will be no liberty, no equality, no social justice without democracy, and there will be no democracy without citizens and the schools that forge civic identity and democratic responsibility. If I am wrong (I'd like to be), my error will be easy to discern, for before the year is out we will put education first on the nation's agenda. We will put it ahead of the deficit, for if the future is finished before it starts, the deficit doesn't matter. Ahead of defense, for without democracy, what liberties will be left to defend? Ahead of all the other public issues and public goods, for without public education there can be no public and hence no truly public issues or public goods to advance. When the polemics are spent and we are through hyperventilating about the crisis in education, there is only one question worth asking: are we serious? If we are, we can begin by honoring that old folk homily and put our money where for much too long our common American mouth has been. Our kids, for once, might even be grateful.

9. French philosopher and political and social theorist (1712–1778).

QUESTIONS

1. What is the function of Barber's Real-World Cultural Literacy Test in the larger argument of his essay?

2. Write three additional questions for the Real-World Cultural Literacy Test.

3. Mark some of the passages in which Barber expresses strong feelings about American education. What are some characteristic ways he expresses these feelings?

4. What is "civic literacy"? How does Barber define it? Why is it so important to him? Do you share his sense of its importance? Why or why not?

CAROLINE BIRD   *College Is a Waste of Time and Money*

A GREAT MAJORITY of our nine million college students are not in school because they want to be or because they want to learn. They are there because it has become the thing to do or because college is a pleasant place to be; because it's the only way they can get parents or taxpayers to support them without working at a job they don't like; because Mother wanted them to go, or some other reason entirely irrelevant to the course of studies for which college is supposedly organized.

From Bird's book The Case Against College *(1975).*

As I crisscross the United States lecturing on college campuses, I am dismayed to find that professors and administrators, when pressed for a candid opinion, estimate that no more than 25 percent of their students are turned on by classwork. For the rest, college is at best a social center or aging vat, and at worst a young folks' home or even a prison that keeps them out of the mainstream of economic life for a few more years.

The premise—which I no longer accept—that college is the best place for all high-school graduates grew out of a noble American ideal. Just as the United States was the first nation to aspire to teach every small child to read and write, so, during the 1950s, we became the first and only great nation to aspire to higher education for all. During the '60s we damned the expense and built great state university systems as fast as we could. And adults—parents, employers, high-school counselors—began to push, shove and cajole youngsters to "get an education."

It became a mammoth industry, with taxpayers footing more than half the bill. By 1970, colleges and universities were spending more than 30 billion dollars annually. But still only half our high-school graduates were going on. According to estimates made by the economist Fritz Machlup, if we had been educating every young person until age 22 in that year of 1970, the bill for higher education would have reached 47.5 billion dollars, 12.5 billion more than the total corporate profits for the year.

5   Figures such as these have begun to make higher education for all look financially prohibitive, particularly now when colleges are squeezed by the pressures of inflation and a drop-off in the growth of their traditional market.

Predictable demography has caught up with the university empire builders. Now that the record crop of postwar babies has graduated from college, the rate of growth of the student population has begun to decline. To keep their mammoth plants financially solvent, many institutions have begun to use hard-sell, Madison-Avenue techniques to attract students. They sell college like soap, promoting features they think students want: innovative programs, an environment conducive to meaningful personal relationships, and a curriculum so free that it doesn't sound like college at all.

Pleasing the customers is something new for college administrators. Colleges have always known that most students don't like to study, and that at least part of the time they are ambivalent about college, but before the student riots of the 1960s educators never thought it either right or necessary to pay any attention to student feelings. But when students rebelling against the Vietnam war and the draft discovered they could disrupt a campus completely, administrators had to act on some student complaints. Few understood that the protests had tapped the basic discontent with college itself, a discontent that did not go away when the riots subsided.

Today students protest individually rather than in concert. They turn inward and withdraw from active participation. They drop out to travel to India or to feed themselves on subsistence farms. Some refuse to go to college at all. Most, of course, have neither the funds nor the self-confidence for constructive articulation of their discontent. They simply hang around college unhappily and reluctantly.

All across the country, I have been overwhelmed by the prevailing sadness on American campuses. Too many young people speak little, and then only in drowned voices. Sometimes the mood surfaces as diffidence, wariness, or coolness, but whatever its form, it looks like a defense mechanism, and that rings a bell. This is the way it used to be with women, and just as society had systematically damaged women by insisting that their proper place was in the home, so we may be systematically damaging 18-year-olds by insisting that their proper place is in college.

Campus watchers everywhere know what I mean when I say students are sad, but they don't agree on the reason for it. During the Vietnam war some ascribed the sadness to the draft; now others blame affluence, or say it has something to do with permissive upbringing.   10

Not satisfied with any of these explanations, I looked for some answers with the journalistic tools of my trade—scholarly studies, economic analyses, the historical record, the opinions of the especially knowledgeable, conversations with parents, professors, college administrators, and employers, all of whom spoke as alumni too. Mostly I learned from my interviews with hundreds of young people on and off campuses all over the country.

My unnerving conclusion is that students are sad because they are not needed. Somewhere between the nursery and the employment office, they become unwanted adults. No one has anything in particular against them. But no one knows what to do with them either. We already have too many people in the world of the 1970s, and there is no room for so many newly minted 18-year-olds. So we temporarily get them out of the way by sending them to college where in fact only a few belong.

To make it more palatable, we fool ourselves into believing that we are sending them there for their own best interests, and that it's good for them, like spinach. Some, of course, learn to like it, but most wind up preferring green peas.

Educators admit as much. Nevitt Sanford, distinguished student of higher education, says students feel they are "capitulating to a kind of voluntary servitude." Some of them talk about their time in college as if it were a sentence to be served. I listened to a 1970 Mount Holyoke graduate: "For two years I was really interested in science, but in my junior and senior years I just kept saying, 'I've done two years; I'm going to finish.' When I got out I made up my mind that I wasn't going to school anymore because so many of my courses had been bullshit."

But bad as it is, college is often preferable to a far worse fate. It is better   15
than the drudgery of an uninspiring nine-to-five job, and better than doing nothing when no jobs are available. For some young people, it is a graceful way to get away from home and become independent without losing the financial support of their parents. And sometimes it is the only alternative to an intolerable home situation.

It is difficult to assess how many students are in college reluctantly. The conservative Carnegie Commission estimates from 5 to 30 percent. Sol Linowitz, who was once chairman of a special committee on campus tension of the American Council on Education, found that "a significant number were not happy with their college experience because they felt they were there only in order to get the 'ticket to the big show' rather than to spend the years as productively as they otherwise could."

Older alumni will identify with Richard Baloga, a policeman's son, who stayed in school even though he "hated it" because he thought it would do him some good. But fewer students each year feel this way. Daniel Yankelovich has surveyed undergraduate attitudes for a number of years, and reported in 1971 that 74 percent thought education was "very important." But just two years earlier, 80 percent thought so.

The doubters don't mind speaking up. Leon Lefkowitz, chairman of the department of social studies at Central High School in Valley Stream, New York, interviewed 300 college students at random, and reports that 200 of them didn't think that the education they were getting was worth the effort. "In two years I'll pick up a diploma," said one student, "and I can honestly say it was a waste of my father's bread."

Nowadays, says one sociologist, you don't have to have a reason for going to college; it's an institution. His definition of an institution is an arrangement everyone accepts without question; the burden of proof is not on why you go, but why anyone thinks there might be a reason for not going. The implication is that an 18-year-old is too young and confused to know what he wants to do, and that he should listen to those who know best and go to college.

20   I don't agree. I believe that college has to be judged not on what other people think is good for students, but on how good it feels to the students themselves.

I believe that people have an inside view of what's good for them. If a child doesn't want to go to school some morning, better let him stay at home, at least until you find out why. Maybe he knows something you don't. It's the same with college. If high-school graduates don't want to go, or if they don't want to go right away, they may perceive more clearly than their elders that college is not for them. It is no longer obvious that adolescents are best off studying a core curriculum that was constructed when all educated men could agree on what made them educated, or that professors, advisors, or parents can be of any particular help to young people in choosing a major or a career. High-school graduates see college graduates driving cabs, and decide it's not worth going. College students find no intellectual stimulation in their studies and drop out.

If students believe that college isn't necessarily good for them, you can't expect them to stay on for the general good of mankind. They don't go to school to beat the Russians to Jupiter, improve the national defense, increase the GNP, or create a new market for the arts—to mention some of the benefits taxpayers are supposed to get for supporting higher education.

Nor should we expect to bring about social equality by putting all young people through four years of academic rigor. At best, it's a roundabout and ex-pensive way to narrow the gap between the highest and lowest in our society anyway. At worst, it is unconsciously elitist. Equalizing opportunity through universal higher education subjects the whole population to the intellectual mode natural only to a few. It violates the fundamental egalitarian principle of respect for the differences between people.

Of course, most parents aren't thinking of the "higher" good at all. They send their children to college because they are convinced young people benefit financially from those four years of higher education. But if money is the only goal, college is the dumbest investment you can make. I say this because a young banker in Poughkeepsie, New York, Stephen G. Necel, used a computer to compare college as an investment with other investments available in 1974 and college did not come out on top.

For the sake of argument, the two of us invented a young man whose rich   25
uncle gave him, in cold cash, the cost of a four-year education at any college he chose, but the young man didn't have to spend the money on college. After bales of computer paper, we had our mythical student write to his uncle: "Since you said I could spend the money foolishly if I wished, I am going to blow it all on Princeton."

The much respected financial columnist Sylvia Porter echoed the common assumption when she said last year, "A college education is among the very best investments you can make in your entire life." But the truth is not quite so rosy, even if we assume that the Census Bureau is correct when it says that as of 1972, a man who completed four years of college would expect to earn $199,000 more between the ages of 22 and 64 than a man who had only a high-school diploma.

If a 1972 Princeton-bound high-school graduate had put the $34,181 that his four years of college would have cost him into a savings bank at 7.5 per cent interest compounded daily, he would have had at age 64 a total of $1,129,200, or $528,200 more than the earnings of a male college graduate, and more than five times as much as the $199,000 extra the more educated man could expect to earn between 22 and 64.

The big advantage of getting your college money in cash now is that you can invest it in something that has a higher return than a diploma. For instance, a Princeton-bound high-school graduate of 1972 who liked fooling around with cars could have banked his $34,181, and gone to work at the local garage at close to $1,000 more per year than the average high-school graduate. Meanwhile, as he was learning to be an expert auto mechanic, his money would be ticking away in the bank. When he became 28, he would have earned $7,199 less on his job from age 22 to 28 than his college-educated friend, but he would have had $73,113 in his passbook—enough to buy out his boss, go into the used-car business, or acquire his own new-car dealership. If successful in business, he could expect to make more than the average college graduate. And if he had the brains to get into Princeton, he would be just as likely to make money without the four years spent on campus. Unfortunately, few college-bound high-school graduates get the opportunity to bank such a large sum of money, and then wait for it to make them rich. And few parents are sophisticated enough to understand that in financial returns alone, their children would be better off with the money than with the education.

Rates of return and dollar signs on education are fascinating brain teasers, but obviously there is a certain unreality to the game. Quite aside from the noneconomic benefits of college, and these should loom larger once the dollars are cleared away, there are grave difficulties in assigning a dollar value to college at all.

30   In fact there is no real evidence that the higher income of college graduates is due to college. College may simply attract people who are slated to earn more money anyway; those with higher IQs, better family backgrounds, a more enterprising temperament. No one who has wrestled with the problem is prepared to attribute all of the higher income to the impact of college itself.

Christopher Jencks, author of *Inequality*, a book that assesses the effect of family and schooling in America, believes that education in general accounts for less than half of the difference in income in the American population. "The biggest single source of income differences," writes Jencks, "seems to be the fact that men from high-status families have higher incomes than men from low-status families even when they enter the same occupations, have the same amount of education, and have the same test scores."

Jacob Mincer of the National Bureau of Economic Research and Columbia University states flatly that of "20 to 30 percent of students at any level, the additional schooling has been a waste, at least in terms of earnings." College fails to work its income-raising magic for almost a third of those who go. More than half of those people in 1972 who earned $15,000 or more reached that comfortable bracket without the benefit of a college diploma. Jencks says that financial success in the U.S. depends a good deal on luck, and the most sophisticated regression analyses have yet to demonstrate otherwise.

But most of today's students don't go to college to earn more money anyway. In 1968, when jobs were easy to get, Daniel Yankelovich made his first nationwide survey of students. Sixty-five percent of them said they "would welcome less emphasis on money." By 1973, when jobs were scarce, that figure jumped to 80 percent.

The young are not alone. Americans today are all looking less to the pay of a job than to the work itself. They want "interesting" work that permits them "to make a contribution," "express themselves" and "use their special abilities," and they think college will help them find it.

35   Jerry Darring of Indianapolis knows what it is to make a dollar. He worked with his father in the family plumbing business, on the line at Chevrolet, and in the Chrysler foundry. He quit these jobs to enter Wright State University in Dayton, Ohio, because "in a job like that a person only has time to work, and after that he's so tired that he can't do anything else but come home and go to sleep."

Jerry came to college to find work "helping people." And he is perfectly willing to spend the dollars he earns at dull, well-paid work to prepare for lower-paid work that offers the reward of service to others.

Jerry's case is not unusual. No one works for money alone. In order to deal with the nonmonetary rewards of work, economists have coined the concept of "psychic income," which according to one economic dictionary means "income that is reckoned in terms of pleasure, satisfaction, or general feelings of euphoria."

Psychic income is primarily what college students mean when they talk about getting a good job. During the most affluent years of the late 1960s and early 1970s college students told their placement officers that they wanted to be researchers, college professors, artists, city planners, social workers, poets, book publishers, archeologists, ballet dancers, or authors.

The psychic income of these and other occupations popular with students is so high that these jobs can be filled without offering high salaries. According to one study, 93 percent of urban university professors would choose the same vocation again if they had the chance, compared with only 16 per cent of unskilled auto workers. Even though the monetary gap between college professor and auto worker is now surprisingly small, the difference in psychic income is enormous.

But colleges fail to warn students that jobs of these kinds are hard to come by, even for qualified applicants, and they rarely accept the responsibility of helping students choose a career that will lead to a job. When a young person says he is interested in helping people, his counselor tells him to become a psychologist. But jobs in psychology are scarce. The Department of Labor, for instance, estimates there will be 4,300 new jobs for psychologists in 1975 while colleges are expected to turn out 58,430 B.A.s in psychology that year.   40

Of 30 psych majors who reported back to Vassar what they were doing a year after graduation in 1972, only five had jobs in which they could possibly use their courses in psychology, and two of these were working for Vassar.

The outlook isn't much better for students majoring in other psychic-pay disciplines: sociology, English, journalism, anthropology, forestry, education. Whatever college graduates want to do, most of them are going to wind up doing what there is to do.

John Shingleton, director of placement at Michigan State University, accuses the academic community of outright hypocrisy. "Educators have never said, 'Go to college and get a good job,' but this has been implied, and now students expect it. . . . If we care what happens to students after college, then let's get involved with what should be one of the basic purposes of education: career preparation."

In the 1970s, some of the more practical professors began to see that jobs for graduates meant jobs for professors too. Meanwhile, students themselves reacted to the shrinking job market, and a "new vocationalism" exploded on campus. The press welcomed the change as a return to the ethic of achievement and service. Students were still idealistic, the reporters wrote, but they now saw that they could best make the world better by healing the sick as physicians or righting individual wrongs as lawyers.

But there are no guarantees in these professions either. The American Enterprise Institute estimated in 1971 that there would be more than the target ratio of 100 doctors for every 100,000 people in the population by 1980. And   45 the odds are little better for would-be lawyers. Law schools are already graduating twice as many new lawyers every year as the Department of Labor thinks will be needed, and the oversupply is growing every year.

And it's not at all apparent that what is actually learned in a "professional" education is necessary for success. Teachers, engineers and others I talked to said they find that on the job they rarely use what they learned in school. In order to see how well college prepared engineers and scientists for actual paid work in their fields, The Carnegie Commission queried all the employees with degrees in these fields in two large firms. Only one in five said the work they were doing bore a "very close relationship" to their college studies, while almost a third saw "very little relationship at all." An overwhelming majority could think of many people who were doing their same work, but had majored in different fields.

Majors in nontechnical fields report even less relationship between their studies and their jobs. Charles Lawrence, a communications major in college and now the producer of "Kennedy & Co.," the Chicago morning television show, says, "You have to learn all that stuff and you never use it again. I learned my job doing it." Others employed as architects, nurses, teachers and other members of the so-called learned professions report the same thing.

Most college administrators admit that they don't prepare their graduates for the job market. "I just wish I had the guts to tell parents that when you get out of this place you aren't prepared to do anything," the academic head of a famous liberal-arts college told us. Fortunately, for him, most people believe that you don't have to defend a liberal-arts education on those grounds. A liberal-arts education is supposed to provide you with a value system, a standard, a set of ideas, not a job. "Like Christianity, the liberal arts are seldom practiced and would probably be hated by the majority of the populace if they were," said one defender.

The analogy is apt. The fact is, of course, that the liberal arts are a religion in every sense of that term. When people talk about them, their language becomes elevated, metaphorical, extravagant, theoretical and reverent. And faith in personal salvation by the liberal arts is professed in a creed intoned on ceremonial occasions such as commencements.

50   If the liberal arts are a religious faith, the professors are its priests. But disseminating ideas in a four-year college curriculum is slow and most expensive. If you want to learn about Milton, Camus, or even Margaret Mead you can find them in paperback books, the public library, and even on television.

And when most people talk about the value of a college education, they are not talking about great books. When at Harvard commencement, the president welcomes the new graduates into "the fellowship of educated men and women," what he could be saying is, "Here is a piece of paper that is a passport to jobs, power and instant prestige." As Glenn Bassett, a personnel specialist at G.E. says, "In some parts of G.E., a college degree appears completely irrelevant to selection to, say, a manager's job. In most, however, it is a ticket of admission."

But now that we have doubled the number of young people attending college, a diploma cannot guarantee even that. The most charitable conclusion we can reach is that college probably has very little, if any, effect on people and things at all. Today, the false premises are easy to see:

First, college doesn't make people intelligent, ambitious, happy, or liberal. It's the other way around. Intelligent, ambitious, happy, liberal people are attracted to higher education in the first place.

Second, college can't claim much credit for the learning experiences that really change students while they are there. Jobs, friends, history, and most of all the sheer passage of time have as big an impact as anything even indirectly related to the campus.

Third, colleges have changed so radically that a freshman entering in the   55
fall of 1974 can't be sure to gain even the limited value research studies assigned to colleges in the '60s. The sheer size of undergraduate campuses of the 1970s makes college even less stimulating now than it was 10 years ago. Today even motivated students are disappointed with their college courses and professors.

Finally, a college diploma no longer opens as many vocational doors. Employers are beginning to realize that when they pay extra for someone with a diploma, they are paying only for an empty credential. The fact is that most of the work for which employers now expect college training is now or has been capably done in the past by people without higher educations.

College, then, may be a good place for those few young people who are really drawn to academic work, who would rather read than eat, but it has become too expensive, in money, time, and intellectual effort to serve as a holding pen for large numbers of our young. We ought to make it possible for those reluctant, unhappy students to find alternative ways of growing up, and more realistic preparation for the years ahead.

QUESTIONS

1. Much of Bird's article focuses on the economic value (or lack thereof) of a college education. Are there other reasons, beyond (or in addition to) economics, why you or your classmates are attending college? To what extent does Bird consider or ignore these other reasons for attending college?

2. In paragraphs 48–50, Bird compares liberal arts education to religion. Why does she make this comparison? What do you think her attitude is toward the liberal arts? Is it similar to or different from yours?

3. In paragraphs 5–6, Bird discusses the hard-sell advertising techniques of many academic institutions. Look into your own school's "advertising techniques" (view books, pamphlets, information sent to homes and high schools, Web site, etc.). How do these sources present the school to parents and potential students? Write an analysis of one of these sources.

JAMES THURBER   *University Days*

I PASSED ALL the other courses that I took at my university, but I could never pass botany. This was because all botany students had to spend several hours a week in a laboratory looking through a microscope at plant cells, and I could never see through a microscope. I never once saw a cell through a microscope. This used to enrage my instructor. He would wander around the laboratory pleased with the progress all the students were making in drawing the involved and, so I am told, interesting structure of flower cells, until he came to me. I would just be standing there. "I can't see anything," I would say. He would begin patiently enough, explaining how anybody can see through a microscope, but he would always end up in a fury, claiming that I could *too* see through a microscope but just pretended that I couldn't. "It takes away from the beauty of flowers anyway," I used to tell him. "We are not concerned with beauty in this course," he would say. "We are concerned solely with what I may call the *mechanics* of flars." "Well," I'd say, "I can't see anything." "Try it just once again," he'd say, and I would put my eye to the microscope and see nothing at all, except now and again a nebulous milky substance—a phenomenon of maladjustment. You were supposed to see a vivid, restless clockwork of sharply defined plant cells. "I see what looks like a lot of milk," I would tell him. This, he claimed, was the result of my not having adjusted the microscope properly, so he would readjust it for me, or rather, for himself. And I would look again and see milk.

I finally took a deferred pass, as they called it, and waited a year and tried again. (You had to pass one of the biological sciences or you couldn't graduate.) The professor had come back from vacation brown as a berry, bright-eyed, and eager to explain cell-structure again to his classes. "Well," he said to me, cheerily, when we met in the first laboratory hour of the semester, "we're going to see cells this time, aren't we?" "Yes, sir," I said. Students to right of me and to left of me and in front of me were seeing cells; what's more, they were quietly drawing pictures of them in their notebooks. Of course, I didn't see anything.

"We'll try it," the professor said to me, grimly, "with every adjustment of the microscope known to man. As God is my witness, I'll arrange this glass so that you see cells through it or I'll give up teaching. In twenty-two years of botany, I—" He cut off abruptly for he was beginning to quiver all over, like Lionel Barrymore,[1] and he genuinely wished to hold onto his temper; his scenes with me had taken a great deal out of him.

So we tried it with every adjustment of the microscope known to man. With only one of them did I see anything but blackness or the familiar lacteal

From My Life and Hard Times *(1933), Thurber's collection of autobiographical essays.*

1. American actor (1878–1954), especially noted for elderly roles.

opacity, and that time I saw, to my pleasure and amazement, a variegated constellation of flecks, specks,
and dots. These I hastily drew. The instructor,
noting my activity, came back from an adjoining
desk, a smile on his lips and his eyebrows high
in hope. He looked at my cell drawing. "What's
that?" he demanded, with a hint of a squeal in
his voice. "That's what I saw," I said. "You didn't,
you didn't, you *didn't!*" he screamed, losing control of his temper instantly, and he bent over and
squinted into the microscope. His head snapped up.
"That's your eye!" he shouted. "You've fixed the lens so
that it reflects! You've drawn your eye!"

He was beginning to
quiver all over like
Lionel Barrymore.

Another course that I didn't like, but somehow
managed to pass, was economics. I went to that class
straight from the botany class, which didn't help me
any in understanding either subject. I used to get
them mixed up. But not as mixed up as another student in my economics class who came there direct
from a physics laboratory. He was a tackle on the
football team, named Bolenciecwcz. At that time Ohio
State University had one of the best football teams in
the country, and Bolenciecwcz was one of its outstanding stars. In order to be eligible to play it was
necessary for him to keep up in his studies, a very difficult matter, for while he was not dumber than an ox
he was not any smarter. Most of his professors were lenient and helped him
along. None gave him more hints in answering questions or asked him simpler
ones than the economics professor, a thin, timid man named Bassum. One day
when we were on the subject of transportation and distribution, it came Bolenciecwcz's turn to answer a question. "Name one means of transportation,"
the professor said to him. No light came into the big tackle's eyes. "Just any
means of transportation," said the professor. Bolenciecwcz sat staring at him.
"That is," pursued the professor, "any medium, agency, or method of going
from one place to another." Bolenciecwcz had the look of a man who is being
led into a trap. "You may choose among steam, horsedrawn, or electrically propelled vehicles," said the instructor. "I might suggest the one which we commonly take in making long journeys across land." There was a profound
silence in which everybody stirred uneasily, including Bolenciecwcz and Mr.
Bassum. Mr. Bassum abruptly broke this silence in an amazing manner.
"Choo-choo-choo," he said, in a low voice, and turned instantly scarlet. He
glanced appealingly around the room. All of us, of course, shared Mr. Bassum's desire that Bolenciecwcz should stay abreast of the class in economics,
for the Illinois game, one of the hardest and most important of the season, was
only a week off. "Toot, toot, too-tooooooot!" some student with a deep voice
moaned, and we all looked encouragingly at Bolenciecwcz. Somebody else

gave a fine imitation of a locomotive letting off steam. Mr. Bassum himself rounded off the little show. "Ding, dong, ding, dong," he said, hopefully. Bolenciecwcz was staring at the floor now, trying to think, his great brow furrowed, his huge hands rubbing together, his face red.

"How did you come to college this year, Mr. Bolenciecwcz?" asked the professor. "*Chuffa* chuffa, *chuffa* chuffa."

"M'father sent me," said the football player.

"What on?" asked Bassum.

"I git an 'lowance," said the tackle, in a low, husky voice, obviously embarrassed.

10   "No, no," said Bassum. "Name a means of transportation. What did you *ride* here on?"

"Train," said Bolenciecwcz.

"Quite right," said the professor. "Now, Mr. Nugent, will you tell us—"

If I went through anguish in botany and economics—for different reasons—gymnasium work was even worse. I don't even like to think about it. They wouldn't let you play games or join in the exercises with your glasses on and I couldn't see with mine off. I bumped into professors, horizontal bars, agricultural students, and swinging iron rings. Not being able to see, I could take it but I couldn't dish it out. Also, in order to pass

Bolenciecwcz was trying to think.

gymnasium (and you had to pass it to graduate) you had to learn to swim if you didn't know how. I didn't like the swimming pool, I didn't like swimming, and I didn't like the swimming instructor, and after all these years I still don't. I never swam but I passed my gym work anyway, by having another student give my gymnasium number (978) and swim across the pool in my place. He was a quiet, amiable blond youth, number 473, and he would have seen through a microscope for me if we could have got away with it, but we couldn't get away with it. Another thing I didn't like about gymnasium work was that they made you strip the day you registered. It is impossible for me to be happy when I am stripped and being asked a lot of questions. Still, I did better than a lanky agricultural student who was cross-examined just before I was. They asked each student what college he was in—that is, whether Arts, Engineering, Commerce, or Agriculture. "What college are you in?" the instructor snapped at the youth in front of me. "Ohio State University," he said promptly.

It wasn't that agricultural student but it was another a whole lot like him who decided to take up journalism, possibly on the ground that when farming went to hell he could fall back on newspaper work. He didn't realize, of course, that that would be very much like falling back full-length on a kit of carpenter's tools. Haskins didn't seem cut out for journalism, being too embarrassed to talk to anybody and unable to use a typewriter, but the editor of the college paper assigned him to the cow barns, the sheep house, the horse pavilion, and the animal husbandry department generally. This was a genuinely big "beat," for it took up five times as much ground and got ten times as great a legislative appropriation as the College of Liberal Arts. The agricultural student knew animals, but nevertheless his stories were dull and colorlessly written. He took all afternoon on each of them, on account of having to hunt for each letter on the typewriter. Once in a while he had to ask somebody to help him hunt. "C" and "L," in particular, were hard letters for him to find. His editor finally got pretty much annoyed at the farmer-journalist because his pieces were so uninteresting. "See here, Haskins," he snapped at him one day, "why is it we never have anything hot from you on the horse pavilion? Here we have two hundred head of horses on this campus—more than any other university in the Western Conference[2] except Purdue—and yet you never get any real lowdown on them. Now shoot over to the horse barns and dig up something lively." Haskins shambled out and came back in about an hour; he said he had something. "Well, start it off snappily," said the editor. "Something people will read." Haskins set to work and in a couple of hours brought a sheet of typewritten paper to the desk; it was a two-hundred-word story about some disease that had broken out among the horses. Its opening sentence was simple but arresting. It read: "Who has noticed the sores on the tops of the horses in the animal husbandry building?"

Ohio State was a land grant university and therefore two years of military drill was compulsory. We drilled with old Springfield rifles and studied the tactics of the Civil War even though the World War was going on at the time. At 11 o'clock each morning thousands of freshmen and sophomores used to deploy over the campus, moodily creeping up on the old chemistry building. It was good training for the kind of warfare that was waged at Shiloh[3] but it had no connection with what was going on in Europe. Some people used to think there was German money behind it, but they didn't dare say so or they would have been thrown in jail as German spies. It was a period of muddy thought and marked, I believe, the decline of higher education in the Middle West.

As a soldier I was never any good at all. Most of the cadets were glumly indifferent soldiers, but I was no good at all. Once General Littlefield, who was commandant of the cadet corps, popped up in front of me during regimental drill and snapped, "You are the main trouble with this university!" I think he meant that my type was the main trouble with the university but he may have meant me individually. I was mediocre at drill, certainly—that is, until my senior year. By that time I had drilled longer than anybody else in the Western Conference, having failed at military at the end of each preceding year so that I had to do it all over again. I was the only senior still in uniform. The uniform which, when new, had made me look like an interurban railway conductor, now that it had become faded and too tight made me look like Bert

2. The Big Ten.
3. In southwestern Tennessee, site of an 1862 Union victory.

Williams[4] in his bellboy act. This had a definitely bad effect on my morale. Even so, I had become by sheer practice little short of wonderful at squad maneuvers.

One day General Littlefield picked our company out of the whole regiment and tried to get it mixed up by putting it through one movement after another as fast as we could execute them: squads right, squads left, squads on right into line, squads right about, squads left front into line, etc. In about three minutes one hundred and nine men were marching in one direction and I was marching away from them at an angle of forty degrees, all alone. "Company, halt!" shouted General Littlefield. "That man is the only man who has it right!" I was made a corporal for my achievement.

The next day General Littlefield summoned me to his office. He was swatting flies when I went in. I was silent and he was silent too, for a long time; I don't think he remembered me or why he had sent for me, but he didn't want to admit it. He swatted some more flies, keeping his eyes on them narrowly before he let go with the swatter. "Button up your coat!" he snapped. Looking back on it now I can see that he meant me although he was looking at a fly, but I just stood there. Another fly came to rest on a paper in front of the general and began rubbing its hind legs together. The general lifted the swatter cautiously. I moved restlessly and the fly flew away. "You startled him!" barked General Littlefield, looking at me severely. I said I was sorry. "That won't help the situation!" snapped the General, with cold military logic. I didn't see what I could do except offer to chase some more flies toward his desk, but I didn't say anything. He stared out the window at the faraway figures of co-eds crossing the campus toward the library. Finally, he told me I could go. So I went. He either didn't know which cadet I was or else he forgot what he wanted to see me about. It may have been that he wished to apologize for having called me the main trouble with the university; or maybe he had decided to compliment me on my brilliant drilling of the day before and then at the last minute decided not to. I don't know. I don't think about it much any more.

4. African American vaudeville star (1874?–1922).

QUESTIONS

1. Analyze how Thurber creates a comic persona by using his literal and metaphoric blindness. What, in the various anecdotes that constitute the essay, does he not see?

2. In an essay called "Some Remarks on Humor," E. B. White says: "Humorists fatten on trouble. . . . You find them wrestling with foreign languages, fighting folding ironing boards and swollen drainpipes, suffering the terrible discomfort of tight boots. They pour out their sorrows profitably, in a form that is not quite fiction nor quite fact either. Beneath the sparkling surface of these dilemmas flows the strong tide of human woe." Discuss the relevance of this quotation to Thurber's essay.

3. Ethnic stereotypes are often a staple of humor: in this essay, Bolenciecwcz, the dumb football player, is Polish American. Is the anecdote offensive? Would it be more or less offensive if he were African American? Why?

4. Find some incident that will yield to a Thurberesque treatment, that is, that can be told from the point of view of a "blind" narrator, and write about it.

WILLIAM ZINSSER   *College Pressures*

Dear Carlos: I desperately need a dean's excuse for my chem midterm which will begin in about 1 hour. All I can say is that I totally blew it this week. I've fallen incredibly, inconceivably behind.

Carlos: Help! I'm anxious to hear from you. I'll be in my room and won't leave it until I hear from you. Tomorrow is the last day for . . .

Carlos: I left town because I started bugging out again. I stayed up all night to finish a take-home make-up exam & am typing it to hand in on the 10th. It was due on the 5th. P.S. I'm going to the dentist. Pain is pretty bad.

Carlos: Probably by Friday I'll be able to get back to my studies. Right now I'm going to take a long walk. This whole thing has taken a lot out of me.

Carlos: I'm really up the proverbial creek. The problem is I really *bombed* the history final. Since I need that course for my major I . . .

Carlos: Here follows a tale of woe. I went home this weekend, had to help my Mom, & caught a fever so didn't have much time to study. My professor . . .

Carlos: Aargh! Trouble. Nothing original but everything's piling up at once. To be brief, my job interview . . .

Hey Carlos, good news! I've got mononucleosis.

Who are these wretched supplicants, scribbling notes so laden with anxiety, seeking such miracles of postponement and balm? They are men and women who belong to Branford College, one of the twelve residential colleges at Yale University, and the messages are just a few of the hundreds that they left for their dean, Carlos Hortas—often slipped under his door at 4 A.M.—last year.

But students like the ones who wrote those notes can also be found on campuses from coast to coast—especially in New England and at many other private colleges across the country that have high academic standards and highly motivated students. Nobody could doubt that the notes are real. In their urgency and their gallows humor they are authentic voices of a generation that is panicky to succeed.

Written when Zinsser was Master (head) of a Yale residential college and published in a small circulation bimonthly magazine about rural life, Blair and Ketchum's Country Journal *(April 1979), which has since ceased publication.*

My own connection with the message writers is that I am master of Branford College. I live in its Gothic quadrangle and know the students well. (We have 485 of them.) I am privy to their hopes and fears—and also to their stereo music and their piercing cries in the dead of night ("Does anybody ca-a-are?"). If they went to Carlos to ask how to get through tomorrow, they come to me to ask how to get through the rest of their lives.

Mainly I try to remind them that the road ahead is a long one and that it will have more unexpected turns than they think. There will be plenty of time to change jobs, change careers, change whole attitudes and approaches. They don't want to hear such liberating news. They want a map—right now—that they can follow unswervingly to career security, financial security, Social Security and, presumably, a prepaid grave.

5   What I wish for all students is some release from the clammy grip of the future. I wish them a chance to savor each segment of their education as an experience in itself and not as a grim preparation for the next step. I wish them the right to experiment, to trip and fall, to learn that defeat is as instructive as victory and is not the end of the world.

My wish, of course, is naive. One of the few rights that America does not proclaim is the right to fail. Achievement is the national god, venerated in our media—the million-dollar athlete, the wealthy executive—and glorified in our praise of possessions. In the presence of such a potent state religion, the young are growing up old.

I see four kinds of pressure working on college students today: economic pressure, parental pressure, peer pressure, and self-induced pressure. It is easy to look around for villains—to blame the colleges for charging too much money, the professors for assigning too much work, the parents for pushing their children too far, the students for driving themselves too hard. But there are no villains; only victims.

"In the late 1960s," one dean told me, "the typical question that I got from students was 'Why is there so much suffering in the world?' or 'How can I make a contribution?' Today it's 'Do you think it would look better for getting into law school if I did a double major in history and political science, or just majored in one of them?'" Many other deans confirmed this pattern. One said: "They're trying to find an edge—the intangible something that will look better on paper if two students are about equal."

Note the emphasis on looking better. The transcript has become a sacred document, the passport to security. How one appears on paper is more important than how one appears in person. A is for Admirable and B is for Borderline, even though, in Yale's official system of grading, A means "excellent" and B means "very good." Today, looking very good is no longer good enough, especially for students who hope to go on to law school or medical school. They know that entrance into the better schools will be an entrance into the better law firms and better medical practices where they will make a lot of money. They also know that the odds are harsh. Yale Law School, for instance, matricu-

lates 170 students from an applicant pool of 3,700; Harvard enrolls 550 from
a pool of 7,000.

It's all very well for those of us who write letters of recommendation for   10
our students to stress the qualities of humanity that will make them good
lawyers or doctors. And it's nice to think that admission officers are really
reading our letters and looking for the extra dimension of commitment or concern. Still, it would be hard for a student not to visualize these officers shuffling so many transcripts studded with As that they regard a B as positively
shameful.

The pressure is almost as heavy on students who just want to graduate
and get a job. Long gone are the days of the "gentleman's C," when students
journeyed through college with a certain relaxation, sampling a wide variety of
courses—music, art, philosophy, classics, anthropology, poetry, religion—that
would send them out as liberally educated men and women. If I were an em-
ployer I would rather employ graduates who have this range and curiosity than
those who narrowly pursued safe subjects and high grades. I know countless
students whose inquiring minds exhilarate me. I like to hear the play of their
ideas. I don't know if they are getting As or Cs, and I don't care. I also like
them as people. The country needs them, and they will find satisfying jobs. I
tell them to relax. They can't.

Nor can I blame them. They live in a brutal economy. Tuition, room, and
board at most private colleges now comes to at least $7,000, not counting
books and fees. This might seem to suggest that the colleges are getting rich.
But they are equally battered by inflation. Tuition covers only 60 percent of
what it costs to educate a student, and ordinarily the remainder comes from
what colleges receive in endowments, grants, and gifts. Now the remainder
keeps being swallowed by the cruel costs—higher every year—of just opening
the doors. Heating oil is up. Insurance is up. Postage is up. Health-premium
costs are up. Everything is up. Deficits are up. We are witnessing in America
the creation of a brotherhood of paupers—colleges, parents, and students,
joined by the common bond of debt.

Today it is not unusual for a student, even if he works part time at college
and full time during the summer, to accrue $5,000 in loans after four years—
loans that he must start to repay within one year after graduation. Exhorted at
commencement to go forth into the world, he is already behind as he goes
forth. How could he not feel under pressure throughout college to prepare for
this day of reckoning? I have used "he," incidentally, only for brevity. Women at
Yale are under no less pressure to justify their expensive education to themselves, their parents, and society. In fact, they are probably under more pressure. For although they leave college superbly equipped to bring fresh
leadership to traditionally male jobs, society hasn't yet caught up with this fact.

Along with economic pressure goes parental pressure. Inevitably, the two are
deeply intertwined.

I see many students taking pre-medical courses with joyless tenacity. They   15 go off to their labs as if they were going to the dentist. It saddens me because I know them in other corners of their life as cheerful people.

"Do you want to go to medical school?" I ask them.

"I guess so," they say, without conviction, or "Not really."

"Then why are you going?"

"Well, my parents want me to be a doctor. They're paying all this money and . . ."

20   Poor students, poor parents. They are caught in one of the oldest webs of love and duty and guilt. The parents mean well; they are trying to steer their sons and daughters toward a secure future. But the sons and daughters want to major in history or classics or philosophy—subjects with no "practical" value. Where's the payoff on the humanities? It's not easy to persuade such loving parents that the humanities do indeed pay off. The intellectual faculties developed by studying subjects like history and classics—an ability to synthesize and relate, to weigh cause and effect, to see events in perspective—are just the faculties that make creative leaders in business or almost any general field. Still, many fathers would rather put their money on courses that point toward a specific profession—courses that are pre-law, pre-medical, pre-business, or, as I sometimes heard it put, "pre-rich."

But the pressure on students is severe. They are truly torn. One part of them feels obligated to fulfill their parents' expectations; after all, their parents are older and presumably wiser. Another part tells them that the expectations that are right for their parents are not right for them.

I know a student who wants to be an artist. She is very obviously an artist and will be a good one—she has already had several modest local exhibits. Meanwhile she is growing as a well-rounded person and taking humanistic subjects that will enrich the inner resources out of which her art will grow. But her father is strongly opposed. He thinks that an artist is a "dumb" thing to be. The student vacillates and tries to please everybody. She keeps up with her art somewhat furtively and takes some of the "dumb" courses her father wants her to take—at least they are dumb courses for her. She is a free spirit on a campus of tense students—no small achievement in itself—and she deserves to follow her muse.

Peer pressure and self-induced pressure are also intertwined, and they begin almost at the beginning of freshman year.

"I had a freshman student I'll call Linda," one dean told me, "who came in and said she was under terrible pressure because her roommate, Barbara, was much brighter and studied all the time. I couldn't tell her that Barbara had come in two hours earlier to say the same thing about Linda."

25   The story is almost funny—except that it's not. It's symptomatic of all the pressures put together. When every student thinks every other student is working harder and doing better, the only solution is to study harder still. I see students going off to the library every night after dinner and coming back when it closes at midnight. I wish they would sometimes forget about their peers and go to a movie. I hear the clacking of typewriters in the hours before dawn. I

see the tension in their eyes when exams are approaching and papers are due: "*Will I get everything done?*"

Probably they won't. They will get sick. They will get "blocked." They will sleep. They will oversleep. They will bug out. *Hey Carlos, help!*

Part of the problem is that they do more than they are expected to do. A professor will assign five-page papers. Several students will start writing ten-page papers to impress him. Then more students will write ten-page papers, and a few will raise the ante to fifteen. Pity the poor student who is still just doing the assignment.

"Once you have twenty or thirty percent of the student population deliberately overexerting," one dean points out, "it's bad for everybody. When a teacher gets more and more effort from his class, the student who is doing normal work can be perceived as not doing well. The tactic works, psychologically."

Why can't the professor just cut back and not accept longer papers? He can, and he probably will. But by then the term will be half over and the damage done. Grade fever is highly contagious and not easily reversed. Besides, the professor's main concern is with his course. He knows his students only in relation to the course and doesn't know that they are also overexerting in their other courses. Nor is it really his business. He didn't sign up for dealing with the student as a whole person and with all the emotional baggage the student brought along from home. That's what deans, masters, chaplains, and psychiatrists are for.

To some extent this is nothing new: a certain number of professors have always been self-contained islands of scholarship and shyness, more comfortable with books than with people. But the new pauperism has widened the gap still further, for professors who actually like to spend time with students don't have as much time to spend. They also are overexerting. If they are young, they are busy trying to publish in order not to perish, hanging by their finger nails onto a shrinking profession. If they are old and tenured, they are buried under the duties of administering departments—as departmental chairmen or members of committees—that have been thinned out by the budgetary axe. 30

Ultimately it will be the students' own business to break the circles in which they are trapped. They are too young to be prisoners of their parents' dreams and their classmates' fears. They must be jolted into believing in themselves as unique men and women who have the power to shape their own future.

"Violence is being done to the undergraduate experience," says Carlos Hortas. "College should be open-ended: at the end it should open many, many roads. Instead, students are choosing their goal in advance, and their choices narrow as they go along. It's almost as if they think that the country has been codified in the type of jobs that exist—that they've got to fit into certain slots. Therefore, fit into the best-paying slot.

"They ought to take chances. Not taking chances will lead to a life of colorless mediocrity. They'll be comfortable. But something in the spirit will be missing."

I have painted too drab a portrait of today's students, making them seem a solemn lot. That is only half of their story; if they were so dreary I wouldn't so thoroughly enjoy their company. The other half is that they are easy to like. They are quick to laugh and to offer friendship. They are not introverts. They are unusually kind and are more considerate of one another than any student generation I have known.

35   Nor are they so obsessed with their studies that they avoid sports and extracurricular activities. On the contrary, they juggle their crowded hours to play on a variety of teams, perform with musical and dramatic groups, and write for campus publications. But this in turn is one more cause of anxiety. There are too many choices. Academically, they have 1,300 courses to select from; outside class they have to decide how much spare time they can spare and how to spend it.

This means that they engage in fewer extracurricular pursuits than their predecessors did. If they want to row on the crew and play in the symphony they will eliminate one; in the '60s they would have done both. They also tend to choose activities that are self-limiting. Drama, for instance, is flourishing in all twelve of Yale's residential colleges as it never has before. Students hurl themselves into these productions—as actors, directors, carpenters, and technicians—with a dedication to create the best possible play, knowing that the day will come when the run will end and they can get back to their studies.

They also can't afford to be the willing slave of organizations like the *Yale Daily News*. Last spring at the one-hundredth anniversary banquet of that paper—whose past chairmen include such once and future kings as Potter Stewart, Kingman Brewster, and William F. Buckley, Jr.—much was made of the fact that the editorial staff used to be small and totally committed and that "newsies" routinely worked fifty hours a week. In effect they belonged to a club; Newsies is how they defined themselves at Yale. Today's student will write one or two articles a week, when he can, and he defines himself as a student. I've never heard the word Newsie except at the banquet.

If I have described the modern undergraduate primarily as a driven creature who is largely ignoring the blithe spirit inside who keeps trying to come out and play, it's because that's where the crunch is, not only at Yale but throughout American education. It's why I think we should all be worried about the values that are nurturing a generation so fearful of risk and so goal-obsessed at such an early age.

I tell students that there is no one "right" way to get ahead—that each of them is a different person, starting from a different point and bound for a different destination. I tell them that change is a tonic and that all the slots are not codified nor the frontiers closed. One of my ways of telling them is to invite men and women who have achieved success outside the academic world to come and talk informally with my students during the year. They are heads of companies or ad agencies, editors of magazines, politicians, public officials, television magnates, labor leaders, business executives, Broadway producers, artists, writers, economists, photographers, scientists, historians—a mixed bag of achievers.

I ask them to say a few words about how they got started. The students assume that they started in their present profession and knew all along that it was what they wanted to do. Luckily for me, most of them got into their field by a circuitous route, to their surprise, after many detours. The students are startled. They can hardly conceive of a career that was not pre-planned. They can hardly imagine allowing the hand of God or chance to nudge them down some unforeseen trail.

40

QUESTIONS

1. What are the four kinds of pressure Zinsser describes for the 1970s? Are they the same kinds of pressure that trouble students today? Or have new ones taken their place?

2. Some people believe that students perform best when subjected to pressure, others that they perform best when relatively free of pressure. How do you respond to pressure? How much pressure is enough? How much is too much?

3. Write an essay in which you compare your expectations of college pressures with the reality as you have experienced it to date.

ADRIENNE RICH   *Taking Women Students Seriously*

I SEE MY FUNCTION here today as one of trying to create a context, delineate a background, against which we might talk about women as students and students as women. I would like to speak for a while about this background, and then I hope that we can have, not so much a question period, as a raising of concerns, a sharing of questions for which we as yet may have no answers, an opening of conversations which will go on and on.

When I went to teach at Douglass, a women's college,[1] it was with a particular background which I would like briefly to describe to you. I had graduated from an all-girls' school in the 1940s, where the head and the majority of the faculty were independent, unmarried women. One or two held doctorates, but had been forced by the Depression (and by the fact that they were

The talk that follows was addressed to teachers of women. . . . It was given for the New Jersey College and University Coalition on Women's Education, May 9, 1978 [Rich's note]. Reprinted in On Lies, Secrets, and Silence: Selected Prose, *1966–1978 (1979).*

1. Part of Rutgers University in New Jersey.

women) to take secondary school teaching jobs. These women cared a great deal about the life of the mind, and they gave a great deal of time and energy—beyond any limit of teaching hours—to those of us who showed special intellectual interest or ability. We were taken to libraries, art museums, lectures at neighboring colleges, set to work on extra research projects, given extra French or Latin reading. Although we sometimes felt "pushed" by them, we held those women in a kind of respect which even then we dimly perceived was not generally accorded to women in the world at large. They were vital individuals, defined not by their relationships but by their personalities; and although under the pressure of the culture we were all certain we wanted to get married, their lives did not appear empty or dreary to us. In a kind of cognitive dissonance, we knew they were "old maids" and therefore supposed to be bitter and lonely; yet we saw them vigorously involved with life. But despite their existence as alternate models of women, the *content* of the education they gave us in no way prepared us to survive as women in a world organized by and for men.

From that school, I went on to Radcliffe, congratulating myself that now I would have great men as my teachers. From 1947 to 1951, when I graduated, I never saw a single woman on a lecture platform, or in front of a class, except when a woman graduate student gave a paper on a special topic. The "great men" talked of other "great men," of the nature of Man, the history of Mankind, the future of Man; and never again was I to experience, from a teacher, the kind of prodding, the insistence that my best could be even better, that I had known in high school. Women students were simply not taken very seriously. Harvard's message to women was an elite mystification: we were, of course, part of Mankind; we were special, achieving women, or we would not have been there; but of course our real goal was to marry—if possible, a Harvard graduate.

In the late sixties, I began teaching at the City College of New York—a crowded, public, urban, multiracial institution as far removed from Harvard as possible. I went there to teach writing in the SEEK Program,[2] which predated Open Admissions and which was then a kind of model for programs designed to open up higher education to poor, black, and Third World students. Although during the next few years we were to see the original concept of SEEK diluted, then violently attacked and betrayed, it was for a short time an extraordinary and intense teaching and learning environment. The characteristics of this environment were a deep commitment on the part of teachers to the minds of their students; a constant, active effort to create or discover the conditions for learning, and to educate ourselves to meet the needs of the new college population; a philosophical attitude based on open discussion of racism, oppression, and the politics of literature and language; and a belief that learning in the classroom could not be isolated from the student's experience as a member of an urban mi-

---

2. SEEK is an acronym for "Search for Education, Elevation, and Knowledge"; the instructors in the program included not only college teachers but also creative artists and writers.

nority group in white America. Here are some of the kinds of questions we, as teachers of writing, found ourselves asking:

(1) What has been the student's experience of education in the inadequate, often abusively racist public school system, which rewards passivity and treats a questioning attitude or independent mind as a behavior problem? What has been her or his experience in a society that consistently undermines the selfhood of the poor and the nonwhite? How can such a student gain that sense of self which is necessary for active participation in education? What does all this mean for us as teachers?

(2) How do we go about teaching a canon of literature which has consistently excluded or depreciated nonwhite experience?

(3) How can we connect the process of learning to write well with the student's own reality, and not simply teach her/him how to write acceptable lies in standard English?

When I went to teach at Douglass College in 1976, and in teaching women's writing workshops elsewhere, I came to perceive stunning parallels to the questions I had first encountered in teaching the so-called disadvantaged students at City. But in this instance, and against the specific background of the women's movement, the questions framed themselves like this:

(1) What has been the student's experience of education in schools which reward female passivity, indoctrinate girls and boys in stereotypic sex roles, and do not take the female mind seriously? How does a woman gain a sense of her *self* in a system—in this case, patriarchal capitalism— which devalues work done by women, denies the importance and uniqueness of female experience, and is physically violent toward women? What does this mean for a woman teacher?

(2) How do we, as women, teach women students a canon of literature which has consistently excluded or depreciated female experience, and which often expresses hostility to women and validates violence against us?

(3) How can we teach women to move beyond the desire for male approval and getting "good grades" and seek and write their own truths that the culture has distorted or made taboo? (For women, of course, language itself is exclusive: I want to say more about this further on.)

In teaching women, we have two choices: to lend our weight to the forces that indoctrinate women to passivity, self-depreciation, and a sense of powerlessness, in which case the issue of "taking women students seriously" is a moot one; or to consider what we have to work against, as well as with, in ourselves, in our students, in the content of the curriculum, in the structure of the institution, in the society at large. And this means, first of all, taking ourselves seriously: Recognizing that central responsibility of a woman to herself, without which we remain always the Other, the defined, the object, the victim; believing that there is a unique quality of validation, affirmation, challenge, support, that one woman can offer another. Believing in the value and significance of women's experience, traditions, perceptions. Thinking of ourselves seriously, not as one of the boys, not as neuters, or androgynes, but *as women.*

Suppose we were to ask ourselves, simply: What does a woman need to know? Does she not, as a self-conscious, self-defining human being, need a knowledge of her own history, her much-politicized biology, an awareness of the creative work of women of the past, the skills and crafts and techniques and powers exercised by women in different times and cultures, a knowledge of women's rebellions and organized movements against our oppression and how they have been routed or diminished? Without such knowledge women live and have lived without context, vulnerable to the projections of male fantasy, male prescriptions for us, estranged from our own experience because our education has not reflected or echoed it. I would suggest that not biology, but ignorance of our selves, has been the key to our powerlessness.

But the university curriculum, the high-school curriculum, do not provide this kind of knowledge for women, the knowledge of Womankind, whose experience has been so profoundly different from that of Mankind. Only in the precariously budgeted, much-condescended-to area of women's studies is such knowledge available to women students. Only there can they learn about the lives and work of women other than the few select women who are included in the "mainstream" texts, usually misrepresented even when they do appear. Some students, at some institutions, manage to take a majority of courses in women's studies, but the message from on high is that this is self-indulgence, soft-core education: the "real" learning is the study of Mankind.

If there is any misleading concept, it is that of "coeducation": that because women and men are sitting in the same classrooms, hearing the same lectures, reading the same books, performing the same laboratory experiments, they are receiving an equal education. They are not, first because the content of education itself validates men even as it invalidates women. Its very message is that men have been the shapers and thinkers of the world, and that this is only natural. The bias of higher education, including the so-called sciences, is white and male, racist and sexist; and this bias is expressed in both subtle and blatant ways. I have mentioned already the exclusiveness of grammar itself: "The student should test himself on the above questions"; "The poet is representative. He stands among partial men for the complete man." Despite a few half-hearted departures from custom, what the linguist Wendy Martyna has named "He-Man" grammar prevails throughout the culture. The efforts of feminists to reveal the profound ontological implications of sexist grammar are routinely ridiculed by academicians and journalists, including the professedly liberal *Times* columnist, Tom Wicker, and the professed humanist, Jacques Barzun. Sexist grammar burns into the brains of little girls and young women a message that the male is the norm, the standard, the central figure beside which we are the deviants, the marginal, the dependent variables. It lays the foundation for androcentric thinking, and leaves men safe in their solipsistic tunnel-vision.

Women and men do not receive an equal education because outside the classroom women are perceived not as sovereign beings but as prey. The growing incidence of rape on and off the campus may or may not be fed by the proliferations of pornographic magazines and X-rated films available to young males in fraternities and student unions; but it is certainly occurring in a context of widespread images of sexual violence against women, on billboards and in so-called high art. More subtle, more daily than rape is the verbal abuse experienced by the woman student on many campuses—Rutgers for example—where, traversing a street lined with fraternity houses, she must run a gauntlet of male commentary and verbal assault. The undermining of self, of a woman's sense of her right to occupy space and walk freely in the world, is deeply relevant to education. The capacity to think independently, to take intellectual risks, to assert ourselves mentally, is inseparable from our physical way of being in the world, our feelings of personal integrity. If it is dangerous for me to walk home late of an evening from the library, *because I am a woman and can be raped,* how self-possessed, how exuberant can I feel as I sit working in that library? how much of my working energy is drained by the subliminal knowledge that, as a woman, I test my physical right to exist each time I go out alone? Of this knowledge, Susan Griffin has written:

> . . . more than rape itself, the fear of rape permeates our lives. And what does one do from day to day, with *this* experience, which says, without words and directly to the heart, *your existence, your experience, may end at any moment.* Your experience may end, and the best defense against this is not to be, to deny being in the body, as a self, to . . . avert your gaze, make yourself, as a presence in the world, less felt.[3]

Finally, rape of the mind. Women students are more and more often now reporting sexual overtures by male professors—one part of our overall growing consciousness of sexual harassment in the workplace. At Yale a legal suit has been brought against the university by a group of women demanding an explicit policy against sexual advances toward female students by male professors. Most young women experience a profound mixture of humiliation and intellectual self-doubt over seductive gestures by men who have the power to award grades, open doors to grants and graduate school, or extend special knowledge and training. Even if turned aside, such gestures constitute mental rape, destructive to a woman's ego. They are acts of domination, as despicable as the molestation of the daughter by the father.

But long before entering college the woman student has experienced her alien identity in a world which misnames her, turns her to its own uses, denying her the resources she needs to become self-affirming, self-defined. The nuclear family teaches her that relationships are more important than selfhood

3. Rich is quoting from the manuscript of Griffin's *Rape: The Power of Consciousness* (New York, 1979).

or work; that "whether the phone rings for you, and how often," having the right clothes, doing the dishes, take precedence over study or solitude; that too much intelligence or intensity may make her unmarriageable; that marriage and children—service to others—are, finally, the points on which her life will be judged a success or a failure. In high school, the polarization between feminine attractiveness and independent intelligence comes to an absolute. Meanwhile, the culture resounds with messages. During Solar Energy Week in New York I saw young women wearing "ecology" T-shirts with the legend: CLEAN, CHEAP AND AVAILABLE; a reminder of the 1960s antiwar button which read: CHICKS SAY YES TO MEN WHO SAY NO. Department store windows feature female mannequins in chains, pinned to the wall with legs spread, smiling in positions of torture. Feminists are depicted in the media as "shrill," "strident," "puritanical," or "humorless," and the lesbian choice—the choice of the woman-identified woman—as pathological or sinister. The young woman sitting in the philosophy classroom, the political science lecture, is already gripped by tensions between her nascent sense of self-worth, and the battering force of messages like these.

Look at a classroom: look at the many kinds of women's faces, postures, expressions. Listen to the women's voices. Listen to the silences, the unasked questions, the blanks. Listen to the small, soft voices, often courageously trying to speak up, voices of women taught early that tones of confidence, challenge, anger, or assertiveness, are strident and unfeminine. Listen to the voices of the women and the voices of the men; observe the space men allow themselves, physically and verbally, the male assumption that people will listen, even when the majority of the group is female. Look at the faces of the silent, and of those who speak. Listen to a woman groping for language in which to express what is on her mind, sensing that the terms of academic discourse are not her language, trying to cut down her thought to the dimensions of a discourse not intended for her (*for it is not fitting that a woman speak in public*); or reading her paper aloud at breakneck speed, throwing her words away, deprecating her own work by a reflex prejudgment: *I do not deserve to take up time and space.*

As women teachers, we can either deny the importance of this context in which women students think, write, read, study, project their own futures; or try to work with it. We can either teach passively, accepting these conditions, or actively, helping our students identify and resist them.

15   One important thing we can do is *discuss* the context. And this need not happen only in a women's studies course; it can happen anywhere. We can refuse to accept passive, obedient learning and insist upon critical thinking. We can become harder on our women students, giving them the kinds of "cultural prodding" that men receive, but on different terms and in a different style. Most young women need to have their intellectual lives, their work, legitimized against the claims of family, relationships, the old message that a woman is always available for service to others. We need to keep our standards very high, not to accept a woman's preconceived sense of her limitations; we need to be hard to please, while supportive of risk-taking, because self-respect

often comes only when exacting standards have been met. At a time when adult literacy is generally low, we need to demand more, not less, of women, both for the sake of their futures as thinking beings, and because historically women have always had to be better than men to do half as well. A romantic sloppiness, an inspired lack of rigor, a self-indulgent incoherence, are symptoms of female self-depreciation. We should help our women students to look very critically at such symptoms, and to understand where they are rooted.

Nor does this mean we should be training women students to "think like men." Men in general think badly: in disjuncture from their personal lives, claiming objectivity where the most irrational passions seethe, losing, as Virginia Woolf[4] observed, their senses in the pursuit of professionalism. It is not easy to think like a woman in a man's world, in the world of the professions; yet the capacity to do that is a strength which we can try to help our students develop. To think like a woman in a man's world means thinking critically, refusing to accept the givens, making connections between facts and ideas which men have left unconnected. It means remembering that every mind resides in a body; remaining accountable to the female bodies in which we live; constantly retesting given hypotheses against lived experience. It means a constant critique of language, for as Wittgenstein[5] (no feminist) observed, "The limits of my language are the limits of my world." And it means that most difficult thing of all: listening and watching in art and literature, in the social sciences, in all the descriptions we are given of the world, for the silences, the absences, the nameless, the unspoken, the encoded—for there we will find the true knowledge of women. And in breaking those silences, naming our selves, uncovering the hidden, making ourselves present, we begin to define a reality which resonates to *us*, which affirms *our* being, which allows the woman teacher and the woman student alike to take ourselves, and each other, seriously: meaning, to begin taking charge of our lives.

4. British novelist, essayist, and feminist (1882–1941).
5. Ludwig Wittgenstein (1889–1951), Austrian-born British philosopher.

QUESTIONS

1. Rich discusses the importance of listening to silences and of paying attention to absences. In one of your classes, listen and observe; take note of who speaks and who doesn't; and watch for responses from the instructor. What sense can you make of these silences and absences? Do your conclusions correspond to Rich's, or do they differ?

2. Rich and David Brooks (in "The Gender Gap at School" in the Op Eds section) come to very different conclusions. What do you think accounts for their differences?

3. In paragraph 10, Rich discusses the relationship between intellectual independence and physical safety. Do some research on the public safety policies on your own campus (escorts, lighting, etc.) and also consider your own experiences. Do you feel safe walking alone on campus? To what extent does your sense of physical safety affect your intellectual work? Write a journal entry or article for your school's newspaper on these issues.

WILLIAM GOLDING *Thinking as a Hobby*

WHILE I WAS STILL A BOY, I came to the conclusion that there were three grades of thinking; and since I was later to claim thinking as my hobby, I came to an even stranger conclusion—namely, that I myself could not think at all.

I must have been an unsatisfactory child for grown-ups to deal with. I remember how incomprehensible they appeared to me at first, but not, of course, how I appeared to them. It was the headmaster of my grammar school who first brought the subject of thinking before me—though neither in the way, nor with the result he intended. He had some stat-uettes in his study. They stood on a high cupboard behind his desk. One was a lady wearing nothing but a bath towel. She seemed frozen in an eternal panic lest the bath towel slip down any farther; and since she had no arms, she was in an unfortunate position to pull the towel up again. Next to her, crouched the statuette of a leopard, ready to spring down at the top drawer of a filing cabinet labeled A-AH. My innocence interpreted this as the victim's last, de-spairing cry. Beyond the leopard was a naked, muscular gentleman, who sat, looking down, with his chin on his fist and his elbow on his knee. He seemed utterly miserable.

Some time later, I learned about these statuettes. The headmaster had placed them where they would face delinquent children, because they symbol-ized to him the whole of life. The naked lady was the Venus of Milo. She was Love. She was not worried about the towel. She was just busy being beautiful. The leopard was Nature, and he was being natural. The naked, muscular gen-tleman was not miserable. He was Rodin's Thinker, an image of pure thought.[1] It is easy to buy small plaster models of what you think life is like.

I had better explain that I was a frequent visitor to the headmaster's study, because of the latest thing I had done or left undone. As we now say, I was not integrated. I was, if anything, disintegrated; and I was puzzled. Grownups never made sense. Whenever I found myself in a penal position before the headmas-ter's desk, with the statuettes glimmering whitely above him, I would sink my head, clasp my hands behind my back and writhe one shoe over the other.

5   The headmaster would look opaquely at me through flashing spectacles.

"What are we going to do with you?"

Well, what *were* they going to do with me? I would writhe my shoe some more and stare down at the worn rug.

First published in Holiday *(August 1961), a popular monthly travel magazine.*

1. François-Auguste-René Rodin (1840–1917), French sculptor whose famous *The Thinker* was originally created as part of a larger bronze piece, *The Gates of Hell* (1880). The sculpture was meant to represent Dante in front of the Gates of Hell pondering his great poem *Inferno*, but is now generally interpreted, as Golding suggests, as "an image of pure thought."

"Look up, boy! Can't you look up?"

Then I would look up at the cupboard, where the naked lady was frozen in her panic and the muscular gentleman contemplated the hindquarters of the leopard in endless gloom. I had nothing to say to the headmaster. His spectacles caught the light so that you could see nothing human behind them. There was no possibility of communication.

"Don't you ever think at all?"   10

No, I didn't think, wasn't thinking, couldn't think—I was simply waiting in anguish for the interview to stop.

"Then you'd better learn—hadn't you?"

On one occasion the headmaster leaped to his feet, reached up and plonked Rodin's masterpiece on the desk before me.

"That's what a man looks like when he's really thinking."

I surveyed the gentleman without interest or comprehension.   15

"Go back to your class."

Clearly there was something missing in me. Nature had endowed the rest of the human race with a sixth sense and left me out. This must be so, I mused, on my way back to the class, since whether I had broken a window, or failed to remember Boyle's Law, or been late for school, my teachers produced me one, adult answer: "Why can't you think?"

As I saw the case, I had broken the window because I had tried to hit Jack Arney with a cricket ball and missed him; I could not remember Boyle's Law because I had never bothered to learn it; and I was late for school because I preferred looking over the bridge into the river. In fact, I was wicked. Were my teachers, perhaps, so good that they could not understand the depths of my depravity? Were they clear, untormented people who could direct their every action by this mysterious business of thinking? The whole thing was incomprehensible. In my earlier years, I found even the statuette of the Thinker confusing. I did not believe any of my teachers were naked, ever. Like someone born deaf, but bitterly determined to find out about sound, I watched my teachers to find out about thought.

There was Mr. Houghton. He was always telling me to think. With a modest satisfaction, he would tell me that he had thought a bit himself. Then why did he spend so much time drinking? Or was there more sense in drinking than there appeared to be? But if not, and if drinking were in fact ruinous to health—and Mr. Houghton was ruined, there was no doubt about that—why was he always talking about the clean life and the virtues of fresh air? He would spread his arms wide with the action of a man who habitually spent his time striding along mountain ridges.

"Open air does me good, boys—I know it!"   20

Sometimes, exalted by his own oratory, he would leap from his desk and hustle us outside into a hideous wind.

"Now, boys! Deep breaths! Feel it right down inside you—huge draughts of God's good air!"

He would stand before us, rejoicing in his perfect health, an open-air man. He would put his hands on his waist and take a tremendous breath. You could hear the wind, trapped in the cavern of his chest and struggling with all the unnatural impediments. His body would reel with shock and his ruined face go white at the unaccustomed visitation. He would stagger back to his desk and collapse there, useless for the rest of the morning.

Mr. Houghton was given to high-minded monologues about the good life, sexless and full of duty. Yet in the middle of one of these monologues, if a girl passed the window, tapping along on her neat little feet, he would interrupt his discourse, his neck would turn of itself and he would watch her out of sight. In this instance, he seemed to me ruled not by thought but by an invisible and irresistible spring in his nape.

25   His neck was an object of great interest to me. Normally it bulged a bit over his collar. But Mr. Houghton had fought in the First World War alongside both Americans and French, and had come—by who knows what illogic?—to a settled detestation of both countries. If either country happened to be prominent in current affairs, no argument could make Mr. Houghton think well of it. He would bang the desk, his neck would bulge still further and go red. "You can say what you like," he would cry, "but I've thought about this—and I know what I think!"

Mr. Houghton thought with his neck.

There was Miss Parsons. She assured us that her dearest wish was our welfare, but I knew even then, with the mysterious clairvoyance of childhood, that what she wanted most was the husband she never got. There was Mr. Hands—and so on.

I have dealt at length with my teachers because this was my introduction to the nature of what is commonly called thought. Through them I discovered that thought is often full of unconscious prejudice, ignorance and hypocrisy. It will lecture on disinterested purity while its neck is being remorselessly twisted toward a skirt. Technically, it is about as proficient as most businessmen's golf, as honest as most politicians' intentions, or—to come near my own preoccupation—as coherent as most books that get written. It is what I came to call grade-three thinking, though more properly, it is feeling, rather than thought.

True, often there is a kind of innocence in prejudices, but in those days I viewed grade-three thinking with an intolerant contempt and an incautious mockery. I delighted to confront a pious lady who hated the Germans with the proposition that we should love our enemies. She taught me a great truth in dealing with grade-three thinkers; because of her, I no longer dismiss lightly a mental process which for nine-tenths of the population is the nearest they will ever get to thought. They have immense solidarity. We had better respect them, for we are outnumbered and surrounded. A crowd of grade-three thinkers, all shouting the same thing, all warming their hands at the fire of their own prejudices, will not thank you for pointing out the contradictions in their beliefs. Man is a gregarious animal, and enjoys agreement as cows will graze all the same way on the side of a hill.

30   Grade-two thinking is the detection of contradictions. I reached grade two when I trapped the poor, pious lady. Grade-two thinkers do not stampede easily, though often they fall into the other fault and lap behind. Grade-two think-

ing is a withdrawal, with eyes and ears open. It became my hobby and brought satisfaction and loneliness in either hand. For grade-two thinking destroys without having the power to create. It set me watching the crowds cheering His Majesty and King and asking myself what all the fuss was about, without giving me anything positive to put in the place of that heady patriotism. But there were compensations. To hear people justify their habit of hunting foxes and tearing them to pieces by claiming that the foxes liked it. To hear our Prime Minister talk about the great benefit we conferred on India by jailing people like Pandit Nehru and Gandhi. To hear American politicians talk about peace in one sentence and refuse to join the League of Nations in the next. Yes, there were moments of delight.

But I was growing toward adolescence and had to admit that Mr. Houghton was not the only one with an irresistible spring in his neck. I, too, felt the compulsive hand of nature and began to find that pointing out contradiction could be costly as well as fun. There was Ruth, for example, a serious and attractive girl. I was an atheist at the time. Grade-two thinking is a menace to religion and knocks down sects like skittles. I put myself in a position to be converted by her with an hypocrisy worthy of grade three. She was a Methodist—or at least, her parents were, and Ruth had to follow suit. But, alas, instead of relying on the Holy Spirit to convert me, Ruth was foolish enough to open her pretty mouth in argument. She claimed that the Bible (King James Version) was literally inspired. I countered by saying that the Catholics believed in the literal inspiration of Saint Jerome's *Vulgate*,[2] and the two books were different. Argument flagged.

At last she remarked that there were an awful lot of Methodists, and they couldn't be wrong, could they—not all those millions? That was too easy, said I restively (for the nearer you were to Ruth, the nicer she was to be near to) since there were more Roman Catholics than Methodists anyway; and they couldn't be wrong, could they—not all those hundreds of millions? An awful flicker of doubt appeared in her eyes. I slid my arm around her waist and murmured breathlessly that if we were counting heads, the Buddhists were the boys for my money. But Ruth had *really* wanted to do me good, because I was so nice. She fled. The combination of my arm and those countless Buddhists was too much for her.

That night her father visited my father and left, red-cheeked and indignant. I was given the third degree to find out what had happened. It was lucky we were both of us only fourteen. I lost Ruth and gained an undeserved reputation as a potential libertine.

So grade-two thinking could be dangerous. It was in this knowledge, at the age of fifteen, that I remember making a comment from the heights of grade two, on the limitations of grade three. One evening I found myself alone

2. The King James Bible (1611) is the authorized text for English-speaking Protestants, so-called because King James I of England (1566–1625) commissioned its translation; the Vulgate is the Latin Bible revised in the fourth century C.E. by Jerome and used thereafter as the authoritative text for Roman Catholics.

in the school hall, preparing it for a party. The door of the headmaster's study was open. I went in. The headmaster had ceased to thump Rodin's Thinker down on the desk as an example to the young. Perhaps he had not found any more candidates, but the statuettes were still there, glimmering and gathering dust on top of the cupboard. I stood on a chair and rearranged them. I stood Venus in her bath towel on the filing cabinet, so that now the top drawer caught its breath in a gasp of sexy excitement. "A-ah!" The portentous Thinker I placed on the edge of the cupboard so that he looked down at the bath towel and waited for it to slip.

35   Grade-two thinking, though it filled life with fun and excitement, did not make for content. To find out the deficiencies of our elders bolsters the young ego but does not make for personal security. I found that grade two was not only the power to point out contradictions. It took the swimmer some distance from the shore and left him there, out of his depth. I decided that Pontius Pilate[3] was a typical grade-two thinker. "What is truth?" he said, a very common grade-two thought, but one that is used always as the end of an argument instead of the beginning. There is still a higher grade of thought which says, "What is truth?" and sets out to find it.

But these grade-one thinkers were few and far between. They did not visit my grammar school in the flesh though they were there in books. I aspired to them, partly because I was ambitious and partly because I now saw my hobby as an unsatisfactory thing if it went no further. If you set out to climb a mountain, however high you climb, you have failed if you cannot reach the top.

I *did* meet an undeniably grade-one thinker in my first year at Oxford. I was looking over a small bridge in Magdalen Deer Park, and a tiny mustached and hatted figure came and stood by my side. He was a German who had just fled from the Nazis to Oxford as a temporary refuge. His name was Einstein.

But Professor Einstein knew no English at that time and I knew only two words of German. I beamed at him, trying wordlessly to convey by my bearing all the affection and respect that the English felt for him. It is possible—and I have to make the admission—that I felt here were two grade-one thinkers standing side by side; yet I doubt if my face conveyed more than a formless awe. I would have given my Greek and Latin and French and a good slice of my English for enough German to communicate. But we were divided; he was as inscrutable as my headmaster. For perhaps five minutes we stood together on the bridge, undeniable grade-one thinker and breathless aspirant. With true greatness, Professor Einstein realized that any contact was better than none. He pointed to a trout wavering in midstream.

He spoke: *"Fisch."*

40   My brain reeled. Here I was, mingling with the great, and yet helpless as the veriest grade-three thinker. Desperately I sought for some sign by which I might convey that I, too, revered pure reason. I nodded vehemently. In a brilliant flash I used up half of my German vocabulary.

"Fisch. Ja Ja."

---

3. The Roman procurator who ruled Judaea from 26 to 36 C.E. and oversaw the trial of Jesus.

For perhaps another five minutes we stood side by side. Then Professor Einstein, his whole figure still conveying good will and amiability, drifted away out of sight.

I, too, would be a grade-one thinker. I was irreverent at the best of times. Political and religious systems, social customs, loyalties and traditions, they all came tumbling down like so many rotten apples off a tree. This was a fine hobby and a sensible substitute for cricket, since you could play it all the year round. I came up in the end with what must always remain the justification for grade-one thinking, its sign, seal and charter. I devised a coherent system for living. It was a moral system, which was wholly logical. Of course, as I readily admitted, conversion of the world to my way of thinking might be difficult, since my system did away with a number of trifles, such as big business, centralized government, armies, marriage. . . .

It was Ruth all over again. I had some very good friends who stood by me, and still do. But my acquaintances vanished, taking the girls with them. Young women seemed oddly contented with the world as it was. They valued the meaningless ceremony with a ring. Young men, while willing to concede the chaining sordidness of marriage, were hesitant about abandoning the organizations which they hoped would give them a career. A young man on the first rung of the Royal Navy, while perfectly agreeable to doing away with big business and marriage, got as rednecked as Mr. Houghton when I proposed a world without any battleships in it.

Had the game gone too far? Was it a game any longer? In those prewar days, I stood to lose a great deal, for the sake of a hobby.   45

Now you are expecting me to describe how I saw the folly of my ways and came back to the warm nest, where prejudices are so often called loyalties, where pointless actions are hallowed into custom by repetition, where we are content to say we think when all we do is feel.

But you would be wrong. I dropped my hobby and turned professional.

If I were to go back to the headmaster's study and find the dusty statuettes still there, I would arrange them differently. I would dust Venus and put her aside, for I have come to love her and know her for the fair thing she is. But I would put the Thinker, sunk in his desperate thought, where there were shadows before him—and at his back, I would put the leopard, crouched and ready to spring.

QUESTIONS

1. Trace Golding's reflections on the statues in his headmaster's office throughout the essay. In what ways do these reflections reflect Golding's changing understanding of "thought"?

2. Define Golding's three grades of thinking. Which grade is most clear to you? Which could use further explanation?

3. Write a personal essay in which you, like Golding, use personal experience to illustrate your developing understanding of "thought" or some other abstraction (such as "love," "faith," "independence," or "growth").

WILLIAM G. PERRY JR. *Examsmanship and the Liberal Arts: A Study in Educational Epistemology*

"Bʊт sɪʀ, I don't think I really deserve it, it was mostly bull, really." This disclaimer from a student whose examination we have awarded a straight "A" is wondrously depressing. Alfred North Whitehead[1] invented its only possible rejoinder: "Yes sir, what you wrote is nonsense, utter nonsense. But ah! Sir! It's the right *kind* of nonsense!"

Bull, in this university,[2] is customarily a source of laughter, or a problem in ethics. I shall step a little out of fashion to use the subject as a take-off point for a study in comparative epistemology. The phenomenon of bull, in all the honor and opprobrium with which it is regarded by students and faculty, says something, I think, about our theories of knowledge. So too, the grades which we assign on examinations communicate to students what these theories may be.

We do not have to be out-and-out logical-positivists[3] to suppose that we have something to learn about "what we think knowledge is" by having a good look at "what we do when we go about measuring it." We know the straight "A" examination when we see it, of course, and we have reason to hope that the student will understand why his work receives our recognition. He doesn't always. And those who receive lesser honor? Perhaps an understanding of certain anomalies in our customs of grading good bull will explain the students' confusion.

I must beg patience, then, both of the reader's humor and of his morals. Not that I ask him to suspend his sense of humor but that I shall ask him to go beyond it. In a great university the picture of a bright student attempting to outwit his professor while his professor takes pride in not being outwitted is certainly ridiculous. I shall report just such a scene, for its implications bear upon my point. Its comedy need not present a serious obstacle to thought.

5   As for the ethics of bull, I must ask for a suspension of judgment. I wish that students could suspend theirs. Unlike humor, moral commitment is hard to think beyond. Too early a moral judgment is precisely what stands between many able students and a liberal education. The stunning realization that the Harvard Faculty will often accept, as evidence of knowledge, the cerebrations

From Examining in Harvard College *(1964), a collection of studies by faculty members about Harvard's testing programs.*

1. British philosopher (1861–1947), later a Harvard professor.
2. Harvard.
3. Mid-twentieth-century philosophers concerned not with abstract notions of what a thing is but with empirical observation of what it does.

of a student who has little data at his disposal, confronts every student with an ethical dilemma. For some it forms an academic focus for what used to be thought of as "adolescent disillusion." It is irrelevant that rumor inflates the phenomenon to mythical proportions. The students know that beneath the myth there remains a solid and haunting reality. The moral "bind" consequent on this awareness appears most poignantly in serious students who are reluctant to concede the competitive advantage to the bullster and who yet feel a deep personal shame when, having succumbed to "temptation," they themselves receive a high grade for work they consider "dishonest."

I have spent many hours with students caught in this unwelcome bitterness. These hours lend an urgency to my theme. I have found that students have been able to come to terms with the ethical problem, to the extent that it is real, only after a refined study of the true nature of bull and its relation to "knowledge." I shall submit grounds for my suspicion that we can be found guilty of sharing the students' confusion of moral and epistemological issues.

I

I present as my "premise," then, an amoral *fabliau*.[4] Its hero-villain is the Abominable Mr. Metzger '47. Since I celebrate his virtuosity, I regret giving him a pseudonym, but the peculiar style of his bravado requires me to honor also his modesty. Bull in pure form is rare; there is usually some contamination by data. The community has reason to be grateful to Mr. Metzger for having created an instance of laboratory purity, free from any adulteration by matter. The more credit is due him, I think, because his act was free from premeditation, deliberation, or hope of personal gain.

Mr. Metzger stood one rainy November day in the lobby of Memorial Hall.[5] A junior, concentrating in mathematics, he was fond of diverting himself by taking part in the drama, a penchant which may have had some influence on the events of the next hour. He was waiting to take part in a rehearsal in Sanders Theatre, but, as sometimes happens, no other players appeared. Perhaps the rehearsal had been canceled without his knowledge? He decided to wait another five minutes.

Students, meanwhile, were filing into the Great Hall opposite, and taking seats at the testing tables. Spying a friend crossing the lobby toward the Great Hall's door, Metzger greeted him and extended appropriate condolences. He inquired, too, what course his friend was being tested in. "Oh, Soc. Sci. something-or-other." "What's it all about?" asked Metzger, and this, as Homer remarked of Patroclus,[6] was the beginning of evil for him.

4. A short, often coarse French medieval tale.

5. Large building at Harvard where examinations took place; inside Memorial Hall is Sanders Theatre, site of musical performances.

6. In Homer's *Iliad*, Achilles refused to fight, but his friend Patroclus persuaded him to let him wear his armor and lead his troops. Achilles agreed, and the Greeks won, but Patroclus was slain by Hector. This made Achilles decide to avenge Patroclus's death, and the eventual result was the fall of Troy.

10   "It's about Modern Perspectives on Man and Society and All That," said
      his friend. "Pretty interesting, really."
            "Always wanted to take a course like that," said Metzger. "Any good
      reading?"
            "Yeah, great. There's this book"—his friend did not have time to finish.
            "Take your seats please," said a stern voice beside them. The idle conver-
      sation had somehow taken the two friends to one of the tables in the Great
      Hall. Both students automatically obeyed; the proctor put blue books before
      them; another proctor presented them with copies of the printed hour-test.
            Mr. Metzger remembered afterwards a brief misgiving that was suddenly
      overwhelmed by a surge of curiosity and puckish glee. He wrote "George
      Smith" on the blue book, opened it, and addressed the first question.
15   I must pause to exonerate the Management. The Faculty has a rule that
      no student may attend an examination in a course in which he is not enrolled.
      To the wisdom of this rule the outcome of this deplorable story stands witness.
      The Registrar, charged with the enforcement of the rule, has developed an or-
      ganization with procedures which are certainly the finest to be devised. In No-
      vember, however, class rosters are still shaky, and on this particular day
      another student, named Smith, was absent. As for the culprit, we can reduce
      his guilt no further than to suppose that he was ignorant of the rule, or, in the
      face of the momentous challenge before him, forgetful.
            We need not be distracted by Metzger's performance on the "objective" or
      "spot" questions on the test. His D on these sections can be explained by those
      versed in the theory of probability. Our interest focuses on the quality of his
      essay. It appears that when Metzger's friend picked up his own blue book a few
      days later, he found himself in company with a large proportion of his section
      in having received on the essay a C+. When he quietly picked up "George
      Smith's" blue book to return it to Metzger, he observed that the grade for the
      essay was A. In the margin was a note in the section man's hand. It read "Ex-
      cellent work. Could you have pinned these observations down a bit more
      closely? Compare . . . in . . . pp. . . . ."
            Such news could hardly be kept quiet. There was a leak, and the whole
      scandal broke on the front page of Tuesday's *Crimson*.[7] With the press
      Metzger was modest, as becomes a hero. He said that there had been nothing
      to it at all, really. The essay question had offered a choice of two books, Mar-
      garet Mead's *And Keep Your Powder Dry* or Geoffrey Gorer's *The American
      People*. Metzger reported that having read neither of them, he had chosen the
      second "because the title gave me some notion as to what the book might
      be about." On the test, two critical comments were offered on each book, one
      favorable, one unfavorable. The students were asked to "discuss." Metzger
      conceded that he had played safe in throwing his lot with the more
      laudatory of the two comments, "but I did not forget to be balanced."
            I do not have Mr. Metzger's essay before me except in vivid memory. As
      I recall, he took his first cue from the name Geoffrey, and committed his

      ---

      7. Harvard's college newspaper.

strategy to the premise that Gorer was born into an "Anglo-Saxon" culture, probably English, but certainly "English speaking." Having heard that Margaret Mead was a social anthropologist, he inferred that Gorer was the same. He then entered upon his essay, centering his inquiry upon what he supposed might be the problems inherent in an anthropologist's observation of a culture which was his own, or nearly his own. Drawing in part from memories of table-talk on cultural relativity[8] and in part from creative logic, he rang changes on the relation of observer to observed, and assessed the kind and degree of objectivity which might accrue to an observer through training as an anthropologist. He concluded that the book in question did in fact contribute a considerable range of " 'objective,' and even 'fresh,' " insights into the nature of our culture. "At the same time," he warned, "these observations must be understood within the context of their generation by a person only partly freed from his embeddedness in the culture he is observing, and limited in his capacity to transcend those particular tendencies and biases which he has himself developed as a personality in his interraction with this culture since his birth. In this sense the book portrays as much the character of Geoffrey Gorer as it analyzes that of the American people." It is my regrettable duty to report that at this moment of triumph Mr. Metzger was carried away by the temptations of parody and added, "We are thus much the richer."

In any case, this was the essay for which Metzger received his honor grade and his public acclaim. He was now, of course, in serious trouble with the authorities.

I shall leave him for the moment to the mercy of the Administrative Board 20 of Harvard College and turn the reader's attention to the section man who ascribed the grade. He was in much worse trouble. All the consternation in his immediate area of the Faculty and all the glee in other areas fell upon his unprotected head. I shall now undertake his defense.

I do so not simply because I was acquainted with him and feel a respect for his intelligence; I believe in the justice of his grade! Well, perhaps "justice" is the wrong word in a situation so manifestly absurd. This is more a case in "equity." That is, the grade is equitable if we accept other aspects of the situation which are equally absurd. My proposition is this: if we accept as valid those C grades which were accorded students who, like Metzger's friend, demonstrated a thorough familiarity with the details of the book without relating their critique to the methodological problems of social anthropology, then "George Smith" deserved not only the same, but better.

The reader may protest that the C's given to students who showed evidence only of diligence were indeed not valid and that both these students and "George Smith" should have received E's.[9] To give the diligent E is of course not in accord with custom. I shall take up this matter later. For now, were I to

8. "An important part of Harvard's education takes place during meals in the Houses" [Perry's note]. The houses are dormitory complexes.
9. A failing grade, now usually indicated by an "F."

allow the protest, I could only restate my thesis: that "George Smith's" E would, in a college of liberal arts, be properly a "better" E.

At this point I need a short-hand. It is a curious fact that there is no academic slang for the presentation of evidence of diligence alone. "Parroting" won't do; it is possible to "parrot" bull. I must beg the reader's pardon, and, for reasons almost too obvious to bear, suggest "cow."

Stated as nouns, the concepts look simple enough:

> cow (pure): data, however relevant, without relevancies.
> bull (pure): relevancies, however relevant, without data.

25   The reader can see all too clearly where this simplicity would lead. I can assure him that I would not have imposed on him this way were I aiming to say that knowledge in this university is definable as some neuter compromise between cow and bull, some infertile hermaphrodite. This is precisely what many diligent students seem to believe: that what they must learn to do is to "find the right mean" between "amounts" of detail and "amounts" of generalities. Of course this is not the point at all. The problem is not quantitative, nor does its solution lie on a continuum between the particular and the general. Cow and bull are not poles of a single dimension. A clear notion of what they really are is essential to my inquiry, and for heuristic purposes I wish to observe them further in the celibate state.

When the pure concepts are translated into verbs, their complexities become apparent in the assumptions and purposes of the students as they write:

To cow (*v. intrans.*) or the act of cowing:
    To list data (or perform operations) without awareness of, or comment upon, the contexts, frames of reference, or points of observation which determine the origin, nature, and meaning of the data (or procedures). To write on the assumption that "a fact is a fact." To present evidence of hard work as a substitute for understanding, without any intent to deceive.

To bull (*v. intrans.*) or the act of bulling:
    To discourse upon the contexts, frames of reference and points of observation which would determine the origin, nature, and meaning of data if one had any. To present evidence of an understanding of form in the hope that the reader may be deceived into supposing a familiarity with content.

At the level of conscious intent, it is evident that cowing is more moral, or less immoral, than bulling. To speculate about unconscious intent would be either an injustice or a needless elaboration of my theme. It is enough that the impression left by cow is one of earnestness, diligence, and painful naiveté. The grader may feel disappointment or even irritation, but these feelings are usually balanced by pity, compassion, and a reluctance to hit a man when he's both down and moral. He may feel some challenge to his teaching, but none whatever to his one-ups-manship. He writes in the margin: "See me."

We are now in a position to understand the anomaly of custom: As instructors, we always assign bull an E, *when we detect it*; whereas we usually give cow a C, *even though it is always obvious*.

After all, we did not ask to be confronted with a choice between morals and understanding (or did we?). We evince a charming humanity, I think, in our decision to grade in favor of morals and pathos. "I simply *can't* give this student an E after he has *worked* so hard." At the same time we tacitly express our respect for the bullster's strength. We recognize a colleague. If he knows so well how to dish it out, we can be sure that he can also take it.

Of course it is just possible that we carry with us, perhaps from our own school-days, an assumption that if a student is willing to work hard and collect "good hard facts" he can always be taught to understand their relevance, whereas a student who has caught onto the forms of relevance without working at all is a lost scholar.

But this is not in accord with our experience.

It is not in accord either, as far as I can see, with the stated values of a liberal education. If a liberal education should teach students "how to think," not only in their own fields but in fields outside their own—that is, to understand "how the other fellow orders knowledge," then bulling, even in its purest form, expresses an important part of what a pluralist university holds dear, surely a more important part than the collecting of "facts that are facts" which school-boys learn to do. Here then, good bull appears not as ignorance at all but as an aspect of knowledge. It is both relevant and "true." In a university setting good bull is therefore of more value than "facts," which, without a frame of reference, are not even "true" at all.

Perhaps this value accounts for the final anomaly: as instructors, we are inclined to reward bull highly, *where we do not detect its intent,* to the consternation of the bullster's acquaintances. And often we do not examine the matter too closely. After a long evening of reading blue books full of cow, the sudden meeting with a student who at least understands the problems of one's field provides a lift like a draught of refreshing wine, and a strong disposition toward trust.

This was, then, the sense of confidence that came to our unfortunate section man as he read "George Smith's" sympathetic considerations.

II

In my own years of watching over students' shoulders as they work, I have come to believe that this feeling of trust has a firmer basis than the confidence generated by evidence of diligence alone. I believe that the theory of a liberal education holds. Students who have dared to understand man's real relation to his knowledge have shown themselves to be in a strong position to learn content rapidly and meaningfully, and to retain it. I have learned to be less concerned about the education of a student who has come to understand the nature of man's knowledge, even though he has not yet committed himself to hard work, than I am about the education of the student who, after one or two terms at Harvard, is working desperately hard and still believes that collected "facts" constitute knowledge. The latter, when I try to explain to him, too often understands me to be saying that he "doesn't *put in enough generalities.*" Surely he has "put in *enough* facts."

I have come to see such quantitative statements as expressions of an entire, coherent epistemology. In grammar school the student is taught that Columbus discovered America in 1492. The *more* such items he gets "right" on a given test the more he is credited with "knowing." From years of this sort of thing it is not unnatural to develop the conviction that knowledge consists of the accretion of hard facts by hard work.

The student learns that the more facts and procedures he can get "right" in a given course, the better will be his grade. The more courses he takes, the more subjects he has "had," the more credits he accumulates, the more diplomas he will get, until, after graduate school, he will emerge with his doctorate, a member of the community of scholars.

The foundation of this entire life is the proposition that a fact is a fact. The necessary correlate of this proposition is that a fact is either right or wrong. This implies that the standard against which the rightness or wrongness of a fact may be judged exists *someplace*—perhaps graven upon a tablet in a Platonic world[10] outside and above *this* cave of tears. In grammar school it is evident that the tablets which enshrine the spelling of a word or the answer to an arithmetic problem are visible to my teacher, who need only compare my offerings to it. In high school I observe that my English teachers disagree. This can only mean that the tablets in such matters as the goodness of a poem are distant and obscured by clouds. They surely exist. The pleasing of befuddled English teachers degenerates into assessing their prejudices, a game in which I have no protection against my competitors more glib of tongue. I respect only my science teachers, authorities who *really know*. Later I learn from them that "this is only what we think *now*." But eventually, surely. . . . Into this epistemology of education, apparently shared by teachers in such terms as "credits," "semester hours" and "years of French" the student may invest his ideals, his drive, his competitiveness, his safety, his self-esteem, and even his love.

College raises other questions: by whose calendar is it proper to say that Columbus discovered America in 1492? How, when and by whom was the year 1 established in this calendar? What of other calendars? In view of the evidence for Leif Ericson's previous visit (and the American Indians), what historical ethnocentrism is suggested by the use of the word "discover" in this sentence? As for Leif Ericson, in accord with what assumptions do you order the evidence?

40

These questions and their answers are not "more" knowledge. They are devastation. I do not need to elaborate upon the epistemology, or rather epistemologies, they imply. A fact has become at last "an observation or an operation performed in a frame of reference." A liberal education is founded in an awareness of frame of reference even in the most immediate and empirical examination of data. Its acquirement involves relinquishing hope of absolutes and of the protection they afford against doubt and the glib-tongued competitor. It demands an ever widening sophistication about systems of thought and observation. It leads, not away from, but *through* the arts of gamesmanship to a new trust.

10. In, for example, Plato's intellectual world; see "The Allegory of the Cave" (p. 1128).

This trust is in the value and integrity of systems, their varied character, and the way their apparently incompatible metaphors enlighten, from complementary facets, the particulars of human experience. As one student said to me: "I used to be cynical about intellectual games. Now I want to know them thoroughly. You see I came to realize that it was only when I knew the rules of the game cold that I could tell whether what I was saying was tripe."

We too often think of the bullster as cynical. He can be, and not always in a light-hearted way. We have failed to observe that there can lie behind cow the potential of a deeper and more dangerous despair. The moralism of sheer work and obedience can be an ethic that, unwilling to face a despair of its ends, glorifies its means. The implicit refusal to consider the relativity of both ends and means leaves the operator in an unconsidered proprietary absolutism. History bears witness that in the pinches this moral superiority has no recourse to negotiation, only to force.

A liberal education proposes that man's hope lies elsewhere: in the negotiability that can arise from an understanding of the integrity of systems and of their origins in man's address to his universe. The prerequisite is the courage to accept such a definition of knowledge. From then on, of course, there is nothing incompatible between such an epistemology and hard work. Rather the contrary.

I can now at last let bull and cow get together. The reader knows best how a productive wedding is arranged in his own field. This is the nuptial he celebrates with a straight A on examinations. The masculine context must embrace the feminine particular, though itself "born of woman." Such a union is knowledge itself, and it alone can generate new contexts and new data which can unite in their turn to form new knowledge.

In this happy setting we can congratulate in particular the Natural Sciences, long thought to be barren ground to the bullster. I have indeed drawn my examples of bull from the Social Sciences, and by analogy from the Humanities. Essay-writing in these fields has long been thought to nurture the art of bull to its prime. I feel, however, that the Natural Sciences have no reason to feel slighted. It is perhaps no accident that Metzger was a mathematician. As part of my researches for this paper, furthermore, a student of considerable talent has recently honored me with an impressive analysis of the art of amassing "partial credits" on examinations in advanced physics. Though beyond me in some respects, his presentation confirmed my impression that instructors of Physics frequently honor on examinations operations structurally similar to those requisite in a good essay.

The very qualities that make the Natural Sciences fields of delight for the eager gamesman have been essential to their marvelous fertility.

III

As priests of these mysteries, how can we make our rites more precisely expressive? The student who merely cows robs himself, without knowing it, of his education and his soul. The student who only bulls robs himself, as he

45

knows full well, of the joys of inductive discovery—that is, of engagement. The introduction of frames of reference in the new curricula of Mathematics and Physics in the schools is a hopeful experiment. We do not know yet how much of these potent revelations the very young can stand, but I suspect they may rejoice in them more than we have supposed. I can't believe they have never wondered about Leif Ericson and that word "discovered," or even about 1492. They have simply been too wise to inquire.

Increasingly in recent years better students in the better high schools and preparatory schools *are* being allowed to inquire. In fact they appear to be receiving both encouragement and training in their inquiry. I have the evidence before me.

Each year for the past five years all freshmen entering Harvard and Radcliffe have been asked in freshman week to "grade" two essays answering an examination question in History. They are then asked to give their reasons for their grades. One essay, filled with dates, is 99% cow. The other, with hardly a date in it, is a good essay, easily mistaken for bull. The "official" grades of these essays are, for the first (alas!) C+ "because he has worked so hard," and for the second (soundly, I think) B+. Each year a larger majority of freshmen evaluate these essays as would the majority of the faculty, and for the faculty's reasons, and each year a smaller minority give the higher honor to the essay offering data alone. Most interesting, a larger number of students each year, while not overrating the second essay, award the first the straight E appropriate to it in a college of liberal arts.

50   For us who must grade such students in a university, these developments imply a new urgency, did we not feel it already. Through our grades we describe for the students, in the showdown, what we believe about the nature of knowledge. The subtleties of bull are not peripheral to our academic concerns. That they penetrate to the center of our care is evident in our feelings when a student whose good work we have awarded a high grade reveals to us that he does not feel he deserves it. Whether he disqualifies himself because "there's too much bull in it," or worse because "I really don't think I've worked that hard," he presents a serious educational problem. Many students feel this sleaziness; only a few reveal it to us.

We can hardly allow a mistaken sense of fraudulence to undermine our students' achievements. We must lead students beyond their concept of bull so that they may honor relevancies that are really relevant. We can willingly acknowledge that, in lieu of the date 1492, a consideration of calendars and of the word "discovered" may well be offered with intent to deceive. We must insist that this does not make such considerations intrinsically immoral, and that, contrariwise, the date 1492 may be no substitute for them. Most of all, we must convey the impression that we grade understanding qua understanding. To be convincing, I suppose we must concede to ourselves in advance that a bright student's understanding is understanding even if he achieved it by osmosis rather than by hard work in our course.

These are delicate matters. As for cow, its complexities are not what need concern us. Unlike good bull, it does not represent partial knowledge at all. It belongs to a different theory of knowledge entirely. In our theories of knowledge it represents total ignorance, or worse yet, a knowledge downright inimical to understanding. I even go so far as to propose that we award no more C's for cow. To do so is rarely, I feel, the act of mercy it seems. Mercy lies in clarity.

The reader may be afflicted by a lingering curiosity about the fate of Mr. Metzger. I hasten to reassure him. The Administrative Board of Harvard College, whatever its satanic reputations, is a benign body. Its members, to be sure, were on the spot. They delighted in Metzger's exploit, but they were responsible to the Faculty's rule. The hero stood in danger of probation. The debate was painful. Suddenly one member, of a refined legalistic sensibility, observed that the rule applied specifically to "examinations" and that the occasion had been simply an hour-test. Mr. Metzger was merely "admonished."

QUESTIONS

1. Perry divides this essay into four sections, an introduction and sections numbered I, II, and III. Identify the focus of each and its relation to what precedes and what follows.

2. Perry makes the point that "bull" and "cow" are not the equivalent of generalizations and particulars, not "poles of a single dimension" (paragraph 25). Explain how, according to Perry, they differ from generalizations and particulars.

3. Perry's essay appeared in a volume on examinations, written by members of the Harvard University faculty and presumably addressed to them and to others like them. How does Perry address his audience? What kind of persona does he construct? Point to evidence and examples of it.

4. Have you found the grading practices of your teachers mysterious or confusing? Write an essay in which you describe the practices of two or three of your teachers and try to discern the theories of knowledge that account for them.

5. Perry proposes that his colleagues "award no more C's for cow" (paragraph 52). Write an essay in which you argue for or against his proposal.

LANGUAGE AND
COMMUNICATION

GLORIA NAYLOR *"Mommy, What Does 'Nigger' Mean?"*

Language is the subject. It is the written form with which I've managed to keep the wolf away from the door and, in diaries, to keep my sanity. In spite of this, I consider the written word inferior to the spoken, and much of the frustration experienced by novelists is the awareness that whatever we manage to capture in even the most transcendent passages falls far short of the richness of life. Dialogue achieves its power in the dynamics of a fleeting moment of sight, sound, smell and touch.

I'm not going to enter the debate here about whether it is language that shapes reality or vice versa. That battle is doomed to be waged whenever we seek intermittent reprieve from the chicken and egg dispute. I will simply take the position that the spoken word, like the written word, amounts to a nonsensical arrangement of sounds or letters without a consensus that assigns "meaning." And building from the meanings of what we hear, we order reality. Words themselves are innocuous; it is the consensus that gives them true power.

I remember the first time I heard the word nigger. In my third-grade class, our math tests were being passed down the rows, and as I handed the papers to a little boy in back of me, I remarked that once again he had received a much lower mark than I did. He snatched his test from me and spit out that word. Had he called me a nymphomaniac or a necrophiliac, I couldn't have been more puzzled. I didn't know what a nigger was, but I knew that whatever it meant, it was something he shouldn't have called me. This was verified when I raised my hand, and in a loud voice repeated what he had said and watched the teacher scold him for using a "bad" word. I was later to go home and ask the inevitable question that every black parent must face—"Mommy, what does 'nigger' mean?"

And what exactly did it mean? Thinking back, I realize that this could not have been the first time the word was used in my presence. I was part of a large extended family that had migrated from the rural South after World War II and formed a close-knit network that gravitated around my maternal grandparents. Their ground-floor apartment in one of the buildings they

Originally published in the "Hers" column of the New York Times *(February 20, 1986), which featured essays and commentary by women writers.*

owned in Harlem was a weekend mecca for my immediate family, along with countless aunts, uncles and cousins who brought along assorted friends. It was a bustling and open house with assorted neighbors and tenants popping in and out to exchange bits of gossip, pick up an old quarrel or referee the ongoing checkers game in which my grandmother cheated shamelessly. They were all there to let down their hair and put up their feet after a week of labor in the factories, laundries and shipyards of New York.

Amid the clamor, which could reach deafening proportions—two or three conversations going on simultaneously, punctuated by the sound of a baby's crying somewhere in the back rooms or out on the street—there was still a rigid set of rules about what was said and how. Older children were sent out of the living room when it was time to get into the juicy details about "you-know-who" up on the third floor who had gone and gotten herself "p-r-e-g-n-a-n-t!" But my parents, knowing that I could spell well beyond my years, always demanded that I follow the others out to play. Beyond sexual misconduct and death, everything else was considered harmless for our young ears. And so among the anecdotes of the triumphs and disappointments in the various workings of their lives, the word nigger was used in my presence, but it was set within contexts and inflections that caused it to register in my mind as something else.

In the singular, the word was always applied to a man who had distinguished himself in some situation that brought their approval for his strength, intelligence or drive:

"Did Johnny really do that?"

"I'm telling you, that nigger pulled in $6,000 of overtime last year. Said he got enough for a down payment on a house."

When used with a possessive adjective by a woman—"my nigger"—it became a term of endearment for husband or boyfriend. But it could be more than just a term applied to a man. In their mouths it became the pure essence of manhood—a disembodied force that channeled their past history of struggle and present survival against the odds into a victorious statement of being: "Yeah, that old foreman found out quick enough—you don't mess with a nigger."

In the plural, it became a description of some group within the community that had overstepped the bounds of decency as my family defined it: Parents who neglected their children, a drunken couple who fought in public, people who simply refused to look for work, those with excessively dirty mouths or unkempt households were all "trifling niggers." This particular circle could forgive hard times, unemployment, the occasional bout of depression—they had gone through all of that themselves—but the unforgivable sin was lack of self-respect.

A woman could never be a "nigger" in the singular, with its connotation of confirming worth. The noun girl was its closest equivalent in that sense, but only when used in direct address and regardless of the gender doing the addressing. "Girl" was a token of respect for a woman. The one-syllable word was drawn out to sound like three in recognition of the extra ounce of wit, nerve or daring that the woman had shown in the situation under discussion.

"G-i-r-l, stop. You mean you said that to his face?"

But if the word was used in a third-person reference or shortened so that it almost snapped out of the mouth, it always involved some element of communal disapproval. And age became an important factor in these exchanges. It was only between individuals of the same generation, or from an older person to a younger (but never the other way around), that "girl" would be considered a compliment.

I don't agree with the argument that use of the word nigger at this social stratum of the black community was an internalization of racism. The dynamics were the exact opposite: the people in my grandmother's living room took a word that whites used to signify worthlessness or degradation and rendered it impotent. Gathering there together, they transformed "nigger" to signify the varied and complex human beings they knew themselves to be. If the word was to disappear totally from the mouths of even the most liberal of white society, no one in that room was naïve enough to believe it would disappear from white minds. Meeting the word head-on, they proved it had absolutely nothing to do with the way they were determined to live their lives.

15   So there must have been dozens of times that the word "nigger" was spoken in front of me before I reached the third grade. But I didn't "hear" it until it was said by a small pair of lips that had already learned it could be a way to humiliate me. That was the word I went home and asked my mother about. And since she knew that I had to grow up in America, she took me in her lap and explained.

QUESTIONS

1. In her opening paragraph, Naylor writes that she considers "the written word inferior to the spoken." In what ways does she demonstrate the superiority of the spoken word in this essay?

2. Naylor claims that "[w]ords themselves are innocuous; it is consensus that gives them true power" (paragraph 2). As a class, brainstorm a list of words that can have different meanings and connotations, depending on who uses the words.

3. Think of a word that has several different meanings in your own family or community. Write a personal essay in which you detail those meanings. Like Naylor, use grammatical terms (as well as age- and gender-specifics, if applicable) to categorize the different meanings.

MAXINE HONG KINGSTON *Tongue-Tied*

L ONG AGO IN CHINA, knot-makers tied string into buttons and frogs, and rope into bell pulls. There was one knot so complicated that it blinded the knot-maker. Finally an emperor outlawed this cruel knot, and the nobles could not order it anymore. If I had lived in China, I would have been an outlaw knot-maker.

Maybe that's why my mother cut my tongue. She pushed my tongue up and sliced the frenum.[1] Or maybe she snipped it with a pair of nail scissors. I don't remember her doing it, only her telling me about it, but all during childhood I felt sorry for the baby whose mother waited with scissors or knife in hand for it to cry—and then, when its mouth was wide open like a baby bird's, cut. The Chinese say "a ready tongue is an evil."

I used to curl up my tongue in front of the mirror and tauten my frenum into a white line, itself as thin as a razor blade. I saw no scars in my mouth. I thought perhaps I had had two frena, and she had cut one. I made other children open their mouths so I could compare theirs to mine. I saw perfect pink membranes stretching into precise edges that looked easy enough to cut. Sometimes I felt very proud that my mother committed such a powerful act upon me. At other times I was terrified—the first thing my mother did when she saw me was to cut my tongue.

"Why did you do that to me, Mother?"

"I told you."   5

"Tell me again."

"I cut it so that you would not be tongue-tied. Your tongue would be able to move in any language. You'll be able to speak languages that are completely different from one another. You'll be able to pronounce anything. Your frenum looked too tight to do those things, so I cut it."

"But isn't 'a ready tongue an evil'?"

"Things are different in this ghost country."[2]

"Did it hurt me? Did I cry and bleed?"   10

"I don't remember. Probably."

She didn't cut the other children's. When I asked cousins and other Chinese children whether their mothers had cut their tongues loose, they said, "What?"

"Why didn't you cut my brothers' and sisters' tongues?"

"They didn't need it."

Published as the first chapter of The Woman Warrior: Memoirs of a Girlhood among Ghosts *(1976), Kingston's highly acclaimed account of her Asian American girlhood and her family history.*

1. The connecting fold of membrane on the underside of the tongue.

2. In Kingston's story, the Chinese immigrants see white Americans as "ghosts," whose language and values they must adopt to become American.

15   "Why not? Were theirs longer than mine?"

"Why don't you quit blabbering and get to work?"

If my mother was not lying she should have cut more, scraped away the rest of the frenum skin, because I have a terrible time talking. Or she should not have cut at all, tampering with my speech. When I went to kindergarten and had to speak English for the first time, I became silent. A dumbness—a shame—still cracks my voice in two, even when I want to say "hello" casually, or ask an easy question in front of the check-out counter, or ask directions of a bus driver. I stand frozen, or I hold up the line with the complete, grammatical sentence that comes squeaking out at impossible length. "What did you say?" says the cab driver, or "Speak up," so I have to perform again, only weaker the second time. A telephone call makes my throat bleed and takes up that day's courage. It spoils my day with self-disgust when I hear my broken voice come skittering out into the open. It makes people wince to hear it. I'm getting better, though. Recently I asked the postman for special-issue stamps; I've waited since childhood for postmen to give me some of their own accord. I am making progress, a little every day.

My silence was thickest—total—during the three years that I covered my school paintings with black paint. I painted layers of black over houses and flowers and suns, and when I drew on the blackboard, I put a layer of chalk on top. I was making a stage curtain, and it was the moment before the curtain parted or rose. The teachers called my parents to school, and I saw they had been saving my pictures, curling and cracking, all alike and black. The teachers pointed to the pictures and looked serious, talked seriously too, but my parents did not understand English. ("The parents and teachers of criminals were executed," said my father.) My parents took the pictures home. I spread them out (so black and full of possibilities) and pretended the curtains were swinging open, flying up, one after another, sunlight underneath, mighty operas.

During the first silent year I spoke to no one at school, did not ask before going to the lavatory, and flunked kindergarten. My sister also said nothing for three years, silent in the playground and silent at lunch. There were other quiet Chinese girls not of our family, but most of them got over it sooner than we did. I enjoyed the silence. At first it did not occur to me I was supposed to talk or to pass kindergarten. I talked at home and to one or two of the Chinese kids in class. I made motions and even made some jokes. I drank out of a toy saucer when the water spilled out of the cup, and everybody laughed, pointing at me, so I did it some more. I didn't know that Americans don't drink out of saucers.

20   I liked the Negro students (Black Ghosts) best because they laughed the loudest and talked to me as if I were a daring talker too. One of the Negro girls had her mother coil braids over her ears Shanghai-style like mine; we were Shanghai twins except that she was covered with black like my paintings. Two Negro kids enrolled in Chinese school, and the teachers gave them Chinese names. Some Negro kids walked me to school and home, protecting me from the Japanese kids, who hit me and chased me and stuck gum in my ears. The

Japanese kids were noisy and tough. They appeared one day in kindergarten, released from concentration camp,[3] which was a tic-tac-toe mark, like barbed wire, on the map.

It was when I found out I had to talk that school became a misery, that the silence became a misery. I did not speak and felt bad each time that I did not speak. I read aloud in first grade, though, and heard the barest whisper with little squeaks come out of my throat. "Louder," said the teacher, who scared the voice away again. The other Chinese girls did not talk either, so I knew the silence had to do with being a Chinese girl.

Reading out loud was easier than speaking because we did not have to make up what to say, but I stopped often, and the teacher would think I'd gone quiet again. I could not understand "I." The Chinese "I" had seven strokes, intricacies. How could the American "I," assuredly wearing a hat like the Chinese, have only three strokes, the middle so straight? Was it out of politeness that this writer left off strokes the way a Chinese has to write her own name small and crooked? No, it was not politeness; "I" is a capital and "you" is a lower-case. I stared at that middle line and waited so long for its black center to resolve into tight strokes and dots that I forgot to pronounce it. The other troublesome word was "here," no strong consonant to hang on to, and so flat, when "here" is two mountainous ideographs. The teacher, who had already told me every day how to read "I" and "here," put me in the low corner under the stairs again, where the noisy boys usually sat.

When my second grade class did a play, the whole class went to the auditorium except the Chinese girls. The teacher, lovely and Hawaiian, should have understood about us, but instead left us behind in the classroom. Our voices were too soft or nonexistent, and our parents never signed the permission slips anyway. They never signed anything unnecessary. We opened the door a crack and peeked out, but closed it again quickly. One of us (not me) won every spelling bee, though.

I remember telling the Hawaiian teacher, "We Chinese can't sing 'land where our fathers died.' " She argued with me about politics, while I meant because of curses. But how can I have that memory when I couldn't talk? My mother says that we, like the ghosts, have no memories.

After American school, we picked up our cigar boxes, in which we had   25
arranged books, brushes, and an inkbox neatly, and went to Chinese school, from 5:00 to 7:30 P.M. There we chanted together, voices rising and falling, loud and soft, some boys shouting, everybody reading together, reciting together and not alone with one voice. When we had a memorization test, the teacher let each of us come to his desk and say the lesson to him privately, while the rest of the class practiced copying or tracing. Most of the teachers were men. The boys who were so well behaved in the American school played tricks on them and talked back to them. The girls were not mute. They screamed and yelled during recess, when there were no rules; they had fist-

---

3. During World War II, more than 100,000 Japanese Americans were imprisoned in "War Relocation Camps" in the United States.

fights. Nobody was afraid of children hurting themselves or of children hurt-ing school property. The glass doors to the red and green balconies with the gold joy symbols were left wide open so that we could run out and climb the fire escapes. We played capture-the-flag in the auditorium, where Sun Yat-sen and Chiang Kai-shek's[4] pictures hung at the back of the stage, the Chinese flag on their left and the American flag on their right. We climbed the teak cere-monial chairs and made flying leaps off the stage. One flag headquarters was behind the glass door and the other on stage right. Our feet drummed on the hollow stage. During recess the teachers locked themselves up in their office with the shelves of books, copybooks, inks from China. They drank tea and warmed their hands at a stove. There was no play supervision. At recess we had the school to ourselves, and also we could roam as far as we could go—downtown, Chinatown stores, home—as long as we returned before the bell rang.

At exactly 7:30 the teacher again picked up the brass bell that sat on his desk and swung it over our heads, while we charged down the stairs, our cheering magnified in the stairwell. Nobody had to line up.

Not all of the children who were silent at American school found voice at Chinese school. One new teacher said each of us had to get up and recite in front of the class, who was to listen. My sister and I had memorized the lesson perfectly. We said it to each other at home, one chanting, one listening. The teacher called on my sister to recite first. It was the first time a teacher had called on the second-born to go first. My sister was scared. She glanced at me and looked away; I looked down at my desk. I hoped that she could do it because if she could, then I wouldn't have to. She opened her mouth and a voice came out that wasn't a whisper, but it wasn't a proper voice either. I hoped that she would not cry, fear breaking up her voice like twigs underfoot. She sounded as if she were trying to sing through weeping and strangling. She did not pause or stop to end the embarrassment. She kept going until she said the last word, and then she sat down. When it was my turn, the same voice came out, a crippled animal running on broken legs. You could hear splinters in my voice, bones rubbing jagged against one another. I was loud, though. I was glad I didn't whisper. There was one little girl who whispered.

4. Sun Yat-sen (1866–1925) and his successor, Chiang Kai-shek (1888–1975), led the Guomindang (or Nationalist party) campaign to unify China in the 1920s and 1930s.

QUESTIONS

1. Like Gloria Anzaldúa in "How to Tame a Wild Tongue" (p. 523), Kingston uses the tongue as both a physical body part and a metaphor for speech. Locate examples of these uses of "tongue" and explain them.

2. Why does Kingston call non-Asians "ghosts"? Are these the only ghosts Kingston confronts? Discuss her usage of this term in the essay and in the subtitle of her auto-biography, *Memoirs of a Girlhood among Ghosts*.

3. If you have had difficulty speaking up or if you have faced a language problem in your past, write about it in an essay that explains your experience in terms of a family or social context.

RICHARD RODRIGUEZ *Aria*

Supporters of bilingual education today imply that students like me miss a great deal by not being taught in their family's language. What they seem not to recognize is that, as a socially disadvantaged child, I considered Spanish to be a private language. What I needed to learn in school was that I had the right—and the obligation—to speak the public language of *los gringos*. The odd truth is that my first-grade classmates could have become bilingual, in the conventional sense of that word, more easily than I. Had they been taught (as upper-middle-class children are often taught early) a second language like Spanish or French, they could have regarded it simply as that: another public language. In my case such bilingualism could not have been so quickly achieved. What I did not believe was that I could speak a single public language.

Without question, it would have pleased me to hear my teachers address me in Spanish when I entered the classroom. I would have felt much less afraid. I would have trusted them and responded with ease. But I would have delayed—for how long postponed?—having to learn the language of public society. I would have evaded—and for how long could I have afforded to delay?—learning the great lesson of school, that I had a public identity.

Fortunately, my teachers were unsentimental about their responsibility. What they understood was that I needed to speak a public language. So their voices would search me out, asking me questions. Each time I'd hear them, I'd look up in surprise to see a nun's face frowning at me. I'd mumble, not really meaning to answer. The nun would persist, "Richard, stand up. Don't look at the floor. Speak up. Speak to the entire class, not just to me!" But I couldn't believe that the English language was mine to use. (In part, I did not want to believe it.) I continued to mumble. I resisted the teacher's demands. (Did I somehow suspect that once I learned public language my pleasing family life would be changed?) Silent, waiting for the bell to sound, I remained dazed, diffident, afraid.

Because I wrongly imagined that English was intrinsically a public language and Spanish an intrinsically private one, I easily noted the difference between classroom language and the language of home. At school, words were directed to a general audience of listeners. ("Boys and girls.") Words were

From Hunger of Memory: The Education of Richard Rodriguez (1982), *an autobiography of Rodriguez's experiences as a student, including his controversial argument against bilingual education.*

meaningfully ordered. And the point was not self-expression alone but to make oneself understood by many others. The teacher quizzed: "Boys and girls, why do we use that word in this sentence? Could we think of a better word to use there? Would the sentence change its meaning if the words were differently arranged? And wasn't there a better way of saying much the same thing?" (I couldn't say. I wouldn't try to say.)

5   Three months. Five. Half a year passed. Unsmiling, ever watchful, my teachers noted my silence. They began to connect my behavior with the difficult progress my older sister and brother were making. Until one Saturday morning three nuns arrived at the house to talk to our parents. Stiffly, they sat on the blue living room sofa. From the doorway of another room, spying the visitors, I noted the incongruity—the clash of two worlds, the faces and voices of school intruding upon the familiar setting of home. I overheard one voice gently wondering, "Do your children speak only Spanish at home, Mrs. Rodriguez?" While another voice added, "That Richard especially seems so timid and shy."

That Rich-heard!

With great tact the visitors continued, "Is it possible for you and your husband to encourage your children to practice their English when they are home?" Of course, my parents complied. What would they not do for their children's well-being? And how could they have questioned the Church's authority which those women represented? In an instant, they agreed to give up the language (the sounds) that had revealed and accentuated our family's closeness. The moment after the visitors left, the change was observed. "*Ahora,* speak to us *en inglés,*"[1] my father and mother united to tell us.

At first, it seemed a kind of game. After dinner each night, the family gathered to practice "our" English. (It was still then *inglés,* a language foreign to us, so we felt drawn as strangers to it.) Laughing, we would try to define words we could not pronounce. We played with strange English sounds, often overanglicizing our pronunciations. And we filled the smiling gaps of our sentences with familiar Spanish sounds. But that was cheating, somebody shouted. Everyone laughed. In school, meanwhile, like my brother and sister, I was required to attend a daily tutoring session. I needed a full year of special attention. I also needed my teachers to keep my attention from straying in class by calling out, *Rich-heard*—their English voices slowly prying loose my ties to my other name, its three notes, *Ri-car-do.* Most of all I needed to hear my mother and father speak to me in a moment of seriousness in broken—suddenly heartbreaking—English. The scene was inevitable: One Saturday morning I entered the kitchen where my parents were talking in Spanish. I did not realize that they were talking in Spanish however until, at the moment they saw me, I heard their voices change to speak English. Those *gringo* sounds they uttered startled me. Pushed me away. In that moment of trivial misunderstanding and profound insight, I felt my throat twisted by unsounded grief. I turned quickly and left the room. But I had no place to escape to with

1. "*Now,* speak to us *in English.*"

Spanish. (The spell was broken.) My brother and sisters were speaking English in another part of the house.

Again and again in the days following, increasingly angry, I was obliged to hear my mother and father: "Speak to us *en inglés.*" (*Speak.*) Only then did I determine to learn classroom English. Weeks after, it happened: One day in school I raised my hand to volunteer an answer. I spoke out in a loud voice. And I did not think it remarkable when the entire class understood. That day, I moved very far from the disadvantaged child I had been only days earlier. The belief, that calming assurance that I belonged in public, had at last taken hold.

Shortly after, I stopped hearing the high and loud sounds of *los gringos.* A more and more confident speaker of English, I didn't trouble to listen to *how* strangers sounded, speaking to me. And there simply were too many English-speaking people in my day for me to hear American accents anymore. Conversations quickened. Listening to persons who sounded eccentrically pitched voices, I usually noted their sounds for an initial few seconds before I concentrated on *what* they were saying. Conversations became content-full. Transparent. Hearing someone's *tone* of voice—angry or questioning or sarcastic or happy or sad—I didn't distinguish it from the words it expressed. Sound and word were thus tightly wedded. At the end of a day, I was often bemused, always relieved, to realize how "silent," though crowded with words, my day in public had been. (This public silence measured and quickened the change in my life.)

At last, seven years old, I came to believe what had been technically true since my birth: I was an American citizen.

But the special feeling of closeness at home was diminished by then. Gone was the desperate, urgent, intense feeling of being at home; rare was the experience of feeling myself individualized by family intimates. We remained a loving family, but one greatly changed. No longer so close; no longer bound tight by the pleasing and troubling knowledge of our public separateness. Neither my older brother nor sister rushed home after school anymore. Nor did I. When I arrived home there would often be neighborhood kids in the house. Or the house would be empty of sounds.

Following the dramatic Americanization of their children, even my parents grew more publicly confident. Especially my mother. She learned the names of all the people on our block. And she decided we needed to have a telephone installed in the house. My father continued to use the word *gringo.* But it was no longer charged with the old bitterness or distrust. (Stripped of any emotional content, the word simply became a name for those Americans not of Hispanic descent.) Hearing him, sometimes, I wasn't sure if he was pronouncing the Spanish word *gringo* or saying gringo in English.

Matching the silence I started hearing in public was a new quiet at home. The family's quiet was partly due to the fact that, as we children learned more and more English, we shared fewer and fewer words with our parents. Sentences needed to be spoken slowly when a child addressed his mother or father. (Often the parent wouldn't understand.) The child would need to repeat

10

himself. (Still the parent misunderstood.) The young voice, frustrated, would end up saying, "Never mind"—the subject was closed. Dinners would be noisy with the clinking of knives and forks against dishes. My mother would smile softly between her remarks; my father at the other end of the table would chew and chew at his food, while he stared over the heads of his children.

15   My *mother*! My *father*! After English became my primary language, I no longer knew what words to use in addressing my parents. The old Spanish words (those tender accents of sound) I had used earlier—*mamá* and *papá*—I couldn't use anymore. They would have been too painful reminders of how much had changed in my life. On the other hand, the words I heard neighborhood kids call *their* parents seemed equally unsatisfactory. *Mother* and *Father*; *Ma, Papa, Pa, Dad, Pop* (how I hated the all American sound of that last word especially)—all these terms I felt were unsuitable, not really terms of address for *my* parents. As a result, I never used them at home. Whenever I'd speak to my parents, I would try to get their attention with eye contact alone. In public conversations, I'd refer to "my parents" or "my mother and father."

My mother and father, for their part, responded differently, as their children spoke to them less. She grew restless, seemed troubled and anxious at the scarcity of words exchanged in the house. It was she who would question me about my day when I came home from school. She smiled at small talk. She pried at the edges of my sentences to get me to say something more. (What?) She'd join conversations she overheard, but her intrusions often stopped her children's talking. By contrast, my father seemed reconciled to the new quiet. Though his English improved somewhat, he retired into silence. At dinner he spoke very little. One night his children and even his wife helplessly giggled at his garbled English pronunciation of the Catholic Grace before Meals. Thereafter he made his wife recite the prayer at the start of each meal, even on formal occasions, when there were guests in the house. Hers became the public voice of the family. On official business, it was she, not my father, one would usually hear on the phone or in stores, talking to strangers. His children grew so accustomed to his silence that, years later, they would speak routinely of his shyness. (My mother would often try to explain: Both his parents died when he was eight. He was raised by an uncle who treated him like little more than a menial servant. He was never encouraged to speak. He grew up alone. A man of few words.) But my father was not shy, I realized, when I'd watch him speaking Spanish with relatives. Using Spanish, he was quickly effusive. Especially when talking with other men, his voice would spark, flicker, flare alive with sounds. In Spanish, he expressed ideas and feelings he rarely revealed in English. With firm Spanish sounds, he conveyed confidence and authority English would never allow him.

The silence at home, however, was finally more than a literal silence. Fewer words passed between parent and child, but more profound was the silence that resulted from my inattention to sounds. At about the time I no longer bothered to listen with care to the sounds of English in public, I grew careless about listening to the sounds family members made when they spoke. Most of the time I heard someone speaking at home and didn't distinguish his sounds from the words people uttered in public. I didn't even pay much attention to my parents' accented and ungrammatical speech. At least not at home. Only when I was with them in public would I grow alert to their accents. Though, even then, their sounds caused me less and less concern. For I was increasingly confident of my own public identity.

I would have been happier about my public success had I not sometimes recalled what it had been like earlier, when my family had conveyed its intimacy through a set of conveniently private sounds. Sometimes in public, hearing a stranger, I'd hark back to my past. A Mexican farmworker approached me downtown to ask directions to somewhere, "¡Hijito . . . ? "[2] he said. And his voice summoned deep longing. Another time, standing beside my mother in the visiting room of a Carmelite convent,[3] before the dense screen which rendered the nuns shadowy figures, I heard several Spanish-speaking nuns—their busy, singsong overlapping voices—assure us that yes, yes, we were remembered, all our family was remembered in their prayers. (Their voices echoed faraway family sounds.) Another day, a dark-faced old woman—her hand light on my shoulder—steadied herself against me as she boarded a bus. She murmured something I couldn't quite comprehend. Her Spanish voice came near, like the face of a never-before-seen relative in the instant before I was kissed. Her voice, like so many of the Spanish voices I'd hear in public, recalled the golden age of my youth. Hearing Spanish then, I continued to be a careful, if sad, listener to sounds. Hearing a Spanish-speaking family walking behind me, I turned to look. I smiled for an instant, before my glance found the Hispanic-looking faces of strangers in the crowd going by.

Today I hear bilingual educators say that children lose a degree of "individuality" by becoming assimilated into public society. (Bilingual schooling was popularized in the seventies, that decade when middle-class ethnics began to resist the process of assimilation—the American melting pot.) But the bilingualists simplistically scorn the value and necessity of assimilation. They do not seem to realize that there are *two* ways a person is individualized. So they do not realize that while one suffers a diminished sense of *private* individuality by becoming assimilated into public society, such assimilation makes possible the achievement of *public* individuality.

The bilingualists insist that a student should be reminded of his difference from others in mass society, his heritage. But they equate mere separateness with individuality. The fact is that only in private—with intimates—is separateness from the crowd a prerequisite for individuality. (An intimate draws me apart, tells me that I am unique, unlike all others.) In public, by contrast, full individuality is achieved, paradoxically, by those who are able to consider themselves members of the crowd. Thus it happened for me: Only when I was able to think of myself as an American, no longer an alien in *gringo* society, could I seek the rights and opportunities necessary for full public indi-

20

2. "Little boy . . . ?"
3. Of the Catholic Order of Our Lady of Mount Carmel.

viduality. The social and political advantages I enjoy as a man result from the day that I came to believe that my name, indeed, is *Rich-heard Road-ree-guess*. It is true that my public society today is often impersonal. (My public society is usually mass society). Yet despite the anonymity of the crowd and despite the fact that the individuality I achieve in public is often tenuous—because it depends on my being one in a crowd—I celebrate the day I acquired my new name. Those middle-class ethnics who scorn assimilation seem to me filled with decadent self-pity, obsessed by the burden of public life. Dangerously, they romanticize public separateness and they trivialize the dilemma of the socially disadvantaged.

My awkward childhood does not prove the necessity of bilingual education. My story discloses instead an essential myth of childhood—inevitable pain. If I rehearse here the changes in my private life after my Americanization, it is finally to emphasize the public gain. The loss implies the gain: The house I returned to each afternoon was quiet. Intimate sounds no longer rushed to the door to greet me. There were other noises inside. The telephone rang. Neighborhood kids ran past the door of the bedroom where I was reading my schoolbooks—covered with shopping-bag paper. Once I learned public language, it would never again be easy for me to hear intimate family voices. More and more of my day was spent hearing words. But that may only be a way of saying that the day I raised my hand in class and spoke loudly to an entire roomful of faces, my childhood started to end.

QUESTIONS

1. What, according to Rodriguez, did he lose because he attended an English-speaking (Catholic) school without a bilingual program? What did he gain?

2. Rodriguez frames this section of his autobiography with an argument against bilingual education. How convincing is his evidence? Does he claim that all nonnative speakers of English educated in English would have the same losses and gains as he did?

3. According to Rodriguez, what are the differences between private and public languages, private and public individuality? Can both exist when the family language and the school language are English? How might a native speaker of English describe the differences?

4. Make a case, in writing, for or against bilingual education using material from Gloria Naylor's "Mommy, What Does 'Nigger' Mean?" (p. 510), Maxine Hong Kingston's "Tongue-Tied" (p. 513), Gloria Anzaldúa's "How to Tame a Wild Tongue" (p. 523), and Majorie Agosín's "Always Living in Spanish" (p. 532), as well as your own experience, observation, and reading.

GLORIA ANZALDÚA *How to Tame a Wild Tongue*

"WE'RE GOING TO have to control your tongue," the dentist says, pulling out all the metal from my mouth. Silver bits plop and tinkle into the basin. My mouth is a motherlode.

The dentist is cleaning out my roots. I get a whiff of the stench when I gasp. "I can't cap that tooth yet, you're still draining," he says.

"We're going to have to do something about your tongue," I hear the anger rising in his voice. My tongue keeps pushing out the wads of cotton, pushing back the drills, the long thin needles. "I've never seen anything as strong or as stubborn," he says. And I think, how do you tame a wild tongue, train it to be quiet, how do you bridle and saddle it? How do you make it lie down?

> "Who is to say that robbing a people of
> its language is less violent than war?"
>
> —RAY GWYN SMITH[1]

I remember being caught speaking Spanish at recess—that was good for three licks on the knuckles with a sharp ruler. I remember being sent to the corner of the classroom for "talking back" to the Anglo teacher when all I was trying to do was tell her how to pronounce my name. "If you want to be American, speak 'American.' If you don't like it, go back to Mexico where you belong."

"I want you to speak English. *Pa'hallar buen trabajo tienes que saber hablar el inglés bien. Qué vale toda tu educación si todavía hablas inglés con un* 'accent,' " my mother would say, mortified that I spoke English like a Mexican. At Pan American University, I, and all Chicano students were required to take two speech classes. Their purpose: to get rid of our accents.

Attacks on one's form of expression with the intent to censor are a violation of the First Amendment. *El Anglo con cara de inocente nos arrancó la lengua.* Wild tongues can't be tamed, they can only be cut out.

Overcoming the Tradition of Silence

> *Ahogadas, escupimos el oscuro.*
> *Peleando con nuestra propia sombra*
> *el silencio nos sepulta.*

En boca cerrada no entran moscas. "Flies don't enter a closed mouth" is a saying I kept hearing when I was a child. *Ser habladora* was to be a gossip and

5

From Borderlands/La Frontera *(1987), a collection of experimental essays and memoirs that combine English, Spanish, and Chicano Spanish. All notes are the author's. The author has asked that no translations of Spanish or Chicano Spanish be included.*

1. Ray Gwyn Smith, Moorland Is Cold Country, unpublished book.

a liar, to talk too much. *Muchachitas bien criadas,* well-bred girls don't answer back. *Es una falta de respeto* to talk back to one's mother or father. I remember one of the sins I'd recite to the priest in the confession box the few times I went to confession: talking back to my mother, *hablar pa' 'trás, repelar. Hocicona, repelona, chismosa,* having a big mouth, questioning, carrying tales are all signs of being *mal criada.* In my culture they are all words that are derogatory if applied to women—I've never heard them applied to men.

The first time I heard two women, a Puerto Rican and a Cuban, say the word *"nosotras,"* I was shocked. I had not known the word existed. Chicanas use *nosotros* whether we're male or female. We are robbed of our female being by the masculine plural. Language is a male discourse.

> And our tongues have become
> dry   the wilderness has
> dried out our tongues   and
> we have forgotten speech.
>   —IRENA KLEPFISZ[2]

Even our own people, other Spanish speakers *nos quieren poner candados en la boca.* They would hold us back with their bag of *reglas de academia.*

Oyé como ladra: el lenguaje de la frontera

> *Quien tiene boca se equivoca.*
>   —MEXICAN SAYING

10   "*Pocho,* cultural traitor, you're speaking the oppressor's language by speaking English, you're ruining the Spanish language," I have been accused by various Latinos and Latinas. Chicano Spanish is considered by the purist and by most Latinos deficient, a mutilation of Spanish.

But Chicano Spanish is a border tongue which developed naturally. Change, *evolución, enriquecimiento de palabras nuevas por invención o adopción* have created variants of Chicano Spanish, *un nuevo lenguaje. Un lenguaje que corresponde a un modo de vivir.* Chicano Spanish is not incorrect, it is a living language.

For a people who are neither Spanish nor live in a country in which Spanish is the first language; for a people who live in a country in which English is the reigning tongue but who are not Anglo; for a people who cannot entirely identify with either standard (formal, Castillian) Spanish nor standard English, what recourse is left to them but to create their own language? A language which they can connect their identity to, one capable of communicating the realities and values true to themselves—a language with terms that are

---

2. Irena Klepfisz, "*Di rayze aheym*/The Journey Home," in <u>The Tribe of Dina: A Jewish Women's Anthology</u>, Melanie Kaye/Kantrowitz and Irena Klepfisz, eds. (Montpelier, VT: Sinister Wisdom Books, 1986), 49.

neither *español ni inglés,* but both. We speak a patois, a forked tongue, a variation of two languages.

Chicano Spanish sprang out of the Chicanos' need to identify ourselves as a distinct people. We needed a language with which we could communicate with ourselves, a secret language. For some of us, language is a homeland closer than the Southwest—for many Chicanos today live in the Midwest and the East. And because we are a complex, heterogeneous people, we speak many languages. Some of the languages we speak are:

1. Standard English
2. Working class and slang English
3. Standard Spanish
4. Standard Mexican Spanish
5. North Mexican Spanish dialect
6. Chicano Spanish (Texas, New Mexico, Arizona and California have regional variations)
7. Tex-Mex
8. *Pachuco* (called *caló*)

My "home" tongues are the languages I speak with my sister and brothers, with my friends. They are the last five listed, with 6 and 7 being closest to my heart. From school, the media and job situations, I've picked up standard and working class English. From Mamagrande Locha and from reading Spanish and Mexican literature, I've picked up Standard Spanish and Standard Mexican Spanish. From *los recién llegados,* Mexican immigrants, and *braceros,* I learned the North Mexican dialect. With Mexicans I'll try to speak either Standard Mexican Spanish or the North Mexican dialect. From my parents and Chicanos living in the Valley, I picked up Chicano Texas Spanish, and I speak it with my mom, younger brother (who married a Mexican and who rarely mixes Spanish with English), aunts and older relatives.

With Chicanas from *Nuevo México* or *Arizona* I will speak Chicano Spanish a little, but often they don't understand what I'm saying. With most California Chicanas I speak entirely in English (unless I forget). When I first moved to San Francisco, I'd rattle off something in Spanish, unintentionally embarrassing them. Often it is only with another Chicana *tejana* that I can talk freely.   15

Words distorted by English are known as anglicisms or *pochismos.* The *pocho* is an anglicized Mexican or American of Mexican origin who speaks Spanish with an accent characteristic of North Americans and who distorts and reconstructs the language according to the influence of English.[3] Tex-Mex, or Spanglish, comes most naturally to me. I may switch back and forth from En-

---

3. R. C. Ortega, *Dialectología Del Barrio,* trans. Hortencia S. Alwan (Los Angeles, CA: R. C. Ortega Publisher & Bookseller, 1977), 132.

glish to Spanish in the same sentence or in the same word. With my sister and my brother Nune and with Chicano *tejano* contemporaries I speak in Tex-Mex.

From kids and people my own age I picked up *Pachuco. Pachuco* (the language of the zoot suiters) is a language of rebellion, both against Standard Spanish and Standard English. It is a secret language. Adults of the culture and outsiders cannot understand it. It is made up of slang words from both English and Spanish. *Ruca* means girl or woman, *vato* means guy or dude, *chale* means no, *simón* means yes, *churo* is sure, talk is *periquiar, pigionear* means petting, *que gacho* means how nerdy, *ponte águila* means watch out, death is called *la pelona.* Through lack of practice and not having others who can speak it, I've lost most of the *Pachuco* tongue.

Chicano Spanish

Chicanos, after 250 years of Spanish/Anglo colonization have developed significant differences in the Spanish we speak. We collapse two adjacent vowels into a single syllable and sometimes shift the stress in certain words such as *maíz/maiz, cohete/cuete.* We leave out certain consonants when they appear between vowels: *lado/lao, mojado/mojao.* Chicanos from South Texas pronounced *f* as *j* as in *jue (fue).* Chicanos use "archaisms," words that are no longer in the Spanish language, words that have been evolved out. We say *semos, truje, haiga, ansina,* and *naiden.* We retain the "archaic" *j,* as in *jalar,* that derives from an earlier *h* (the French *halar* or the Germanic *halon* which was lost to standard Spanish in the 16th century), but which is still found in several regional dialects such as the one spoken in South Texas. (Due to geography, Chicanos from the Valley of South Texas were cut off linguistically from other Spanish speakers. We tend to use words that the Spaniards brought over from Medieval Spain. The majority of the Spanish colonizers in Mexico and the Southwest came from Extremadura—Hernán Cortés was one of them—and Andalucía. Andalucians pronounce *ll* like a *y,* and their *d*'s tend to be absorbed by adjacent vowels: *tirado* becomes *tirao.* They brought *el lenguaje popular, dialectos y regionalismos.*[4])

Chicanos and other Spanish speakers also shift *ll* to *y* and *z* to *s.*[5] We leave out initial syllables, saying *tar* for *estar, toy* for *estoy, hora* for *ahora (cubanos* and *puertorriqueños* also leave out initial letters of some words.) We also leave out the final syllable such as *pa* for *para.* The intervocalic *y,* the *ll* as in *tortilla, ella, botella,* gets replaced by *tortia* or *tortiya, ea, botea.* We add an additional syllable at the beginning of certain words: *atocar* for *tocar, agastar* for *gastar.* Sometimes we'll say *lavaste las vacijas,* other times *lavates* (substituting the *ates* verb endings for the *aste*).

20   We use anglicisms, words borrowed from English: *bola* from ball, *carpeta* from carpet, *máchina de lavar* (instead of *lavadora*) from washing machine.

---

4. Eduardo Hernandéz-Chávez, Andrew D. Cohen, and Anthony F. Beltramo, *El Lenguaje de los Chicanos: Regional and Social Characteristics of Language Used By Mexican Americans* (Arlington, VA: Center for Applied Linguistics, 1975), 39.

5. Hernandéz-Chávez, xvii.

Tex-Mex argot, created by adding a Spanish sound at the beginning or end of an English word such as *cookiar* for cook, *watchar* for watch, *parkiar* for park, and *rapiar* for rape, is the result of the pressures on Spanish speakers to adapt to English.

We don't use the word *vosotros/as* or its accompanying verb form. We don't say *claro* (to mean yes), *imagínate*, or *me emociona*, unless we picked up Spanish from Latinas, out of a book, or in a classroom. Other Spanish-speaking groups are going through the same, or similar, development in their Spanish.

Linguistic Terrorism

> *Deslenguadas. Somos los del español deficiente.* We are your linguistic night-mare, your linguistic aberration, your linguistic *mestizaje*, the subject of your *burla*. Because we speak with tongues of fire we are culturally cruci-fied. Racially, culturally and linguistically *somos huérfanos*—we speak an or-phan tongue.

Chicanas who grew up speaking Chicano Spanish have internalized the belief that we speak poor Spanish. It is illegitimate, a bastard language. And because we internalize how our language has been used against us by the dominant culture, we use our language differences against each other.

Chicana feminists often skirt around each other with suspicion and hesi-tation. For the longest time I couldn't figure it out. Then it dawned on me. To be close to another Chicana is like looking into the mirror. We are afraid of what we'll see there. *Pena.* Shame. Low estimation of self. In childhood we are told that our language is wrong. Repeated attacks on our native tongue dimin-ish our sense of self. The attacks continue throughout our lives.

Chicanas feel uncomfortable talking in Spanish to Latinas, afraid of their censure. Their language was not outlawed in their countries. They had a whole lifetime of being immersed in their native tongue; generations, cen-turies in which Spanish was a first language, taught in school, heard on radio and TV, and read in the newspaper.

If a person, Chicana or Latina, has a low estimation of my native tongue, she also has a low estimation of me. Often with *mexicanas y latinas* we'll speak English as a neutral language. Even among Chicanas we tend to speak English at parties or conferences. Yet, at the same time, we're afraid the other will think we're *agringadas* because we don't speak Chicano Spanish. We oppress each other trying to out-Chicano each other, vying to be the "real" Chicanas, to speak like Chicanos. There is no one Chicano language just as there is no one Chicano experience. A monolingual Chicana whose first language is En-glish or Spanish is just as much a Chicana as one who speaks several variants of Spanish. A Chicana from Michigan or Chicago or Detroit is just as much a Chicana as one from the Southwest. Chicano Spanish is as diverse linguisti-cally as it is regionally.

By the end of this century, Spanish speakers will comprise the biggest minority group in the U.S., a country where students in high schools and colleges are encouraged to take French classes because French is con-sidered more "cultured." But for a language to remain alive it must be

25

used.[6] By the end of this century English, and not Spanish, will be the mother tongue of most Chicanos and Latinos.

So, if you want to really hurt me, talk badly about my language. Ethnic identity is twin skin to linguistic identity—I am my language. Until I can take pride in my language, I cannot take pride in myself. Until I can accept as legitimate Chicano Texas Spanish, Tex-Mex and all the other languages I speak, I cannot accept the legitimacy of myself. Until I am free to write bilingually and to switch codes without having always to translate, while I still have to speak English or Spanish when I would rather speak Spanglish, and as long as I have to accommodate the English speakers rather than having them accommodate me, my tongue will be illegitimate.

I will no longer be made to feel ashamed of existing. I will have my voice: Indian, Spanish, white. I will have my serpent's tongue—my woman's voice, my sexual voice, my poet's voice. I will overcome the tradition of silence.

> My fingers
> move sly against your palm
> Like women everywhere, we speak in code . . . .
> —MELANIE KAYE/KANTROWITZ[7]

"Vistas," corridos, y comida: My Native Tongue

In the 1960s, I read my first Chicano novel. It was *City of Night* by John Rechy, a gay Texan, son of a Scottish father and a Mexican mother. For days I walked around in stunned amazement that a Chicano could write and could get published. When I read *I Am Joaquín*[8] I was surprised to see a bilingual book by a Chicano in print. When I saw poetry written in Tex-Mex for the first time, a feeling of pure joy flashed through me. I felt like we really existed as a people. In 1971, when I started teaching High School English to Chicano students, I tried to supplement the required texts with works by Chicanos, only to be reprimanded and forbidden to do so by the principal. He claimed that I was supposed to teach "American" and English literature. At the risk of being fired, I swore my students to secrecy and slipped in Chicano short stories, poems, a play. In graduate school, while working toward a Ph.D., I had to "argue" with one advisor after the other, semester after semester, before I was allowed to make Chicano literature an area of focus.

30   Even before I read books by Chicanos or Mexicans, it was the Mexican movies I saw at the drive-in—the Thursday night special of $1.00 a carload— that gave me a sense of belonging. *"Vámonos a las vistas,"* my mother would call out and we'd all—grandmother, brothers, sister and cousins—squeeze into

6. Irena Klepfisz, "Secular Jewish Identity: Yidishkayt in America," in The Tribe of Dina, Kaye/Kantrowitz and Klepfisz, eds., 43.

7. Melanie Kaye/Kantrowitz, "Sign," in We Speak in Code: Poems and Other Writings (Pittsburgh, PA: Motheroot Publications, Inc., 1980), 85.

8. Rodolfo Gonzales, I Am Joaquín / Yo Soy Joaquín (New York, NY: Bantam Books, 1972). It was first published in 1967.

the car. We'd wolf down cheese and bologna white bread sandwiches while watching Pedro Infante in melodramatic tear-jerkers like *Nosotros los pobres,* the first "real" Mexican movie (that was not an imitation of European movies). I remember seeing *Cuando los hijos se van* and surmising that all Mexican movies played up the love a mother has for her children and what ungrateful sons and daughters suffer when they are not devoted to their mothers. I remember the singing-type "westerns" of Jorge Negrete and Miguel Aceves Mejía. When watching Mexican movies, I felt a sense of homecoming as well as alienation. People who were to amount to something didn't go to Mexican movies, or *bailes* or tune their radios to *bolero, rancherita,* and *corrido* music.

The whole time I was growing up, there was *norteño* music sometimes called North Mexican border music, or Tex-Mex music, or Chicano music, or *cantina* (bar) music. I grew up listening to *conjuntos,* three- or four-piece bands made up of folk musicians playing guitar, *bajo sexto,* drums and button accordion, which Chicanos had borrowed from the German immigrants who had come to Central Texas and Mexico to farm and build breweries. In the Rio Grande Valley, Steve Jordan and Little Joe Hernández were popular, and Flaco Jiménez was the accordion king. The rhythms of Tex-Mex music are those of the polka, also adapted from the Germans, who in turn had borrowed the polka from the Czechs and Bohemians.

I remember the hot, sultry evenings when *corridos*—songs of love and death on the Texas-Mexican borderlands—reverberated out of cheap amplifiers from the local *cantinas* and wafted in through my bedroom window.

Corridos first became widely used along the South Texas/Mexican border during the early conflict between Chicanos and Anglos. The *corridos* are usually about Mexican heroes who do valiant deeds against the Anglo oppressors. Pancho Villa's song, "*La cucaracha*," is the most famous one. *Corridos* of John F. Kennedy and his death are still very popular in the Valley. Older Chicanos remember Lydia Mendoza, one of the great border *corrido* singers who was called *la Gloria de Tejas.* Her "*El tango negro*," sung during the Great Depression, made her a singer of the people. The everpresent *corridos* narrated one hundred years of border history, bringing news of events as well as entertaining. These folk musicians and folk songs are our chief cultural mythmakers, and they made our hard lives seem bearable.

I grew up feeling ambivalent about our music. Country-western and rock-and-roll had more status. In the 50s and 60s, for the slightly educated and *agringado* Chicanos, there existed a sense of shame at being caught listening to our music. Yet I couldn't stop my feet from thumping to the music, could not stop humming the words, nor hide from myself the exhilaration I felt when I heard it.

There are more subtle ways that we internalize identification, especially in the forms of images and emotions. For me food and certain smells are tied to my identity, to my homeland. Woodsmoke curling up to an immense blue sky; woodsmoke perfuming my grandmother's clothes, her skin. The stench of cow manure and the yellow patches on the ground; the crack of a .22 rifle and the

35

reek of cordite. Homemade white cheese sizzling in a pan, melting inside a folded *tortilla*. My sister Hilda's hot, spicy *menudo, chile colorado* making it deep red, pieces of *panza* and hominy floating on top. My brother Carito barbecuing *fajitas* in the backyard. Even now and 3,000 miles away, I can see my mother spicing the ground beef, pork and venison with *chile*. My mouth salivates at the thought of the hot steaming *tamales* I would be eating if I were home.

Si le preguntas a mi mamá, "¿Qué eres?"

> "Identity is the essential core of who
> we are as individuals, the conscious
> experience of the self inside."
>
> —KAUFMAN[9]

Nosotros los Chicanos straddle the borderlands. On one side of us, we are constantly exposed to the Spanish of the Mexicans, on the other side we hear the Anglos' incessant clamoring so that we forget our language. Among ourselves we don't say *nosotros los americanos, o nosotros los españoles, o nosotros los hispanos*. We say *nosotros los mexicanos* (by *mexicanos* we do not mean citizens of Mexico; we do not mean a national identity, but a racial one). We distinguish between *mexicanos del otro lado* and *mexicanos de este lado*. Deep in our hearts we believe that being Mexican has nothing to do with which country one lives in. Being Mexican is a state of soul—not one of mind, not one of citizenship. Neither eagle nor serpent, but both. And like the ocean, neither animal respects borders.

> *Dime con quien andas y te diré quien eres.*
> (Tell me who your friends are and I'll tell you who you are.)
>
> —MEXICAN SAYING

Si le preguntas a mi mamá, "¿Qué eres?" te dirá, "Soy mexicana." My brothers and sister say the same. I sometimes will answer "soy mexicana" and at others will say "soy Chicana" o "soy tejana." But I identified as "Raza" before I ever identified as "mexicana" or "Chicana."

As a culture, we call ourselves Spanish when referring to ourselves as a linguistic group and when copping out. It is then that we forget our predominant Indian genes. We are 70 to 80% Indian.[10] We call ourselves Hispanic[11] or Spanish-American or Latin American or Latin when linking ourselves to other Spanish-speaking peoples of the Western hemisphere and when copping out. We call ourselves Mexican-American[12] to signify we are neither Mexican nor

9. Kaufman, 68.
10. Chávez, 88–90.
11. "Hispanic" is derived from *Hispanis* (*España*, a name given to the Iberian Peninsula in ancient times when it was a part of the Roman Empire) and is a term designated by the U.S. government to make it easier to handle us on paper.
12. The Treaty of Guadalupe Hidalgo created the Mexican-American in 1848.

American, but more the noun "American" than the adjective "Mexican" (and when copping out).

Chicanos and other people of color suffer economically for not acculturating. This voluntary (yet forced) alienation makes for psychological conflict, a kind of dual identity—we don't identify with the Anglo-American cultural values and we don't totally identify with the Mexican cultural values. We are a synergy of two cultures with various degrees of Mexicanness or Angloness. I have so internalized the borderland conflict that sometimes I feel like one cancels out the other and we are zero, nothing, no one. *A veces no soy nada ni nadie. Pero hasta cuando no lo soy, lo soy.*

When not copping out, when we know we are more than nothing, we call   40
ourselves Mexican, referring to race and ancestry; *mestizo* when affirming both our Indian and Spanish (but we hardly ever own our Black ancestry); Chicano when referring to a politically aware people born and/or raised in the U.S.; *Raza* when referring to Chicanos; *tejanos* when we are Chicanos from Texas.

Chicanos did not know we were a people until 1965 when Cesar Chavez and the farmworkers united and *I Am Joaquín* was published and *la Raza Unida* party was formed in Texas. With that recognition, we became a distinct people. Something momentous happened to the Chicano soul—we became aware of our reality and acquired a name and a language (Chicano Spanish) that reflected that reality. Now that we had a name, some of the fragmented pieces began to fall together—who we were, what we were, how we had evolved. We began to get glimpses of what we might eventually become.

Yet the struggle of identities continues, the struggle of borders is our reality still. One day the inner struggle will cease and a true integration take place. In the meantime, *tenemos que hacerla lucha. ¿Quién está protegiendo los ranchos de mi gente? ¿Quién está tratando de cerrar la fisura entre la india y el blanco en nuestra sangre? El Chicano, sí, el Chicano que anda como un ladrón en su propia casa.*

Los Chicanos, how patient we seem, how very patient. There is the quiet of the Indian about us.[13] We know how to survive. When other races have given up their tongue, we've kept ours. We know what it is to live under the hammer blow of the dominant *norteamericano* culture. But more than we count the blows, we count the days the weeks the years the centuries the eons until the white laws and commerce and customs will rot in the deserts they've created, lie bleached. *Humildes* yet proud, *quietos* yet wild, *nosotros los mexicanos*-Chicanos will walk by the crumbling ashes as we go about our

13. Anglos, in order to alleviate their guilt for dispossessing the Chicano, stressed the Spanish part of us and perpetrated the myth of the Spanish Southwest. We have accepted the fiction that we are Hispanic, that is Spanish, in order to accommodate ourselves to the dominant culture and its abhorrence of Indians. Chávez, 88–91.

business. Stubborn, persevering, impenetrable as stone, yet possessing a malleability that renders us unbreakable, we, the *mestizas* and *mestizos*, will remain.

QUESTIONS

1. Anzaldúa includes many Spanish words and phrases, some of which she explains, others which she leaves untranslated. Why? What different responses might bilingual versus English-only readers have to her writing?

2. The essay begins with an example of Anzaldúa's "untamed tongue." What meanings, many metaphoric, does Anzaldúa give for "tongue" or "wild tongue"? How does the essay develop these meanings?

3. Anzaldúa speaks of Chicano Spanish as a "living language" (paragraph 11). What does she mean? What is her evidence for this point? What other languages do you know that are living, and how do you know they are living?

4. If you speak or write more than one language, or if you come from a linguistic community that has expressions specific to itself, write an essay in which you incorporate that language and/or alternate it with English. Think about the ways that Anzaldúa uses both English and Spanish.

MARJORIE AGOSÍN *Always Living in Spanish*

I N THE EVENINGS in the northern hemisphere, I repeat the ancient ritual that I observed as a child in the southern hemisphere: going out while the night is still warm and trying to recognize the stars as it begins to grow dark silently. In the sky of my country, Chile, that long and wide stretch of land that the poets blessed and dictators abused, I could easily name the stars: the three Marias, the Southern Cross, and the three Lilies, names of beloved and courageous women.

But here in the United States, where I have lived since I was a young girl, the solitude of exile makes me feel that so little is mine, that not even the sky has the same constellations, the trees and the fauna the same names or sounds, or the rubbish the same smell. How does one recover the familiar? How does one name the unfamiliar? How can one be another or live in a foreign language? These are the dilemmas of one who writes in Spanish and lives in translation.

Published in Poets & Writers (*March–April 1999*), *by a professor of Spanish at Wellesley College in Massachusetts. The magazine is the publication of Poets & Writers, Inc., an organization that provides "information, support and guidance for creative writers."*

Since my earliest childhood in Chile I lived with the tempos and the melodies of a multiplicity of tongues: German, Yiddish,[1] Russian, Turkish, and many Latin songs. Because everyone was from somewhere else, my relatives laughed, sang, and fought in a Babylon of languages. Spanish was reserved for matters of extreme seriousness, for commercial transactions, or for illnesses, but everyone's mother tongue was always associated with the memory of spaces inhabited in the past: the shtetl,[2] the flowering and vast Vienna avenues, the minarets of Turkey, and the Ladino[3] whispers of Toledo. When my paternal grandmother sang old songs in Turkish, her voice and body assumed the passion of one who was there in the city of Istanbul, gazing by turns toward the west and the east.

Destiny and the always ambiguous nature of history continued my family's enforced migration, and because of it I, too, became one who had to live and speak in translation. The disappearances, torture, and clandestine deaths in my country in the early seventies drove us to the United States, that other America that looked with suspicion at those who did not speak English and especially those who came from the supposedly uncivilized regions of Latin America. I had left a dangerous place that was my home, only to arrive in a dangerous place that was not: a high school in the small town of Athens, Georgia, where my poor English and my accent were the cause of ridicule and insult. The only way I could recover my usurped country and my Chilean childhood was by continuing to write in Spanish, the same way my grandparents had sung in their own tongues in diasporic[4] sites.

5

The new and learned English language did not fit with the visceral emotions and themes that my poetry contained, but by writing in Spanish I could recover fragrances, spoken rhythms, and the passion of my own identity. Daily I felt the need to translate myself for the strangers living all around me, to tell them why we were in Georgia, why we ate differently, why we had fled, why my accent was so thick, and why I did not look Hispanic. Only at night, writing poems in Spanish, could I return to my senses, and soothe my own sorrow over what I had left behind.

This is how I became a Chilean poet who wrote in Spanish and lived in the southern United States. And then, one day, a poem of mine was translated and published in the English language. Finally, for the first time since I had left Chile, I felt I didn't have to explain myself. My poem, expressed in another language, spoke for itself . . . and for me.

Sometimes the austere sounds of English help me bear the solitude of knowing that I am foreign and so far away from those about whom I write. I must

1. A Germanic language with a Hebrew alphabet, spoken by the Ashkenazi Jews who once populated Eastern Europe.

2. Yiddish word meaning "small town."

3. A nearly extinct language, based on Spanish and spoken by Sephardic Jews who fled Spain and settled in North Africa and the Balkans.

4. Relating to a diaspora, or the spread of a people out from a single geographic area.

admit I would like more opportunities to read in Spanish to people whose language and culture is also mine, to join in our common heritage and in the feast of our sound. I would also like readers of English to understand the beauty of the spoken word in Spanish, that constant flow of oxytonic and paraoxytonic[5] syllables (*Verde que te quiero verde*),[6] the joy of writing—of dancing—in another language. I believe that many exiles share the unresolvable torment of not being able to live in the language of their childhood.

I miss that undulating and sensual language of mine, those baroque descriptions, the sense of being and feeling that Spanish gives me. It is perhaps for this reason that I have chosen and will always choose to write in Spanish. Nothing else from my childhood world remains. My country seems to be frozen in gestures of silence and oblivion. My relatives have died, and I have grown up not knowing a young generation of cousins and nieces and nephews. Many of my friends were disappeared, others were tortured, and the most fortunate, like me, became guardians of memory. For us, to write in Spanish is to always be in active pursuit of memory. I seek to recapture a world lost to me on that sorrowful afternoon when the blue electric sky and the Andean cordillera[7] bade me farewell. On that, my last Chilean day, I carried under my arm my innocence recorded in a little blue notebook I kept even then. Gradually that diary filled with memoranda, poems written in free verse, descriptions of dreams and of the thresholds of my house surrounded by cherry trees and gardenias. To write in Spanish is for me a gesture of survival. And because of translation, my memory has now become a part of the memory of many others.

Translators are not traitors, as the proverb says, but rather splendid friends in this great human community of language.

5. Oxytonic: term for the stress falling on the last syllable of a word; paraoxytonic: term for the stress falling on the next-to-last syllable of a word.
6. Spanish: "Green, how I want you green." This opening line of a poem by Frederico Garcia Lorca illustrates oxytonic and paraoxytonic stress.
7. Spanish: a mountain range with a string of summits.

QUESTIONS

1. Agosín obviously knows English, but she continues to write in Spanish. What is her reason for doing so? What do you think of such a practice?

2. Compare Agosín's attitude toward the Spanish of her youth to Anzaldúa's (p. 523) or Rodriguez's (p. 517). What do they have in common? What are their differences? Which attitude attracts you more? Why?

3. Agosín writes of a Babylon of language, a concept that has negative connotations. What is wrong with so many languages being used? Can you see how some could find it distasteful, while others would celebrate diversity? Write about where you stand on this question.

Garrison Keillor *How to Write a Letter*

WE SHY PERSONS need to write a letter now and then, or else we'll dry up and blow away. It's true. And I speak as one who loves to reach for the phone, dial the number, and talk. I say, "Big Bopper[1] here— what's shakin', babes?" The telephone is to shyness what Hawaii is to February, it's a way out of the woods, *and yet*: a letter is better.

Such a sweet gift—a piece of handmade writing, in an envelope that is not a bill, sitting in our friend's path when she trudges home from a long day spent among wahoos and savages, a day our words will help repair. They don't need to be immortal, just sincere. She can read them twice and again tomorrow: *You're someone I care about, Corinne, and think of often and every time I do you make me smile.*

We need to write, otherwise nobody will know who we are. They will have only a vague impression of us as A Nice Person, because, frankly, we don't shine at conversation, we lack the confidence to thrust our faces forward and say, "Hi, I'm Heather Hooten; let me tell you about my week." Mostly we say "Uh-huh" and "Oh, really." People smile and look over our shoulder, looking for someone else to meet.

So a shy person sits down and writes a letter. To be known by another person—to meet and talk freely on the page—to be close despite distance. To escape from anonymity and be our own sweet selves and express the music of our souls.

Same thing that moves a giant rock star to sing his heart out in front of 123,000 people moves us to take ballpoint in hand and write a few lines to our dear Aunt Eleanor. *We want to be known.* We want her to know that we have fallen in love, that we quit our job, that we're moving to New York, and we want to say a few things that might not get said in casual conversation: *Thank you for what you've meant to me, I am very happy right now.* 5

The first step in writing letters is to get over the guilt of *not* writing. You don't "owe" anybody a letter. Letters are a gift. The burning shame you feel when you see unanswered mail makes it harder to pick up a pen and makes for a cheerless letter when you finally do. *I feel bad about not writing, but I've been so busy,* etc. Skip this. Few letters are obligatory, and they are *Thanks for the wonderful gift* and *I am terribly sorry to hear about George's death* and *Yes, you're welcome to stay with us next month,* and not many more than that. Write those promptly if you want to keep your friends. Don't worry about the others, except love letters, of course. When your true love writes, *Dear Light of My*

From We Are Still Married *(1989), a collection of Keillor's stories, letters, and skits. Many of Keillor's humorous pieces are aired on his popular radio program,* A Prairie Home Companion.

1. American disc-jockey turned rock star (1930–1959), popular in the late 1950s.

Life, Joy of My Heart, O Lovely Pulsating Core of My Sensate Life, some response is called for.

Some of the best letters are tossed off in a burst of inspiration, so keep your writing stuff in one place where you can sit down for a few minutes and (*Dear Roy, I am in the middle of a book entitled* We Are Still Married *but thought I'd drop you a line. Hi to your sweetie, too*) dash off a note to a pal. Envelopes, stamps, address book, everything in a drawer so you can write fast when the pen is hot.

A blank white eight-by-eleven sheet can look as big as Montana if the pen's not so hot—try a smaller page and write boldly. Or use a note card with a piece of fine art on the front; if your letter ain't good, at least they get the Matisse.[2] Get a pen that makes a sensuous line, get a comfortable typewriter, a friendly word processor—which feels easy to the hand.

Sit for a few minutes with the blank sheet in front of you, and meditate on the person you will write to, let your friend come to mind until you can almost see her or him in the room with you. Remember the last time you saw each other and how your friend looked and what you said and what perhaps was unsaid between you, and when your friend becomes real to you, start to write.

10   Write the salutation—*Dear* You—and take a deep breath and plunge in. A simple declarative sentence will do, followed by another and another and another. Tell us what you're doing and tell it like you were talking to us. Don't think about grammar, don't think about lit'ry style, don't try to write dramatically, just give us your news. Where did you go, who did you see, what did they say, what do you think?

If you don't know where to begin, start with the present moment: *I'm sitting at the kitchen table on a rainy Saturday morning. Everyone is gone and the house is quiet*. Let your simple description of the present moment lead to something else, let the letter drift gently along.

The toughest letter to crank out is one that is meant to impress, as we all know from writing job applications; if it's hard work to slip off a letter to a friend, maybe you're trying too hard to be terrific. A letter is only a report to someone who already likes you for reasons other than your brilliance. Take it easy.

Don't worry about form. It's not a term paper. When you come to the end of one episode, just start a new paragraph. You can go from a few lines about the sad state of pro football to the fight with your mother to your fond memories of Mexico to your cat's urinary-tract infection to a few thoughts on personal indebtedness and on to the kitchen sink and what's in it. The more you write, the easier it gets, and when you have a True True Friend to write to, a *compadre*, a soul sibling, then it's like driving a car down a country road, you just get behind the keyboard and press on the gas.

Don't tear up the page and start over when you write a bad line—try to write your way out of it. Make mistakes and plunge on. Let the letter cook along and let yourself be bold. Outrage, confusion, love—whatever is in your mind, let it find a way to the page. Writing is a means of discovery, always, and

2. French painter (1869–1954).

when you come to the end and write *Yours ever* or *Hugs and kisses*, you'll know something you didn't when you wrote *Dear Pal*.

Probably your friend will put your letter away, and it'll be read again a few years from now—and it will improve with age. And forty years from now, your friend's grandkids will dig it out of the attic and read it, a sweet and precious relic of the ancient eighties that gives them a sudden clear glimpse of you and her and the world we old-timers knew. You will then have created an object of art. Your simple lines about where you went, who you saw, what they said, will speak to those children and they will feel in their hearts the humanity of our times.

You can't pick up a phone and call the future and tell them about our times. You have to pick up a piece of paper.

Postcards

A postcard takes about fifty words gracefully, which is how to write one. A few sweet strokes in a flowing hand—pink roses, black-face sheep in a wet meadow, the sea, the Swedish coast—your friend in Washington gets the idea. She doesn't need your itinerary to know that you remember her.

Fifty words is a strict form but if you write tiny and sneak over into the address side to squeeze in a hundred, the grace is gone and the result is not a poem but notes for a letter you don't have time to write, which will make her feel cheated.

So many persons traveling to a strange land are inclined to see its life so clearly, its essential national character, they could write a book about it as other foreign correspondents have done ("highly humorous . . . definitely a must"), but fifty words is a better length for what you really know.

Fifty words and a picture. Say you are in Scotland, the picture is of your hotel, a stone pile looking across the woods of Druimindarroch to Loch Nan Uamh near the village of Arisaig. You've never seen this country. For the past year you've worked like a prisoner in the mines. Write.

Scotland is the most beautiful country in the world and I am drinking coffee in the library of what once was the manor of people who inherited everything and eventually lost it. Thus it became a hotel. I'm with English people whose correctness is overpowering. What wild good luck to be here. And to be an American! I'm so happy, bubba.

In the Highlands, many one-lane roads which widen at curves and hills—a driving thrill, especially when following a native who drives like hell—you stick close to him, like the second car of the roller-coaster, but lose your nerve. Sixty mph down a one-lane winding road. I prefer a career.

The arrogance of Americans who, without so much as a *"mi scusi"* or *"bitte"* or *"s'il vous plaît,"* words that a child could learn easily, walk up to a stranger and say, "Say, where's the museum?" as if English and rudeness rule the world, never ceases to amaze. You hear the accent and sink under the table.

Woke up at six, dark. Switzerland. Alps. Raining. Lights of villages high in the sky. Too dark to see much so snoozed awhile. Woke up in sunny Italy. Field after field of corn, like Iowa in August. Mamas, papas, grammas, grampas, little babies. Skinny trees above the whitewashed houses.

Arrived in Venice. A pipe had burst at the hotel and we were sent to another not as good. Should you spend time arguing for a refund? Went to San Marco,[1] on which the doges overspent. A cash register in the sanctuary: five hundred lire to see the gold altar. Now we understand the Reformation.

10   On the train to Vienna, she, having composed the sentences carefully from old memory of intermediate German, asked the old couple if the train went to Vienna. *"Ja, ja!"* Did we need to change trains? *"Nein."* Later she successfully ordered dinner and registered at the hotel. *Mein wundercompanion.*

People take me for an American tourist and stare at me, maybe because I walk slow and stare at them, so today I walked like a bat out of hell along the Ringstrasse, past the Hofburg Palace to Stephans Platz and back, and if anyone stared, I didn't notice. Didn't see much of Vienna but felt much better.

One week in a steady drizzle of German and now I am starting to lose my grip on English, I think. Don't know what to write. How are you? Are the Twins going to be in the World Series?

You get to Mozart's apartment[2] through the back door of a restaurant. Kitchen smells, yelling, like at Burger King. The room where he wrote *Figaro* is bare, as if he moved out this morning. It's a nice apartment. His grave at the cemetery is now marked, its whereabouts being unknown. Mozart our brother.

Copenhagen is raining and all the Danes seem unperturbed. A calm humorous people. Kids are the same as anywhere, wild, and nobody hits them. Men wear pastels, especially turquoise. Narrow streets, no cars, little shops, and in the old square a fruit stand and an old woman with flowers yelling, "WŌSA FOR TEW-VA!"

1. The Basilica di San Marco of Venice, a magnificent hodgepodge of Byzantine domes, mosaics, and plundered treasure from the Near East and Asia, is one of the largest and most famous cathedrals in the world.
2. Mozart's "Figarohaus," where he lived from October 1784 to April 1787, is behind St. Stephen's Cathedral in Vienna.

Sunbathing yesterday. A fine woman took off her shirt, jeans, pants, nearby,   15
and lay on her belly, then turned over. Often she sat up to apply oil. Today my
back is burned bright red (as St. Paul warns) from my lying and looking at her
so long but who could ignore such beauty and *so generous*.

QUESTION

1. In "How to Write a Letter," Keillor offers several suggestions. Make a list of the suggestions that seem most helpful. Why might Keillor have included the other, less practical suggestions?

2. Keillor addresses "How to Write a Letter" to shy people (a group in which he includes himself—"We shy persons . . ."). Does his advice also apply to those who are not
shy? Why or why not?

3. Analyze the progression of "Postcards." How is the piece organized? Why do you
think Keillor chose this organization?

4. Keillor wrote these pieces in the 1980s before people communicated by email. Does
any of his advice fit email correspondence? Write a how-to piece entitled "How to Write
an Email." Email it to the class.

5. Pick up several postcards from your college bookstore. Write fifty-word messages on
each and send them to family and friends—or, if assigned—to your classmates and
teacher.

BENJAMIN FRANKLIN *Learning to Write*

ABOUT THIS TIME I met with an odd Volume of the *Spectator*.[1] I had never before seen any of them. I bought it,
read it over and over, and was much delighted with it.
I thought the Writing excellent, and wish'd if possible
to imitate it. With that View, I took some of the Papers, and making short Hints of the Sentiment in
each Sentence, laid them by a few Days, and then without looking at the
Book, tried to complete the Papers again, by expressing each hinted Sentiment
at length and as fully as it had been express'd before in any suitable Words that
should come to hand.

Then I compar'd my *Spectator* with the Original, discover'd some of my
Faults and corrected them. But I found I wanted a Stock of Words or a Readi-

Drawn from Franklin's Autobiography, *his classic account of his life, first published in
1791.*

1. Daily English periodical noted for its excellence in prose.

ness in recollecting and using them which I thought I should have acquir'd before that time, if I had gone on making Verses, since the continual Occasion for Words of the same Import but of different Length, to suit the Measure,[2] or of different Sound for the Rhyme, would have laid me under a constant Necessity of searching for Variety, and also have tended to fix that Variety in my Mind, and make me Master of it. Therefore I took some of the Tales and turn'd them into Verse: And after a time, when I had pretty well forgotten the Prose, turn'd them back again. I also sometimes jumbled my Collections of Hints into Confusion, and after some Weeks, endeavor'd to reduce them into the best Order, before I began to form the full Sentences, and complete the Paper. This was to teach me Method in the Arrangement of Thoughts. By comparing my Work afterwards with the original, I discover'd many faults and amended them; but I sometimes had the Pleasure of Fancying that in certain Particulars of small Import, I had been lucky enough to improve the Method or the Language and this encourag'd me to think I might possibly in time come to be a tolerable English Writer, of which I was extremely ambitious.

My Time for these Exercises and for Reading, was at Night after Work, or before Work began in the Morning; or on Sundays, when I contrived to be in the Printing-House alone, evading as much as I could the common Attendance on public Worship, which my Father used to exact of me when I was under his Care: And which indeed I still thought a Duty; tho' I could not, as it seemed to me, afford the Time to practice it.

When about 16 Years of Age, I happen'd to meet with a Book written by one Tryon,[3] recommending a Vegetable Diet. I determined to go into it. My Brother being yet unmarried, did not keep House, but boarded himself and his Apprentices in another Family. My refusing to eat Flesh occasioned an Inconveniency, and I was frequently chid for my singularity. I made myself acquainted with Tryon's Manner of preparing some of his Dishes, such as Boiling Potatoes or Rice, making Hasty Pudding,[4] and a few others, and then propos'd to my Brother, that if he would give me Weekly half the Money he paid for my Board, I would board myself. He instantly agreed to it, and I presently found that I could save half what he paid me. This was an additional Fund for buying Books: But I had another Advantage in it. My Brother and the rest going from the Printing-House to their Meals, I remain'd there alone, and dispatching presently my light Repast, (which often was no more than a Biscuit or a Slice of Bread, a Handful of Raisins or a Tart from the Pastry Cook's, and a Glass of Water) had the rest of the Time till their Return, for Study, in which I made the greater Progress from that greater Clearness of Head and quicker Apprehension which usually attend Temperance in Eating and Drinking. And now it was that being on some Occasion made asham'd of my Ignorance in Figures; which I had twice fail'd in learning when at School, I took

2. Meter.
3. Thomas Tryon (1634–1703), author of *Way to Health and Happiness* (1682).
4. Cornmeal mush.

Cocker's Book of Arithmetic,[5] and went thro' the whole by myself with great Ease. I also read Seller's[6] and Sturmy's[7] Books of Navigation, and became acquainted with the little Geometry they contain, but never proceeded far in that Science. And I read about this Time Locke on Human Understanding and the Art of Thinking by Messrs. du Port Royal.[8]

While I was intent on improving my Language, I met with an English Grammar (I think it was Greenwood's[9]) at the End of which there were two little Sketches of the Arts of Rhetoric and Logic, the latter finishing with a Specimen of a Dispute in the Socratic Method. And soon after I procur'd Xenophon's Memorable Things of Socrates,[10] wherein there are many Instances of the same Method. I was charm'd with it, adopted it, dropped my abrupt Contradiction and positive Argumentation, and put on the humble Enquirer and Doubter. And being then, from reading Shaftesbury[11] and Collins,[12] became a real Doubter in many Points of our Religious Doctrine. I found this Method safest for myself and very embarrassing to those against whom I used it, therefore I took a Delight in it, practic'd it continually and grew very artful and expert in drawing People even of superior Knowledge into Concessions the Consequences of which they did not foresee, entangling them in Difficulties out of which they could not extricate themselves, and so obtaining Victories that neither myself nor my Cause always deserved. I continu'd this Method some few Years, but gradually left it, retaining only the Habit of expressing myself in Terms of modest Diffidence, never using when I advance any thing that may possibly be disputed, the Words, *Certainly, undoubtedly*, or any others that give the Air of Positiveness to an Opinion; but rather say, *I conceive*, or *I apprehend* a Thing to be so or so. *It appears to me*, or *I should think it so or so for such and such Reasons*, or *I imagine* it to be so, or *it is so if I am not mistaken*. This Habit I believe has been of great Advantage to me, when I have had occasion to inculcate my Opinions and persuade Men into Measures that I have been from time to time engag'd in promoting. And as the chief Ends of Conversation are to *inform*, or to be *informed*, to *please* or to *persuade*, I wish well-meaning sensible Men would not lessen their Power of doing Good

5. Well-known textbook, first published in 1677.

6. John Seller (c. 1658–1698), author of *Practical Navigation* (1694).

7. Samuel Sturmy (1633–1669), author of *The Mariner's Magazine* (1699).

8. John Locke (1632–1704), British philosopher and author of *An Essay Concerning Human Understanding* (1690); Pierre Nicole (1625–1695) of Port Royal published his book in 1662; it was translated into English as *Logic: Or the Art of Thinking* in 1687.

9. James Greenwood (d. 1737), author of *An Essay towards a Practical English Grammar* (1711).

10. Xenophon's (c. 430–355 B.C.E.) *The Memorable Things of Socrates* was published in English translation by Edward Bysshe in 1712.

11. Anthony Ashley Cooper, earl of Shaftesbury (1671–1713), famous for his *Characteristics of Men, Manners, Opinions, Times* (1711).

12. Anthony Collins (1676–1729), a friend of Locke; author of *A Discourse of Free Thinking* (1713).

by a Positive assuming Manner that seldom fails to disgust, tends to create Opposition, and to defeat every one of those Purposes for which Speech was given us, to wit, giving or receiving Information, or Pleasure: For if you would *inform*, a positive dogmatical Manner in advancing your Sentiments, may provoke Contradiction and prevent a candid Attention. If you wish Information and Improvement from the Knowledge of others and yet at the same time express yourself as firmly fix'd in your present Opinions, modest sensible Men, who do not love Disputation, will probably leave you undisturb'd in the Possession of your Error; and by such a Manner you can seldom hope to recommend yourself in *pleasing* your Hearers, or to persuade those whose Concurrence you desire. Pope says, judiciously,

> Men should be taught as if you taught them not,
> And things unknown propos'd as things forgot,

farther recommending it to us,

> To speak tho' sure, with seeming Diffidence.[13]

And he might have coupled with this Line that which he has coupled with another, I think less properly,

> For want of Modesty is want of Sense.

If you ask why *less properly*, I must repeat the Lines;

> "Immodest Words admit of *no* Defence;
> For Want of Modesty is Want of Sense."[14]

Now is not *Want of Sense*, (where a Man is so unfortunate as to want it) some Apology for his *Want of Modesty?* and would not the Lines stand more justly thus?

> Immodest Words admit *but this* Defence.
> That Want of Modesty is Want of Sense.

This however I should submit to better Judgments.

13. Adapted from Alexander Pope's (1688–1744) *An Essay on Criticism* (1711).
14. Franklin wrongly attributes these two lines to Pope. They are by Wentworth Dillon (1633?–1685), from his *Essay on Translated Verse* (1684). The second line should read "For want of Decency is want of Sense."

QUESTIONS

1. Franklin describes his youthful practice of imitating successful writers' sentences. Have you ever done this? What do you think of the practice? What are writers likely to learn from such a practice?

2. When he was sixteen, Franklin read a book about vegetarian diets and immediately was converted. Write about how you or someone you know was converted to following a distinct path, either religious, ethical, or physical (examples you might choose: a religious sect, a strict diet, exercise). Did the conversion happen suddenly, as it did with Franklin, or did it take place slowly, over time? How long did the conversion last?

3. Franklin is a classic auto-didact, a self-teacher. Recount what Franklin learned in this manner, and note what he failed to teach himself. What kinds of knowledge did Franklin seek to acquire? Was his learning broad or narrow? What kinds of endeavors was this knowledge most suited for?

PATRICIA WILLIAMS *The Death of the Profane:*
The Rhetoric of Race and Rights

BUZZERS ARE BIG IN NEW YORK CITY. Favored particularly by smaller stores and boutiques, merchants throughout the city have installed them as screening devices to reduce the incidence of robbery: if the face at the door looks desirable, the buzzer is pressed and the door is unlocked. If the face is that of an undesirable, the door stays locked. Predictably, the issue of undesirability has revealed itself to be a racial determination. While controversial enough at first, even civil-rights organizations backed down eventually in the face of arguments that the buzzer system is a "necessary evil," that it is a "mere inconvenience" in comparison to the risks of being murdered, that suffering discrimination is not as bad as being assaulted, and that in any event it is not all blacks who are barred, just "17-year-old black males wearing running shoes and hooded sweatshirts."[1]

The installation of these buzzers happened swiftly in New York; stores that had always had their doors wide open suddenly became exclusive or received people by appointment only. I discovered them and their meaning one Saturday in 1986. I was shopping in Soho and saw in a store window a sweater that I wanted to buy for my mother. I pressed my round brown face to the window and my finger to the buzzer, seeking admittance. A narrow-eyed, white teenager wearing running shoes and feasting on bubble gum glared out, evaluating me for signs that would pit me against the limits of his social under-

A chapter in Williams's book The Alchemy of Race and Rights *(1991), which probes the roots of racism through anecdote and personal witness, as well as scholarly analysis of the law's inadequacies. All notes in the essay are the author's.*

1. "When 'By Appointment' Means Keep Out," *New York Times*, December 17, 1986, p. B1. Letter to the Editor from Michael Levin and Marguerita Levin, *New York Times*, January 11, 1987, p. E32.

standing. After about five seconds, he mouthed "We're closed," and blew pink rubber at me. It was two Saturdays before Christmas, at one o'clock in the afternoon; there were several white people in the store who appeared to be shopping for things for *their* mothers.

I was enraged. At that moment I literally wanted to break all the windows of the store and *take* lots of sweaters for my mother. In the flicker of his judgmental gray eyes, that saleschild had transformed my brightly sentimental, joy-to-the-world, pre-Christmas spree to a shambles. He snuffed my sense of humanitarian catholicity, and there was nothing I could do to snuff his, without making a spectacle of myself.

I am still struck by the structure of power that drove me into such a blizzard of rage. There was almost nothing I could do, short of physically intruding upon him, that would humiliate him the way he humiliated me. No words, no gestures, no prejudices of my own would make a bit of difference to him; his refusal to let me into the store—it was Benetton's, whose colorfully punnish ad campaign is premised on wrapping every one of the world's peoples in its cottons and woolens—was an outward manifestation of his never having let someone like me into the realm of his reality. He had no compassion, no remorse, no reference to me; and no desire to acknowledge me even at the estranged level of arm's-length transactor. He saw me only as one who would take his money and therefore could not conceive that I was there to give him money.

5   In this weird ontological imbalance, I realized that buying something in that store was like bestowing a gift, the gift of my commerce, the lucre of my patronage. In the wake of my outrage, I wanted to take back the gift of appreciation that my peering in the window must have appeared to be. I wanted to take it back in the form of unappreciation, disrespect, defilement. I wanted to work so hard at wishing he could feel what I felt that he would never again mistake my hatred for some sort of plaintive wish to be included. I was quite willing to disenfranchise myself, in the heat of my need to revoke the flattery of my purchasing power. I was willing to boycott Benetton's, random white-owned businesses, and anyone who ever blew bubble gum in my face again.

My rage was admittedly diffuse, even self-destructive, but it was symmetrical. The perhaps loose-ended but utter propriety of that rage is no doubt lost not just to the young man who actually barred me, but to those who would appreciate my being barred only as an abstract precaution, who approve of those who would bar even as they deny that they would bar *me*.

The violence of my desire to burst into Benetton's is probably quite apparent. I often wonder if the violence, the exclusionary hatred, is equally apparent in the repeated public urgings that blacks understand the buzzer system by putting themselves in the shoes of white storeowners—that, in effect, blacks look into the mirror of frightened white faces for the reality of their undesirability; and that then blacks would "just as surely conclude that [they] would not let [themselves] in under similar circumstances."[2] (That some blacks might agree merely shows that some of us have learned too well the lessons of

2. *New York Times*, January 11, 1987, p. E32.

privatized intimacies of self-hatred and rationalized away the fullness of our public, participatory selves.)

On the same day I was barred from Benetton's, I went home and wrote the above impassioned account in my journal. On the day after that, I found I was still brooding, so I turned to a form of catharsis I have always found healing. I typed up as much of the story as I have just told, made a big poster of it, put a nice colorful border around it, and, after Benetton's was truly closed, stuck it to their big sweater-filled window. I exercised my first-amendment right to place my business with them right out in the street.

So that was the first telling of this story. The second telling came a few months later, for a symposium on Excluded Voices sponsored by a law review. I wrote an essay summing up my feelings about being excluded from Benetton's and analyzing "how the rhetoric of increased privatization, in response to racial issues, functions as the rationalizing agent of public unaccountability and, ultimately, irresponsibility." Weeks later, I received the first edit. From the first page to the last, my fury had been carefully cut out. My rushing, run-on-rage had been reduced to simple declarative sentences. The active personal had been inverted in favor of the passive impersonal. My words were different; they spoke to me upsidedown. I was afraid to read too much of it at a time—meanings rose up at me oddly, stolen and strange.

A week and a half later, I received the second edit. All reference to Benetton's had been deleted because, according to the editors and the faculty adviser, it was defamatory; they feared harassment and liability; they said printing it would be irresponsible. I called them and offered to supply a footnote attesting to this as my personal experience at one particular location and of a buzzer system not limited to Benetton's; the editors told me that they were not in the habit of publishing things that were unverifiable. I could not but wonder, in this refusal even to let me file an affadavit, what it would take to make my experience verifiable. The testimony of an independent white bystander? (a requirement in fact imposed in U.S. Supreme Court holdings through the first part of the century[3]).

Two days *after* the piece was sent to press, I received copies of the final page proofs. All reference to my race had been eliminated because it was against "editorial policy" to permit descriptions of physiognomy. "I realize," wrote one editor, "that this was a very personal experience, but any reader will know what you must have looked like when standing at that window." In a telephone conversation to them, I ranted wildly about the significance of such an omission. "It's irrelevant," another editor explained in a voice gummy with soothing and patience; "It's nice and poetic," but it doesn't "advance the discussion of any principle . . . This is a law review, after all." Frustrated, I accused him of censorship; calmly he assured me it was not. "This is just a matter of style," he said with firmness and finality.

Ultimately I did convince the editors that mention of my race was central

3. See generally *Blyew v. U.S.*, 80 U.S. 581 (1871), upholding a state's right to forbid blacks to testify against whites.

to the whole sense of the subsequent text; that my story became one of extreme paranoia without the information that I am black; or that it became one in which the reader had to fill in the gap by assumption, presumption, prejudgment, or prejudice. What was most interesting to me in this experience was how the blind application of principles of neutrality, through the device of omission, acted either to make me look crazy or to make the reader participate in old habits of cultural bias.

That was the second telling of my story. The third telling came last April, when I was invited to participate in a law-school conference on Equality and Difference. I retold my sad tale of exclusion from Soho's most glitzy boutique, focusing in this version on the law-review editing process as a consequence of an ideology of style rooted in a social text of neutrality. I opined:

> Law and legal writing aspire to formalized, color-blind, liberal ideals. Neutrality is the standard for assuring these ideals; yet the adherence to it is often determined by reference to an aesthetic of uniformity, in which difference is simply omitted. For example, when segregation was eradicated from the American lexicon, its omission led many to actually believe that racism therefore no longer existed. Race-neutrality in law has become the presumed antidote for race bias in real life. With the entrenchment of the notion of race-neutrality came attacks on the concept of affirmative action and the rise of reverse discrimination suits. Blacks, for so many generations deprived of jobs based on the color of our skin, are now told that we ought to find it demeaning to be hired, based on the color of our skin. Such is the silliness of simplistic either-or inversions as remedies to complex problems.
>
> What is truly demeaning in this era of double-speak-no-evil is going on interviews and not getting hired because someone doesn't think we'll be comfortable. It is demeaning not to get promoted because we're judged "too weak," then putting in a lot of energy the next time and getting fired because we're "too strong." It is demeaning to be told what we find demeaning. It is very demeaning to stand on street corners unemployed and begging. It is downright demeaning to have to explain why we haven't been employed for months and then watch the job go to someone who is "more experienced." It is outrageously demeaning that none of this can be called racism, even if it happens only to, or to large numbers of, black people; as long as it's done with a smile, a handshake and a shrug; as long as the phantom-word "race" is never used.
>
> The image of race as a phantom-word came to me after I moved into my late godmother's home. In an attempt to make it my own, I cleared the bedroom for painting. The following morning the room asserted itself, came rushing and raging at me through the emptiness, exactly as it had been for twenty-five years. One day filled with profuse and overwhelming complexity, the next day filled with persistently recurring memories. The shape of the past came to haunt me, the shape of the emptiness confronted me each time I was about to enter the room. The force of its spirit still drifts like an odor throughout the house.
>
> The power of that room, I have thought since, is very like the power of racism as status quo: it is deep, angry, eradicated from view, but strong enough to make everyone who enters the room walk around the bed that isn't there, avoiding the phantom as they did the substance, for fear of bodily harm. They do not even know they are avoiding; they defer to the unseen

shapes of things with subtle responsiveness, guided by an impulsive aware-ness of nothingness, and the deep knowledge and denial of witchcraft at work.

The phantom room is to me symbolic of the emptiness of formal equal opportunity, particularly as propounded by President Reagan, the Reagan Civil Rights Commission and the Reagan Supreme Court. Blindly formal-ized constructions of equal opportunity are the creation of a space that is filled in by a meandering stream of unguided hopes, dreams, fantasies, fears, recollections. They are the presence of the past in imaginary, imagis-tic form—the phantom-roomed exile of our longing.

It is thus that I strongly believe in the efficacy of programs and para-digms like affirmative action. Blacks are the objects of a constitutional omission which has been incorporated into a theory of neutrality. It is thus that omission is really a form of expression, as oxymoronic as that sounds: racial omission is a literal part of original intent; it is the fixed, reiterated prophecy of the Founding Fathers. It is thus that affirmative ac-tion is an affirmation; the affirmative act of hiring—or hearing—blacks is a recognition of individuality that re-places blacks as a social statistic, that is profoundly interconnective to the fate of blacks and whites either as sub-groups or as one group. In this sense, affirmative action is as mys-tical and beyond-the-self as an initiation ceremony. It is an act of verifi-cation and of vision. It is an act of social as well as professional responsi-bility.

The following morning I opened the local newspaper, to find that the event of my speech had commanded two columns on the front page of the Metro section. I quote only the opening lines: "Affirmative action promotes prejudice by denying the status of women and blacks, instead of affirming them as its name suggests. So said New York City attorney Patricia Williams to an audience Wednesday."[4]

I clipped out the article and put it in my journal. In the margin there is a note to myself: eventually, it says, I should try to pull all these threads together into yet another law-review article. The problem, of course, will be that in the hierarchy of law-review citation, the article in the newspaper will have more authoritative weight about me, as a so-called "primary resource," than I will have; it will take precedence over my own citation of the unverifiable testi-mony of my speech. 15

I have used the Benetton's story a lot, in speaking engagements at various schools. I tell it whenever I am too tired to whip up an original speech from scratch. Here are some of the questions I have been asked in the wake of its telling:

Am I not privileging a racial perspective, by considering only the black point of view? Don't I have an obligation to include the "salesman's side" of the story?

Am I not putting the salesman on trial and finding him guilty of racism without giving him a chance to respond to or cross-examine me?

4. "Attorney Says Affirmative Action Denies Racism, Sexism," *Dominion Post* (Morgan-town, West Virginia), April 8, 1988, p. B1.

Am I not using the store window as a "metaphorical fence" against the potential of his explanation in order to represent my side as "authentic"?

20   How can I be sure I'm right?

What makes my experience the real black one anyway?

Isn't it possible that another black person would disagree with my experience? If so, doesn't that render my story too unempirical and subjective to pay any attention to?

Always a major objection is to my having put the poster on Benetton's window. As one law professor put it: "It's one thing to publish this in a law review, where no one can take it personally, but it's another thing altogether to put your own interpretation right out there, just like that, uncontested, I mean, with nothing to counter it."*

*At the end of her essay, Williams added these observations. "These questions put me on trial—an imaginary trial where it is I who have the burden of proof—and proof being nothing less than the testimony of the salesman actually confessing yes yes I am a racist. These questions question my own ability to know, to assess, to be objective. And of course, since anything that happens to me is inherently subjective, they take away my power to know what happens to me in the world. Others, by this standard, will always know better than I. And my insistence on recounting stories from my own perspective will be treated as presumption, slander, paranoid hallucination, or just plain lies.

"Recently I got an urgent call from Thomas Grey of Stanford Law School. He had used this piece in his jurisprudence class, and a rumor got started that the Benetton's story wasn't true, that I had made it up, that it was a fantasy, a lie that was probably the product of a diseased mind trying to make all white people feel guilty. At this point I realized it almost didn't make any difference whether I was telling the truth or not—that the greater issue I had to face was the overwhelming weight of a disbelief that goes beyond mere disinclination to believe and becomes active suppression of anything I might have to say. The greater problem is a powerfully oppressive mechanism for denial of black self-knowledge and expression. And this denial cannot be separated from the simultaneously pathological willingness to believe certain things about blacks—not to believe them, but things about them.

"When students in Grey's class believed and then claimed that I had made it all up, they put me in a position like that of Tawana Brawley [a black woman who falsely claimed she was abducted and raped by white men (eds.)]. I mean that specifically: the social consequence of concluding that we are liars operates as a kind of public absolution of racism—the conclusion is not merely that we are troubled or that I am eccentric, but that we, as liars, are the norm. Therefore, the nonbelievers can believe, things of this sort really don't happen (even in the face of statistics to the contrary). Racism or rape is all a big fantasy concocted by troublesome minorities and women. It is interesting to recall the outcry in every national medium, from the *New York Post* to the *Times* to the major networks, in the wake of the Brawley case: who will ever again believe a black woman who cries rape by a white man? Now shift the frame a bit, and imagine a white male facing a consensus that he lied. Would there be a difference? Consider Charles Stuart, for example, the white Bostonian who accused a black man of murdering his pregnant wife and whose brother later alleged that in fact the brothers had conspired to murder her. Most people and the media not only did not claim but actively resisted believing that Stuart represented any kind of "white male" norm. Instead he was written off as a troubled weirdo, a deviant—again even in the face of spousal-abuse statistics to the contrary. There was not a story I could find that carried on about "who will ever believe" the next white man who cries murder."

QUESTIONS

1. Williams's essay is about how the "objective," "neutral" forms writing often takes can drain away the significance of a particular person's story. Can you find examples of this phenomenon in other writing you read? Or can you find examples of it on TV or radio talk shows, for instance?

2. How does Williams move from the Benetton story to her larger point?

3. How would you characterize the tone of Williams's essay? Does any of her original rage remain?

4. What do you think of Williams's posting her reaction on the Benetton window? Write your opinion of the function and effectiveness of this action.

ANNE FADIMAN   *The His'er Problem*

WHEN I WAS NINETEEN, William Shawn[1] interviewed me for a summer job at *The New Yorker*. To grasp the full import of what follows, you should know that I considered *The New Yorker* a cathedral and Mr. Shawn a figure so godlike that I expected a faint nimbus to emanate from his ruddy head. During the course of our conversation, he asked me what other magazines I hoped to write for.

"Um, *Esquire*, the *Saturday Review*, and—"

I wanted to say "*Ms.*," but my lips had already butted against the *M*—too late for a politic retreat—when I realized I had no idea how to pronounce it. Lest you conclude that I had been raised in Ulan Bator,[2] I might remind you that in 1973, when I met Mr. Shawn, *Ms.* magazine had been published for scarcely a year, and most people, including me, had never heard the word *Ms.* used as a term of address. (Mr. Shawn had called me Miss Fadiman. *He* was so venerated by his writers that "Mister" had virtually become part of his name.) Its pronunciation, reflexive now, was not as obvious as you might think. After all, *Mr.* is not pronounced "Mir," and *Mrs.* is not pronounced "Mirz." Was it "Mzzzzz"? "Miz"? "Muz"?

In that apocalyptic split second, I somehow alighted on "Em Ess," which I knew to be the correct pronunciation of *ms.*, or manuscript.

Mr. Shawn didn't blink. He gave no indication that I had said anything un-   5

Published as an essay in Fadiman's collection Ex Libris *(1998). The title is a Latin phrase meaning "from the library of," which is often used on bookplates before the owner's name. The subtitle,* Confessions of a Common Reader, *suggests reading for the pure love of books, rather than for scholarly analysis.*

1. Editor of the *New Yorker* magazine from 1952 to 1987 (d. 1992).
2. The capital of Mongolia.

toward. In fact, he calmly proceeded to discuss the new feminist magazine—its history, its merits, its demerits, the opportunities it might offer a young writer like me—for four or five minutes *without ever mentioning its name.*

Since that time, whenever I have heard anyone talk about civility, I have thought of Mr. Shawn, a man so civil that, in order to spare me embarrassment, he succeeded in crossing an entire minefield of potential *Ms.*'s without detonating a single one. I consider his feat comparable to that of Georges Perec, the experimental French writer who composed a 311-page novel without using the letter *e*. After I left the building, I called a friend. ("How do you say that new little word? . . . Oh my God, no!") That was a terrible moment, but as Mr. Shawn had surmised, wanting to die in a telephone booth was greatly preferable to wanting to die in his office.

In twenty-three years—an eyeblink in our linguistic history—the new little word has evolved from a cryptic buzz to an automatism. From the beginning, I saw its logic and fairness. Why should people instantly know if a woman, but not a man, was married? Why should they care? The need for *Ms.* was indisputable. The hitch was feeling comfortable *saying* it. It sounded too much like a lawn mower. Gradually, my ear returned. Now, although it's probably a moot point—everyone except telephone solicitors calls me Anne—I am, by process of elimination, Ms. Fadiman. I can't be Miss Fadiman because I'm married. I can't be Mrs. Fadiman because my husband is Mr. Colt. I can't be Mrs. Colt because my name is still Fadiman. I am, to my surprise, the very woman for whom *Ms.* was invented.

On the sanguinary fields of gender politics, *Ms.* has scored a clear victory. I wish I could say the same of, say, the United Church of Christ's new "inclusive" hymnal, in which "Dear Lord and Father of Mankind" has been replaced by "Dear God, Embracing Humankind." The end is estimable; it's the means that chafe. I'm not sure I want to be embraced by an Almighty with so little feeling for poetry. Yet, having heard the new version, I can't say I feel entirely happy with the old one either. As is all too often the case these days, I find my peace as a reader and writer rent by a war between two opposing semantic selves, one feminist and one reactionary. Most people who have written about questions of gender bias in language have belonged to one camp or the other. Either they want to change everything, or they don't see what all the fuss is about. Am I the only one who feels torn?

Verbally speaking, as in other areas, my feminist self was born of a simple desire for parity. The use of gender-neutral terms like *flight attendant, firefighter,* and *police officer* seems to me an unambiguous step forward, part of the same process that has euthanized such terminal patients as *authoress* and *sculptress*—good riddance!—and is even now working on the gaggingly adorable *-ette* words: *usherettes* are being promoted to *ushers, suffragettes* to *suffragists.* (I have been particularly sensitive to words that make women sound little and cute ever since the day my college roommates and I sat around discussing which animals we all resembled. I'd hoped for something majestic—an eland, perhaps, or a great horned owl—but was unanimously declared a gopher. Given that history, it's a wonder no one has ever called me an authorette.)

My reactionary self, however, prevails when I hear someone attempt to   10
purge the bias from "to each his own" by substituting "to each their own." The
disagreement between pronoun and antecedent is more than I can bear. To
understand how I feel about grammar, you need to remember that I come
from the sort of family in which, at the age of ten, I was told I must always say
hoi polloi, never "the *hoi polloi*," because *hoi* meant "the," and two "the's" were
redundant—indeed something only hoi polloi would say. (Why any ten-year-
old would say *hoi polloi* in the first place is another, more pathological matter,
but we won't go into that here.)

I call the "to each his own" quandary the His'er Problem, after a solution originally proposed by Chicago school superintendent Ella Young in 1912: "To
each his'er own." I'm sorry. I just can't. My reactionary self has aesthetic as
well as grammatical standards, and *his'er* is hideous. Unlike *Ms.*, *his'er* could
never become reflexive. (I might interject here that when I posed the His'er
Problem to my brother, who was raised in the same grammatical hothouse as
I, he surprised me by saying, "I won't say *his'er*. That would be a capitulation
to barbarism. But I would be willing to consider a more rhythmically acceptable neologism such as *hyr* or *hes*, which would be preferable to having to
avoid *his* by plotting each sentence in advance like a military campaign." My
brother clearly doesn't warm to the same challenges as Messrs. Shawn and
Perec.)
     What about "to each his or her own"? I do resort to that construction oc-
casionally, but I find the double pronoun an ungainly burden. More frequently
I recast the entire sentence in the plural, although "to all their own" is slightly
off pitch. Even a phrase that is not stylistically disfigured—for example, "all
writers worth their salt," which is only marginally more lumpish than "every
writer worth his salt"—loses its specificity, that fleeting moment in which the
reader conjures up an individual writer (Isaiah Berlin in one mind's eye,
Robert James Waller in another)[3] instead of a faceless throng.
     But I can't go back. I said "to each his own" until about five years ago, be-
lieving what my sixth-grade grammar textbook, *Easy English Exercises*, had told
me: that "or her" was "understood," just as womankind was understood to be
lurking somewhere within "mankind." I no longer understand. The other day I
came across the following sentence by my beloved role model, E. B. White:[4]
"There is one thing the essayist cannot do—he cannot indulge himself in deceit
or concealment, for he will be found out in no time." I felt the door slamming in
my face so fast I could feel the wind against my cheek. "But he *meant* to include
you!" some of you may be murmuring. "It was understood!"
     I don't think so. Long ago, my father wrote something similar: "The best

3. Berlin (1909–1997), British historian and writer; Waller (b. 1939), American writer,
author of *The Bridges of Madison County* (1992).
4. American essayist (1899–1985) and coauthor with William Strunk of the famous
handbook *The Elements of Style* (often referred to as "Strunk and White" rather than by
its title).

essays [do not] develop original themes. They develop original men, their com-posers." Since my father, unlike E. B. White, is still around to testify, I called him up last night and said, "Be honest. What was really in your mind when you wrote those sentences?" He replied, "Males. I was thinking about males. I viewed the world of literature—indeed, the entire world of artistic creation—as a world of males, and so did most writers. Any writer of fifty years ago who denies that is lying. Any male writer, I mean."

15   I believe that although my father and E. B. White were not misogynists, they didn't really *see* women, and their language reflected and reinforced that blind spot. Our invisibility was brought home to me fifteen years ago, after *Thunder Out of China*, a 1946 best-seller about China's role in the Second World War, was reissued in paperback. Its co-authors were Theodore H. White and Annalee Jacoby, my mother. In his foreword to the new edition, Harrison Salisbury mentioned White nineteen times and my mother once. His first sen-tence was "There is, in the end, no substitute for the right man in the right place at the right moment." I wrote to Salisbury, suggesting that sometimes—for example, in half of *Thunder Out of China*—there is no substitute for the right woman in the right place at the right moment. To his credit, he re-sponded with the following mea culpa:[5] "Oh, oh, oh! You are totally right. I am entirely guilty. You are the second person who has pointed that out to me. What can I say? It is just one of those totally dumb things which I do some-times." I believe that Salisbury was motivated by neither malice nor premedi-tated sexism; my mother, by being a woman, just happened to be in the wrong place at the wrong moment.

        For as long as anyone can remember, my father has called every woman who is more than ten years his junior a girl. Since he is now ninety-one, that covers a lot of women. He would never call a man over the age of eighteen a boy. I have tried to persuade him to mend his ways, but the word is ingrained, and he means it gallantly. He truly believes that inside every stout, white-haired woman of eighty there is the glimmer of that fresh and lissome thing, a girl.

        If my father were still writing essays, every full-grown "girl" would proba-bly be transformed by an editor's pencil into a "woman." The same thing would happen to E. B. White. In an essay called "The Sea and the Wind That Blows," White described a small sailing craft as "shaped less like a box than like a fish or a bird or a girl." I don't think he meant a ten-year-old girl. I think he meant a girl old enough to be called a woman. But if he had compared that boat to a woman, his slim little craft, as well as his sentence, would have been forever slowed.

        What I am saying here is very simple: Changing our language to make men and women equal has a cost. That doesn't mean it shouldn't be done. High prices are attached to many things that are on the whole worth doing. It does mean that the loss of our heedless grace should be mourned, and then accepted with all the civility we can muster, by every writer worth his'er salt.

5. Latin for "my fault."

QUESTIONS

1. Why does Fadiman begin with an incident from her personal history, in which she struggles with the pronunciation of Ms.? What facts about herself and about linguistic history does the incident allow her to convey?

2. In Fadiman's estimate, the use of gender-neutral language has both pros and cons. List some of each, and decide on which side she ends up—pro or con.

3. If you are using a handbook in your writing course or if your college has an official style sheet, consult its section on gender-neutral language. What recommendations does it have for the usage problems that Fadiman raises? With which do you side— Fadiman or the handbook? Write an essay in which you explain the differences and your stance on the issues.

LEWIS THOMAS   *Notes on Punctuation*

THERE ARE NO precise rules about punctuation (Fowler[1] lays out some general advice (as best he can under the complex circumstances of English prose (he points out, for example, that we possess only four stops (the comma, the semicolon, the colon and the period (the question mark and exclamation point are not, strictly speaking, stops; they are indicators of tone (oddly enough, the Greeks employed the semicolon for their question mark (it produces a strange sensation to read a Greek sentence which is a straightforward question: Why weepest thou; (instead of Why weepest thou? (and, of course, there are parentheses (which are surely a kind of punctuation making this whole much more complicated by having to count up the left-handed parentheses in order to be sure of closing with the right number (but if the parentheses were left out, with nothing to work with but the stops, we would have considerably more flexibility in the deploying of layers of meaning than if we tried to separate all the clauses by physical barriers (and in the latter case, while we might have more precision and exactitude for our meaning, we would lose the essential flavor of language, which is its wonderful ambiguity)))))))))))).

The commas are the most useful and usable of all the stops. It is highly important to put them in place as you go along. If you try to come back after doing a paragraph and stick them in the various spots that tempt you you will discover that they tend to swarm like minnows into all sorts of crevices whose existence you hadn't realized and before you know it the whole long sentence

From The Medusa and the Snail: More Notes of a Biology Watcher *(1979), a collection of science writing.*

1. H. W. Fowler, author of *Modern English Usage* (1926).

becomes immobilized and lashed up squirming in commas. Better to use them sparingly, and with affection, precisely when the need for each one arises, nicely, by itself.

I have grown fond of semicolons in recent years. The semicolon tells you that there is still some question about the preceding full sentence; something needs to be added; it reminds you sometimes of the Greek usage. It is almost always a greater pleasure to come across a semicolon than a period. The period tells you that that is that; if you didn't get all the meaning you wanted or expected, anyway you got all the writer intended to parcel out and now you have to move along. But with a semicolon there you get a pleasant little feeling of expectancy; there is more to come; read on; it will get clearer.

Colons are a lot less attractive, for several reasons: firstly, they give you the feeling of being rather ordered around, or at least having your nose pointed in a direction you might not be inclined to take if left to yourself, and, secondly, you suspect you're in for one of those sentences that will be labeling the points to be made: firstly, secondly and so forth, with the implication that you haven't sense enough to keep track of a sequence of notions without having them numbered. Also, many writers use this system loosely and incompletely, starting out with number one and number two as though counting off on their fingers but then going on and on without the succession of labels you've been led to expect, leaving you floundering about searching for the ninthly or seventeenthly that ought to be there but isn't.

5   Exclamation points are the most irritating of all. Look! they say, look at what I just said! How amazing is my thought! It is like being forced to watch someone else's small child jumping up and down crazily in the center of the living room shouting to attract attention. If a sentence really has something of importance to say, something quite remarkable, it doesn't need a mark to point it out. And if it is really, after all, a banal sentence needing more zing, the exclamation point simply emphasizes its banality!

Quotation marks should be used honestly and sparingly, when there is a genuine quotation at hand, and it is necessary to be very rigorous about the words enclosed by the marks. If something is to be quoted, the *exact* words must be used. If part of it must be left out because of space limitations, it is good manners to insert three dots to indicate the omission, but it is unethical to do this if it means connecting two thoughts which the original author did not intend to have tied together. Above all, quotation marks should not be used for ideas that you'd like to disown, things in the air so to speak. Nor should they be put in place around clichés; if you want to use a cliché you must take full responsibility for it yourself and not try to job it off on anon., or on society. The most objectionable misuse of quotation marks, but one which illustrates the dangers of misuse in ordinary prose, is seen in advertising, especially in advertisements for small restaurants, for example "just around the corner," or "a good place to eat." No single, identifiable, citable person ever really said, for the record, "just around the corner," much less "a good place to eat," least likely of all for restaurants of the type that use this type of prose.

The dash is a handy device, informal and essentially playful, telling you that you're about to take off on a different tack but still in some way connected with the present course—only you have to remember that the dash is there, and either put a second dash at the end of the notion to let the reader know that he's back on course, or else end the sentence, as here, with a period.

The greatest danger in punctuation is for poetry. Here it is necessary to be as economical and parsimonious with commas and periods as with the words themselves, and any marks that seem to carry their own subtle meanings, like dashes and little rows of periods, even semicolons and question marks, should be left out altogether rather than inserted to clog up the thing with ambiguity. A single exclamation point in a poem, no matter what else the poem has to say, is enough to destroy the whole work.

The things I like best in T. S. Eliot's poetry, especially in the *Four Quartets,* are the semicolons. You cannot hear them, but they are there, laying out the connections between the images and the ideas. Sometimes you get a glimpse of a semicolon coming, a few lines farther on, and it is like climbing a steep path through woods and seeing a wooden bench just at a bend in the road ahead, a place where you can expect to sit for a moment, catching your breath.

Commas can't do this sort of thing; they can only tell you how the different parts of a complicated thought are to be fitted together, but you can't sit, not even take a breath, just because of a comma, 10

Questions

1. The title of this piece begins with the word "notes." Is that the right word? Is this a series of notes or something else?

2. How long did it take you to realize that Thomas is playing a kind of game with his readers? (For instance, paragraph 1 is a single sentence.) Is punctuation the kind of thing people usually play games with?

3. Choose one or two writers from the next section, "An Album of Styles," and describe how they employ commas, colons, and semicolons. Do any of the semicolons serve as "a wooden bench just at a bend in the road ahead" (paragraph 9)?

4. Compare Thomas's technique of illustrating his points as he explains them with Garrison Keillor's similar technique in "Postcards" (p. 537). What other forms of writing might be treated this way? Find other examples that, like Thomas's "Notes" or Keillor's "Postcards," merge form and content.

ELLEN LUPTON AND *Period Styles: A Punctuated History*
J. ABBOTT MILLER

GREEKANDLATINMANUSCRIPTSWEREUSUALLYWRITTENWITHNOSPACE
BETWEENWORDS UNTIL AROUND THE NINTH CENTURY AD ALTHOUGH·
ROMAN·INSCRIPTIONS·LIKE·THE·FAMOUS·TRAJAN·COLUMN·SOMETIMES·
SEPARATED·WORDS·WITH·A·CENTERED·DOT·   EVEN AFTER SPACING BECAME
COMMON IT REMAINED HAPHAZARD   FOREXAMPLE OFTEN A PREPOSITION
WAS LINKEDTO ANOTHER WORD   EARLY GREEK WRITING RAN IN LINES
ALTERNATING FROM LEFT TO RIGHT AND RIGHT TO LEFT   THIS CONVENTION
ƧAW TI   ƧWO⅃ꟼ XO ƎHT ƧA ꟼNINAƎM NOꟼƎHꟼƎЯTƧUOꟼ ꟼƎ⅃⅃AƆ ƧAW
CONVENIENT FOR LARGE CARVED MONUMENTS   BUT BOUSTREPHEDON
HINDERED THE READING AND WRITING OF SMALLER TEXTS AND SO THE
LEFT TO RIGHT DIRECTION BECAME DOMINANT   A CENTERED DOT DIVID·
ED WORDS WHICH SPLIT AT THE END OF A LINE IN EARLY GREEK AND LATIN
MANUSCRIPTS   IN THE ELEVENTH CENTURY A MARK SIMILAR TO THE MOD-
ERN HYPHEN WAS INTRODUCED   MEDIEVAL SCRIBES OFTEN FILLED⁝°/⁝°(;](;]
SHORT LINES WITH MARKS AND ORNAMENTS   THE PERFECTLY JUSTIFIED
LINE BECAME THE STANDARD AFTER THE INVENTION OF PRINTING
THE EARLIEST GREEK LITERARY TEXTS WERE DIVIDED INTO UNITS WITH A
HORIZONTAL LINE CALLED A PARAGRAPHOS   PARAGRAPHING REMAINS OUR
CENTRAL METHOD OF ORGANIZING PROSE AND YET ALTHOUGH PARAGRAPHS
ARE ANCIENT THEY ARE NOT GRAMMATICALLY ESSENTIAL THE CORRECTNESS
OF A PARAGRAPH IS A MATTER OF STYLE HAVING NO STRICT RULES

LATER GREEK DOCUMENTS SOMETIMES MARKED PARAGRAPHS BY PLACING THE
FIRST LETTER OF THE NEW LINE IN THE MARGIN   THIS LETTER COULD BE
ENLARGED COLORED OR ORNATE

TODAY THE OUTDENT IS OFTEN USED FOR LISTS WHOSE ITEMS ARE IDENTIFIED
ALPHABETICALLY AS IN DICTIONARIES OR BIBLIOGRAPHIES ¶ A MARK
CALLED CAPITULUM WAS INTRODUCED IN EARLY LATIN MANUSCRIPTS ⸓ IT
FUNCTIONED VARIOUSLY AS A POINTER OR SEPARATOR ⸓ IT USUALLY

*As leading experts in the field of graphic design, Lupton and Miller publish frequently on
authorship and issues of design. This illustrative essay was published in their book* Design,
Writing, Research *(1996), which is also the name of their studio.*

OCCURRED INSIDE A RUNNING BLOCK OF TEXT WHICH DID NOT BREAK ONTO A NEW LINE • THIS TECHNIQUE SAVED SPACE • IT ALSO PRESERVED THE VISUAL DENSITY OF THE PAGE WHICH EMULATED THE CONTINUOUS UNBROKEN FLOW OF SPEECH

BY THE SEVENTEENTH CENTURY THE INDENT WAS THE STANDARD PARAGRAPH BREAK IN WESTERN PROSE   THE RISE OF PRINTING ENCOURAGED THE USE OF SPACE TO ORGANIZE TEXTS   A GAP IN A PRINTED PAGE FEELS MORE DELIBERATE THAN A GAP IN A MANUSCRIPT BECAUSE IT IS MADE BY A SLUG OF LEAD RATHER THAN A FLUX IN HANDWRITING

EVEN AFTER THE ASCENDENCE OF THE INDENT THE CAPITULUM REMAINED IN USE FOR IDENTIFYING SECTIONS AND CHAPTERS ALONG WITH OTHER MARKS LIKE THE SECTION § THE DAGGER † THE DOUBLE DAGGER ‡ THE ASTERISK * AND NUMEROUS LESS CONVENTIONAL ORNAMENTS § SUCH MARKS HAVE BEEN USED SINCE THE MIDDLE AGES FOR CITING PASSAGES AND KEYING MARGINAL REFERENCES † THE INVENTION OF PRINTING MADE MORE ELABORATE AND PRECISE REFERENCING POSSIBLE BECAUSE THE PAGES OF A TEXT WERE CONSISTENT FROM ONE COPY TO THE NEXT ‡

ALL PUNCTUATION WAS USED IDIOSYNCRATICALLY UNTIL AFTER THE INVENTION OF PRINTING WHICH REVOLUTIONIZED WRITING BY DISSEMINATING GRAMMATICAL AND TYPOGRAPHICAL STANDARDS   BEFORE PRINTING PUNCTUATION VARIED WILDLY FROM REGION TO REGION AND SCRIBE TO SCRIBE   THE LIBRARIAN AT ALEXANDRIA WHO WAS NAMED ARISTOPHANES DESIGNED A GREEK PUNCTUATION SYSTEM CIRCA 260 BC   HIS SYSTEM MARKED THE SHORTEST SEGMENTS OF DISCOURSE WITH A CENTERED DOT · CALLED A COMMA · AND MARKED THE LONGER SECTIONS WITH A LOW DOT CALLED A COLON . A HIGH DOT SET OFF THE LONGEST UNIT · HE CALLED IT PERIODOS · THE THREE DOTS WERE EASILY DISTINGUISHED FROM ONE ANOTHER BECAUSE ALL THE LETTERS WERE THE SAME HEIGHT · PROVIDING A CONSISTENT FRAME OF REFERENCE · LIKE A MUSICAL STAFF ·

ALTHOUGH THE TERMS COMMA · COLON · AND PERIOD PERSIST · THE SHAPE OF THE MARKS AND THEIR FUNCTION TODAY ARE DIFFERENT · DURING THE SEVENTH AND EIGHTH CENTURIES NEW MARKS APPEARED IN SOME MANUSCRIPTS INCLUDING THE SEMICOLON ; THE INVERTED SEMICOLON ⁏ AND A QUESTION MARK THAT RAN HORIZONTALLY ⌣ A THIN

5

DIAGONAL SLASH / CALLED A VIRGULE / WAS SOMETIMES USED LIKE A COMMA IN MEDIEVAL MANUSCRIPTS AND EARLY PRINTED BOOKS . SUCH MARKS ARE THOUGHT TO HAVE BEEN CUES FOR READING ALOUD ; THEY INDICATED A RISING , FALLING , OR LEVEL TONE OF VOICE . THE USE OF PUNCTUATION BY SCRIBES AND THEIR INTERPRETATION BY READERS WAS BY NO MEANS CONSISTENT , HOWEVER , AND MARKS MIGHT BE ADDED TO A MANUSCRIPT BY ANOTHER SCRIBE WELL AFTER IT WAS WRITTEN .

EARLY PUNCTUATION WAS LINKED TO ORAL DELIVERY. FOR EXAMPLE THE TERMS COMMA, COLON, AND PERIODOS, AS THEY WERE USED BY ARISTOPHANES, COME FROM THE THEORY OF RHETORIC, WHERE THEY REFER TO RHYTHMICAL UNITS OF SPEECH. AS A SOURCE OF RHETORICAL RATHER THAN GRAMMATICAL CUES, PUNCTUATION SERVED TO REGULATE PACE AND GIVE EMPHASIS TO PARTICULAR PHRASES, RATHER THAN TO MARK THE LOGICAL STRUCTURE OF SENTENCES. MANY OF THE PAUSES IN RHETORICAL DELIVERY, HOWEVER, NATURALLY CORRESPOND WITH GRAMMATICAL STRUCTURE: FOR EXAMPLE, WHEN A PAUSE FALLS BETWEEN TWO CLAUSES OR SENTENCES.

THE SYSTEM OF ARISTOPHANES WAS RARELY USED BY THE GREEKS, BUT IT WAS REVIVED BY THE LATIN GRAMMARIAN DONATUS IN THE FOURTH CENTURY A.D. ACCORDING TO DONATUS PUNCTUATION SHOULD FALL WHEREVER THE SPEAKER WOULD NEED A MOMENT'S REST; IT PROVIDED BREATHING CUES FOR READING ALOUD. SOME LATER WRITERS MODIFIED THE THEORIES OF DONATUS, RETURNING TO A RHETORICAL APPROACH TO PUNCTUATION, IN WHICH THE MARKS SERVED TO CONTROL RHYTHM AND EMPHASIS. AFTER THE INVENTION OF PRINTING, GRAMMARIANS BEGAN TO BASE PUNCTUATION ON STRUCTURE RATHER THAN ON SPOKEN SOUND: MARKS SUCH AS THE COMMA, COLON, AND PERIOD SIGNALLED SOME OF THE GRAMMATICAL PARTS OF A SENTENCE. THUS PUNCTUATION CAME TO BE DEFINED ARCHITECTURALLY RATHER THAN ORALLY. THE COMMA BECAME A MARK OF SEPARATION, AND THE SEMICOLON WORKED AS A JOINT BETWEEN INDEPENDENT CLAUSES; THE COLON INDICATED GRAMMATICAL DISCONTINUITY: WRITING WAS SLOWLY DISTANCED FROM SPEECH.

10   RHETORIC, STRUCTURE, AND PACE ARE ALL AT WORK IN MODERN ENGLISH PUNCTUATION, WHOSE RULES WERE ESTABLISHED BY THE END OF THE EIGHTEENTH CENTURY. ALTHOUGH STRUCTURE IS THE STRONGEST

RATIONALE TODAY, PUNCTUATION REMAINS A LARGELY INTUITIVE ART. A WRITER CAN OFTEN CHOOSE AMONG SEVERAL CORRECT WAYS TO PUNCTUATE A PASSAGE, EACH WITH A SLIGHTLY DIFFERENT RHYTHM AND MEANING.

THERE WAS NO CONSISTENT MARK FOR QUOTATIONS BEFORE THE SEVENTEENTH CENTURY. DIRECT SPEECH WAS USUALLY ANNOUNCED ONLY BY PHRASES LIKE HE SAID. ,,SOMETIMES A DOUBLE COMMA WAS USED IN MANUSCRIPTS TO POINT OUT IMPORTANT SENTENCES AND WAS LATER USED TO ENCLOSE "QUOTATIONS." ENGLISH PRINTERS BEFORE THE NINETEENTH
" CENTURY OFTEN EDGED ONE MARGIN OF A QUOTE WITH DOUBLE COMMAS.
" THIS CONVENTION PRESENTED TEXT AS A SPATIAL PLANE RATHER THAN A
" TEMPORAL LINE, FRAMING THE QUOTED PASSAGE LIKE A PICTURE.
" PRINTING, BY PRODUCING IDENTICAL COPIES OF A TEXT, ENCOURAGED
" THE STANDARDIZATION OF QUOTATION MARKS. PRINTED BOOKS COM-
" MONLY INCORPORATED MATERIAL FROM OTHER SOURCES.

BOTH THE GREEK AND ROMAN ALPHABETS WERE ORIGINALLY MAJUSCULE: ALL LETTERS WERE THE SAME HEIGHT. greek and roman minuscule letters developed out of rapidly written scripts called cursive, which were used for business correspondence. minuscule characters have limbs extending above and below a uniform body. alcuin, advisor to charlemagne, introduced the "carolingian" minuscule, which spread rapidly through europe between the eighth and twelfth centuries. during the dissemination of the carolingian script, condensed, black minuscule styles of handwriting, now called "gothic," were also developing; they eventually replaced the classical carolingian.

A carolingian manuscript sometimes marked the beginning of a sentence with an enlarged letter. This character was often a majuscule, presaging the modern use of minuscule and majuscule as double features of the same alphabet. Both scripts were still considered separate manners of writing, however.

> "As he Sets on, he [the printer] considers
> how to Point his Work,
> viz. when to Set, where; where. where to make ( ) where [ ]
> and when to make a Break....
> When he meets with proper Names of Persons or Places
> he Sets them in Italick...

and Sets the first Letter with a Capital,
or as the Person or Place he finds
the purpose of the Author to dignifie, all Capitals;
but then, if he conveniently can,
he will Set a Space between every Letter...
to make it shew more Graceful and Stately."
JOSEPH MOXON 1683

In the fifteenth century, the Carolingian script was revived by the Italian humanists. The new script, called "lettera antica," was paired with classical roman capitals. It became the basis of the roman typefaces, which were established as a European norm by the mid-sixteenth century. The terms "uppercase" and "lowercase" refer to the drawers in a printing shop that hold the two fonts. Until recently, Punctuation was an Intuitive Art, ruled by convenience and Intuition. A Printer could Liberally Capitalize the Initial of Any word She deemed worthy of Distinction, as well as Proper Names. The printer was Free to set some Words entirely in C A P I T A L S and to add further emphasis with extra S P A C E S.

The roman typefaces were based on a formal script used for books. *The cursive, rapidly written version of the Carolingian minuscule was employed for business and also for books sold in the less expensive writing shops. Called "antica corsiva" or "cancelleresca," this style of handwriting was the model for the italic typefaces cut for Aldus Manutius in Venice in 1500. Aldus Manutius was a scholar, printer, and businessman. Italic script conserved space, and Aldus developed it for his internationally distributed series of small, inexpensive books. The Aldine italic was paired with Roman capitals. The Italian typographer Tagliente advocated Italic Capitals in the early sixteenth century. Aldus set entire books in italic; it was an autonomous type style, unrelated to roman.* In France, however, the roman style was becoming the neutral, generic norm, with *italic* played against it for *contrast*. The pairs UPPER-CASE/lowercase and roman/*italic* each add an inaudible, non-phonetic dimension to the alphabet. Before *italic* became the official auxiliary of roman, scribes and printers had other techniques for marking emphasis, including enlarged, **heavy**, colored, or **gothic** letters. Underlining appeared in some medieval manuscripts, and today it is the conventional substitute for italics in handwritten and typewritten texts. S p a c e is sometimes inserted between letters to declare e m p h a s i s in German and Eastern European book t y p o g r a p h y . **Boldface** fonts were not common until the nineteenth century, when display advertising created a demand for **big, black** types. Most book faces designed since the early twentieth century belong to families of four: roman, *italic*, **bold roman**, and ***bold italic***. These are used for systematically marking different kinds of copy, such as headings, captions, body text, notes, and references.

Since the rise of digital production, printed texts have become more visually elaborate—typographic variations are now routinely available to writers and designers. Some recent fonts contain only ornaments and symbols; Carlos Segura's typeface Dingura (✕ẟ ϫϫ⅄⅄ ↵ẟ ⇆⅄⅄ ⅄⇲⅂ẟ⅄ ☉) consists of mysterious runes that recall the era of manuscript production. During the e-mail incunabula, writers and designers have been using punctuation marks for expressive ends. Punctuated portraits found in electronic correspondence range from the simple "smiley" :-) to such subtle constructions as $-) [yuppie] or :-I [indifferent].

15

QUESTIONS

1. Throughout their essay Lupton and Miller explain by illustrating. What do their illustrations teach the reader about paragraphs, punctuation marks, and print typefaces?

2. In "Notes on Punctuation" (p. 553) Lewis Thomas also illustrates punctuation usage. How is Thomas's approach similar to, yet different from, Lupton and Miller's? What usage issues does Thomas cover that they do not?

3. Choose one or two writers from the next section, "An Album of Styles," especially writers from an earlier century, and describe how they use commas, colons, semicolons, and other punctuation marks. If there are variations, what do you think explains them?

KITTY BURNS FLOREY *Sister Bernadette's Barking Dog*

IAGRAMMING SENTENCES is one of those lost skills, like darning socks or playing the sackbut, that no one seems to miss. Invented, or at least codified, in an 1877 text called *Higher Lessons in English,* by Alonzo Reed and Brainerd Kellogg, it swept through American public schools like the measles, and was embraced by teachers as the way to reform students who were engaged in "the cold-blooded murder of the English tongue" (to take Henry Higgins slightly out of context). By promoting the beautifully logical rules of syntax, diagramming would root out evils like "it's me" and "I ain't got none," until everyone wrote like Ralph Waldo Emerson, or at least James Fenimore Cooper.

In my own youth, many years after 1877, diagramming was still serious business. I learned it in the sixth grade from Sister Bernadette. I can still see her: a tiny nun with a sharp pink nose, confidently drawing a dead-straight horizontal line like a highway across the blackboard, flourishing her chalk in the air at the end of it, her veil flipping out behind her as she turned back to the class. "We begin," she said, "with a straight line." And then, in her firm and saintly script, she put words on the line, a noun and a verb—probably something like *dog barked.* Between the words she drew a short vertical slash, bisecting the line. Then she made a road that forked off at an angle—a short country lane under the word *dog*—and on it she wrote *The.*

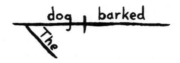

That was it: subject, predicate, and the little modifying article that civilized the sentence—all of it made into a picture that was every bit as clear and informative as an actual portrait of a beagle in mid-woof. The thrilling part was that this was a picture not of the animal but of the words that stood for the animal and its noises. It was a representation of something both concrete and abstract. The diagram was a bit like art, a bit like mathematics. It was much more than words uttered or words written: it was a picture of language.

I was hooked. So, it seems, were many of my contemporaries. Among the myths that have attached themselves to memories of being educated in the fifties is the notion that activities like diagramming sentences (along with

This essay appeared on Florey's Web site (kittyburnsflorey.com)*, as well as in* Vocabulary Review *(November 2004) and* Harper's Magazine *(December 2004). It is a section of Florey's most recent book,* Sister Bernadette's Barking Dog: The Quirky History and Lost Art of Diagramming Sentences *(2006).*

memorizing poems and adding long columns of figures without a calculator) were pointless and monotonous. I thought diagramming was fun, and most of my friends who were subjected to it look back with varying degrees of delight. Some of us were better at it than others, but it was considered a kind of treat, a game that broke up the school day. You took a sentence, threw it against the wall, picked up the pieces, and put them together again, slotting each word into its pigeonhole. When you got it right, you made order and sense out of what we used all the time and took for granted: sentences.

Gertrude Stein, of all people, was a great fan of diagramming. "I really do not know that anything has ever been more exciting than diagramming sentences," she wrote in the early 1930s. "I like the feeling the everlasting feeling of sentences as they diagram themselves."

In my experience they didn't exactly diagram themselves; they had to be coaxed, if not wrestled. But—the feeling the everlasting feeling: if Gertrude Stein wasn't just riffing on the words, the love-song sound of them, she must have meant the glorious definiteness of the process. I remember loving the look of the sentences, short or long, once they were tidied into diagrams— the curious maplike shapes they made, the way the words settled primly along their horizontals like houses on a road, the way some roads were culs-de-sac and some were long meandering interstates with many exit ramps and scenic lookouts. And the clarity of it all, the ease with which—once they were laid open, their secrets exposed—those sentences could be comprehended.

On a more trivial level, part of the fun was being summoned to the blackboard to show off. There you stood, chalk in hand, while, with a glint in her eye, Sister Bernadette read off an especially tricky sentence. Compact, fastidious handwriting was an asset. A good spatial sense helped you arrange things so that the diagram didn't end up with the words jammed together against the edge of the blackboard like commuters in a subway car. The trick was to think fast, write fast, and not get rattled if you failed in the attempt.

As we became more proficient, the tasks got harder. There was great appeal in the Shaker-like simplicity of sentences like *The dog chased a rabbit* (subject, predicate, direct object), with their plain, no-nonsense diagrams:

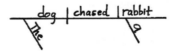

But there were also lovable subtleties, like the way the line that set off a predicate adjective slanted back like a signpost toward the subject it modified:

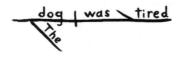

Or the thorny rosebush created by diagramming a prepositional phrase modifying another prepositional phrase:

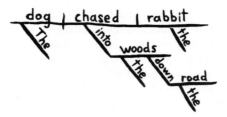

Or the elegant absence of the preposition when using an indirect object, indicated by a short road with no house on it:

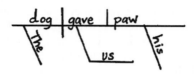

The missing preposition—in this case *to*—could also be placed on that road in parentheses, but this always seemed to me a clumsy solution, right up there with explaining a pun. In a related situation, however, the void where the subject of an imperative sentence would go was better filled, to my mind, with the graphic and slightly menacing parenthesized pronoun, as in:

Questions were a special case. For diagramming, they had to be turned inside out, the way a sock has to be eased onto a foot: *What is the dog doing?* transformed into the more dramatic *The dog is doing what?*

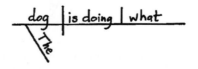

10   Mostly we diagrammed sentences out of a grammar book, but sometimes we were assigned the task of making up our own, taking pleasure in coming up with wild Proustian wanderings that—kicking and screaming—had to be corralled, harnessed, and made to trot into the barn in neat rows.

Part of the fun of diagramming sentences was that it didn't matter what they said. The dog could bark, chew gum, play chess—in the world of diagramming, sentences weren't about meaning so much as they were about subject, predicate, object, and their various dependents or modifiers. If they were diagrammed properly, they always illustrated correct syntax, no matter how silly their content. We hung those sentences out like a wash until we understood every piece of them. We could see for ourselves the difference between *who* and *whom*. We knew what an adverb was, and we knew where in a sentence it went, and why it went there. We were aware of dangling modifiers because we could see them, quite literally, dangle.

Today, diagramming is not exactly dead, but for many years it has been in sharp decline. This is partly because diagramming sentences seems to double the task of the student, who has to learn a whole new set of rules—where does that pesky line go, and which way does it slant?—in order to illustrate a set of rules that, in fact, has been learned pretty thoroughly simply by immersion in the language from birth. It's only the subtleties that are difficult—*who* versus *whom*, adjective versus adverb, *it's I* versus *it's me*—and most of those come from the mostly doomed attempt, in the early days of English grammar, to stuff English into the well-made boxes of Latin and Greek, which is something like forcing a struggling cat into the carrier for a trip to the vet.

Another problem is that teachers—and certainly students—have become more willing to accept the idea that the sentences that can be popped into a diagram aren't always sentences anyone wants to write. One writer friend of mine says that she disliked diagramming because it meant "forcing sentences into conformity." And indeed language can be more supple and interesting than the patterns that perfect syntax forces on it. An attempt to diagram a sentence by James Joyce, or one by Henry James (whose style H. G. Wells compared so memorably to "a magnificent but painful hippopotamus resolved at any cost . . . upon picking up a pea"), will quickly demonstrate the limitations of Sister Bernadette's methods. Diagramming may have taught us to write more correctly—and maybe even to think more logically—but I don't think anyone would claim that it taught us to write well. And besides, any writer knows that the best way to learn to write good sentences is not to diagram them but to read them.

Still, like pocket watches and Gilbert and Sullivan operas, diagramming persists, alternately reviled and championed by linguists and grammarians. It can be found in university linguistics courses and on the Web sites of a few diehard enthusiasts. There are teachers' guides, should any teacher want one; it's taught in ESL courses and in progressive private schools. There's a video, *English Grammar: The Art of Diagramming Sentences*, that features a very 1950s-looking teacher named Miss Lamb working at a blackboard. There's even a computer program, apparently, that diagrams.

Sometimes, on a slow subway or a boring car trip, I mentally diagram a sentence, just as I occasionally try to remember the declension of *hic, haec, hoc* or the words to the second verse of "The Star-Spangled Banner." I have no illusions that diagramming sentences in my youth did anything for me, practi-

15

cally speaking. But in an occasional fit of nostalgia, I like to bring back those golden afternoons when

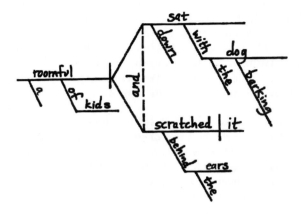

QUESTIONS

1. Florey writes, "I have no illusions that diagramming sentences in my youth did anything for me, practically speaking" (paragraph 15). If that is the case, why is she so fond of the skill she's mastered? What values or pleasures does her essay reveal?

2. This essay compares diagramming sentences to "lost skills, like darning socks or playing the sackbutt, that no one seems to miss" (paragraph 1). Write about a "lost skill" that you or someone you know possesses, describing the skill itself and speculating on why it has gone out of fashion.

3. Write about the memory of learning something in school, and, like Florey, try to capture the satisfaction you got out of your newfound mastery.

WAYNE C. BOOTH *Boring from Within:*
The Art of the Freshman Essay

L AST WEEK I had for about the hundredth time an experience that always disturbs me. Riding on a train, I found myself talking with my seat-mate, who asked me what I did for a living. "I teach English." Do you have any trouble predicting his response? His face fell, and he groaned, "Oh, dear, I'll have to watch my language." In my experience there are only two other possible reactions. The first

Adapted by Booth from a speech delivered in May 1963 to the Illinois Council of College Teachers of English.

is even less inspiriting: "I hated English in school; it was my worst subject." The second, so rare as to make an honest English teacher almost burst into tears of gratitude when it occurs, is an animated conversation about literature, or ideas, or the American language—the kind of conversation that shows a continuing respect for "English" as something more than being sure about *who* and *whom, lie* and *lay.*

Unless the people you meet are a good deal more tactful or better liars than the ones I meet, you've had the two less favorable experiences many times. And it takes no master analyst to figure out why so many of our fellow citizens think of us as unfriendly policemen: it is because too many of us have seen ourselves as unfriendly policemen. I know of a high school English class in Indiana in which the students are explicitly told that their paper grades will not be affected by anything they say; required to write a paper a week, they are graded simply on the number of spelling and grammatical errors. What is more, they are given a standard form for their papers: each paper is to have three paragraphs, a beginning, a middle, and an end—or is it an introduction, a body, and a conclusion? The theory seems to be that if the student is not troubled about having to say anything, or about discovering a good way of saying it, he can then concentrate on the truly important matter of avoiding mistakes.

What's wrong with such assignments? What's wrong with getting the problem of correctness focused sharply enough so that we can really work on it? After all, we do have the job of teaching correct English, don't we? We can't possibly teach our hordes of students to be colorful writers, but by golly, we can beat the bad grammar out of them. Leaving aside the obvious fact that we *can't* beat the bad grammar out of them, not by direct assault, let's think a bit about what that kind of assignment does to the poor teacher who gives it. Those papers must be read, by someone, and unless the teacher has more trained assistance than you and I have, *she's* the victim. She can't help being bored silly by her own paper-reading, and we all know what an evening of being bored by a class's papers does to our attitude toward that class the next day. The old formula of John Dewey was that any teaching that bores the student is likely to fail. The formula was subject to abuse, quite obviously, since interest in itself is only one of many tests of adequate teaching. A safer formula, though perhaps also subject to abuse, might be: Any teaching that bores the teacher is sure to fail. And I am haunted by the picture of that poor woman in Indiana, week after week reading batches of papers written by students who have been told that nothing they say can possibly affect her opinion of those papers. Could any hell imagined by Dante or Jean-Paul Sartre[1] match this self-inflicted futility?

I call it self-inflicted, as if it were a simple matter to avoid receiving papers that bore us. But unfortunately it is not. It may be a simple matter to avoid the *total* meaninglessness that the students must give that Indiana

---

1. Booth refers to the elaborately described hell of the *Inferno,* by the fourteenth-century Italian poet Dante Alighieri, and to the banal locked room in which the characters of Sartre's *No Exit* discover that hell is "other people."

teacher, but we all know that it is no easy matter to produce interesting papers; our pet cures for boredom never work as well as they ought to. Every beginning teacher learns quickly and painfully that nothing works with all students, and that on bad days even the most promising ideas work with nobody.

5   As I try to sort out the various possible cures for those batches of boredom—in ink, double-spaced, on one side of the sheet, only, please—I find them falling into three groups: efforts to give the students a sharper sense of writing to an audience, efforts to give them some substance to express, and efforts to improve their habits of observation and of approach to their task—what might be called improving their mental personalities.

This classification, both obvious and unoriginal, is a useful one not only because it covers—at least I hope it does—all of our efforts to improve what our students can do but also because it reminds us that no one of the three is likely to work unless it is related to each of the others. In fact each of the three types of cure— "develop an awareness of audience," "give them something to say," and "enliven their writing personalities"—threatens us with characteristic dangers and distortions; all three together are indispensable to any lasting cure.

Perhaps the most obvious omission in that Indiana teacher's assignments is all sense of an audience to be persuaded, of a serious rhetorical purpose to be achieved. One tempting cure for this omission is to teach them to put a controversial edge on what they say. So we ask them to write a three-page paper arguing that China should be allowed into the UN or that women are superior to men or that American colleges are failing in their historic task. Then we are surprised when the papers turn out to be as boring as ever. The papers on Red China are full of abstract pomposities that the students themselves obviously do not understand or care about, since they have gleaned them in a desperate dash through the most readily available sources listed in the *Readers' Guide*. Except for the rare student who has some political background and awareness, and who thus might have written on the subject anyway, they manage to convey little more than their resentment at the assignment and their boredom in carrying it out. One of the worst batches of papers I ever read came out of a good idea we had at Earlham College for getting the whole student body involved in controversial discussion about world affairs. We required them to read Barbara Ward's *Five Ideas that Change the World*; we even had Lady Jackson[2] come to the campus and talk to everyone about her concern for the backward nations. The papers, to our surprise, were a discouraging business. We found ourselves in desperation collecting the boners that are always a sure sign, when present in great numbers, that students are thoroughly disengaged. "I think altruism is all right, so long as we practice it in our own interest." "I would be willing to die for anything fatal." "It sure is a doggie dog world."

It is obvious what had gone wrong: though we had ostensibly given the

2. English title of Barbara Ward (1914–1981), economist.

student a writing purpose, it had not become *his* purpose, and he was really no better off, perhaps worse, than if we had him writing about, say, piccolos or pizza. We might be tempted in revulsion from such overly ambitious failures to search for controversy in the students' own mundane lives. This may be a good move, but we should not be surprised when the papers on "Let's clean up the campus" or "Why must we have traffic fatalities?" turn out to be just as empty as the papers on the UN or the Congo. They may have more exclamation points and underlined adjectives, but they will not interest any teacher who would like to read papers for his own pleasure or edification. "People often fail to realize that nearly 40,000 people are killed on our highways each year. Must this carnage continue?" Well, I suppose it must, until people who write about it learn to see it with their own eyes, and hearts, instead of through a haze of cliché. The truth is that to make students assume a controversial pose before they have any genuine substance to be controversial about is to encourage dishonesty and slovenliness, and to ensure our own boredom. It may very well lead them into the kind of commercial concern for the audience which makes almost every *Reader's Digest* article intelligible to everyone over the chronological age of ten and boring to everyone over the mental age of fifteen. *Newsweek* magazine recently had a readability survey conducted on itself. It was found to be readable by the average twelfth grader, unlike *Time,* which is readable by the average eleventh grader. The editors were advised, and I understand are taking the advice, that by improving their "readability" by one year they could improve their circulation by several hundred thousand. Whether they will thereby lop off a few thousand adult readers in the process was not reported.

The only protection from this destructive type of concern for the audience is the control of substance, of having something solid to say. Our students bore us, even when they take a seemingly lively controversial tone, because they have nothing to say, to us or to anybody else. If and when they discover something to say, they will no longer bore us, and our comments will no longer bore them. Having something to say, they will be interested in learning how to say it better. Having something to say, they can be taught how to give a properly controversial edge to what will by its nature be controversial—nothing, after all, is worth saying that everybody agrees on already.

When we think of providing substance, we are perhaps tempted first to find 　10 some way of filling students' minds with a goodly store of general ideas, available on demand. This temptation is not necessarily a bad one. After all, if we think of the adult writers who interest us, most of them have such a store; they have read and thought about man's major problems, and they have opinions and arguments ready to hand about how men ought to live, how society ought to be run, how literature ought to be written. Edmund Wilson, for example, one of the most consistently interesting men alive, seems to have an inexhaustible flow of reasoned opinions on any subject that comes before him.[3] Obviously our students are not going to interest us until they too have some ideas.

3. Wilson was an American man of letters (1895–1972), actively writing when Booth gave this speech.

But it is not easy to impart ideas. It is not even easy to impart opinions, though a popular teacher can usually manage to get students to parrot his views. But ideas—that is, opinions backed with genuine reasoning—are extremely difficult to develop. If they were not, we wouldn't have a problem in the first place; we could simply send our students off with an assignment to prove their conviction that God does or does not exist or that the American high school system is the best on God's earth, and the interesting arguments would flow.

There is, in fact, no short cut to the development of reasoned ideas. Years and years of daily contact with the world of ideas are required before the child can be expected to begin formulating his own ideas and his own reasons. And for the most part the capacity to handle abstract ideas comes fairly late. I recently saw a paper of a bright high school sophomore, from a good private school, relating the economic growth of China and India to their political development and relative supply of natural resources. It was a terrible paper; the student's hatred of the subject, his sense of frustration in trying to invent generalizations about processes that were still too big for him, showed in every line. The child's parent told me that when the paper was returned by the geography teacher, he had pencilled on the top of one page, "Why do you mix so many bad ideas with your good ones?" The son was almost in tears, his father told me, with anger and helplessness. "He talks as if I'd put bad ideas in on purpose. *I* don't know a bad idea from a good one on this subject."

Yet with all this said, I am still convinced that general ideas are not only a resource but also a duty that cannot be dodged just because it is a dangerous one. There is nothing we touch, as English teachers, that is immune to being tainted by our touch; all the difference lies in how we go about it.

Ideas are a resource because adolescents are surprisingly responsive to any real encouragement to think for themselves, *if* methods of forced feeding are avoided. The seventeen-year-old who has been given nothing but commonplaces and clichés all his life and who finally discovers a teacher with ideas of his own may have his life changed, and, as I shall say in my final point, when his life is changed his writing is changed. Perhaps some of you can remember, as I can, a first experience with a teacher who could think for himself. I can remember going home from a conversation with my high school chemistry teacher and audibly vowing to myself: "Someday I'm going to be able to think for myself like that." There was nothing especially unconventional about Luther Gidding's ideas—at least I can remember few of them now. But what I cannot forget is the way he had with an idea, the genuine curiosity with which he approached it, the pause while he gave his little thoughtful cough, and then the bulldog tenacity with which he would argue it through. And I am convinced that though he never required me to write a line, he did more to improve my writing during the high school years than all of my English teachers put together. The diary I kept to record my sessions with him, never read by anyone, was the best possible writing practice.

15   If ideas, in this sense of speculation backed up with an attempt to think about things rigorously and constructively, are a great and often neglected re-

source, they are also our civic responsibility—a far more serious responsibility than our duty to teach spelling and grammar. It is a commonplace to say that democracy depends for its survival on an informed citizenry, but we all know that mere information is not what we are talking about when we say such things. What we mean is that democracy depends on a citizenry that can reason for themselves, on men who know whether a case has been proved, or at least made probable. Democracy depends, if you will forgive some truisms for a moment, on free choices, and choices cannot be in any sense free if they are made blind: free choice is, in fact, choice that is based on knowledge—not just opinions, but knowledge in the sense of reasoned opinion. And if that half of our population who do not go beyond high school do not learn from us how to put two and two together and how to test the efforts of others to do so, and if the colleges continue to fail with most of the other half, we are doomed to become even more sheeplike, as a nation, than we are already.

Papers about ideas written by sheep are boring; papers written by thinking boys and girls are interesting. The problem is always to find ideas at a level that will allow the student to *reason,* that is, to provide support for his ideas, rather than merely assert them in half-baked form. And this means something that is all too often forgotten by the most ambitious teachers—namely, that whatever ideas the student writes about must somehow be connected with his own experience. Teaching machines will never be able to teach the kind of writing we all want, precisely because no machine can ever know which general ideas relate, for a given student, to some meaningful experience. In the same class we'll have one student for whom philosophical and religious ideas are meaningful, another who can talk with confidence about entropy and the second law of thermodynamics, a third who can write about social justice, and a fourth who can discuss the phony world of Holden Caulfield.[4] Each of them can do a good job on his own subject, because he has as part of his equipment a growing awareness of how conclusions in that subject are related to the steps of argument that support conclusions. Ideally, each of these students ought to have the personal attention of a tutor for an hour or so each week, someone who can help him sharpen those connections, and not force him to write on topics not yet appropriate to his interests or experience. But when these four are in a class of thirty or forty others, taught by a teacher who has three or four other similar sections, we all know what happens: the teacher is forced by his circumstances to provide some sort of mold into which all of the students can be poured. Although he is still better able to adapt to individual differences than a machine, he is unfortunately subject to boredom and fatigue, as a machine would not be. Instead of being the philosopher, scientist, political analyst, and literary critic that these four students require him to be, teaching them and learning from them at the same time, the teacher is almost inevitably tempted to force them all to write about the ideas he himself knows best. The result is that at least three of the four must write out of ignorance.

Now clearly the best way out of this impasse would be for legislatures and

4. The hero of *The Catcher in the Rye* (1951) by J. D. Salinger (b. 1919).

school boards and college presidents to recognize the teaching of English for what it is: the most demanding of all teaching jobs, justifying the smallest sections and the lightest course loads. No composition teacher can possibly concentrate on finding special interests, making imaginative assignments, and testing the effectiveness and cogency of papers if he has more than seventy-five students at a time; the really desirable limit would be about forty-five—three sections of fifteen students each. Nobody would ever expect a piano teacher, who has no themes to read, to handle the great masses of pupils that we handle. Everyone recognizes that for all other technical skills individual attention is required. Yet for this, the most delicate of all skills, the one requiring the most subtle interrelationships of training, character, and experience, we fling students and teachers into hopelessly impersonal patterns.

But if I'm not careful I'll find myself saying that our pupils bore us because the superintendents and college presidents hire us to be bored. Administrative neglect and misallocation of educational funds are basic to our problem, and we should let the citizenry know of the scandal on every occasion. But meanwhile, back at the ranch, we are faced with the situation as it now is: we must find some way to train a people to write responsibly even though the people, as represented, don't want this service sufficiently to pay for it.

The tone of political exhortation into which I have now fallen leads me to one natural large source of ideas as we try to encourage writing that is not just lively and controversial but informed and genuinely persuasive. For many students there is obviously more potential interest in social problems and forces, political controversy, and the processes of everyday living around them than in more general ideas. The four students I described a moment ago, students who can say something about philosophy, science, general political theory, or literary criticism, are rare. But most students, including these four, can in theory at least be interested in meaningful argument about social problems in which they are personally involved.

20   As a profession we have tried, over the past several decades, a variety of approaches attempting to capitalize on such interests. Papers on corruption in TV, arguments about race relations, analyses of distortions in advertising, descriptions of mass communication—these have been combined in various quantities with traditional subjects like grammar, rhetoric, and literature. The "communications" movement, which looked so powerful only a few years ago and which now seems almost dead, had at its heart a perfectly respectable notion, a notion not much different from the one I'm working with today: get them to write about something they know about, and make sure that they see their writing as an act of communication, not as a meaningless exercise. And what better material than other acts of communication.

The dangers of such an approach are by now sufficiently understood. As subject matter for the English course, current "communications media" can at best provide only a supplement to literature and analysis of ideas. But they can be a valuable supplement. Analysis in class of the appeals buried in a *New Yorker* or *Life* advertisement followed by a writing assignment requiring similar analyses can be a far more interesting introduction to the intricacies of style than assignments out of a language text on levels of usage or emotion-charged adjectives. Analysis of a *Time* magazine account, purporting to be objective news but in actual fact a highly emotional editorial, can be not only a valuable experience in itself, but it can lead to papers in which the students do say something to us. Stylistic analysis of the treatment of the same news events by two newspapers or weeklies of different editorial policy can lead to an intellectual awakening of great importance, and thus to papers that will not, cannot, bore the teacher. But this will happen only if the students' critical powers are genuinely developed. It will not do simply to teach the instructor's own prejudices.

There was a time in decades not long past when many of the most lively English teachers thought of their job as primarily to serve as handmaids to liberalism. I had one teacher in college who confessed to me that his overriding purpose was to get students to read and believe *The Nation*[5] rather than the editorials of their daily paper. I suppose that his approach was not entirely valueless. It seems preferable to the effort to be noncontroversial that marks too many English teachers in the '60s, and at least it stirred some of us out of our dogmatic slumbers. But unfortunately it did nothing whatever about teaching us to think critically. Though we graduated from his course at least aware—as many college graduates do not seem to be today—that you can't believe anything you read in the daily press until you have analyzed it and related it to your past experience and to other accounts, it failed to teach us that you can't believe what you read in *The Nation* either. It left the job undone of training our ability to think, because it concentrated too heavily on our opinions. The result was, as I remember, that my own papers in that course were generally regurgitated liberalism. I was excited by them, and that was something. But I can't believe that the instructor found reading them anything other than a chore. There was nothing in them that came from my own experience, my own notions of what would constitute evidence for my conclusions. There I was, in Utah in the depths of the depression, writing about the Okies when I could have been writing about the impoverished farmers all around me. I wrote about race relations in the south without ever having talked with a Negro in my life and without recognizing that the bootblack I occasionally saw in Salt Lake City in the Hotel Utah was in any way related to the problem of race relations.

The third element that accounts for our boring papers is the lack of character and personality in the writer. My life, my observations, my insights were not included in those papers on the Okies and race relations and the New Deal. Every opinion was derivative, every observation second-hand. I had no real opinions of my own, and my eyes were not open wide enough for me to make first-hand observations on the world around me. What I wrote was therefore characterless, without true personality, though often full of personal pronouns. My opinions had been changed, my *self* had not. The style was the

5. A liberal weekly magazine that features politics and cultural affairs.

boy, the opinionated, immature, uninformed boy; whether my teacher knew it or not—and apparently he did not—his real job was to make a man of me if he wanted me to write like a man.

Putting the difficulty in this way naturally leads me to what perhaps many of you have been impatient about from the beginning. Are not the narrative arts, both as encountered in great literature and as practiced by the students themselves, the best road to the infusion of individuality that no good writing can lack? Would not a real look at the life of that bootblack, and an attempt to deal with him in narrative, have led to a more interesting paper than all of my generalized attacks on the prejudiced southerners?

25   I think it would, but once again I am almost more conscious of the dangers of the cure than of the advantages. As soon as we make our general rule something like, "Have the students write a personal narrative on what they know about, what they can see and feel at first hand," we have opened the floodgates for those dreadful assignments that we all find ourselves using, even though we know better: "My Summer Vacation," "Catching My First Fish," and "Our Trip to the Seattle World's Fair." Here are personal experiences that call for personal observation and narration. What's wrong with them?

Quite simply, they invite triviality, superficiality, puerility. Our students have been writing essays on such non-subjects all their lives, and until they have developed some sort of critical vision, some way of looking at the world they passed through on their vacations or fishing trips, they are going to feed us the same old bromides that have always won their passing grades. "My Summer Vacation" is an invitation to a grocery list of items, because it implies no audience, no point to be made, no point of view, no character in the speaker. A bright student will make something of such an invitation, by dramatizing the comic family quarrel that developed two days out, or by comparing his view of the American motel system with Nabokov's in *Lolita*, or by remembering the types of people seen in the campgrounds. If he had his own eyes and ears open he might have seen, in a men's room in Grand Canyon last summer, a camper with a very thick French accent trying to convert a Brooklyn Jew into believing the story of the Mormon gold plates.[6] Or he could have heard, at Mesa Verde, a young park ranger, left behind toward the end of the season by all of the experienced rangers, struggling ungrammatically through a set speech on the geology of the area and finally breaking down in embarrassment over his lack of education. Such an episode, really *seen*, could be used narratively to say something to other high school students about what education really is.

But mere narration can be in itself just as dull as the most abstract theorizing about the nature of the universe or the most derivative opinion-mongering about politics. Even relatively skilful narration, used too obviously as a gimmick to catch interest, with no real relation to the subject, can be as

6. Bearing, according to Mormon tradition, the Book of Mormon, divinely revealed to the prophet Joseph Smith in upstate New York in 1827.

dull as the most abstract pomposities. We all know the student papers that begin like *Reader's Digest* articles, with stereotyped narration that makes one
doubt the event itself: "On a dark night last January, two teenagers were seen
etc., etc." One can open any issue of *Time* and find this so-called narrative interest plastered throughout. From the March 29 issue I find, among many others, the following bits of fantasy: #1: "A Bolivian father sadly surveyed his
nation's seven universities, then made up his mind. 'I don't want my son mixed
up in politics.' . . . So saying, he sent his son off to West Germany to college."
So writing, the author sends me into hysterical laughter: the quote is phony,
made up for the occasion to disguise the generality of the news item. #2:
"Around 12:30 P.M. every Monday and Friday, an aging Cubana Airlines turbo-
prop Britannia whistles to a halt at Mexico City's International Airport. Squads
of police stand by. All passengers . . . without diplomatic or Mexican passports
are photographed and questioned. . . . They always dodge questions. 'Why are
you here? Where are you going?' ask the Mexicans. 'None of your business,'
answer the secretive travelers." "Why should I go on reading?" ask I. #3: "At
6:30 one morning early this month, a phone shrilled in the small office off the
bedroom of Egypt's President . . . Nasser. [All early morning phones "shrill" for
Time.] Already awake, he lifted the receiver to hear exciting news: a military
coup had just been launched against the anti-Nasser government of Syria. The
phone rang again. It was the Minister of Culture. . . . How should Radio Cairo
handle the Syrian crisis? 'Support the rebels,' snapped Nasser." Oh lucky reporter, I sigh, to have such an efficient wiretapping service. #4: "In South Korea last week, a farmer named Song Kyu Il traveled all the way from the
southern provinces to parade before Seoul's Duk Soo Palace with a placard
scrawled in his own blood. . . . Farmer Song was thrown in jail, along with
some 200 other demonstrators." That's the last we hear of Song, who is invented as an individual for this opening and then dropped. #5: "Defense Secretary Robert McNamara last spring stood beside President Kennedy on the
tenth-deck bridge of the nuclear-powered carrier *Enterprise*. For as far as the
eye could see, other U.S. ships deployed over the Atlantic seascape." Well,
maybe. But for as far as the eye can see, the narrative clichés are piled, rank
on rank. At 12:00 midnight last Thursday a gaunt, harried English professor
could be seen hunched over his typewriter, a pile of *Time* magazines beside
him on the floor. "What," he murmured to himself, sadly, "Whatever can we do
about this trashy imitation of narration?"

Fortunately there is something we can do, and it is directly within our
province. We can subject our students to models of genuine narration, with
the sharp observation and penetrating critical judgment that underlies all good
story telling, whether reportorial or fictional.

> It is a truth universally acknowledged, that a single man in possession
> of a good fortune must be in want of a wife.
> However little known the feelings or views of such a man may be on
> his first entering a neighborhood, this truth is so well fixed in the minds of
> the surrounding families, that he is considered as the rightful property of
> someone or other of their daughters.

> "My dear Mr. Bennet," said his lady to him one day, "have you heard
> that Netherfield Park is let at last?"

And already we have a strong personal tone established, a tone of mocking
irony which leaves Jane Austen's Mrs. Bennet[7] revealed before us as the grasping, silly gossip she is. Or try this one:

> I am an American, Chicago-born—Chicago, that somber city—and go
> at things as I have taught myself, free-style, and will make the record in my
> own way: first to knock, first admitted; sometimes an innocent knock,
> sometimes a not so innocent. But a man's character is his fate, says Hera-
> clitus, and in the end there isn't any way to disguise the nature of the
> knocks by acoustical work on the door or gloving the knuckles.
> Everybody knows there is no fineness or accuracy of suppression; if
> you hold down one thing you hold down the adjoining.
> My own parents were not much to me, though I cared for my mother.
> She was simple-minded, and what I learned from her was not what she
> taught. . . .

Do you catch the accent of Saul Bellow here, beneath the accent of his
Augie March?[8] You do, of course, but the students, many of them, do not.
How do you know, they will ask, that Jane Austen is being ironic? How do you
know, they ask again, that Augie is being characterized by his author through
what he says? In teaching them how we know, in exposing them to the great
narrative voices, ancient and modern, and in teaching them to hear these
voices accurately, we are, of course, trying to change their lives, to make them
new, to raise their perceptions to a new level altogether. Nobody can really
catch these accents who has not grown up sufficiently to see through cheap
substitutes. Or, to put it another way, a steady exposure to such voices is the
very thing that will produce the maturity that alone can make our students
ashamed of beclouded, commercial, borrowed spectacles for viewing the
world.

30   It is true that exposure to good fiction will not in itself transform our students into good writers. Even the best-read student still needs endless hours
and years of practice, with rigorous criticism. Fiction will not do the job of discipline in reasoned argument and of practice in developing habits of addressing a living audience. But in the great fiction they will learn what it means to
look at something with full attention, what it means to see beneath the surface
of society's platitudes. If we then give them practice in writing about things
close to the home base of their own honest observations, constantly stretching
their powers of generalization and argument but never allowing them to drift
into pompous inanities or empty controversiality, we may have that rare but
wonderful pleasure of witnessing the miracle: a man and a style where before
there was only a bag of wind or a bundle of received opinions. Even when, as
with most of our students, no miracles occur, we can hope for papers that we

7. In *Pride and Prejudice*, published in 1813.
8. In *The Adventures of Augie March*, published in 1953.

can enjoy reading. And as a final bonus, we might hope that when our students encounter someone on a train who says that he teaches English, their automatic response may be something other than looks of pity or cries of mock alarm.

QUESTIONS

1. What is the occasion for Booth's address? How does it shape his language, structure, and evidence?

2. Divide the essay into sections and explain what Booth does in each and how each functions as part of the whole.

3. Select three essays from other sections of *The Norton Reader* that you think would engage Booth. Explain his criteria and how the essays meet them.

4. When you write, do you consciously attempt not to bore your reader? If so, list your strategies. Or, if the obligation not to bore your reader is a new idea to you, think of some strategies you might employ and list them. Use the list to develop an essay on strategies for generating interest and the circumstances in which they are appropriate.

DENNIS BARON   *When Professors Get A's and Machines Get F's*

I T'S TIME TO put a stop to talk about new computer programs that can grade student's essays with less effort and more accuracy than any teacher could— and do so more cheaply and quickly, to boot. Such programs are neither necessary nor desirable. I'm not worried that computers will replace teachers. Technology, used well, can enhance the human aspects of learning. But I am concerned that essay-grading programs may give both students and teachers a false picture of how readers evaluate what they read, and that in turn will lead to false ideas about how we should write.

According to its promoters, the Intelligent Essay Assessor, this year's entry in the grading-software sweepstakes, can scan essays and reliably identify what students have learned in seconds. Like older grading programs, it can measure the length of words and sentences and analyze punctuation. But it also does something its developers call "latent semantic analysis." By searching for keywords and their synonyms, it can tell whether a student is on the right topic

Published in the Chronicle of Higher Education (*November 20, 1998*) by a professor of English. The Chronicle, *a weekly newspaper for college administrators and faculty, often includes articles written by its readers.*

and how much information the essay contains compared to stored samples of essays on the topic. It can tell students what they've left out, and it can signal instructors that a student may have plagiarized. The program looks not just for single words, but for word patterns and phrases, so students can't fool it by parroting lists of concepts. And the program can learn what's good by being fed model essays, written by experts and professionals, on the topic in question.

Pitted against human graders, we are told, this software program gives grades that mirror those of real teachers. The program won't do away with teachers, but it will allow them to escape the drudgery of reading essays and to spend more time with students. The program also promises to be more consistent than human readers, who are notoriously inconsistent.

Teachers often insist that an objective standard of reading does indeed exist, that they can reward good writing in the same way that they can recognize a literary masterpiece. But in spite of such assurances, students know how erratic their teachers can be. From the students' point of view, every teacher seems to have a different set of expectations when it comes to written work. Students spend half their lives trying to figure out what each new teacher wants from a writing assignment, and the rest of their time trying to figure out how to adapt their writing to those ever-shifting expectations. The Intelligent Essay Assessor would assure students that they would be held to the same standard—time after time, class after class. In theory, the program could rank the 100 best student essays much as a Random House panel recently ranked the 100 best English-language novels of the 20th century.

5   I'm not convinced the program can perform consistently, and I don't think consistency, if it could be achieved, would improve the assessment of written assignments. Teachers believe in standards for grading, but they don't all share the same standard. Every teacher can tell a good essay from a bad one, a C paper from an A or an F. They can do so blindfolded, upside down, underwater, with both hands tied behind their backs. What they can't do is agree unanimously on which paper deserves the A, the C, or the F. Give a group of teachers an essay to grade, and, among them, they will manage to assign it every grade on the scale, citing plenty of reasons to back up their decisions.

The consistent grades that the computer promises to award may be comforting to students, to their parents, and to deans, but consistency in reading is not a human trait. That is why teachers don't share a common standard for evaluating writing. Such a standard is not something we should either expect or strive for in education, since it's not something students will encounter in their out-of-school writing.

Students may complain that their roommate's freshman-composition teacher is an easier grader than the one they're stuck with, or that their mother thinks the essay they got a C-minus on is really worth an A. But both the history of reading and our everyday experience confirm that even the most rigorous and attentive of readers will disagree over texts. If we've learned anything about reading and writing in the past 20 years, it is that each person brings to the activities such individual perspectives that it's amazing readers can agree on any aspect of the meaning or value of texts at all. Heraclitus, commenting on the vagaries of life in Greece in the 6th and 5th centuries B.C.E., said you can't put your foot into the same river twice, since it is always changing. Some wag amended this to claim you can't even put your foot into the same river once.

No two readers approach a text in exactly the same way; even the same person reading a text repeatedly will come away with different feelings each time. Like it or not, students must learn that their human readers will be inconsistent, a hard and frustrating lesson.

Writers learn to take their best shot, but they all know it is impossible to predict a reader's response with complete accuracy. Professional readers are no more consistent or predictable than any others. As a writer, I know I can send a manuscript to one editor and get it back by return mail—by return e-mail these days—with a polite, "Not for us, thanks," while another editor will pounce on the same piece and rush it into print. As a manuscript reader, I know I've accepted essays for publication that others have rejected, while ones I've turned down have found their way into print, where they have been well received.

Writers and editors learn that this is part of the natural give and take of the word game. It is harder, and often more frustrating, for teachers to face up to the fact that they too disagree over the relative value of different texts, whether they are student-generated essays or lists of great books produced by the cultural elite. That realization may not change how teachers grade, but acknowledging it would help them teach their students to expect real, rather than ideal, readings of their work.

Teachers want to grade less, but I doubt many will want computers to do their reading for them. We don't always relish grading student essays, but neither do we want to give up the insights that reading students' work gives us into how they are thinking.

I don't think student writers will be happy with computer-graded essays either. Students may be content filling in machine-gradeable sheets for multiple-choice tests, but they don't want their written work read and graded by machines. After years of being reminded by teachers to consider their audience, students don't want that audience to be a silicon chip. They want to know that there's a real person out there responding to them, even if that reader isn't predictable or knowable.

I asked students in my "Literacy and Technology" class, who are more committed than not to the new technologies, how they felt about the Intelligent Essay Assessor, and they were not encouraging. One student pointed out that computers won't be able to tell if their essays have improved over time, while another wondered if the program could detect and reward students who go way beyond what the question calls for, or who answer a better question that they have posed themselves.

The World-Wide Web site for the Intelligent Essay Assessor allows writers to submit their own answers to several set essay questions. To test the efficacy of the program, I submitted the essay you are reading (concluding with the paragraph above) for evaluation. None of the essay questions on the site matched my topic very well, but that did not prove a great obstacle for the virtual grader. I tried submitting my work as a response to a question in the Graduate Management Admission Test that asked for an evaluation of a particular kind of business practice. It crunched my essay in a couple of seconds, rating it a 3.36 on a six-point scale. The program assured me its score was valid, adding, "None of the confidence measures detected anything inappropriate with this essay."

15   Knowing my essay was completely inappropriate, since it didn't address the required topic at all, I resubmitted it, this time as a response to another set GMAT topic—an analysis of a marketing campaign. The program quickly slapped on a grade of 4.82. This time, the program acknowledged that it had low confidence in the assigned grade, presumably because my essay was once again completely off the topic. Nonetheless, it did give me a fairly high mark (I actually think it deserves more), and added this message: "In a real grading situation, this essay would likely be forwarded to a human grader for verification." Note that referral to a human grader would be likely, not certain. Interestingly, my off-topic essay got a high score when submitted as a response to one topic and a lower score as a response to a different topic. The program showed an inconsistency approaching that of human readers after all. So much for a gold standard of consistency in grading.

When I submitted the essay a third time, as the answer to a question for a freshman class on the function of the heart and circulatory system, the computer finally realized something was amiss and responded to my writing sample with the wry comment: "A very ZEN essay. Your emptiness impresses me." Apparently grading machines can get testy, too.

Perhaps it is wrong for me to stand in the way of technological progress. After all, technology serves students as well as teachers; Web sites now offer students the ability to download term papers free. If we're going to eliminate the human reader, why not eliminate the writer as well, and let the computer grading program interface directly with the computer-generated essay? In a way, they deserve each other. Besides, eliminating the drudgery of writing would allow students more free time that they could then spend with their newly leisured instructors.

In any case, until the virtual writing and reading technology is perfected, my advice to teachers, students, and people about to take the GMAT is, Don't quit your day job.

QUESTIONS

1. In your experience, is Baron right about the inconsistency among teachers when they grade papers? If so, how has such inconsistency affected you?

2. What is Baron's main argument against machine grading of student writing? What evidence does he give in support of his position?

3. Write about a time when you had to produce some high-stakes writing. What thoughts went through your mind? How did you prepare for the task? What did you write? What was the outcome?

Politics and the English Language

MOST PEOPLE who bother with the matter at all would admit that the English language is in a bad way, but it is generally assumed that we cannot by conscious action do anything about it. Our civilization is decadent and our language—so the argument runs—must inevitably share in the general collapse. It follows that any struggle against the abuse of language is a sentimental archaism, like preferring candles to electric light or hansom cabs to aeroplanes. Underneath this lies the half-conscious belief that language is a natural growth and not an instrument which we shape for our own purposes.

Now, it is clear that the decline of a language must ultimately have political and economic causes: it is not due simply to the bad influence of this or that individual writer. But an effect can become a cause, reinforcing the original cause and producing the same effect in an intensified form, and so on indefinitely. A man may take to drink because he feels himself to be a failure, and then fail all the more completely because he drinks. It is rather the same thing that is happening to the English language. It becomes ugly and inaccurate because our thoughts are foolish, but the slovenliness of our language makes it easier for us to have foolish thoughts. The point is that the process is reversible. Modern English, especially written English, is full of bad habits which spread by imitation and which can be avoided if one is willing to take the necessary trouble. If one gets rid of these habits one can think more clearly, and to think clearly is a necessary first step towards political regeneration: so that the fight against bad English is not frivolous and is not the exclusive concern of professional writers. I will come back to this presently, and I hope that by that time the meaning of what I have said here will have become clearer. Meanwhile, here are five specimens of the English language as it is now habitually written.

These five passages have not been picked out because they are especially bad—I could have quoted far worse if I had chosen—but because they illustrate various of the mental vices from which we now suffer. They are a little below the average, but are fairly representative samples. I number them so that I can refer back to them when necessary:

> "(1) I am not, indeed, sure whether it is not true to say that the Milton who once seemed not unlike a seventeenth-century Shelley had not become, out of an experience ever more bitter in each year, more alien [*sic*] to the founder of that Jesuit sect which nothing could induce him to tolerate."
>
> PROFESSOR HAROLD LASKI (ESSAY IN *FREEDOM OF EXPRESSION*).

From Shooting an Elephant, and Other Essays *(1950), a collection of Orwell's best-known essays. "Politics and the English Language" is the most famous modern argument for a clear, unadorned writing style—not only as a matter of good sense, but as a political virtue.*

"(2) Above all, we cannot play ducks and drakes with a native battery of idioms which prescribes such egregious collocations of vocables as the Basic *put up with* for *tolerate* or *put at a loss* for *bewilder.*"

PROFESSOR LANCELOT HOGBEN (INTERGLOSSA).

"(3) On the one side we have the free personality: by definition it is not neurotic, for it has neither conflict nor dream. Its desires, such as they are, are transparent, for they are just what institutional approval keeps in the forefront of consciousness; another institutional pattern would alter their number and intensity; there is little in them that is natural, irreducible, or culturally dangerous. But *on the other side,* the social bond itself is nothing but the mutual reflection of these self-secure integrities. Recall the definition of love. Is not this the very picture of a small academic? Where is there a place in this hall of mirrors for either personality or fraternity?"

ESSAY ON PSYCHOLOGY IN POLITICS (NEW YORK).

"(4) All the 'best people' from the gentlemen's clubs, and all the frantic fascist captains, united in common hatred of Socialism and bestial horror of the rising tide of the mass revolutionary movement, have turned to acts of provocation, to foul incendiarism, to medieval legends of poisoned wells, to legalize their own destruction of proletarian organizations, and rouse the agitated petty-bourgeoisie to chauvinistic fervour on behalf of the fight against the revolutionary way out of the crisis."

COMMUNIST PAMPHLET.

"(5) If a new spirit *is* to be infused into this old country, there is one thorny and contentious reform which must be tackled, and that is the humanization and galvanization of the B.B.C. Timidity here will bespeak cancer and atrophy of the soul. The heart of Britain may be sound and of strong beat, for instance, but the British lion's roar at present is like that of Bottom in Shakespeare's *Midsummer Night's Dream*—as gentle as any sucking dove. A virile new Britain cannot continue indefinitely to be traduced in the eyes or rather ears, of the world by the effete languors of Langham Place, brazenly masquerading as 'standard English'. When the Voice of Britain is heard at nine o'clock, better far and infinitely less ludicrous to hear aitches honestly dropped than the present priggish, inflated, inhibited, school-ma'amish arch braying of blameless bashful mewing maidens!"

LETTER IN TRIBUNE.

Each of these passages has faults of its own, but, quite apart from avoidable ugliness, two qualities are common to all of them. The first is staleness of imagery; the other is lack of precision. The writer either has a meaning and cannot express it, or he inadvertently says something else, or he is almost indifferent as to whether his words mean anything or not. This mixture of vagueness and sheer incompetence is the most marked characteristic of modern English prose, and especially of any kind of political writing. As soon as certain topics are raised, the concrete melts into the abstract and no one seems able to think of turns of speech that are not hackneyed: prose consists less and less of *words* chosen for the sake of their meaning, and more and more of *phrases* tacked together like the sections of a prefabricated henhouse. I list below, with notes and examples, various of the tricks by means of which the work of prose-construction is habitually dodged:

DYING METAPHORS

A newly invented metaphor assists thought by evoking a visual image, while on the other hand a metaphor which is technically "dead" (e.g. *iron resolution*) has in effect reverted to being an ordinary word and can generally be used without loss of vividness. But in between these two classes there is a huge dump of worn-out metaphors which have lost all evocative power and are merely used because they save people the trouble of inventing phrases for themselves. Examples are: *Ring the changes on, take up the cudgels for, toe the line, ride roughshod over, stand shoulder to shoulder with, play into the hands of, no axe to grind, grist to the mill, fishing in troubled waters, on the order of the day, Achilles' heel, swan song, hotbed.* Many of these are used without knowledge of their meaning (what is a "rift," for instance?), and incompatible metaphors are frequently mixed, a sure sign that the writer is not interested in what he is saying. Some metaphors now current have been twisted out of their original meaning without those who use them even being aware of the fact. For example, *toe the line* is sometimes written *tow the line.* Another example is *the hammer and the anvil,* now always used with the implication that the anvil gets the worst of it. In real life it is always the anvil that breaks the hammer, never the other way about: a writer who stopped to think what he was saying would be aware of this, and would avoid perverting the original phrase.

OPERATORS OR VERBAL FALSE LIMBS

These save the trouble of picking out appropriate verbs and nouns, and at the same time pad each sentence with extra syllables which give it an appearance of symmetry. Characteristic phrases are: *render inoperative, militate against, make contact with, be subjected to, give rise to, give grounds for, have the effect of, play a leading part (role) in, make itself felt, take effect, exhibit a tendency to, serve the purpose of,* etc., etc. The keynote is the elimination of simple verbs. Instead of being a single word, such as *break, stop, spoil, mend, kill,* a verb becomes a *phrase,* made up of a noun or adjective tacked on to some general-purposes verb such as *prove, serve, form, play, render.* In addition, the passive voice is wherever possible used in preference to the active, and noun constructions are used instead of gerunds (*by examination of* instead of *by examining*). The range of verbs is further cut down by means of the *-ize* and *de-* formation, and the banal statements are given an appearance of profundity by means of the *not un-* formation. Simple conjunctions and prepositions are replaced by such phrases as *with respect to, having regard to, the fact that, by dint of, in view of, in the interests of, on the hypothesis that;* and the ends of sentences are saved from anticlimax by such resounding commonplaces as *greatly to be desired, cannot be left out of account, a development to be expected in the near future, deserving of serious consideration, brought to a satisfactory conclusion,* and so on and so forth.

PRETENTIOUS DICTION

Words like *phenomenon, element, individual* (as noun), *objective, categorical, effective, virtual, basic, primary, promote, constitute, exhibit, exploit, utilize, eliminate, liquidate,* are used to dress up simple statements and give an air of scientific impartiality to biased judgments. Adjectives like *epoch-making, epic, historic, unforgettable, triumphant, age-old, inevitable, inexorable, veritable,* are used to dignify the sordid processes of international politics, while writing that aims at glorifying war usually takes on an archaic colour, its characteristic words being: *realm, throne, chariot, mailed fist, trident, sword, shield, buckler, banner, jackboot, clarion.* Foreign words and expressions such as *cul de sac, ancien régime, deus ex machina, mutatis mutandis, status quo, gleichschaltung, weltanschauung,* are used to give an air of culture and elegance. Except for the useful abbreviations *i.e., e.g.,* and *etc.,* there is no real need for any of the hundreds of foreign phrases now current in English. Bad writers, and especially scientific, political and sociological writers, are nearly aways haunted by the notion that Latin or Greek words are grander than Saxon ones, and unnecessary words like *expedite, ameliorate, predict, extraneous, deracinated, clandestine, subaqueous* and hundreds of others constantly gain ground from their Anglo-Saxon opposite numbers.[1] The jargon peculiar to Marxist writing (*hyena, hangman, cannibal, petty bourgeois, these gentry, lackey, flunkey, mad dog, White Guard,* etc.) consists largely of words and phrases translated from Russian, German or French; but the normal way of coining a new word is to use a Latin or Greek root with the appropriate affix and, where necessary, the *-ize* formation. It is often easier to make up words of this kind (*deregionalize, impermissible, extramarital, nonfragmentatory* and so forth) than to think up the English words that will cover one's meaning. The result, in general, is an increase in slovenliness and vagueness.

MEANINGLESS WORDS

In certain kinds of writing, particularly in art criticism and literary criticism, it is normal to come across long passages which are almost completely lacking in meaning.[2] Words like *romantic, plastic, values, human, dead, sentimental, natural, vitality,* as used in art criticism, are strictly meaningless in the sense that

1. An interesting illustration of this is the way in which the English flower names which were in use till very recently are being ousted by Greek ones, *snapdragon* becoming *antirrhinum, forget-me-not* becoming *myosotis,* etc. It is hard to see any practical reason for this change of fashion: it is probably due to an instinctive turning-away from the more homely word and a vague feeling that the Greek word is scientific [Orwell's note].

2. Example: "Comfort's catholicity of perception and image, strangely Whitmanesque in range, almost the exact opposite in aesthetic compulsion, continues to evoke that trembling atmospheric accumulative hinting at a cruel, an inexorably serene timelessness. . . . Wrey Gardiner scores by aiming at simple bull's-eyes with precision. Only they are not so simple, and through this contented sadness runs more than the surface bittersweet of resignation" (*Poetry Quarterly*) [Orwell's note].

they not only do not point to any discoverable object, but are hardly ever expected to do so by the reader. When one critic writes, "The outstanding feature of Mr. X's work is its living quality," while another writes, "The immediately striking thing about Mr. X's work is its peculiar deadness," the reader accepts this as a simple difference of opinion. If words like *black* and *white* were involved, instead of the jargon words *dead* and *living*, he would see at once that language was being used in an improper way. Many political words are similarly abused. The word *Fascism* has now no meaning except in so far as it signifies "something not desirable." The words *democracy, socialism, freedom, patriotic, realistic, justice,* have each of them several different meanings which cannot be reconciled with one another. In the case of a word like *democracy,* not only is there no agreed definition, but the attempt to make one is resisted from all sides. It is almost universally felt that when we call a country democratic we are praising it: consequently the defenders of every kind of régime claim that it is a democracy, and fear that they might have to stop using the word if it were tied down to any one meaning. Words of this kind are often used in a consciously dishonest way. That is, the person who uses them has his own private definition, but allows his hearer to think he means something quite different. Statements like *Marshal Pétain was a true patriot, The Soviet Press is the freest in the world, The Catholic Church is opposed to persecution,* are almost always made with intent to deceive. Other words used in variable meanings, in most cases more or less dishonestly, are: *class, totalitarian, science, progressive, reactionary, bourgeois, equality.*

Now that I have made this catalogue of swindles and perversions, let me give another example of the kind of writing that they lead to. This time it must of its nature be an imaginary one. I am going to translate a passage of good English into modern English of the worst sort. Here is a well-known verse from *Ecclesiastes:*

> "I returned and saw under the sun, that the race is not to the swift, nor the battle to the strong, neither yet bread to the wise, nor yet riches to men of understanding, nor yet favour to men of skill; but time and chance happeneth to them all."

Here it is in modern English: 10

> "Objective consideration of contemporary phenomena compels the conclusion that success or failure in competitive activities exhibits no tendency to be commensurate with innate capacity, but that a considerable element of the unpredictable must invariably be taken into account."

This is a parody, but not a very gross one. Exhibit (3), above, for instance, contains several patches of the same kind of English. It will be seen that I have not made a full translation. The beginning and ending of the sentence follow the original meaning fairly closely, but in the middle the concrete illustrations—race, battle, bread—dissolve into the vague phrase "success or failure in competitive activities." This had to be so, because no modern writer of the kind I am discussing—no one capable of using phrases like "objective consideration of contemporary phenomena"—would ever tabulate his thoughts in that precise and detailed way. The whole tendency of modern prose is away from concreteness. Now analyse these two sentences a little more closely. The first contains forty-nine words but only sixty syllables, and all its words are those of everyday life. The second contains thirty-eight words of ninety syllables: eighteen of its words are from Latin roots, and one from Greek. The first sentence contains six vivid images, and only one phrase ("time and chance") that could be called vague. The second contains not a single fresh, arresting phrase, and in spite of its ninety syllables it gives only a shortened version of the meaning contained in the first. Yet without a doubt it is the second kind of sentence that is gaining ground in modern English. I do not want to exaggerate. This kind of writing is not yet universal, and outcrops of simplicity will occur here and there in the worst-written page. Still, if you or I were told to write a few lines on the uncertainty of human fortunes, we should probably come much nearer to my imaginary sentence than to the one from *Ecclesiastes*.

As I have tried to show, modern writing at its worst does not consist in picking out words for the sake of their meaning and inventing images in order to make the meaning clearer. It consists in gumming together long strips of words which have already been set in order by someone else, and making the results presentable by sheer humbug. The attraction of this way of writing is that it is easy. It is easier—even quicker, once you have the habit—to say *In my opinion it is a not unjustifiable assumption that* than to say *I think*. If you use ready-made phrases, you not only don't have to hunt about for words; you also don't have to bother with the rhythms of your sentences, since these phrases are generally so arranged as to be more or less euphonious. When you are composing in a hurry—when you are dictating to a stenographer, for instance, or making a public speech—it is natural to fall into a pretentious, Latinized style. Tags like *a consideration which we should do well to bear in mind* or *a conclusion to which all of us would readily assent* will save many a sentence from coming down with a bump. By using stale metaphors, similes and idioms, you save much mental effort, at the cost of leaving your meaning vague, not only for your reader but for yourself. This is the significance of mixed metaphors. The sole aim of a metaphor is to call up a visual image. When these images clash—as in *The Fascist octopus has sung its swan song, the jackboot is thrown into the melting pot*—it can be taken as certain that the writer is not seeing a mental image of the objects he is naming; in other words he is not really thinking. Look again at the examples I gave at the beginning of this essay. Professor Laski (1) uses five negatives in fifty-three words. One of these is superfluous, making nonsense of the whole passage, and in addition there is the slip *alien* for akin, making further nonsense, and several avoidable pieces of clumsiness which increase the general vagueness. Professor Hogben (2) plays ducks and drakes with a battery which is able to write prescriptions, and, while disapproving of the everyday phrase *put up with,* is unwilling to look *egregious* up in the dictionary and see what it means. (3), if one takes an uncharitable attitude towards it, is simply meaningless: probably one could work out its intended meaning by reading the whole of the article in which it occurs. In (4), the writer knows more or less what he wants to say, but an accumulation of stale phrases chokes him like tea leaves blocking a sink. In (5), words and meaning have almost parted company. People who write in this manner usually have a general emotional meaning—they dislike one thing and want to express solidarity with another—but they are not interested in the detail of what they are saying. A scrupulous writer, in every sentence that he writes, will ask himself at least four questions, thus: What am I trying to say? What words will express it? What image or idiom will make it clearer? Is this image fresh enough to have an effect? And he will probably ask himself two more: Could I put it more shortly? Have I said anything that is avoidably ugly? But you are not obliged to go to all this trouble. You can shirk it by simply throwing your mind open and letting the ready-made phrases come crowding in. They will construct your sentences for you—even think your thoughts for you, to a certain extent—and at need they will perform the important service of partially concealing your meaning even from yourself. It is at this point that the special connection between politics and the debasement of language becomes clear.

In our time it is broadly true that political writing is bad writing. Where it is not true, it will generally be found that the writer is some kind of rebel, expressing his private opinions and not a "party line." Orthodoxy, of whatever colour, seems to demand a lifeless, imitative style. The political dialects to be found in pamphlets, leading articles, manifestos, White Papers and the speeches of under-secretaries do, of course, vary from party to party, but they are all alike in that one almost never finds in them a fresh, vivid, homemade turn of speech. When one watches some tired hack on the platform mechanically repeating the familiar phrases—*bestial atrocities, iron heel, blood-stained tyranny, free peoples of the world, stand shoulder to shoulder*—one often has a curious feeling that one is not watching a live human being but some kind of dummy: a feeling which suddenly becomes stronger at moments when the light catches the speaker's spectacles and turns them into blank discs which seem to have no eyes behind them. And this is not altogether fanciful. A speaker who uses that kind of phraseology has gone some distance towards turning himself into a machine. The appropriate noises are coming out of his larynx, but his brain is not involved as it would be if he were choosing his words for himself. If the speech he is making is one that he is accustomed to make over and over again, he may be almost unconscious of what he is saying, as one is when one utters the responses in church. And this reduced state of consciousness, if not indispensable, is at any rate favourable to political conformity.

In our time, political speech and writing are largely the defence of the indefensible. Things like the continuance of British rule in India, the Russian purges and deportations, the dropping of the atom bombs on Japan, can indeed be defended, but only by arguments which are too brutal for most people to face, and which do not square with the professed aims of political parties. Thus political language has to consist largely of euphemism, question-begging and sheer cloudy vagueness. Defenceless villages are bombarded from the air, the inhabitants driven out into the countryside, the cattle machine-gunned, the huts set on fire with incendiary bullets: this is called *pacification*. Millions of peasants are robbed of their farms and sent trudging along the roads with no more than they can carry: this is called *transfer of population* or *rectification of frontiers*. People are imprisoned for years without trial, or shot in the back of the neck or sent to die of scurvy in Arctic lumber camps: this is called *elimination of unreliable elements*. Such phraseology is needed if one wants to name things without calling up mental pictures of them. Consider for instance some comfortable English professor defending Russian totalitarianism. He cannot say outright, "I believe in killing off your opponents when you can get good results by doing so." Probably, therefore, he will say something like this:

15   "While freely conceding that the Soviet régime exhibits certain features which the humanitarian may be inclined to deplore, we must, I think, agree that a certain curtailment of the right to political opposition is an unavoidable concomitant of transitional periods, and that the rigors which the Russian people have been called upon to undergo have been amply justified in the sphere of concrete achievement."

The inflated style is itself a kind of euphemism. A mass of Latin words falls upon the facts like soft snow, blurring the outlines and covering up all the details. The great enemy of clear language is insincerity. When there is a gap between one's real and one's declared aims, one turns as it were instinctively to long words and exhausted idioms, like a cuttlefish squirting out ink. In our age there is no such thing as "keeping out of politics." All issues are political issues, and politics itself is a mass of lies, evasions, folly, hatred and schizophrenia. When the general atmosphere is bad, language must suffer. I should expect to find—this is a guess which I have not sufficient knowledge to verify—that the German, Russian and Italian languages have all deteriorated in the last ten or fifteen years, as a result of dictatorship.

But if thought corrupts language, language can also corrupt thought. A bad usage can spread by tradition and imitation, even among people who should and do know better. The debased language that I have been discussing is in some ways very convenient. Phrases like *a not unjustifiable assumption, leaves much to be desired, would serve no good purpose, a consideration which we should do well to bear in mind,* are a continuous temptation, a packet of aspirins always at one's elbow. Look back through this essay, and for certain you will find that I have again and again committed the very faults I am protesting against. By this morning's post I have received a pamphlet dealing with conditions in Germany. The author tells me that he "felt impelled" to write it. I open it at random, and here is almost the first sentence that I see: "(The Allies) have an opportunity not only of achieving a radical transformation of Germany's social and political structure in such a way as to avoid a nationalistic reaction in Germany itself, but at the same time of laying the foundations of a co-operative and unified Europe." You see, he "feels impelled" to write—feels, presumably, that he has something new to say—and yet his words, like cavalry horses answering the bugle, group themselves automatically into the familiar dreary pattern. This invasion of one's mind by ready-made phrases (*lay the foundations, achieve a radical transformation*) can only be prevented if one is constantly on guard against them, and every such phrase anaesthetizes a portion of one's brain.

I said earlier that the decadence of our language is probably curable. Those who deny this would argue, if they produced an argument at all, that language merely reflects existing social conditions, and that we cannot influence its development by any direct tinkering with words and constructions. So far as the general tone or spirit of a language goes, this may be true, but it is not true in detail. Silly words and expressions have often disappeared, not through any evolutionary process but owing to the conscious action of a minority. Two recent examples were *explore every avenue* and *leave no stone unturned*, which were killed by the jeers of a few journalists. There is a long list of fly-blown metaphors which could similarly be got rid of if enough people would interest themselves in the job; and it should also be possible to laugh the *not un-* formation out of existence,[3] to reduce the amount of Latin and Greek in the average sentence, to drive out foreign phrases and strayed scientific words, and, in general, to make pretentiousness unfashionable. But all these are minor points. The defence of the English language implies more than this, and perhaps it is best to start by saying what it does *not* imply.

To begin with it has nothing to do with archaism, with the salvaging of obsolete words and turns of speech, or with the setting up of a "standard English" which must never be departed from. On the contrary, it is especially concerned with the scrapping of every word or idiom which has outworn its usefulness. It has nothing to do with correct grammar and syntax, which are of no importance so long as one makes one's meaning clear, or with the avoidance of Americanisms, or with having what is called a "good prose style." On the other hand it is not concerned with fake simplicity and the attempt to make written English colloquial. Nor does it even imply in every case preferring the Saxon word to the Latin one, though it does imply using the fewest and shortest words that will cover one's meaning. What is above all needed is to let the meaning choose the word, and not the other way about. In prose, the worst thing one can do with words is to surrender to them. When you think of a concrete object, you think wordlessly, and then, if you want to describe the thing you have been visualizing you probably hunt about till you find the exact words that seem to fit. When you think of something abstract you are more inclined to use words from the start, and unless you make a conscious effort to prevent it, the existing dialect will come rushing in and do the job for you, at the expense of blurring or even changing your meaning. Probably it is better to put off using words as long as possible and get one's meaning as clear as one can through pictures or sensations. Afterwards one can choose—not simply *accept*—the phrases that will best cover the meaning, and then switch round and decide what impression one's words are likely to make on another person. This last effort of the mind cuts out all stale or mixed images, all prefabricated

3. One can cure oneself of the *not un-* formation by memorizing this sentence: *A not unblack dog was chasing a not unsmall rabbit across a not ungreen field* [Orwell's note].

phrases, needless repetitions, and humbug and vagueness generally. But one can often be in doubt about the effect of a word or a phrase, and one needs rules that one can rely on when instinct fails. I think the following rules will cover most cases:

(i)   Never use a metaphor, simile or other figure of speech which you are used to seeing in print.

(ii)   Never use a long word where a short one will do.

(iii)   If it is possible to cut a word out, always cut it out.

(iv)   Never use the passive where you can use the active.

(v)   Never use a foreign phrase, a scientific word or a jargon word if you can think of an everyday English equivalent.

(vi)   Break any of these rules sooner than say anything outright barbarous.

These rules sound elementary, and so they are, but they demand a deep change of attitude in anyone who has grown used to writing in the style now fashionable. One could keep all of them and still write bad English, but one could not write the kind of stuff that I quoted in those five specimens at the beginning of this article.

20   I have not here been considering the literary use of language, but merely language as an instrument for expressing and not for concealing or preventing thought. Stuart Chase[4] and others have come near to claiming that all abstract words are meaningless, and have used this as a pretext for advocating a kind of political quietism. Since you don't know what Fascism is, how can you struggle against Fascism? One need not swallow such absurdities as this, but one ought to recognize that the present political chaos is connected with the decay of language, and that one can probably bring about some improvement by starting at the verbal end. If you simplify your English, you are freed from the worst follies of orthodoxy. You cannot speak any of the necessary dialects, and when you make a stupid remark its stupidity will be obvious, even to yourself. Political language—and with variations this is true of all political parties, from Conservatives to Anarchists—is designed to make lies sound truthful and murder respectable, and to give an appearance of solidity to pure wind. One cannot change this all in a moment, but one can at least change one's own habits, and from time to time one can even, if one jeers loudly enough, send some worn-out and useless phrase—some *jackboot, Achilles' heel, hotbed, melting pot, acid test, veritable inferno* or other lump of verbal refuse—into the dustbin where it belongs.

4. Chase (in *The Tyranny of Words* [1938] and *The Power of Words* [1954]) and S. I. Hayakawa (in *Language in Action* [1939]) popularized the semantic theories of Alfred Korzybski.

QUESTIONS

1. State Orwell's main point as precisely as possible.

2. What kinds of prose does Orwell analyze in this essay? Look, in particular, at the passages he quotes in paragraph 3. Where would you find their contemporary equivalents?

3. Apply Orwell's rule iv, "Never use the passive where you can use the active" (paragraph 19), to paragraph 14 of his essay. What happens when you change his passive constructions to active? Has Orwell forgotten rule iv or is he covered by rule vi, "Break any of these rules sooner than say anything outright barbarous"?

4. Orwell wrote this essay in 1946. Choose at least two examples of political discourse from current media and discuss, in an essay, whether Orwell's analysis of the language of politics is still valid. If it is, which features that he singles out for criticism appear most frequently in your examples?

AN ALBUM OF
STYLES

W hat is style? The question eludes easy an-
swers. "Le style est l'homme même," the
Count de Buffon observed in 1753, in an address on his admission to the French
Academy. His words, translated into English, have become proverbial: "The style
is the man." (To avoid the false generic man, we might translate his statement as
"The style is the person.")

Buffon's words suggest that we can gain insight into a person's character by
considering the mode of self-presentation, whether in action or in words. A
writer's style is a recognizable expression of self that permeates a text, the clear,
distinct, and individual voice that readers "hear" when they read an essay. We
can work toward an understanding of a writer's style by examining the elements
that create it—words, metaphors, syntax, rhetorical techniques and maneuvers.

Although a writer's style reflects an individual personality and a personal set
of preferences, it is also influenced by the historical context in which the writer
lives. Different historical periods privileged different prose styles. For example,
the "Metaphysical" writers of the early seventeenth century used elaborate
metaphors, or "conceits." This stylistic preference appears in the selection from
John Donne's meditation "No Man Is an Island," where Donne reflects on the interconnectedness of all humankind by positing that each of us is part of a continent or mainland, no one an "island, entire of itself." The "Augustan" writers of
the eighteenth century preferred periodic sentences—sentences that used frequent parallel construction; introductory, dependent clauses before the main, independent clause; and balanced correlatives such as neither and nor, not only
with but also, or both and and. Examples of the periodic style appear in the ex-
cerpts from Samuel Johnson and Mary Wollstonecraft—as in Johnson's final
sentence, which balances the verbs "imagine" and "dream" in the opening
dependent clause and the verbs "survey" and "confess" in the main clause: "Whoever thou art, that, not content with a moderate condition, imaginest happiness
in royal magnificence, and dreamest that command or riches can feed the appetite of novelty with perpetual gratifications, survey the pyramids, and confess
thy folly!" When Wollstonecraft uses the periodic sentence in A Vindication of
the Rights of Woman (1792), she is not only expressing her feminist sentiments
but also demonstrating her mastery of the dominant literary style of the day.

Modern American writers tend to appear—at least to our contemporary
eyes—more simple, direct, and concise than their literary predecessors. No doubt
Ernest Hemingway's crisp, precise style—dominated by strong nouns and verbs,
virtually free of adjectives—has influenced recent generations of American writers. But before concluding that modern styles are less elaborate, more straightfor-
word than older ones, we should study carefully the prose patterns of Terry

Tempest Williams, who sometimes uses short, simple observations ("I love sitting by the river") but also creates longer, more intricate sentences that mimic the movement of flowing water: "Around and around, a cottonwood leaf spins; a breeze gives it a nudge, and it glides downriver, this river braided with light."

Reading the prose and studying the style of authors, both old and new, can help aspiring writers develop their own styles. Ben Franklin tells us in his Auto-biography *that, as a young man, he would read the essays of Joseph Addison and Richard Steele, then close his book and try to write out the essays in his (and their) best style. Ben Jonson advises us, in the selection "To Write Well" from his commonplace book,* Timber, or Discoveries, *"For a man to write well, there are required three necessaries: to read the best authors, observe the best speakers, and much exercise of his own style." As usual, Samuel Johnson's reflection on writing speaks volumes: "What is written without effort is in general read without pleasure."*

Francis Bacon: *Of Youth and Age*

A man that is young in years may be old in hours, if he have lost no time. But that happeneth rarely. Generally, youth is like the first cogitations, not so wise as the second. For there is a youth in thoughts as well as in ages. And yet the invention of young men is more lively than that of old, and imaginations stream into their minds better, and as it were more divinely. Natures that have much heat, and great and violent desires and perturbations, are not ripe for action till they have passed the meridian of their years: as it was with Julius Caesar,[1] and Septimius Severus. Of the latter of whom it is said, *Juventutem egit erroribus, imo furoribus, plenam:*[2] and yet he was the ablest emperor, almost, of all the list. But reposed natures may do well in youth. As it is seen in Augustus Caesar, Cosmus, Duke of Florence, Gaston de Foix,[3] and others. On the other side, heat and vivacity in age is an excellent composition for business. Young men are fitter to invent than to judge, fitter for execution than for counsel, and fitter for new projects than for settled business. For the experience of age, in things that fall within the compass of it, directeth them, but in new things abuseth them. The errors of young men are the ruin of business; but the errors of aged men amount but to this, that more might have been done, or sooner. Young men, in the conduct and manage of actions, embrace more than they can hold; stir more than they can quiet; fly to the end, without consideration of the

From Bacon's Essays, *the first edition of which appeared in 1597, with augmented and revised editions in 1612 and 1625. Bacon's essays are known for their objective, judicial style.*

1. Julius Caesar (100–44 B.C.E.) became dictator of Rome in 49 B.C.E.
2. Severus (145/6–211 C.E.) became emperor of Rome in 193 C.E. "He passed a youth full of folly, or rather of madness," according to Spartianus (*Life of Severus*).
3. Augustus Caesar (63 B.C.E.–14 C.E.) became ruler of Rome in 27 B.C.E.; Cosimo de' Medici (1519–1574) became ruler of Florence in 1537; Gaston de Foix, duke of Nemours and nephew of Louis XII of France, died in battle in 1512, at twenty-two.

means and degrees; pursue some few principles which they have chanced upon absurdly; care not to innovate,[4] which draws unknown inconveniences; use extreme remedies at first; and, that which doubleth all errors, will not acknowledge or retract them; like an unready horse that will neither stop nor turn. Men of age object too much, consult too long, adventure too little, repent too soon, and seldom drive business home to the full period, but content themselves with a mediocrity of success. Certainly it is good to compound employments of both; for that will be good for the present, because the virtues of either age may correct the defects of both; and good for succession, that young men may be learners while men in age are actors; and, lastly, good for extern accidents, because authority followeth old men, and favour and popularity youth. But for the moral part, perhaps youth will have the pre-eminence, as age hath for the politic. A certain rabbin, upon the text, *Your young men shall see visions, and your old men shall dream dreams,*[5] inferreth that young men are admitted nearer to God than old, because vision is a clearer revelation than a dream. And certainly, the more a man drinketh of the world, the more it intoxicateth; and age doth profit rather in the powers of understanding than in the virtues of the will and affections. There be some have an over-early ripeness in their years, which fadeth betimes. These are, first, such as have brittle wits, the edge whereof is soon turned; such as was Hermogenes the rhetorician, whose books are exceeding subtle, who afterwards waxed stupid.[6] A second sort is of those that have some natural dispositions which have better grace in youth than in age, such as is a fluent and luxuriant speech, which becomes youth well, but not age: so Tully saith of Hortensius, *Idem manebat, neque idem docebat.*[7] The third is of such as take too high a strain at the first, and are magnanimous more than tract of years can uphold. As was Scipio Africanus, of whom Livy saith in effect, *Ultima primis cedebant.*[8]

4. Are not careful about innovating.

5. Joel 2.28. "Rabbin" means "rabbi."

6. Hermogenes, Greek rhetorician of the 2nd century c.e., is said to have lost his memory when young.

7. "He remained the same when the same style no longer became him" (Cicero, *Brutus*); said by Cicero (or Tully) of a rival orator.

8. "His last actions were not the equal of his first" (*Heroides* 9); Bacon quotes from the poet Ovid (43 b.c.e.–17 c.e.) to express the gist of what the historian Livy (59 b.c.e.–17 c.e.) said of Africanus (236–183 or 184 b.c.e.), Roman conqueror of Africa.

Ben Jonson: *To Write Well*

For a man to write well, there are required three necessaries: to read the best authors, observe the best speakers, and much exercise of his own style. In style to consider what ought to be written, and after what manner; he

From Timber, or Discoveries, Made upon men and matter, as they have flowed each out of his daily readings, or had their reflux to his peculiar notion of the times, *printed in 1740 and containing notes, extracts, and reflections on miscellaneous subjects.*

must first think and excogitate his matter, then choose his words, and examine the weight of either. Then take care in placing and ranking both matter and words, that the composition be comely, and to do this with diligence and often. No matter how slow the style be at first, so it be laboured and accurate; seek the best, and be not glad of the froward conceits, or first words, that offer themselves to us; but judge of what we invent, and order what we approve. Repeat often what we have formerly written; which beside that it helps the consequence, and makes the juncture better, it quickens the heat of imagination, that often cools in the time of setting down, and gives it new strength, as if it grew lustier by the going back. As we see in the contention of leaping, they jump farthest, that fetch their race largest: or, as in throwing a dart or javelin, we force back our arms, to make our loose the stronger. Yet, if we have a fair gale of wind, I forbid not the steering out of our sail, so the favour of the gale deceive us not. For all that we invent doth please us in conception of birth, else we would never set it down. But the safest is to return to our judgement, and handle over again those things, the easiness of which might make them justly suspected. So did the best writers in their beginnings; they imposed upon themselves care and industry; they did nothing rashly: they obtained first to write well, and then custom made it easy and a habit. By little and little their matter shewed itself to them more plentifully; their words answered, their composition followed; and all, as in a well-ordered family, presented itself in the place. So that the sum of all is, ready writing makes not good writing; but good writing brings on ready writing: yet, when we think we have got the faculty, it is even then good to resist it; as to give a horse a check sometimes with a bit, which doth not so much stop his course, as stir his mettle. Again, whether a man's genius is best able to reach thither, it should more and more contend, lift, and dilate itself, as men of low stature raise themselves on their toes, and so oft-times get even, if not eminent. Besides, as it is fit for grown and able writers to stand of themselves, and work with their own strength, to trust and endeavour by their own faculties: so it is fit for the beginner and learner to study others and the best. For the mind and memory are more sharply exercised in comprehending another man's things than our own; and such as accustom themselves, and are familiar with the best authors, shall ever and anon find somewhat of them in themselves, and in the expression of their minds, even when they feel it not, be able to utter something like theirs, which hath an authority above their own. Nay, sometimes it is the reward of a man's study, the praise of quoting another man fitly: and though a man be more prone, and able for one kind of writing than another, yet he must exercise all. For as in an instrument, so in style, there must be a harmony and consent of parts.

JOHN DONNE: *No Man Is an Island*

No man is an island, entire of itself; every man is a piece of the continent, a part of the main.[1] If a clod be washed away by the sea, Europe is the less, as well as if a promontory were, as well as if a manor of thy friend's or of thine own were. Any man's death diminishes me, because I am involved in mankind; and therefore never send to know for whom the bell tolls; it tolls for thee.[2]

Originally given as a sermon; later published as Meditation 17 *of Donne's* Devotions upon Emergent Occasions *(1623).*

1. Mainland.
2. Church bells were rung to mark the death of parishoners.

SAMUEL JOHNSON: *The Pyramids*

Of the wall [of China] it is very easy to assign the motives. It secured a wealthy and timorous nation from the incursions of Barbarians, whose unskillfulness in arts made it easier for them to supply their wants by rapine than by industry, and who from time to time poured in upon the habitations of peaceful commerce, as vultures descend upon domestic fowl. Their celerity and fierceness made the wall necessary, and their ignorance made it efficacious.

But for the pyramids no reason has ever been given adequate to the cost and labor of the work. The narrowness of the chambers proves that it could afford no retreat from enemies, and treasures might have been reposited at far less expense with equal security. It seems to have been erected only in compliance with that hunger of imagination which preys incessantly upon life, and must be always appeased by some employment. Those who have already all that they can enjoy, must enlarge their desires. He that has built for use, till use is supplied, must begin to build for vanity, and extend his plan to the utmost power of human performance, that he may not be soon reduced to form another wish.

I consider this mighty structure as a monument of the insufficiency of human enjoyments. A king, whose power is unlimited, and whose treasures surmount all real and imaginary wants, is compelled to solace, by the erection of a pyramid, the satiety of dominion and tastelessness of pleasures, and to amuse the tediousness of declining life, by seeing thousands laboring without end, and one stone, for no purpose, laid upon another. Whoever thou art, that, not content with a moderate condition, imaginest happiness in royal magnificence, and dreamest that command or riches can feed the appetite of novelty with perpetual gratifications, survey the pyramids, and confess thy folly!

From Rasselas *(1759), a didactic tale about an emperor's son who grows weary of life in the "happy valley" where he was born and who sets out to study the conditions of other men's lives.*

Benjamin Franklin: from *Poor Richard's Almanack*

Light purse, heavy heart.   1733
He's a fool that makes his doctor his heir.
Love well, whip well.

Hunger never saw bad bread.
Fools make feasts, and wise men eat 'em.
He that lies down with dogs, shall rise up with fleas.
He is ill clothed, who is bare of virtue.
There is no little enemy.

Without justice courage is weak.   1734
Where there's marriage without love, there will be love
    without marriage.
Do good to thy friend to keep him, to thy enemy to gain him.
He that cannot obey, cannot command.
Marry your son when you will, but your daughter when you can.

Approve not of him who commends all you say.   1735
Necessity never made a good bargain.
Be slow in choosing a friend, slower in changing.
Three may keep a secret, if two of them are dead.
Deny self for self's sake.
To be humble to superiors is duty, to equals courtesy, to inferiors
    nobleness.

Fish and visitors stink in three days.   1736
Do not do that which you would not have known.
Bargaining has neither friends nor relations.
Now I've a sheep and a cow, every body bids me good morrow.
God helps them that help themselves.
He that speaks much, is much mistaken.
God heals, and the doctor takes the fees.

There are no ugly loves, nor handsome prisons.   1737
Three good meals a day is bad living.

Who has deceiv'd thee so oft as thyself?   1738
Read much, but not many books.
Let thy vices die before thee.

From Poor Richard's Almanack, *the composite name given to the yearly almanacs Franklin
printed between 1732 and 1757. From 1732 to 1747 their title was* Poor Richard; *from
1748 on they were called* Poor Richard Improved.

He that falls in love with himself, will have no rivals.   1739
Sin is not hurtful because it is forbidden, but it is forbidden because
    it's hurtful.

An empty bag cannot stand upright.   1740

Learn of the skilful: he that teaches himself, hath a fool for his
    master.   1741

Death takes no bribes.   1742

An old man in a house is a good sign.   1744
Fear God, and your enemies will fear you.

He's a fool that cannot conceal his wisdom.   1745
Many complain of their memory, few of their judgment.

When the well's dry, we know the worth of water.   1746
The sting of a reproach is the truth of it.

Write injuries in dust, benefits in marble.   1747

Nine men in *ten* are suicides.   1749
A man in a passion rides a mad horse.

He is a governor that governs his passions, and he is a servant that
    serves them.   1750
Sorrow is good for nothing but sin.

Calamity and prosperity are the touchstones of integrity.   1752
Generous minds are all of kin.

Haste makes waste.   1753

The doors of wisdom are never shut.   1755

The way to be safe, is never to be secure.   1757

William Blake: *Proverbs of Hell*

In seed time learn, in harvest teach, in winter enjoy.
Drive your cart and your plough over the bones of the dead.
The road of excess leads to the palace of wisdom.
Prudence is a rich, ugly old maid courted by Incapacity.
He who desires but acts not, breeds pestilence.   5
The cut worm forgives the plough.
Dip him in the river who loves water.
A fool sees not the same tree that a wise man sees.
He whose face gives no light, shall never become a star.
Eternity is in love with the productions of time.   10
The busy bee has no time for sorrow.
The hours of folly are measur'd by the clock; but of wisdom, no clock can
    measure.
All wholesome food is caught without a net or a trap.
Bring out number, weight, and measure in a year of dearth.
No bird soars too high, if he soars with his own wings.   15
A dead body revenges not injuries.
The most sublime act is to set another before you.
If the fool would persist in his folly he would become wise.
Folly is the cloak of knavery.
Shame is Pride's cloak.   20
Prisons are built with stones of Law, brothels with bricks of Religion.
The pride of the peacock is the glory of God.
The lust of the goat is the bounty of God.
The wrath of the lion is the wisdom of God.
The nakedness of woman is the work of God.   25
Excess of sorrow laughs. Excess of joy weeps.
The roaring of lions, the howling of wolves, the raging of the stormy sea, and
    the destructive sword are portions of eternity too great for the eye of man.
The fox condemns the trap, not himself.
Joys impregnate. Sorrows bring forth.
Let man wear the fell of the lion, woman the fleece of the sheep.   30
The bird a nest, the spider a web, man friendship.
The selfish, smiling fool, and the sullen, frowning fool shall be both thought
    wise, that they may be a rod.
What is now proved was once only imagin'd.
The rat, the mouse, the fox, the rabbit watch the roots; the lion, the tiger, the
    horse, the elephant watch the fruits.
The cistern contains: the fountain overflows.   35
One thought fills immensity.
Always be ready to speak your mind, and a base man will avoid you.

From The Marriage of Heaven and Hell (1790), *a book in which Blake sets forth his doctrine of Contraries.*

Everything possible to be believ'd is an image of truth.

The eagle never lost so much time as when he submitted to learn of the crow.

40   The fox provides for himself; but God provides for the lion.

Think in the morning. Act in the noon. Eat in the evening. Sleep in the night.

He who has suffer'd you to impose on him, knows you.

As the plough follows words, so God rewards prayers.

The tigers of wrath are wiser than the horses of instruction.

45   Expect poison from the standing water.

You never know what is enough unless you know what is more than enough.

Listen to the fool's reproach! it is a kingly title!

The eyes of fire, the nostrils of air, the mouth of water, the beard of earth.

The weak in courage is strong in cunning.

50   The apple tree never asks the beech how he shall grow; nor the lion, the horse,
       how he shall take his prey.

The thankful receiver bears a plentiful harvest.

If others had not been foolish, we should be so.

The soul of sweet delight can never be defil'd.

When thou seest an eagle, thou seest a portion of Genius; lift up thy head!

55   As the caterpillar chooses the fairest leaves to lay her eggs on, so the priest
       lays his curse on the fairest joys.

To create a little flower is the labor of ages.

Damn braces. Bless relaxes.

The best wine is the oldest, the best water the newest.

Prayers plough not! Praises reap not!

60   Joys laugh not! Sorrows weep not!

The head Sublime, the heart Pathos, the genitals Beauty, the hands and feet
       Proportion.

As the air to a bird or the sea to a fish, so is contempt to the contemptible.

The crow wish'd everything was black, the owl that everything was white.

Exuberance is Beauty.

65   If the lion was advised by the fox, he would be cunning.

Improvement makes straight roads; but the crooked roads without
       improvement are roads of Genius.

Sooner murder an infant in its cradle than nurse unacted desires.

Where man is not, nature is barren.

Truth can never be told so as to be understood, and not be believ'd.

70   Enough! or Too much.

AMBROSE BIERCE: from *The Devil's Dictionary*

abdication, *n.* An act whereby a sovereign attests his sense of the high tem-
    perature of the throne.

abscond, *v.i.* To "move in a mysterious way," commonly with the property of
    another.

From The Devil's Dictionary (1906).

absent, *adj.* Peculiarly exposed to the tooth of detraction; vilified; hopelessly in the wrong; superseded in the consideration and affection of another.

accident, *n.* An inevitable occurrence due to the action of immutable natural laws.

accordion, *n.* An instrument in harmony with the sentiments of an assassin.

achievement, *n.* The death of endeavor and the birth of disgust.

admiration, *n.* Our polite recognition of another's resemblance to ourselves.

alone, *adj.* In bad company.

applause, *n.* The echo of a platitude.

ardor, *n.* The quality that distinguishes love without knowledge.

bore, *n.* A person who talks when you wish him to listen.

cemetery, *n.* An isolated suburban spot where mourners match lies, poets write at a target and stone-cutters spell for a wager. The inscription following will serve to illustrate the success attained in these Olympian games:

> His virtues were so conspicuous that his enemies, unable to overlook them, denied them, and his friends, to whose loose lives they were a rebuke, represented them as vices. They are here commemorated by his family, who shared them.

childhood, *n.* The period of human life intermediate between the idiocy of infancy and the folly of youth—two removes from the sin of manhood and three from the remorse of age.

Christian, *n.* One who believes that the New Testament is a divinely inspired book admirably suited to the spiritual needs of his neighbor. One who follows the teachings of Christ in so far as they are not inconsistent with a life of sin.

compulsion, *n.* The eloquence of power.

congratulation, *n.* The civility of envy.

conservative, *n.* A statesman who is enamored of existing evils, as distinguished from the Liberal, who wishes to replace them with others.

consult, *v.t.* To seek another's approval of a course already decided on.

contempt, *n.* The feeling of a prudent man for an enemy who is too formidable safely to be opposed.

coward, *n.* One who in a perilous emergency thinks with his legs.

debauchee, *n.* One who has so earnestly pursued pleasure that he has had the misfortune to overtake it.

destiny, *n.* A tyrant's authority for crime and a fool's excuse for failure.

diplomacy, *n.* The patriotic art of lying for one's country.

distance, *n.* The only thing that the rich are willing for the poor to call theirs and keep.

duty, *n.* That which sternly impels us in the direction of profit, along the line of desire.

education, *n.* That which discloses to the wise and disguises from the foolish their lack of understanding.

erudition, *n.* Dust shaken out of a book into an empty skull.

extinction, *n.* The raw material out of which theology created the future state.

faith, *n.* Belief without evidence in what is told by one who speaks without knowledge, of things without parallel.

genealogy, *n.* An account of one's descent from an ancestor who did not particularly care to trace his own.

ghost, *n.* The outward and visible sign of an inward fear.

habit, *n.* A shackle for the free.

heaven, *n.* A place where the wicked cease from troubling you with talk of their personal affairs, and the good listen with attention while you expound your own.

historian, *n.* A broad-gauge gossip.

hope, *n.* Desire and expectation rolled into one.

hypocrite, *n.* One who, professing virtues that he does not respect, secures the advantage of seeming to be what he despises.

impiety, *n.* Your irreverence toward my deity.

impunity, *n.* Wealth.

language, *n.* The music with which we charm the serpents guarding another's treasure.

logic, *n.* The art of thinking and reasoning in strict accordance with the limitations and incapacities of the human misunderstanding. The basis of logic is the syllogism, consisting of a major and a minor premise and a conclusion—thus:

> *Major Premise:* Sixty men can do a piece of work sixty times as quickly as one man.
> *Minor Premise:* One man can dig a post-hole in sixty seconds; therefore—
> *Conclusion:* Sixty men can dig a post-hole in one second. This may be called the syllogism arithmetical, in which, by combining logic and mathematics, we obtain a double certainty and are twice blessed.

love, *n.* A temporary insanity curable by marriage or by removal of the patient from the influences under which he incurred the disorder. This disease, like *caries* and many other ailments, is prevalent only among civilized races living under artificial conditions; barbarous nations breathing pure air and eating simple food enjoy immunity from its ravages. It is sometimes fatal, but more frequently to the physician than to the patient.

miracle, *n.* An act or event out of the order of nature and unaccountable, as beating a normal hand of four kings and an ace with four aces and a king.

monkey, *n.* An arboreal animal which makes itself at home in genealogical trees.

mouth, *n.* In man, the gateway to the soul; in woman, the outlet of the heart.

non-combatant, *n.* A dead Quaker.

platitude, *n.* The fundamental element and special glory of popular literature. A thought that snores in words that smoke. The wisdom of a million fools in the diction of a dullard. A fossil sentiment in artificial rock. A moral without the fable. All that is mortal of a departed truth. A demitasse of milk-and-morality. The Pope's-nose of a featherless peacock. A jelly-fish withering on the shore of the sea of thought. The cackle surviving the egg. A dessicated epigram.

pray, *v.* To ask that the laws of the universe be annulled in behalf of a single petitioner confessedly unworthy.

presidency, *n.* The greased pig in the field game of American politics.

prude, *n.* A bawd hiding behind the back of her demeanor.

rapacity, *n.* Providence without industry. The thrift of power.

reason, *v.i.* To weigh probabilities in the scales of desire.

religion, *n.* A daughter of Hope and Fear, explaining to Ignorance the nature of the Unknowable.

resolute, *adj.* Obstinate in a course that we approve.

retaliation, *n.* The natural rock upon which is reared the Temple of Law.

saint, *n.* A dead sinner revised and edited.

> The Duchess of Orleans relates that the irreverent old calumniator, Marshal Villeroi, who in his youth had known St. Francis de Sales, said, on hearing him called saint: "I am delighted to hear that Monsieur de Sales is a saint. He was fond of saying indelicate things, and used to cheat at cards. In other respects he was a perfect gentleman, though a fool."

valor, *n.* A soldierly compound of vanity, duty and the gambler's hope:

> "Why have you halted?" roared the commander of a division at Chicka-mauga, who had ordered a charge; "move forward, sir, at once."
> "General," said the commander of the delinquent brigade, "I am persuaded that any further display of valor by my troops will bring them into collision with the enemy."

MARY WOLLSTONECRAFT: from *A Vindication of the Rights of Woman*

The education of women has, of late, been more attended to than formerly; yet they are still reckoned a frivolous sex, and ridiculed or pitied by the writers who endeavour by satire or instruction to improve them. It is acknowledged that they spend many of the first years of their lives in acquiring a smattering of accomplishments; meanwhile strength of body and mind are sacrificed to libertine notions of beauty, to the desire of establishing themselves,—the only way women can rise in the world,—by marriage. And this desire making mere animals of them, when they marry they act as such children may be expected to act:—they dress; they paint, and nickname God's creatures.[1]—Surely these weak beings are only fit for a seraglio!—Can they be expected to govern a family with judgment, or take care of the poor babes whom they bring into the world?

From A Vindication of the Rights of Woman *(1792), written after the publication of* Thomas Paine's A Vindication of the Rights of Man *(1790) as an argument for the extension of political, legal, and educational rights to women.*

1. In Shakespeare's *Hamlet* (III.i.143–45), the hero accuses Ophelia: "You jig, you amble, and you lisp, and nickname God's creatures, and make your wantonness your ignorance"—a sequence of feminine faults that Wollstonecraft echoes.

If then it can be fairly deduced from the present conduct of the sex, from the prevalent fondness for pleasure which takes place of ambition and those nobler passions that open and enlarge the soul; that the instruction which women have hitherto received has only tended, with the constitution of civil society, to render them insignificant objects of desire—mere propagators of fools!—if it can be proved that in aiming to accomplish them, without cultivating their understandings, they are taken out of their sphere of duties, and made ridiculous and useless when the short-lived bloom of beauty is over,[2] I presume that *rational* men will excuse me for endeavouring to persuade them to become more masculine and respectable.

Indeed the word masculine is only a bugbear: there is little reason to fear that women will acquire too much courage or fortitude; for their apparent inferiority with respect to bodily strength, must render them, in some degree, dependent on men in the various relations of life, but why should it be increased by prejudices that give a sex to virtue, and confound simple truths with sensual reveries?

Women are, in fact, so much degraded by mistaken notions of female excellence, that I do not mean to add a paradox when I assert, that this artificial weakness produces a propensity to tyrannize, and gives birth to cunning, the natural opponent of strength, which leads them to play off those contemptible infantine airs that undermine esteem even whilst they excite desire. Let men become more chaste and modest, and if women do not grow wiser in the same ratio, it will be clear that they have weaker understandings. It seems scarcely necessary to say, that I now speak of the sex in general. Many individuals have more sense than their male relatives; and, as nothing preponderates where there is a constant struggle or an equilibrium, without it has[3] naturally more gravity, some women govern their husbands without degrading themselves, because intellect will always govern.

2. "A lively writer, I cannot recollect his name, asks what business women turned of forty have to do in the world?" [Wollstonecraft's note].

3. Unless it has.

John Henry Newman: *Knowledge and Virtue*

Knowledge is one thing, virtue is another; good sense is not conscience, refinement is not humility, nor is largeness and justness of view faith. Philosophy, however enlightened, however profound, gives no command over the passions, no influential motives, no vivifying principles. Liberal Education makes not the Christian, not the Catholic, but the gentleman. It is well to be a gentleman, it is well to have a cultivated intellect, a delicate taste, a candid, eq-

From The Idea of a University Defined and Illustrated *(1852), Newman's classic statement on the role and value of education. The book emerged from Newman's work as rector of a new Catholic University in Dublin and his various lectures and articles on university education.*

uitable, dispassionate mind, a noble and courteous bearing in the conduct of life—these are the connatural qualities of a large knowledge; they are the objects of a University; I am advocating, I shall illustrate and insist upon them; but still, I repeat, they are no guarantee for sanctity or even for conscientiousness, they may attach to the man of the world, to the profligate, to the heartless, pleasant, alas, and attractive as he shows when decked out in them. Taken by themselves, they do but seem to be what they are not; they look like virtue at a distance, but they are detected by close observers, and on the long run; and hence it is that they are popularly accused of pretense and hypocrisy, not, I repeat, from their own fault, but because their professors and their admirers persist in taking them for what they are not, and are officious in arrogating for them a praise to which they have no claim. Quarry the granite rock with razors, or moor the vessel with a thread of silk; then may you hope with such keen and delicate instruments as human knowledge and human reason to contend against those giants, the passion and the pride of man.

Abraham Lincoln: *The Gettysburg Address*

Four score and seven years ago our fathers brought forth on this continent, a new nation, conceived in Liberty, and dedicated to the proposition that all men are created equal.

Now we are engaged in a great civil war, testing whether that nation, or any nation so conceived and so dedicated, can long endure. We are met on a great battlefield of that war. We have come to dedicate a portion of that field, as a final resting place for those who here gave their lives that that nation might live. It is altogether fitting and proper that we should do this.

But, in a larger sense, we can not dedicate—we can not consecrate—we can not hallow—this ground. The brave men, living and dead, who struggled here, have consecrated it, far above our poor power to add or detract. The world will little note, nor long remember what we say here, but it can never forget what they did here. It is for us the living, rather, to be dedicated here to the unfinished work which they who fought here have thus far so nobly advanced. It is rather for us to be here dedicated to the great task remaining before us—that from these honored dead we take increased devotion to that cause for which they gave the last full measure of devotion—that we here highly resolve that these dead shall not have died in vain—that this nation, under God, shall have a new birth of freedom—and that government of the people, by the people, for the people, shall not perish from the earth.

A presidential address delivered on November 19, 1863, during the height of the American Civil War, on the battlefield at Gettysburg, Pennsylvania.

Ernest Hemingway: from A *Farewell to Arms*

I was always embarrassed by the words sacred, glorious, and sacrifice and the expression in vain. We had heard them, sometimes standing in the rain almost out of earshot, so that only the shouted words came through, and had read them, on proclamations that were slapped up by billposters over other proclamations, now for a long time, and I had seen nothing sacred, and the things that were glorious had no glory and the sacrifices were like the stockyards at Chicago if nothing was done with the meat except to bury it. There were many words that you could not stand to hear and finally only the names of places had dignity. Certain numbers were the same way and certain dates and these with the names of places were all you could say and have them mean anything. Abstract words such as glory, honor, courage, or hallow were obscene beside the concrete names of villages, the numbers of roads, the names of rivers, the numbers of regiments and the dates.

From A Farewell to Arms *(1929), a novel depicting the tragedy and destructiveness, personal and cultural, of World War I.*

E. B. White: *Progress and Change*

In resenting progress and change, a man lays himself open to censure. I suppose the explanation of anyone's defending anything as rudimentary and cramped as a Pullman berth is that such things are associated with an earlier period in one's life and that this period in retrospect seems a happy one. People who favor progress and improvements are apt to be people who have had a tough enough time without any extra inconvenience. Reactionaries who pout at innovations are apt to be well-heeled sentimentalists who had the breaks. Yet for all that, there is always a subtle danger in life's refinements, a dim degeneracy in progress. I have just been refining the room in which I sit, yet I sometimes doubt that a writer should refine or improve his workroom by so much as a dictionary: one thing leads to another and the first thing you know he has a stuffed chair and is fast asleep in it. Half a man's life is devoted to what he calls improvements, yet the original had some quality which is lost in the process. There was a fine natural spring of water on this place when I bought it. Our drinking water had to be lugged in a pail, from a wet glade of alder and tamarack. I visited the spring often in those first years, and had friends there—a frog, a woodcock, and an eel which had churned its way all the way up through the pasture creek to enjoy the luxury of pure water. In the normal course of development, the spring was rocked up, fitted with a concrete curb, a copper pipe, and an electric pump. I have visited it only once or twice since. This year my only gesture was the purely perfunctory one of send-

From White's regular column, "One Man's Meat," in Harper's Magazine *(December 1938), an American monthly founded in 1850 to explore issues in politics, science, and the arts.*

ing a sample to the state bureau of health for analysis. I felt cheap, as though I were smelling an old friend's breath.

JOHN UPDIKE: *Beer Can*

This seems to be an era of gratuitous inventions and negative improvements. Consider the beer can. It was beautiful—as beautiful as the clothespin, as inevitable as the wine bottle, as dignified and reassuring as the fire hydrant. A tranquil cylinder of delightfully resonant metal, it could be opened in an instant, requiring only the application of a handy gadget freely dispensed by every grocer. Who can forget the small, symmetrical thrill of those two triangular punctures, the dainty *pffff*, the little crest of suds that foamed eagerly in the exultation of release? Now we are given, instead, a top beetling with an ugly, shmoo-shaped "tab,"[1] which, after fiercely resisting the tugging, bleeding fingers of the thirsty man, threatens his lips with a dangerous and hideous hole. However, we have discovered a way to thwart Progress, usually so unthwartable. *Turn the beer can upside down and open the bottom.* The bottom is still the way the top used to be. True, this operation gives the beer an unsettling jolt, and the sight of a consistently inverted beer can might make people edgy, not to say queasy. But the latter difficulty could be eliminated if manufacturers would design cans that looked the same whichever end was up, like playing cards. What we need is Progress with an escape hatch.

Originally published in the New Yorker *(January 18, 1964), an American magazine of literature, politics, the arts, and culture.*

1. The first tabs, made of plastic, reminded Updike of shmoos, bloblike creatures invented by Al Capp in the comic strip *Li'l Abner.*

TERRY TEMPEST WILLIAMS: *River Music*

River. The river is brown is red is green is turquoise. On any given day, the river is light, liquid light, a traveling mirror in the desert.

> Love this river, stay by it, learn from it. . . . It seemed to him that whoever understood this river and its secrets, would understand much more, many secrets, all secrets. —SIDDHARTHA

I love sitting by the river. A deep calm washes over me in the face of this fluid continuity where it always appears the same, yet I know each moment of the Rio Colorado is new.

"Have you learned that secret from the river; that there is no such thing as time?"

From the author's 2001 book Red: Passion and Patience in the Desert.

May 28, 2000—a relatively uneventful day. A few herons fly by, a few mergansers. Two rafts float through the redrock corridor. I wave. They wave back. One man is playing a harmonica, the oars resting on his lap as he coasts through flat water.

Sweet echoes continue to reach me.

I sit on the fine pink sand, still damp from high water days, and watch the river flow, the clouds shift, and the colors of the cliffs deepen from orange to red to maroon.

Present. Completely present. My eyes focus on one current in particular, a small eddy that keeps circling back on itself. Around and around, a cottonwood leaf spins; a breeze gives it a nudge, and it glides downriver, this river braided with light.

The eddy continues to coil the currents.

Boredom could catch up with me. But it never does, only the music, river music, the continual improvisation of water. Perhaps the difference between repetition and boredom lies in our willingness to believe in surprise, the subtle shifts of form that loom large in a trained and patient eye.

I think about a night of lovemaking with the man I live with, how it is that a body so known and familiar can still take my breath all the way down, then rise and fall, the river that flows through me, through him, this river, the Colorado River keeps moving, beckoning us to do the same, nothing stagnant, not today, not ever, as my mind moves as the river moves.

"To find one's own equilibrium" he tells me this morning by the river. "That is what I want to learn."

He finds rocks that stand on their own and bear the weight of others. An exercise in balance and form. Down river, I watch him place a thin slab of sandstone on a rock pedestal, perfectly poised. He continues placing pebbles on top, testing the balance. In another sculpture, he leans two flat rocks against each other like hands about to pray.

The stillness of stones, their silence, is a rest note against the music of the river.

Our shadows on the moving water are no different than those cast by the boulders on the bank. Composition. What is the composition of the river, these boulders, these birds, our own flesh? What is the composition of a poem except a series of musical lines?

River. River music. Day and night. Shadow and light. The roar and roll of cobbles being churned by the current is strong. This river has muscle when flexed against stone carved stone, stones that appear as waves of rock, secret knowledge known only through engagement. I am no longer content to sit, but stand and walk, walk to the river, enter the river, surrender my body to water now red, red is the Colorado, blood of my veins.

Questions on An Album of Styles

1. For any selection: What kinds of words does the writer use? From what sources (Anglo-Saxon, Latin, Greek, French, and so on)? (Most good collegiate dictionaries list word origins.) What effects are created by the writer's choice of words?

2. For any selection: What types of sentences does the writer prefer? Long or short? Loose or carefully balanced? What effects does the writer achieve with sentence form and length?

3. For any selection: What metaphors or similes does the writer use? Are they fundamental to the argument or primarily ornamental?

4. For any selection: What is the writer's characteristic voice or tone? What kind of person do you imagine this writer to be?

5. Which selection do you like best? Why? Identify and analyze those aspects of style that create this positive impression.

Nature and the Environment

Rachel Carson   *Tides*

> In every country the moon keeps ever the rule of
> alliance with the sea which it once for all has agreed
> upon.   — The Venerable Bede[1]

THERE IS NO drop of water in the ocean, not even in the deepest parts of the abyss, that does not know and respond to the mysterious forces that create the tide. No other force that affects the sea is so strong. Compared with the tide the wind-created waves are surface movements felt, at most, no more than a hundred fathoms below the surface. So, despite their impressive sweep, are the planetary currents, which seldom involve more than the upper several hundred fathoms. The masses of water affected by the tidal movement are enormous, as will be clear from one example. Into one small bay on the east coast of North America—Passamaquoddy—2 billion tons of water are carried by the tidal currents twice each day; into the whole Bay of Fundy, 100 billion tons.

Here and there we find dramatic illustration of the fact that the tides affect the whole ocean, from its surface to its floor. The meeting of opposing tidal currents in the Strait of Messina creates whirlpools (one of them is Charybdis of classical fame)[2] which so deeply stir the waters of the strait that fish bearing all the marks of abyssal existence, their eyes atrophied or abnormally large, their bodies studded with phosphorescent organs, frequently are cast up on the lighthouse beach, and the whole area yields a rich collection of deep-sea fauna for the Institute of Marine Biology at Messina.

The tides are a response of the mobile waters of the ocean to the pull of the moon and the more distant sun. In theory, there is a gravitational attraction between every drop of sea water and even the outermost star of the universe. In practice, however, the pull of the remote stars is so slight as to be

A chapter from Carson's best-selling book The Sea Around Us *(1951), which won the National Book Award and the John Burroughs Medal, the latter awarded annually to a distinguished book of natural history.*

1. British Benedictine monk and scholar (673–735), canonized in 1899.
2. The Strait of Messina lies between Sicily and the Italian mainland; thought to be the original of Scylla and Charybdis, i.e., the rocks and the whirlpool in Homer's *Odyssey*.

obliterated in the vaster movements by which the ocean yields to the moon and the sun. Anyone who has lived near tidewater knows that the moon, far more than the sun, controls the tides. He has noticed that, just as the moon rises later each day by fifty minutes, on the average, than the day before, so, in most places, the time of high tide is correspondingly later each day. And as the moon waxes and wanes in its monthly cycle, so the height of the tide varies. Twice each month, when the moon is a mere thread of silver in the sky, and again when it is full, we have the highest of the high tides, called the springs. At these times sun, moon, and earth are directly in line and the pull of the two heavenly bodies is added together to bring the water high on the beaches, and send its surf leaping upward against the sea cliffs, and draw a brimming tide into the harbors so that the boats float high beside their wharfs. And twice each month, at the quarters of the moon, when sun, moon, and earth lie at the apexes of a triangle, and the pull of sun and moon are opposed, we have the least tides of the lunar month, called the neaps.

That the sun, with a mass 27 million times that of the moon, should have less influence over the tides than a small satellite of the earth is at first surprising. But in the mechanics of the universe, nearness counts for more than distant mass, and when all the mathematical calculations have been made we find that the moon's power over the tides is more than twice that of the sun.

The tides are enormously more complicated than all this would suggest. The influence of sun and moon is constantly changing, varying with the phases of the moon, with the distance of moon and sun from the earth, and with the position of each to north or south of the equator. They are complicated further by the fact that every body of water, whether natural or artificial, has its own period of oscillation. Disturb its waters and they will move with a seesaw or rocking motion, with the most pronounced movement at the ends of the container, the least motion at the center. Tidal scientists now believe that the ocean contains a number of "basins," each with its own period of oscillation determined by its length and depth. The disturbance that sets the water in motion is the attracting force of the moon and sun. But the kind of motion, that is, the period of the swing of the water, depends upon the physical dimensions of the basin. What this means in terms of actual tides we shall presently see.

The tides present a striking paradox, and the essence of it is this: the force that sets them in motion is cosmic, lying wholly outside the earth and presumably acting impartially on all parts of the globe, but the nature of the tide at any particular place is a local matter, with astonishing differences occurring within a very short geographic distance. When we spend a long summer holiday at the seashore we may become aware that the tide in our cove behaves very differently from that at a friend's place twenty miles up the coast, and is strikingly different from what we may have known in some other locality. If we are summering on Nantucket Island our boating and swimming will be little disturbed by the tides, for the range between high water and low is only about a foot or two. But if we choose to vacation near the upper part of the Bay of Fundy, we must accommodate ourselves to a rise and fall of 40 to 50 feet, although both places are included within the same body of water—the Gulf of

Maine. Or if we spend our holiday on Chesapeake Bay we may find that the time of high water each day varies by as much as 12 hours in different places on the shores of the same bay.

The truth of the matter is that local topography is all-important in determining the features that to our minds make "the tide." The attractive force of the heavenly bodies sets the water in motion, but how, and how far, and how strongly it will rise depend on such things as the slope of the bottom, the depth of a channel, or the width of a bay's entrance.

If the history of the earth's tides should one day be written by some observer of the universe, it would no doubt be said that they reached their greatest grandeur and power in the younger days of Earth, and that they slowly grew feebler and less imposing until one day they ceased to be. For the tides were not always as they are today, and as with all that is earthly, their days are numbered.

In the days when the earth was young, the coming in of the tide must have been a stupendous event. If the moon was * * * formed by the tearing away of a part of the outer crust of the earth, it must have remained for a time very close to its parent. Its present position is the consequence of being pushed farther and farther away from the earth for some 2 billion years. When it was half its present distance from the earth, its power over the ocean tides was eight times as great as now, and the tidal range may even then have been several hundred feet on certain shores. But when the earth was only a few million years old, assuming that the deep ocean basins were then formed, the sweep of the tides must have been beyond all comprehension. Twice each day, the fury of the incoming waters would inundate all the margins of the continents. The range of the surf must have been enormously extended by the reach of the tides, so that the waves would batter the crests of high cliffs and sweep inland to erode the continents. The fury of such tides would contribute not a little to the general bleakness and grimness and uninhabitability of the young earth.

10   Under such conditions, no living thing could exist on the shores or pass beyond them, and, had conditions not changed, it is reasonable to suppose that life would have evolved no further than the fishes. But over the millions of years the moon has receded, driven away by the friction of the tides it creates. The very movement of the water over the bed of the ocean, over the shallow edges of the continents, and over the inland seas carries within itself the power that is slowly destroying the tides, for tidal friction is gradually slowing down the rotation of the earth. In those early days we have spoken of, it took the earth a much shorter time—perhaps only about 4 hours—to make a complete rotation on its axis. Since then, the spinning of the globe has been so greatly slowed that a rotation now requires, as everyone knows, about 24 hours. This retarding will continue, according to mathematicians, until the day is about 50 times as long as it is now.

And all the while the tidal friction will be exerting a second effect, pushing the moon farther away, just as it has already pushed it out more than 200,000 miles. As the moon recedes, it will, of course, have less power over

the tides and they will grow weaker. It will also take the moon longer to complete its orbit around the earth. When finally the length of the day and of the
month coincide, the moon will no longer rotate relatively to the earth, and
there will be no lunar tides.

All this, of course, will require time on a scale the mind finds it difficult to
conceive, and before it happens it is quite probable that the human race will
have vanished from the earth. This may seem, then, like a Wellsian fantasy[3] of
a world so remote that we may dismiss it from our thoughts. But already, even
in our allotted fraction of earthly time, we can see some of the effects of these
cosmic processes. Our day is believed to be several seconds longer than that of
Babylonian times. Britain's Astronomer Royal recently called the attention of
the American Philosophical Society to the fact that the world will soon have to
choose between two kinds of time. The tide-induced lengthening of the day
has already complicated the problems of human systems of keeping time. Conventional clocks, geared to the earth's rotation, do not show the effect of the
lengthening days. New atomic clocks now being constructed will show actual
time and will differ from other clocks.

Although the tides have become tamer, and their range is now measured
in tens instead of hundreds of feet, mariners are nevertheless greatly concerned not only with the stages of the tide and the set of the tidal currents, but
with the many violent movements and disturbances of the sea that are indirectly related to the tides. Nothing the human mind has invented can tame a
tide rip or control the rhythm of the water's ebb and flow, and the most modern instruments cannot carry a vessel over a shoal until the tide has brought a
sufficient depth of water over it. Even the *Queen Mary* waits for slack water to
come to her pier in New York; otherwise the set of the tidal current might
swing her against the pier with enough force to crush it. On the Bay of Fundy,
because of the great range of tide, harbor activities follow a pattern as rhythmic as the tides themselves, for vessels can come to the docks to take on or
discharge cargo during only a few hours on each tide, leaving promptly to
avoid being stranded in mud at low water.

In the confinement of narrow passages or when opposed by contrary
winds and swells, the tidal currents often move with uncontrollable violence,
creating some of the most dangerous waterways of the world. It is only necessary to read the Coast Pilots and Sailing Directions for various parts of the
world to understand the menace of such tidal currents to navigation.

"Vessels around the Aleutians are in more danger from tidal currents than
from any other cause, save the lack of surveys," says the postwar edition of the
Alaska Pilot. Through Unalga and Akutan Passes, which are among the most-
used routes for vessels entering the Bering Sea from the Pacific, strong tidal
currents pour, making their force felt well offshore and setting vessels
unexpectedly against the rocks. Through Akun Strait the flood tide has the ve-
locity of a mountain torrent, with dangerous swirls and over-falls. In each of
these passes the tide will raise heavy, choppy seas if opposed by wind or swells.

15

3. H. G. Wells (1866–1946), British author whose works include science fiction.

"Vessels must be prepared to take seas aboard," warns the *Pilot,* for a 15-foot wave of a tide rip may suddenly rise and sweep across a vessel, and more than one man has been carried off to his death in this way.

On the opposite side of the world, the tide setting eastward from the open Atlantic presses between the islands of the Shetlands and Orkneys into the North Sea, and on the ebb returns through the same narrow passages. At certain stages of the tide these waters are dotted with dangerous eddies, with strange upward domings, or with sinister pits or depressions. Even in calm weather boats are warned to avoid the eddies of Pentland Firth, which are known as the Swilkie; and with an ebb tide and a northwest wind the heavy breaking seas of the Swilkie are a menace to vessels "which few, having once experienced, would be rash enough to encounter a second time."

* * *

The influence of the tide over the affairs of sea creatures as well as men may be seen all over the world. The billions upon billions of sessile animals, like oysters, mussels, and barnacles, owe their very existence to the sweep of the tides, which brings them the food which they are unable to go in search of. By marvelous adaptations of form and structure, the inhabitants of the world between the tide lines are enabled to live in a zone where the danger of being dried up is matched against the danger of being washed away, where for every enemy that comes by sea there is another that comes by land, and where the most delicate of living tissues must somehow withstand the assault of storm waves that have the power to shift tons of rock or to crack the hardest granite.

The most curious and incredibly delicate adaptations, however, are the ones by which the breeding rhythm of certain marine animals is timed to coincide with the phases of the moon and the stages of the tide. In Europe it has been well established that the spawning activities of oysters reach their peak on the spring tides, which are about two days after the full or the new moon. In the waters of northern Africa there is a sea urchin that, on the nights when the moon is full and apparently only then, releases its reproductive cells into the sea. And in tropical waters in many parts of the world there are small marine worms whose spawning behavior is so precisely adjusted to the tidal calendar that, merely from observing them, one could tell the month, the day, and often the time of day as well.

Near Samoa in the Pacific, the palolo worm lives out its life on the bottom of the shallow sea, in holes in the rocks and among the masses of corals. Twice each year, during the neap tides of the moon's last quarter in October and November, the worms forsake their burrows and rise to the surface in swarms that cover the water. For this purpose, each worm has literally broken its body in two, half to remain in its rocky tunnel, half to carry the reproductive products to the surface and there to liberate the cells. This happens at dawn on the day before the moon reaches its last quarter, and again on the following day; on the second day of the spawning the quantity of eggs liberated is so great that the sea is discolored.

The Fijians, whose waters have a similar worm, call them "Mbalolo" and have designated the periods of their spawning "Mbalolo lailai" (little) for October and "Mbalolo levu" (large) for November. Similar forms near the Gilbert Islands respond to certain phases of the moon in June and July; in the Malay Archipelago a related worm swarms at the surface on the second and third nights after the full moon of March and April, when the tides are running highest. A Japanese palolo swarms after the new moon and again after the full moon in October and November.

Concerning each of these, the question recurs but remains unanswered: is it the state of the tides that in some unknown way supplies the impulse from which springs this behavior, or is it, even more mysteriously, some other influence of the moon? It is easier to imagine that it is the press and the rhythmic movement of the water that in some way brings about this response. But why is it only certain tides of the year, and why for some species is it the fullest tides of the month and for others the least movements of the waters that are related to the perpetuation of the race? At present, no one can answer.

No other creature displays so exquisite an adaptation to the tidal rhythm as the grunion—a small, shimmering fish about as long as a man's hand. Through no one can say what processes of adaptation, extending over no one knows how many millennia, the grunion has come to know not only the daily rhythm of the tides, but the monthly cycle by which certain tides sweep higher on the beaches than others. It has so adapted its spawning habits to the tidal cycle that the very existence of the race depends on the precision of this adjustment.

Shortly after the full moon of the months from March to August, the grunion appear in the surf on the beaches of California. The tide reaches flood stage, slackens, hesitates, and begins to ebb. Now on these waves of the ebbing tide the fish begin to come in. Their bodies shimmer in the light of the moon as they are borne up the beach on the crest of a wave, they lie glittering on the wet sand for a perceptible moment of time, then fling themselves into the wash of the next wave and are carried back to sea. For about an hour after the turn of the tide this continues, thousands upon thousands of grunion coming up onto the beach, leaving the water, returning to it. This is the spawning act of the species.

During the brief interval between successive waves, the male and female have come together in the wet sand, the one to shed her eggs, the other to fertilize them. When the parent fish return to the water, they have left behind a mass of eggs buried in the sand. Succeeding waves on that night do not wash out the eggs because the tide is already ebbing. The waves of the next high tide will not reach them, because for a time after the full of the moon each tide will halt its advance a little lower on the beach than the preceding one. The eggs, then, will be undisturbed for at least a fortnight. In the warm, damp, incubating sand they undergo their development. Within two weeks the magic change from fertilized egg to larval fishlet is completed, the perfectly formed little grunion still confined within the membranes of the egg, still buried in the sand, waiting for release. With the tides of the new moon it comes. Their waves wash over the places where the little masses of the grunion eggs were buried, the swirl and rush of the surf stirring the sand deeply. As the sand is washed away, and the eggs feel the touch of the cool sea water, the membranes rupture, the fishlets hatch, and the waves that released them bear them away to the sea.

But the link between tide and living creature I like best to remember is that of a very small worm, flat of body, with no distinction of appearance, but with one unforgettable quality. The name of this worm is *Convoluta roscoffensis*, and it lives on the sandy beaches of northern Brittany and the Channel Islands. Convoluta has entered into a remarkable partnership with a green alga, whose cells inhabit the body of the worm and lend to its tissues their own green color. The worm lives entirely on the starchy products manufactured by its plant guest, having become so completely dependent upon this means of nutrition that its digestive organs have degenerated. In order that the algal cells may carry on their function of photosynthesis (which is dependent upon sunlight) Convoluta rises from the damp sands of the intertidal zone as soon as the tide has ebbed, the sand becoming spotted with large green patches composed of thousands of the worms. For the several hours while the tide is out, the worms lie thus in the sun, and the plants manufacture their starches and sugars; but when the tide returns, the worms must again sink into the sand to avoid being washed away, out into deep water. So the whole lifetime of the worm is a succession of movements conditioned by the stages of the tide—upward into sunshine on the ebb, downward on the flood.

What I find most unforgettable about Convoluta is this: sometimes it happens that a marine biologist, wishing to study some related problem, will transfer a whole colony of the worms into the laboratory, there to establish them in an aquarium, where there are no tides. But twice each day Convoluta rises out of the sand on the bottom of the aquarium, into the light of the sun. And twice each day it sinks again into the sand. Without a brain, or what we would call a memory, or even any very clear perception, Convoluta continues to live out its life in this alien place, remembering, in every fiber of its small green body, the tidal rhythm of the distant sea.

QUESTIONS

1. No one would call Carson's prose style lively. (Look closely, for example, at her verbs.) How, then, does this piece work? What accounts for its overall impact?

2. *The Sea Around Us* was translated into over thirty languages. Do you think it was easy or difficult to translate? On what characteristics of Carson's writing do you base your opinion?

3. Write about a common natural phenomenon like tides, using research or personal knowledge or both.

JOHN MUIR   *A Wind-Storm in the Forests*

T HE MOUNTAIN WINDS, like the dew and rain, sunshine and snow, are measured and bestowed with love on the forests to develop their strength and beauty. However restricted the scope of other forest influences, that of the winds is universal. The snow bends and trims the upper forests every winter, the lightning strikes a single tree here and there, while avalanches mow down thousands at a swoop as a gardener trims out a bed of flowers. But the winds go to every tree, fingering every leaf and branch and furrowed bole; not one is forgotten; the Mountain Pine towering with outstretched arms on the rugged buttresses of the icy peaks, the lowliest and most retiring tenant of the dells; they seek and find them all, caressing them tenderly, bending them in lusty exercise, stimulating their growth, plucking off a leaf or limb as required, or removing an entire tree or grove, now whispering and cooing through the branches like a sleepy child, now roaring like the ocean; the winds blessing the forests, the forests the winds, with ineffable beauty and harmony as the sure result.

After one has seen pines six feet in diameter bending like grasses before a mountain gale, and ever and anon some giant falling with a crash that shakes the hills, it seems astonishing that any, save the lowest thickset trees, could ever have found a period sufficiently stormless to establish themselves; or, once established, that they should not, sooner or later, have been blown down. But when the storm is over, and we behold the same forests tranquil again, towering fresh and unscathed in erect majesty, and consider what centuries of storms have fallen upon them since they were first planted,—hail, to break the tender seedlings; lightning, to scorch and shatter; snow, winds, and avalanches, to crush and overwhelm,—while the manifest result of all this wild storm-culture is the glorious perfection we behold; then faith in Nature's forestry is established, and we cease to deplore the violence of her most destructive gales, or of any other storm-implement whatsoever.

There are two trees in the Sierra forests that are never blown down, so long as they continue in sound health. These are the Juniper and the Dwarf Pine of the summit peaks. Their stiff, crooked roots grip the storm-beaten ledges like eagles' claws, while their lithe, cord-like branches bend round compliantly, offering but slight holds for winds, however violent. The other alpine conifers—the Needle Pine, Mountain Pine, Two-leaved Pine, and Hemlock Spruce—are never thinned out by this agent to any destructive extent, on account of their admirable toughness and the closeness of their growth. In general the same is true of the giants of the lower zones. The kingly Sugar Pine, towering aloft to a height of more than 200 feet, offers a fine mark to storm-

From Muir's classic account The Mountains of California *(1894), a book of scientific observation and personal memoir.*

A wind-storm in the California forests (after a sketch by the author)

winds: but it is not densely foliaged, and its long, horizontal arms swing round compliantly in the blast, like tresses of green, fluent algæ in a brook; while the Silver Firs in most places keep their ranks well together in united strength. The Yellow or Silver Pine is more frequently overturned than any other tree on the Sierra, because its leaves and branches form a larger mass in proportion to its height, while in many places it is planted sparsely, leaving open lanes through which storms may enter with full force. Furthermore, because it is distributed along the lower portion of the range, which was the first to be left bare on the breaking up of the ice-sheet at the close of the glacial winter, the soil it is growing upon has been longer exposed to post-glacial weathering, and consequently is in a more crumbling, decayed condition than the fresher soils farther up the range, and therefore offers a less secure anchorage for the roots.

While exploring the forest zones of Mount Shasta, I discovered the path of a hurricane strewn with thousands of pines of this species. Great and small had been uprooted or wrenched off by sheer force, making a clean gap, like that made by a snow avalanche. But hurricanes capable of doing this class of work are rare in the Sierra, and when we have explored the forests from one extremity of the range to the other, we are compelled to believe that they are the most beautiful on the face of the earth, however we may regard the agents that have made them so.

5   There is always something deeply exciting, not only in the sounds of winds in the woods, which exert more or less influence over every mind, but in their varied waterlike flow as manifested by the movements of the trees, especially those of the conifers. By no other trees are they rendered so extensively and impressively visible, not even by the lordly tropic palms or tree-ferns responsive to the gentlest breeze. The waving of a forest of the giant Sequoias is indescribably impressive and sublime, but the pines seem to me the best interpreters of winds. They are mighty waving goldenrods, ever in tune, singing and writing wind-music all their long century lives. Little, however, of this noble tree-waving and tree-music will you see or hear in the strictly alpine portion of the forests. The burly Juniper, whose girth sometimes more than equals its

height, is about as rigid as the rocks on which it grows. The slender lash-like sprays of the Dwarf Pine stream out in wavering ripples, but the tallest and slenderest are far too unyielding to wave even in the heaviest gales. They only shake in quick, short vibrations. The Hemlock Spruce, however, and the Mountain Pine, and some of the tallest thickets of the Two-leaved species bow in storms with considerable scope and gracefulness. But it is only in the lower and middle zones that the meeting of winds and woods is to be seen in all its grandeur.

One of the most beautiful and exhilarating storms I ever enjoyed in the Sierra occurred in December, 1874, when I happened to be exploring one of the tributary valleys of the Yuba River. The sky and the ground and the trees had been thoroughly rain-washed and were dry again. The day was intensely pure, one of those incomparable bits of California winter, warm and balmy and full of white sparkling sunshine, redolent of all the purest influences of the spring, and at the same time enlivened with one of the most bracing wind-storms conceivable. Instead of camping out, as I usually do, I then chanced to be stopping at the house of a friend. But when the storm began to sound, I lost no time in pushing out into the woods to enjoy it. For on such occasions Nature has always something rare to show us, and the danger to life and limb is hardly greater than one would experience crouching deprecatingly beneath a roof.

It was still early morning when I found myself fairly adrift. Delicious sunshine came pouring over the hills, lighting the tops of the pines, and setting free a stream of summery fragrance that contrasted strangely with the wild tones of the storm. The air was mottled with pine-tassels and bright green plumes, that went flashing past in the sunlight like birds pursued. But there was not the slightest dustiness, nothing less pure than leaves, and ripe pollen, and flecks of withered bracken and moss. I heard trees falling for hours at the rate of one every two or three minutes; some uprooted, partly on account of the loose, water-soaked condition of the ground; others broken straight across, where some weakness caused by fire had determined the spot. The gestures of the various trees made a delightful study. Young Sugar Pines, light and feathery as squirrel-tails, were bowing almost to the ground; while the grand old patriarchs, whose massive boles had been tried in a hundred storms, waved solemnly above them, their long, arching branches streaming fluently on the gale, and every needle thrilling and ringing and shedding off keen lances of light like a diamond. The Douglas Spruces,[1] with long sprays drawn out in level tresses, and needles massed in a gray, shimmering glow, presented a most striking appearance as they stood in bold relief along the hilltops. The madroños[2] in the dells, with their red bark and large glossy leaves tilted every way, reflected the sunshine in throbbing spangles like those one so often sees on the rippled surface of a glacier lake. But the Silver Pines were now the most impressively beautiful of all. Colossal spires 200 feet in height waved like sup-

---

1. Another name for Douglas fir.
2. A type of evergreen tree.

ple goldenrods chanting and bowing low as if in worship, while the whole mass of their long, tremulous foliage was kindled into one continuous blaze of white sun-fire. The force of the gale was such that the most steadfast monarch of them all rocked down to its roots with a motion plainly perceptible when one leaned against it. Nature was holding high festival, and every fiber of the most rigid giants thrilled with glad excitement.

I drifted on through the midst of this passionate music and motion, across many a glen, from ridge to ridge; often halting in the lee of a rock for shelter, or to gaze and listen. Even when the grand anthem had swelled to its highest pitch, I could distinctly hear the varying tones of individual trees,—Spruce, and Fir, and Pine, and leafless Oak—and even the infinitely gentle rustle of the withered grasses at my feet. Each was expressing itself in its own way,— singing its own song, and making its own peculiar gestures,—manifesting a richness of variety to be found in no other forest I have yet seen. The coniferous woods of Canada, and the Carolinas, and Florida, are made up of trees that resemble one another about as nearly as blades of grass, and grow close together in much the same way. Coniferous trees, in general, seldom possess individual character, such as is manifest among Oaks and Elms. But the California forests are made up of a greater number of distinct species than any other in the world. And in them we find, not only a marked differentiation into special groups, but also a marked individuality in almost every tree, giving rise to storm effects indescribably glorious.

Toward midday, after a long, tingling scramble through copses of hazel and ceanothus,[3] I gained the summit of the highest ridge in the neighborhood; and then it occurred to me that it would be a fine thing to climb one of the trees to obtain a wider outlook and get my ear close to the Æolian music[4] of its topmost needles. But under the circumstances the choice of a tree was a serious matter. One whose instep was not very strong seemed in danger of being blown down, or of being struck by others in case they should fall; another was branchless to a considerable height above the ground, and at the same time too large to be grasped with arms and legs in climbing; while others were not favorably situated for clear views. After cautiously casting about, I made choice of the tallest of a group of Douglas Spruces that were growing close together like a tuft of grass, no one of which seemed likely to fall unless all the rest fell with it. Though comparatively young, they were about 100 feet high, and their lithe, brushy tops were rocking and swirling in wild ecstasy. Being accustomed to climb trees in making botanical studies, I experienced no difficulty in reaching the top of this one, and never before did I enjoy so noble an exhilaration of motion. The slender tops fairly flapped and swished in the passionate torrent, bending and swirling backward and forward, round and round, tracing indescribable combinations of vertical and horizontal curves, while I clung with muscles firm braced, like a bobolink on a reed.

3. A type of evergreen shrub.
4. Music made by the wind, from Aeolus, the Greek god of the winds, the strings of whose harp were sounded by the wind.

In its widest sweeps my tree-top described an arc of from twenty to thirty 10
degrees, but I felt sure of its elastic temper, having seen others of the same
species still more severely tried—bent almost to the ground indeed, in heavy
snows—without breaking a fiber. I was therefore safe, and free to take the
wind into my pulses and enjoy the excited forest from my superb outlook. The
view from here must be extremely beautiful in any weather. Now my eye roved
over the piny hills and dales as over fields of waving grain, and felt the light
running in ripples and broad swelling undulations across the valleys from ridge
to ridge, as the shining foliage was stirred by corresponding waves of air. Oftentimes these waves of reflected light would break up suddenly into a kind of
beaten foam, and again, after chasing one another in regular order, they would
seem to bend forward in concentric curves, and disappear on some hillside,
like sea-waves on a shelving shore. The quantity of light reflected from the
bent needles was so great as to make whole groves appear as if covered with
snow, while the black shadows beneath the trees greatly enhanced the effect
of the silvery splendor.

Excepting only the shadows there was nothing somber in all this wild sea
of pines. On the contrary, notwithstanding this was the winter season, the colors were remarkably beautiful. The shafts of the pine and libocedrus[5] were
brown and purple, and most of the foliage was well tinged with yellow; the laurel groves, with the pale undersides of their leaves turned upward, made masses
of gray; and then there was many a dash of chocolate color from clumps of
manzanita,[6] and jet of vivid crimson from the bark of the madroños, while the
ground on the hillsides, appearing here and there through openings between
the groves, displayed masses of pale purple and brown.

The sounds of the storm corresponded gloriously with this wild exuberance of light and motion. The profound bass of the naked branches and boles
booming like waterfalls; the quick, tense vibrations of the pine-needles, now
rising to a shrill, whistling hiss, now falling to a silky murmur; the rustling of
laurel groves in the dells, and the keen metallic click of leaf on leaf—all this
was heard in easy analysis when the attention was calmly bent.

The varied gestures of the multitude were seen to fine advantage, so that
one could recognize the different species at a distance of several miles by this
means alone, as well as by their forms and colors, and the way they reflected
the light. All seemed strong and comfortable, as if really enjoying the storm,
while responding to its most enthusiastic greetings. We hear much nowadays
concerning the universal struggle for existence, but no struggle in the common
meaning of the word was manifest here; no recognition of danger by any tree;
no deprecation; but rather an invincible gladness as remote from exultation as
from fear.

I kept my lofty perch for hours, frequently closing my eyes to enjoy the
music by itself, or to feast quietly on the delicious fragrance that was stream-

5. A genus of cedar trees. In the Sierra Nevada, *Libocedrus decurans* often reaches a
height of 150 feet.
6. A type of evergreen shrub.

ing past. The fragrance of the woods was less marked than that produced during warm rain, when so many balsamic buds and leaves are steeped like tea; but, from the chafing of resiny branches against each other, and the incessant attrition of myriads of needles, the gale was spiced to a very tonic degree. And besides the fragrance from these local sources there were traces of scents brought from afar. For this wind came first from the sea, rubbing against its fresh, briny waves, then distilled through the redwoods, threading rich ferny gulches, and spreading itself in broad undulating currents over many a flower-enameled ridge of the coast mountains, then across the golden plains, up the purple foot-hills, and into these piny woods with the varied incense gathered by the way.

15   Winds are advertisements of all they touch, however much or little we may be able to read them; telling their wanderings even by their scents alone. Mariners detect the flowery perfume of land-winds far at sea, and sea-winds carry the fragrance of dulse and tangle far inland, where it is quickly recognized, though mingled with the scents of a thousand land-flowers. As an illustration of this, I may tell here that I breathed sea-air on the Firth of Forth, in Scotland, while a boy; then was taken to Wisconsin, where I remained nineteen years; then, without in all this time having breathed one breath of the sea, I walked quietly, alone, from the middle of the Mississippi Valley to the Gulf of Mexico, on a botanical excursion, and while in Florida, far from the coast, my attention wholly bent on the splendid tropical vegetation about me, I suddenly recognized a sea-breeze, as it came sifting through the palmettos and blooming vine-tangles, which at once awakened and set free a thousand dormant associations, and made me a boy again in Scotland, as if all the intervening years had been annihilated.

Most people like to look at mountain rivers, and bear them in mind; but few care to look at the winds, though far more beautiful and sublime, and though they become at times about as visible as flowing water. When the north winds in winter are making upward sweeps over the curving summits of the High Sierra, the fact is sometimes published with flying snow-banners a mile long. Those portions of the winds thus embodied can scarce be wholly invisible, even to the darkest imagination. And when we look around over an agitated forest, we may see something of the wind that stirs it, by its effects upon the trees. Yonder it descends in a rush of water-like ripples, and sweeps over the bending pines from hill to hill. Nearer, we see detached plumes and leaves, now speeding by on level currents, now whirling in eddies, or, escaping over the edges of the whirls, soaring aloft on grand, upswelling domes of air, or tossing on flame-like crests. Smooth, deep currents, cascades, falls, and swirling eddies, sing around every tree and leaf, and over all the varied topography of the region with telling changes of form, like mountain rivers conforming to the features of their channels.

After tracing the Sierra streams from their fountains to the plains, marking where they bloom white in falls, glide in crystal plumes, surge gray and foam-filled in boulder-choked gorges, and slip through the woods in long, tranquil reaches—after thus learning their language and forms in detail, we may at length hear them chanting all together in one grand anthem, and comprehend them all in clear inner vision, covering the range like lace. But even this spectacle is far less sublime and not a whit more substantial than what we may behold of these storm-streams of air in the mountain woods.

We all travel the milky way together, trees and men; but it never occurred to me until this stormday, while swinging in the wind, that trees are travelers, in the ordinary sense. They make many journeys, not extensive ones, it is true; but our own little journeys, away and back again, are only little more than tree-wavings—many of them not so much.

When the storm began to abate, I dismounted and sauntered down through the calming woods. The storm-tones died away, and, turning toward the east, I beheld the countless hosts of the forests hushed and tranquil, towering above one another on the slopes of the hills like a devout audience. The setting sun filled them with amber light, and seemed to say, while they listened, "My peace I give unto you."

As I gazed on the impressive scene, all the so-called ruin of the storm was forgotten, and never before did these noble woods appear so fresh, so joyous, so immortal.   20

QUESTIONS

1. What preconceptions did you bring to Muir's title, "A Wind-Storm in the Forests"? How does the opening sentence—indeed, the entire opening paragraph—suggest a different perspective?

2. The central adventure in this essay occurs when Muir climbs a Douglas Spruce (paragraph 9). Why does Muir undertake this climb? What does he wish to experience?

3. Write about an experience you have had in nature, whether dramatic (as in Muir's essay) or more quiet (as in Aldo Leopold's, also in this section).

EDWARD ABBEY   *The Serpents of Paradise*

THE APRIL MORNINGS are bright, clear and calm. Not until the afternoon does the wind begin to blow, raising dust and sand in funnel-shaped twisters that spin across the desert briefly, like dancers, and then collapse—whirlwinds from which issue no voice or word except the forlorn moan of the elements under stress. After the reconnoitering dust devils comes the real, the serious wind, the voice of the desert rising to a demented howl and blotting out sky

From Abbey's classic book Desert Solitaire: A Season in the Wilderness *(1968). Drawings by Peter Parnall were added in the 1990 edition and are included here.*

and sun behind yellow clouds of dust, sand, confusion, embattled birds, last year's scrub-oak leaves, pollen, the husks of locusts, bark of juniper. . . .

Time of the red eye, the sore and bloody nostril, the sand-pitted windshield, if one is foolish enough to drive his car into such a storm. Time to sit indoors and continue that letter which is never finished—while the fine dust forms neat little windrows under the edge of the door and on the windowsills. Yet the springtime winds are as much a part of the canyon country as the silence and the glamorous distances; you learn, after a number of years, to love them also.

The mornings therefore, as I started to say and meant to say, are all the sweeter in the knowledge of what the afternoon is likely to bring. Before beginning the morning chores I like to sit on the sill of my doorway, bare feet planted on the bare ground and a mug of hot coffee in hand, facing the sunrise. The air is gelid, not far above freezing, but the butane heater inside the trailer keeps my back warm, the rising sun warms the front, and the coffee warms the interior.

Perhaps this is the loveliest hour of the day, though it's hard to choose. Much depends on the season. In midsummer the sweetest hour begins at sundown, after the awful heat of the afternoon. But now, in April, we'll take the opposite, that hour beginning with the sunrise. The birds, returning from wherever they go in winter, seem inclined to agree. The pinyon jays are whirling in garrulous, gregarious flocks from one stunted tree to the next and back again, erratic exuberant games without any apparent practical function. A few big ravens hang around and croak harsh clanking statements of smug satisfaction from the rimrock, lifting their greasy wings now and then to probe for lice. I can hear but seldom see the canyon wrens singing their distinctive song from somewhere up on the cliffs: a flutelike descent—never ascent—of the whole tone scale. Staking out new nesting claims, I understand. Also invisible but invariably present at some indefinable distance are the mourning doves whose plaintive call suggests irresistibly a kind of seeking out, the attempt by separated souls to restore a lost communion:

5   *Hello . . .* they seem to cry, *who . . . are . . . you?*

And the reply from a different quarter. *Hello . . .* (pause) *where . . . are . . . you?*

No doubt this line of analogy must be rejected. It's foolish and unfair to impute to the doves, with serious concerns of their own, an interest in questions more appropriate to their human kin. Yet their song, if not a mating call or a warning, must be what it sounds like, a brooding meditation on space, on solitude. The game.

Other birds, silent, which I have not yet learned to identify, are also lurking in the vicinity, watching me. What the ornithologist terms l.g.b.'s—little gray birds—they flit about from point to point on noiseless wings, their origins obscure.

* * * I share the housetrailer with a number of mice. I don't know how many but apparently only a few, perhaps a single family. They don't disturb me and are welcome to my crumbs and leavings. Where they came from, how they got into the trailer, how they survived before my arrival (for the trailer had been locked up for six months), these are puzzling matters I am not prepared to resolve. My only reservation concerning the mice is that they do attract rattlesnakes.

I'm sitting on my doorstep early one morning, facing the sun as usual, drinking coffee, when I happen to look down and see almost between my bare feet, only a couple of inches to the rear of my heels, the very thing I had in mind. No mistaking that wedgelike head, that tip of horny segmented tail peeping out of the coils. He's under the doorstep and in the shade where the ground and air remain very cold. In his sluggish condition he's not likely to strike unless I rouse him by some careless move of my own.

There's a revolver inside the trailer, a huge British Webley .45, loaded, but it's out of reach. Even if I had it in my hands I'd hesitate to blast a fellow creature at such close range, shooting between my own legs at a living target flat on solid rock thirty inches away. It would be like murder; and where would I set my coffee? My cherrywood walking stick leans against the trailerhouse wall only a few feet away, but I'm afraid that in leaning over for it I might stir up the rattler or spill some hot coffee on his scales.

Other considerations come to mind. Arches National Monument[1] is meant to be among other things a sanctuary for wildlife—for all forms of wildlife. It is

1. Near Moab, Utah, in the spectacular Canyonlands region, where Abbey lived at the time.

my duty as a park ranger to protect, preserve and defend all living things within the park
boundaries, making no exceptions. Even if this were not the
case I have personal convictions
to uphold. Ideals, you might
say. I prefer not to kill animals.
I'm a humanist; I'd rather kill a
man than a snake.

What to do. I drink some
more coffee and study the dormant reptile at my heels. It is
not after all the mighty dia-
mondback, *Crotalus atrox,* I'm
confronted with but a smaller
species known locally as the
horny rattler or more precisely as the Faded Midget. An insulting name for a
rattlesnake, which may explain the Faded Midget's alleged bad temper. But
the name is apt: he is small and dusty-looking, with a little knob above each
eye—the horns. His bite though temporarily disabling would not likely kill a
full-grown man in normal health. Even so I don't really want him around. Am
I to be compelled to put on boots or shoes every time I wish to step outside?
The scorpions, tarantulas, centipedes, and black widows are nuisance
enough.

I finish my coffee, lean back and swing my feet up and inside the doorway
of the trailer. At once there is a buzzing sound from below and the rattler lifts
his head from his coils, eyes brightening, and extends his narrow black tongue
to test the air.

After thawing out my boots over the gas flame I pull them on and come
back to the doorway. My visitor is still waiting beneath the doorstep, basking in
the sun, fully alert. The trailerhouse has two doors. I leave by the other and
get a long-handled spade out of the bed of the government pickup. With this
tool I scoop the snake into the open. He strikes, I can hear the click of the
fangs against steel, see the stain of venom. He wants to stand and fight, but I
am patient; I insist on herding him well away from the trailer. On guard, head
aloft—that evil slit-eyed weaving head shaped like the ace of spades—tail
whirring, the rattler slithers sideways, retreating slowly before me until he
reaches the shelter of a sandstone slab. He backs under it.

You better stay there, cousin, I warn him; if I catch you around the trailer
again I'll chop your head off.

A week later he comes back. If not him his twin brother. I spot him one
morning under the trailer near the kitchen drain, waiting for a mouse. I have
to keep my promise.

This won't do. If there are midget rattlers in the area there may be dia-
mondbacks too—five, six or seven feet long, thick as a man's wrist, dangerous.

I don't want them camping under my home. It looks as though I'll have to trap the mice.

However, before being forced to take that step I am lucky enough to capture a gopher snake. Burning garbage one morning at the park dump, I see a long slender yellow-brown snake emerge from a mound of old tin cans and plastic picnic plates and take off down the sandy bed of a gulch. There is a burlap sack in the cab of the truck which I carry when plucking Kleenex flowers from the brush and cactus along the road; I grab that and my stick, run after the snake and corner it beneath the exposed roots of a bush. Making sure it's a gopher snake and not something less useful, I open the neck of the sack and with a great deal of coaxing and prodding get the snake into it. The gopher snake, *Drymarchon corais couperi,* or bull snake, has a reputation as the enemy of rattlesnakes, destroying or driving them away whenever encountered.

Hoping to domesticate this sleek, handsome and docile reptile, I release   20
him inside the trailerhouse and keep him there for several days. Should I attempt to feed him? I decide against it—let him eat mice. What little water he may need can also be extracted from the flesh of his prey.

The gopher snake and I get along nicely. During the day he curls up like a cat in the warm corner behind the heater and at night he goes about his business. The mice, singularly quiet for a change, make themselves scarce. The snake is passive, apparently contented, and makes no resistance when I pick him up with my hands and drape him over an arm or around my neck. When I take him outside into the wind and sunshine his favorite place seems to be inside my shirt, where he wraps himself around my waist and rests on my belt. In this position he sometimes sticks his head out between shirt buttons for a survey of the weather, astonishing and delighting any tourists who may happen to be with me at the time. The scales of a snake are dry and smooth, quite pleasant to the touch. Being a cold blooded creature, of, course, he takes his temperature from that of the immediate environment—in this case my body.

We are compatible. From my point of view, friends. After a week of close association I turn him loose on the warm sandstone at my doorstep and leave for a patrol of the park. At noon when I return he is gone. I search everywhere beneath, nearby and inside the trailerhouse, but my companion has disappeared. Has he left the area entirely or is he hiding somewhere close by? At any rate I am troubled no more by rattlesnakes under the door.

The snake story is not yet ended.

In the middle of May, about a month after the gopher snake's disappearance, in the evening of a very hot day, with all the rosy desert cooling like a griddle with the fire turned off, he reappears. This time with a mate.

I'm in the stifling heat of the trailer opening a can of beer, barefooted,   25
about to go outside and relax after a hard day watching cloud formations. I happen to glance out the little window near the refrigerator and see two gopher snakes on my verandah engaged in what seems to be a kind of ritual dance. Like a living caduceus they wind and unwind about each other in undulant, graceful, perpetual motion, moving slowly across a dome of sandstone. Invisible but tangible as music is the passion which joins them—sexual? com-

bative? both? A shameless *voyeur,* I stare at the lovers, and then to get a closer view run outside and around the trailer to the back. There I get down on hands and knees and creep toward the dancing snakes, not wanting to frighten or disturb them. I crawl to within six feet of them and stop, flat on my belly, watching from the snake's eye level. Obsessed with their ballet, the serpents seem unaware of my presence.

The two gopher snakes are nearly identical in length and coloring; I cannot be certain that either is actually my former household pet. I cannot even be sure that they are male and female, though their performance resembles so strongly a *pas de deux*[2] by formal lovers. They intertwine and separate, glide side by side in perfect congruence, turn like mirror images of each other and glide back again, wind and unwind again. This is the basic pattern but there is a variation: at regular intervals the snakes elevate their heads, facing one another, as high as they can go, as if each is trying to outreach or overawe the other. Their heads and bodies rise, higher and higher, then topple together and the rite goes on.

I crawl after them, determined to see the whole thing. Suddenly and simultaneously they discover me, prone on my belly a few feet away. The dance stops. After a moment's pause the two snakes come straight toward me, still in flawless unison, straight toward my face, the forked tongues flickering, their intense wild yellow eyes staring directly into my eyes. For an instant I am paralyzed by wonder; then, stung by a fear too ancient and powerful to overcome I scramble back, rising, to my knees. The snakes veer and turn and race away from me in parallel motion, their lean elegant bodies making a soft hissing noise as they slide over the sand and stone. I follow them for a short distance, still plagued by curiosity, before remembering my place and the requirements of common courtesy. For godsake let them go in peace, I tell myself. Wish them luck and (if lovers) innumerable offspring, a life of happily ever after. Not for their sake alone but for your own.

In the long hot days and cool evenings to come I will not see the gopher snakes again. Nevertheless I will feel their presence watching over me like totemic deities, keeping the rattlesnakes far back in the brush where I like them best, cropping off the surplus mouse population, maintaining useful connections with the primeval. Sympathy, mutual aid, symbiosis, continuity.

How can I descend to such anthropomorphism? Easily—but is it, in this case, entirely false? Perhaps not. I am not attributing human motives to my snake and bird acquaintances. I recognize that when and where they serve purposes of mine they do so for beautifully selfish reasons of their own. Which is exactly the way it should be. I suggest, however, that it's a foolish, simpleminded rationalism which denies any form of emotion to all animals but man and his dog. This is no more justified than the Moslems are in denying souls to women. It seems to me possible, even probable, that many of the nonhuman undomesticated animals experience emotions unknown to us. What do the coyotes mean when they yodel at the moon? What are the dolphins trying so

2. Literally, step for two (French), a dance for two dancers.

patiently to tell us? Precisely what did those two enraptured gopher snakes have in mind when they came gliding toward my eyes over the naked sandstone? If I had been as capable of trust as I am susceptible to fear I might have learned something new or some truth so very old we have all forgotten it.

> They do not sweat and whine about their condition.
> They do not lie awake in the dark and weep for their sins.[3]

All men are brothers, we like to say, half-wishing sometimes in secret it   30
were not true. But perhaps it is true. And is the evolutionary hue from protozoan to Spinoza[4] any less certain? That also may be true. We are obliged, therefore, to spread the news, painful and bitter though it may be for some to hear, that all living things on hand are kindred. . . .

3. From Walt Whitman's *Song of Myself*, sec. 32.
4. Baruch Spinoza (1632–1677), Dutch philosopher known today for his writings on the doctrine of pantheism.

QUESTIONS

1. Why is the word "paradise" included in the title? What does it reveal about Abbey's attitude toward the desert in which he lives?

2. "I'd rather kill a *man* than a snake," writes Abbey in paragraph 12; yet several paragraphs later he threatens, "if I catch you around the trailer again I'll chop your head off" (paragraph 16). What are the rhetorical purposes of these statements? How do they articulate the thematic concerns of the essay?

3. Write an essay in which you use your own experience in nature to defend an ecological or environmental cause.

4. Write about your own encounter with an animal, whether domesticated or wild.

ALLISON WALLACE   *The Work of Honeybees*

IT IS MEASURED in droplets, flakes, grains: all natural materials, some produced by their own bodies. The work of bees aims at mass, strength, durability, longevity—achieving these with particles that, taken alone, would blow away in the slightest breeze. The work of bees appears in constant need of doing, though once they've established a solidly respectable colonial home, it's hard to see why. I peer into one of my hives—a marvelous, multichambered palace

Published in the Georgia Review *(Spring 2003), a quarterly magazine that includes creative personal essays and informed, thesis-driven essays, as well as poetry, short fiction, book reviews, and art.*

weighing a hundred pounds in wax, honey, pollen, and stored brood—and say
aloud, "Look, gang, time to kick back and take it easy for a bit, don't you
think? Haven't you earned a break?" But no: they're as hard at it as ever, every
one of these thousands of murmuring engines roaming across the comb on her
particular mission of the moment. And if ever this hive begins to feel too
small, if the volume of the bees' work begins to push uncomfortably at the
sturdy pine walls and inner cover, about half of them will take to the sky in
search of nature's vacant lots for sale or rent, some hollow in a tree or rock
overhang where a new colony can be established. The work of bees can slow
down, can pause (during a northern winter, for example), but it can never really cease. And though most of us know it not, we have reason to be deeply
grateful this is so.

Every morning for a whole school year, the same thin-shouldered college boy
could be found swabbing the tiled stairway separating me from my office when
I arrived for work. Generally embarrassed with people doing any kind of cleaning on my behalf, I would tiptoe self-consciously onto the damp tile, apologize
("Sure, no prob"), and occasionally try to offer some variation on your basic
"Nice work." By degrees I came to realize that he worked some afternoon
shifts, too, when once again he plied his mop over every step, perhaps ticking
them off one, two, three in his head as he slicked them. Ignorant of the young
man's name, I was free to think of him as Sisyphus.[1] He may have been fortunate in having only to drag a mop down the stairs rather than push a rock up,
but there still remained for him the daily problem of ruined work in need of
doing all over again. No matter that he'd left the tile a shiny chocolate brown
before heading to class: every following morning and many afternoons there
they'd be, a set of stairs newly begritted and grimed.

   As I say, I was myself arriving for work each morning that I encountered
this fellow. And how many student essays had I already marked in my time,
how many classes taught, meetings attended, sloppy committee reports
mopped up? It did not much matter, since there was always another one waiting—and by some grace or other I never thought to drive myself daft ticking
them off one at a time.

   Such appears to be the futile nature of most work: for every floor
scrubbed, shirt sewn, wall painted, brick laid, wire strung, bale tossed, net
hauled, baby delivered, engine tuned, meal prepared, report written, form
processed, purchase order filled, confession heard, steer branded, or broken
bone set, another just behind awaits its turn. The fact may be the sweetest
dream that labor knows (as Frost put it),[2] but let's not be fooled: each fact
achieved by work *is* nevertheless a dream, a dissolution in the making, a ruin
waiting to unfold. There is no such thing as work done that *stays* done: even

---

1. A figure in Greek mythology condemned, in the afterlife, to push a rock up a hill forever.
2. Robert Frost (1874–1963), American poet. Wallace is adapting a line from "Mowing," published in 1913: "The fact is the sweetest dream that labor knows."

God—or if you prefer, organic evolution—seems not to have called it a day (not on the seventh, not on the six million and seventh), called it good, and given up tinkering. For mere mortals, the impermanence of achievement is an old, familiar grief. Listen to the Preacher:[3]

> Then I looked on all the works that my hands had wrought,
> And on the labor that I had labored to do,
> And, behold, all was vanity and vexation of spirit,
> And there was no profit under the sun.

Fast-forward a few hundred years toward our own time, and here comes the thin, robed figure of Gandhi[4] stepping up to say, maddeningly, that although everything I do will be insignificant, I must do it anyway. Stopping short, I peer into the apparition of his raisin-brown face: *But why?*

Animals generally and insects in particular appear not the least afflicted   5
by such questions, though their work, too, is consistently undone by the same law of entropy that has set a shoulder against permanent human achievement. Those bees of mine, for example, and their exquisitely built environment inside the hive: they tend it endlessly because it is endlessly subject to the vicissitudes of temperature, humidity, and the differential pressure exerted by thousands of tiny, hairy, honeybee feet. To leave off housekeeping for even a day would be to court disaster, since the hive (especially in summer) is a very active nursery, where the near-constant birthing of bee babies makes for a constant mess in need of tidying up.

The great majority of honeybees in a given colony are infertile females, and there's a reason they're called "worker" bees; there's reason in the phrase, "busy as a bee." While the males or drones have their one job of mating with queens from other colonies (outside the hive, high up in the air), and while the queen has her one job of laying eggs (as many as two thousand on a really good summer's day), each worker bee has nearly a dozen jobs. Certain tasks are usually taken up as she reaches a certain age, and she usually takes them up in roughly the same sequence followed by her sisters, though the overall condition of the colony can affect these patterns somewhat: the colony's needs always take precedence over any one worker bee's "need" to fulfill a given role. Like human children in a well-ordered home, the workers have their various chores, all of them assigned according to the bees' ages and abilities, or more precisely, their degree of physiological development. But unlike children's growth, honeybee development appears to hasten or slow down as the colony's well-being demands. Imagine being able, at will, to turn your toddlers into teenagers overnight, just because the housework has come to include some heavy lifting.

3. The speaker in the biblical Book of Ecclesiastes. Wallace quotes Ecclesiastes 2.11 (KJV).
4. Mahatma Gandhi (1869–1948), Indian political and spiritual leader who championed nonviolence.

Suppose it's high summer. In some nondescript region of honeycomb in one of my hives, a newly matured worker bee is chewing and pawing her way out of the wax cell in which she has been nestled, growing, for a couple of weeks. In order to keep up with her in the throng of bees she's about to join, let's daub a bit of fluorescent orange paint on her back, and for ease of reference, let's call her Bella. Finally freed from her chamber, the first thing she does is turn around and clean it of any debris she may have left behind, like a newborn tidying up its own afterbirth. She soon moves on to do the same for other brood (larvae) cells, joining thousands of newborns who are similarly occupied, many of whom will poke around in Bella's cell too, to be sure it's clean. (Honeybees are nothing if not thorough.) Bella and her young sisters may keep this up for only a day, or for as many as thirty days in rare instances. During this time many will also begin capping brood or nursery cells—that is, sealing off with a wax cap the larvae that are ready to pupate.[5] The wax has come afresh from the bees' own bodies—one flake at a time emerging from their upper abdomens like paper from a fax machine, in response to glandular signals. Or it could be that some of the caps are recent castoffs from newly emptied cells; recycling of this sort saves precious energy in the present moment.

Before long Bella's body has responded to further physiological prompting and has begun to produce "brood food," a glandular secretion mixed with a bit of honey, water, and digestive enzymes. (As larvae age, they will also be fed some pollen, important to them for its protein.) This brood food she will dole out in tiny, one-droplet doses at the inner edges of larval cells, each time she pokes her head into one and determines the larva therein is deservedly hungry. By no means does she often reach that conclusion: she's at once a fussy and a stingy sort of nanny, unable to refrain from constantly looking in on the babes, yet rarely willing to dispense warm bottles of formula. Which is just as well, since, again, Bella is one of thousands doing the nursery rounds at all hours, making honeybee young among nature's most doted upon.

Days pass. Having reared her share of brats in her time, Bella's about ready to move up into royal service—tending the queen. The lady of the hive must needs be frequently stroked, petted, and generously fed mouth-to-mouth helpings of brood food. She must also have her chamber pot emptied—that is, her feces carried away. Her every need anticipated by Bella and a half dozen or more daughters who keep close beside her, she moves steadily all the while over the brood comb, looking for clean, empty beds in the nursery to fill with more eggs. (And although her majesty seems to reign over the scene, let her fail regularly in this, her one grave duty, and the otherwise servile worker bees will forthwith have off with her head, trotting in a replacement they will have raised themselves.) Now Bella is more heavily drenched in the queen's perfume—her special pheromone—than usual. This substance Bella and the other royal attendants will unwittingly spread out among the rest of the colony, giving all the bees there a sense of family identity. They may *look* like any other honeybees on the block, but they won't *smell* like them.

5. Become a pupa, one phase in the development of insects.

Bella may now be ten to twenty or perhaps even thirty days old. She's   10
cleaning the hive of debris, such as dead bees, of which there are always some;
the queen's egg laying occurs as steadily as it does precisely because there's always a certain amount of dying going on here, as each bee's life runs its
course. Bella is also building comb—again, with wax she's produced herself,
forming near-perfect hexagonal cells, each of which shares its walls with adjacent hexagonals, a geometric miracle that maximizes space and architectural
strength to a degree that circles or squares could not. And she's helping to
process the nectar and pollen that are coming into the hive via the foraging
bees. The pollen storage is begun by the foragers themselves, who scrape it off
of their back legs where they had stored it temporarily, during flight, in the
middle of some hairs that curl around to form a kind of basket. Look—there's
one scraping herself clean now. And here comes Bella, the bee with the orange
spot on her back. Her newest job is to moisten the pollen pellets with saliva
and regurgitated honey and to pack them into solid plugs securely within their
cells. As for the nectar arriving daily, that too is Bella's responsibility now,
whenever a returning forager gets her attention. Taking the nectar into her
mouth from the regurgitating bee, she spends a few minutes opening and closing her mouth around it (presumably to begin the evaporation process), then
tucks it into a cell well above the brood nest, where it will undergo further
evaporation before being sealed off later on with a wax cap. To aid in this all-
important evaporation period (nectar must lose eighty-two percent of its water
content to become honey), Bella and thousands of sisters fan their wings over
the cells here at the top of the hive; at other times, they do the same down below, at the hive entrance, helping in the process to air-condition the whole
building.

A few more days pass. Soon Bella is at the entrance regularly, getting a
glimpse of the wide world while she now serves sentry duty: each bee alighting
at the entrance and seeking admission had better have about her a whiff of
this hive's pheromone, or Bella will turn bouncer.

Having reached her prime anywhere between as few as a dozen and as
many as forty to sixty days old, Bella gets ready to fly. The glands that had produced wax and brood food now atrophy. In her first attempts—very short "orientation" flights only, to be sure she's got landmarks by which to find the hive
again later—Bella's brain actually undergoes subtle changes, and at this time
(oh, finally!) she gets to eliminate her own feces, something she hasn't been
willing to do indoors. (Just causes more work for everybody, and who needs
that?) Flying and foraging for water, nectar, pollen, and propolis—plant resins
that bees use as "glue" within the hive—making dozens of trips daily between
the hive and the surrounding fields and woods: all of this will take every mite
of energy she can summon over the next several days. And then it will kill her,
essentially by wearing her out. Here lies Bella the bee, a hard worker gone to
a deserving rest.

At the risk of stating the obvious, one might observe that work is not generally easy: some etymologists contend that we derive the word "labor," ultimately, from the Latin verb *labi*, to slip or fail, to stagger under a weight.

Sisyphus growing ever more fatigued with each upward shove of the rock;
Bella wearing her wings and her life away fighting the wind that would bar her
way back to the hive. The same Latin root gives us *lapse*. Not for nothing is it
said, then, that after their great lapse, Adam and Eve[6] were made to labor for
the rest of their days. If we may compare small things with great, Bella and all
her laboring kin are in esteemed company.

Yet she *did* get quite a lot of rest during her short summer weeks of life,
prior to flying anyway. Perhaps the honeybee's best kept secret is that, though
she appears to work like the dickens around the clock, she actually gets in a
good deal of strolling or loitering on comb corners during part of every hour.
How can this be, you ask, since so much astonishing work really does get
done—many hundreds of wax cells built, many thousands of larvae reared,
many pounds of honey put up in storage one drop at a time? It would appear,
as the old saw tells us, that many hands (or feet) do indeed make light work:
with up to eighty thousand bees looking after business in a strong colony at
the height of summer, the real wonder is that they don't make a mess of the
job, getting in each other's way.

15   Bella's wintertime sisters get even more rest, since numerous tasks, especially foraging tasks, aren't begging for attention at that time of year. Most of
these girls' work consists in keeping each other and the precious queen warm,
not by hibernating, as many believe, but by drawing tightly together into a ball
with the queen near the center, and keeping the ball in slow, constant motion
all winter long—the toasty bees on the inside gradually moving to the outside
to take the places of the chilled ones, who in turn move in for a brief stay near
the colony's inner fire. The extra rest these winter workers get appears to mean
longer life, as many as three or four months above and beyond that of the
summer bees. Even so, a single worker bee, no matter what time of year she's
born, doesn't live to celebrate a birthday.

For all the work performed in a normal hive throughout most weeks of the
year, the rub still is—you guessed it—the fact that every bit of it has to be
done countless times over. Every task completed will have to be taken up
anew, if not by this worker bee then by that one, if not this summer season
then the next. *Everything you do will be insignificant, but you must do it anyway.* The question persists: what in the world *for*?

For the sake of the world itself, it seems, for starters. For the very *formation* of the world. Scott Russell Sanders[7] speaks of the "force of spirit" in a recent book by that title, but I find myself dwelling on the force of form—on
the force with which spirit demands manifestation. The unspeakably powerful spirit of life comes we know not whence and goes we know not where, but
it always does so in *forms*—a wax cell here, a beaver lodge there; an orchard
heavy with fruit, a stream dammed into habitat for water striders and wading

6. "Lapse" refers to the fall in the Garden of Eden of Adam and Eve, the biblical parents of all humanity.
7. American essayist (b. 1946).

birds. A world built and rebuilt, world without end, so long as bees and beavers go about their work. Things do not fall altogether apart[8]—at least, not right away, and not until some other creature comes along, say a bacterium of some kind, whose own special work it is to dismantle the world. And even then, the scattering of molecules out there in the fallen leaves is prelude to some new construction project or other. The center does hold,[9] as long as every being at the periphery keeps to its given work, its given activity, its own in*form*ation.

That is, while at work a creature is not just shaping its own little corner of the world: it is also forming itself, coming into its own (we might say), living out its own form's dictates. In his wonderful little book *The Hungry Soul*, Leon Kass[10] writes that, "To be something, to be a particular animal in the full sense, is to be that animal-at-work: Really to be a squirrel means to be actively engaged in the constellation of activities we can call 'squirreling.' . . ." "Do your work," wrote Emerson[11] in a similar vein, "and I shall know you. Do your work, and you shall reinforce yourself." For us as for animals, the work we undertake is a major key to our identity: if we're lucky, we do work that we have been formed *for*. (If only each of us could know what that is, as easily as a squirrel or a honeybee knows!) It would seem that a big reason we work is just to realize something of who we are—to find out what we're made of, what we're capable of. Be we tinker, tailor, soldier, or spy, we yearn to find out which of the world's countless itches we were born to scratch.

For work can only be performed upon the world, in response to problems (using the word loosely here) presented by other forms, by phenomena lying outside ourselves. Just as the eye sees only when it encounters an object to be seen, just as the tongue tastes only in the presence of flavor, so the elements of identity—will, energy, brain, opposable thumbs in a person, compound eyes in a honeybee—join forces and go to work only when some part of the world presents itself in invitation. A flower oozes sweet, minute droplets of nectar; another flower sheds its golden dust, a little of which the visiting bee will accidentally deposit on the next flower over, cradled in a branch just inches away, in the course of her work. And all so that spirit may soon say *peach*. *Orange*. *Almond*. *Pecan*. Behold, all work is vanity and vexation of spirit—but first it is beauty, spirit's good news. Creation itself, shining wet and new as youth and maiden on that first day of their perfect, prelapsarian[12] beginning.

"The forms of beauty fall naturally around the path of him who is in the performance of his proper work; as the curled shaving drop from the plane, and borings cluster around the auger," wrote Thoreau.[13] Thus will

20

---

8. Wallace is quoting "The Second Coming," a 1920 poem by the Irish poet William Butler Yeats (1865–1939), who writes, "Things fall apart; the centre does not hold."

9. Wallace is playing on Yeats's line (above).

10. American professor, physician, and biologist (b. 1939).

11. Ralph Waldo Emerson (1803–1882), American poet, essayist, and philosopher.

12. Before the fall in Eden.

13. Henry David Thoreau (1817–1862), American writer and philosopher.

the neighborhood of honeybees grow fatly into an orchard, and the orchard will nourish children and squirrels and juncos and mushrooms and earthworms and springtails. And these in their turn will do unto the world as it has been done unto them, for good and for ill, and always in spirit's fantastic guises.

QUESTIONS

1. Popular expressions and maxims comment on the work of bees—for example, "Busy as a bee" or "The busy bee has no time for sorrow"—usually to encourage human beings to work hard, too. Wallace begins with the ceaseless work of honeybees (paragraph 1) and then compares it to human work (paragraphs 2–5). What parallels does she suggest? What differences?

2. The middle section of Wallace's essay (paragraphs 6–15) describes the life cycle of a worker bee, whom she calls "Bella." Retrace that life cycle, looking for periods of rest as well as work. What implicit model is Wallace suggesting for human life, too?

3. In the final section (paragraph 18), Wallace writes that the bee is "not just shaping its own little corner of the world: it is also forming itself, coming into its own." What does she mean? How does she suggest that work can be a mode of self-formation for humans, too?

4. Write a descriptive essay about an animal, large or small, that draws parallels to or shows differences from human life.

ALEXANDER PETRUNKEVITCH *The Spider and the Wasp*

IN THE FEEDING and safeguarding of their progeny insects and spiders exhibit some interesting analogies to reasoning and some crass examples of blind instinct. The case I propose to describe here is that of the tarantula spiders and their archenemy, the digger wasps of the genus Pepsis. It is a classic example of what looks like intelligence pitted against instinct—a strange situation in which the victim, though fully able to defend itself, submits unwittingly to its destruction.

Most tarantulas live in the tropics, but several species occur in the temperate zone and a few are common in the southern U.S. Some varieties are large and have powerful fangs with which they can inflict a deep wound. These formidable looking spiders do not, however, attack man; you can hold one in your hand, if you are gentle, without being bitten. Their bite is danger-

Published as an article in Scientific American *(August 1952), America's leading scientific monthly for nonspecialist readers. The illustrations appeared with the original article.*

ous only to insects and small mammals such as mice; for man it is no worse than a hornet's sting.

Tarantulas customarily live in deep cylindrical burrows, from which they emerge at dusk and into which they retire at dawn. Mature males wander about after dark in search of females and occasionally stray into houses. After mating, the male dies in a few weeks, but a female lives much longer and can mate several years in succession. In a Paris museum is a tropical specimen which is said to have been living in captivity for 25 years.

A fertilized female tarantula lays from 200 to 400 eggs at a time; thus it is possible for a single tarantula to produce several thousand young. She takes no care of them beyond weaving a cocoon of silk to enclose the eggs. After they hatch, the young walk away, find convenient places in which to dig their burrows and spend the rest of their lives in solitude. The eyesight of tarantulas is poor, being limited to a sensing of change in the intensity of light and to the perception of moving objects. They apparently have little or no sense of hearing, for a hungry tarantula will pay no attention to a loudly chirping cricket placed in its cage unless the insect happens to touch one of its legs.

But all spiders, and especially hairy ones, have an extremely delicate sense 5
of touch. Laboratory experiments prove that tarantulas can distinguish three types of touch: pressure against the body wall, stroking of the body hair, and riffling of certain very fine hairs on the legs called trichobothria. Pressure against the body, by the finger or the end of a pencil, causes the tarantula to move off slowly for a short distance. The touch excites no defensive response unless the approach is from above where the spider can see the motion, in which case it rises on its hind legs, lifts its front legs, opens its fangs and holds this threatening posture as long as the object continues to move.

The entire body of a tarantula, especially its legs, is thickly clothed with hair. Some of it is short and wooly, some long and stiff. Touching this body hair produces one of two distinct reactions. When the spider is hungry, it responds with an immediate and swift attack. At the touch of a cricket's antennae the tarantula seizes the insect so swiftly that a motion picture taken at the rate of 64 frames per second shows only the result and not the process of capture. But when the spider is not hungry, the stimulation of its hairs merely causes it to shake the touched limb. An insect can walk under its hairy belly unharmed.

The trichobothria, very fine hairs growing from dislike[1] membranes on the legs, are sensitive only to air movement. A light breeze makes them vibrate slowly, without disturbing the common hair. When one blows gently on the trichobothria, the tarantula reacts with a quick jerk of its four front legs. If the front and hind legs are stimulated at the same time, the spider makes a sudden jump. This reaction is quite independent of the state of its appetite.

These three tactile responses—to pressure on the body wall, to moving of the common hair, and to flexing of the trichobothria—are so different from one another that there is no possibility of confusing them. They serve the

1. Unlike or dissimilar.

tarantula adequately for most of its needs and enable it to avoid most annoyances and dangers. But they fail the spider completely when it meets its deadly enemy, the digger wasp Pepsis.

These solitary wasps are beautiful and formidable creatures. Most species are either a deep shiny blue all over, or deep blue with rusty wings. The largest have a wing span of about four inches. They live on nectar. When excited, they give off a pungent odor—a warning that they are ready to attack. The sting is much worse than that of a bee or common wasp, and the pain and swelling last longer. In the adult stage the wasp lives only a few months. The female produces but a few eggs, one at a time at intervals of two or three days. For each egg the mother must provide one adult tarantula, alive but paralyzed. The mother wasp attaches the egg to the paralyzed spider's abdomen. Upon hatching from the egg, the larva is many hundreds of times smaller than its living but helpless victim. It eats no other food and drinks no water. By the time it has finished its single Gargantuan meal and become ready for wasphood, nothing remains of the tarantula but its indigestible chitinous skeleton.

10   The mother wasp goes tarantula-hunting when the egg in her ovary is almost ready to be laid. Flying low over the ground late on a sunny afternoon,

SPIDER AND WASP are the tarantula *Cyrtopholis portoricae* (*top*) and the digger wasp *Pepsis marginata* (*bottom*). The tarantula is shown in an attitude of defense. The wasps of the genus Pepsis are either a deep blue or blue with rust-colored wings. The largest species of the genus have a wingspread of about four inches.

the wasp looks for its victim or for the mouth of a tarantula burrow, a round hole edged by a bit of silk. The sex of the spider makes no difference, but the mother is highly discriminating as to species. Each species of Pepsis requires a certain species of tarantula, and the wasp will not attack the wrong species. In a cage with a tarantula which is not its normal prey, the wasp avoids the spider and is usually killed by it in the night.

Yet when a wasp finds the correct species, it is the other way about. To identify the species the wasp apparently must explore the spider with her antennae. The tarantula shows an amazing tolerance to this exploration. The wasp crawls under it and walks over it without evoking any hostile response. The molestation is so great and so persistent that the tarantula often rises on all eight legs, as if it were on stilts. It may stand this way for several minutes. Meanwhile the wasp, having satisfied itself that the victim is of the right species, moves off a few inches to dig the spider's grave. Working vigorously with legs and jaws, it excavates a hole 8 to 10 inches deep with a diameter slightly larger than the spider's girth. Now and again the wasp pops out of the hole to make sure that the spider is still there.

When the grave is finished, the wasp returns to the tarantula to complete her ghastly enterprise. First she feels it all over once more with her antennae. Then her behavior becomes more aggressive. She bends her abdomen, protruding her sting, and searches for the soft membrane at the point where the spider's legs join its body—the only spot where she can penetrate the horny skeleton. From time to time, as the exasperated spider slowly shifts ground, the wasp turns on her back and slides along with the aid of her wings, trying to get under the tarantula for a shot at the vital spot. During all this maneuvering, which can last for several minutes, the tarantula makes no move to save itself. Finally the wasp corners it against some obstruction and grasps one of its legs in her powerful jaws. Now at last the harassed spider tries a desperate but vain defense. The two contestants roll over and over on the ground. It is a terrifying sight and the outcome is always the same. The wasp finally manages to thrust her sting into the soft spot and holds it there for a few seconds while she pumps in the poison. Almost immediately the tarantula falls paralyzed on its back. Its legs stop twitching; its heart stops beating. Yet it is not dead, as is shown by the fact that if taken from the wasp it can be restored to some sensitivity by being kept in a moist chamber for several months.

After paralyzing the tarantula, the wasp cleans herself by dragging her body along the ground and rubbing her feet, sucks the drop of blood oozing from the wound in the spider's abdomen, then grabs a leg of the flabby, helpless animal in her jaws and drags it down to the bottom of the grave. She stays there for many minutes, sometimes for several hours, and what she does all that time in the dark we do not know. Eventually she lays her egg and attaches it to the side of the spider's abdomen with a sticky secretion. Then she emerges, fills the grave with soil carried bit by bit in her jaws, and finally tramples the ground all around to hide any trace of the grave from prowlers. Then she flies away, leaving her descendant safely started in life.

DEATH OF THE SPIDER is shown in these drawings. In the first drawing the wasp digs a grave, occasionally looking out.

In all this the behavior of the wasp evidently is qualitatively different from that of the spider. The wasp acts like an intelligent animal. This is not to say that instinct plays no part or that she reasons as man does. But her actions are to the point; they are not automatic and can be modified to fit the situation. We do not know for certain how she identifies the tarantula—probably it is by some olfactory or chemo-tactile sense—but she does it purposefully and does not blindly tackle a wrong species.

15   On the other hand, the tarantula's behavior shows only confusion. Evidently the wasp's pawing gives it no pleasure, for it tries to move away. That the wasp is not simulating sexual stimulation is certain because male and female tarantulas react in the same way to its advances. That the spider is not anesthetized by some odorless secretion is easily shown by blowing lightly at the tarantula and making it jump suddenly. What, then, makes the tarantula behave as stupidly as it does?

No clear, simple answer is available. Possibly the stimulation by the wasp's antennae is masked by a heavier pressure on the spider's body, so that it reacts as when prodded by a pencil. But the explanation may be much more complex. Initiative in attack is not in the nature of tarantulas; most species fight only when cornered so that escape is impossible. Their inherited patterns of behavior apparently prompt them to avoid problems rather than attack them. For example, spiders always weave their webs in three dimensions, and when a spider finds that there is insufficient space to attach certain threads in the third dimension, it leaves the place and seeks another, instead of finishing the web in a single plane. This urge to escape seems to arise under all circumstances, in all phases of life, and to take the place of reasoning. For a spider to change the pattern of its web is as impossible as for an inexperienced man to build a bridge across a chasm obstructing his way.

In a way the instinctive urge to escape is not only easier but often more efficient than reasoning. The tarantula does exactly what is most efficient in all cases except in an encounter with a ruthless and determined attacker dependent for the existence of her own species on killing as many tarantulas

The spider stands with its legs extended after raising its body so the wasp could pass under it. In the second drawing the wasp stings the spider, which falls on its back. In the third the wasp licks a drop of blood from the wound. In the final drawing the spider lies in its grave with the egg of the wasp on its abdomen.

as she can lay eggs. Perhaps in this case the spider follows its usual pattern of trying to escape, instead of seizing and killing the wasp, because it is not aware of its danger. In any case, the survival of the tarantula species as a whole is protected by the fact that the spider is much more fertile than the wasp.

QUESTIONS

1. Why is Petrunkevitch's initial description of the tarantula longer than his initial description of the wasp?

2. What are the major points of contrast between the spider and the wasp? Why does Petrunkevitch emphasize these particular points rather than others?

3. Petrunkevitch suggests more than one hypothesis for the behavior of the tarantula; indeed, he says that "no clear, simple answer is available" (paragraph 16). How does he test the possible explanations? Which one do you think he prefers?

4. What evidence is there that Petrunkevitch sees the tarantula and the wasp at least partly in human terms? In a brief essay explain why you think this is or is not a legitimate perspective for a scientist.

CHIEF SEATTLE   *Letter to President Pierce, 1855*

W
E KNOW THAT the white man does not understand our ways. One portion of the land is the same to him as the next, for he is a stranger who comes in the night and takes from the land whatever he needs. The earth is not his brother, but his enemy, and when he has conquered it, he moves on. He leaves his fathers' graves, and his children's birthright is forgotten. The sight of your cities pains the eyes of the red man. But perhaps it is because the red man is a savage and does not understand.

There is no quiet place in the white man's cities. No place to hear the leaves of spring or the rustle of insects' wings. But perhaps because I am a savage and do not understand, the clatter only seems to insult the ears. The Indian prefers the soft sound of the wind darting over the face of the pond, the smell of the wind itself cleansed by a mid-day rain, or scented with the piñon pine. The air is precious to the red man. For all things share the same breath—the beasts, the trees, the man. Like a man dying for many days, he is numb to the stench.

What is man without the beasts? If all the beasts were gone, men would die from great loneliness of spirit, for whatever happens to the beasts also happens to man. All things are connected. Whatever befalls the earth befalls the sons of the earth.

It matters little where we pass the rest of our days; they are not many. A few more hours, a few more winters, and none of the children of the great tribes that once lived on this earth, or that roamed in small bands in the woods, will be left to mourn the graves of a people once as powerful and hopeful as yours.

5   The whites, too, shall pass—perhaps sooner than other tribes. Continue to contaminate your bed, and you will one night suffocate in your own waste. When the buffalo are all slaughtered, the wild horses all tamed, the secret corners of the forest heavy with the scent of many men, and the view of the ripe hills blotted by talking wires,[1] where is the thicket? Gone. Where is the eagle? Gone. And what is it to say goodby to the swift and the hunt, the end of living and the beginning of survival? We might understand if we knew what it was that the white man dreams, what he describes to his children on the long winter nights, what visions he burns into their minds, so they will wish for tomorrow. But we are savages. The white man's dreams are hidden from us.

Because of its origin as an oration given in Salish, there are many different versions of Chief Seattle's speech; this one comes from Native American Testimony: An Anthology of Indian and White Relations, *edited by Peter Nabokov (1977).*

1. I.e., the telegraph.

642

Questions

1. Chief Seattle repeatedly refers to the red man as "a savage" who "does not understand," yet in the course of this letter he gives evidence of a great deal of understanding. What is the purpose of such ironic comments and apparently self-disparaging remarks?

2. Scholars have recently suggested that Chief Seattle's "Letter" is in fact the creation of a white man, based on Seattle's public oratory. If so, what rhetorical techniques does the white editor associate with Indian speech? Why might he have done so?

3. A surprisingly modern note of ecological awareness resounds in the statement "[W]hatever happens to the beasts also happens to man. All things are connected" (paragraph 3). Locate two or three similar observations, and explain their effectiveness.

4. Chief Seattle says that the red man might understand the white man better "if we knew what it was that the white man dreams, what he describes to his children on the long winter nights, what visions he burns into their minds, so they will wish for tomorrow" (paragraph 5). Write a short essay explaining, either straightforwardly or ironically, how "the white man" might reply. If you prefer, write the reply itself.

ALDO LEOPOLD   *Marshland Elegy*

A DAWN WIND STIRS on the great marsh. With almost imperceptible slowness it rolls a bank of fog across the wide morass. Like the white ghost of a glacier the mists advance, riding over phalanxes of tamarack, sliding across bog-meadows heavy with dew. A single silence hangs from horizon to horizon.

Out of some far recess of the sky a tinkling of little bells falls soft upon the listening land. Then again silence. Now comes a baying of some sweet-throated hound, soon the clamor of a responding pack. Then a far clear blast of hunting horns, out of the sky into the fog.

High horns, low horns, silence, and finally a pandemonium of trumpets, rattles, croaks, and cries that almost shakes the bog with its nearness, but without yet disclosing whence it comes. At last a glint of sun reveals the approach of a great echelon of birds. On motionless wing they emerge from the lifting mists, sweep a final arc of sky, and settle in clangorous descending spirals to their feeding grounds. A new day has begun on the crane marsh.

A sense of time lies thick and heavy on such a place. Yearly since the ice age it has awakened each spring to the clangor of cranes. The peat layers that com-

First appeared in American Forests *(October 1937), a century-old journal that calls itself "the quarterly magazine of trees and forests"; later reprinted in Leopold's classic book of nature writing* A Sand County Almanac *(1949).*

prise the bog are laid down in the basin of an ancient lake. The cranes stand, as it were, upon the sodden pages of their own history. These peats are the compressed remains of the mosses that clogged the pools, of the tamaracks that spread over the moss, of the cranes that bugled over the tamaracks since the retreat of the ice sheet. An endless caravan of generations has built of its own bones this bridge into the future, this habitat where the oncoming host again may live and breed and die.

5   To what end? Out on the bog a crane, gulping some luckless frog, springs his ungainly hulk into the air and flails the morning sun with mighty wings. The tamaracks re-echo with his bugled certitude. He seems to know.

Our ability to perceive quality in nature begins, as in art, with the pretty. It expands through successive stages of the beautiful to values as yet uncaptured by language. The quality of cranes lies, I think, in this higher gamut, as yet beyond the reach of words.

This much, though, can be said: our appreciation of the crane grows with the slow unraveling of earthly history. His tribe, we now know, stems out of the remote Eocene.[1] The other members of the fauna in which he originated are long since entombed within the hills. When we hear his call we hear no mere bird. We hear the trumpet in the orchestra of evolution. He is the symbol of our untamable past, of that incredible sweep of millennia which underlies and conditions the daily affairs of birds and men.

And so they live and have their being—these cranes—not in the constricted present, but in the wider reaches of evolutionary time. Their annual return is the ticking of the geologic clock. Upon the place of their return they confer a peculiar distinction. Amid the endless mediocrity of the commonplace, a crane marsh holds a palentological patent of nobility, won in the march of aeons, and revocable only by shotgun. The sadness discernible in some marshes arises, perhaps, from their once having harbored cranes. Now, they stand humbled, adrift in history.

Some sense of this quality in cranes seems to have been felt by sportsmen and ornithologists of all ages. Upon such quarry as this the Holy Roman Emperor Frederick loosed his gyrfalcons.[2] Upon such quarry as this once swooped the hawks of Kublai Khan. Marco Polo tells us: "He derives the highest amusement from sporting with gyrfalcons and hawks. At Changanor the Khan has a great Palace surrounded by a fine plain where are found cranes in great numbers. He causes millet and other grains to be sown in order that the birds may not want."[3]

1. The epoch forty to fifty-five million years ago, when mammals first appeared.
2. Frederick (c. 1123–1190), Holy Roman Emperor (1152–90), known as Frederick Barbarossa; gyrfalcon, a large white falcon used for hunting.
3. Kublai Khan (1215–1294), Chinese emperor, founder of the Mongol dynasty; Marco Polo (c. 1254–1324), Italian traveler to China during Kublai Khan's reign; chapter 56 of Marco Polo's *Travels* describes the Khan's palace at Changanor, where he maintained a marsh for cranes so that he could hunt them.

The ornithologist Bengt Berg,[4] seeing cranes as a boy upon the Swedish   10
heaths, forthwith made them his life work. He followed them to Africa and
discovered their winter retreat on the White Nile. He says of his first encounter: "It was a spectacle which eclipsed the flight of the roc in the Thousand and One Nights."[5]

When the glacier came down out of the north, crunching hills and gouging
valleys, some adventuring rampart of the ice climbed the Baraboo Hills[6] and
fell back into the outlet gorge of the Wisconsin River. The swollen waters
backed up and formed a lake half as long as the state, bordered on the east by
cliffs of ice, and fed by the torrents that fell from melting mountains. The
shorelines of this old lake are still visible; its bottom is the bottom of the great
marsh.

The lake rose through the centuries, finally spilling over east of the Baraboo range. There it cut a new channel for the river, and thus drained itself. To
the residual lagoons came the cranes, bugling the defeat of the retreating winter, summoning the on-creeping host of living things to their collective task of
marsh-building. Floating bogs of sphagnum moss clogged the lowered waters,
filled them. Sedge and leatherleaf, tamarack and spruce successively advanced
over the bog, anchoring it by their root fabric, sucking out its water, making
peat. The lagoons disappeared, but not the cranes. To the moss-meadows that
replaced the ancient waterways they returned each spring to dance and bugle
and rear their gangling sorrel-colored young. These, albeit birds, are not properly called chicks, but *colts*. I cannot explain why. On some dewy June morning watch them gambol over their ancestral pastures at the heels of the roan
mare, and you will see for yourself.

One year not long ago a French trapper in buckskins pushed his canoe up
one of the moss-clogged creeks that thread the great marsh. At this attempt to
invade their miry stronghold the cranes gave vent to loud and ribald laughter.
A century or two later Englishmen came in covered wagons. They chopped
clearings in the timbered moraines that border the marsh, and in them planted
corn and buckwheat. They did not intend, like the Great Khan at Changanor,
to feed the cranes. But the cranes do not question the intent of glaciers, emperors, or pioneers. They ate the grain, and when some irate farmer failed to
concede their usufruct in his corn, they trumpeted a warning and sailed across
the marsh to another farm.

There was no alfalfa in those days, and the hill-farms made poor hay land,
especially in dry years. One dry year someone set a fire in the tamaracks. The
burn grew up quickly to bluejoint grass,[7] which, when cleared of dead trees,
made a dependable hay meadow. After that, each August, men appeared to cut

4. Swedish ornithologist and nature photographer (1885–1967).

5. Roc is the giant Arabian bird who carries off Sinbad in *The Thousand and One
Nights*, the famous Middle Eastern collection of tales.

6. A range in south-central Wisconsin.

7. A reed grass that grows rapidly on soil that has been burned.

hay. In winter, after the cranes had gone South, they drove wagons over the frozen bogs and hauled the hay to their farms in the hills. Yearly they plied the marsh with fire and axe, and in two short decades hay meadows dotted the whole expanse.

15   Each August when the haymakers came to pitch their camps, singing and drinking and lashing their teams with whip and tongue, the cranes whinnied to their colts and retreated to the far fastnesses. "Red shitepokes" the haymakers called them, from the rusty hue which at that season often stains the battleship-gray of crane plumage. After the hay was stacked and the marsh again their own, the cranes returned, to call down out of October skies the migrant flocks from Canada. Together they wheeled over the new-cut stubbles and raided the corn until frosts gave the signal for the winter exodus.

These haymeadow days were the Arcadian age[8] for marsh dwellers. Man and beast, plant and soil lived on and with each other in mutual toleration, to the mutual benefit of all. The marsh might have kept on producing hay and prairie chickens, deer and muskrat, crane-music and cranberries forever.

The new overlords did not understand this. They did not include soil, plants, or birds in their ideas of mutuality. The dividends of such a balanced economy were too modest. They envisaged farms not only around, but *in* the marsh. An epidemic of ditch-digging and land-booming set in. The marsh was gridironed with drainage canals, speckled with new fields and farmsteads.

But crops were poor and beset by frosts, to which the expensive ditches added an aftermath of debt. Farmers moved out. Peat beds dried, shrank, caught fire. Sun-energy out of the Pleistocene[9] shrouded the countryside in acrid smoke. No man raised his voice against the waste, only his nose against the smell. After a dry summer not even the winter snows could extinguish the smoldering marsh. Great pockmarks were burned into field and meadow, the scars reaching down to the sands of the old lake, peat-covered these hundred centuries. Rank weeds sprang out of the ashes, to be followed after a year or two by aspen scrub. The cranes were hard put, their numbers shrinking with the remnants of unburned meadow. For them, the song of the power shovel came near being an elegy. The high priests of progress knew nothing of cranes, and cared less. What is a species more or less among engineers? What good is an undrained marsh anyhow?

For a decade or two crops grew poorer, fires deeper, wood-fields larger, and cranes scarcer, year by year. Only reflooding, it appeared, could keep the peat from burning. Meanwhile cranberry growers had, by plugging drainage ditches, reflooded a few spots and obtained good yields. Distant politicians bugled about marginal land, over-production, unemployment relief, conservation. Economists and planners came to look at the marsh. Surveyors, technicians, CCC's,[10] buzzed about. A counter-epidemic of reflooding set in.

8. An era of innocent peace and contentment.

9. The epoch beginning two million years ago and ending about ten thousand years ago; this era saw the last Ice Age and the first appearance of modern humans.

10. Civilian Conservation Corps, a Depression-era agency that sent the unemployed to work in forests and wild areas.

Government bought land, resettled farmers, plugged ditches wholesale. Slowly the bogs are re-wetting. The fire-pocks become ponds. Grass fires still burn, but they can no longer burn the wetted soil.

All this, once the CCC camps were gone, was good for cranes, but not so   20
the thickets of scrub popple that spread inexorably over the old burns, and still less the maze of new roads that inevitably follow governmental conservation. To build a road is so much simpler than to think of what the country really needs. A roadless marsh is seemingly as worthless to the alphabetical conservationist as an undrained one was to the empire-builders. Solitude, the one natural resource still undowered of alphabets, is so far recognized as valuable only by ornithologists and cranes.

Thus always does history, whether of marsh or market place, end in paradox. The ultimate value in these marshes is wildness, and the crane is wildness incarnate. But all conservation of wildness is self-defeating, for to cherish we must see and fondle, and when enough have seen and fondled, there is no wilderness left to cherish.

Some day, perhaps in the very process of our benefactions, perhaps in the fullness of geologic time, the last crane will trumpet his farewell and spiral skyward from the great marsh. High out of the clouds will fall the sound of hunting horns, the baying of the phantom pack, the tinkle of little bells, and then a silence never to be broken, unless perchance in some far pasture of the Milky Way.

QUESTIONS

1. Why does Leopold connect cranes with significant historical figures and epochs?

2. Leopold employs white spaces in addition to normal paragraph divisions. Can you explain how these white spaces work in his essay?

3. Is the last paragraph a kind of warning about increased hunting? Fifty years after Leopold's essay, have other dangers to marshlands become more worrisome?

4. Write your own account of a natural phenomenon that has disappeared in your lifetime—or that is in the process of disappearing.

MARY OLIVER   *Waste Land: An Elegy*

At our town's old burn dump, not officially used for years, discarded peppermint and raspberries reconnected their roots to the gravelly earth and went on growing; a couple of apple trees blossomed and bore each year a bushel of green and bumpy fruit. Blackberries drifted up and down the slopes; thistles, Bouncing Bet, everlasting, goldenrod, wild carrot lifted their leaves and then their flowers and then their rafts of seeds. Honeysuckle, in uplifted waves, washed toward some pink roses, no longer a neat and civilized hedge but a thorny ledge, with darkness at its hem. Now the burn dump is no more. The old world had its necessities; presently there are new ones, and they are not so simply met—nor will the old parcels of land suffice. On these few acres of land, and more, will be established the heartland of our town's sewage, where the buried pipes will converge with the waste of our lives. What a sad hilarity! I want to talk about flowers, but the necessity has become, for our visitor-rich town, how to deal with the daily sewage of, it may be, sixty thousand souls. At least that was a weekend estimate a few years ago. They come, to this last town on the long Cape,[1] in good part for the very beauty that their numbers imperil. They come for fellowship, the beaches and the sun, the entertainment, the shops and restaurants. They inhabit old captains' houses turned into inns, or the condominiums ever rising along newly created streets and crowded cul-de-sacs. So, this is an elegy.

In the summers, black snakes swirled among the creamy blossoms of the honeysuckle and the pink-petaled roses. When I walked through the grass, their black faces appeared, like exotic flowers. There were almost always two of them, sometimes three. One had eyes the color of garnets. It gave no greeting, only a long, motionless gaze. And they were brave, those snakes. Occasionally when I came upon a pair sleeping in the sun, on stones or a heap of old asphalt shingles, one of them would streak toward me and fling itself against my body, before it turned and followed the other away, whipping after it into the shadows under the roses.

Soon they will be off, hunting another place to live. Which may not be so easy, for the world today is nothing if it is not sprawl, and this not only within the residential areas but the seemingly endless facilities such settlements need. And we do need them. (So, this is an elegy.) Box turtles nested here, and painted turtles also. Out of the shallow ponds below the crest of the hill, snapping turtles crawled to lay their pale, leathery eggs. Raccoons aspire to them; many of the nests were ransacked as soon as the turtle had

Published in Orion *magazine (September/October 2003) just before the appearance of Oliver's book collection,* Long Life: Essays and Other Writings *(2004).*

1. Cape Cod, Massachusetts.

shuffled away. Foxes left their dainty tracks, and in summer the red-coated deer.

The toad was always here, with his gold-rimmed eyes.

And, in a certain shaded place nearby, the uncommon, cool and gleaming   5
bunchberry.

For years there were signs posted, prohibitions against leaving trash. In more recent years another sign designated the area a motorcycle and motor-bike course. The bikes appeared most often in the afternoons; they snarled over the field, they cut ruts along the trails, they raced with a furious, uncontainable form of boy-energy and noise. I hated it, yet did not resent it. There must be a place for boys and their trappings, though surely it should not have been here, on one of the few town-owned woodlands fresh and untrammeled except for its polluted center. Also it joined seamlessly with the National Seashore, and what young boy hunched over the handlebars of his bike could remember that invisible line? So sections of the park's shady paths also became rutted by tires and besotted by blown trash. But when space is limited for recreations of such different kinds, compatibility is given improbable tasks.

As for the trash, which gathered in spite of the signs, it did what trash does and ever will do; it lay there, and did not grow thin or fade or even, much of it, rot. Old stoves were predominant. And dozens of tires, lining the bike track, the standing water within them breeding uncountable numbers of mosquitoes.

And yet, at certain hours, in the absence of boys and their bikes, I could walk here and see birds I found nowhere else: the indigo bunting, for example, and the black-billed cuckoo. And their more findable associates: goldfinches, catbirds, the brown thrasher, the yellowthroat, palm warblers, the grosbeak. The ruby-throated hummingbird nested here, but even now I will not tell you in precisely what tree. It was a secret to be kept then, so why not keep it still, now that the birds and the tree itself have vanished? And there were daisies, and butter-and-eggs, and milkweed with its mauve pendants, and Black-eyed Susans. There were rugosas, white and red. In the summer light they shot upward heavy with buds and pleated, glossy leaves. Then sagged under their own sweet weight.

But this is an elegy. Now there are buildings to take care of this new and important work. A brick building, neat and Cape Cod enough that it could almost be a bank! And behind it a huge, circular, cement construction—I cannot call it a building—round and thick-walled: not built for beauty, and not yet finished. Piles of pipes are everywhere. The blackberries that climbed up and down the hill, the goldenrod, the honeysuckle are gone; the pink roses are gone; the fox tracks are gone.

The land itself has been capped against the poisons that have been seep-   10
ing all these years into the ground, from the fires, from the unknown elements cast away: oils and paints and car batteries and a hundred offensive substances more. And, imagine! for what unaware years I picked the blackberries and the raspberries, and thought them sweet and fine—thought them good

fortune. And found, on the rubbled hillsides, strange shapes of old jars, glass bent and reshaped by the flames. Nuggets of deep blue from medicine containers; once a glass airplane that originally held candy, with a chip missing from one wing.

But, this is an elegy. A part of the book of not-wanting-to-let-go. And, go it must; and go it has. The pink roses and the toad with gold-rimmed eyes. The young boys on bikes who in fact are men now. Even the tires are gone. The town government has made its not unreasonable decision. We cannot continue with failing cesspools; we cannot condone seepage into the water supply, or into the blue harbor that lies along the town's frontage. And, we are so many.

In May the moccasin flowers blossomed, even in this thin soil, extravagantly. They stood in gatherings of six or seven, like small choirs getting ready to sing. Very rarely, one flower would rise pure white.

I do not like what has happened. I do not hold the loss lightly. I wish to be reasonable; I know I must be amenable to what is necessary. But—such few choices! I apologize to the hummingbird. I hope the snakes have found a new home. I hope the new system works. I am glad that I have a good memory; I will not forget the dainty tracks of the fox, or the goldfinches, or the everlasting. I think I know what our manifest, tree-filled, creature-lively world is—our garden and our pasture and our recreation. Also it is our schoolhouse, courthouse, church, graveyard, and the soft breath of eternity.

I walk in the world to love it. Only one question, really, frightens me. I wonder why, in all the years I walked in the old burn dump—this waste place, this secret garden—I never met another soul there, who had come forth for a like reason.

QUESTIONS

1. An elegy is a lament for something lost, often for the death of a person. What losses does Oliver write about in this essay?

2. At the end of a traditional elegy, the poet or writer offers consolation to the bereaved or hope for the future. Does Oliver offer consolation, or does she leave the reader with a sense of loss? Locate the places in the ending (paragraphs 13–14) that support your response.

3. Other authors in *The Norton Reader* write about dumps—Wallace Stegner in "The Dump Ground" and Lars Eighner in "On Dumpster Diving" (see Personal Report). Write an essay in which you compare Oliver's experience and interest in her town dump with one of their essays.

WILLIAM CRONON *The Trouble with Wilderness*

RESERVING WILDERNESS has for decades been a fundamental tenet—indeed, a passion—of the environmental movement, especially in the United States. For many Americans, wilderness stands as the last place where civilization, that all-too-human disease, has not fully infected the earth. It is an island in the polluted sea of urban-industrial modernity, a refuge we must somehow recover to save the planet. As Henry David Thoreau famously declared, "In Wildness is the preservation of the World."

But is it? The more one knows of its peculiar history, the more one realizes that wilderness is not quite what it seems. Far from being the one place on earth that stands apart from humanity, it is quite profoundly a human creation—indeed, the creation of very particular human cultures at very particular moments in human history. It is not a pristine sanctuary where the last remnant of an endangered but still transcendent nature can be encountered without the contaminating taint of civilization. Instead, it is a product of that civilization. As we gaze into the mirror it holds up for us, we too easily imagine that what we behold is nature when in fact we see the reflection of our own longings and desires. Wilderness can hardly be the solution to our culture's problematic relationship with the nonhuman world, for wilderness is itself a part of the problem.

To assert the unnaturalness of so natural a place may seem perverse: we can all conjure up images and sensations that seem all the more hauntingly real for having engraved themselves so indelibly on our memories. Remember this? The torrents of mist shooting out from the base of a great waterfall in the depths of a Sierra Nevada canyon, the droplets cooling your face as you listen to the roar of the water and gaze toward the sky through a rainbow that hovers just out of reach. Or this: Looking out across a desert canyon in the evening air, the only sound a lone raven calling in the distance, the rock walls dropping away into a chasm so deep that its bottom all but vanishes as you squint into the amber light of the setting sun. Remember the feelings of such moments, and you will know as well as I do that you were in the presence of something irreducibly nonhuman, something profoundly Other than yourself. Wilderness is made of that too.

And yet: what brought each of us to the places where such memories became possible is entirely a cultural invention.

For the Americans who first celebrated it, wilderness was tied to the myth of the frontier. The historian Frederick Jackson Turner wrote the classic academic statement of this myth in 1893, but it had been part of American thought for well over a century. As Turner described the process, Easterners and European immigrants, in moving to the wild lands of the frontier, shed the

5

Cronon published a number of versions of this essay, each aimed at a different audience. This version comes from the New York Times *(August 13, 1995); another version appears as the introduction to his book* Uncommon Ground: Toward Reinventing Nature *(1995).*

trappings of civilization and thereby gained an energy, an independence and a creativity that were the sources of American democracy and national character. Seen this way, wilderness became a place of religious redemption and national renewal, the quintessential location for experiencing what it meant to be an American.

Those who celebrate the frontier almost always look backward, mourning an older, simpler world that has disappeared forever. That world and all its attractions, Turner said, depended on free land—on wilderness. It is no accident that the movement to set aside national parks and wilderness areas gained real momentum just as laments about the vanishing frontier reached their peak. To protect wilderness was to protect the nation's most sacred myth of origin.

The decades following the Civil War saw more and more of the nation's wealthiest citizens seeking out wilderness for themselves. The passion for wild land took many forms: enormous estates in the Adirondacks and elsewhere (disingenuously called "camps" despite their many servants and amenities); cattle ranches for would-be roughriders on the Great Plains; guided big-game hunting trips in the Rockies. Wilderness suddenly emerged as the landscape of choice for elite tourists. For them, it was a place of recreation.

In just this way, wilderness came to embody the frontier myth, standing for the wild freedom of America's past and seeming to represent a highly attractive natural alternative to the ugly artificiality of modern civilization. The irony, of course, was that in the process wilderness came to reflect the very civilization its devotees sought to escape. Ever since the nineteenth century, celebrating wilderness has been an activity mainly for well-to-do city folks. Country people generally know far too much about working the land to regard unworked land as their ideal.

There were other ironies as well. The movement to set aside national parks and wilderness areas followed hard on the heels of the final Indian wars, in which the prior human inhabitants of these regions were rounded up and moved onto reservations so that tourists could safely enjoy the illusion that they were seeing their nation in its pristine, original state—in the new morning of God's own creation. Meanwhile, its original inhabitants were kept out by dint of force, their earlier uses of the land redefined as inappropriate or even illegal. To this day, for instance, the Blackfeet continue to be accused of "poaching" on the lands of Glacier National Park, in Montana, that originally belonged to them and that were ceded by treaty only with the proviso that they be permitted to hunt there.

10   The removal of Indians to create an "uninhabited wilderness" reminds us just how invented and how constructed the American wilderness really is. One of the most striking proofs of the cultural invention of wilderness is its thoroughgoing erasure of the history from which it sprang. In virtually all its manifestations, wilderness represents a flight from history. Seen as the original garden, it is a place outside time, from which human beings had to be ejected before the fallen world of history could properly begin.[1] Seen as

1. According to the Bible, Adam and Eve were ejected from the Garden of Eden for disobeying God's command.

the frontier, it is a savage world at the dawn of civilization, whose transformation represents the very beginning of the national historical epic. Seen as sacred nature, it is the home of a God who transcends history, untouched by time's arrow. No matter what the angle from which we regard it, wilderness offers us the illusion that we can escape the cares and troubles of the world in which our past has ensnared us. It is the natural, unfallen antithesis of an unnatural civilization that has lost its soul, the place where we can see the world as it really is, and so know ourselves as we really are—or ought to be.

The trouble with wilderness is that it reproduces the very values its devotees seek to reject. It offers the illusion that we can somehow wipe clean the slate of our past and return to the tabula rasa[2] that supposedly existed before we began to leave our marks on the world. The dream of an unworked natural landscape is very much the fantasy of people who have never themselves had to work the land to make a living—urban folk for whom food comes from a supermarket or a restaurant instead of a field, and for whom the wooden houses in which they live and work apparently have no meaningful connection to the forests in which trees grow and die. Only people whose relation to the land was already alienated could hold up wilderness as a model for human life in nature, for the romantic ideology of wilderness leaves no place in which human beings can actually make their living from the land.

We live in an urban-industrial civilization, but too often pretend to ourselves that our real home is in the wilderness. We work our nine-to-five jobs, we drive our cars (not least to reach the wilderness), we benefit from the intricate and all too invisible networks with which society shelters us, all the while pretending that these things are not an essential part of who we are. By imagining that our true home is in the wilderness, we forgive ourselves for the homes we actually inhabit. In its flight from history, in its siren song[3] of escape, in its reproduction of the dangerous dualism that sets human beings somehow outside nature—in all these ways, wilderness poses a threat to responsible environmentalism at the end of the twentieth century.

Do not misunderstand me. What I criticize here is not wild nature, but the alienated way we often think of ourselves in relation to it. Wilderness can still teach lessons that are hard to learn anywhere else. When we visit wild places, we find ourselves surrounded by plants and animals and landscapes whose otherness compels our attention. In forcing us to acknowledge that they are not of our making, that they have little or no need for humanity, they recall for us a creation far greater than our own. In wilderness, we need no reminder that a tree has its own reasons for being, quite apart from us—proof that ours is not the only presence in the universe.

We get into trouble only if we see the tree in the garden as wholly artificial and the tree in the wilderness as wholly natural. Both trees in some ultimate sense are wild; both in a practical sense now require our care. We need to rec-

2. Clean slate (Latin).
3. In Homer's *Odyssey*, the Sirens use irresistible songs to tempt Odysseus and his crew to steer their ship toward destruction, so a siren song is an alluring but deceptive appeal.

oncile them, to see a natural landscape that is also cultural, in which city, sub-urb, countryside and wilderness each has its own place. We need to discover a middle ground in which all these things, from city to wilderness, can somehow be encompassed in the word "home." Home, after all, is the place where we live. It is the place for which we take responsibility, the place we try to sustain so we can pass on what is best in it (and in ourselves) to our children.

15   Learning to honor the wild—learning to acknowledge the autonomy of the other—means striving for critical self-consciousness in all our actions. It means that reflection and respect must accompany each act of use, and means we must always consider the possibility of nonuse. It means looking at the part of nature we intend to turn toward our own ends and asking whether we can use it again and again and again—sustainably—without diminishing it in the process. Most of all, it means practicing remembrance and gratitude for the nature, culture and history that have come together to make the world as we know it. If wildness can stop being (just) out there and start being (also) in here, if it can start being as humane as it is natural, then perhaps we can get on with the unending task of struggling to live rightly in the world—not just in the garden, not just in the wilderness, but in the home that encompasses them both.

QUESTIONS

1. In paragraph 12 Cronon writes: "We live in an urban-industrial civilization, but too often pretend to ourselves that our real home is in the wilderness." Cronon gives no ex-amples. What examples might back up Cronon's statement? Can you think of counter-examples as well?

2. Who is Cronon's "we" throughout his essay? Why does he use "we" so fre-quently?

3. Paragraph 2 raises the issue of whether wilderness provides us with a "mirror." Look through the essay for similar visual imagery; then explain the role that such imagery plays.

4. If you found significant counterexamples in response to Question 1, write a letter to the editor in which you question or object to one aspect of Cronon's argument.

JOSEPH WOOD KRUTCH *The Most Dangerous Predator*

I N THE UNITED STATES the slaughter of wild animals for fun is subject to certain restrictions fairly well enforced. In Mexico the laws are less strict and in many regions there is little or no machinery for enforcement. Hence an automobile club in southern California distributes to its members an outline map of Baja[1] purporting to indicate in detail just where various large animals not yet quite extinct may be found by those eager to do their bit toward eliminating them completely. This map gives the impression that pronghorn antelopes, mountain sheep, and various other "game animals" abound.

In actual fact, the country can never have supported very many such and today the traveler accustomed to the open country of our own Southwest would be struck by the fact that, except for sea birds, sea mammals and fish, wildlife of any kind is far scarcer than at home. This is no doubt due in part to American hunters but also in part to the fact that native inhabitants who once could not afford the cartridges to shoot anything they did not intend to eat now get relatively cheap ammunition from the United States and can indulge in what seems to be the almost universal human tendency to kill anything that moves.

Someday—probably a little too late—the promoters of Baja as a resort area will wake up to the fact that wildlife is a tourist attraction and that though any bird or beast can be observed or photographed an unlimited number of times it can be shot only once. The Mexican government is cooperating with the government of the United States in a successful effort to save the gray whale and the sea elephant but to date does not seem much interested in initiating its own measures of protection. As long ago as 1947, Lewis Wayne Walker (who guided me on our innocent hunt for the boojum trees he had previously photographed) wrote for *Natural History Magazine* a survey of the situation, particularly as it concerns the pronghorn and the mountain sheep. A quarter of a century before, herds of antelope were to be found within thirty or forty miles of the United States border. But by 1933 they had all, so a rancher told him, been killed after a party of quail hunters had discovered them. In the roadless areas some bands of mountain sheep still existed (and doubtless do even today) but the water holes near traversable areas were already deserted by the mid forties. All the large animals of a given region must come to drink at the only pool or spring for many miles around, hence a single party need only wait beside it to exterminate the entire population inhabiting that area. Though Walker had driven more than ten thousand miles on the Baja trails

From The Forgotten Peninsula *(1961); later included in a collection,* The Best Nature Writing of Joseph Wood Krutch *(1969).*

1. The Mexican peninsula extending some 760 miles south from the U.S. border and separating the Gulf of California from the Pacific Ocean.

during the two years preceding the writing of his letter, he saw only one deer, no sheep, and no antelope. Despite the publicity given it, "Baja is," he wrote, "the poorest game area I have ever visited."

The depredations of the hunter are not always the result of any fundamental blood lust. Perhaps he is only, more often than not, merely lacking in imagination. The exterminator of the noble animals likes the out-of-doors and thrills at the sight of something which suggests the world as it once was. But contemplation is not widely recognized as an end in itself. Having seen the antelope or the sheep, he must "do something about it." And the obvious thing to do is to shoot.

5   In the *Sea of Cortez* John Steinbeck[2] describes how a Mexican rancher invited his party to a sheep hunt. They were reluctant to accept until they realized that the rancher himself didn't really want to kill the animals—he merely didn't know what other excuse to give for seeking them out. When his Indians returned empty-handed he said with only mild regret: "If they had killed one we could have had our pictures taken with it." Then Steinbeck adds: "They had taught us the best of all ways to go hunting and we shall never use any other. We have, however, made one slight improvement on their method; we shall not take a gun, thereby obviating the last remote possibility of having the hunt cluttered up with game. We have never understood why men mount the heads of animals and hang them up to look down on their conquerors. Possibly it feels good to these men to be superior to animals but it does seem that if they were sure of it they would not have to prove it." Later, when one of the Indians brought back some droppings which he seemed to treasure and presented a portion of them to the white men, Steinbeck adds: "Where another man can say, 'there was an animal but because I am greater than he, he is dead and I am alive and there is his head to prove it' we can say, 'there was an animal, and for all we know there still is and here is proof of it. He was very healthy when we last heard of him.' "

"Very pretty," so the tough-minded will say, "but hardly realistic. Man is a predator, to be sure, but he isn't the only one. The mountain lion killed sheep long before even the Indian came to Baja. The law of life is also a law of death. Nature is red in tooth and claw. You can't get away from that simple fact and there is no use in trying. Whatever else he may be, man is an animal; and like the other animals he is the enemy of all other living things. You talk of 'the balance of nature' but we are an element in it. As we increase, the mountain sheep disappear. The fittest, you know, survive."

Until quite recent times this reply would have been at least a tenable one. Primitive man seems to have been a rather unsuccessful animal, few in numbers and near the ragged edge of extinction. But gradually the balance shifted. He held his own; then he increased in numbers; then he developed techniques of aggression as well as of protection incomparably more effective than any

2. American author (1902–1968). California, Steinbeck's birthplace, was the setting for many of his books.

which nature herself had ever been able to devise before the human mind intervened. Up until then, animals had always been a match, one for another.
But they were no match for him. The balance no longer worked. Though for
another 500,000 years "coexistence" still seemed to be a *modus vivendi*[3] the
time came, only a short while ago, when man's strength, his numbers, and his
skill made him master and tyrant. He now dominated the natural world of
which he had once been only a part. Now for the first time he could exterminate, if he wished to do so, any other living creature—perhaps even (as we
learned just yesterday) his fellow man. What this means in a specific case,
what the difference is between nature, however red she may be in tooth and
claw, and the terrifying predator who is no longer subject to the limitations she
once imposed, can readily be illustrated on the Baja peninsula. In neither case
is the story a pretty one. Both involve a ruthless predator and the slaughter of
innocents. But nature's far from simple plan does depend upon a coexistence.
Man is, on the other hand, the only animal who habitually exhausts or exter-
minates what he has learned to exploit.

Let us, then, take first a typical dog-eat-story as nature tells it, year after year,
on Rasa Island, where confinement to a small area keeps it startlingly simple,
without any of these sub-plots which make nature's usual stories so endlessly
complicated.
    This tiny island—less than a mile square in area and barely one hundred
feet above sea level at its highest point—lies in the Gulf fifteen or twenty miles
away from the settlement at Los Angeles Bay. It is rarely visited because even
in fair weather the waters round about it are treacherous. Currents up to eight
knots create whirlpools between it and other small islands and there is a tide
drop of twelve to thirty feet, depending upon the season. It is almost bare of
vegetation except for a little of the salt weed or Salicornia which is found in so
many of the saline sands in almost every climate. But it is the nesting place of
thousands of Heermann gulls who, after the young are able to fend for themselves, migrate elswhere—a few southward as far as Central America but most
of them north to various points on the Pacific coast. A few of the latter take
the shortest route across the Baja peninsula but most take what seems an absurd detour by going first some 450 miles south to the tip of Baja and then the
eight hundred or a thousand miles up its west coast to the United States—perhaps, as seems to be the case in various other paradoxes of migration—because they are following some ancestral habit acquired when the climate or
the lay of the land was quite different.
    My travels in Baja are, I hope, not finished, and I intend someday to   10
set foot on Rasa to see what goes on there for myself. So far, however, I have
observed the huge concentration of birds only from a low-flying plane and
what I have to describe is what Walker has told me and what he wrote some
ten years ago in an illustrated account for the *National Geographic Magazine*.
    In late April, when the breeding season is at its height, the ground is

3. Way of getting along (Latin).

crowded with innumerable nests—in some places no more than a yard apart, nowhere with more than twenty feet between them. Because man has so seldom disturbed the gulls here they show little fear of him though once they have reached the northern shore they rise and fly out to sea at the first sight of a human being.

If this were all there was to tell, Rasa might seem to realize that idyllic state of nature of which man, far from idyllic though he has made his own society, often loves to dream. Though on occasion gulls are predators as well as scavengers they respect one another's eggs and offspring on Rasa and live together in peace. But like most animals (and like most men) they are ruthless in their attitude toward other species though too utterly nature's children to rationalize as man does that ruthlessness. They know in their nerves and muscles without even thinking about it that the world was made for the exclusive use and convenience of gulls.

In the present case the victims of that egomania of the species are the two kinds of tern which share the island with them and have chosen to lay their eggs in a depression surrounded by gulls.

Here Walker had best tell his own story: "In the early morning of the second day a few eggs were seen under the terns but even as we watched, several were stolen by gulls. By late afternoon not an egg remained. Nightfall brought on an influx of layers, and morning found twice as many eggs dotting the ground. By dusk only a fraction of the number in the exact center of the plot had escaped the inroads of the egg-eating enemy.

15   "The new colony had now gained a permanent foothold. Accordion-like it expanded during the night, contracted by evening. Each twenty-four hour period showed a gain for the terns and a corresponding retreat in the waiting ranks of the killing gulls.

"By the end of a week the colony had expanded from nothing to approximately four hundred square feet of egg-spotted ground and it continued to spread. The gulls seemed to be losing their appetites. Like children sated with ice cream, they had found that a single diet can be over-done."

What an absurd—some would say what a horrid—story that is. How decisively it gives the lie to what the earliest idealizers of nature called her "social union." How difficult it makes it to believe that some all-good, omnipotent, conscious, and transcendental power consciously chose to set up a general plan of which this is a typical detail. How much more probable it makes it seem that any purpose that may exist in the universe is one emerging from a chaos rather than one which had deliberately created that chaos.

But a fact remains: one must recognize that the scheme works—for the terns as well as for the gulls. If it is no more than the mechanism which so many call it, then it is at least (to use the newly current terminology) a cybernetic or self-regulating mechanism. If the gulls destroyed so many eggs that the tern population began to decline, then the gulls, deprived of their usual food supply, would also decline in numbers and the terns would again increase until the balance had been reached. "How careful of the type she seems; how careless of the single life"—as Tennyson observed some years before Darwin[4] made the same humanly disturbing fact a cornerstone of his theories.

Absurd as the situation on Rasa may seem, it has probably existed for thousands of years and may well continue for thousands more—if left to itself, undisturbed by the only predator who almost invariably renders the "cybernetic" system inoperable.

Consider now the case of the elephant seal, a great sea beast fourteen to sixteen feet long and nearly three tons in weight. Hardly more than a century ago it bred in enormous numbers on the rocky coast and on the islands from Point Reyes, just north of San Francisco, almost to the Magdalena Bay on the Pacific coast of Baja. Like the gray whale it was preyed upon by the ferocious killer whale which is, perhaps, the most formidable of all the predators of the sea. But a balance had been reached and the two coexisted in much the same fashion as the gulls and the terns of Rasa.

Unfortunately (at least for them) human enterprise presently discovered that sea elephants could become a source of oil second in importance to the whale alone. And against this new predator nature afforded no protection. The elephant seals had learned to be wary of the killer whale but they had known no enemy on land and they feared none. Because instinct is slow while the scheming human brain works fast, those who must depend upon instinct are lost before it can protect them against any new threat. Captain Scammon, always clear, vivid, and businesslike, describes how easy and how profitable it was to bring the seals as near to extinction as the gray whales were brought at approximately the same time:

"The mode of capturing them is thus; the sailors get between the herd and the water; then raising all possible noise by shouting, and at the same time flourishing clubs, guns, and lances, the party advances slowly towards the rookery, when the animals will retreat, appearing in a state of great alarm. Occasionally, an overgrown male will give battle, or attempt to escape; but a musket ball through the brain dispatches it; or someone checks its progress by thrusting a lance into the roof of its mouth, which causes it to settle on its haunches, when two men with heavy oaken clubs give the creature repeated blows about the head, until it is stunned or killed. After securing those that are disposed to showing resistance, the party rush on the main body. The onslaught creates such a panic among these peculiar creatures, that, losing all control of their actions, they climb, roll, and tumble over each other, when prevented from further retreat by the projecting cliffs. We recollect in one instance, where sixty-five were captured, that several were found showing no signs of having been either clubbed or lanced but were smothered by numbers of their kind heaped upon them. The whole flock, when attacked, manifested alarm by their peculiar roar, the sound of which, among the largest males, is

20

4. Alfred, Lord Tennyson (1809–1892), English poet; Charles Darwin (1809–1882), English naturalist whose *Origin of Species* (1859) and *The Descent of Man* (1871) set forth his theory of evolution.

nearly as loud as the lowing of an ox, but more prolonged in one strain, accompanied by a rattling noise in the throat. The quantity of blood in this species of the seal tribe is supposed to be double that contained in an ox, in proportion to its size.

"After the capture, the flay begins. First, with a large knife, the skin is ripped along the upper side of the body its whole length, and then cut down as far as practicable, without rolling it over; then the coating of fat that lies between the skin and flesh—which may be from one to seven inches in thickness, according to the size and condition of the animal—is cut into 'horse pieces,' about eight inches wide and twelve to fifteen long, and a puncture is made in each piece sufficiently large to pass a rope through. After flensing the upper portion of the body, it is rolled over, and cut all around as above described. Then the 'horse pieces' are strung on a raft rope (a rope three fathoms long, with an eye splice in one end) and taken to the edge of the surf; a long line is made fast to it, the end of which is thrown to a boat lying just outside of the breakers; they are then hauled through the rollers and towed to the vessel, where the oil is tried out by boiling the blubber, or fat, in large pots set in a brick furnace. . . . The oil produced is superior to whale oil for lubricating purposes. Owing to the continual pursuit of the animals, they have become nearly if not quite extinct on the California coast, or the few remaining have fled to some unknown point for security."

Captain Scammon's account was first published in the *Overland Monthly* in 1870. A few members of the herds he had helped to slaughter must have survived because in 1884 the zoologist Charles Haskins Townsend accompanied a party of sealers who hunted for two months and succeeded in killing sixty. Then, eight years later, he found eight elephant seals on Guadalupe, the lonely lava-capped island twenty-two by seven miles in extent which lies 230 miles southwest of Ensenada in Baja and is the most westerly of Mexican possessions.

25   It seems to be a biological law that if a given species diminishes in numbers, no matter how slowly, it presently reaches a point of no return from which even the most careful fostering cannot bring it back. Eight elephant seals would probably have been far too few to preserve the species; but there must have been others somewhere because when Townsend visited the islands again in 1911 he found 125, and in 1922 scientists from the Scripps Institution and the California Academy of Sciences counted 264 males at a time of year when the females had already left the breeding grounds.

Had Guadalupe not happened to be one of the most remote and inaccessible islands in our part of the world, the few refugees could hardly have survived. By the time it became known that on Guadalupe they had not only survived but multiplied into the hundreds, sealers would almost certainly have sought them out again to finish the job of extermination had not the Mexican government agreed to make Guadalupe a closed area. Because the elephant seal has again no enemy except the killer whale it now occupies all the beaches of the island to which it fled and has established new colonies on various other small islands in the same Pacific area, especially on the San Benitos group nearly two hundred miles to the east. By 1950 the total population was estimated at one thousand.

The earliest voyagers described Guadalupe, rising majestically from the sea to its four-thousand-foot summit, as a true island paradise and also, like other isolated islands, so rich in the unique forms of life which had been slowly evolved in isolation that half the birds and half the plants were unknown anywhere else. So far, I know it only by reputation and have not even seen it, as I have seen Rasa, from the air; but it is said to be very far from a paradise today. Though inhabited only by a few officers of the Mexican Navy who operate a meteorological station, whalers had begun to visit it as early as 1700 and disastrously upset the balance of nature by intentionally introducing goats to provide food for subsequent visits and unintentionally allowing cats and rats to escape from their ships. Several thousand wild goats as well as innumerable cats and rats now manage to exist there, but it is said that almost nothing of the original flora and fauna remains. Most of the unique birds are extinct; the goats have nibbled the trees as high as they are able to reach, and have almost completely destroyed all other plant life. In the absence of the natural predators necessary to establish a tolerable balance, many of the goats are said to die of starvation every year for the simple reason that any animal population will ultimately destroy its own food supply unless multiplication is regulated by either natural or artificial means. Guadalupe is, in short, a perfect demonstration of three truths: (1) That nature left to herself establishes a *modus vivendi* which may be based upon tooth and claw but which nevertheless does permit a varied flora and fauna to live and flourish; (2) that man easily upsets the natural balance so quickly and drastically that nature herself cannot reestablish it in any fashion so generally satisfactory as that which prevailed before the balance was destroyed; (3) that man, if he wishes, can mitigate to some extent the destructive effects of his intervention by intervening again to save some individual species as he seems now to have saved the gray whale and the elephant seal.

How important is it that he should come to an adequate realization of these three truths? Of the second he must take some account if he is not, like the goats of Guadalupe, to come up against the fact that any species may become so "successful" that starvation is inevitable as the ultimate check upon its proliferation and that from this fate not even his technology can save him ultimately, because even those cakes of sewage-grown algae with which he is already experimenting could do no more than postpone a little longer the final day of reckoning. He has proved himself so much cleverer than nature that, once he has intervened, she can no longer protect him just as she could not protect either the life indigenous to Guadalupe or the goats man had introduced there. Having decided to go it alone, he needs for his survival to become more clever still and, especially, more farseeing.

On the other hand, and if he so wishes, he can, perhaps, disregard the other two laws that prevent the gradual disappearance of every area which illustrates the profusion and variety which nature achieves by her own methods and he may see no reason why he should preserve from extinction the elephant seal, which will probably never again be commercially valuable, or for that matter any other of the plants and animals which supply none of his physical needs. None of them may be necessary to his survival, all of them merely "beautiful" or "curious," rather than "useful."

30   Many arguments have been advanced by those who would persuade him to take some thought before it is too late. But the result may depend less upon arguments than upon the attitudes which are essentially emotional and aesthetic.

Thoreau[5]—perhaps the most eloquent exponent we have ever had of the practical, the aesthetic, and the mystical goods which man can receive from the contemplation of the natural as opposed to the man-made or man-managed—once wrote as follows:

"When I consider that the nobler animals have been exterminated here— the cougar, the panther, lynx, wolverine, wolf, bear, moose, deer, the beaver, the turkey and so forth and so forth, I cannot but feel as if I lived in a tamed and, as it were, emasculated country. . . . Is it not a maimed and imperfect nature that I am conversing with? As if I were to study a tribe of Indians that had lost all its warriors. . . . I take infinite pains to know all the phenomena of the spring, for instance, thinking that I have here the entire poem, and then, to my chagrin, I hear that it is but an imperfect copy that I possess and have read, that my ancestors had torn out many of the first leaves and grandest passages, and mutilated it in many places. I should not like to think that some demigod had come before me and picked out some of the best of the stars. I wish to know an entire heaven and an entire earth."

To what proportion of the human race such a statement is, or could be made, meaningful I do not know. But upon the answer that time is already beginning to give will depend how much, if any, of the "poem" will be legible even a few generations hence.

Many of us now talk as if, until recently, there was no need to talk about "conservation." Probably there are today more men than ever before who could answer in the affirmative Emerson's[6] question:

> "Hast thou named all the birds without a gun?
> "Loved the wild rose, and left it on its stalk?"

35   But in absolute rather than relative numbers there are vastly more men today equipped with vastly more efficient instruments of destruction than there ever were before and many of them respect neither the bird nor the wild rose. As of this moment it is they who are winning against everything those of us who would like to preserve the poem are able to say or do.

---

5. Henry David Thoreau (1817–1862), American author and naturalist.
6. Ralph Waldo Emerson (1803–1882), American poet and essayist.

QUESTIONS

1. What is the distinction Krutch makes between predation within the non-human world of nature and predation on the creatures of that world by humans?

2. Krutch obviously feels disdain for those who shoot and kill wild animals. Locate sentences in which he expresses disdain, and analyze how they work.

3. Krutch wrote this essay over forty years ago. Have any of the facts changed? If he were writing today, would he need to modify any of the conclusions he draws in paragraph 27?

4. Taking the gulls and terns as a kind of model, explore the similarities and differences between their relationship and some other relationship of predation—for instance, birds and mosquitoes, mosquitoes and people, hunters and deer—and write a brief account of how the relationship works.

SANDRA STEINGRABER *Tune of the Tuna Fish*

To COMMEMORATE my daughter's first piano recital last spring, my mother sent a package of old songbooks and sheet music that she had scooped from the bench of my own childhood piano, where they had undoubtedly sat for more than thirty years. Faith immediately seized on *The Red Book*, one of my very first lesson books, and began to sight-read some of the pieces. Her favorite was "Tune of the Tuna Fish" (copyright 1945), which introduces the key of F major. The cartoon drawing accompanying the song depicts a yodeling fish. The lyrics are as follows:

> Tuna fish! Tuna fish! Sing a tune of tuna fish!
> Tuna fish! Tuna fish! It's a favorite dish.
> Everybody likes it so. From New York to Kokomo.
> Tuna fish! Tuna fish! It's a favorite dish.

After we belted the song out a few times together, Faith asked, "Mama, what is a tuna fish? Have I ever eaten one?" In fact, she hadn't. Although tuna salad sandwiches were a mainstay of my own childhood diet, tuna has, during the time period between my childhood and my daughter's, become so contaminated with mercury that I choose not to buy it.

A few weeks later, at a potluck picnic, an elderly woman offered Faith a tuna salad sandwich. She loved it. On the ride home, she announced that she

Published in Orion (February 2006), a magazine founded in 1982 to explore "an emerging alternative worldview informed by a growing ecological awareness and the need for cultural change"; the magazine includes photos and paintings as well as essays.

would like tuna sandwiches for her school lunches. She wants to eat one *every* *day*. I smiled that noncommittal motherly smile and said, "We'll see." She broke into song, "Everybody likes it so. From New York to Kokomo. . . ."

A month after that, Faith walked up to me with an alarmed look. Is it true, she wanted to know, that tuna fish have mercury in them? And mercury poisons children? Will she die from eating that sandwich at the picnic? I was able to reassure her that she was fine, but I was left wondering where she'd heard all this. Then I noticed that I'd left out on my office desk a copy of an article about the impact of mercury on fetal brain growth and development. It was one that I myself had authored. Could she have seen it? At age six, can she read well enough to have figured it out?

Other than the twenty-three chromosomes that each of us parents contributes to our offspring during the moment of conception, their growing bodies are entirely made up of rearranged molecules of air, food, and water. Our children are the jet stream, the food web, and the water cycle. Whatever is in the environment is also in them. We know that this now includes hundreds of industrial pollutants. A recent study of umbilical cord blood, collected by the Red Cross from ten newborns and analyzed in two different laboratories, revealed the presence of pesticides, stain removers, wood preservatives, heavy metals, and industrial lubricants, as well as the wastes from burning coal, garbage, and gasoline. Of the 287 chemicals detected, 180 were suspected carcinogens, 217 were toxic to the brain and nervous system, and 208 have been linked to abnormal development and birth defects in lab animals.

5   One of these chemicals was methylmercury, the form of mercury found in fish. Its presence in umbilical cord blood is especially troubling because methylmercury has been shown to paralyze migrating fetal brain cells and halt their cell division. As a result, the architecture of the brain is subtly altered in ways that can lead to learning disabilities, delayed mental development, and shortened attention spans in later childhood. Moreover, the placenta actively pumps methylmercury into the umbilical cord, raising the concentration of mercury in fetal blood above that of the mother's own blood. Most pregnant mothers probably don't realize that when they eat tuna, the mercury within is transferred to and concentrated in the blood of their unborn babies.

Recently, I've been talking with my children about why we buy organically grown food. I've explained to Faith and her younger brother, Elijah, that I like to give my food dollars to farmers who sustain the soil, are kind to their animals, and don't use chemicals that poison birds, fish, and toads. I add that I like to buy food that is grown right here in our own county. It tastes better and doesn't require lots of gasoline to get to our house. I haven't shared with them the results of the 2003 Seattle study, which revealed that children with conventional diets had, on average, nine times more insecticide residues in their urine than those who ate organic produce.

But there is no "organic" option for buying tuna. No mercury-free tuna exists. When mercury from coal-burning power plants rains down from the atmosphere into the world's oceans, ancient anaerobic bacteria found in marine sediments transform this heavy metal into methylmercury, which is quickly siphoned up the food chain. Because tuna is a top-of-the-food chain predator, methylmercury inexorably concentrates in the flesh of its muscle tissue. There is no special way of cleaning or cooking tuna that would lower its body burden. Nor is there any way of keeping mercury from trespassing into a child's brain, once he or she consumes the tuna. Nor is there a way of preventing those molecules of mercury from interfering with brain cell functioning. In that sense, the problem of tuna fish is more akin to the problem of air and water pollution: it is not a problem we can shop our way out of.

Recognizing the potential for methylmercury to create neurological problems in children, the U.S. Food and Drug Administration has now promulgated advisories and guidelines on how much tuna is safe for pregnant women and children—as well as nursing mothers and women who might become pregnant—to eat in a month's time. There is debate about whether these current restrictions are protective enough. But even if they are sufficient, I find them highly impractical. Children do not want to eat a food they like once a month, or even once a week. In my experience, when children discover a new food item to their liking, they want it all the time. They want it for breakfast, lunch, and dinner from here to Sunday. Children's dining habits are, for mysterious reasons, highly ritualized. Elijah, for example, consumed two avocados a day for the better part of his second year. I vaguely recall one summer when I, at about age seven, ate liver sausage on Saltines as part of every meal.

How, then, do you explain to a young child with a tuna jones that she'll have to wait until next month before she can have her favorite dish again? Do you tell her that she's already consumed her monthly quota of a known brain poison, as determined by the federal government? Or do you make up some other excuse?

I eventually sat down with Faith and showed her the article I had written. I said that I was working hard to stop the mercury contamination of seafood so that she could someday enjoy tuna without needing to worry. I said that keeping mercury out of tuna required generating electricity in some way other than burning coal, which is why her father and I support solar energy and wind power.

Soon after, we went hiking in the woods near the day camp she had attended earlier in the summer. Faith summarized for me the history of the old stone building where snakes and turtles are housed in one wing and bunk beds fill the other. It was originally built, she explained, as a *pre-ven-tor-i-um*. Children whose parents were sick with tuberculosis were brought there to live so they wouldn't get sick, too. In fact, I already knew the history of the Cayuga Nature Center but was, nonetheless, amazed at my daughter's ability to recount this information. I tried to gauge whether she was worried about the idea of children being separated from their families because of disease. "You know," I said, "we don't have to worry about tuberculosis anymore. We fixed

10

that problem." She said she knew that. That's why the building had been turned into a camp for everyone.

The top of the hill offered a view across Cayuga Lake. On the far bank floated the vaporous emissions from New York State Electric and Gas Corporation's Cayuga Plant, whose coal-burning stacks were plainly visible against an otherwise cloudless sky. It's one of the state's biggest emitters of mercury. In the year my daughter was born, the Cayuga facility released 323 pounds of mercury into the environment. Pointing it out to Faith, I said that's where the mercury comes from that gets inside the fish. I said that I hoped one day we could fix that problem, too. She thought about it a minute and said, then they can do something else with the building.

QUESTIONS

1. Steingraber's essay informs readers of the high levels of mercury in fish and the dangers of eating a tuna fish sandwich. Why, then, does she begin with her daughter's piano playing? What roles do her daughter, Faith, and later her son, Elijah, play in this essay?

2. What facts about industrial pollutants, including methylmercury, does Steingraber provide? Where do they appear in the essay? How do they relate—structurally and conceptually—to the episodes with her daughter?

3. Does Steingraber suggest a solution to the problem of industrial pollutants? In terms of the environment, does the essay end on a hopeful or despairing note?

4. Write an essay about another kind of environmental problem, ideally one with personal or local significance. Interweave facts with examples or short narratives.

TERRY TEMPEST WILLIAMS *The Clan of One-Breasted Women*

I BELONG TO a Clan of One-breasted Women. My mother, my grandmothers, and six aunts have all had mastectomies. Seven are dead. The two who survive have just completed rounds of chemotherapy and radiation.

I've had my own problems: two biopsies for breast cancer and a small tumor between my ribs diagnosed as "a border-line malignancy."

This is my family history.

Most statistics tell us breast cancer is genetic, hereditary, with rising per-

From the winter 1989 issue of the Witness, *a small circulation journal that calls itself "a feisty, independent, provocative, intelligent, feminist voice of Christian social conscience"; later included in* Refuge: An Unnatural History of Family and Place *(1991).*

centages attached to fatty diets, childlessness, or becoming pregnant after thirty. What they don't say is living in Utah may be the greatest hazard of all.

We are a Mormon family with roots in Utah since 1847. The word-of-wisdom, a religious doctrine of health, kept the women in my family aligned with good foods: no coffee, no tea, tobacco, or alcohol. For the most part, these women were finished having their babies by the time they were thirty. And only one faced breast cancer prior to 1960. Traditionally, as a group of people, Mormons have a low rate of cancer.

Is our family a cultural anomaly? The truth is we didn't think about it. Those who did, usually the men, simply said, "bad genes." The women's attitude was stoic. Cancer was part of life. On February 16, 1971, the eve before my mother's surgery, I accidently picked up the telephone and overheard her ask my grandmother what she could expect.

"Diane, it is one of the most spiritual experiences you will ever encounter."

I quietly put down the receiver.

Two days later, my father took my three brothers and me to the hospital to visit her. She met us in the lobby in a wheelchair. No bandages were visible. I'll never forget her radiance, the way she held herself in a purple velour robe and how she gathered us around her.

"Children, I am fine. I want you to know I felt the arms of God around me."

We believed her. My father cried. Our mother, his wife, was thirty-eight years old.

Two years ago, after my mother's death from cancer, my father and I were having dinner together. He had just returned from St. George where his construction company was putting in natural gas lines for towns in southern Utah. He spoke of his love for the country: the sandstoned landscape, bare-boned and beautiful. He had just finished hiking the Kolob trail in Zion National Park. We got caught up in reminiscing, recalling with fondness our walk up Angel's Landing on his fiftieth birthday and the years our family had vacationed there. This was a remembered landscape where we had been raised.

Over dessert, I shared a recurring dream of mine. I told my father that for years, as long as I could remember, I saw this flash of light in the night in the desert. That this image had so permeated my being, I could not venture south without seeing it again, on the horizon, illuminating buttes and mesas.

"You did see it," he said.

"Saw what?" I asked, a bit tentative.

"The bomb. The cloud. We were driving home from Riverside, California. You were sitting on your mother's lap. She was pregnant. In fact, I remember the date, September 7, 1957. We had just gotten out of the Service. We were driving north, past Las Vegas. It was an hour or so before dawn, when this explosion went off. We not only heard it, but felt it. I thought the oil tanker in front of us had blown up. We pulled over and suddenly, rising from the desert floor, we saw it, clearly, this golden-stemmed cloud, the mushroom. The sky seemed to vibrate with an eerie pink glow. Within a few minutes, a light ash was raining on the car."

I stared at my father. This was new information to me.

"I thought you knew that," my father said. "It was a common occurrence in the fifties."

It was at this moment I realized the deceit I had been living under. Children growing up in the American Southwest, drinking contaminated milk from contaminated cows, even from the contaminated breasts of their mother, my mother—members, years later, of the Clan of One-breasted Women.

20   It is a well-known story in the Desert West, "The Day We Bombed Utah," or perhaps, "The Years We Bombed Utah."[1] Above ground atomic testing in Nevada took place from January 27, 1951, through July 11, 1962. Not only were the winds blowing north, covering "low use segments of the population" with fallout and leaving sheep dead in their tracks, but the climate was right.[2] The United States of the 1950s was red, white, and blue. The Korean War was raging. McCarthyism was rampant. Ike was it and the Cold War was hot.[3] If you were against nuclear testing, you were for a Communist regime.

Much has been written about this "American nuclear tragedy." Public health was secondary to national security. The Atomic Energy Commissioner, Thomas Murray said, "Gentlemen, we must not let anything interfere with this series of tests, nothing."[4]

Again and again, the American public was told by its government, in spite of burns, blisters, and nausea, "It has been found that the tests may be conducted with adequate assurance of safety under conditions prevailing at the bombing reservations."[5] Assuaging public fears was simply a matter of public relations. "Your best action," an Atomic Energy Commission booklet read, "is not to be worried about fallout." A news release typical of the times stated, "We find no basis for concluding that harm to any individual has resulted from radioactive fallout."[6]

1. Fuller, John G., *The Day We Bombed Utah* (New York: New American Library, 1984) [Williams's note].

2. Discussion on March 14, 1988, with Carole Gallagher, photographer and author, *American Ground Zero: The Secret Nuclear War*, published by Random House, 1994 [Williams's note].

3. Events and figures of the 1950s: the Korean War (1950–53) pitted the combined forces of the Republic of Korea and the United Nations (primarily the United States) against the invading armies of Communist North Korea; McCarthyism, after Republican senator Joseph S. McCarthy, refers to the Communist "witch-hunt" led by the senator; Ike is the nickname of Dwight D. Eisenhower, president from 1953 to 1961; the Cold War refers to the power struggle between the Western powers and the Communist bloc that began at the end of World War II.

4. Szasz, Ferenc M., "Downwind From the Bomb," *Nevada Historical Society Quarterly*, Fall 1987, Vol. XXX, No. 3, p. 185 [Williams's note].

5. Fradkin, Philip L., *Fallout* (Tucson: University of Arizona Press, 1989), 98 [Williams's note].

6. Ibid., 109 [Williams's note].

On August 30, 1979, during Jimmy Carter's presidency, a suit was filed entitled "Irene Allen vs. the United States of America." Mrs. Allen was the first to be alphabetically listed with twenty-four test cases, representative of nearly 1200 plaintiffs seeking compensation from the United States government for cancers caused from nuclear testing in Nevada.

Irene Allen lived in Hurricane, Utah. She was the mother of five children and had been widowed twice. Her first husband with their two oldest boys had watched the tests from the roof of the local high school. He died of leukemia in 1956. Her second husband died of pancreatic cancer in 1978.

In a town meeting conducted by Utah Senator Orrin Hatch, shortly be-   25
fore the suit was filed, Mrs. Allen said, "I am not blaming the government, I want you to know that, Senator Hatch. But I thought if my testimony could help in any way so this wouldn't happen again to any of the generations coming up after us . . . I am really happy to be here this day to bear testimony of this."[7]

God-fearing people. This is just one story in an anthology of thousands.

On May 10, 1984, Judge Bruce S. Jenkins handed down his opinion. Ten of the plaintiffs were awarded damages. It was the first time a federal court had determined that nuclear tests had been the cause of cancers. For the remaining fourteen test cases, the proof of causation was not sufficient. In spite of the split decision, it was considered a landmark ruling.[8] It was not to remain so for long.

In April, 1987, the 10th Circuit Court of Appeals overturned Judge Jenkins' ruling on the basis that the United States was protected from suit by the legal doctrine of sovereign immunity, the centuries-old idea from England in the days of absolute monarchs.[9]

In January, 1988, the Supreme Court refused to review the Appeals Court decision. To our court system, it does not matter whether the United States Government was irresponsible, whether it lied to its citizens or even that citizens died from the fallout of nuclear testing. What matters is that our government is immune. "The King can do no wrong."

In Mormon culture, authority is respected, obedience is revered, and inde-   30
pendent thinking is not. I was taught as a young girl not to "make waves" or "rock the boat."

"Just let it go—" my mother would say. "You know how you feel, that's what counts."

For many years, I did just that—listened, observed, and quietly formed my own opinions within a culture that rarely asked questions because they had all the answers. But one by one, I watched the women in my family die common, heroic deaths. We sat in waiting rooms hoping for good news, always receiving

7. Town meeting held by Senator Orrin Hatch in St. George, Utah, April 17, 1979, transcript, 26–28 [Williams's note].

8. Fradkin, Op. cit., 228 [Williams's note].

9. U.S. vs. Allen, 816 Federal Reporter, 2d/1417 (10th Circuit Court 1987), cert. denied, 108 S. CT. 694 (1988) [Williams's note].

the bad. I cared for them, bathed their scarred bodies and kept their secrets. I watched beautiful women become bald as cytoxan, cisplatin and adriamycin were injected into their veins. I held their foreheads as they vomited green-black bile and I shot them with morphine when the pain became inhuman. In the end, I witnessed their last peaceful breaths, becoming a midwife to the re-birth of their souls. But the price of obedience became too high.

The fear and inability to question authority that ultimately killed rural communities in Utah during atmospheric testing of atomic weapons was the same fear I saw being held in my mother's body. Sheep. Dead sheep. The evidence is buried.

I cannot prove that my mother, Diane Dixon Tempest, or my grandmothers, Lettie Romney Dixon and Kathryn Blackett Tempest, along with my aunts contracted cancer from nuclear fallout in Utah. But I can't prove they didn't.

35   My father's memory was correct, the September blast we drove through in 1957 was part of Operation Plumbbob, one of the most intensive series of bomb tests to be initiated. The flash of light in the night in the desert I had always thought was a dream developed into a family nightmare. It took fourteen years, from 1957 to 1971, for cancer to show up in my mother—the same time, Howard L. Andrews, an authority on radioactive fallout at the National Institutes of Health, says radiation cancer requires to become evident.[10] The more I learn about what it means to be a "downwinder," the more questions I drown in.

What I do know, however, is that as a Mormon woman of the fifth generation of "Latter-Day-Saints," I must question everything, even if it means losing my faith, even if it means becoming a member of a border tribe among my own people. Tolerating blind obedience in the name of patriotism or religion ultimately takes our lives.

When the Atomic Energy Commission described the country north of the Nevada Test Site as "virtually uninhabited desert terrain," my family members were some of the "virtual uninhabitants."

One night, I dreamed women from all over the world circling a blazing fire in the desert. They spoke of change, of how they hold the moon in their bellies and wax and wane with its phases. They mocked at the presumption of even-tempered beings and made promises that they would never fear the witch inside themselves. The women danced wildly as sparks broke away from the flames and entered the night sky as stars.

And they sang a song given to them by Shoshoni grandmothers:

> *Ah ne nah, nah*
> *nin nah nah—*
> *Ah ne nah, nah*
> *nin nah nah—*
> *Nyaga mutzi*

10. Fradkin, Op. cit., 116 [Williams's note].

oh ne nay—
Nyaga mutzi
oh ne nay—[11]

The women danced and drummed and sang for weeks, preparing them-   40
selves for what was to come. They would reclaim the desert for the sake of
their children, for the sake of the land.

A few miles downwind from the fire circle, bombs were being tested. Rabbits felt the tremors. Their soft leather pads on paws and feet recognized the
shaking sands while the roots of mesquite and sage were smoldering. Rocks
were hot from the inside out and dust devils hummed unnaturally. And each
time there was another nuclear test, ravens watched the desert heave. Stretch
marks appeared. The land was losing its muscle.

The women couldn't bear it any longer. They were mothers. They had suffered labor pains but always under the promise of birth. The red hot pains beneath the desert promised death only as each bomb became a stillborn. A
contract had been broken between human beings and the land. A new contract was being drawn by the women who understood the fate of the earth as
their own.

Under the cover of darkness, ten women slipped under the barbed wire
fence and entered the contaminated country. They were trespassing. They
walked toward the town of Mercury in moonlight, taking their cues from coy-
ote, kit fox, antelope squirrel, and quail. They moved quietly and deliberately
through the maze of Joshua trees. When a hint of daylight appeared they
rested, drinking tea and sharing their rations of food. The women closed their
eyes. The time had come to protest with the heart, that to deny one's genealogy with the earth was to commit treason against one's soul.

At dawn, the women draped themselves in mylar, wrapping long streamers
of silver plastic around their arms to blow in the breeze. They wore clear
masks that became the faces of humanity. And when they arrived on the edge
of Mercury, they carried all the butterflies of a summer day in their wombs.
They paused to allow their courage to settle.

The town which forbids pregnant women and children to enter because of   45
radiation risks to their health was asleep. The women moved through the
streets as winged messengers, twirling around each other in slow motion,
peeking inside homes and watching the easy sleep of men and women. They
were astonished by such stillness and periodically would utter a shrill note or
low cry just to verify life.

The residents finally awoke to what appeared as strange apparitions. Some
simply stared. Others called authorities, and in time, the women were appre-
hended by wary soldiers dressed in desert fatigues. They were taken to a white,

11. This song was sung by the Western Shoshone women as they crossed the line at
the Nevada Test Site on March 18, 1988, as part of their "Reclaim the Land" action.
The translation they gave was: "Consider the rabbits how gently they walk on the earth.
Consider the rabbits how gently they walk on the earth. We remember them. We can
walk gently also. We remember them. We can walk gently also" [Williams's note].

square building on the other edge of Mercury. When asked who they were and why they were there, the women replied, "We are mothers and we have come to reclaim the desert for our children."

The soldiers arrested them. As the ten women were blindfolded and hand-cuffed, they began singing:

> You can't forbid us everything
> You can't forbid us to think—
> You can't forbid our tears to flow
> And you can't stop the songs that we sing.

The women continued to sing louder and louder, until they heard the voices of their sisters moving across the mesa.

> Ah ne nah, nah
> nin nah nah—
> Ah ne nah, nah
> nin nah nah—
> Nyaga mutzi
> oh ne nay—
> Nyaga mutzi
> oh ne nay—

"Call for re-enforcement," one soldier said.

50   "We have," interrupted one woman. "We have—and you have no idea of our numbers."

On March 18, 1988, I crossed the line at the Nevada Test Site and was ar-rested with nine other Utahns for trespassing on military lands. They are still conducting nuclear tests in the desert. Ours was an act of civil disobedience. But as I walked toward the town of Mercury, it was more than a gesture of peace. It was a gesture on behalf of the Clan of One-Breasted Women.

As one officer cinched the handcuffs around my wrists, another frisked my body. She found a pen and a pad of paper tucked inside my left boot.

"And these?" she asked sternly.

"Weapons," I replied.

55   Our eyes met. I smiled. She pulled the leg of my trousers back over my boot.

"Step forward, please," she said as she took my arm.

We were booked under an afternoon sun and bussed to Tonapah, Nevada. It was a two-hour ride. This was familiar country to me. The Joshua trees standing their ground had been named by my ancestors who believed they looked like prophets pointing west to the promised land. These were the same trees that bloomed each spring, flowers appearing like white flames in the Mo-jave. And I recalled a full moon in May when my mother and I had walked among them, flushing out mourning doves and owls.

The bus stopped short of town. We were released. The officials thought it was a cruel joke to leave us stranded in the desert with no way to get home. What they didn't realize is that we were home, soul-centered and strong, women who recognized the sweet smell of sage as fuel for our spirits.

QUESTIONS

1. Williams uses a variety of evidence in this essay, including personal memory, family history, government documents, and other sources. List the evidence and the order in which she uses it. Why does Williams present her material in this order?

2. The essay begins with a description of what Williams later calls a "family nightmare" and ends with a dream vision. What is the rhetorical effect of this interactive opening and closing?

3. What does Williams mean by the statement "I must question everything" (paragraph 36)?

4. Do some research on an environmental issue that affects you or your family, and, using Williams as a model, write an essay that combines your personal experience and your research.

ETHICS

LORD CHESTERFIELD *Letter to His Son*

London, October 16, O.S. 1747

DEAR BOY

The art of pleasing is a very necessary one to possess, but a very difficult one to acquire. It can hardly be reduced to rules; and your own good sense and observation will teach you more of it than I can. "Do as you would be done by," is the surest method that I know of pleasing. Observe carefully what pleases you in others, and probably the same things in you will please others. If you are pleased with the complaisance and attention of others to your humors, your tastes, or your weaknesses, depend upon it, the same complaisance and attention on your part to theirs will equally please them. Take the tone of the company that you are in, and do not pretend to give it; be serious, gay, or even trifling, as you find the present humor of the company; this is an attention due from every individual to the majority. Do not tell stories in company; there is nothing more tedious and disagreeable; if by chance you know a very short story, and exceedingly applicable to the present subject of conversation, tell it in as few words as possible; and even then, throw out that you do not love to tell stories, but that the shortness of it tempted you.

Of all things banish the egotism out of your conversation, and never think of entertaining people with your own personal concerns or private affairs; though they are interesting to you, they are tedious and impertinent to everybody else; besides that, one cannot keep one's own private affairs too secret. Whatever you think your own excellencies may be, do not affectedly display them in company; nor labor, as many people do, to give that turn to the conversation, which may supply you with an opportunity of exhibiting them. If they are real, they will infallibly be discovered, without your pointing them out yourself, and with much more advantage. Never maintain an argument with heat and clamor, though you think or know yourself to be in the right; but give your opinion modestly and coolly, which is the only way to convince; and, if that does not do, try to change the conversation, by saying, with good-humor, "We shall hardly convince one another; nor is it necessary that we should, so let us talk of something else."

Remember that there is a local propriety to be observed in all companies; and that what is extremely proper in one company may be, and often is, highly improper in another.

Not originally intended for publication, Lord Chesterfield's letters to his son Philip were begun in 1737 and first published in 1774 as Letters. *Both celebrated and controversial in their day, the letters reveal the author's political attitudes, his views on good breeding, and his lessons in etiquette and the social arts.*

The jokes, the *bon-mots*,[1] the little adventures, which may do very well in one company, will seem flat and tedious, when related in another. The particular characters, the habits, the cant of one company may give merit to a word, or a gesture, which would have none at all if divested of those accidental circumstances. Here people very commonly err; and fond of something that has entertained them in one company, and in certain circumstances, repeat it with emphasis in another, where it is either insipid, or, it may be, offensive, by being ill-timed or misplaced. Nay, they often do it with this silly preamble: "I will tell you an excellent thing," or, "I will tell you the best thing in the world." This raises expectations, which, when absolutely disappointed, make the relator of this excellent thing look, very deservedly, like a fool.

If you would particularly gain the affection and friendship of particular people, whether men or women, endeavor to find out their predominant excellency, if they have one, and their prevailing weakness, which everybody has; and do justice to the one, and something more than justice to the other. Men have various objects in which they may excel, or at least would be thought to excel; and, though they love to hear justice done to them, where they know that they excel, yet they are most and best flattered upon those points where they wish to excel, and yet are doubtful whether they do or not. As for example: Cardinal Richelieu, who was undoubtedly the ablest statesman of his time, or perhaps of any other, had the idle vanity of being thought the best poet too; he envied the great Corneille his reputation, and ordered a criticism to be written upon the *Cid*.[2] Those, therefore, who flattered skillfully, said little to him of his abilities in state affairs, or at least but *en passant*,[3] and as it might naturally occur. But the incense which they gave him, the smoke of which they knew would turn his head in their favor, was as a *bel esprit*[4] and a poet. Why? Because he was sure of one excellency, and distrustful as to the other.

You will easily discover every man's prevailing vanity by observing his favorite topic of conversation; for every man talks most of what he has most a mind to be thought to excel in. Touch him but there, and you touch him to the quick. The late Sir Robert Walpole[5] (who was certainly an able man) was little open to flattery upon that head, for he was in no doubt himself about it; but his prevailing weakness was, to be thought to have a polite and happy turn to gallantry—of which he had undoubtedly less than any man living. It was his favorite and frequent subject of conversation, which proved to those who had any penetration that it was his prevailing weakness, and they applied to it with success.

1. Clever sayings; literally, good words (French).
2. When the French classic tragedy *The Cid*, founded upon the legendary exploits of the medieval Castilian warrior-hero, was published in 1636 by its author Pierre Corneille (1606–1684), it was the subject of violent criticism, led by the French minister of state Richelieu (1585–1642).
3. Casually or in passing (French).
4. Beautiful spirit (French).
5. For two decades a powerful prime minister, Walpole (1676–1745) was also a patron of the arts and prided himself on his taste.

Women have, in general, but one object, which is their beauty; upon which scarce any flattery is too gross for them to follow. Nature has hardly formed a woman ugly enough to be insensible to flattery upon her person; if her face is so shocking that she must, in some degree, be conscious of it, her figure and air, she trusts, make ample amends for it. If her figure is deformed, her face, she thinks, counterbalances it. If they are both bad, she comforts herself that she has graces, a certain manner, a *je ne sais quoi*[6] still more engaging than beauty. This truth is evident from the studied and elaborate dress of the ugliest woman in the world. An undoubted, uncontested, conscious beauty is, of all women, the least sensible of flattery upon that head; she knows it is her due, and is therefore obliged to nobody for giving it her. She must be flattered upon her understanding; which, though she may possibly not doubt of herself, yet she suspects that men may distrust.

Do not mistake me, and think that I mean to recommend to you abject and criminal flattery: no; flatter nobody's vices or crimes: on the contrary, abhor and discourage them. But there is no living in the world without a complaisant indulgence for people's weaknesses, and innocent, though ridiculous vanities. If a man has a mind to be thought wiser, and a woman handsomer, than they really are, their error is a comfortable one to themselves, and an innocent one with regard to other people; and I would rather make them my friends by indulging them in it, than my enemies by endeavoring (and that to no purpose) to undeceive them.

There are little attentions, likewise, which are infinitely engaging, and which sensibly affect that degree of pride and self-love, which is inseparable from human nature, as they are unquestionable proofs of the regard and consideration which we have for the persons to whom we pay them. As, for example, to observe the little habits, the likings, the antipathies, and the tastes of those whom we would gain; and then take care to provide them with the one, and to secure them from the other; giving them, genteelly, to understand, that you had observed they liked such a dish, or such a room, for which reason you had prepared it: or, on the contrary, that having observed they had an aversion to such a dish, a dislike to such a person, etc., you had taken care to avoid presenting them. Such attention to such trifles flatters self-love much more than greater things, as it makes people think themselves almost the only objects of your thoughts and care.

10 These are some of the arcana necessary for your initiation in the great society of the world. I wish I had known them better at your age; I have paid the price of three and fifty years for them, and shall not grudge it if you reap the advantage. Adieu.

6. A certain inexpressible quality; literally, I do not know what (French).

QUESTIONS

1. Chesterfield recommends to his son the rule "Do as you would be done by" (paragraph 1). What kind of behavior does Chesterfield suggest? How does his injunction differ from Jesus' injunction "Therefore all things whatsoever ye would that men should do to you, do ye so unto them" (Matthew 7.12; see also Luke 6.31)?

2. Chesterfield does not recommend "abject and criminal flattery" of vices and crimes but rather "complaisant indulgence for people's weaknesses, and innocent, though ridiculous vanities" (paragraph 8). Make a short list of what you consider vices and crimes and another of what you consider weaknesses and vanities. Be prepared to defend your distinctions.

3. Rewrite Chesterfield's "Letter to His Son" for a modern reader.

MARK TWAIN   *Advice to Youth*

BEING TOLD I WOULD be expected to talk here, I inquired what sort of a talk I ought to make. They said it should be something suitable to youth—something didactic, instructive, or something in the nature of good advice. Very well. I have a few things in my mind which I have often longed to say for the instruction of the young; for it is in one's tender early years that such things will best take root and be most enduring and most valuable. First, then, I will say to you, my young friends—and I say it beseechingly, urgingly—

Always obey your parents, when they are present. This is the best policy in the long run, because if you don't they will make you. Most parents think they know better than you do, and you can generally make more by humoring that superstition than you can by acting on your own better judgment.

Be respectful to your superiors, if you have any, also to strangers, and sometimes to others. If a person offend you, and you are in doubt as to whether it was intentional or not, do not resort to extreme measures; simply watch your chance and hit him with a brick. That will be sufficient. If you shall find that he had not intended any offense, come out frankly and confess yourself in the wrong when you struck him; acknowledge it like a man and say you didn't mean to. Yes, always avoid violence; in this age of charity and kindliness, the time has gone by for such things. Leave dynamite to the low and unrefined.

Go to bed early, get up early—this is wise. Some authorities say get up with the sun; some others say get up with one thing, some with another. But a lark is really the best thing to get up with. It gives you a splendid reputation with everybody to know that you get up with the lark; and if you get the right

Text of a lecture given by Twain (a.k.a. Samuel Clemens) in 1882. The original audience and occasion for this lecture remain unknown.

kind of a lark, and work at him right, you can easily train him to get up at half past nine, every time—it is no trick at all.

5   Now as to the matter of lying. You want to be very careful about lying; otherwise you are nearly sure to get caught. Once caught, you can never again be, in the eyes of the good and the pure, what you were before. Many a young person has injured himself permanently through a single clumsy and illfinished lie, the result of carelessness born of incomplete training. Some authorities hold that the young ought not to lie at all. That, of course, is putting it rather stronger than necessary; still, while I cannot go quite so far as that, I do maintain, and I believe I am right, that the young ought to be temperate in the use of this great art until practice and experience shall give them that confidence, elegance, and precision which alone can make the accomplishment graceful and profitable. Patience, diligence, painstaking attention to detail—these are the requirements; these, in time, will make the student perfect; upon these, and upon these only, may he rely as the sure foundation for future eminence. Think what tedious years of study, thought, practice, experience, went to the equipment of that peerless old master who was able to impose upon the whole world the lofty and sounding maxim that "truth is mighty and will prevail"—the most majestic compound fracture of fact which any of woman born has yet achieved. For the history of our race, and each individual's experience, are sown thick with evidence that a truth is not hard to kill and that a lie told well is immortal. There is in Boston a monument of the man who discovered anaesthesia; many people are aware, in these latter days, that that man didn't discover it at all, but stole the discovery from another man. Is this truth mighty, and will it prevail? Ah no, my hearers, the monument is made of hardy material, but the lie it tells will outlast it a million years. An awkward, feeble, leaky lie is a thing which you ought to make it your unceasing study to avoid; such a lie as that has no more real permanence than an average truth. Why, you might as well tell the truth at once and be done with it. A feeble, stupid, preposterous lie will not live two years—except it be a slander upon somebody. It is indestructible, then, of course, but that is no merit of yours. A final word: begin your practice of this gracious and beautiful art early—begin now. If I had begun earlier, I could have learned how.

Never handle firearms carelessly. The sorrow and suffering that have been caused through the innocent but heedless handling of firearms by the young! Only four days ago, right in the next farmhouse to the one where I am spending the summer, a grandmother, old and gray and sweet, one of the loveliest spirits in the land, was sitting at her work, when her young grandson crept in and got down an old, battered, rusty gun which had not been touched for many years and was supposed not to be loaded, and pointed it at her, laughing and threatening to shoot. In her fright she ran screaming and pleading toward the door on the other side of the room; but as she passed him he placed the gun almost against her very breast and pulled the trigger! He had supposed it was not loaded. And he was right—it wasn't. So there wasn't any harm done. It is the only case of that kind I ever heard of. Therefore, just the same, don't you meddle with old unloaded firearms; they are the most deadly and unerring things that have ever been created by man. You don't have to take any pains at all with them; you don't have to have a rest, you don't have to have any sights on the gun, you don't have to take aim, even. No, you just pick out a relative and bang away, and you are sure to get him. A youth who can't hit a cathedral at thirty yards with a Gatling gun in three-quarters of an hour, can take up an old empty musket and bag his grandmother every time, at a hundred. Think what Waterloo[1] would have been if one of the armies had been boys armed with old muskets supposed not to be loaded, and the other army had been composed of their female relations. The very thought of it makes one shudder.

There are many sorts of books; but good ones are the sort for the young to read. Remember that. They are a great, an inestimable, an unspeakable means of improvement. Therefore be careful in your selection, my young friends; be very careful; confine yourselves exclusively to Robertson's Sermons, Baxter's *Saint's Rest, The Innocents Abroad,* and works of that kind.[2]

But I have said enough. I hope you will treasure up the instructions which I have given you, and make them a guide to your feet and a light to your understanding. Build your character thoughtfully and painstakingly upon these precepts, and by and by, when you have got it built, you will be surprised and gratified to see how nicely and sharply it resembles everybody else's.

1. The bloody battle (1815) in which Napoleon suffered his final defeat at the hands of English and German troops under the Duke of Wellington.
2. The five volumes of sermons by Frederick William Robertson (1816–1853), an English clergyman, and Richard Baxter's *Saints' Everlasting Rest* (1650) were well-known religious works; *The Innocents Abroad* is Twain's own collection of humorous travel sketches.

QUESTIONS

1. Underline the various pieces of "serious" advice that Twain offers and notice where and how he begins to turn each one upside down.

2. Mark Twain was already known as a comic author when he delivered "Advice to Youth" as a lecture in 1882; it was not published until 1923. We do not know the circumstances under which he delivered it or to whom. Using evidence from the text, imagine both the circumstances and the audience.

3. Rewrite "Advice to Youth" for a modern audience, perhaps as a lecture for a school assembly or a commencement address.

JONATHAN RAUCH *In Defense of Prejudice*

T
HE WAR ON PREJUDICE is now, in all likelihood, the most uncontroversial social movement in America. Opposition to "hate speech," formerly identified with the liberal left, has become a bipartisan piety. In the past year, groups and factions that agree on nothing else have agreed that the public expression of any and all prejudices must be forbidden. On the left, protesters and editorialists have insisted that Francis L. Lawrence resign as president of Rutgers University for describing blacks as "a disadvantaged population that doesn't have that genetic, hereditary background to have a higher average." On the other side of the ideological divide, Ralph Reed, the executive director of the Christian Coalition, responded to criticism of the religious right by calling a press conference to denounce a supposed outbreak of "name-calling, scapegoating, and religious bigotry." Craig Rogers, an evangelical Christian student at California State University, recently filed a $2.5 million sexual-harassment suit against a lesbian professor of psychology, claiming that anti-male bias in one of her lectures violated campus rules and left him feeling "raped and trapped."

In universities and on Capitol Hill, in workplaces and newsrooms, authorities are declaring that there is no place for racism, sexism, homophobia, Christian-bashing, and other forms of prejudice in public debate or even in private thought. "Only when racism and other forms of prejudice are expunged," say the crusaders for sweetness and light, "can minorities be safe and society be fair." So sweet, this dream of a world without prejudice. But the very last thing society should do is seek to utterly eradicate racism and other forms of prejudice.

I suppose I should say, in the customary I-hope-I-don't-sound-too-defensive tone, that I am not a racist and that this is not an article favoring racism or any other particular prejudice. It is an article favoring intellectual pluralism, which permits the expression of various forms of bigotry and always will. Although we like to hope that a time will come when no one will believe that people come in types and that each type belongs with its own kind, I doubt such a day will ever arrive. By all indications, *Homo sapiens* is a tribal species for whom "us versus them" comes naturally and must be continually pushed back. Where there is genuine freedom of expression, there will be racist expression. There will also be people who believe that homosexuals are sick or threaten children or—especially among teenagers—are rightful targets of manly savagery. Homosexuality will always be incomprehensible to most people, and what is incomprehensible is feared. As for anti-Semitism, it appears to be a hardier virus than influenza. If you want pluralism, then you get racism and sexism and homophobia, and communism and fascism and xeno-

Originally published in Harper's Magazine *(May 1995) with the subtitle "Why Incendiary Speech Must Be Protected." Articles in* Harper's *focus on current issues in politics, science, and the arts.*

phobia and tribalism, and that is just for a start. If you want to believe in intellectual freedom and the progress of knowledge and the advancement of science and all those other good things, then you must swallow hard and accept this: for as thickheaded and wayward an animal as us, the realistic question is how to make the best of prejudice, not how to eradicate it.

Indeed, "eradicating prejudice" is so vague a proposition as to be meaningless. Distinguishing prejudice reliably and nonpolitically from nonprejudice, or even defining it crisply, is quite hopeless. We all feel we know prejudice when we see it. But do we? At the University of Michigan, a student said in a classroom discussion that he considered homosexuality a disease treatable with therapy. He was summoned to a formal disciplinary hearing for violating the school's policy against speech that "victimizes" people based on "sexual orientation." Now, the evidence is abundant that this particular hypothesis is wrong, and any American homosexual can attest to the harm that the student's hypothesis has inflicted on many real people. But was it a statement of prejudice or of misguided belief? Hate speech or hypothesis? Many Americans who do not regard themselves as bigots or haters believe that homosexuality is a treatable disease. They may be wrong, but are they all bigots? I am unwilling to say so, and if you are willing, beware. The line between a prejudiced belief and a merely controversial one is elusive, and the harder you look the more elusive it becomes. "God hates homosexuals" is a statement of fact, not of bias, to those who believe it; "American criminals are disproportionately black" is a statement of bias, not of fact, to those who disbelieve it.

Who is right? You may decide, and so may others, and there is no need to   5
agree. That is the great innovation of intellectual pluralism (which is to say, of post-Enlightenment science, broadly defined). We cannot know in advance or for sure which belief is prejudice and which is truth, but to advance knowledge we don't need to know. The genius of intellectual pluralism lies not in doing away with prejudices and dogmas but in channeling them—making them socially productive by pitting prejudice against prejudice and dogma against dogma, exposing all to withering public criticism. What survives at the end of the day is our base of knowledge.

What they told us in high school about this process is very largely a lie. The Enlightenment tradition taught us that science is orderly, antiseptic, rational, the province of detached experimenters and high-minded logicians. In the popular view, science stands for reason against prejudice, openmindedness against dogma, calm consideration against passionate attachment—all personified by pop-science icons like the magisterially deductive Sherlock Holmes, the coolly analytic Mr. Spock, the genially authoritative Mr. Science (from our junior-high science films). Yet one of science's dirty secrets is that although science as a whole is as unbiased as anything human can be, scientists are just as biased as anyone else, sometimes more so. "One of the strengths of science," writes the philosopher of science David L. Hull, "is that it does not require that scientists be unbiased, only that different scientists have different biases." Another dirty secret is that, no less than the rest of us, scientists can be dogmatic and pigheaded. "Although this pigheadedness often damages the careers of individual scientists," says Hull, "it is beneficial for the manifest goal of science," which relies on people to invest years in their ideas and defend them passionately. And the dirtiest secret of all, if you believe in the antiseptic popular view of science, is that this most ostensibly rational of enterprises depends on the most irrational of motives—ambition, narcissism, animus, even revenge. "Scientists acknowledge that among their motivations are natural curiosity, the love of truth, and the desire to help humanity, but other inducements exist as well, and one of them is to 'get that son of a bitch,' " says Hull. "Time and again, scientists whom I interviewed described the powerful spur that 'showing that son of a bitch' supplied to their own research."

Many people, I think, are bewildered by this unvarnished and all too human view of science. They believe that for a system to be unprejudiced, the people in it must also be unprejudiced. In fact, the opposite is true. Far from eradicating ugly or stupid ideas and coarse or unpleasant motives, intellectual pluralism relies upon them to excite intellectual passion and redouble scientific effort. I know of no modern idea more ugly and stupid than that the Holocaust never happened, nor any idea more viciously motivated. Yet the deniers' claims that the Auschwitz gas chambers could not have worked led to closer study and, in 1993, research showing, at last, how they actually did work. Thanks to prejudice and stupidity, another opening for doubt has been shut.

An enlightened and efficient intellectual regime lets a million prejudices bloom, including many that you or I may regard as hateful or grotesque. It avoids any attempt to stamp out prejudice, because stamping out prejudice really means forcing everyone to share the same prejudice, namely that of whoever is in authority. The great American philosopher Charles Sanders Peirce wrote in 1877: "When complete agreement could not otherwise be reached, a general massacre of all who have not thought in a certain way has proved a very effective means of settling opinion in a country." In speaking of "settling opinion," Peirce was writing about one of the two or three most fundamental problems that any human society must confront and solve. For most societies down through the centuries, this problem was dealt with in the manner he described: errors were identified by the authorities—priests, politburos, dictators—or by mass opinion, and then the error-makers were eliminated along with their putative mistakes. "Let all men who reject the established belief be terrified into silence," wrote Peirce, describing this system. "This method has, from the earliest times, been one of the chief means of upholding correct theological and political doctrines."

Intellectual pluralism substitutes a radically different doctrine: we kill our mistakes rather than each other. Here I draw on another great philosopher, the late Karl Popper, who pointed out that the critical method of science "consists in letting our hypotheses die in our stead." Those who are in error are not (or are not supposed to be) banished or excommunicated or forced to sign a renunciation or required to submit to "rehabilitation" or sent for psychological counseling. It is the error we punish, not the errant. By letting people make errors—even mischievous, spiteful errors (as, for instance, Galileo's insistence on Copernicanism was taken to be in 1633)—pluralism creates room to challenge orthodoxy, think imaginatively, experiment boldly. Brilliance and bigotry are empowered in the same stroke.

Pluralism is the principle that protects and makes a place in human company for that loneliest and most vulnerable of all minorities, the minority who is hounded and despised among blacks and whites, gays and straights, who is suspect or criminal among every tribe and in every nation of the world, and yet on whom progress depends: the dissident. I am not saying that dissent is always or even usually enlightened. Most of the time it is foolish and self-serving. No dissident has the right to be taken seriously, and the fact that Aryan Nation[1] racists or Nation of Islam[2] anti-Semites are unorthodox does not entitle them to respect. But what goes around comes around. As a supporter of gay marriage, for example, I reject the majority's view of family, and as a Jew I reject its view of God. I try to be civil, but the fact is that most Americans regard my views on marriage as a reckless assault on the most fundamental of all institutions, and many people are more than a little discomfited by the statement, "Jesus Christ was no more divine than anybody else" (which is why so few people ever say it). Trap the racists and anti-Semites, and you lay a trap for me too. Hunt for them with eradication in your mind, and you have brought dissent itself within your sights.

The new crusade against prejudice waves aside such warnings. Like earlier crusades against antisocial ideas, the mission is fueled by good (if cocksure) intentions and a genuine sense of urgency. Some kinds of error are held to be intolerable, like pollutants that even in small traces poison the water for a whole town. Some errors are so pernicious as to damage real people's lives, so wrongheaded that no person of right mind or goodwill could support them. Like their forebears of other stripe—the Church in its campaigns against heretics, the McCarthyites in their campaigns against Communists[3]—the modern anti-racist and anti-sexist and anti-homophobic campaigners are totalists, demanding not that misguided ideas and ugly expressions be corrected or criticized but that they be eradicated. They make war not on errors but on error, and like other totalists they act in the name of public safety—the safety, especially, of minorities.

The sweeping implications of this challenge to pluralism are not, I think, well enough understood by the public at large. Indeed, the new brand of totalism has yet even to be properly named. "Multiculturalism," for instance, is much

1. A white separatist religious group in the United States.

2. An African American religious organization in the United States that combines some of the practices and beliefs of Islam with a philosophy of black separatism.

3. In the early 1950s, Senator Joseph McCarthy pursued suspected Communists in the government and throughout the nation. Although his "Fight for America" did not result in a single conviction, he and his followers ruined the lives and careers of many they investigated. McCarthy was later condemned for "conduct contrary to Senatorial traditions."

too broad. "Political correctness" comes closer but is too trendy and snide. For lack of anything else, I will call the new anti-pluralism "purism," since its major tenet is that society cannot be just until the last traces of invidious prejudice have been scrubbed away. Whatever you call it, the purists' way of seeing things has spread through American intellectual life with remarkable speed, so much so that many people will blink at you uncomprehendingly or even call you a racist (or sexist or homophobe, etc.) if you suggest that expressions of racism should be tolerated or that prejudice has its part to play.

The new purism sets out, to begin with, on a campaign against words, for words are the currency of prejudice, and if prejudice is hurtful then so must be prejudiced words. "We are not safe when these violent words are among us," wrote Mari Matsuda, then a UCLA law professor. Here one imagines gangs of racist words swinging chains and smashing heads in back alleys. To suppress bigoted language seems, at first blush, reasonable, but it quickly leads to a curious result. A peculiar kind of verbal shamanism takes root, as though certain expressions, like curses or magical incantations, carry in themselves the power to hurt or heal—as though words were bigoted rather than people. "Context is everything," people have always said. The use of the word "nigger" in *Huckleberry Finn*[4] does not make the book an "act" of hate speech—or does it? In the new view, this is no longer so clear. The very utterance of the word "nigger" (at least by a non-black) is a racist act. When a *Sacramento Bee* cartoonist put the word "nigger" mockingly in the mouth of a white supremacist, there were howls of protest and 1,400 canceled subscriptions and an editorial apology, even though the word was plainly being invoked against racists, not against blacks.

Faced with escalating demands of verbal absolutism, newspapers issue lists of forbidden words. The expressions "gyp" (derived from "Gypsy") and "Dutch treat" were among the dozens of terms stricken as "offensive" in a much-ridiculed (and later withdrawn) *Los Angeles Times* speech code. The University of Missouri journalism school issued a *Dictionary of Cautionary Words and Phrases*, which included "*Buxom*: Offensive reference to a woman's chest. Do not use. See 'Woman.' *Codger*: Offensive reference to a senior citizen."

15   As was bound to happen, purists soon discovered that chasing around after words like "gyp" or "buxom" hardly goes to the roots of the problem. As long as they remain bigoted, bigots will simply find other words. If they can't call you a kike then they will say Jewboy, Judas, or Hebe, and when all those are banned they will press words like "oven" and "lampshade" into their service. The vocabulary of hate is potentially as rich as your dictionary, and all you do by banning language used by cretins is to let them decide what the rest of us may say. The problem, some purists have concluded, must therefore go much deeper than laws: it must go to the deeper level of ideas. Racism, sexism, homophobia, and the rest must be built into the very structure of American society and American patterns of thought, so pervasive yet so insidious

4. Mark Twain's 1889 novel includes coarse language, some of it now called racist.

that, like water to a fish, they are both omnipresent and unseen. The mere existence of prejudice constructs a society whose very nature is prejudiced.

This line of thinking was pioneered by feminists, who argued that pornography, more than just being expressive, is an act by which men construct an
oppressive society. Racial activists quickly picked up the argument. Racist expressions are themselves acts of oppression, they said. "All racist speech constructs the social reality that constrains the liberty of nonwhites because of
their race," wrote Charles R. Lawrence III, then a law professor at Stanford.
From the purist point of view, a society with even one racist is a racist society,
because the idea itself threatens and demeans its targets. They cannot feel
wholly safe or wholly welcome as long as racism is present. Pluralism says:
There will always be some racists. Marginalize them, ignore them, exploit
them, ridicule them, take pains to make their policies illegal, but otherwise
leave them alone. Purists say: That's not enough. Society cannot be just until
these pervasive and oppressive ideas are searched out and eradicated.

And so what is now under way is a growing drive to eliminate prejudice
from every corner of society. I doubt that many people have noticed how far-
reaching this anti-pluralist movement is becoming.

In universities: Dozens of universities have adopted codes proscribing
speech or other expression that (this is from Stanford's policy, which is more
or less representative) "is intended to insult or stigmatize an individual or a
small number of individuals on the basis of their sex, race, color, handicap, religion, sexual orientation or national and ethnic origin." Some codes punish
only persistent harassment of a targeted individual, but many, following the
purist doctrine that even one racist is too many, go much further. At Penn, an
administrator declared: "We at the University of Pennsylvania have guaranteed
students and the community that they can live in a community free of sexism,
racism, and homophobia." Here is the purism that gives "political correctness"
its distinctive combination of puffy high-mindedness and authoritarian zeal.

In school curricula: "More fundamental than eliminating racial segregation has to be the removal of racist thinking, assumptions, symbols, and materials in the curriculum," writes theorist Molefi Kete Asante. In practice, the
effort to "remove racist thinking" goes well beyond striking egregious references from textbooks. In many cases it becomes a kind of mental engineering
in which students are encouraged to see prejudice.

Ah, but the task of scouring minds clean is Augean.[5] "Nobody escapes,"   20
said a Rutgers University report on campus prejudice. Bias and prejudice, it
found, cross every conceivable line, from sex to race to politics: "No matter
who you are, no matter what the color of your skin, no matter what your gender or sexual orientation, no matter what you believe, no matter how you behave, there is somebody out there who doesn't like people of your kind."

---

5. In Greek mythology, Heracles was assigned twelve difficult and dangerous tasks, referred to as the Labors of Heracles. One task required cleaning the enormous stables of
Augeas, king of Elis, which Heracles did by diverting the rivers Alpheus and Peneus so
that they flowed through the stables and swept them clean.

Charles Lawrence writes: "Racism is ubiquitous. We are all racists." If he means that most of us think racist thoughts of some sort at one time or another, he is right. If we are going to "eliminate prejudices and biases from our society," then the work of the prejudice police is unending. They are doomed to hunt and hunt, scour and scour and scour.

What is especially dismaying is that the purists pursue prejudice in the name of protecting minorities. In order to protect people like me (homosexual), they must pursue people like me (dissident). In order to bolster minority self-esteem, they suppress minority opinion. There are, of course, all kinds of practical and legal problems with the purists' campaign: the incursions against the First Amendment; the inevitable abuses by prosecutors and activists who define as "hateful" or "violent" whatever speech they dislike or can score points off of; the lack of any evidence that repressing prejudice eliminates rather than inflames it. But minorities, of all people, ought to remember that by definition we cannot prevail by numbers, and we generally cannot prevail by force. Against the power of ignorant mass opinion and group prejudice and superstition, we have only our voices. If you doubt that minorities' voices are powerful weapons, think of the lengths to which Southern officials went to silence the Reverend Martin Luther King Jr. (recall that the city commissioner of Montgomery, Alabama, won a $500,000 libel suit, later overturned in *New York Times v. Sullivan* [1964], regarding an advertisement in the *Times* placed by civil-rights leaders who denounced the Montgomery police). Think of how much gay people have improved their lot over twenty-five years simply by refusing to remain silent. Recall the Michigan student who was prosecuted for saying that homosexuality is a treatable disease, and notice that he was black. Under that Michigan speech code, more than twenty blacks were charged with racist speech, while no instance of racist speech by whites was punished. In Florida, the hate-speech law was invoked against a black man who called a policeman a "white cracker"; not so surprisingly, in the first hate-crimes case to reach the Supreme Court, the victim was white and the defendant black.

In the escalating war against "prejudice," the right is already learning to play by the rules that were pioneered by the purist activists of the left. Last year leading Democrats, including the President, criticized the Republican Party for being increasingly in the thrall of the Christian right. Some of the rhetoric was harsh ("fire-breathing Christian radical right"), but it wasn't vicious or even clearly wrong. Never mind: when Democratic Representative Vic Fazio said Republicans were "being forced to the fringes by the aggressive political tactics of the religious right," the chairman of the Republican National Committee, Haley Barbour, said, "Christian-bashing" was "the left's preferred form of religious bigotry." Bigotry! Prejudice! "Christians active in politics are now on the receiving end of an extraordinary campaign of bias and prejudice," said the conservative leader William J. Bennett. One discerns, here, where the new purism leads. Eventually, any criticism of any group will be "prejudice."

Here is the ultimate irony of the new purism: words, which pluralists hope can be substituted for violence, are redefined by purists *as* violence. "The experience of being called 'nigger,' 'spic,' 'Jap,' or 'kike' is like receiving a slap in the face," Charles Lawrence wrote in 1990. "Psychic injury is no less an injury than being struck in the face, and it often is far more severe." This kind of talk is commonplace today. Epithets, insults, often even polite expressions of what's taken to be prejudice are called by purists "assaultive speech," "words that wound," "verbal violence." "To me, racial epithets are not speech," one University of Michigan law professor said. "They are bullets." In her speech accepting the 1993 Nobel Prize for Literature in Stockholm, Sweden, the author Toni Morrison[6] said this: "Oppressive language does more than represent violence; it is violence."

It is not violence. I am thinking back to a moment on the subway in Washington, a little thing. I was riding home late one night and a squad of noisy kids, maybe seventeen or eighteen years old, noisily piled into the car. They yelled across the car and a girl said, "Where do we get off?"

A boy said, "Farragut North."   25

The girl: "*Faggot* North!"

The boy: "Yeah! Faggot North!"

General hilarity.

First, before the intellect resumes control, there is a moment of fear, an animal moment. Who are they? How many of them? How dangerous! Where is the way out? All of these things are noted preverbally and assessed by the gut. Then the brain begins an assessment: they are sober, this is probably too public a place for them to do it, there are more girls than boys, they were just talking, it is probably nothing.

They didn't notice me and there was no incident. The teenage babble   30
flowed on, leaving me to think. I became interested in my own reaction: the jump of fear out of nowhere like an alert animal, the sense for a brief time that one is naked and alone and should hide or run away. For a time, one ceases to be a human being and becomes instead a faggot.

The fear engendered by these words is real. The remedy is as clear and as imperfect as ever: protect citizens against violence. This, I grant, is something that American society has never done very well and now does quite poorly. It is no solution to define words as violence or prejudice as oppression, and then by cracking down on words or thoughts pretend that we are doing something about violence and oppression. No doubt it is easier to pass a speech code or hate-crimes law and proclaim the streets safer than actually to make the streets safer, but the one must never be confused with the other. Every cop or prosecutor chasing words is one fewer chasing criminals. In a world rife with real violence and oppression, full of Rwandas and Bosnias and eleven-year-olds spraying bullets at children in Chicago and in turn being executed by gang lords, it is odious of Toni Morrison to say that words are violence.

Indeed, equating "verbal violence" with physical violence is a treacherous, mischievous business. Not long ago a writer was charged with viciously and

6. African American author (b. 1931).

gratuitously wounding the feelings and dignity of millions of people. He was charged, in effect, with exhibiting flagrant prejudice against Muslims and outrageously slandering their beliefs. "What is freedom of expression?" mused Salman Rushdie[7] a year after the ayatollahs sentenced him to death and put a price on his head. "Without the freedom to offend, it ceases to exist." I can think of nothing sadder than that minority activists, in their haste to make the world better, should be the ones to forget the lesson of Rushdie's plight: for minorities, pluralism, not purism, is the answer. The campaigns to eradicate prejudice—all of them, the speech codes and workplace restrictions and mandatory therapy for accused bigots and all the rest—should stop, now. The whole objective of eradicating prejudice, as opposed to correcting and criticizing it, should be repudiated as a fool's errand. Salman Rushdie is right, Toni Morrison wrong, and minorities belong at his side, not hers.

7. British novelist of Indian descent (b. 1947). Muslims condemned Rushdie's novel *The Satanic Verses* (1988) as an attack on the Islamic faith; in 1989, Iran's Ayatollah Khomeini declared that Rushdie and everyone involved in the book's publication should be put to death; the death sentence was lifted in 1998.

QUESTIONS

1. Rauch advances a controversial argument: that we should allow prejudice to be expressed rather than seek to repress or eradicate it. How, in the opening paragraphs, does he establish himself as a reasonable, even likable person whose views should be heard? Where else in the essay does he create this persona? Why is persona (or *ethos*) important in ethical argument?

2. What does Rauch mean by "intellectual pluralism" (paragraph 3)? Where does he come closest to giving a definition? How does he use examples to imply a definition?

3. In the third section of the essay (paragraphs 12–20), Rauch defines the position antithetical to his own as "purism." Why does he choose this term rather than another? What does it mean?

4. What are some counterarguments to Rauch's position? How many of these arguments does Rauch himself raise and refute? How effective is he at refuting them?

5. Rauch ends with quotations from Toni Morrison and Salman Rushdie. Why? What do their experiences as writers add to his argument?

Michael Levin   *The Case for Torture*

I
T IS GENERALLY assumed that torture is impermissible, a throwback to a more brutal age. Enlightened societies reject it outright, and regimes suspected of using it risk the wrath of the United States.

I believe this attitude is unwise. There are situations in which torture is not merely permissible but morally mandatory. Moreover, these situations are moving from the realm of imagination to fact.

Death: Suppose a terrorist has hidden an atomic bomb on Manhattan Island which will detonate at noon on July 4 unless . . . (here follow the usual demands for money and release of his friends from jail). Suppose, further, that he is caught at 10 a.m. of the fateful day, but—preferring death to failure—won't disclose where the bomb is. What do we do? If we follow due process—wait for his lawyer, arraign him—millions of people will die. If the only way to save those lives is to subject the terrorist to the most excruciating possible pain, what grounds can there be for not doing so? I suggest there are none. In any case, I ask you to face the question with an open mind.

Torturing the terrorist is unconstitutional? Probably. But millions of lives surely outweigh constitutionality. Torture is barbaric? Mass murder is far more barbaric. Indeed, letting millions of innocents die in deference to one who flaunts his guilt is moral cowardice, an unwillingness to dirty one's hands. If *you* caught the terrorist, could you sleep nights knowing that millions died because you couldn't bring yourself to apply the electrodes?

Once you concede that torture is justified in extreme cases, you have admitted that the decision to use torture is a matter of balancing innocent lives against the means needed to save them. You must now face more realistic cases involving more modest numbers. Someone plants a bomb on a jumbo jet. He alone can disarm it, and his demands cannot be met (or if they can, we refuse to set a precedent by yielding to his threats). Surely we can, we must, do anything to the extortionist to save the passengers. How can we tell 300, or 100, or 10 people who never asked to be put in danger, "I'm sorry, you'll have to die in agony, we just couldn't bring ourselves to . . ."

Here are the results of an informal poll about a third, hypothetical, case. Suppose a terrorist group kidnapped a newborn baby from a hospital. I asked four mothers if they would approve of torturing kidnappers if that were necessary to get their own newborns back. All said yes, the most "liberal" adding that she would like to administer it herself.

I am not advocating torture as punishment. Punishment is addressed to deeds irrevocably past. Rather, I am advocating torture as an acceptable measure for preventing future evils. So understood, it is far less objectionable

5

Originally published in Newsweek *in the "My Turn" column on June 7, 1982. The magazine introduced the column in 1972 to encourage members of the general public, as well as professional writers, to voice their views on current events and issues.*

689

than many extant punishments. Opponents of the death penalty, for example, are forever insisting that executing a murderer will not bring back his victim (as if the purpose of capital punishment were supposed to be resurrection, not deterrence or retribution). But torture, in the cases described, is intended not to bring anyone back but to keep innocents from being dispatched. The most powerful argument against using torture as a punishment or to secure confessions is that such practices disregard the rights of the individual. Well, if the individual is all that important—and he is—it is correspondingly important to protect the rights of individuals threatened by terrorists. If life is so valuable that it must never be taken, the lives of the innocents must be saved even at the price of hurting the one who endangers them.

Better precedents for torture are assassination and pre-emptive attack. No Allied leader would have flinched at assassinating Hitler, had that been possible. (The Allies did assassinate Heydrich.)[1] Americans would be angered to learn that Roosevelt could have had Hitler killed in 1943—thereby shortening the war and saving millions of lives—but refused on moral grounds. Similarly, if nation A learns that nation B is about to launch an unprovoked attack, A has a right to save itself by destroying B's military capability first. In the same way, if the police can by torture save those who would otherwise die at the hands of kidnappers or terrorists, they must.

Idealism: There is an important difference between terrorists and their victims that should mute talk of the terrorists' "rights." The terrorist's victims are at risk unintentionally, not having asked to be endangered. But the terrorist knowingly initiated his actions. Unlike his victims, he volunteered for the risks of his deed. By threatening to kill for profit or idealism, he renounces civilized standards, and he can have no complaint if civilization tries to thwart him by whatever means necessary.

10   Just as torture is justified only to save lives (not extort confessions or recantations), it is justifiably administered only to those *known* to hold innocent lives in their hands. Ah, but how can the authorities ever be sure they have the right malefactor? Isn't there a danger of error and abuse? Won't We turn into Them?

Questions like these are disingenuous in a world in which terrorists proclaim themselves and perform for television. The name of their game is public recognition. After all, you can't very well intimidate a government into releasing your freedom fighters unless you announce that it is your group that has seized its embassy. "Clear guilt" is difficult to define, but when 40 million people see a group of masked gunmen seize an airplane on the evening news, there is not much question about who the perpetrators are. There will be hard cases where the situation is murkier. Nonetheless, a line demarcating the legitimate use of torture can be drawn. Torture only the obviously guilty, and only for the sake of saving innocents, and the line between Us and Them will remain clear.

1. Reinhard Heydrich (1904–1942), German head of the Nazi SS who was shot by Czech resistance fighters.

There is little danger that the Western democracies will lose their way if they choose to inflict pain as one way of preserving order. Paralysis in the face of evil is the greater danger. Some day soon a terrorist will threaten tens of thousands of lives, and torture will be the only way to save them. We had better start thinking about this.

QUESTIONS

1. On what assumptions about torture (and its efficacy) does Levin's argument rest? Do you agree with his assumptions? Why or why not?

2. What support does Levin provide for his position? List the key evidence that Levin gives, and analyze how it is or is not compelling.

3. Write your own argument for or against the use of torture. Be sure to consider how you will support your position and how you will answer readers who hold a different view.

TOM REGAN   *The Case for Animal Rights*

I REGARD MYSELF as an advocate of animal rights—as a part of the animal rights movement. That movement, as I conceive it, is committed to a number of goals, including:

- the total abolition of the use of animals in science;
- the total dissolution of commercial animal agriculture;
- the total elimination of commercial and sport hunting and trapping.

There are, I know, people who profess to believe in animal rights but do not avow these goals. Factory farming, they say, is wrong—it violates animals' rights—but traditional animal agriculture is all right. Toxicity tests of cosmetics on animals violates their rights, but important medical research—cancer research, for example—does not. The clubbing of baby seals is abhorrent, but not the harvesting of adult seals. I used to think I understood this reasoning. Not any more. You don't change unjust institutions by tidying them up.

What's wrong—fundamentally wrong—with the way animals are treated isn't the details that vary from case to case. It's the whole system. The forlorn-

From In Defense of Animals (1985), *one of several books Regan has published on this ethical issue. Others include* The Case for Animal Rights (1983) *and* Defending Animal Rights (2001).

ness of the veal calf is pathetic, heart-wrenching; the pulsing pain of the chimp with electrodes planted deep in her brain is repulsive; the slow, tortuous death of the racoon caught in the leg-hold trap is agonizing. But what is wrong isn't the pain, isn't the suffering, isn't the deprivation. These compound what's wrong. Sometimes—often—they make it much, much worse. But they are not the fundamental wrong.

The fundamental wrong is the system that allows us to view animals as *our resources*, here for *us*—to be eaten, or surgically manipulated, or exploited for sport or money. Once we accept this view of animals—as our resources—the rest is as predictable as it is regrettable. Why worry about their loneliness, their pain, their death? Since animals exist for us, to benefit us in one way or another, what harms them really doesn't matter—or matters only if it starts to bother us, makes us feel a trifle uneasy when we eat our veal escalope, for example. So, yes, let us get veal calves out of solitary confinement, give them more space, a little straw, a few companions. But let us keep our veal escalope.

But a little straw, more space and a few companions won't eliminate—won't even touch—the basic wrong that attaches to our viewing and treating these animals as our resources. A veal calf killed to be eaten after living in close confinement is viewed and treated in this way: but so, too, is another who is raised (as they say) "more humanely." To right the wrong of our treatment of farm animals requires more than making rearing methods "more humane"; it requires the total dissolution of commercial animal agriculture.

5   How we do this, whether we do it or, as in the case of animals in science, whether and how we abolish their use—these are to a large extent political questions. People must change their beliefs before they change their habits. Enough people, especially those elected to public office, must believe in change—must want it—before we will have laws that protect the rights of animals. This process of change is very complicated, very demanding, very exhausting, calling for the efforts of many hands in education, publicity, political organization and activity, down to the licking of envelopes and stamps. As a trained and practicing philosopher, the sort of contribution I can make is limited but, I like to think, important. The currency of philosophy is ideas—their meaning and rational foundation—not the nuts and bolts of the legislative process, say, or the mechanics of community organization. That's what I have been exploring over the past ten years or so in my essays and talks and, most recently, in my book, *The Case for Animal Rights*. I believe the major conclusions I reach in the book are true because they are supported by the weight of the best arguments. I believe the idea of animal rights has reason, not just emotion, on its side.

In the space I have at my disposal here I can only sketch, in the barest outline, some of the main features of the book. Its main themes—and we should not be surprised by this—involve asking and answering deep, foundational moral questions about what morality is, how it should be understood and what is the best moral theory, all considered. I hope I can convey something of the shape I think this theory takes. The attempt to do this will be (to use a word a friendly critic once used to describe my work) cerebral, perhaps too cerebral. But this is misleading. My feelings about how animals are sometimes treated run just as deep and just as strong as those of my more volatile compatriots. Philosophers do—to use the jargon of the day—have a right side to their brains. If it's the left side we contribute (or mainly should), that's because what talents we have reside there.

How to proceed? We begin by asking how the moral status of animals has been understood by thinkers who deny that animals have rights. Then we test the mettle of their ideas by seeing how well they stand up under the heat of fair criticism. If we start our thinking in this way, we soon find that some people believe that we have no duties directly to animals, that we owe nothing to them, that we can do nothing that wrongs them. Rather, we can do wrong acts that involve animals, and so we have duties regarding them, though none to them. Such views may be called indirect duty views. By way of illustration: suppose your neighbor kicks your dog. Then your neighbor has done something wrong. But not to your dog. The wrong that has been done is a wrong to you. After all, it is wrong to upset people, and your neighbor's kicking your dog upsets you. So you are the one who is wronged, not your dog. Or again: by kicking your dog your neighbor damages your property. And since it is wrong to damage another person's property, your neighbor has done something wrong— to you, of course, not to your dog. Your neighbor no more wrongs your dog than your car would be wronged if the wind-shield were smashed. Your neighbor's duties involving your dog are indirect duties to you. More generally, all of our duties regarding animals are indirect duties to one another—to humanity.

How could someone try to justify such a view? Someone might say that your dog doesn't feel anything and so isn't hurt by your neighbor's kick, doesn't care about the pain since none is felt, is as unaware of anything as is your windshield. Someone might say this, but no rational person will, since, among other considerations, such a view will commit anyone who holds it to the position that no human being feels pain either—that human beings also don't care about what happens to them. A second possibility is that though both humans and your dog are hurt when kicked, it is only human pain that matters. But, again, no rational person can believe this. Pain is pain wherever it occurs. If your neighbor's causing you pain is wrong because of the pain that is caused, we cannot rationally ignore or dismiss the moral relevance of the pain that your dog feels.

Philosophers who hold indirect duty views—and many still do—have come to understand that they must avoid the two defects just noted: that is, both the view that animals don't feel anything as well as the idea that only human pain can be morally relevant. Among such thinkers the sort of view now favored is one or other form of what is called *contractarianism*.

Here, very crudely, is the root idea: morality consists of a set of rules that individuals voluntarily agree to abide by, as we do when we sign a contract (hence the name contractarianism). Those who understand and accept the terms of the contract are covered directly; they have rights created and recognized by, and protected in, the contract and these contractors can also have protection spelled out for others who, though they lack the ability to under-

10

stand morality and so cannot sign the contract themselves, are loved or cherished by those who can. Thus young children, for example, are unable to sign contracts and lack rights. But they are protected by the contract none the less because of the sentimental interests of others, most notably their parents. So we have, then, duties involving these children, duties regarding them, but no duties to them. Our duties in their case are indirect duties to other human beings, usually their parents.

As for animals, since they cannot understand contracts, they obviously cannot sign; and since they cannot sign, they have no rights. Like children, however, some animals are the objects of the sentimental interest of others. You, for example, love your dog or cat. So those animals that enough people care about (companion animals, whales, baby seals, the American bald eagle), though they lack rights themselves, will be protected because of the sentimental interests of people. I have, then, according to contractarianism, no duty directly to your dog or any other animal, not even the duty not to cause them pain or suffering; my duty not to hurt them is a duty I have to those people who care about what happens to them. As for other animals, where no or little sentimental interest is present—in the case of farm animals, for example, or laboratory rats—what duties we have grow weaker and weaker, perhaps to vanishing point. The pain and death they endure, though real, are not wrong if no one cares about them.

When it comes to the moral status of animals, contractarianism could be a hard view to refute if it were an adequate theoretical approach to the moral status of human beings. It is not adequate in this latter respect, however, which makes the question of its adequacy in the former case, regarding animals, utterly moot. For consider: morality, according to the (crude) contractarian position before us, consists of rules that people agree to abide by. What people? Well, enough to make a difference—enough, that is, *collectively* to have the power to enforce the rules that are drawn up in the contract. This is very well and good for the signatories but not so good for anyone who is not asked to sign. And there is nothing in contractarianism of the sort we are discussing that guarantees or requires that everyone will have a chance to participate equally in framing the rules of morality. The result is that this approach to ethics could sanction the most blatant forms of social, economic, moral and political injustice, ranging from a repressive caste system to systematic racial or sexual discrimination. Might, according to this theory, does make right. Let those who are the victims of injustice suffer as they will. It matters not so long as no one else—no contractor, or too few of them—cares about it. Such a theory takes one's moral breath away . . . as if, for example, there would be nothing wrong with apartheid in South Africa if few white South Africans were upset by it. A theory with so little to recommend it at the level of the ethics of our treatment of our fellow humans cannot have anything more to recommend it when it comes to the ethics of how we treat our fellow animals.

The version of contractarianism just examined is, as I have noted, a crude variety, and in fairness to those of a contractarian persuasion it must be noted that much more refined, subtle and ingenious varieties are possible. For example, John Rawls,[1] in his A *Theory of Justice*, sets forth a version of contractarianism that forces contractors to ignore the accidental features of being a human being—for example, whether one is white or black, male or female, a genius or of modest intellect. Only by ignoring such features, Rawls believes, can we ensure that the principles of justice that contractors would agree upon are not based on bias or prejudice. Despite the improvement a view such as Rawls's represents over the cruder forms of contractarianism, it remains deficient: it systematically denies that we have direct duties to those human beings who do not have a sense of justice—young children, for instance, and many mentally retarded humans. And yet it seems reasonably certain that, were we to torture a young child or a retarded elder, we would be doing something that wronged him or her, not something that would be wrong if (and only if) other humans with a sense of justice were upset. And since this is true in the case of these humans, we cannot rationally deny the same in the case of animals.

Indirect duty views, then, including the best among them, fail to command our rational assent. Whatever ethical theory we should accept rationally, therefore, it must at least recognize that we have some duties directly to animals, just as we have some duties directly to each other. The next two theories I'll sketch attempt to meet this requirement.

The first I call the cruelty-kindness view. Simply stated, this says that we have a direct duty to be kind to animals and a direct duty not to be cruel to them. Despite the familiar, reassuring ring of these ideas, I do not believe that this view offers an adequate theory. To make this clearer, consider kindness. A kind person acts from a certain kind of motive—compassion or concern, for example. And that is a virtue. But there is no guarantee that a kind act is a right act. If I am a generous racist, for example, I will be inclined to act kindly towards members of my own race, favoring their interests above those of others. My kindness would be real and, so far as it goes, good. But I trust it is too obvious to require argument that my kind acts may not be above moral reproach—may, in fact, be positively wrong because rooted in injustice. So kindness, notwithstanding its status as a virtue to be encouraged, simply will not carry the weight of a theory of right action.

Cruelty fares no better. People or their acts are cruel if they display either a lack of sympathy for or, worse, the presence of enjoyment in another's suffering. Cruelty in all its guises is a bad thing, a tragic human failing. But just as a person's being motivated by kindness does not guarantee that he or she does what is right, so the absence of cruelty does not ensure that he or she avoids doing what is wrong. Many people who perform abortions, for example, are not cruel, sadistic people. But that fact alone does not settle the terribly difficult question of the morality of abortion. The case is no different when we examine the ethics of our treatment of animals. So, yes, let us be for kindness and against cruelty. But let us not suppose that being for the one and against the other answers questions about moral right and wrong.

15

1. American philosopher (1921–2002).

Some people think that the theory we are looking for is utilitarianism. A utilitarian accepts two moral principles. The first is that of equality: everyone's interests count, and similar interests must be counted as having similar weight or importance. White or black, American or Iranian, human or animal—everyone's pain or frustration matter, and matter just as much as the equivalent pain or frustration of anyone else. The second principle a utilitarian accepts is that of utility: do the act that will bring about the best balance between satisfaction and frustration for everyone affected by the outcome.

As a utilitarian, then, here is how I am to approach the task of deciding what I morally ought to do: I must ask who will be affected if I choose to do one thing rather than another, how much each individual will be affected, and where the best results are most likely to lie—which option, in other words, is most likely to bring about the best results, the best balance between satisfaction and frustration. That option, whatever it may be, is the one I ought to choose. That is where my moral duty lies.

The great appeal of utilitarianism rests with its uncompromising *egalitarianism*: everyone's interests count and count as much as the like interests of everyone else. The kind of odious discrimination that some forms of contractarianism can justify—discrimination based on race or sex, for example—seems disallowed in principle by utilitarianism, as is speciesism, systematic discrimination based on species membership.

20   The equality we find in utilitarianism, however, is not the sort an advocate of animal or human rights should have in mind. Utilitarianism has no room for the equal moral rights of different individuals because it has no room for their equal inherent value or worth. What has value for the utilitarian is the satisfaction of an individual's interests, not the individual whose interests they are. A universe in which you satisfy your desire for water, food and warmth is, other things being equal, better than a universe in which these desires are frustrated. And the same is true in the case of an animal with similar desires. But neither you nor the animal have any value in your own right. Only your feelings do.

Here is an analogy to help make the philosophical point clearer: a cup contains different liquids, sometimes sweet, sometimes bitter, sometimes a mix of the two. What has value are the liquids: the sweeter the better, the bitterer the worse. The cup, the container, has no value. It is what goes into it, not what they go into, that has value. For the utilitarian you and I are like the cup; we have no value as individuals and thus no equal value. What has value is what goes into us, what we serve as receptacles for; our feelings of satisfaction have positive value, our feelings of frustration negative value.

Serious problems arise for utilitarianism when we remind ourselves that it enjoins us to bring about the best consequences. What does this mean? It doesn't mean the best consequences for me alone, or for my family or friends, or any other person taken individually. No, what we must do is, roughly, as follows: we must add up (somehow!) the separate satisfactions and frustrations of everyone likely to be affected by our choice, the satisfactions in one column, the frustrations in the other. We must total each column for each of the options before us. That is what it means to say the theory is aggregative. And then we must choose that option which is most likely to bring about the best balance of totaled satisfactions over totaled frustrations. Whatever act would lead to this outcome is the one we ought morally to perform—it is where our moral duty lies. And that act quite clearly might not be the same one that would bring about the best results for me personally, or for my family or friends, or for a lab animal. The best aggregated consequences for everyone concerned are not necessarily the best for each individual.

That utilitarianism is an aggregative theory—different individuals' satisfactions or frustrations are added, or summed, or totaled—is the key objection to this theory. My Aunt Bea is old, inactive, a cranky, sour person, though not physically ill. She prefers to go on living. She is also rather rich. I could make a fortune if I could get my hands on her money, money she intends to give me in any event, after she dies, but which she refuses to give me now. In order to avoid a huge tax bite, I plan to donate a handsome sum of my profits to a local children's hospital. Many, many children will benefit from my generosity, and much joy will be brought to their parents, relatives and friends. If I don't get the money rather soon, all these ambitions will come to naught. The once-in-a-lifetime opportunity to make a real killing will be gone. Why, then, not kill my Aunt Bea? Oh, of course I *might* get caught. But I'm no fool and, besides, her doctor can be counted on to cooperate (he has an eye for the same investment and I happen to know a good deal about his shady past). The deed can be done . . . professionally, shall we say. There is *very* little chance of getting caught. And as for my conscience being guilt-ridden, I am a resourceful sort of fellow and will take more than sufficient comfort—as I lie on the beach at Acapulco—in contemplating the joy and health I have brought to so many others.

Suppose Aunt Bea is killed and the rest of the story comes out as told. Would I have done anything wrong? Anything immoral? One would have thought that I had. Not according to utilitarianism. Since what I have done has brought about the best balance between totaled satisfaction and frustration for all those affected by the outcome, my action is not wrong. Indeed, in killing Aunt Bea the physician and I did what duty required.

This same kind of argument can be repeated in all sorts of cases, illustrating, time after time, how the utilitarian's position leads to results that impartial people find morally callous. It *is* wrong to kill my Aunt Bea in the name of bringing about the best results for others. A good end does not justify an evil means. Any adequate moral theory will have to explain why this is so. Utilitarianism fails in this respect and so cannot be the theory we seek.

What to do? Where to begin anew? The place to begin, I think, is with the utilitarian's view of the value of the individual—or, rather, lack of value. In its place, suppose we consider that you and I, for example, do have value as individuals—what we'll call *inherent value*. To say we have such value is to say that we are something more than, something different from, mere receptacles. Moreover, to ensure that we do not pave the way for such injustices as slavery or sexual discrimination, we must believe that all who have inherent value

25

have it equally, regardless of their sex, race, religion, birthplace and so on. Similarly to be discarded as irrelevant are one's talents or skills, intelligence and wealth, personality or pathology, whether one is loved and admired or despised and loathed. The genius and the retarded child, the prince and the pauper, the brain surgeon and the fruit vendor, Mother Teresa[2] and the most unscrupulous used-car salesman—all have inherent value, all possess it equally, and all have an equal right to be treated with respect, to be treated in ways that do not reduce them to the status of things, as if they existed as resources for others. My value as an individual is independent of my usefulness to you. Yours is not dependent on your usefulness to me. For either of us to treat the other in ways that fail to show respect for the other's independent value is to act immorally, to violate the individual's rights.

Some of the rational virtues of this view—what I call the rights view—should be evident. Unlike (crude) contractarianism, for example, the rights view *in principle* denies the moral tolerability of any and all forms of racial, sexual or social discrimination; and unlike utilitarianism, this view *in principle* denies that we can justify good results by using evil means that violate an individual's rights—denies, for example, that it could be moral to kill my Aunt Bea to harvest beneficial consequences for others. That would be to sanction the disrespectful treatment of the individual in the name of the social good, something the rights view will not—categorically will not—ever allow.

The rights view, I believe, is rationally the most satisfactory moral theory. It surpasses all other theories in the degree to which it illuminates and explains the foundation of our duties to one another—the domain of human morality. On this score it has the best reasons, the best arguments, on its side. Of course, if it were possible to show that only human beings are included within its scope, then a person like myself, who believes in animal rights, would be obliged to look elsewhere.

But attempts to limit its scope to humans only can be shown to be rationally defective. Animals, it is true, lack many of the abilities humans possess. They can't read, do higher mathematics, build a bookcase or make *baba ghanoush*.[3] Neither can many human beings, however, and yet we don't (and shouldn't) say that they (these humans) therefore have less inherent value, less of a right to be treated with respect, than do others. It is the *similarities* between those human beings who most clearly, most noncontroversially have such value (the people reading this, for example), not our differences, that matter most. And the really crucial, the basic similarity is simply this: we are each of us the experiencing subject of a life, a conscious creature having an individual welfare that has importance to us whatever our usefulness to others. We want and prefer things, believe and feel things, recall and expect things. And all these dimensions of our life, including our pleasure and pain, our enjoyment and suffering, our satisfaction and frustration, our continued exis-

2. Nun (1910–1998) who founded the Missionaries of Charity in Calcutta, India, and is now proverbially known as the ultimate good person.
3. An eggplant-sesame spread or dip popular in the Middle East.

tence or our untimely death—all make a difference to the quality of our life as lived, as experienced, by us as individuals. As the same is true of those animals that concern us (the ones that are eaten and trapped, for example), they too must be viewed as the experiencing subjects of a life, with inherent value of their own.

Some there are who resist the idea that animals have inherent value. "Only humans have such value," they profess. How might this narrow view be defended? Shall we say that only humans have the requisite intelligence, or autonomy, or reason? But there are many, many humans who fail to meet these standards and yet are reasonably viewed as having value above and beyond their usefulness to others. Shall we claim that only humans belong to the right species, the species *Homo sapiens*?[4] But this is blatant speciesism. Will it be said, then, that all—and only—humans have immortal souls? Then our opponents have their work cut out for them. I am myself not ill-disposed to the proposition that there are immortal souls. Personally, I profoundly hope I have one. But I would not want to rest my position on a controversial ethical issue on the even more controversial question about who or what has an immortal soul. That is to dig one's hole deeper, not to climb out. Rationally, it is better to resolve moral issues without making more controversial assumptions than are needed. The question of who has inherent value is such a question, one that is resolved more rationally without the introduction of the idea of immortal souls than by its use.

Well, perhaps some will say that animals have some inherent value, only less than we have. Once again, however, attempts to defend this view can be shown to lack rational justification. What could be the basis of our having more inherent value than animals? Their lack of reason, or autonomy, or intellect? Only if we are willing to make the same judgment in the case of humans who are similarly deficient. But it is not true that such humans—the retarded child, for example, or the mentally deranged—have less inherent value than you or I. Neither, then, can we rationally sustain the view that animals like them in being the experiencing subjects of a life have less inherent value. *All* who have inherent value have it *equally*, whether they be human animals or not.

Inherent value, then, belongs equally to those who are the experiencing subjects of a life. Whether it belongs to others—to rocks and rivers, trees and glaciers, for example—we do not know and may never know. But neither do we need to know, if we are to make the case for animal rights. We do not need to know, for example, how many people are eligible to vote in the next presidential election before we can know whether I am. Similarly, we do not need to know how many individuals have inherent value before we can know that some do. When it comes to the case for animal rights, then, what we need to know is whether the animals that, in our culture, are routinely eaten, hunted and used in our laboratories, for example, are like us in being subjects of a life.

30

---

4. Latin for "man with intellect," the taxonomic designation for the modern human species.

And we do know this. We do know that many—literally, billions and billions—of these animals are the subjects of a life in the sense explained and so have inherent value if we do. And since, in order to arrive at the best theory of our duties to one another, we must recognize our equal inherent value as individuals, reason—not sentiment, not emotion—reason compels us to recognize the equal inherent value of these animals and, with this, their equal right to be treated with respect.

That, *very* roughly, is the shape and feel of the case for animal rights. Most of the details of the supporting argument are missing. They are to be found in the book to which I alluded earlier. Here, the details go begging, and I must, in closing, limit myself to four final points.

The first is how the theory that underlies the case for animal rights shows that the animal rights movement is a part of, not antagonistic to, the human rights movement. The theory that rationally grounds the rights of animals also grounds the rights of humans. Thus those involved in the animal rights movement are partners in the struggle to secure respect for human rights—the rights of women, for example, or minorities, or workers. The animal rights movement is cut from the same moral cloth as these.

35   Second, having set out the broad outlines of the rights view, I can now say why its implications for farming and science, among other fields, are both clear and uncompromising. In the case of the use of animals in science, the rights view is categorically abolitionist. Lab animals are not our tasters; we are not their kings. Because these animals are treated routinely, systematically as if their value were reducible to their usefulness to others, they are routinely, systematically treated with a lack of respect, and thus are their rights routinely, systematically violated. This is just as true when they are used in trivial, duplicative, unnecessary or unwise research as it is when they are used in studies that hold out real promise of human benefits. We can't justify harming or killing a human being (my Aunt Bea, for example) just for these sorts of reason. Neither can we do so even in the case of so lowly a creature as a laboratory rat. It is not just refinement or reduction that is called for, not just larger, cleaner cages, not just more generous use of anaesthetic or the elimination of multiple surgery, not just tidying up the system. It is complete replacement. The best we can do when it comes to using animals in science is—not to use them. That is where our duty lies, according to the rights view.

As for commercial animal agriculture, the rights view takes a similar abolitionist position. The fundamental moral wrong here is not that animals are kept in stressful close confinement or in isolation, or that their pain and suffering, their needs and preferences are ignored or discounted. All these *are* wrong, of course, but they are not the fundamental wrong. They are symptoms and effects of the deeper, systematic wrong that allows these animals to be viewed and treated as lacking independent value, as resources for us—as, indeed, a renewable resource. Giving farm animals more space, more natural environments, more companions does not right the fundamental wrong, any more than giving lab animals more anaesthesia or bigger, cleaner cages would right the fundamental wrong in their case. Nothing less than the total dissolution of commercial animal agriculture will do this, just as, for similar reasons I won't develop at length here, morality requires nothing less than the total elimination of hunting and trapping for commercial and sporting ends. The rights view's implications, then, as I have said, are clear and uncompromising.

My last two points are about philosophy, my profession. It is, most obviously, no substitute for political action. The words I have written here and in other places by themselves don't change a thing. It is what we do with the thoughts that the words express—our acts, our deeds—that changes things. All that philosophy can do, and all I have attempted, is to offer a vision of what our deeds should aim at. And the why. But not the how.

Finally, I am reminded of my thoughtful critic, the one I mentioned earlier, who chastised me for being too cerebral. Well, cerebral I have been: indirect duty views, utilitarianism, contractarianism—hardly the stuff deep passions are made of. I am also reminded, however, of the image another friend once set before me—the image of the ballerina as expressive of disciplined passion. Long hours of sweat and toil, of loneliness and practice, of doubt and fatigue: those are the discipline of her craft. But the passion is there too, the fierce drive to excel, to speak through her body, to do it right, to pierce our minds. That is the image of philosophy I would leave with you, not "too cerebral" but *disciplined passion*. Of the discipline enough has been seen. As for the passion: there are times, and these not infrequent, when tears come to my eyes when I see, or read, or hear of the wretched plight of animals in the hands of humans. Their pain, their suffering, their loneliness, their innocence, their death. Anger. Rage. Pity. Sorrow. Disgust. The whole creation groans under the weight of the evil we humans visit upon these mute, powerless creatures. It *is* our hearts, not just our heads, that call for an end to it all, that demand of us that we overcome, for them, the habits and forces behind their systematic oppression. All great movements, it is written, go through three stages: ridicule, discussion, adoption. It is the realization of this third stage, adoption, that requires both our passion and our discipline, our hearts and our heads. The fate of animals is in our hands. God grant we are equal to the task.

QUESTIONS

1. Regan argues against four views that deny rights to animals: indirect duty, contractarianism, cruelty-kindness, and utilitarianism. Locate his account of each and explain his objections to it.

2. Regan then argues for what he calls a "rights view," which is, he claims, "rationally the most satisfactory moral theory" (paragraph 28). Explain both his view and his claim.

3. What are the advantages of arguing for views that conflict with one's own before arguing for one's own? What are the disadvantages?

4. Regan includes among his goals "the total dissolution of commercial animal agriculture" and "the total elimination of commercial and sport hunting and trapping" (para-

graph 1). Do these goals include vegetarianism? If so, why does he not use the word "vegetarian"?

5. Write an essay in which you take a position on an issue about which you have strong feelings. Following Regan's example, focus on argument while both acknowledging and excluding your feelings.

MICHAEL POLLAN   *An Animal's Place*

THE FIRST TIME I opened Peter Singer's *Animal Liberation*, I was dining alone at the Palm,[1] trying to enjoy a rib-eye steak cooked medium-rare. If this sounds like a good recipe for cognitive dissonance (if not indigestion), that was sort of the idea. Preposterous as it might seem, to supporters of animal rights, what I was doing was tantamount to reading *Uncle Tom's Cabin* on a plantation in the Deep South in 1852.

Singer and the swelling ranks of his followers ask us to imagine a future in which people will look back on my meal, and this steakhouse, as relics of an equally backward age. Eating animals, wearing animals, experimenting on animals, killing animals for sport: all these practices, so resolutely normal to us, will be seen as the barbarities they are, and we will come to view "speciesism"—a neologism I had encountered before only in jokes—as a form of discrimination as indefensible as racism or anti-Semitism.

Even in 1975, when *Animal Liberation* was first published, Singer, an Australian philosopher now teaching at Princeton, was confident that he had the wind of history at his back. The recent civil rights past was prologue, as one liberation movement followed on the heels of another. Slowly but surely, the white man's circle of moral consideration was expanded to admit first blacks, then women, then homosexuals. In each case, a group once thought to be so different from the prevailing "we" as to be undeserving of civil rights was, after a struggle, admitted to the club. Now it was animals' turn.

That animal liberation is the logical next step in the forward march of moral progress as no longer the fringe idea it was back in 1975. A growing and increasingly influential group of philosophers, ethicists, law professors and activists are convinced that the great moral struggle of our time will be for the rights of animals.

5   So far the movement has scored some of its biggest victories in Europe. Earlier this year, Germany became the first nation to grant animals a constitu-

Published on November 10, 2002, in the New York Times Magazine, *a supplement to the Sunday newspaper.*

1. Famous New York City steakhouse.

tional right: the words "and animals" were added to a provision obliging the state to respect and protect the dignity of human beings. The farming of animals for fur was recently banned in England. In several European nations, sows may no longer be confined to crates nor laying hens to "battery cages"— stacked wired cages so small the birds cannot stretch their wings. The Swiss are amending their laws to change the status of animals from "things" to "beings."

Though animals are still very much "things" in the eyes of American law, change is in the air. Thirty-seven states have recently passed laws making some forms of animal cruelty a crime, twenty-one of them by ballot initiative. Following protests by activists, McDonald's and Burger King forced significant improvements in the way the U.S. meat industry slaughters animals. Agribusiness and the cosmetics and apparel industries are all struggling to defuse mounting public concerns over animal welfare.

Once thought of as a left-wing concern, the movement now cuts across ideological lines. Perhaps the most eloquent recent plea on behalf of animals, a new book called *Dominion*, was written by a former speechwriter for President Bush. And once outlandish ideas are finding their way into mainstream opinion. A recent Zogby poll found that fifty-one percent of Americans believe that *primates* are entitled to the same rights as human children.

What is going on here? A certain amount of cultural confusion, for one thing. For at the same time many people seem eager to extend the circle of our moral consideration to animals, in our factory farms and laboratories we are inflicting more suffering on more animals than at any time in history. One by one, science is dismantling our claims to uniqueness as a species, discovering that such things as culture, toolmaking, language and even possibly self-consciousness are not the exclusive domain of *Homo sapiens*. Yet most of the animals we kill lead lives organized very much in the spirit of Descartes,[2] who famously claimed that animals were mere machines, incapable of thought or feeling. There's a schizoid quality to our relationship with animals, in which sentiment and brutality exist side by side. Half the dogs in America will receive Christmas presents this year, yet few of us pause to consider the miserable life of the pig—an animal easily as intelligent as a dog—that becomes the Christmas ham.

We tolerate this disconnect because the life of the pig has moved out of view. When's the last time you saw a pig? (Babe doesn't count.) Except for our pets, real animals—animals living and dying—no longer figure in our everyday lives. Meat comes from the grocery store, where it is cut and packaged to look as little like parts of animals as possible. The disappearance of animals from our lives has opened a space in which there's no reality check, either on the sentiment or the brutality. This is pretty much where we live now, with respect to animals, and it is a space in which the Peter Singers and Frank Perdues of the world can evidently thrive equally well.

Several years ago, the English critic John Berger wrote an essay, "Why   10

2. René Descartes (1596–1650), French philosopher.

Look at Animals?," in which he suggested that the loss of everyday contact between ourselves and animals—and specifically the loss of eye contact—has left
us deeply confused about the terms of our relationship to other species. That
eye contact, always slightly uncanny, had provided a vivid daily reminder that
animals were at once crucially like and unlike us; in their eyes we glimpsed
something unmistakably familiar (pain, fear, tenderness) and something irre-
trievably alien. Upon this paradox people built a relationship in which they felt
they could both honor and eat animals without looking away. But that accommodation has pretty much broken down; nowadays, it seems, we either look
away or become vegetarians. For my own part, neither option seemed especially appetizing. Which might explain how I found myself reading *Animal
Liberation* in a steakhouse.

This is not something I'd recommend if you're determined to continue eating
meat. Combining rigorous philosophical argument with journalistic description, *Animal Liberation* is one of those rare books that demand that you either
defend the way you live or change it. Because Singer is so skilled in argument,
for many readers it is easier to change. His book has converted countless thousands to vegetarianism, and it didn't take long for me to see why: within a few
pages, he had succeeded in throwing me on the defensive.

Singer's argument is disarmingly simple and, if you accept its premises,
difficult to refute. Take the premise of equality, which most people readily accept. Yet what do we really mean by it? People are not, as a matter of fact,
equal at all—some are smarter than others, better looking, more gifted.
"Equality is a moral idea," Singer points out, "not an assertion of fact." The
moral idea is that everyone's interests ought to receive equal consideration, regardless of "what abilities they may possess." Fair enough; many philosophers
have gone this far. But fewer have taken the next logical step. "If possessing a
higher degree of intelligence does not entitle one human to use another for his
or her own ends, how can it entitle humans to exploit nonhumans for the
same purpose?"

This is the nub of Singer's argument, and right around here I began scribbling objections in the margin. *But humans differ from animals in morally significant ways.* Yes they do, Singer acknowledges, which is why we shouldn't
treat pigs and children alike. Equal consideration of interests is not the same
as equal treatment, he points out: children have an interest in being educated;
pigs, in rooting around in the dirt. But where their interests are the same, the
principle of equality demands they receive the same consideration. And the
one all-important interest that we share with pigs, as with all sentient creatures, is an interest in avoiding pain.

Here Singer quotes a famous passage from Jeremy Bentham, the
eighteenth-century utilitarian philosopher, that is the wellspring of the animal
rights movement. Bentham was writing in 1789, soon after the French
colonies freed black slaves, granting them fundamental rights. "The day *may*
come," he speculates, "when the rest of the animal creation may acquire those
rights." Bentham then asks what characteristic entitles any being to moral

consideration. "Is it the faculty of reason or perhaps the faculty of discourse?" Obviously not, since "a full-grown horse or dog is beyond comparison a more rational, as well as a more conversable animal, than an infant." He concludes: "The question is not, Can they *reason*? nor, Can they *talk*? but, Can they *suffer*?"

Bentham here is playing a powerful card philosophers call the "argument from marginal cases," or AMC for short. It goes like this: There are humans— infants, the severely retarded, the demented—whose mental function cannot match that of a chimpanzee. Even though these people cannot reciprocate our moral attentions, we nevertheless include them in the circle of our moral consideration. So on what basis do we exclude the chimpanzee?   15

Because he's a chimp, I furiously scribbled in the margin, *and they're human!* For Singer that's not good enough. To exclude the chimp from moral consideration simply because he's not human is no different from excluding the slave simply because he's not white. In the same way we'd call that exclusion racist, the animal rightist contends that it is speciesist to discriminate against the chimpanzee solely because he's not human.

But the differences between blacks and whites are trivial compared with the differences between my son and a chimp. Singer counters by asking us to imagine a hypothetical society that discriminates against people on the basis of something nontrivial—say, intelligence. If that scheme offends our sense of equality, then why is the fact that animals lack certain human characteristics any more just as a basis for discrimination? Either we do not owe any justice to the severely retarded, he concludes, or we do owe it to animals with higher capabilities.

This is where I put down my fork. If I believe in equality, and equality is based on interests rather than characteristics, then I have to either take the interests of the steer I'm eating into account or concede that I am a speciesist. For the time being, I decided to plead guilty as charged. I finished my steak.

But Singer had planted a troubling notion, and in the days afterward, it grew and grew, watered by the other animal rights thinkers I began reading: the philosophers Tom Regan and James Rachels; the legal theorist Steven M. Wise; the writers Joy Williams and Matthew Scully. I didn't *think* I minded being a speciesist, but could it be, as several of these writers suggest, that we will someday come to regard speciesism as an evil comparable to racism? Will history someday judge us as harshly as it judges the Germans who went about their ordinary lives in the shadow of Treblinka? Precisely that question was recently posed by J. M. Coetzee, the South African novelist, in a lecture delivered at Princeton; he answered it in the affirmative. If animal rightists are right, "a crime of stupefying proportions" (in Coetzee's words) is going on all around us every day, just beneath our notice.

It's an idea almost impossible to entertain seriously, much less to accept,   20 and in the weeks following my restaurant face-off between Singer and the steak, I found myself marshaling whatever mental power I could muster to try to refute it. Yet Singer and his allies managed to trump almost all my objections.

My first line of defense was obvious. *Animals kill one another all the time. Why treat animals more ethically than they treat one another?* (Ben Franklin tried this one long before me: during a fishing trip, he wondered, "If you eat one another, I don't see why we may not eat you." He admits, however, that the rationale didn't occur to him until the fish were in the frying pan, smelling "admirably well." The advantage of being a "reasonable creature," Franklin remarks, is that you can find a reason for whatever you want to do.) To the "they do it too" defense, the animal rightist has a devastating reply: Do you really want to base your morality on the natural order? Murder and rape are natural too. Besides, humans don't need to kill other creatures in order to survive; animals do. (Though if my cat, Otis, is any guide, animals sometimes kill for sheer pleasure.)

This suggests another defense. *Wouldn't life in the wild be worse for these farm animals?* "Defenders of slavery imposed on black Africans often made a similar point," Singer retorts. "The life of freedom is to be preferred."

But domesticated animals can't survive in the wild; in fact, without us they wouldn't exist at all. Or as one nineteenth-century political philosopher put it, "The pig has a stronger interest than anyone in the demand for bacon. If all the world were Jewish, there would be no pigs at all." But it turns out that this would be fine by the animal rightists: for if pigs don't exist, they can't be wronged.

Animals on factory farms have never known any other life. Singer replies that "animals feel a need to exercise, stretch their limbs or wings, groom themselves and turn around, whether or not they have ever lived in conditions that permit this." The measure of their suffering is not their prior experiences but the unremitting daily frustration of their instincts.

25   *OK, the suffering of animals is a legitimate problem, but the world is full of problems, and surely human problems must come first!* Sounds good, and yet all the animal people are asking me to do is to stop eating meat and wearing animal furs and hides. There's no reason I can't devote myself to solving humankind's problems while being a vegetarian who wears synthetics.

But doesn't the fact that we could choose to forgo meat for moral reasons point to a crucial moral difference between animals and humans? As Kant pointed out, the human being is the only moral animal, the only one even capable of entertaining a concept of "rights." What's wrong with reserving moral consideration for those able to reciprocate it? Right here is where you run smack into the AMC: the moral status of the retarded, the insane, the infant and the Alzheimer's patient. Such "marginal cases," in the detestable argot of modern moral philosophy, cannot participate in moral decision-making any more than a monkey can, yet we nevertheless grant them rights.

That's right, I respond, for the simple reason that they're one of us. And all of us have been, and will probably once again be, marginal cases ourselves. What's more, these people have fathers and mothers, daughters and sons, which makes our interest in their welfare deeper than our interest in the welfare of even the most brilliant ape.

Alas, none of these arguments evade the charge of speciesism; the racist, too, claims that it's natural to give special consideration to one's own kind. A utilitarian like Singer would agree, however, that the feelings of relatives do count for something. Yet the principle of equal consideration of interests demands that, given the choice between performing a painful medical experiment on a severely retarded orphan and on a normal ape, we must sacrifice the child. Why? Because the ape has a greater capacity for pain.

Here in a nutshell is the problem with the AMC: it can be used to help the animals, but just as often it winds up hurting the marginal cases. Giving up our speciesism will bring us to a moral cliff from which we may not be prepared to jump, even when logic is pushing us.

And yet this isn't the moral choice I am being asked to make. (Too bad; it   30
would be so much easier!) In everyday life, the choice is not between babies and chimps but between the pork and the tofu. Even if we reject the "hard utilitarianism" of a Peter Singer, there remains the question of whether we owe animals that can feel pain *any* moral consideration, and this seems impossible to deny. And if we do owe them moral consideration, how can we justify eating them?

This is why killing animals for meat (and clothing) poses the most difficult animal rights challenge. In the case of animal testing, all but the most radical animal rightists are willing to balance the human benefit against the cost to the animals. That's because the unique qualities of human consciousness carry weight in the utilitarian calculus: human pain counts for more than that of a mouse, since our pain is amplified by emotions like dread; similarly, our deaths are worse than an animal's because we understand what death is in a way they don't. So the argument over animal testing is really in the details: Is this particular procedure or test *really* necessary to save human lives? (Very often it's not, in which case we probably shouldn't do it:) But if humans no longer need to eat meat or wear skins, then what exactly are we putting on the human side of the scale to outweigh the interests of the animal?

I suspect that this is finally why the animal people managed to throw me on the defensive. It's one thing to choose between the chimp and the retarded child or to accept the sacrifice of all those pigs surgeons practiced on to develop heart-bypass surgery. But what happens when the choice is between "a lifetime of suffering for a nonhuman animal and the gastronomic preference of a human being?" You look away—or you stop eating animals. And if you don't want to do either? Then you have to try to determine if the animals you're eating have really endured "a lifetime of suffering."

Whether our interest in eating animals outweighs their interest in not being eaten (assuming for the moment that is their interest) turns on the vexed question of animal suffering. Vexed, because it is impossible to know what really goes on in the mind of a cow or a pig or even an ape. Strictly speaking, this is true of other humans, too, but since humans are all basically wired the same way, we have excellent reason to assume that other people's experience of pain feels much like our own. Can we say that about animals? Yes and no.

I have yet to find anyone who still subscribes to Descartes's belief that animals cannot feel pain because they lack a soul. The general consensus among scientists and philosophers is that when it comes to pain, the higher animals are wired much the way we are for the same evolutionary reasons, so we should take the writhings of the kicked dog at face value. Indeed, the very premise of a great deal of animal testing—the reason it has value—is that animals' experience of physical and even some psychological pain closely resembles our own. Otherwise, why would cosmetics testers drip chemicals into the eyes of rabbits to see if they sting? Why would researchers study head trauma by traumatizing chimpanzee heads? Why would psychologists attempt to induce depression and "learned helplessness" in dogs by exposing them to ceaseless random patterns of electrical shock?

35   That said, it can be argued that human pain differs from animal pain by an order of magnitude. This qualitative difference is largely the result of our possession of language and, by virtue of language, an ability to have thoughts about thoughts and to imagine alternatives to our current reality. The philosopher Daniel C. Dennett suggests that we would do well to draw a distinction between pain, which a great many animals experience, and suffering, which depends on a degree of self-consciousness only a few animals appear to command. Suffering, in this view, is not just lots of pain but pain intensified by human emotions like loss, sadness, worry, regret, self-pity, shame, humiliation and dread.

Consider castration. No one would deny the procedure is painful to animals, yet animals appear to get over it in a way humans do not. (Some rhesus monkeys competing for mates will bite off a rival's testicle; the very next day the victim may be observed mating, seemingly little the worse for wear.) Surely the suffering of a man able to comprehend the full implications of castration, to anticipate the event and contemplate its aftermath, represents an agony of another order.

By the same token, however, language and all that comes with it can also make certain kinds of pain *more* bearable. A trip to the dentist would be a torment for an ape that couldn't be made to understand the purpose and duration of the procedure.

As humans contemplating the pain and suffering of animals, we do need to guard against projecting onto them what the same experience would feel like to us. Watching a steer force-marched up the ramp to the kill-floor door, as I have done, I need to remind myself that this is not Sean Penn in *Dead Man Walking*, that in a bovine brain the concept of nonexistence is blissfully absent. "If we fail to find suffering in the [animal] lives we can see," Dennett writes in *Kinds of Minds*, "we can rest assured there is no invisible suffering somewhere in their brains. If we find suffering, we will recognize it without difficulty."

Which brings us—reluctantly, necessarily—to the American factory farm, the place where all such distinctions turn to dust. It's not easy to draw lines between pain and suffering in a modern egg or confinement hog operation. These are places where the subtleties of moral philosophy and animal cognition mean less than nothing, where everything we've learned about animals at least since Darwin has been simply . . . set aside. To visit a modern CAFO (Confined Animal Feeding Operation) is to enter a world that, for all its technological sophistication, is still designed according to Cartesian principles: animals are machines incapable of feeling pain. Since no thinking person can possibly believe this anymore, industrial animal agriculture depends on a suspension of disbelief on the part of the people who operate it and a willingness to avert your eyes on the part of everyone else.

From everything I've read, egg and hog operations are the worst. Beef cattle in America at least still live outdoors, albeit standing ankle deep in their own waste, eating a diet that makes them sick. And broiler chickens, although they do get their beaks snipped off with a hot knife to keep them from cannibalizing one another under the stress of their confinement, at least don't spend their eight-week lives in cages too small to ever stretch a wing. That fate is reserved for the American laying hen, who passes her brief span piled together with a half-dozen other hens in a wire cage whose floor a single page of this magazine could carpet. Every natural instinct of this animal is thwarted, leading to a range of behavioral "vices" that can include cannibalizing her cagemates and rubbing her body against the wire mesh until it is featherless and bleeding. Pain? Suffering? Madness? The operative suspension of disbelief depends on more neutral descriptors, like "vices" and "stress." Whatever you want to call what's going on in those cages, the ten percent or so of hens that can't bear it and simply die is built into the cost of production. And when the output of the others begins to ebb, the hens will be "force-molted"—starved of food and water and light for several days in order to stimulate a final bout of egg-laying before their life's work is done.

Simply reciting these facts, most of which are drawn from poultry-trade magazines, makes me sound like one of those animal people, doesn't it? I don't mean to, but this is what can happen when . . . you look. It certainly wasn't my intention to ruin anyone's breakfast. But now that I probably have spoiled the eggs, I do want to say one thing about the bacon, mention a single practice (by no means the worst) in modern hog production that points to the compound madness of an impeccable industrial logic.

Piglets in confinement operations are weaned from their mothers ten days after birth (compared with thirteen weeks in nature) because they gain weight faster on their hormone- and antibiotic-fortified feed. This premature weaning leaves the pigs with a life-long craving to suck and chew, a desire they gratify in confinement by biting the tail of the animal in front of them. A normal pig would fight off his molester, but a demoralized pig has stopped caring. "Learned helplessness" is the psychological term, and it's not uncommon in confinement operations, where tens of thousands of hogs spend their entire lives ignorant of sunshine or earth or straw, crowded together beneath a metal roof upon metal slats suspended over a manure pit. So it's not surprising that an animal as sensitive and intelligent as a pig would get depressed, and a depressed pig will allow his tail to be chewed on to the point of infection. Sick pigs, being underperforming "production units," are clubbed to death on the

40

spot. The USDA's recommended solution to the problem is called "tail dock-ing." Using a pair of pliers (and no anesthetic), most but not all of the tail is snipped off. Why the little stump? Because the whole point of the exercise is not to remove the object of tail-biting so much as to render it *more* sensitive. Now, a bite on the tail is so painful that even the most demoralized pig will mount a struggle to avoid it.

Much of this description is drawn from *Dominion*, Matthew Scully's re-cent book in which he offers a harrowing description of a North Carolina hog operation. Scully, a Christian conservative, has no patience for lefty rights talk, arguing instead that while God did give man "dominion" over animals ("Every moving thing that liveth shall be meat for you"), he also admonished us to show them mercy. "We are called to treat them with kindness, not because they have rights or power or some claim to equality but . . . because they stand unequal and powerless before us."

Scully calls the contemporary factory farm "our own worst nightmare" and, to his credit, doesn't shrink from naming the root cause of this evil: unfettered capitalism. (Perhaps this explains why he resigned from the Bush administra-tion just before his book's publication.) A tension has always existed between the capitalist imperative to maximize efficiency and the moral imperatives of re-ligion or community which have historically served as a counterweight to the moral blindness of the market. This is one of "the cultural contradictions of capitalism"—the tendency of the economic impulse to erode the moral under-pinnings of society. Mercy toward animals is one such casualty.

45   More than any other institution, the American industrial animal farm of-fers a nightmarish glimpse of what capitalism can look like in the absence of moral or regulatory constraint. In these places life itself is redefined—as pro-tein production—and with it suffering. *That* venerable word becomes "stress," an economic problem in search of a cost-effective solution, like tail-docking or beak-clipping or, in the industry's latest plan, by simply engineering the "stress gene" out of pigs and chickens. "Our own worst nightmare" such a place may well be; it is also real life for the billions of animals unlucky enough to have been born beneath these grim steel roofs, into the brief, pitiless life of a "pro-duction unit" in the days before the suffering gene was found.

Vegetarianism doesn't seem an unreasonable response to such an evil. Who would want to be made complicit in the agony of these animals by eating them? You want to throw *something* against the walls of those infernal sheds, whether it's the Bible, a new constitutional right or a whole platoon of animal rightists bent on breaking in and liberating the inmates. In the shadow of these factory farms, Coetzee's notion of a "stupefying crime" doesn't seem far-fetched at all.

But before you swear off meat entirely, let me describe a very different sort of animal farm. It is typical of nothing, and yet its very existence puts the whole moral question of animal agriculture in a different light. Polyface Farm occupies 550 acres of rolling grassland and forest in the Shenandoah Valley of Virginia. Here, Joel Salatin and his family raise six different food animals—

cattle, pigs, chickens, rabbits, turkeys and sheep—in an intricate dance of symbiosis designed to allow each species, in Salatin's words, "to fully express its physiological distinctiveness."

What this means in practice is that Salatin's chickens live like chickens; his cows, like cows; pigs, pigs. As in nature, where birds tend to follow herbivores, once Salatin's cows have finished grazing a pasture, he moves them out and tows in his "eggmobile," a portable chicken coop that houses several hundred laying hens—roughly the natural size of a flock. The hens fan out over the pasture, eating the short grass and picking insect larvae out of the cowpats—all the while spreading the cow manure and eliminating the farm's parasite problem. A diet of grubs and grass makes for exceptionally tasty eggs and contented chickens, and their nitrogenous manure feeds the pasture. A few weeks later, the chickens move out and the sheep come in, dining on the lush new growth as well as on the weed species (nettles, nightshade) that the cattle and chickens won't touch.

Meanwhile, the pigs are in the barn turning the compost. All winter long, while the cattle were indoors, Salatin layered their manure with straw, wood chips—and corn. By March, this steaming compost layer cake stands three feet high, and the pigs, whose powerful snouts can sniff out and retrieve the fermented corn at the bottom, get to spend a few happy weeks rooting through the pile, aerating it as they work. All you can see of these pigs, intently nosing out the tasty alcoholic morsels, are their upturned pink hams and corkscrew tails churning the air. The finished compost will go to feed the grass; the grass, the cattle; the cattle, the chickens; and eventually all of these animals will feed us.

I thought a lot about vegetarianism and animal rights during the day I spent on Joel Salatin's extraordinary farm. So much of what I'd read, so much of what I'd accepted, looked very different from here. To many animal rightists, even Polyface Farm is a death camp. But to look at these animals is to see this for the sentimental conceit it is. In the same way that we can probably recognize animal suffering when we see it, animal happiness is unmistakable, too, and here I was seeing it in abundance.

For any animal, happiness seems to consist in the opportunity to express its creaturely character—its essential pigness or wolfness or chickenness. Aristotle speaks of each creature's "characteristic form of life." For domesticated species, the good life, if we can call it that, cannot be achieved apart from humans—apart from our farms and, therefore, our meat-eating. This, it seems to me, is where animal rightists betray a profound ignorance about the workings of nature. To think of domestication as a form of enslavement or even exploitation is to misconstrue the whole relationship, to project a human idea of power onto what is, in fact, an instance of mutualism between species. Domestication is an evolutionary, rather than a political, development. It is certainly not a regime humans imposed on animals some ten thousand years ago.

Rather, domestication happened when a small handful of especially opportunistic species discovered through Darwinian trial and error that they were more likely to survive and prosper in an alliance with humans than on

50

their own. Humans provided the animals with food and protection, in exchange for which the animals provided the humans their milk and eggs and—
yes—their flesh. Both parties were transformed by the relationship: animals
grew tame and lost their ability to fend for themselves (evolution tends to edit
out unneeded traits), and humans gave up their hunter-gatherer ways for the
settled life of agriculturists. (Humans changed biologically too, evolving such
new traits as a tolerance for lactose as adults.)

From the animals' point of view, the bargain with humanity has been a
great success, at least until our own time. Cows, pigs, dogs, cats and chickens
have thrived, while their wild ancestors have languished. (There are ten thousand wolves in North America, fifty million dogs.) Nor does their loss of autonomy seem to trouble these creatures. It is wrong, the rightists say, to treat
animals as "means" rather than "ends," yet the happiness of a working animal
like the dog consists precisely in serving as a "means." Liberation is the last
thing such a creature wants. To say of one of Joel Salatin's caged chickens that
"the life of freedom is to be preferred" betrays an ignorance about chicken
preferences—which on this farm are heavily focused on not getting their
heads bitten off by weasels.

But haven't these chickens simply traded one predator for another—
weasels for humans? True enough, and for the chickens this is probably not a
bad deal. For brief as it is, the life expectancy of a farm animal would be considerably briefer in the world beyond the pasture fence or chicken coop. A
sheep farmer told me that a bear will eat a lactating ewe alive, starting with
her udders. "As a rule," he explained, "animals don't get 'good deaths' surrounded by their loved ones."

55   The very existence of predation—animals eating animals—is the cause of
much anguished hand-wringing in animal rights circles. "It must be admitted,"
Singer writes, "that the existence of carnivorous animals does pose one problem for the ethics of Animal Liberation, and that is whether we should do anything about it." Some animal rightists train their dogs and cats to become
vegetarians. (Note: cats will require nutritional supplements to stay healthy.)
Matthew Scully calls predation "the intrinsic evil in nature's design . . . among
the hardest of all things to fathom." *Really?* A deep Puritan streak pervades animal rights activists, an abiding discomfort not only with our animality but
with the animals' animality too.

However it may appear to us, predation is not a matter of morality or politics; it, also, is a matter of symbiosis. Hard as the wolf may be on the deer he
eats, the herd depends on him for its well-being; without predators to cull the
herd, deer overrun their habitat and starve. In many places, human hunters
have taken over the predator's ecological role. Chickens also depend for their
continued well-being on their human predators—not individual chickens, but
chickens as a species. The surest way to achieve the extinction of the chicken
would be to grant chickens a "right to life."

Yet here's the rub: the animal rightist is not concerned with species, only
individuals. Tom Regan, author of *The Case for Animal Rights*, bluntly asserts
that because "species are not individuals . . . the rights view does not recognize

the moral rights of species to anything, including survival." Singer concurs, insisting that only sentient individuals have interests. But surely a species can have interests—in its survival, say—just as a nation or community or a corporation can. The animal rights movement's exclusive concern with individual animals makes perfect sense given its roots in a culture of liberal individualism, but does it make any sense in nature?

Consider this hypothetical episode: In 1611 Juan da Goma (a.k.a. Juan the Disoriented) made accidental landfall on Wrightson Island, a six-square-mile rock in the Indian Ocean. The island's sole distinction is as the only known home of the Arcania tree and the bird that nests in it, the Wrightson giant sea sparrow. Da Goma and his crew stayed a week, much of that time spent in a failed bid to recapture the ship's escaped goat—who happened to be pregnant. Nearly four centuries later, Wrightson Island is home to 380 goats that have consumed virtually every scrap of vegetation in their reach. The youngest Arcania tree on the island is more than three hundred years old, and only fifty-two sea sparrows remain. In the animal rights view, any one of those goats have at least as much right to life as the last Wrightson sparrow on earth, and the trees, because they are not sentient, warrant no moral consideration whatsoever. (In the mid-1980s a British environmental group set out to shoot the goats, but was forced to cancel the expedition after the Mammal Liberation Front bombed its offices.)

The story of Wrightson Island (invented by the biologist David Ehrenfeld in *Beginning Again*) suggests at the very least that a human morality based on individual rights makes for an awkward fit when applied to the natural world. This should come as no surprise: morality is an artifact of human culture, devised to help us negotiate social relations. It's very good for that. But just as we recognize that nature doesn't provide an adequate guide for human social conduct, isn't it anthropocentric to assume that our moral system offers an adequate guide for nature? We may require a different set of ethics to guide our dealings with the natural world, one as well suited to the particular needs of plants and animals and habitats (where sentience counts for little) as rights suit us humans today.

To contemplate such questions from the vantage of a farm is to appreciate just   60
how parochial and urban an ideology animal rights really is. It could thrive only in a world where people have lost contact with the natural world, where animals no longer pose a threat to us and human mastery of nature seems absolute. "In our normal life," Singer writes, "there is no serious clash of interests between human and nonhuman animals." Such a statement assumes a decidedly urbanized "normal life," one that certainly no farmer would recognize.

The farmer would point out that even vegans have a "serious clash of interests" with other animals. The grain that the vegan eats is harvested with a combine that shreds field mice, while the farmer's tractor crushes woodchucks in their burrows, and his pesticides drop songbirds from the sky. Steve Davis, an animal scientist at Oregon State University, has estimated that if America were to adopt a strictly vegetarian diet, the total number of animals killed every year would actually *increase*, as animal pasture gave way to row crops. Davis contends that if our goal is to kill as few animals as possible, then people should eat the largest possible animal that can live on the least intensively cultivated land: grass-fed beef for everybody. It would appear that killing animals is unavoidable no matter what we choose to eat.

When I talked to Joel Salatin about the vegetarian utopia, he pointed out that it would also condemn him and his neighbors to importing their food from distant places, since the Shenandoah Valley receives too little rainfall to grow many row crops. Much the same would hold true where I live, in New England. We get plenty of rain, but the hilliness of the land has dictated an agriculture based on animals since the time of the Pilgrims. The world is full of places where the best, if not the only, way to obtain food from the land is by grazing animals on it—especially ruminants, which alone can transform grass into protein and whose presence can actually improve the health of the land.

The vegetarian utopia would make us even more dependent than we already are on an industrialized national food chain. That food chain would in turn be even more dependent than it already is on fossil fuels and chemical fertilizer, since food would need to travel farther and manure would be in short supply. Indeed, it is doubtful that you can build a more sustainable agriculture without animals to cycle nutrients and support local food production. If our concern is for the health of nature—rather than, say, the internal consistency of our moral code or the condition of our souls—then eating animals may sometimes be the most ethical thing to do.

There is, too, the fact that we humans have been eating animals as long as we have lived on this earth. Humans may not need to eat meat in order to survive, yet doing so is part of our evolutionary heritage, reflected in the design of our teeth and the structure of our digestion. Eating meat helped make us what we are, in a social and biological sense. Under the pressure of the hunt, the human brain grew in size and complexity, and around the fire where the meat was cooked, human culture first flourished. Granting rights to animals may lift us up from the brutal world of predation, but it will entail the sacrifice of part of our identity—our own animality.

65 Surely this is one of the odder paradoxes of animal rights doctrine. It asks us to recognize all that we share with animals and then demands that we act toward them in a most unanimalistic way. Whether or not this is a good idea, we should at least acknowledge that our desire to eat meat is not a trivial matter, no mere "gastronomic preference." We might as well call sex—also now technically unnecessary—a mere "recreational preference." Whatever else it is, our meat-eating is something very deep indeed.

Are any of these good enough reasons to eat animals? I'm mindful of Ben Franklin's definition of the reasonable creature as one who can come up with reasons for whatever he wants to do. So I decided I would track down Peter Singer and ask him what he thought. In an e-mail message, I described Polyface and asked him about the implications for his position of the Good Farm—

one where animals got to live according to their nature and to all appearances did not suffer.

"I agree with you that it is better for these animals to have lived and died than not to have lived at all," Singer wrote back. Since the utilitarian is concerned exclusively with the sum of happiness and suffering and the slaughter of an animal that doesn't comprehend that death need not involve suffering, the Good Farm adds to the total of animal happiness, provided you replace the slaughtered animal with a new one. However, he added, this line of thinking doesn't obviate the wrongness of killing an animal that "has a sense of its own existence over time and can have preferences for its own future." In other words, it's OK to eat the chicken, but he's not so sure about the pig. Yet, he wrote, "I would not be sufficiently confident of my arguments to condemn someone who purchased meat from one of these farms."

Singer went on to express serious doubts that such farms could be practical on a large scale, since the pressures of the marketplace will lead their owners to cut costs and corners at the expense of the animals. He suggested, too, that killing animals is not conducive to treating them with respect. Also, since humanely raised food will be more expensive, only the well-to-do can afford morally defensible animal protein. These are important considerations, but they don't alter my essential point: what's wrong with animal agriculture—with eating animals—is the practice, not the principle.

What this suggests to me is that people who care should be working not for animal rights but animal welfare—to ensure that farm animals don't suffer and that their deaths are swift and painless. In fact, the decent-life-merciful-death line is how Jeremy Bentham justified his own meat-eating. Yes, the philosophical father of animal rights was himself a carnivore. In a passage rather less frequently quoted by animal rightists, Bentham defended eating animals on the grounds that "we are the better for it, and they are never the worse . . . The death they suffer in our hands commonly is, and always may be, a speedier and, by that means, a less painful one than that which would await them in the inevitable course of nature."

My guess is that Bentham never looked too closely at what happens in a   70
slaughterhouse, but the argument suggests that, in theory at least, a utilitarian can justify the killing of humanely treated animals—for meat or, presumably, for clothing. (Though leather and fur pose distinct moral problems. Leather is a byproduct of raising domestic animals for food, which can be done humanely. However, furs are usually made from wild animals that die brutal deaths—usually in leg-hold traps—and since most fur species aren't domesticated, raising them on farms isn't necessarily more humane.) But whether the issue is food or fur or hunting, what should concern us is the suffering, not the killing. All of which I was feeling pretty good about—until I remembered that utilitarians can also justify killing retarded orphans. Killing just isn't the problem for them that it is for other people, including me.

During my visit to Polyface Farm, I asked Salatin where his animals were slaughtered. He does the chickens and rabbits right on the farm, and would do the cattle, pigs and sheep there too if only the USDA would let him. Salatin showed me the open-air abattoir he built behind the farmhouse—a sort of outdoor kitchen on a concrete slab, with stainless-steel sinks, scalding tanks, a feather-plucking machine and metal cones to hold the birds upside down while they're being bled. Processing chickens is not a pleasant job, but Salatin insists on doing it himself because he's convinced he can do it more humanely and cleanly than any processing plant. He slaughters every other Saturday through the summer. Anyone's welcome to watch.

I asked Salatin how he could bring himself to kill a chicken.

"People have a soul; animals don't," he said. "It's a bedrock belief of mine." Salatin is a devout Christian. "Unlike us, animals are not created in God's image, so when they die, they just die."

The notion that only in modern times have people grown uneasy about killing animals is a flattering conceit. Taking a life is momentous, and people have been working to justify the slaughter of animals for thousands of years. Religion and especially ritual has played a crucial part in helping us reckon the moral costs. Native Americans and other hunter-gatherers would give thanks to their prey for giving up its life so the eater might live (sort of like saying grace). Many cultures have offered sacrificial animals to the gods, perhaps as a way to convince themselves that it was the gods' desires that demanded the slaughter, not their own. In ancient Greece, the priests responsible for the slaughter (priests!—now we entrust the job to minimum-wage workers) would sprinkle holy water on the sacrificial animal's brow. The beast would promptly shake its head, and this was taken as a sign of assent. Slaughter doesn't necessarily preclude respect. For all these people, it was the ceremony that allowed them to look, then to eat.

75   Apart from a few surviving religious practices, we no longer have any rituals governing the slaughter or eating of animals, which perhaps helps to explain why we find ourselves where we do, feeling that our only choice is to either look away or give up meat. Frank Perdue is happy to serve the first customer; Peter Singer, the second.

Until my visit to Polyface Farm, I had assumed these were the only two options. But on Salatin's farm, the eye contact between people and animals whose loss John Berger mourned is still a fact of life—and of death, for neither the lives nor the deaths of these animals have been secreted behind steel walls. "Food with a face," Salatin likes to call what he's selling, a slogan that probably scares off some customers. People see very different things when they look into the eyes of a pig or a chicken or a steer—a being without a soul, a "subject of a life" entitled to rights, a link in a food chain, a vessel for pain and pleasure, a tasty lunch. But figuring out what we do think, and what we can eat, might begin with the looking.

We certainly won't philosophize our way to an answer. Salatin told me the story of a man who showed up at the farm one Saturday morning. When Salatin noticed a PETA bumper sticker on the man's car, he figured he was in for it. But the man had a different agenda. He explained that after sixteen years as a vegetarian, he had decided that the only way he could ever eat meat again was if he killed the animal himself. He had come to *look*.

"Ten minutes later we were in the processing shed with a chicken," Salatin recalled. "He slit the bird's throat and watched it die. He saw that the animal did not look at him accusingly, didn't do a Disney double take. The animal had been treated with respect when it was alive, and he saw that it could also have a respectful death—that it wasn't being treated as a pile of protoplasm."

Salatin's open-air abattoir is a morally powerful idea. Someone slaughtering a chicken in a place where he can be watched is apt to do it scrupulously, with consideration for the animal as well as for the eater. This is going to sound quixotic, but maybe all we need to do to redeem industrial animal agriculture in this country is to pass a law requiring that the steel and concrete walls of the CAFOs and slaughterhouses be replaced with . . . glass. If there's any new "right" we need to establish, maybe it's this one: the right to look.

No doubt the sight of some of these places would turn many people into vegetarians. Many others would look elsewhere for their meat, to farmers like Salatin. There are more of them than I would have imagined. Despite the relentless consolidation of the American meat industry, there has been a revival of small farms where animals still live their "characteristic form of life." I'm thinking of the ranches where cattle still spend their lives on grass, the poultry farms where chickens still go outside and the hog farms where pigs live as they did fifty years ago—in contact with the sun, the earth and the gaze of a farmer. 80

For my own part, I've discovered that if you're willing to make the effort, it's entirely possible to limit the meat you eat to nonindustrial animals. I'm tempted to think that we need a new dietary category, to go with the vegan and lactovegetarian and piscatorian. I don't have a catchy name for it yet (humanocarnivore?), but this is the only sort of meat-eating I feel comfortable with these days. I've become the sort of shopper who looks for labels indicating that his meat and eggs have been humanely grown (the American Humane Association's new "Free Farmed" label seems to be catching on), who visits the farms where his chicken and pork come from and who asks kinky-sounding questions about touring slaughterhouses. I've actually found a couple of small processing plants willing to let a customer onto the kill floor, including one, in Cannon Falls, Minnesota, with a glass abattoir.

The industrialization—and dehumanization—of American animal farming is a relatively new, evitable and local phenomenon: no other country raises and slaughters its food animals quite as intensively or as brutally as we do. Were the walls of our meat industry to become transparent, literally or even figuratively, we would not long continue to do it this way. Tail-docking and sow crates and beak-clipping would disappear overnight, and the days of slaughtering four hundred head of cattle an hour would come to an end. For who could stand the sight? Yes, meat would get more expensive. We'd probably eat less of it, too, but maybe when we did eat animals, we'd eat them with the consciousness, ceremony and respect they deserve.

QUESTIONS

1. Precisely how much of the Animal Liberation approach has Pollan accepted? How can you tell?

2. Things change when Pollan visits Polyface farm, the humane operation run by Joel Salatin. What about the farm convinces Pollan that it represents an alternative to Peter Singer's approach?

3. Describe the structure of Pollan's essay. How does he introduce Animal Liberation and how does he argue against it?

CARL COHEN

The Case for the Use of Animals in Biomedical Research

USING ANIMALS as research subjects in medical investigations is widely condemned on two grounds: first, because it wrongly violates the *rights* of animals,[1] and second, because it wrongly imposes on sentient creatures much avoidable *suffering*.[2] Neither of these arguments is sound. The first relies on a mistaken understanding of rights; the second relies on a mistaken calculation of consequences. Both deserve definitive dismissal.

WHY ANIMALS HAVE NO RIGHTS

A right, properly understood, is a claim, or potential claim, that one party may exercise against another. The target against whom such a claim may be registered can be a single person, a group, a community, or (perhaps) all humankind. The content of rights claims also varies greatly: repayment of loans, nondiscrimination by employers, noninterference by the state, and so on. To comprehend any genuine right fully, therefore, we must know *who* holds the right, *against whom* it is held, and *to what* it is a right.

Alternative sources of rights add complexity. Some rights are grounded in constitution and law (e.g., the right of an accused to trial by jury); some rights are moral but give no legal claims (e.g., my right to your keeping the promise you gave me); and some rights (e.g., against theft or assault) are rooted both in morals and in law.

The different targets, contents, and sources of rights, and their inevitable conflict, together weave a tangled web. Notwithstanding all such complications, this much is clear about rights in general: they are in every case claims, or potential claims, within a community of moral agents. Rights arise, and can

Published in the New England Journal of Medicine *(October 1986), a scholarly periodical known primarily for research articles but that also prints editorials on topics important to medicine and medical research. The author's notes are collected at the end as "References," as is the custom in this scientific journal.*

be intelligibly defended, only among beings who actually do, or can, make moral claims against one another. Whatever else rights may be, therefore, they are necessarily human; their possessors are persons, human beings.

The attributes of human beings from which this moral capability arises have been described variously by philosophers, both ancient and modern: the inner consciousness of a free will (Saint Augustine);[3] the grasp, by human reason, of the binding character of moral law (Saint Thomas);[4] the self-conscious participation of human beings in an objective ethical order (Hegel);[5] human membership in an organic moral community (Bradley);[6] the development of the human self through the consciousness of other moral selves (Mead);[7] and the underivative, intuitive cognition of the rightness of an action (Prichard).[8] Most influential has been Immanuel Kant's emphasis on the universal human possession of a uniquely moral will and the autonomy its use entails.[9] Humans confront choices that are purely moral; humans—but certainly not dogs or mice—lay down moral laws, for others and for themselves. Human beings are self-legislative, morally *autonomous*.

Animals (that is, nonhuman animals, the ordinary sense of that word) lack this capacity for free moral judgment. They are not beings of a kind capable of exercising or responding to moral claims. Animals therefore have no rights, and they can have none. This is the core of the argument about the alleged rights of animals. The holders of rights must have the capacity to comprehend rules of duty, governing all including themselves. In applying such rules, the holders of rights must recognize possible conflicts between what is in their own interest and what is just. Only in a community of beings capable of self-restricting moral judgments can the concept of a right be correctly invoked.

Humans have such moral capacities. They are in this sense self-legislative, are members of communities governed by moral rules, and do possess rights. Animals do not have such moral capacities. They are not morally self-legislative, cannot possibly be members of a truly moral community, and therefore cannot possess rights. In conducting research on animal subjects, therefore, we do not violate their rights, because they have none to violate.

To animate life, even in its simplest forms, we give a certain natural reverence. But the possession of rights presupposes a moral status not attained by the vast majority of living things. We must not infer, therefore, that a live being has, simply in being alive, a "right" to its life. The assertion that all animals, only because they are alive and have interests, also possess the "right to life"[10] is an abuse of that phrase, and wholly without warrant.

It does not follow from this, however, that we are morally free to do anything we please to animals. Certainly not. In our dealings with animals, as in our dealings with other human beings, we have obligations that do not arise from claims against us based on rights. Rights entail obligations, but many of the things one ought to do are in no way tied to another's entitlement. Rights and obligations are not reciprocals of one another, and it is a serious mistake to suppose that they are.

Illustrations are helpful. Obligations may arise from internal commitments made: physicians have obligations to their patients not grounded merely in their patients' rights. Teachers have such obligations to their students, shepherds to their dogs, and cowboys to their horses. Obligations may arise from differences of status: adults owe special care when playing with young children, and children owe special care when playing with young pets. Obligations may arise from special relationships: the payment of my son's college tuition is something to which he may have no right, although it may be my obligation to bear the burden if I reasonably can; my dog has no right to daily exercise and veterinary care, but I do have the obligation to provide these things for her. Obligations may arise from particular acts or circumstances: one may be obliged to another for a special kindness done, or obliged to put an animal out of its misery in view of its condition—although neither the human benefactor nor the dying animal may have had a claim of right.

Plainly, the grounds of our obligations to humans and to animals are manifold and cannot be formulated simply. Some hold that there is a general obligation to do no gratuitous harm to sentient creatures (the principle of nonmaleficence); some hold that there is a general obligation to do good to sentient creatures when that is reasonably within one's power (the principle of beneficence). In our dealings with animals, few will deny that we are at least obliged to act humanely—that is, to treat them with the decency and concern that we owe, as sensitive human beings, to other sentient creatures. To treat animals humanely, however, is not to treat them as humans or as the holders of rights.

A common objection, which deserves a response, may be paraphrased as follows:

> If having rights requires being able to make moral claims, to grasp and apply moral laws, then many humans—the brain-damaged, the comatose, the senile—who plainly lack those capacities must be without rights. But that is absurd. This proves [the critic concludes] that rights do not depend on the presence of moral capacities.[1,10]

This objection fails; it mistakenly treats an essential feature of humanity as though it were a screen for sorting humans. The capacity for moral judgment that distinguishes humans from animals is not a test to be administered to human beings one by one. Persons who are unable, because of some disability, to perform the full moral functions natural to human beings are certainly not for that reason ejected from the moral community. The issue is one of kind. Humans are of such a kind that they may be the subject of experiments only with their voluntary consent. The choices they make freely must be respected. Animals are of such a kind that it is impossible for them, in principle, to give or withhold voluntary consent or to make a moral choice. What humans retain when disabled, animals have never had.

A second objection, also often made, may be paraphrased as follows:

> Capacities will not succeed in distinguishing humans from the other animals. Animals also reason; animals also communicate with one another; animals also care passionately for their young; animals also exhibit desires and preferences.[11,12] Features of moral relevance—rationality, interdependence,

and love—are not exhibited uniquely by human beings. Therefore [this critic concludes], there can be no solid moral distinction between humans and other animals.[10]

This criticism misses the central point. It is not the ability to communicate or to reason, or dependence on one another, or care for the young, or the exhibition of preference, or any such behavior that marks the critical divide. Analogies between human families and those of monkeys, or between human communities and those of wolves, and the like, are entirely beside the point. Patterns of conduct are not at issue. Animals do indeed exhibit remarkable behavior at times. Conditioning, fear, instinct, and intelligence all contribute to species survival. Membership in a community of moral agents nevertheless remains impossible for them. Actors subject to moral judgment must be capable of grasping the generality of an ethical premise in a practical syllogism. Humans act immorally often enough, but only they—never wolves or monkeys—can discern, by applying some moral rule to the facts of a case, that a given act ought or ought not to be performed. The moral restraints imposed by humans on themselves are thus highly abstract and are often in conflict with the self-interest of the agent. Communal behavior among animals, even when most intelligent and most endearing, does not approach autonomous morality in this fundamental sense.

15

Genuinely moral acts have an internal as well as an external dimension. Thus, in law, an act can be criminal only when the guilty deed, the actus reus, is done with a guilty mind, mens rea. No animal can ever commit a crime; bringing animals to criminal trial is the mark of primitive ignorance. The claims of moral right are similarly inapplicable to them. Does a lion have a right to eat a baby zebra? Does a baby zebra have a right not to be eaten? Such questions, mistakenly invoking the concept of right where it does not belong, do not make good sense. Those who condemn biomedical research because it violates "animal rights" commit the same blunder.

In Defense of "Speciesism"

Abandoning reliance on animal rights, some critics resort instead to animal sentience—their feelings of pain and distress. We ought to desist from imposition of pain insofar as we can. Since all or nearly all experimentation on animals does impose pain and could be readily forgone, say these critics, it should be stopped. The ends sought may be worthy, but those ends do not justify imposing agonies on humans, and by animals the agonies are felt no less. The laboratory use of animals (these critics conclude) must therefore be ended—or at least very sharply curtailed.

Argument of this variety is essentially utilitarian, often expressly so;[13] it is based on the calculation of the net product, in pains and pleasures, resulting from experiments on animals. Jeremy Bentham, comparing horses and dogs with other sentient creatures, is thus commonly quoted: "The question is not, Can they reason? nor Can they talk? but, Can they suffer?"[14]

Animals certainly can suffer and surely ought not to be made to suffer needlessly. But in inferring, from these uncontroversial premises, that biomedical research causing animal distress is largely (or wholly) wrong, the critic commits two serious errors.

20   The first error is the assumption, often explicitly defended, that all sentient animals have equal moral standing. Between a dog and a human being, according to this view, there is no moral difference; hence the pains suffered by dogs must be weighed no differently from the pains suffered by humans. To deny such equality, according to this critic, is to give unjust preference to one species over another; it is "speciesism." The most influential statement of this moral equality of species was made by Peter Singer:

> The racist violates the principle of equality by giving greater weight to the interests of members of his own race when there is a clash between their interests and the interests of those of another race. The sexist violates the principle of equality by favoring the interests of his own sex. Similarly the speciesist allows the interests of his own species to override the greater interests of members of other species. The pattern is identical in each case.[2]

This argument is worse than unsound; it is atrocious. It draws an offensive moral conclusion from a deliberately devised verbal parallelism that is utterly specious. Racism has no rational ground whatever. Differing degrees of respect or concern for humans for no other reason than that they are members of different races is an injustice totally without foundation in the nature of the races themselves. Racists, even if acting on the basis of mistaken factual beliefs, do grave moral wrong precisely because there is no morally relevant distinction among the races. The supposition of such differences has led to outright horror. The same is true of the sexes, neither sex being entitled by right to greater respect or concern than the other. No dispute here.

Between species of animate life, however—between (for example) humans on the one hand and cats or rats on the other—the morally relevant differences are enormous, and almost universally appreciated. Humans engage in moral reflection; humans are morally autonomous; humans are members of moral communities, recognizing just claims against their own interest. Human beings do have rights; theirs is a moral status very different from that of cats or rats.

I am a speciesist. Speciesism is not merely plausible; it is essential for right conduct, because those who will not make the morally relevant distinctions among species are almost certain, in consequence, to misapprehend their true obligations. The analogy between speciesism and racism is insidious. Every sensitive moral judgment requires that the differing natures of the beings to whom obligations are owed be considered. If all forms of animate life—or vertebrate animal life?—must be treated equally, and if therefore in evaluating a research program the pains of a rodent count equally with the pains of a human, we are forced to conclude (1) that neither humans nor rodents possess rights, or (2) that rodents possess all the rights that humans possess. Both alternatives are absurd. Yet one or the other must be swallowed if the moral equality of all species is to be defended.

Humans owe to other humans a degree of moral regard that cannot be owed to animals. Some humans take on the obligation to support and heal others, both humans and animals, as a principal duty in their lives; the fulfillment of that duty may require the sacrifice of many animals. If biomedical investigators abandon the effective pursuit of their professional objectives because they are convinced that they may not do to animals what the service of humans requires, they will fail, objectively, to do their duty. Refusing to recognize the moral differences among species is a sure path to calamity. (The largest animal rights group in the country is People for the Ethical Treatment of Animals; its codirector, Ingrid Newkirk, calls research using animal subjects "fascism" and "supremacism." "Animal liberationists do not separate out the *human* animal," she says, "so there is no rational basis for saying that a human being has special rights. A rat is a pig is a dog is a boy. They're all mammals.")[15]

Those who claim to base their objection to the use of animals in biomedical research on their reckoning of the net pleasures and pains produced make a second error, equally grave. Even if it were true—as it is surely not—that the pains of all animal beings must be counted equally, a cogent utilitarian calculation requires that we weigh all the consequences of the use, and of the nonuse, of animals in laboratory research. Critics relying (however mistakenly) on animal rights may claim to ignore the beneficial results of such research, rights being trump cards to which interest and advantage must give way. But an argument that is explicitly framed in terms of interest and benefit for all over the long run must attend also to the disadvantageous consequences of not using animals in research, and to all the achievements attained and attainable only through their use. The sum of the benefits of their use is utterly beyond quantification. The elimination of horrible disease, the increase of longevity, the avoidance of great pain, the saving of lives, and the improvement of the quality of lives (for humans and for animals) achieved through research using animals is so incalculably great that the argument of these critics, systematically pursued, establishes not their conclusion but its reverse: to refrain from using animals in biomedical research is, on utilitarian grounds, morally wrong.

When balancing the pleasures and pains resulting from the use of animals in research, we must not fail to place on the scales the terrible pains that would have resulted, would be suffered now, and would long continue had animals not been used. Every disease eliminated, every vaccine developed, every method of pain relief devised, every surgical procedure invented, every prosthetic device implanted—indeed, virtually every modern medical therapy is due, in part or in whole, to experimentation using animals. Nor may we ignore, in the balancing process, the predictable gains in human (and animal) well-being that are probably achievable in the future but that will not be achieved if the decision is made now to desist from such research or to curtail it.

Medical investigators are seldom insensitive to the distress their work may cause animal subjects. Opponents of research using animals are frequently insensitive to the cruelty of the results of the restrictions they would impose.[2] Untold numbers of human beings—real persons, although not now identifiable—would suffer grievously as the consequence of this well-meaning but shortsighted tenderness. If the morally relevant differences between humans and animals are borne in mind, and if all relevant considerations are weighed, the calculation of long-term consequences must give overwhelming support for biomedical research using animals.

CONCLUDING REMARKS

Substitution.

The humane treatment of animals requires that we desist from experimenting on them if we can accomplish the same result using alternative methods—in vitro experimentation, computer simulation, or others. Critics of some experiments using animals rightly make this point.

It would be a serious error to suppose, however, that alternative techniques could soon be used in most research now using live animal subjects. No other methods now on the horizon—or perhaps ever to be available—can fully replace the testing of a drug, a procedure, or a vaccine, in live organisms. The flood of new medical possibilities being opened by the successes of recombinant DNA technology will turn to a trickle if testing on live animals is forbidden. When initial trials entail great risks, there may be no forward movement whatever without the use of live animal subjects. In seeking knowledge that may prove critical in later clinical applications, the unavailability of animals for inquiry may spell complete stymie. In the United States, federal regulations require the testing of new drugs and other products on animals, for efficacy and safety, before human beings are exposed to them.[16,17] We would not want it otherwise.

30   Every new advance in medicine—every new drug, new operation, new therapy of any kind—must sooner or later be tried on a living being for the first time. That trial, controlled or uncontrolled, will be an experiment. The subject of that experiment, if it is not an animal, will be a human being. Prohibiting the use of live animals in biomedical research, therefore, or sharply restricting it, must result either in the blockage of much valuable research or in the replacement of animal subjects with human subjects. These are the consequences—unacceptable to most reasonable persons—of not using animals in research.

Reduction.

Should we not at least reduce the use of animals in biomedical research? No, we should increase it, to avoid when feasible the use of humans as experimental subjects. Medical investigations putting human subjects at some risk are numerous and greatly varied. The risks run in such experiments are usually unavoidable, and (thanks to earlier experiments on animals) most such risks are minimal or moderate. But some experimental risks are substantial.

When an experimental protocol that entails substantial risk to humans comes before an institutional review board, what response is appropriate? The investigation, we may suppose, is promising and deserves support, so long as its human subjects are protected against unnecessary dangers. May not the investigators be fairly asked, Have you done all that you can do to eliminate risk to humans by the extensive testing of that drug, that procedure, or that device on animals? To achieve maximal safety for humans we are right to require thorough experimentation on animal subjects before humans are involved.

Opportunities to increase human safety in this way are commonly missed; trials in which risks may be shifted from humans to animals are often not devised, sometimes not even considered. Why? For the investigator, the use of animals as subjects is often more expensive, in money and time, than the use of human subjects. Access to suitable human subjects is often quick and convenient, whereas access to appropriate animal subjects may be awkward, costly, and burdened with red tape. Physician-investigators have often had more experience working with human beings and know precisely where the needed pool of subjects is to be found and how they may be enlisted. Animals, and the procedures for their use, are often less familiar to these investigators. Moreover, the use of animals in place of humans is now more likely to be the target of zealous protests from without. The upshot is that humans are sometimes subjected to risks that animals could have borne, and should have borne, in their place. To maximize the protection of human subjects, I conclude, the wide and imaginative use of live animal subjects should be encouraged rather than discouraged. This enlargement in the use of animals is our obligation.

Consistency.

Finally, inconsistency between the profession and the practice of many who oppose research using animals deserves comment. This frankly ad hominem observation aims chiefly to show that a coherent position rejecting the use of animals in medical research imposes costs so high as to be intolerable even to the critics themselves.

One cannot coherently object to the killing of animals in biomedical investigations while continuing to eat them. Anesthetics and thoughtful animal husbandry render the level of actual animal distress in the laboratory generally lower than that in the abattoir. So long as death and discomfort do not substantially differ in the two contexts, the consistent objector must not only refrain from all eating of animals but also protest as vehemently against others eating them as against others experimenting on them. No less vigorously must the critic object to the wearing of animal hides in coats and shoes, to employment in any industrial enterprise that uses animal parts, and to any commercial development that will cause death or distress to animals.

Killing animals to meet human needs for food, clothing, and shelter is judged entirely reasonable by most persons. The ubiquity of these uses and the virtual universality of moral support for them confront the opponent of research using animals with an inescapable difficulty. How can the many common uses of animals be judged morally worthy, while their use in scientific investigation is judged unworthy?

The number of animals used in research is but the tiniest fraction of the total used to satisfy assorted human appetites. That these appetites, often base and satisfiable in other ways, morally justify the far larger consumption of animals, whereas the quest for improved human health and understanding cannot justify the far smaller, is wholly implausible. Aside from the numbers of animals involved, the distinction in terms of worthiness of use, drawn with regard to any single animal, is not defensible. A given sheep is surely not more justifiably used to put lamb chops on the supermarket counter than to serve in testing a new contraceptive or a new prosthetic device. The needless killing of animals is wrong; if the common killing of them for our food or convenience is right, the less common but more humane uses of animals in the service of medical science are certainly not less right.

Scrupulous vegetarianism, in matters of food, clothing, shelter, commerce, and recreation, and in all other spheres, is the only fully coherent position the critic may adopt. At great human cost, the lives of fish and crustaceans must also be protected, with equal vigor, if speciesism has been forsworn. A very few consistent critics adopt this position. It is the reductio ad absurdum of the rejection of moral distinctions between animals and human beings.

Opposition to the use of animals in research is based on arguments of two different kinds—those relying on the alleged rights of animals and those relying on the consequences for animals. I have argued that arguments of both kinds must fail. We surely do have obligations to animals, but they have, and can have, no rights against us on which research can infringe. In calculating the consequences of animal research, we must weigh all the long-term benefits of the results achieved—to animals and to humans—and in that calculation we must not assume the moral equality of all animate species.

REFERENCES

1. Regan T. The case for animal rights. Berkeley, Calif.: University of California Press, 1983.
2. Singer P. Animal liberation. New York: Avon Books, 1977.
3. St. Augustine. Confessions. Book Seven. A.D. 397. New York: Pocket Books, 1957:104–26.
4. St. Thomas Aquinas. Summa theologica. A.D. 1273. Philosophic texts. New York. Oxford University Press, 1960:353–66.
5. Hegel GWF. Philosophy of right. 1821. London: Oxford University Press, 1952:105–10.
6. Bradley FH. Why should I be moral? 1876. In: Melden AI, ed. Ethical theories. New York: Prentice Hall, 1950:345–59.
7. Mead GH. The genesis of the self and social control. 1925. In: Reck AJ, ed. Selected writings. Indianapolis: Bobbs-Merrill, 1964:264–93.
8. Prichard HA. Does moral philosophy rest on a mistake? 1912. In: Cellars W, Hospers J, eds. Readings in ethical theory. New York: Appleton-Century-Crofts, 1952:149–63.
9. Kant I. Fundamental principles of the metaphysic of morals. 1785. New York: Liberal Arts Press, 1949.
10. Rollin BE. Animal rights and human morality. New York: Prometheus Books, 1981.

11. Hoff C. Immoral and moral uses of animals. N Engl J Med 1980; 302:115–8.

12. Jamieson D. Killing persons and other beings. In: Miller HB, Williams WH, eds. Ethics and animals. Clifton, N.J.: Humana Press, 1983:135–46.

13. Singer P. Ten years of animal liberation. New York Review of Books. 1985; 31:46–52.

14. Bentham J. Introduction to the principles of morals and legislation. London: Athlone Press, 1970.

15. McCabe K. Who will live, who will die? Washingtonian Magazine. August 1986:115.

16. U.S. Code of Federal Regulations, Title 21, Sect. 505(i). Food, drug and cosmetic regulations.

17. U.S. Code of Federal Regulations, Title 16, Sect. 1500.40–2. Consumer product regulations.

QUESTIONS

1. Cohen limits his argument to the use of animals in biomedical research. What are the advantages of this limitation? What are the disadvantages?

2. Cohen defends speciesism; Tom Regan, in "The Case for Animal Rights" (p. 691), condemns it. What are the issues at stake between them?

3. "Neither of these arguments is sound," Cohen opines. "The first relies on a mistaken understanding of rights; the second relies on a mistaken calculation of consequences" (paragraph 1). Find other examples of the language Cohen uses to dismiss arguments in opposition to his own. How do you respond to it? Is it the kind of language you would use in your own writing? Explain.

4. Write an essay in which you argue for or against speciesism. Be sure to define it. You may use Regan's and Cohen's arguments (with proper credit) in support of your own, but you need not.

NORA EPHRON   *The Boston Photographs*

"I MADE ALL KINDS of pictures because I thought it would be a good rescue shot over the ladder . . . never dreamed it would be anything else. . . . I kept having to move around because of the light set. The sky was bright and they were in deep shadow. I was making pictures with a motor drive and he, the fire fighter, was reaching up and, I don't know, everything started falling. I followed the girl down taking pictures . . . I made three or four frames. I realized

Originally written for Ephron's column on the media in Esquire (November 1975), *this essay later appeared in her collection* Scribble, Scribble: Notes on the Media *(1978).*

what was going on and I completely turned around, because I didn't want to see her hit."

You probably saw the photographs. In most newspapers, there were three of them. The first showed some people on a fire escape—a fireman, a woman and a child. The fireman had a nice strong jaw and looked very brave. The woman was holding the child. Smoke was pouring from the building behind them. A rescue ladder was approaching, just a few feet away, and the fireman had one arm around the woman and one arm reaching out toward the ladder. The second picture showed the fire escape slipping off the building. The child had fallen on the escape and seemed about to slide off the edge. The woman was grasping desperately at the legs of the fireman, who had managed to grab

the ladder. The third picture showed the woman and child in midair, falling to
the ground. Their arms and legs were outstretched, horribly distended. A pot-
ted plant was falling too. The caption said that the woman, Diana Bryant,
nineteen, died in the fall. The child landed on the woman's body and lived.

The pictures were taken by Stanley Forman, thirty, of the *Boston Herald
American*. He used a motor-driven Nikon F set at 1/250, f 5.6–8. Because of
the motor, the camera can click off three frames a second. More than four
hundred newspapers in the United States alone carried the photographs; the
tear sheets from overseas are still coming in. The *New York Times* ran them on
the first page of its second section; a paper in south Georgia gave them nineteen columns; the *Chicago Tribune*, the *Washington Post* and the *Washington*

Star filled almost half their front pages, the *Star* under a somewhat redundant headline that read: SENSATIONAL PHOTOS OF RESCUE ATTEMPT THAT FAILED.

The photographs are indeed sensational. They are pictures of death in action, of that split second when luck runs out, and it is impossible to look at them without feeling their extraordinary impact and remembering, in an almost subconscious way, the morbid fantasy of falling, falling off a building, falling to one's death. Beyond that, the pictures are classics, old-fashioned but perfect examples of photojournalism at its most spectacular. They're throwbacks, really, fire pictures, 1930s tabloid shots; at the same time they're technically superb and thoroughly modern—the sequence could not have been taken at all until the development of the motor-driven camera some sixteen years ago.

Most newspaper editors anticipate some reader reaction to photographs   5
like Forman's; even so, the response around the country was enormous, and almost all of it was negative. I have read hundreds of the letters that were printed in letters-to-the-editor sections, and they repeat the same points. "Invading the privacy of death." "Cheap sensationalism." "I thought I was reading the *National Enquirer.*" "Assigning the agony of a human being in terror of imminent death to the status of a side-show act." "A tawdry way to sell newspapers." The *Seattle Times* received sixty letters and calls; its managing editor even got a couple of them at home. A reader wrote the *Philadelphia Inquirer:* "*Jaws* and *Towering Inferno* are playing downtown; don't take business away from people who pay good money to advertise in your own paper." Another reader wrote the *Chicago Sun-Times:* "I shall try to hide my disappointment that Miss Bryant wasn't wearing a skirt when she fell to her death. You could have had some award-winning photographs of her underpants as her skirt billowed over her head, you voyeurs." Several newspaper editors wrote columns defending the pictures: Thomas Keevil of the *Costa Mesa* (California) *Daily Pilot* printed a ballot for readers to vote on whether they would have printed the pictures; Marshall L. Stone of Maine's *Bangor Daily News*, which refused to print the famous assassination picture of the Vietcong prisoner in Saigon, claimed that the Boston pictures showed the dangers of fire escapes and raised questions about slumlords. (The burning building was a five-story brick apartment house on Marlborough Street in the Back Bay section of Boston.)[1]

For the last five years, the *Washington Post* has employed various journalists as ombudsmen, whose job is to monitor the paper on behalf of the public. The *Post's* current ombudsman is Charles Seib, former managing editor of the *Washington Star*; the day the Boston photographs appeared, the paper received over seventy calls in protest. As Seib later wrote in a column about the pictures, it was "the largest reaction to a published item that I have experienced in eight months as the *Post's* ombudsman. . . .

"In the *Post's* newsroom, on the other hand, I found no doubts, no second thoughts . . . the question was not whether they should be printed but how they should be displayed. When I talked to editors . . . they used words like 'interesting' and 'riveting' and 'gripping' to describe them. The pictures told something about life in the ghetto, they said (although the neighborhood where the tragedy occurred is not a ghetto, I am told). They dramatized the need to check on the safety of fire escapes. They dramatically conveyed something that had happened, and that is the business we're in. They were news. . . .

"Was publication of that [third] picture a bow to the same taste for the morbidly sensational that makes gold mines of disaster movies? Most papers will not print the picture of a dead body except in the most unusual circumstances. Does the fact that the final picture was taken a millisecond before the

---

1. Since 1975 Marlborough Street has been gentrified; it is now one of Boston's most sought-after addresses.

young woman died make a difference? Most papers will not print a picture of
a bare female breast. Is that a more inappropriate subject for display than the
picture of a human being's last agonized instant of life?" Seib offered no answers to the questions he raised, but he went on to say that although as an editor he would probably have run the pictures, as a reader he was "revolted by
them."

In conclusion, Seib wrote: "Any editor who decided to print those pictures
without giving at least a moment's thought to what purpose they served and
what their effect was likely to be on the reader should ask another question:
Have I become so preoccupied with manufacturing a product according to
professional traditions and standards that I have forgotten about the consumer, the reader?"

10   It should be clear that the phone calls and letters and Seib's own reaction
were occasioned by one factor alone: the death of the woman. Obviously, had
she survived the fall, no one would have protested; the pictures would have had
a completely different impact. Equally obviously, had the child died as well—or
instead—Seib would undoubtedly have received ten times the phone calls he
did. In each case, the pictures would have been exactly the same—only the captions, and thus the responses, would have been different.

But the questions Seib raises are worth discussing—though not exactly
for the reasons he mentions. For it may be that the real lesson of the Boston
photographs is not the danger that editors will be forgetful of reader reaction,
but that they will continue to censor pictures of death precisely because of
that reaction. The protests Seib fielded were really a variation on an old
theme—and we saw plenty of it during the Nixon-Agnew years—the "Why
doesn't the press print the good news?" argument. In this case, of course, the
objections were all dressed up and cleverly disguised as righteous indignation
about the privacy of death. This is a form of puritanism that is often justifiable; just as often it is merely puritanical.

Seib takes it for granted that the widespread though fairly recent newspaper policy against printing pictures of dead bodies is a sound one; I don't
know that it makes any sense at all. I recognize that printing pictures of
corpses raises all sorts of problems about taste and titillation and sensationalism; the fact is, however, that people die. Death happens to be one of life's
main events. And it is irresponsible—and more than that, inaccurate—for
newspapers to fail to show it, or to show it only when an astonishing set of
photos comes in over the Associated Press wire. Most papers covering fatal automobile accidents will print pictures of mangled cars. But the significance of
fatal automobile accidents is not that a great deal of steel is twisted but that
people die. Why not show it? That's what accidents are about. Throughout the
Vietnam war, editors were reluctant to print atrocity pictures. Why *not* print
them? That's what that war was about. Murder victims are almost never photographed; they are granted their privacy. But their relatives are relentlessly
pictured on their way in and out of hospitals and morgues and funerals.

I'm not advocating that newspapers print these things in order to teach
their readers a lesson. The *Post* editors justified their printing of the Boston

pictures with several arguments in that direction; every one of them is irrelevant. The pictures don't show anything about slum life; the incident could have happened anywhere, and it did. It is extremely unlikely that anyone who saw them rushed out and had his fire escape strengthened. And the pictures were not news—at least they were not national news. It is not news in Washington, or New York, or Los Angeles that a woman was killed in a Boston fire. The only newsworthy thing about the pictures is that they were taken. They deserve to be printed because they are great pictures, breathtaking pictures of something that happened. That they disturb readers is exactly as it should be: that's why photojournalism is often more powerful than written journalism.

QUESTIONS

1. Why does Ephron begin with the words of the photographer Stanley Forman? What information—as well as perspective—does her opening paragraph convey?

2. What was public reaction to the publication of the Boston photographs? What reasons did newspeople give for printing them? How does Ephron arrange these responses?

3. What conclusions does Ephron reach about the ethics of publishing sensational photographs? Does she offer ethical guidelines?

4. Find a startling photograph recently printed in a newspaper or magazine, and argue for or against its publication, using Ephron's terms and your own.

5. Examine the Vietcong assassination photo on p. 819 (in H. Bruce Franklin's "From Realism to Virtual Reality"). Were the issues about publishing this photo the same as those for the Boston photographs Ephron discusses? Were they different? Or different enough? Write an essay about the issues surrounding the two photo publications.

ALDO LEOPOLD   *The Land Ethic*

WHEN GOD-LIKE ODYSSEUS returned from the wars in Troy, he hanged all on one rope a dozen slave-girls of his household whom he suspected of misbehavior during his absence.

This hanging involved no question of propriety. The girls were property. The disposal of property was then, as now, a matter of expediency, not of right and wrong.

Concepts of right and wrong were not lacking from Odysseus' Greece: witness the fidelity of his wife through the long years before at last his black-

The final essay in Leopold's A Sand County Almanac *(1949), which combines journal entries and essays on his home in Wisconsin to reflect on nature and environmental issues.*

prowed galleys clove the wine-dark seas for home. The ethical structure of that day covered wives, but had not yet been extended to human chattels. During the three thousand years which have since elapsed, ethical criteria have been extended to many fields of conduct, with corresponding shrinkages in those judged by expediency only.

THE ETHICAL SEQUENCE

This extension of ethics, so far studied only by philosophers, is actually a process in ecological evolution. Its sequences may be described in ecological as well as in philosophical terms. An ethic, ecologically, is a limitation on freedom of action in the struggle for existence. An ethic, philosophically, is a differentiation of social from anti-social conduct. These are two definitions of one thing. The thing has its origin in the tendency of interdependent individuals or groups to evolve modes of co-operation. The ecologist calls these symbioses. Politics and economics are advanced symbioses in which the original free-for-all competition has been replaced, in part, by co-operative mechanisms with an ethical content.

5   The complexity of co-operative mechanisms has increased with population density, and with the efficiency of tools. It was simpler, for example, to define the anti-social uses of sticks and stones in the days of the mastodons than of bullets and billboards in the age of motors.

The first ethics dealt with the relation between individuals; the Mosaic Decalogue[1] is an example. Later accretions dealt with the relation between the individual and society. The Golden Rule tries to integrate social organization to the individual.

There is as yet no ethic dealing with man's relation to land and to the animals and plants which grow upon it. Land, like Odysseus' slave-girls, is still property. The land-relation is still strictly economic, entailing privileges but not obligations.

The extension of ethics to this third element in human environment is, if I read the evidence correctly, an evolutionary possibility and an ecological necessity. It is the third step in a sequence. The first two have already been taken. Individual thinkers since the days of Ezekiel and Isaiah[2] have asserted that the despoliation of land is not only inexpedient but wrong. Society, however, has not yet affirmed their belief. I regard the present conservation movement as the embryo of such an affirmation.

An ethic may be regarded as a mode of guidance for meeting ecological situations so new or intricate, or involving such deferred reactions, that the path of social expediency is not discernible to the average individual. Animal instincts are modes of guidance for the individual in meeting such situations. Ethics are possibly a kind of community instinct in-the-making.

---

1. The Ten Commandments.
2. Ezekiel (sixth century B.C.E.) and Isaiah (eighth century B.C.E.) were prophets of ancient Israel; the biblical books Ezekiel and Isaiah were named after them.

THE COMMUNITY CONCEPT

All ethics so far evolved rest upon a single premise: that the individual is a   10
member of a community of interdependent parts. His instincts prompt him to
compete for his place in that community, but his ethics prompt him also to cooperate (perhaps in order that there may be a place to compete for).

The land ethic simply enlarges the boundaries of the community to include soils, waters, plants, and animals, or collectively: the land.

This sounds simple: do we not already sing our love for and obligation to
the land of the free and the home of the brave? Yes, but just what and whom
do we love? Certainly not the soil, which we are sending helter-skelter downriver. Certainly not the waters, which we assume have no function except to
turn turbines, float barges, and carry off sewage. Certainly not the plants, of
which we exterminate whole communities without batting an eye. Certainly
not the animals, of which we have already extirpated many of the largest and
most beautiful species. A land ethic of course cannot prevent the alteration,
management, and use of these "resources," but it does affirm their right to
continued existence, and, at least in spots, their continued existence in a natural state.

In short, a land ethic changes the role of *Homo sapiens* from conqueror of
the land-community to plain member and citizen of it. It implies respect for
his fellow-members, and also respect for the community as such.

In human history, we have learned (I hope) that the conqueror role is
eventually self-defeating. Why? Because it is implicit in such a role that the
conqueror knows, *ex cathedra*,[3] just what makes the community clock tick,
and just what and who is valuable, and what and who is worthless, in community life. It always turns out that he knows neither, and this is why his con-
quests eventually defeat themselves.

In the biotic community, a parallel situation exists. Abraham knew exactly   15
what the land was for: it was to drip milk and honey into Abraham's mouth. At
the present moment, the assurance with which we regard this assumption is
inverse to the degree of our education.

The ordinary citizen today assumes that science knows what makes the
community clock tick; the scientist is equally sure that he does not. He knows
that the biotic mechanism is so complex that its workings may never be fully
understood.

That man is, in fact, only a member of a biotic team is shown by an ecological interpretation of history. Many historical events, hitherto explained
solely in terms of human enterprise, were actually biotic interactions between
people and land. The characteristics of the land determined the facts quite as
potently as the characteristics of the men who lived on it.

Consider, for example, the settlement of the Mississippi valley. In the
years following the Revolution, three groups were contending for its control:
the native Indian, the French and English traders, and the American settlers.
Historians wonder what would have happened if the English at Detroit had

3. From the official throne of the bishop; hence, with authority.

thrown a little more weight into the Indian side of those tipsy scales which decided the outcome of the colonial migration into the cane-lands of Kentucky.
It is time now to ponder the fact that the cane-lands, when subjected to the
particular mixture of forces represented by the cow, plow, fire, and axe of the
pioneer, became bluegrass. What if the plant succession inherent in this dark
and bloody ground had, under the impact of these forces, given us some
worthless sedge, shrub, or weed? Would Boone and Kenton[4] have held out?
Would there have been any overflow into Ohio, Indiana, Illinois, and Missouri? Any Louisiana Purchase? Any transcontinental union of new states? Any
Civil War?

Kentucky was one sentence in the drama of history. We are commonly
told what the human actors in this drama tried to do, but we are seldom told
that their success, or the lack of it, hung in large degree on the reaction of
particular soils to the impact of the particular forces exerted by their occupancy. In the case of Kentucky, we do not even know where the bluegrass
came from—whether it is a native species, or a stowaway from Europe.

20   Contrast the cane-lands with what hindsight tells us about the Southwest,
where the pioneers were equally brave, resourceful, and persevering. The impact of occupancy here brought no bluegrass, or other plant fitted to withstand the bumps and buffetings of hard use. This region, when grazed by
livestock, reverted through a series of more and more worthless grasses,
shrubs, and weeds to a condition of unstable equilibrium. Each recession of
plant types bred erosion; each increment to erosion bred a further recession
of plants. The result today is a progressive and mutual deterioration, not only
of plants and soils, but of the animal community subsisting thereon. The early
settlers did not expect this: on the ciénegas[5] of New Mexico some even cut
ditches to hasten it. So subtle has been its progress that few residents of the
region are aware of it. It is quite invisible to the tourist who finds this wrecked
landscape colorful and charming (as indeed it is, but it bears scant resemblance to what it was in 1848).

This same landscape was "developed" once before, but with quite different results. The Pueblo Indians settled the Southwest in pre-Columbian
times,[6] but they happened *not* to be equipped with range livestock. Their civilization expired, but not because their land expired.

In India, regions devoid of any sod-forming grass have been settled, apparently without wrecking the land, by the simple expedient of carrying the grass
to the cow, rather than vice versa. (Was this the result of some deep wisdom,
or was it just good luck? I do not know.)

In short, the plant succession steered the course of history; the pioneer
simply demonstrated, for good or ill, what successions inhered in the land. Is

---

4. Daniel Boone (1734–1820), American frontiersman who explored and helped settle
the West; Simon Kenton (1755–1836), frontiersman and friend of Daniel Boone, famous for his miraculous escape from the Shawnee Indians.

5. Marshes, swamps (Spanish).

6. Before the arrival of Christopher Columbus in the New World.

history taught in this spirit? It will be, once the concept of land as a community really penetrates our intellectual life.

THE ECOLOGICAL CONSCIENCE

Conservation is a state of harmony between men and land. Despite nearly a century of propaganda, conservation still proceeds at a snail's pace; progress still consists largely of letterhead pieties and convention oratory. On the back forty[7] we still slip two steps backward for each forward stride.

The usual answer to this dilemma is "more conservation education." No one will debate this, but is it certain that only the *volume* of education needs stepping up? Is something lacking in the *content* as well?

It is difficult to give a fair summary of its content in brief form, but, as I understand it, the content is substantially this: obey the law, vote right, join some organizations, and practice what conservation is profitable on your own land; the government will do the rest.

Is not this formula too easy to accomplish anything worth-while? It defines no right or wrong, assigns no obligation, calls for no sacrifice, implies no change in the current philosophy of values. In respect of land-use, it urges only enlightened self-interest. Just how far will such education take us? An example will perhaps yield a partial answer.

By 1930 it had become clear to all except the ecologically blind that southwestern Wisconsin's topsoil was slipping seaward. In 1933 the farmers were told that if they would adopt certain remedial practices for five years, the public would donate CCC[8] labor to install them, plus the necessary machinery and materials. The offer was widely accepted, but the practices were widely forgotten when the five-year contract period was up. The farmers continued only those practices that yielded an immediate and visible economic gain for themselves.

This led to the idea that maybe farmers would learn more quickly if they themselves wrote the rules. Accordingly the Wisconsin Legislature in 1937 passed the Soil Conservation District Law. This said to farmers, in effect: *We, the public, will furnish you free technical service and loan you specialized machinery, if you will write your own rules for land-use. Each county may write its own rules, and these will have the force of law.* Nearly all the counties promptly organized to accept the proffered help, but after a decade of operation, *no county has yet written a single rule.* There has been visible progress in such practices as strip-cropping, pasture renovation, and soil liming, but none in fencing woodlots against grazing, and none in excluding plow and cow from steep slopes. The farmers, in short, have selected those remedial practices which were profitable anyhow, and ignored those which were profitable to the community, but not clearly profitable to themselves.

When one asks why no rules have been written, one is told that the com-

7. Acres of a farm.

8. Civilian Conservation Corps, established in 1933 during the Great Depression to employ thousands of unemployed young men and send them into battle against the destruction of America's natural resources.

munity is not yet ready to support them; education must precede rules. But the education actually in progress makes no mention of obligations to land over and above those dictated by self-interest. The net result is that we have more education but less soil, fewer healthy woods, and as many floods as in 1937.

The puzzling aspect of such situations is that the existence of obligations over and above self-interest is taken for granted in such rural community enterprises as the betterment of roads, schools, churches, and baseball teams. Their existence is not taken for granted, nor as yet seriously discussed, in bettering the behavior of the water that falls on the land, or in the preserving of the beauty or diversity of the farm landscape. Land-use ethics are still governed wholly by economic self-interest, just as social ethics were a century ago.

To sum up: we asked the farmer to do what he conveniently could to save his soil, and he has done just that, and only that. The farmer who clears the woods off a 75 per cent slope, turns his cows into the clearing, and dumps its rainfall, rocks, and soil into the community creek, is still (if otherwise decent) a respected member of society. If he puts lime on his fields and plants his crops on contour, he is still entitled to all the privileges and emoluments of his Soil Conservation District. The District is a beautiful piece of social machinery, but it is coughing along on two cylinders because we have been too timid, and too anxious for quick success, to tell the farmer the true magnitude of his obligations. Obligations have no meaning without conscience, and the problem we face is the extension of the social conscience from people to land.

No important change in ethics was ever accomplished without an internal change in our intellectual emphasis, loyalties, affections, and convictions. The proof that conservation has not yet touched these foundations of conduct lies in the fact that philosophy and religion have not yet heard of it. In our attempt to make conservation easy, we have made it trivial.

THE OUTLOOK

It is inconceivable to me that an ethical relation to land can exist without love, respect, and admiration for land, and a high regard for its value. By value, I of course mean something far broader than mere economic value; I mean value in the philosophical sense.

35   Perhaps the most serious obstacle impeding the evolution of a land ethic is the fact that our educational and economic system is headed away from, rather than toward, an intense consciousness of land. Your true modern is separated from the land by many middlemen, and by innumerable physical gadgets. He has no vital relation to it; to him it is the space between cities on which crops grow. Turn him loose for a day on the land, and if the spot does not happen to be a golf links or a "scenic" area, he is bored stiff. If crops could be raised by hydroponics instead of farming, it would suit him very well. Synthetic substitutes for wood, leather, wool, and other natural land products suit him better than the originals. In short, land is something he has "outgrown."

Almost equally serious as an obstacle to a land ethic is the attitude of the farmer for whom the land is still an adversary, or a taskmaster that keeps him in slavery. Theoretically, the mechanization of farming ought to cut the farmer's chains, but whether it really does is debatable.

One of the requisites for an ecological comprehension of land is an understanding of ecology, and this is by no means co-extensive with "education"; in fact, much higher education seems deliberately to avoid ecological concepts. An understanding of ecology does not necessarily originate in courses bearing ecological labels; it is quite as likely to be labeled geography, botany, agronomy, history, or economics. This is as it should be, but whatever the label, ecological training is scarce.

The case for a land ethic would appear hopeless but for the minority which is in obvious revolt against these "modern" trends.

The "key-log" which must be moved to release the evolutionary process for an ethic is simply this: quit thinking about decent land-use as solely an economic problem. Examine each question in terms of what is ethically and esthetically right, as well as what is economically expedient. A thing is right when it tends to preserve the integrity, stability, and beauty of the biotic community. It is wrong when it tends otherwise.

It of course goes without saying that economic feasibility limits the tether of what can or cannot be done for land. It always has and it always will. The fallacy the economic determinists have tied around our collective neck, and which we now need to cast off, is the belief that economics determines *all* land-use. This is simply not true. An innumerable host of actions and attitudes, comprising perhaps the bulk of all land relations, is determined by the land-users' tastes and predilections, rather than by his purse. The bulk of all land relations hinges on investments of time, forethought, skill, and faith rather than on investments of cash. As a land-user thinketh, so is he.

I have purposely presented the land ethic as a product of social evolution because nothing so important as an ethic is ever "written." Only the most superficial student of history supposes that Moses "wrote" the Decalogue; it evolved in the minds of a thinking community, and Moses wrote a tentative summary of it for a "seminar." I say tentative because evolution never stops.

The evolution of a land ethic is an intellectual as well as emotional process. Conservation is paved with good intentions which prove to be futile, or even dangerous, because they are devoid of critical understanding either of the land, or of economic land-use. I think it is a truism that as the ethical frontier advances from the individual to the community, its intellectual content increases.

The mechanism of operation is the same for any ethic: social approbation for right actions: social disapproval for wrong actions.

By and large, our present problem is one of attitudes and implements. We are remodeling the Alhambra[9] with a steam-shovel, and we are proud of our yardage. We shall hardly relinquish the shovel, which after all has many good points, but we are in need of gentler and more objective criteria for its successful use.

9. Moorish palace in Grenada, Spain, built between 1338 and 1390.

QUESTIONS

1. Leopold begins with a story of the Greek hero Odysseus returning from the Trojan War and executing "a dozen slave-girls of his household." What relevance does this story have to his argument about progress in human ethics?

2. What is the "ethical sequence"? What three aspects or stages of ethical development does Leopold include?

3. How does the concept of a biotic community alter the relationship of humans to the land? Why does Leopold use the Latin designation *Homo sapiens* in paragraph 13 as he redefines this relationship?

4. What problems does Leopold anticipate in putting a land ethic into effect? Do environmentalists face the same or different problems today?

5. How far have Americans come since 1949, when Leopold's essay was published? If your course includes a research paper, consider writing on contemporary responses to problems that Leopold enumerated in his day.

MARY GORDON   *A Moral Choice*

I AM HAVING LUNCH with six women. What is unusual is that four of them are in their seventies, two of them widowed, the other two living with husbands beside whom they've lived for decades. All of them have had children. Had they been men, they would have published books and hung their paintings on the walls of important galleries. But they are women of a certain generation, and their lives were shaped around their families and personal relations. They are women you go to for help and support. We begin talking about the latest legislative act that makes abortion more difficult for poor women to obtain. An extraordinary thing happens. Each of them talks about the illegal abortions she had during her young womanhood. Not one of them was spared the experience. Any of them could have died on the table of whatever person (not a doctor in any case) she was forced to approach, in secrecy and in terror, to end a pregnancy that she felt would blight her life.

I mention this incident for two reasons: first as a reminder that all kinds of women have always had abortions; second because it is essential that we remember that an abortion is performed on a living woman who has a life in which a terminated pregnancy is only a small part. Morally speaking, the decision to have an abortion doesn't take place in a vacuum. It is connected to other choices that a woman makes in the course of an adult life.

Published in the Atlantic Monthly *(April 1990), one of America's oldest and most prestigious magazines of literature, culture, and politics.*

Anti-choice propagandists paint pictures of women who choose to have abortions as types of moral callousness, selfishness, or irresponsibility. The woman choosing to abort is the dressed-for-success yuppie who gets rid of her baby so that she won't miss her Caribbean vacation or her chance for promotion. Or she is the feckless, promiscuous ghetto teenager who couldn't bring herself to just say no to sex. A third, purportedly kinder, gentler picture has recently begun to be drawn. The woman in the abortion clinic is there because she is misinformed about the nature of the world. She is having an abortion because society does not provide for mothers and their children, and she mistakenly thinks that another mouth to feed will be the ruin of her family, not understanding that the temporary truth of family unhappiness doesn't stack up beside the eternal verity that abortion is murder. Or she is the dupe of her husband or boyfriend, who talks her into having an abortion because a child will be a drag on his life-style. None of these pictures created by the anti-choice movement assumes that the decision to have an abortion is made responsibly, in the context of a morally lived life, by a free and responsible moral agent.

THE ONTOLOGY OF THE FETUS

How would a woman who habitually makes choices in moral terms come to the decision to have an abortion? The moral discussion of abortion centers on the issue of whether or not abortion is an act of murder. At first glance it would seem that the answer should follow directly upon two questions: Is the fetus human? and Is it alive? It would be absurd to deny that a fetus is alive or that it is human. What would our other options be—to say that it is inanimate or belongs to another species? But we habitually use the terms "human" and "live" to refer to parts of our body—"human hair," for example, or "live red-blood cells"—and we are clear in our understanding that the nature of these objects does not rank equally with an entire personal existence. It then seems important to consider whether the fetus, this alive human thing, is a *person*, to whom the term "murder" could sensibly be applied. How would anyone come to a decision about something so impalpable as personhood? Philosophers have struggled with the issue of personhood, but in language that is so abstract that it is unhelpful to ordinary people making decisions in the course of their lives. It might be more productive to begin thinking about the status of the fetus by examining the language and customs that surround it. This approach will encourage us to focus on the choosing, acting woman, rather than the act of abortion—as if the act were performed by abstract forces without bodies, histories, attachments.

This focus on the acting woman is useful because a pregnant woman has   5 an identifiable, consistent ontology,[1] and a fetus takes on different ontological identities over time. But common sense, experience, and linguistic usage point clearly to the fact that we habitually consider, for example, a seven-week-old

1. Concerned with existence or being.

fetus to be different from a seven-month-old one. We can tell this by the way we respond to the involuntary loss of one as against the other. We have different language for the experience of the involuntary expulsion of the fetus from the womb depending upon the point of gestation at which the experience occurs. If it occurs early in the pregnancy, we call it a miscarriage; if late, we call it a stillbirth.

We would have an extreme reaction to the reversal of those terms. If a woman referred to a miscarriage at seven weeks as a stillbirth, we would be alarmed. It would shock our sense of propriety; it would make us uneasy; we would find it disturbing, misplaced—as we do when a bag lady sits down in a restaurant and starts shouting, or an octogenarian arrives at our door in a sailor suit. In short, we would suspect that the speaker was mad. Similarly, if a doctor or a nurse referred to the loss of a seven-month-old fetus as a miscarriage, we would be shocked by that person's insensitivity: could she or he not understand that a fetus that age is not what it was months before?

Our ritual and religious practices underscore the fact that we make distinctions among fetuses. If a woman took the bloody matter—indistinguishable from a heavy period—of an early miscarriage and insisted upon putting it in a tiny coffin and marking its grave, we would have serious concerns about her mental health. By the same token, we would feel squeamish about flushing a seven-month-old fetus down the toilet—something we would quite normally do with an early miscarriage. There are no prayers for the matter of a miscarriage, nor do we feel there should be. Even a Catholic priest would not baptize the issue of an early miscarriage.

The difficulties stem, of course, from the odd situation of a fetus's ontology: a complicated, differentiated, and nuanced response is required when we are dealing with an entity that changes over time. Yet we are in the habit of making distinctions like this. At one point we know that a child is no longer a child but an adult. That this question is vexed and problematic is clear from our difficulty in determining who is a juvenile offender and who is an adult criminal and at what age sexual intercourse ceases to be known as statutory rape. So at what point, if any, do we on the pro-choice side say that the developing fetus is a person, with rights equal to its mother's?

The anti-choice people have one advantage over us; their monolithic position gives them unity on this question. For myself, I am made uneasy by third-trimester abortions, which take place when the fetus could live outside the mother's body, but I also know that these are extremely rare and often performed on very young girls who have had difficulty comprehending the realities of pregnancy. It seems to me that the question of late abortions should be decided case by case, and that fixation on this issue is a deflection from what is most important: keeping early abortions, which are in the majority by far, safe and legal. I am also politically realistic enough to suspect that bills restricting late abortions are not good-faith attempts to make distinctions about the nature of fetal life. They are, rather, the cynical embodiments of the hope among anti-choice partisans that technology will be on their side and that medical science's ability to create situations in which younger fetuses are viable outside their mothers' bodies will increase dramatically in the next few years. Ironically, medical science will probably make the issue of abortion a minor one in the near future. The RU-486 pill, which can induce abortion early on, exists, and whether or not it is legally available (it is not on the market here, because of pressure from anti-choice groups), women will begin to obtain it. If abortion can occur through chemical rather than physical means, in the privacy of one's home, most people not directly involved will lose interest in it. As abortion is transformed from a public into a private issue, it will cease to be perceived as political; it will be called personal instead.

AN EQUIVOCAL GOOD

But because abortion will always deal with what it is to create and sustain life,   10
it will always be a moral issue. And whether we like it or not, our moral thinking about abortion is rooted in the shifting soil of perception. In an age in which much of our perception is manipulated by media that specialize in the sound bite and the photo op, the anti-choice partisans have a twofold advantage over us on the pro-choice side. The pro-choice moral position is more complex, and the experience we defend is physically repellent to contemplate. None of us in the pro-choice movement would suggest that abortion is not a regrettable occurrence. Anti-choice proponents can offer pastel photographs of babies in buntings, their eyes peaceful in the camera's gaze. In answer, we can't offer the material of an early abortion, bloody, amorphous in a paper cup, to prove that what has just been removed from the woman's body is not a child, not in the same category of being as the adorable bundle in an adoptive mother's arms. It is not a pleasure to look at the physical evidence of abortion, and most of us don't get the opportunity to do so.

The theologian Daniel Maguire, uncomfortable with the fact that most theological arguments about the nature of abortion are made by men who have never been anywhere near an actual abortion, decided to visit a clinic and observe abortions being performed. He didn't find the experience easy, but he knew that before he could in good conscience make a moral judgment on abortion, he needed to experience through his senses what an aborted fetus is like: he needed to look at and touch the controversial entity. He held in his hand the bloody fetal stuff; the eight-week-old fetus fit in the palm of his hand, and it certainly bore no resemblance to either of his two children when he had held them moments after their birth. He knew at that point what women who have experienced early abortions and miscarriages know: that some event occurred, possibly even a dramatic one, but it was not the death of a child.

Because issues of pregnancy and birth are both physical and metaphorical, we must constantly step back and forth between ways of perceiving the world. When we speak of gestation, we are often talking in terms of potential, about events and objects to which we attach our hopes, fears, dreams, and ideals. A mother can speak to the fetus in her uterus and name it; she and her mate may decorate a nursery according to their vision of the good life; they may choose for an embryo a college, a profession, a dwelling. But those of us who are trying to think morally about pregnancy and birth must remember that these feelings are our own projections onto what is in reality an inappropriate object. However charmed we may be by an expectant father's buying a little football for something inside his wife's belly, we shouldn't make public policy based on such actions, nor should we force others to live their lives conforming to our fantasies.

As a society, we are making decisions that pit the complicated future of a complex adult against the fate of a mass of cells lacking cortical development. The moral pressure should be on distinguishing the true from the false, the real suffering of living persons from our individual and often idiosyncratic dreams and fears. We must make decisions on abortion based on an understanding of how people really do live. We must be able to say that poverty is worse than not being poor, that having dignified and meaningful work is better than working in conditions of degradation, that raising a child one loves and has desired is better than raising a child in resentment and rage, that it is better for a twelve-year-old not to endure the trauma of having a child when she is herself a child.

When we put these ideas against the ideas of "child" or "baby," we seem to be making a horrifying choice of life-style over life. But in fact we are telling the truth of what it means to bear a child, and what the experience of abortion really is. This is extremely difficult, for the object of the discussion is hidden, changing, potential. We make our decisions on the basis of approximate and inadequate language, often on the basis of fantasies and fears. It will always be crucial to try to separate genuine moral concern from phobia, punitiveness, superstition, anxiety, a desperate search for certainty in an uncertain world.

15   One of the certainties that is removed if we accept the consequences of the pro-choice position is the belief that the birth of a child is an unequivocal good. In real life we act knowing that the birth of a child is not always a good thing: people are sometimes depressed, angry, rejecting, at the birth of a child. But this is a difficult truth to tell; we don't like to say it, and one of the fears preyed on by anti-choice proponents is that if we cannot look at the birth of a child as an unequivocal good, then there is nothing to look toward. The desire for security of the imagination, for typological fixity, particularly in the area of "the good," is an understandable desire. It must seem to some anti-choice people that we on the pro-choice side are not only murdering innocent children but also murdering hope. Those of us who have experienced the birth of a desired child and felt the joy of that moment can be tempted into believing that it was the physical experience of the birth itself that was the joy. But it is crucial to remember that the birth of a child itself is a neutral occurrence emotionally: the charge it takes on is invested in it by the people experiencing or observing it.

THE FEAR OF SEXUAL AUTONOMY

These uncertainties can lead to another set of fears, not only about abortion but about its implications. Many anti-choice people fear that to support abortion is to cast one's lot with the cold and technological rather than with the warm and natural, to head down the slippery slope toward a brave new world where handicapped children are left on mountains to starve and the old are put out in the snow. But if we look at the history of abortion, we don't see the embodiment of what the anti-choice proponents fear. On the contrary, excepting the grotesque counterexample of the People's Republic of China (which practices forced abortion), there seems to be a real link between repressive anti-abortion stances and repressive governments. Abortion was banned in Fascist Italy and Nazi Germany; it is illegal in South Africa and in Chile. It is paid for by the governments of Denmark, England, and the Netherlands, which have national health and welfare systems that foster the health and well-being of mothers, children, the old, and the handicapped.

Advocates of outlawing abortion often refer to women seeking abortion as self-indulgent and materialistic. In fact these accusations mask a discomfort with female sexuality, sexual pleasure, and sexual autonomy. It is possible for a woman to have a sexual life unriddled by fear only if she can be confident that she need not pay for a failure of technology or judgment (and who among us has never once been swept away in the heat of a sexual moment?) by taking upon herself the crushing burden of unchosen motherhood.

It is no accident, therefore, that the increased appeal of measures to restrict maternal conduct during pregnancy—and a new focus on the physical autonomy of the pregnant woman—have come into public discourse at precisely the time when women are achieving unprecedented levels of economic and political autonomy. What has surprised me is that some of this new anti-autonomy talk comes to us from the left. An example of this new discourse is an article by Christopher Hitchens that appeared in *The Nation* last April, in which the author asserts his discomfort with abortion. Hitchens's tone is impeccably British: arch, light, we're men of the left.

> Anyone who has ever seen a sonogram or has spent even an hour with a textbook on embryology knows that the emotions are not the deciding factor. In order to terminate a pregnancy, you have to still a heartbeat, switch off a developing brain, and whatever the method, break some bones and rupture some organs. As to whether this involves pain on the "Silent Scream" scale, I have no idea. The "right to life" leadership, again, has cheapened everything it touches.

"It is a pity," Hitchens goes on to say, "that . . . the majority of feminists and their allies have stuck to the dead ground of 'Me Decade' possessive individualism, an ideology that has more in common than it admits with the prehistoric right, which it claims to oppose but has in fact encouraged." Hitchens proposes, as an alternative, a program of social reform that would make contraception free and support a national adoption service. In his opinion, it would seem, women have abortions for only two reasons: because they are selfish or because they are poor. If the state will take care of the economic problems and the bureaucratic messiness around adoption, it remains only for the possessive individualists to get their act together and walk with their babies into the communal utopia of the future. Hitchens would allow victims of rape or incest to have free abortions, on the grounds that since they didn't choose to have sex, the women should not be forced to have the babies. This would seem to put the issue of volition in a wrong and telling place. To Hitchens's mind, it would appear, if a woman chooses to have sex, she can't choose whether or not to have a baby. The implications of this are clear. If a woman is consciously and volitionally sexual, she should be prepared to take her medicine. And what medicine must the consciously sexual male take? Does Hitchens really believe, or want us to believe, that every male who has unintentionally impregnated a woman will be involved in the lifelong responsibility for the upbringing of the engendered child? Can he honestly say that he has observed this behavior—or, indeed, would want to see it observed—in the world in which he lives?

REAL CHOICES

20   It is essential for a moral decision about abortion to be made in an atmosphere of open, critical thinking. We on the pro-choice side must accept that there are indeed anti-choice activists who take their position in good faith. I believe, however, that they are people for whom childbirth is an emotionally overladen topic, people who are susceptible to unclear thinking because of their unrealistic hopes and fears. It is important for us in the pro-choice movement to be open in discussing those areas involving abortion which are nebulous and unclear. But we must not forget that there are some things that we know to be undeniably true. There are some undeniable bad consequences of a woman's being forced to bear a child against her will. First is the trauma of going through a pregnancy and giving birth to a child who is not desired, a trauma more long-lasting than that experienced by some (only some) women who experience an early abortion: The grief of giving up a child at its birth—and at nine months it is a child whom one has felt move inside one's body—is underestimated both by anti-choice partisans and by those for whom access to adoptable children is important. This grief should not be forced on any woman—or, indeed, encouraged by public policy.

We must be realistic about the impact on society of millions of unwanted children in an overpopulated world. Most of the time, human beings have sex not because they want to make babies. Yet throughout history sex has resulted in unwanted pregnancies. And women have always aborted. One thing that is not hidden, mysterious, or debatable is that making abortion illegal will result in the deaths of women, as it has always done. Is our historical memory so short that none of us remember aunts, sisters, friends, or mothers who were killed or rendered sterile by septic abortions?[2] Does no one in the anti-choice movement remember stories or actual experiences of midnight drives to filthy rooms from which aborted women were sent out, bleeding, to their fate? Can anyone genuinely say that it would be a moral good for us as a society to return to those conditions?

---

2. Leading to bacterial infection.

Thinking about abortion, then, forces us to take moral positions as adults who understand the complexities of the world and the realities of human suffering, to make decisions based on how people actually live and choose, and not on our fears, prejudices, and anxieties about sex and society, life and death.

QUESTIONS

1. How would you characterize Gordon's tone throughout the essay, keeping in mind that she is dealing with a hotly debated topic?

2. Gordon takes on only some of the arguments against abortion. Why do you think she leaves many arguments out?

3. Make an outline of Gordon's arguments. Which strikes you as the most important? Why?

4. Write an essay in which you compare Gordon's position on abortion with that of Sallie Tisdale in the next essay, "We Do Abortions Here: A Nurse's Story."

SALLIE TISDALE   *We Do Abortions Here: A Nurse's Story*

WE DO ABORTIONS here; that is all we do. There are weary, grim moments when I think I cannot bear another basin of bloody remains, utter another kind phrase of reassurance. So I leave the procedure room in the back and reach for a new chart. Soon I am talking to an eighteen-year-old woman pregnant for the fourth time. I push up her sleeve to check her blood pressure and find row upon row of needle marks, neat and parallel and discolored. She has been so hungry for her drug for so long that she has taken to using the loose skin of her upper arms; her elbows are already a permanent ruin of bruises. She is surprised to find herself nearly four months pregnant. I suspect she is often surprised, in a mild way, by the blows she is dealt. I prepare myself for another basin, another brief and chafing loss.

"How can you stand it?" Even the clients ask. They see the machine, the strange instruments, the blood, the final stroke that wipes away the promise of pregnancy. Sometimes I see that too: I watch a woman's swollen abdomen sink to softness in a few stuttering moments and my own belly flip-flops with sorrow. But all it takes for me to catch my breath is another interview, one more

From Harper's Magazine *(October 1990), a monthly that includes fiction, essays, reviews, and commentary on American politics and culture.*

story that sounds so much like the last one. There is a numbing sameness lurking in this job: the same questions, the same answers, even the same trembling tone in the voices. The worst is the sameness of human failure, of inadequacy in the face of each day's dull demands.

In describing this work, I find it difficult to explain how much I enjoy it most of the time. We laugh a lot here, as friends and as professional peers. It's nice to be with women all day. I like the sudden, transient bonds I forge with some clients: moments when I am in my strength, remembering weakness, and a woman in weakness reaches out for my strength. What I offer is not power, but solidness, offered almost eagerly. Certain clients waken in me every tender urge I have—others make me wince and bite my tongue. Both challenge me to find a balance. It is a sweet brutality we practice here, a stark and loving dispassion.

I look at abortion as if I am standing on a cliff with a telescope, gazing at some great vista. I can sweep the horizon with both eyes, survey the scene in all its distance and size. Or I can put my eye to the lens and focus on the small details, suddenly so close. In abortion the absolute must always be tempered by the contextual, because both are real, both valid, both hard. How can we do this? How can we refuse? Each abortion is a measure of our failure to protect, to nourish our own. Each basin I empty is a promise—but a promise broken a long time ago.

5   I grew up on the great promise of birth control. Like many women my age, I took the pill as soon as I was sexually active. To risk pregnancy when it was so easy to avoid seemed stupid, and my contraceptive success, as it were, was part of the promise of social enlightenment. But birth control fails, far more frequently than laboratory trials predict. Many of our clients take the pill; its failure to protect them is a shocking realization. We have clients who have been sterilized, whose husbands have had vasectomies; each one is a statistical misfit, fine print come to life. The anger and shame of these women I hold in one hand, and the basin in the other. The distance between the two, the length I pace and try to measure, is the size of an abortion.

The procedure is disarmingly simple. Women are surprised, as though the mystery of conception, a dark and hidden genesis, requires an elaborate finale. In the first trimester of pregnancy, it's a mere few minutes of vacuuming, a neat tidying up. I give a woman a small yellow Valium, and when it has begun to relax her, I lead her into the back, into bareness, the stirrups. The doctor reaches in her, opening the narrow tunnel to the uterus with a succession of slim, smooth bars of steel. He inserts a plastic tube and hooks it to a hose on the machine. The woman is framed against white paper that crackles as she moves, the light bright in her eyes. Then the machine rumbles low and loud in the small windowless room; the doctor moves the tube back and forth with an efficient rhythm, and the long tail of it fills with blood that spurts and stumbles along into a jar. He is usually finished in a few minutes. They are long minutes for the woman; her uterus frequently reacts to its abrupt emptying with a powerful, unceasing cramp, which cuts off the blood vessels and enfolds the irritated, bleeding tissue.

I am learning to recognize the shadows that cross the faces of the women I hold. While the doctor works between her spread legs, the paper drape hiding his intent expression, I stand beside the table. I hold the woman's hands in mine, resting them just below her ribs. I watch her eyes, finger her necklace, stroke her hair. I ask about her job, her family; in a haze she answers me; we chatter, faces close, eyes meeting and sliding apart.

I watch the shadows that creep up unnoticed and suddenly darken her face as she screws up her features and pushes a tear out each side to slide down her cheeks. I have learned to anticipate the quiver of chin, the rapid intake of breath and the surprising sobs that rise soon after the machine starts to drum. I know this is when the cramp deepens, and the tears are partly the tears that follow pain—the sharp, childish crying when one bumps one's head on a cabinet door. But a well of woe seems to open beneath many women when they hear that thumping sound. The anticipation of the moment has finally come to fruit; the moment has arrived when the loss is no longer an imagined one. It has come true.

I am struck by the sameness and I am struck every day by the variety here—how this commonplace dilemma can so display the differences of women. A twenty-one-year-old woman, unemployed, uneducated, without family, in the fifth month of her fifth pregnancy. A forty-two-year-old mother of teenagers, shocked by her condition, refusing to tell her husband. A twenty-three-year-old mother of two having her seventh abortion, and many women in their thirties having their first. Some are stoic, some hysterical, a few giggle uncontrollably, many cry.

I talk to a sixteen-year-old uneducated girl who was raped. She has gonorrhea. She describes blinding headaches, attacks of breathlessness, nausea. "Sometimes I feel like two different people," she tells me with a calm smile, "and I talk to myself."   10

I pull out my plastic models. She listens patiently for a time, and then holds her hands wide in front of her stomach.

"When's the baby going to go up into my stomach?" she asks.

I blink. "What do you mean?"

"Well," she says, still smiling, "when women get so big, isn't the baby in your stomach? Doesn't it hatch out of an egg there?"

My first question in an interview is always the same. As I walk down the hall with the woman, as we get settled in chairs and I glance through her files, I am trying to gauge her, to get a sense of the words, and the tone, I should use. With some I joke, with others I chat, sometimes I fall into a brisk, business-like patter. But I ask every woman, "Are you sure you want to have an abortion?" Most nod with grim knowing smiles. "Oh, yes," they sigh. Some seek forgiveness, offer excuses. Occasionally a woman will flinch and say, "Please don't use that word."   15

Later I describe the procedure to come, using care with my language. I don't say "pain" any more than I would say "baby." So many are afraid to ask how much it will hurt. "My sister told me—" I hear. "A friend of mine said—" and the dire expectations unravel. I prick the index finger of a woman for a drop of blood to test, and as the tiny lancet approaches the skin she averts her eyes, holding her trembling hand out to me and jumping at my touch.

It is when I am holding a plastic uterus in one hand, a suction tube in the other, moving them together in imitation of the scrubbing to come, that women ask the most secret question. I am speaking in a matter-of-fact voice about "the tissue" and "the contents" when the woman suddenly catches my eye and asks, "How big is the baby now?" These words suggest a quiet need for a definition of the boundaries being drawn. It isn't so odd, after all, that she feels relief when I describe the growing bud's bulbous shape, its miniature nature. Again I gauge, and sometimes lie a little, weaseling around its infantile features until its clinging power slackens.

But when I look in the basin, among the curdlike blood clots, I see an elfin thorax, attenuated, its pencilline ribs all in parallel rows with tiny knobs of spine rounding upwards. A translucent arm and hand swim beside.

A sleepy-eyed girl, just fourteen, watched me with a slight and goofy smile all through her abortion. "Does it have little feet and little fingers and all?" she'd asked earlier. When the suction was over she sat up woozily at the end of the table and murmured, "Can I see it?" I shook my head firmly.

20   "It's not allowed," I told her sternly, because I knew she didn't really want to see what was left. She accepted this statement of authority, and a shadow of confused relief crossed her plain, pale face.

Privately, even grudgingly, my colleagues might admit the power of abortion to provoke emotion. But they seem to prefer the broad view and disdain the telescope. Abortion is a matter of choice, privacy, control. Its uncertainty lies in specific cases: retarded women and girls too young to give consent for surgery, women who are ill or hostile or psychotic. Such common dilemmas are met with both compassion and impatience: they slow things down. We are too busy to chew over ethics. One person might discuss certain concerns, behind closed doors, or describe a particularly disturbing dream. But generally there is to be no ambivalence.

Every day I take calls from women who are annoyed that we cannot see them, cannot do their abortion today, this morning, now. They argue the price, demand that we stay after hours to accommodate their job or class schedule. Abortion is so routine that one expects it to be like a manicure: quick, cheap, and painless.

Still, I've cultivated a certain disregard. It isn't negligence, but I don't always pay attention. I couldn't be here if I tried to judge each case on its merits; after all, we do over a hundred abortions a week. At some point each individual in this line of work draws a boundary and adheres to it. For one physician the boundary is a particular week of gestation; for another, it is a certain number of repeated abortions. But these boundaries can be fluid too: one physician overruled his own limit to abort a mature but severely malformed fetus. For me, the limit is allowing my clients to carry their own burden, shoulder the responsibility themselves. I shoulder the burden of trying not to judge them.

This city has several "crisis pregnancy centers" advertised in the Yellow Pages. They are small offices staffed by volunteers, and they offer free pregnancy testing, glossy photos of dead fetuses, and movies. I had a client recently whose mother is active in the anti-abortion movement. The young woman went to the local crisis center and was told that the doctor would make her touch her dismembered baby, that the pain would be the most horrible she could imagine, and that she might, after an abortion, never be able to have children. All lies. They called her at home and at work, over and over and over, but she had been wise enough to give a false name. She came to us a fugitive. We who do abortions are marked, by some, as impure. It's dirty work.

When a deliveryman comes to the sliding glass window by the reception   25
desk and tilts a box toward me, I hesitate. I read the packing slip, assess the shape and weight of the box in light of its supposed contents. We request familiar faces. The doors are carefully locked; I have learned to half glance around at bags and boxes, looking for a telltale sign. I register with security when I arrive, and I am careful not to bang a door. We are all a little on edge here.

Concern about size and shape seem to be natural, and so is the relief that follows. We make the powerful assumption that the fetus is different from us, and even when we admit the similarities, it is too simplistic to be seduced by form alone. But the form is enormously potent—humanoid, powerless, palm-sized, and pure, it evokes an almost fierce tenderness when viewed simply as what it appears to be. But appearance, and even potential, aren't enough. The fetus, in becoming itself, can ruin others; its utter dependence has a sinister side. When I am struck in the moment by the contents in the basin, I am careful to remember the context, to note the tearful teenager and the woman sighing with something more than relief. One kind of question, though, I find considerably trickier.

"Can you tell what it is?" I am asked, and this means gender. This question is asked by couples, not women alone. Always couples would abort a girl and keep a boy. I have been asked about twins, and even if I could tell what race the father was.

An eighteen-year-old woman with three daughters brought her husband to the interview. He glared first at me, then at his wife, as he sank lower and lower in the chair, picking his teeth with a toothpick. He interrupted a conversation with his wife to ask if I could tell whether the baby would be a boy or a girl. I told him I could not.

"Good," he replied in a slow and strangely malevolent voice, " 'cause if it was a boy I'd wring her neck."

In a literal sense, abortion exists because we are able to ask such questions,   30
able to assign a value to the fetus which can shift with changing circumstances. If the human bond to a child were as primitive and unflinchingly narrow as that of other animals, there would be no abortion. There would be no abortion because there would be nothing more important than caring for the young and perpetuating the species, no reason for sex but to make babies. I sense this sometimes, this wordless organic duty, when I do ultrasounds.

We do ultrasound, a sound-wave test that paints a faint, gray picture of the fetus, whenever we're uncertain of gestation. Age is measured by the width of the skull and confirmed by the length of the femur or thighbone; we speak of a pregnancy as being a certain "femur length" in weeks. The usual concern is whether a pregnancy is within the legal limit for an abortion. Women this far along have bellies which swell out round and tight like trim muscles. When they lie flat, the mound rises softly above the hips, pressing the umbilicus upward.

It takes practice to read an ultrasound picture, which is grainy and etched as though in strokes of charcoal. But suddenly a rapid rhythmic motion appears—the beating heart. Nearby is a soft oval, scratched with lines—the skull. The leg is harder to find, and then suddenly the fetus moves, bobbing in the surf. The skull turns away, an arm slides across the screen, the torso rolls. I know the weight of a baby's head on my shoulder, the whisper of lips on ears, the delicate curve of a fragile spine in my hand. I know how heavy and correct a newborn cradled feels. The creature I watch in secret requires nothing from me but to be left alone, and that is precisely what won't be done.

These inadvertently made beings are caught in a twisting web of motive and desire. They are at least inconvenient, sometimes quite literally dangerous in the womb, but most often they fall somewhere in between—consequences never quite believed in come to roost. Their virtue rises and falls outside their own nature: they become only what we make them. A fetus created by accident is the most absolute kind of surprise. Whether the blame lies in a failed IUD, a slipped condom, or a false impression of safety, that fetus is a thing whose creation has been actively worked against. Its existence is an error. I think this is why so few women, even late in a pregnancy, will consider giving a baby up for adoption. To do so means making the fetus real—imagining it as something whole and outside oneself. The decision to terminate a pregnancy is sometimes so difficult and confounding that it creates an enormous demand for immediate action. The decision is a rejection; the pregnancy has become something to be rid of, a condition to be ended. It is a burden, a weight, a thing separate.

Women have abortions because they are too old, and too young, too poor, and too rich, too stupid, and too smart. I see women who berate themselves with violent emotions for their first and only abortion, and others who return three times, five times, hauling two or three children, who cannot remember to take a pill or where they put the diaphragm. We talk glibly about choice. But the choice for what? I see all the broken promises in lives lived like a series of impromptu obstacles. There are the sweet, light promises of love and intimacy, the glittering promise of education and progress, the warm promise of safe families, long years of innocence and community. And there is the promise of freedom: freedom from failure, from faithlessness. Freedom from biology. The early feminist defense of abortion asked many questions, but the one I remember is this: Is biology destiny? And the answer is yes, sometimes it is. Women who have the fewest choices of all exercise their right to abortion the most.

35   Oh, the ignorance. I take a woman to the back room and ask her to undress; a few minutes later I return and find her positioned discreetly behind a

drape, still wearing underpants. "Do I have to take these off too?" she asks, a little shocked. Some swear they have not had sex, many do not know what a uterus is, how sperm and egg meet, how sex makes babies. Some late seekers do not believe themselves pregnant; they believe themselves *impregnable*. I was chastised when I began this job for referring to some clients as girls: it is a feminist heresy. They come so young, snapping gum, sockless and sneakered, and their shakily applied eyeliner smears when they cry. I call them girls with maternal benignity. I cannot imagine them as mothers.

The doctor seats himself between the woman's thighs and reaches into the di-lated opening of a five-month pregnant uterus. Quickly he grabs and crushes the fetus in several places, and the room is filled with a low clatter and snap of forceps, the click of the tanaculum, and a pulling, sucking sound. The paper crinkles as the drugged and sleepy woman shifts, the nurse's low, honey-brown voice explains each step in delicate words.

I have fetus dreams, we all do here: dreams of abortions one after the other; of buckets of blood splashed on the walls; trees full of crawling fetuses. I dreamed that two men grabbed me and began to drag me away. "Let's do an abortion," they said with a sickening leer, and I began to scream, plunged into a vision of sucking, scraping pain, of being spread and torn by impartial instru-ments that do only what they are bidden. I woke from this dream barely able to breathe and thought of kitchen tables and coat hangers, knitting needles striped with blood, and women all alone clutching a pillow in their teeth to keep the screams from piercing the apartment-house walls. Abortion is the narrowest edge between kindness and cruelty. Done as well as it can be, it is still violence—merciful violence, like putting a suffering animal to death.

Maggie, one of the nurses, received a call at midnight not long ago. It was a woman in her twentieth week of pregnancy; the necessarily gradual process of cervical dilation begun the day before had stimulated labor, as it sometimes does. Maggie and one of the doctors met the woman at the office in the night. Maggie helped her onto the table, and as she lay down the fetus was delivered into Maggie's hands. When Maggie told me about it the next day, she cupped her hands into a small bowl—"It was just like a little kitten," she said softly, wonderingly. "Everything was still attached."

At the end of the day I clean out the suction jars, pouring blood into the sink, splashing the sides with flecks of tissue. From the sink rises a rich and humid smell, hot, earthy, and moldering; it is the smell of something recently alive beginning to decay. I take care of the plastic tub on the floor, filled with pieces too big to be trusted to the trash. The law defines the contents of the bucket I hold protectively against my chest as "tissue." Some would say my complicity in filling that bucket gives me no right to call it anything else. I slip the tissue gently into a bag and place it in the freezer, to be burned at another time. Abortion requires of me an entirely new set of assumptions. It requires a willingness to live with conflict, fearlessness, and grief. As I close the freezer door, I imagine a world where this won't be necessary, and then return to the world where it is.

QUESTIONS

1. Tisdale speaks of taking both broad views—"as if I am standing on a cliff with a telescope"—and narrow views—"I can put my eye to the lens and focus on the small details" (paragraph 4). Choose one section of this essay (such as the second, third, or fourth) and mark the passages you would describe as taking broad views and the passages you would describe as taking narrow views. What is the effect of Tisdale's going back and forth between them? How does she manage transitions?

2. "We are too busy to chew over ethics" (paragraph 21), Tisdale observes. What does she mean by ethics? Does she engage with what you consider ethical issues in this essay? Explain.

3. Although Tisdale takes a pro-choice position, a pro-lifer could use parts of her essay against her. What parts? What are the advantages and disadvantages of including material that could be used in support of the opposition?

4. Write a pro-choice or pro-life essay of your own. Include material that could be used in support of the opposition. You may use Tisdale's essay (with proper credit), but you need not.

STEPHEN JAY GOULD *The Terrifying Normalcy of AIDS*

DISNEY'S EPCOT CENTER in Orlando, Fla., is a technological tour de force and a conceptual desert. In this permanent World's Fair, American industrial giants have built their versions of an unblemished future. These masterful entertainments convey but one message, brilliantly packaged and relentlessly expressed: progress through technology is the solution to all human problems. G.E. proclaims from Horizons: "If we can dream it, we can do it." A.T.&T. speaks from on high within its giant golf ball: We are now "unbounded by space and time." United Technologies bubbles from the depths of Living Seas: "With the help of modern technology, we feel there's really no limit to what can be accomplished."

Yet several of these exhibits at the Experimental Prototype Community of Tomorrow, all predating last year's space disaster, belie their stated message from within by using the launch of the shuttle as a visual metaphor for technological triumph. The Challenger disaster[1] may represent a general malaise, but it remains an incident. The AIDS pandemic, an issue that may

From the New York Times Magazine (*April 19, 1987), a weekly supplement to the Sunday edition that includes regular columns and original articles on contemporary issues.*

1. In January 1986, when the space shuttle *Challenger* exploded after launching, seven astronauts were killed.

rank with nuclear weaponry as the greatest danger of our era, provides a more striking proof that mind and technology are not omnipotent and that we have not canceled our bond to nature.

In 1984, John Platt, a biophysicist who taught at the University of Chicago for many years, wrote a short paper for private circulation. At a time when most of us were either ignoring AIDS, or viewing it as a contained and peculiar affliction of homosexual men, Platt recognized that the limited data on the origin of AIDS and its spread in America suggested a more frightening prospect: we are all susceptible to AIDS, and the disease has been spreading in a simple exponential manner.

Exponential growth is a geometric increase. Remember the old kiddy problem: if you place a penny on square one of a checkerboard and double the number of coins on each subsequent square—2, 4, 8, 16, 32 . . . —how big is the stack by the 64th square? The answer: about as high as the universe is wide. Nothing in the external environment inhibits this increase, thus giving to exponential processes their relentless character. In the real, noninfinite world, of course, some limit will eventually arise, and the process slows down, reaches a steady state, or destroys the entire system: the stack of pennies falls over, the bacterial cells exhaust their supply of nutrients.

Platt noticed that data for the initial spread of AIDS fell right on an expo-   5
nential curve. He then followed the simplest possible procedure of extrapolating the curve unabated into the 1990's. Most of us were incredulous, accusing Platt of the mathematical gamesmanship that scientists call "curve fitting." After all, aren't exponential models unrealistic? Surely we are not all susceptible to AIDS. Is it not spread only by odd practices to odd people? Will it not, therefore, quickly run its short course within a confined group?

Well, hello 1987—worldwide data still match Platt's extrapolated curve. This will not, of course, go on forever. AIDS has probably already saturated the African areas where it probably originated, and where the sex ratio of afflicted people is 1-to-1, male-female. But AIDS still has far to spread, and may be moving exponentially, through the rest of the world. We have learned enough about the cause of AIDS to slow its spread, if we can make rapid and fundamental changes in our handling of that most powerful part of human biology—our own sexuality. But medicine, as yet, has nothing to offer as a cure and precious little even for palliation.

This exponential spread of AIDS not only illuminates its, and our, biology, but also underscores the tragedy of our moralistic misperception. Exponential processes have a definite time and place of origin, an initial point of "inoculation"—in this case, Africa. We didn't notice the spread at first. In a population of billions, we pay little attention when 1 increases to 2, or 8 to 16, but when 1 million becomes 2 million, we panic, even though the *rate* of doubling has not increased.

The infection has to start somewhere, and its initial locus may be little more than an accident of circumstance. For a while, it remains confined to those in close contact with the primary source, but only by accident of proximity, not by intrinsic susceptibility. Eventually, given the power and lability of human sexuality, it spreads outside the initial group and into the general population. And now AIDS has begun its march through our own heterosexual community.

What a tragedy that our moral stupidity caused us to lose precious time, the greatest enemy in fighting an exponential spread, by downplaying the danger because we thought that AIDS was a disease of three irregular groups of minorities: minorities of life style (needle users), of sexual preference (homosexuals) and of color (Haitians). If AIDS had first been imported from Africa into a Park Avenue apartment, we would not have dithered as the exponential march began.

10   The message of Orlando—the inevitability of technological solutions—is wrong, and we need to understand why.

Our species has not won its independence from nature, and we cannot do all that we can dream. Or at least we cannot do it at the rate required to avoid tragedy, for we are not unbounded from time. Viral diseases are preventable in principle, and I suspect that an AIDS vaccine will one day be produced. But how will this discovery avail us if it takes until the millennium, and by then AIDS has fully run its exponential course and saturated our population, killing a substantial percentage of the human race? A fight against an exponential enemy is primarily a race against time.

We must also grasp the perspective of ecology and evolutionary biology and recognize, once we reinsert ourselves properly into nature, that AIDS represents the ordinary workings of biology, not an irrational or diabolical plague with a moral meaning. Disease, including epidemic spread, is a natural phenomenon, part of human history from the beginning. An entire subdiscipline of my profession, paleopathology, studies the evidence of ancient diseases preserved in the fossil remains of organisms. Human history has been marked by episodic plagues. More native peoples died of imported disease than ever fell before the gun during the era of colonial expansion. Our memories are short, and we have had a respite, really, only since the influenza pandemic at the end of World War I, but AIDS must be viewed as a virulent expression of an ordinary natural phenomenon.

I do not say this to foster either comfort or complacency. The evolutionary perspective is correct, but utterly inappropriate for our human scale. Yes, AIDS is a natural phenomenon, one of a recurring class of pandemic diseases. Yes, AIDS may run through the entire population, and may carry off a quarter or more of us. Yes, it may make no *biological* difference to Homo sapiens in the long run: there will still be plenty of us left and we can start again. Evolution cares as little for its agents—organisms struggling for reproductive success—as physics cares for individual atoms of hydrogen in the sun. But *we* care. These atoms are our neighbors, our lovers, our children and ourselves. AIDS is both a natural phenomenon and, potentially, the greatest natural tragedy in human history.

The cardboard message of Epcot fosters the wrong attitudes; we must both reinsert ourselves into nature and view AIDS as a natural phenomenon in order to fight properly. If we stand above nature and if technology is all-powerful, then AIDS is a horrifying anomaly that must be trying to tell us something. If so, we can adopt one of two attitudes, each potentially fatal. We can either become complacent, because we believe the message of Epcot and assume that medicine will soon generate a cure, or we can panic in confusion and seek a scapegoat for something so irregular that it must have been visited upon us to teach us a moral lesson.   15

But AIDS is not irregular. It is part of nature. So are we. This should galvanize us and give us hope, not prompt the worst of all responses: a kind of "new-age" negativism that equates natural with what we must accept and cannot, or even should not, change. When we view AIDS as natural, and when we recognize both the exponential property of its spread and the accidental character of its point of entry into America, we can break through our destructive tendencies to blame others and to free ourselves of concern.

If AIDS is natural, then there is no *message* in its spread. But by all that science has learned and all that rationality proclaims, AIDS works by a *mechanism*—and we can discover it. Victory is not ordained by any principle of progress, or any slogan of technology, so we shall have to fight like hell, and be watchful. There is no message, but there is a mechanism.

QUESTIONS

1. Gould uses current events, historical information, and scientific data to make his case. Identify examples of each.

2. What case does Gould make?

3. Why is this essay in the section called "Ethics" rather than in the section called "Science and Technology"?

4. Gould uses Disney's Epcot Center in Orlando, Florida, as a symbol of our belief in technology. Find another symbol of this belief and, in a brief essay, describe and interpret it.

The Shatterer of Worlds

BEFORE THAT MORNING in 1945 only a few conventional bombs, none of which did any great damage, had fallen on the city. Fleets of U.S. bombers had, however, devastated many cities round about, and Hiroshima had begun a program of evacuation which had reduced its population from 380,000 to some 245,000. Among the evacuees were Emiko and her family.

"We were moved out to Otake, a town about an hour's train-ride out of the city," Emiko told me. She had been a fifteen-year-old student in 1945. Fragile and vivacious, versed in the gentle traditions of the tea ceremony and flower arrangement, Emiko still had an air of the frail school-child when I talked with her. Every day, she and her sister Hideko used to commute into Hiroshima to school. Hideko was thirteen. Their father was an antique-dealer and he owned a house in the city, although it was empty now. Tetsuro, Emiko's thirteen-year-old brother, was at the Manchurian front with the Imperial Army. Her mother was kept busy looking after the children, for her youngest daughter Eiko was sick with heart trouble, and rations were scarce. All of them were undernourished.

The night of August 5, 1945, little Eiko was dangerously ill. She was not expected to live. Everybody took turns watching by her bed, soothing her by massaging her arms and legs. Emiko retired at 8:30 (most Japanese people go to bed early) and at midnight was roused to take her turn with the sick girl. At 2 A.M. she went back to sleep.

While Emiko slept, the *Enola Gay*, a U.S. B-29 carrying the world's first operational atom bomb, was already in the air. She had taken off from the Pacific island of Iwo Jima at 1:45 A.M., and now Captain William Parsons, U.S.N. ordnance expert, was busy in her bomb-hold with the final assembly of Little Boy. Little Boy looked much like an outsize T.N.T. block-buster but the crew knew there was something different about him. Only Parsons and the pilot, Colonel Paul Tibbets, knew exactly in what manner Little Boy was different. Course was set for Hiroshima.

5   Emiko slept.

On board the *Enola Gay* co-pilot Captain Robert Lewis was writing up his personal log. "After leaving Iwo," he recorded, "we began to pick up some low stratus and before very long we were flying on top of an under-cast. Outside of a thin, high cirrus and the low stuff, it's a very beautiful day."

Emiko and Hideko were up at six in the morning. They dressed in the uniform of their women's college—white blouse, quilted hat, and black skirt—breakfasted and packed their aluminum lunch-boxes with white rice and eggs. These they stuffed into their shoulder bags as they hurried for the seven-o'-clock train to Hiroshima. Today there would be no classes. Along with many women's groups, high school students, and others, the sisters were going to

From Dobbs's 1968 book Reading the Time, *a collection of autobiographical, travel, and literary essays.*

work on demolition. The city had begun a project of clearance to make fire-breaks in its downtown huddle of wood and paper buildings.

It was a lovely morning.

While the two young girls were at breakfast, Captain Lewis, over the Pacific, had made an entry in his log. "We are loaded. The bomb is now alive, and it's a funny feeling knowing it's right in back of you. Knock wood!"

In the train Hideko suddenly said she was hungry. She wanted to eat her lunch. Emiko dissuaded her: she'd be much hungrier later on. The two sisters argued, but Hideko at last agreed to keep her lunch till later. They decided to meet at the main station that afternoon and catch the five-o'clock train home. By now they had arrived at the first of Hiroshima's three stations. This was where Hideko got off, for she was to work in a different area from her sister. "Sayonara!" she called. "Goodbye." Emiko never saw her again.

There had been an air-raid at 7 A.M., but before Emiko arrived at Hiroshima's main station, two stops farther on, the sirens had sounded the all-clear. Just after eight, Emiko stepped off the train, walked through the station, and waited in the morning sunshine for her streetcar.

At about the same moment Lewis was writing in his log. "There'll be a short intermission while we bomb our target."

It was hot in the sun, Emiko saw a class-mate and greeted her. Together they moved back into the shade of a high concrete wall to chat. Emiko looked up at the sky and saw, far up in the cloudless blue, a single B-29.

It was exactly 8:10 A.M. The other people waiting for the streetcar saw it too and began to discuss it anxiously. Emiko felt scared. She felt that at all costs she must go on talking to her friend. Just as she was thinking this, there was a tremendous greenish-white flash in the sky. It was far brighter than the sun. Emiko afterwards remembered vaguely that there was a roaring or a rushing sound as well, but she was not sure, for just at that moment she lost consciousness.

"About 15 seconds after the flash," noted Lewis, 30,000 feet high and several miles away, "there were two very distinct slaps on the ship from the blast and the shock wave. That was all the physical effect we felt. We turned the ship so that we could observe the results."

When Emiko came to, she was lying on her face about forty feet away from where she had been standing. She was not aware of any pain. Her first thought was: "I'm alive!" She lifted her head slowly and looked about her.

It was growing dark. The air was seething with dust and black smoke. There was a smell of burning. Emiko felt something trickle into her eyes, tested it in her mouth. Gingerly she put a hand to her head, then looked at it. She saw with a shock that it was covered with blood.

She did not give a thought to Hideko. It did not occur to her that her sister who was in another part of the city could possibly have been in danger. Like most of the survivors, Emiko assumed she had been close to a direct hit by a conventional bomb. She thought it had fallen on the post-office next to the station. With a hurt child's panic, Emiko, streaming with blood from gashes in her scalp, ran blindly in search of her mother and father.

10

15

The people standing in front of the station had been burned to death instantly (a shadow had saved Emiko from the flash). The people inside the station had been crushed by falling masonry. Emiko heard their faint cries, saw hands scrabbling weakly from under the collapsed platform. All around her the maimed survivors were running and stumbling away from the roaring furnace that had been a city. She ran with them toward the mountains that ring the landward side of Hiroshima.

20   From the *Enola Gay,* the strangers from North America looked down at their handiwork. "There, in front of our eyes," wrote Lewis, "was without a doubt the greatest explosion man had ever witnessed. The city was nine-tenths covered with smoke of a boiling nature, which seemed to indicate buildings blowing up, and a large white cloud which in less than three minutes reached 30,000 feet, then went to at least 50,000 feet."

Far below, on the edge of this cauldron of smoke, at a distance of some 2,500 yards from the blast's epicenter, Emiko ran with the rest of the living. Some who could not run limped or dragged themselves along. Others were carried. Many, hideously burned, were screaming with pain; when they tripped they lay where they had fallen. There was a man whose face had been ripped open from mouth to ear, another whose forehead was a gaping wound. A young soldier was running with a foot-long splinter of bamboo protruding from one eye. But these, like Emiko, were the lightly wounded.

Some of the burned people had been literally roasted. Skin hung from their flesh like sodden tissue paper. They did not bleed but plasma dripped from their seared limbs.

The *Enola Gay,* mission completed, was returning to base. Lewis sought words to express his feelings, the feelings of all the crew. "I might say," he wrote, "I might say `My God! What have we done?' "

Emiko ran. When she had reached the safety of the mountain she remembered that she still had her shoulder bag. There was a small first-aid kit in it and she applied ointment to her wounds and to a small cut in her left hand. She bandaged her head.

25   Emiko looked back at the city. It was a lake of fire. All around her the burned fugitives cried out in pain. Some were scorched on one side only. Others, naked and flayed, were burned all over. They were too many to help and most of them were dying. Emiko followed the walking wounded along a back road, still delirious, expecting suddenly to meet her father and mother.

The thousands dying by the roadside called feebly for help or water. Some of the more lightly injured were already walking in the other direction, back towards the flames. Others, with hardly any visible wounds, stopped, turned ashy pale, and died within minutes. No one knew then that they were victims of radiation.

Emiko reached the suburb of Nakayama.

Far off in the *Enola Gay,* Lewis, who had seen none of this, had been writing, "If I live a hundred years, I'll never get those few minutes out of my mind. Looking at Captain Parsons, why he is as confounded as the rest, and he is supposed to have known everything and expected this to happen. . . ."

At Nakayama, Emiko stood in line at a depot where rice-balls were being distributed. Though it distressed her that the badly maimed could hardly feed themselves, the child found she was hungry. It was about 6 P.M. now. A little farther on, at Gion, a farmer called her by name. She did not recognize him, but it seemed he came monthly to her home to collect manure. The farmer took Emiko by the hand, led her to his own house, where his wife bathed her and fed her a meal of white rice. Then the child continued on her way. She passed another town where there were hundreds of injured. The dead were being hauled away in trucks. Among the injured a woman of about forty-five was waving frantically and muttering to herself. Emiko brought this woman a little water in a pumpkin leaf. She felt guilty about it; the schoolgirls had been warned not to give water to the seriously wounded. Emiko comforted herself with the thought that the woman would die soon anyway.

At Koi, she found standing-room in a train. It was heading for Otake with 30 a full load of wounded. Many were put off at Ono, where there was a hospital; and two hours later the train rolled into Otake station. It was around 10 P.M.

A great crowd had gathered to look for their relations. It was a nightmare, Emiko remembered years afterwards; people were calling their dear kinfolk by name, searching frantically. It was necessary to call them by name, since most were so disfigured as to be unrecognizable. Doctors in the town council offices stitched Emiko's head-wounds. The place was crowded with casualties lying on the floor. Many died as Emiko watched.

The town council authorities made a strange announcement. They said a new and mysterious kind of bomb had fallen in Hiroshima. People were advised to stay away from the ruins.

Home at midnight, Emiko found her parents so happy to see her that they could not even cry. They could only give thanks that she was safe. Then they asked, "Where is your sister?"

For ten long days, while Emiko walked daily one and a half miles to have her wounds dressed with fresh gauze, her father searched the rubble of Hiroshima for his lost child. He could not have hoped to find her alive. All, as far as the eye could see, was a desolation of charred ashes and wreckage, relieved only by a few jagged ruins and by the seven estuarial rivers that flowed through the waste delta. The banks of these rivers were covered with the dead and in the rising tidal waters floated thousands of corpses. On one broad street in the Hakushima district the crowds who had been thronging there were all naked and scorched cadavers. Of thousands of others there was no trace at all. A fire several times hotter than the surface of the sun had turned them instantly to vapor.

On August 11 came the news that Nagasaki had suffered the same fate as 35 Hiroshima; it was whispered that Japan had attacked the United States mainland with similar mysterious weapons. With the lavish circumstantiality of rumor, it was said that two out of a fleet of six-engined trans-Pacific bombers had failed to return. But on August 15, speaking for the first time over the radio to his people, the Emperor Hirohito announced his country's surrender. Emiko heard him. No more bombs! she thought. No more fear! The family did not learn till June the following year that this very day young Tetsuro had been killed in action in Manchuria.

Emiko's wounds healed slowly. In mid-September they had closed with a thin layer of pinkish skin. There had been a shortage of antiseptics and Emiko was happy to be getting well. Her satisfaction was short-lived. Mysteriously she came down with diarrhea and high fever. The fever continued for a month. Then one day she started to bleed from the gums, her mouth and throat became acutely inflamed, and her hair started to fall out. Through her delirium the child heard the doctors whisper by her pillow that she could not live. By now the doctors must have known that ionizing radiation caused such destruction of the blood's white cells that victims were left with little or no resistance against infection.

Yet Emiko recovered.

The wound on her hand, however, was particularly troublesome and did not heal for a long time.

As she got better, Emiko began to acquire some notion of the fearful scale of the disaster. Few of her friends and acquaintances were still alive. But no one knew precisely how many had died in Hiroshima. To this day the claims of various agencies conflict.

40
    According to General Douglas MacArthur's headquarters, there were 78,150 dead and 13,083 missing.[1] The United States Atomic Bomb Casualty Commission claims there were 79,000 dead. Both sets of figures are probably far too low. There's reason to believe that at the time of the surrender Japanese authorities lied about the number of survivors, exaggerating it to get extra medical supplies. The Japanese welfare ministry's figures of 260,000 dead and 163,263 missing may well be too high. But the very order of such discrepancies speaks volumes about the scale of the catastrophe. The dead were literally uncountable.

This appalling toll of human life had been exacted from a city that had been prepared for air attack in a state of full wartime readiness. All civil-defense services had been overwhelmed from the first moment and it was many hours before any sort of organized rescue and relief could be put into effect.

It's true that single raids using so-called conventional weapons on other cities such as Tokyo and Dresden inflicted far greater casualties. And that it could not matter much to a victim whether he was burnt alive by a fire-storm caused by phosphorus, or by napalm or by nuclear fission. Yet in the whole of human history so savage a massacre had never before been inflicted with a single blow. And modern thermonuclear weapons are upwards of 1,000 times more powerful and deadly than the Hiroshima bomb.

The white scar I saw on Emiko's small, fine-boned hand was a tiny metaphor, a faint but eloquent reminder of the scar on humanity's conscience.

---

1. MacArthur (1880–1964), American army officer, Allied Supreme Commander in the Southwest Pacific (1942) and of occupied Japan following World War II (1945–1951).

QUESTIONS

1. Dobbs moves between one narrative, Emiko's story, and another, the bombing mission of the *Enola Gay*; in film this technique is called cross-cutting. What effect does this cross-cutting have on you as you read this essay?

2. Consider the differences between the visible accumulation of information in Paul Fussell's "Thank God for the Atom Bomb" (below), which acknowledges sources (e.g., paragraphs 25–26), and Dobbs's you-are-there reconstruction, mostly without sources. What effect does each have on you as a reader? What are the advantages and disadvantages of each technique?

3. Dobbs waits until the final paragraph to make explicit the moral judgments that have been implicit throughout his essay. Write an essay of your own in which the narrative speaks for itself, without your intervention or interpretations, until the very end.

PAUL FUSSELL   *Thank God for the Atom Bomb*

MANY YEARS AGO in New York I saw on the side of a bus a whiskey ad I've remembered all this time. It's been for me a model of the short poem, and indeed I've come upon few short poems subsequently that exhibited more poetic talent. The ad consisted of two eleven-syllable lines of "verse," thus:

In life, experience is the great teacher.
In Scotch, Teacher's is the great experience.

For present purposes we must jettison the second line (licking our lips, to be sure, as it disappears), leaving the first to register a principle whose banality suggests that it enshrines a most useful truth. I bring up the matter because, writing on the forty-second anniversary of the atom-bombing of Hiroshima and Nagasaki, I want to consider something suggested by the long debate about the ethics, if any, of that ghastly affair. Namely, the importance of experience, sheer, vulgar experience, in influencing, if not determining, one's views about that use of the atom bomb.

The experience I'm talking about is having to come to grips, face to face, with an enemy who designs your death. The experience is common to those in the marines and the infantry and even the line navy, to those, in short, who fought the Second World War mindful always that their mission was, as they were repeatedly assured, "to close with the enemy and destroy him." *Destroy*, notice: not hurt, frighten, drive away, or capture. I think there's something to be learned about that war, as well as about the tendency of historical memory

Originally published as an article in the New Republic *(August 22, 1981); later included in Fussell's* Thank God for the Atom Bomb, and Other Essays *(1988).*

unwittingly to resolve ambiguity and generally clean up the premises, by considering the way testimonies emanating from real war experience tend to complicate attitudes about the most cruel ending of that most cruel war.

"What did you do in the Great War, Daddy?" The recruiting poster deserves ridicule and contempt, of course, but here its question is embarrassingly relevant, and the problem is one that touches on the dirty little secret of social class in America. Arthur T. Hadley said recently that those for whom the use of the A-bomb was "wrong" seem to be implying "that it would have been better to allow thousands on thousands of American and Japanese infantrymen to die in honest hand-to-hand combat on the beaches than to drop those two bombs." People holding such views, he notes, "do not come from the ranks of society that produce infantrymen or pilots." And there's an eloquence problem: most of those with firsthand experience of the war at its worst were not elaborately educated people. Relatively inarticulate, most have remained silent about what they know. That is, few of those destined to be blown to pieces if the main Japanese islands had been invaded went on to become our most effective men of letters or impressive ethical theorists or professors of contemporary history or of international law. The testimony of experience has tended to come from rough diamonds—James Jones[1] is an example—who went through the war as enlisted men in the infantry or the Marine Corps.

Anticipating objections from those without such experience, in his book *WWII* Jones carefully prepares for his chapter on the A-bombs by detailing the plans already in motion for the infantry assaults on the home islands of Kyushu (thirteen divisions scheduled to land in November 1945) and ultimately Honshu (sixteen divisions scheduled for March 1946). Planners of the invasion assumed that it would require a full year, to November 1946, for the Japanese to be sufficiently worn down by land-combat attrition to surrender. By that time, one million American casualties was the expected price. Jones observes that the forthcoming invasion of Kyushu "was well into its collecting and stockpiling stages before the war ended." (The island of Saipan was designated a main ammunition and supply base for the invasion, and if you go there today you can see some of the assembled stuff still sitting there.) "The assault troops were chosen and already in training," Jones reminds his readers, and he illuminates by the light of experience what this meant:

> What it must have been like to some old-timer buck sergeant or staff sergeant who had been through Guadalcanal or Bougainville or the Philippines, to stand on some beach and watch this huge war machine beginning to stir and move all around him and know that he very likely had survived this far only to fall dead on the dirt of Japan's home islands, hardly bears thinking about.

5   Another bright enlisted man, this one an experienced marine destined for the assault on Honshu, adds his testimony. Former Pfc. E. B. Sledge, author

1. American novelist (1921–1977), author of *From Here to Eternity* (1951), the first volume in a trilogy about World War II.

of the splendid memoir *With the Old Breed at Peleliu and Okinawa*, noticed at the time that the fighting grew "more vicious the closer we got to Japan," with the carnage of Iwo Jima and Okinawa worse than what had gone before. He points out that

> what we had *experienced* [my emphasis] in fighting the Japs (pardon the expression) on Peleliu and Okinawa caused us to formulate some very definite opinions that the invasion . . . would be a ghastly bloodletting. . . . It would shock the American public and the world. [Every Japanese] soldier, civilian, woman, and child would fight to the death with whatever weapons they had, rifle, grenade, or bamboo spear.

The Japanese pre-invasion patriotic song, "One Hundred Million Souls for the Emperor," says Sledge, "meant just that." Universal national kamikaze was the point. One kamikaze pilot, discouraged by his unit's failure to impede the Americans very much despite the bizarre casualties it caused, wrote before diving his plane onto an American ship, "I see the war situation becoming more desperate. All Japanese must become soldiers and die for the Emperor." Sledge's First Marine Division was to land close to the Yokosuka Naval Base, "one of the most heavily defended sectors of the island." The marines were told, he recalls, that

> due to the strong beach defenses, caves, tunnels, and numerous Jap suicide torpedo boats and manned mines, few Marines in the first five assault waves would get ashore alive—my company was scheduled to be in the first and second waves. The veterans in the outfit felt we had already run out of luck anyway. . . . We viewed the invasion with complete resignation that we would be killed—either on the beach or inland.

And the invasion was going to take place: there's no question about that. It was not theoretical or merely rumored in order to scare the Japanese. By July 10, 1945, the prelanding naval and aerial bombardment of the coast had begun, and the battleships *Iowa, Missouri, Wisconsin*, and *King George V* were steaming up and down the coast, softening it up with their sixteen-inch shells.

On the other hand, John Kenneth Galbraith[2] is persuaded that the Japanese would have surrendered surely by November without an invasion. He thinks the A-bombs were unnecessary and unjustified because the war was ending anyway. The A-bombs meant, he says, "a difference, at most, of two or three weeks." But at the time, with no indication that surrender was on the way, the kamikazes were sinking American vessels, the *Indianapolis* was sunk (880 men killed), and Allied casualties were running to over 7,000 per week. "Two or three weeks," says Galbraith. Two weeks more means 14,000 more killed and wounded, three weeks more, 21,000. Those weeks mean the world if you're one of those thousands or related to one of them. During the time be-

---

2. American economist and professor of economics at Harvard University (1908–2006). During World War II he was in charge of wartime price control, and after the war he went to Japan with other economists to study the economic and social conditions.

tween the dropping of the Nagasaki bomb on August 9 and the actual surrender on the fifteenth, the war pursued its accustomed course: on the twelfth of August eight captured American fliers were executed (heads chopped off); the fifty-first United States submarine, *Bonefish*, was sunk (all aboard drowned); the destroyer *Callaghan* went down, the seventieth to be sunk, and the Destroyer Escort *Underhill* was lost. That's a bit of what happened in six days of the two or three weeks posited by Galbraith. What did he do in the war? He worked in the Office of Price Administration in Washington. I don't demand that he experience having his ass shot off. I merely note that he didn't.

Likewise, the historian Michael Sherry, author of a recent book on the rise of the American bombing mystique, *The Creation of Armageddon*, argues that we didn't delay long enough between the test explosion in New Mexico and the mortal explosions in Japan. More delay would have made possible deeper moral considerations and perhaps laudable second thoughts and restraint. "The risks of delaying the bomb's use," he says, "would have been small—not the thousands of casualties expected of invasion but only a few days or weeks of relatively routine operations." While the mass murders represented by these "relatively routine operations" were enacting, Michael Sherry was safe at home. Indeed, when the bombs were dropped he was going on eight months old, in danger only of falling out of his pram. In speaking thus of Galbraith and Sherry, I'm aware of the offensive implications *ad hominem*.[3] But what's at stake in an infantry assault is so entirely unthinkable to those without the experience of one, or several, or many, even if they possess very wide-ranging imaginations and warm sympathies, that experience is crucial in this case.

10   In general, the principle is, the farther from the scene of horror, the easier the talk. One young combat naval officer close to the action wrote home in the fall of 1943, just before the marines underwent the agony of Tarawa: "When I read that we will fight the Japs for years if necessary and will sacrifice hundreds of thousands if we must, I always like to check from where he's talking: it's seldom out here." That was Lieutenant (j.g.) John F. Kennedy. And Winston Churchill, with an irony perhaps too broad and easy, noted in Parliament that the people who preferred invasion to A-bombing seemed to have "no intention of proceeding to the Japanese front themselves."

A remoteness from experience like Galbraith's and Sherry's, and a similar rationalistic abstraction from actuality, seem to motivate the reaction of an anonymous reviewer of William Manchester's *Goodbye Darkness: A Memoir of the Pacific War* for *The New York Review of Books*. The reviewer naturally dislikes Manchester's still terming the enemy Nips or Japs, but what really shakes him (her?) is this passage of Manchester's:

> After Biak the enemy withdrew to deep caverns. Rooting them out became a bloody business which reached its ultimate horrors in the last months of the war. You think of the lives which would have been lost in an invasion of Japan's home islands—a staggering number of Americans but millions more of Japanese—and you thank God for the atomic bomb.

---

3. Marked by an attack on an opponent's character; literally, to the man (Latin).

Thank God for the atom bomb. From this, "one recoils," says the reviewer. One does, doesn't one?

And not just a staggering number of Americans would have been killed in the invasion. Thousands of British assault troops would have been destroyed too, the anticipated casualties from the almost 200,000 men in the six divisions (the same number used to invade Normandy) assigned to invade the Malay Peninsula on September 9. Aimed at the reconquest of Singapore, this operation was expected to last until about March 1946—that is, seven more months of infantry fighting. "But for the atomic bombs," a British observer intimate with the Japanese defenses notes, "I don't think we would have stood a cat in hell's chance. We would have been murdered in the biggest massacre of the war. They would have annihilated the lot of us."

The Dutchman Laurens van der Post had been a prisoner of the Japanese for three and a half years. He and thousands of his fellows, enfeebled by beriberi and pellagra, were being systematically starved to death, the Japanese rationalizing this treatment not just because the prisoners were white men but because they had allowed themselves to be captured at all and were therefore moral garbage. In the summer of 1945 Field Marshal Terauchi issued a significant order: at the moment the Allies invaded the main islands, all prisoners were to be killed by the prison-camp commanders. But thank God that did not happen. When the A-bombs were dropped, van der Post recalls, "This cataclysm I was certain would make the Japanese feel that they could withdraw from the war without dishonor, because it would strike them, as it had us in the silence of our prison night, as something supernatural."

In an exchange of views not long ago in *The New York Review of Books*, Joseph Alsop and David Joravsky set forth the by now familiar argument on both sides of the debate about the "ethics" of the bomb. It's not hard to guess which side each chose once you know that Alsop experienced capture by the Japanese at Hong Kong early in 1942, while Joravsky came into no deadly contact with the Japanese: a young, combat-innocent soldier, he was on his way to the Pacific when the war ended. The editors of *The New York Review* gave the debate the tendentious title "Was the Hiroshima Bomb Necessary?" surely an unanswerable question (unlike "Was It Effective?") and one precisely indicating the intellectual difficulties involved in imposing *ex post facto*[4] a rational and even a genteel ethics on this event. In arguing the acceptability of the bomb, Alsop focuses on the power and fanaticism of War Minister Anami, who insisted that Japan fight to the bitter end, defending the main islands with the same techniques and tenacity employed at Iwo and Okinawa. Alsop concludes: "Japanese surrender could never have been obtained, at any rate without the honor-satisfying bloodbath envisioned by . . . Anami, if the hideous destruction of Hiroshima and Nagasaki had not finally galvanized the peace advocates into tearing up the entire Japanese book of rules." The Japanese plan to deploy the undefeated bulk of their ground forces, over two million men, plus 10,000 kamikaze planes, plus the elderly and all the women and children with sharp-

_____

4. After the fact (Latin).

ened spears they could muster in a suicidal defense makes it absurd, says Alsop, to "hold the common view, by now hardly challenged by anyone, that the decision to drop the two bombs on Japan was wicked in itself, and that President Truman and all others who joined in making or who [like Robert Oppenheimer][5] assented to this decision shared in the wickedness." And in explanation of "the two bombs," Alsop adds: "The true, climactic, and successful effort of the Japanese peace advocates . . . did not begin in deadly earnest until *after* the second bomb had destroyed Nagasaki. The Nagasaki bomb was thus the trigger to all the developments that led to peace." At this time the army was so unready for surrender that most looked forward to the forthcoming invasion as an indispensable opportunity to show their mettle, enthusiastically agreeing with the army spokesman who reasoned early in 1945, "Since the retreat from Guadalcanal, the Army has had little opportunity to engage the enemy in land battles. But when we meet in Japan proper, our Army will demonstrate its invincible superiority." This possibility foreclosed by the Emperor's post-A-bomb surrender broadcast, the shocked, disappointed officers of one infantry battalion, anticipating a professionally impressive defense of the beaches, killed themselves in the following numbers: one major, three captains, ten first lieutenants, and twelve second lieutenants.

15   David Joravsky, now a professor of history at Northwestern, argued on the other hand that those who decided to use the A-bombs on cities betray defects of "reason and self-restraint." It all needn't have happened, he says, "if the U.S. government had been willing to take a few more days and to be a bit more thoughtful in opening up the age of nuclear warfare." I've already noted what "a few more days" would mean to the luckless troops and sailors on the spot, and as to being thoughtful when "opening up the age of nuclear warfare," of course no one was focusing on anything as portentous as that, which reflects a historian's tidy hind-sight. The U.S. government was engaged not in that sort of momentous thing but in ending the war conclusively, as well as irrationally Remembering Pearl Harbor with a vengeance. It didn't know then what everyone knows now about leukemia and various kinds of carcinoma and birth defects. Truman was not being sly or coy when he insisted that the bomb was "only another weapon." History, as Eliot's "Gerontion" notes,

> . . . has many cunning passages, contrived corridors
> And issues, deceives with whispering ambitions,
> Guides us by vanities. . . .
>   Think

5. J. Robert Oppenheimer (1904–1967), American physicist and organizer of the research station at Los Alamos, New Mexico, that developed the atomic bomb, and after World War II, chair of the U.S. Atomic Energy Commission. As chair of the AEC, he opposed developing even more powerful hydrogen bombs but conceded when President Truman approved the legislation to do so.

> Neither fear nor courage saves us.
>   Unnatural vices
> Are fathered by our heroism. Virtues
> Are forced upon us by our impudent crimes.

Understanding the past requires pretending that you don't know the present. It requires feeling its own pressure on your pulses without any *ex post facto* illumination. That's a harder thing to do than Joravsky seems to think.

The Alsop-Joravsky debate, reduced to a collision between experience and theory, was conducted with a certain civilized respect for evidence. Not so the way the scurrilous, agitprop *New Statesman* conceives those justifying the dropping of the bomb and those opposing. They are, on the one hand, says Bruce Page, "the imperialist class-forces acting through Harry Truman" and, on the other, those representing "the humane, democratic virtues"—in short, "fascists" as opposed to "populists." But ironically the bomb saved the lives not of any imperialists but only of the low and humble, the quintessentially democratic huddled masses—the conscripted enlisted men manning the fated invasion divisions and the sailors crouching at their gun-mounts in terror of the Kamikazes. When the war ended, Bruce Page was nine years old. For someone of his experience, phrases like "imperialist class forces" come easily, and the issues look perfectly clear.

He's not the only one to have forgotten, if he ever knew, the unspeakable savagery of the Pacific war. The dramatic postwar Japanese success at hustling and merchandising and tourism has (happily, in many ways) effaced for most people the vicious assault context in which the Hiroshima horror should be viewed. It is easy to forget, or not to know, what Japan was like before it was first destroyed, and then humiliated, tamed, and constitutionalized by the West. "Implacable, treacherous, barbaric"—those were Admiral Halsey's characterizations of the enemy, and at the time few facing the Japanese would deny that they fit to a T. One remembers the captured American airmen—the lucky ones who escaped decapitation—locked for years in packing crates. One remembers the gleeful use of bayonets on civilians, on nurses and the wounded, in Hong Kong and Singapore. Anyone who actually fought in the Pacific recalls the Japanese routinely firing on medics, killing the wounded (torturing them first, if possible), and cutting off the penises of the dead to stick in the corpses' mouths. The degree to which Americans register shock and extraordinary shame about the Hiroshima bomb correlates closely with lack of information about the Pacific war.

And of course the brutality was not just on one side. There was much sadism and cruelty, undeniably racist, on ours. (It's worth noting in passing how few hopes blacks could entertain of desegregation and decent treatment when the U.S. Army itself slandered the enemy as "the little brown Jap.") Marines and soldiers could augment their view of their own invincibility by possessing a well-washed Japanese skull, and very soon after Guadalcanal it was common to treat surrendering Japanese as handy rifle targets. Plenty of Japanese gold teeth were extracted—some from still living mouths—with Ma-

rine Corps Ka-Bar Knives,[6] and one of E. B. Sledge's fellow marines went
around with a cut-off Japanese hand. When its smell grew too offensive and
Sledge urged him to get rid of it, he defended his possession of this trophy
thus: "How many Marines you reckon that hand pulled the trigger on?" (It's
hardly necessary to observe that a soldier in the ETO would probably not have
dealt that way with a German or Italian—that is, a "white person's"—hand.) In
the Pacific the situation grew so public and scandalous that in September
1942, the Commander in Chief of the Pacific Fleet issued this order: "No part
of the enemy's body may be used as a souvenir. Unit Commanders will take
stern disciplinary action. . . ."

Among Americans it was widely held that the Japanese were really subhu-
man, little yellow beasts, and popular imagery depicted them as lice, rats, bats,
vipers, dogs, and monkeys. What was required, said the Marine Corps journal
The Leatherneck in May 1945, was "a gigantic task of extermination." The
Japanese constituted a "pestilence," and the only appropriate treatment was
"annihilation." Some of the marines landing on Iwo Jima had "Rodent Exterminator" written on their helmet covers, and on one American flagship the
naval commander had erected a large sign enjoining all to "KILL JAPS! KILL
JAPS! KILL MORE JAPS!" Herman Wouk remembers the Pacific war scene
correctly while analyzing Ensign Keith in *The Caine Mutiny*: "Like most of the
naval executioners of Kwajalein, he seemed to regard the enemy as a species of
animal pest." And the feeling was entirely reciprocal: "From the grim and desperate taciturnity with which the Japanese died, they seemed on their side to
believe that they were contending with an invasion of large armed ants." Hiroshima seems to follow in natural sequence: "This obliviousness of both sides
to the fact that the opponents were human beings may perhaps be cited as the
key to the many massacres of the Pacific war." Since the Jap vermin resist so
madly and have killed so many of us, let's pour gasoline into their bunkers and
light it and then shoot those afire who try to get out. Why not? Why not blow
them all up, with satchel charges or with something stronger? Why not, indeed, drop a new kind of bomb on them, and on the un-uniformed ones too,
since the Japanese government has announced that women from ages of seventeen to forty are being called up to repel the invasion? The intelligence officer of the U.S. Fifth Air Force declared on July 21, 1945, that "the entire
population of Japan is a proper military target," and he added emphatically,
"There are no civilians in Japan." Why delay and allow one more American
high school kid to see his own intestines blown out of his body and spread before him in the dirt while he screams and screams when with the new bomb
we can end the whole thing just like that?

20   On Okinawa, only weeks before Hiroshima, 123,000 Japanese and Americans *killed* each other. (About 140,000 Japanese died at Hiroshima.) "Just
awful" was the comment on the Okinawa slaughter not of some pacifist but of
General MacArthur. On July 14, 1945, General Marshall sadly informed the

---

6. High-carbon steel knives carried by Marines (officers and gunners) who did not
carry bayonet-bearing rifles.

Combined Chiefs of Staff—he was not trying to scare the Japanese—that it's "now clear . . . that in order to finish with the Japanese quickly, it will be necessary to invade the industrial heart of Japan." The invasion was definitely on, as I know because I was to be in it.

When the atom bomb ended the war, I was in the Forty-fifth Infantry Division, which had been through the European war so thoroughly that it had needed to be reconstituted two or three times. We were in a staging area near Rheims, ready to be shipped back across the United States for refresher training at Fort Lewis, Washington, and then sent on for final preparation in the Philippines. My division, like most of the ones transferred from Europe, was to take part in the invasion of Honshu. (The earlier landing on Kyushu was to be carried out by the 700,000 infantry already in the Pacific, those with whom James Jones has sympathized.) I was a twenty-one-year-old second lieutenant of infantry leading a rifle platoon. Although still officially fit for combat, in the German war I had already been wounded in the back and the leg badly enough to be adjudged, after the war, 40 percent disabled. But even if my leg buckled and I fell to the ground whenever I jumped out of the back of a truck, and even if the very idea of more combat made me breathe in gasps and shake all over, my condition was held to be adequate for the next act. When the atom bombs were dropped and news began to circulate that "Operation Olympic" would not, after all, be necessary, when we learned to our astonishment that we would not be obliged in a few months to rush up the beaches near Tokyo assault-firing while being machine-gunned, mortared, and shelled, for all the practiced phlegm of our tough façades we broke down and cried with relief and joy. We were going to live. We were going to grow to adulthood after all. The killing was all going to be over, and peace was actually going to be the state of things. When the *Enola Gay* dropped its package, "There were cheers," says John Toland, "over the intercom; it meant the end of the war." Down on the ground the reaction of Sledge's marine buddies when they heard the news was more solemn and complicated. They heard about the end of the war

> with quiet disbelief coupled with an indescribable sense of relief. We thought the Japanese would never surrender. Many refused to believe it. . . . Sitting in stunned silence, we remembered our dead. So many dead. So many maimed. So many bright futures consigned to the ashes of the past. So many dreams lost in the madness that had engulfed us. Except for a few widely scattered shouts of joy, the survivors of the abyss sat hollow-eyed and silent, trying to comprehend a world without war.

These troops who cried and cheered with relief or who sat stunned by the weight of their experience are very different from the high-minded, guilt-ridden GIs we're told about by J. Glenn Gray in his sensitive book *The Warriors*. During the war in Europe Gray was an interrogator in the Army Counterintelligence Corps, and in that capacity he experienced the war at Division level. There's no denying that Gray's outlook on everything was admirably noble, elevated, and responsible. After the war he became a much-admired professor of philosophy at Colorado College and an esteemed editor of Heidegger.[7] But *The Warriors*, his meditation on the moral and psychological dimensions of modern soldiering, gives every sign of error occasioned by remoteness from experience. Division headquarters is miles—*miles*—behind the line where soldiers experience terror and madness and relieve those pressures by crazy brutality and sadism. Indeed, unless they actually encountered the enemy during the war, most "soldiers" have very little idea what "combat" was like. As William Manchester says, "All who wore uniforms are called veterans, but more than 90 percent of them are as uninformed about the killing zones as those on the home front." Manchester's fellow marine E. B. Sledge thoughtfully and responsibly invokes the terms *drastically* and *totally* to underline the differences in experience between front and rear, and not even the far rear, but the close rear. "Our code of conduct toward the enemy," he notes, "differed drastically from that prevailing back at the division CP." (He's describing gold-tooth extraction from still-living Japanese.) Again he writes: "We existed in an environment totally incomprehensible to men behind the lines . . . ," even, he would insist, to men as intelligent and sensitive as Glenn Gray, who missed seeing with his own eyes Sledge's marine friends sliding under fire down a shell-pocked ridge slimy with mud and liquid dysentery shit into the maggoty Japanese and USMC corpses at the bottom, vomiting as the maggots burrowed into their own foul clothing. "We didn't talk about such things," says Sledge. "They were too horrible and obscene even for hardened veterans. . . . Nor do authors normally write about such vileness; unless they have seen it with their own eyes, it is too preposterous to think that men could actually live and fight for days and nights on end under such terrible conditions and not be driven insane." And Sledge has added a comment on such experience and the insulation provided by even a short distance: "Often people just behind our rifle companies couldn't understand what we knew." Glenn Gray was not in a rifle company, or even just behind one. "When the news of the atomic bombing of Hiroshima and Nagasaki came," he asks us to believe, "many an American soldier felt shocked and ashamed." Shocked, OK, but why ashamed? Because we'd destroyed civilians? We'd been doing that for years, in raids on Hamburg and Berlin and Cologne and Frankfurt and Mannheim and Dresden, and Tokyo, and besides, the two A-bombs wiped out 10,000 Japanese troops, not often thought of now, John Hersey's[8] kindly physicians and Jesuit priests being more touching. If around division headquarters some of the people Gray talked to felt ashamed, down in the rifle companies no one did, despite Gray's assertions. "The combat soldier," he says,

> knew better than did Americans at home what those bombs meant in suffering and injustice. The man of conscience realized intuitively that the vast majority of Japanese in both cities were no more, if no less, guilty of the war than were his own parents, sisters, or brothers.

7. Martin Heidegger (1889–1976), German existentialist philosopher.

8. American fiction and nonfiction writer (1914–1993), author of *Hiroshima* (1946), a moving account of the devastation and human suffering caused by the atomic bomb.

I find this canting nonsense. The purpose of the bombs was not to "punish" people but to stop the war. To intensify the shame Gray insists we feel, he seems willing to fiddle the facts. The Hiroshima bomb, he says, was dropped "without any warning." But actually, two days before, 720,000 leaflets were dropped on the city urging everyone to get out and indicating that the place was going to be (as the Potsdam Declaration[9] had promised) obliterated. Of course few left.

Experience whispers that the pity is not that we used the bomb to end the Japanese war but that it wasn't ready in time to end the German one. If only it could have been rushed into production faster and dropped at the right moment on the Reich Chancellery or Berchtesgaden or Hitler's military headquarters in East Prussia (where Colonel Stauffenberg's July 20 bomb didn't do the job because it wasn't big enough), much of the Nazi hierarchy could have been pulverized immediately, saving not just the embarrassment of the Nuremberg trials but the lives of around four million Jews, Poles, Slavs, and gypsies, not to mention the lives and limbs of millions of Allied and German soldiers. If the bomb had only been ready in time, the young men of my infantry platoon would not have been so cruelly killed and wounded.

All this is not to deny that like the Russian Revolution, the atom-bombing of Japan was a vast historical tragedy, and every passing year magnifies the dilemma into which it has lodged the contemporary world. As with the Russian Revolution, there are two sides—that's why it's a tragedy instead of a disaster—and unless we are, like Bruce Page, simple-mindedly unimaginative and cruel, we will be painfully aware of both sides at once. To observe that from the viewpoint of the war's victims-to-be the bomb seemed precisely the right thing to drop is to purchase no immunity from horror. To experience both sides, one might study the book *Unforgettable Fire: Pictures Drawn by Atomic Bomb Survivors,* which presents a number of amateur drawings and watercolors of the Hiroshima scene made by middle-aged and elderly survivors for a peace exhibition in 1975. In addition to the almost unbearable pictures, the book offers brief moments of memoir not for the weak-stomached:

> While taking my severely wounded wife out to the river bank . . . , I was horrified indeed at the sight of a stark naked man standing in the rain with his eyeball in his palm. He looked to be in great pain but there was nothing that I could do for him. I wonder what became of him. Even today, I vividly remember the sight. I was simply miserable.

These childlike drawings and paintings are of skin hanging down, breasts torn off, people bleeding and burning, dying mothers nursing dead babies. A bloody woman holds a bloody child in the ruins of a house, and the artist remembers her calling, "Please help this child! Someone, please help this child.

9. An agreement signed on July 26, 1945, by the president of the United States and the prime minister of Great Britain, with the concurrence of Generalissimo Chiang Kaishek of Nationalist China, that mandated Japanese surrender, offering them a choice between unconditional surrender and total destruction, and that set forth the principles under which the defeated Axis territories would be governed and rebuilt.

Please help! Someone, please." As Samuel Johnson said of the smothering of
Desdemona, the innocent in another tragedy, "It is not to be endured." Nor, it
should be noticed, is an infantryman's account of having his arm blown off in
the Arno Valley in Italy in 1944:

> I wanted to die and die fast. I wanted to forget this miserable world. I
> cursed the war, I cursed the people who were responsible for it, I cursed
> God for putting me here . . . to suffer for something I never did or knew
> anything about.

(A good place to interrupt and remember Glenn Gray's noble but hopelessly one-sided remarks about "injustice," as well as "suffering.")

"For this was hell," the soldier goes on,

> and I never imagined anything or anyone could suffer so bitterly. I
> screamed and cursed. Why? What had I done to deserve this? But no an-
> swer came. I yelled for medics, because subconsciously I wanted to live. I
> tried to apply my right hand over my bleeding stump, but I didn't have the
> strength to hold it. I looked to the left of me and saw the bloody mess that
> was once my left arm; its fingers and palm were turned upward, like a
> flower looking to the sun for its strength.

The future scholar-critic who writes *The History of Canting in the Twentieth Century* will find much to study and interpret in the utterances of those
who dilate on the special wickedness of the A-bomb-droppers. He will realize
that such utterance can perform for the speaker a valuable double function.
First, it can display the fineness of his moral weave. And second, by implication it can also inform the audience that during the war he was not socially so
unfortunate as to find himself down there with the ground forces, where he
might have had to compromise the purity and clarity of his moral system by
the experience of weighing his own life against someone else's. Down there,
which is where the other people were, is the place where coarse self-interest is
the rule. When the young soldier with the wild eyes comes at you, firing, do
you shoot him in the foot, hoping he'll be hurt badly enough to drop or mis-
aim the gun with which he's going to kill you, or do you shoot him in the chest
(or, if you're a prime shot, in the head) and make certain that you and not he
will be the survivor of that mortal moment?

30   It would be not just stupid but would betray a lamentable want of human
experience to expect soldiers to be very sensitive humanitarians. The Glenn
Grays of this world need to have their attention directed to the testimony of
those who know, like, say, Admiral of the Fleet Lord Fisher, who said, "Moder-
ation in war is imbecility," or Sir Arthur Harris, director of the admittedly
wicked aerial-bombing campaign designed, as Churchill put it, to "dehouse"
the German civilian population, who observed that "War is immoral," or our
own General W. T. Sherman: "War is cruelty, and you cannot refine it." Lord
Louis Mountbatten, trying to say something sensible about the dropping of the
A-bomb, came up only with "War is crazy." Or rather, it requires choices
among crazinesses. "It would seem even more crazy," he went on, "if we were
to have more casualties on our side to save the Japanese." One of the unpleasant facts for anyone in the ground armies during the war was that you had to
become pro tem[10] a subordinate of the very uncivilian George S. Patton[11] and

respond somehow to his unremitting insistence that you embrace his view of things. But in one of his effusions he was right, and his observation tends to suggest the experimental dubiousness of the concept of "just wars." "War is not a contest with gloves," he perceived. "It is resorted to only when laws, which are rules, have failed." Soldiers being like that, only the barest decencies should be expected of them. They did not start the war, except in the terrible sense hinted at in Frederic Manning's observation based on his front-line experience in the Great War: "War is waged by men; not by beasts, or by gods. It is a peculiarly human activity. To call it a crime against mankind is to miss at least half its significance; it is also the punishment of a crime." Knowing that unflattering truth by experience, soldiers have every motive for wanting a war stopped, by any means.

The stupidity, parochialism, and greed in the international mismanagement of the whole nuclear challenge should not tempt us to misimagine the circumstances of the bomb's first "use." Nor should our well-justified fears and suspicions occasioned by the capture of the nuclear-power trade by the inept and the mendacious (who have fucked up the works at Three Mile Island, Chernobyl, etc.)[12] tempt us to infer retrospectively extraordinary corruption, imbecility, or motiveless malignity in those who decided, all things considered, to drop the bomb. Times change. Harry Truman * * * knew war, and he knew better than some of his critics then and now what he was doing and why he was doing it. "Having found the bomb," he said, "we have used it. . . . We have used it to shorten the agony of young Americans."

The past, which as always did not know the future, acted in ways that ask to be imagined before they are condemned. Or even simplified.

10. Short for *pro tempore*: temporarily; literally, for the time being (Latin).

11. American general who served in North Africa and Sicily in World War II before becoming commander of the Third Army, which drove the Nazis from France and back into Germany (1885–1945).

12. Two disasters at nuclear power plants: the first, near Harrisburg, Pennsylvania, occurred in the spring of 1979; the second, in the Soviet Union, occurred in the spring of 1986.

QUESTIONS

1. Note the places where Fussell includes personal experience in this essay. How much is his own, how much belongs to others? Why does he include both kinds?

2. Fussell dismisses with contempt those who disagree with him. Locate some examples. How do you respond to them? Would you use Fussell's strategies to dismiss those who disagree with you? Explain.

3. Mark some instances of Fussell's "voice." What kind of voice does he adopt? What kind of person does he present himself as?

4. Write a similarly argumentative essay in which you take a strong position. Include your own experience and the experience of others if appropriate.

HISTORY

<hr>

HENRY DAVID THOREAU *The Battle of the Ants*

O NE DAY WHEN I went out to my wood-pile, or rather my pile of stumps, I observed two large ants, the one red, the other much larger, nearly half an inch long, and black, fiercely contending with one another. Having once got hold they never let go, but struggled and wrestled and rolled on the chips incessantly. Looking farther, I was surprised to find that the chips were covered with such combatants, that it was not a *duellum*, but a *bellum*, a war between two races of ants, the red always pitted against the black, and frequently two red ones to one black. The legions of these Myrmidons[1] covered all the hills and vales in my wood-yard, and the ground was already strewn with the dead and dying, both red and black. It was the only battle which I have ever witnessed, the only battle-field I ever trod while the battle was raging; internecine war; the red republicans on the one hand, and the black imperialists on the other. On every side they were engaged in deadly combat, yet without any noise that I could hear, and human soldiers never fought so resolutely. I watched a couple that were fast locked in each other's embraces, in a little sunny valley amid the chips, now at noonday prepared to fight till the sun went down, or life went out. The smaller red champion had fastened himself like a vice to his adversary's front, and through all the tumblings on that field never for an instant ceased to gnaw at one of his feelers near the root, having already caused the other to go by the board; while the stronger black one dashed him from side to side, and, as I saw on looking nearer, had already divested him of several of his members. They fought with more pertinacity than bulldogs. Neither manifested the least disposition to retreat. It was evident that their battle-cry was "Conquer or die." In the meanwhile there came along a single red ant on the hillside of this valley, evidently full of excitement, who either had despatched his foe, or had not yet taken part in the battle; probably the latter, for he had lost none of his limbs; whose mother had charged him to return with his shield or upon it. Or perchance he was some Achilles, who had nourished his wrath apart, and had now come to avenge or rescue his Patroclus.[2] He saw

<hr>

From Thoreau's most famous book, Walden (1854), *an account of his life in a small cabin on Walden Pond, outside the village of Concord, Massachusetts.*

1. The reference is to the powerful soldiers of Achilles in Homer's *Iliad*.
2. In the *Iliad*, the Greek warrior and friend whose death Achilles avenges. Achilles had previously refused to fight after a falling-out with Agamemnon, the leader of the Greek army.

this unequal combat from afar—for the blacks were nearly twice the size of the red—he drew near with rapid pace till he stood on his guard within half an inch of the combatants; then, watching his opportunity, he sprang upon the black warrior, and commenced his operations near the root of his right fore leg, leaving the foe to select among his own members; and so there were three united for life, as if a new kind of attraction had been invented which put all other locks and cements to shame. I should not have wondered by this time to find that they had their respective musical bands stationed on some eminent chip, and playing their national airs the while, to excite the slow and cheer the dying combatants. I was myself excited somewhat even as if they had been men. The more you think of it, the less the difference. And certainly there is not the fight recorded in Concord history, at least, if in the history of America, that will bear a moment's comparison with this, whether for the numbers engaged in it, or for the patriotism and heroism displayed. For numbers and for carnage it was an Austerlitz or Dresden.[3] Concord Fight! Two killed on the patriots' side, and Luther Blanchard wounded! Why here every ant was a Buttrick—"Fire! for God's sake fire!"—and thousands shared the fate of Davis and Hosmer. There was not one hireling there. I have no doubt that it was a principle they fought for, as much as our ancestors, and not to avoid a three-penny tax on their tea; and the results of this battle will be as important and memorable to those whom it concerns as those of the battle of Bunker Hill, at least.

I took up the chip on which the three I have particularly described were struggling, carried into my house, and placed it under a tumbler on my window-sill, in order to see the issue. Holding a microscope to the first-mentioned red ant, I saw that, though he was assiduously gnawing at the near fore leg of his enemy, having severed his remaining feeler, his own breast was all torn away, exposing what vitals he had there to the jaws of the black warrior, whose breastplate was apparently too thick for him to pierce; and the dark carbuncles of the sufferer's eyes shone with ferocity such as war only could excite. They struggled half an hour longer under the tumbler, and when I looked again the black soldier had severed the heads of his foes from their bodies, and the still living heads were hanging on either side of him like ghastly trophies at his saddle-bow, still apparently as firmly fastened as ever, and he was endeavoring with feeble struggles, being without feelers, and with only the remnant of a leg, and I know not how many other wounds, to divest himself of them; which at length, after half an hour more, he accomplished. I raised the glass, and he went off over the window-sill in that crippled state. Whether he finally survived that combat, and spent the remainder of his days in some Hôtel des Invalides,[4] I do not know; but I thought that his industry would not be worth much thereafter. I never learned which party was victorious, nor the cause of the war, but I felt for the rest of that day as if I had my feelings excited and

3. Austerlitz and Dresden were bloody Napoleonic victories. The battles at Lexington and Concord, opening the American Revolution, took place on April 19, 1775; the names that follow are those of men who took part, and the words "Fire! for God's sake fire!" were those that, by popular account, started the war.
4. A French hospital for wounded soldiers and sailors.

harrowed by witnessing the struggle, the ferocity and carnage, of a human battle before my door.

Kirby and Spence tell us that the battles of ants have long been celebrated
and the date of them recorded, though they say that Huber[5] is the only modern author who appears to have witnessed them. "Aeneas Sylvius," say they,
"after giving a very circumstantial account of one contested with great obsti-
nacy by a great and small species on the trunk of a pear tree," adds that " 'this
action was fought in the pontificate of Eugenius the Fourth, in the presence of
Nicholas Pistoriensis, an eminent lawyer, who related the whole history of the
battle with the greatest fidelity.' A similar engagement between great and small
ants is recorded by Olaus Magnus, in which the small ones, being victorious,
are said to have buried the bodies of their own soldiers, but left those of their
giant enemies a prey to the birds. This event happened previous to the expulsion of the tyrant Christiern the Second from Sweden." The battle which I
witnessed took place in the Presidency of Polk, five years before the passage of
Webster's Fugitive-Slave Bill.[6]

5. Kirby and Spence were nineteenth-century American entomologists; François Huber
(1750–1831) was a great Swiss entomologist.
6. Passed in 1851.

QUESTIONS

1. Thoreau uses the Latin word *bellum* to describe the battle of the ants and follows it
with a reference to the Myrmidons, the soldiers of Achilles in Homer's *Iliad*. Locate additional examples of this kind of allusion. How does it work? Why does Thoreau compare the ants to Greek soldiers?

2. Ordinarily we speak of accounts of natural events as "natural history" and accounts
of human events as "history." How does Thoreau, in this selection, blur the distinction?
To what effect?

3. Look up a description of the behavior of ants in a book by one of the entomologists
Thoreau refers to or in another scientific text. Compare the scientist's style with
Thoreau's. Take another event in nature and describe it twice, once in scientific and
once in allusive language. Or write an essay in which you describe and analyze the differences between the scientist's style and Thoreau's.

BARBARA TUCHMAN *"This Is the End of the World":*
The Black Death

I N OCTOBER 1347, two months after the fall of Calais,[1] Genoese trading ships put into the harbor of Messina in Sicily with dead and dying men at the oars. The ships had come from the Black Sea port of Caffa (now Feodosiya) in the Crimea, where the Genoese maintained a trading post. The diseased sailors showed strange black swellings about the size of an egg or an apple in the armpits and groin. The swellings oozed blood and pus and were followed by spreading boils and black blotches on the skin from internal bleeding. The sick suffered severe pain and died quickly within five days of the first symptoms. As the disease spread, other symptoms of continuous fever and spitting of blood appeared instead of the swellings or buboes. These victims coughed and sweated heavily and died even more quickly, within three days or less, sometimes in 24 hours. In both types everything that issued from the body— breath, sweat, blood from the buboes and lungs, bloody urine, and blood-blackened excrement—smelled foul. Depression and despair accompanied the physical symptoms, and before the end "death is seen seated on the face."

The disease was bubonic plague, present in two forms: one that infected the bloodstream, causing the buboes and internal bleeding, and was spread by contact; and a second, more virulent pneumonic type that infected the lungs and was spread by respiratory infection. The presence of both at once caused the high mortality and speed of contagion. So lethal was the disease that cases were known of persons going to bed well and dying before they woke, of doctors catching the illness at a bedside and dying before the patient. So rapidly did it spread from one to another that to a French physician, Simon de Covino, it seemed as if one sick person "could infect the whole world." The malignity of the pestilence appeared more terrible because its victims knew no prevention and no remedy.

The physical suffering of the disease and its aspect of evil mystery were expressed in a strange Welsh lament which saw "death coming into our midst like black smoke, a plague which cuts off the young, a rootless phantom which has no mercy for fair countenance. Woe is me of the shilling in the armpit! It is seething, terrible . . . a head that gives pain and causes a loud cry . . . a painful angry knob . . . Great is its seething like a burning cinder . . . a grievous thing of ashy color." Its eruption is ugly like the "seeds of black peas, broken fragments of brittle sea-coal . . . the early ornaments of black death,

From A Distant Mirror: The Calamitous Fourteenth Century (1978), *in which Tuchman presents a vivid picture of life in medieval France and draws parallels between the disasters of that time and those in our own.*

1. After a year-long siege, the French citizens of Calais surrendered to Edward III, king of England and self-declared king of France.

The Triumph of Death. A detail from a fresco by Francesco Traini in the Camposanto, Pisa, c. 1350.

cinders of the peelings of the cockle weed, a mixed multitude, a black plague like halfpence, like berries. . . ."

Rumors of a terrible plague supposedly arising in China and spreading through Tartary (Central Asia) to India and Persia, Mesopotamia, Syria, Egypt, and all of Asia Minor had reached Europe in 1346. They told of a death toll so devastating that all of India was said to be depopulated, whole territories covered by dead bodies, other areas with no one left alive. As added up by Pope Clement VI at Avignon, the total of reported dead reached 23,840,000. In the absence of a concept of contagion, no serious alarm was felt in Europe until the trading ships brought their black burden of pestilence into Messina while other infected ships from the Levant carried it to Genoa and Venice.

By January 1348 it penetrated France via Marseille, and North Africa via Tunis. Shipborne along coasts and navigable rivers, it spread westward from Marseille through the ports of Languedoc to Spain and northward up the Rhône to Avignon, where it arrived in March. It reached Narbonne, Montpellier, Carcassonne, and Toulouse between February and May, and at the same time in Italy spread to Rome and Florence and their hinterlands. Between June and August it reached Bordeaux, Lyon, and Paris, spread to Burgundy and Normandy, and crossed the Channel from Normandy into southern England. From Italy during the same summer it crossed the Alps into Switzerland and reached eastward to Hungary.

In a given area the plague accomplished its kill within four to six months and then faded, except in the larger cities, where, rooting into the close-

Burial of the plague victim. From *Annales de Gilles li Muisis.*

quartered population, it abated during the winter, only to reappear in spring and rage for another six months.

In 1349 it resumed in Paris, spread to Picardy, Flanders, and the Low Countries, and from England to Scotland and Ireland as well as to Norway, where a ghost ship with a cargo of wool and a dead crew drifted offshore until it ran aground near Bergen. From there the plague passed into Sweden, Denmark, Prussia, Iceland, and as far as Greenland. Leaving a strange pocket of immunity in Bohemia, and Russia unattacked until 1351, it had passed from most of Europe by mid-1350. Although the mortality rate was erratic, ranging from one fifth in some places to nine tenths or almost total elimination in others, the overall estimate of modern demographers has settled—for the area extending from India to Iceland—around the same figure expressed in Froissart's casual words: "a third of the world died." His estimate, the common one at the time, was not an inspired guess but a borrowing of St. John's figure for mortality from plague in Revelation, the favorite guide to human affairs of the Middle Ages.

A third of Europe would have meant about 20 million deaths. No one knows in truth how many died. Contemporary reports were an awed impression, not an accurate count. In crowded Avignon, it was said, 400 died daily; 7,000 houses emptied by death were shut up; a single graveyard received 11,000 corpses in six weeks; half the city's inhabitants reportedly died, including 9 cardinals or one third of the total, and 70 lesser prelates. Watching the endlessly passing death carts, chroniclers let normal exaggeration take wings and put the Avignon death toll at 62,000 and even at 120,000, although the city's total population was probably less than 50,000.

When graveyards filled up, bodies at Avignon were thrown into the Rhône until mass burial pits were dug for dumping the corpses. In London in such pits corpses piled up in layers until they overflowed. Everywhere reports speak of the sick dying too fast for the living to bury. Corpses were dragged out of homes and left in front of doorways. Morning light revealed new piles of bodies. In Florence the dead were gathered up by the Compagnia della Misericordia—founded in 1244 to care for the sick—whose members wore red robes and hoods masking the face except for the eyes. When their efforts failed, the dead lay putrid in the streets for days at a time. When no coffins were to be had, the bodies were laid on boards, two or three at once, to be carried to graveyards or common pits. Families dumped their own relatives into the pits, or buried them so hastily and thinly "that dogs dragged them forth and devoured their bodies."

10   Amid accumulating death and fear of contagion, people died without last rites and were buried without prayers, a prospect that terrified the last hours of the stricken. A bishop in England gave permission to laymen to make confession to each other as was done by the Apostles, "or if no man is present then even to a woman," and if no priest could be found to administer extreme unction, "then faith must suffice." Clement VI found it necessary to grant remissions of sin to all who died of the plague because so many were unattended by priests. "And no bells tolled," wrote a chronicler of Siena, "and nobody wept no matter what his loss because almost everyone expected death. . . . And people said and believed, 'This is the end of the world.' "

In Paris, where the plague lasted through 1349, the reported death rate was 800 a day, in Pisa 500, in Vienna 500 to 600. The total dead in Paris numbered 50,000 or half the population. Florence, weakened by the famine of 1347, lost three to four fifths of its citizens, Venice two thirds, Hamburg and Bremen, though smaller in size, about the same proportion. Cities, as centers of transportation, were more likely to be affected than villages, although once a village was infected, its death rate was equally high. At Givry, a prosperous village in Burgundy of 1,200 to 1,500 people, the parish register records 615 deaths in the space of fourteen weeks, compared to an average of thirty deaths a year in the previous decade. In three villages of Cambridgeshire, manorial records show a death rate of 47 percent, 57 percent, and in one case 70 percent. When the last survivors, too few to carry on, moved away, a deserted village sank back into the wilderness and disappeared from the map altogether, leaving only a grass-covered ghostly outline to show where mortals once had lived.

In enclosed places such as monasteries and prisons, the infection of one person usually meant that of all, as happened in the Franciscan convents of Carcassonne and Marseille, where every inmate without exception died. Of the 140 Dominicans at Montpellier only seven survived. Petrarch's[2] brother Gherardo, member of a Carthusian monastery, buried the prior and 34 fellow monks one by one, sometimes three a day, until he was left alone with his dog and fled to look for a place that would take him in. Watching every comrade

---

2. Francesco Petrarch (1304–1374), Italian writer whose sonnets to "my lady Laura" influenced a tradition of European love poetry for centuries.

die, men in such places could not but wonder whether the strange peril that filled the air had not been sent to exterminate the human race. In Kilkenny, Ireland, Brother John Clyn of the Friars Minor, another monk left alone among dead men, kept a record of what had happened lest "things which should be remembered perish with time and vanish from the memory of those who come after us." Sensing "the whole world, as it were, placed within the grasp of the Evil One," and waiting for death to visit him too, he wrote, "I leave parchment to continue this work, if perchance any man survive and any of the race of Adam escape this pestilence and carry on the work which I have begun." Brother John, as noted by another hand, died of the pestilence, but he foiled oblivion.

The largest cities of Europe, with populations of about 100,000, were Paris and Florence, Venice and Genoa. At the next level, with more than 50,000, were Ghent and Bruges in Flanders, Milan, Bologna, Rome, Naples, and Palermo, and Cologne. London hovered below 50,000, the only city in England except York with more than 10,000. At the level of 20,000 to 50,000 were Bordeaux, Toulouse, Montpellier, Marseille, and Lyon in France, Barcelona, Seville, and Toledo in Spain, Siena, Pisa, and other secondary cities in Italy, and the Hanseatic trading cities of the Empire. The plague raged through them all, killing anywhere from one third to two thirds of their inhabitants. Italy, with a total population of 10 to 11 million, probably suffered the heaviest toll. Following the Florentine bankruptcies, the crop failures and workers' riots of 1346–47, the revolt of Cola di Rienzi that plunged Rome into anarchy, the plague came as the peak of successive calamities. As if the world were indeed in the grasp of the Evil One, its first appearance on the European mainland in January 1348 coincided with a fearsome earthquake that carved a path of wreckage from Naples up to Venice. Houses collapsed, church towers toppled, villages were crushed, and the destruction reached as far as Germany and Greece. Emotional response, dulled by horrors, underwent a kind of atrophy epitomized by the chronicler who wrote, "And in these days was burying without sorrowe and wedding without friendschippe."

In Siena, where more than half the inhabitants died of the plague, work was abandoned on the great cathedral, planned to be the largest in the world, and never resumed, owing to loss of workers and master masons and "the melancholy and grief" of the survivors. The cathedral's truncated transept still stands in permanent witness to the sweep of death's scythe. Agnolo di Tura, a chronicler of Siena, recorded the fear of contagion that froze every other instinct. "Father abandoned child, wife husband, one brother another," he wrote, "for this plague seemed to strike through the breath and sight. And so they died. And no one could be found to bury the dead for money or friendship. . . . And I, Agnolo di Tura, called the Fat, buried my five children with my own hands, and so did many others likewise."

There were many to echo his account of inhumanity and few to balance it, for the plague was not the kind of calamity that inspired mutual help. Its loathsomeness and deadliness did not herd people together in mutual distress, but only prompted their desire to escape each other. "Magistrates and notaries

15

refused to come and make the wills of the dying," reported a Franciscan friar of Piazza in Sicily; what was worse, "even the priests did not come to hear their confessions." A clerk of the Archbishop of Canterbury reported the same of English priests who "turned away from the care of their benefices from fear of death." Cases of parents deserting children and children their parents were reported across Europe from Scotland to Russia. The calamity chilled the hearts of men, wrote Boccaccio[3] in his famous account of the plague in Florence that serves as introduction to the *Decameron*. "One man shunned another . . . kinsfolk held aloof, brother was forsaken by brother, oftentimes husband by wife; nay, what is more, and scarcely to be believed, fathers and mothers were found to abandon their own children to their fate, untended, unvisited as if they had been strangers." Exaggeration and literary pessimism were common in the 14th century, but the Pope's physician, Guy de Chauliac, was a sober, careful observer who reported the same phenomenon: "A father did not visit his son, nor the son his father. Charity was dead."

Yet not entirely. In Paris, according to the chronicler Jean de Venette, the nuns of the Hôtel Dieu or municipal hospital, "having no fear of death, tended the sick with all sweetness and humility." New nuns repeatedly took the places of those who died, until the majority "many times renewed by death now rest in peace with Christ as we may piously believe."

When the plague entered northern France in July 1348, it settled first in Normandy and, checked by winter, gave Picardy a deceptive interim until the next summer. Either in mourning or warning, black flags were flown from church towers of the worst-stricken villages of Normandy. "And in that time," wrote a monk of the abbey of Fourcarment, "the mortality was so great among the people of Normandy that those of Picardy mocked them." The same unneighborly reaction was reported of the Scots, separated by a winter's immunity from the English. Delighted to hear of the disease that was scourging the "southrons," they gathered forces for an invasion, "laughing at their enemies." Before they could move, the savage mortality fell upon them too, scattering some in death and the rest in panic to spread the infection as they fled.

In Picardy in the summer of 1349 the pestilence penetrated the castle of Coucy to kill Enguerrand's[4] mother, Catherine, and her new husband. Whether her nine-year-old son escaped by chance or was perhaps living elsewhere with one of his guardians is unrecorded. In nearby Amiens, tannery workers, responding quickly to losses in the labor force, combined to bargain for higher wages. In another place villagers were seen dancing to drums and trumpets, and on being asked the reason, answered that, seeing their neighbors die day by day while their village remained immune, they believed they could keep the plague from entering "by the jollity that is in us. That is why we

3. Giovanni Boccaccio (1313–1375), Italian writer best known for his collection of stories, *The Decameron*, in which seven young ladies and three young men flee from Florence to escape the Black Death and tell stories to while away the time.

4. Enguerrand de Coucy, a French nobleman, is the historical figure around whom Tuchman constructs her account of the fourteenth century.

dance." Further north in Tournai on the border of Flanders, Gilles li Muisis, Abbot of St. Martin's, kept one of the epidemic's most vivid accounts. The passing bells rang all day and all night, he recorded, because sextons were anxious to obtain their fees while they could. Filled with the sound of mourning, the city became oppressed by fear, so that the authorities forbade the tolling of bells and the wearing of black and restricted funeral services to two mourners. The silencing of funeral bells and of criers' announcements of deaths was ordained by most cities. Siena imposed a fine on the wearing of mourning clothes by all except widows.

Flight was the chief recourse of those who could afford it or arrange it. The rich fled to their country places like Boccaccio's young patricians of Florence, who settled in a pastoral palace "removed on every side from the roads" with "wells of cool water and vaults of rare wines." The urban poor died in their burrows, "and only the stench of their bodies informed neighbors of their death." That the poor were more heavily afflicted than the rich was clearly remarked at the time, in the north as in the south. A Scottish chronicler, John of Fordun, stated flatly that the pest "attacked especially the meaner sort and common people—seldom the magnates." Simon de Covino of Montpellier made the same observation. He ascribed it to the misery and want and hard lives that made the poor more susceptible, which was half the truth. Close contact and lack of sanitation was the unrecognized other half. It was noticed too that the young died in greater proportion than the old; Simon de Covino compared the disappearance of youth to the withering of flowers in the fields.

In the countryside peasants dropped dead on the roads, in the fields, in their houses. Survivors in growing helplessness fell into apathy, leaving ripe wheat uncut and livestock untended. Oxen and asses, sheep and goats, pigs and chickens ran wild and they too, according to local reports, succumbed to the pest. English sheep, bearers of the precious wool, died throughout the country. The chronicler Henry Knighton, canon of Leicester Abbey, reported 5,000 dead in one field alone, "their bodies so corrupted by the plague that neither beast nor bird would touch them," and spreading an appalling stench. In the Austrian Alps wolves came down to prey upon sheep and then, "as if alarmed by some invisible warning, turned and fled back into the wilderness." In remote Dalmatia bolder wolves descended upon a plague-stricken city and attacked human survivors. For want of herdsmen, cattle strayed from place to place and died in hedgerows and ditches. Dogs and cats fell like the rest.

The dearth of labor held a fearful prospect because the 14th century lived close to the annual harvest both for food and for next year's seed. "So few servants and laborers were left," wrote Knighton, "that no one knew where to turn for help." The sense of a vanishing future created a kind of dementia of despair. A Bavarian chronicler of Neuberg on the Danube recorded that "Men and women . . . wandered around as if mad" and let their cattle stray "because no one had any inclination to concern themselves about the future." Fields went uncultivated, spring seed unsown. Second growth with nature's awful energy crept back over cleared land, dikes crumbled, salt water reinvaded and soured the lowlands. With so few hands remaining to restore the work of cen-

20

turies, people felt, in Walsingham's words, that "the world could never again regain its former prosperity."

Though the death rate was higher among the anonymous poor, the known and the great died too. King Alfonso XI of Castile was the only reigning monarch killed by the pest, but his neighbor King Pedro of Aragon lost his wife, Queen Leonora, his daughter Marie, and a niece in the space of six months. John Cantacuzene, Emperor of Byzantium, lost his son. In France the lame Queen Jeanne and her daughter-in-law Bonne de Luxemburg, wife of the Dauphin, both died in 1349 in the same phase that took the life of Enguerrand's mother. Jeanne, Queen of Navarre, daughter of Louis X, was another victim. Edward III's second daughter, Joanna, who was on her way to marry Pedro, the heir of Castile, died in Bordeaux. Women appear to have been more vulnerable than men, perhaps because, being more housebound, they were more exposed to fleas. Boccaccio's mistress Fiammetta, illegitimate daughter of the King of Naples, died, as did Laura, the beloved—whether real or fictional—of Petrarch. Reaching out to us in the future, Petrarch cried, "Oh happy posterity who will not experience such abysmal woe and will look upon our testimony as a fable."

In Florence Giovanni Villani, the great historian of his time, died at 68 in the midst of an unfinished sentence: "*. . . e dure questo pistolenza fino a . . .* (in the midst of this pestilence there came to an end . . .)." Siena's master painters, the brothers Ambrogio and Pietro Lorenzetti, whose names never appear after 1348, presumably perished in the plague, as did Andrea Pisano, architect and sculptor of Florence. William of Ockham and the English mystic Richard Rolle of Hampole both disappear from mention after 1349. Francisco Datini, merchant of Prato, lost both his parents and two siblings. Curious sweeps of mortality afflicted certain bodies of merchants in London. All eight wardens of the Company of Cutters, all six wardens of the Hatters, and four wardens of the Goldsmiths died before July 1350. Sir John Pulteney, master draper and four times Mayor of London, was a victim, likewise Sir John Montgomery, Governor of Calais.

Among the clergy and doctors the mortality was naturally high because of the nature of their professions. Out of 24 physicians in Venice, 20 were said to have lost their lives in the plague, although, according to another account, some were believed to have fled or to have shut themselves up in their houses. At Montpellier, site of the leading medieval medical school, the physician Simon de Covino reported that, despite the great number of doctors, "hardly one of them escaped." In Avignon, Guy de Chauliac confessed that he performed his medical visits only because he dared not stay away for fear of infamy, but "I was in continual fear." He claimed to have contracted the disease but to have cured himself by his own treatment; if so, he was one of the few who recovered.

25   Clerical mortality varied with rank. Although the one-third toll of cardinals reflects the same proportion as the whole, this was probably due to their concentration in Avignon. In England, in strange and almost sinister procession, the Archbishop of Canterbury, John Stratford, died in August 1348, his appointed successor died in May 1349, and the next appointee three months

later, all three within a year. Despite such weird vagaries, prelates in general managed to sustain a higher survival rate than the lesser clergy. Among bishops the deaths have been estimated at about one in twenty. The loss of priests, even if many avoided their fearful duty of attending the dying, was about the same as among the population as a whole.

Government officials, whose loss contributed to the general chaos, found, on the whole, no special shelter. In Siena four of the nine members of the governing oligarchy died, in France one third of the royal notaries, in Bristol 15 out of the 52 members of the Town Council or almost one third. Tax-collecting obviously suffered, with the result that Philip VI was unable to collect more than a fraction of the subsidy granted him by the Estates in the winter of 1347–48.

Lawlessness and debauchery accompanied the plague as they had during the great plague of Athens of 430 B.C., when according to Thucydides, men grew bold in the indulgence of pleasure: "For seeing how the rich died in a moment and those who had nothing immediately inherited their property, they reflected that life and riches were alike transitory and they resolved to enjoy themselves while they could." Human behavior is timeless. When St. John had his vision of plague in Revelation, he knew from some experience or race memory that those who survived "repented not of the work of their hands. . . . Neither repented they of their murders, nor of their sorceries, nor of their fornication, nor of their thefts."

Ignorance of the cause augmented the sense of horror. Of the real carriers, rats and fleas, the 14th century had no suspicion, perhaps because they were so familiar. Fleas, though a common household nuisance, are not once mentioned in contemporary plague writings, and rats only incidentally, although folklore commonly associated them with pestilence. The legend of the Pied Piper arose from an outbreak of 1284. The actual plague bacillus, *Pasturella pestis,* remained undiscovered for another 500 years. Living alternately in the stomach of the flea and the bloodstream of the rat who was the flea's host, the bacillus in its bubonic form was transferred to humans and animals by the bite of either rat or flea. It traveled by virtue of *Rattus rattus,* the small medieval black rat that lived on ships, as well as by the heavier brown or sewer rat. What precipitated the turn of the bacillus from innocuous to virulent form is unknown, but the occurrence is now believed to have taken place not in China but somewhere in central Asia and to have spread along the caravan routes. Chinese origin was a mistaken notion of the 14th century based on real but belated reports of huge death tolls in China from drought, famine, and pestilence which have since been traced to the 1330s, too soon to be responsible for the plague that appeared in India in 1346.

The phantom enemy had no name. Called the Black Death only in later recurrences, it was known during the first epidemic simply as the Pestilence or Great Mortality. Reports from the East, swollen by fearful imaginings, told of strange tempests and "sheets of fire" mingled with huge hailstones that "slew almost all," or a "vast rain of fire" that burned up men, beasts, stones, trees, villages, and cities. In another version, "foul blasts of wind" from the fires carried the infection to Europe "and now as some suspect it cometh round the seacoast." Accurate observation in this case could not make the mental jump to ships and rats because no idea of animal- or insect-borne contagion existed.

30   The earthquake was blamed for releasing sulfurous and foul fumes from the earth's interior, or as evidence of a titanic struggle of planets and oceans causing waters to rise and vaporize until fish died in masses and corrupted the air. All these explanations had in common a factor of poisoned air, of miasmas and thick, stinking mists traced to every kind of natural or imagined agency from stagnant lakes to malign conjunction of the planets, from the hand of the Evil One to the wrath of God. Medical thinking, trapped in the theory of astral influences, stressed air as the communicator of disease, ignoring sanitation or visible carriers. The existence of two carriers confused the trail, the more so because the flea could live and travel independently of the rat for as long as a month and, if infected by the particularly virulent septicemic form of the bacillus, could infect humans without reinfecting itself from the rat. The simultaneous presence of the pneumonic form of the disease, which was indeed communicated through the air, blurred the problem further.

The mystery of the contagion was "the most terrible of all the terrors," as an anonymous Flemish cleric in Avignon wrote to a correspondent in Bruges. Plagues had been known before, from the plague of Athens (believed to have been typhus) to the prolonged epidemic of the 6th century A.D., to the recurrence of sporadic outbreaks in the 12th and 13th centuries, but they had left no accumulated store of understanding. That the infection came from contact with the sick or with their houses, clothes, or corpses was quickly observed but not comprehended. Gentile da Foligno, renowned physician of Perugia and doctor of medicine at the universities of Bologna and Padua, came close to respiratory infection when he surmised that poisonous material was "communicated by means of air breathed out and in." Having no idea of microscopic carriers, he had to assume that the air was corrupted by planetary influences. Planets, however, could not explain the ongoing contagion. The agonized search for an answer gave rise to such theories as transference by sight. People fell ill, wrote Guy de Chauliac, not only by remaining with the sick but "even by looking at them." Three hundred years later Joshua Barnes, the 17th-century biographer of Edward III, could write that the power of infection had entered into beams of light and "darted death from the eyes."

Doctors struggling with the evidence could not break away from the terms of astrology, to which they believed all human physiology was subject. Medicine was the one aspect of medieval life, perhaps because of its links with the Arabs, not shaped by Christian doctrine. Clerics detested astrology, but could not dislodge its influence. Guy de Chauliac, physician to three popes in succession, practiced in obedience to the zodiac. While his *Cirurgia* was the major treatise on surgery of its time, while he understood the use of anesthesia made from the juice of opium, mandrake, or hemlock, he nevertheless prescribed bleeding and purgatives by the planets and divided chronic from acute diseases on the basis of one being under the rule of the sun and the other of the moon.

In October 1348 Philip VI asked the medical faculty of the University of

Paris for a report on the affliction that seemed to threaten human survival. With careful thesis, antithesis, and proofs, the doctors ascribed it to a triple conjunction of Saturn, Jupiter, and Mars in the 40th degree of Aquarius said to have occurred on March 20, 1345. They acknowledged, however, effects "whose cause is hidden from even the most highly trained intellects." The verdict of the masters of Paris became the official version. Borrowed, copied by scribes, carried abroad, translated from Latin into various vernaculars, it was everywhere accepted, even by the Arab physicians of Cordova and Granada, as the scientific if not the popular answer. Because of the terrible interest of the subject, the translations of the plague tracts stimulated use of national languages. In that one respect, life came from death.

To the people at large there could be but one explanation—the wrath of God. Planets might satisfy the learned doctors, but God was closer to the average man. A scourge so sweeping and unsparing without any visible cause could only be seen as Divine punishment upon mankind for its sins. It might even be God's terminal disappointment in his creature. Matteo Villani compared the plague to the Flood in ultimate purpose and believed he was recording "the extermination of mankind." Efforts to appease Divine wrath took many forms, as when the city of Rouen ordered that everything that could anger God, such as gambling, cursing, and drinking, must be stopped. More general were the penitent processions authorized at first by the Pope, some lasting as long as three days, some attended by as many as 2,000, which everywhere accompanied the plague and helped to spread it.

 Barefoot in sackcloth, sprinkled with ashes, weeping, praying, tearing their hair, carrying candles and relics, sometimes with ropes around their necks or beating themselves with whips, the penitents wound through the streets, imploring the mercy of the Virgin and saints at their shrines. In a vivid illustration for the *Très Riches Heures* of the Duc de Berry, the Pope is shown in a penitent procession attended by four cardinals in scarlet from hat to hem. He raises both arms in supplication to the angel on top of the Castel Sant' Angelo, while white-robed priests bearing banners and relics in golden cases turn to look as one of their number, stricken by the plague, falls to the ground, his face contorted with anxiety. In the rear, a gray-clad monk falls beside another victim already on the ground as the townspeople gaze in horror. (Nominally the illustration represents a 6th century plague in the time of Pope Gregory the Great, but as medieval artists made no distinction between past and present, the scene is shown as the artist would have seen it in the 14th century.) When it became evident that these processions were sources of infection, Clement VI had to prohibit them.

 In Messina, where the plague first appeared, the people begged the Archbishop of neighboring Catania to lend them the relics of St. Agatha. When the Catanians refused to let the relics go, the Archbishop dipped them in holy water and took the water himself to Messina, where he carried it in a procession with prayers and litanies through the streets. The demonic, which shared the medieval cosmos with God, appeared as "demons in the shape of dogs" to ter-

35

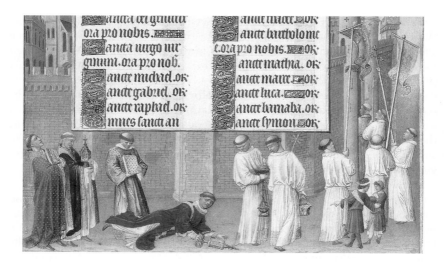

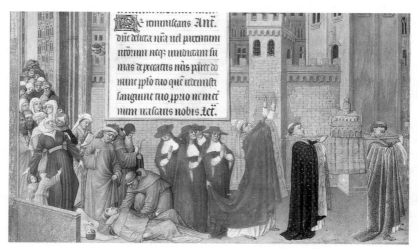

Penitential procession led by the Pope during the plague (pictured in 14th century Rome although it purports to illustrate the 6th century plague under Gregory the Great). By Pol de Limbourg for the *Très Riches Heures* of the Duc de Berry, c. 1410.

rify the people. "A black dog with a drawn sword in his paws appeared among them, gnashing his teeth and rushing upon them and breaking all the silver vessels and lamps and candlesticks on the altars and casting them hither and thither. . . . So the people of Messina, terrified by this prodigious vision, were all strangely overcome by fear."

The apparent absence of earthly cause gave the plague a supernatural and sinister quality. Scandinavians believed that a Pest Maiden emerged from the mouth of the dead in the form of a blue flame and flew through the air to infect the next house. In Lithuania the Maiden was said to wave a red scarf through the door or window to let in the pest. One brave man, according to legend, deliberately waited at his open window with drawn sword and, at the fluttering of the scarf, chopped off the hand. He died of his deed, but his village was spared and the scarf long preserved as a relic in the local church.

Beyond demons and superstition the final hand was God's. The Pope acknowledged it in a Bull of September 1348, speaking of the "pestilence with which God is afflicting the Christian people." To the Emperor John Cantacuzene it was manifest that a malady of such horrors, stenches, and agonies, and especially one bringing the dismal despair that settled upon its victims before they died, was not a plague "natural" to mankind but "a chastisement from Heaven." To Piers Plowman[5] "these pestilences were for pure sin."

The general acceptance of this view created an expanded sense of guilt, for if the plague were punishment there had to be terrible sin to have occasioned it. What sins were on the 14th century conscience? Primarily greed, the sin of avarice, followed by usury, worldliness, adultery, blasphemy, falsehood, luxury, irreligion. Giovanni Villani, attempting to account for the cascade of calamity that had fallen upon Florence, concluded that it was retribution for the sins of avarice and usury that oppressed the poor. Pity and anger about the condition of the poor, especially victimization of the peasantry in war, was often expressed by writers of the time and was certainly on the conscience of the century. Beneath it all was the daily condition of medieval life, in which hardly an act or thought, sexual, mercantile, or military, did not contravene the dictates of the Church. Mere failure to fast or attend mass was sin. The result was an underground lake of guilt in the soul that the plague now tapped.

That the mortality was accepted as God's punishment may explain in part   40
the vacuum of comment that followed the Black Death. An investigator has noticed that in the archives of Périgord references to the war are innumerable, to the plague few. Froissart mentions the great death but once, Chaucer gives it barely a glance. Divine anger so great that it contemplated the extermination of man did not bear close examination.

5. The main character (and title) of a fourteenth-century poem by the English poet William Langland (c. 1330–c. 1386).

QUESTIONS

1. Why does Tuchman begin with the account of the Genoese trading ships?

2. What ways does Tuchman find to group related facts together—in other words, what categories does she develop? Suggest other categories that Tuchman might have used in arranging her facts. What would she have gained or lost by using such categories?

3. Can you determine a basis for Tuchman's decision sometimes to quote a source, sometimes to recount it in her own words?

4. Write a brief account of a modern disaster, based on research from several sources.

PHILIP ALCABES *The Bioterrorism Scare:*
A Historical Perspective

SINCE THE FALL OF 2001, when America embarked
on a "war on terrorism" and federal officials
started warning us about the next plague, here are
some events that have not happened: a U.S. epidemic of sudden acute respiratory syndrome
(SARS),[1] a widespread anthrax outbreak, any small-
pox attack, the discovery of hard evidence of a biological weapons program in
Iraq. Yet the talk about "biopreparedness" continues. Some people in Washington want the Centers for Disease Control and Prevention to be transferred
from the Department of Health and Human Services to Homeland Security.
There is even a professional journal, *Biosecurity and Bioterrorism*, devoted to
learned discussions of the topic. Is it sound public policy to rush to protect the
country against the threat of attack with germs that could cause an epidemic?
Does the bio in biosecurity mean that we should turn our public health into a
matter of civil defense? Or have we Americans been sold a bill of goods?

Throughout history, the responses to both actual communicable disease
and the threat of it have been guided by the metaphor of the stranger as the
spreader of contagion. Allegations that epidemic disease was caused by foreigners are ancient. Thucydides[2] reported that his contemporaries, in the fifth
century B.C., attributed the Plague of Athens[3] to Ethiopians. Later on, such
thinking was refined to impute causation specifically to enemy foreigners.
Many European and American authors still believe that the Black Death[4] entered western Europe after the Mongols, besieging the city of Kefe (or Kaffa,
now Feodosiya in Ukraine) in 1346, catapulted into the European-held city
the corpses of comrades who had died of plague. When the siege was lifted,
the theory goes, the disease reached Genoa aboard ships. Although Kefe
clearly experienced plague in 1346, the story of its source is almost certainly
apocryphal: Xenopsylla cheopis, the flea that usually carries the plague bacillus, has affinity only for warm bodies and will desert a corpse within hours of
death. But the myth's persistence attests to the readiness of some, even centuries later, to believe that epidemics were caused by enemies.

Published in the American Scholar, *the magazine of the Phi Beta Kappa Society (Spring
2004).*

1. Severe Acute Respiratory Syndrome, a pneumonia-like condition that broke out in
Singapore and China in 2002.

2. Greek historian (c. 460–400 B.C.E.).

3. An epidemic that struck Athens in 430 B.C.E. during the second year of the Pelopon-
nesian War against Sparta.

4. An epidemic of bubonic plague that struck Europe in the fourteenth century, killing
approximately one-third of the population.

Similarly, Londoners believed that the Great Plague of 1665[5] was brought by the Dutch, with whom England was then at war (echoes of that belief appear in both Defoe's *Journal of the Plague Year* and Samuel Pepys's *Diary*),[6] although there is no evidence that plague in fact came to England from Holland. The great influenza pandemic of 1918–19, which killed more than 20 million people—possibly as many as 40 million—in a world at war, was attributed to various enemies. In fact, the name by which we remember this epidemic, "Spanish Flu," seems to have been a compromise acceptable to the warring parties (Spain was neutral in the war). And in a telling instance, very shortly after Germany broke its pact with the Soviet Union and invaded its former ally, Hitler[7] used the term Pestherd—"plague focus"—to refer to Russia, accusing the Soviets of infecting Europe with Jewish "bacilli." It was the metaphor of foreign culpability for disease turned inside out, Hitler imputing pathogenic properties to Jews and creating a new enemy by alleging that it was Russia that had spawned them. More recently, Tanzanians attributed the high death rate from AIDS in their Kagera province to HIV infections brought by Idi Amin's[8] Ugandan troops, who crossed the border into Tanzania in the late 1970s. "It made sense, then," Laurie Garrett[9] writes in *The Coming Plague*, "to assume that the new disease came from old enemies." When West Nile encephalitis made its Western hemisphere debut in New York in 1999, epidemiologists received calls from the FBI; they (and the CIA, too) were concerned that it might be the work of foreign bioterrorists.

The Stranger Spreading Germs shows up often in literature and film. Alessandro Manzoni's[10] 1821 novel, *I Promessi Sposi*, attributes the advance of plague in 1629 to the German army, then campaigning through the valleys of northern Italy in the Thirty Years' War. In the novel, foreigners, particularly the French, come under suspicion in plague-ridden Milan, where they are accused of "daubing" plague-inducing substances on walls or sprinkling plague powders on the streets; those found guilty of such felonious behavior are tortured to death. In F. W. Murnau's[11] classic silent film *Nosferatu*, plague arrives in Bremen by sea, brought from the East by the odious Other, the undead Nos-

---

5. An epidemic of bubonic plague that hit London in the seventeenth century, killing up to a fifth of the population.

6. Daniel Defoe (1660–1731), British writer best known for his novel *Robinson Crusoe* (1719); Pepys (1633–1703), British naval administrator and politician known for his diary written in code.

7. Adolf Hitler (1889–1945), Austrian-born Chancellor of Germany, leader of the Nazi party, and perpetrator of World War II.

8. Dictatorial Ugandan president (1924–2003) who ruled during the 1970s.

9. Pulitzer Prize–winning science writer and author of *The Coming Plague* (1994) and *Betrayal of Trust: The Collapse of Global Public Health* (2000).

10. Italian writer (1775–1883) whose novel *I Promessi Sposi* (translated into English as "The Betrothed") includes a detailed description of the plague that Milan suffered in 1630.

11. German film director (1888–1931) who based his film *Nosferatu* (1922) on Bram Stoker's novel *Dracula* (1897).

feratu. In 1922, just after the carnage of World War I and the far greater mortality of the Spanish Flu pandemic, Murnau depicted Evil as the man who was beyond death, the inscrutable and indomitable being who brings pestilence from the benighted Ausland.[12]

5   Sometimes, of course, epidemics have come from the enemy foreigner. Clearly, Cortes[13] was able to conquer Mexico because of smallpox. The disease appeared among the Taino[14] on Hispaniola in 1518, brought by Spaniards who had colonized the island; later, it would contribute to the Taino's extinction. By 1519 smallpox was in Cuba. Cortes, who was secretary to the governor of Cuba, left to take Tenochtitlan from the Aztec chief Montezuma;[15] either Cortes's Spanish troops or those of Narvaez,[16] who led a relief expedition against the Aztecs after they repulsed Cortes's initial sallies, brought smallpox to the Aztecs. The disease, to which the Aztecs were immunologically naive, so diminished their numbers that Cortes had only to finish them off. Smallpox thence spread southward, killing the Incan emperor Huayna Capac[17] and then his son in 1524–25, and plunging their people into civil war. Francisco Pizarro had little more to do to vanquish the Incas than march into Cuzco.[18]

It is unlikely that the Spaniards infected the American natives deliberately—and the Aztecs, at least, seemed to interpret the devastation as evidence of divine disfavor, not treachery on the part of Spain. But in the French and Indian War, in the early 1760s, smallpox does seem to have been spread deliberately. During the conflict known as Pontiac's Rebellion, Sir Jeffrey Amherst, the British commanding general, approved a plan to distribute smallpox-contaminated blankets "to innoculate the Indians" besieging Fort Pitt, at the fork of the Ohio River. That epidemic smallpox occurred in the Ohio Valley at the time is an established fact.

Around the same time, the Polish army considered producing cannon shells filled with the saliva of rabid dogs, in an attempt to poison the air the enemy breathed. Later, during World War I, the German biological warfare program sought to create animal epidemics—epizootics, in the lingo of epidemiology—that would diminish their enemies' ability to fight. German agents deliberately infected their neutral trading partners' livestock and animal feed with the agents of glanders (principally an equine disease) and anthrax. Ro-

12. German for "foreign country."

13. Hernando Cortes (1485–1547), Spanish conquistador who brought about the demise of the Aztec Empire in present-day Mexico.

14. Natives of Cuba, Haiti, the Dominican Republic, Puerto Rico, and Jamaica, whom Columbus encountered upon his arrival in the Americas.

15. Tenochtitlan: capital of the Aztec Empire, which was destroyed by conquering Spaniards and became the site of present-day Mexico City; Montezuma (c. 1466–1520), emperor of the Aztecs at the beginning of the Spanish conquest.

16. Panfilo de Narvaez (1470–1528), Spanish conquistador.

17. Chief of the Incas (1493–1527), a people native to South America.

18. Pizarro (1475–1541), Spanish conquistador who helped bring about the demise of the Inca Empire; Cuzco was its capital.

manian sheep were infected with both microbes in 1916 before export to Russia; more than two hundred Argentine mules intended as dray animals[19] for Allied forces died after being inoculated with both bacteria; French cavalry horses were infected with glanders; and attempts were made to contaminate animal feed in the United States. During World War II, the Third Reich avowedly eschewed use of biological warfare, but one report holds that Colorado beetles were dropped by German airplanes on potato crops in southern England. The U.S. Army claims that the retreating Wehrmacht[20] contaminated a reservoir in Bohemia with sewage, presumably to produce disease in the advancing Soviet army.

The best documented, and most successful, deliberately caused human epidemic was set by the infamous Unit 731 of the Japanese Imperial Army, stationed in conquered China during World War II. In addition to numerous heinous medical "experiments"—tortures, really—the unit dropped plague-carrying fleas on eleven Chinese towns. The number of Chinese who died of plague was probably about seven hundred. Unit 731 also produced cholera. In fact, Japanese soldiers, whom the unit had failed to warn or prepare, died in large numbers after entering Chinese areas seeded with Vibrio cholerae.[21] Some historians put the total number of deaths attributable to the unit's intentional contaminations, including others involving anthrax and typhoid, in the thousands.

In connection with humans deliberately causing epidemics, the smallpox germ, variola virus, is the one we hear most about. It enjoyed a five-hundred-year career as a natural epidemic pathogen, from roughly the late fifteenth century until the late twentieth. Then smallpox was eradicated from the earth. Variola killed several hundred million people in the first half of the twentieth century alone—a public-health menace to be reckoned with. No doubt because of its fearsome reputation, it is the subject of a great number of speculative scenarios about how it might be resurrected as an epidemic scourge.

In fact, though, none of those scenarios is even remotely likely. First, not many people have access to viable smallpox stocks. Second, the disease that variola virus produces is fairly easy to diagnose. Third, vaccination will prevent disease even in already-infected contacts of smallpox cases, and vaccine stocks are reasonably large nowadays. The hubbub about smallpox has had the effect of sharpening physicians' diagnostic skills (indeed, so much so that instances of overdiagnosis produce false alarms) and expanding the supply of available vaccine. At this point, standard public-health procedures, including case diagnosis, contact investigation, and immunization of possibly infected individuals, would be adequate to prevent an outbreak in the unlikely event that some individuals were deliberately infected.

Anthrax is the second most popular topic of bioterrorism conversation. We have seen intentional anthrax infection—the much-ballyhooed postal an-

10

19. Animals used to move wagons, such as horses, oxen, and mules.
20. German for "defense force," the name of the German army under Adolf Hitler.
21. The bacterium that causes cholera.

thrax events that took place in the fall of 2001. Three characteristics of that outbreak are of note: very few people became ill; very, very few died; and it was almost certainly not produced by a stranger. Environmental studies in mail-rooms indicated that many hundreds of people were probably exposed to an-thrax spores that fall, yet only twenty-two people got sick. And of those twenty-two, half had cutaneous anthrax, the rarely-life-threatening skin form of the disease. Only five died. In the jargon of epidemiology, anthrax turned out to be neither very infectious nor very pathogenic. That experience should tell us that spraying anthrax spores from crop dusters or releasing them from aerosol cans into the subway is highly unlikely to make many people ill. Spec-ulation about subway attacks stems from a real event in March 1995, when the Japanese religious cult Aum Shinrikyo released the nerve toxin sarin in the Tokyo subway system. Twelve people died. Two subsequent attempts to release toxins in the Tokyo subways were foiled. Note that Aum was using a gas, which does not have to be sprayed; it diffuses by itself. This is not how germs are dis-seminated, and it is a distinction worth bearing in mind. And even that ignores the more central question of likelihood. Large-scale poisonings are not easy to carry out well. The light death toll from mailed anthrax was a result of the low pathogenicity of the bacteria—half the cases were not pulmonary and were therefore unlikely to be fatal—and the comparative treatability of anthrax dis-ease once detected. Do five deaths constitute a public-health crisis? Along with his colleagues, Victor Sidel, Distinguished Professor of Social Medicine at Albert Einstein College of Medicine in New York, has noted that a fraction of our nation's expenditure on biopreparedness would pay for effective treat-ment of tuberculosis for all of the two million people who get TB each year in India, thereby preventing close to half a million deaths a year. Half a mil-lion deaths because commonly available antibiotics are not affordable—now there's a public-health problem.

The other microbe that is on the lists of virtually all the bioterrorism watchers is the plague bacillus. It is true that Unit 731 produced plague out-breaks in China by dropping infected fleas on towns. But at that time plague was a recurring problem in Asia: a ferocious epidemic struck Manchuria in 1910, and another occurred in 1921. (It still is a problem: a large outbreak caused many deaths in India as recently as 1994.) By contrast, despite the presence of Yersinia pestis, the plague bacterium, in wild rodents in the West-ern Hemisphere, there has never been an extensive epidemic of human plague in this country. Even when plague epidemics moved out of Asia through much of South America, circa 1900, the U.S. saw only a small outbreak in San Fran-cisco's Chinatown. The reason is not that Americans are immune to plague; it is that the urban arrangements that we have been accustomed to for the past two hundred years are inhospitable to the rat-flea-bacillus ecosystem. Such re-forms as garbage removal, pest control, and better housing explain why plague disappeared from eastern Europe in the early 1700s and has never troubled us seriously here. Since epidemics of plague are unlikely, should we then worry that terrorists will produce isolated cases? Perhaps, but garden-variety anti-biotics are very effective at treating the disease and interrupting transmission. There is no potential for the next catastrophe there.

Other pathogens have been mentioned as possible bioweapons—for example, the agents of tularemia, botulism, and Q fever.[22] These organisms are not generally transmitted from person to person, so they carry little or no outbreak potential. Hemorrhagic fever viruses are sometimes transmitted by mosquitoes or by the bite of infected animals. It has never been shown that they can be manipulated into transportable weapons and then elude standard mosquito- and animal-control programs.

All in all, there is little evidence that terrorists are more likely, or better able, to use microbes as part of their armamentarium than ever before. If there were evidence, would editorialists in the nation's most prestigious medical journal need to argue, as they did in the context of the purported smallpox threat, that public-health decisions should rely on "theoretical data"? Consider the ratio of known success to attempts at bioterrorism. Jessica Stern reports in *The Ultimate Terrorists* that the Aura Shinrikyo cult drove three trucks set up to spray botulinum toxin through Tokyo in 1990, but no cases of botulism resulted. Judith Miller, William Broad, and Stephen Engelberg report in their book, *Germs*, that Aura sprayed anthrax spores from the roof of its building in Tokyo in 1993. This apparently killed some birds, but no humans got sick. Aum members also reportedly tried to procure Ebola virus in the 1990s from what was then Zaire, but if they were able to get the virus, they were unable to produce any cases of Ebola.

In the 1960s, a Japanese researcher purposely contaminated food with Salmonella typhi,[23] producing outbreaks of typhoid fever and dysentery, but no deaths. In 1970, four Canadian students got sick after eating food that had been deliberately contaminated with pig ringworm ova. A neo-Nazi group in the U.S. stockpiled the typhoid bacterium in 1972, with the intent of contaminating the water supplies of midwestern cities. They failed. In 1984, members of the Rajneeshee cult[24] contaminated ten Oregon salad bars with Salmonella typhimurium, which causes diarrhea. Federal investigators located 751 cases of salmonellosis, but no deaths occurred. In 1996, twelve people in Texas developed dysentery after eating doughnuts or muffins purposely contaminated with shigella bacteria[25] by a disgruntled lab worker. Again, no deaths.

Presumably, these initiatives represent only a small subset—the known ones—of all attempts to cause mayhem by deliberately introducing germs into a population. Indeed, one systematic study uncovered twenty-nine such attempts to use germs to harm others, although a large proportion seemed to have been perpetrated by single individuals whose aims were against other in-

15

22. Tularemia: highly infectious disease with flulike symptoms; botulism: an often food-borne illness that can cause paralysis; Q fever: short for "Query Fever," an extremely infectious illness that can be contracted through inhalation of bacteria, so called because its discoverer could not recognize it.

23. The bacterium responsible for typhoid fever and salmonellosis.

24. Followers of the controversial cult leader Rajneesh Chandra Mohan Jain.

25. A family of bacteria, named for the Japanese scientist Shiga who discovered it, that causes diarrhea, fever, and stomach cramps.

dividuals rather than the population. No doubt there are still more instances, unknown because they were unsuccessful. And yet we can enumerate on the fingers of one hand the deadly epidemics that have in fact been caused deliberately. In the creation of epidemics, the gap between intention and the deed itself is a wide one.

Americans began looking at new infectious diseases as a grave social menace in the early 1990s, and that anxiety resonated loudly after the publication of Laurie Garrett's *Coming Plague* in 1994. In a sense, the relatively recent worry about bioterrorism is a spin-off of the past decade's concern about the "coming plague." In reality, the intensity of even naturally occurring new epidemics never matches that anticipation.

Our most recent experience with so-called emerging infections has been SARS. It appeared suddenly in southern China in late 2002, the causative virus probably having entered the human population through people who had substantial contact with domestic animals. Although SARS affected more than 8,000 people worldwide and killed more than 700, it was a negligible problem in the U.S. (eight cases, no deaths) and produced no more than a mild epidemic in most other countries: despite the high case-fatality ratio (people diagnosed with SARS had about one chance in ten of dying from the disease), only in China, Hong Kong, Singapore, and Canada were there more than five SARS deaths. Only nineteen countries saw more than a single SARS case. In all the affected areas, the outbreak was brought under control within about six months of its onset.

Two aspects of the SARS experience are important. First, though it is easy to acquire the virus by inhaling respiratory secretions from a SARS sufferer, it also turns out to be easy to prevent or control an outbreak. The key is to use standard infectious-disease-control measures, including case finding and reporting, active surveillance at points of entry to the country, isolation of possible cases, and recommendations against travel to heavily affected regions. None of these measures requires cutting-edge technology; all have been used in controlling communicable disease for well over a century.

20   Second, SARS made news partly because it was not the expected epidemic. For six months before the advent of SARS, Americans had been worrying very publicly about smallpox. Urged toward apprehension by the federal government, we had alarmed ourselves about the possibility that the long-defunct disease would be reborn in the hands of bioterrorists. The administration made ready, in mid-2002, to vaccinate half a million armed-services personnel and half a million health-care workers. The former plan it came close to accomplishing; the latter was abandoned because so many health-care workers refused to show up for vaccination. All of it repeatedly made the headlines and the evening news reports. Yet what happened in the end was not smallpox, or smallpox prevention; it was SARS. Had our faces not already been turned toward epidemic disease and our anxieties about infection elevated, had the news hours not been hungry for new news after a month of relentless coverage of the Iraq war, SARS might not have made such big headlines.

The lesson we should learn from our experience with SARS is that if we are vigilant about spotting new disease outbreaks and equally vigilant about applying public-health programs to curtail their spread, we can limit them, although we cannot ward them off completely. We cannot make life risk-free. Had we dealt with AIDS and West Nile encephalitis the way we dealt with SARS (which, of course, may return in the future and therefore requires continued vigilance), their course might have been different. West Nile, ending only its fifth season in the U.S. as I write, is already virtually a national epidemic; AIDS went national within six or seven years of its appearance. But in its initial season, 1999, in New York City, West Nile virus caused forty-six cases of encephalitis and seven deaths: not negligible, but a public-health problem more minor than Lyme disease (and far less extensive, in New York, than asthma or lead poisoning). AIDS began with a handful of cases—there were only a few hundred in 1981, the first year it was recognized—and the U.S. might have kept the toll fairly small had we had the political nerve to do something about it at the time. The point is that, at the outset, none of these "plagues" were cataclysmic. Epidemics do not work that way. Errant microbes do not find their way into the human ecosystem and wipe out most of the population unannounced. The Andromeda Strain[26] is fantasy.

The crystal ball with which we divine epidemic mayhem is no clearer now than it used to be, and no clearer than the vision with which we try to foresee the coming plague. No one can dispute, after the events of September 11, 2001, that some people wish us harm. However, that harm is not likely to come from bioterrorism. To worry that the Middle Easterner, the Arab, or any Muslim—however the Stranger is configured—will use germs to attack us would be to pretend that we can indeed foresee great epidemics. For two reasons, that is certainly not the case. First, humans, even ill-tempered and badly behaved humans, have never been able to use germs or weapons to the terrible degree of mortal effect that nature always has been able to use germs. Just four communicable diseases—malaria, smallpox, AIDS, and tuberculosis—killed well over half a billion people in the twentieth century, or about ten times the combined tolls of World Wars I and II, history's bloodiest conflicts. Even today, with good vaccines and effective antibiotics to stop them, infectious diseases kill about 10 million people each year.

The worst catastrophes the world has seen have been not the genocides, however gruesome, but the cataclysmic disease outbreaks. When a few million people are killed by design with Zyklon B,[27] the machete, or the machine gun, it is a horror and an outrage; it shakes our moral faith. But the Black Death killed a third of Europe's population in just four years in the mid-1300s. Smallpox wiped out entire tribes of American natives after Europeans arrived in the 1500s. Plague killed over 50,000 in Moscow alone in just a few months in 1771. The Spanish Flu killed between 20 and 40 million in sixteen months in 1918–19.

26. A contagious illness of extraterrestrial origin and boundless danger, invented by novelist Michael Crichton in his book of the same title.
27. A cyanide-based insecticide with which the Nazis killed millions in gas chambers.

And that suddenness is the second point. Prevision is of little help against epidemic disasters. Each of the disasters I just mentioned, and every other great epidemic of history, was unimaginable until the moment it began. But neither is prescience necessary: each epidemic, even the ones that turned out to be most terrible, began slowly, percolated a while, and could have been stopped with conventional public-health responses had anyone acted in time. SARS reminded us of that.

25   Whether or not the Stranger is an enemy avowedly bent on terror, casting him in the role of microbial evildoer has the perilous effect of distracting us from realizing two truths: the disheartening one that the epidemic crystal ball is always cloudy, and the uncomfortable one that it is usually social circumstances that make epidemics possible and public-health funding that stops them.

Worrying about the germ-bearing Stranger, we forgo the upkeep of a workaday public-health apparatus in favor of fabricating modern wonders. The CDC now operates what it calls a "war room." From there, it can coordinate activities around SARS, West Nile virus, and other infections, as well as bioterrorism—if it can be found—using high-tech communications equipment. The war room is in an "undisclosed location." Once, CDC[28] officials knew they were running a public-health agency. Now, apparently, they must act as if they are in charge of national defense. After the U.S. Department of Health and Human Services scotched the 2002 plan to vaccinate health-care workers, the CDC announced it would continue its effort to vaccinate police officers and firefighters, despite numerous reasons to stop: several deaths directly attributable to the vaccine; several more possibly attributable; evidence that people who might be predisposed to heart disease (something like 10 or 15 percent of the middle-aged population) can be harmed by the vaccination; certainty that people with HIV infection (a sizable percentage of the adult population in some big-city neighborhoods) must not be vaccinated; and of course the complete absence of natural smallpox infection anywhere in the world for the past twenty-five years.

Federal grant money, under President Bush's multimillion-dollar Project BioShield program, has been allocated to technologic innovation for bioterrorism prevention. By 2003, according to *The Chronicle of Higher Education*, the National Institutes of Health were supporting almost seventy extramural research projects on anthrax alone. The NIH has funded two new National Biocontainment Laboratories and new facilities at Regional Biocontainment Laboratories, most at major universities, to the tune of $360 million in start-up costs. The University of Pittsburgh just lured the top staff of the Center for Civilian Biodefense Strategies away from Johns Hopkins by offering to set up a Center for Biosecurity with a $12 million endowment. The University of South Florida recently received $5 million in federal grant money for its Center for Biological Defense, which has projects like "Photocatalytic Air Disinfection" and "Aquatic Real-time Monitoring System (ARMS) for Bioterrorism Events." And Auburn University received a million-dollar federal bioprepared-

---

28. Centers for Disease Control and Prevention.

ness grant for something called a Canine Detection Center. When Harvard received a $1.2 million federal grant in 2002 to set up a program for detecting "events possibly related to bioterrorism" by electronically linking 20 million patient-care records from around the country (an endeavor called syndromic surveillance), the grant was a mere drop in the bucket: Congress soon allotted $420 million to Homeland Security for a larger linked health-monitoring network. A consortium led by the New York Academy of Medicine then developed software for syndromic surveillance. The new software allows public health officials to monitor what are called "aberrant clusters health events"—translation: more than the expected number of cases of some symptom that might be related to a disease that might be produced by an organism that might be in the possession of terrorists. Syndromic surveillance works fine if someone knows what to look for. But it is of no help at all with the unexpected. When there really was bioterrorism in the U.S.—the anthrax attacks in fall 2001—linked databases were useless; it took a smart clinician to figure out that anthrax was around, and old-fashioned shoe-leather epidemiology quickly worked out which people had been affected. West Nile virus, ditto. A friend who is an official of a local health department tells me that the syndromic surveillance experts find it works well for predicting the first influenza outbreak each year. But anyone's grandmother can predict the first influenza outbreak where I live, in the New York City area, since the symptoms are always the same and flu always starts here in the two weeks preceding Thanksgiving. For all its meager productivity, the syndromic surveillance software also throws out plenty of false-positive "clusters" that waste investigators' time. It is our new and expensive white elephant, justified by the fear of evildoers and germs.

It all sounds a little phantasmagoric.

In "The Expose of 1935," Walter Benjamin[29] identified certain phantasmagorias of modern life as Wunschbilder, "wish symbols," that seek to "transfigure the . . . inadequacies in the social organization." Benjamin was concerned with phantasmagorias as magical images, as he put it in his Passagen-Werk, "residues of a dream world," revelations of unfulfilled wishes. In this sense we might ask whether the many projects of the Bioshield—the electronic anthrax detectors, the hyperdatabanks, the supersecure biohazard-level-4 labs, the men and women in full-body protective suits, the urban-evacuation exercises, whatever it is they are doing with dogs at Auburn University, and so on—are emblems of some shared desire to feel that all the effort America expends on technology development protects us from something. We might ask whether the something is the Stranger Spreading Germs. And we must ask what the cost is.

The core issue here is that the Stranger Spreading Germs is a metaphor, 30 and largely an empty one. Bioterrorism is not a public-health problem, and will not become one. The next plague, whatever it is, will not decimate us unheralded. In signing the contract on biopreparedness, we have bought a confection, a defense against the chimeric stranger with the metaphorical germs.

29. German literary critic and philosopher (1892–1940).

And the costs of buy-in? When our public-health "leaders" corroborate government rhetoric about bioterrorists by reassuring us that our state or municipal health department is ready for any smallpox, anthrax, or plague attack, they legitimate both their own efforts and the standing of their offices. The planned result is that we will not question spending tax dollars so those officials can continue to defend us, even when it means closing down municipal clinics or shortchanging programs for the poor, and even if such biodefense is not what we most need or want.

The biopreparedness campaign goes to work. It discredits the simple logic of public health. Lose the distinction between the minuscule risk of dying in an intentional outbreak and the millionfold-higher chance of dying in a natural pandemic, it says. Ignore the hundredfold-higher-still chance of dying of cancer or heart disease. Defund the prenatal-care clinics, the chest clinics, the exercise and cancer screening and lead abatement programs. Ignore the lessons of history: forget that human attempts to create epidemics have almost always failed, and dismiss the repeated ability of a well-funded public-health apparatus to control epidemic disease with time-tested measures. Just think about germs, and tremble.

The lesson of history that we ignore at our peril is this: nobody can tell us how the next epidemic will happen. New germs come and go, epidemics wax and wane, but national catastrophes happen rarely. And when they do, it is never because of a stranger spreading germs. Anyone who promises certain protection from the next plague is selling us a bill of goods.

QUESTIONS

1. Philip Alcabes argues that, historically, most plagues and epidemics have been wrongly interpreted in terms of "the stranger as the spreader of contagion" (paragraph 2). What historical evidence does he supply to support this claim in the opening paragraphs (1–9)? Why does he wish to refute the belief that strangers are the source of disease, plagues, epidemics, and other such biological invasions?

2. What role have books, films, and other fictional media played in past and current "bioterrorism scares"? Locate Alcabes's examples of fictional scare tactics, and analyze his treatment of these media.

3. Instead of buying into the current "bioterrorism scare," what does Alcabes suggest Americans do? What does he, as a professor of urban public health, advance as an appropriate set of actions?

4. Test Alcabes's claim that a "core issue [in the current bioterrorism scare] is that the Stranger Spreading Germs is a metaphor, and largely an empty one" (paragraph 30) by examining newspaper and magazine articles about SARS, anthrax, or other scares. Write up what you find about the use of this metaphor and/or other metaphors in these articles.

WALT WHITMAN   *Death of Abraham Lincoln*

I SHALL NOT easily forget the first time I ever saw Abraham Lincoln. It must have been about the 18th or 19th of February, 1861. It was rather a pleasant afternoon, in New York City, as he arrived there from the West, to remain a few hours, and then pass on to Washington, to prepare for his inauguration. I saw him in Broadway, near the site of the present Post-office. He came down, I think from Canal street, to stop at the Astor House. The broad spaces, sidewalks, and streets in the neighborhood, and for some distance, were crowded with solid masses of people, many thousands. The omnibuses and other vehicles had all been turn'd off, leaving an unusual hush in that busy part of the city. Presently two or three shabby hack barouches made their way with some difficulty through the crowd, and drew up at the Astor House entrance. A tall figure stepp'd out of the centre of these barouches, paus'd leisurely on the sidewalk, look'd up at the granite walls and looming architecture of the grand old hotel—then, after a relieving stretch of arms and legs, turn'd round for over a minute to slowly and good-humoredly scan the appearance of the vast and silent crowds. There were no speeches—no compliments—no welcome—as far as I could hear, not a word said. Still much anxiety was conceal'd in the quiet. Cautious persons had fear'd some mark'd insult or indignity to the President-elect—for he possess'd no personal popularity at all in New York City, and very little political. But it was evidently tacitly agreed that if the few political supporters of Mr. Lincoln present would entirely abstain from any demonstration on their side, the immense majority, who were anything but supporters, would abstain on their sides also. The result was a sulky, unbroken silence, such as certainly never before characterized so great a New York crowd.

Almost in the same neighborhood I distinctly remember'd seeing Lafayette on his visit to America in 1825. I had also personally seen and heard, various years afterward, how Andrew Jackson, Clay, Webster, Hungarian Kossuth, Filibuster Walker, the Prince of Wales[1] on his visit, and other *célèbres*, native and foreign, had been welcom'd there—all that indescribable human roar and magnetism, unlike any other sound in the universe—the glad exulting thunder-shouts of countless unloos'd throats of men! But on this oc-

From Whitman's collection of prose writings, Specimen Days *(1882).*

1. Marquis de Lafayette (1757–1834), French statesman and general who fought for the United States in the War of Independence; Jackson (1767–1845), seventh president of the United States, 1829–37; Henry Clay (1777–1852), American statesman and orator; Daniel Webster (1782–1852), American statesman and orator; Lajos Kossuth (1802–1894), Hungarian patriot and statesman; William Walker (1824–1860), an American who filibustered (i.e., undertook unsanctioned revolutionary activities) in Central America; the future Edward VII (1841–1910), Queen Victoria's son.

casion, not a voice—not a sound. From the top of an omnibus, (driven up one side, close by, and block'd by the curbstone and the crowds), I had, I say, a capital view of it all, and especially of Mr. Lincoln, his look and gait—his perfect composure and coolness—his unusual and uncouth height, his dress of complete black, stovepipe hat push'd back on the head, dark-brown complexion, seam'd and wrinkled yet canny-looking face, black, bushy head of hair, disproportionately long neck, and his hands held behind as he stood observing the people. He look'd with curiosity upon that immense sea of faces, and the sea of faces return'd the look with similar curiosity. In both there was a dash of comedy, almost farce, such as Shakspere puts in his blackest tragedies. The crowd that hemm'd around consisted I should think of thirty to forty thousand men, not a single one his personal friend—while I have no doubt, (so frenzied were the ferments of the time,) many an assassin's knife and pistol lurk'd in hip or breast-pocket there, ready, soon as break and riot came.

But no break or riot came. The tall figure gave another relieving stretch or two of arms and legs; then with moderate pace, and accompanied by a few unknown-looking persons, ascended the portico-steps of the Astor House, disappear'd through its broad entrance—and the dumb-show ended.

I saw Abraham Lincoln often the four years following that date. He changed rapidly and much during his Presidency—but this scene, and him in it, are indelibly stamp'd upon my recollection. As I sat on the top of my omnibus, and had a good view of him, the thought, dim and inchoate then, has since come out clear enough, that four sorts of genius, four mighty and primal hands, will be needed to the complete limning of this man's future portrait—the eyes and brains and finger-touch of Plutarch and Eschylus and Michel Angelo, assisted now by Rabelais.[2]

5   And now—(Mr. Lincoln passing on from this scene to Washington, where he was inaugurated, amid armed cavalry, and sharpshooters at every point—the first instance of the kind in our history—and I hope it will be the last)—now the rapid succession of well-known events, (too well-known—I believe, these days, we almost hate to hear them mention'd)—the national flag fired on at Sumter—the uprising of the North, in paroxysms of astonishment and rage—the chaos of divided councils—the call for troops—the first Bull Run—the stunning cast-down, shock, and dismay of the North—and so in full flood the Secession war. Four years of lurid, bleeding, murky, murderous war. Who paint those years, with all their scenes?—the hard-fought engagements—the defeats, plans, failures—the gloomy hours, days, when our Nationality seem'd hung in pall of doubt, perhaps death—the Mephistophelean sneers of foreign lands and attachés—the dreaded Scylla of European interference, and the Charybdis of the tremendously dangerous latent strata of secession sympathiz-

2. Plutarch (46?–120 C.E.), Greek author who wrote the histories of famous Greeks and Romans; Aeschylus (525–456 B.C.E.), Greek tragic dramatist; Michelangelo Buonarroti (1475–1574), Italian architect, painter, sculptor, and poet; François Rabelais (1493–1553), French author who created the giants Gargantua and Pantagruel.

ers throughout the free States,[3] (far more numerous than is supposed)—the long marches in summer—the hot sweat, and many a sunstroke, as on the rush to Gettysburg in '63—the night battles in the woods, as under Hooker at Chancellorsville—the camps in winter—the military prisons—the hospitals—(alas! alas! the hospitals.)

The Secession war? Nay, let me call it the Union war. Though whatever call'd, it is even yet too near us—too vast and too closely overshadowing—its branches unform'd yet, (but certain,) shooting too far into the future—and the most indicative and mightiest of them yet ungrown. A great literature will yet arise out of the era of those four years, those scenes—era compressing centuries of native passion, first-class pictures, tempests of life and death—an inexhaustible mine for the histories, drama, romance, and even philosophy, of peoples to come—indeed the verteber[4] of poetry and art, (of personal character too,) for all future America—far more grand, in my opinion, to the hands capable of it, than Homer's siege of Troy, or the French wars to Shakspere.[5]

But I must leave these speculations, and come to the theme I have assign'd and limited myself to. Of the actual murder of President Lincoln, though so much has been written, probably the facts are yet very indefinite in most persons' minds. I read from my memoranda, written at the time, and revised frequently and finally since.

The day, April 14, 1865, seems to have been a pleasant one throughout the whole land—the moral atmosphere pleasant too—the long storm, so dark, so fratricidal, full of blood and doubt and gloom, over and ended at last by the sunrise of such an absolute National victory, and utter break-down of Secessionism—we almost doubted our own senses! Lee had capitulated beneath the apple-tree of Appomattox. The other armies, the flanges of the revolt, swiftly follow'd. And could it really be, then? Out of all the affairs of this world of woe and failure and disorder, was there really come the confirm'd, unerring sign of plan, like a shaft of pure light—of rightful rule—of God? So the day, as I say, was propitious. Early herbage, early flowers, were out. (I remember where I was stopping at the time, the season being advanced, there were many lilacs in full bloom. By one of those caprices that enter and give tinge to events without being at all a part of them, I find myself always reminded of the great tragedy of that day by the sight and odor of these blossoms.[6] It never fails.)

But I must not dwell on accessories. The deed hastens. The popular after-

---

3. Mephistopheles is the name of an evil spirit to whom men legendarily sell their souls in exchange for something they desire; the character appears in European literature most frequently in tales and drama about Faust, a German conjurer who lived from about 1488 to 1541. In Homer's *Odyssey*, Scylla and Charybdis are the rocks and the whirlpool between which Odysseus must navigate.

4. Vertebra.

5. In the *Iliad* and in Shakespeare's history plays.

6. Cf. Whitman's elegy on Lincoln, "When Lilacs Last in the Dooryard Bloom'd" (1865–66).

noon paper of Washington, the little *Evening Star,* has spatter'd all over its third page, divided among the advertisements in a sensational manner, in a hundred different places, *"The President and his Lady will be at the Theatre this evening. . . ."* (Lincoln was fond of the theatre. I have myself seen him there several times. I remember thinking how funny it was that he, in some respects the leading actor in the stormiest drama known to real history's stage through centuries, should sit there and be so completely interested and absorb'd in those human jackstraws, moving about with their silly little gestures, foreign spirit, and flatulent text.)

10   On this occasion the theatre was crowded, many ladies in rich and gay costumes, officers in their uniforms, many well-known citizens, young folks, the usual clusters of gas-lights, the usual magnetism of so many people, cheerful, with perfumes, music of violins and flutes—(and over all, and saturating all, that vast, vague wonder, *Victory,* the nation's victory, the triumph of the Union, filling the air, the thought, the sense, with exhilaration more than all music and perfumes.)

The President came betimes, and, with his wife, witness'd the play from the large stage-boxes of the second tier, two thrown into one, and profusely drap'd with the national flag. The acts and scenes of the piece—one of those singularly written compositions which have at least the merit of giving entire relief to an audience engaged in mental action or business excitements and cares during the day, as it makes not the slightest call on either the moral, emotional, esthetic, or spiritual nature—a piece, (*Our American Cousin,*)[7] in which, among other characters so call'd, a Yankee, certainly such a one as was never seen, or the least like it ever seen, in North America, is introduced in England, with a varied fol-de-rol of talk, plot, scenery, and such phantasmagoria as goes to make up a modern popular drama—had progress'd through perhaps a couple of its acts, when in the midst of this comedy, or non-such, or whatever it is to be call'd, and to offset it, or finish it out, as if in Nature's and the great Muse's mockery of those poor mimes, came interpolated that scene, not really or exactly to be described at all, (for on the many hundreds who were there it seems to this hour to have left a passing blur, a dream, a blotch)—and yet partially to be described as I now proceed to give it. There is a scene in the play representing a modern parlor, in which two unprecedented English ladies are inform'd by the impossible Yankee that he is not a man of fortune, and therefore undesirable for marriage-catching purposes; after which, the comments being finish'd, the dramatic trio make exit, leaving the stage clear for a moment. At this period came the murder of Abraham Lincoln. Great as all its manifold train, circling round it, and stretching into the future for many a century, in the politics, history, art &c., of the New World, in point of fact the main thing, the actual murder, transpired with the quiet and simplicity of any commonest occurrence—the bursting of a bud or pod in the growth of vegetation, for instance. Through the general hum following the stage pause, with the change of positions, came the muffled sound of a pistol-

7. By the British playwright Tom Taylor (1817–1880).

shot, which not one-hundredth part of the audience heard at the time—and yet a moment's hush—somehow, surely, a vague startled thrill—and then, through the ornamented, draperied, starr'd and striped space-way of the President's box, a sudden figure, a man, raises himself with hands and feet, stands a moment on the railing, leaps below to the stage, (a distance of perhaps fourteen or fifteen feet), falls out of position, catching his boot-heel in the copious drapery, (the American flag,) falls on one knee, quickly recovers himself, rises as if nothing had happen'd, (he really sprains his ankle, but unfelt then)—and so the figure, Booth,[8] the murderer, dress'd in plain black broadcloth, bareheaded, with full, glossy, raven hair, and his eyes like some mad animal's flashing with light and resolution, yet with a certain strange calmness, holds aloft in one hand a large knife—walks along not much back from the footlights—turns fully toward the audience his face of statuesque beauty, lit by those basilisk eyes, flashing with desperation, perhaps insanity—launches out in a firm and steady voice the words *Sic semper tyrannis*[9]—and then walks with neither slow nor very rapid pace diagonally across to the back of the stage, and disappears. (Had not all this terrible scene—making the mimic ones preposterous—had it not all been rehears'd, in blank, by Booth, beforehand?)

A moment's hush—a scream—the cry of *"murder"*—Mrs. Lincoln leaning out of the box, with ashy cheeks and lips, with involuntary cry, pointing to the retreating figure, *"He has kill'd the President."* And still a moment's strange, incredulous suspense—and then the deluge! then that mixture of horror, noises, uncertainty—(the sound, somewhere back, of a horse's hoofs clattering with speed)—the people burst through chairs and railings, and break them up—there is inextricable confusion and terror—women faint—quite feeble persons fall, and are trampl'd on—many cries of agony are heard—the broad stage suddenly fills to suffocation with a dense and motley crowd, like some horrible carnival—the audience rush generally upon it, at least the strong men do—the actors and actresses are all there in their playcostumes and painted faces, with mortal fright showing through the rouge—the screams and calls, confused talk—redoubled, trebled—two or three manage to pass up water from the stage to the President's box—others try to clamber up—&c., &c.

In the midst of all this, the soldiers of the President's guard, with others, suddenly drawn to the scene, burst in—(some two hundred altogether)—they storm the house, through all the tiers, especially the upper ones, inflam'd with fury, literally charging the audience with fix'd bayonets, muskets, and pistols, shouting *"Clear out! clear out! you sons of ———"*. . . . Such a wild scene, or a suggestion of it rather, inside the play-house that night.

Outside, too, in the atmosphere of shock and craze, crowds of people, fill'd with frenzy, ready to seize any outlet for it, come near committing murder several times on innocent individuals. One such case was especially exciting. The infuriated crowd, through some chance, got started against one man, either for words he utter'd, or perhaps without any cause at all, and were pro-

8. John Wilkes Booth (1835–1865).
9. "Thus always to tyrants," the motto of the state of Virginia.

ceeding at once to actually hang him on a neighboring lamp-post, when he was rescued by a few heroic policemen, who placed him in their midst, and fought their way slowly and amid great peril toward the station-house. It was a fitting episode of the whole affair. The crowd rushing and eddying to and fro—the night, the yells, the pale faces, many frighten'd people trying in vain to extricate themselves—the attack'd man, not yet freed from the jaws of death, looking like a corpse—the silent, resolute, half-dozen policemen, with no weapons but their little clubs, yet stern and steady through all those eddying swarms—made a fitting side-scene to the grand tragedy of the murder. They gain'd the station house with the protected man, whom they placed in security for the night, and discharged him in the morning.

15 And in the midst of that pandemonium, infuriated soldiers, the audience and the crowd, the stage, and all its actors and actresses, its paint-pots, spangles, and gas-lights—the life blood from those veins, the best and sweetest of the land, drips slowly down, and death's ooze already begins its little bubbles on the lips.

Thus the visible incidents and surroundings of Abraham Lincoln's murder, as they really occur'd. Thus ended the attempted secession of these States: thus the four years' war. But the main things come subtly and invisibly afterward, perhaps long afterward—neither military, political, nor (great as those are,) historical. I say, certain secondary and indirect results, out of the tragedy of this death, are, in my opinion, greatest. Not the event of the murder itself. Not that Mr. Lincoln strings the principal points and personages of the period, like beads, upon the single string of his career. Not that his idiosyncrasy, in its sudden appearance and disappearance, stamps this Republic with a stamp more mark'd and enduring than any yet given by any one man—(more even than Washington's;)—but, join'd with these, the immeasurable value and meaning of that whole tragedy lies, to me, in senses finally dearest to a nation, (and here all our own)—the imaginative and artistic senses—the literary and dramatic ones. Not in any common or low meaning of those terms, but a meaning precious to the race, and to every age. A long and varied series of contradictory events arrives at last at its highest poetic, single, central, pictorial *dénouement*. The whole involved, baffling, multiform whirl of the secession period comes to a head, and is gather'd in one brief flash of lightning-illumination—one simple, fierce deed. Its sharp culmination, and as it were solution, of so many bloody and angry problems, illustrates those climax-moments on the stage of universal Time, where the historic Muse at one entrance, and the tragic Muse at the other, suddenly ringing down the curtain, close an immense act in the long drama of creative thought, and give it radiation, tableau, stranger than fiction. Fit radiation—fit close! How the imagination—how the student loves these things! America, too, is to have them. For not in all great deaths, not far or near—not Caesar in the Roman senate-house, or Napoleon passing away in the wild night-storm at St. Helena—not Paleologus,[10] falling, desperately fighting, piled over dozens deep with Grecian

10. Emperor Constantine XI, who yielded Constantinople to the Turks in 1453.

corpses—not calm old Socrates, drinking the hemlock—outvies that terminus of the secession war, in one man's life, here in our midst, in our time—that seal of the emancipation of three million slaves—that parturition and delivery of our at last really free Republic, born again, henceforth to commence its career of genuine homogeneous Union, compact, consistent with itself.

Nor will ever future American Patriots and Unionists, indifferently over the whole land, or North or South, find a better moral to their lesson. The final use of the greatest men of a Nation is, after all, not with reference to their deeds in themselves, or their direct bearing on their times or lands. The final use of a heroic-eminent life—especially of a heroic-eminent death—is its indirect filtering into the nation and the race, and to give, often at many removes, but unerringly, age after age, color and fibre to the personalism of the youth and maturity of that age, and of mankind. Then, there is a cement to the whole people, subtler, more underlying, than any thing in written constitution, or courts or armies—namely, the cement of a death identified thoroughly with that people, at its head, and for its sake. Strange, (is it not?) that battles, martyrs, agonies, blood, even assassination, should so condense—perhaps only really, lastingly condense—a Nationality.

I repeat it—the grand deaths of the race—the dramatic deaths of every nationality—are its most important inheritance-value—in some respects beyond its literature and art—(as the hero is beyond his finest portrait, and the battle itself beyond its choicest song or epic.) Is not here indeed the point underlying all tragedy? the famous pieces of the Grecian masters—and all masters? Why, if the old Greeks had had this man, what trilogies of plays—what epics—would have been made out of him! How the rhapsodes would have recited him! How quickly that quaint tall form would have enter'd into the region where men vitalize gods, and gods divinify men! But Lincoln, his times, his death—great as any, any age—belong altogether to our own, and are autochthonic.[11] (Sometimes indeed I think our American days, our own stage—the actors we know and have shaken hands, or talk'd with—more fateful than any thing in Eschylus—more heroic than the fighters around Troy—afford kings of men for our Democracy prouder than Agamemnon—models of character cute and hardy as Ulysses—deaths more pitiful than Priam's.)[12]

When centuries hence, (as it must, in my opinion, be centuries hence before the life of these States, or of Democracy, can be really written and illustrated,) the leading historians and dramatists seek for some personage, some special event, incisive enough to mark with deepest cut, and mnemonize, this turbulent nineteenth century of ours, (not only these States, but all over the political and social world)—something, perhaps, to close that gorgeous procession of European feudalism, with all its pomp and caste-prejudices, (of whose

11. Native, indigenous.
12. Eschylus (i.e., Aeschylus), Greek tragic dramatist (525–456 B.C.E.) whose plays, like Homer's epics, deal with such figures of the Trojan War as Agamemnon, leader of the Greek forces; Ulysses (Odysseus), whose return to Ithaca after the war took ten years; and Priam, slaughtered king of Troy. "Cute" here means "acute."

long train we in America are yet so inextricably the heirs)—something to identify with terrible identification, by far the greatest revolutionary step in the history of the United States, (perhaps the greatest of the world, our
century)—the absolute extirpation and erasure of slavery from the States—
those historians will seek in vain for any point to serve more thoroughly their
purpose, than Abraham Lincoln's death.

20   Dear to the Muse—thrice dear to Nationality—to the whole human race—
precious to this Union—precious to Democracy—unspeakably and forever
precious—their first great Martyr Chief.

QUESTIONS

1. Whitman delivered this piece as a lecture. What features suggest a lecture? How
might it have differed if he had composed it as an essay to be read rather than a lecture
to be heard?

2. The events of the assassination lead Whitman to mention his perception of Lincoln's
fondness for the theater. How does he make this observation serve a larger purpose?

3. At the end of this speech, Whitman speaks grandly of Lincoln's significance for far
more than the citizens of the United States. As he sees it, what do all these people have
in common that allows for Lincoln's more-than-national significance?

4. How does Whitman convey the sense of horror and confusion in the scene when
Lincoln is shot? Using some of Whitman's techniques, write an account of a similar
scene that produces a strong emotional effect.

H. BRUCE FRANKLIN *From Realism to Virtual Reality: Images of America's Wars*

THE INDUSTRIAL REVOLUTION was only about one
century old when modern technological warfare
burst upon the world in the US Civil War. During that
century human progress had already been manifested
in the continually increasing deadliness and range of
weapons, as well as in other potential military bene-
fits of industrial capitalism. But it was the Civil War that actually demonstrated industrialism's ability to produce carnage and devastation on an unprecedented scale, thus foreshadowing a future more and more dominated by
what we have come to call *technowar*. For the first time, immense armies had
been transported by railroad, coordinated by telegraph, and equipped with an

From Georgia Review *(Spring 1994), a small circulation quarterly published by the University of Georgia.*

ever-evolving arsenal of mass-produced weapons designed by scientists and engineers. The new machines of war—such as the repeating rifle, the primitive machine gun, the submarine, and the steam-powered, ironclad warship—were being forged by other machines. Industrial organization was essential, therefore, not only in the factories where the technoweapons were manufactured but also on the battlefields and waters where these machines destroyed each other and slaughtered people.

Prior to the Civil War, visual images of America's wars were almost without exception expressions of romanticism and nationalism. Paintings, lithographs, woodcuts, and statues displayed a glorious saga of thrilling American heroism from the Revolution through the Mexican War. Drawing on their imagination, artists could picture action-filled scenes of heroic events, such as Emmanuel Leutze's 1851 painting *Washington Crossing the Delaware*.[1]

Literature, however, was the only art form capable of projecting the action of warfare as temporal flow and movement. Using words as a medium, writers had few limitations on how they chose to paint this action, and their visions had long covered a wide spectrum. One of the Civil War's most distinctively modern images was expressed by Herman Melville in his poem "A Utilitarian View of the Monitor's Fight." Melville sees the triumph of "plain mechanic power" placing war "Where War belongs— / Among the trades and artisans," depriving it of "passion": "all went on by crank, / Pivot, and screw, / And calculations of caloric." Since "warriors / Are now but operatives," he hopes that "War's made / Less grand than Peace."

The most profoundly deglamorizing images of that war, however, were produced not by literature but directly by technology itself. The industrial processes and scientific knowledge that created technowar had also brought forth a new means of perceiving its devastation. Industrial chemicals, manufactured metal plates, lenses, mirrors, bellows, and actuating mechanisms—all were essential to the new art and craft of photography. Thus the Civil War was the first truly modern war—both in how it was fought and in how it was imaged. The romantic images of warfare projected by earlier visual arts were now radically threatened by images of warfare introduced by photography.

Scores of commercial photographers, seeking authenticity and profits, followed the Union armies into battle. Although evidently more than a million photographs of the Civil War were taken, hardly any show actual combat or other exciting action typical of the earlier paintings.[2] The photographers' need to stay close to their cumbersome horse-drawn laboratory wagons usually kept them from the thick of battle, and the collodion wet-plate process, which demanded long exposures, forced them to focus on scenes of stillness rather

5

---

1. See especially Alan Trachtenberg, *Reading American Photographs: Images as History, Mathew Brady to Walker Evans* (New York: Hill and Wang, 1989), p. 74; and William A. Frassanito, *Antietam: The Photographic Legacy of America's Bloodiest Day* (New York: Charles Scribner's Sons, 1978), pp. 27–28 [Franklin's note].

2. William C. Davis, "Finding the Hidden Images of the Civil War," *Civil War Times Illustrated*, 21 (1982, #2), 9 [Franklin's note].

Figure 1. "A Harvest of Death, Gettysburg," 1863 photograph by Timothy O'Sullivan.

than action. Among all human subjects, those who stayed most perfectly still for the camera were the dead. Hence Civil War photography, dominated by images of death, inaugurated a grim, profoundly antiromantic realism.

Perhaps the most widely reproduced photo from the war, Timothy O'Sullivan's "A Harvest of Death, Gettysburg," contains numerous corpses of Confederate soldiers, rotting after lying two days in the rain (see *Figure 1*). Stripped of their shoes and with their pockets turned inside out, the bodies stretch into the distance beyond the central corpse, whose mouth gapes gruesomely.

The first of such new images of war were displayed for sale to the public by Mathew Brady at his Broadway gallery in October 1862. Brady entitled his show "The Dead of Antietam." *The New York Times* responded in an awed editorial:

> The living that throng Broadway care little perhaps for the Dead at Antietam, but we fancy they would jostle less carelessly down the great thoroughfare . . . were a few dripping bodies, fresh from the field, laid along the pavement. . . .
> Mr. Brady has done something to bring home to us the terrible reality and earnestness of war. If he has not brought bodies and laid them in our dooryards and along the streets, he has done something very like it. At the door of his gallery hangs a little placard, "The Dead of Antietam." Crowds of people are constantly going up the stairs; follow them, and you find them bending over photographic views of that fearful battle-field, taken immediately after the action. . . . You will see hushed, reverent groups standing around these weird copies of carnage, bending down to look in the pale faces of the dead, chained by the strange spell that dwells in dead men's eyes.[3]

3. "Brady's Photographs: Pictures of the Dead at Antietam," *The New York Times,* 20 October 1862 [Franklin's note].

Oliver Wendell Holmes went further in explicating the meaning of the exhibition, which gives "some conception of what a repulsive, brutal, sickening, hideous thing it is, this dashing together of two frantic mobs to which we give the name of armies." He continues: "Let him who wishes to know what war is look at this series of illustrations. These wrecks of manhood thrown together in careless heaps or ranged in ghastly rows for burial were alive but yesterday. . . ."[4]

Nevertheless, three decades after the end of the Civil War the surging forces of militarism and imperialism were reimaging the conflict as a glorious episode in America's history. The disgust, shame, guilt, and deep national divisions that had followed this war—just like those a century later that followed the Vietnam War—were being buried under an avalanche of jingoist culture, the equivalent of contemporary Ramboism, even down to the cult of muscularism promulgated by Teddy Roosevelt.

It was in this historical context that Stephen Crane used realism, then flourishing as a literary mode, to assault just such treacherous views of war. Although *The Red Badge of Courage* is generally viewed as the great classic novel of the Civil War, it can be read much more meaningfully as Crane's response to the romantic militarism that was attempting to erase from the nation's memory the horrifying lessons taught by the war's realities.[5] Crane, not subject to the technological limitations of the slow black-and-white photographs that had brought home glimpses of the war's sordid repulsiveness, was able to image the animal frenzy that masqueraded as heroic combat and even to add color and tiny moving details to his pictures of the dead:

> The corpse was dressed in a uniform that once had been blue but was now faded to a melancholy shade of green. The eyes, staring at the youth, had changed to the dull hue to be seen on the side of a dead fish. The mouth was opened. Its red had changed to an appalling yellow. Over the grey skin of the face ran little ants. One was trundling some sort of a bundle along the upper lip.[6]

Other literary reactions to the new militarism looked even further backward to project images of a future dominated by war. Melville's *Billy Budd,* completed in 1891, envisions this triumph of violence in the aftermath of the American Revolution on the (aptly named) British warship HMS *Bellipotent,* where the best of humanity is hanged to death by the logic of war, the com-

10

4. Oliver Wendell Holmes's "Doings of the Sunbeam," *Atlantic Monthly* (July 1863), p. 12 [Franklin's note]. Holmes (1809–1894) was an American physician, writer, and frequent contributor to the *Atlantic Monthly,* an American magazine founded in 1857 and still famous for its coverage of politics and the arts.

5. This concept is developed most effectively by Amy Kaplan in "The Spectacle of War in Crane's Revision of History," *New Essays on "The Red Badge of Courage,"* ed. Lee Clark Mitchell (Cambridge: Cambridge University Press, 1986), pp. 77–108 [Franklin's note].

6. Stephen Crane, *"The Red Badge of Courage": An Episode in the American Civil War,* ed. Henry Binder (New York: Avon Books, 1983), p. 37 [Franklin's note].

mon people are turned into automatons "dispersed to the places allotted them when not at the guns," and the final image is of a sterile, lifeless, inorganic mass of "smooth white marble."[7]

In *A Connecticut Yankee in King Arthur's Court* (1889), Mark Twain recapitulates the development of industrial capitalism and extrapolates its future in a vision of apocalyptic technowar. Hank Morgan and his young disciples have run "secret wires" to dynamite deposits under all their "vast factories, mills, workshops, magazines, etc." and have connected them to a single command button so that nothing can stop them "when we want to blow up our civilization." When Hank does initiate this instantaneous push-button war, "In that explosion all our noble civilization-factories went up in the air and disappeared from the earth." Beyond an electrified fence, the technowarriors have prepared a forty-foot-wide belt of land mines. The first wave of thousands of knights triggers a twentieth-century-style explosion: "As to destruction of life, it was amazing. Moreover, it was beyond estimate. Of course we could not *count* the dead, because they did not exist as individuals, but merely as homogeneous protoplasm, with alloys of iron and buttons."

After Hank and his boys trap the rest of the feudal army inside their electric fence, Hank electrocutes the first batch, a flood is released on the survivors, and the boys man machine guns that "vomit death" into their ranks: "Within ten short minutes after we had opened fire, armed resistance was totally annihilated. . . . Twenty-five thousand men lay dead around us."[8] That number of dead, it is worth noting, matches exactly the total casualties in America's costliest day of war, the battle of Antietam, and thus recalls Brady's exhibition, "The Dead of Antietam." Twain's vision is even more horrific, for the victors themselves are conquered by "the poisonous air bred by those dead thousands." All that remains of this first experiment in industrialized warfare is a desolate landscape pockmarked by craters and covered with unburied, rotting corpses.

Twain's vision of the future implicit in industrial capitalism began to materialize in the First World War, when armies slaughtered each other on an unprecedented scale, sections of Europe were turned into a wasteland, and weapons of mass destruction first seemed capable of actually destroying civilization. Meanwhile, the scientific, engineering, and organizational progress that had produced the modern machine gun, long-range artillery, poison gas, and fleets of submarines and warplanes had also created a new image-making technology that broke through the limits of still photography. Just as the Civil War was the first to be extensively photographed, the "War to End All Wars" was the first to be extensively imaged in motion pictures.[9]

---

7. H. Bruce Franklin, "From Empire to Empire: *Billy Budd, Sailor,*" in *Herman Melville: Reassessments,* ed. A. Robert Lee (London: Vision Press, 1984), pp. 199–216 [Franklin's note].

8. Mark Twain, *A Connecticut Yankee in King Arthur's Court,* ed. Bernard L. Stein (Berkeley: University of California Press, 1979), pp. 466–86 [Franklin's note].

9. During the Spanish-American War, the Edison Company had recorded some motion pictures of the embarking troops but was unable to obtain any battle footage. Later the

World War I, of course, generated millions of still photographs, many showing scenes at least as ghastly as the corpse-strewn battlefields of the Civil War, and now there was also authentic documentary film of live action. But for various reasons the most influential photographic images from World War I, though realistic in appearance, displayed not reality but fantasy. Filmmakers who wished to record actual combat were severely restricted by the various governments and military authorities. At the same time, powerful forces were making a historic discovery: the tremendous potential of movies for propaganda and for profits. This was the dawn of twentieth-century image-making.

In the United States the most important photographic images were movies designed to inflame the nation, first to enter the war and then to support it. Probably the most influential was *The Battle Cry of Peace*, a 1915 smash hit that played a crucial role in rousing the public against Germany by showing realistic scenes of the invasion and devastation of America by a rapacious Germanic army. Once the US entered the war, the American public got to view an endless series of feature movies, such as *To Hell with the Kaiser*; *The Kaiser, the Beast of Berlin*; and *The Claws of the Hun*—each outdoing its predecessors in picturing German bestiality. Erich von Stroheim's career began with his portrayal of the archetypal sadistic German officer in films like *The Unbeliever* and *Heart of Humanity*, where in his lust to rape innocent young women he murders anyone who gets in the way—even the crying baby of one intended victim. This genre is surveyed by Larry Wayne Ward, who describes the 1918 Warner Brothers hit *My Four Years in Germany*, which opens with a title card telling the audience they are seeing "Fact Not Fiction":

> After the brutal conquest of Belgium, German troops are shown slaughtering innocent refugees and tormenting prisoners of war. Near the end of the film one of the German officials boasts that "America Won't Fight," a title which dissolves into newsreel footage of President Wilson and marching American soldiers. Soon American troops are seen fighting their way across the European battlefields. As he bayonets another German soldier, a young American doughboy turns to his companions and says, "I promised Dad I'd get six."[10]

Before the end of World War I, the motion picture had already proved to be a more effective vehicle for romanticizing and popularizing war than the antebellum school of heroic painting that had been partly debunked by Civil War photography. Indeed, the audiences that thronged to *My Four Years in Germany* frequently burned effigies of the kaiser outside the theaters and in some cases turned into angry mobs that had to be dispersed by police.

To restore the glamour of preindustrial war, however, it would take more

15

---

company re-created battle scenes in a mountain reservation near Edison's headquarters in Essex County, New Jersey. See "Historian Remembers the Maine, Spain-America Conflict," Newark (NJ) *Star Ledger* 11 February 1992 [Franklin's note].

10. Larry Wayne Ward, *The Motion Picture Goes to War: The U.S. Government Film Effort during World War I* (Ann Arbor: UMI Research Press, 1985), pp. 55–56 [Franklin's note].

than glorifying the men fighting on the ground or even the aviators supposedly dueling like medieval knights high above the battlefield. What was necessary to reverse Melville's "utilitarian" view of industrial warfare was the romanticizing of machines of war themselves.

The airplane was potentially an ideal vehicle for this romance. But photographic technology had to develop a bit further to bring home the thrills generated by destruction from the sky, because it needed to be seen *from* the sky, not from the ground where its reality was anything but glamorous. The central figure in America's romance with warplanes (as I have discussed at length elsewhere)[11] was Billy Mitchell, who also showed America and the world how to integrate media imagery with technowar.

In 1921, Mitchell staged a historic event by using bombers to sink captured German warships and turning the action into a media bonanza. His goal was to hit the American public with immediate, nationwide images of the airplane's triumph over the warship. The audacity of this enterprise in 1921 was remarkable. There were no satellites to relay images, and no television; in fact, the first experimental radio broadcast station had begun operation only in November 1920.

20   Back in 1919, Mitchell had given the young photographer George Goddard his own laboratory where, with assistance from Eastman Kodak, Goddard developed high-resolution aerial photography. As soon as Mitchell won the opportunity to bomb the German ships, he put Goddard in command of a key unit: a team of aerial photographers provided with eighteen airplanes and a dirigible. Mitchell's instructions were unambiguous: "I want newsreels of those sinking ships in every theater in the country, just as soon as we can get 'em there." This demanded more than mere picture taking. With his flair for public relations, Mitchell explained to Goddard: "Most of all I need you to handle the newsreel and movie people. They're temperamental, and we've got to get all we can out of them."[12] Goddard had to solve unprecedented logistical problems, flying the film first to Langley Field and thence to Bolling Field for pickup by the newsreel people who would take it to New York for development and national distribution. The sinking of each ship, artfully filmed by relays of Goddard's planes, was screened the very next day in big-city theaters across the country.

This spectacular media coup implanted potent images of the warplane in the public mind, and Mitchell himself became an overnight national hero as millions watched the death of great warships on newsreel screens. Mitchell was a prophet. The battleship was doomed. The airplane would rule the world.

America was now much closer to the 1990 media conception of the Gulf War than to Melville's "Utilitarian View of the Monitor's Fight." Melville's vision of technowar as lacking "passion" was becoming antiquated, for what could be more thrilling—even erotic—than aerial war machines? The evi-

11. H. Bruce Franklin, *War Stars: The Superweapon and the American Imagination* (New York: Oxford University Press, 1988), chapter 15 [Franklin's note].

12. Burke Davis, *The Billy Mitchell Affair* (New York: Random House, 1967), p. 16 [Franklin's note].

dence is strewn throughout modern America: the warplane models assembled by millions of boys and young men during World War II; the thousands of warplane magazines and books filled with glossy photographs that some find as stimulating as those in "men's" magazines; and Hollywood's own warplane romances, such as *Top Gun*—one of the most popular movies of the 1980's— or *Strategic Air Command*, in which Jimmy Stewart's response to his first sight of a B-47 nuclear bomber is, "She's the most beautiful thing I've ever seen in my life."

One of the warplane's great advantages as a vehicle of romance is its distance from its victims. From the aircraft's perspective, even the most grotesque slaughter it inflicts is sufficiently removed so that it can be imaged aesthetically. The aesthetics of aerial bombing in World War II were prefigured in 1937 by Mussolini's son Vittorio, whose ecstasy about his own experience bombing undefended Ethiopian villages was expressed in his image of his victims "bursting out like a rose after I had landed a bomb in the middle of them."[13] These aesthetics were consummated at the end of World War II by the mushroom clouds that rose over Hiroshima and Nagasaki.

Bracketed by these images, the aerial bombing of World War II has been most insightfully explored in *Catch-22* by Joseph Heller, a bombardier with sixty combat missions. The novel envisions the political and cultural triumph of fascism through the very means used to defeat it militarily. The turning point in Heller's work is the annihilation of an insignificant antifascist Italian mountain village, an event which allows fascist forces, embodied by US Air Corps officers, to gain total control.[14] The sole purpose of the American bombing of the village is image-making. The novel's General Peckem privately admits that bombing this "tiny undefended village, reducing the whole community to rubble" is "entirely unnecessary," but it will allow him to extend his power over the bombing squadrons. He has convinced them that he will measure their success by "a neat aerial photograph" of their *bomb pattern*—"a term I dreamed up," he confides, that "means nothing." The briefing officer tells the crews:

> Colonel Cathcart wants to come out of this mission with a good clean aerial photograph he won't be ashamed to send through channels. Don't forget that General Peckem will be here for the full briefing, and you know how he feels about bomb patterns.[15]

Pictures of bomb patterns were not, of course, the most influential American photographic image-making in World War II. The still photos published

25

13. *Voli sulle ambe* (Florence, 1937), a book Vittorio Mussolini wrote to convince Italian boys they should all try war, "the most beautiful and complete of all sports." Quoted by Denis Mack Smith, *Mussolini's Roman Empire* (New York: Viking, 1976), p. 75 [Franklin's note].

14. For extended analyses of the significance of this event, see Franklin, *War Stars*, pp. 123–27, and Clinton Burhans Jr., "Spindrift and the Sea: Structural Patterns and Unifying Elements in *Catch-22*," *Twentieth Century Literature*, 19 (1973), 239–50 [Franklin's note].

15. Joseph Heller, *Catch-22* (New York: Dell, 1962), pp. 334–37 [Franklin's note].

in *Life* alone could be the subject of several dissertations, and World War II feature movies about strategic bombing have been discussed at length by myself and many others. Indeed, in 1945 one might have wondered how the camera could possibly play a more important role in war.

The answer came in Vietnam, the first war to be televised directly into tens of millions of homes.[16] Television's glimpses of the war's reality were so horrendous and so influential that these images have been scapegoated as one of the main causes of the United States' defeat. Indeed, the Civil War still photographs of corpses seem innocuous when compared to the Vietnam War's on-screen killings, as well as live-action footage of the bulldozing of human carcasses into mass graves, the napalming of children, and the ravaging of villages by American soldiers.

As appalling as these public images were, however, few had meanings as loathsome as the pictures that serve as the central metaphor of Stephen Wright's novel *Meditations in Green*. The hero of the novel has the job that the author had in Vietnam: he works as a photoanalyst in an intelligence unit whose mission is to aid the torture and assassination campaign known as Operation Phoenix, the ecocidal defoliation campaign originally designated Operation Hades, and the genocidal bombing. His official job as "image interpreter" is to scrutinize reconnaissance films to find evidence of life so that it can be eliminated. Not just humans are targets to be erased by bombing; trees themselves become the enemy. Anyone in the unit who has qualms about such genocide and ecocide is defined—in a revealing term—as a "smudge," thus becoming another target for elimination. The perfect image, it is implied, should have nothing left of the human or the natural. From the air, the unit's own base looks like "a concentration camp or a movie lot." The climax of the novel comes when the base is devastated by an enemy attack intercut with scenes from *Night of the Living Dead*, that ghoulish 1968 vision of America which is simultaneously being screened as entertainment.[17]

One of the most influential and enduring single images from the Vietnam War—certainly the most contested—exploded into the consciousness of millions of Americans in February 1968 when they actually watched, within the comfort of their own homes, as the chief of the Saigon national police executed a manacled NLF[18] prisoner. In a perfectly framed sequence, the notorious General Nguyen Ngoc Loan unholsters a snub-nosed revolver and places its muzzle to the prisoner's right temple. The prisoner's head jolts, a sudden spurt of blood gushes straight out of his right temple, and he collapses in death. The next morning, newspaper readers were confronted with AP photog-

---

16. When the Korean War began in mid-1950, there were fewer than ten million television sets in the United States. Americans' principal visual images of that war came from newsreels shown before feature films in movie theaters and from still photos in magazines [Franklin's note].

17. Stephen Wright, *Meditations in Green* (New York: Bantam, 1984) [Franklin's note].

18. National Liberation Front, opponents of the government of South Vietnam who were allied with the North Vietnamese.

Figure 2. General Nguyen Ngoc Loan, head of South Vietnam's police and intelligence, executing a prisoner: 1968 photograph by Eddie Adams.

rapher Eddie Adams' potent stills of the execution (see *Figure* 2). The grim ironies of the scene were accentuated by the cultural significance of the weapon itself: a revolver, a somewhat archaic handgun, symbolic of the American West.

Precisely one decade later this image, with the roles now reversed, was transformed into the dominant metaphor of a Hollywood production presenting a new version of the Vietnam War: *The Deer Hunter.* This lavishly financed movie, which the New York Film Critics' Circle designated the best English-language film of 1978 and which received four Academy Awards, including Best Picture of 1978, succeeded not only in radically reimaging the war but in transforming prisoners of war (POW's) into central symbols of American manhood for the 1980's and 1990's.

The manipulation of familiar images—some already accruing symbolic power—was blatant, though most critics at the time seemed oblivious to it. The basic technique was to take images of the war that had become deeply embedded in America's consciousness and transform them into their opposites. For example, in the film's first scene in Vietnam, a uniformed soldier throws a grenade into an underground village shelter harboring women and children, and then with his automatic rifle mows down a woman and her baby.

30

Figure 3. In *The Deer Hunter* (1978), General Loan's revolver metamorphoses into a North Vietnamese revolver, and his NLF prisoner is replaced by South Vietnamese and US prisoners forced to play Russian roulette.

Although the scene resembles the familiar TV sequence of GI's in Vietnamese villages (as well as *Life*'s photographs of the My Lai massacre), the soldier turns out to be not American but North Vietnamese. In turn he is killed by a lone guerrilla—who is not a Viet Cong but our Special Forces hero, played by Robert DeNiro. Later, when two men plummet from a helicopter, the images replicate a familiar telephotographic sequence showing an NLF prisoner being pushed from a helicopter to make other prisoners talk;[19] but the falling men in the movie are American POW's attempting to escape from their murderous North Vietnamese captors.

The structuring metaphor of the film is the Russian roulette that the sadistic Asian Communists force their prisoners to play. The crucial torture scene consists of sequence after sequence of images replicating and replacing the infamous killing of the NLF prisoner by General Nguyen Ngoc Loan. Prisoner after prisoner is hauled out of the tiger cages (which also serve as a substitute image for the tiger cages of the Saigon government) and then forced by the demonic North Vietnamese officer in charge (who always stands to the prisoner's right, our left) to place a revolver to his own right temple. Then the

19. "How Helicopter Dumped a Viet Captive to Death," *Chicago Sun-Times*, 29 November 1969; "Death of a Prisoner," *San Francisco Chronicle*, 29 November 1969 [Franklin's note].

Figure 4. *P.O.W.: The Escape* (1986) transforms the South Vietnamese execution of a prisoner into a North Vietnamese prison commander's murder of a US prisoner.

image is framed to eliminate the connection between the prisoner's body and the arm holding the revolver, thus bringing the image closer to the famous execution image (see *Figure 3*). One sequence even replicates the blood spurting out of the victim's right temple.

The Deer Hunter's manipulation of this particular image to reverse the roles of victim and victimizer was used again and again in the 1980's by other vehicles of the militarization of American culture from movies to comic books. Take, for example, *P.O.W.: The Escape*, an overtly militaristic 1986 POW rescue movie, inspired by *Rambo* and starring David Carradine as superhero. The bestiality of the Asian Communists is here embodied by a North Vietnamese prison-camp commander who executes an American prisoner with a revolver shot to the right temple in a tableau modeled even more precisely than *The Deer Hunter's* on the original execution of the NLF prisoner in Saigon (see *Figure 4*). Then—just in case viewers missed it—this scene is replayed later as the movie's only flashback.

Toward the end of the 1980's, however, the infamous execution got manipulated incredibly further, actually shifting the role of the most heartless shooter (originally a South Vietnamese official) from the Vietnamese Communists to the photographers themselves! For example, the cover story of the November 1988 issue of the popular comic book *The 'Nam* portrays the photojournalists, both still photographers and TV cameramen, as the real enemies because they had placed the image on the "front page of every newspaper in the states!" The cover literally reverses the original image by showing the execution scene from a position behind the participants (*Figure 5*). This offers a frontal view of the photographer, whose deadly camera conceals his face and

Figure 5. Cover story of the November 1988 issue of *The 'Nam*,
glorifying General Nguyen Ngoc Loan and making the
photographer into the villain.

occupies the exact center of the picture. The prisoner appears merely as an
arm, shoulder, and sliver of a body on the left. The only face shown belongs to
the chief of the security police, who displays the righteous—even heroic—indignation that has led him to carry out this justifiable revenge against the
treacherous actions of the "Viet Cong" pictured in the story. The climactic image (*Figure 6*) is a full page in which the execution scene appears as a reflection in the gigantic lens of the camera above the leering mouth of the
photographer, from which comes a bubble with his greedy words, "Keep shooting! Just keep shooting!" "Shooting" a picture here has become synonymous
with murder and treason. In the next panel, two GI's register their shock—not
at the execution, but at a TV cameraman focusing on the dead body:

> "Front page of every newspaper in the states!"
> "Geez . . ."

Figure 6. *The 'Nam* images the photographer as the
shooter—and the camera as the most destructive weapon.

One can hardly imagine a more complete reversal of the acclaim accorded to
Civil War photographers for bringing the reality of war and death home to the
American people.

The logic of this comic-book militarism, put into practice for each of
America's wars since Vietnam, is inescapable: photographers must be allowed
to image for the public only what the military deems suitable. Non-military
photographers and all journalists were simply banished from the entire war
zone during the 1983 invasion of Grenada. Partly as a result of this treatment,
the major media accepted a pool system for the 1989 invasion of Panama—
and meekly went along with the military's keeping even these selected journalists confined to a US base throughout most of the conflict. (A European
reporter who attempted to report directly from the scene was actually shot to
death when the military unit sent to arrest him became involved in "friendly
fire" with another group of US soldiers.)

The almost complete absence of photographic images was quite conven-   35
ient for the Grenada and Panama invasions, which were carried out so swiftly
and with such minimal military risk that they required no Congressional or
public endorsement. And for the first several days after US troops had been dispatched to confront Iraq in August 1990, Secretary of Defense Dick Cheney refused to allow journalists to accompany them. The Pentagon seemed to be
operating under the belief that photographic and televised images had helped
bring about the US defeat in Vietnam. But for the Gulf War, with its long

buildup, its potential for significant casualties, and its intended international and domestic political purposes, *some* effective images proved to be essential.

To control these images, the US government set up pools of selected reporters and photographers, confined them to certain locations, required them to have military escorts when gathering news, established stringent guidelines limiting what could be reported or photographed, and subjected all written copy, photographs, and videotape to strict censorship.[20] Most of those admitted to the pools, it is interesting to note, represented the very newspapers and TV networks that were simultaneously mounting a major campaign to build support for the war. Journalists were forced to depend on military briefings, where they were often fed deliberately falsified information. Immediately after the ground offensive began, all press briefings and pool reports were indefinitely suspended. In a most revealing negation of the achievement of Civil War photography, with its shocking disclosure of the reality of death, the Pentagon banned the press entirely from Dover Air Force Base during the arrival of the bodies of those killed in the war. Responding to an ACLU legal argument that it was attempting to shield the public from disturbing images, the Pentagon replied that it was merely protecting the privacy of grieving relatives.[21]

Although the media were largely denied access to the battlefields, the Gulf War nevertheless gained the reputation of the first "real-time" television war, and the images projected into American homes helped to incite the most passionate war fever since World War II. These screened images ranged from the most traditional to the most innovative modes of picturing America's wars. Even the antiquated icon of the heroic commanding general, missing for about forty years, was given new life. Although hardly as striking a figure as the commander in Leutze's *Washington Crossing the Delaware* or the posed picture of General Douglas MacArthur returning to the Philippines during World War II, a public idol took shape in the corpulent form of General Norman Schwarzkopf in his fatigues, boots, and jaunty cap.

But perhaps the most potent images combined techniques pioneered by Billy Mitchell with General Peckem's quest for aerial photos of perfect bomb patterns, the medium of television, and the technological capabilities of the weapons themselves. After all, since one of the main goals of the warmakers was to create the impression of a "clean" technowar—almost devoid of human suffering and death, conducted with surgical precision by wondrous mechanisms—why not project the war from the point of view of the weapons? And so the most thrilling images were transmitted directly by the laser-guidance systems of missiles and by those brilliant creations, "smart" bombs. Fascinated and excited, tens of millions of Americans stared at their screens, sharing the experience of these missiles and bombs unerringly guided by the wonders of American technology to a target identified by a narrator as an important military installation. The generation raised in video arcades and on Nintendo

---

20. Everette E. Dennis et al., *The Media at War: The Press and the Persian Gulf Conflict* (New York: Gannett Foundation, 1991), pp. 17–18 [Franklin's note].

21. Dennis, pp. 21–22 [Franklin's note].

Figure 7. Technowar triumphs in TV sequence of a smart bomb destroying an Iraqi building.

could hardly be more satisfied. The target got closer and closer, larger and larger (*Figure* 7). And then everything ended with the explosion. There were no bloated human bodies, as in the photographs of the battlefields of Antietam and Gettysburg—and none of the agony of the burned and wounded glimpsed on television relays from Vietnam. There was just nothing at all. In this magnificent triumph of technowar, America's images of its wars had seemingly reached perfection.

QUESTIONS

1. Franklin tells a double story of technological advances in making war and in making images. Trace each stage of both narratives. Explain, at each stage, how he links them.

2. Franklin includes seven illustrations in this essay. Explain his choice of each. Are there others he mentions that you wish he had included? Why? (Locating them might be a class project.)

3. Take one of the illustrations in this essay and write an essay in which you offer an alternative interpretation of it as a counterargument to Franklin's interpretation.

4. Franklin includes references to literature (fiction, primarily, but also poetry), films, television, and comic books. How does he present the differences among them? Compare the powers he attributes to words and the powers he attributes to images.

5. Choose a recent U.S. war (or military action) and reconstruct your sense of it and how you acquired that sense. Locate some of the images you remember, and write an essay comparing your memory of them with the images as you see them now. Or, if you had no sense of the event when it occurred, locate some of the important images of it, and write an essay comparing how you think you would have seen them then and how you see them now.

HANNAH ARENDT *Deportations from Western Europe*

AT THE WANNSEE CONFERENCE,[1] Martin Luther, of the Foreign Office, warned of great difficulties in the Scandinavian countries, notably in Norway and Denmark. (Sweden was never occupied, and Finland, though in the war on the side of the Axis, was one country the Nazis never even approached on the Jewish question. This surprising exception of Finland, with some two thousand Jews, may have been due to Hitler's great esteem for the Finns, whom perhaps he did not want to subject to threats and humiliating blackmail.) Luther proposed postponing evacuations from Scandinavia for the time being, and as far as Denmark was concerned, this really went without saying, since the country retained its independent government, and was respected as a neutral state, until the fall of 1943, although it, along with Norway, had been invaded by the German Army in April, 1940. There existed no Fascist or Nazi movement in Denmark worth mentioning, and therefore no collaborators. In Norway, however, the Germans had been able to find enthusiastic supporters; indeed, Vidkun Quisling, leader of the pro-Nazi and anti-Semitic Norwegian party, gave his name to what later became known as a "quisling government." The bulk of Norway's seventeen hundred Jews were stateless, refugees from Germany; they were seized and interned in a few lightning operations in October and November, 1942. When Eichmann's[2] office ordered their deportation to Auschwitz, some of Quisling's own men resigned their government posts. This may not have come as a surprise to Mr. Luther and the Foreign Office, but what was much more serious, and certainly totally unexpected, was that Sweden imme-

Originally published in the "Reporter at Large" section of the New Yorker *(February–March 1963), Arendt's articles covered the trial of Adolf Eichmann, the Nazi lieutenant colonel responsible for transporting countless Jews to concentration camps. This selection comes from the book version of her account,* Eichmann in Jerusalem: A Report on the Banality of Evil *(1963), which, beyond reportage, raises larger questions about the crime of genocide and the nature of totalitarianism.*

1. A meeting of German officials on "the Jewish question."
2. Adolf Eichmann (1906–1962), German Nazi in charge of the execution of Jews (1942–45).

diately offered asylum, and even Swedish nationality, to all who were persecuted. Dr. Ernst von Weizsäcker, Undersecretary of State of the Foreign Office, who received the proposal, refused to discuss it, but the offer helped
nevertheless. It is always relatively easy to get out of a country illegally,
whereas it is nearly impossible to enter the place of refuge without permission
and to dodge the immigration authorities. Hence, about nine hundred people,
slightly more than half of the small Norwegian community, could be smuggled
into Sweden.

It was in Denmark, however, that the Germans found out how fully justified the Foreign Office's apprehensions had been. The story of the Danish
Jews is *sui generis*,[3] and the behavior of the Danish people and their government was unique among all the countries in Europe—whether occupied, or a
partner of the Axis, or neutral and truly independent. One is tempted to recommend the story as required reading in political science for all students who
wish to learn something about the enormous power potential inherent in nonviolent action and in resistance to an opponent possessing vastly superior
means of violence. To be sure, a few other countries in Europe lacked proper
"understanding of the Jewish question," and actually a majority of them were
opposed to "radical" and "final" solutions. Like Denmark, Sweden, Italy, and
Bulgaria proved to be nearly immune to anti-Semitism, but of the three that
were in the German sphere of influence, only the Danes dared speak out on
the subject to their German masters. Italy and Bulgaria sabotaged German orders and indulged in a complicated game of double-dealing and double-cross-
ing, saving their Jews by a tour de force of sheer ingenuity, but they never
contested the policy as such. That was totally different from what the Danes
did. When the Germans approached them rather cautiously about introducing
the yellow badge, they were simply told that the King would be the first to
wear it, and the Danish government officials were careful to point out that
anti-Jewish measures of any sort would cause their own immediate resignation. It was decisive in this whole matter that the Germans did not even succeed in introducing the vitally important distinction between native Danes of
Jewish origin, of whom there were about sixty-four hundred, and the fourteen
hundred German Jewish refugees who had found asylum in the country prior
to the war and who now had been declared stateless by the German government. This refusal must have surprised the Germans no end, since it appeared
so "illogical" for a government to protect people to whom it had categorically
denied naturalization and even permission to work. (Legally, the prewar situation of refugees in Denmark was not unlike that in France, except that the
general corruption in the Third Republic's civil services enabled a few of them
to obtain naturalization papers, through bribes or "connections," and most
refugees in France could work illegally, without a permit. But Denmark, like
Switzerland, was no country *pour se débrouiller*.)[4] The Danes, however, explained to the German officials that because the stateless refugees were no

3. Unique; literally, of its own kind (Latin).
4. For wangling—using bribery to circumvent bureaucratic regulations.

longer German citizens, the Nazis could not claim them without Danish assent. This was one of the few cases in which statelessness turned out to be an asset, although it was of course not statelessness per se that saved the Jews but, on the contrary, the fact that the Danish government had decided to protect them. Thus, none of the preparatory moves, so important for the bureaucracy of murder, could be carried out, and operations were postponed until the fall of 1943.

What happened then was truly amazing; compared with what took place in other European countries, everything went topsy-turvy. In August, 1943—after the German offensive in Russia had failed, the Afrika Korps had surrendered in Tunisia, and the Allies had invaded Italy—the Swedish government canceled its 1940 agreement with Germany which had permitted German troops the right to pass through the country. Thereupon, the Danish workers decided that they could help a bit in hurrying things up; riots broke out in Danish shipyards, where the dock workers refused to repair German ships and then went on strike. The German military commander proclaimed a state of emergency and imposed martial law, and Himmler[5] thought this was the right moment to tackle the Jewish question, whose "solution" was long overdue. What he did not reckon with was that—quite apart from Danish resistance—the German officials who had been living in the country for years were no longer the same. Not only did General von Hannecken, the military commander, refuse to put troops at the disposal of the Reich plenipotentiary, Dr. Werner Best; the special S.S. units (*Einsatzkommandos*) employed in Denmark very frequently objected to "the measures they were ordered to carry out by the central agencies"—according to Best's testimony of Nuremberg. And Best himself, an old Gestapo man and former legal adviser to Heydrich, author of a then famous book on the police, who had worked for the military government in Paris to the entire satisfaction of his superiors, could no longer be trusted, although it is doubtful that Berlin ever learned the extent of his unreliability. Still, it was clear from the beginning that things were not going well, and Eichmann's office sent one of its best men to Denmark—Rolf Günther, whom no one had ever accused of not possessing the required "ruthless toughness." Günther made no impression on his colleagues in Copenhagen, and now von Hannecken refused even to issue a decree requiring all Jews to report for work.

Best went to Berlin and obtained a promise that all Jews from Denmark would be sent to Theresienstadt[6] regardless of their category—a very important concession, from the Nazis' point of view. The night of October 1 was set for their seizure and immediate departure—ships were ready in the harbor—and since neither the Danes nor the Jews nor the German troops stationed in Denmark could be relied on to help, police units arrived from Germany for a

5. Heinrich Himmler (1900–1945), high-ranking official in Nazi Germany who organized the SS (*Schutzstaffel*, Elite Guard) in 1929 and the Gestapo in 1933.
6. A camp for certain classes of prisoners who were supposed to receive special treatment.

door-to-door search. At the last moment, Best told them that they were not permitted to break into apartments, because the Danish police might then interfere, and they were not supposed to fight it out with the Danes. Hence they could seize only those Jews who voluntarily opened their doors. They found exactly 477 people, out of a total of more than 7,800, at home and willing to let them in. A few days before the date of doom, a German shipping agent, Georg F. Duckwitz, having probably been tipped off by Best himself, had revealed the whole plan to Danish government officials, who, in turn, had hurriedly informed the heads of the Jewish community. They, in marked contrast to Jewish leaders in other countries, had then communicated the news openly in the synagogues on the occasion of the New Year services. The Jews had just time enough to leave their apartments and go into hiding, which was very easy in Denmark, because, in the words of the judgment, "all sections of the Danish people, from the King down to simple citizens," stood ready to receive them.

They might have remained in hiding until the end of the war if the Danes had not been blessed with Sweden as a neighbor. It seemed reasonable to ship the Jews to Sweden, and this was done with the help of the Danish fishing fleet. The cost of transportation for people without means—about a hundred dollars per person—was paid largely by wealthy Danish citizens, and that was perhaps the most astounding feat of all, since this was a time when Jews were paying for their own deportation, when the rich among them were paying fortunes for exit permits (in Holland, Slovakia, and, later, in Hungary) either by bribing the local authorities or by negotiating "legally" with the S.S., who accepted only hard currency and sold exit permits, in Holland, to the tune of five or ten thousand dollars per person. Even in places where Jews met with genuine sympathy and a sincere willingness to help, they had to pay for it, and the chances poor people had of escaping were nil.

It took the better part of October to ferry all the Jews across the five to fifteen miles of water that separates Denmark from Sweden. The Swedes received 5,919 refugees, of whom at least 1,000 were of German origin, 1,310 were half-Jews, and 686 were non-Jews married to Jews. (Almost half the Danish Jews seem to have remained in the country and survived the war in hiding.) The non-Danish Jews were better off than ever before; they all received permission to work. The few hundred Jews whom the German police had been able to arrest were shipped to Theresienstadt. They were old or poor people, who either had not received the news in time or had not been able to comprehend its meaning. In the ghetto, they enjoyed greater privileges than any other group because of the never-ending "fuss" made about them by Danish institutions and private persons. Forty-eight persons died, a figure that was not particularly high, in view of the average age of the group. When everything was over, it was the considered opinion of Eichmann that "for various reasons the action against the Jews in Denmark has been a failure," whereas the curious Dr. Best declared that "the objective of the operation was not to seize a great number of Jews but to clean Denmark of Jews, and this objective has now been achieved."

Politically and psychologically, the most interesting aspect of this incident is perhaps the role played by the German authorities in Denmark, their obvious sabotage of orders from Berlin. It is the only case we know of in which the Nazis met with *open* native resistance, and the result seems to have been that those exposed to it changed their minds. They themselves apparently no longer looked upon the extermination of a whole people as a matter of course. They had met resistance based on principle, and their "toughness" had melted like butter in the sun; they had even been able to show a few timid beginnings of genuine courage. That the ideal of "toughness," except, perhaps, for a few half-demented brutes, was nothing but a myth of self-deception, concealing a ruthless desire for conformity at any price, was clearly revealed at the Nuremberg Trials, where the defendants accused and betrayed each other and assured the world that they "had always been against it" or claimed, as Eichmann was to do, that their best qualities had been "abused" by their superiors. (In Jerusalem, he accused "those in power" of having abused his "obedience." "The subject of a good government is lucky, the subject of a bad government is unlucky. I had no luck.") The atmosphere had changed, and although most of them must have known that they were doomed, not a single one of them had the guts to defend the Nazi ideology. Werner Best claimed at Nuremberg that he had played a complicated double role and that it was thanks to him that the Danish officials had been warned of the impending catastrophe; documentary evidence showed, on the contrary, that he himself had proposed the Danish operation in Berlin, but he explained that this was all part of the game. He was extradited to Denmark and there condemned to death, but he appealed the sentence, with surprising results; because of "new evidence," his sentence was commuted to five years in prison, from which he was released soon afterward. He must have been able to prove to the satisfaction of the Danish court that he really had done his best.

QUESTIONS

1. Why do you think the Danes spoke out against anti-Semitism when other countries under German influence chose different methods of response or resistance? What details or hints does Arendt provide?

2. In paragraph 7, Arendt writes about Nazis who, when "met with open native resistance," changed their minds. What possible reasons does Arendt offer for this change? Are there other reasons you can think of for such change?

3. In paragraph 2, Arendt writes about "the enormous power potential inherent in nonviolent action and in resistance to an opponent possessing vastly superior means of violence." Research a more recent political situation in which you think a government or group of people could productively respond in a nonviolent manner, and write about it.

World War II: Victims, Villains, Heroes

MATT BAI   *He Said No to Internment*

In February 1942, a little more than two months after the attack on Pearl Harbor,[1] Franklin Roosevelt signed Executive Order 9066, which effectively decreed that West Coast residents of Japanese ancestry—whether American citizens or not—were now "enemy aliens." More than 100,000 Japanese-

Fred Korematsu, b. 1919.

Americans reported to government staging areas, where they were processed and taken off to 10 internment camps. Fred Korematsu, the son of Japanese immigrants, was at the time a 23-year-old welder at Bay Area shipyards. His parents left their home and reported to a racetrack south of San Francisco, but Korematsu chose not to follow them. He stayed behind in Oakland with his Italian-American girlfriend and then fled, even having plastic surgery on his eyes to avoid recognition. In May 1942, he was arrested and branded a spy in the newspapers.

In search of a test case, Ernest Besig, then the executive director of the American Civil Liberties Union for Northern California, went to see Korematsu in jail and asked if he would be willing to challenge the internment policy in court. Korematsu said he would. Besig posted $5,000 bail, but instead of freeing him, federal authorities sent him to the internment camp at Topaz, Utah. He and Besig sued the government, appealing their case all the way to the Supreme Court, which in a 6-to-3 decision that stands as

The New York Times Magazine *published these three short biographies of World War II survivors in a special issue (December 25, 2005) on known and unknown heroes who had died during the year.*

1. The Japanese attacked this American military base in Honolulu, on the island of Oahu, on December 7, 1941, prompting America to enter World War II. Franklin Roosevelt (1882–1945) was then president of the United States.

one of the most ignoble in its history, rejected his argument and upheld the government's right to intern its citizens.

After the war, Korematsu married, returned to the Bay Area and found work as a draftsman. He might have been celebrated in his community, the Rosa Parks[2] of Japanese-American life; in fact, he was shunned. Even during his time in Topaz, other prisoners refused to talk to him. "All of them turned their backs on me at that time because they thought I was a troublemaker," he later recalled. His ostracism didn't end with the war. The overwhelming majority of Japanese-Americans had reacted to the internment by acquiescing to the government's order, hoping to prove their loyalty as Americans. To them, Korematsu's opposition was treacherous to both his country and his community.

In the years after the war, details of the internment were lost behind a wall of repression. It was common for Japanese-American families not to talk about the experience, or to talk about it only obliquely. Korematsu, too, remained silent, but for different reasons. "He felt responsible for the internment in a sort of backhanded way, because his case had been lost in the Supreme Court," Peter Irons, a legal historian, recalled in a PBS documentary. Korematsu's own daughter has said she didn't learn of his wartime role until she was a junior in high school.

5   Korematsu might have faded into obscurity had it not been for Irons, who in 1981 asked the Justice Department for the original documents in the Korematsu case. Irons found a memo in which a government lawyer had accused the solicitor general of lying to the Supreme Court about the danger posed by Japanese-Americans. Irons tracked down Korematsu and asked if he would be willing, once again, to go to court.

Perhaps Korematsu had been waiting all those years for a chance to clear his name. Or maybe he saw, in Irons's entreaty, an opportunity to vindicate himself with other Japanese-Americans. Whatever his thinking, not only did Korematsu agree to return to court but he also became an ardent public critic of the internment. When government lawyers offered Korematsu a pardon, he refused. "As long as my record stands in federal court," Korematsu, then 64, said in an emotional courtroom oration, "any American citizen can be held in prison or concentration camps without a trial or a hearing." The judged agreed, ruling from the bench that Korematsu had been innocent. Just like that, the legality of the internment was struck down forever.

In the last decade of his life, Korematsu became, for some Americans, a symbol of principled resistance. President Clinton[3] awarded Korematsu the Presidential Medal of Freedom in 1998. Six years later, outraged by the prolonged detention of prisoners at Guantánamo Bay,[4] Korematsu filed an amicus

---

2. Parks (1913–2005), African-American civil rights activist whose refusal to give up her bus seat for a white passenger became an iconic moment in the U.S. history of civil rights.

3. William Jefferson Clinton (b. 1946), president of the United States from 1993 to 2001.

4. Site of a U.S.-owned prison in Cuba where militants from Iraq and Afghanistan are currently being detained.

brief with the Supreme Court, warning that the mistakes of the internment were being repeated. Still, Korematsu's place among contemporaries in his own community remained obscured by lingering resentments and a reluctance to revisit the past. When he died from a respiratory illness in March [2005], not a single public building or landmark bore his name. It wasn't until last month [November 2005] that officials in Davis, Calif., dedicated the Fred Korematsu Elementary School. It was an especially fitting tribute for Korematsu, whose legacy rested with a generation of Japanese-Americans who were beginning to remember, at long last, what their parents had labored to forget.

QUESTIONS

1. Many Americans do not know the history of the government's internment of its own citizens during World War II. Where does Matt Bai provide the necessary background so that the reader understands this history? Where does he supply the after-events of the history?

2. Was Fred Korematsu a hero? What responses to this question does Bai provide in his biography? What is his opinion as biographer? How do you know?

3. Interview someone—a family member, a neighbor, an older person on your campus—who has lived through an important era of American history. Write a short biography in which you interweave his or her experience with facts and background information about that era.

SARA CORBETT   *Saved by Strangers*

He was prodded to his feet by rifle barrels. This was northern Tunisia, Nov. 29, 1942. Just after midnight, following faulty intelligence, he had led his men into enemy territory. Now he stood surrounded, trembling, sickened by the gravity of his mistake. A German sergeant jammed a pistol into Joe Frelinghuysen's gut and joked that he'd been easier to catch than a rabbit.

This indignity stayed with him. He was flown to Italy and put in a series of Fascist-run prison camps in a mountainous area northeast of Rome. There he studied the walls, filled with self-recrimination.

He had been easier to catch than a rabbit. It wouldn't happen again. He nourished himself with potato peels sneaked from the cook's garbage. He did push-ups, paced the fence line of the camp. A guard gave him an Italian grammar book, which he studied feverishly, memorizing 30 words a day.

He had been imprisoned nearly 10 months—had lost 70 pounds and was tormented by nightmares—when Dick Rossbach showed up. Rossbach didn't give a damn. He had tried to escape twice already, once by flinging himself out the window of a moving train near the Austrian border. Fear, Rossbach liked to say, was better than a martini.   5

Nine days later, they left together, wriggling in the twilight under one barbed-wire fence, then another, then under two more and finally scaled a wall. They climbed a dark mountain and did not look back. Life from here on out boiled down to one thing: not getting caught.

With his grasp of Italian, Frelinghuysen was in charge of begging for food. In a small, silent village, he encountered an old woman who, upon seeing him, gathered her skirts and fled. The Germans had posted signs: anyone caught helping a prisoner would be shot. So they slept in caves and in clearings in the woods. The only warm night came when a sympathetic shepherd allowed them to sleep pressed up against his pregnant sow. They ate what was handed to them: apples, cheese, a sheep's lung wrapped in newspaper.

What felt perverse was how beautiful the setting was. Frelinghuysen would later describe in his memoir the stunning beech and oak forests of those valleys in the region called Abruzzi—the flaming colors of autumn and the toylike villages stacked into the hills.

After three weeks, it felt like the end. Rossbach had damaged his knee and could barely walk. Their skin was filthy; their bodies were malnourished. If this was freedom, they were ready to trade it for something that less approximated a slow, limping death.

But then, high in the Apennine mountains, more than an hour's walk from the nearest road, they came upon a stooped man with a black mustache, working his fields with a hoe. He wore a sweat-stained hat and smiled easily. When they asked for food, he directed them toward a stone farmhouse.

10   Being hunted by soldiers with dogs can kill a person's faith, but there are simple things that revive it. Inside the farmhouse, Rosa DiGiacomantonio— the wife of the man with the hoe—served them sausage with steaming polenta, scooped from an iron caldron on the hearth, flavored with garlic and pepper, drizzled with rich olive oil. She poured two glasses of red wine.

Already, she had fed dozens of these filthy, starved men. She'd chopped, simmered and ladled up just about everything her family had harvested that summer. But the prisoners kept coming. The farmhouse sat on a grassy saddle between mountain ranges, a natural stopping point for P.O.W.'s picking their way south toward the Allies. The only things she wouldn't share were the chickens' eggs, which she fed to Letizia, her hugely pregnant daughter-in-law. That night, when the two fugitives asked for a barn to sleep in, Antonio, Rosa's husband, led them instead to a candlelit room with a double bed and spotless white sheets and a pink blanket. He all but tucked them in.

Back home, Joe Frelinghuysen had a wife named Emily and two small children who wouldn't recognize him. To think of them was painful, so he avoided it. But for more than two weeks in October 1943, he and Rossbach had the DiGiacomantonios, who fed and helped shelter them and who jubilantly shared a bottle of tawny wine with them on the night when Letizia, cloistered upstairs, gave birth to a son. Letizia's husband, Berardino, became a friend—traveling to town to gather news of the war, arranging for a doctor to look at Rossbach's knee. The doctor wrapped his knee, but there was no time for it to mend. Nazi patrols were now searching houses in the valleys below.

One day when the two Americans were out doing reconnaissance, they were surrounded by three German soldiers on a hillside. Rossbach grabbed the barrel of the corporal's gun and pointed it to his chest, announcing that he was injured and demanding that they shoot him right there. It was grand theater—Frelinghuysen knew this—a diversion so that he, the only one able, could run. When the soldiers marched them inside a nearby hut, Rossbach offered food to their bewildered captors. When the Germans set down their rifles to eat, Rossbach looked impatiently at Frelinghuysen, then at the door.

Letizia and Berardino DiGiacomantonio, at home in Raritan, N.J., risked their lives to save Frelinghuysen from the Nazis in Italy. He gave them their start in America.

He ran like hell. Leaving his friend to an uncertain fate, he hurled himself outside and down a slick embankment. He ran for miles, soaked by a hard, cold rain. For a while, they chased him. Their bullets ricocheted off the trees. He ran, then walked, then finally dragged himself toward safety. He crossed into British territory 12 days later on Nov. 15, 1943.

He returned to his house in New Jersey—to Emily and the kids, to his 1937 Dodge and his job in insurance. He was snappish, disoriented. This time he had made it—and still he was full of self-recrimination.

15

Some soldiers put war behind them, and others live it forever. Joe Frelinghuysen wanted only to make amends. He tracked down Dick Rossbach, who had been badly beaten by the three soldiers and then trucked to German prisons, eventually landing in a Russian camp. Undaunted, Rossbach escaped again, talking his way to the American Embassy in Moscow. When Frelinghuysen unloaded his guilt over having abandoned him, Rossbach dismissed it. "Oh, for God's sake, Joe," he said. For many years they met regularly in Manhattan for lunch.

The DiGiacomantonios survived the war, though German soldiers lined up 26 people against a stone wall in a nearby village and shot them for helping prisoners. In 1956, Frelinghuysen returned to the farmhouse, carrying a gift of gold rosary beads for Rosa. While his parents were content to stay on the farm, Berardino expressed a desire to emigrate. Frelinghuysen found a way, creating a position in his family's dairy business for an Italian cheesemaker. He settled Berardino, Letizia and their children into a home near his own, and over time, let go of his guilt.

They live there still, Berardino and his wife. During 1943 and 1944, they say, their family harbored more than 100 escaped American and British soldiers. They can recall the desperation and hunger and nervous gratitude these men showed at the time. But only one found them again after the war. No one else even sent a letter.

QUESTIONS

1. Who are the heroes in this historical vignette: Joe Frelinghuysen and Dick Rossbach? Rosa and Antonio DiGiacomantonio? Are there any anti-heroes? Find the evidence that Corbett includes to support your answer.

2. Corbett's essay ponders the question: What turns an ordinary person into a hero? What answers does she provide, either directly or indirectly?

3. Write a mini-biography or short narrative of someone you think is an ordinary hero. Use Sara Corbett's piece or one of the others in this section as a model.

DANIEL BERGNER   *Chasing Evil*

Peter Malkin wore a pair of fur-lined leather gloves when he seized Adolf Eichmann[1] on a street in suburban Buenos Aires. It was 1960. For 15 years, one of the chief engineers of Hitler's Final Solution[2] had escaped capture. Now Malkin, the point man of a small team of clandestine Israeli agents, helped to wrestle him into the back of a waiting car and, Malkin would recount in his memoir, "Eichmann in My Hands," written with Harry Stein, pressed his hand over Eichmann's mouth so he could not scream. Malkin wore the gloves, he wrote, because "the thought of placing my bare hand over the mouth that had ordered the death of millions, of feeling the hot breath and saliva on my skin, filled me with an overwhelming sense of revulsion." But the leather and fur weren't enough. They were quickly "soaked through with his spittle."

It was the beginning of strange intimacy. Malkin—whose sister had been killed along with her children in Poland during the Holocaust, after Malkin, his two brothers and his parents managed to flee to Palestine—had already prepared a bedroom for Eichmann in the safe house where the agents would keep him hidden until, against international law, they could spirit him out of Argentina to stand trial in Israel. Malkin had made the bed with fresh sheets and laid out a towel and toiletries and a pair of striped pajamas. The room, where Malkin would spend much of the next 10 days in solo shifts watching over one of the 20th century's greatest murderers, was spare and tiny; captor and captive, alone, were never more than two or three steps apart. A blanket covered the only window.

Malkin would wash and shave Eichmann's face, tracing, over and over, the contours of his cheeks and jaw. Malkin fed him, lifting a spoon to his lips,

---

1. Eichmann (1906–1962), the German Nazi who organized the deportation of thousands of Jews to Nazi death camps.
2. The "final solution to the Jewish question," engineered by German leader Adolf Hitler (1889–1945), was genocide against Jews in German-occupied territories.

and dressed and undressed him. (The memoir implies that Eichmann's hands were kept loosely bound, yet the leader of the Israeli team, Rafi Eitan, told me recently that, after the first day, Eichmann's hands were not bound during the daytime.) Malkin held Eichmann's hands, aiding him as he did deep knee bends for exercise.

And when Eichmann said that he adored fine red wine, Malkin stole an expensive bottle that another agent had been saving for the Sabbath. He served him wine and played him music—a flamenco, a tango—on an old wind-up record player.

Partly, Malkin wrote, his ministering to Eichmann was an attempt to preserve him for public justice. In captivity, Eichmann became passive and seemed utterly incapable of caring for himself (Malkin had to bark orders at him to get him to move his bowels), and Malkin worried that his body and mind

THE PROVINCIAL TERRITORIAL DIVISION OF
ARGENTINA

Malkin's drawing of Eichmann after he was caught by Israeli agents in Argentina.

would deteriorate irreparably before he could be put on trial. Partly, too, Malkin's caring was calculated seduction: he hoped that Eichmann would reveal the whereabouts of the fugitive Nazi doctor Josef Mengele, and that Eichmann would sign a document stating that he was traveling to Israel to stand trial of his own free will. But meanwhile, in a way, the killer became Malkin's muse.

Malkin—an explosives specialist in the fight for Israeli statehood before he was recruited into the Israeli intelligence services—was an expert in disguises and an amateur painter, avid and skilled. Within the room's close walls, with oil-based pencils from his disguise kit, he began to evoke Eichmann on the pages of a guidebook to South America, which he'd brought along on the mission. The first portrait (above) was done in black and gray on a map of Argentina. Eichmann might simply be a tired clerk, an accountant worn down by numbers, with just a tentative suggestion of emotional depth, of self-reflection, of conscience, in the blurred black irises of the eyes.

"Then I flipped the page and did him in his SS regalia,"[3] Malkin wrote. "I

---

3. Short for *Schutzstaffel*, German for "protective echelon," SS refers to the military and security organization that worked for Hitler's Nazi government.

continued drawing in a kind of frenzy. Now I had him watching a railroad train, counting the cars; now in abstract, lying prone atop a flatcar, bearing a machine gun; now, on facing pages, appeared Hitler and Mussolini;[4] now my parents and, in muted pastels, her eyes immense and brooding, my sister, Fruma."

As days and nights went by, Malkin told none of the other agents about his portraits of their prisoner; Eichmann was the only one who knew, remarking, when Malkin turned the guidebook and showed him a work in progress, an image of himself, "Nice. Very nice." Nor, at first, did Malkin tell anyone about their conversations: dialogues spurred by Malkin's questions about the killer's motives; talks driven by the prisoner's fear for his family; chats about music or the pair's "shared love of nature and the wild." Malkin wasn't supposed to converse with Eichmann at all; talk was to be left to sessions with the team's official, harsh-tongued interrogator. And except as Eichmann ate or went to the bathroom, he was supposed to be kept blindfolded. Malkin broke this rule as well. "We found ourselves co-conspirators of a sort," he wrote. "He knew as well as I did to fall silent at the sound of approaching footsteps."

The touching of the face; the portraiture; the talks of Eichmann's beloved young son and of all the children, like Fruma's, he had sent to death (discussions during which Malkin barely controlled his voice and his rage, as he strained to coax words from Eichmann that would somehow offer explanation of his deeds); the removal of the blindfold—Malkin wanted desperately to see into him. By the end of the 10 days, the memoir relates, another of the agents, the team's only woman, would accuse Malkin: "You act like you're in love with him." But the object of desire was elusive. In words, Eichmann gave up little beyond versions of what he would ultimately claim in court in Jerusalem, that in orchestrating the killing of millions he had merely followed orders. And in art, Malkin could create of Eichmann only unyielding surfaces.

10   During the years to come, Malkin would rise to be chief of operations in the Mossad, Israel's famed intelligence agency. Later, in retirement, he devoted himself to his art. He collected and painted on maps from all over the world. Israel Perry, the owner of the Manhattan gallery that represents Malkin's work, told me that Malkin used the maps for inspiration, to pull himself back into the past, back toward people and scenes that had floated by in his widely traveled, covert life. In this way, he found other subjects, other faces besides Eichmann's; in this way, perhaps, he found other, easier paths to the human soul.

4. Benito Mussolini (1883–1945), fascist Italian dictator from 1922 until 1945.

QUESTIONS

1. Bergner's mini-biography of Peter Malkin is based on a memoir, *Eichmann in My Hands*, written by Malkin himself. Where does Bergner draw on that memoir for his mini-biography? Where does he provide other information or offer his own interpretation?

2. In paragraph 9, Bergner quotes a female Israeli agent, who accuses Malkin: "You act like you're in love with him." What evidence does Bergner supply that might support this accusation? Does he agree with it, or does the final paragraph offer another interpretation of Malkin's actions?

3. Read Peter Malkin's memoir, *Eichmann in My Hands*, and/or other accounts of the capture and trial of Adolf Eichmann. Write your own explanation of why Malkin and other members of the Israeli team found it essential to capture and bring Eichmann to trial.

Philip Gourevitch *After the Genocide*

IN THE PROVINCE of Kibungo, in eastern Rwanda, in the swamp- and pasture-land near the Tanzanian border, there's a rocky hill called Nyarubuye with a church where many Tutsis were slaughtered in mid-April of 1994. A year after the killing I went to Nyarubuye with two Canadian military officers. We flew in a United Nations helicopter, traveling low over the hills in the morning mists, with the banana trees like green starbursts dense over the slopes. The uncut grass blew back as we dropped into the center of the parish schoolyard. A lone soldier materialized with his Kalashnikov, and shook our hands with stiff, shy formality. The Canadians presented the paperwork for our visit, and I stepped up into the open doorway of a classroom.

At least fifty mostly decomposed cadavers covered the floor, wadded in clothing, their belongings strewn about and smashed. Macheted skulls had rolled here and there.

The dead looked like pictures of the dead. They did not smell. They did not buzz with flies. They had been killed thirteen months earlier, and they hadn't been moved. Skin stuck here and there over the bones, many of which lay scattered away from the bodies, dismembered by the killers, or by scavengers—birds, dogs, bugs. The more complete figures looked a lot like people, which they were once. A woman in a cloth wrap printed with flowers lay near the door. Her fleshless hip bones were high and her legs slightly spread, and a child's skeleton extended between them. Her torso was hollowed out. Her ribs and spinal column poked through the rotting cloth. Her head was tipped back and her mouth was open: a strange image—half agony, half repose.

I had never been among the dead before. What to do? Look? Yes. I wanted to see them, I suppose; I had come to see them—the dead had been left unburied at Nyarubuye for memorial purposes—and there they were, so inti-

Gourevitch spent nine months in Rwanda chronicling the 1994 massacre of over 800,000 people. His resulting New Yorker *article, "After the Genocide" (December 18, 1995), was a finalist for the Overseas Press Club Award.*

mately exposed. I didn't need to see them. I already knew, and believed, what had happened in Rwanda. Yet looking at the buildings and the bodies, and hearing the silence of the place, with the grand Italianate basilica standing there deserted, and beds of exquisite, decadent, death-fertilized flowers blooming over the corpses, it was still strangely unimaginable. I mean one still had to imagine it.

5   Those dead Rwandans will be with me forever, I expect. That was why I had felt compelled to come to Nyarubuye: to be stuck with them—not with their experience, but with the experience of looking at them. They had been killed there, and they were dead there. What else could you really see at first? The Bible bloated with rain lying on top of one corpse or, littered about, the little woven wreaths of thatch which Rwandan women wear as crowns to balance the enormous loads they carry on their heads, and the water gourds, and the Converse tennis sneaker stuck somehow in a pelvis.

The soldier with the Kalashnikov—Sergeant Francis of the Rwandese Patriotic Army, a Tutsi whose parents had fled to Uganda with him when he was a boy, after similar but less extensive massacres in the early 1960s, and who had fought his way home in 1994 and found it like this—said that the dead in this room were mostly women who had been raped before being murdered. Sergeant Francis had high, rolling girlish hips, and he walked and stood with his butt stuck out behind him, an oddly purposeful posture, tipped forward, driven. He was, at once, candid and briskly official. His English had the punctilious clip of military drill, and after he told me what I was looking at I looked instead at my feet. The rusty head of a hatchet lay beside them in the dirt.

A few weeks earlier, in Bukavu, Zaire, in the giant market of a refugee camp that was home to many Rwandan Hutu militiamen, I had watched a man butchering a cow with a machete. He was quite expert at his work, taking big precise strokes that made a sharp hacking noise. The rallying cry to the killers during the genocide was "Do your work!" And I saw that it *was* work, this butchery; hard work. It took many hacks—two, three, four, five hard hacks—to chop through the cow's leg. How many hacks to dismember a person?

Considering the enormity of the task, it is tempting to play with theories of collective madness, mob mania, a fever of hatred erupted into a mass crime of passion, and to imagine the blind orgy of the mob, with each member killing one or two people. But at Nyarubuye, and at thousands of other sites in this tiny country, on the same days of a few months in 1994, hundreds of thousands of Hutus had worked as killers in regular shifts. There was always the next victim, and the next. What sustained them, beyond the frenzy of the first attack, through the plain physical exhaustion and mess of it?

The pygmy in Gikongoro said that humanity is part of nature and that we must go against nature to get along and have peace. But mass violence, too, must be organized; it does not occur aimlessly. Even mobs and riots have a design, and great and sustained destruction requires great ambition. It must be conceived as the means toward achieving a new order, and although the idea behind that new order may be criminal and objectively very stupid, it must also be compellingly simple and at the same time absolute. The ideology of genocide is all of those things, and in Rwanda it went by the bald name of Hutu Power. For those who set about systematically exterminating an entire people—even a fairly small and unresisting subpopulation of perhaps a million and a quarter men, women, and children, like the Tutsis in Rwanda—blood lust surely helps. But the engineers and perpetrators of a slaughter like the one just inside the door where I stood need not enjoy killing, and they may even find it unpleasant. What is required above all is that they want their victims dead. They have to want it so badly that they consider it a necessity.

So I still had much to imagine as I entered the classroom and stepped carefully between the remains. These dead and their killers had been neighbors, schoolmates, colleagues, sometimes friends, even in-laws. The dead had seen their killers training as militias in the weeks before the end, and it was well known that they were training to kill Tutsis; it was announced on the radio, it was in the newspapers, people spoke of it openly. The week before the massacre at Nyarubuye, the killing began in Rwanda's capital, Kigali. Hutus who opposed the Hutu Power ideology were publicly denounced as "accomplices" of the Tutsis and were among the first to be killed as the extermination got under way. In Nyarubuye, when Tutsis asked the Hutu Power mayor how they might be spared, he suggested that they seek sanctuary at the church. They did, and a few days later the mayor came to kill them. He came at the head of a pack of soldiers, policemen, militiamen, and villagers; he gave out arms and orders to complete the job well. No more was required of the mayor, but he was also said to have killed a few Tutsis himself.

The killers killed all day at Nyarubuye. At night they cut the Achilles tendons of survivors and went off to feast behind the church, roasting cattle looted from their victims in big fires, and drinking beer. (Bottled beer, banana beer—Rwandans may not drink more beer than other Africans, but they drink prodigious quantities of it around the clock.) And, in the morning, still drunk after whatever sleep they could find beneath the cries of their prey, the killers at Nyarubuye went back and killed again. Day after day, minute to minute, Tutsi by Tutsi: all across Rwanda, they worked like that. "It was a process," Sergeant Francis said. I can see that it happened, I can be told how, and after nearly three years of looking around Rwanda and listening to Rwandans, I can tell you how, and I will. But the horror of it—the idiocy, the waste, the sheer wrongness—remains uncircumscribable.

Like Leontius, the young Athenian in Plato,[1] I presume that you are reading this because you desire a closer look, and that you, too, are properly disturbed by your curiosity. Perhaps, in examining this extremity with me, you hope for some understanding, some insight, some flicker of self-knowledge—a moral, or a lesson, or a clue about how to behave in this world: some such information. I don't discount the possibility, but when it comes to genocide, you already know right from wrong. The best reason I have come up with for look-

10

---

1. In Plato's *Republic*, Leontius struggles over whether to stare at corpses left by the executioner. He wants to look but knows that his curiosity is wrong. He gives in to the temptation.

ing closely into Rwanda's stories is that ignoring them makes me even more uncomfortable about existence and my place in it. The horror, as horror, interests me only insofar as a precise memory of the offense is necessary to understand its legacy.

The dead at Nyarubuye were, I'm afraid, beautiful. There was no getting around it. The skeleton is a beautiful thing. The randomness of the fallen forms, the strange tranquillity of their rude exposure, the skull here, the arm bent in some uninterpretable gesture there—these things were beautiful, and their beauty only added to the affront of the place. I couldn't settle on any meaningful response: revulsion, alarm, sorrow, grief, shame, incomprehension, sure, but nothing truly meaningful. I just looked, and I took photographs, because I wondered whether I could really see what I was seeing while I saw it, and I wanted also an excuse to look a bit more closely.

We went on through the first room and out the far side. There was another room and another and another and another. They were all full of bodies, and more bodies were scattered in the grass and there were stray skulls in the grass, which was thick and wonderfully green. Standing outside, I heard a crunch. The old Canadian colonel stumbled in front of me, and I saw, though he did not notice, that his foot had rolled on a skull and broken it. For the first time at Nyarubuye my feelings focused, and what I felt was a small but keen anger at this man. Then I heard another crunch, and felt a vibration underfoot. I had stepped on one, too.

15   Rwanda is spectacular to behold. Throughout its center, a winding succession of steep, tightly terraced slopes radiates out from small roadside settlements and solitary compounds. Gashes of red clay and black loam mark fresh hoe work; eucalyptus trees flash silver against brilliant green tea plantations; banana trees are everywhere. On the theme of hills, Rwanda produces countless variations: jagged rain forests, round-shouldered buttes, undulating moors, broad swells of savanna, volcanic peaks sharp as filed teeth. During the rainy season, the clouds are huge and low and fast, mists cling in highland hollows, lightning flickers through the nights, and by day the land is lustrous. After the rains, the skies lift, the terrain takes on a ragged look beneath the flat unvarying haze of the dry season, and in the savannas of the Akagera Park wildlife blackens the hills.

One day, when I was returning to Kigali from the south, the car mounted a rise between two winding valleys, the windshield filled with purple-bellied clouds, and I asked Joseph, the man who was giving me a ride, whether Rwandans realize what a beautiful country they have. "Beautiful?" he said. "You think so? After the things that happened here? The people aren't good. If the people were good, the country might be OK." Joseph told me that his brother and sister had been killed, and he made a soft hissing click with his tongue against his teeth. "The country is empty," he said. "Empty!"

It was not just the dead who were missing. The genocide had been brought to a halt by the Rwandese Patriotic Front, a rebel army led by Tutsi refugees from past persecutions, and as the RPF advanced through the country in the summer of 1994, some two million Hutus had fled into exile at the behest of the same leaders who had urged them to kill. Yet except in some rural areas in the south, where the desertion of Hutus had left nothing but bush to reclaim the fields around crumbling adobe houses, I, as a newcomer, could not see the emptiness that blinded Joseph to Rwanda's beauty. Yes, there were grenade-flattened buildings, burnt homesteads, shot-up facades, and mortar-pitted roads. But these were the ravages of war, not of genocide, and by the summer of 1995, most of the dead had been buried. Fifteen months earlier, Rwanda had been the most densely populated country in Africa. Now the work of the killers looked just as they had intended: invisible.

From time to time, mass graves were discovered and excavated, and the remains would be transferred to new, properly consecrated mass graves. Yet even the occasionally exposed bones, the conspicuous number of amputees and people with deforming scars, and the superabundance of packed orphanages could not be taken as evidence that what had happened to Rwanda was an attempt to eliminate a people. There were only people's stories.

"Every survivor wonders why he is alive," Abbé Modeste, a priest at the cathedral in Butare, Rwanda's second-largest city, told me. Abbé Modeste had hidden for weeks in his sacristy, eating communion wafers, before moving under the desk in his study, and finally into the rafters at the home of some neighboring nuns. The obvious explanation of his survival was that the RPF had come to the rescue. But the RPF didn't reach Butare till early July, and roughly seventy-five percent of the Tutsis in Rwanda had been killed by early May. In this regard, at least, the genocide had been entirely successful: to those who were targeted, it was not death but life that seemed an accident of fate.

"I had eighteen people killed at my house," said Etienne Niyonzima, a former businessman who had become a deputy in the National Assembly. "Everything was totally destroyed—a place of fifty-five meters by fifty meters. In my neighborhood they killed six hundred and forty-seven people. They tortured them, too. You had to see how they killed them. They had the number of everyone's house, and they went through with red paint and marked the homes of all the Tutsis and of the Hutu moderates. My wife was at a friend's, shot with two bullets. She is still alive, only"—he fell quiet for a moment—"she has no arms. The others with her were killed. The militia left her for dead. Her whole family of sixty-five in Gitarama were killed." Niyonzima was in hiding at the time. Only after he had been separated from his wife for three months did he learn that she and four of their children had survived. "Well," he said, "one son was cut in the head with a machete. I don't know where he went." His voice weakened, and caught. "He disappeared." Niyonzima clicked his tongue, and said, "But the others are still alive. Quite honestly, I don't understand at all how I was saved."

Laurent Nkongoli attributed his survival to "Providence, and also good neighbors, an old woman who said, 'Run away, we don't want to see your corpse.' " Nkongoli, a lawyer, who had become the vice president of the National Assembly after the genocide, was a robust man, with a taste for double-

20

breasted suit jackets and lively ties, and he moved, as he spoke, with a brisk determination. But before taking his neighbor's advice, and fleeing Kigali in late April of 1994, he said, "I had accepted death. At a certain moment this happens. One hopes not to die cruelly, but one expects to die anyway. Not death by machete, one hopes, but with a bullet. If you were willing to pay for it, you could often ask for a bullet. Death was more or less normal, a resignation. You lose the will to fight. There were four thousand Tutsis killed here at Kacyiru"—a neighborhood of Kigali. "The soldiers brought them here, and told them to sit down because they were going to throw grenades. And they sat."

"Rwandan culture is a culture of fear," Nkongoli went on. "I remember what people said." He adopted a pipey voice, and his face took on a look of disgust: " 'Just let us pray, then kill us,' or 'I don't want to die in the street, I want to die at home.' " He resumed his normal voice. "When you're that resigned and oppressed you're already dead. It shows the genocide was prepared for too long. I detest this fear. These victims of genocide had been psychologically prepared to expect death just for being Tutsi. They were being killed for so long that they were already dead."

I reminded Nkongoli that, for all his hatred of fear, he had himself accepted death before his neighbor urged him to run away. "Yes," he said. "I got tired in the genocide. You struggle so long, then you get tired."

Every Rwandan I spoke with seemed to have a favorite, unanswerable question. For Nkongoli, it was how so many Tutsis had allowed themselves to be killed. For François Xavier Nkurunziza, a Kigali lawyer, whose father was Hutu and whose mother and wife were Tutsi, the question was how so many Hutus had allowed themselves to kill. Nkurunziza had escaped death only by chance as he moved around the country from one hiding place to another, and he had lost many family members. "Conformity is very deep, very developed here," he told me. "In Rwandan history, everyone obeys authority. People revere power, and there isn't enough education. You take a poor, ignorant population, and give them arms, and say, 'It's yours. Kill.' They'll obey. The peasants, who were paid or forced to kill, were looking up to people of higher socio-economic standing to see how to behave. So the people of influence, or the big financiers, are often the big men in the genocide. They may think they didn't kill because they didn't take life with their own hands, but the people were looking to them for their orders. And, in Rwanda, an order can be given very quietly."

As I traveled around the country, collecting accounts of the killing, it almost seemed as if, with the machete, the *masu*—a club studded with nails—a few well-placed grenades, and a few bursts of automatic-rifle fire, the quiet orders of Hutu Power had made the neutron bomb[2] obsolete.

"Everyone was called to hunt the enemy," said Theodore Nyilinkwaya, a survivor of the massacres in his home village of Kimbogo, in the southwestern province of Cyangugu. "But let's say someone is reluctant. Say that guy comes with a stick. They tell him, 'No, get a *masu*.' So, OK, he does, and he runs along with the rest, but he doesn't kill. They say, 'Hey, he might denounce us

2. A nuclear device designed to kill people while leaving structures relatively intact.

later. He must kill. Everyone must help to kill at least one person.' So this person who is not a killer is made to do it. And the next day it's become a game for him. You don't need to keep pushing him."

At Nyarubuye, even the little terracotta votive statues in the sacristy had been methodically decapitated. "They were associated with Tutsis," Sergeant Francis explained.

QUESTIONS

1. In paragraph 10 Gourevitch says, "So I still had much to imagine . . ." What does he believe he needs to imagine? And why do you think an act of imagination is so important to him?

2. As paragraph 12 opens, the pronouns change, moving from the first person "I" to the second person "you," in a direct address to us, the readers. What is the effect of this pronoun shift here? Can the author "presume" to know why we are reading?

3. This essay has two sections, separated by a white space. How can the two sections be compared? What do they have in common? Do you note any parallels?

4. Plan and then write two different descriptive paragraphs that both lead up to highly significant last lines, as in Gourevitch's paragraphs 14 and 27. Consider what kinds of writing such conclusions might be best suited for.

FRANCES FITZGERALD *Rewriting American History*

THOSE OF US who grew up in the fifties believed in the permanence of our American-history textbooks. To us as children, those texts were the truth of things: they were American history. It was not just that we read them before we understood that not everything that is printed is the truth, or the whole truth. It was that they, much more than other books, had the demeanor and trappings of authority. They were weighty volumes. They spoke in measured cadences: imperturbable, humorless, and as distant as Chinese emperors. Our teachers treated them with respect, and we paid them abject homage by memorizing a chapter a week. But now the textbook histories have changed, some of them to such an extent that an adult would find them unrecognizable.

One current junior-high-school American history begins with a story about a Negro cowboy called George McJunkin. It appears that when McJunkin was riding down a lonely trail in New Mexico one cold spring morn-

From America Revised: History Schoolbooks in the Twentieth Century *(1979), FitzGerald's analysis of how textbook interpretations of key moments in American history have changed over time.*

ing in 1925 he discovered a mound containing bones and stone implements, which scientists later proved belonged to an Indian civilization ten thousand years old. The book goes on to say that scientists now believe there were people in the Americas at least twenty thousand years ago. It discusses the Aztec, Mayan, and Incan civilizations and the meaning of the word "culture" before introducing the European explorers.

Another history text—this one for the fifth grade—begins with the story of how Henry B. Gonzalez, who is a member of Congress from Texas, learned about his own nationality. When he was ten years old, his teacher told him he was an American because he was born in the United States. His grandmother, however, said, "The cat was born in the oven. Does that make him bread?" After reporting that Mr. Gonzalez eventually went to college and law school, the book explains that "the melting pot idea hasn't worked out as some thought it would," and that now "some people say that the people of the United States are more like a salad bowl than a melting pot."

Poor Columbus! He is a minor character now, a walk-on in the middle of American history. Even those books that have not replaced his picture with a Mayan temple or an Iroquois mask do not credit him with discovering America—even for the Europeans. The Vikings, they say, preceded him to the New World, and after that the Europeans, having lost or forgotten their maps, simply neglected to cross the ocean again for five hundred years. Columbus is far from being the only personage to have suffered from time and revision. Captain John Smith, Daniel Boone, and Wild Bill Hickok—the great self-promoters of American history—have all but disappeared, taking with them a good deal of the romance of the American frontier. General Custer has given way to Chief Crazy Horse; General Eisenhower no longer liberates Europe single-handed; and, indeed, most generals, even to Washington and Lee, have faded away, as old soldiers do, giving place to social reformers such as William Lloyd Garrison and Jacob Riis. A number of black Americans have risen to prominence: not only George Washington Carver but Frederick Douglass and Martin Luther King, Jr. W. E. B. Du Bois now invariably accompanies Booker T. Washington. In addition, there is a mystery man called Crispus Attucks, a fugitive slave about whom nothing seems to be known for certain except that he was a victim of the Boston Massacre and thus became one of the first casualties of the American Revolution. Thaddeus Stevens[1] has been reconstructed—his character changed, as it were, from black to white, from cruel and vindictive to persistent and sincere. As for Teddy Roosevelt, he now champions the issue of conservation instead of charging up San Juan Hill. No single President really stands out as a hero, but all Presidents—except certain unmentionables in the second half of the nineteenth century—seem to have done as well as could be expected, given difficult circumstances.

5   Of course, when one thinks about it, it is hardly surprising that modern scholarship and modern perspectives have found their way into children's

---

1. Congressman (1792–1868) who urged Lincoln to emancipate the slaves during the Civil War and advocated strict federal control of the South after the war.

books. Yet the changes remain shocking. Those who in the sixties complained of the bland optimism, the chauvinism, and the materialism of their old civics text did so in the belief that, for all their protests, the texts would never change. The thought must have had something reassuring about it, for that generation never noticed when its complaints began to take effect and the songs about radioactive rainfall and houses made of ticky-tacky began to appear in the textbooks. But this is what happened.

The history texts now hint at a certain level of unpleasantness in American history. Several books, for instance, tell the story of Ishi, the last "wild" Indian in the continental United States, who, captured in 1911 after the massacre of his tribe, spent the final four and a half years of his life in the University of California's museum of anthropology, in San Francisco. At least three books show the same stunning picture of the breaker boys, the child coal miners of Pennsylvania—ancient children with deformed bodies and blackened faces who stare stupidly out from the entrance to a mine. One book quotes a soldier on the use of torture in the American campaign to pacify the Philippines at the beginning of the century. A number of books say that during the American Revolution the patriots tarred and feathered those who did not support them, and drove many of the loyalists from the country. Almost all the present-day history books note that the United States interned Japanese-Americans in detention camps during the Second World War.

Ideologically speaking, the histories of the fifties were implacable, seamless. Inside their covers, America was perfect: the greatest nation in the world, and the embodiment of democracy, freedom, and technological progress. For them, the country never changed in any important way: its values and its political institutions remained constant from the time of the American Revolution. To my generation—the children of the fifties—these texts appeared permanent just because they were so self-contained. Their orthodoxy, it seemed, left no handholds for attack, no lodging for decay. Who, after all, would dispute the wonders of technology or the superiority of the English colonists over the Spanish? Who would find fault with the pastorale of the West or the Old South? Who would question the anti-Communist crusade? There was, it seemed, no point in comparing these visions with reality, since they were the public truth and were thus quite irrelevant to what existed and to what anyone privately believed. They were—or so it seemed—the permanent expression of mass culture in America.

But now the texts have changed, and with them the country that American children are growing up into. The society that was once uniform is now a patchwork of rich and poor, old and young, men and women, blacks, whites, Hispanics, and Indians. The system that ran so smoothly by means of the Constitution under the guidance of benevolent conductor Presidents is now a rattletrap affair. The past is no highway to the present; it is a collection of issues and events that do not fit together and that lead in no single direction. The word "progress" has been replaced by the word "change": children, the modern texts insist, should learn history so that they can adapt to the rapid changes taking place around them. History is proceeding in spite of us. The present, which was once portrayed in the concluding chapters as a peaceful haven of scientific advances and Presidential inaugurations, is now a tangle of problems: race problems, urban problems, foreign-policy problems, problems of pollution, poverty, energy depletion, youthful rebellion, assassination, and drugs. Some books illustrate these problems dramatically. One, for instance, contains a picture of a doll half buried in a mass of untreated sewage; the caption reads, "Are we in danger of being overwhelmed by the products of our society and wastage created by their production? Would you agree with this photographer's interpretation?" Two books show the same picture of an old black woman sitting in a straight chair in a dingy room, her hands folded in graceful resignation; the surrounding text discusses the problems faced by the urban poor and by the aged who depend on Social Security. Other books present current problems less starkly. One of the texts concludes sagely:

> Problems are part of life. Nations face them, just as people face them, and try to solve them. And today's Americans have one great advantage over past generations. Never before have Americans been so well equipped to solve their problems. They have today the means to conquer poverty, disease, and ignorance. The technetronic age has put that power into their hands.

Such passages have a familiar ring. Amid all the problems, the deus ex machina[2] of science still dodders around in the gloaming of pious hope.

Even more surprising than the emergence of problems is the discovery that the great unity of the texts has broken. Whereas in the fifties all texts represented the same political view, current texts follow no pattern of orthodoxy. Some books, for instance, portray civil-rights legislation as a series of actions taken by a wise, paternal government; others convey some suggestion of the social upheaval involved and make mention of such people as Stokely Carmichael and Malcolm X.[3] In some books, the Cold War has ended; in others, it continues, with Communism threatening the free nations of the earth.

10   The political diversity in the books is matched by a diversity of pedagogical approach. In addition to the traditional narrative histories, with their endless streams of facts, there are so-called "discovery," or "inquiry," texts, which deal with a limited number of specific issues in American history. These texts do not pretend to cover the past; they focus on particular topics, such as "stratification in Colonial society" or "slavery and the American Revolution," and illustrate them with documents from primary and secondary sources. The chapters in these books amount to something like case studies, in that they include testimony from people with different perspectives or conflicting views on a single subject. In addition, the chapters provide background information, explanatory notes, and a series of questions for the student. The questions are the heart of

2. God from a machine. A reference to early plays in which a god, lowered to the stage by mechanical means, solved the drama's problems; thus, an artificial solution to a difficulty.

3. Carmichael (1941–1998) and Malcolm X (1925–1965) were radical black leaders of the 1960s.

the matter, for when they are carefully selected they force students to think much as historians think: to define the point of view of the speaker, analyze the ideas presented, question the relationship between events, and so on. One text, for example, quotes Washington, Jefferson, and John Adams on the question of foreign alliances and then asks, "What did John Adams assume that the international situation would be after the American Revolution? What did Washington's attitude toward the French alliance seem to be? How do you account for his attitude?" Finally, it asks, "Should a nation adopt a policy toward alliances and cling to it consistently, or should it vary its policies toward other countries as circumstances change?" In these books, history is clearly not a list of agreed-upon facts or a sermon on politics but a babble of voices and a welter of events which must be ordered by the historian.

In matters of pedagogy, as in matters of politics, there are not two sharply differentiated categories of books; rather, there is a spectrum. Politically, the books run from moderate left to moderate right; pedagogically, they run from the traditional history sermons, through a middle ground of narrative texts with inquiry-style questions and of inquiry texts with long stretches of narrative, to the most rigorous of case-study books. What is common to the current texts—and makes all of them different from those of the fifties—is their engagement with the social sciences. In eighth-grade histories, the "concepts" of social sciences make fleeting appearances. But these "concepts" are the very foundation stones of various elementary-school social-studies series. The 1970 Harcourt Brace Jovanovich[4] series, for example, boasts in its preface of "a horizontal base or ordering of conceptual schemes" to match its "vertical arm of behavioral themes." What this means is not entirely clear, but the books do proceed from easy questions to hard ones, such as—in the sixth-grade book—"How was interaction between merchants and citizens different in the Athenian and Spartan social systems?" Virtually all the American-history texts for older children include discussions of "role," "status," and "culture." Some of them stage debates between eminent social scientists in roped-off sections of the text; some include essays on economics or sociology; some contain pictures and short biographies of social scientists of both sexes and of diverse races. Many books seem to accord social scientists a higher status than American Presidents.

Quite as striking as these political and pedagogical alterations is the change in the physical appearance of the texts. The schoolbooks of the fifties showed some effort in the matter of design: they had maps, charts, cartoons, photographs, and an occasional four-color picture to break up the columns of print. But beside the current texts they look as naïve as Soviet fashion magazines. The print in the fifties books is heavy and far too black, the colors muddy. The photographs are conventional news shots—portraits of Presidents in three-quarters profile, posed "action" shots of soldiers. The other illustrations tend to be Socialist-realist-style[5] drawings (there are a lot of hefty

---

4. Major textbook publisher.

5. Socialist realism, which originated in the Soviet Union, is a style of art that glorifies the communal labor of farmers and industrial workers in works of posterlike simplicity.

farmers with hoes in the Colonial-period chapters) or incredibly vulgar made-
for-children paintings of patriotic events. One painting shows Columbus
standing in full court dress on a beach in the New World from a perspective
that could have belonged only to the Arawaks.[6] By contrast, the current texts
are paragons of sophisticated modern design. They look not like *People* or
Family Circle but, rather, like *Architectural Digest* or *Vogue.* * * * The amount
of space given to illustrations is far greater than it was in the fifties; in fact, in
certain "slow-learner" books the pictures far outweigh the text in importance.
However, the illustrations have a much greater historical value. Instead of
made-up paintings or anachronistic sketches, there are cartoons, photographs,
and paintings drawn from the periods being treated. The chapters on the
Colonial period will show, for instance, a ship's carved prow, a Revere bowl, a
Copley painting[7]—a whole gallery of Early Americana. The nineteenth century
is illustrated with nineteenth-century cartoons and photographs—and the
photographs are all of high artistic quality. As for the twentieth-century chapters, they are adorned with the contents of a modern-art museum.

The use of all this art and high-quality design contains some irony. The
nineteenth-century photographs of child laborers or urban slum apartments
are so beautiful that they transcend their subjects. To look at them, or at the
Victor Gatto painting of the Triangle shirtwaist-factory fire,[8] is to see not misery or ugliness but an art object. In the modern chapters, the contrast between
style and content is just as great: the color photographs of junk yards
or polluted rivers look as enticing as *Gourmet's* photographs of food. The book
that is perhaps the most stark in its description of modern problems
illustrates the horrors of nuclear testing with a pretty Ben Shahn picture
of the Bikini explosion,[9] and the potential for global ecological disaster
with a color photograph of the planet swirling its mantle of white clouds.
Whereas in the nineteen-fifties the texts were childish in the sense that
they were naïve and clumsy, they are now childish in the sense that they are
polymorphous-perverse. American history is not dull any longer; it is a sensuous experience.

The surprise that adults feel in seeing the changes in history texts must
come from the lingering hope that there is, somewhere out there, an objective
truth. The hope is, of course, foolish. All of us children of the twentieth century know, or should know, that there are no absolutes in human affairs, and

6. A Native American tribe, then inhabiting the Caribbean area.

7. Paul Revere (1735–1818), American craftsman and patriot, known both for his fine
silver bowls and for his famous midnight ride from Boston to Lexington, on April 18–
19, 1775, on the eve of the American Revolutionary War. John Singleton Copley
(1738–1815), greatest of the American old masters; he specialized in portraits and historical paintings.

8. In 1941 Victor Joseph Gatto (1893–1965) painted this fire, which occurred on
March 25, 1911, when he was eighteen.

9. Ben Shahn (1898–1969) was an American painter and graphic artist with strong social and political concerns; the Bikini atoll, part of the Marshall Islands in the Pacific,
was the site of American nuclear bomb testing from 1946 to 1958.

thus there can be no such thing as perfect objectivity. We know that each historian in some degree creates the world anew and that all history is in some degree contemporary history. But beyond this knowledge there is still a hope for some reliable authority, for some fixed stars in the universe. We may know that journalists cannot be wholly unbiased and that "balance" is an imaginary point between two extremes, and yet we hope that Walter Cronkite[10] will tell us the truth of things. In the same way, we hope that our history will not change—that we learned the truth of things as children. The texts, with their impersonal voices, encourage this hope, and therefore it is particularly disturbing to see how they change, and how fast.

Slippery history! Not every generation but every few years the content of   15
American-history books for children changes appreciably. Schoolbooks are not, like trade books,[11] written and left to their fate. To stay in step with the cycles of "adoption"[12] in school districts across the country, the publishers revise most of their old texts or substitute new ones every three or four years. In the process of revision, they not only bring history up to date but make changes—often substantial changes—in the body of the work. History books for children are thus more contemporary than any other form of history. How should it be otherwise? Should students read histories written ten, fifteen, thirty years ago? In theory, the system is reasonable—except that each generation of children reads only one generation of schoolbooks. The transient history is those children's history forever—their particular version of America.

10. Anchor (b. 1916) of the *CBS Evening News* from 1952 to 1981.
11. Books written for a general audience, as opposed to textbooks.
12. The choosing of required textbooks by teachers and school boards.

QUESTIONS

1. What differences does FitzGerald find between the American history textbooks of the 1950s and those of the 1970s? In what ways—according to what she states or implies—have they been improved? Does she see any changes for the worse?

2. FitzGerald's *America Revised* was published in 1979, and textbooks, she argues, change rapidly (paragraph 15). Have American history textbooks changed since the late 1970s and, if so, in what ways? What do you remember of the American history textbooks you used in school—and when did you use them? What kind of American history textbooks are being used today? On your own or in a group, write a brief essay updating FitzGerald.

3. By "rewriting," FitzGerald does not mean changing the facts of American history. What is the relationship between the facts of history and history textbooks?

4. FitzGerald says that in the new texts "the word 'progress' has been replaced by the word 'change' " (paragraph 8). Write an essay in which you consider the difference between these two words and the changes that the replacement of one by the other reflects.

POLITICS AND GOVERNMENT

GEORGE ORWELL *Shooting an Elephant*

I N MOULMEIN, in Lower Burma, I was hated by large numbers of people—the only time in my life that I have been important enough for this to happen to me. I was sub-divisional police officer of the town, and in an aimless, petty kind of way anti-European feeling was very bitter. No one had the guts to raise a riot, but if a European woman went through the bazaars alone somebody would probably spit betel juice over her dress. As a police officer I was an obvious target and was baited whenever it seemed safe to do so. When a nimble Burman tripped me up on the football field and the referee (another Burman) looked the other way, the crowd yelled with hideous laughter. This happened more than once. In the end the sneering yellow faces of young men that met me everywhere, the insults hooted after me when I was at a safe distance, got badly on my nerves. The young Buddhist priests were the worst of all. There were several thousands of them in the town and none of them seemed to have anything to do except stand on street corners and jeer at Europeans.

All this was perplexing and upsetting. For at that time I had already made up my mind that imperialism was an evil thing and the sooner I chucked up my job and got out of it the better. Theoretically—and secretly, of course—I was all for the Burmese and all against their oppressors, the British. As for the job I was doing, I hated it more bitterly than I can perhaps make clear. In a job like that you see the dirty work of Empire at close quarters. The wretched prisoners huddling in the stinking cages of the lock-ups, the grey, cowed faces of the long-term convicts, the scarred buttocks of the men who had been flogged with bamboos—all these oppressed me with an intolerable sense of guilt. But I could get nothing into perspective. I was young and ill-educated and I had had to think out my problems in the utter silence that is imposed on every Englishman in the East. I did not even know that the British Empire is dying, still less did I know that it is a great deal better than the younger empires that are going to supplant it. All I knew was that I was stuck between my hatred of the empire I served and my rage against the evil-spirited little beasts who tried

First published in the periodical New Writing *(Fall 1936), at the beginning of Orwell's writing career and soon after his novel* Burmese Days *(1934) appeared. The essay later became the title piece in a collection,* Shooting an Elephant, and Other Essays *(1950).*

to make my job impossible. With one part of my mind I thought of the British Raj[1] as an unbreakable tyranny, as something clamped down, in *saecula saeculorum*,[2] upon the will of prostrate peoples; with another part I thought that the greatest joy in the world would be to drive a bayonet into a Buddhist priest's guts. Feelings like these are the normal by-products of imperialism; ask any Anglo-Indian official, if you can catch him off duty.

One day something happened which in a roundabout way was enlightening. It was a tiny incident in itself, but it gave me a better glimpse than I had had before of the real nature of imperialism—the real motives for which despotic governments act. Early one morning the sub-inspector at a police station the other end of the town rang me up on the 'phone and said that an elephant was ravaging the bazaar. Would I please come and do something about it? I did not know what I could do, but I wanted to see what was happening and I got on to a pony and started out. I took my rifle, an old .44 Winchester and much too small to kill an elephant, but I thought the noise might be useful *in terrorem*. Various Burmans stopped me on the way and told me about the elephant's doings. It was not, of course, a wild elephant, but a tame one which had gone "must."[3] It had been chained up, as tame elephants always are when their attack of "must" is due, but on the previous night it had broken its chain and escaped. Its mahout, the only person who could manage it when it was in that state, had set out in pursuit, but had taken the wrong direction and was now twelve hours' journey away, and in the morning the elephant had suddenly reappeared in the town. The Burmese population had no weapons and were quite helpless against it. It had already destroyed somebody's bamboo hut, killed a cow and raided some fruit-stalls and devoured the stock; also it had met the municipal rubbish van and, when the driver jumped out and took to his heels, had turned the van over and inflicted violences upon it.

The Burmese sub-inspector and some Indian constables were waiting for me in the quarter where the elephant had been seen. It was a very poor quarter, a labyrinth of squalid bamboo huts, thatched with palm-leaf, winding all over a steep hillside. I remember that it was a cloudy, stuffy morning at the beginning of the rains. We began questioning the people as to where the elephant had gone and, as usual, failed to get any definite information. That is invariably the case in the East; a story always sounds clear enough at a distance, but the nearer you get to the scene of events the vaguer it becomes. Some of the people said that the elephant had gone in one direction, some said that he had gone in another, some professed not even to have heard of any elephant. I had almost made up my mind that the whole story was a pack of lies, when we heard yells a little distance away. There was a loud, scandalized cry of "Go away, child! Go away this instant!" and an old woman with a switch in her hand came round the corner of a hut, violently shooing away a crowd of naked children. Some more women followed, clicking their tongues

1. The imperial government of British India and Burma.
2. Forever and ever.
3. Gone into sexual heat.

and exclaiming; evidently there was something that the children ought not to have seen. I rounded the hut and saw a man's dead body sprawling in the mud. He was an Indian, a black Dravidian coolie,[4] almost naked, and he could not have been dead many minutes. The people said that the elephant had come suddenly upon him round the corner of the hut, caught him with its trunk, put its foot on his back and ground him into the earth. This was the rainy season and the ground was soft, and his face had scored a trench a foot deep and a couple of yards long. He was lying on his belly with arms crucified and head sharply twisted to one side. His face was coated with mud, the eyes wide open, the teeth bared and grinning with an expression of unendurable agony. (Never tell me, by the way, that the dead look peaceful. Most of the corpses I have seen looked devilish.) The friction of the great beast's foot had stripped the skin from his back as neatly as one skins a rabbit. As soon as I saw the dead man I sent an orderly to a friend's house nearby to borrow an elephant rifle. I had already sent back the pony, not wanting it to go mad with fright and throw me if it smelt the elephant.

5   The orderly came back in a few minutes with a rifle and five cartridges, and meanwhile some Burmans had arrived and told us that the elephant was in the paddy fields below, only a few hundred yards away. As I started forward practically the whole population of the quarter flocked out of the houses and followed me. They had seen the rifle and were all shouting excitedly that I was going to shoot the elephant. They had not shown much interest in the elephant when he was merely ravaging their homes, but it was different now that he was going to be shot. It was a bit of fun to them, as it would be to an English crowd; besides they wanted the meat. It made me vaguely uneasy. I had no intention of shooting the elephant—I had merely sent for the rifle to defend myself if necessary—and it is always unnerving to have a crowd following you. I marched down the hill, looking and feeling a fool, with the rifle over my shoulder and an ever-growing army of people jostling at my heels. At the bottom, when you got away from the huts, there was a metalled road and beyond that a miry waste of paddy fields a thousand yards across, not yet ploughed but soggy from the first rains and dotted with coarse grass. The elephant was standing eight yards from the road, his left side towards us. He took not the slightest notice of the crowd's approach. He was tearing up bunches of grass, beating them against his knees to clean them and stuffing them into his mouth.

I had halted on the road. As soon as I saw the elephant I knew with perfect certainty that I ought not to shoot him. It is a serious matter to shoot a working elephant—it is comparable to destroying a huge and costly piece of machinery—and obviously one ought not to do it if it can possibly be avoided. And at that distance, peacefully eating, the elephant looked no more dangerous than a cow. I thought then and I think now that his attack of "must" was already passing off; in which case he would merely wander harmlessly about until the mahout came back and caught him. Moreover, I did not in the least

4. A hired worker from southern India, one speaking a Dravidian language. The word "coolie" comes from Koli, or Kuli, the name of an aboriginal race of western India.

want to shoot him. I decided that I would watch him for a little while to make sure that he did not turn savage again, and then go home.

But at that moment I glanced round at the crowd that had followed me. It was an immense crowd, two thousand at the least and growing every minute. It blocked the road for a long distance on either side. I looked at the sea of yellow faces above the garish clothes—faces all happy and excited over this bit of fun, all certain that the elephant was going to be shot. They were watching me as they would watch a conjurer about to perform a trick. They did not like me, but with the magical rifle in my hands I was momentarily worth watching. And suddenly I realized that I should have to shoot the elephant after all. The people expected it of me and I had got to do it; I could feel their two thousand wills pressing me forward, irresistibly. And it was at this moment, as I stood there with the rifle in my hands, that I first grasped the hollowness, the futility of the white man's dominion in the East. Here was I, the white man with his gun, standing in front of the unarmed native crowd—seemingly the leading actor of the piece; but in reality I was only an absurd puppet pushed to and fro by the will of those yellow faces behind. I perceived in this moment that when the white man turns tyrant it is his own freedom that he destroys. He becomes a sort of hollow, posing dummy, the conventionalized figure of a sahib. For it is the condition of his rule that he shall spend his life in trying to impress the "natives," and so in every crisis he has got to do what the "natives" expect of him. He wears a mask, and his face grows to fit it. I had got to shoot the elephant. I had committed myself to doing it when I sent for the rifle. A sahib has got to act like a sahib; he has got to appear resolute, to know his own mind and do definite things. To come all that way, rifle in hand, with two thousand people marching at my heels, and then to trail feebly away, having done nothing— no, that was impossible. The crowd would laugh at me. And my whole life, every white man's life in the East, was one long struggle not to be laughed at.

But I did not want to shoot the elephant. I watched him beating his bunch of grass against his knees, with that preoccupied grandmotherly air that elephants have. It seemed to me that it would be murder to shoot him. At that age I was not squeamish about killing animals, but I had never shot an elephant and never wanted to. (Somehow it always seems worse to kill a *large* animal.) Besides, there was the beast's owner to be considered. Alive, the elephant was worth at least a hundred pounds; dead, he would only be worth the value of his tusks, five pounds, possibly. But I had got to act quickly. I turned to some experienced-looking Burmans who had been there when we arrived, and asked them how the elephant had been behaving. They all said the same thing: he took no notice of you if you left him alone, but he might charge if you went too close to him.

It was perfectly clear to me what I ought to do. I ought to walk up to within, say, twenty-five yards of the elephant and test his behavior. If he charged, I could shoot; if he took no notice of me, it would be safe to leave him until the mahout came back. But also I knew that I was going to do no such thing. I was a poor shot with a rifle and the ground was soft mud into which one would sink at every step. If the elephant charged and I missed him,

I should have about as much chance as a toad under a steam-roller. But even then I was not thinking particularly of my own skin, only of the watchful yellow faces behind. For at that moment, with the crowd watching me, I was not afraid in the ordinary sense, as I would have been if I had been alone. A white man mustn't be frightened in front of "natives"; and so, in general, he isn't frightened. The sole thought in my mind was that if anything went wrong those two thousand Burmans would see me pursued, caught, trampled on and reduced to a grinning corpse like that Indian up the hill. And if that happened it was quite probable that some of them would laugh. That would never do. There was only one alternative. I shoved the cartridges into the magazine and lay down on the road to get a better aim.

10   The crowd grew very still, and a deep, low, happy sigh, as of people who see the theatre curtain go up at last, breathed from innumerable throats. They were going to have their bit of fun after all. The rifle was a beautiful German thing with cross-hair sights. I did not then know that in shooting an elephant one would shoot to cut an imaginary bar running from ear-hole to ear-hole. I ought, therefore, as the elephant was sideways on, to have aimed straight at his ear-hole; actually I aimed several inches in front of this, thinking the brain would be further forward.

When I pulled the trigger I did not hear the bang or feel the kick—one never does when a shot goes home—but I heard the devilish roar of glee that went up from the crowd. In that instant, in too short a time, one would have thought, even for the bullet to get there, a mysterious, terrible change had come over the elephant. He neither stirred nor fell, but every line of his body had altered. He looked suddenly stricken, shrunken, immensely old, as though the frightful impact of the bullet had paralysed him without knocking him down. At last, after what seemed a long time—it might have been five seconds, I dare say—he sagged flabbily to his knees. His mouth slobbered. An enormous senility seemed to have settled upon him. One could have imagined him thousands of years old. I fired again into the same spot. At the second shot he did not collapse but climbed with desperate slowness to his feet and stood weakly upright, with legs sagging and head drooping. I fired a third time. That was the shot that did for him. You could see the agony of it jolt his whole body and knock the last remnant of strength from his legs. But in falling he seemed for a moment to rise, for as his hind legs collapsed beneath him he seemed to tower upward like a huge rock toppling, his trunk reaching skywards like a tree. He trumpeted, for the first and only time. And then down he came, his belly towards me, with a crash that seemed to shake the ground even where I lay.

I got up. The Burmans were already racing past me across the mud. It was obvious that the elephant would never rise again, but he was not dead. He was breathing very rhythmically with long rattling gasps, his great mound of a side painfully rising and falling. His mouth was wide open—I could see far down into caverns of pale pink throat. I waited a long time for him to die, but his breathing did not weaken. Finally I fired my two remaining shots into the spot where I thought his heart must be. The thick blood welled out of him like red velvet, but still he did not die. His body did not even jerk when the shots hit him, the tortured breathing continued without a pause. He was dying, very slowly and in great agony, but in some world remote from me where not even a bullet could damage him further. I felt that I had got to put an end to that dreadful noise. It seemed dreadful to see the great beast lying there, powerless to move and yet powerless to die, and not even to be able to finish him. I sent back for my small rifle and poured shot after shot into his heart and down his throat. They seemed to make no impression. The tortured gasps continued as steadily as the ticking of a clock.

In the end I could not stand it any longer and went away. I heard later that it took him half an hour to die. Burmans were bringing dahs[5] and baskets even before I left, and I was told they had stripped his body almost to the bones by the afternoon.

Afterwards, of course, there were endless discussions about the shooting of the elephant. The owner was furious, but he was only an Indian and could do nothing. Besides, legally I had done the right thing, for a mad elephant has to be killed, like a mad dog, if its owner fails to control it. Among the Europeans opinion was divided. The older men said I was right, the younger men said it was a damn shame to shoot an elephant for killing a coolie, because an elephant was worth more than any damn Coringhee coolie.[6] And afterwards I was very glad that the coolie had been killed; it put me legally in the right and it gave me a sufficient pretext for shooting the elephant. I often wondered whether any of the others grasped that I had done it solely to avoid looking a fool.

5. Butcher knives.
6. A hired worker from the seaport of Coringa, in Madras, India.

Questions

1. Why did Orwell shoot the elephant? Account for the motives that led him to shoot. Then categorize them as personal motives, circumstantial motives, social motives, or political motives. Is it easy to assign his motives to categories? Why or why not?

2. In this essay the proportion of narrative to analysis is high. Mark each paragraph as narrative or analytic, and note, in particular, how much analysis Orwell places in the middle of the essay. What are the advantages and disadvantages of having it there rather than at the beginning or the end of the essay?

3. Facts ordinarily do not speak for themselves. How does Orwell present his facts to make them speak in support of his analytic points? Look, for example, at the death of the elephant (paragraphs 11 to 13).

4. Write an essay in which you present a personal experience that illuminates a larger issue: schooling, or affirmative action, or homelessness, or law enforcement, or taxes, or some other local or national issue.

Jonathan Swift *A Modest Proposal*

For Preventing the Children of Poor People in Ireland
from Being a Burden to Their Parents or Country,
and for Making Them Beneficial to the Public

I T IS A MELANCHOLY object to those who walk through this great town[1] or travel in the country, when they see the streets, the roads, and cabin doors, crowded with beggars of the female-sex, followed by three, four, or six children, all in rags and importuning every passenger for an alms. These mothers, instead of being able to work for their honest livelihood, are forced to employ all their time in strolling to beg sustenance for their helpless infants, who, as they grow up, either turn thieves for want of work, or leave their dear native country to fight for the Pretender in Spain, or sell themselves to the Barbadoes.[2]

I think it is agreed by all parties that this prodigious number of children in the arms, or on the backs, or at the heels of their mothers, and frequently of their fathers, is in the present deplorable state of the kingdom a very great additional grievance; and therefore whoever could find out a fair, cheap, and easy method of making these children sound, useful members of the commonwealth would deserve so well of the public as to have his statue set up for a preserver of the nation.

But my intention is very far from being confined to provide only for the children of professed beggars; it is of a much greater extent, and shall take in the whole number of infants at a certain age who are born of parents in effect as little able to support them as those who demand our charity in the streets.

As to my own part, having turned my thoughts for many years upon this important subject, and maturely weighed the several schemes of other projectors,[3] I have always found them grossly mistaken in their computation. It is true, a child just dropped from its dam may be supported by her milk for a solar year, with little other nourishment; at most not above the value of two shillings,[4] which the mother may certainly get, or the value in scraps, by her

Printed in 1729 as a pamphlet, a form commonly used for political debate in the eighteenth century.

1. Dublin.
2. Many poor Irish sought to escape poverty by emigrating to the Barbadoes and other western English colonies, paying for transport by binding themselves to work for a landowner there for a period of years. The Pretender, claimant to the English throne, was barred from succession after his father, King James II, was deposed in a Protestant revolution; thereafter, many Irish Catholics joined the Pretender in his exile in France and Spain and in his unsuccessful attempts at counterrevolution.
3. People with projects; schemers.
4. A shilling used to be worth about twenty-five cents.

858

lawful occupation of begging; and it is exactly at one year old that I propose to provide for them in such a manner as instead of being a charge upon their parents or the parish, or wanting food and raiment for the rest of their lives, they shall on the contrary contribute to the feeding, and partly to the clothing, of many thousands.

There is likewise another great advantage in my scheme, that it will prevent those voluntary abortions, and that horrid practice of women murdering their bastard children, alas, too frequent among us, sacrificing the poor innocent babes, I doubt, more to avoid the expense than the shame, which would move tears and pity in the most savage and inhuman breast.

The number of souls in this kingdom being usually reckoned one million and a half, of these I calculate there may be about two hundred thousand couple whose wives are breeders; from which number I subtract thirty thousand couples who are able to maintain their own children, although I apprehend there cannot be so many under the present distresses of the kingdom; but this being granted, there will remain an hundred and seventy thousand breeders. I again subtract fifty thousand for those women who miscarry, or whose children die by accident or disease within the year. There only remain an hundred and twenty thousand children of poor parents annually born. The question therefore is, how this number shall be reared and provided for, which, as I have already said, under the present situation of affairs, is utterly impossible by all the methods hitherto proposed. For we can neither employ them in handicraft or agriculture; we neither build houses (I mean in the country) nor cultivate land. They can very seldom pick up a livelihood by stealing till they arrive at six years old, except where they are of towardly parts;[5] although I confess they learn the rudiments much earlier, during which time they can however be looked upon only as probationers, as I have been informed by a principal gentleman in the county of Cavan, who protested to me that he never knew above one or two instances under the age of six, even in a part of the kingdom so renowned for the quickest proficiency in that art.

I am assured by our merchants that a boy or a girl before twelve years old is no salable commodity; and even when they come to this age they will not yield above three pounds, or three pounds and half a crown[6] at most on the Exchange; which cannot turn to account either to the parents or the kingdom, the charge of nutriment and rags having been at least four times that value.

I shall now therefore humbly propose my own thoughts, which I hope will not be liable to the least objection.

I have been assured by a very knowing American of my acquaintance in London, that a young healthy child well nursed is at a year old a most delicious, nourishing, and wholesome food, whether stewed, roasted, baked, or boiled; and I make no doubt that it will equally serve in a fricassee or a ragout.

I do therefore humbly offer it to public consideration that of the hundred and twenty thousand children, already computed, twenty thousand may be re-

5. Promising abilities.
6. A crown was one quarter of a pound.

served for breed, whereof only one fourth part to be males, which is more than we allow to sheep, black cattle, or swine; and my reason is that these children are seldom the fruits of marriage, a circumstance not much regarded by our savages, therefore one male will be sufficient to serve four females. That the remaining hundred thousand may at a year old be offered in sale to the persons of quality and fortune through the kingdom, always advising the mother to let them suck plentifully in the last month, so as to render them plump and fat for a good table. A child will make two dishes at an entertainment for friends; and when the family dines alone, the fore or hind quarter will make a reasonable dish, and seasoned with a little pepper or salt will be very good boiled on the fourth day, especially in winter.

I have reckoned upon a medium that a child just born will weigh twelve pounds, and in a solar year if tolerably nursed increaseth to twenty-eight pounds.

I grant this food will be somewhat dear, and therefore very proper for landlords, who, as they have already devoured most of the parents, seem to have the best title to the children.

Infant's flesh will be in season throughout the year, but more plentiful in March, and a little before and after. For we are told by a grave author, an eminent French physician,[7] that fish being a prolific diet, there are more children born in Roman Catholic countries about nine months after Lent than at any other season; therefore, reckoning a year after Lent, the markets will be more glutted than usual, because the number of popish infants is at least three to one in this kingdom; and therefore it will have one other collateral advantage, by lessening the number of Papists among us.[8]

I have already computed the charge of nursing a beggar's child (in which list I reckon all cottagers, laborers, and four fifths of the farmers) to be about two shillings per annum, rags included; and I believe no gentleman would repine to give ten shillings for the carcass of a good fat child, which, as I have said, will make four dishes of excellent nutritive meat, when he hath only some particular friend or his own family to dine with him. Thus the squire will learn to be a good landlord, and grow popular among the tenants; the mother will have eight shillings net profit, and be fit for work till she produces another child.

15   Those who are more thrifty (as I must confess the times require) may flay the carcass; the skin of which artificially[9] dressed will make admirable gloves for ladies, and summer boots for fine gentlemen.

As to our city of Dublin, shambles[10] may be appointed for this purpose in the most convenient parts of it, and butchers we may be assured will not be wanting; although I rather recommend buying the children alive, and dressing them hot from the knife as we do roasting pigs.

---

7. The comic writer François Rabelais (1483–1553).

8. The speaker is addressing Protestant Anglo-Irish, who were the chief landowners and administrators, and his views of Catholicism in Ireland and abroad echo theirs.

9. Skillfully.

10. Slaughterhouses.

A very worthy person, a true lover of his country, and whose virtues I highly esteem, was lately pleased in discoursing on this matter to offer a refinement upon my scheme. He said that many gentlemen of this kingdom, having of late destroyed their deer, he conceived that the want of venison might be well supplied by the bodies of young lads and maidens, not exceeding fourteen years of age nor under twelve, so great a number of both sexes in every county being now ready to starve for want of work and service; and these to be disposed of by their parents, if alive, or otherwise by their nearest relations. But with due deference to so excellent a friend and so deserving a patriot, I cannot be altogether in his sentiments; for as to the males, my American acquaintance assured me from frequent experience that their flesh was generally tough and lean, like that of our schoolboys, by continual exercise, and their taste disagreeable; and to fatten them would not answer the charge. Then as to the females, it would, I think with humble submission, be a loss to the public, because they soon would become breeders themselves: and besides, it is not improbable that some scrupulous people might be apt to censure such a practice (although indeed very unjustly) as a little bordering upon cruelty; which, I confess, hath always been with me the strongest objection against any project, how well soever intended.

But in order to justify my friend, he confessed that this expedient was put into his head by the famous Psalmanazar, a native of the island Formosa,[11] who came from thence to London above twenty years ago, and in conversation told my friend that in his country when any young person happened to be put to death, the executioner sold the carcass to persons of quality as a prime dainty; and that in his time the body of a plump girl of fifteen, who was crucified for an attempt to poison the emperor, was sold to his Imperial Majesty's prime minister of state, and other great mandarins of the court, in joints from the gibbet, at four hundred crowns. Neither indeed can I deny that if the same use were made of several plump young girls in this town, who without one single groat[12] to their fortunes cannot stir abroad without a chair,[13] and appear at the playhouse and assemblies in foreign fineries which they never will pay for, the kingdom would not be the worse.

Some persons of a desponding spirit are in great concern about that vast number of poor people who are aged, diseased, or maimed, and I have been desired to employ my thoughts what course may be taken to ease the nation of so grievous an encumbrance. But I am not in the least pain upon that matter, because it is very well known that they are every day dying and rotting by cold and famine, and filth and vermin, as fast as can be reasonably expected. And as to the younger laborers, they are now in almost as hopeful a condition. They cannot get work, and consequently pine away for want of nourishment to

11. Actually a Frenchman, George Psalmanazar had passed himself off as from Formosa (now Taiwan) and had written a fictitious book about his "homeland," with descriptions of human sacrifice and cannibalism.
12. A coin worth about four English pennies.
13. A sedan chair.

a degree that if at any time they are accidentally hired to common labor, they have not strength to perform it; and thus the country and themselves are happily delivered from the evils to come.

20   I have too long digressed, and therefore shall return to my subject. I think the advantages by the proposal which I have made are obvious and many, as well as of the highest importance.

For first, as I have already observed, it would greatly lessen the number of Papists, with whom we are yearly overrun, being the principal breeders of the nation as well as our most dangerous enemies; and who stay at home on purpose to deliver the kingdom to the Pretender, hoping to take their advantage by the absence of so many good Protestants, who have chosen rather to leave their country than to stay at home and pay tithes against their conscience to an Episcopal curate.

Secondly, the poorer tenants will have something valuable of their own, which by law may be made liable to distress,[14] and help to pay their landlord's rent, their corn and cattle being already seized and money a thing unknown.

Thirdly, whereas the maintenance of an hundred thousand children, from two years old and upwards, cannot be computed at less than ten shillings a piece per annum, the nation's stock will be thereby increased fifty thousand pounds per annum, besides the profit of a new dish introduced to the tables of all gentlemen of fortune in the kingdom who have any refinement in taste. And the money will circulate among ourselves, the goods being entirely of our own growth and manufacture.

Fourthly, the constant breeders, besides the gain of eight shillings sterling per annum by the sale of their children, will be rid of the charge of maintaining them after the first year.

25   Fifthly, this food would likewise bring great custom to taverns, where the vintners will certainly be so prudent as to procure the best receipts for dressing it to perfection, and consequently have their houses frequented by all the fine gentlemen, who justly value themselves upon their knowledge in good eating; and a skillful cook, who understands how to oblige his guests, will contrive to make it as expensive as they please.

Sixthly, this would be a great inducement to marriage, which all wise nations have either encouraged by rewards or enforced by laws and penalties. It would increase the care and tenderness of mothers toward their children, when they were sure of a settlement for life to the poor babes, provided in some sort by the public, to their annual profit instead of expense. We should see an honest emulation among the married women, which of them could bring the fattest child to the market. Men would become as fond of their wives during the time of their pregnancy as they are now of their mares in foal, their cows in calf, or sows when they are ready to farrow; nor offer to beat or kick them (as is too frequent a practice) for fear of a miscarriage.

Many other advantages might be enumerated. For instance, the addition of some thousand carcasses in our exportation of barreled beef, the propaga-

14. Seizure for the payment of debts.

tion of swine's flesh, and improvement in the art of making good bacon, so much wanted among us by the great destruction of pigs, too frequent at our tables, which are no way comparable in taste or magnificence to a well-grown, fat, yearling child, which roasted whole will make a considerable figure at a lord mayor's feast or any other public entertainment. But this and many others I omit, being studious of brevity.

Supposing that one thousand families in this city would be constant customers for infants' flesh, besides others who might have it at merry meetings, particularly weddings and christenings, I compute that Dublin would take off annually about twenty thousand carcasses, and the rest of the kingdom (where probably they will be sold somewhat cheaper) the remaining eighty thousand.

I can think of no one objection that will possibly be raised against this proposal, unless it should be urged that the number of people will be thereby much lessened in the kingdom. This I freely own, and it was indeed one principal design in offering it to the world. I desire the reader will observe, that I calculate my remedy for this one individual kingdom of Ireland and for no other that ever was, is, or I think ever can be upon earth. Therefore let no man talk to me of other expedients: of taxing our absentees at five shillings a pound: of using neither clothes nor household furniture except what is of our own growth and manufacture: of utterly rejecting the materials and instruments that promote foreign luxury: of curing the expensiveness of pride, vanity, idleness, and gaming in our women: of introducing a vein of parsimony, prudence, and temperance: of learning to love our country, in the want of which we differ even from Laplanders and the inhabitants of Topinamboo:[15] of quitting our animosities and factions, nor acting any longer like the Jews, who were murdering one another at the very moment their city was taken: of being a little cautious not to sell our country and conscience for nothing: of teaching landlords to have at least one degree of mercy toward their tenants: lastly, of putting a spirit of honesty, industry, and skill into our shopkeepers; who, if a resolution could now be taken to buy only our native goods, would immediately unite to cheat and exact upon us in the price, the measure, and the goodness, nor could ever yet be brought to make one fair proposal of just dealing, though often and earnestly invited to it.[16]

Therefore I repeat, let no man talk to me of these and the like expedients, till he hath at least some glimpse of hope that there will ever be some hearty and sincere attempt to put them in practice.   30

But as to myself, having been wearied out for many years with offering vain, idle, visionary thoughts, and at length utterly despairing of success, I fortunately fell upon this proposal, which, as it is wholly new, so it hath something solid and real, of no expense and little trouble, full in our own power, and whereby we can incur no danger in disobliging England. For this kind of commodity will not bear exportation, the flesh being of too tender a consis-

15. A district in Brazil.
16. Swift himself had made these proposals seriously in various previous works, but to no avail.

tence to admit a long continuance in salt, although perhaps I could name a country[17] which would be glad to eat up our whole nation without it.

After all, I am not so violently bent upon my own opinion as to reject any offer proposed by wise men, which shall be found equally innocent, cheap, easy, and effectual. But before something of that kind shall be advanced in contradiction to my scheme, and offering a better, I desire the author or authors will be pleased maturely to consider two points. First, as things now stand, how they will be able to find food and raiment for an hundred thousand useless mouths and backs. And secondly, there being a round million of creatures in human figure throughout this kingdom, whose sole subsistence put into a common stock would leave them in debt two millions of pounds sterling, adding those who are beggars by profession to the bulk of farmers, cottagers, and laborers, with their wives and children who are beggars in effect; I desire those politicians who dislike my overture, and may perhaps be so bold to attempt an answer, that they will first ask the parents of these mortals whether they would not at this day think it a great happiness to have been sold for food at a year old in the manner I prescribe, and thereby have avoided such a perpetual scene of misfortunes as they have since gone through by the oppression of landlords, the impossibility of paying rent without money or trade, the want of common sustenance, with neither house nor clothes to cover them from the inclemencies of the weather, and the most inevitable prospect of entailing the like or greater miseries upon their breed forever.

I profess, in the sincerity of my heart, that I have not the least personal interest in endeavoring to promote this necessary work, having no other motive than the public good of my country, by advancing our trade, providing for infants, relieving the poor, and giving some pleasure to the rich. I have no children by which I can propose to get a single penny; the youngest being nine years old, and my wife past childbearing.

17. England.

QUESTIONS

1. Identify examples of the reasonable voice of Swift's authorial persona, such as the title of the essay itself.

2. Look, in particular, at instances in which Swift's authorial persona proposes shocking things. How does the style of the "Modest Proposal" affect its content?

3. Verbal irony consists of saying one thing and meaning another. At what point in this essay do you begin to suspect that Swift is using irony? What additional evidence of irony can you find?

4. Write a modest proposal of your own in the manner of Swift to remedy a real problem; that is, propose an outrageous remedy in a reasonable voice.

Niccolò Machiavelli *The Morals of the Prince*

On the Reasons Why Men Are Praised or Blamed— Especially Princes

I T REMAINS now to be seen what style and principles a prince ought to adopt in dealing with his subjects and friends. I know the subject has been treated frequently before, and I'm afraid people will think me rash for trying to do so again, especially since I intend to differ in this discussion from what others have said. But since I intend to write something useful to an understanding reader, it seemed better to go after the real truth of the matter than to repeat what people have imagined. A great many men have imagined states and princedoms such as nobody ever saw or knew in the real world, for there's such a difference between the way we really live and the way we ought to live that the man who neglects the real to study the ideal will learn how to accomplish his ruin, not his salvation. Any man who tries to be good all the time is bound to come to ruin among the great number who are not good. Hence a prince who wants to keep his post must learn how not to be good, and use that knowledge, or refrain from using it, as necessity requires.

Putting aside, then, all the imaginary things that are said about princes, and getting down to the truth, let me say that whenever men are discussed (and especially princes because they are prominent), there are certain qualities that bring them either praise or blame. Thus some are considered generous, others stingy (I use a Tuscan term, since "greedy" in our speech means a man who wants to take other people's goods. We call a man "stingy" who clings to his own); some are givers, others grabbers; some cruel, others merciful; one man is treacherous, another faithful; one is feeble and effeminate, another fierce and spirited; one humane, another proud; one lustful, another chaste; one straightforward, another sly; one harsh, another gentle; one serious, another playful; one religious, another skeptical, and so on. I know everyone will agree that among these many qualities a prince certainly ought to have all those that are considered good. But since it is impossible to have and exercise them all, because the conditions of human life simply do not allow it, a prince must be shrewd enough to avoid the public disgrace of those vices that would lose him his state. If he possibly can, he should also guard against vices that will not lose him his state; but if he cannot prevent them, he should not be too worried about indulging them. And furthermore, he should not be too worried about incurring blame for any vice without which he would find it hard to save his state. For if you look at matters carefully, you will see that something resembling virtue, if you follow it, may be your ruin, while some-

From The Prince *(1513), a book on statecraft written for Giuliano de' Medici (1479–1516), a member of one of the most famous and powerful families of Renaissance Italy. Excerpted from an edition translated and edited by Robert M. Adams (1977).*

thing else resembling vice will lead, if you follow it, to your security and well-being.

ON LIBERALITY AND STINGINESS

Let me begin, then, with the first of the qualities mentioned above, by saying that a reputation for liberality is doubtless very fine; but the generosity that earns you that reputation can do you great harm. For if you exercise your generosity in a really virtuous way, as you should, nobody will know of it, and you cannot escape the odium of the opposite vice. Hence if you wish to be widely known as a generous man, you must seize every opportunity to make a big display of your giving. A prince of this character is bound to use up his entire revenue in works of ostentation. Thus, in the end, if he wants to keep a name for generosity, he will have to load his people with exorbitant taxes and squeeze money out of them in every way he can. This is the first step in making him odious to his subjects; for when he is poor, nobody will respect him. Then, when his generosity has angered many and brought rewards to a few, the slightest difficulty will trouble him, and at the first approach of danger, down he goes. If by chance he foresees this, and tries to change his ways, he will immediately be labeled a miser.

Since a prince cannot use this virtue of liberality in such a way as to become known for it unless he harms his own security, he won't mind, if he judges prudently of things, being known as a miser. In due course he will be thought the more liberal man, when people see that his parsimony enables him to live on his income, to defend himself against his enemies, and to undertake major projects without burdening his people with taxes. Thus he will be acting liberally toward all those people from whom he takes nothing (and there are an immense number of them), and in a stingy way toward those people on whom he bestows nothing (and they are very few). In our times, we have seen great things being accomplished only by men who have had the name of misers; all the others have gone under. Pope Julius II, though he used his reputation as a generous man to gain the papacy, sacrificed it in order to be able to make war; the present king of France has waged many wars without levying a single extra tax on his people, simply because he could take care of the extra expenses out of the savings from his long parsimony. If the present king of Spain had a reputation for generosity, he would never have been able to undertake so many campaigns, or win so many of them.

5   Hence a prince who prefers not to rob his subjects, who wants to be able to defend himself, who wants to avoid poverty and contempt, and who doesn't want to become a plunderer, should not mind in the least if people consider him a miser; this is simply one of the vices that enable him to reign. Someone may object that Caesar used a reputation for generosity to become emperor, and many other people have also risen in the world, because they were generous or were supposed to be so. Well, I answer, either you are a prince already, or you are in the process of becoming one; in the first case, this reputation for generosity is harmful to you, in the second case it is very necessary. Caesar

was one of those who wanted to become ruler in Rome; but after he had reached his goal, if he had lived, and had not cut down on his expenses, he would have ruined the empire itself. Someone may say: there have been plenty of princes, very successful in warfare, who have had a reputation for generosity. But I answer: either the prince is spending his own money and that of his subjects, or he is spending someone else's. In the first case, he ought to be sparing; in the second case, he ought to spend money like water. Any prince at the head of his army, which lives on loot, extortion, and plunder, disposes of other people's property, and is bound to be very generous; otherwise, his soldiers would desert him. You can always be a more generous giver when what you give is not yours or your subjects'; Cyrus, Caesar, and Alexander[1] were generous in this way. Spending what belongs to other people does no harm to your reputation, rather it enhances it; only spending your own substance harms you. And there is nothing that wears out faster than generosity; even as you practice it, you lose the means of practicing it, and you become either poor and contemptible or (in the course of escaping poverty) rapacious and hateful. The thing above all against which a prince must protect himself is being contemptible and hateful; generosity leads to both. Thus, it's much wiser to put up with the reputation of being a miser, which brings you shame without hate, than to be forced—just because you want to appear generous—into a reputation for rapacity, which brings shame on you and hate along with it.

ON CRUELTY AND CLEMENCY: WHETHER IT IS BETTER TO BE LOVED OR FEARED

Continuing now with our list of qualities, let me say that every prince should prefer to be considered merciful rather than cruel, yet he should be careful not to mismanage this clemency of his. People thought Cesare Borgia[2] was cruel, but that cruelty of his reorganized the Romagna, united it, and established it in peace and loyalty. Anyone who views the matter realistically will see that this prince was much more merciful than the people of Florence, who, to avoid the reputation of cruelty, allowed Pistoia to be destroyed.[3] Thus, no prince should mind being called cruel for what he does to keep his subjects united and loyal; he may make examples of a very few, but he will be more merciful in reality than those who, in their tenderheartedness, allow disorders to occur, with their attendant murders and lootings. Such turbulence brings harm to an entire community, while the executions ordered by a prince affect only one individual at a time. A new prince, above all others, cannot possibly avoid a name for cruelty, since new states are always in danger. And Virgil, speaking through the mouth of Dido,[4] says:

1. Persian, Roman, and Macedonian conquerors and rulers in ancient times.
2. The son of Pope Alexander VI; he was duke of Romagna, which he subjugated in 1499–1502.
3. By unchecked rioting between opposing factions in 1502.
4. Queen of Carthage and tragic heroine of Virgil's epic, the *Aeneid*.

> My cruel fate
> And doubts attending an unsettled state
> Force me to guard my coast from foreign foes.

Yet a prince should be slow to believe rumors and to commit himself to action on the basis of them. He should not be afraid of his own thoughts; he ought to proceed cautiously, moderating his conduct with prudence and humanity, allowing neither overconfidence to make him careless, nor overtimidity to make him intolerable.

Here the question arises: is it better to be loved than feared, or vice versa? I don't doubt that every prince would like to be both; but since it is hard to accommodate these qualities, if you have to make a choice, to be feared is much safer than to be loved. For it is a good general rule about men, that they are ungrateful, fickle, liars and deceivers, fearful of danger and greedy for gain. While you serve their welfare, they are all yours, offering their blood, their belongings, their lives, and their children's lives, as we noted above—so long as the danger is remote. But when the danger is close at hand, they turn against you. Then, any prince who has relied on their words and has made no other preparations will come to grief; because friendships that are bought at a price, and not with greatness and nobility of soul, may be paid for but they are not acquired, and they cannot be used in time of need. People are less concerned with offending a man who makes himself loved than one who makes himself feared: the reason is that love is a link of obligation which men, because they are rotten, will break any time they think doing so serves their advantage; but fear involves dread of punishment, from which they can never escape.

Still, a prince should make himself feared in such a way that, even if he gets no love, he gets no hate either; because it is perfectly possible to be feared and not hated, and this will be the result if only the prince will keep his hands off the property of his subjects or citizens, and off their women. When he does have to shed blood, he should be sure to have a strong justification and manifest cause; but above all, he should not confiscate people's property, because men are quicker to forget the death of a father than the loss of a patrimony. Besides, pretexts for confiscation are always plentiful, it never fails that a prince who starts living by plunder can find reasons to rob someone else. Excuses for proceeding against someone's life are much rarer and more quickly exhausted.

But a prince at the head of his armies and commanding a multitude of soldiers should not care a bit if he is considered cruel; without such a reputation, he could never hold his army together and ready for action. Among the marvelous deeds of Hannibal,[5] this was prime: that, having an immense army, which included men of many different races and nations, and which he led to battle in distant countries, he never allowed them to fight among themselves

---

5. Carthaginian general who led a massive but unsuccessful invasion of Rome in 218–203 B.C.E.

or to rise against him, whether his fortune was good or bad. The reason for this could only be his inhuman cruelty, which, along with his countless other talents, made him an object of awe and terror to his soldiers; and without the cruelty, his other qualities would never have sufficed. The historians who pass snap judgments on these matters admire his accomplishments and at the same time condemn the cruelty which was their main cause.

When I say, "His other qualities would never have sufficed," we can see that this is true from the example of Scipio,[6] an outstanding man not only among those of his own time, but in all recorded history; yet his armies revolted in Spain, for no other reason than his excessive leniency in allowing his soldiers more freedom than military discipline permits. Fabius Maximus rebuked him in the senate for this failing, calling him the corrupter of the Roman armies. When a lieutenant of Scipio's plundered the Locrians,[7] he took no action in behalf of the people, and did nothing to discipline that insolent lieutenant; again, this was the result of his easygoing nature. Indeed, when someone in the senate wanted to excuse him on this occasion, he said there are many men who knew better how to avoid error themselves than how to correct error in others. Such a soft temper would in time have tarnished the fame and glory of Scipio, had he brought it to the office of emperor; but as he lived under the control of the senate, this harmful quality of his not only remained hidden but was considered creditable.

Returning to the question of being feared or loved, I conclude that since men love at their own inclination but can be made to fear at the inclination of the prince, a shrewd prince will lay his foundations on what is under his own control, not on what is controlled by others. He should simply take pains not to be hated, as I said.

The Way Princes Should Keep Their Word

How praiseworthy it is for a prince to keep his word and live with integrity rather than by craftiness, everyone understands; yet we see from recent experience that those princes have accomplished most who paid little heed to keeping their promises, but who knew how craftily to manipulate the minds of men. In the end, they won out over those who tried to act honestly.

You should consider then, that there are two ways of fighting, one with laws and the other with force. The first is properly a human method, the second belongs to beasts. But as the first method does not always suffice, you sometimes have to turn to the second. Thus a prince must know how to make good use of both the beast and the man. Ancient writers made subtle note of this fact when they wrote that Achilles and many other princes of antiquity were sent to be reared by Chiron the centaur, who trained them in his disci-

10

6. The Roman general whose successful invasion of Carthage in 203 b.c.e. caused Hannibal's army to be recalled from Rome. The episode described here occurred in 206 b.c.e.
7. Fabius Maximus, not only a senator but also a high public official and general who had fought against Hannibal in Italy; Locrians, people of Sicily defeated by Scipio in 205 b.c.e. and placed under Q. Pleminius.

pline.[8] Having a teacher who is half man and half beast can only mean that a prince must know how to use both these two natures, and that one without the other has no lasting effect.

Since a prince must know how to use the character of beasts, he should pick for imitation the fox and the lion. As the lion cannot protect himself from traps, and the fox cannot defend himself from wolves, you have to be a fox in order to be wary of traps, and a lion to overawe the wolves. Those who try to live by the lion alone are badly mistaken. Thus a prudent prince cannot and should not keep his word when to do so would go against his interest, or when the reasons that made him pledge it no longer apply. Doubtless if all men were good, this rule would be bad; but since they are a sad lot, and keep no faith with you, you in your turn are under no obligation to keep it with them.

15   Besides, a prince will never lack for legitimate excuses to explain away his breaches of faith. Modern history will furnish innumerable examples of this behavior, showing how many treaties and promises have been made null and void by the faithlessness of princes, and how the man succeeded best who knew best how to play the fox. But it is a necessary part of this nature that you must conceal it carefully; you must be a great liar and hypocrite. Men are so simple of mind, and so much dominated by their immediate needs, that a deceitful man will always find plenty who are ready to be deceived. One of many recent examples calls for mention. Alexander VI[9] never did anything else, never had another thought, except to deceive men, and he always found fresh material to work on. Never was there a man more convincing in his assertions, who sealed his promises with more solemn oaths, and who observed them less. Yet his deceptions were always successful, because he knew exactly how to manage this sort of business.

In actual fact, a prince may not have all the admirable qualities we listed, but it is very necessary that he should seem to have them. Indeed, I will venture to say that when you have them and exercise them all the time, they are harmful to you; when you just seem to have them, they are useful. It is good to appear merciful, truthful, humane, sincere, and religious; it is good to be so in reality. But you must keep your mind so disposed that, in case of need, you can turn to the exact contrary. This has to be understood: a prince, and especially a new prince, cannot possibly exercise all those virtues for which men are called "good." To preserve the state, he often has to do things against his word, against charity, against humanity, against religion. Thus he has to have a mind ready to shift as the winds of fortune and the varying circumstances of life may dictate. And as I said above, he should not depart from the good if he can hold to it, but he should be ready to enter on evil if he has to.

Hence a prince should take great care never to drop a word that does not seem imbued with the five good qualities noted above; to anyone who sees or

8. Achilles was foremost among the Greek heroes in the Trojan War. Half man and half horse, the mythical Chiron was said to have taught the arts of war and peace, including hunting, medicine, music, and prophecy.
9. Pope from 1492 to 1503.

hears him, he should appear all compassion, all honor, all humanity, all integrity, all religion. Nothing is more necessary than to seem to have this last virtue. Men in general judge more by the sense of sight than by the sense of touch, because everyone can see but only a few can test by feeling. Everyone sees what you seem to be, few know what you really are; and those few do not dare take a stand against the general opinion, supported by the majesty of the government. In the actions of all men, and especially of princes who are not subject to a court of appeal, we must always look to the end. Let a prince, therefore, win victories and uphold his state; his methods will always be considered worthy, and everyone will praise them, because the masses are always impressed by the superficial appearance of things, and by the outcome of an enterprise. And the world consists of nothing but the masses; the few who have no influence when the many feel secure. A certain prince of our own time, whom it's just as well not to name,[10] preaches nothing but peace and mutual trust, yet he is the determined enemy of both; and if on several different occasions he had observed either, he would have lost both his reputation and his throne.

10. Probably Ferdinand of Spain, then allied with the house of Medici.

QUESTIONS

1. This selection contains four sections of *The Prince*: "On the Reasons Why Men Are Praised or Blamed—Especially Princes"; "On Liberality and Stinginess"; "On Cruelty and Clemency: Whether It Is Better to Be Loved or Feared"; and "The Way Princes Should Keep Their Word." How, in each section, does Machiavelli contrast the ideal and the real, what he calls "the way we really live and the way we ought to live" (paragraph 1)? Mark some of the sentences in which he expresses these contrasts.

2. Rewrite some of Machiavelli's advice to princes less forcibly and shockingly, and more palatably. For example, "Any man who tries to be good all the time is bound to come to ruin among the great number who are not good" (paragraph 1) might be rewritten as "Good men are often taken advantage of and harmed by men who are not good."

3. Describe Machiavelli's view of human nature. How do his views of government follow from it?

4. Machiavelli might be described as a sixteenth-century spin doctor teaching a ruler how to package himself. Adapt his advice to a current figure in national, state, or local politics and write about that figure in a brief essay.

Thomas Jefferson *Original Draft of the*
Declaration of Independence

A DECLARATION OF THE REPRESENTATIVES OF THE UNITED STATES OF
AMERICA, IN GENERAL CONGRESS ASSEMBLED.

W HEN IN THE COURSE of human events it becomes necessary for a people to advance from that subordination in which they have hitherto remained, & to assume among the powers of the earth the equal & independant station to which the laws of nature & of nature's god entitle them, a decent respect to the opinions of mankind requires that they should declare the causes which impel them to the change.

We hold these truths to be sacred & undeniable; that all men are created equal & independant, that from that equal creation they derive rights inherent & inalienable, among which are the preservation of life, & liberty, & the spirit of happiness; that to secure these ends, governments are instituted among men, deriving their just powers from the consent of the governed; that whenever any form of government shall become destructive of these ends, it is the right of the people to alter or to abolish it, & to institute new government, laying its foundation on such principles & organising it's powers in such form, as to them shall seem most likely to effect their safety & happiness. prudence indeed will dictate that governments long established should not be changed for light & transient causes: and accordingly all experience hath shewn that mankind are more disposed to suffer while evils are sufferable, than to right themselves by abolishing the forms to which they are accustomed. but when a long train of abuses & usurpations, begun at a distinguished period, & pursuing invariably the same object, evinces a design to subject them to arbitrary power, it is their right, it is their duty, to throw off such government & to provide new guards for their future security. such has been the patient sufferance of these colonies; & such is now the necessity which constrains them to expunge their former systems of government. The history of his present majesty, is a history of unremitting injuries and usurpations, among which no one fact stands single or solitary to contradict the uniform tenor of the rest, all of which have in direct object the establishment of an absolute tyranny over these states. to prove this, let facts be submitted to a candid world, for the truth of which we pledge a faith yet unsullied by falsehood.

he has refused his assent to laws the most wholesome and necessary for the public good:

On June 11, 1776, Jefferson was elected by the Second Continental Congress to join John Adams, Benjamin Franklin, Roger Sherman, and Robert Livingston in drafting a declaration of independence. The draft presented to Congress on June 28 was primarily the work of Jefferson.

872

he has forbidden his governors to pass laws of immediate & pressing importance, unless suspended in their operation till his assent should be obtained; and when so suspended, he has neglected utterly to attend to them.

he has refused to pass other laws for the accommodation of large districts of people unless those people would relinquish the right of representation, a right inestimable to them, & formidable to tyrants alone:[1]

he has dissolved Representative houses repeatedly & continually, for opposing with manly firmness his invasions on the rights of the people:

he has refused for a long space of time to cause others to be elected, whereby the legislative powers, incapable of annihilation, have returned to the people at large for their exercise, the state remaining in the mean time exposed to all the dangers of invasion from without, &, convulsions within:

he has suffered the administration of justice totally to cease in some of these colonies, refusing his assent to laws for establishing judiciary powers:

he has made our judges dependant on his will alone, for the tenure of their offices, and amount of their salaries:

he has erected a multitude of new offices by a self-assumed power, & sent hither swarms of officers to harrass our people & eat out their substance: he has kept among us in times of peace standing armies & ships of war:

he has affected[2] to render the military, independent of & superior to the civil power:

he has combined with others to subject us to a jurisdiction foreign to our constitutions and unacknowledged by our laws; giving his assent to their pretended acts of legislation, for quartering large bodies of armed troops among us;

for protecting them by a mock-trial from punishment for any murders they should commit on the inhabitants of these states;

for cutting off our trade with all parts of the world;

for imposing taxes on us without our consent;

for depriving us of the benefits of trial by jury

he has endeavored to prevent the population of these states; for that purpose obstructing the laws for naturalization of foreigners; refusing to pass others to encourage their migrations hither; & raising the conditions of new appropriations of lands;

---

1. At this point in the manuscript a strip containing the following clause is inserted: "He called together legislative bodies at places unusual, unco[mfortable, & distant from] the depository of their public records for the sole purpose of fatiguing [them into compliance] with his measures." Missing parts in the Library of Congress text are supplied from the copy made by Jefferson for George Wythe. This copy is in the New York Public Library. The fact that this passage was omitted from John Adams's transcript suggests that it was not a part of Jefferson's original rough draft.

2. Tried.

for transporting us beyond seas to be tried for pretended offences:
for taking away our charters & altering fundamentally the forms of our
governments;
for suspending our own legislatures & declaring themselves invested
with power to legislate for us in all cases whatsoever:
he has abdicated government here, withdrawing his governors, & declaring us out of his allegiance & protection:
he has plundered our seas, ravaged our coasts, burnt our towns &
destroyed the lives of our people:
he is at this time transporting large armies of foreign mercenaries to compleat the works of death, desolation & tyranny, already begun with
circumstances of cruelty & perfidy unworthy the head of a civilized nation:
he has endeavored to bring on the inhabitants of our frontiers the merciless Indian savages, whose known rule of warfare is an undistinguished
destruction of all ages, sexes, & conditions of existence:
he has incited treasonable insurrections of our fellow-citizens, with the allurements of forfeiture & confiscation of our property:
he has waged cruel war against human nature itself, violating it's most sacred rights of life & liberty in the persons of a distant people who never
offended him, captivating & carrying them into slavery in another
hemisphere, or to incur miserable death in their transportation thither.
this piratical warfare, the opprobrium of *infidel* powers, is the warfare
of the CHRISTIAN king of Great Britain. determined to keep open a
market where MEN should be bought & sold; he has prostituted his
negative for suppressing every legislative attempt to prohibit or to restrain this execrable commerce: and that this assemblage of horrors
might want no fact of distinguished die, he is now exciting those very
people to rise in arms among us, and to purchase that liberty of which
he has deprived them, by murdering the people upon whom *he* also obtruded them; thus paying off former crimes committed against the *liberties* of one people, with crimes which he urges them to commit
against the *lives* of another.

in every stage of these oppressions we have petitioned for redress in the most
humble terms; our repeated petitions have been answered by repeated injury. a
prince whose character is thus marked by every act which may define a tyrant,
is unfit to be the ruler of a people who mean to be free. future ages will scarce
believe that the hardiness of one man, adventured within the short compass of
twelve years only, on so many acts of tyranny without a mask, over a people
fostered & fixed in principles of liberty.

Nor have we been wanting in attentions to our British brethren. we have
warned them from time to time of attempts by their legislature to extend a jurisdiction over these our states. we have reminded them of the circumstances
of our emigration & settlement here, no one of which could warrant so strange
a pretension: that these were effected at the expence of our own blood & trea-

sure, unassisted by the wealth or the strength of Great Britain: that in constituting indeed our several forms of government, we had adopted one common king, thereby laying a foundation for perpetual league & amity with them; but that submission to their [Parliament, was no Part of our Constitution, nor ever in Idea, if History may be][3] credited: and we appealed to their native justice & magnanimity, as to the ties of our common kindred to disavow these usurpations which were likely to interrupt our correspondence & connection. they too have been deaf to the voice of justice & of consanguinity, & when occasions have been given them, by the regular course of their laws, of removing from their councils the disturbers of our harmony, they have by their free election re-established them in power. at this very time too they are permitting their chief magistrate to send over not only soldiers of our common blood, but Scotch & foreign mercenaries to invade & deluge us in blood. these facts have given the last stab to agonizing affection, and manly spirit bids us to renounce for ever these unfeeling brethren. we must endeavor to forget our former love for them, and to hold them as we hold the rest of mankind, enemies in war, in peace friends. we might have been a free & a great people together; but a communication of grandeur & of freedom it seems is below their dignity. be it so, since they will have it: the road to glory & happiness is open to us too; we will climb it in a separate state, and acquiesce in the necessity which pronounces our everlasting Adieu!

We therefore the representatives of the United States of America in General Congress assembled do, in the name & by authority of the good people of these states, reject and renounce all allegiance & subjection to the kings of Great Britain & all others who may hereafter claim by, through, or under them; we utterly dissolve & break off all political connection which may have heretofore subsisted between us & the people or parliament of Great Britain; and finally we do assert and declare these colonies to be free and independant states, and that as free & independant states they shall hereafter have power to levy war, conclude peace, contract alliances, establish commerce, & to do all other acts and things which independant states may of right do. And for the support of this declaration we mutually pledge to each other our lives, our fortunes, & our sacred honour.

3. A passage illegible in the original is supplied from John Adams's transcription.

QUESTIONS

1. Note the stylistic differences (including choices of grammar and punctuation) between the original draft of the Declaration of Independence and the revised draft. What effect do those differences have?

2. Choose one or two significant revisions that Jefferson made between the draft and the final version of the Declaration, and explain why they are significant in a short essay.

THOMAS JEFFERSON AND OTHERS *The Declaration of Independence*

IN CONGRESS, JULY 4, 1776
THE UNANIMOUS DECLARATION OF THE
THIRTEEN UNITED STATES OF AMERICA

WHEN IN THE Course of human events it becomes necessary for one people to dissolve the political bands which have connected them with another, and to assume among the powers of the earth, the separate and equal station to which the Laws of Nature and of Nature's God entitle them, a decent respect to the opinions of mankind requires that they should declare the causes which impel them to the separation.

We hold these truths to be self-evident, that all men are created equal, that they are endowed by their Creator with certain unalienable Rights, that among these are Life, Liberty and the pursuit of Happiness. That to secure these rights, Governments are instituted among Men, deriving their just powers from the consent of the governed. That whenever any Form of Government becomes destructive of these ends, it is the Right of the People to alter or to abolish it, and to institute new Government, laying its foundation on such principles and organizing its powers in such form, as to them shall seem most likely to effect their Safety and Happiness. Prudence, indeed, will dictate that Governments long established should not be changed for light and transient causes; and accordingly all experience hath shewn that mankind are more disposed to suffer, while evils are sufferable, than to right themselves by abolishing the forms to which they are accustomed. But when a long train of abuses and usurpations, pursuing invariably the same Object evinces a design to reduce them under absolute Despotism, it is their right, it is their duty, to throw off such Government, and to provide new Guards for their future security. Such has been the patient sufferance of these Colonies; and such is now the necessity which constrains them to alter their former Systems of Government. The history of the present King of Great Britain is a history of repeated injuries and usurpations, all having in direct object the establishment of an absolute Tyranny over these States. To prove this, let Facts be submitted to a candid world.

He has refused his Assent to Laws, the most wholesome and necessary for the public good.

He has forbidden his Government to pass laws of immediate and pressing importance, unless suspended in their operation till his Assent should be obtained; and when so suspended, he has utterly neglected to attend to them.

This final version of the Declaration of Independence resulted from revisions made to Jefferson's original draft by members of the committee to draft the declaration, including John Adams and Benjamin Franklin, and by members of the Continental Congress.

He has refused to pass other Laws for the accommodation of large districts   5
of people, unless those people would relinquish the right of Representation in
the Legislature, a right inestimable to them and formidable to tyrants only.

He has called together legislative bodies at places unusual, uncomfortable, and distant from the depository of their Public Records, for the sole purpose of fatiguing them into compliance with his measures.

He has dissolved Representative Houses repeatedly, for opposing with
manly firmness his invasions on the rights of the people.

He has refused for a long time, after such dissolutions, to cause others to
be elected; whereby the Legislative Powers, incapable of Annihilation, have returned to the People at large for their exercise; the State remaining in the
mean time exposed to all the dangers of invasion from without, and convulsions within.

He has endeavored to prevent the population of these States; for that purpose obstructing the Laws for Naturalization of Foreigners; refusing to pass
others to encourage their migration hither, and raising the conditions of new
Appropriations of Lands.

He has obstructed the Administration of Justice, by refusing his Assent to   10
Laws for establishing Judiciary Powers.

He has made Judges dependent on his Will alone, for the tenure of their
offices, and the amount and payment of their salaries.

He has erected a multitude of New Offices, and sent hither swarms of Officers to harass our people, and eat out their substance.

He has kept among us, in times of peace, Standing Armies without the
Consent of our legislatures.

He has affected to render the Military independent of and superior to the
Civil Power.

He has combined with others to subject us to a jurisdiction foreign to our   15
constitution, and unacknowledged by our laws; giving his Assent to their Acts
of pretended Legislation: For quartering large bodies of armed troops among
us: For protecting them, by a mock Trial, from punishment for any Murders
which they should commit on the Inhabitants of these States: For cutting off
our Trade with all parts of the world: For imposing Taxes on us without our
Consent: For depriving us in many cases, of the benefits of Trial by Jury: For
transporting us beyond Seas to be tried for pretended offenses: For abolishing
the free System of English Laws in a neighboring Province, establishing
therein an Arbitrary government, and enlarging its Boundaries so as to render
it at once an example and fit instrument for introducing the same absolute
rule into these Colonies: For taking away our Charters, abolishing our most
valuable Laws, and altering fundamentally the Forms of our Governments: For
suspending our own Legislatures, and declaring themselves invested with
power to legislate for us in all cases whatsoever.

He has abdicated Government here, by declaring us out of his Protection
and waging War against us.

He has plundered our seas, ravaged our Coasts, burnt our towns, and destroyed the lives of our people.

He is at this time transporting large Armies of foreign Mercenaries to complete the works of death, desolation and tyranny, already begun with circumstances of Cruelty & Perfidy scarcely paralleled in the most barbarous ages, and totally unworthy the Head of a civilized nation.

He has constrained our fellow Citizens taken Captive on the high Seas to bear Arms against their Country, to become the executioners of their friends and Brethren, or to fall themselves by their Hands.

20   He has excited domestic insurrections amongst us, and has endeavored to bring on the inhabitants of our frontiers, the merciless Indian Savages, whose known rule of warfare, is an undistinguished destruction of all ages, sexes, and conditions.

In every stage of these Oppressions We have Petitioned for Redress in the most humble terms: Our repeated Petitions have been answered only by repeated injury. A Prince, whose character is thus marked by every act which may define a Tyrant, is unfit to be the ruler of a free people.

Nor have We been wanting in attention to our British brethren. We have warned them from time to time of attempts by their legislature to extend an unwarrantable jurisdiction over us. We have reminded them of the circumstances of our emigration and settlement here. We have appealed to their native justice and magnanimity, and we have conjured them by the ties of our common kindred to disavow these usurpations, which would inevitably interrupt our connections and correspondence. They too have been deaf to the voice of justice and of consanguinity. We must, therefore, acquiesce in the necessity, which denounces our Separation, and hold them, as we hold the rest of mankind, Enemies in War, in Peace Friends.

We, THEREFORE the Representatives of the UNITED STATES OF AMERICA, in General Congress, Assembled, appealing to the Supreme Judge of the world for the rectitude of our intentions, do, in the Name, and by Authority of the good People of these Colonies, solemnly publish and declare, That these United Colonies are, and of Right ought to be FREE AND INDEPENDENT STATES; that they are Absolved from all Allegiance to the British Crown, and that all political connection between them and the State of Great Britain, is and ought to be totally dissolved; and that as Free and Independent States, they have full Power to levy War, conclude Peace, contract Alliances, establish Commerce, and to do all other Acts and Things which Independent States may of right do. And for the support of this Declaration, with a firm reliance on the protection of Divine Providence, we mutually pledge to each other our Lives, our Fortunes, and our sacred Honor.

QUESTIONS

1. The Declaration of Independence is an example of deductive argument: Jefferson sets up general principles, details particular instances, and then draws conclusions. In both the original and the final drafts, locate the three sections of the declaration that use deduction. Explain how they work as argument.

2. Locate the general principles (or "truths") that Jefferson sets up in the first section of both the original and the final drafts. Mark the language he uses to describe them: for example, he calls them "sacred & undeniable" in the original draft, "self-evident" in the final draft. What kinds of authority does his language appeal to? Why might he or others have revised the language?

3. Write an essay explaining Jefferson's views on the nature of humankind, the function of government, and the relationship between morality and political life, as expressed in the Declaration of Independence. What assumptions are necessary to make these views, as he says in the final draft, "self-evident"?

ELIZABETH CADY STANTON *Declaration of Sentiments and Resolutions*

WHEN, IN THE course of human events, it becomes necessary for one portion of the family of man to assume among the people of the earth a position different from that which they have hitherto occupied, but one to which the laws of nature and of nature's God entitle them, a decent respect to the opinions of mankind requires that they should declare the causes that impel them to such a course.

We hold these truths to be self-evident: that all men and women are created equal; that they are endowed by their Creator with certain inalienable rights; that among these are life, liberty, and the pursuit of happiness; that to secure these rights governments are instituted, deriving their just powers from the consent of the governed. Whenever any form of government becomes destructive of these ends, it is the right of those who suffer from it to refuse allegiance to it, and to insist upon the institution of a new government, laying its foundation on such principles, and organizing its powers in such form, as to them shall seem most likely to effect their safety and happiness. Prudence indeed, will dictate that governments long established should not be changed for light and transient causes; and accordingly all experience hath shown that mankind are more disposed to suffer, while evils are sufferable, than to right themselves by abolishing the forms to which they were accustomed. But when a long train of abuses and usurpations, pursuing invariably the same object evinces a design to reduce them under absolute despotism, it is their duty to throw off such government, and to provide new guards for their future security. Such has been the patient sufferance of the women under this government, and such is now the necessity which constrains them to demand the equal station to which they are entitled.

Written and presented at the first U.S. women's rights convention, in Seneca Falls, New York, in 1848. Stanton published this version in A History of Woman Suffrage *(1881), edited by herself, Susan B. Anthony, and Matilda Joslyn Gage, all prominent leaders of the American women's movement.*

The history of mankind is a history of repeated injuries and usurpations on the part of man toward woman, having in direct object the establishment of an absolute tyranny over her. To prove this, let facts be submitted to a candid world.

He has never permitted her to exercise her inalienable right to the elective franchise.

5   He has compelled her to submit to laws, in the formation of which she had no voice.

He has withheld from her rights which are given to the most ignorant and degraded men—both natives and foreigners.

Having deprived her of this first right of a citizen, the elective franchise, thereby leaving her without representation in the halls of legislation, he has oppressed her on all sides.

He has made her, if married, in the eye of the law, civilly dead.

He has taken from her all right in property, even to the wages she earns.

10   He has made her, morally, an irresponsible being, as she can commit many crimes with impunity, provided they be done in the presence of her husband. In the covenant of marriage, she is compelled to promise obedience to her husband, he becoming, to all intents and purposes, her master—the law giving him power to deprive her of her liberty, and to administer chastisement.

He has so framed the laws of divorce, as to what shall be the proper causes, and in case of separation, to whom the guardianship of the children shall be given, as to be wholly regardless of the happiness of women—the law, in all cases, going upon a false supposition of the supremacy of man, and giving all power into his hands.

After depriving her of all rights as a married woman, if single, and the owner of property, he has taxed her to support a government which recognizes her only when her property can be made profitable to it.

He has monopolized nearly all the profitable employments, and from those she is permitted to follow, she receives but a scanty remuneration. He closes against her all the avenues to wealth and distinction which he considers most honorable to himself. As a teacher of theology, medicine, or law, she is not known.

He has denied her the facilities for obtaining a thorough education, all colleges being closed against her.

15   He allows her in Church, as well as State, but a subordinate position, claiming Apostolic authority for her exclusion from the ministry, and, with some exceptions, from any public participation in the affairs of the Church.

He has created a false public sentiment by giving to the world a different code of morals for men and women, by which moral delinquencies which exclude women from society, are not only tolerated, but deemed of little account in man.

He has usurped the prerogative of Jehovah himself, claiming it as his right to assign for her a sphere of action, when that belongs to her conscience and to her God.

He has endeavored, in every way that he could, to destroy her confidence in her own powers, to lessen her self-respect, and to make her willing to lead a dependent and abject life.

Now, in view of this entire disfranchisement of one-half the people of this country, their social and religious degradation—in view of the unjust laws above mentioned, and because women do feel themselves aggrieved, oppressed, and fraudulently deprived of their most sacred rights, we insist that they have immediate admission to all the rights and privileges which belong to them as citizens of the United States.

In entering upon the great work before us, we anticipate no small amount   20
of misconception, misrepresentation, and ridicule; but we shall use every instrumentality within our power to effect our object. We shall employ agents, circulate tracts, petition the State and National legislatures, and endeavor to enlist the pulpit and the press in our behalf. We hope this Convention will be followed by a series of Conventions embracing every part of the country.

QUESTIONS

1. Stanton imitates both the argument and the style of the Declaration of Independence. Where does her declaration diverge from Jefferson's? For what purpose?

2. Stanton's declaration was presented at the first conference on women's rights, in Seneca Falls, New York, in 1848. Using books or Web resources, do research on this conference; then use your research to explain the political aims of one of the resolutions.

3. Write your own "declaration" of political, educational, or social rights, using the declarations of Jefferson and Stanton as models.

ABRAHAM LINCOLN *Second Inaugural Address*

A T THIS SECOND appearing to take the oath of the presidential office, there is less occasion for an extended address than there was at the first. Then a statement, somewhat in detail, of a course to be pursued, seemed fitting and proper. Now, at the expiration of four years, during which public declarations have been constantly called forth on every point and phase of the great contest which still absorbs the attention, and engrosses the energies of the nation, little that is new could be presented. The progress of our arms, upon which all else chiefly depends, is as well known to the public as to myself; and it is, I

Delivered on March 4, 1865, as Lincoln took office for a second term as America's sixteenth president. In the nineteenth century U.S. presidents took office in March, not in January as they do today.

trust, reasonably satisfactory and encouraging to all. With high hope for the future, no prediction in regard to it is ventured.

On the occasion corresponding to this four years ago, all thoughts were anxiously directed to an impending civil war. All dreaded it—all sought to avert it. While the inaugural address was being delivered from this place, devoted altogether to *saving* the Union without war, insurgent agents were in the city seeking to *destroy* it without war—seeking to dissolve the Union, and divide effects, by negotiation. Both parties deprecated war; but one of them would *make* war rather than let the nation survive; and the other would *accept* war rather than let it perish. And the war came.

One-eighth of the whole population were colored slaves, not distributed generally over the Union, but localized in the Southern part of it. These slaves constituted a peculiar and powerful interest. All knew that this interest was, somehow, the cause of the war. To strengthen, perpetuate, and extend this interest was the object for which the insurgents would rend the Union, even by war; while the government claimed no right to do more than to restrict the territorial enlargement of it. Neither party expected for the war, the magnitude, or the duration, which it has already attained. Neither anticipated that the *cause* of the conflict might cease with, or even before, the conflict itself should cease. Each looked for an easier triumph, and a result less fundamental and astounding. Both read the same Bible, and pray to the same God; and each invokes His aid against the other. It may seem strange that any men should dare to ask a just God's assistance in wringing their bread from the sweat of other men's faces; but let us judge not that we be not judged.[1] The prayers of both could not be answered; that of neither has been answered fully. The Almighty has His own purposes. "Woe unto the world because of offenses! for it must needs be that offenses come; but woe to that man by whom the offense cometh!"[2] If we shall suppose that American slavery is one of those offenses which, in the providence of God, must needs come, but which, having continued through His appointed time, He now wills to remove, and that He gives to both North and South, this terrible war, as the woe due to those by whom the offense came, shall we discern therein any departure from those divine attributes which the believers in a Living God always ascribe to Him? Fondly do we hope—fervently do we pray—that this mighty scourge of war may speedily pass away. Yet, if God wills that it continue, until all the wealth piled by the bondman's two hundred and fifty years of unrequited toil shall be sunk, and until every drop of blood drawn with the lash, shall be paid by another drawn with the sword, as was said three thousand years ago, so still it must be said "the judgments of the Lord are true and righteous altogether."[3]

With malice toward none; with charity for all; with firmness in the right,

---

1. Lincoln alludes to Jesus' statement in the Sermon on the Mount—"Judge not, that ye be not judged" (Matthew 7.1)—and to God's curse on Adam—"In the sweat of thy face shalt thou eat bread, till thou return unto the ground" (Genesis 3.19).
2. From Jesus' speech to his disciples (Matthew 18.7).
3. Psalms 19.9.

as God gives us to see the right, let us strive on to finish the work we are in; to bind up the nation's wounds; to care for him who shall have borne the battle, and for his widow, and his orphan—to do all which may achieve and cherish a just, and a lasting peace, among ourselves, and with all nations.

Questions

1. Lincoln's speech includes both allusions to and direct quotations from the Bible. What argument does he use these references to support? Why are biblical references important as a persuasive technique?

2. In paragraphs 1–2, Lincoln reflects on his first inaugural speech in order to set the stage for his present speech. Find a copy of the first inaugural speech online or in the library. In what ways does that thirty-five-paragraph speech help inform this four-paragraph speech? What aspects of the Second Inaugural Address does it clarify?

3. Read the text of a more recent presidential address and compare or contrast it to Lincoln's address. (John F. Kennedy's inaugural address is included in this section; others can be found online.) Does the more recent address use a similar style, language, or set of allusions? How does it differ?

John F. Kennedy   *Inaugural Address*

We observe today not a victory of a party but a celebration of freedom—symbolizing an end as well as a beginning—signifying renewal as well as change. For I have sworn before you and Almighty God the same solemn oath our forebears prescribed nearly a century and three quarters ago.

The world is very different now. For man holds in his mortal hands the power to abolish all forms of human poverty and all forms of human life. And yet the same revolutionary beliefs for which our forebears fought are still at issue around the globe—the belief that the rights of man come not from the generosity of the state but from the hand of God.

We dare not forget today that we are the heirs of that first revolution. Let the word go forth from this time and place, to friend and foe alike, that the torch has been passed to a new generation of Americans—born in this century, tempered by war, disciplined by a hard and bitter peace, proud of our ancient heritage—and unwilling to witness or permit the slow undoing of those human rights to which this nation has always been committed, and to which we are committed today at home and around the world.

The inaugural address of John F. Kennedy (1917–1963), America's thirty-fifth president, delivered on January 21, 1961.

Let every nation know, whether it wishes us well or ill, that we shall pay any price, bear any burden, meet any hardship, support any friend, oppose any foe to assure the survival and success of liberty.

This much we pledge—and more.

To those old allies whose cultural and spiritual origins we share, we pledge the loyalty of faithful friends. United, there is little we cannot do in a host of cooperative ventures. Divided, there is little we can do—for we dare not meet a powerful challenge at odds and split asunder.

To those new states whom we welcome to the ranks of the free, we pledge our word that one form of colonial control shall not have passed away merely to be replaced by a far more iron tyranny. We shall not always expect to find them supporting our view. But we shall always hope to find them strongly supporting their own freedom—and to remember that, in the past, those who foolishly sought power by riding the back of the tiger ended up inside.

To those peoples in the huts and villages of half the globe struggling to break the bonds of mass misery, we pledge our best efforts to help them help themselves, for whatever period is required—not because the Communists may be doing it, not because we seek their votes, but because it is right. If a free society cannot help the many who are poor, it cannot save the few who are rich.

To our sister republics south of our border,[1] we offer a special pledge—to convert our good words into good deeds—in a new alliance for progress—to assist free men and free governments in casting off the chains of poverty. But this peaceful revolution of hope cannot become the prey of hostile powers. Let all our neighbors know that we shall join with them to oppose aggression or subversion anywhere in the Americas. And let every other power know that this hemisphere intends to remain the master of its own house.

To that world assembly of sovereign states, the United Nations, our last best hope in an age where the instruments of war have far outpaced the instruments of peace, we renew our pledge of support—to prevent it from becoming merely a forum for invective—to strengthen its shield of the new and the weak—and to enlarge the area in which its writ may run.

Finally, to those nations who would make themselves our adversary, we offer not a pledge but a request: that both sides begin anew the quest for peace, before the dark powers of destruction unleashed by science[2] engulf all humanity in planned or accidental self-destruction.

We dare not tempt them with weakness. For only when our arms are sufficient beyond doubt can we be certain beyond doubt that they will never be employed.

But neither can two great and powerful groups of nations take comfort from our present course—both sides overburdened by the cost of modern weapons, both rightly alarmed by the steady spread of the deadly atom, yet both racing to alter that uncertain balance of terror that stays the hand of mankind's final war.

1. This paragraph is laced with references to Cuba, which by 1961 had turned to socialism under Fidel Castro and had allied itself with the Soviet Union.

2. A reference to atomic weapons.

So let us begin anew—remembering on both sides that civility is not a sign of weakness, and sincerity is always subject to proof. Let us never negotiate out of fear. But let us never fear to negotiate.

Let both sides explore what problems unite us instead of belaboring those problems which divide us. Let both sides, for the first time, formulate serious and precise proposals for the inspection and control of arms—and bring the absolute power to destroy other nations under the absolute control of all nations.

Let both sides seek to invoke the wonders of science instead of its terrors. Together let us explore the stars, conquer the deserts, eradicate disease, tap the ocean depths, and encourage the arts and commerce.

Let both sides unite to heed in all corners of the earth the command of Isaiah—to "undo the heavy burdens and to let the oppressed go free."[3]

And if a beachhead of cooperation may push back the jungle of suspicion, let both sides join in creating a new endeavor—not a new balance of power but a new world of law, where the strong are just and the weak secure and the peace preserved.

All this will not be finished in the first one hundred days. Nor will it be finished in the first one thousand days, nor in the life of this administration, nor even perhaps in our lifetime on this planet. But let us begin.

In your hands, my fellow citizens, more than mine, will rest the final success or failure of our course. Since this country was founded, each generation of Americans has been summoned to give testimony to its national loyalty. The graves of young Americans who answered the call to service surround the globe.

Now the trumpet summons us again—not as a call to bear arms, though arms we need—not as a call to battle, though embattled we are—but a call to bear the burden of a long twilight struggle, year in and year out, "rejoicing in hope, patient in tribulation"[4]—a struggle against the common enemies of man: tyranny, poverty, disease, and war itself.

Can we forge against these enemies a grand and global alliance, North and South, East and West, that can assure a more fruitful life for all mankind? Will you join in that historic effort?

In the long history of the world, only a few generations have been granted the role of defending freedom in its hour of maximum danger. I do not shrink from this responsibility—I welcome it. I do not believe that any of us would exchange places with any other people or any other generation. The energy, the faith, the devotion which we bring to this endeavor will light our country and all who serve it—and the glow from that fire can truly light the world.

And so, my fellow Americans, ask not what your country can do for you—ask what you can do for your country.

My fellow citizens of the world, ask not what America will do for you, but what together we can do for the freedom of man.

3. Isaiah 58.6.
4. Romans 12.12.

Finally, whether you are citizens of America or citizens of the world, ask of us here the same high standards of strength and sacrifice which we ask of you. With a good conscience our only sure reward, with history the final judge of our deeds, let us go forth to lead the land we love, asking His blessing and His help, but knowing that here on earth God's work must truly be our own.

QUESTIONS

1. Choose three rhetorical devices from this speech and show how they are constructed. What are their common elements? Their differences?

2. On what level of generality is Kennedy operating? When does he get specific?

3. Kennedy was the youngest man to be elected president. Speculate on how that fact might be reflected in this speech.

LANI GUINIER   *The Tyranny of the Majority*

I HAVE ALWAYS WANTED to be a civil rights lawyer. This lifelong ambition is based on a deep-seated commitment to democratic fair play—to playing by the rules as long as the rules are fair. When the rules seem unfair, I have worked to change them, not subvert them. When I was eight years old, I was a Brownie. I was especially proud of my uniform, which represented a commitment to good citizenship and good deeds. But one day, when my Brownie group staged a hatmaking contest, I realized that uniforms are only as honorable as the people who wear them. The contest was rigged. The winner was assisted by her milliner mother, who actually made the winning entry in full view of all the participants. At the time, I was too young to be able to change the rules, but I was old enough to resign, which I promptly did.

To me, fair play means that the rules encourage everyone to play. They should reward those who win, but they must be acceptable to those who lose. The central theme of my academic writing is that not all rules lead to elemental fair play. Some even commonplace rules work against it.

The professional milliner competing with amateur Brownies stands as an example of rules that are patently rigged or patently subverted. Yet, sometimes, even when rules are perfectly fair in form, they serve in practice to exclude particular groups from meaningful participation. When they do not encourage everyone to play, or when, over the long haul, they do not make the losers feel

From The Tyranny of the Majority *(1994), a collection of essays on affirmative action published after Guinier's unsuccessful nomination for assistant attorney general for civil rights in 1993. In it she clarifies her views on democracy, political equality, and majority rule.*

as good about the outcomes as the winners, they can seem as unfair as the milliner who makes the winning hat for her daughter.

Sometimes, too, we construct rules that force us to be divided into winners and losers when we might have otherwise joined together. This idea was cogently expressed by my son, Nikolas, when he was four years old, far exceeding the thoughtfulness of his mother when she was an eight-year-old Brownie. While I was writing one of my law journal articles, Nikolas and I had a conversation about voting prompted by a *Sesame Street Magazine* exercise. The magazine pictured six children: four children had raised their hands because they wanted to play tag; two had their hands down because they wanted to play hide-and-seek. The magazine asked its readers to count the number of children whose hands were raised and then decide what game the children would play.

Nikolas quite realistically replied, "They will play both. First they will play tag. Then they will play hide-and-seek." Despite the magazine's "rules," he was right. To children, it is natural to take turns. The winner may get to play first or more often, but even the "loser" gets something. His was a positive-sum solution that many adult rule-makers ignore.

The traditional answer to the magazine's problem would have been a zero-sum solution: "The children—all the children—will play tag, and only tag." As a zero-sum solution, everything is seen in terms of "I win; you lose." The conventional answer relies on winner-take-all majority rule, in which the tag players, as the majority, win the right to decide for all the children what game to play. The hide-and-seek preference becomes irrelevant. The numerically more powerful majority choice simply subsumes minority preferences.

In the conventional case, the majority that rules gains all the power and the minority that loses gets none. For example, two years ago Brother Rice High School in Chicago held two senior proms. It was not planned that way. The prom committee at Brother Rice, a boys' Catholic high school, expected just one prom when it hired a disc jockey, picked a rock band, and selected music for the prom by consulting student preferences. Each senior was asked to list his three favorite songs, and the band would play the songs that appeared most frequently on the lists.

Seems attractively democratic. But Brother Rice is predominantly white, and the prom committee was all white. That's how they got two proms. The black seniors at Brother Rice felt so shut out by the "democratic process" that they organized their own prom. As one black student put it: "For every vote we had, there were eight votes for what they wanted. . . . [W]ith us being in the minority we're always outvoted. It's as if we don't count."

Some embittered white seniors saw things differently. They complained that the black students should have gone along with the majority: "The majority makes a decision. That's the way it works."

In a way, both groups were right. From the white students' perspective, this was ordinary decisionmaking. To the black students, majority rule sent the message: "we don't count" is the "way it works" for minorities. In a racially divided society, majority rule may be perceived as majority tyranny.

That is a large claim, and I do not rest my case for it solely on the actions

5

10

of the prom committee in one Chicago high school. To expand the range of the argument, I first consider the ideal of majority rule itself, particularly as reflected in the writings of James Madison[1] and other founding members of our Republic. These early democrats explored the relationship between majority rule and democracy. James Madison warned, "If a majority be united by a common interest, the rights of the minority will be insecure." The tyranny of the majority, according to Madison, requires safeguards to protect "one part of the society against the injustice of the other part."

For Madison, majority tyranny represented the great danger to our early constitutional democracy. Although the American revolution was fought against the tyranny of the British monarch, it soon became clear that there was another tyranny to be avoided. The accumulations of all powers in the same hands, Madison warned, "whether of one, a few, or many, and whether hereditary, self-appointed, or elective, may justly be pronounced the very definition of tyranny."

As another colonist suggested in papers published in Philadelphia, "We have been so long habituated to a jealousy of tyranny from monarchy and aristocracy, that we have yet to learn the dangers of it from democracy." Despotism had to be opposed "whether it came from Kings, Lords or the people."

The debate about majority tyranny reflected Madison's concern that the majority may not represent the whole. In a homogeneous society, the interest of the majority would likely be that of the minority also. But in a heterogeneous community, the majority may not represent all competing interests. The majority is likely to be self-interested and ignorant or indifferent to the concerns of the minority. In such case, Madison observed, the assumption that the majority represents the minority is "altogether fictitious."

15   Yet even a self-interested majority can govern fairly if it cooperates with the minority. One reason for such cooperation is that the self-interested majority values the principle of reciprocity. The self-interested majority worries that the minority may attract defectors from the majority and become the next governing majority. The Golden Rule principle of reciprocity functions to check the tendency of a self-interested majority to act tyrannically.

So the argument for the majority principle connects it with the value of reciprocity: You cooperate when you lose in part because members of the current majority will cooperate when they lose. The conventional case for the fairness of majority rule is that it is not really the rule of a fixed group—The Majority—on all issues; instead it is the rule of shifting majorities, as the losers at one time or on one issue join with others and become part of the governing coalition at another time or on another issue. The result will be a fair system of mutually beneficial cooperation. I call a majority that rules but does not dominate a Madisonian Majority.

The problem of majority tyranny arises, however, when the self-interested majority does not need to worry about defections. When the majority is fixed

---

1. Founding Father (1751–1836) and fourth president of the United States, from 1809 to 1817.

and permanent, there are no checks on its ability to be overbearing. A majority that does not worry about defectors is a majority with total power.

In such a case, Madison's concern about majority tyranny arises. In a heterogeneous community, any faction with total power might subject "the minority to the caprice and arbitrary decisions of the majority, who instead of consulting the interest of the whole community collectively, attend sometimes to partial and local advantages."

"What remedy can be found in a republican Government, where the majority must ultimately decide," argued Madison, but to ensure "that no one common interest or passion will be likely to unite a majority of the whole number in an unjust pursuit." The answer was to disaggregate the majority to ensure checks and balances or fluid, rotating interests. The minority needed protection against an overbearing majority, so that "a common sentiment is less likely to be felt, and the requisite concert less likely to be formed, by a majority of the whole."

Political struggles would not be simply a contest between rulers and people; the political struggles would be among the people themselves. The work of government was not to transcend different interests but to reconcile them. In an ideal democracy, the people would rule, but the minorities would also be protected against the power of majorities. Again, where the rules of decision-making protect the minority, the Madisonian Majority rules without dominating.   20

But if a group is unfairly treated, for example, when it forms a racial minority, *and* if the problems of unfairness are not cured by conventional assumptions about majority rule, then what is to be done? The answer is that we may need an *alternative* to winner-take-all majoritarianism. In this book, a collection of my law review articles, I describe the alternative, which, with Nikolas's help, I now call the "principle of taking turns." In a racially divided society, this principle does better than simple majority rule if it accommodates the values of self-government, fairness, deliberation, compromise, and consensus that lie at the heart of the democratic ideal.

In my legal writing, I follow the caveat of James Madison and other early American democrats. I explore decisionmaking rules that might work in a multi-racial society to ensure that majority rule does not become majority tyranny. I pursue voting systems that might disaggregate The Majority so that it does not exercise power unfairly or tyrannically. I aspire to a more cooperative political style of decisionmaking to enable all of the students at Brother Rice to feel comfortable attending the same prom. In looking to create Madisonian Majorities, I pursue a positive-sum, taking-turns solution.

Structuring decisionmaking to allow the minority "a turn" may be necessary to restore the reciprocity ideal when a fixed majority refuses to cooperate with the minority. If the fixed majority loses its incentive to follow the Golden Rule principle of shifting majorities, the minority never gets to take a turn. Giving the minority a turn does not mean the minority gets to rule; what it does mean is that the minority gets to influence decisionmaking and the majority rules more legitimately.

Instead of automatically rewarding the preferences of the monolithic majority, a taking-turns approach anticipates that the majority rules, but is not overbearing. Because those with 51 percent of the votes are not assured 100 percent of the power, the majority cooperates with, or at least does not tyrannize, the minority.

25   The sports analogy of "I win; you lose" competition within a political hierarchy makes sense when only one team can win; Nikolas's intuition that it is often possible to take turns suggests an alternative approach. Take family decisionmaking, for example. It utilizes a taking-turns approach. When parents sit around the kitchen table deciding on a vacation destination or activities for a rainy day, often they do not simply rely on a show of hands, especially if that means that the older children always prevail or if affinity groups among the children (those who prefer movies to video games, or those who prefer baseball to playing cards) never get to play their activity of choice. Instead of allowing the majority simply to rule, the parents may propose that everyone take turns, going to the movies one night and playing video games the next. Or as Nikolas proposes, they might do both on a given night.

Taking turns attempts to build consensus while recognizing political or social differences, and it encourages everyone to play. The taking-turns approach gives those with the most support more turns, but it also legitimates the outcome from each individual's perspective, including those whose views are shared only by a minority.

In the end, I do not believe that democracy should encourage rule by the powerful—even a powerful majority. Instead, the idea of democracy promises a fair discussion among self-defined equals about how to achieve our common aspirations. To redeem that promise, we need to put the idea of taking turns and disaggregating the majority at the center of our conception of representation. Particularly as we move into the twenty-first century as a more highly diversified citizenry, it is essential that we consider the ways in which voting and representational systems succeed or fail at encouraging Madisonian Majorities.

To use Nikolas's terminology, "it is no fair" if a fixed, tyrannical majority excludes or alienates the minority. It is no fair if a fixed, tyrannical majority monopolizes all the power all the time. It is no fair if we engage in the periodic ritual of elections, but only the permanent majority gets to choose who is elected. Where we have tyranny by The Majority, we do not have genuine democracy.

QUESTIONS

1. Throughout her essay, Guinier uses personal anecdotes to support and illustrate her argument. Which one do you think best supports her points? Why?

2. In her final paragraph Guinier repeats the phrase "it is no fair" three times in three successive sentences. Why does Guinier deliberately repeat this phrase? What is the effect?

3. Think of a time when you—in either a majority or a minority position—used cooperation or "turn-taking" to build consensus. Write an essay about that experience.

E. B. WHITE *Democracy*

WE RECEIVED a letter from the Writers' War Board the other day asking for a statement on "The Meaning of Democracy." It presumably is our duty to comply with such a request, and it is certainly our pleasure.

Surely the Board knows what democracy is. It is the line that forms on the right. It is the don't in don't shove. It is the hole in the stuffed shirt through which the sawdust slowly trickles; it is the dent in the high hat. Democracy is the recurrent suspicion that more than half of the people are right more than half of the time. It is the feeling of privacy in the voting booths, the feeling of communion in the libraries, the feeling of vitality everywhere. Democracy is a letter to the editor. Democracy is the score at the beginning of the ninth. It is an idea which hasn't been disproved yet, a song the words of which have not gone bad. It's the mustard on the hot dog and the cream in the rationed coffee. Democracy is a request from a War Board, in the middle of a morning in the middle of a war, wanting to know what democracy is.

First appeared in the New Yorker *during World War II (July 3, 1943); later reprinted in* The Wild Flag *(1946).*

QUESTIONS

1. Consult a standard desk dictionary for the definition of "democracy." Of the several meanings given, which one best encompasses White's definitions? What other meanings do his definitions engage?

2. Translate White's examples into nonmetaphoric language. For example, "It is the line that forms on the right" might be translated as "It has no special privileges." Can "It is the don't in don't shove" also be translated as "It has no special privileges"? Consider what is lost in translation or, more important, what is gained by metaphor.

3. Using White's technique, write a definition for an abstract term; you might consider such terms as "generosity," "love," "sophistication," "tolerance," "virtue."

MARTIN LUTHER KING JR. *Letter from Birmingham Jail*[1]

MY DEAR FELLOW CLERGYMEN:

While confined here in the Birmingham city jail, I came across your recent statement calling my present activities "unwise and untimely." Seldom do I pause to answer criticism of my work and ideas. If I sought to answer all the criticisms that cross my desk, my secretaries would have little time for anything other than such correspondence in the course of the day, and I would have no time for constructive work. But since I feel that you are men of genuine good will and that your criticisms are sincerely set forth, I want to try to answer your statement in what I hope will be patient and reasonable terms.

I think I should indicate why I am here in Birmingham, since you have been influenced by the view which argues against "outsiders coming in." I have the honor of serving as president of the Southern Christian Leadership Conference, an organization operating in every southern state, with headquarters in Atlanta, Georgia. We have some eighty-five affiliated organizations across the South, and one of them is the Alabama Christian Movement for Human Rights. Frequently we share staff, educational, and financial resources with our affiliates. Several months ago the affiliate here in Birmingham asked us to be on call to engage in a nonviolent direct-action program if such were deemed necessary. We readily consented, and when the hour came we lived up to our promise. So I, along with several members of my staff, am here because I was invited here. I am here because I have organizational ties here.

But more basically, I am in Birmingham because injustice is here. Just as the prophets of the eighth century B.C. left their villages and carried their "thus saith the Lord" far beyond the boundaries of their home towns, and just as the Apostle Paul left his village of Tarsus and carried the gospel of Jesus Christ to the far corners of the Greco-Roman world, so am I compelled to carry the gospel of freedom beyond my own home town. Like Paul, I must constantly respond to the Macedonian call for aid.

Moreover, I am cognizant of the interrelatedness of all communities and states. I cannot sit idly by in Atlanta and not be concerned about what hap-

---

Written on April 16, 1963, while King was jailed for civil disobedience; subsequently published in Why We Can't Wait *(1964).*

1. This response to a published statement by eight fellow clergymen from Alabama (Bishop C. C. J. Carpenter, Bishop Joseph A. Durick, Rabbi Milton L. Grafman, Bishop Paul Hardin, Bishop Holan B. Harmon, the Reverend George M. Murray, the Reverend Edward V. Ramage and the Reverend Earl Stallings) was composed under somewhat constricting circumstances. Begun on the margins of the newspaper in which the statement appeared while I was in jail, the letter was continued on scraps of writing paper supplied by a friendly Negro trusty, and concluded on a pad my attorneys were eventually permitted to leave me. Although the text remains in substance unaltered, I have indulged in the author's prerogative of polishing it for publication [King's note].

pens in Birmingham. Injustice anywhere is a threat to justice everywhere. We are caught in an inescapable network of mutuality, tied in a single garment of destiny. Whatever affects one directly, affects all indirectly. Never again can we afford to live with the narrow, provincial "outside agitator" idea. Anyone who lives inside the United States can never be considered an outsider anywhere within its bounds.

You deplore the demonstrations taking place in Birmingham. But your statement, I am sorry to say, fails to express a similar concern for the conditions that brought about the demonstrations. I am sure that none of you would want to rest content with the superficial kind of social analysis that deals merely with effects and does not grapple with underlying causes. It is unfortunate that demonstrations are taking place in Birmingham, but it is even more unfortunate that the city's white power structure left the Negro community with no alternative.

In any nonviolent campaign there are four basic steps: collection of the facts to determine whether injustices exist; negotiation; self-purification; and direct action. We have gone through all these steps in Birmingham. There can be no gainsaying the fact that racial injustice engulfs this community. Birmingham is probably the most thoroughly segregated city in the United States. Its ugly record of brutality is widely known. Negroes have experienced grossly unjust treatment in the courts. There have been more unsolved bombings of Negro homes and churches in Birmingham than in any other city in the nation. These are the hard, brutal facts of the case. On the basis of these conditions, Negro leaders sought to negotiate with the city fathers. But the latter consistently refused to engage in good-faith negotiation.

Then, last September, came the opportunity to talk with leaders of Birmingham's economic community. In the course of the negotiations, certain promises were made by the merchants—for example, to remove the stores' humiliating racial signs. On the basis of these promises, the Reverend Fred Shuttlesworth and the leaders of the Alabama Christian Movement for Human Rights agreed to a moratorium on all demonstrations. As the weeks and months went by, we realized that we were the victims of a broken promise. A few signs, briefly removed, returned; the others remained.

As in so many past experiences, our hopes had been blasted, and the shadow of deep disappointment settled upon us. We had no alternative except to prepare for direct action, whereby we would present our very bodies as a means of laying our case before the conscience of the local and the national community. Mindful of the difficulties involved, we decided to undertake a process of self-purification. We began a series of workshops on nonviolence, and we repeatedly asked ourselves: "Are you able to accept blows without retaliating?" "Are you able to endure the ordeal of jail?" We decided to schedule our direct-action program for the Easter season, realizing that except for Christmas, this is the main shopping period of the year. Knowing that a strong economic-withdrawal program would be the by-product of direct action, we felt that this would be the best time to bring pressure to bear on the merchants for the needed change.

5

Then it occurred to us that Birmingham's mayoral election was coming up in March, and we speedily decided to postpone action until after election day. When we discovered that the Commissioner of Public Safety, Eugene "Bull" Connor, had piled up enough votes to be in the run-off, we decided again to postpone action until the day after the run-off so that the demonstrations could not be used to cloud the issues. Like many others, we wanted to see Mr. Connor defeated, and to this end we endured postponement after postponement. Having aided in this community need, we felt that our direct-action program could be delayed no longer.

10   You may well ask, "Why direct action? Why sit-ins, marches, and so forth? Isn't negotiation a better path?" You are quite right in calling for negotiation. Indeed, this is the very purpose of direct action. Nonviolent direct action seeks to create such a crisis and foster such a tension that a community which has constantly refused to negotiate is forced to confront the issue. It seeks so to dramatize the issue that it can no longer be ignored. My citing the creation of tension as part of the work of the nonviolent-resister may sound rather shocking. But I must confess that I am not afraid of the word "tension." I have earnestly opposed violent tension, but there is a type of constructive, nonviolent tension which is necessary for growth. Just as Socrates felt that it was necessary to create a tension in the mind so that individuals could rise from the bondage of myths and half-truths to the unfettered realm of creative analysis and objective appraisal, so must we see the need for nonviolent gadflies to create the kind of tension in society that will help men rise from the dark depths of prejudice and racism to the majestic heights of understanding and brotherhood.

The purpose of our direct-action program is to create a situation so crisis-packed that it will inevitably open the door to negotiation. I therefore concur with you in your call for negotiation. Too long has our beloved Southland been bogged down in a tragic effort to live in monologue rather than dialogue.

One of the basic points in your statement is that the action that I and my associates have taken in Birmingham is untimely. Some have asked: "Why didn't you give the new city administration time to act?" The only answer that I can give to this query is that the new Birmingham administration must be prodded about as much as the outgoing one, before it will act. We are sadly mistaken if we feel that the election of Albert Boutwell as mayor will bring the millennium to Birmingham. While Mr. Boutwell is a much more gentle person than Mr. Connor, they are both segregationists, dedicated to maintenance of the status quo. I have hoped that Mr. Boutwell will be reasonable enough to see the futility of massive resistance to desegregation. But he will not see this without pressure from devotees of civil rights. My friends, I must say to you that we have not made a single gain in civil rights without determined legal and nonviolent pressure. Lamentably, it is an historical fact that privileged groups seldom give up their privileges voluntarily. Individuals may see the moral light and voluntarily give up their unjust posture; but, as Reinhold Niebuhr[2] has reminded us, groups tend to be more immoral than individuals.

---

2. American Protestant theologian (1892–1971).

We know through painful experience that freedom is never voluntarily given by the oppressor; it must be demanded by the oppressed. Frankly, I have yet to engage in a direct-action campaign that was "well timed" in the view of those who have not suffered unduly from the disease of segregation. For years now I have heard the word "Wait!" It rings in the ear of every Negro with piercing familiarity. This "Wait" has almost always meant "Never." We must come to see, with one of our distinguished jurists, that "justice too long delayed is justice denied."

We have waited for more than 340 years for our constitutional and God-given rights. The nations of Asia and Africa are moving with jetlike speed toward gaining political independence, but we still creep at horse-and-buggy pace toward gaining a cup of coffee at a lunch counter. Perhaps it is easy for those who have never felt the stinging darts of segregation to say, "Wait." But when you have seen vicious mobs lynch your mothers and fathers at will and drown your sisters and brothers at whim; when you have seen hate-filled policemen curse, kick, and even kill your black brothers and sisters; when you see the vast majority of your twenty million Negro brothers smothering in an airtight cage of poverty in the midst of an affluent society; when you suddenly find your tongue twisted and your speech stammering as you seek to explain to your six-year-old daughter why she can't go to the public amusement park that has just been advertised on television, and see tears welling up in her eyes when she is told that Funtown is closed to colored children, and see ominous clouds of inferiority beginning to form in her little mental sky, and see her beginning to distort her personality by developing an unconscious bitterness toward white people; when you have to concoct an answer for a five-year-old son who is asking, "Daddy, why do white people treat colored people so mean?"; when you take a cross-country drive and find it necessary to sleep night after night in the uncomfortable corners of your automobile because no motel will accept you; when you are humiliated day in and day out by nagging signs reading "white" and "colored"; when your first name becomes "nigger," your middle name becomes "boy" (however old you are) and your last name becomes "John," and your wife and mother are never given the respected title "Mrs."; when you are harried by day and haunted by night by the fact that you are a Negro, living constantly at tiptoe stance, never quite knowing what to expect next, and are plagued with inner fears and outer resentments; when you are forever fighting a degenerating sense of "nobodiness"—then you will understand why we find it difficult to wait. There comes a time when the cup of endurance runs over, and men are no longer willing to be plunged into the abyss of despair. I hope, sirs, you can understand our legitimate and unavoidable impatience.

You express a great deal of anxiety over our willingness to break laws. This   15 is certainly a legitimate concern. Since we so diligently urge people to obey the Supreme Court's decision of 1954 outlawing segregation in the public schools, at first glance it may seem rather paradoxical for us consciously to break laws. One may well ask: "How can you advocate breaking some laws and obeying others?" The answer lies in the fact that there are two types of laws: just and unjust. I would be the first to advocate obeying just laws. One has not only a legal but a moral responsibility to obey just laws. Conversely, one has a moral responsibility to disobey unjust laws. I would agree with St. Augustine[3] that "an unjust law is no law at all."

Now, what is the difference between the two? How does one determine whether a law is just or unjust? A just law is a man-made code that squares with the moral law or the law of God. An unjust law is a code that is out of harmony with the moral law. To put it in the terms of St. Thomas Aquinas:[4] An unjust law is a human law that is not rooted in eternal law and natural law. Any law that uplifts human personality is just. Any law that degrades human personality is unjust. All segregation statutes are unjust because segregation distorts the soul and damages the personality. It gives the segregator a false sense of superiority and the segregated a false sense of inferiority. Segregation, to use the terminology of the Jewish philosopher Martin Buber,[5] substitutes an "I-it" relationship for an "I-thou" relationship and ends up relegating persons to the status of things. Hence segregation is not only politically, economically, and sociologically unsound, it is morally wrong and sinful. Paul Tillich[6] has said that sin is separation. Is not segregation an existential expression of man's tragic separation, his awful estrangement, his terrible sinfulness? Thus it is that I can urge men to obey the 1954 decision of the Supreme Court, for it is morally right; and I can urge them to disobey segregation ordinances, for they are morally wrong.

Let us consider a more concrete example of just and unjust laws. An unjust law is a code that a numerical or power majority group compels a minority group to obey but does not make binding on itself. This is *difference* made legal. By the same token, a just law is a code that a majority compels a minority to follow and that it is willing to follow itself. This is *sameness* made legal.

Let me give another explanation. A law is unjust if it is inflicted on a minority that, as a result of being denied the right to vote, had no part in enacting or devising the law. Who can say that the legislature of Alabama which set up that state's segregation laws was democratically elected? Throughout Alabama all sorts of devious methods are used to prevent Negroes from becoming registered voters, and there are some counties in which, even though Negroes constitute a majority of the population, not a single Negro is registered. Can any law enacted under such circumstances be considered democratically structured?

Sometimes a law is just on its face and unjust in its application. For instance, I have been arrested on a charge of parading without a permit. Now, there is nothing wrong in having an ordinance which requires a permit for a parade. But such an ordinance becomes unjust when it is used to maintain segregation and to deny citizens the First-Amendment privilege of peaceful assembly and protest.

3. Early Christian church father (354–430).
4. Christian philosopher and theologian (1225–1274).
5. German-born Israeli philosopher (1878–1965).
6. German-born American Protestant theologian (1886–1965).

I hope you are able to see the distinction I am trying to point out. In no sense do I advocate evading or defying the law, as would the rabid segregationist. That would lead to anarchy. One who breaks an unjust law must do so openly, lovingly, and with a willingness to accept the penalty. I submit that an individual who breaks a law that conscience tells him is unjust, and who willingly accepts the penalty of imprisonment in order to arouse the conscience of the community over its injustice, is in reality expressing the highest respect for law.

Of course, there is nothing new about this kind of civil disobedience. It was evidenced sublimely in the refusal of Shadrach, Meshach, and Abednego to obey the laws of Nebuchadnezzar,[7] on the ground that a higher moral law was at stake. It was practiced superbly by the early Christians, who were willing to face hungry lions and the excruciating pain of chopping blocks rather than submit to certain unjust laws of the Roman Empire. To a degree, academic freedom is a reality today because Socrates practiced civil disobedience.[8] In our own nation, the Boston Tea Party represented a massive act of civil disobedience.

We should never forget that everything Adolf Hitler did in Germany was "legal" and everything the Hungarian freedom fighters[9] did in Hungary was "illegal." It was "illegal" to aid and comfort a Jew in Hitler's Germany. Even so, I am sure that, had I lived in Germany at the time, I would have aided and comforted my Jewish brothers. If today I lived in a Communist country where certain principles dear to the Christian faith are suppressed, I would openly advocate disobeying that country's anti-religious laws.

I must make two honest confessions to you, my Christian and Jewish brothers. First, I must confess that over the past few years I have been gravely disappointed with the white moderate. I have almost reached the regrettable conclusion that the Negro's great stumbling block in his stride toward freedom is not the White Citizen's Counciler or the Ku Klux Klanner, but the white moderate, who is more devoted to "order" than to justice; who prefers a negative peace which is the absence of tension to a positive peace which is the presence of justice; who constantly says, "I agree with you in the goal you seek, but I cannot agree with your methods of direct action"; who paternalistically believes he can set the timetable for another man's freedom; who lives by a mythical concept of time and who constantly advises the Negro to wait for a "more convenient season." Shallow understanding from people of good will is more frustrating than absolute misunderstanding from people of ill will. Lukewarm acceptance is much more bewildering than outright rejection.

I had hoped that the white moderate would understand that law and order exist for the purpose of establishing justice and that when they fail in this pur-

7. Their story is told in Daniel 3.
8. The ancient Greek philosopher Socrates was tried by the Athenians for corrupting their youth through his skeptical, questioning manner of teaching. He refused to change his ways and was condemned to death.
9. In the anti-Communist revolution of 1956, which was quickly put down by the Soviet army.

pose they become the dangerously structured dams that block the flow of social progress. I had hoped that the white moderate would understand that the
present tension in the South is a necessary phase of the transition from an obnoxious negative peace, in which the Negro passively accepted his unjust
plight, to a substantive and positive peace, in which all men will respect the
dignity and worth of human personality. Actually, we who engage in nonviolent
direct action are not the creators of tension. We merely bring to the surface
the hidden tension that is already alive. We bring it out in the open, where it
can be seen and dealt with. Like a boil that can never be cured so long as it is
covered up but must be opened with all its ugliness to the natural medicines
of air and light, injustice must be exposed, with all the tension its exposure
creates, to the light of human conscience and the air of national opinion, before it can be cured.

25   In your statement you assert that our actions, even though peaceful, must
be condemned because they precipitate violence. But is this a logical assertion? Isn't this like condemning a robbed man because his possession of
money precipitated the evil act of robbery? Isn't this like condemning Socrates because his unswerving commitment to truth and his philosophical inquiries precipitated the act by the misguided populace in which they made
him drink hemlock? Isn't this like condemning Jesus because his unique God-
consciousness and never-ceasing devotion to God's will precipitated the evil
act of crucifixion? We must come to see that, as the federal courts have consistently affirmed, it is wrong to urge an individual to cease his efforts to gain
his basic constitutional rights because the quest may precipitate violence. Society must protect the robbed and punish the robber.

I had also hoped that the white moderate would reject the myth concerning time in relation to the struggle for freedom. I have just received a letter
from a white brother in Texas. He writes: "All Christians know that the colored
people will receive equal rights eventually, but it is possible that you are in too
great a religious hurry. It has taken Christianity almost two thousand years to
accomplish what it has. The teachings of Christ take time to come to earth."
Such an attitude stems from a tragic misconception of time, from the
strangely irrational notion that there is something in the very flow of time that
will inevitably cure all ills. Actually, time itself is neutral; it can be used either
destructively or constructively. More and more I feel that the people of ill will
have used time much more effectively than have the people of good will. We
will have to repent in this generation not merely for the hateful words and actions of the bad people, but for the appalling silence of the good people. Human progress never rolls in on wheels of inevitability; it comes through the
tireless efforts of men willing to be co-workers with God, and without this
hard work, time itself becomes an ally of the forces of social stagnation. We
must use time creatively, in the knowledge that the time is always ripe to do
right. Now is the time to make real the promise of democracy and transform
our pending national elegy into a creative psalm of brotherhood. Now is the
time to lift our national policy from the quicksand of racial injustice to the
solid rock of human dignity.

You speak of our activity in Birmingham as extreme. At first I was rather disappointed that fellow clergymen would see my nonviolent efforts as those of an extremist. I began thinking about the fact that I stand in the middle of two opposing forces in the Negro community. One is a force of complacency, made up in part of Negroes who, as a result of long years of oppression, are so drained of self-respect and a sense of "somebodiness" that they have adjusted to segregation; and in part of a few middle-class Negroes who, because of a degree of academic and economic security and because in some ways they profit by segregation, have become insensitive to the problems of the masses. The other force is one of bitterness and hatred, and it comes perilously close to advocating violence. It is expressed in the various black nationalist groups that are springing up across the nation, the largest and best-known being Elijah Muhammad's Muslim movement.[10] Nourished by the Negro's frustration over the continued existence of racial discrimination, this movement is made up of people who have lost faith in America, who have absolutely repudiated Christianity, and who have concluded that the white man is an incorrigible "devil."

I have tried to stand between these two forces, saying that we need emulate neither the "do-nothingism" of the complacent nor the hatred and despair of the black nationalist. For there is the more excellent way of love and nonviolent protest. I am grateful to God that, through the influence of the Negro church, the way of nonviolence became an integral part of our struggle.

If this philosophy had not emerged, by now many streets of the South would, I am convinced, be flowing with blood. And I am further convinced that if our white brothers dismiss as "rabblerousers" and "outside agitators" those of us who employ nonviolent direct action, and if they refuse to support our nonviolent efforts, millions of Negroes will, out of frustration and despair, seek solace and security in black-nationalist ideologies—a development that would inevitably lead to a frightening racial nightmare.

Oppressed people cannot remain oppressed forever. The yearning for freedom eventually manifests itself, and that is what has happened to the American Negro. Something within has reminded him of his birthright of freedom, and something without has reminded him that it can be gained. Consciously or unconsciously, he has been caught up by the *Zeitgeist*,[11] and with his black brothers of Africa and his brown and yellow brothers of Asia, South America, and the Caribbean, the United States Negro is moving with a sense of great urgency toward the promised land of racial justice. If one recognizes this vital urge that has engulfed the Negro community, one should readily understand why public demonstrations are taking place. The Negro has many pent-up resentments and latent frustrations, and he must release them. So let him march; let him make prayer pilgrimages to the city hall; let him go on freedom rides—and try to understand why he must do so. If his repressed emotions are not released in nonviolent ways, they will seek expression through violence;

10. Elijah Muhammed (1897–1975) succeeded to the leadership of the Nation of Islam in 1934.
11. The spirit of the times.

this is not a threat but a fact of history. So I have not said to my people, "Get rid of your discontent." Rather, I have tried to say that this normal and healthy discontent can be channeled into the creative outlet of nonviolent direct action. And now this approach is being termed extremist.

But though I was initially disappointed at being categorized as an extremist, as I continued to think about the matter I gradually gained a measure of satisfaction from the label. Was not Jesus an extremist for love: "Love your enemies, bless them that curse you, do good to them that hate you, and pray for them which despitefully use you, and persecute you." Was not Amos an extremist for justice: "Let justice roll down like waters and righteousness like an ever-flowing stream." Was not Paul an extremist for the Christian gospel: "I bear in my body the marks of the Lord Jesus." Was not Martin Luther an extremist: "Here I stand; I cannot do otherwise, so help me God." And John Bunyan:[12] "I will stay in jail to the end of my days before I make a butchery of my conscience." And Abraham Lincoln: "This nation cannot survive half slave and half free." And Thomas Jefferson: "We hold these truths to be self-evident, that all men are created equal. . . ." So the question is not whether we will be extremists, but what kind of extremists we will be. Will we be extremists for hate or for love? Will we be extremists for the preservation of injustice or for the extension of justice? In that dramatic scene on Calvary's hill three men were crucified. We must never forget that all three were crucified for the same crime—the crime of extremism. Two were extremists for immorality, and thus fell below their environment. The other, Jesus Christ, was an extremist for love, truth, and goodness, and thereby rose above his environment. Perhaps the South, the nation, and the world are in dire need of creative extremists.

I had hoped that the white moderate would see this need. Perhaps I was too optimistic; perhaps I expected too much. I suppose I should have realized that few members of the oppressor race can understand the deep groans and passionate yearnings of the oppressed race, and still fewer have the vision to see that injustice must be rooted out by strong, persistent, and determined action. I am thankful, however, that some of our white brothers in the South have grasped the meaning of this social revolution and committed themselves to it. They are still all too few in quantity, but they are big in quality. Some—such as Ralph McGill, Lillian Smith, Harry Golden, James McBridge Dabbs, Ann Braden, and Sarah Patton Boyle—have written about our struggle in eloquent and prophetic terms. Others have marched with us down nameless streets of the South. They have languished in filthy, roach-infested jails, suffering the abuse and brutality of policemen who view them as "dirty nigger-lovers." Unlike so many of their moderate brothers and sisters, they have recognized the urgency of the moment and sensed the need for powerful "action" antidotes to combat the disease of segregation.

Let me take note of my other major disappointment. I have been so

12. Amos was an Old Testament prophet; Paul a New Testament apostle; Luther (1483–1546), German Protestant reformer; Bunyan, English preacher and author (1628–1688).

greatly disappointed with the white church and its leadership. Of course, there are some notable exceptions. I am not unmindful of the fact that each of you has taken some significant stands on this issue. I commend you, Reverend Stallings, for your Christian stand on this past Sunday, in welcoming Negroes to your worship service on a nonsegregated basis. I commend the Catholic leaders of this state for integrating Spring Hill College several years ago.

But despite these notable exceptions, I must honestly reiterate that I have been disappointed with the church. I do not say this as one of those negative critics who can always find something wrong with the church. I say this as a minister of the gospel, who loves the church; who was nurtured in its bosom; who has been sustained by its spiritual blessings and who will remain true to it as long as the cord of life shall lengthen.

When I was suddenly catapulted into the leadership of the bus protest in   35
Montgomery, Alabama, a few years ago,[13] I felt we would be supported by the white church. I felt that the white ministers, priests, and rabbis of the South would be among our strongest allies. Instead, some have been outright opponents, refusing to understand the freedom movement and misrepresenting its leaders; all too many others have been more cautious than courageous and have remained silent behind the anesthetizing security of stained-glass windows.

In spite of my shattered dreams, I came to Birmingham with the hope that the white religious leadership of this community would see the justice of our cause and, with deep moral concern, would serve as the channel through which our just grievances could reach the power structure. I had hoped that each of you would understand. But again I have been disappointed.

I have heard numerous southern religious leaders admonish their worshipers to comply with a desegregation decision because it is the law, but I have longed to hear white ministers declare: "Follow this decree because integration is morally right and because the Negro is your brother." In the midst of blatant injustices inflicted upon the Negro, I have watched white churchmen stand on the sideline and mouth pious irrelevancies and sanctimonious trivialities. In the midst of a mighty struggle to rid our nation of racial and economic injustice, I have heard many ministers say: "Those are social issues, with which the gospel has no real concern." And I have watched many churches commit themselves to a completely otherworldly religion which makes a strange, un-Biblical distinction between body and soul, between the sacred and the secular.

I have traveled the length and breadth of Alabama, Mississippi, and all the other southern states. On sweltering summer days and crisp autumn mornings I have looked at the South's beautiful churches with their lofty spires pointing heavenward. I have beheld the impressive outlines of her massive religious-education buildings. Over and over I have found myself asking: "What kind of people worship here? Who is their God? Where were their voices when the lips of Governor Barnett dripped with words of interposition and nullification?

13. In December 1955, when Rosa Parks refused to move to the back of a bus.

Where were they when Governor Wallace gave a clarion call for defiance and hatred?[14] Where were their voices of support when bruised and weary Negro men and women decided to rise from the dark dungeons of complacency to the bright hills of creative protest?"

Yes, these questions are still in my mind. In deep disappointment I have wept over the laxity of the church. But be assured that my tears have been tears of love. There can be no deep disappointment where there is not deep love. Yes, I love the church. How could I do otherwise? I am in the rather unique position of being the son, the grandson, and the great-grandson of preachers. Yes, I see the church as the body of Christ. But, oh! How we have blemished and scarred that body through social neglect and through fear of being nonconformists.

40   There was a time when the church was very powerful—in the time when the early Christians rejoiced at being deemed worthy to suffer for what they believed. In those days the church was not merely a thermometer that recorded the ideas and principles of popular opinion; it was a thermostat that transformed the mores of society. Whenever the early Christians entered a town, the people in power became disturbed and immediately sought to convict the Christians for being "disturbers of the peace" and "outside agitators." But the Christians pressed on, in the conviction that they were "a colony of heaven," called to obey God rather than man. Small in number, they were big in commitment. They were too God-intoxicated to be "astronomically intimidated." By their effort and example they brought an end to such ancient evils as infanticide and gladiatorial contests.

Things are different now. So often the contemporary church is a weak, ineffectual voice with an uncertain sound. So often it is an archdefender of the status quo. Far from being disturbed by the presence of the church, the power structure of the average community is consoled by the church's silent—and often even vocal—sanction of things as they are.

But the judgment of God is upon the church as never before. If today's church does not recapture the sacrificial spirit of the early church, it will lose its authenticity, forfeit the loyalty of millions, and be dismissed as an irrelevant social club with no meaning for the twentieth century. Every day I meet young people whose disappointment with the church has turned into outright disgust.

Perhaps I have once again been too optimistic. Is organized religion too inextricably bound to the status quo to save our nation and the world? Perhaps I must turn my faith to the inner spiritual church, the church within the church, as the true *ekklesia*[15] and the hope of the world. But again I am thankful to God that some noble souls from the ranks of organized religion have broken loose from the paralyzing chains of conformity and joined us as active

14. Ross Barnett (1898–1988), governor of Mississippi, opposed James Meredith's admission to the University of Mississippi; George Wallace (1919–1998), governor of Alabama, opposed admission of several black students to the University of Alabama.
15. The Greek New Testament word for the early Christian church.

partners in the struggle for freedom. They have left their secure congregations and walked the streets of Albany, Georgia, with us. They have gone down the highways of the South on tortuous rides for freedom. Yes, they have gone to jail with us. Some have been dismissed from their churches, have lost the support of their bishops and fellow ministers. But they have acted in the faith that right defeated is stronger than evil triumphant. Their witness has been the spiritual salt that has preserved the true meaning of the gospel in these troubled times. They have carved a tunnel of hope through the dark mountain of disappointment.

I hope the church as a whole will meet the challenge of this decisive hour. But even if the church does not come to the aid of justice, I have no despair about the future. I have no fear about the outcome of our struggle in Birmingham, even if our motives are at present misunderstood. We will reach the goal of freedom in Birmingham and all over the nation, because the goal of America is freedom. Abused and scorned though we may be, our destiny is tied up with America's destiny. Before the pilgrims landed at Plymouth, we were here. Before the pen of Jefferson etched the majestic words of the Declaration of Independence across the pages of history, we were here. For more than two centuries our forebears labored in this country without wages; they made cotton king; they built the homes of their masters while suffering gross injustice and shameful humiliation—and yet out of a bottomless vitality they continued to thrive and develop. If the inexpressible cruelties of slavery could not stop us, the opposition we now face will surely fail. We will win our freedom because the sacred heritage of our nation and the eternal will of God are embodied in our echoing demands.

Before closing I feel impelled to mention one other point in your statement that has troubled me profoundly. You warmly commended the Birmingham police force for keeping "order" and "preventing violence." I doubt that you would have so warmly commended the police force if you had seen its dogs sinking their teeth into unarmed, nonviolent Negroes. I doubt that you would so quickly commend the policemen if you were to observe their ugly and inhumane treatment of Negroes here in the city jail; if you were to watch them push and curse old Negro women and young Negro girls; if you were to see them slap and kick old Negro men and young boys; if you were to observe them, as they did on two occasions, refuse to give us food because we wanted to sing our grace together. I cannot join you in your praise of the Birmingham police department.

It is true that the police have exercised a degree of discipline in handling the demonstrators. In this sense they have conducted themselves rather "nonviolently" in public. But for what purpose? To preserve the evil system of segregation. Over the past few years I have consistently preached that nonviolence demands that the means we use must be as pure as the ends we seek. I have tried to make clear that it is wrong to use immoral means to attain moral ends. But now I must affirm that it is just as wrong, or perhaps even more so, to use moral means to preserve immoral ends. Perhaps Mr. Connor and his policemen have been rather nonviolent in public, as was Chief Pritchett in Albany, Geor-

45

gia, but they have used the moral means of nonviolence to maintain the immoral end of racial injustice. As T. S. Eliot has said, "The last temptation is the greatest treason: To do the right deed for the wrong reason."[16]

I wish you had commended the Negro sit-inners and demonstrators of Birmingham for their sublime courage, their willingness to suffer, and their amazing discipline in the midst of great provocation. One day the South will recognize its real heroes. They will be the James Merediths,[17] with the noble sense of purpose that enables them to face jeering and hostile mobs, and with the agonizing loneliness that characterizes the life of the pioneer. They will be old, oppressed, battered Negro women, symbolized in a seventy-two-year-old woman in Montgomery, Alabama, who rose up with a sense of dignity and with her people decided not to ride segregated buses, and who responded with ungrammatical profundity to one who inquired about her weariness: "My feets is tired, but my soul is at rest." They will be the young high school and college students, the young ministers of the gospel and a host of their elders, courageously and nonviolently sitting in at lunch counters and willingly going to jail for conscience' sake. One day the South will know that when these disinherited children of God sat down at lunch counters, they were in reality standing up for what is best in the American dream and for the most sacred values in our Judaeo-Christian heritage, thereby bringing our nation back to those great wells of democracy which were dug deep by the founding fathers in their formulation of the Constitution and the Declaration of Independence.

Never before have I written so long a letter. I'm afraid it is much too long to take your precious time. I can assure you that it would have been much shorter if I had been writing from a comfortable desk, but what else can one do when he is alone in a narrow jail cell, other than write long letters, think long thoughts, and pray long prayers?

If I have said anything in this letter that overstates the truth and indicates an unreasonable impatience, I beg you to forgive me. If I have said anything that understates the truth and indicates my having a patience that allows me to settle for anything less than brotherhood, I beg God to forgive me.

50   I hope this letter finds you strong in the faith. I also hope that circumstances will soon make it possible for me to meet each of you, not as an integrationist or a civil-rights leader but as a fellow clergyman and a Christian brother. Let us all hope that the dark clouds of racial prejudice will soon pass away and the deep fog of misunderstanding will be lifted from our feardrenched communities, and in some not too distant tomorrow the radiant stars of love and brotherhood will shine over our great nation with all their scintillating beauty.

Yours for the cause of Peace and Brotherhood,
MARTIN LUTHER KING, JR.

16. American-born English poet (1888–1965); the lines are from his play *Murder in the Cathedral*.
17. Meredith was the first black to enroll at the University of Mississippi.

QUESTIONS

1. King addressed the "Letter from Birmingham Jail" to eight fellow clergymen who had written a statement criticizing his activities (see note 1). Where and how, in the course of the "Letter," does he attempt to make common cause with them?

2. King was trained in oral composition, that is, in composing and delivering sermons. One device he uses as an aid to oral comprehension is prediction: he announces, in advance, the organization of what he is about to say. Locate examples of prediction in the "Letter."

3. Describe King's theory of nonviolent resistance.

4. Imagine an unjust law that, to you, would justify civil disobedience. Describe the law, the form your resistance would take, and the penalties you would expect to incur.

PROSE FORMS:
SPOKEN WORDS

T he six selections gathered here represent highly characteristic examples of prominent speech types: an address at a civil rights demonstration, a speech at a rally, a position statement to the United Nations, a PowerPoint demonstration on a university campus, a formal acceptance speech for the Nobel Prize, and a Sunday sermon. Most of us have sat through or heard examples of some of them; we know how they should go, what they should sound like, and even how long they should take. What we do not know is how they will move us and the crowd assembled to listen.

Rhetoricians, people who think professionally about how speeches work, divide orations into three main categories: forensic, for use at a trial, where the issue is innocence or guilt; deliberative, for use in a legislative body, where the issue is what shall be done; and ceremonial, for use on celebratory or commemorative occasions, where the issue is how the audience should think and behave. Most of the speeches here are ceremonial, closely tied either to momentous occasions (an awards banquet) or to calls for personal commitment (demonstration, sermon). Ceremonial oratory tends toward the ornate, toward complex, full-dress language and sentiments. Its aim is to move the listeners, to make them believe or act in a certain way, through the power of words.

With ceremonial oratory, the occasion itself works to produce a particular kind of speech. In her address to the United Nations, Eleanor Roosevelt did not attempt to convince by logic or to argue fine points of policy. Instead, her speech does its work through simple words and complex, high-flown rhetoric; it mixes short sentences whose words are straightforward with a complex syntax and the official style of the Declaration of Human Rights. The tone is formal, but Roosevelt includes plenty of rhetorical flourishes intended to strike every reader and listener as especially memorable.

Great leaders are created through both deeds and words. If the words are faulty or inadequate, then there is something missing in the leadership. Martin Luther King Jr., William Lloyd Garrison, and Al Gore recognized this fact in their speeches: King's "I Have a Dream," Garrison's "No Compromise with Slavery," and Gore's "The Climate Emergency." These speakers are asserting leadership, deliberately stirring the listeners' emotions and preparing them for action. As you read, look for the emotional pressure points, the parts that seem deliberately designed to be repeated by listeners or remembered long after the speech is done. Success in these speeches comes from a combination of a strong stand and memorable expression.

For less politically charged ceremonial occasions, such as an awards banquet or a Sunday sermon, the speaker becomes a leader of a different type: an educator, actively teaching the audience or congregation about values and be-

*havior. Such an occasion calls for memorable language, too, though somewhat
less elaborate or high flown. The stakes may be very high—how to wite novels in
a postwar era, how to regard a confrontation with death—but if the talk turns
into a lecture or a harangue, much of its rhetorical impact will be lost.*

*These six orations have plenty of company in other parts of The Norton
Reader, where every section carries pieces that had their start as speeches. The
selections here are pure examples of the form, genuine representatives of the
high rhetorical mode that has characterized formal speeches for centuries. They
are a powerful introduction to a particular genre, one that has been influential
for over two thousand years.*

Martin Luther King Jr.: *I Have a Dream*

Five score years ago,[1] a great American, in whose symbolic shadow we
stand, signed the Emancipation Proclamation. This momentous decree
came as a great beacon light of hope to millions of Negro slaves who had been
seared in the flames of withering injustice. It came as a joyous daybreak to end
the long night of captivity.

But one hundred years later, we must face the tragic fact that the Negro is
still not free. One hundred years later, the life of the Negro is still sadly crippled by the manacles of segregation and the chains of discrimination. One
hundred years later, the Negro lives on a lonely island of poverty in the midst
of a vast ocean of material prosperity. One hundred years later, the Negro is
still languishing in the corners of American society and finds himself an exile
in his own land. So we have come here today to dramatize an appalling
condition.

In a sense we have come to our nation's capital to cash a check. When the
architects of our republic wrote the magnificent words of the Constitution and
the Declaration of Independence, they were signing a promissory note to
which every American was to fall heir. This note was a promise that all men
would be guaranteed the inalienable rights of life, liberty, and the pursuit of
happiness.

It is obvious today that America has defaulted on this promissory note insofar as her citizens of color are concerned. Instead of honoring this sacred
obligation, America has given the Negro people a bad check which has come
back marked "insufficient funds." But we refuse to believe that the bank of
justice is bankrupt. We refuse to believe that there are insufficient funds in
the great vaults of opportunity of this nation. So we have come to cash this
check—a check that will give us upon demand the riches of freedom and the
security of justice. We have also come to this hallowed spot to remind America

---

*Delivered on the steps of the Lincoln Memorial in Washington, D.C., on August 28, 1963,
at one of the largest civil rights demonstrations in U.S. history.*

1. An echo of Lincoln's Gettysburg Address, "Four score . . ."

of the fierce urgency of *now*. This is no time to engage in the luxury of cooling off or to take the tranquilizing drug of gradualism. *Now* is the time to rise from the dark and desolate valley of segregation to the sunlit path of racial justice. *Now* is the time to open the doors of opportunity to all of God's children. *Now* is the time to lift our nation from the quicksands of racial injustice to the solid rock of brotherhood.

5   It would be fatal for the nation to overlook the urgency of the moment and to underestimate the determination of the Negro. This sweltering summer of the Negro's legitimate discontent[2] will not pass until there is an invigorating autumn of freedom and equality. Nineteen sixty-three is not an end, but a beginning. Those who hope that the Negro needed to blow off steam and will now be content will have a rude awakening if the nation returns to business as usual. There will be neither rest nor tranquility in America until the Negro is granted his citizenship rights. The whirlwinds of revolt will continue to shake the foundations of our nation until the bright day of justice emerges.

But there is something that I must say to my people who stand on the warm threshold which leads into the palace of justice. In the process of gaining our rightful place we must not be guilty of wrongful deeds. Let us not seek to satisfy our thirst for freedom by drinking from the cup of bitterness and hatred.

We must forever conduct our struggle on the high plane of dignity and discipline. We must not allow our creative protest to degenerate into physical violence. Again and again we must rise to the majestic heights of meeting physical force with soul force. The marvelous new militancy which has engulfed the Negro community must not lead us to distrust of all white people, for many of our white brothers, as evidenced by their presence here today, have come to realize that their destiny is tied up with our destiny and their freedom is inextricably bound to our freedom. We cannot walk alone.

And as we walk, we must make the pledge that we shall march ahead. We cannot turn back. There are those who are asking the devotees of civil rights, "When will you be satisfied?" We can never be satisfied as long as our bodies, heavy with the fatigue of travel, cannot gain lodging in the motels of the highways and the hotels of the cities. We cannot be satisfied as long as the Negro's basic mobility is from a smaller ghetto to a larger one. We can never be satisfied as long as a Negro in Mississippi cannot vote and a Negro in New York believes he has nothing for which to vote. No, no, we are not satisfied, and we will not be satisfied until justice rolls down like waters and righteousness like a mighty stream.

I am not unmindful that some of you have come here out of great trials and tribulations. Some of you have come fresh from narrow cells. Some of you have come from areas where your quest for freedom left you battered by the storms of persecution and staggered by the winds of police brutality. You have been the veterans of creative suffering. Continue to work with the faith that unearned suffering is redemptive.

2. An echo of Shakespeare's *Richard III*: "Now is the winter of our discontent."

Go back to Mississippi, go back to Alabama, go back to Georgia, go back   10
to Louisiana, go back to the slums and ghettos of our northern cities, knowing
that somehow this situation can and will be changed. Let us not wallow in the
valley of despair.

I say to you today, my friends, that in spite of the difficulties and frustrations of the moment, I still have a dream. It is a dream deeply rooted in the
American dream.

I have a dream that one day this nation will rise up and live out the true
meaning of its creed: "We hold these truths to be self-evident: that all men are
created equal."

I have a dream that one day on the red hills of Georgia the sons of former
slaves and the sons of former slaveowners will be able to sit down together at
a table of brotherhood.

I have a dream that one day even the state of Mississippi, a desert state,
sweltering with the heat of injustice and oppression, will be transformed into
an oasis of freedom and justice.

I have a dream that my four children will one day live in a nation where   15
they will not be judged by the color of their skin but by the content of their
character.

I have a dream today.

I have a dream that one day the state of Alabama, whose governor's lips
are presently dripping with the words of interposition and nullification,[3] will
be transformed into a situation where little black boys and black girls will be
able to join hands with little white boys and white girls and walk together as
sisters and brothers.

I have a dream today.

I have a dream that one day every valley shall be exalted, every hill and
mountain shall be made low, the rough places will be made plain, and the
crooked places will be made straight, and the glory of the Lord shall be revealed, and all flesh shall see it together.[4]

This is our hope. This is the faith with which I return to the South. With   20
this faith we will be able to hew out of the mountain of despair a stone of
hope. With this faith we will be able to transform the jangling discords of our
nation into a beautiful symphony of brotherhood. With this faith we will be
able to work together, to pray together, to struggle together, to go to jail together, to stand up for freedom together, knowing that we will be free one day.

This will be the day when all of God's children will be able to sing with a
new meaning, "My country, 'tis of thee, sweet land of liberty, of thee I sing.
Land where my fathers died, land of the pilgrim's pride, from every mountainside, let freedom ring."

And if America is to be a great nation this must become true. So let free-

3. George Wallace (1919–1998), Alabama's segregationist governor, used big legal
terms such as "interposition" and "nullification" in his unsuccessful attempt to prevent
the integration of the University of Alabama.
4. From Isaiah 40.4–5, familiar to many through Handel's *Messiah.*

dom ring from the prodigious hilltops of New Hampshire. Let freedom ring from the mighty mountains of New York. Let freedom ring from the heightening Alleghenies of Pennsylvania!

Let freedom ring from the snowcapped Rockies of Colorado!

Let freedom ring from the curvaceous peaks of California!

25   But not only that; let freedom ring from Stone Mountain of Georgia![5]

Let freedom ring from Lookout Mountain of Tennessee![6]

Let freedom ring from every hill and every molehill of Mississippi. From every mountainside, let freedom ring.

When we let freedom ring, when we let it ring from every village and every hamlet, from every state and every city, we will be able to speed up that day when all of God's children, black men and white men, Jews and Gentiles, Protestants and Catholics, will be able to join hands and sing in the words of the old Negro spiritual, "Free at last! free at last! thank God Almighty, we are free at last!"

5. Site of a large Confederate memorial near Atlanta.

6. Site of a Civil War battle, now part of Chickamauga-Chattanooga Military Park.

QUESTIONS

1. What elements of a sermon do you notice in King's speech?

2. What are the benefits King derives from posing matters in the form of a dream? Are there any losses?

3. King's address has a "modular" form, meaning it has distinct, separate parts. What are the "modules" in King's speech? What would be changed if some parts were omitted?

WILLIAM LLOYD GARRISON: *No Compromise with Slavery*

L et me define my positions, and at the same time challenge anyone to show wherein they are untenable.

I am a believer in that portion of the Declaration of American Independence in which it is set forth, as among self-evident truths, "that all men are created equal; that they are endowed by their Creator with certain inalienable rights; that among these are life, liberty, and the pursuit of happiness." Hence, I am an abolitionist. Hence, I cannot but regard oppression in every form—and most of all, that which turns a man into a thing—with indignation and abhorrence. Not to cherish these feelings would be recreancy to principle. They who desire me to be dumb on the subject of slavery, unless I will open my mouth in its defense, ask me to give the lie to my professions, to degrade my manhood,

Delivered as a speech in 1854. Garrison also expressed his strong antislavery views in his weekly newspaper, The Liberator, *published from 1831 to 1865.*

and to stain my soul. I will not be a liar, a poltroon, or a hypocrite, to accommodate any party, to gratify any sect, to escape any odium or peril, to save any interest, to preserve any institution, or to promote any object. Convince me that one man may rightfully make another man his slave, and I will no longer subscribe to the Declaration of Independence. Convince me that liberty is not the inalienable birthright of every human being, of whatever complexion or clime, and I will give that instrument to the consuming fire. I do not know how to espouse freedom and slavery together. I do not know how to worship God and Mammon at the same time. If other men choose to go upon all fours, I choose to stand erect, as God designed every man to stand. If, practically falsifying its heaven-attested principles, this nation denounces me for refusing to imitate its example, then, adhering all the more tenaciously to those principles, I will not cease to rebuke it for its guilty inconsistency. Numerically, the contest may be an unequal one, for the time being; but the author of liberty and the source of justice, the adorable God, is more than multitudinous, and he will defend the right. My crime is that I will not go with the multitude to do evil. My singularity is that when I say that freedom is of God and slavery is of the devil, I mean just what I say. My fanaticism is that I insist on the American people abolishing slavery or ceasing to prate of the rights of man. * * *

* * *

The abolitionism which I advocate is as absolute as the law of God, and as unyielding as his throne. It admits of no compromise. Every slave is a stolen man; every slaveholder is a man stealer. By no precedent, no example, no law, no compact, no purchase, no bequest, no inheritance, no combination of circumstances, is slaveholding right or justifiable. While a slave remains in his fetters, the land must have no rest. Whatever sanctions his doom must be pronounced accursed. The law that makes him a chattel is to be trampled underfoot; the compact that is formed at his expense, and cemented with his blood, is null and void; the church that consents to his enslavement is horribly atheistical; the religion that receives to its communion the enslaver is the embodiment of all criminality. Such, at least, is the verdict of my own soul, on the supposition that I am to be the slave; that my wife is to be sold from me for the vilest purposes; that my children are to be torn from my arms, and disposed of to the highest bidder, like sheep in the market. And who am I but a man? What right have I to be free, that another man cannot prove himself to possess by nature? Who or what are my wife and children, that they should not be herded with four-footed beasts, as well as others thus sacredly related? * * *

* * *

* * * If the slaves are not men; if they do not possess human instincts, passions, faculties, and powers; if they are below accountability, and devoid of reason; if for them there is no hope of immortality, no God, no heaven, no hell; if, in short, they are what the slave code declares them to be, rightly "deemed, sold, taken, reputed and adjudged in law to be chattels personal in the hands of their owners and possessors, and their executors, administrators and assigns, to all intents, constructions, and purposes whatsoever"; then, undeniably, I am mad, and can no longer discriminate between a man and a

beast. But, in that case, away with the horrible incongruity of giving them oral instruction, of teaching them the catechism, of recognizing them as suitably qualified to be members of Christian churches, of extending to them the ordinance of baptism, and admitting them to the communion table, and enumerating many of them as belonging to the household of faith! Let them be no more included in our religious sympathies or denominational statistics than are the dogs in our streets, the swine in our pens, or the utensils in our dwellings. It is right to own, to buy, to sell, to inherit, to breed, and to control them, in the most absolute sense. All constitutions and laws which forbid their possession ought to be so far modified or repealed as to concede the right.

5   But, if they are men; if they are to run the same career of immortality with ourselves; if the same law of God is over them as over all others; if they have souls to be saved or lost; if Jesus included them among those for whom he laid down his life; if Christ is within many of them "the hope of glory"; then, when I claim for them all that we claim for ourselves, because we are created in the image of God, I am guilty of no extravagance, but am bound, by every principle of honor, by all the claims of human nature, by obedience to Almighty God, to "remember them that are in bonds as bound with them,"[1] and to demand their immediate and unconditional emancipation.

* * *

These are solemn times. It is not a struggle for national salvation; for the nation, as such, seems doomed beyond recovery. The reason why the South rules, and the North falls prostrate in servile terror, is simply this: with the South, the preservation of slavery is paramount to all other considerations—above party success, denominational unity, pecuniary interest, legal integrity, and constitutional obligation. With the North, the preservation of the Union is placed above all other things—above honor, justice, freedom, integrity of soul, the Decalogue and the Golden Rule[2]—the infinite God himself. All these she is ready to discard for the Union. Her devotion to it is the latest and the most terrible form of idolatry. She has given to the slave power a carte blanche,[3] to be filled as it may dictate—and if, at any time, she grows restive under the yoke, and shrinks back aghast at the new atrocity contemplated, it is only necessary for that power to crack the whip of disunion over her head, as it has done again and again, and she will cower and obey like a plantation slave—for has she not sworn that she will sacrifice everything in heaven and on earth, rather than the Union?

What then is to be done? Friends of the slave, the question is not whether by our efforts we can abolish slavery, speedily or remotely—for duty is ours, the result is with God; but whether we will go with the multitude to do evil, sell our birthright for a mess of pottage,[4] cease to cry aloud and spare not, and

1. Hebrews 13.3.

2. Decalogue, the Ten Commandments; Golden Rule, Matthew 7.12: "Therefore all things whatsoever ye would that men should do to you, do ye even so to them."

3. Blank check.

4. Reference to Genesis 25; trading something that will become valuable later for something of less value that you want right now. Pottage is soup.

remain in Babylon[5] when the command of God is "Come out of her, my people, that ye be not partakers of her sins, and that ye receive not of her plagues." Let us stand in our lot, "and having done all, to stand."[6] At least, a remnant shall be saved. Living or dying, defeated or victorious, be it ours to exclaim, "No compromise with slavery! Liberty for each, for all, forever! Man above all institutions! The supremacy of God over the whole earth!"

5. Where the Israelites were kept in slavery.
6. Revelation 18.4 and Ephesians 6.13. The first is a reference to God's command to escape the Harlot of Babylon, a great evildoer. In the second, Paul exhorts the early Christians to be brave warriors.

QUESTIONS

1. As an abolitionist, Garrison argues that Americans should not allow slavery in any form within the United States. What evidence does his speech include to support this position?

2. Garrison includes a critique of both the North and the South (paragraph 6). Against what standard does he measure both? How do they fall short?

3. Write a speech in which you take a firm position on some contemporary event or debate. Include the basis (the standard) of your position and give evidence to support it.

ELEANOR ROOSEVELT: *On the Universal Declaration of Human Rights*

The long and meticulous study and debate of which this Universal Declaration of Human Rights is the product means that it reflects the composite views of the many men and governments who have contributed to its formulation. Not every man nor every government can have what he wants in a document of this kind. There are of course particular provisions in the declaration before us with which we are not fully satisfied. I have no doubt this is true of other delegations, but taken as a whole the Delegation of the United States[1] believes that this [is] a good document—even a great document—and we propose to give it our full support. The position of the United States on the various parts of the declaration is a matter of record in the Third Committee. I shall not burden the Assembly, and particularly my colleagues of the Third Committee, with a restatement of that position here.

Given before the General Assembly of the United Nations on December 9, 1948, the day before the UN adopted the "Universal Declaration of Human Rights." The speaker was the wife of the late president Franklin Delano Roosevelt and U.S. delegate to the UN. The "Preamble to the Universal Declaration" is reprinted after the speech.

1. The representatives of the United States to the United Nations.

Certain provisions of the declaration are stated in such broad terms as to be acceptable only because of the limitations in article 29[2] providing for limitation on the exercise of the rights for the purpose of meeting the requirements of morality, public order, and the general welfare. An example of this is the provision that everyone has the right of equal access to the public service in his country. The basic principle of equality and of nondiscrimination as to public employment is sound, but it cannot be accepted without limitations. My government, for example, would consider that this is unquestionably subject to limitation in the interest of public order and the general welfare. It would not consider that the exclusion from public employment of persons holding subversive political beliefs and not loyal to the basic principles and practices of the constitution and laws of the country would in any way infringe upon this right.

Likewise, my Government has made it clear in the course of the development of the declaration that it does not consider that the economic and social and cultural rights stated in the declaration imply an obligation on governmental action. This was made quite clear in the Human Rights Commission text of article 23[3] which served as a so-called "umbrella" article to the articles on economic and social rights. We consider that the principle has not been affected by the fact that this article no longer contains a reference to the articles which follow it. This in no way affects our whole-hearted support for the basic principles of economic, social, and cultural rights set forth in these articles.

In giving our approval to the declaration today it is of primary importance that we keep clearly in mind the basic character of the document. It is not a treaty; it is not an international agreement. It is not and does not purport to be a statement of basic principles of law or legal obligation. It is a declaration of basic principles of human rights and freedoms, to be stamped with the approval of the General Assembly[4] by formal vote of its members, and to serve as a common standard of achievement for all peoples of all nations.

5   We stand today at the threshold of a great event both in the life of the United Nations and in the life of mankind, that is the approval by the General Assembly of the Universal Declaration of Human Rights recommended by the Third Committee. This declaration may well become the international Magna Carta[5] of all men everywhere.

2. One of thirty articles in the Declaration.

3. Article 23 states: "1. Everyone has the right to work, to free choice of employment, to just and favourable conditions of work and to protection against unemployment. 2. Everyone, without any discrimination, has the right to equal pay for equal work. 3. Everyone who works has the right to just and favourable remuneration ensuring for himself and his family an existence worthy of human dignity, and supplemented, if necessary, by other means of social protection. 4. Everyone has the right to form and to join trade unions for the protection of his interests."

4. A gathering of representatives from all United Nations constituents and the site of debate and decision-making for the organization.

5. Englishs legal document, written in 1215, that bound the king to law and thus laid the foundation for constitutional government.

Eleanor Roosevelt and United Nations Universal Declaration of Human Rights in Spanish text.

We hope its proclamation by the General Assembly will be an event comparable to the proclamation of the Declaration of the Rights of Man by the French people in 1789,[6] the adoption of the Bill of Rights by the people of the United States,[7] and the adoption of comparable declarations at different times in other countries. At a time when there are so many issues on which we find it difficult to reach a common basis of agreement, it is a significant fact that 58 states[8] have found such a large measure of agreement in the complex field of human rights. This must be taken as testimony of our common aspiration first voiced in the Charter of the United Nations[9] to lift men everywhere to a higher standard of life and to a greater enjoyment of freedom.

Man's desire for peace lies behind this declaration.

The realization that the flagrant violation of human rights by Nazi and Fascist countries[10] sowed the seeds of the last world war has supplied the impetus for the work which brings us to the moment of achievement here today.

6. French legal document, adopted in 1789, proclaiming the existence of inalienable human rights and thereby setting the stage for the French Revolution.

7. The first ten amendments to the American Constitution, drafted by James Madison in 1789.

8. I.e., nations, countries.

9. The constitution of the United Nations, which lays out the rules that bind the constituent countries and states that those rules trump those set forth in other treaties.

10. Primarily Germany and Italy.

In a recent speech in Canada, Gladstone Murray[11] said: "The central fact is that man is fundamentally a moral being, that the light we have is imperfect does not matter so long as we are always trying to improve it . . . we are equal in sharing the moral freedom that distinguishes us as men. Man's status makes each individual an end in himself. No man is by nature simply the servant of the state or of another man . . . the ideal and fact of freedom—and not technology—are the true distinguishing marks of our civilization."

10   This declaration is based upon the spiritual fact that man must have freedom in which to develop his full stature and through common effort to raise the level of human dignity.

We have much to do to fully achieve and to assure the rights set forth in this declaration. But having them put before us with the moral backing of 58 nations will be a great step forward.

As we here bring to fruition our labors on this Declaration of Human Rights, we must at the same time rededicate ourselves to the unfinished task which lies before us. We can now move on with new courage and inspiration to the completion of an international covenant on human rights and of measures for the implementation of human rights.

In conclusion I feel that I cannot do better than to repeat the call to action by Secretary Marshall[12] in his opening statement to this Assembly:

> "Let this third regular session of the General Assembly approve by an overwhelming majority the Declaration of Human Rights as a statement of conduct for all; and let us, as Members of the United Nations, conscious of our own short-comings and imperfections, join our effort in all faith to live up to this high standard."

PREAMBLE TO THE UNIVERSAL DECLARATION OF HUMAN RIGHTS

Whereas recognition of the inherent dignity and of the equal and inalienable rights of all members of the human family is the foundation of freedom, justice and peace in the world,

Whereas disregard and contempt for human rights have resulted in barbarous acts which have outraged the conscience of mankind, and the advent of a world in which human beings shall enjoy freedom of speech and belief and freedom from fear and want has been proclaimed as the highest aspiration of the common people,

Whereas it is essential, if man is not to be compelled to have recourse, as a last resort, to rebellion against tyranny and oppression, that human rights should be protected by the rule of law,

11. First General Manager of the Canadian Broadcasting Corporation.

12. George Marshall (1880–1959), American military leader and Secretary of State, was also author of the Marshall Plan, which helped reconstruct Europe after World War II.

Whereas it is essential to promote the development of friendly relations between nations,

Whereas the peoples of the United Nations have in the Charter reaffirmed   5
their faith in fundamental human rights, in the dignity and worth of the human person and in the equal rights of men and women and have determined to promote social progress and better standards of life in larger freedom,

Whereas Member States have pledged themselves to achieve, in cooperation with the United Nations, the promotion of universal respect for and observance of human rights and fundamental freedoms,

Whereas a common understanding of these rights and freedoms is of the greatest importance for the full realization of this pledge,

Now, therefore, The General Assembly proclaims This Universal Declaration of Human Rights.

QUESTIONS

1. In this speech, Eleanor Roosevelt is not expressing her own personal opinions but is representing the United States as a delegate to the United Nations. How, in her opening remarks, does she make clear her government's position on the declaration? Why does she begin with these qualifying remarks?

2. In explaining the importance of the declaration, Roosevelt makes comparisons with other historical documents: the Magna Carta (paragraph 4), the Declaration of the Rights of Man (paragraph 5), the Bill of Rights (paragraph 5), and the Charter of the United Nations (paragraph 5). Why does she choose these documents? What effect do her comparisons have?

3. Toward the middle of the speech, Roosevelt proclaims: "Man's desire for peace lies behind this declaration" (paragraph 7). How does the end of the speech develop this theme?

4. Compare and contrast this speech with another speech given on an official occasion (for example, Abraham Lincoln's second inaugural address or John F. Kennedy's inaugural address, both in Politics and Government). What similar techniques do you find? What differences?

Al Gore: *The Climate Emergency*

April 13, 2004

I'm Al Gore. I used to be the next president of the United States.[1] This has been an interesting period of my life. I wanted to start by inviting you to put yourselves in my shoes for a minute. It hasn't been easy, you know. For eight years I flew on Air Force II,[2] and now I have to take off my shoes to get on an airplane.

Not long after Tipper[3] and I left the White House, we were driving from our home in Nashville to a small farm we have fifty miles east of Nashville. We were driving ourselves. I looked in the rear view mirror and all of a sudden it just hit me that there was no motorcade. Some of you may have heard of phantom limb pain.[4]

It was mealtime, so we looked for a place to eat. We pulled off the interstate highway and finally found a Shoney's Restaurant, a low-cost, family restaurant chain. We walked in and sat down. The waitress came over and made a big commotion over Tipper. She took our order and then went to the couple in the booth next to us, and lowered her voice so much I had to really strain to hear what she was saying: "Yes, that's former Vice President Al Gore and his wife Tipper." And the man said, "He's come down a long way, hasn't he?"

The very next day, continuing a true story, I got on a plane and flew to Africa, to Nigeria, to the city of Lagos, to make a speech about energy. I began my speech by telling that story, that had just happened the day before back in Tennessee, and I told it pretty much the same way I just told it here. They laughed. Then I went on and gave my speech and went back to the airport and flew back toward the U.S. I fell asleep on the plane, and was awakened in the middle of the night when we were landing on the Azores Islands out in the middle of the Atlantic. They opened the door of the plane to let some fresh air in, and I looked out, and here came a man running across the runway waving a piece of paper saying "Call Washington, call Washington."

Gore gave this speech during the 2004 presidential campaign; it became the basis of his documentary film and book, An Inconvenient Truth *(2006). This version was given with extensive illustrations, charts, and graphs on April 13, 2004, at the Yale School of Forestry and Environmental Science, and was included in a collection of speeches,* Red, White, Blue and Green: Politics and the Environment in the 2004 Election *(2004), edited by members of YSFES, James R. Lyons, Heather S. Kaplan, Fred Strebeigh, and Kathleen E. Campbell.*

1. Gore ran for president in 2000 and won more popular votes than George W. Bush, who was nonetheless elected because of his majority in the electoral college.
2. Part of the presidential fleet of airplanes.
3. Gore's wife, Tipper Gore (b. 1948).
4. The sensation of pain in a missing limb.

I thought—what in the world, in the middle of the night, in the middle of   5
the Atlantic, what in the world could be wrong in Washington? And then I remembered it could be a bunch of things. But what it turned out to be was that
my staff back in Washington was very, very upset. A wire service reporter in
Lagos had written a story about my speech, and it had already been transmitted to the U.S. and printed all over the country. The story began: "Former Vice
President Al Gore announced in Nigeria yesterday 'My wife Tipper and I
opened a low-cost family restaurant named Shoney's and we are running it
ourselves.' " Before I could get back to U.S. soil, the late-night comics Leno
and Letterman[5] had already started in on me. They had me in a big white
chef's hat and Tipper was taking orders—"One more with fries!" Three days
later I got a nice long handwritten letter from my friend Bill Clinton[6] that said
"Congratulations on the new restaurant, Al!" We like to celebrate each other's
successes in life.

Anyway, it really is an honor to be here and to share some words about the
climate issue. The title I chose for this speech is not a misprint. The phrase
"climate emergency" is intended to convey what it conveys—that this is a crisis with an unusual sense of urgency attached to it, and we should see it as an
emergency. The fact that we don't, or that most people don't, is part of what I
want to cover here.

CLIMATE CHANGE: IMPACTS AND EVIDENCE

There is a very famous picture called Earth Rise. A young astronaut named
William Anders took it on December 24, 1968.[7] This mission, Apollo 7, was
the first one to go around the moon. It went on Christmas Eve, and they had
just been on the dark side of the moon, coming back around, seeing the earth
for the first time. Anders—the rookie astronaut, without a big fancy camera—
took this snapshot and it instantly became an icon. Many people believe that
this one picture, Earth Rise, in many ways was responsible for the birth of the
modern environmental movement. Less than two years after this picture was
printed, the first Earth Day[8] was organized. This picture became a powerful
force in changing the way people thought about the earth and about the environment.

The environment is often felt to be relatively invulnerable because the
earth is so big. People tend to assume that the earth is so big that we as hu-

5. Jay Leno (b. 1950) and David Letterman (b. 1947), contemporary American comedians.
6. Bill Clinton (b. 1946), forty-second American president (1993–2001); Gore was his
vice president.
7. William Anders (b. 1933), United States Air Force officer and astronaut on the
Apollo 8 (not 7) mission, took this famous photograph depicting the moon, partially in
light, off the edge of the earth.
8. An annual celebration of the environment, intended to increase awareness and activism, and held at different points around the world.

man beings can't possibly have any impact on it. That is a mistake. The most vulnerable part of earth's environment is the atmosphere. It's astonishingly thin, as any image from space shows. The space is so small that we are able to fill it up with greenhouse gases, such as CO_2,[9] which form a thick blanket of gas surrounding the earth, trapping some of the sun's radiation. This process, called the "greenhouse effect," is what leads to increased global temperatures or what most refer to as climate change.

In Europe during the summer of 2003, we experienced an extreme heat wave that killed an estimated 20,000 people, and many predict such events will be much more commonplace as a result of increasing temperatures. The anomaly was extreme, particularly in France, with consequences that were well reported in the press. Year-to-year, decade-to-decade there's variation, but the overall upward trend worldwide since the American Civil War is really clear and really obvious, at least to me.

10   If you look at the glaciers around the world, you see that many are melting away. A friend of mine named Lonnie Thompson of Ohio State studies glaciers, and he reports that 15 to 20 years from now there will be no more snows of Kilimanjaro. This shrinking of glaciers is happening all around the world, including Latin America, China, and the U.S. In our own Glacier National Park, all of the glaciers are predicted to be gone within 15 to 20 years.

One of the remarkable things about glaciers is that they really could care less about politics. They either melt or freeze. Rhetoric has no impact on them whatsoever. A few years ago some hikers in the Alps between Austria and Italy were walking along and they ran across what looked like a 5,000-year-old man. Actually he was from 3,000 B.C., and you don't see that every day. The reason you don't is that the ice there hasn't melted for 5,000 years. Every mountain glacier in the entire world, with the exception of a few in Scandinavia that are affected by the Gulf Stream patterns, is melting rapidly.

Lonnie Thompson and his team of researchers don't just watch glaciers melt. They drill down into the glaciers and pull up columns of ice. Then they study the bubbles of air trapped in the ice, and they can do that year by year because every year there's a new layer. In Antarctica the layers are paper-thin and they stack up 400,000 years back. Ninety-five percent of all the fresh water in the world is locked up as ice in Antarctica. It's two miles high.

When Lonnie and his team drill down through Antarctica, they're able to get 400,000 years worth of ice. They can then look at the little bubbles of atmosphere and measure the CO_2 content, and they can also measure temperature by comparing the ratio of different oxygen isotopes.[10] However that works, it's extremely accurate and not controversial. And here's what that record shows where carbon dioxide is concerned:

9. Carbon dioxide.
10. Different forms of chemical elements.

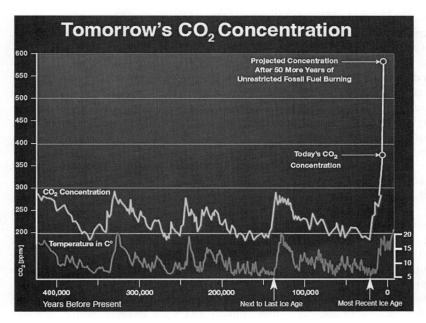

Now, there are two points here. The first is: Do those lines—the line for level of temperature and the line for concentration of CO_2—look like they go together to you? They do to me. The second point is: Here in New Haven,[11] on the temperature line, the difference of approximately 15°C of average temperature is the difference between a nice day and having one mile of ice over your head. What has been happening lately is that the concentration of CO_2 is approaching 380 parts per million. So that's way, way above anything that has been seen for as far back as we can measure—400,000 years. And within fifty years it's going to approach 600 parts per million. So if a difference of approximately 200 parts per million of CO_2 on the cold side is a mile of ice over your head, what does that much difference represent on the warm side?

Or to state the question another way, is it perfectly sane and rational and reasonable to go ahead and do this? Or is it in fact crazy? It is crazy, but that is what the world is doing right now. And fifty years is not a long time. Unless we make decisions very soon, we will reach much higher levels. So, when I use the phrase *climate emergency*, I have partly in mind the fact that this is happening right now. And it carries with it, unless we do something, catastrophic consequences for all civilization.

In Antarctica you've heard about ice shelves the size of Rhode Island[12] coming off and calving. There are actually a bunch of them in the Antarctic, and also in Greenland. Incidentally, there was a flurry of publicity on April 9th

11. City in Connecticut where this speech was given.
12. Rhode Island is about 37 miles wide by 48 miles long.

15

about a new study showing that if greenhouse gas emissions continue to rise at current rates the disappearance of Greenland's ice sheet is inevitable, unless we act fairly soon.

When ice melts in mountains and in Antarctica and Greenland—when land-based ice melts—it raises sea level. When you have rivers that are close to the ocean like the Thames River in London, the water level goes up, and it threatens the lower lying areas. London, in 1983, built barriers to protect the city against flooding from higher sea level and thus higher storm surges. These barriers had to be closed only once in 1983. Twenty years later, in 2003, they were closed 19 times. Again, the same pattern shows up wherever you look.

An area of Bangladesh is due to be flooded where ten million people live. A large area of Florida is due to be flooded. The Florida Keys are very much at risk. The Everglades are at risk.

Now the Arctic is very different from the Antarctic because, while the Antarctic is land surrounded by ocean, the Arctic is ocean surrounded by land. And the ice in the Arctic is floating on top of the ocean, so it doesn't get nearly as thick. Instead of two miles thick, it's only ten feet thick—that is, it used to be ten feet. Just in the last few decades it has melted quite a bit. I went up there twice in a submarine. They have these specially designed submarines where the wings rotate vertically so that they can cut through the ice. Ice in water, or thinner ice, melts more rapidly and leads to temperature increases because, as soon as a little bit of ice melts, the water absorbs a lot more temperature. This effect is now happening to the entire Arctic Ocean. The Arctic ice cap has thinned by 40 percent in the last 40 years. Let me repeat that. Listen to that number. The Arctic ice cap has thinned 40 percent in 40 years. Within 50 years it may be entirely gone.

20   That's a big problem because when the sun hits the ice cap, 95 percent of the energy bounces off like a big mirror. But when it hits the open ocean more than 90 percent is absorbed. So it's a phase change, it's not a gradual change. Ice is that way—the difference between 33F° and 31F° is not just two degrees. That puts more energy into the system and it changes the amount of evaporation off the oceans, so you get more rain and snow but it comes at different times and you get more soil erosion as well. You get simultaneously more flooding and more droughts, which is really a bad thing. You get more precipitation in one-time storm events. More of it comes at one time in big storms.

The trend is very clear. What's behind it all? I've come to believe that global warming, the disappearance of the ocean fisheries, the destruction of the rain forests, the stratospheric ozone depletion problem, the extinction crisis, all of these are really symptoms of an underlying cause. The underlying cause is a collision between our civilization and the earth. The relationship between the human species and our planet has been completely changed. All of our culture, all of our literature, all of our history, everything we've learned, was premised on one relationship between the earth and us, and now we have a different one.

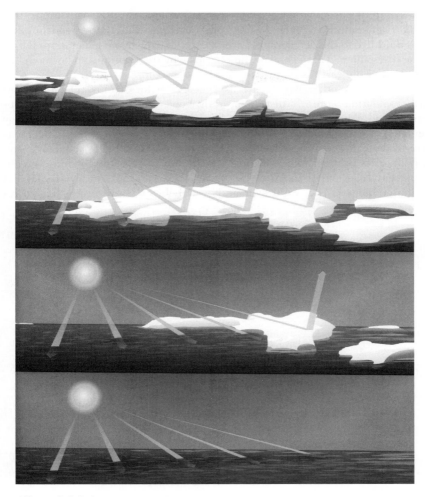

Effect of global warming on Arctic ice cap.

THREE LEADING CAUSES: POPULATION GROWTH, TECHNOLOGY, AND OUR WAY OF THINKING

The new relationship between humankind and the earth has been caused by a confluence of three factors.

The first is population, which has been growing rapidly. The population crisis has actually been a success story in some ways. We've slowed it down, but the momentum of the population increases is really incredible. Say the scientists are right and we emerged as a species 160,000 years ago. It took from that time, almost 160,000 years until the end of World War II, before we got to a population of 2 billion. Since I've been alive, as part of the baby boom generation, it has gone from 2 billion to 6.3 billion. So if it takes more than 10,000 generations to reach 2 billion and one human lifetime to go from 2 to 6, and if I live to the demographic average of the baby boom generation, it'll go close to 9 billion. That is one of the reasons why the relationship between our species and the earth is different now than ever before.

Some of the other global patterns, species loss for example, match the human population pattern. Most importantly, however, the increase in the population of developing nations is driving food demand, water demand, and energy demand, creating intense pressures on human resources. We are seeing a pattern of devastation and destruction that is simply driven by those factors. And it really is a political issue. We in the U.S. are responsible for more greenhouse gas emissions than Africa, South America, Central America, India, and China combined. The world average is way below where we are. Just to re-

| First modern humans | | | | | | |
| 160,000 BC | 100,000 BC | 10,000 BC | 7000 BC | 6000 BC | 5000 BC | 4000 BC |

Population Growth Throughout History

cap—this is 1,000 years of carbon emissions, CO_2 concentrations, and temperature. This is not rocket science. Those lines match up.

The second factor that changes the relationship between humans and the   25
earth is technology. In many ways, it is more powerful and significant than the
population explosion because new technologies have increased our power beyond imagination. That's a good thing often in areas like medicine or communications—you can fill in the blanks. There are all kinds of great things that
represent progress. Even cleaning up the environment with new technology.
There are a lot of great things that have come out of this, but when we don't
examine habits that have persisted for a long time, and then use the same
habits with new technology and don't take into account the new power that we
have, then the consequences can get away from us. One quick example: warfare was one thing with swords and bows and arrows and even muskets, but

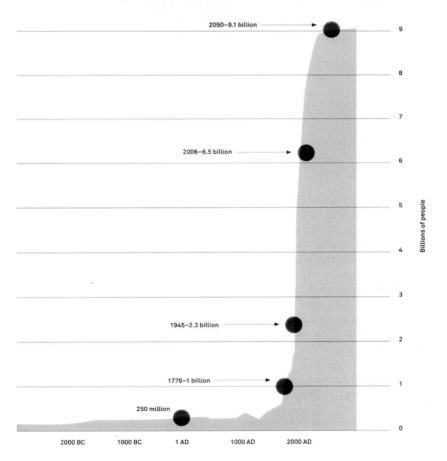

2.3%
CANADA

30.3%[*]
UNITED STATES

*INCLUDES ALASKA AND HAWAII

3.8%
CENTRAL AMERICA
SOUTH AMERICA

CONTRIBUTIONS TO GLOBAL WARMING

■ United States   ▩ Other industrialized nations   ■ Developing nations

when nuclear weapons were created, the consequences of war were utterly transformed. So we had to think differently about war. And what happened? The cold war emerged and unfortunately the other kind didn't completely go away, but we're in the midst of rethinking that age-old habit of warfare. We just have to, because the new technologies make it unthinkable to continue as we were doing in the past.

Now think about that pattern: old habits, new technologies. Think about the subsistence that we have always drawn from the earth. The plow was a great advance, as was irrigation. But then we began to get more powerful with these tools. At the Aral Sea[13] in Russia, something as simple as irrigation on a large scale led to the virtual disappearance of the fourth largest inland body of water in the world. We're changing the surface of the earth, and technology sometimes seems to dwarf our human scale. We now have to try to change this pattern.

The third factor is our way of thinking. We have to change our way of thinking. One illustration comes from the fact that, as I said earlier, we have these big assumptions that we don't question. I had a classmate in the sixth grade. Every time our geography teacher put a map of the world up he would mutter. One time, he got up his courage and pointed to the outline of South

13. A landlocked Central Asian sea.

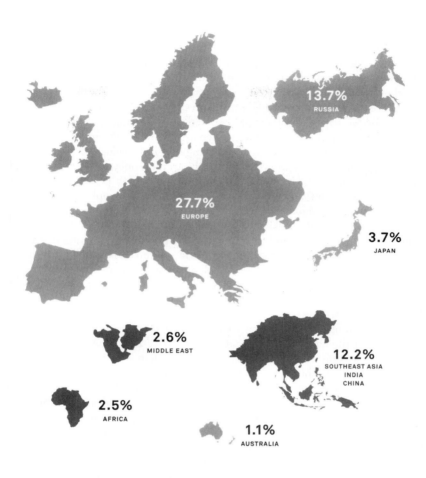

13.7%
RUSSIA

27.7%
EUROPE

3.7%
JAPAN

2.6%
MIDDLE EAST

12.2%
SOUTHEAST ASIA
INDIA
CHINA

2.5%
AFRICA

1.1%
AUSTRALIA

SOURCE: U.S. DEPARTMENT OF ENERGY, ENERGY INFORMATION ADMINISTRATION, CARBON DIOXIDE INFORMATION ANALYSIS CENTER

America and the outline of Africa and said, "Did they ever fit together?" And the teacher said "Of course not. That's the most ridiculous thing I've ever heard." In fact, until about the 1960s, the guy who talked about continental drift was thought to be a kook because he said that Africa and South America fit together. It turns out that they did, but the teacher in this story had an assumption in his mind. Continents are so big they obviously don't move, thereby illustrating the old philosopher's saying that "What gets us into trouble is not what we don't know. It's what we know for sure that just ain't so" (Yogi Berra).[14] We know for sure that the earth is so big we can't have a big impact on it, but that's just not so.

You know this cliché, I'm sure: That a frog's nervous system is such that if

14. Berra (b. 1925), famous New York Yankee and wordsmith.

it's dropped into a pot of boiling water it will jump right out because it perceives the contrast, but if it's put in a pot of tepid water which is slowly heated, it doesn't jump out unless it's rescued. Here's the deeper meaning of that cliché: the frog did perceive the sudden boiling water, but did not perceive the slow process.

Global warming seems to be gradual in the context of a human life, but it is actually fairly sudden. Another problem with our thinking is that there are people who are paid money by some coal companies and oil companies to go out and pretend that the science says something that it doesn't say. These are scientific camp followers who are willing to do things for money. And some of the very same individuals who are doing this now (i.e., trying to persuade people that global warming is not a problem) were some of the same people who took money from the tobacco companies after the Surgeon General's report came out warning of the dangers of smoking. The tobacco companies hired these scientific camp followers to go out and try to confuse the public into thinking that the science wasn't clear. They produced marketing campaigns like "More doctors smoke Camels." On a similar note, the Republican pollster Frank Luntz advised the White House that the issue of the environment is important, but the way to deal with it is to make the lack of scientific certainly a primary issue by finding people who are willing to say that it's confusing when it's really not.

30   There's another assumption that needs to be questioned. In contrast to the idea that the earth is so big that we can't have any impact on it, there are others who assume that the climate change problem is so big we can't solve it. I, however, believe that we can if we put our minds to it. We had a problem with the ozone hole, a big global problem that seemed too big to solve. In response, we had political leadership and the world passed a treaty outlawing chlorofluorocarbons, the chemicals that caused this problem.

The United States led the way, and we brought about a dramatic drop in CFCs and are now in the process of solving that problem. We now have the ability to buy hybrid cars like the Toyota Prius and the marketplace for new sources of energy is increasing dramatically. We're also seeing new efficiencies with energy savings. If we have political leadership and the collective political will to say it is important to solve this problem, we can not only solve it, we can create more jobs, we can create higher incomes, a better way of life, and a higher quality of life by solving the problem.

And finally, it's an issue of values. Back when I was in the Senate, the first President Bush[15] was trying to fend off some of the attacks by myself and many others in Congress who were saying we have to solve this global warming problem. So they had a White House conference on global stewardship. One of their view graphs caught my attention. Their view of the global environmental crisis was represented by a scale with money, in the form of gold bars on one side, and on the other side of the scales was the entire planet. The point they were trying to make was that we have to find a balance between our monetary wealth and the well being of the entire planet. Boy, that's a tough

15. George H. W. Bush (b. 1924), forty-first American president; his son, George W. Bush (b. 1946), followed in his footsteps as forty-third president.

one! It's a false choice—because you're not going to have much wealth if you lose the planet and there is wealth to be made in saving it. We have to get our perspective right.

Everything we have ever known—and Carl Sagan[16] made a beautiful long statement about this—all the wars, all the heartbreak, all the romance, every triumph, every mistake, everything we've ever known is contained in this small planet. If we keep the right perspective and keep our eyes on the prize, we *can* solve this problem, we *will* solve this problem, we *must* solve this problem. It really is up to you.

16. American astronomer (1934–1996).

QUESTIONS

1. This speech begins with a self-introduction. Why does Al Gore, a well-known public figure, introduce himself to the audience? How do his humorous tactics aid in his presentation of the serious part of his speech?

2. Gore's serious presentation of the climate emergency begins with the section "Climate Change: Impacts and Evidence." (The section headings were added by the editors of *Red, White, Blue and Green*.) Where does he define "climate emergency"? What examples does he give as evidence?

3. Gore introduces and interprets a graph to make a point about temperature change (paragraphs 12–14)—a technique used in scientific writing. Yet Gore's interpretation is not "scientific" in style. How does he make clear to the audience the meaning of this graph?

4. Gore gives three leading causes of the climate emergency: population growth, technology, and our way of thinking. List the kinds of evidence and examples he uses in this part of his speech, and suggest how the diversity of evidence and examples helps him communicate with his audience.

5. Write a speech about a current crisis, drawing on a variety of examples and, if possible, using illustrations, charts, and graphs.

WILLIAM FAULKNER: *Nobel Prize Award Speech*

I feel that this award was not made to me as a man but to my work—a life's work in the agony and sweat of the human spirit, not for glory and least of all for profit, but to create out of the materials of the human spirit something which did not exist before. So this award is only mine in trust. It will not be difficult to find a dedication for the money part of it commensurate with the

On acceptance of the Nobel Prize in Literature for 1949, Faulkner gave this speech at a banquet in City Hall, Stockholm, Sweden, on December 10, 1850 (the anniversary of the death of Alfred Nobel, founder of the prize). The Nobel Prizes are presented by the king of Sweden, then King Gustaf VI Adolf (1882–1973).

purpose and significance of its origin. But I would like to do the same with the acclaim too, by using this moment as a pinnacle from which I might be listened to by the young men and women already dedicated to the same anguish and travail, among whom is already that one who will some day stand here where I am standing.

Our tragedy today is a general and universal physical fear so long sustained by now that we can even bear it. There are no longer problems of the spirit. There is only the question: When will I be blown up? Because of this, the young man or woman writing today has forgotten the problems of the human heart in conflict with itself which alone can make good writing because only that is worth writing about, worth the agony and the sweat.

He must learn them again. He must teach himself that the basest of all things is to be afraid; and, teaching himself that, forget it forever, leaving no room in his workshop for anything but the old verities and truths of the heart, the old universal truths lacking which any story is ephemeral and doomed— love and honor and pity and pride and compassion and sacrifice. Until he does so, he labors under a curse. He writes not of love but of lust, of defeats in which nobody loses anything of value, of victories without hope and, worst of all, without pity or compassion. His griefs grieve on no universal bones leaving no scars. He writes not of the heart but of the glands.

Until he relearns these things, he will write as though he stood alone and watched the end of man. I decline to accept the end of man. It is easy enough to say that man is immortal simply because he will endure; that when the last ding-dong of doom has clanged and faded from the last worthless rock hanging tideless in the last red and dying evening, that even then there will still be one more sound: that of his puny inexhaustible voice, still talking. I refuse to accept this. I believe that man will not merely endure; he will prevail. He is immortal, not because he alone among creatures has an inexhaustible voice but because he has a soul, a spirit capable of compassion and sacrifice and endurance. The poet's, the writer's, duty is to write about these things. It is his privilege to help man endure by lifting his heart, by reminding him of the courage and honor and hope and pride and compassion and pity and sacrifice which have been the glory of his past. The poet's voice need not merely be the record of man, it can be one of the props, the pillars to help him endure and prevail.

QUESTIONS

1. Writers accepting the Nobel Prize in literature usually feel obligated to explain what literature and the arts can do for humankind. How does Faulkner's speech meet this obligation?

2. Faulkner gave his speech in the aftermath of World War II. How does he address, directly or indirectly, the work of writers in healing the scars of war?

3. Choose a writer you admire, and write a speech that you imagine expresses that writer's sense of the value of literature.

James Van Tholen: *Surprised by Death*

> While we were still weak, at the right time Christ died for the ungodly. . . . But God proves his love for us in that while we still were sinners God died for us.
>
> — ROMANS 5:6, 8, NRSV[1]

This is a strange day—for all of us. Most of you know that today marks my return to this pulpit after seven months of dealing with an aggressive and deadly form of cancer. Now, with the cancer vacationing for a little while, I am back. And of course, I'm glad to be back. But I can't help feeling how strange this day is—especially because I want to ignore my absence, and I want to pretend everybody has forgotten the reason for it.

But we can't do that. We can't ignore what has happened. We can rise above it; we can live through it; but we can't ignore it. If we ignore the threat of death as too terrible to talk about, then the threat wins. Then we are overwhelmed by it, and our faith doesn't apply to it. And if that happens, we lose hope.

We want to worship God in this church, and for our worship to be real, it doesn't have to be fun, and it doesn't have to be guilt-ridden. But it does have to be honest, and it does have to hope in God. We have to be honest about a world of violence and pain, a world that scorns faith and smashes hope and rebuts love. We have to be honest about the world, and honest about the difficulties of faith within it. And then we still have to hope in God.

So let me start with the honesty. The truth is that for seven months I have been scared. Not of the cancer, not really. Not even of death. Dying is another matter—how long it will take and how it will go. Dying scares me. But when I say that I have been scared, I don't mean that my thoughts have centered on dying. My real fear has centered somewhere else. Strange as it may sound, I have been scared of meeting God.

How could this be so? How could I have believed in the God of grace and still have dreaded to meet him? Why did I stand in this pulpit and preach grace to you over and over, and then, when I myself needed the grace so much, why did I discover fear where the grace should have been?

I think I know the answer now. As the wonderful preacher John Timmer[2] has taught me over the years, the answer is that grace is a scandal. Grace is hard to believe. Grace goes against the grain. The gospel of grace says that there is nothing I can *do* to get right with God, but that God has made himself right with me through Jesus' bloody death. And that is a scandalous thing to believe.

5

A 1999 Sunday sermon, preached as Van Tholen returned to his Rochester, N.Y., pulpit after months of cancer treatment. He died eighteen months later. His sermon was published in Christianity Today, *a moderate evangelical weekly; it was reprinted in* Best American Spiritual Writing *(2001).*

1. New Revised Standard Version, a modern translation of the Bible.
2. Pastor of the Christian Reformed Church; author of many books of sermons.

God comes to us before we go to him. John Timmer used to say that this is God's habit. God came to Abraham when there was nothing to come to, just an old man at a dead end. But that's God for you. That's the way God likes to work. He comes to old men and to infants, to sinners and to losers. That's grace, and a sermon without it is no sermon at all.

So I've tried to preach grace, to fill my sermons up with grace, to persuade you to believe in grace. And it's wonderful work to have—that is, to stand here and preach grace to people. I got into this pulpit and talked about war and homosexuality and divorce. I talked about death before I knew what death really was. And I tried to bring the gospel of grace to these areas when I preached. I said that God goes to people in trouble, that God receives people in trouble, that God is a God who *gets* into trouble because of his grace. I said what our Heidelberg Catechism[3] says: that our only comfort in life and in death is that we are not our own but belong to our faithful Savior, Jesus Christ.

I said all those things, and I meant them. But that was before I faced death myself. So now I have a silly thing to admit: I don't think I ever realized the shocking and radical nature of God's grace—even as I preached it. And the reason I didn't get it where grace is concerned, I think, is that I assumed I still had about forty years left. Forty years to unlearn my bad habits. Forty years to let my sins thin down and blow away. Forty years to be good to animals and pick up my neighbors' mail for them when they went on vacation.

10   But that's not how it's going to go. Now I have months, not years. And now I have to meet my creator who is also my judge—I have to meet God not later, but sooner. I haven't enough time to undo my wrongs, not enough time to straighten out what's crooked, not enough time to clean up my life.

And that's what has scared me.

So now, for the first time, I have to preach grace and know what I'm talking about. I have to preach grace and not only believe it, but rest on it, depend on it, stake my life on it. And as I faced the need to do this I remembered one of the simplest, most powerful statements in the entire Bible.

You may have thought that the reason for my choice of Romans 5 lay in the wonderful words about how suffering produces endurance, and endurance produces character, and character produces hope. Those are beautiful words, true words, but I'm not so sure they apply to me. I'm not sure I've suffered so much or so faithfully to claim that my hope has arisen through the medium of good character. No, many of you know far more about good character than I do, and more about suffering, too.

It wasn't that beautiful chain with character as the main link that drew my attention to Romans 5; instead, it was just one little word in verses 6 and 8. It's the Greek word *eti*, and it has brought comfort to my soul. The word means "yet" or "still," and it makes all the difference between sin and grace.

3. One of the major statements of faith of the Christian Reformed Church in Europe and the United States. It received its name from the place of its origin, Heidelberg, Germany.

Paul writes that "while we were *still* weak Christ died for the ungodly." He wants us to marvel at the Christ of the gospel, who comes to us in our weakness and in our need. Making sure we get the point, Paul uses the word twice in verse 6 in a repetitious and ungrammatical piling up of his meaning: "*Still* while we were *still* weak, at the right time Christ died for the ungodly."

I'm physically weak, but that's not my main weakness, my most debilitating weakness. What the last half year has proved to me is that my weakness is more of the soul than the body. This is what I've come to understand as I have dwelled on one question: How will I explain myself to my God? How can I ever claim to have been what he called me to be?

And, of course, the scary truth is that I can't. That's the kind of weakness Paul is talking about. And that's where *eti* comes in—while we were *still* weak, while we were *still* sinners, while we were *still* enemies of God, we were reconciled with him through the death of his Son. I find it unfathomable that God's love propelled him to reach into our world with such scandalous grace, such a way out, such hope. No doubt God has done it, because there's no hope anywhere else. I know. I've been looking. And I have come to see that the hope of the world lies only inside the cradle of God's grace.

This truth has come home to me as I've been thinking what it will mean to die. The same friends I enjoy now will get together a year, and three years, and twenty years from now, and I will not be there, not even in the conversation. Life will go on. In this church you will call a new minister with new gifts and a new future, and eventually I'll fade from your mind and memory. I understand. The same thing has happened to my own memories of others. When I was saying something like this a few months ago to a friend of mine, he reminded me of those poignant words of Psalm 103:15–16: "As for mortals, their days are like grass; they flourish like a flower of the field; for the wind passes over it, and it is gone, and its place knows it no more." For the first time I felt those words in my gut; I understood that my place would know me no more.

In his poem "Adjusting to the Light," Miller Williams[4] explores the sense of awkwardness among Lazarus's friends and neighbors just after Jesus has resuscitated him. Four days after his death, Lazarus returns to the land of the living and finds that people have moved on from him. Now they have to scramble to fit him back in:

> Lazarus, listen, we have things to tell you.
> We killed the sheep you meant to take to market.
> We couldn't keep the old dog, either.
> He minded you. The rest of us he barked at.
> Rebecca, who cried two days, has given her hand
> to the sandalmaker's son. Please understand
> we didn't know that Jesus could do this.

4. Professor at the University of Arkansas (b. 1930) who read one of his poems at President Clinton's second inauguration, in 1997.

15

We're glad you're back. But give us time to think.
Imagine our surprise. . . . We want to say
we're sorry for all of that. And one thing more.
We threw away the lyre. But listen, we'll pay
whatever the sheep was worth. The dog, too.
And put your room the way it was before.

Miller Williams has it just right. After only a few days, Lazarus's place knew him no more. Before cancer, I liked Williams's poem, but now I'm living it. Believe me: hope doesn't lie in our legacy; it doesn't lie in our longevity; it doesn't lie in our personality or our career or our politics or our children or, heaven knows, our goodness. Hope lies in *eti*.

20   So please don't be surprised when in the days ahead I don't talk about my cancer very often. I've told a part of my story today, because it seemed right to do it on the first day back after seven months. But what we must talk about here is not me. I cannot be our focus, because the center of my story—*our* story—is that the grace of Jesus Christ carries us beyond every cancer, every divorce, every sin, every trouble that comes to us. The Christian gospel is the story of Jesus, and that's the story I'm called to tell.

I'm dying. Maybe it will take longer instead of shorter; maybe I'll preach for several months, and maybe for a bit more. But I am dying. I know it, and I hate it, and I'm still frightened by it. But there is hope, unwavering hope. I have hope not in something I've done, some purity I've maintained, or some sermon I've written. I hope in God—the God who reaches out for an enemy, saves a sinner, dies for the weak.

That's the gospel, and I can stake my life on it. I must. And so must you.

QUESTIONS

1. Many sermons and speeches have a "modular" form, meaning they are made up of distinct, separate parts. Choose two speeches from this section and note the "modules" they use. How are they organized? Why do you suppose the speaker chose this order?

2. Compare the rhetorical devices used in two speeches—particularly strategies that help the listener follow the argument or that move the listener to agree or take action. Consider, for example, repeated key words, pronouns that include or exclude, series of sentences with parallel constructions, and quotations from esteemed sources. What rhetorical elements do the two speeches have in common? What are their differences?

3. Listen to a speech, either in person or on television or video. What rhetorical techniques did the speaker use that you noticed in the "Spoken Words" of this section? Write a brief description of the speech, noting its effective techniques.

SCIENCE AND TECHNOLOGY

JACOB BRONOWSKI *The Nature of Scientific Reasoning*

WHAT IS THE INSIGHT in which the scientist tries to see into nature? Can it indeed be called either imaginative or creative? To the literary man the question may seem merely silly. He has been taught that science is a large collection of facts; and if this is true, then the only seeing which scientists need to do is, he supposes, seeing the facts. He pictures them, the colorless professionals of science, going off to work in the morning into the universe in a neutral, unexposed state. They then expose themselves like a photographic plate. And then in the darkroom or laboratory they develop the image, so that suddenly and startlingly it appears, printed in capital letters, as a new formula for atomic energy.

Men who have read Balzac and Zola[1] are not deceived by the claims of these writers that they do no more than record the facts. The readers of Christopher Isherwood[2] do not take him literally when he writes "I am a camera." Yet the same readers solemnly carry with them from their school-days this foolish picture of the scientist fixing by some mechanical process the facts of nature. I have had of all people a historian tell me that science is a collection of facts, and his voice had not even the ironic rasp of one filing cabinet reproving another.

It seems impossible that this historian had ever studied the beginnings of a scientific discovery. The Scientific Revolution can be held to begin in the year 1543 when there was brought to Copernicus, perhaps on his deathbed, the first printed copy of the book he had finished about a dozen years earlier. The thesis of this book is that the earth moves around the sun. When did Copernicus go out and record this fact with his camera? What appearance in nature prompted his outrageous guess? And in what odd sense is this guess to be called a neutral record of fact?

First delivered as a lecture at the Massachusetts Institute of Technology and then reprinted as part of Bronowski's book Science and Human Values *(1956).*

1. Honoré de Balzac (1799–1850) and Émile Zola (1840–1902), nineteenth-century French novelists.
2. English novelist and playwright (1904–1986) whose writing was the basis for the musical *Cabaret*.

Less than a hundred years after Copernicus, Kepler published (between 1609 and 1619) the three laws which describe the paths of the planets. The work of Newton and with it most of our mechanics spring from these laws.[3] They have a solid, matter-of-fact sound. For example, Kepler says that if one squares the year of a planet, one gets a number which is proportional to the cube of its average distance from the sun. Does anyone think that such a law is found by taking enough readings and then squaring and cubing everything in sight? If he does, then, as a scientist, he is doomed to a wasted life; he has as little prospect of making a scientific discovery as an electronic brain has.

5   It was not this way that Copernicus and Kepler thought, or that scientists think today. Copernicus found that the orbits of the planets would look simpler if they were looked at from the sun and not from the earth. But he did not in the first place find this by routine calculation. His first step was a leap of imagination—to lift himself from the earth, and put himself wildly, speculatively into the sun. "The earth conceives from the sun," he wrote; and "the sun rules the family of stars." We catch in his mind an image, the gesture of the virile man standing in the sun, with arms outstretched, overlooking the planets. Perhaps Copernicus took the picture from the drawings of the youth with outstretched arms which the Renaissance teachers put into their books on the proportions of the body. Perhaps he had seen Leonardo's[4] drawings of his loved pupil Salai. I do not know. To me, the gesture of Copernicus, the shining youth looking outward from the sun, is still vivid in a drawing which William Blake[5] in 1780 based on all these: the drawing which is usually called *Glad Day.*

Kepler's mind, we know, was filled with just such fanciful analogies; and we know what they were. Kepler wanted to relate the speeds of the planets to the musical intervals. He tried to fit the five regular solids into their orbits. None of these likenesses worked, and they have been forgotten; yet they have been and they remain the stepping stones of every creative mind. Kepler felt for his laws by way of metaphors, he searched mystically for likenesses with what he knew in every strange corner of nature. And when among these guesses he hit upon his laws, he did not think of their numbers as the balancing of a cosmic bank account, but as a revelation of the unity in all nature. To us, the analogies by which Kepler listened for the movement of the planets in the music of the spheres are farfetched. Yet are they more so than the wild leap by which Rutherford and Bohr[6] in our own century found a model for the atom in, of all places, the planetary system?

---

3. Nicolaus Copernicus (1473–1543), Polish astronomer; Johannes Kepler (1571–1630), German astronomer; Isaac Newton (1642–1727), English physicist and mathematician.

4. Leonardo da Vinci (1452–1519), Italian artist, inventor, and designer.

5. English poet, artist, and engraver (1757–1827).

6. Ernest Rutherford (1871–1937), British physicist; Niels Bohr (1885–1962), Danish physicist.

No scientific theory is a collection of facts. It will not even do to call a theory true or false in the simple sense in which every fact is either so or not so. The Epicureans held that matter is made of atoms two thousand years ago and we are now tempted to say that their theory was true. But if we do so we confuse their notion of matter with our own. John Dalton[7] in 1808 first saw the structure of matter as we do today, and what he took from the ancients was not their theory but something richer, their image: the atom. Much of what was in Dalton's mind was as vague as the Greek notion, and quite as mistaken. But he suddenly gave life to the new facts of chemistry and the ancient theory together, by fusing them to give what neither had: a coherent picture of how matter is linked and built up from different kinds of atoms. The act of fusion is the creative act.

All science is the search for unity in hidden likenesses. The search may be on a grand scale, as in the modern theories which try to link the fields of gravitation and electromagnetism. But we do not need to be browbeaten by the scale of science. There are discoveries to be made by snatching a small likeness from the air too, if it is bold enough. In 1935 the Japanese physicist Hideki Yukawa wrote a paper which can still give heart to a young scientist. He took as his starting point the known fact that waves of light can sometimes behave as if they were separate pellets. From this he reasoned that the forces which hold the nucleus of an atom together might sometimes also be observed as if they were solid pellets. A schoolboy can see how thin Yukawa's analogy is, and his teacher would be severe with it. Yet Yukawa without a blush calculated the mass of the pellet he expected to see, and waited. He was right; his meson was found, and a range of other mesons, neither the existence nor the nature of which had been suspected before. The likeness had borne fruit.

The scientist looks for order in the appearances of nature by exploring such likenesses. For order does not display itself of itself; if it can be said to be there at all, it is not there for the mere looking. There is no way of pointing a finger or camera at it; order must be discovered and, in a deep sense, it must be created. What we see, as we see it, is mere disorder.

This point has been put trenchantly in a fable by Karl Popper.[8] Suppose   10
that someone wished to give his whole life to science. Suppose that he therefore sat down, pencil in hand, and for the next twenty, thirty, forty years recorded in notebook after notebook everything that he could observe. He may be supposed to leave out nothing: today's humidity, the racing results, the level of cosmic radiation and the stockmarket prices and the look of Mars, all would be there. He would have compiled the most careful record of nature that has ever been made; and, dying in the calm certainty of a life well spent, he would of course leave his notebooks to the Royal Society. Would the Royal Society thank him for the treasure of a lifetime of observation? It would not. The Royal Society would treat his notebooks exactly as the English bishops have

7. British chemist and physicist (1766–1844) who developed the atomic theory of matter and thus is considered a father of modern physical science.
8. Austrian-born British philosopher (1902–1994).

treated Joanna Southcott's box.[9] It would refuse to open them at all, because it would know without looking that the notebooks contain only a jumble of disorderly and meaningless items.

Science finds order and meaning in our experience, and sets about this in quite a different way. It sets about it as Newton did in the story which he himself told in his old age, and of which the schoolbooks give only a caricature. In the year 1665, when Newton was twenty-two, the plague broke out in southern England, and the University of Cambridge was closed. Newton therefore spent the next eighteen months at home, removed from traditional learning, at a time when he was impatient for knowledge and, in his own phrase, "I was in the prime of my age for invention." In this eager, boyish mood, sitting one day in the garden of his widowed mother, he saw an apple fall. So far the books have the story right; we think we even know the kind of apple; tradition has it that it was a Flower of Kent. But now they miss the crux of the story. For what struck the young Newton at the sight was not the thought that the apple must be drawn to the earth by gravity; that conception was older than Newton. What struck him was the conjecture that the same force of gravity, which reaches to the top of the tree, might go on reaching out beyond the earth and its air, endlessly into space. Gravity might reach the moon: this was Newton's new thought; and it might be gravity which holds the moon in her orbit. There and then he calculated what force from the earth (falling off as the square of the distance) would hold the moon, and compared it with the known force of gravity at tree height. The forces agreed; Newton says laconically, "I found them answer pretty nearly." Yet they agreed only nearly: the likeness and the approximation go together, for no likeness is exact. In Newton's science modern science is full grown.

It grows from a comparison. It has seized a likeness between two unlike appearances; for the apple in the summer garden and the grave moon overhead are surely as unlike in their movements as two things can be. Newton traced in them two expressions of a single concept, gravitation: and the concept (and the unity) are in that sense his free creation. The progress of science is the discovery at each step of a new order which gives unity to what had long seemed unlike.

* * *

9. Southcott was a nineteenth-century English farm servant who claimed to be a prophet. She left behind a box that was to be opened in a time of national emergency in the presence of all the English bishops. In 1927, a bishop agreed to officiate; when the box was opened, it was found to contain only some odds and ends.

QUESTIONS

1. Mark the generalizations Bronowski makes in the course of "The Nature of Scientific Reasoning"; for example, "No scientific theory is a collection of facts" (paragraph 7). Where is the information that supports them?

2. Bronowski tells the well-known story of Newton and the apple (paragraphs 11–12). How many of his generalizations does it exemplify, and how?

3. "The scientist," Bronowski observes, "looks for order in the appearances of nature" (paragraph 9). Is this operation unique to scientists? Consider the operations of "knowers" in humanities and social science disciplines such as history, literature, psychology, and sociology.

4. Bronowski sets up an adversary, a literary person who believes that scientists observe, collect, and record facts, and writes his essay as a refutation. Adapt his rhetorical strategy in an essay of your own: explain your beliefs about something by refuting the beliefs of someone who disagrees with them.

ISAAC ASIMOV   *The Eureka Phenomenon*

IN THE OLD DAYS, when I was writing a great deal of fiction, there would come, once in a while, moments when I was stymied. Suddenly, I would find I had written myself into a hole and could see no way out. To take care of that, I developed a technique which invariably worked.

It was simply this—I went to the movies. Not just any movie. I had to pick a movie which was loaded with action but which made no demands on the intellect. As I watched, I did my best to avoid any conscious thinking concerning my problem, and when I came out of the movie I knew exactly what I would have to do to put the story back on the track.

It never failed.

In fact, when I was working on my doctoral dissertation, too many years ago, I suddenly came across a flaw in my logic that I had not noticed before and that knocked out everything I had done. In utter panic, I made my way to a Bob Hope movie—and came out with the necessary change in point of view.

It is my belief, you see, that thinking is a double phenomenon like breathing.   5

You can control breathing by deliberate voluntary action: you can breathe deeply and quickly, or you can hold your breath altogether, regardless of the body's needs at the time. This, however, doesn't work well for very long. Your chest muscles grow tired, your body clamors for more oxygen, or less, and you relax. The automatic involuntary control of breathing takes over, adjusts it to the body's needs and unless you have some respiratory disorder, you can forget about the whole thing.

Well, you can think by deliberate voluntary action, too, and I don't think it is much more efficient on the whole than voluntary breath control is. You can deliberately force your mind through channels of deductions and associations

From The Left Hand of the Electron, *Asimov's 1971 collection of popular scientific essays.*

in search of a solution to some problem and before long you have dug mental furrows for yourself and find yourself circling round and round the same limited pathways. If those pathways yield no solution, no amount of further conscious thought will help.

On the other hand, if you let go, then the thinking process comes under automatic involuntary control and is more apt to take new pathways and make erratic associations you would not think of consciously. The solution will then come while you *think* you are *not* thinking.

The trouble is, though, that conscious thought involves no muscular action and so there is no sensation of physical weariness that would force you to quit. What's more, the panic of necessity tends to force you to go on uselessly, with each added bit of useless effort adding to the panic in a vicious cycle.

10   It is my feeling that it helps to relax, deliberately, by subjecting your mind to material complicated enough to occupy the voluntary faculty of thought, but superficial enough not to engage the deeper involuntary one. In my case, it is an action movie; in your case, it might be something else.

I suspect it is the involuntary faculty of thought that gives rise to what we call "a flash of intuition," something that I imagine must be merely the result of unnoticed thinking.

Perhaps the most famous flash of intuition in the history of science took place in the city of Syracuse in third-century B.C. Sicily. Bear with me and I will tell you the story—

About 250 B.C., the city of Syracuse was experiencing a kind of Golden Age. It was under the protection of the rising power of Rome, but it retained a king of its own and considerable self-government; it was prosperous; and it had a flourishing intellectual life.

The king was Hieron II, and he had commissioned a new golden crown from a goldsmith, to whom he had given an ingot of gold as raw material. Hieron, being a practical man, had carefully weighed the ingot and then weighed the crown he received back. The two weights were precisely equal. Good deal!

15   But then he sat and thought for a while. Suppose the goldsmith had subtracted a little bit of the gold, not too much, and had substituted an equal weight of the considerably less valuable copper. The resulting alloy would still have the appearance of pure gold, but the goldsmith would be plus a quantity of gold over and above his fee. He would be buying gold with copper, so to speak, and Hieron would be neatly cheated.

Hieron didn't like the thought of being cheated any more than you or I would, but he didn't know how to find out for sure if he had been. He could scarcely punish the goldsmith on mere suspicion. What to do?

Fortunately, Hieron had an advantage few rulers in the history of the world could boast. He had a relative of considerable talent. The relative was named Archimedes and he probably had the greatest intellect the world was to see prior to the birth of Newton.

Archimedes was called in and was posed the problem. He had to determine whether the crown Hieron showed him was pure gold, or was gold to which a small but significant quantity of copper had been added.

If we were to reconstruct Archimedes' reasoning, it might go as follows. Gold was the densest known substance (at that time). Its density in modern terms is 19.3 grams per cubic centimeter. This means that a given weight of gold takes up less volume than the same weight of anything else! In fact, a given weight of pure gold takes up less volume than the same weight of *any* kind of impure gold.

The density of copper is 8.92 grams per cubic centimeter, just about half   20
that of gold. If we consider 100 grams of pure gold, for instance, it is easy to calculate it to have a volume of 5.18 cubic centimeters. But suppose that 100 grams of what looked like pure gold was really only 90 grams of gold and 10 grams of copper. The 90 grams of gold would have a volume of 4.66 cubic centimeters, while the 10 grams of copper would have a volume of 1.12 cubic centimeters; for a total value of 5.78 cubic centimeters.

The difference between 5.18 cubic centimeters and 5.78 cubic centimeters is quite a noticeable one, and would instantly tell if the crown were of pure gold, or if it contained 10 per cent copper (with the missing 10 per cent of gold tucked neatly in the goldsmith's strongbox).

All one had to do, then, was measure the volume of the crown and compare it with the volume of the same weight of pure gold.

The mathematics of the time made it easy to measure the volume of many simple shapes: a cube, a sphere, a cone, a cylinder, any flattened object of simple regular shape and known thickness, and so on.

We can imagine Archimedes saying, "All that is necessary, sire, is to pound that crown flat, shape it into a square of uniform thickness, and then I can have the answer for you in a moment."

Whereupon Hieron must certainly have snatched the crown away and said,   25
"No such thing. I can do that much without you; I've studied the principles of mathematics, too. This crown is a highly satisfactory work of art and I won't have it damaged. Just calculate its volume without in any way altering it."

But Greek mathematics had no way of determining the volume of anything with a shape as irregular as the crown, since integral calculus had not yet been invented (and wouldn't be for two thousand years, almost). Archimedes would have had to say, "There is no known way, sire, to carry through a nondestructive determination of volume."

"Then think of one," said Hieron testily.

And Archimedes must have set about thinking of one, and gotten nowhere. Nobody knows how long he thought, or how hard, or what hypotheses he considered and discarded, or any of the details.

What we do know is that, worn out with thinking, Archimedes decided to visit the public baths and relax. I think we are quite safe in saying that Archimedes had no intention of taking his problem to the baths with him. It would be ridiculous to imagine he would, for the public baths of a Greek metropolis weren't intended for that sort of thing.

The Greek baths were a place for relaxation. Half the social aristocracy of   30
the town would be there and there was a great deal more to do than wash. One steamed one's self, got a massage, exercised, and engaged in general socializing. We can be sure that Archimedes intended to forget the stupid crown for a while.

One can envisage him engaging in light talk, discussing the latest news from Alexandria and Carthage, the latest scandals in town, the latest funny jokes at the expense of the country-squire Romans—and then he lowered himself into a nice hot bath which some bumbling attendant had filled too full.

The water in the bath slopped over as Archimedes got in. Did Archimedes notice that at once, or did he sigh, sink back, and paddle his feet awhile before noting the water-slop. I guess the latter. But, whether soon or late, he noticed, and that one fact, added to all the chains of reasoning his brain had been working on during the period of relaxation when it was unhampered by the comparative stupidities (even in Archimedes) of voluntary thought, gave Archimedes his answer in one blinding flash of insight.

Jumping out of the bath, he proceeded to run home at top speed through the streets of Syracuse. He did *not* bother to put on his clothes. The thought of Archimedes running naked through Syracuse has titillated dozens of generations of youngsters who have heard this story, but I must explain that the ancient Greeks were quite lighthearted in their attitude toward nudity. They thought no more of seeing a naked man on the streets of Syracuse, than we would on the Broadway stage.

And as he ran, Archimedes shouted over and over, "I've got it! I've got it!" Of course, knowing no English, he was compelled to shout it in Greek, so it came out, "*Eureka! Eureka!*"

35   Archimedes' solution was so simple that anyone could understand it—once Archimedes explained it.

If an object that is not affected by water in any way, is immersed in water, it is bound to displace an amount of water equal to its own volume, since two objects cannot occupy the same space at the same time.

Suppose, then, you had a vessel large enough to hold the crown and suppose it had a small overflow spout set into the middle of its side. And suppose further that the vessel was filled with water exactly to the spout, so that if the water level were raised a bit higher, however slightly, some would overflow.

Next, suppose that you carefully lower the crown into the water. The water level would rise by an amount equal to the volume of the crown, and that volume of water would pour out the overflow and be caught in a small vessel. Next, a lump of gold, known to be pure and exactly equal in weight to the crown, is also immersed in the water and again the level rises and the overflow is caught in a second vessel.

If the crown were pure gold, the overflow would be exactly the same in each case, and the volume of water caught in the two small vessels would be equal. If, however, the crown were of alloy, it would produce a larger overflow than the pure gold would and this would be easily noticeable.

40   What's more, the crown would in no way be harmed, defaced, or even as much as scratched. More important, Archimedes had discovered the "principle of buoyancy."

And was the crown pure gold? I've heard that it turned out to be alloy and that the goldsmith was executed, but I wouldn't swear to it.

How often does this "Eureka phenomenon" happen? How often is there this flash of deep insight during a moment of relaxation, this triumphant cry of

"I've got it! I've got it!" which must surely be a moment of the purest ecstasy this sorry world can afford?

I wish there were some way we could tell. I suspect that in the history of science it happens *often;* I suspect that very few significant discoveries are made by the pure technique of voluntary thought; I suspect that voluntary thought may possibly prepare the ground (if even that), but that the final touch, the real inspiration, comes when thinking is under involuntary control.

But the world is in a conspiracy to hide the fact. Scientists are wedded to reason, to the meticulous working out of consequences from assumptions to the careful organization of experiments designed to check those consequences. If a certain line of experiments ends nowhere, it is omitted from the final report. If an inspired guess turns out to be correct, it is *not* reported as an inspired guess. Instead, a solid line of voluntary thought is invented after the fact to lead up to the thought, and that is what is inserted in the final report.

The result is that anyone reading scientific papers would swear that *noth-*   45
ing took place but voluntary thought maintaining a steady clumping stride from origin to destination, and that just can't be true.

It's such a shame. Not only does it deprive science of much of its glamour (how much of the dramatic story in Watson's *Double Helix* do you suppose got into the final reports announcing the great discovery of the structure of DNA?),[1] but it hands over the important process of "insight," "inspiration," "revelation" to the mystic.

The scientist actually becomes ashamed of having what we might call a revelation, as though to have one is to betray reason—when actually what we call revelation in a man who has devoted his life to reasoned thought, is after all merely reasoned thought that is not under voluntary control.

Only once in a while in modern times do we ever get a glimpse into the workings of involuntary reasoning, and when we do, it is always fascinating. Consider, for instance, the case of Friedrich August Kekule von Stradonitz.

In Kekule's time, a century and a quarter ago, a subject of great interest to chemists was the structure of organic molecules (those associated with living tissue). Inorganic molecules were generally simple in the sense that they were made up of few atoms. Water molecules, for instance, are made up of two atoms of hydrogen and one of oxygen (H_2O). Molecules of ordinary salt are made up of one atom of sodium and one of chlorine ($NaCl$), and so on.

Organic molecules, on the other hand, often contained a large number of   50
atoms. Ethyl alcohol molecules have two carbon atoms, six hydrogen atoms, and an oxygen atom (C_2H_6O); the molecule of ordinary cane sugar is $C_{12}H_{22}O_{11}$, and other molecules are even more complex.

Then, too, it is sufficient, in the case of inorganic molecules generally, merely to know the kinds and numbers of atoms in the molecule; in organic molecules, more is necessary. Thus, dimethyl ether has the formula C_2H_6O, just as ethyl alcohol does, and yet the two are quite different in properties. Ap-

1. I'll tell you, in case you're curious. None! [Asimov's note]. How Francis Crick and James Watson discovered the molecular structure of this vital substance is told in Watson's autobiographical book, *The Double Helix.*

parently, the atoms are arranged differently within the molecules—but how to determine the arrangements?

In 1852, an English chemist, Edward Frankland, had noticed that the atoms of a particular element tended to combine with a fixed number of other atoms. This combining number was called "valence." Kekule in 1858 reduced this notion to a system. The carbon atom, he decided (on the basis of plenty of chemical evidence) had a valence of four; the hydrogen atom, a valence of one; and the oxygen atom, a valence of two (and so on).

Why not represent the atoms as their symbols plus a number of attached dashes, that number being equal to the valence. Such atoms could then be put together as though they were so many Tinker Toy units and "structural formulas" could be built up.

It was possible to reason out that the structural formula of ethyl alcohol was

$$\begin{array}{ccc} \text{H} & \text{H} \\ | & | \\ \text{H—C—C—O—H,} \\ | & | \\ \text{H} & \text{H} \end{array}$$

while that of dimethyl ether was

$$\begin{array}{ccc} \text{H} & \text{H} \\ | & | \\ \text{H—C—O—C—H.} \\ | & | \\ \text{H} & \text{H} \end{array}$$

55   In each case, there were two carbon atoms, each with four dashes attached; six hydrogen atoms, each with one dash attached; and an oxygen atom with two dashes attached. The molecules were built up of the same components, but in different arrangements.

Kekule's theory worked beautifully. It has been immensely deepened and elaborated since his day, but you can still find structures very much like Kekule's Tinker Toy formulas in any modern chemical textbook. They represent oversimplifications of the true situation, but they remain extremely useful in practice even so.

The Kekule structures were applied to many organic molecules in the years after 1858 and the similarities and contrasts in the structures neatly matched similarities and contrasts in properties. The key to the rationalization of organic chemistry had, it seemed, been found.

Yet there was one disturbing fact. The well-known chemical benzene wouldn't fit. It was known to have a molecule made up of equal numbers of carbon and hydrogen atoms. Its molecular weight was known to be 78 and a single carbon-hydrogen combination had a weight of 13. Therefore, the benzene molecule had to contain six carbon-hydrogen combinations and its formula had to be C_6H_6.

But that meant trouble. By the Kekule formulas, the hydrocarbons (molecules made up of carbon and hydrogen atoms only) could easily be envisioned as chains of carbon atoms with hydrogen atoms attached. If all the valences of the carbon atoms were filled with hydrogen atoms, as in "hexane," whose molecule looks like this—

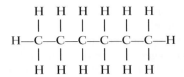

the compound is said to be saturated. Such saturated hydrocarbons were found to have very little tendency to react with other substances.

If some of the valences were not filled, unused bonds were added to those   60
connecting the carbon atoms. Double bonds were formed as in "hexene"—

$$\begin{array}{ccccccccccc}
\text{H} & & \text{H} & & \text{H} & & \text{H} & & \text{H} & & \text{H} \\
| & & | & & | & & | & & | & & | \\
\text{H}-\text{C}- & & \text{C}- & & \text{C} & = & \text{C}- & & \text{C}- & & \text{C}-\text{H} \\
| & & | & & | & & | & & | & & | \\
\text{H} & & \text{H} & & & & & & \text{H} & & \text{H}
\end{array}$$

Hexene is unsaturated, for that double bond has a tendency to open up and add other atoms. Hexene is chemically active.

When six carbons are present in a molecule, it takes fourteen hydrogen atoms to occupy all the valence bonds and make it inert—as in hexane. In hexene, on the other hand, there are only twelve hydrogens. If there were still fewer hydrogen atoms, there would be more than one double bond; there might even be triple bonds, and the compound would be still more active than hexene.

Yet benzene, which is C_6H_6 and has eight fewer hydrogen atoms than hexane, is *less* active than hexene, which has only two fewer hydrogen atoms than hexane. In fact, benzene is even less active than hexane itself. The six hydrogen atoms in the benzene molecule seem to satisfy the six carbon atoms to a greater extent than do the fourteen hydrogen atoms in hexane.

For heaven's sake, why?

This might seem unimportant. The Kekule formulas were so beautifully suitable in the case of so many compounds that one might simply dismiss benzene as an exception to the general rule.

65   Science, however, is not English grammar. You can't just categorize something as an exception. If the exception doesn't fit into the general system, then the general system must be wrong.

Or, take the more positive approach. An exception can often be made to fit into a general system, provided the general system is broadened. Such broadening generally represents a great advance and for this reason, exceptions ought to be paid great attention.

For some seven years, Kekule faced the problem of benzene and tried to puzzle out how a chain of six carbon atoms could be completely satisfied with as few as six hydrogen atoms in benzene and yet be left unsatisfied with twelve hydrogen atoms in hexene.

Nothing came to him!

And then one day in 1865 (he tells the story himself) he was in Ghent, Belgium, and in order to get to some destination, he boarded a public bus. He was tired and, undoubtedly, the droning beat of the horses' hooves on the cobblestones, lulled him. He fell into a comatose half-sleep.

70   In that sleep, he seemed to see a vision of atoms attaching themselves to each other in chains that moved about. (Why not? It was the sort of thing that constantly occupied his waking thoughts.) But then one chain twisted in such a way that head and tail joined, forming a ring—and Kekule woke with a start.

To himself, he must surely have shouted "Eureka," for indeed he had it. The six carbon atoms of benzene formed a ring and not a chain, so that the structural formula looked like this:

To be sure, there were still three double bonds, so you might think the molecule had to be very active—but now there was a difference. Atoms in a ring might be expected to have different properties from those in a chain and double bonds in one case might not have the properties of those in the other. At least, chemists could work on that assumption and see if it involved them in contradictions.

It didn't. The assumption worked excellently well. It turned out that organic molecules could be divided into two groups: aromatic and aliphatic. The former had the benzene ring (or certain other similar rings) as part of the structure and the latter did not. Allowing for different properties within each group, the Kekule structures worked very well.

For nearly seventy years, Kekule's vision held good in the hard field of actual chemical techniques, guiding the chemist through the jungle of reactions that led to the synthesis of more and more molecules. Then, in 1932, Linus Pauling applied quantum mechanics to chemical structure with sufficient subtlety to explain just why the benzene ring was so special and what had proven correct in practice proved correct in theory as well.

Other cases? Certainly.   75

In 1764, the Scottish engineer James Watt was working as an instrument maker for the University of Glasgow. The university gave him a model of a Newcomen steam engine, which didn't work well, and asked him to fix it. Watt fixed it without trouble, but even when it worked perfectly, it didn't work well. It was far too inefficient and consumed incredible quantities of fuel. Was there a way to improve that?

Thought didn't help; but a peaceful, relaxed walk on a Sunday afternoon did. Watt returned with the key notion in mind of using two separate chambers, one for steam only and one for cold water only, so that the same chamber did not have to be constantly cooled and reheated to the infinite waste of fuel.

The Irish mathematician William Rowan Hamilton worked up a theory of "quaternions" in 1843 but couldn't complete that theory until he grasped the fact that there were conditions under which $p \times q$ was *not* equal to $q \times p$. The necessary thought came to him in a flash one time when he was walking to town with his wife.

The German physiologist Otto Loewi was working on the mechanism of nerve action, in particular, on the chemicals produced by nerve endings. He awoke at 3 A.M. one night in 1921 with a perfectly clear notion of the type of experiment he would have to run to settle a key point that was puzzling him. He wrote it down and went back to sleep. When he woke in the morning, he found he couldn't remember what his inspiration had been. He remembered he had written it down, but he couldn't read his writing.

The next night, he woke again at 3 A.M. with the clear thought once more   80
in mind. This time, he didn't fool around. He got up, dressed himself, went straight to the laboratory and began work. By 5 A.M. he had proved his point and the consequences of his findings became important enough in later years so that in 1936 he received a share in the Nobel prize in medicine and physiology.

How very often this sort of thing must happen, and what a shame that scientists are so devoted to their belief in conscious thought that they so consistently obscure the actual methods by which they obtain their results.

QUESTIONS

1. Consider Asimov's narrative of Archimedes' and Kekule's discoveries. What elements does he heighten and how? How does he include the scientific information necessary to understand them? How does he make (or attempt to make) this information accessible to nonscientists?

2. Scientists, Asimov concludes, "are so devoted to their belief in conscious thought that they . . . consistently obscure the actual methods by which they obtain their results" (paragraph 81). Consider your own experiments in science courses and the way you have been taught to report them. Do you agree or disagree with Asimov? Why?

3. Have you ever had a "Eureka" experience? Does Asimov's account of the "Eureka phenomenon" help you to understand it? Write about your experience with reference to Asimov's essay.

THOMAS S. KUHN   *The Route to Normal Science*

I N THIS ESSAY, "normal science" means research firmly based upon one or more past scientific achievements, achievements that some particular scientific community acknowledges for a time as supplying the foundation for its further practice. Today such achievements are recounted, though seldom in their original form, by science textbooks, elementary and advanced. These textbooks expound the body of accepted theory, illustrate many or all of its successful applications, and compare these applications with exemplary observations and experiments. Before such books became popular early in the nineteenth century (and until even more recently in the newly matured sciences), many of the famous classics of science fulfilled a similar function. Aristotle's *Physica*, Ptolemy's *Almagest*, Newton's *Principia* and *Opticks*, Franklin's *Electricity*, Lavoisier's *Chemistry*, and Lyell's *Geology*—these and many other works served for a time implicitly to define the legitimate problems and methods of a research field for succeeding generations of practitioners. They were able to do so because they shared two essential characteristics. Their achievement was sufficiently unprecedented to attract an enduring group of adherents away from competing modes of scientific activity. Simultaneously, it was sufficiently open-ended to leave all sorts of problems for the redefined group of practitioners to resolve.

Achievements that share these two characteristics I shall henceforth refer to as "paradigms," a term that relates closely to "normal science." By choosing it, I mean to suggest that some accepted examples of actual scientific practice—examples which include law, theory, application, and instrumentation to-

From The Structure of Scientific Revolutions (1962), *one of the most influential books ever written on the history and philosophy of science.*

gether—provide models from which spring particular coherent traditions of scientific research. These are the traditions which the historian describes under such rubrics as "Ptolemaic astronomy" (or "Copernican"), "Aristotelian dynamics" (or "Newtonian"), "corpuscular optics" (or "wave optics"), and so on. The study of paradigms, including many that are far more specialized than those named illustratively above, is what mainly prepares the student for membership in the particular scientific community with which he will later practice. Because he there joins men who learned the bases of their field from the same concrete models, his subsequent practice will seldom evoke overt disagreement over fundamentals. Men whose research is based on shared paradigms are committed to the same rules and standards for scientific practice. That commitment and the apparent consensus it produces are prerequisites for normal science, i.e., for the genesis and continuation of a particular research tradition.

Because in this essay the concept of a paradigm will often substitute for a variety of familiar notions, more will need to be said about the reasons for its introduction. Why is the concrete scientific achievement, as a locus of professional commitment, prior to the various concepts, laws, theories, and points of view that may be abstracted from it? In what sense is the shared paradigm a fundamental unit for the student of scientific development, a unit that cannot be fully reduced to logically atomic components which might function in its stead? There can be a sort of scientific research without paradigms, or at least without any so unequivocal and so binding as the ones named above. Acquisition of a paradigm and of the more esoteric type of research it permits is a sign of maturity in the development of any given scientific field.

If the historian traces the scientific knowledge of any selected group of related phenomena backward in time, he is likely to encounter some minor variant of a pattern here illustrated from the history of physical optics. Today's physics textbooks tell the student that light is photons, i.e., quantum-mechanical entities that exhibit some characteristics of waves and some of particles. Research proceeds accordingly, or rather according to the more elaborate and mathematical characterization from which this usual verbalization is derived. That characterization of light is, however, scarcely half a century old. Before it was developed by Planck, Einstein, and others early in this century, physics texts taught that light was transverse wave motion, a conception rooted in a paradigm that derived ultimately from the optical writings of Young and Fresnel in the early nineteenth century.[1] Nor was the wave theory the first to be embraced by almost all practitioners of optical science. During the eighteenth century the paradigm for this field was provided by Newton's *Opticks*, which taught that light was material corpuscles. At that time physicists sought evidence, as the early wave theorists had not, of the pressure exerted by light

---

1. Max Planck (1858–1947), German physicist; Albert Einstein (1879–1955), German physicist famous for his theory of relativity; Thomas Young (1773–1829), English physician and physicist; Augustin-Jean Fresnel (1788–1827), French physicist.

particles impinging on solid bodies.

These transformations of the paradigms of physical optics are scientific
5   revolutions, and the successive transition from one paradigm to another via
revolution is the usual developmental pattern of mature science. It is not,
however, the pattern characteristic of the period before Newton's work, and
that is the contrast that concerns us here. No period between remote antiquity
and the end of the seventeenth century exhibited a single generally accepted
view about the nature of light. Instead there were a number of competing
schools and sub-schools, most of them espousing one variant or another of
Epicurean, Aristotelian, or Platonic theory.[2] One group took light to be particles emanating from material bodies; for another it was a modification of the
medium that intervened between the body and the eye; still another explained
light in terms of an interaction of the medium with an emanation from the
eye; and there were other combinations and modifications besides. Each of
the corresponding schools derives strength from its relation to some particular
metaphysic, and each emphasized, as paradigmatic observations, the particular cluster of optical phenomena that its own theory could do most to explain.
Other observations were dealt with by *ad hoc*[3] elaborations, or they remained
as outstanding problems for further research.

At various times all these schools made significant contributions to the
body of concepts, phenomena, and techniques from which Newton drew the
first nearly uniformly accepted paradigm for physical optics. Any definition of
the scientist that excludes at least the more creative members of these various
schools will exclude their modern successors as well. Those men were scientists. Yet anyone examining a survey of physical optics before Newton may well
conclude that, though the field's practitioners were scientists, the net result of
their activity was something less than science. Being able to take no common
body of belief for granted, each writer on physical optics felt forced to build
his field anew from its foundations. In doing so, his choice of supporting observation and experiment was relatively free, for there was no standard set of
methods or of phenomena that every optical writer felt forced to employ and
explain. Under these circumstances, the dialogue of the resulting books was
often directed as much to the members of other schools as it was to nature.
That pattern is not unfamiliar in a number of creative fields today, nor is it incompatible with significant discovery and invention. It is not, however, the
pattern of development that physical optics acquired after Newton and that
other natural sciences make familiar today.

The history of electrical research in the first half of the eighteenth century
provides a more concrete and better known example of the way a science develops before it acquires its first universally received paradigm. During that period
there were almost as many views about the nature of electricity as there were
important electrical experimenters, men like Hauksbee, Gray, Desaguliers, Du
Fay, Nollett, Watson, Franklin,[4] and others. All their numerous concepts of

2. The reference is to the three principal worldviews of ancient Greek philosophy.
3. For a particular purpose; literally, toward this (Latin).

electricity had something in common—they were partially derived from one or another version of the mechanico-corpuscular philosophy that guided all scientific research of the day. In addition, all were components of real scientific theories, of theories that had been drawn in part from experiment and observation and that partially determined the choice and interpretation of additional problems undertaken in research. Yet though all the experiments were electrical and though most of the experimenters read each other's works, their theories had no more than a family resemblance.

One early group of theories, following seventeenth-century practice, regarded attraction and frictional generation as the fundamental electrical phenomena. This group tended to treat repulsion as a secondary effect due to some sort of mechanical rebounding and also to postpone for as long as possible both discussion and systematic research on Gray's newly discovered effect, electrical conduction. Other "electricians" (the term is their own) took attraction and repulsion to be equally elementary manifestations of electricity and modified their theories and research accordingly. (Actually, this group is remarkably small—even Franklin's theory never quite accounted for the mutual repulsion of two negatively charged bodies.) But they had as much difficulty as the first group in accounting simultaneously for any but the simplest conduction effects. Those effects, however, provided the starting point for still a third group, one which tended to speak of electricity as a "fluid" that could run through conductors rather than as an "effluvium" that emanated from non-conductors. This group, in its turn, had difficulty reconciling its theory with a number of attractive and repulsive effects. Only through the work of Franklin and his immediate successors did a theory arise that could account with something like equal facility for very nearly all these effects and that therefore could and did provide a subsequent generation of "electricians" with a common paradigm for its research.

Excluding those fields, like mathematics and astronomy, in which the first firm paradigms date from prehistory and also those, like biochemistry, that arose by division and recombination of specialties already matured, the situations outlined above are historically typical. Though it involves my continuing to employ the unfortunate simplification that tags an extended historical episode with a single and somewhat arbitrarily chosen name (e.g., Newton or Franklin), I suggest that similar fundamental disagreements characterized, for example, the study of motion before Aristotle and of statics before Archimedes, the study of heat before Black, of chemistry before Boyle and Boerhaave, and of historical geology before Hutton.[5] In parts of biology—the study of heredity, for example—the first universally received paradigms are still

4. Francis Hauksbee the Elder (d. c. 1713) and Francis Hauksbee the Younger (1687–1763), Stephen Gray (1666–1736), Jean-Théophile Desaguliers (1683–1744), Charles-François de Cisternay Du Fay (1698–1739), Jean-Antoine Nollet (1700–1770), William Watson (1715–1787), and Benjamin Franklin (1706–1790) all made important discoveries about electricity.

5. The scientists referred to include the Greek philosopher-physicists Aristotle (384–322 B.C.E.) and Archimedes (c. 287–211 B.C.E), the British chemists Joseph Black

more recent; and it remains an open question what parts of social science have yet acquired such paradigms at all. History suggests that the road to a firm research consensus is extraordinarily arduous.

History also suggests, however, some reasons for the difficulties encountered on the road. In the absence of a paradigm or some candidate for paradigm, all of the facts that could possibly pertain to the development of a given science are likely to seem equally relevant. As a result, early fact-gathering is a far more nearly random activity than the one that subsequent scientific development makes familiar. Futhermore, in the absence of a reason for seeking some particular form of more recondite information, early fact-gathering is usually restricted to the wealth of data that lie ready to hand. The resulting pool of facts contains those accessible to casual observation and experiment together with some of the more esoteric data retrievable from established crafts like medicine, calendar making, and metallurgy. Because the crafts are one readily accessible source of facts that could not have been casually discovered, technology has often played a vital role in the emergence of new sciences.

But though this sort of fact-collecting has been essential to the origin of many significant sciences, anyone who examines, for example, Pliny's encyclopedic writings or the Baconian[6] natural histories of the seventeenth century will discover that it produces a morass. One somehow hesitates to call the literature that results scientific. The Baconian "histories" of heat, color, wind, mining, and so on, are filled with information, some of it recondite. But they juxtapose facts that will later prove revealing (e.g., heating by mixture) with others (e.g., the warmth of dung heaps) that will for some time remain too complex to be integrated with theory at all. In addition, since any description must be partial, the typical natural history often omits from its immensely circumstantial accounts just those details that later scientists will find sources of important illumination. Almost none of the early "histories" of electricity, for example, mention that chaff, attracted to a rubbed glass rod, bounces off again. That effect seemed mechanical, not electrical. Moreover, since the casual fact-gatherer seldom possesses the time or the tools to be critical, the natural histories often juxtapose descriptions like the above with others, say, heating by antiperistasis (or by cooling), that we are now quite unable to confirm.[7] Only very occasionally, as in the cases of ancient statics, dynamics, and geometrical optics, do facts collected with so little guidance from pre-established theory speak with sufficient clarity to permit the emergence of a first paradigm.

This is the situation that creates the schools characteristic of the early

---

(1728–1799) and Robert Boyle (1627–1691), the Dutch physician and chemist Hermann Boerhaave (1668–1738), and the Scottish geologist James Hutton (1726–1797).

6. *Historia naturalis*, the one surviving work of the Roman naturalist Pliny the Elder (c. 23–79 B.C.E.), attempts to deal with the physical universe, geography, anthropology, zoology, botany, and mineralogy. In *Novum Organum*, the English philosopher, essayist, and statesman Francis Bacon (1561–1626) presented his scientific method.

7. Bacon [in the *Novum Organum*] says, "Water slightly warm is more easily frozen than quite cold" [Kuhn's note]; antiperistasis: an old word meaning a reaction caused by the action of an opposite quality or principle—here, heating through cooling.

stages of a science's development. No natural history can be interpreted in the absence of at least some implicit body of intertwined theoretical and method-ological belief that permits selection, evaluation, and criticism. If that body of belief is not already implicit in the collection of facts—in which case more than "mere facts" are at hand—it must be externally supplied, perhaps by a current metaphysic, by another science, or by personal and historical accident. No wonder, then, that in the early stages of the development of any science different men confronting the same range of phenomena, but not usually all the same particular phenomena, describe and interpret them in different ways. What is surprising, and perhaps also unique in its degree to the fields we call science, is that such initial divergences should ever largely disappear.

For they do disappear to a very considerable extent and then apparently once and for all. Furthermore, their disappearance is usually caused by the triumph of one of the pre-paradigm schools, which, because of its own char-acteristic beliefs and pre-conceptions, emphasized only some special part of the too sizable and inchoate pool of information. Those electricians who thought electricity a fluid and therefore gave particular emphasis to conduc-tion provide an excellent case in point. Led by this belief, which could scarcely cope with the known multiplicity of attractive and repulsive effects, several of them conceived the idea of bottling the electrical fluid. The imme-diate fruit of their efforts was the Leyden jar,[8] a device which might never have been discovered by a man exploring nature casually or at random, but which was in fact independently developed by at least two investigators in the early 1740's. Almost from the start of his electrical researches, Franklin was particularly concerned to explain that strange and, in the event, particularly revealing piece of special apparatus. His success in doing so provided the most effective of the arguments that made his theory a paradigm, though one that was still unable to account for quite all the known cases of electrical re-pulsion.[9] To be accepted as a paradigm, a theory must seem better than its competitors, but it need not, and in fact never does, explain all the facts with which it can be confronted.

What the fluid theory of electricity did for the subgroup that held it, the Franklinian paradigm later did for the entire group of electricians. It suggested which experiments would be worth performing and which, because directed to secondary or to overly complex manifestations of electricity, would not. Only the paradigm did the job far more effectively, partly because the end of inter-school debate ended the constant reiteration of fundamentals and partly be-cause the confidence that they were on the right track encouraged scientists to undertake more precise, esoteric, and consuming sorts of work.[10] Freed from the concern with any and all electrical phenomena, the united group of elec-

8. A kind of capacitor (or condenser), a device for storing electrical charge.

9. The troublesome case was the mutual repulsion of negatively charged bodies [Kuhn's note].

10. It should be noted that the acceptance of Franklin's theory did not end quite all de-bate. In 1759 Robert Symmer proposed a two-fluid version of that theory, and for many

tricians could pursue selected phenomena in far more detail, designing much special equipment for the task and employing it more stubbornly and systematically than electricians had ever done before. Both fact collection and theory articulation became highly directed activities. The effectiveness and efficiency of electrical research increased accordingly, providing evidence for a societal version of Francis Bacon's acute methodological dictum: "Truth emerges more readily from error than from confusion."

15   We shall be examining the nature of this highly directed or paradigm-based research in the next section, but must first note briefly how the emergence of a paradigm affects the structure of the group that practices the field. When, in the development of a natural science, an individual or group first produces a synthesis able to attract most of the next generation's practitioners, the older schools gradually disappear. In part their disappearance is caused by their members' conversion to the new paradigm. But there are always some men who cling to one or another of the older views, and they are simply read out of the profession, which thereafter ignores their work. The new paradigm implies a new and more rigid definition of the field. Those unwilling or unable to accommodate their work to it must proceed in isolation or attach themselves to some other group.[11] Historically, they have often simply stayed in the departments of philosophy from which so many of the special sciences have been spawned. As these indications hint, it is sometimes just its reception of a paradigm that transforms a group previously interested merely in the study of nature into a profession or, at least, a discipline. In the sciences (though not in fields like medicine, technology, and law, of which the principal *raison d'être*[12] is an external social need), the formation of specialized journals, the foundation of specialists' societies, and the claim for a special place in the curriculum have usually been associated with a group's first reception of a single paradigm. At least this was the case between the time, a century and a half ago, when the institutional pattern of scientific specialization first developed and the very recent

years thereafter electricians were divided about whether electricity was a single fluid or two. But the debates on this subject only confirm what has been said above about the manner in which a universally recognized achievement unites the profession. Electricians, though they continued divided on this point, rapidly concluded that no experimental tests could distinguish the two versions of the theory and that they were therefore equivalent. After that, both schools could and did exploit all the benefits that the Franklinian theory provided [Kuhn's note].

11. The history of electricity provides an excellent example which could be duplicated from the careers of Priestley, Kelvin, and others. Franklin reports that Nollet, who at mid-century was the most influential of the Continental electricians, "lived to see himself the last of his Sect, except Mr. B.—his *Eleve* [pupil] and immediate Disciple." More interesting, however, is the endurance of whole schools in increasing isolation from professional science. Consider, for example, the case of astrology, which was once an integral part of astronomy. Or consider the continuation in the late eighteenth and early nineteenth centuries of a previously respected tradition of "romantic" chemistry [Kuhn's note].

12. Reason for being (French).

time when the paraphernalia of specialization acquired a prestige of their own.

The more rigid definition of the scientific group has other consequences. When the individual scientist can take a paradigm for granted, he need no longer, in his major works, attempt to build his field anew, starting from first principles and justifying the use of each concept introduced. That can be left to the writer of textbooks. Given a textbook, however, the creative scientist can begin his research where it leaves off and thus concentrate exclusively upon the subtlest and most esoteric aspects of the natural phenomena that concern his group. And as he does this, his research communiqués will begin to change in ways whose evolution has been too little studied but whose modern end products are obvious to all and oppressive to many. No longer will his researches usually be embodied in books addressed, like Franklin's *Experiments . . . on Electricity* or Darwin's *Origin of Species*, to anyone who might be interested in the subject matter of the field. Instead they will usually appear as brief articles addressed only to professional colleagues, the men whose knowledge of a shared paradigm can be assumed and who prove to be the only ones able to read the papers addressed to them.

Today in the sciences, books are usually either texts or retrospective reflections upon one aspect or another of the scientific life. The scientist who writes one is more likely to find his professional reputation impaired than enhanced. Only in the earlier, pre-paradigm, stages of the development of the various sciences did the book ordinarily possess the same relation to professional achievement that it still retains in other creative fields. And only in those fields that still retain the book, with or without the article, as a vehicle for research communication are the lines of professionalization still so loosely drawn that the layman may hope to follow progress by reading the practitioners' original reports. Both in mathematics and astronomy, research reports had ceased already in antiquity to be intelligible to a generally educated audience. In dynamics, research became similarly esoteric in the latter Middle Ages, and it recaptured general intelligibility only briefly during the early seventeenth century when a new paradigm replaced the one that had guided medieval research. Electrical research began to require translation for the layman before the end of the eighteenth century, and most other fields of physical science ceased to be generally accessible in the nineteenth. During the same two centuries similar transitions can be isolated in the various parts of the biological sciences. In parts of the social sciences they may well be occurring today. Although it has become customary, and is surely proper, to deplore the widening gulf that separates the professional scientist from his colleagues in other fields, too little attention is paid to the essential relationship between that gulf and the mechanisms intrinsic to scientific advance.

Ever since prehistoric antiquity one field of study after another has crossed the divide between what the historian might call its prehistory as a science and its history proper. These transitions to maturity have seldom been so sudden or so unequivocal as my necessarily schematic discussion may have implied. But neither have they been historically gradual, coextensive, that is to say, with the entire development of the fields within which they occurred. Writers on elec-

tricity during the first four decades of the eighteenth century possessed far
more information about electrical phenomena than had their sixteenth-century
predecessors. During the half-century after 1740, few new sorts of electrical
phenomena were added to their lists. Nevertheless, in important respects, the
electrical writings of Cavendish, Coulomb, and Volta[13] in the last third of the
eighteenth century seem further removed from those of Gray, Du Fay, and even
Franklin than are the writings of these early eighteenth-century electrical discoverers from those of the sixteenth century.[14] Sometime between 1740 and
1780, electricians were for the first time enabled to take the foundations of
their field for granted. From that point they pushed on to more concrete and
recondite problems, and increasingly they then reported their results in articles
addressed to other electricians rather than in books addressed to the learned
world at large. As a group they achieved what had been gained by astronomers
in antiquity and by students of motion in the Middle Ages, of physical optics in
the late seventeenth century, and of historical geology in the early nineteenth.
They had, that is, achieved a paradigm that proved able to guide the whole
group's research. Except with the advantage of hindsight, it is hard to find another criterion that so clearly proclaims a field a science.

13. Henry Cavendish (1731–1810), Charles-Augustin de Coulomb (1736–1806), and
Alessandro Giuseppe Antonio Anastasio Volta (1745–1827) made important discoveries
about electricity.
14. The post-Franklinian developments include an immense increase in the sensitivity
of charge detectors, the first reliable and generally diffused techniques for measuring
charge, the evolution of the concept of capacity and its relation to a newly refined notion of electric tension, and the quantification of electrostatic force [Kuhn's note].

QUESTIONS

1. Mark the important terms in this selection from *The Structure of Scientific Revolutions* and Kuhn's definitions of them. How many terms does he illustrate as well as define? Why does he both define and illustrate?

2. What are prevailing paradigms in sciences other than those Kuhn discusses? You
might consider biology, chemistry, psychology, and sociology. Are you aware of older paradigms in these sciences, or have they and the work based on them, as Kuhn says (paragraph 15), disappeared?

3. Without a paradigm, Kuhn writes, "all of the facts that could possibly pertain to the
development of a given science are likely to seem equally relevant" (paragraph 10). What,
according to Edward O. Wilson in "Intelligent Evolution" (p. 1007) or Stephen Jay Gould
in "Darwin's Middle Road" (p, 1018), was the paradigm that enabled Darwin to discriminate among his facts? How can he be said to have made a "scientific revolution"?

DAVID BALTIMORE *Limiting Science:*
A Biologist's Perspective

ONTEMPORARY RESEARCH in molecular biology has grown up in an era of almost complete permissiveness. Its practitioners have been allowed to decide their own priorities and have met with virtually no restraints on the types of work they can do. Viewed as a whole, the field has not even met with fiscal restraints because, relative to "big science," molecular biology has been a relatively cheap enterprise.

Some of the funds that fueled the initial, seminal investigations in molecular biology were granted because of the medical implications of work in basic biology. Most continue to come from agencies concerned with health. Although basic research in biology has yet to have a major impact on the prevention and treatment of human disease, a backlash already seems to be developing in which various groups in our society question whether the freedom that has characteristically been granted to research biologists by a permissive public requires modification. Among the numerous elements prompting this questioning are impatience with the lack of practical results, and fears that direct hazards might result from the experimentation, that basic research may not be an appropriate investment of significant funds, and that dangerous new technologies may flow from discoveries in basic biology. Lay critics as well as a few members of the profession have argued that molecular biologists should concentrate their efforts in certain areas of research, like fertility mechanisms, while other areas, like genetics or aging, are possibly dangerous and certainly not worthy of financial support from the public. These critics believe that they can channel contemporary biology to fit their own conception of appropriate research.

I wish to argue that the traditional pact between society and its scientists, in which the scientist is given the responsibility for determining the direction of his work, is a necessary relationship if basic science is to be an effective endeavor. This does not mean that society is at the mercy of science, but rather that society, while it must determine the pace of basic scientific innovation, should not attempt to prescribe its directions.

What we call molecular biology today had its origins in individual decisions of a small number of scientists during the period from the late 1930s through the early 1950s. These people were trained in diverse fields, among them physics, medicine, microbiology, and crystallography.[1] They created mo-

Written by a Nobel Prize–winning scientist and originally published in Dædalus *(Spring 1978), the professional journal of the American Academy of Arts and Sciences; the Academy re-published the essay in* Dædalus *(Fall 2005).*

1. The science of the formation and structure of crystals.

lecular biology out of the realization that the problems posed by genetics were central to understanding the structures of living systems. No one channeled them towards this line of thinking, no one cajoled them to tackle these problems; rather, their own curiosity and sense of timing led them to try to elucidate these mysteries. This history provides a model of how the most effective science is done.

5   It is partly the successes of molecular biology that have brought on the questioning of whether scientists should be allowed their freedom of decision. It is therefore worthwhile tracing the development of concerns about whether certain areas of science should be closed to investigation. Molecular biology is the science that has revealed to us the nature of one of the most fundamental of all substances of life, the gene. There is a very simple underlying reality to the transmission of characteristics from parents to children: a code based on four different chemicals, denoted by the letters A, T, G, and C,[2] is used to store the information of heredity. The order in which these four chemicals appear in a virtually endless polymer, called DNA,[3] is the language of life.

Knowing that DNA was the physical storehouse of the genes, Watson and Crick in 1953 first solved the problem of how the DNA is organized to assure that information is transferred with almost perfect reliability from parent cells to progeny cells.[4] They showed that DNA is made of two strands intertwined together into a helix and also that the four sub-units in DNA are physically related so that only A and T form a specific pair as do G and C. The two strands are held together by this specific pairing so that the two strands carry redundant information. Each gene is thus really a gene and a mirror-gene; this self-complementarity allows DNA to repair itself—and therefore maintain the fidelity of its information—and also to duplicate itself, sending identical copies into the two daughter cells resulting from a round of cell division.

Following the monumental discovery of the structure of DNA, many scientists have contributed to learning how to make DNA, how to read DNA, how to cut DNA, how to rejoin DNA, and in general, how to manipulate at will the genes of very simple organisms.

What good has all of this new knowledge brought to the average person? First and of great importance is the contribution that scientific advances make to human culture. The continued accumulation of knowledge about ourselves and our environment is a crucial cultural aspect of contemporary life. Science as well as art illuminates man's view of himself and his relation to others. Our knowledge of how we work, how one person differs from and is similar to another, what is health and what disease, what we need to support health, and so

2. Short for adenine, thymine, guanine, cytosine, the main four substances that make up DNA and RNA.

3. Polymer: a molecule that comprises many repeating units; DNA: Deoxyribonucleic acid, which contains genetic information that determines the characteristics of living organisms.

4. James Watson (b. 1928) and Francis Crick (1916–2004), discoverers of DNA's double-helix structure. Parent cells are the units of life that, in cell division, create progeny cells.

on, helps to set the ground rules for the debates of politics and the productions of art.

The more practical benefits of biology can be expected to come in the future in the form of medical advances, or increases in food production, or in other manipulations of life processes that will be able to provide positive contributions to civilization. But molecular biology, for all of its power as a basic science, has not been easily translated into tangible benefits. This is a situation that could change very soon. New discoveries are rapidly bringing molecular biology closer to an ability to affect the lives of the general public.

Of the advances that have occurred, a critical one has been the development 10 of a process called recombinant DNA research. This is a technique whereby different pieces of DNA are sewn together using enzymes;[5] the chimeric DNA is then inserted into a bacterium where it can be multiplied indefinitely. Because the method allows genes from any species in the world to be put into a common type of bacterium, there is a theoretical possibility of hazard in this research. The potential for unforeseen occurrences led a number of scientists, including me, to issue in 1974 a call for restraint in the application of these new methods. We were addressing a limited problem, whether there could be a recognizable hazard in the performance of certain experiments. That limited question opened a floodgate; other questions came pouring out and are still coming. They have led to front-cover stories in weekly magazines, to serious attempts at federal legislation, to a demoralization of some of the community of basic research biologists, and, most significantly, to a deep questioning of whether further advances in biology are likely to be beneficial or harmful to our society.

Much of the discussion about recombinant DNA research has centered on whether the work is likely to create hazardous organisms. The mayor of Cambridge, Massachusetts, raised the specter of Frankenstein monsters emerging from MIT and Harvard laboratories, and speculations about the possibility of inadvertent development of a destructive organism like the fictitious Andromeda Strain have been much in the news.[6] I am personally satisfied that most of such talk is simply science fiction and that the research can be made as safe as any other research. The people who understand infectious diseases best make the arguments most strongly that recombinant DNA research is not going to create monsters. But rather than defend my judgment that the safety issue has been blown out of proportion, I want to consider some of the more general issues that have been raised by the controversy.

If safety were the most important consideration behind the debate about recombinant DNA, then we might expect the debate to focus on the hazards of

5. Proteins that facilitate chemical reactions.
6. In Mary Shelley's 1818 novel, *Frankenstein*, Dr. Frankenstein creates a terrifying, not-quite-human monster through scientific manipulation; in *The Andromeda Strain*, Michael Crichton's 1969 science fiction novel, an extraterrestrial disease causes fatal blood clots.

doing recombinant DNA experiments. Instead, many of the discussions that start considering such questions soon turn to a consideration of genetic engineering.

Two techniques labeled genetic engineering exist. Both originated because not everybody's genes are perfectly designed for the job of being a functioning human being, so that many instances of blood disorders, mental problems, and a host of other disabilities are traceable to a malfunctioning gene. It would be a triumph of medicine if the effects of such genes could be countered, and two approaches for countering them have been considered, both of which are called genetic engineering. One approach involves altering some cells of the body so that they can carry out the needed function. A patient could, for instance, be treated in this way for a blood disease caused by an abnormal protein made by a mutant gene. A normal gene would be inserted into the precursor cells—immature bone marrow cells that ultimately develop into functioning blood cells. In this way, a normal protein could be made in place of, or along with, the aberrant protein. The genetically altered blood cell precursor could then cure the patient's disease. But the malfunctioning gene would still be transmitted to the patient's offspring. Because this form of genetic engineering would not change the gene pool of the species and because it may prove an effective medical treatment of disease, it does not present the same moral problem as the other form. It is likely to be the first type of genetic engineering tried on human beings, and might be tried within the next five years.

The second type of genetic engineering presents more of a dilemma because it could change the human gene pool. This would involve replacement of genes in the germ cells, cells that transmit their genes to our offspring. Such a change would represent a permanent alteration of the types of the genetic information that constitutes our species. Replacement of germ cell genes would be very difficult and is, I suspect, at least twenty years away. It presents no theoretical problems, only formidable logistic problems.

15   Both forms of genetic engineering, but especially the engineering of germ cells, present two very deep and perplexing problems: who is to decide, and how shall they decide what genes are malfunctional? Decisions about which genes are good and which bad truly represent decisions of morality and are therefore highly subjective. Fear that dictators will decide which genes should be suppressed and which promoted, and that their criteria for decision will be how best to maintain their own power, has made the phrase "genetic engineering" symbolic of the moral problems that can be created by modern biology.

Genetic engineering of human beings is not the same as recombinant DNA research. Genetic engineering is a process carried out on human beings; recombinant DNA methods are ways to purify genes. Such genes might be used in genetic engineering procedures but are much more likely to be used as tools in studies of biological organization or as elements in a biological manufacturing process. Although genetic engineering is not the same as recombinant DNA research, the two are rightly linked because recombinant DNA work is hastening the day when genetic engineering will be a feasible process for use on certain human diseases. Since recombinant DNA work is also bringing closer the discovery of many other possible new medical treatments, and is likely to bring other new capabilities, why is there so much focus on genetic engineering? I believe that genetic engineering, because of its tabloid appeal, has become a symbol to many people of the frightening potential of modern-day technology. Rather than seeing in molecular biology the same complex mixtures of appropriate and inappropriate applications that characterize all powerful sciences, many people have allowed the single negative catch phrase "genetic engineering" to dominate discussions. People worry that if the possibility of curing a genetic defect by gene therapy should ever become a reality, the inevitable result would be "people made to order." It is argued that unless we block recombinant DNA research now, we will never have another chance to control our fate.

To see the form of the argument against recombinant DNA research most clearly and to highlight its danger to intellectual freedom and creativity, we should realize that similar arguments have been put forward relative to other areas of basic biology. One of the most respected critics of recombinant DNA research, Robert Sinsheimer, has for instance, made comparable analyses of two other research topics, research on aging and attempts to contact extraterrestrial beings.[7] He argues that if research on aging were to be successful, people could live to much older ages and the changed age structure of the population would bring serious stresses to society. His fear about searching for extraterrestrial beings is, again, that we could be successful, and he considers that the discovery of civilizations much more advanced than ours would have effects on us like those the Europeans had on native Americans after the discovery of the New World. In the case of recombinant DNA research as well as the other topics, Dr. Sinsheimer says we should avoid studying these areas of science. Rather, he believes, we should put our resources into investigating areas of proven need, such as fertility control.

These examples—and I could choose many others, especially outside of biology—have the same general form: certain people believe that there are areas of research that should be taboo because their outcome might be, or in some scenarios will be, detrimental to the stable relationships that characterize contemporary society. I have heard the argument in a different and more pernicious form from members of a Boston area group called Science for the People. They argue that some research in genetics should not go on because its findings might be detrimental to the relationships they believe should characterize a just society. Such arguments are reminiscent of those surrounding the eugenics[8] movements that developed in Germany and Russia in the 1920s.

7. R. L. Sinsheimer, "Inquiry to Inquiry: Two Opposing Views," *The Hastings Center Report* 6 (4) (1976): 18 [Baltimore's note].

8. A philosophy (or program) advocating the adjustment or improvement of inherited human traits through genetic manipulation.

After a period of intense debate, these countries with opposing ideologies settled on opposing analyses of the role of genetics in determining human diversity.[9] German scientists and politicians espoused a theory of racial purification by selective breeding, while Russia accepted the Lamarckian principle of transmission of acquired characteristics.[10] In both cases, science was forced into a mold created by political and social ideology, and in both cases the results were disastrous.

As I see it, we are being faced today with the following question: should limits be placed on biological research because of the danger that new knowledge can present to the established or desired order of our society? Having thus posed the question, I believe that there are two simple, and almost universally applicable, answers. First, the criteria determining what areas to restrain inevitably express certain sociopolitical attitudes that reflect a dominant ideology. Such criteria cannot be allowed to guide scientific choices. Second, attempts to restrain directions of scientific inquiry are more likely to be generally disruptive of science than to provide the desired specific restraints. These answers to the question of whether limits should be imposed can be stated in two arguments. One is that science should not be the servant of ideology, because ideology assumes answers, but science asks questions. The other is that attempts to make science serve ideology will merely make science impotent without assuring that only desired questions are investigated. I am stating simply that we should not control the direction of science and, moreover, that we cannot do so with any precision.

20   Before trying to substantiate these arguments I must make a crucial distinction. The arguments pertain to basic scientific research, not to the technological applications of science. As we go from the fundamental to the applied, my arguments fall away. There is every reason why technology should and must serve specific needs. Conversely, there are many technological possibilities that ought to be restrained.

To return to basic research, let me first consider the danger of restricting types of investigation because their outcome could be disruptive to society. There are three aspects of danger. One is the fallacy that you can predict what society will be like even in the near future. To say, for instance, that it would be bad for Americans to live longer assumes that the birth rate will stay near where it is. But what happens if the birth rate falls even lower than it is now in the United States and also stabilizes elsewhere in the world? We might welcome a readjustment of the life span. In any case, we have built a world around a given human life span; we could certainly adjust to a longer span, and it would be hard to predict whether in the long run the results would be better or worse.

9. L. R. Graham, "Political Ideology and Genetic Theory: Russia and Germany in the 1920's," *The Hastings Center Report* 7 (5) (1977): 30–39 [Baltimore's note].

10. Based on the philosophy of Jean-Baptiste Pierre Antoine de Monet, Chevalier de Lamarck (1744–1829), who believed that living creatures could inherit acquired traits.

In a general form, I would call this argument for restricting research the Error of Futurism. The futurist believes that the present holds enough readable clues about the future to provide a good basis for prediction. I doubt this assumption; to think that the data of today can be analyzed well enough to predict the future with any accuracy seems nonsensical to me.

The second danger in restricting areas of scientific investigation is more crucial: although we often worry most about keeping society stable, in fact societies need certain kinds of upheaval and renewal to stay vital. The new ideas and insights of science, much as we may fight against them, provide an important part of the renewal process that maintains the fascination of life. Freedom is the range of opportunities available to an individual—the more he has to choose from, the freer his choice. Science creates freedom by widening our range of understanding and therefore the possibilities from which we can choose.

Finally, attempts to dictate scientific limits on political or social considerations have another disastrous implication. Scientific orthodoxy is usually dictated by the state when its leaders fear that truths could undermine their power. Their repressive dicta are interpreted by the citizens as an admission of the leaders' insecurity and may thus lead to unrest requiring further repression. A social system that leaves science free to explore, and encourages scientific discoveries rather than trying to make science serve it by producing the truths necessary for its stability, transmits to the members of that society strength, not fear, and can endure.

The other argument I mentioned in opposing imposition of orthodoxy on science is the practical impossibility of stopping selected areas of research. Take aging as a prime example. It is one of the mystery areas of modern biology. The questions are clear. Why do we get older? Why do organ systems slowly fail? Why does one species of animal live three years and another live for one hundred? These seemingly straightforward questions are unapproachably difficult for modern biology. Not only can we not understand events that occur over years, but we even have difficulty understanding questions about events that require minutes to transpire. In fact, molecular biologists are really only experts in the millisecond range of time. Such times are those of chemical reactions; to understand events in longer time frames probably requires knowing how individual reactions are integrated to produce clocks that measure time in seconds to years. Clues to the great mysteries of biology—memory, aging, and differentiation—lie in understanding how biological systems tell time.

There are a few hints about where answers to the puzzle of aging might be found, but they are only the vaguest suggestions. In such an area of science, history tells us that successes are likely to come from unpredictable directions. A scientist working on vitamins or viruses or even plants is just as likely to find a clue to the problem of aging as is a scientist working on the problem directly. In fact, someone outside the field is more likely to make a revolutionary discovery than someone inside the field.

Another example will help to show the generality of this contention. Imag-

25

ine that we were living at the turn of the last century and had wanted to help medical diagnosis by devising a method of seeing into the insides of people. We would probably have decided to fund medical scientists to learn how to use bright lights to see through patients' skin. Little would we have guessed that the solution would be revolutionary and would come, not from a medical research scientist, but from a physicist who would discover a new form of radiation, X-rays.[11]

Major breakthroughs cannot be programmed. They come from people and areas of research that are not predictable. So if you wanted to cut off an area of fundamental research, how would you be able to devise the controls? I contend that it would be impossible. You could close the National Institute of Aging Research, but I doubt that any major advance in that field *could* be prevented. Only the shutdown of all scientific research can guarantee such an outcome.

Although they would fail to produce their desired result, attempts explicitly to control the directions of basic research would hardly be benign. Instead, disruption and demoralization would follow from attempts to determine when a scientist was doing work in approved directions and when he was not. Creative people would shun whole areas of science if they knew that in those areas their creativity would be channeled, judged, and limited. The net effect of constraining biologists to approved lines of investigation would be to degrade the effectiveness of the whole science of biology.

30   Put this way, the penalty for trying to control lines of investigation seems to me greater than any conceivable benefit. I conclude that society can choose to have either more science or less science, but choosing *which* science to have is not a feasible alternative.

I must repeat a qualification of this broad generalization: the less basic the research area in which controls are imposed, the less general disruption will be caused by the controls. The development of a specific sweetener, pesticide, or weapon could be prevented with little generalized effect.

While it seems necessary that scientific research be free of overt restraints, it would be naive to think that science is not directed at all. Many crucial decisions are made about general directions of science, usually by the control of available resources. Again, the formula I used before is applicable: the less basic the area of research, the easier it is to target the problems. A fallacy behind some of the hopes for the "War on Cancer" was the assumption that the problems to be solved were sufficiently well defined to allow a targeted, applied approach to the disease. Some problems could be defined and those were appropriate targets for a war on the disease, but the deeper mysteries of cancer are so close to the frontiers of biology that targets are hard to discern.

I have painted a picture of inexorable, uncontrollable development of basic scientific knowledge. The response of many people to such a vision might well

11. Dr. Mahlon Hoagland first suggested to me this example [Baltimore's note].

be "If we can't put any controls on research, maybe we shouldn't have any research." I see the rationale in this criticism because it is conceivable that the rate of accretion of knowledge could become so high that a brake might be needed. A way exists to produce a slowdown, that is, by controlling the overall availability of resources. A nonselective brake on fundamental biology would decrease productivity without the disruptive and dangerous effects of trying to halt one area and advance another.

Because such a brake was applied in the late 1960s, today we have less basic research, measured in constant dollars spent on it, than we had then. As a result of the slowdown, the danger seen by many is not that we have too much basic research, but rather that we are living on our intellectual capital and that an infusion of funds into basic areas of research is needed before these scientific resources are exhausted. It must also be realized that our commitment to the solution of problems like cancer requires that we develop much more basic knowledge.

I may seem to have strayed from my topic of recombinant DNA research, but I think not. In 1977, there was a draft bill in the U.S. Senate to set up a National Commission on Recombinant DNA Research. The charge to this commission discussed mainly questions of safety, but at the end of the bill questions of ethics and morality entered. The bill was a clear invitation to begin the process of deciding what research shall be allowed and what research prevented. The battle to stop the creation of this commission was waged by scientists, university presidents, and other concerned individuals across the country. I believe that the long-term success or failure of these efforts will determine whether America continues to have a tradition of free inquiry into matters of science or falls under the fist of orthodoxy.

To finish this discussion, let me quote from the most eloquent analyst of contemporary biology, Lewis Thomas,[12] the president of the Memorial Sloan-Kettering Cancer Center in New York. Writing in the *New England Journal of Medicine* about the recombinant DNA issue, Dr. Thomas ended with this analysis of the role of scientific research in the life of the mind:

> Is there something fundamentally unnatural, or intrinsically wrong, or hazardous for the species, in the ambition that drives us all to reach a comprehensive understanding of nature, including ourselves? I cannot believe it. It would seem to me a more unnatural thing, and more of an offense against nature, for us to come on the same scene endowed as we are with curiosity, filled to overbrimming as we are with questions, and naturally talented as we are for the asking of clear questions, and then for us to do nothing about it, or worse, to try to suppress the questions. This is the greater danger for our species, to try to pretend that we are another kind of animal, that we do not need to satisfy our curiosity, exploration, and experimentation, and that the human mind can rise above its ignorance by simply asserting that there are things it has no need to know.[13]

35

---

12. American physician, educator, and science writer (1913–1993).

13. Lewis Thomas in the *New England Journal of Medicine* 296 (1977): 328 [Baltimore's note].

QUESTIONS

1. David Baltimore argues that scientists must have the freedom to pursue their research without governmental or societal interference. Where does he state this argument? What function does the paragraph preceding it have?

2. Why does Baltimore give a history of the discovery of DNA? What evidence does that history supply in support of his argument?

3. Midway through his argument, Baltimore acknowledges the difficulties that genetic engineering raises. Why does he describe two different forms of genetic engineering? What careful distinctions does he make between them—and why?

4. Write an essay in which you support or disagree with Baltimore's argument, in terms of contemporary issues in biological research. Incorporate, as Baltimore does, definitions and careful distinctions as you support your position.

MATT RIDLEY   *Genome*

> All forms that perish other forms supply,
> (By turns we catch the vital breath and die)
> Like bubbles on the sea of matter borne,
> They rise, they break, and to that sea return.
>   —ALEXANDER POPE,
>   *An Essay on Man*

IN THE BEGINNING was the word. The word proselytized the sea with its message, copying itself unceasingly and forever. The word discovered how to rearrange chemicals so as to capture little eddies in the stream of entropy and make them live. The word transformed the land surface of the planet from a dusty hell to a verdant paradise. The word eventually blossomed and became sufficiently ingenious to build a porridgy contraption called a human brain that could discover and be aware of the word itself.

My porridgy contraption boggles every time I think this thought. In four thousand million years of earth history, I am lucky enough to be alive today. In five million species, I was fortunate enough to be born a conscious human being. Among six thousand million people on the planet, I was privileged enough to be born in the country where the word was discovered. In all of the earth's history, biology and geography, I was born just five years after the moment when, and just two hundred miles from the place where, two

Published as the first chapter of Genome: The Autobiography of a Species in Twenty-Three Chapters *(2000).*

1. Deoxyribonucleic acid, which contains genetic information that determines characteristics of living organisms.

members of my own species discovered the structure of DNA[1] and hence uncovered the greatest, simplest and most surprising secret in the universe. Mock my zeal if you wish; consider me a ridiculous materialist for investing such enthusiasm in an acronym. But follow me on a journey back to the very origin of life, and I hope I can convince you of the immense fascination of the word.

"As the earth and ocean were probably peopled with vegetable productions long before the existence of animals; and many families of these animals long before the other families of them, shall we conjecture that one and the same kind of living filaments is and has been the cause of all organic life?" asked the polymathic poet and physician Erasmus Darwin in 1794.[2] It was a startling guess for the time, not only in its bold conjecture that all organic life shared the same origin, sixty-five years before his grandson Charles' book on the topic, but for its weird use of the word "filaments." The secret of life is indeed a thread.

Yet how can a filament make something live? Life is a slippery thing to define, but it consists of two very different skills: the ability to replicate, and the ability to create order. Living things produce approximate copies of themselves: rabbits produce rabbits, dandelions make dandelions. But rabbits do more than that. They eat grass, transform it into rabbit flesh and somehow build bodies of order and complexity from the random chaos of the world. They do not defy the second law of thermodynamics, which says that in a closed system everything tends from order towards disorder, because rabbits are not closed systems. Rabbits build packets of order and complexity called bodies but at the cost of expending large amounts of energy. In Erwin Schrödinger's phrase,[3] living creatures "drink orderliness" from the environment.

The key to both of these features of life is information. The ability to replicate is made possible by the existence of a recipe, the information that is needed to create a new body. A rabbit's egg carries the instructions for assembling a new rabbit. But the ability to create order through metabolism also depends on information—the instructions for building and maintaining the equipment that creates the order. An adult rabbit, with its ability to both reproduce and metabolize, is prefigured and presupposed in its living filaments in the same way that a cake is prefigured and presupposed in its recipe. This is an idea that goes right back to Aristotle, who said that the "concept" of a chicken is implicit in an egg, or that an acorn was literally "informed" by the plan of an oak tree. When Aristotle's dim perception of information theory,[4] buried under generations of chemistry and physics, re-emerged amid the discoveries of modern genetics, Max Delbruck joked that

5

---

2. Darwin, E. (1794). *Zoonomia: or the laws of organic life.* Vol. II, p. 244. Third edition (1801). J. Johnson, London [Ridley's note]. "Polymathic": having many interests and abilities. Erasmus Darwin (1731–1802), grandfather of Charles Darwin (1809–1882), theorized that living creatures evolve through natural selection.

3. Austrian physicist (1887–1961).

4. Aristotle (c. 384–322 B.C.E.), ancient Greek philosopher and teacher. "Information theory": relates to the possibilities and problems involved in data transmission.

the Greek sage should be given a posthumous Nobel prize for the discovery of DNA.[5]

The filament of DNA is information, a message written in a code of chemicals, one chemical for each letter. It is almost too good to be true, but the code turns out to be written in a way that we can understand. Just like written English, the genetic code is a linear language, written in a straight line. Just like written English, it is digital, in that every letter bears the same importance. Moreover, the language of DNA is considerably simpler than English, since it has an alphabet of only four letters, conventionally known as A, C, G and T.[6]

Now that we know that genes are coded recipes, it is hard to recall how few people even guessed such a possibility. For the first half of the twentieth century, one question reverberated unanswered through biology: what is a gene? It seemed almost impossibly mysterious. Go back not to 1953, the year of the discovery of DNA's symmetrical structure, but ten years further, to 1943. Those who will do most to crack the mystery, a whole decade later, are working on other things in 1943. Francis Crick[7] is working on the design of naval mines near Portsmouth. At the same time James Watson is just enrolling as an undergraduate at the precocious age of fifteen at the University of Chicago; he is determined to devote his life to ornithology. Maurice Wilkins is helping to design the atom bomb in the United States. Rosalind Franklin is studying the structure of coal for the British government.[8]

In Auschwitz in 1943, Josef Mengele[9] is torturing twins to death in a grotesque parody of scientific inquiry. Mengele is trying to understand heredity, but his eugenics[10] proves not to be the path to enlightenment. Mengele's results will be useless to future scientists.

In Dublin in 1943, a refugee from Mengele and his ilk, the great physicist Erwin Schrödinger is embarking on a series of lectures at Trinity College entitled "What is life?" He is trying to define a problem. He knows that chromosomes contain the secret of life, but he cannot understand how: "It is these chromosomes . . . that contain in some kind of code-script the entire pattern of the individual's future development and of its functioning in the mature state." The gene, he says, is too small to be anything other than a large mole-

5. Campbell, J. (1983). *Grammatical man: information, entropy, language and life.* Allen Lane, London [Ridley's note]. Max Delbruck (1906–1981), German-Austrian physicist.

6. Short for adenine, cytosine, thymine, guanine; four of the main substances that make up DNA and RNA.

7. British co-discoverer (1916–2004), with James Watson (b. 1928), of the structure of DNA.

8. Maurice Wilkins (1916–2004), New Zealand-born physicist; Rosalind Franklin (1920–1958), British chemist and crystallographer, also discovered the structure of DNA.

9. German physician and SS officer (1911–1979), employed at Auschwitz, a German death camp during World War II.

10. A philosophy (or program) advocating the adjustment or improvement of inherited human traits through genetic manipulation.

cule, an insight that will inspire a generation of scientists, including Crick, Watson, Wilkins and Franklin, to tackle what suddenly seems like a tractable problem. Having thus come tantalizingly close to the answer, though, Schrödinger veers off track. He thinks that the secret of this molecule's ability to carry heredity lies in his beloved quantum theory,[11] and is pursuing that obsession down what will prove to be a blind alley. The secret of life has nothing to do with quantum states. The answer will not come from physics.[12]

In New York in 1943, a sixty-six-year-old Canadian scientist, Oswald Avery, is putting the finishing touches to an experiment that will decisively identify DNA as the chemical manifestation of heredity. He has proved in a series of ingenious experiments that a pneumonia bacterium can be transformed from a harmless to a virulent strain merely by absorbing a simple chemical solution. By 1943, Avery has concluded that the transforming substance, once purified, is DNA. But he will couch his conclusions in such cautious language for publication that few will take notice until much later. In a letter to his brother Roy written in May 1943, Avery is only slightly less cautious:[13]

> If we are right, and of course that's not yet proven, then it means that nucleic acids [DNA] are not merely structurally important but functionally active substances in determining the biochemical activities and specific characteristics of cells—and that by means of a known chemical substance it is possible to induce predictable and hereditary changes in cells. That is something that has long been the dream of geneticists.

Avery is almost there, but he is still thinking along chemical lines. "All life is chemistry," said Jan Baptista van Helmont in 1648, guessing. At least some life is chemistry, said Friedrich Wöhler in 1828[14] after synthesizing urea from ammonium chloride and silver cyanide, thus breaking the hitherto sacrosanct divide between the chemical and biological worlds: urea was something that only living things had produced before. That life is chemistry is true but boring, like saying that football is physics. Life, to a rough approximation, consists of the chemistry of three atoms, hydrogen, carbon and oxygen, which between them make up ninety-eight per cent of all atoms in living beings. But it is the emergent properties of life—such as heritability—not the constituent parts that are interesting. Avery cannot conceive what it is about DNA that enables it to hold the secret of heritable properties. The answer will not come from chemistry.

In Bletchley, in Britain, in 1943, in total secrecy, a brilliant mathematician, Alan Turing,[15] is seeing his most incisive insight turned into physical re-

11. A theory of physics that surpasses the limitations of classical mechanics.

12. Schrödinger, E. (1967). *What is life? Mind and matter.* Cambridge University Press, Cambridge [Ridley's note].

13. Quoted in Judson, H. F. (1979). *The eighth day of creation.* Jonathan Cape, London [Ridley's note].

14. Jan Baptista van Helmont (1577–1644), Flemish physician, chemist, and physiologist; Friedrich Wöhler (1800–1882), German chemist.

15. British cryptographer, mathematician, and logician (1912–1954).

ality. Turing has argued that numbers can compute numbers. To crack the Lorentz encoding machines[16] of the German forces, a computer called Colossus has been built based on Turing's principles: it is a universal machine with a modifiable stored program. Nobody realizes it at the time, least of all Turing, but he is probably closer to the mystery of life than anybody else. Heredity is a modifiable stored program; metabolism is a universal machine. The recipe that links them is a code, an abstract message that can be embodied in a chemical, physical or even immaterial form. Its secret is that it can cause itself to be replicated. Anything that can use the resources of the world to get copies of itself made is alive; the most likely form for such a thing to take is a digital message—a number, a script or a word.[17]

In New Jersey in 1943, a quiet, reclusive scholar named Claude Shannon[18] is ruminating about an idea he had first had at Princeton a few years earlier. Shannon's idea is that information and entropy are opposite faces of the same coin and that both have an intimate link with energy. The less entropy a system has, the more information it contains. The reason a steam engine can harness the energy from burning coal and turn it into rotary motion is because the engine has high information content—information injected into it by its designer. So does a human body. Aristotle's information theory meets Newton's physics in Shannon's brain. Like Turing, Shannon has no thoughts about biology. But his insight is of more relevance to the question of what is life than a mountain of chemistry and physics. Life, too, is digital information written in DNA.[19]

In the beginning was the word. The word was not DNA. That came afterwards, when life was already established, and when it had divided the labor between two separate activities: chemical work and information storage, metabolism and replication. But DNA contains a record of the word, faithfully transmitted through all subsequent aeons to the astonishing present.

Imagine the nucleus of human egg beneath the microscope. Arrange the twenty-three chromosomes, if you can, in order of size, the biggest on the left and the smallest on the right. Now zoom in on the largest chromosome, the one called, for purely arbitrary reasons, chromosome 1. Every chromosome has a long arm and a short arm separated by a pinch point known as a centromere. On the long arm of chromosome 1, close to the centromere, you will find, if you read it carefully, that there is a sequence of 120 letters—As, Cs, Gs and Ts—that repeats over and over again. Between each repeat there lies a stretch of more random text, but the 120-letter paragraph keeps coming back like a familiar theme tune, in all more than 100 times. This short paragraph is perhaps as close as we can get to an echo of the original word.

15   This "paragraph" is a small gene, probably the single most active gene in

16. German cipher machines used during World War II.

17. Hodges, A. (1997). *Turing*. Phoenix, London [Ridley's note].

18. American engineer and mathematician (1916–2001).

19. Campbell, J. (1983). *Grammatical man: information, entropy, language and life*. Allen Lane, London [Ridley's note].

the human body. Its 120 letters are constantly being copied into a short filament of RNA.[20] The copy is known as 5S RNA. It sets up residence with a lump of proteins and other RNAs, carefully intertwined, in a ribosome, a machine whose job is to translate DNA recipes into proteins. And it is proteins that enable DNA to replicate. To paraphrase Samuel Butler,[21] a protein is just a gene's way of making another gene; and a gene is just a protein's way of making another protein. Cooks need recipes, but recipes also need cooks. Life consists of the interplay of two kinds of chemicals: proteins and DNA.

Protein represents chemistry, living, breathing, metabolism and behaviour—what biologists call the phenotype. DNA represents information, replication, breeding, sex—what biologists call the genotype. Neither can exist without the other. It is the classic case of chicken and egg: which came first, DNA or protein? It cannot have been DNA, because DNA is a helpless, passive piece of mathematics, which catalyzes no chemical reactions. It cannot have been protein, because protein is pure chemistry with no known way of copying itself accurately. It seems impossible either that DNA invented protein or vice versa. This might have remained a baffling and strange conundrum had not the word left a trace of itself faintly drawn on the filament of life. Just as we now know that eggs came long before chickens (the reptilian ancestors of all birds laid eggs), so there is growing evidence that RNA came before proteins.

RNA is a chemical substance that links the two worlds of DNA and protein. It is used mainly in the translation of the message from the alphabet of DNA to the alphabet of proteins. But in the way it behaves, it leaves little doubt that it is the ancestor of both. RNA was Greece to DNA's Rome: Homer to her Virgil.[22]

RNA was the word. RNA left behind five little clues to its priority over both protein and DNA. Even today, the ingredients of DNA are made by modifying the ingredients of RNA, not by a more direct route. Also DNA's letter Ts are made from RNA's letter Us. Many modern enzymes, though made of protein, rely on small molecules of RNA to make them work. Moreover, RNA, unlike DNA and protein, can copy itself without assistance: give it the right ingredients and it will stitch them together into a message. Wherever you look in the cell, the most primitive and basic functions require the presence of RNA. It is an RNA-dependent enzyme that takes the message, made of RNA, from the gene. It is an RNA-containing machine, the ribosome, that translates that message, and it is a little RNA molecule that fetches and carries the amino acids for the translation of the gene's message. But above all, RNA— unlike DNA—can act as a catalyst, breaking up and joining other molecules including RNAs themselves. It can cut them up, join the ends together, make some of its own building blocks, and elongate a chain of RNA. It can even op-

20. Ribonucleic acid, which enables the translation of genes into proteins.
21. Novelist, satirist, and popularizer of Lamarckian evolutionary theory (1835–1902).
22. Homer (prob. eighth c. B.C.E.), Greek epic poet; Virgil (70–19 B.C.E.), Roman epic poet.

erate on itself, cutting out a chunk of text and splicing the free ends together again.[23]

The discovery of these remarkable properties of RNA in the early 1980s, made by Thomas Cech and Sidney Altman,[24] transformed our understanding of the origin of life. It now seems probable that the very first gene, the "ur-gene," was a combined replicator—catalyst, a word that consumed the chemicals around it to duplicate itself. It may well have been made of RNA. By repeatedly selecting random RNA molecules in the test tube based on their ability to catalyze reactions, it is possible to "evolve" catalytic RNAs from scratch—almost to rerun the origin of life. And one of the most surprising results is that these synthetic RNAs often end up with a stretch of RNA text that reads remarkably like part of the text of a ribosomal RNA gene such as the 5S gene on chromosome 1.

20   Back before the first dinosaurs, before the first fishes, before the first worms, before the first plants, before the first fungi, before the first bacteria, there was an RNA world—probably somewhere around four billion years ago, soon after the beginning of planet earth's very existence and when the universe itself was only ten billion years old. We do not know what these "ribo-organisms" looked like. We can only guess at what they did for a living, chemically speaking. We do not know what came before them. We can be pretty sure that they once existed, because of the clues to RNA's role that survive in living organisms today.[25]

These ribo-organisms had a big problem. RNA is an unstable substance, which falls apart within hours. Had these organisms ventured anywhere hot, or tried to grow too large, they would have faced what geneticists call an error catastrophe—a rapid decay of the message in their genes. One of them invented by trial and error a new and tougher version of RNA called DNA and a system for making RNA copies from it, including a machine we'll call the proto-ribosome. It had to work fast and it had to be accurate. So it stitched together genetic copies three letters at a time, the better to be fast and accurate. Each threesome came flagged with a tag to make it easier for the proto-ribosome to find, a tag that was made of amino acid. Much later, those tags themselves became joined together to make proteins and the three-letter word became a form of code for the proteins—the genetic code itself. (Hence to this day, the genetic code consists of three-letter words, each spelling out a particular one of twenty amino acids as part of a recipe for a protein.) And so was born a more sophisticated creature that stored its genetic recipe on DNA, made its working machines of protein and used RNA to bridge the gap between them.

23. Joyce, G. F. (1989). RNA evolution and the origins of life. *Nature* 338: 217–24; Unrau, P. J. and Bartel, D. P. (1998). RNA-catalysed nucleotide sythesis. *Nature* 395 260–63 [Ridley's note].

24. Thomas Cech (b. 1947), American chemist, and Sidney Altman (b. 1939), Canadian-born Yale molecular biologist, won the 1989 Nobel Prize for their work on DNA.

25. Gesteland, R. F. and Atkins, J. F. (eds) (1993). *The RNA world.* Cold Spring Harbor Laboratory Press, Cold Spring Harbor, New York [Ridley's note].

Her name was Luca, the Last Universal Common Ancestor. What did she look like, and where did she live? The conventional answer is that she looked like a bacterium and she lived in a warm pond, possibly by a hot spring, or in a marine lagoon. In the last few years it has been fashionable to give her a more sinister address, since it became clear that the rocks beneath the land and sea are impregnated with billions of chemical-fueled bacteria. Luca is now usually placed deep underground, in a fissure in hot igneous rocks, where she fed on sulphur, iron, hydrogen and carbon. To this day, the surface life on earth is but a veneer. Perhaps ten times as much organic carbon as exists in the whole biosphere is in thermophilic bacteria deep beneath the surface, where they are possibly responsible for generating what we call natural gas.[26]

There is, however, a conceptual difficulty about trying to identify the earliest forms of life. These days it is impossible for most creatures to acquire genes except from their parents, but that may not always have been so. Even today, bacteria can acquire genes from other bacteria merely by ingesting them. There might once have been widespread trade, even burglary, of genes. In the deep past chromosomes were probably numerous and short, containing just one gene each, which could be lost or gained quite easily. If this was so, Carl Woese[27] points out, the organism was not yet an enduring entity. It was a temporary team of genes. The genes that ended up in all of us may therefore have come from lots of different "species" of creature and it is futile to try to sort them into different lineages. We are descended not from one ancestral Luca, but from the whole community of genetic organisms. Life, says Woese, has a physical history, but not a genealogical one.[28]

You can look on such a conclusion as a fuzzy piece of comforting, holistic, communitarian philosophy—we are all descended from society, not from an individual species—or you can see it as the ultimate proof of the theory of the selfish gene: in those days, even more than today, the war was carried on between genes, using organisms as temporary chariots and forming only transient alliances; today it is more of a team game. Take your pick.

Even if there were lots of Lucas, we can still speculate about where they lived and what they did for a living. This is where the second problem with the thermophilic bacteria arises. Thanks to some brilliant detective work by three New Zealanders published in 1998, we can suddenly glimpse the possibility that the tree of life, as it appears in virtually every textbook, may be upside down. Those books assert that the first creatures were like bacteria, simple cells with single copies of circular chromosomes, and that all other living things came about when teams of bacteria ganged together to make complex cells. It may much more plausibly be the exact reverse. The very first modern

25

26. Gold, T. (1992). The deep, hot biosphere. *Proceedings of the National Academy of Sciences of the USA* 89: 6045–49; Gold, T. (1997). An unexplored habitat for life in the universe? *American Scientist* 84: 408–11. [Ridley's note].

27. American microbiologist (b. 1928).

28. Woese, C. (1998). The universal ancestor. *Proceedings of the National Academy of Sciences of the USA* 95: 6854–9 [Ridley's note].

organisms were not like bacteria; they did not live in hot springs or deep-sea volcanic vents. They were much more like protozoa: with genomes fragmented into several linear chromosomes rather than one circular one, and "polypoid"—that is, with several spare copies of every gene to help with the correction of spelling errors. Moreover, they would have liked cool climates. As Patrick Forterre[29] has long argued, it now looks as if bacteria came later, highly specialized and simplified descendants of the Lucas, long after the invention of the DNA-protein world. Their trick was to drop much of the equipment of the RNA world specifically to enable them to live in hot places. It is we that have retained the primitive molecular features of the Lucas in our cells; bacteria are much more "highly evolved" than we are.

This strange tale is supported by the existence of molecular "fossils"—little bits of RNA that hang about inside the nucleus of your cells doing unnecessary things such as splicing themselves out of genes: guide RNA, vault RNA, small nuclear RNA, small nucleolar RNA, self-splicing introns. Bacteria have none of these, and it is more parsimonious to believe that they dropped them rather than we invented them. (Science, perhaps surprisingly, is supposed to treat simple explanations as more probable than complex ones unless given reason to think otherwise; the principle is known in logic as Occam's razor.) Bacteria dropped the old RNAs when they invaded hot places like hot springs or subterranean rocks where temperatures can reach 170°C—to minimize mistakes caused by heat, it paid to simplify the machinery. Having dropped the RNAs, bacteria found their new streamlined cellular machinery made them good at competing in niches where speed of reproduction was an advantage—such as parasitic and scavenging niches. We retained those old RNAs, relics of machines long superseded, but never entirely thrown away. Unlike the massively competitive world of bacteria, we—that is all animals, plants and fungi—never came under such fierce competition to be quick and simple. We put a premium instead on being complicated, in having as many genes as possible, rather than a streamlined machine for using them.[30]

The three-letter words of the genetic code are the same in every creature. CGA means arginine and GCG means alanine—in bats, in beetles, in beech trees, in bacteria. They even mean the same in the misleadingly named archaebacteria living at boiling temperatures in sulphurous springs thousands of feet beneath the surface of the Atlantic ocean or in those microscopic capsules of deviousness called viruses. Wherever you go in the world, whatever animal, plant, bug or blob you look at, if it is alive, it will use the same dictionary and know the same code. All life is one. The genetic code, bar a few tiny local aberrations, mostly for unexplained reasons in the ciliate protozoa,[31] is the same in every creature. We all use exactly the same language.

---

29. French evolutionary biologist (b. 1949).

30. Poole, A. M., Jeffares, D. C. and Penny, D. (1998). The path from the RNA world. *Journal of the Molecular Evolution* 46: 1–17; Jaffares, D. C., Poole, A. M. and Penny, D. (1998). Relics from the RNA world. *Journal of Molecular Evolution* 46: 18–36 [Ridley's note].

31. A single-celled organism featuring cilia, hairlike organelles, on its outside.

This means—and religious people might find this a useful argument—that there was only one creation, one single event when life was born. Of course, that life might have been born on a different planet and seeded here by spacecraft, or there might even have been thousands of kinds of life at first, but only Luca survived in the ruthless free-for-all of the primeval soup. But until the genetic code was cracked in the 1960s, we did not know what we now know: that all life is one; seaweed is your distant cousin and anthrax one of your advanced relatives. The unity of life is an empirical fact. Erasmus Darwin was outrageously close to the mark: "One and the same kind of living filaments has been the cause of all organic life."

In this way simple truths can be read from the book that is the genome: the unity of all life, the primacy of RNA, the chemistry of the very earliest life on the planet, the fact that large, single-celled creatures were probably the ancestors of bacteria, not vice versa. We have no fossil record of the way life was four billion years ago. We have only this great book of life, the genome. The genes in the cells of your little finger are the direct descendants of the first replicator molecules; through an unbroken chain of tens of billions of copyings, they come to us today, still bearing a digital message that has traces of those earliest struggles of life. If the human genome can tell us things about what happened in the primeval soup, how much more can it tell us about what else happened during the succeeding four million millennia. It is a record of our history written in the code for a working machine.

QUESTIONS

1. Matt Ridley's essay gives two histories: a history of the discovery of DNA (paragraphs 7–12) and a history of the origin of life (paragraphs 13–25). What facts does he supply for each? What speculations does he make? Why must the second history be more speculative than the first?

2. Popular writers on science often "translate" difficult scientific concepts into terms that a general reader can understand. Find two or three places where Ridley provides this sort of translation—for example, paragraph 14, where he asks us to "imagine the nucleus of a human egg," or paragraph 22, where he introduces us to Luca, "the Last Universal Common Ancestor." Explain how his translation works, including its advantages and limitations.

3. "In the beginning was the word": Ridley introduces his essay with this sentence and repeats it in paragraph 13. In so doing, he quotes a famous verse of the New Testament (John 1.1). What implicit point is Ridley making by quoting a biblical passage in a scientific essay about the origins of life?

4. Choose a concept from science or technology and explain it to a general, nonspecialist reader. Think about how you will "translate" the concept from a specialized to a general audience.

HENRY WECHSLER, ANDREA DAVENPORT,
GEORGE DOWDALL, BARBARA MOEYKENS,
AND SONIA CASTILLO

Health and Behavioral Consequences of Binge Drinking in College: A National Survey of Students at 140 Campuses

Objective.—To examine the extent of binge drinking by college students and the ensuing health and behavioral problems that binge drinkers create for themselves and others on their campus.

Design.—Self-administered survey mailed to a national representative sample of US 4-year college students.

Setting.—One hundred forty US 4-year colleges in 1993.

Participants.—A total of 17,592 college students.

Main Outcome Measures.—Self-reports of drinking behavior, alcohol-related health problems, and other problems.

Results.—Almost half (44%) of college students responding to the survey were binge drinkers, including almost one fifth (19%) of the students who were frequent binge drinkers. Frequent binge drinkers are more likely to experience serious health and other consequences of their drinking behavior than other students. Almost half (47%) of the frequent binge drinkers experienced five or more different drinking-related problems, including injuries and engaging in unplanned sex, since the beginning of the school year. Most binge drinkers do not consider themselves to be problem drinkers and have not sought treatment for an alcohol problem. Binge drinkers create problems for classmates who are not binge drinkers. Students who are not binge drinkers at schools with higher binge rates were more likely than students at schools with lower binge rates to experience problems such as being pushed, hit, or assaulted or experiencing an unwanted sexual advance.

Conclusions.—Binge drinking is widespread on college campuses. Programs aimed at reducing this problem should focus on frequent binge drinkers, refer them to treatment or educational programs, and emphasize the harm they cause for students who are not binge drinkers (*JAMA,* 1994; 272:1672–1677).

Heavy episodic or binge drinking poses a danger of serious health and other consequences for alcohol abusers and for others in the immediate environment. Alcohol contributes to the leading causes of accidental death in the United States, such as motor vehicle crashes and falls.[1] Alcohol abuse is seen as contributing to almost half of motor vehicle fatalities, the most important cause of death among young Americans.[2] Unsafe sex—a growing threat with the spread of acquired immunodeficiency syndrome (AIDS) and other sexually transmitted diseases—and unintentional injuries have been associated with alcohol intoxication.[3–5] These findings support the view of college presidents who believe that alcohol abuse is the No. 1 problem on campus.[6]

Originally published as "Health and Behavioral Consequences of Binge Drinking in College," Journal of the American Medical Association *(December 7, 1994). The authors' notes are collected at the end as "References," in the style of* JAMA.

976

Despite the fact that alcohol is illegal for most undergraduates, alcohol continues to be widely used on most college campuses today. Since the national study by Straus and Bacon in 1949,[7] numerous subsequent surveys have documented the overwhelming use of alcohol by college students and have pointed to problem drinking among this group.[8–10] Most previous studies of drinking by college students have been conducted on single college campuses and have not used random sampling of students.[9–12] While these studies are in general agreement about the prevalence and consequences of binge drinking, they do not provide a national representative sample of college drinking.

A few large-scale, multicollege surveys have been conducted in recent years. However, these have not selected a representative national sample of colleges, but have used colleges in one state[3] or those participating in a federal program,[5] or have followed a sample of high school seniors through college.[1,3]

In general, studies of college alcohol use have consistently found higher rates of binge drinking among men than women. However, these studies used the same definition of binge drinking for men and women, without taking into account sex differences in metabolism of ethanol or in body mass.[3,5,9–12,14–17]

The consequences of binge drinking often pose serious risks for drinkers and for others in the college environment. Binge drinking has been associated with unplanned and unsafe sexual activity, physical and sexual assault, unintentional injuries, other criminal violations, interpersonal problems, physical or cognitive impairment, and poor academic performance.[3–5]

This study examines the nature and extent of binge drinking among a representative national sample of students at 140 US 4-year colleges and details the problems such drinking causes for drinkers themselves and for others on their college campus. Binge drinking is defined through a sex-specific mea-sure to take into account sex differences in the dosage effects of ethanol.

METHODS

The Colleges

A national sample of 179 colleges was selected from the American Council on Education's list of 4-year colleges and universities accredited by one of the six regional bodies covering the United States. The sample was selected using probability proportionate to enrollment size sampling. All full-time undergraduate students at a university were eligible to be chosen for this study, regardless of the college in which they were enrolled. This sample contained few women-only colleges and few colleges with less than 1000 students. To correct for this problem, an oversample of 15 additional colleges with enrollments of less than 1000 students and 10 all-women's colleges were added to the sample. Nine colleges were subsequently dropped because they were considered inappropriate. These included seminary schools, military schools, and allied health schools.

One hundred forty (72%) of the final sample of 195 colleges agreed to participate. The primary reason stated for nonparticipation by college administrators was inability to provide a random sample of students and their addresses within the time requirements of the study. The 140 participating colleges are located in 40 states and the District of Columbia. They represent a cross-section of US higher education. Two thirds of the colleges sampled are public and one third are private. Approximately two thirds are located in a suburban or urban setting and one third in a small town/rural setting. Four percent are women-only, and 4% are predominantly black institutions.

When the 55 nonparticipating schools were compared with the 140 in the study, the only statistically significant difference found was in terms of enrollment size. Proportionately fewer small colleges (fewer than 1000 students) participated in the study. Since these were oversampled, sufficient numbers are present for statistical analysis.

Sampling Procedures

10   Colleges were sent a set of specific guidelines for drawing a random sample of students based on the total enrollment of full-time undergraduates. Depending on enrollment size, every xth student was selected from the student registry using a random starting point. A sample of undergraduate students was provided by each of the 140 participating colleges: 215 students at each of 127 colleges, and 108 at each of 13 colleges (12 of which were in the oversample). The final student sample included 28,709 students.

The Questionnaire

The 20-page survey instrument asked students a number of questions about their drinking behavior as well as other health issues. Whenever possible, the survey instrument included questions that had been used previously in other national or large-scale epidemiological studies.[13,14] A drink was defined as a 12-oz (360-mL) can (or bottle) of beer, a 4-oz (120-mL) glass of wine, a 12-oz (360-mL) bottle (or can) of wine cooler, or a shot (1.25 oz [37-mL]) of liquor straight or in a mixed drink. The following four questions were used to assess binge drinking: (1) sex; (2) recency of last drink ("never," "not in past year," "within last year but more than 30 days ago," "within 30 days but more than 1 week ago," or "within week"); (3) "Think back over the last two weeks. How many times have you had five or more drinks in a row?" (The use of this question, without specification of time elapsed in a drinking episode, is consistent with standard practice in recent research on alcohol use among this population.[3,5,13,18]); and (4) "During the last two weeks, how many times have you had four drinks in a row (but no more than that) (for women)?" Missing responses to any of these four questions excluded the student from the binging analyses.

Students were also asked the extent to which they had experienced any of the following 12 problems as a consequence of their drinking since the beginning of the school year: have a hangover; miss a class; get behind in schoolwork; do something you later regretted; forget where you were or what you did; argue with friends; engage in unplanned sexual activity; not use protection when you had sex; damage property; get into trouble with campus or local police; get hurt or injured; or require medical treatment for an alcohol overdose. They were also asked if, since the beginning of the school year, they had experienced any of the following eight problems caused by other students' drinking: been insulted or humiliated; had a serious argument or quarrel; been pushed, hit, or assaulted; had your property damaged; had to "babysit" or take care of another student who drank too much; had your studying or sleep interrupted; experienced an unwanted sexual advance; or had been a victim of sexual assault or date rape.

The Mailing

The initial mailing of questionnaires to students began on February 5, 1993. By the end of March, 87% of the final group of questionnaires had been received, with another 10% in April and 2% in May and June. There are no discernible differences in binging rates among questionnaires received in each of the 5 months of the survey. Mailings were modified to take into account spring break, so that students would be responding about their binge drinking behavior during a 2-week time on campus. Responses were voluntary and anonymous. Four separate mailings, usually 10 days apart, were sent at each college: a questionnaire, a reminder postcard, a second questionnaire, and a second reminder postcard. To encourage students to respond, the following cash awards were offered: one $1000 award to a student whose name was drawn from among students responding within 1 week, and one $500 award and ten $100 awards to students selected from all those who responded.

The Response Rate

The questionnaires were mailed to 28,709 students. Overall, 3,082 students were eliminated from the sample because of school reports of incorrect addresses, withdrawal from school, or leaves of absence, reducing the sample size to 25,627. A total of 17,592 students returned questionnaires, yielding an overall student response rate of approximately 69%. The response rate is likely to be underestimated since it does not take into account all of the students who may not have received questionnaires. At 104 of the colleges, response rates were between 60% and 80%, and only six colleges had response rates less than 50%. Response rate was not associated with the binging rate (i.e., the Pearson correlation coefficient between the binge drinking rate at the college and the response rate was 0.06 with a P value of .46).

When responses of early and late responders to the survey were compared, there were no significant differences in the percent of nondrinkers, nonbinge drinkers, and binge drinkers. In the case of 11,557 students who could be classified as early or late responders, there was no significant differences in terms of binge drinking (43% for the early responders vs 42% for the late responders). An additional short form of the questionnaire was mailed to a segment of students who had failed to return the questionnaire. The rate of binge drinking of these nonresponders did not differ from that of responders to the original student survey.

15

Data Analysis

All statistical analyses were carried out using the current version of SAS.[19]* Comparisons of unweighted and weighted sample results suggested little difference between them, so unweighted results are reported here. Chi-square analyses among students who had a drink in the past year were used to compare nonbinge drinkers, infrequent binge drinkers, and binge drinkers. Binge drinking was defined as the consumption of five or more drinks in a row for men and four or more drinks in a row for women during the 2 weeks prior to the survey. An extensive analysis showed that this sex-specific measure accurately indicates an equivalent likelihood of alcohol-related problems. In this article, the term "binge drinker" is used to refer to students who binged at least once in the previous 2 weeks. Frequent binge drinkers were defined as those who binged three or more times in the past 2 weeks and infrequent binge drinkers as those who binged one or two times in the past 2 weeks. Nonbinge drinkers were those who had consumed alcohol in the past year, but had not binged.

Logistic regression analyses were used to examine how much more likely frequent binge drinkers were to experience an alcohol-related problem or driving behavior compared with nonbinge drinkers, and to compare infrequent binge drinkers with nonbinge drinkers. Odds ratios were adjusted for age, sex, race, marital status, and parents' college education.

In examining secondary binge effects, schools were divided into three groups on the basis of the percentage of students who were binge drinkers at each school. The responses of students who had not binged in the past 2 weeks (including those who had never had a drink) and who resided in dormitories, fraternities, or sororities were compared through χ^2† analyses across the three school types. High-level binge schools (where 51% or more students were binge drinkers) included 44 schools with 6,084 students; middle-level binge schools (36% to 50% of students were binge drinkers) included 53 schools with 6,455 students; and low-level binge schools (35% or less of students were binge drinkers) included 43 schools with 5,043 students (for 10 students, information regarding school of attendance was missing). For two of the problems that occurred primarily or almost exclusively to women (sexual assault and experiencing an unwanted sexual advance), only women were included in the analyses.

RESULTS

Characteristics of the Student Sample

This analysis is based on data from 17,592 undergraduate students at 140 US 4-year colleges. The student sample includes more women (58%) than men (42%), due in part to the inclusion of six all-women's institutions. This compares with national 1991 data that report 51% of undergraduates at 4-year institutions are women.[20] The sample is predominantly white (81%). This

---

* A standard social science statistical program.

† Chi-square.

coincides exactly with national 1991 data that report 81% of undergraduates at 4-year institutions are white.[20] Minority groups included Asian/Pacific Islander (7%), Spanish/Hispanic (7%), black/African American (6%), and Native American (1%). The age of the students was distributed as follows: 45% younger than 21 years, 38% aged 21 to 23 years, and 17% aged 24 years or more. There were slightly more juniors (25%) and seniors (26%) in the sample than freshmen (20%) and sophomores (19%), probably because 30% of the students were transfers from other institutions. Ten percent of the students were in their fifth undergraduate year of school or beyond. Religious affiliation was discerned by asking students in which of the following religions they were raised: Protestant (44%), Catholic (36%), Jewish (3%), Muslim (1%), other (4%), and none (12%). Religion was cited as an important to very important activity among 36% of the students. Approximately three of five students (59%) worked for pay. Approximately half (49%) of the students had a grade-point average of A, A–, or B+.

Extent of Binge Drinking

Because of missing responses, there were 496 students excluded from binging analyses (i.e., 17,096 were included). Most students drank alcohol during the past year. Only about one of six (16%) were nondrinkers (15% of the men and 16% of the women). About two of five students (41%) drank but were non-binge drinkers (35% of the men and 45% of the women). Slightly fewer than half (44%) of the students were binge drinkers (50% of the men and 39% of the women). About half of this group of binge drinkers, or about one in five students (19%) overall, were frequent binge drinkers (overall, 23% of the men and 17% of the women).

Binge Drinking Rates at Colleges

The Figure shows that binge drinking rates vary extensively among the 140 colleges in the study. While 1% of the students were binge drinkers at the school with the lowest rate of binge drinkers, 70% of students were binge drinkers at the school with the highest rate. At 44 schools, more than half of the responding students were binge drinkers.

When the 140 colleges were divided into levels of binging rate, χ^2 analyses showed that several college characteristics were individually associated (at $P < .05$) with binging rate. Colleges located in the Northeast or North Central regions of the United States (compared with those in the West or South) or those that were residential (compared with commuter schools, where 90% or more of the students lived off campus)[21] tended to have higher rates of binging. In addition, traditionally black institutions and women's colleges had lower binge rates than schools that were not traditionally black or were coeducational colleges. Other characteristics, such as whether the college was public or private and its enrollment size, were not related to binge drinker rates.

Examination of whether college alcohol programs and policies have any association with binge drinking will be presented in a separate publication. There is little evidence to conclude that current policies have had strong im-

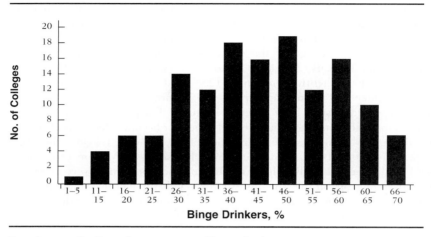

Distribution of colleges by percentage of binge drinkers.

pacts on overall drinking levels. Preliminary analyses suggest that individual binge drinking is less likely if the institution does not have any alcohol outlets within 1 mile of campus, or if it prohibits alcohol use for all persons (even those older than 21 years) on campus.

Drinking Patterns of Binge Drinkers

Table 1 indicates that our designations of binge drinker and frequent binge drinker are strongly indicative of a drinking style that involves more frequent and heavier drinking. Furthermore, intoxication (often intentional) is associated with binge drinking in men and women.

25   Binge drinking is related to age. Students who are in the predominant college age group (between 17 and 23 years) have much higher binging rates than older students. However, within the predominant college age group, students who are younger than the legal drinking age of 21 years do not differ in binging rates from students aged 21 to 23 years. In contrast to the modest effects of age, there is no relationship between year in school and binging, with rates of binge drinking virtually identical among students across the years of college attendance.

Alcohol-Related Health and Other Problems

There is a strong, positive relationship between the frequency of binge drinking and alcohol-related health and other problems reported by the students (Table 2). Among the more serious alcohol-related problems, the frequent binge drinkers were seven to 10 times more likely than the nonbinge drinkers to not use protection when having sex, to engage in unplanned sexual activity, to get into trouble with campus police, to damage property, or to get hurt or injured. A similar comparison between the infrequent binge drinkers and nonbinge drinkers also shows a strong relationship.

TABLE I

DRINKING STYLES OF STUDENTS WHO WERE NONBINGE DRINKERS,
INFREQUENT BINGE DRINKERS, OR FREQUENT BINGE DRINKERS*

Drinking Styles	Nonbinge Drinkers, %†		Infrequent Binge Drinkers, %‡		Frequent Binge Drinkers, %§	
	Men (n=2,539)	Women (n=4,400)	Men (n=1,968)	Women (n=2,130)	Men (n=1,630)	Women (n=1,684)
Drank on 10 or more occasions in the past 30 days‖	3	1	11	6	61	39
Usually binges when drinks	4	4	43	45	83	82
Was drunk three or more times in past month	2	1	17	13	70	55
Drinks to get drunk¶	22	18	49	44	73	68

*Chi-square comparisons of students who were nonbinge drinkers, infrequent binge drinkers, and frequent binge drinkers and each of the four drinking styles were significant for men and women separately at P<.001. Sample sizes vary slightly for each question because of missing values. Binging is defined as four or more drinks for women and five or more drinks for men.

†Students who consumed alcohol in the past year, but did not binge.

‡Students who binged one or two times in a 2-week period.

§Students who binged three or more times in a 2-week period.

‖Question asked, "On how many occasions have you had a drink of alcohol in the past 30 days?" Response categories were 1 to 2 occasions, 3 to 5 occasions, 6 to 9 occasions, 10 to 19 occasions, 20 to 39 occasions, and 40 or more occasions.

¶Says that to get drunk is an important reason for drinking.

TABLE 2

RISK OF ALCOHOL-RELATED PROBLEMS COMPARING STUDENTS WHO WERE INFREQUENT BINGE DRINKERS OR FREQUENT BINGE DRINKERS WITH STUDENTS WHO WERE NONBINGE DRINKERS AMONG COLLEGE STUDENTS WHO HAD A DRINK IN THE PAST YEAR*

Reporting Problem	Nonbinge Drinkers, % (n=6,894)	Infrequent Binge Drinkers		Frequent Binge Drinkers	
		% (n=4,090)	Adjusted OR (95% CI)†	% (n=3,291)	Adjusted OR (95% CI)‡
Have a hangover	30	75	6.28 (5.73–6.87)	90	17.62 (15.20–20.04)
Do something you regret	14	37	3.31 (3.00–3.64)	63	8.98 (8.11–9.95)
Miss a class	8	30	4.66 (4.15–5.24)	61	16.58 (14.73–18.65)
Forget where you were or what you did	8	26	3.62 (3.22–4.06)	54	11.23 (10.05–12.65)
Get behind in school work	6	21	3.70 (3.26–4.20)	46	11.43 (10.09–12.94)
Argue with friends	8	22	3.06 (2.72–3.46)	42	7.77 (6.90–8.74)
Engage in unplanned sexual activity	8	20	2.78 (2.46–3.13)	41	7.17 (6.37–8.06)
Get hurt or injured	2	9	3.65 (3.01–4.13)	23	10.43 (8.70–12.52)
Damage property	2	8	3.09 (2.53–3.77)	22	9.49 (7.86–11.43)
Not use protection when having sex	4	10	2.90 (2.45–3.42)	22	7.11 (6.07–8.34)
Get into trouble with campus or local police	1	4	2.50 (1.92–3.26)	11	6.92 (5.44–8.81)
Require medical treatment of alcohol overdose	<1	<1	NS	1	2.81 (1.39–5.68)
Have five or more alcohol-related problems since the beginning of the school year§	3	14	4.95 (4.17–5.89)	47	25.10 (21.30–29.58)

*Problem occurred not at all or one or more times. Chi-square comparisons of nonbinge drinkers, infrequent binge drinkers, and frequent binge drinkers and each of the problems are significant at P<.001, except for alcohol overdose (P=.002). Sample sizes vary slightly for each problem of missing values. OR indicates odds ratio; CI, confidence interval. See Table 1 for explanation of drinking classification.

†Adjusted ORs of infrequent binge drinkers vs. nonbinge drinkers are significant at P<.001.

‡Adjusted ORs of frequent binge drinkers vs. nonbinge drinkers are significant at P<.001, except for alcohol overdose, P<.01.

§Excludes hangover and includes driving after drinking as one of the problems.

TABLE 3

ALCOHOL-RELATED DRIVING BEHAVIOR FOR A 30-DAY PERIOD COMPARING STUDENTS WHO WERE INFREQUENT BINGE DRINKERS OR FREQUENT BINGE DRINKERS WITH STUDENTS WHO WERE NONBINGE DRINKERS*

Drinking Behavior	Nonbinge Drinkers		Infrequent Binge Drinkers			Frequent Binge Drinkers		
	Men, % (n=2,531)	Women, % (n=4,393)	Men, % (n=1,975)	Women, % (n=2,132)	Adjusted OR 95% CI†	Men, % (n=1,630)	Women, % (n=1,684)	Adjusted OR (95% CI)‡
Drove after drinking alcohol	20	13	47	33	5.13 (4.67–5.64)	62	49	10.33 (9.34–11.42)
Drove after having five or more drinks	2	1	18	7	22.23 (16.89–29.26)	40	21	74.30 (56.56–97.58)
Rode with a driver who was high or drunk	7	7	23	22	4.73 (4.20–5.32)	†53	48	15.97 (14.22–17.95)

*Chi-square comparisons of nonbinge drinkers, infrequent binge drinkers, and frequent binge drinkers and each of the three driving behaviors were all significant for men and women separately at P<.001. Sample sizes vary slightly for each question because of missing values. OR indicates odds ratio; CI, confidence interval. See Table 1 for explanation of drinking classification.

†Adjusted OR of infrequent binge drinkers vs nonbinge drinkers (sex combined) are significant at P<.001.

‡Adjusted OR of frequent binge drinkers vs nonbinge drinkers (sex combined) are significant at P<.001.

Men and women reported similar frequencies for most of the problems, except for damaging property or getting into trouble with the campus police. Among the frequent binge drinkers, 35% of the men and 9% of the women reported damaging property, and 16% of the men and 6% of the women reported getting into trouble with the campus police.

Drinking and Driving

There is also a positive relationship between binge drinking and driving under the influence of alcohol (Table 3). A large proportion of the student population reported driving after drinking alcohol. Binge drinkers, particularly frequent binge drinkers, reported significantly ($P<.001$) higher frequencies of dangerous driving behaviors than nonbinge drinkers.

Number of Problems

Nearly half (47%) of the frequent binge drinkers reported having experienced five or more of the 12 problems listed in Table 2 (omitting hangover and including driving after drinking) since the beginning of the school year, compared with 14% of infrequent binge drinkers and 3% of nonbinge drinkers. The adjusted odds ratios indicate that frequent binge drinkers were 25 times more likely than nonbinge drinkers to experience five or more of these problems, while the infrequent binge drinkers were five times more likely than nonbinge drinkers to experience five or more problems.

Self-assessment of Drinking Problem

30 Few students describe themselves as having a drinking problem. When asked to classify themselves in terms of their current alcohol use, less than 1% of the total sample (0.2%), including only 0.6% of the frequent binge drinkers, designated themselves as problem drinkers. In addition, few students have ever sought treatment for a problem with alcohol.

A somewhat larger proportion of students indicated that they had ever had a drinking problem. Slightly more than one fifth (22%) of the frequent binge drinkers thought that they ever had a drinking problem, compared with 12% of the infrequent binge drinkers and 7% of the nonbinge drinkers.

Secondary Binge Effects

Table 4 reports on the percentage of nonbinging students who experienced "secondary binge effects," each of eight types of problems due to other students' drinking at each of the three different school types (i.e., schools with high, middle, and low binge levels). For seven of the eight problems studied, students at schools with high and middle binge levels were more likely than students at schools with low binge levels to experience problems as a result of the drinking behaviors of others. Odds ratios (adjusted for age, sex, race, marital status, and parents' college education) indicated that nonbinging students at schools with the high binge levels were more likely than nonbinging students at schools with low binge levels to experience secondary binge effects.

The odds of experiencing at least one of the eight problems was roughly

4:1 when students at schools with high binge levels were compared with students at schools with low binge levels.

TABLE 4

STUDENTS EXPERIENCING SECONDARY BINGE EFFECTS
(BASED ON STUDENTS WHO WERE NOT BINGE DRINKERS AND LIVING
IN DORMITORIES, FRATERNITIES, OR SORORITIES)*

| | | School's Binging Level | | | |
| | | Middle | | High | |
Secondary Binge Effect	Low, % (n=801)	% (n=1,115)	Adjusted OR (95% CI)†	% (n=1,064)	Adjusted OR (95% CI)‡
Been insulted or humiliated	21	30	1.6 (1.3-2.1)	34	1.9 (1.5-2.3)
Had a serious argument or quarrel	13	18	1.3 (1.0-1.7)	20	1.5 (1.1-2.0)
Been pushed, hit, or assaulted	7	10	1.4 (1.0-2.1)	13	2.0 (1.4-2.8)
Had your property damaged	6	13	2.0 (1.4-2.8)	15	2.3 (1.6-3.2)
Had to take care of drunken student	31	47	1.9 (1.6-2.3)	54	2.5 (2.0-3.0)
Had your study/sleep interrupted	42	64	2.3 (1.9-2.8)	68	2.6 (2.2-3.2)
Experienced an unwanted sexual advance§	15	21	1.7 (1.2-2.3)	26	2.1 (1.5-2.8)
Been a victim of sexual assault or date rape§	2	1	NS	2	NS
Experienced at least one of the above problems	62	82	2.8 (2.3-3.5)	87	4.1 (3.2-5.2)

*OR indicates odds ratio; CI, confidence interval.
†Adjusted OR of students at schools with middle levels of binging vs. students at schools with low levels are significant at P<.05.
‡Adjusted OR of students at schools with high levels of binging vs. students at schools with low levels are significant at P<.05.
§Based on women only.

Binge Drinking in High School

Most students reported the same drinking behavior in high school as in college. Almost half (47%) had not been binge drinkers in high school and did not binge in college, while one fifth (22%) binged in high school and in college. One fifth (22%) of the students were binge drinkers in college but not in high school, while 10% were not binge drinkers at the time of the survey in college, but reported having been binge drinkers in high school.

COMMENT

To our knowledge, this is the first study that has used a representative national sample, and the first large-scale study to measure binge drinking under a sex-specific definition. Forty-four percent of the college students in this study were classified as binge drinkers. This finding is consistent with the findings of

35

other national studies such as the University of Michigan's Monitoring the Future Project, which found that 41% of college students were binge drinkers,[1,3] and the Core Alcohol and Drug Survey, which found that 42% of college students were binge drinkers.[5] All three studies used a definition of binging over a 2-week period, but the other studies used the same five-drink measure for both sexes. Binge drinking was defined in terms of the number of drinks consumed in a single episode. No attempt was made to specify the duration of time for each episode. Future research might examine whether subgroup differences exist in duration and whether such differences are linked to outcomes.

A possible limitation of surveys using self-reports of drinking behavior pertains to the validity of responses; however, a number of studies have confirmed the validity of self-reported of alcohol and substance use.[22–24] Findings indicate that if a self-report bias exists, it is largely limited to the heaviest use group[2,5] and should not affect such a conservative estimate of heavy volume as five drinks.

The results confirm that binge drinking is widespread on college campuses. Overall, almost half of all students were binge drinkers. One fifth of all students were frequent binge drinkers (had three or more binge drinking occasions in the past 2 weeks) and were deeply involved in a lifestyle characterized by frequent and deliberate intoxication. Frequent binge drinkers are much more likely to experience serious health and other consequences of their drinking behavior than other students. Almost half of them have experienced five or more alcohol-related problems since the beginning of the school year, one of three report they were hurt or injured, and two in five engaged in unplanned sexual activity. Frequent binge drinkers also report drinking and driving. Three of five male frequent binge drinkers drove after drinking some alcohol in the 30 days prior to the survey, and two of five drove after having five or more drinks. A recent national report that reviewed published studies concluded that alcohol was involved in two thirds of college student suicides, in 90% of campus rapes, and in 95% of violent crime on campus.[2,6]

Almost a third of the colleges in the study have a majority of students who binge. Not only do these binge drinkers put themselves at risk, they also create problems for their fellow students who are not binge drinking. Students who did not binge and who reside at schools with high levels of binge drinkers were up to three times as likely to report being bothered by the drinking-related behaviors of other students than students who did not binge and who reside at schools with lower levels of binge drinkers. These problems included being pushed, hit, or assaulted and experiencing an unwanted sexual advance.

Effective interventions face a number of challenges. Drinking is not typically a behavior learned in college and often continues patterns established earlier. In fact, one of three students in the present study was already a binge drinker in the year before college.

40   The prominence of drinking on college campuses reflects its importance in the wider society, but drinking has traditionally occupied a unique place in campus life. Despite the overall decline in drinking in US society, recent time-

trend studies have failed to show a corresponding decrease in binge drinking on college campuses.[3,13] The variation in binge drinking rates among the colleges in this study suggests that colleges may create and unwittingly perpetuate their own drinking cultures through selection, tradition, policy, and other strategies. On many campuses, drinking behavior that would elsewhere be classified as alcohol abuse may be socially acceptable, or even socially attractive, despite its documented implication in automobile crashes, other injury, violence, suicide, and high-risk sexual behavior.

The scope of the problem makes immediate results of any interventions highly unlikely. Colleges need to be committed to large-scale and long-term behavior change strategies, including referral of alcohol abusers to appropriate treatment. Frequent binge drinkers on college campuses are similar to other alcohol abusers elsewhere in their tendency to deny that they have a problem. Indeed, their youth, the visibility of others who drink the same way, and the shelter of the college community may make them less likely to recognize the problem. In addition to addressing the health problems of alcohol abusers, a major effort should address the large group of students who are not binge drinkers on campus who are adversely affected by the alcohol-related behavior of binge drinkers.

This study was supported by the Robert Wood Johnson Foundation. We wish to thank the following persons who assisted with the project: Lloyd Johnston, PhD, Thomas J. Mangione, PhD, Anthony M. Roman, MD, Nan Laird, PhD, Jeffrey Hansen, Avtar Khalsa, MSW, and Marianne Lee, MPA.

REFERENCES

1. US Dept of Health and Human Services, *Alcohol and Health.* Rockville, Md: National Institute on Alcohol Abuse and Alcoholism: 1990.

2. Robert Wood Johnson Foundation. *Substance Abuse: The Nation's Number One Health Problem. Key Indicators for Policy.* Princeton, NJ: Robert Wood Johnson Foundation; October 1993.

3. Wechsler H, Isaac N. 'Binge' drinkers at Massachusetts colleges: prevalence, drinking styles, time trends, and associated problems. *JAMA.* 1992;267:2929–2931.

4. Hanson DJ, Engs RC. College students' drinking problems: a national study, 1982–1991. *Psychol Rep.* 1992;71:39–42.

5. Presley CA, Meilman PW, Lyerla R. *Alcohol and Drugs on American College Campuses: Use, Consequence, and Perceptions of the Campus Environment, Volume I: 1989–1991.* Carbondale, Ill: The Core Institute: 1993.

6. The Carnegie Foundation for the Advancement of Teaching. *Campus Life: In Search of Community.* Princeton, NJ: Princeton University Press: 1990.

7. Straus R, Bacon SD. *Drinking in College.* New Haven, Conn: Yale University Press: 1953.

8. Berkowitz AD, Perkins HW. Problem drinking among college students: a review of recent research. *J Am Coll Health.* 1986;35:21–28.

9. Saltz R, Elandt D. College student drinking studies: 1976–1986. *Contemp Drug Probl.* 1986;13:117–157.

10. Haworth-Hoeppner S, Globetti G, Stem J, Morasco F. The quantity and frequency of drinking among undergraduates at a southern university. *Int J Addict.* 1989; 24:829–857.

11. Liljestrand P. Quality in college student drinking research: conceptual and methodological issues. *J Alcohol Drug Educ.* 1993;38:1–36.

12. Hughes S, Dodder R. Alcohol consumption patterns among college populations. *J Coll Student Personnel.* 1983;20:257–264.

13. Johnston LD, O'Malley PM, Bachman JG. *Drug Use Among American High School Seniors, College Students, and Young Adults, 1975–1990,* Volume 2. Washington, DC: Government Printing Office; 1991. US Dept of Health and Human Services publication ADM 91-1835.

14. Wechsler H, McFadden M. Drinking among college students in New England. *J Stud Alcohol.* 1979;40:969–996.

15. O'Hare TM. Drinking in college: consumption patterns, problems, sex differences, and legal drinking age. *J Stud Alcohol.* 1990;51:536–541.

16. Engs RC, Hanson DJ. The drinking patterns and problems of college students: 1983. *J Alcohol Drug Educ.* 1985;31:65–83.

17. Brennan AF, Walfish S, AuBuchon P. Alcohol use and abuse in college students, I: a review of individual and personality correlates. *Int J Addict.* 1986;21:449–474.

18. Room R. Measuring alcohol consumption in the US: methods and rationales. In: Clark WB, Hilton ME, eds. *Alcohol in America: Drinking Practices and Problems.* Albany: State University of New York Press, 1991:26–50.

19. SAS Institute Inc. *SAS/STAT User's Guide, Release 6.03* ed. Cary, NC: SAS Institute Inc; 1988.

20. US Dept of Education. *Digest of Educational Statistics.* Washington, DC: National Center of Educational Statistics: 1993:180,205.

21. *Barron's Profiles of American Colleges.* Hauppauge, NY: Barron's Educational Series Inc: 1992.

22. Midanik L. Validity of self-reported alcohol use: a literature review and assessment. *Br J Addict.* 1988;83:1019–1030.

23. Cooper AM, Sobell MB, Sobell LC, Maisto SA. Validity of alcoholics' self-reports: duration data. *Int J Addict.* 1981;16:401–406.

24. Reinisch OJ, Bell RM, Ellickson PL. *How Accurate Are Adolescent Reports of Drug Use?* Santa Monica, Calif: RAND; 1991. RAND publication N-3189-CHF.

25. Room R. Survey vs sales data for the US. *Drink Drug Pract Surv.* 1971;3:15–16.

26. CASA Commission on Substance Abuse at Colleges and Universities. *Rethinking Rites of Passage: Substance Abuse on America's Campuses.* New York, NY: Columbia University; June 1994.

QUESTIONS

1. This article's conclusions depend on the wording of the questions asked. A central question is "Think back over the last two weeks. How many times have you had five or more drinks in a row?" What do you think "in a row" means? Do you think the question is precise or fuzzy? Why was it asked this way?

2. How do you and people you know define "binge drinking"? How close is your definition to the definition used by Wechsler et al.?

3. At 44 of the 140 colleges surveyed, more than 50 percent of the students were binge drinkers. Does that sound alarming? Accurate? What might some of those colleges be?

4. Compare this scientific article with the Op-Ed Wechsler and his colleagues wrote for the *Chronicle of Higher Education* (p. 417). Note the important changes you see between this article and the Op-Ed. Are they changes in style? In audience? In format? In details? Which changes matter most to the overall impact of the essays?

MELVIN KONNER *Why the Reckless Survive*

IN A RECENT ELECTION Massachusetts rescinded its seat-belt law.[1] As a result some hundreds of citizens of that commonwealth have in the past year gone slamming into windshields instead of getting a pain in the neck from the shoulder belt. Quite a few are unnecessarily brain-damaged or dead. Such laws in fact make a difference. Americans in general use seat belts at a rate of about 20 percent; but in Texas, where failure to wear one can cost you not only your life but also fifty dollars, nearly seven people in ten wear them habitually—a fivefold increase since the law was passed in 1985. Having lived in Massachusetts for fifteen years, I considered it—wrongly, perhaps—the most sensible state in the union, so I was rather amazed by its recent collective decision.

But I shouldn't have been. All I needed to do was to look at my own behavior. I have, while coauthoring a book on health, sat at my word processor at three A.M. guzzling coffee and gobbling Oreo cookies by the dozen, pecking solemnly away about our need to take better care of ourselves. I could almost feel the fat from the cookies sinking into the arteries of my brain, the coffee laying the groundwork for future cardiac arrhythmias.

Why can't we follow our own advice, or others', even when we know it's right? Is it the heedless child in us, or the perverse, destructive teenager, or only the antiauthoritarian, freedom-loving adult that says, *I will do as I please, thank you*? Or could it be that there is something inevitable—even something good—about the taking of all these chances?

People don't think clearly about risk. This is no mere insult, but a conclusion that emerges from attempts by behavioral scientists to understand how people make decisions. In part these studies were sparked by the unprecedented demand for risk reduction that has emerged in recent years. How many cases of cancer do people consider acceptable nationally as a result of the widespread

From Konner's book Why the Reckless Survive, and Other Secrets of Human Nature *(1990), an anthropological analysis of risk taking and adventure seeking.*

1. Massachusetts rescinded its seat-belt law in 1986, reimposed it in 1994.

use of a food additive or an industrial chemical? None. How many accidents or near-accidents at nuclear power plants? None. How many airline crashes per decade? Basically, none.

5   We may consider the change good: doesn't it reflect a healthy increase in awareness of real risks? But consider that this is the same American public that, after years of education, wears seat belts at the rate of 20 percent and has reduced its cigarette smoking only somewhat. The widespread success of lotteries alone shows that people do not think or act rationally, even in their own self-interest.

So we ignore some risks and overestimate others. The conundrum for an evolutionist is simple. Natural selection should have relentlessly culled systematic biases in decision making, producing a rational organism that hews to the order of real cost-benefit analysis—an organism that behaves efficiently to minimize those ratios. How can evolution, with its supposedly relentless winnowing out of error, have preserved this bewildering array of dangerous habits?

We are highly sensitive to certain dangers. A Harris poll conducted in 1980 showed that 78 percent of the American public (as opposed to roughly half of business and government leaders) thought that risks in general were greater than they had been twenty years before. The greatest perceived risks were in the areas of crime and personal safety, international and domestic political stability, energy sources, and "the chemicals we use." Comfortable majorities of the general public (but only small minorities of the leadership groups) agreed with the statements "Society has only perceived the tip of the iceberg with regard to the risks associated with modern technology" and "Unless technological development is restrained, the overall safety of society will be jeopardized significantly in the next twenty years."

But the logic of our concerns is problematic. People are willing to pay indirectly large sums of money to reduce the risk of a nuclear accident or a cancer death from a chemical to levels they consider acceptably low. But they will not pay a much smaller amount for air bags in automobiles, that, inflating on impact, will save many more lives; and they will not stop smoking, although this risk-reducing measure would actually save money, both immediately and in the long term.

Apparently, irrational factors are at work. But before we consider them, and why we may be subject to them, it is worth looking at the realities of risk. John Urquhart and Klaus Heilmann, both physicians, have reviewed some of these realities in their book *Riskwatch: The Odds of Life*. There is a genuine hierarchy of danger. For example, the number of deaths linked to cigarette smoking in the United States is equivalent to three jumbo jets full of passengers crashing daily, day in and day out. We have fifty thousand traffic fatalities a year—almost the number of deaths we suffered during our entire involvement in Vietnam. Half involve drunk drivers, and a large proportion would be prevented by seat belts or air bags.

10   Yet neither of these sources of risk evokes the interest—indeed the fear—shown in response to possible nuclear accidents, or to toxic-shock syndrome caused by tampons, or even to homicide, all (for most of us) trivial risks by

comparison to smoking or driving. If you tremble when you strap yourself into the seat of an airliner, you ought to really shudder when you climb onto your bicycle, since that is much more dangerous as a regular activity. As for homicide, the people most afraid of it are the ones least likely to be victimized. And the millions of women who stopped taking birth-control pills because of the risk of death from stroke did so in response to an annual probability of dying equal to about one fourth their routine risk of death in an automobile.

Urquhart and Heilmann deal with this quirkiness in our response to risk by developing a Safety-Degree Scale analogous to the Richter scale for earthquake severity. The units are logarithms of the cohort size necessary for one death to occur. Thus lightning, which kills fewer than one person per million exposed, has a safety degree of more than six, while motorcycling, which kills one in a thousand, has a safety degree of three; motorcycling is three orders of magnitude more dangerous. But they aren't perceived in that relation. In general, people will accept one to two orders of magnitude more danger in voluntary risks than they will in involuntary ones. And that is only one aspect of the quirkiness. Risks that result in many deaths at once will be perceived as worse than probabilistically equal risks that kill in a more distributed way. And any bad outcome that is reported unexpectedly—especially if its shock value is exploited—increases fear.

Chronic departures from rationality have been the subject of a major line of thought in economics, in which the most distinguished name is Herbert Simon's. Simon, a winner of the Nobel Memorial prize in economics, has for years criticized and occasionally ridiculed the economic decision theory known as subjective expected utility, or SEU. According to this classic approach, individuals face their life choices with full knowledge of the probability and value of all possible outcomes, and furthermore they possess an unambiguous value scale to measure utility—in plain English, they know a great deal, in advance, about the consequences of their choices, and, more important, they know what they want. In the real world, Simon points out, no such knowledge exists. Whether in the choices of executives or in those of consumers, knowledge is imperfect and values (at least to some extent) indeterminate and mercurial.

A similar point was demonstrated in laboratory experiments by psychologists Amos Tversky and Daniel Kahnemann, in which people are shown to be rather feeble in their abilities to choose among various outcomes. They are readily confused by differences in the language in which a problem is posed. In one study, Tversky and Kahnemann asked physicians to choose among possible programs to combat a hypothetical disease that was on the verge of killing six hundred people. The physicians favored a program guaranteed to save *two hundred lives* over one that had a one-third probability of saving everyone and a two-thirds probability of saving no one. Yet a second group of physicians favored the riskier program over one described as resulting in exactly *four hundred deaths*. They were, of course, rejecting the same alternative the previous group had chosen. The only difference was that it was now being described in terms of victims rather than survivors. Human decision making is

rife with such framing errors, and analyzing them has become a cottage industry.

At least equally interesting is a new psychological view—advanced by Lola
Lopes among others—that certain "errors" may not be errors at all. Lottery
players can be shown to be irrational by multiplying the prize by the probability of winning, and comparing that number to the cost of the ticket. But that
does not take into account the subjective value placed on becoming rich, or
the fact that this may be someone's only chance for that outcome. Nor, of
course, does it consider the thrill of playing.

15   But another aspect of this behavior clearly is irrational: people—especially, but not only, compulsive gamblers—have unrealistically high expectations of winning. On the average, in the larger game of life, they also have
unrealistically high expectations of protection against losing. Linda Perloff and
others have shown that people—average people—think that they will live
longer than average, that they will have fewer diseases than average, and even
that their marriages will last longer than average. Since average people are
likely to have average rates of disease, death, and divorce, they are (in these
studies) underestimating their risks—a tendency Lionel Tiger has summarized
as a ubiquitous, biologically based human propensity to unwarranted optimism.

While these results fit well with the prevalence of risky behavior, they
seem to contradict the findings about people's *over*estimate of the risk of violent crime, or terrorist attacks, or airline crashes, or nuclear-plant accidents.
Part of this is resolvable by reference to the principle that risks beyond our
control are more frightening than those we consider ourselves in charge of. So
we drink and drive, and buckle the seat belt behind us, and light up another
cigarette, on the strength of the illusion that to *these* risks at least, we are invulnerable; and we cancel the trip to Europe on the one-in-a-million chance of
an Arab terrorist attack.

Three patterns, then, emerge in our misestimates. First, we prefer voluntary risks to involuntary ones—or, put another way, risks that we feel we have
some control over to those that we feel we don't. By the way we drive and react to cues on the road, we think, we reduce our risk to such a low level that
seat belts add little protection. But in the case of the terrorist attack or the nuclear-plant accident, we feel we have no handle on the risks. (We seem especially to resent and fear risks that are imposed on us by others, especially if for
their own benefit. If I want to smoke myself to death, we seem to say, it's my
own business; but if some company is trying to put something over on me with
asbestos or nerve gas, I'll be furious.)

Second, we prefer familiar risks to strange ones. The homicide during a
mugging, or the airliner hijacked in Athens, or the nerve gas leaking from an
armed forces train, get our attention and so loom much larger in our calculations than they should in terms of real risk. Third, deaths that come in
bunches—the jumbo-jet crash of the disaster movie—are more frightening
than those that come in a steady trickle, even though the latter may add up to
more risk when the counting is done. This principle may be related in some

way to the common framing error in which people in Tversky and Kahne-mann's studies will act more strongly to prevent two hundred deaths in six hundred people than they will to guarantee four hundred survivors from the same group. Framing the risk in terms of death rather than survival biases judgment.

But there is yet another, more interesting complication. "The general public," "average people," "human" rational or irrational behavior—these categories obscure the simple fact that people differ in these matters.

Average people knowingly push their cholesterol levels upward, but only a third pay essentially no attention to doctors' orders when it comes to modifying their behavior (smoking, or eating a risky diet) in the setting of an established illness worsened by that behavior. Average people leave their seat belts unbuckled, but only some people ride motorcycles, and fewer still race or do stunts with them. Average people play lotteries, friendly poker, and church bingo, but an estimated one to four million Americans are pathological gamblers, relentlessly destroying their lives and the lives of those close to them by compulsively taking outrageous financial risks.

Psychologists have only begun to address these individual differences, but several different lines of research suggest that there is such a thing as a risk-taking or sensation-seeking personality. For example, studies of alcohol, tobacco, and caffeine abuse have found these three forms of excess to be correlated, and also to be related to various other measures of risk taking.

For many years psychologist Marvin Zuckerman, of the University of Delaware, and his colleagues have been using the Sensation Seeking Scale, a questionnaire designed to address these issues directly. Empirically, the questions fall along four dimensions: *thrill and adventure seeking,* related to interest in physical risk taking, as in skydiving and mountain climbing; *experience seeking,* reflecting a wider disposition to try new things, in art, music, travel, friendship, or even drugs; *disinhibition,* the hedonistic pursuit of pleasure through activities like social drinking, partying, sex, and gambling; and *boredom susceptibility,* an aversion to routine work and dull people.

At least the first three of these factors have held up in many samples, of both sexes and various ages, in England and America, but there are systematic differences. Males always exceed females, and sensation seeking in general declines in both sexes with age. There is strongly suggestive evidence of a genetic predisposition: 233 pairs of identical twins had a correlation of 0.60 in sensation seeking, while 138 nonidentical twin pairs had a corresponding correlation of only 0.21.

More interesting than these conventional calculations is a series of studies showing that sensation seeking, as measured by the questionnaire, has significant physiological correlates. For example, heart-rate change in reaction to novelty is greater in sensation seekers, as is brain-wave response to increasingly intense stimulation. The activity of monoamine oxidase (MAO), an enzyme that breaks down certain neurotransmitters (the chemicals that transmit signals between brain cells), is another correlate. Sensation seekers have less

20

MAO activity, suggesting that neurotransmitters that might be viewed as stimulants may persist longer in their brains. Finally, the sex hormones, testosterone and estrogen, show higher levels in sensation seekers.

25   But in addition this paper-and-pencil test score correlates with real behavior. High scores engage in more frequent, more promiscuous, and more unusual sex; consume more drugs, alcohol, cigarettes, and even spicy food; volunteer more for experiments and other unusual activities; gamble more; and court more physical danger. In the realm of the abnormal, the measure is correlated with hypomania, and in the realm of the criminal, with psychopathy.

In other words, something measured by this test has both biological and practical significance. Furthermore, independent studies by Frank Farley and his colleagues at the University of Wisconsin, using a different instrument and a somewhat distinct measure they call thrill seeking, have confirmed and extended these findings. For example, in prison populations fighting and escape attempts are higher in those who score high on thrill seeking. But Farley also emphasizes positive outcomes—a well-established correlation between sensation seeking and the extraverted personality underscores the possibility that some such people are well primed for leadership.

We can now return to the main question: how could all this irrationality have been left untouched by natural selection? Herbert Simon, in an accessible, even lyrical, summary of his thought, the 1983 book *Reason in Human Affairs*, surprised some of us in anthropology and biology who are more or less constantly railing against the un-Darwinian musings of social scientists. He shows a quite incisive understanding of Darwin's theories and of very recent significant refinements of them.

But my own anthropological heart was most warmed by passages such as this one: "If this [situation] is not wholly descriptive of the world we live in today . . . it certainly describes the world in which human rationality evolved: the world of the cavemen's ancestors, and of the cavemen themselves. In that world . . . periodically action had to be taken to deal with hunger, or to flee danger, or to secure protection against the coming winter. Rationality could focus on dealing with one or a few problems at a time. . . ." The appeal to the world of our ancestors, the hunters and gatherers, is as explicit as I could wish. As Simon recognizes, this is the world in which our rationality, limited as it is, evolved. It could not be much better now than it needed to be then, because less perfect rationality would not have been selected against; and we, the descendants of those hunters and gatherers, would have inherited their imperfections.

The result is what Simon calls "bounded rationality"—a seat-of-the-pants, day-by-day sort of problem solving that, far from pretending to assess all possible outcomes against a clear spectrum of values, attempts no more than to get by. "Putting out fires" is another way of describing it; and it follows directly from the concept of economic behavior that made Simon famous: "satisficing," the notion that people are just trying to solve the problem at hand in a way that is "good enough"—his practical answer to those too-optimistic constructions of economists, "maximizing" and "optimizing."

Simon has perceived that the basic human environment did not call for optimal decision making, in the modern risk-benefit sense of the phrase; thus our imperfection, this "bounded rationality." But this does not explain the systematic departures from rationality—the preference for "controllable" or familiar rather than "uncontrollable" or strange risks, or the particular fear attached to large disasters. And it does not explain, especially, the sense of invulnerability of risk takers. Certain kinds of recklessness are easy to handle by looking at the specific evolutionary provenance of certain motives. Kristin Luker, a sociologist at the University of California at San Diego, studied contraceptive risk taking and uncovered what often seemed an unconscious desire for a baby. It is no challenge to reconcile this with evolutionary theory; a Darwinian couple ought to take such risks right and left. Sexual indiscretions in general could be covered by a similar line of argument: sexy sensation seekers perpetuate their genes. Slightly more interesting are the specific risks involved in certain human culinary preferences. We overdo it on fats and sweets because our ancestors were rewarded for such excesses with that inch of insulation needed to carry them through shortages. Death by atherosclerosis may be a pervasive threat today, but for most of the past three million years it was a consummation devoutly to be wished.

But we are still far from the comprehensive explanation of recklessness we need. For this we must look to the darker side of human nature, as expressed in that same ancestral environment. Martin Daly and Margo Wilson, both psychologists at McMaster University in Ontario, explore this matter directly in a book called *Homicide*. Although their analysis is restricted to only one highly dramatic form of risk taking, it is paradigmatic of the problem.

Homicides occur in all human societies, and a frequent cause is a quarrel over something seemingly trivial—an insult, a misunderstanding, a disagreement about a fact neither combatant cares about. Of course, these conflicts are never *really* trivial; they are about status and honor—which in practical terms means whether and how much you can be pushed around. And on this will depend your access to food, land, women (the participants are almost always male)—in short, most of what matters in life and in natural selection. In societies where heads are hunted or coups counted, the process is more formalized, but the principle is similar.

If you simulate, as Daly and Wilson do, a series of fights in which individuals with different risk propensities—low, medium, and high—encounter each other, the high-risk individuals invariably have the highest mortality. But any assumption that winning increases Darwinian fitness—virtually certain to be correct in most environments—leads to predominance of high- or medium-risk individuals. Their candles burn at both ends, but they leave more genes.

The underlying assumption is that the environment is a dangerous one, but this assumption is sensible. The environments of our ancestors must have been full of danger. "Nothing ventured, nothing gained" must have been a cardinal rule; and yet venturing meant exposure to grave risk: fire, heights, cold, hunger, predators, human enemies. And all this risk has to be seen against a background of mortality from causes outside of human control—especially

30

disease. With an average life expectancy at birth of thirty years, with a constant high probability of dying from pneumonia or malaria—the marginal utility, in economic terms, of strict avoidance of danger would have been much lower than it is now, perhaps negligible. In Oscar Lewis's studies of the Mexican "culture of poverty" and in Eliot Liebow's studies of poor black street-corner men, the point is clearly made: the failure of such people to plan for the future is not irrational—they live for the day because they know that they have no future.

35   To die, in Darwinian terms, is not to lose the game. Individuals risk or sacrifice their lives for their kin. Sacrifice for offspring is ubiquitous in the animal world, and the examples of maternal defense of the young in mammals and male death in the act of copulation in insects have become familiar. But great risks are taken and sacrifices made for other relatives as well. Consider the evisceration of the worker honeybee in the act of stinging an intruder and the alarm call of a bird or ground squirrel, calling the predator's attention to itself while warning its relatives. During our own evolution small, kin-based groups might have gained much from having a minority of reckless sensation seekers in the ranks—people who wouldn't hesitate to snatch a child from a pack of wild dogs or to fight an approaching grass fire with a counterfire.

In any case, both sensation seekers and people in general should have taken their risks selectively. They may have found it advantageous to take risks with the seemingly controllable and familiar, even while exaggerating the risk of the unknown, and hedging it around with all sorts of taboo and ritual. It is difficult to imagine a successful encounter with a volcano, but an early human would have had at least a fighting chance against a lion. And we, their descendants, fear toxic nuclear waste but leave our seat belts unbuckled.

Why can't we adjust our personal behavior to our modern middle-class spectrum of risks? Because we are just not built to cut it that finely. We are not designed for perfectly rational calculations, or to calibrate such relatively unimpressive risks. For many of us, life seems compromised by such calculations; they too have a cost—in effort, in freedom, in self-image, in fun. And the fun is not incidental. It is evolution's way of telling us what we were designed for.

Sensation seeking fulfills two of the three cardinal criteria for evolution by natural selection: it varies in the population, and the varieties are to some extent inheritable. In any situation in which the varieties give rise in addition to different numbers of offspring, evolution will occur. The notion that riskier types, because they suffer higher mortality, must slowly disappear is certainly wrong for many environments, and it may still be wrong even for ours.

Ideally, of course, one would want a human organism that could take the risks that—despite the dangers—enhance fitness, and leave aside the risks that don't. But life and evolution are not that perfect. The result of the vastly long evolutionary balancing act is a most imperfect organism. The various forms of personal risk taking often hang together; you probably can't be the sort of person who makes sure to maintain perfectly safe and healthy habits, and yet reflexively take the risks needed to ensure survival and reproductive success in the basic human environment. If you are designed, emotionally, for survival and reproduction, then you are not designed for perfect safety.

So when my father buckles his seat belt behind him, and my brother   40
keeps on smoking, and my friend rides her motorcycle to work every day, it isn't because, or only because, they somewhat underestimate the risks. My father wants the full sense of competence and freedom that he has always had in driving, since long before seat belts were dreamed of. My brother wants the sense of calm that comes out of the cigarette. My friend wants to hear the roar of the Harley and feel the wind in her hair. And they want the risk, because risk taking, for them, is part of being alive.

As for me, when I avoid those risks, I feel safe and virtuous but perhaps a little cramped. And I suspect that, like many people who watch their diet carefully—despite the lapses—and exercise more or less scrupulously and buckle up religiously, I am a little obsessed with immortality, with the prospect of controlling that which cannot be controlled. I know I am doing the sensible thing—my behavior matches, most of the time, the spectrum of real probabilities. But against what scale of value? I sometimes think that the more reckless among us may have something to teach the careful about the sort of immortality that comes from living fully every day.

QUESTIONS

1. Mark the research and the researchers' disciplines that Konner relies on. How many kinds of studies does he bring together? What are they?

2. Konner is interested in the effects of biology on human behavior. Locate the evidence he draws from biology and explain his uses of it.

3. Konner introduces and concludes this essay with autobiographical material; he stations himself with respect to his subject. What does the autobiographical material contribute to this essay?

4. Write an essay in which you describe your own or someone else's irrational behavior and speculate about its causes.

NEIL POSTMAN   *Virtual Students, Digital Classroom*

I F ONE HAS a trusting relationship with one's students (let us say, graduate students), it is not altogether gauche to ask them if they believe in God (with a capital G). I have done this three or four times and most students say they do. Their answer is preliminary to the next question: If someone you love were desperately ill, and you had to choose between praying to God for his or her recovery or administering an antibiotic (as prescribed by a competent physician), which would you choose?

Most say the question is silly since the alternatives are not mutually exclusive. Of course. But suppose they were—which would you choose? God helps those who help themselves, some say in choosing the antibiotic, therefore getting the best of two possible belief systems. But if pushed to the wall (e.g., God does not always help those who help themselves; God helps those who pray and who believe), most choose the antibiotic, after noting that the question is asinine and proves nothing. Of course, the question was not asked, in the first place, to prove anything but to begin a discussion of the nature of belief. And I do not fail to inform the students, by the way, that there has recently emerged evidence of a "scientific" nature that when sick people are prayed for they do better than those who aren't.

As the discussion proceeds, important distinctions are made among the different meanings of "belief," but at some point it becomes far from asinine to speak of the god of Technology—in the sense that people believe technology works, that they rely on it, that it makes promises, that they are bereft when denied access to it, that they are delighted when they are in its presence, that for most people it works in mysterious ways, that they condemn people who speak against it, that they stand in awe of it and that, in the "born again" mode, they will alter their life-styles, their schedules, their habits, and their relationships to accommodate it. If this be not a form of religious belief, what is?

In all strands of American cultural life, you can find so many examples of technological adoration that it is possible to write a book about it. And I would if it had not already been done so well. But nowhere do you find more enthusiasm for the god of Technology than among educators. In fact, there are those, like Lewis Perelman, who argue (for example, in his book, *School's Out*) that modern information technologies have rendered schools entirely irrelevant since there is now much more information available outside the classroom than inside it. This is by no means considered an outlandish idea. Dr. Diane Ravitch, former Assistant Secretary of Education, envisions, with considerable relish, the challenge that technology presents to the tradition that "children (and adults) should be educated in a specific place, for a certain

Originally published in the liberal weekly The Nation *(October 9, 1995), this article reflects Postman's lifelong interest in the impact of technology on modern culture, as also reflected in his book* Technopoly: The Surrender of Culture to Technology *(1992).*

number of hours, and a certain number of days during the week and year." In other words, that children should be educated in school. Imagining the possibilities of an information superhighway offering perhaps a thousand channels, Dr. Ravitch assures us that:

> In this new world of pedagogical plenty, children and adults will be able to dial up a program on their home television to learn whatever they want to know, at their own convenience. If Little Eva cannot sleep, she can learn algebra instead. At her home-learning station, she will tune in to a series of interesting problems that are presented in an interactive medium, much like video games. . . .
>
> Young John may decide that he wants to learn the history of modern Japan, which he can do by dialing up the greatest authorities and teachers on the subject, who will not only use dazzling graphs and illustrations, but will narrate a historical video that excites his curiosity and imagination.

In this vision there is, it seems to me, a confident and typical sense of unreality. Little Eva can't sleep, so she decides to learn a little algebra? Where does Little Eva come from? Mars? If not, it is more likely she will tune in to a good movie. Young John decides that he wants to learn the history of modern Japan? How did young John come to this point? How is it that he never visited a library up to now? Or is it that he, too, couldn't sleep and decided that a little modern Japanese history was just what he needed?

What Ravitch is talking about here is not a new technology but a new species of child, one who, in any case, no one has seen up to now. Of course, new technologies do make new kinds of people, which leads to a second objection to Ravitch's conception of the future. There is a kind of forthright determinism about the imagined world described in it. The technology is here or will be; we must use it because it is there; we will become the kind of people the technology requires us to be, and whether we like it or not, we will remake our institutions to accommodate technology. All of this must happen because it is good for us, but in any case, we have no choice. This point of view is present in very nearly every statement about the future relationship of learning to technology. And, as in Ravitch's scenario, there is always a cheery, gee-whiz tone to the prophecies. Here is one produced by the National Academy of Sciences, written by Hugh McIntosh.

> School for children of the Information Age will be vastly different than it was for Mom and Dad.
>
> Interested in biology? Design your own life forms with computer simulation.
>
> Having trouble with a science project? Teleconference about it with a research scientist.
>
> Bored with the real world? Go into a virtual physics lab and rewrite the laws of gravity.
>
> These are the kinds of hands-on learning experiences schools could be providing right now. The technologies that make them possible are already here, and today's youngsters, regardless of economic status, know how to use them. They spend hours with them every week—not in the classroom, but in their own homes and in video game centers at every shopping mall.

5

It is always interesting to attend to the examples of learning, and the motivations that ignite them, in the songs of love that technophiles perform for us. It is, for example, not easy to imagine research scientists all over the world teleconferencing with thousands of students who are having difficulty with their science projects. I can't help thinking that most research scientists would put a stop to this rather quickly. But I find it especially revealing that in the scenario above we have an example of a technological solution to a psychological problem that would seem to be exceedingly serious. We are presented with a student who is "bored with the real world." What does it mean to say someone is bored with the real world, especially one so young? Can a journey into virtual reality cure such a problem? And if it can, will our troubled youngster want to return to the real world? Confronted with a student who is bored with the real world, I don't think we can solve the problem so easily by making available a virtual reality physics lab.

The role that new technology should play in schools or anywhere else is something that needs to be discussed without the hyperactive fantasies of cheerleaders. In particular, the computer and its associated technologies are awesome additions to a culture, and are quite capable of altering the psychic, not to mention the sleeping, habits of our young. But like all important technologies of the past, they are Faustian bargains,[1] giving and taking away, sometimes in equal measure, sometimes more in one way than the other. It is strange—indeed, shocking—that with the twenty-first century so close, we can still talk of new technologies as if they were unmixed blessings—gifts, as it were, from the gods. Don't we all know what the combustion engine has done for us and against us? What television is doing for us and against us? At the very least, what we need to discuss about Little Eva, Young John, and McIntosh's trio is what they will lose, and what we will lose, if they enter a world in which computer technology is their chief source of motivation, authority, and, apparently, psychological sustenance. Will they become, as Joseph Weizenbaum warns,[2] more impressed by calculation than human judgment? Will speed of response become, more than ever, a defining quality of intelligence? If, indeed, the idea of a school will be dramatically altered, what kinds of learning will be neglected, perhaps made impossible? Is virtual reality a new form of therapy? If it is, what are its dangers?

These are serious matters, and they need to be discussed by those who know something about children from the planet Earth, and whose vision of children's needs, and the needs of society, go beyond thinking of school mainly as a place for the convenient distribution of information. Schools are not now and have never been largely about getting information to children. That has been on the schools' agenda, of course, but has always been way down on the

1. The legendary Doctor Faustus exchanged his soul for infinite knowledge in a pact with the Devil.
2. Weizenbaum's 1976 book, *Computer Power and Human Reason: From Judgment to Calculation*, raises these questions.

list. For technological utopians, the computer vaults information access to the top. This reshuffling of priorities comes at a most inopportune time. The goal of giving people greater access to more information faster, more conveniently, and in more diverse forms was the main technological thrust of the nineteenth century. Some folks haven't noticed it but that problem was largely solved, so that for almost a hundred years there has been more information available to the young outside the school than inside. That fact did not make the schools obsolete, nor does it now make them obsolete. Yes, it is true that Little Eva, the insomniac from Mars, could turn on an algebra lesson, thanks to the computer, in the wee hours of the morning. She could also, if she wished, read a book or magazine, watch television, turn on the radio or listen to music. All of this she could have done before the computer. The computer does not solve any problem she has but does exacerbate one. For Little Eva's problem is not how to get access to a well-structured algebra lesson but what to do with all the information available to her during the day, as well as during sleepless nights. Perhaps this is why she couldn't sleep in the first place. Little Eva, like the rest of us, is overwhelmed by information. She lives in a culture that has 260,000 billboards, 17,000 newspapers, 12,000 periodicals, 27,000 video outlets for renting tapes, 400 million television sets, and well over 500 million radios, not including those in automobiles. There are 40,000 new book titles published every year, and each day 41 million photographs are taken. And thanks to the computer, more than 60 billion pieces of advertising junk come into our mailboxes every year. Everything from telegraphy and photography in the nineteenth century to the silicon chip in the twentieth has amplified the din of information intruding on Little Eva's consciousness. From millions of sources all over the globe, through every possible channel and medium—light waves, air waves, ticker tape, computer banks, telephone wires, television cables, satellites, and printing presses—information pours in. Behind it in every imaginable form of storage—on paper, on video, on audiotape, on disks, film, and silicon chips—is an even greater volume of information waiting to be retrieved. In the face of this we might ask. What can schools do for Little Eva besides making still more information available? If there is nothing, then new technologies will indeed make schools obsolete. But in fact, there is plenty.

One thing that comes to mind is that schools can provide her with a serious form of technology education. Something quite different from instruction in using computers to process information, which, it strikes me, is a trivial thing to do, for two reasons. In the first place, approximately 35 million people have already learned how to use computers without the benefit of school instruction. If the schools do nothing, most of the population will know how to use computers in the next ten years, just as most of the population learns how to drive a car without school instruction. In the second place, what we needed to know about cars—as we need to know about computers, television, and other important technologies—is not how to use them but how they use us. In the case of cars, what we needed to think about in the early twentieth century was not how to drive them but what they would do to our air, our landscape, our social relations, our family life, and our cities. Suppose in 1946 we had

10

started to address similar questions about television: What will be its effects on our political institutions, our psychic habits, our children, our religious conceptions, our economy? Would we be better positioned today to control TV's massive assault on American culture? I am talking here about making technology itself an object of inquiry so that Little Eva and Young John are more interested in asking questions about the computer than getting answers from it.

I am not arguing against using computers in school. I am arguing against our sleepwalking attitudes toward it, against allowing it to distract us from important things, against making a god of it. This is what Theodore Roszak warned against in *The Cult of Information*: "Like all cults," he wrote, "this one also has the intention of enlisting mindless allegiance and acquiescence. People who have no clear idea of what they mean by information or why they should want so much of it are nonetheless prepared to believe that we live in an Information Age, which makes every computer around us what the relics of the True Cross were in the Age of Faith: emblems of salvation." To this, I would add the sage observation of Alan Kay of Apple Computer. Kay is widely associated with the invention of the personal computer, and certainly has an interest in schools using them. Nonetheless, he has repeatedly said that any problems the schools cannot solve without computers, they cannot solve with them. What are some of those problems? There is, for example, the traditional task of teaching children how to behave in groups. One might even say that schools have never been essentially about individualized learning. It is true, of course, that groups do not learn, individuals do. But the idea of a school is that individuals must learn in a setting in which individual needs are subordinated to group interests. Unlike other media of mass communication, which celebrate individual response and are experienced in private, the classroom is intended to tame the ego, to connect the individual with others, to demonstrate the value and necessity of group cohesion. At present, most scenarios describing the uses of computers have children solving problems alone; Little Eva, Young John, and the others are doing just that. The presence of other children may, indeed, be an annoyance.

Like the printing press before it, the computer has a powerful bias toward amplifying personal autonomy and individual problem-solving. That is why educators must guard against computer technology's undermining some of the important reasons for having the young assemble (to quote Ravitch) "in a specific place, for a certain number of hours, and a certain number of days during the week and year."

Although Ravitch is not exactly against what she calls "state schools," she imagines them as something of a relic of a pretechnological age. She believes that the new technologies will offer all children equal access to information. Conjuring up a hypothetical Little Mary who is presumably from a poorer home than Little Eva, Ravitch imagines that Mary will have the same opportunities as Eva "to learn any subject, and to learn it from the same master teachers as children in the richest neighborhood." For all of its liberalizing spirit, this scenario makes some important omissions. One is that though new technologies may be a solution to the learning of "subjects," they work against the learning of what are called "social values," including an understanding of democratic processes. If one reads the first chapter of Robert Fulghum's *All I Really Need to Know I Learned in Kindergarten,* one will find an elegant summary of a few things Ravitch's scenario has left out. They include learning the following lessons: Share everything, play fair, don't hit people, put things back where you found them, clean up your own mess, wash your hands before you eat, and, of course, flush. The only thing wrong with Fulghum's book is that no one has learned all these things at kindergarten's end. We have ample evidence that it takes many years of teaching these values in school before they have been accepted and internalized. That is why it won't do for children to learn in "settings of their own choosing." That is also why schools require children to be in a certain place at a certain time and to follow certain rules, like raising their hands when they wish to speak, not talking when others are talking, not chewing gum, not leaving until the bell rings, exhibiting patience toward slower learners, etc. This process is called making civilized people. The god of Technology does not appear interested in this function of schools. At least, it does not come up much when technology's virtues are enumerated.

The god of Technology may also have a trick or two up its sleeve about something else. It is often asserted that new technologies will equalize learning opportunities for the rich and poor. It is devoutly to be wished for, but I doubt it will happen. In the first place, it is generally understood by those who have studied the history of technology that technological change always produces winners and losers. There are many reasons for this, among them economic differences. Even in the case of the automobile, which is a commodity most people can buy (although not all), there are wide differences between the rich and poor in the quality of what is available to them. It would be quite astonishing if computer technology equalized all learning opportunities, irrespective of economic differences. One may be delighted that Little Eva's parents could afford the technology and software to make it possible for her to learn algebra at midnight. But Little Mary's parents may not be able to, may not even know such things are available. And if we say that the school could make the technology available to Little Mary (at least during the day), there may be something else Little Mary is lacking.

It turns out, for example, that Little Mary may be having sleepless nights   15 as frequently as Little Eva but not because she wants to get a leg up on her algebra. Maybe because she doesn't know who her father is, or, if she does, where he is. Maybe we can understand why McIntosh's kid is bored with the real world. Or is the child confused about it? Or terrified? Are there educators who seriously believe that these problems can be addressed by new technologies?

I do not say, of course, that schools can solve the problems of poverty, alienation, and family disintegration, but schools can *respond* to them. And they can do this because there are people in them, because these people are concerned with more than algebra lessons or modern Japanese history, and because these people can identify not only one's level of competence in math but one's level of rage and confusion and depression. I am talking here about children as they really come to us, not children who are invented to show us how computers may enrich their lives. Of course, I suppose it is possible that there are children who, waking at night, want to study algebra or who are so interested in their world that they yearn to know about Japan. If there be such children, and one hopes there are, they do not require expensive computers to satisfy their hunger for learning. They are on their way, with or without computers. Unless, of course, they do not care about others or have no friends, or little respect for democracy or are filled with suspicion about those who are not like them. When we have machines that know how to do something about these problems, that is the time to rid ourselves of the expensive burden of schools or to reduce the function of teachers to "coaches" in the uses of machines (as Ravitch envisions). Until then, we must be more modest about this god of Technology and certainly not pin our hopes on it.

We must also, I suppose, be empathetic toward those who search with good intentions for technological panaceas. I am a teacher myself and know how hard it is to contribute to the making of a civilized person. Can we blame those who want to find an easy way, through the agency of technology? Perhaps not. After all, it is an old quest. As early as 1918, H. L. Mencken[3] (although completely devoid of empathy) wrote, "There is no sure-cure so idiotic that some superintendent of schools will not swallow it. The aim seems to be reduce the whole teaching process to a sort of automatic reaction, to discover some master formula that will not only take the place of competence and resourcefulness in the teacher but that will also create an artificial receptivity in the child."

Mencken was not necessarily speaking of technological panaceas but he may well have been. In the early 1920s a teacher wrote the following poem:

> Mr. Edison says
> That the radio will supplant the teacher.
> Already one may learn languages by means of Victrola records.
> The moving picture will visualize
> What the radio fails to get across.
> Teachers will be relegated to the backwoods,
> With fire-horses,
> And long-haired women;
> Or, perhaps shown in museums.
> Education will become a matter
> Of pressing the button.
> Perhaps I can get a position at the switchboard.

I do not go as far back as the radio and Victrola, but I am old enough to remember when 16-millimeter film was to be the sure-cure. Then closed-circuit television. Then 8-millimeter film. Then teacher-proof textbooks. Now computers.

20   I know a false god when I see one.

3. American journalist (1880–1956).

QUESTIONS

1. In paragraph 10 Postman says that "schools can provide . . . a serious form of technology education" and argues for "making technology itself an object of inquiry." Since this is exactly what Postman does as a writer and professor, is this argument an instance of self-interested special pleading? Why or why not?

2. Consult Postman's biography in the "Authors" section at the back of this book; then look through his essay for evidence of his professional expertise. What kinds of sources does he refer to? What is the range of his reading? Is he writing for a specific community of readers?

3. Write about computers in your own formal education, arguing from your own experiences whether Postman makes a good case or not.

EDWARD O. WILSON *Intelligent Evolution*

> We must acknowledge, as it seems to me, that man with all his noble qualities, with sympathy which feels for the most debased, with benevolence which extends not only to other men but to the humblest living creature, with his god-like intellect which has penetrated into the movements and constitution of the solar system—with all these exalted powers—Man still bears in his bodily frame the indelible stamp of his lowly origin.
>
> —CHARLES DARWIN[1]
> *The Descent of Man, and Selection in Relation to Sex* (1871)

GREAT SCIENTIFIC DISCOVERIES are like sunrises. They illuminate first the steeples of the unknown, then its dark hollows. Such expansive influence has been enjoyed by the scientific writings of Charles Darwin. For over 150 years his books * * * have spread light on the living world and the human condition. They have not lost their freshness: more than any other work in history's scientific canon, they are both timeless and persistently inspirational.

First published in Harvard Magazine *(November/December 2005); a slightly different version appeared as a general introduction to* From So Simple a Beginning: The Four Great Books of Charles Darwin *(2005). The drawings come from the American edition of Charles Darwin's* The Descent of Man, and Selection in Relation to Sex *(1871).*

1. English naturalist (1809–1882) who theorized that living beings evolve through natural selection.

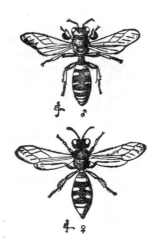

Crabo cribrarius.

The four classics, flowing along one to the next like a well-wrought narrative, trace the development of Darwin's thought across almost all of his adult life. The first, *Voyage of the Beagle* (1845), one of literature's great travel books, is richly stocked with observations in natural history of the kind that were to guide the young Darwin toward his evolutionary worldview. Next comes the "one long argument," as he later put it, of *On the Origin of Species* (1859), arguably history's most influential book. In it the now middle-aged Darwin massively documents the evidences of organic evolution and introduces the theory of natural selection. *The Descent of Man* (1871) then addresses the burning topic foretold in *On the Origin of Species*: "Light will be thrown on the origin of man and his history." Finally, *The Expression of the Emotions in Man and Animals* (1872) draws close to the heart of the matter that concerns us all: the origin and nature of mind, the "citadel" that Darwin could see but knew that science at the time could not conquer.

The adventure that Darwin launched on all our behalf, and which continues into the twenty-first century, is driven by a deceptively simple idea, of which Darwin's friend and staunch supporter Thomas Henry Huxley[2] said, and spoke for many to follow, "How extremely stupid of me not to have thought of that!" Evolution by natural selection is perhaps the only one true law unique to biological systems, as opposed to nonliving physical systems, and in recent decades it has taken on the solidity of a mathematical theorem. It states simply that if a population of organisms contains multiple hereditary variants in some trait (say, red versus blue eyes in a bird population), and if one of these variants succeeds in contributing more offspring to the next generation than the other variants, the overall composition of the population changes, and *evolution has occurred*. Further, if new genetic variants appear regularly in the population (by mutation or immigration), *evolution never ends*. Think of red-eyed and blue-eyed birds in a breeding population, and let the red-eyed birds be better adapted to the environment. The population will in time come to consist mostly or entirely of red-eyed birds. Now let green-eyed mutants appear that are even better adapted to the environment that the red-eyed form. As a consequence the species eventually becomes green-eyed. Evolution has thus taken two more small steps.

2. English scientist (1825–1895) who defended and popularized Darwin's theory of evolution.

The full importance of Darwin's theory can be better understood by realizing that modern biology is guided by two overwhelmingly powerful and creative ideas. The first is that all biological processes are ultimately obedient to even though far from fully explained by, the laws of physics and chemistry. The second is that all biological processes arose through evolution of these physico-chemical systems through natural selection. The first principle is concerned with the *how* of biology. The second is concerned with the ways the systems adapted to the environment over periods of time long enough for evolution to occur—in other words the *why* of biology.

Knowledge addressing the first principle is called functional biology; that addressing the second is called evolutionary biology. If a moving automobile were an organism, functional biology would explain how it is constructed and operates, while evolutionary biology would reconstruct its origin and history—how it came to be made and its journey thus far.

The impact of the theory of evolution by natural selection, nowadays grown very sophisticated (and often referred to as the Modern Synthesis), has been profound. To the extent it can be upheld, and the evidence to date has done so compellingly, we must conclude that life has diversified on Earth autonomously without any kind of external guidance. Evolution in a pure Darwinian world has no goal or purpose: the exclusive driving force is random mutations sorted out by natural selection from one generation to the next.

Top: *Tragelaphus strepsiceros.* Bottom: *Sitana minor* (male with the gular pouch expanded).

What then are we to make of the purposes and goals obviously chosen by human bings? They are, in Darwinian interpretation, processes evolved as adaptive devices by an otherwise purposeless natural selection. Evolution by natural selection means, finally, that the essential qualities of the human mind also evolved autonomously. Humanity was thus born of Earth. However elevated in power over the rest of life, however exalted in self-image, we were descended from animals by the same blind force that created those animals, and we remain a member species of this planet's biosphere.

The revolution in astronomy begun by Nicolaus Copernicus[3] in 1543 proved that Earth is not the center of the universe, nor even the center of the solar system. The revolution begun by Darwin was even more humbling: it showed that humanity is not the center of creation, and not its purpose either. But in freeing our minds from our imagined demigod bondage, even at the price of humility, Darwin turned our attention to the astounding power of the natural creative process and the magnificence of its products:

> There is grandeur in this view of life, with its several powers, having been originally breathed into a few forms or into one; and that, whilst this planet has gone cycling on according to the fixed law of gravity, from so simple a beginning endless forms most beautiful and most wonderful have been, and are being, evolved.
>
> Darwin, *On the Origin of Species* (first edition, 1859)

> If I lived twenty more years and was able to work, how I should have to modify the *Origin*, and how much the views on all points will have to be modified! Well, it is a beginning, and that is something.
>
> —CHARLES DARWIN
> Letter to J. D. Hooker,[4] 1869

Darwin lived thirteen more years after writing this letter to Joseph Hooker, and he did manage to modify the theory of evolution by natural selection, expanding it in *The Descent of Man* (1871) to include human origins and in *The Expression of the Emotions in Man and Animals* (1872) to address the evolution of instinct. The ensuing 130 years have seen an enormous growth of the Darwinian heritage. Joined with molecular and cellular biology, that accumulated knowledge is today a large part of modern biology. Its centrality justifies the famous remark made by the evolutionary geneticist Theodosius Dobzhansky[5] in 1973 that "nothing in biology makes sense except in the light of evolution." In fact, nothing in science as a whole has been more firmly established by interwoven factual documentation, or more illuminating, than the universal occurrence of biological evolution. Further, few natural processes have been more convincingly explained than evolution by the theory of natural selection or, as it is popularly called, Darwinism.

10   Thus it is surpassingly strange that half of Americans recently polled (2004) not only do not believe in evolution by natural selection but do not believe in evolution at all. Americans are certainly capable of belief, and with rocklike conviction if it originates in religious dogma. In evidence is the 60 percent that accept the prophecies of the Book of Revelation[6] as truth, and yet

3. Polish astronomer (1473–1543) who posited that the solar system is heliocentric, with the sun rather than the earth at its center.

4. English botanist (1817–1911) and champion of Darwin's evolutionary theory.

5. Ukrainian evolutionary biologist and geneticist (1900–1975).

6. The final book of the New Testament, which contains visions of apocalypse.

Top: *Cercopithecus petaurista*.
Bottom, from left to right: *Semnopithecus comatus, Cebus capucinus, Ateles marginatus*, and *Cebus vellerosus*.

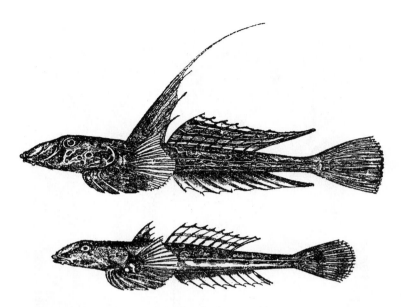

Callionymus lyra (upper figure, male; lower figure, female).

in more evidence is the weight that faith-based positions hold in political life. Most of the religious Right opposes the teaching of evolution in public schools, either by an outright ban on the subject or, at the least, by insisting that it be treated as "only a theory" rather than a "fact."

Yet biologists, particularly those statured by the peer review and publication of substantial personal research on the subject in leading journals of science, are unanimous in concluding that evolution is a *fact*. The evidence they and thousands of others have adduced over 150 years falls together in intricate and interlocking detail. The multitudinous examples range from the small changes in DNA[7] sequences observed as they occur in real time to finely graded sequences within larger evolutionary changes in the fossil record. Further, on the basis of comparably firm evidence, natural selection grows ever stronger as the prevailing explanation of evolution.

Many who accept the fact of evolution cannot, however, on religious grounds, accept the operation of blind chance and the absence of divine purpose implicit in natural selection. They support the alternative explanation of intelligent design. The reasoning they offer is not based on evidence but on the lack of it. The formulation of intelligent design is a default argument advanced in support of a non sequitur. It is in essence the following: There are some phenomena that have not yet been explained and that (and most impor-

---

7. Deoxyribonucleic acid, which contains and encodes genetic information in living organisms.

Dog "in a humble and affectionate frame of mind."

tantly) the critics personally cannot imagine being explained; therefore there must be a supernatural designer at work. The designer is seldom specified, but in the canon of intelligent design it is most certainly not Satan and his angels, nor any god or gods conspicuously different from those accepted in the believer's faith.

Flipping the scientific argument upside down, the intelligent designers join the strict creationists (who insist that no evolution ever occurred in the first place) by arguing that scientists resist the supernatural theory because it is counter to their own personal secular beliefs. This may have a kernel of truth; everybody suffers from some amount of bias. But in this case bias is easily overcome. The critics forget how the reward system in science works. Any researcher who can prove the existence of intelligent design within the accepted framework of science will make history and achieve eternal fame. He will prove at last that *science and religious dogma are compatible!* Even a combined Nobel Prize and Templeton Prize (the latter designed to encourage search for just such harmony) would fall short as proper recognition. Every scientist would like to accomplish such an epoch-making advance. But no one has even come close, because unfortunately there is no evidence, no theory, and no criteria for proof that even marginally might pass for science. There is only the residue of hoped for default, which steadily shrinks as the science of biology expands.

In all of the history of science only one other disparity of comparable magnitude to evolution has occurred between a scientific event and the impact it has had on the public mind. This was the discovery by Copernicus that Earth and therefore humanity are not the center of the universe, and the universe is not a closed spherical bubble. Copernicus delayed publication of his

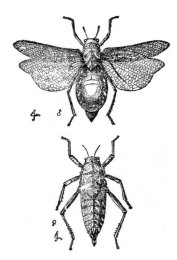

Pneumora.

masterwork *On the Revolution of the Heavenly Spheres* until the year of his death (1543). For his extension of the idea subsequently, Bruno was burned at the stake, and for its documentation Galileo was shown the instruments of torture at Rome and remained under house arrest for the remainder of his life.[8]

Today we live in a less barbaric age, but an otherwise comparable disjunction between science and religion, the one born of Darwinism, still roils the public mind. Why does such intense and pervasive resistance to evolution continue 150 years after the publication of *The Origin of Species*, and in the teeth of the overwhelming accumulated evidence favoring it? The answer is simply that the Darwinian revolution, even more than the Copernican revolution, challenges the prehistoric and still-regnant self-image of humanity. Evolution by natural selection, to be as concise as possible, has changed everything.

In the more than slightly schizophrenic circumstances of the present era, global culture is divided into three opposing images of the human condition, each logically consistent within its own, independent premises. The dominant of these hypotheses, exemplified by the creation myths of the Abrahamic monotheistic religions[9] (Judaism, Christianity, and Islam), sees humanity as a creation of God. He brought us into being and He guides us still as father, judge, and friend. We interpret his will from sacred scriptures and the wisdom of ecclesiastical authorities.

The second worldview is that of political behaviorism. Still beloved by the now rapidly fading Marxist-Leninist[10] states, it says that the brain is largely a blank state devoid of any inborn inscription beyond reflexes and primitive bodily urges. As a consequence the mind originates almost wholly as a result of learning, and it is the product of a culture that itself evolves by historical contingency. Because there is no biologically based "human nature," people can be molded to the best possible political and economic system, namely, as

8. Giordano Bruno (1548–1600), Italian astronomer, priest, and philosopher burned at the stake for his unconventional beliefs, including in the existence of planets outside our solar system; Galileo Galilei (1564–1642), Italian astronomer whose research supported Copernicus's heliocentric view of the universe.

9. Jewish, Christian, and Muslim faiths that trace their lineage to the ancient Hebrew Abraham (ca. 2000 B.C.E.–1500 B.C.E.).

10. Socialist thinking in the style or tradition of German thinker Karl Marx (1818–1883) and Russian politician Vladimir Lenin (1870–1924).

Rhynchaea capensis.

urged upon the world through most of the twentieth century, communism.[11]
In practical politics, this belief has been repeatedly tested and, after economic
collapses and tens of millions of deaths in a dozen dysfunctional states, is generally deemed a failure.

Both of these worldviews, God-centered religion and atheistic communism, are opposed by a third and in some ways more radical worldview, scientific humanism. Still held by only a tiny minority of the world's population, it
considers humanity to be a biological species that evolved over millions of
years in a biological world, acquiring unprecedented intelligence yet still
guided by complex inherited emotions and biased channels of learning. Human nature exists, and it was self-assembled. It is the commonality of the
hereditary responses and propensities that define our species. Having arisen by
evolution during the far simpler conditions in which humanity lived during

---

11. A social philosophy that seeks to eliminate class structure and private property in
favor of common ownership.

more than 99 percent of its existence, it forms the behavioral part of what, in *The Descent of Man*, Darwin called the indelible stamp of our lowly origin.

To understand biological human nature in depth is to drain the fever swamps of religious and blank-slate dogma.[12] But it also imposes the heavy burden of individual choice that goes with intellectual freedom.

20   Such was the long journey for Darwin, the architect of the naturalistic worldview. He began his voyage on the *Beagle* as a devout Christian who trained for the ministry. "Whilst on board the *Beagle* I was quite orthodox," he wrote much later in his autobiography, "and I remember being heartily laughed at by several of the officers (though themselves orthodox) for quoting the Bible as an unanswerable authority on some point of morality." His later drift from the religion of his birth was stepwise and slow. Still on H.M.S. *Beagle* during its circumnavigation of the globe (1831–1836) he came to believe that the "false history" and reports of God's vengeful feelings made the Old Testament "no more to be trusted than the sacred books of the Hindoos,[13] or the beliefs of any barbarian." The miracles of Jesus seemed to him to suggest that people living at the time of the Gospels were "ignorant and credulous to a degree almost incomprehensible by us." The growth of disbelief was so slow that Darwin felt no distress. In a striking passage of his autobiography he expressed his final and complete rejection of Christian dogma based solely on blind faith:

> I can indeed hardly see how anyone ought to wish Christianity to be true; for if so the plain language of the text seems to show that the men who do not believe, and this would include my Father, Brother and almost all my best friends, will be everlastingly punished. And that is a damnable doctrine.

Did Charles Darwin recant in his last days, as some religious critics have hopefully suggested? There is not a shred of evidence that he did or that he was presented with any reason to do so. Further, it would have been wholly contrary to the deliberate, careful manner with which he approached every subject.

The great naturalist did not abandon Abrahamic and other religious dogmas because of his discovery of evolution by natural selection, as one might reasonably suppose. The reverse occurred. The shedding of blind faith gave him the intellectual fearlessness to explore human evolution wherever logic and evidence took him. And so he set forth boldly, in *The Descent of Man* to track the origin of humanity, and in *The Expression of the Emotions in Man and Animals* to address the evolution of instinct. Thus was born scientific humanism, the only worldview compatible with science's growing knowledge of the real world and the laws of nature.

So, will science and religion find common ground, or at least agree to

---

12. The idea that humans are born without personality or knowledge and that their experience is entirely responsible for forming them.

13. Hindus.

divide the fundamentals into mutually exclusive domains? A great many well-meaning scholars believe that such rapprochement is both possible and desirable. A few disagree, and I am one of them. I think Darwin would have held to the same position. The battle line is, as it has ever been, in biology. The inexorable growth of this science continues to widen, not to close, the tectonic gap between science and faith-based religion.

Rapprochement may be neither possible nor desirable. There is something deep in religious belief that divides people and amplifies societal conflict. In the early part of this century, the toxic mix of religion and tribalism has become so dangerous as to justify taking seriously the alternative view, that humanism based on science is the effective antidote, the light and the way at last placed before us.

In any case, the dilemma to be solved is truly profound. On the one side   25
the input of religion on human history has been beneficent in many ways. It has generated much of which is best in culture, including the ideals of altruism and public service. From the beginning of history it has inspired the arts. Creation myths were in a sense the beginning of science itself. Fabricating them was the best the early scribes could do to explain the universe and human existence.

Yet the high risk is the ease with which alliances between religions and tribalism are made. Then comes bigotry and the dehumanization of infidels. Our gods, the true believer asserts, stand against your false idols, our spiritual purity against your corruption, our divinely sanctioned knowledge against your errancy. In past ages the posture provided an advantage. It united each tribe during life-and-death struggles with other tribes. It buoyed the devotees with a sense of superiority. It sacralized tribal laws and mores, and encouraged altruistic behaviors. Through sacred rites it lent solemnity to the passages of life. And it comforted the anxious and afflicted. For all this and more it gave people an identity and purpose, and vouchsafed tribal fitness—yet, unfortunately, at the expense of less united or otherwise less fortunate tribes.

Religions continue both to render their special services and to exact their heavy costs. Can scientific humanism do as well or better, at a lower cost? Surely that ranks as one of the great unanswered questions of philosophy. It is the noble yet troubling legacy that Charles Darwin left us.

QUESTIONS

1. As the contextual note explains, Edward Wilson wrote this essay to introduce a new edition of the scientific works of Charles Darwin. What parts of the essay provide information about Darwin and his work? What parts extend Darwin's theories to present-day debates about evolution and intelligent design? Why does Wilson arrange these parts in the order they appear?

2. Wilson uses similes (comparisons with *like* or *as*) and metaphors (comparisons without connectives) to explain key concepts. Analyze the similes in paragraphs 1 (sunrises), 5 (automobile), and 13 (designers), and explain their function in the argument.

3. In the last section of the essay Wilson defines three worldviews: religious, Marxist-Leninist, and scientific. How does he define each? How do his classifications and definitions help advance his argument in this essay?

4. Choose one of Darwin's four books or one of the scientists Wilson mentions. Do research about your choice, and write a brief account of its importance in the history of science.

STEPHEN JAY GOULD *Darwin's Middle Road*

"WE BEGAN TO SAIL up the narrow strait lamenting," narrates Odysseus. "For on the one hand lay Scylla, with twelve feet all dangling down; and six necks exceeding long, and on each a hideous head, and therein three rows of teeth set thick and close, full of black death. And on the other mighty Charybdis sucked down the salt sea water.[1] As often as she belched it forth, like a cauldron on a great fire she would seethe up through all her troubled deeps." Odysseus managed to swerve around Charybdis, but Scylla grabbed six of his finest men and devoured them in his sight—"the most pitiful thing mine eyes have seen of all my travail in searching out the paths of the sea."

False lures and dangers often come in pairs in our legends and metaphors—consider the frying pan and the fire, or the devil and the deep blue sea. Prescriptions for avoidance either emphasize a dogged steadiness—the straight and narrow of Christian evangelists—or an averaging between unpleasant alternatives—the golden mean of Aristotle. The idea of steering a course between undesirable extremes emerges as a central prescription for a sensible life.

The nature of scientific creativity is both a perennial topic of discussion and a prime candidate for seeking a golden mean. The two extreme positions have not been directly competing for allegiance of the unwary. They have, rather, replaced each other sequentially, with one now in the ascendency, the other eclipsed.

The first—inductivism—held that great scientists are primarily great observers and patient accumulators of information. For new and significant theory, the inductivists claimed, can only arise from a firm foundation of facts. In this architectural view, each fact is a brick in a structure built without blueprints. Any talk or thought about theory (the completed building) is fatuous and premature before the bricks are set. Inductivism once commanded great

For many years Gould wrote a monthly column for the magazine Natural History. *This essay appeared there in December 1979 and was reprinted in Gould's collection* The Panda's Thumb *(1980).*

1. Scylla was a female monster who lived in a cave and threatened Odysseus and his sailors in the *Odyssey*. Located opposite it was Charybdis, a whirlpool in the narrow channel of the Strait of Messina, between Sicily and mainland Italy.

prestige within science, and even represented an "official" position of sorts, for it touted, however falsely, the utter honesty, complete objectivity, and almost automatic nature of scientific progress towards final and incontrovertible truth.

Yet, as its critics so rightly claimed, inductivism also depicted science as a heartless, almost inhuman discipline offering no legitimate place to quirkiness, intuition, and all the other subjective attributes adhering to our vernacular notion of genius. Great scientists, the critics claimed, are distinguished more by their powers of hunch and synthesis, than their skill in experiment or observation. The criticisms of inductivism are certainly valid and I welcome its dethroning during the past thirty years as a necessary prelude to better understanding. Yet, in attacking it so strongly, some critics have tried to substitute an alternative equally extreme and unproductive in its emphasis on the essential subjectivity of creative thought. In this "eureka" view, creativity is an ineffable something, accessible only to persons of genius. It arises like a bolt of lightning, unanticipated, unpredictable and unanalyzable—but the bolts strike only a few special people. We ordinary mortals must stand in awe and thanks. (The name refers, of course, to the legendary story of Archimedes running naked through the streets of Syracuse shouting eureka [I have discovered it] when water displaced by his bathing body washed the scales abruptly from his eyes and suggested a method for measuring volumes.)

I am equally disenchanted by both these opposing extremes. Inductivism reduces genius to dull, rote operations; eurekaism grants it an inaccessible status more in the domain of intrinsic mystery than in a realm where we might understand and learn from it. Might we not marry the good features of each view, and abandon both the elitism of eurekaism and the pedestrian qualities of inductivism? May we not acknowledge the personal and subjective character of creativity, but still comprehend it as a mode of thinking that emphasizes or exaggerates capacities sufficiently common to all of us that we may at least understand if not hope to imitate?

In the hagiography of science, a few men hold such high positions that all arguments must apply to them if they are to have any validity. Charles Darwin, as the principal saint of evolutionary biology, has therefore been presented both as an inductivist and as a primary example of eurekaism. I will attempt to show that these interpretations are equally inadequate, and that recent scholarship on Darwin's own odyssey towards the theory of natural selection supports an intermediate position.

So great was the prestige of inductivism in his own day, that Darwin himself fell under its sway and, as an old man, falsely depicted his youthful accomplishments in its light. In an autobiography, written as a lesson in morality for his children and not intended for publication, he penned some famous lines that misled historians for nearly a hundred years. Describing his path to the theory of natural selection, he claimed: "I worked on true Baconian principles, and without any theory collected facts on a wholesale scale."[2]

2. Francis Bacon (1561–1626), English philosopher, statesman, and essayist, and the first apostle of inductivism.

The inductivist interpretation focuses on Darwin's five years aboard the *Beagle* and explains his transition from a student for the ministry to the nemesis of preachers as the result of his keen powers of observation applied to the whole world. Thus, the traditional story goes, Darwin's eyes opened wider and wider as he saw, in sequence, the bones of giant South American fossil mammals, the turtles and finches of the Galapagos, and the marsupial fauna of Australia. The truth of evolution and its mechanism of natural selection crept up gradually upon him as he sifted facts in a sieve of utter objectivity.

10   The inadequacies of this tale are best illustrated by the falsity of its conventional premier example—the so-called Darwin's finches of the Galapagos. We now know that although these birds share a recent and common ancestry on the South American mainland, they have radiated into an impressive array of species on the outlying Galapagos. Few terrestrial species manage to cross the wide oceanic barrier between South America and the Galapagos. But the fortunate migrants often find a sparsely inhabited world devoid of the competitors that limit their opportunities on the crowded mainland. Hence, the finches evolved into roles normally occupied by other birds and developed their famous set of adaptations for feeding—seed crushing, insect eating, even grasping and manipulating a cactus needle to dislodge insects from plants. Isolation—both of the islands from the mainland and among the islands themselves—provided an opportunity for separation, independent adaptation, and speciation.

According to the traditional view, Darwin discovered these finches, correctly inferred their history, and wrote the famous lines in his notebook: "If there is the slightest foundation for these remarks the zoology of Archipelagoes will be worth examining; for such facts would undermine the stability of Species." But, as with so many heroic tales from Washington's cherry tree to the piety of Crusaders, hope rather than truth motivates the common reading. Darwin found the finches to be sure. But he didn't recognize them as variants of a common stock. In fact, he didn't even record the island of discovery for many of them—some of his labels just read "Galapagos Islands." So much for his immediate recognition of the role of isolation in the formation of new species. He reconstructed the evolutionary tale only after his return to London, when a British Museum ornithologist correctly identified all the birds as finches.

The famous quotation from his notebook refers to Galapagos tortoises and to the claim of native inhabitants that they can "at once pronounce from which Island any Tortoise may have been brought" from subtle differences in size and shape of body and scales. This is a statement of different, and much reduced, order from the traditional tale of finches. For the finches are true and separate species—a living example of evolution. The subtle differences among tortoises represent minor geographic variation within a species. It is a jump in reasoning, albeit a valid one as we now know, to argue that such small differences can be amplified to produce a new species. All creationists, after all, acknowledged geographic variation (consider human races), but argued that it could not proceed beyond the rigid limits of a created archetype.

I don't wish to downplay the pivotal influence of the *Beagle* voyage on Darwin's career. It gave him space, freedom and endless time to think in his favored mode of independent self-stimulation. (His ambivalence towards university life, and his middling performance there by conventional standards, reflected his unhappiness with a curriculum of received wisdom.) He writes from South America in 1834: "I have not one clear idea about cleavage, stratification, lines of upheaval. I have no books, which tell me much and what they do I cannot apply to what I see. In consequence I draw my own conclusions, and most gloriously ridiculous ones they are." The rocks and plants and animals that he saw did provoke him to the crucial attitude of doubt—midwife of all creativity. Sydney, Australia—1836. Darwin wonders why a rational God would create so many marsupials on Australia since nothing about its climate or geography suggests any superiority for pouches: "I had been lying on a sunny bank and was reflecting on the strange character of the animals of this country as compared to the rest of the World. An unbeliever in everything beyond his own reason might exclaim, 'Surely two distinct Creators must have been at work.' "

Nonetheless, Darwin returned to London without an evolutionary theory. He suspected the truth of evolution, but had no mechanism to explain it. Natural selection did not arise from any direct reading of the *Beagle*'s facts, but from two subsequent years of thought and struggle as reflected in a series of remarkable notebooks that have been unearthed and published during the past twenty years. In these notebooks, we see Darwin testing and abandoning a number of theories and pursuing a multitude of false leads—so much for his later claim about recording facts with an empty mind. He read philosophers, poets, and economists, always searching for meaning and insight—so much for the notion that natural selection arose inductively from the *Beagle*'s facts. Later, he labelled one notebook as "full of metaphysics on morals."

Yet if this tortuous path belies the Scylla of inductivism, it has engendered an equally simplistic myth—the Charybdis of eurekaism. In his maddeningly misleading autobiography, Darwin does record a eureka and suggests that natural selection struck him as a sudden, serendipitous flash after more than a year of groping frustration:

15

> In October 1838, that is, fifteen months after I had begun my systematic inquiry, I happened to read for amusement Malthus on Population,[3] and being well prepared to appreciate the struggle for existence which everywhere goes on from long-continued observation of the habits of animals and plants, it at once struck me that under these circumstances favorable variations would tend to be preserved, and unfavorable ones to be destroyed. The result of this would be the formation of new species. Here, then, I had at last got a theory by which to work.

Yet, again, the notebooks belie Darwin's later recollections—in this case by their utter failure to record, at the time it happened, any special exultation

3. Thomas Malthus (1766–1834), whose book *An Essay on the Principle of Population* was published under several titles between 1798 and 1817.

over his Malthusian insight. He inscribes it as a fairly short and sober entry without a single exclamation point, though he habitually used two or three in moments of excitement. He did not drop everything and reinterpret a confusing world in its light. On the very next day, he wrote an even longer passage on the sexual curiosity of primates.

The theory of natural selection arose neither as a workmanlike induction from nature's facts, nor as a mysterious bolt from Darwin's subconscious, triggered by an accidental reading of Malthus. It emerged instead as the result of a conscious and productive search, proceeding in a ramifying but ordered manner, and utilizing both the facts of natural history and an astonishingly broad range of insights from disparate disciplines far from his own. Darwin trod the middle path between inductivism and eurekaism. His genius is neither pedestrian nor inaccessible.

Darwinian scholarship has exploded since the centennial of the *Origin*[4] in 1959. The publication of Darwin's notebooks and the attention devoted by several scholars to the two crucial years between the *Beagle*'s docking and the demoted Malthusian insight has clinched the argument for a "middle path" theory of Darwin's creativity. Two particularly important works focus on the broadest and narrowest scales. Howard E. Gruber's masterful intellectual and psychological biography of this phase in Darwin's life, *Darwin on Man*, traces all the false leads and turning points in Darwin's search. Gruber shows that Darwin was continually proposing, testing, and abandoning hypotheses, and that he never simply collected facts in a blind way. He began with a fanciful theory involving the idea that new species arise with a prefixed life span, and worked his way gradually, if fitfully, towards an idea of extinction by competition in a world of struggle. He recorded no exultation upon reading Malthus, because the jigsaw puzzle was only missing a piece or two at the time.

Silvan S. Schweber has reconstructed, in detail as minute as the record will allow, Darwin's activities during the few weeks before Malthus (The Origin of the *Origin* Revisited, *Journal of the History of Biology*, 1977). He argues that the final pieces arose not from new facts in natural history, but from Darwin's intellectual wanderings in distant fields. In particular, he read a long review of social scientist and philosopher Auguste Comte's most famous work, the *Cours de philosophie positive*. He was particularly struck by Comte's insistence that a proper theory be predictive and at least potentially quantitative. He then turned to Dugald Stewart's *On the Life and Writing of Adam Smith*,[5] and imbibed the basic belief of the Scottish economists that theories of overall social structure must begin by analyzing the unconstrained actions of individuals. (Natural selection is, above all, a theory about the struggle of individual organisms for success in reproduction.) Then, searching for quantification, he read a lengthy analysis of work by the most famous statistician of his time—the Belgian

4. *The Origin of Species* (1859).

5. *Cours de philosophie positive* (Course in positivist philosophy) (1830–42). Dugald Stewart (1753–1828) wrote a brief biography of Adam Smith in 1811, which was frequently included in editions of Smith's *The Wealth of Nations* (1776).

Adolphe Quetelet. In the review of Quetelet, he found, among other things, a forceful statement of Malthus's quantitative claim—that population would grow geometrically and food supplies only arithmetically, thus guaranteeing an intense struggle for existence. In fact, Darwin had read the Malthusian statement several times before; but only now was he prepared to appreciate its significance. Thus, he did not turn to Malthus by accident, and he already knew what it contained. His "amusement," we must assume, consisted only in a desire to read in its original formulation the familiar statement that had so impressed him in Quetelet's secondary account.

In reading Schweber's detailed account of the moments preceding Darwin's formulation of natural selection, I was particularly struck by the absence of deciding influence from his own field of biology. The immediate precipitators were a social scientist, an economist, and a statistician. If genius has any common denominator, I would propose breadth of interest and the ability to construct fruitful analogies between fields.

In fact, I believe that the theory of natural selection should be viewed as an extended analogy—whether conscious or unconscious on Darwin's part I do not know—to the laissez faire economics of Adam Smith. The essence of Smith's argument is a paradox of sorts: if you want an ordered economy providing maximal benefits to all, then let individuals compete and struggle for their own advantages. The result, after appropriate sorting and elimination of the inefficient, will be a stable and harmonious polity. Apparent order arises naturally from the struggle among individuals, not from predestined principles or higher control. Dugald Stewart epitomized Smith's system in the book Darwin read:

> The most effective plan for advancing a people . . . is by allowing every man, as long as he observes the rules of justice, to pursue his own interest in his own way, and to bring both his industry and his capital into the freest competition with those of his fellow citizens. Every system of policy which endeavors . . . to draw towards a particular species of industry a greater share of the capital of the society than would naturally go to it . . . is, in reality, subversive of the great purpose which it means to promote.

As Schweber states: "The Scottish analysis of society contends that the combined effect of individual actions results in the institutions upon which society is based, and that such a society is a stable and evolving one and functions without a designing and directing mind."

We know that Darwin's uniqueness does not reside in his support for the idea of evolution—scores of scientists had preceded him in this. His special contribution rests upon his documentation and upon the novel character of his theory about how evolution operates. Previous evolutionists had proposed unworkable schemes based on internal perfecting tendencies and inherent directions. Darwin advocated a natural and testable theory based on immediate interaction among individuals (his opponents considered it heartlessly mechanistic). The theory of natural selection is a creative transfer to biology of Adam Smith's basic argument for a rational economy: the balance and order of nature does not arise from a higher, external (divine) control, or from the existence of laws operating directly upon the whole, but from struggle among individuals for their own benefits (in modern terms, for the transmission of their genes to future generations through differential success in reproduction).

Many people are distressed to hear such an argument. Does it not compromise the integrity of science if some of its primary conclusions originate by analogy from contemporary politics and culture rather than from data of the discipline itself? In a famous letter to Engels, Karl Marx identified the similarities between natural selection and the English social scene:

> It is remarkable how Darwin recognizes among beasts and plants his English society with its division of labor, competition, opening up of new markets, 'invention,' and the Malthusian 'struggle for existence.' It is Hobbes' *bellum omnium contra omnes* (the war of all against all).[6]

Yet Marx was a great admirer of Darwin—and in this apparent paradox lies resolution. For reasons involving all the themes I have emphasized here—that inductivism is inadequate, that creativity demands breadth, and that analogy is a profound source of insight—great thinkers cannot be divorced from their social background. But the source of an idea is one thing; its truth or fruitfulness is another. The psychology and utility of discovery are very different subjects indeed. Darwin may have cribbed the idea of natural selection from economics, but it may still be right. As the German socialist Karl Kautsky wrote in 1902: "The fact that an idea emanates from a particular class, or accords with their interests, of course proves nothing as to its truth or falsity." In this case, it is ironic that Adam Smith's system of laissez faire does not work in his own domain of economics, for it leads to oligopoly and revolution, rather than to order and harmony. Struggle among individuals does, however, seem to be the law of nature.

Many people use such arguments about social context to ascribe great insights primarily to the indefinable phenomenon of good luck. Thus, Darwin was lucky to be born rich, lucky to be on the *Beagle,* lucky to live amidst the ideas of his age, lucky to trip over Parson Malthus—essentially little more than a man in the right place at the right time. Yet, when we read of his personal struggle to understand, the breadth of his concerns and study, and the directedness of his search for a mechanism of evolution, we understand why Pasteur made his famous quip that fortune favors the prepared mind.[7]

6. From *Leviathan* (1651), by the English philosopher Thomas Hobbes.
7. Louis Pasteur (1822–1895), French chemist and microbiologist.

QUESTIONS

1. What, according to Gould, constituted Darwin's scientific research? How and why did he depict it falsely in his autobiography (paragraph 8)?

2. Rather than isolating scientific research from social and political experience, Darwin, Gould explains, was influenced by a social scientist, an economist, and a statistician (paragraph 20). Identify each one and explain what he contributed to Darwin's theory of natural selection.

3. Consider a recent experience of writing an essay. Did you, thinking and writing, shuttle between inductivism and prediction as Gould claims Darwin did? Describe your experience using Gould's analytic vocabulary.

Literature, the Arts, and Media

Eudora Welty *One Writer's Beginnings*

I LEARNED FROM the age of two or three that any room in our house, at any time of day, was there to read in, or to be read to. My mother read to me. She'd read to me in the big bedroom in the mornings, when we were in her rocker together, which ticked in rhythm as we rocked, as though we had a cricket accompanying the story. She'd read to me in the diningroom on winter afternoons in front of the coal fire, with our cuckoo clock ending the story with "Cuckoo," and at night when I'd got in my own bed. I must have given her no peace. Sometimes she read to me in the kitchen while she sat churning, and the churning sobbed along with *any* story. It was my ambition to have her read to me while *I* churned; once she granted my wish, but she read off my story before I brought her butter. She was an expressive reader. When she was reading "Puss in Boots,"[1] for instance, it was impossible not to know that she distrusted *all* cats.

It had been startling and disappointing to me to find out that story books had been written by *people*, that books were not natural wonders, coming up of themselves like grass. Yet regardless of where they came from, I cannot remember a time when I was not in love with them—with the books themselves, cover and binding and the paper they were printed on, with their smell and their weight and with their possession in my arms, captured and carried off to myself. Still illiterate, I was ready for them, committed to all the reading I could give them.

Neither of my parents had come from homes that could afford to buy many books, but though it must have been something of a strain on his salary, as the youngest officer in a young insurance company, my father was all the while carefully selecting and ordering away for what he and Mother thought we children should grow up with. They bought first for the future.

Besides the bookcase in the livingroom, which was always called "the library," there were the encyclopedia tables and dictionary stand under windows

From a set of three lectures delivered at Harvard University in April 1983, to inaugurate the William E. Massey lecture series, and later published in One Writer's Beginnings *(1984).*

1. A fairy tale.

in our diningroom. Here to help us grow up arguing around the diningroom table were the Unabridged Webster, the Columbia Encyclopedia, Compton's Pictured Encyclopedia, the Lincoln Library of Information, and later the Book of Knowledge. And the year we moved into our new house, there was room to celebrate it with the new 1925 edition of the Britannica, which my father, his face always deliberately turned toward the future, was of course disposed to think better than any previous edition.

In "the library," inside the mission-style bookcase with its three diamond-latticed glass doors, with my father's Morris chair and the glass-shaded lamp on its table beside it, were books I could soon begin on—and I did, reading them all alike and as they came, straight down their rows, top shelf to bottom. There was the set of Stoddard's Lectures, in all its late nineteenth-century vocabulary and vignettes of peasant life and quaint beliefs and customs, with matching halftone illustrations: Vesuvius erupting, Venice by moonlight, gypsies glimpsed by their campfires. I didn't know then the clue they were to my father's longing to see the rest of the world. I read straight through his other love-from-afar: the Victrola Book of the Opera, with opera after opera in synopsis, with portraits in costume of Melba, Caruso, Galli-Curci, and Geraldine Farrar,[2] some of whose voices we could listen to on our Red Seal records.

My mother read secondarily for information; she sank as a hedonist into novels. She read Dickens in the spirit in which she would have eloped with him. The novels of her girlhood that had stayed on in her imagination, besides those of Dickens and Scott and Robert Louis Stevenson,[3] were *Jane Eyre, Trilby, The Woman in White, Green Mansions, King Solomon's Mines.*[4] Marie Corelli's[5] name would crop up but I understood she had gone out of favor with my mother, who had only kept *Ardath* out of loyalty. In time she absorbed herself in Galsworthy, Edith Wharton, above all in Thomas Mann of the *Joseph* volumes.[6]

St. Elmo[7] was not in our house; I saw it often in other houses. This wildly popular Southern novel is where all the Edna Earles in our population started coming from. They're all named for the heroine, who succeeded in bringing a dissolute, sinning roué and atheist of a lover (St. Elmo) to his knees. My mother was able to forgo it. But she remembered the classic advice given to rose growers on how to water their bushes long enough: "Take a chair and *St. Elmo.*"

2. Nellie Melba (1861–1931), Enrico Caruso (1837–1921), Amelita Galli-Curci (1889–1964), Geraldine Farrar (1882–1967), all opera stars.

3. Charles Dickens (1812–1870), Sir Walter Scott (1771–1832), Robert Louis Stevenson (1850–1894). The first was English, the others Scottish.

4. Respectively by Charlotte Brontë (1816–1855), George Du Maurier (1834–1896), Wilkie Collins (1824–1889), William Henry Hudson (1841–1922), Sir H. Rider Haggard (1856–1925). All were British.

5. The pen name of Mary Mills Mackay (1855–1924), a popular and prolific British novelist.

6. John Galsworthy (1867–1933), British; Edith Wharton (1862–1937), American; Thomas Mann (1875–1955), German, whose *Joseph* novels appeared in four parts, from 1933 to 1943.

7. By Augusta Jane Evans (1835–1909).

To both my parents I owe my early acquaintance with a beloved Mark Twain. There was a full set of Mark Twain and a short set of Ring Lardner in our bookcase,[8] and those were the volumes that in time united us all, parents and children.

Reading everything that stood before me was how I came upon a worn old book without a back that had belonged to my father as a child. It was called *Sanford and Merton.* Is there anyone left who recognizes it, I wonder? It is the famous moral tale written by Thomas Day in the 1780s, but of him no mention is made on the title page of *this* book; here it is *Sanford and Merton in Words of One Syllable* by Mary Godolphin. Here are the rich boy and the poor boy and Mr. Barlow, their teacher and interlocutor, in long discourses alternating with dramatic scenes—danger and rescue allotted to the rich and the poor respectively. It may have only words of one syllable, but one of them is "quoth." It ends with not one but two morals, both engraved on rings: "Do what you ought, come what may," and "If we would be great, we must first learn to be good."

10   This book was lacking its front cover, the back held on by strips of pasted paper, now turned golden, in several layers, and the pages stained, flecked, and tattered around the edges; its garish illustrations had come unattached but were preserved, laid in. I had the feeling even in my heedless childhood that this was the only book my father as a little boy had had of his own. He had held onto it, and might have gone to sleep on its coverless face: he had lost his mother when he was seven. My father had never made any mention to his own children of the book, but he had brought it along with him from Ohio to our house and shelved it in our bookcase.

My mother had brought from West Virginia that set of Dickens; those books looked sad, too—they had been through fire and water before I was born, she told me, and there they were, lined up—as I later realized, waiting for *me.*

I was presented, from as early as I can remember, with books of my own, which appeared on my birthday and Christmas morning. Indeed, my parents could not give me books enough. They must have sacrificed to give me on my sixth or seventh birthday—it was after I became a reader for myself—the ten-volume set of Our Wonder World. These were beautifully made, heavy books I would lie down with on the floor in front of the diningroom hearth, and more often than the rest volume 5, *Every Child's Story Book,* was under my eyes. There were the fairy tales—Grimm, Andersen, the English, the French, "Ali Baba and the Forty Thieves"; and there was Aesop and Reynard the Fox; there were the myths and legends, Robin Hood, King Arthur, and St. George and the Dragon, even the history of Joan of Arc; a whack of *Pilgrim's Progress* and a long piece of *Gulliver.*[9] They all carried their classic illustrations. I located myself in these pages and could go straight to the stories and pictures I loved; very often "The Yellow Dwarf" was first choice, with Walter Crane's Yellow

---

8. Mark Twain, the pen name of Samuel Langhorne Clemens (1835–1910); Ring (Ringgold Wilmer) Lardner (1885–1933). Both were American.

9. *The Pilgrim's Progress* by John Bunyan (1628–1688) and *Gulliver's Travels* by Jonathan Swift (1667–1745).

Dwarf in full color making his terrifying appearance flanked by turkeys.[10] Now that volume is as worn and backless and hanging apart as my father's poor *Sanford and Merton*. The precious page with Edward Lear's "Jumblies"[11] on it has been in danger of slipping out for all these years. One measure of my love for Our Wonder World was that for a long time I wondered if I would go through fire and water for it as my mother had done for Charles Dickens; and the only comfort was to think I could ask my mother to do it for me.

I believe I'm the only child I know of who grew up with this treasure in the house. I used to ask others, "Did you have Our Wonder World?" I'd have to tell them The Book of Knowledge could not hold a candle to it.

I live in gratitude to my parents for initiating me—and as early as I begged for it, without keeping me waiting—into knowledge of the word, into reading and spelling, by way of the alphabet. They taught it to me at home in time for me to begin to read before starting to school. I believe the alphabet is no longer considered an essential piece of equipment for traveling through life. In my day it was the keystone to knowledge. You learned the alphabet as you learned to count to ten, as you learned "Now I lay me" and the Lord's Prayer and your father's and mother's name and address and telephone number, all in case you were lost.

My love for the alphabet, which endures, grew out of reciting it but, before that, out of seeing the letters on the page. In my own story books, before I could read them for myself, I fell in love with various winding, enchanting-looking initials drawn by Walter Crane at the heads of fairy tales. In "Once upon a time," an "O" had a rabbit running it as a treadmill, his feet upon flowers. When the day came, years later, for me to see the Book of Kells,[12] all the wizardry of letter, initial, and word swept over me a thousand times over, and the illumination, the gold, seemed a part of the word's beauty and holiness that had been there from the start.

15

Learning stamps you with its moments. Childhood's learning is made up of moments. It isn't steady. It's a pulse.

In a children's art class, we sat in a ring on kindergarten chairs and drew three daffodils that had just been picked out of the yard; and while I was drawing, my sharpened pencil and the cup of the yellow daffodil gave off whiffs just alike. That the pencil doing the drawing should give off the same smell as the flower it drew seemed a part of the art lesson—as shouldn't it be? Children, like animals, use all their senses to discover the world. Then artists come along and discover it the same way, all over again. Here and there, it's the same world. Or now and then we'll hear from an artist who's never lost it.

10. A fairy tale illustrated by Walter Crane (1845–1915), popular illustrator of children's books.

11. A narrative poem about creatures called Jumblies who went to sea in a sieve. Edward Lear (1812–1888), British, wrote nonsense poems for children.

12. An illustrated Irish manuscript of the four Gospels from the eighth or ninth century.

In my sensory education I include my physical awareness of the *word*. Of a certain word, that is; the connection it has with what it stands for. At around age six, perhaps, I was standing by myself in our front yard waiting for supper, just at that hour in a late summer day when the sun is already below the horizon and the risen full moon in the visible sky stops being chalky and begins to take on light. There comes the moment, and I saw it then, when the moon goes from flat to round. For the first time it met my eyes as a globe. The word "moon" came into my mouth as though fed to me out of a silver spoon. Held in my mouth the moon became a word. It had the roundness of a Concord grape Grandpa took off his vine and gave me to suck out of its skin and swallow whole, in Ohio.

This love did not prevent me from living for years in foolish error about the moon. The new moon just appearing in the west was the rising moon to me. The new should be rising. And in early childhood the sun and moon, those opposite reigning powers, I just as easily assumed rose in east and west respectively in their opposite sides of the sky, and like partners in a reel they advanced, sun from the east, moon from the west, crossed over (when I wasn't looking) and went down on the other side. My father couldn't have known I believed that when, bending behind me and guiding my shoulder, he positioned me at our telescope in the front yard and, with careful adjustment of the focus, brought the moon close to me.

20   The night sky over my childhood Jackson[13] was velvety black. I could see the full constellations in it and call their names; when I could read, I knew their myths. Though I was always waked for eclipses, and indeed carried to the window as an infant in arms and shown Halley's Comet[14] in my sleep, and though I'd been taught at our diningroom table about the solar system and knew the earth revolved around the sun, and our moon around us, I never found out the moon didn't come up in the west until I was a writer and Herschel Brickell, the literary critic, told me after I misplaced it in a story. He said valuable words to me about my new profession: "Always be sure you get your moon in the right part of the sky."

My mother always sang to her children. Her voice came out just a little bit in the minor key. "Wee Willie Winkie's" song was wonderfully sad when she sang the lullabies.

"Oh, but now there's a record. She could have her own record to listen to," my father would have said. For there came a Victrola record of "Bobby Shafftoe" and "Rock-a-Bye Baby,"[15] all of Mother's lullabies, which could be played to take her place. Soon I was able to play her my own lullabies all day long.

---

13. Jackson, Mississippi, where Welty grew up.

14. A comet named after Edmund Halley (1656–1742), English astronomer.

15. "Wee Willie Winkie," a nursery rhyme of 1841 in which sleep is personified; "Bobby Shafftoe," a traditional sea chantey dating from about 1750; "Rock-a-Bye Baby," words from *Mother Goose's Melodies* (1765), set to music in 1884.

Our Victrola stood in the diningroom. I was allowed to climb onto the seat of a diningroom chair to wind it, start the record turning, and set the needle playing. In a second I'd jumped to the floor, to spin or march around the table as the music called for—now there were all the other records I could play too. I skinned back onto the chair just in time to lift the needle at the end, stop the record and turn it over, then change the needle. That brass receptacle with a hole in the lid gave off a metallic smell like human sweat, from all the hot needles that were fed it. Winding up, dancing, being cocked to start and stop the record, was of course all in one the act of *listening*—to "Overture to *Daughter of the Regiment*," "Selections from *The Fortune Teller*," "Kiss Me Again," "Gypsy Dance from *Carmen*," "Stars and Stripes Forever," "When the Midnight Choo-Choo Leaves for Alabam," or whatever came next.[16] Movement must be at the very heart of listening.

Ever since I was first read to, then started reading to myself, there has never been a line read that I didn't *hear*. As my eyes followed the sentence, a voice was saying it silently to me. It isn't my mother's voice, or the voice of any person I can identify, certainly not my own. It is human, but inward, and it is inwardly that I listen to it. It is to me the voice of the story or the poem itself. The cadence, whatever it is that asks you to believe, the feeling that resides in the printed word, reaches me through the reader-voice. I have supposed, but never found out, that this is the case with all readers—to read as listeners—and with all writers, to write as listeners. It may be part of the desire to write. The sound of what falls on the page begins the process of testing it for truth, for me. Whether I am right to trust so far I don't know. By now I don't know whether I could do either one, reading or writing, without the other.

My own words, when I am at work on a story, I hear too as they go, in the same voice that I hear when I read in books. When I write and the sound of it comes back to my ears, then I act to make my changes. I have always trusted this voice.

25

16. *Daughter of the Regiment*, an opera (1840) by the Italian composer Gaetano Donizetti; *The Fortune Teller*, an operetta (1898) by the American Victor Herbert; "Kiss Me Again," a song from Herbert's *Mlle. Modiste* (1905); *Carmen*, an opera (1875) by the French composer Georges Bizet; "Stars and Stripes Forever," a march (1897) by the American John Philip Sousa; "When the Midnight Choo-Choo Leaves for Alabam," a popular song (1912) by the American Irving Berlin.

QUESTIONS

1. In the opening paragraphs Welty speaks of what she later calls her "sensory education." What does she mean? What examples does she give?

2. Throughout her essay Welty lists the titles of books that she and her mother read. What is the effect of these lists? Have you read any of the books? Or books like them? How important were they to you?

3. Welty concludes her essay by talking of the writer's voice—of "testing it for truth"

and "trust[ing] this voice" (paragraphs 24 and 25). What meanings does she give the key words "truth" and "trust"?

4. Read John Holt's essay "How Teachers Make Children Hate Reading" (p. 449). Write an essay of your own, entitled "How Children Learn to Love Reading," drawing your evidence from Welty's "One Writer's Beginnings" and your experience, observation, and reading.

5. Welty grew up before the advent of television. How does television affect a child's "sensory education"? Write an essay comparing a modern child's sensory education with Welty's.

VLADIMIR NABOKOV *Good Readers and Good Writers*

"H ow to be a Good Reader" or "Kindness to Authors"—something of that sort might serve to provide a subtitle for these various discussions of various authors, for my plan is to deal lovingly, in loving and lingering detail, with several European masterpieces. A hundred years ago, Flaubert[1] in a letter to his mistress made the following remark: *Comme l'on serait savant si l'on connaissait bien seulement cinq à six livres:* "What a scholar one might be if one knew well only some half a dozen books."

In reading, one should notice and fondle details. There is nothing wrong about the moonshine of generalization when it comes *after* the sunny trifles of the book have been lovingly collected. If one begins with a ready-made generalization, one begins at the wrong end and travels away from the book before one has started to understand it. Nothing is more boring or more unfair to the author than starting to read, say, *Madame Bovary,* with the preconceived notion that it is a denunciation of the bourgeoisie. We should always remember that the work of art is invariably the creation of a new world, so that the first thing we should do is to study that new world as closely as possible, approaching it as something brand new, having no obvious connection with the worlds we already know. When this new world has been closely studied, then and only then let us examine its links with other worlds, other branches of knowledge.

Another question: Can we expect to glean information about places and times from a novel? Can anybody be so naive as to think he or she can learn anything about the past from those buxom best-sellers that are hawked around by book clubs under the heading of historical novels? But what about the mas-

A lecture delivered to Nabokov's undergraduate class at Cornell University, where he taught from 1948 to 1959; published in Lectures on Literature *in 1980.*

1. Gustave Flaubert (1821–1880), French novelist, author of *Madame Bovary.*

terpieces? Can we rely on Jane Austen's[2] picture of landowning England with baronets and landscaped grounds when all she knew was a clergyman's parlor? And *Bleak House*,[3] that fantastic romance within a fantastic London, can we call it a study of London a hundred years ago? Certainly not. And the same holds for other such novels in this series. The truth is that great novels are great fairy tales—and the novels in this series are supreme fairy tales.

Time and space, the colors of the seasons, the movements of muscles and minds, all these are for writers of genius (as far as we can guess and I trust we guess right) not traditional notions which may be borrowed from the circulating library of public truths but a series of unique surprises which master artists have learned to express in their own unique way. To minor authors is left the ornamentation of the commonplace: these do not bother about any reinventing of the world; they merely try to squeeze the best they can out of a given order of things, out of traditional patterns of fiction. The various combinations these minor authors are able to produce within these set limits may be quite amusing in a mild ephemeral way because minor readers like to recognize their own ideas in a pleasing disguise. But the real writer, the fellow who sends planets spinning and models a man asleep and eagerly tampers with the sleeper's rib, that kind of author has no given values at his disposal: he must create them himself. The art of writing is a very futile business if it does not imply first of all the art of seeing the world as the potentiality of fiction. The material of this world may be real enough (as far as reality goes) but does not exist at all as an accepted entirety: it is chaos, and to this chaos the author says "go!" allowing the world to flicker and to fuse. It is now recombined in its very atoms, not merely in its visible and superficial parts. The writer is the first man to map it and to name the natural objects it contains. Those berries there are edible. That speckled creature that bolted across my path might be tamed. That lake between those trees will be called Lake Opal or, more artistically, Dishwater Lake. That mist is a mountain—and that mountain must be conquered. Up a trackless slope climbs the master artist, and at the top, on a windy ridge, whom do you think he meets? The panting and happy reader, and there they spontaneously embrace and are linked forever if the book lasts forever.

One evening at a remote provincial college through which I happened to be jogging on a protracted lecture tour, I suggested a little quiz—ten definitions of a reader, and from these ten the students had to choose four definitions that would combine to make a good reader. I have mislaid the list, but as far as I remember the definitions went something like this. Select four answers to the question what should a reader be to be a good reader:

1. The reader should belong to a book club.

2. The reader should identify himself or herself with the hero or heroine.

2. British novelist (1775–1817).

3. Novel by Charles Dickens (1812–1870) that alternates scenes in London and the country and includes a satire on the British judicial system.

3. The reader should concentrate on the social-economic angle.

4. The reader should prefer a story with action and dialogue to one with none.

5. The reader should have seen the book in a movie.

6. The reader should be a budding author.

7. The reader should have imagination.

8. The reader should have memory.

9. The reader should have a dictionary.

10. The reader should have some artistic sense.

The students leaned heavily on emotional identification, action, and the social-economic or historical angle. Of course, as you have guessed, the good reader is one who has imagination, memory, a dictionary, and some artistic sense—which sense I propose to develop in myself and in others whenever I have the chance.

Incidentally, I use the word *reader* very loosely. Curiously enough, one cannot *read* a book: one can only reread it. A good reader, a major reader, an active and creative reader is a rereader. And I shall tell you why. When we read a book for the first time the very process of laboriously moving our eyes from left to right, line after line, page after page, this complicated physical work upon the book, the very process of learning in terms of space and time what the book is about, this stands between us and artistic appreciation. When we look at a painting we do not have to move our eyes in a special way even if, as in a book, the picture contains elements of depth and development. The element of time does not really enter in a first contact with a painting. In reading a book, we must have time to acquaint ourselves with it. We have no physical organ (as we have the eye in regard to a painting) that takes in the whole picture and then can enjoy its details. But at a second, or third, or fourth reading we do, in a sense, behave towards a book as we do towards a painting. However, let us not confuse the physical eye, that monstrous masterpiece of evolution, with the mind, an even more monstrous achievement. A book, no matter what it is—a work of fiction or a work of science (the boundary line between the two is not as clear as is generally believed)—a book of fiction appeals first of all to the mind. The mind, the brain, the top of the tingling spine, is, or should be, the only instrument used upon a book.

Now, this being so, we should ponder the question how does the mind work when the sullen reader is confronted by the sunny book. First, the sullen mood melts away, and for better or worse the reader enters into the spirit of the game. The effort to begin a book, especially if it is praised by people whom the young reader secretly deems to be too old-fashioned or too serious, this effort is often difficult to make; but once it is made, rewards are various and abundant. Since the master artist used his imagination in creating his book, it is natural and fair that the consumer of a book should use his imagination too.

There are, however, at least two varieties of imagination in the reader's case. So let us see which one of the two is the right one to use in reading a book. First, there is the comparatively lowly kind which turns for support to the simple emotions and is of a definitely personal nature. (There are various subvarieties here, in this first section of emotional reading.) A situation in a book is intensely felt because it reminds us of something that happened to us or to someone we know or knew. Or, again, a reader treasures a book mainly because it evokes a country, a landscape, a mode of living which he nostalgically recalls as part of his own past. Or, and this is the worst thing a reader can do, he identifies himself with a character in the book. This lowly variety is not the kind of imagination I would like readers to use.

So what is the authentic instrument to be used by the reader? It is impersonal imagination and artistic delight. What should be established, I think, is an artistic harmonious balance between the reader's mind and the author's mind. We ought to remain a little aloof and take pleasure in this aloofness while at the same time we keenly enjoy—passionately enjoy, enjoy with tears and shivers—the inner weave of a given masterpiece. To be quite objective in these matters is of course impossible. Everything that is worthwhile is to some extent subjective. For instance, you sitting there may be merely my dream, and I may be your nightmare. But what I mean is that the reader must know when and where to curb his imagination and this he does by trying to get clear the specific world the author places at his disposal. We must see things and hear things, we must visualize the rooms, the clothes, the manners of an author's people. The color of Fanny Price's eyes in *Mansfield Park*[4] and the furnishing of her cold little room are important.

We all have different temperaments, and I can tell you right now that the   10
best temperament for a reader to have, or to develop, is a combination of the artistic and the scientific one. The enthusiastic artist alone is apt to be too subjective in his attitude towards a book, and so a scientific coolness of judgment will temper the intuitive heat. If, however, a would-be reader is utterly devoid of passion and patience—of an artist's passion and a scientist's patience—he will hardly enjoy great literature.

Literature was born not the day when a boy crying wolf, wolf came running out of the Neanderthal valley with a big gray wolf at his heels: literature was born on the day when a boy came crying wolf, wolf and there was no wolf behind him. That the poor little fellow because he lied too often was finally eaten up by a real beast is quite incidental. But here is what is important. Between the wolf in the tall grass and the wolf in the tall story there is a shimmering go-between. That go-between, that prism, is the art of literature.

Literature is invention. Fiction is fiction. To call a story a true story is an insult to both art and truth. Every great writer is a great deceiver, but so is that arch-cheat Nature. Nature always deceives. From the simple deception of propagation to the prodigiously sophisticated illusion of protective colors in

4. Novel by Jane Austen published in 1814.

butterflies or birds, there is in Nature a marvelous system of spells and wiles. The writer of fiction only follows Nature's lead.

Going back for a moment to our wolf-crying woodland little woolly fellow, we may put it this way: the magic of art was in the shadow of the wolf that he deliberately invented, his dream of the wolf; then the story of his tricks made a good story. When he perished at last, the story told about him acquired a good lesson in the dark around the camp fire. But he was the little magician. He was the inventor.

There are three points of view from which a writer can be considered: he may be considered as a storyteller, as a teacher, and as an enchanter. A major writer combines these three—storyteller, teacher, enchanter—but it is the enchanter in him that predominates and makes him a major writer.

15   To the storyteller we turn for entertainment, for mental excitement of the simplest kind, for emotional participation, for the pleasure of traveling in some remote region in space or time. A slightly different though not necessarily higher mind looks for the teacher in the writer. Propagandist, moralist, prophet—this is the rising sequence. We may go to the teacher not only for moral education but also for direct knowledge, for simple facts. Alas, I have known people whose purpose in reading the French and Russian novelists was to learn something about life in gay Paree or in sad Russia. Finally, and above all, a great writer is always a great enchanter, and it is here that we come to the really exciting part when we try to grasp the individual magic of his genius and to study the style, the imagery, the pattern of his novels or poems.

The three facets of the great writer—magic, story, lesson—are prone to blend in one impression of unified and unique radiance, since the magic of art may be present in the very bones of the story, in the very marrow of thought. There are masterpieces of dry, limpid, organized thought which provoke in us an artistic quiver quite as strongly as a novel like *Mansfield Park* does or as any rich flow of Dickensian sensual imagery. It seems to me that a good formula to test the quality of a novel is, in the long run, a merging of the precision of poetry and the intuition of science. In order to bask in that magic a wise reader reads the book of genius not with his heart, not so much with his brain, but with his spine. It is there that occurs the telltale tingle even though we must keep a little aloof, a little detached when reading. Then with a pleasure which is both sensual and intellectual we shall watch the artist build his castle of cards and watch the castle of cards become a castle of beautiful steel and glass.

QUESTIONS

1. Make a list of the qualities that Nabokov believes "good readers" should have; then make a list of the qualities he believes "good writers" should have. Do they correspond? Why or why not?

2. Nabokov, as he points out in the conclusion to his essay (paragraphs 14–16), considers the writer from three points of view: as storyteller, as teacher, and as enchanter. He

has not, however, organized his essay by these points of view. Where and how does he discuss each one? Why does he consider the last the most important?

3. Take Nabokov's quiz (paragraph 5). Write an essay in which you explain your "right" answers (as Nabokov sees "good readers") and defend your "wrong" ones.

4. How would Eudora Welty (see "One Writer's Beginnings," p. 1026) and Katha Pollitt (see "Does a Literary Canon Matter?," p. 1046) do on Nabokov's quiz? Give what you think would be their answers and explain, using information from their essays, what you think their reasons would be.

NORTHROP FRYE   *The Motive for Metaphor*

OR THE PAST twenty-five years I have been teaching and studying English literature in a university. As in any other job, certain questions stick in one's mind, not because people keep asking them, but because they're the questions inspired by the very fact of being in such a place. What good is the study of literature? Does it help us to think more clearly, or feel more sensitively, or live a better life than we could without it? What is the function of the teacher and scholar, or of the person who calls himself, as I do, a literary critic? What difference does the study of literature make in our social or political or religious attitude? In my early days I thought very little about such questions, not because I had any of the answers, but because I assumed that anybody who asked them was naïve. I think now that the simplest questions are not only the hardest to answer, but the most important to ask, so I'm going to raise them and try to suggest what my present answers are. I say try to suggest, because there are only more or less inadequate answers to such questions—there aren't any right answers. The kind of problem that literature raises is not the kind that you ever "solve." Whether my answers are any good or not, they represent a fair amount of thinking about the questions. As I can't see my audience, I have to choose my rhetorical style in the dark, and I'm taking the classroom style, because an audience of students is the one I feel easiest with.

There are two things in particular that I want to discuss with you. In school, and in university, there's a subject called "English" in English-speaking countries. English means, in the first place, the mother tongue. As that, it's the most practical subject in the world: you can't understand anything or take any part in your society without it. Wherever illiteracy is a problem, it's as fundamental a problem as getting enough to eat or a place to sleep. The native language takes precedence over every other subject of study: nothing else can compare with it in its usefulness. But then you find that every mother tongue,

Originally delivered as a speech and then included in Frye's book The Educated Imagination *(1964).*

in any developed or civilized society, turns into something called literature. If you keep on studying "English," you find yourself trying to read Shakespeare and Milton. Literature, we're told, is one of the arts, along with painting and music, and, after you've looked up all the hard words and the Classical allusions and learned what words like imagery and diction are supposed to mean, what you use in understanding it, or so you're told, is your imagination. Here you don't seem to be in quite the same practical and useful area: Shakespeare and Milton, whatever their merits, are not the kind of thing you must know to hold any place in society at all. A person who knows nothing about literature may be an ignoramus, but many people don't mind being that. Every child realizes that literature is taking him in a different direction from the immediately useful, and a good many children complain loudly about this. Two questions I want to deal with, then, are, first: what is the relation of English as the mother tongue to English as a literature? Second: What is the social value of the study of literature, and what is the place of the imagination that literature addresses itself to, in the learning process?

Let's start with the different ways there are of dealing with the world we're living in. Suppose you're shipwrecked on an uninhabited island in the South Seas. The first thing you do is to take a long look at the world around you, a world of sky and sea and earth and stars and trees and hills. You see this world as objective, as something set over against you and not yourself or related to you in any way. And you notice two things about this objective world. In the first place, it doesn't have any conversation. It's full of animals and plants and insects going on with their own business, but there's nothing that responds to you: it has no morals and no intelligence, or at least none that you can grasp. It may have a shape and a meaning, but it doesn't seem to be a human shape or a human meaning. Even if there's enough to eat and no dangerous animals, you feel lonely and frightened and unwanted in such a world.

In the second place, you find that looking at the world, as something set over against you, splits your mind in two. You have an intellect that feels curious about it and wants to study it, and you have feelings or emotions that see it as beautiful or austere or terrible. You know that both these attitudes have some reality, at least for you. If the ship you were wrecked in was a Western ship, you'd probably feel that your intellect tells you more about what's really there in the outer world, and that your emotions tell you more about what's going on inside you. If your background were Oriental, you'd be more likely to reverse this and say that the beauty or terror was what was really there, and that your instinct to count and classify and measure and pull to pieces was what was inside your mind. But whether your point of view is Western or Eastern, intellect and emotion never get together in your mind as long as you're simply looking at the world. They alternate, and keep you divided between them.

5   The language you use on this level of the mind is the language of consciousness or awareness. It's largely a language of nouns and adjectives. You have to have names for things, and you need qualities like "wet" or "green" or "beautiful" to describe how things seem to you. This is the speculative or con-

templative position of the mind, the position in which the arts and sciences begin, although they don't stay there very long. The sciences begin by accepting the facts and the evidence about an outside world without trying to alter them. Science proceeds by accurate measurement and description, and follows the demands of the reason rather than the emotions. What it deals with is there, whether we like it or not. The emotions are unreasonable: for them it's what they like and don't like that comes first. We'd be naturally inclined to think that the arts follow the path of emotion, in contrast to the sciences. Up to a point they do, but there's a complicating factor.

That complicating factor is the contrast between "I like this" and "I don't like this." In this Robinson Crusoe life I've assigned you,[1] you may have moods of complete peacefulness and joy, moods when you accept your island and everything around you. You wouldn't have such moods very often, and when you had them, they'd be moods of identification, when you felt that the island was a part of you and you a part of it. That is not the feeling of consciousness or awareness, where you feel split off from everything that's not your perceiving self. Your habitual state of mind is the feeling of separation which goes with being conscious, and the feeling "this is not a part of me" soon becomes "this is not what I want." Notice the word "want": we'll be coming back to it.

So you soon realize that there's a difference between the world you're living in and the world you want to live in. The world you want to live in is a human world, not an objective one: it's not an environment but a home; it's not the world you see but the world you build out of what you see. You go to work to build a shelter or plant a garden, and as soon as you start to work you've moved into a different level of human life. You're not separating only yourself from nature now, but constructing a human world and separating it from the rest of the world. Your intellect and emotions are now both engaged in the same activity, so there's no longer any real distinction between them. As soon as you plant a garden or a crop, you develop the conception of a "weed," the plant you don't want in there. But you can't say that "weed" is either an intellectual or an emotional conception, because it's both at once. Further, you go to work because you feel you have to, and because you want something at the end of the work. That means that the important categories of your life are no longer the subject and the object, the watcher and the things being watched: the important categories are what you have to do and what you want to do—in other words, necessity and freedom.

One person by himself is not a complete human being, so I'll provide you with another shipwrecked refugee of the opposite sex and an eventual family. Now you're a member of a human society. This human society after a while will transform the island into something with a human shape. What that human shape is, is revealed in the shape of the work you do: the buildings, such as they are, the paths through the woods, the planted crops fenced off against whatever animals want to eat them. These things, these rudiments of city,

1. Referring to *Robinson Crusoe* (1719), a novel by Daniel Defoe (1660–1731) about a man shipwrecked on an island.

highway, garden, and farm, are the human form of nature, or the form of human nature, whichever you like. This is the area of the applied arts and sciences, and it appears in our society as engineering and agriculture and medicine and architecture. In this area we can never say clearly where the art stops and the science begins, or vice versa.

The language you use on this level is the language of practical sense, a language of verbs or words of action and movement. The practical world, however, is a world where actions speak louder than words. In some way it's a higher level of existence than the speculative level, because it's doing something about the world instead of just looking at it, but in itself it's a much more primitive level. It's the process of adapting to the environment, or rather of transforming the environment in the interests of one species, that goes on among animals and plants as well as human beings. The animals have a good many of our practical skills: some insects make pretty fair architects, and beavers know quite a lot about engineering. In this island, probably, and certainly if you were alone, you'd have about the ranking of a second-rate animal. What makes our practical life really human is a third level of the mind, a level where consciousness and practical skill come together.

10   This third level is a vision or model in your mind of what you want to construct. There's that word "want" again. The actions of man are prompted by desire, and some of these desires are needs, like food and warmth and shelter. One of these needs is sexual, the desire to reproduce and bring more human beings into existence. But there's also a desire to bring a social human form into existence: the form of cities and gardens and farms that we call civilization. Many animals and insects have this social form too, but man knows that he has it: he can compare what he does with what he can imagine being done. So we begin to see where the imagination belongs in the scheme of human affairs. It's the power of constructing possible models of human experience. In the world of the imagination, anything goes that's imaginatively possible, but nothing really happens. If it did happen, it would move out of the world of imagination into the world of action.

We have three levels of the mind now, and a language for each of them, which in English-speaking societies means an English for each of them. There's the level of consciousness and awareness, where the most important thing is the difference between me and everything else. The English of this level is the English of ordinary conversation, which is mostly monologue, as you'll soon realize if you do a bit of eavesdropping, or listening to yourself. We can call it the language of self-expression. Then there's the level of social participation, the working or technological language of teachers and preachers and politicians and advertisers and lawyers and journalists and scientists. We've already called this the language of practical sense. Then there's the level of imagination, which produces the literary language of poems and plays and novels. They're not really different languages, of course, but three different reasons for using words.

On this basis, perhaps, we can distinguish the arts from the sciences. Science begins with the world we have to live in, accepting its data and trying to explain its laws. From there, it moves towards the imagination: it becomes a mental construct, a model of a possible way of interpreting experience. The further it goes in this direction, the more it tends to speak the language of mathematics, which is really one of the languages of the imagination, along with literature and music. Art, on the other hand, begins with the world we construct, not with the world we see. It starts with the imagination, and then works towards ordinary experience: that is, it tries to make itself as convincing and recognizable as it can. You can see why we tend to think of the sciences as intellectual and the arts as emotional: one starts with the world as it is, the other with the world we want to have. Up to a point it is true that science gives an intellectual view of reality, and that the arts try to make the emotions as precise and disciplined as sciences do the intellect. But of course it's nonsense to think of the scientist as a cold unemotional reasoner and the artist as somebody who's in a perpetual emotional tizzy. You can't distinguish the arts from the sciences by the mental processes the people in them use: they both operate on a mixture of hunch and common sense. A highly developed science and a highly developed art are very close together, psychologically and otherwise.

Still, the fact that they start from opposite ends, even if they do meet in the middle, makes for one important difference between them. Science learns more and more about the world as it goes on: it evolves and improves. A physicist today knows more physics than Newton did, even if he's not as great a scientist. But literature begins with the possible model of experience, and what it produces is the literary model we call the classic. Literature doesn't evolve or improve or progress. We may have dramatists in the future who will write plays as good as *King Lear*, though they'll be very different ones, but drama as a whole will never get better than *King Lear*. *King Lear* is it, as far as drama is concerned; so is *Oedipus Rex*, written two thousand years earlier than that,[2] and both will be models of dramatic writing as long as the human race endures. Social conditions may improve: most of us would rather live in nineteenth-century United States than in thirteenth-century Italy, and for most of us Whitman's celebration of democracy makes a lot more sense than Dante's *Inferno*.[3] But it doesn't follow that Whitman is a better poet than Dante: literature won't line up with that kind of improvement.

So we find that everything that does improve, including science, leaves the literary artist out in the cold. Writers don't seem to benefit much by the advance of science, although they thrive on superstitions of all kinds. And you certainly wouldn't turn to contemporary poets for guidance or leadership in the twentieth-century world. You'd hardly go to Ezra Pound, with his fascism and social credit and Confucianism and anti-semitism. Or to Yeats, with his spiritualism and fairies and astrology. Or to D. H. Lawrence, who'll tell you

---

2. The first is a tragedy by Shakespeare (1564–1616), the second a tragedy by Sophocles (496?–406? B.C.E.).

3. Walt Whitman (1819–1892), American poet; see "Abraham Lincoln" (p. 112) and "Death of Abraham Lincoln" (p. 803). Dante Alighieri (1265–1321); the *Inferno* is the first part of his *Divine Comedy*.

that it's a good thing for servants to be flogged because that restores the precious current of blood-reciprocity between servant and master. Or to T. S. Eliot, who'll tell you that to have a flourishing culture we should educate an élite, keep most people living in the same spot, and never disestablish the Church of England.[4] The novelists seem to be a little closer to the world they're living in, but not much. When Communists talk about the decadence of bourgeois culture, this is the kind of thing they always bring up. Their own writers don't seem to be any better, though; just duller. So the real question is a bigger one. Is it possible that literature, especially poetry, is something that a scientific civilization like ours will eventually outgrow? Man has always wanted to fly, and thousands of years ago he was making sculptures of winged bulls and telling stories about people who flew so high on artificial wings that the sun melted them off.[5] In an Indian play fifteen hundred years old, *Sakuntala*, there's a god who flies around in a chariot that to a modern reader sounds very much like a private aeroplane. Interesting that the writer had so much imagination, but do we need such stories now that we have private aeroplanes?

15   This is not a new question: it was raised a hundred and fifty years ago by Thomas Love Peacock,[6] who was a poet and novelist himself, and a very brilliant one. He wrote an essay called *Four Ages of Poetry,* with his tongue of course in his cheek, in which he said that poetry was the mental rattle that awakened the imagination of mankind in its infancy, but that now, in an age of science and technology, the poet has outlived his social function. "A poet in our times," said Peacock, "is a semi-barbarian in a civilized community. He lives in the days that are past. His ideas, thoughts, feelings, associations, are all with barbarous manners, obsolete customs, and exploded superstitions. The march of his intellect is like that of a crab, backwards." Peacock's essay annoyed his friend Shelley,[7] who wrote another essay called *A Defence of Poetry* to refute it. Shelley's essay is a wonderful piece of writing, but it's not likely to convince anyone who needs convincing. I shall be spending a good deal of my time on this question of the relevance of literature in the world of today, and I can only indicate the general lines my answer will take. There are two points I can make now, one simple, the other more difficult.

The simple point is that literature belongs to the world man constructs, not to the world he sees; to his home, not his environment. Literature's world is a concrete human world of immediate experience. The poet uses images and

---

4. Ezra Pound (1885–1972), an American-born poet, supported Mussolini's fascist regime in Italy and the right-wing economic doctrine of social credit. William Butler Yeats (1865–1939), Irish poet and dramatist; see, for example, his prose work *A Vision*. D. H. Lawrence (1885–1930), British author; see his short story "The Prussian Officer." T. S. Eliot (1888–1965), American-born poet who emigrated to England; see his prose work *The Idea of a Christian Society*.

5. An allusion to the Greek myth of Icarus, who flew too close to the sun on wings made of wax by his father, Daedalus.

6. British author (1785–1866).

7. Percy Bysshe Shelley (1792–1822), British poet.

objects and sensations much more than he uses abstract ideas; the novelist is concerned with telling stories, not with working out arguments. The world of literature is human in shape, a world where the sun rises in the east and sets in the west over the edge of a flat earth in three dimensions, where the primary realities are not atoms or electrons but bodies, and the primary forces not energy or gravitation but love and death and passion and joy. It's not surprising if writers are often rather simple people, not always what we think of as intellectuals, and certainly not always any freer of silliness or perversity than anyone else. What concerns us is what they produce, not what they are, and poetry, according to Milton,[8] who ought to have known, is "more simple, sensuous and passionate" than philosophy or science.

The more difficult point takes us back to what we said when we were on that South Sea island. Our emotional reaction to the world varies from "I like this" to "I don't like this." The first, we said, was a state of identity, a feeling that everything around us was part of us, and the second is the ordinary state of consciousness, or separation, where art and science begin. Art begins as soon as "I don't like this" turns into "this is not the way I could imagine it." We notice in passing that the creative and the neurotic minds have a lot in common. They're both dissatisfied with what they see; they both believe that something else ought to be there, and they try to pretend it is there or to make it be there. The differences are more important, but we're not ready for them yet.

At the level of ordinary consciousness the individual man is the center of everything, surrounded on all sides by what he isn't. At the level of practical sense, or civilization, there's a human circumference, a little cultivated world with a human shape, fenced off from the jungle and inside the sea and the sky. But in the imagination anything goes that can be imagined, and the limit of the imagination is a totally human world. Here we recapture, in full consciousness, that original lost sense of identity with our surroundings, where there is nothing outside the mind of man, or something identical with the mind of man. Religions present us with visions of eternal and infinite heavens or paradises which have the form of the cities and gardens of human civilization, like the Jerusalem and Eden of the Bible, completely separated from the state of frustration and misery that bulks so large in ordinary life. We're not concerned with these visions as religion, but they indicate what the limits of the imagination are. They indicate too that in the human world the imagination has no limits, if you follow me. We said that the desire to fly produced the aeroplane. But people don't get into planes because they want to fly; they get into planes because they want to get somewhere else faster. What's produced the aeroplane is not so much a desire to fly as a rebellion against the tyranny of time and space. And that's a process that can never stop, no matter how high our Titovs and Glenns[9] may go.

8. John Milton (1608–1674), British poet; from a prose work, *Tractate of Education*.
9. Gherman S. Titov, Russian astronaut, first man to make a multi-orbital flight (1961); John H. Glenn, American astronaut, first American to make an orbital flight (1962), later became a senator from Ohio.

For each of these six talks I've taken a title from some work of literature, and my title for this one is "The Motive for Metaphor," from a poem of Wallace Stevens.[10] Here's the poem:

> You like it under the trees in autumn,
> Because everything is half dead.
> The wind moves like a cripple among the leaves
> And repeats words without meaning.
>
> In the same way, you were happy in spring,
> With the half colors of quarter-things,
> The slightly brighter sky, the melting clouds,
> The single bird, the obscure moon—
>
> The obscure moon lighting an obscure world
> Of things that would never be quite expressed,
> Where you yourself were never quite yourself
> And did not want nor have to be,
>
> Desiring the exhilarations of changes:
> The motive for metaphor, shrinking from
> The weight of primary noon,
> The A B C of being,
>
> The ruddy temper, the hammer
> Of red and blue, the hard sound—
> Steel against intimation—the sharp flash,
> The vital, arrogant, fatal, dominant X.

What Stevens calls the weight of primary noon, the A B C of being, and the dominant X is the objective world, the world set over against us. Outside literature, the main motive for writing is to describe this world. But literature itself uses language in a way which associates our minds with it. As soon as you use associative language, you begin using figures of speech. If you say this talk is dry and dull, you're using figures associating it with bread and breadknives. There are two main kinds of association, analogy and identity, two things that are like each other and two things that are each other. You can say with Burns,[11] "My love's like a red, red rose," or you can say with Shakespeare:

> Thou that art now the world's fresh ornament
> And only herald to the gaudy spring.

One produces the figure of speech called the simile; the other produces the figure called metaphor.

10. American poet (1879–1955).
11. Robert Burns (1759–1796), Scottish poet.

In descriptive writing you have to be careful of associative language. You'll   20
find that analogy, or likeness to something else, is very tricky to handle in description, because the differences are as important as the resemblances. As for
metaphor, where you're really saying "this *is* that," you're turning your back on
logic and reason completely, because logically two things can never be the
same thing and still remain two things. The poet, however, uses these two
crude, primitive, archaic forms of thought in the most uninhibited way, because his job is not to describe nature, but to show you a world completely absorbed and possessed by the human mind. So he produces what Baudelaire[12]
called a "suggestive magic including at the same time object and subject, the
world outside the artist and the artist himself." The motive for metaphor, according to Wallace Stevens, is a desire to associate, and finally to identify, the
human mind with what goes on outside it, because the only genuine joy you
can have is in those rare moments when you feel that although we may know
in part, as Paul says, we are also a part of what we know.[13]

12. Charles Baudelaire (1821–1867), French poet.
13. An allusion to 1 Corinthians 13.9–10: "For we know in part, and we prophecy in
part. But when that which is perfect is come, then that which is in part shall be done
away with."

QUESTIONS

1. At what point in his essay does Frye come to the meaning of his title? What is his
conception of the motive for metaphor? Why does he wait to explain it?

2. Frye describes three kinds of English, or, rather, he describes one English and three
uses to which we put it. What are they?

3. Frye describes metaphor, forcibly, as nonsense (paragraph 20). How, then, do we
make sense of it?

4. Why, according to Frye, doesn't literature improve the way science does? What happens to old science? Read Thomas S. Kuhn's "The Route to Normal Science" (p. 948),
and do additional research if necessary. Then write an essay in which you compare the
fates of old literature and old science.

KATHA POLLITT *Does a Literary Canon Matter?*

OR THE PAST couple of years we've all been witness to a furious debate about the literary canon. What books should be assigned to students? What books should critics discuss? What books should the rest of us read, and who are "we" anyway? Like everyone else, I've given these questions some thought, and when an invitation came my way, I leaped to produce my own manifesto. But to my surprise, when I sat down to write—in order to discover, as E. M. Forster[1] once said, what I really think—I found that I agreed with all sides in the debate at once.

Take the conservatives. Now, this rather dour collection of scholars and diatribists—Allan Bloom, Hilton Kramer, John Silber[2] and so on—are not a particularly appealing group of people. They are arrogant, they are rude, they are gloomy, they do not suffer fools gladly, and everywhere they look, fools are what they see. All good reasons not to elect them to public office, as the voters of Massachusetts recently decided. But what is so terrible, really, about what they are saying? I too believe that some books are more profound, more complex, more essential to an understanding of our culture than others; I too am appalled to think of students graduating from college not having read Homer, Plato, Virgil, Milton, Tolstoy[3]—all writers, dead white Western men though they be, whose works have meant a great deal to me. As a teacher of literature and of writing, I too have seen at first hand how ill-educated many students are, and how little aware they are of this important fact about themselves. Last year I taught a graduate seminar in the writing of poetry. None of my students had read more than a smattering of poems by anyone, male or female, published more than ten years ago. Robert Lowell was as far outside their frame of reference as Alexander Pope.[4] When I gently suggested to one student that it might benefit her to

Pollitt writes a regular column in the Nation, *a liberal weekly magazine. This selection was her contribution for September 23, 1991.*

1. British novelist (1879–1970) and member of the Bloomsbury group.

2. Bloom (1930–1992), professor of political philosophy at the University of Chicago and author of *The Closing of the American Mind* (1987); Kramer, art critic, editor of the *New Criterion*, and author of *The Revenge of the Philistines: Art and Culture, 1972–84* (1985); Silber (b. 1926), president, then chancellor, of Boston University, author of *Straight Shooting: What's Wrong with America and How to Fix It* (1989), ran for governor of Massachusetts.

3. Homer (eighth century B.C.E.), Greek epic poet, author of the *Iliad* and the *Odyssey*; Plato (427–347 B.C.E.), Greek philosopher; Virgil (Publius Vergilius Maro, 70–19 B.C.E.), Roman poet, author of the *Aeneid*; John Milton (1608–1674), British poet, author of *Paradise Lost* (1667); Leo (Count Lev Nikolayevich) Tolstoy (1828–1910), Russian novelist and essayist.

4. Lowell (1917–1977), American poet; Pope (1688–1744), British poet.

read some poetry if she planned to spend her life writing it, she told me that yes, she knew she should read more but when she encountered a really good poem it only made her depressed. That contemporary writing has a history which it profits us to know in some depth, that we ourselves were not born yesterday, seems too obvious even to argue.

But ah, say the liberals, the canon exalted by the conservatives is itself an artifact of history. Sure, some books are more rewarding than others, but why can't we change our minds about which books those are? The canon itself was not always as we know it today: Until the 1920s, *Moby-Dick*[5] was shelved with the boys' adventure stories. If T. S. Eliot could single-handedly dethrone the Romantic poets in favor of the neglected Metaphysicals and place John Webster alongside Shakespeare, why can't we dip into the sea of stories and fish out Edith Wharton or Virginia Woolf?[6] And this position too makes a great deal of sense to me. After all, alongside the many good reasons for a book to end up on the required-reading shelf are some rather suspect reasons for its exclusion: because it was written by a woman and therefore presumed to be too slight; because it was written by a black person and therefore presumed to be too unsophisticated or to reflect too special a case. By all means, say the liberals, let's have great books and a shared culture. But let's make sure that all the different kinds of greatness are represented and that the culture we share reflects the true range of human experience.

If we leave the broadening of the canon up to the conservatives, this will never happen, because to them change only means defeat. Look at the recent fuss over the latest edition of the Great Books series published by *Encyclopaedia Britannica,* headed by that old snake-oil salesman Mortimer Adler. Four women have now been added to the series: Virginia Woolf, Willa Cather, Jane Austen and George Eliot.[7] That's nice, I suppose, but really! Jane Austen has been a certified Great Writer for a hundred years! Lionel Trilling[8] said so! There's something truly absurd about the conservatives earnestly sitting in judgment on the illustrious dead, as though up in Writers' Heaven Jane and George and Willa and Virginia were breathlessly waiting to hear if they'd finally made it into the club, while Henry Fielding, newly dropped from the list, howls in outer darkness and the Brontës,[9] presumably, stamp their feet in frus-

5. Novel by Herman Melville (1819–1891) published in 1851.

6. Eliot (1888–1965), American-born British poet and literary critic; Webster (c. 1578–c. 1632), English playwright; William Shakespeare (1564–1616), English playwright; Wharton (1862–1937), American novelist; Woolf (1882–1941), British novelist and essayist.

7. Cather (1876–1947), American novelist; Austen (1775–1817), British novelist; George Eliot, pseudonym of Mary Ann Evans (1819–1890), British novelist and literary critic.

8. American literary critic (1905–1975) whose important studies *The Opposing Self* (1955) and *Beyond Culture* (1966) include discussions of Jane Austen's novels.

9. Fielding (1707–1754), British novelist; Charlotte (1816–1855), Emily (1818–1848), and Anne (1820–1849) Brontë, authors of *Jane Eyre, Wuthering Heights,* and *Agnes Grey,* respectively.

tration and hope for better luck in twenty years, when *Jane Eyre* and *Wuthering Heights* will suddenly turn out to have qualities of greatness never before detected in their pages. It's like Poets' Corner at Manhattan's Cathedral of St. John the Divine, where mortal men—and a woman or two—of letters actually vote on which immortals to honor with a plaque, a process no doubt complete with electoral campaigns, compromise candidates and all the rest of the underside of the literary life. "No, I'm sorry, I just can't vote for Whitman. I'm a Washington Irving[10] man myself."

5   A liberal is not a very exciting thing to be, and so we have the radicals, who attack the concepts of "greatness," "shared," "culture" and "lists." (I'm overlooking here the ultraradicals, who attack the "privileging" of "texts," as they insist on calling books, and think one might as well spend one's college years deconstructing *Leave It to Beaver*.)[11] Who is to say, ask the radicals, what is a great book? What's so terrific about complexity, ambiguity, historical centrality and high seriousness? If *The Color Purple*,[12] say, gets students thinking about their own experience, maybe they ought to read it and forget about— and here you can fill in the name of whatever classic work you yourself found dry and tedious and never got around to finishing. For the radicals the notion of a shared culture is a lie, because it means presenting as universally meaningful and politically neutral books that reflect the interests and experiences and values of privileged white men at the expense of those of others—women, blacks, Latinos, Asians, the working class, whoever. Why not scrap the one-list-for-everyone idea and let people connect with books that are written by people like themselves about people like themselves? It will be a more accurate reflection of a multifaceted and conflict-ridden society, and will do wonders for everyone's self-esteem, except, of course, living white men—but they have too much self-esteem already.

        Now, I have to say that I dislike the radicals' vision intensely. How foolish to argue that Chekhov[13] has nothing to say to a black woman—or, for that matter, myself—merely because he is Russian, long dead, a man. The notion that one reads to increase one's self-esteem sounds to me like more snake oil. Literature is not an aerobics class or a session at the therapist's. But then I think of myself as a child, leafing through anthologies of poetry for the names of women. I never would have admitted that I needed a role model, even if that awful term had existed back in the prehistory of which I speak, but why was I so excited to find a female name, even when, as was often the case, it was attached to a poem of no interest to me whatsoever? Anna Laetitia Barbauld, author of "Life! I know not what thou art / but know that thou and I

10. Walt Whitman (1819–1892), American poet; Irving (1783–1859), American essayist and fiction writer.

11. Television sitcom popular in the 1950s and 1960s.

12. Novel by Alice Walker (b. 1944), African American fiction writer and essayist, published in 1982.

13. Anton Chekhov (1860–1904), Russian dramatist and fiction writer.

must part!"; Lady Anne Lindsay,[14] writer of languid ballads in incomprehensible Scots dialect; and the other minor female poets included by chivalrous Sir Arthur Quiller-Couch in the old *Oxford Book of English Verse*: I have to admit it, just by their presence in that august volume they did something for me. And although it had nothing to do with reading or writing, it was an important thing they did.

What are we to make of this spluttering debate, in which charges of imperialism are met by equally passionate accusations of vandalism, in which each side hates the others, and yet each one seems to have its share of reason? Perhaps what we have here is one of those debates in which the opposing sides, unbeknownst to themselves, share a myopia that will turn out to be the most telling feature of the whole discussion: a debate, for instance, like that of our Founding Fathers over the nature of the franchise. Think of all the energy and passion spent pondering the question of property qualifications or direct versus legislative elections while all along, unmentioned and unimagined, was the fact—to us so central—that women and slaves were never considered for any kind of vote.

Something is being overlooked: the state of reading, and books, and literature in our country at this time. Why, ask yourself, is everyone so hot under the collar about what to put on the required-reading shelf? It is because while we have been arguing so fiercely about which books make the best medicine, the patient has been slipping deeper and deeper into a coma.

Let us imagine a country in which reading is a popular voluntary activity. There, parents read books for their own edification and pleasure, and are seen by their children at this silent and mysterious pastime. These parents also read to their children, give them books for presents, talk to them about books and underwrite, with their taxes, a public library system that is open all day, every day. In school—where an attractive library is invariably to be found—the children study certain books together but also have an active reading life of their own. Years later it may even be hard for them to remember if they read *Jane Eyre* at home and Judy Blume[15] in class, or the other way around. In college young people continue to be assigned certain books, but far more important are the books they discover for themselves—browsing in the library, in bookstores, on the shelves of friends, one book leading to another, back and forth in history and across languages and cultures. After graduation they continue to read, and in the fullness of time produce a new generation of readers. Oh happy land! I wish we all lived there.

In that other country of real readers—voluntary, active, self-determined readers—a debate like the current one over the canon would not be taking place. Or if it did, it would be as a kind of parlor game: What books would you take to a desert island? Everyone would know that the top-ten list was merely a tiny fraction of the books one would read in a life-time. It would not seem

10

14. Barbauld (1743–1825), British poet; Lady Anne Lindsay Barnard (1750–1825), Scottish poet.

15. American writer (b. 1938) of young adult fiction.

racist or sexist or hopelessly hidebound to put Hawthorne on the syllabus and not Toni Morrison.[16] It would be more like putting oatmeal and not noodles on the breakfast menu—a choice part arbitrary, part a nod to the national past, part, dare one say it, a kind of reverse affirmative action: School might frankly be the place where one read the books that are a little off-putting, that have gone a little cold, that you might pass over because they do not address, in reader-friendly contemporary fashion, the issues most immediately at stake in modern life, but that, with a little study, turn out to have a great deal to say. Being on the list wouldn't mean so much. It might even add to a writer's cachet not to be on the list, to be in one way or another too heady, too daring, too exciting to be ground up into institutional fodder for teenagers. Generations of high school kids have been turned off to George Eliot by being forced to read *Silas Marner* at a tender age. One can imagine a whole new readership for her if grown-ups were left to approach *Middlemarch* and *Daniel Deronda*[17] with open minds, at their leisure.

Of course, they rarely do. In America today the assumption underlying the canon debate is that the books on the list are the only books that are going to be read, and if the list is dropped no books are going to be read. Becoming a textbook is a book's only chance; all sides take that for granted. And so all agree not to mention certain things that they themselves, as highly educated people and, one assumes, devoted readers, know perfectly well. For example, that if you read only twenty-five, or fifty, or a hundred books, you can't understand them, however well chosen they are. And that if you don't have an independent reading life—and very few students do—you won't like reading the books on the list and will forget them the minute you finish them. And that books have, or should have, lives beyond the syllabus—thus, the totally misguided attempt to put current literature in the classroom. How strange to think that people need professorial help to read John Updike[18] or Alice Walker, writers people actually do read for fun. But all sides agree, if it isn't taught, it doesn't count.

Let's look at the canon question from another angle. Instead of asking what books we want others to read, let's ask why we read books ourselves. I think the canon debaters are being a little disingenuous here, are suppressing, in the interest of their own agendas, their personal experience of reading. Sure, we read to understand our American culture and history, and we also read to recover neglected masterpieces, and to learn more about the accomplishments of our subgroup and thereby, as I've admitted about myself, increase our self-esteem. But what about reading for the aesthetic pleasures of language, form, image? What about reading to learn something new, to have a vicarious adventure, to follow the workings of an interesting, if possibly skewed, narrow and ill-tempered mind? What about reading for the story? For

16. Nathaniel Hawthorne (1804–1864), American novelist; Toni Morrison (b. 1931), African American novelist.
17. Novels by George Eliot written in 1861, 1871–72, and 1874–76, respectively.
18. Updike (b. 1932), American fiction writer and literary critic.

an expanded sense of sheer human variety? There are a thousand reasons why a book might have a claim on our time and attention other than its canonization. I once infuriated an acquaintance by asserting that Trollope, although in many ways a lesser writer than Dickens,[19] possessed some wonderful qualities Dickens lacked: a more realistic view of women, a more skeptical view of good intentions, a subtler sense of humor, a drier vision of life which I myself found congenial. You'd think I'd advocated throwing Dickens out and replacing him with a toaster. Because Dickens is a certified Great Writer, and Trollope is not.

Am I saying anything different from what Randall Jarrell[20] said in his great 1953 essay "The Age of Criticism"? Not really, so I'll quote him. Speaking of the literary gatherings of the era, Jarrell wrote:

> If at such parties, you wanted to talk about *Ulysses* or *The Castle* or *The Brothers Karamazov* or *The Great Gatsby* or Graham Greene's last novel— Important books—you were at the right place. (Though you weren't so well off if you wanted to talk about *Remembrance of Things Past*. Important, but too long.) But if you wanted to talk about Turgenev's novelettes, or *The House of the Dead*, or *Lavengro*, or *Life on the Mississippi*, or *The Old Wives' Tale*, or *The Golovlyov Family*, or Cunningham-Grahame's stories, or Saint-Simon's memoirs, or *Lost Illusions*, or *The Beggar's Opera*, or *Eugene Onegin*, or *Little Dorrit*, or the Burnt Njál Saga, or *Persuasion*, or *The Inspector-General*, or *Oblomov*, or *Peer Gynt*, or *Far from the Madding Crowd*, or *Out of Africa*, or the *Parallel Lives*, or *A Dreary Story*, or *Debits and Credits*, or *Arabia Deserta*, or *Elective Affinities*, or *Schweik*, or—any of a thousand good or interesting but Unimportant books, you couldn't expect a very ready knowledge or sympathy from most of the readers there. They had looked at the big sights, the current sights, hard, with guides and glasses; and those walks in the country, over unfrequented or thrice-familiar territory, all alone—those walks from which most of the joy and good of reading come—were walks that they hadn't gone on very often.

I suspect that most canon debaters have taken those solitary rambles, if only out of boredom—how many times, after all, can you reread the *Aeneid*, or *Mrs. Dalloway*, or *Cotton Comes to Harlem*[21] (to pick one book from each column)? But those walks don't count, because of another assumption all sides hold in common, which is that the purpose of reading is none of the many varied and delicious satisfactions I've mentioned; it's medicinal. The chief end of reading is to produce a desirable kind of person and a desirable kind of society. A respectful, high-minded citizen of a unified society for the conservatives, an up-to-date and flexible sort for the liberals, a subgroup-identified, robustly confident one for the radicals. How pragmatic, how moralistic, how American! The culture debaters turn out to share a secret suspicion of culture itself, as

---

19. Anthony Trollope (1815–1882), British novelist; Charles Dickens (1812–1870), British novelist.

20. American poet and literary critic (1914–1965).

21. The *Aeneid* (composed 29–19 B.C.E.), Latin epic poem by Virgil; *Mrs. Dalloway* (1925), novel by Virginia Woolf; *Cotton Comes to Harlem* (1965), detective novel by Chester Himes (1909–1984).

well as the antipornographer's belief that there is a simple, one-to-one correlation between books and behavior. Read the conservatives' list and produce a nation of sexists and racists—or a nation of philosopher kings. Read the liberals' list and produce a nation of spineless relativists—or a nation of open-minded world citizens. Read the radicals' list and produce a nation of psychobabblers and ancestor-worshipers—or a nation of stalwart proud-to-be-me pluralists.

15   But is there any list of a few dozen books that can have such a magical effect, for good or for ill? Of course not. It's like arguing that a perfectly nutritional breakfast cereal is enough food for the whole day. And so the canon debate is really an argument about what books to cram down the resistant throats of a resentful captive populace of students; and the trick is never to mention the fact that, in such circumstances, one book is as good, or as bad, as another. Because, as the debaters know from their own experience as readers, books are not pills that produce health when ingested in measured doses. Books do not shape character in any simple way—if, indeed, they do so at all—or the most literate would be the most virtuous instead of just the ordinary run of humanity with larger vocabularies. Books cannot mold a common national purpose when, in fact, people are honestly divided about what kind of country they want—and are divided, moreover, for very good and practical reasons, as they always have been.

For these burly and energetic purposes, books are all but useless. The way books affect us is an altogether more subtle, delicate, wayward and individual, not to say private, affair. And that reading is being made to bear such an inappropriate and simplistic burden speaks to the poverty both of culture and of frank political discussion in our time.

On his deathbed, Dr. Johnson[22]—once canonical, now more admired than read—is supposed to have said to a friend who was energetically rearranging his bedclothes, "Thank you, this will do all that a pillow can do." One might say that the canon debaters are all asking of their handful of chosen books that they do a great deal more than any handful of books can do.

22. Samuel Johnson (1709–1784), British author and compiler of the *Dictionary of the English Language* (1755).

QUESTIONS

1. Pollitt's strategy of argument is classification; she enunciates three positions on the literary canon. How many times does this three-part classification appear in her essay? Mark them.

2. What are the points of difference among the three positions? More important to Pollitt's own argument, what are their points of similarity?

3. What are the strengths and weaknesses of Pollitt's finding herself in partial agreement with all three positions? You may want to contrast her style of argument with Michael Levin's in "The Case for Torture" (p. 689). Levin, like a debater, argues only his

own position and puts down, entirely, the counterarguments of those who disagree with him. Is Pollitt's or Levin's approach more congenial to you?

4. Write a two- or three-part essay in which you argue the strengths and weaknesses of all three positions outlined by Pollitt.

Ngũgĩ wa Thiong'o *Decolonizing the Mind*

I WAS BORN into a large peasant family: father, four wives and about twenty-eight children. I also belonged, as we all did in those days, to a wider extended family and to the community as a whole.

We spoke Gĩkũyũ[1] as we worked in the fields. We spoke Gĩkũyũ in and outside the home. I can vividly recall those evenings of storytelling around the fireside. It was mostly the grown-ups telling the children but everybody was interested and involved. We children would re-tell the stories the following day to other children who worked in the fields picking the pyrethrum[2] flowers, tea-leaves or coffee beans of our European and African landlords.

The stories, with mostly animals as the main characters, were all told in Gĩkũyũ. Hare, being small, weak but full of innovative wit and cunning, was our hero. We identified with him as he struggled against the brutes of prey like lion, leopard, hyena. His victories were our victories and we learned that the apparently weak can outwit the strong. We followed the animals in their struggle against hostile nature—drought, rain, sun, wind—a confrontation often forcing them to search for forms of co-operation. But we were also interested in their struggles amongst themselves, and particularly between the beasts and the victims of prey. These twin struggles, against nature and other animals, reflected real-life struggles in the human world.

Not that we neglected stories with human beings as the main characters. There were two types of characters in such human-centered narratives: the species of truly human beings with qualities of courage, kindness, mercy, hatred of evil, concern for others; and a man-eat-man two-mouthed species with qualities of greed, selfishness, individualism and hatred of what was good for the larger co-operative community. Co-operation as the ultimate good in a community was a constant theme. It could unite human beings with animals against ogres and beasts of prey, as in the story of how dove, after being fed with castor-oil seeds, was sent to fetch a smith working far away from home

Published in Decolonising the Mind: The Politics of Language in African Literature *(1986), a collection of essays reflecting on the relations of modern African literature to its European heritage and arguing for a new, independent African tradition.*

1. Language spoken by the Kikuyu people, the majority of Kenyans.
2. Type of chrysanthemum, often used as an insecticide or for medicinal purposes.

and whose pregnant wife was being threatened by these man-eating two-mouthed ogres.

There were good and bad story-tellers. A good one could tell the same story over and over again, and it would always be fresh to us, the listeners. He or she could tell a story told by someone else and make it more alive and dramatic. The differences really were in the use of words and images and the inflection of voices to effect different tones.

We therefore learned to value words for their meaning and nuances. Language was not a mere string of words. It had a suggestive power well beyond the immediate and lexical meaning. Our appreciation of the suggestive magical power of language was reinforced by the games we played with words through riddles, proverbs, transpositions of syllables, or through nonsensical but musically arranged words. So we learned the music of our language on top of the content. The language, through images and symbols, gave us a view of the world, but it had a beauty of its own. The home and the field were then our pre-primary school but what is important, for this discussion, is that the language of our evening teach-ins, and the language of our immediate and wider community, and the language of our work in the fields were one.

And then I went to school, a colonial school, and this harmony was broken. The language of my education was no longer the language of my culture. I first went to Kamaandura, missionary run, and then to another called Maanguuū run by nationalists grouped around the Gĩkũyũ Independent and Karinga Schools Association. Our language of education was still Gĩkũyũ. The very first time I was ever given an ovation for my writing was over a composition in Gĩkũyũ. So for my first four years there was still harmony between the language of my formal education and that of the Limuru peasant community.

It was after the declaration of a state of emergency over Kenya in 1952 that all the schools run by patriotic nationalists were taken over by the colonial regime and were placed under District Education Boards chaired by Englishmen. English became the language of my formal education. In Kenya, English became more than a language: it was *the* language, and all the others had to bow before it in deference.

Thus one of the most humiliating experiences was to be caught speaking Gĩkũyũ in the vicinity of the school. The culprit was given corporal punishment—three to five strokes of the cane on bare buttocks—or was made to carry a metal plate around the neck with inscriptions such as I AM STUPID or I AM A DONKEY. Sometimes the culprits were fined money they could hardly afford. And how did the teachers catch the culprits? A button was initially given to one pupil who was supposed to hand it over to whoever was caught speaking his mother tongue. Whoever had the button at the end of the day would sing who had given it to him and the ensuing process would bring out all the culprits of the day. Thus children were turned into witch-hunters and in the process were being taught the lucrative value of being a traitor to one's immediate community.

The attitude to English was the exact opposite: any achievement in spoken or written English was highly rewarded; prizes, prestige, applause; the ticket to higher realms. English became the measure of intelligence and ability in the arts, the sciences, and all the other branches of learning. English became *the* main determinant of a child's progress up the ladder of formal education.

As you may know, the colonial system of education in addition to its apartheid racial demarcation had the structure of a pyramid: a broad primary base, a narrowing secondary middle, and an even narrower university apex. Selections from primary into secondary were through an examination, in my time called Kenya African Preliminary Examination, in which one had to pass six subjects ranging from Maths to Nature Study and Kiswahili.[3] All the papers were written in English. Nobody could pass the exam who failed the English language paper no matter how brilliantly he had done in the other subjects. I remember one boy in my class of 1954 who had distinctions in all subjects except English, which he had failed. He was made to fail the entire exam. He went on to become a turn boy[4] in a bus company. I who had only passes but a credit in English got a place at the Alliance High School, one of the most elitist institutions for Africans in colonial Kenya. The requirements for a place at the University, Makerere University College, were broadly the same: nobody could go on to wear the undergraduate red gown, no matter how brilliantly they had performed in all the other subjects unless they had a credit—not even a simple pass!—in English. Thus the most coveted place in the pyramid and in the system was only available to the holder of an English language credit card. English was the official vehicle and the magic formula to colonial elitedom.

Literary education was now determined by the dominant language while also reinforcing that dominance. Orature (oral literature) in Kenyan languages stopped. In primary school I now read simplified Dickens and Stevenson alongside Rider Haggard. Jim Hawkins, Oliver Twist, Tom Brown[5]—not Hare, Leopard and Lion—were now my daily companions in the world of imagination. In secondary school, Scott and G. B. Shaw vied with more Rider Haggard, John Buchan, Alan Paton, Captain W. E. Johns.[6] At Makerere I read English: from Chaucer to T.S. Eliot with a touch of Grahame Greene.[7]

Thus language and literature were taking us further and further from ourselves to other selves, from our world to other worlds.

3. Swahili, a major East African language.

4. A tout; someone who brings in customers.

5. Charles Dickens (1812–1870), British novelist, author of *Oliver Twist*; Robert Louis Stevenson (1850–1894), Scottish novelist, creator of Jim Hawkins in *Treasure Island*; H. Rider Haggard (1856–1925), British adventure novelist; Tom Brown, chief character in *Tom Brown's Schooldays* in the novel by Thomas Hughes (1822–1896).

6. Sir Walter Scott (1771–1832), Scottish poet and novelist; George Bernard Shaw (1856–1950), Irish-born playwright; Buchan (1875–1940), Scottish adventure novelist, author of *The Thirty-Nine Steps*, and also governor general of Canada; Paton (1903–1988), South African novelist; Johns (1893–1968), British writer, famous for the Biggles stories for boys.

7. Geoffrey Chaucer (c. 1343–1400), English poet, author of *The Canterbury Tales*; Eliot (1888–1965), American-born poet; Greene (1904–1991), British novelist.

What was the colonial system doing to us Kenyan children? What were the consequences of, on the one hand, this systematic suppression of our languages and the literature they carried, and on the other the elevation of English and the literature it carried? To answer those questions, let me first examine the relationship of language to human experience, human culture, and the human perception of reality.

15   Language, any language, has a dual character: it is both a means of communication and a carrier of culture. Take English. It is spoken in Britain and in Sweden and Denmark. But for Swedish and Danish people English is only a means of communication with non-Scandinavians. It is not a carrier of their culture. For the British, and particularly the English, it is additionally, and inseparably from its use as a tool of communication, a carrier of their culture and history. Or take Swahili in East and Central Africa. It is widely used as a means of communication across many nationalities. But it is not the carrier of a culture and history of many of those nationalities. However in parts of Kenya and Tanzania, and particularly in Zanzibar,[8] Swahili is inseparably both a means of communication and a carrier of the culture of those people to whom it is a mother-tongue.

Language as communication has three aspects or elements. There is first what Karl Marx[9] once called the language of real life, the element basic to the whole notion of language, its origins and development: that is, the relations people enter into with one another in the labor process, the links they necessarily establish among themselves in the act of a people, a community of human beings, producing wealth or means of life like food, clothing, houses. A human community really starts its historical being as a community of co-operation in production through the division of labor; the simplest is between man, woman and child within a household; the more complex divisions are between branches of production such as those who are sole hunters, sole gatherers of fruits or sole workers in metal. Then there are the most complex divisions such as those in modern factories where a single product, say a shirt or a shoe, is the result of many hands and minds. Production is co-operation, is communication, is language, is expression of a relation between human beings and it is specifically human.

The second aspect of language as communication is speech and it imitates the language of real life, that is communication in production. The verbal signposts both reflect and aid communication or the relation established between human beings in the production of their means of life. Language as a system of verbal signposts makes that production possible. The spoken word is to relations between human beings what the hand is to the relations between human beings and nature. The hand through tools mediates between human beings and nature and forms the language of real life: spoken words mediate between human beings and form the language of speech.

8. Island off the east coast of Africa; part of Tanzania since 1964.
9. German political philosopher (1818–1883).

The third aspect is the written signs. The written word imitates the spoken. Where the first two aspects of language as communication through the hand and the spoken word historically evolved more or less simultaneously, the written aspect is a much later historical development. Writing is representation of sounds with visual symbols, from the simplest knot among shepherds to tell the number in a herd or the hieroglyphics among the Agĩkũyũ gicaandi[10] singers and poets of Kenya, to the most complicated and different letter and picture writing systems of the world today.

In most societies the written and the spoken languages are the same, in that they represent each other: what is on paper can be read to another person and be received as that language, which the recipient has grown up speaking. In such a society there is broad harmony for a child between the three aspects of language as communication. His interaction with nature and with other men is expressed in written and spoken symbols or signs which are both a result of that double interaction and a reflection of it. The association of the child's sensibility is with the language of his experience of life.

But there is more to it: communication between human beings is also the basis and process of evolving culture. In doing similar kinds of things and actions over and over again under similar circumstances, similar even in their mutability, certain patterns, moves, rhythms, habits, attitudes, experiences and knowledge emerge. Those experiences are handed over to the next generation and become the inherited basis for their further actions on nature and on themselves. There is a gradual accumulation of values which in time become almost self-evident truths governing their conception of what is right and wrong, good and bad, beautiful and ugly, courageous and cowardly, generous and mean in their internal and external relations. Over a time this becomes a way of life distinguishable from other ways of life. They develop a distinctive culture and history. Culture embodies those moral, ethical and aesthetic values, the set of spiritual eyeglasses, through which they come to view themselves and their place in the universe. Values are the basis of a people's identity, their sense of particularity as members of the human race. All this is carried by language. Language as culture is the collective memory bank of a people's experience in history. Culture is almost indistinguishable from the language that makes possible its genesis, growth, banking, articulation and indeed its transmission from one generation to the next.

Language as culture also has three important aspects. Culture is a product of the history which it in turn reflects. Culture in other words is a product and a reflection of human beings communicating with one another in the very struggle to create wealth and to control it. But culture does not merely reflect that history, or rather it does so by actually forming images or pictures of the world of nature and nurture. Thus the second aspect of language as culture is as an image-forming agent in the mind of a child. Our whole conception of ourselves as a people, individually and collectively, is based on those pictures

20

10. Agĩkũyũ, another term for Kikuyu, the group that forms the majority of the Kenyan population; gicaandi, a particular Kenyan song genre.

and images which may or may not correctly correspond to the actual reality of the struggles with nature and nurture which produced them in the first place. But our capacity to confront the world creatively is dependent on how those images correspond or not to that reality, how they distort or clarify the reality of our struggles. Language as culture is thus mediating between me and my own self; between my own self and other selves; between me and nature. Language is mediating in my very being. And this brings us to the third aspect of language as culture. Culture transmits or imparts those images of the world and reality through the spoken and the written language, that is through a specific language. In other words, the capacity to speak, the capacity to order sounds in a manner that makes for mutual comprehension between human beings is universal. This is the universality of language, a quality specific to human beings. It corresponds to the universality of the struggle against nature and that between human beings. But the particularity of the sounds, the words, the word order into phrases and sentences, and the specific manner, or laws, of their ordering is what distinguishes one language from another. Thus a specific culture is not transmitted through language in its universality but in its particularity as the language of a specific community with a specific history. Written literature and orature are the main means by which a particular language transmits the images of the world contained in the culture it carries.

Language as communication and as culture are then products of each other. Communication creates culture: culture is a means of communication. Language carries culture, and culture carries, particularly through orature and literature, the entire body of values by which we come to perceive ourselves and our place in the world. How people perceive themselves affects how they look at their culture, at their politics and at the social production of wealth, at their entire relationship to nature and to other beings. Language is thus inseparable from ourselves as a community of human beings with a specific form and character, a specific history, a specific relationship to the world.

So what was the colonialist imposition of a foreign language doing to us children?

The real aim of colonialism was to control the people's wealth: what they produced, how they produced it, and how it was distributed; to control, in other words, the entire realm of the language of real life. Colonialism imposed its control of the social production of wealth through military conquest and subsequent political dictatorship. But its most important area of domination was the mental universe of the colonized, the control, through culture, of how people perceived themselves and their relationship to the world. Economic and political control can never be complete or effective without mental control. To control a people's culture is to control their tools of self-definition in relationship to others.

25   For colonialism this involved two aspects of the same process: the destruction or the deliberate undervaluing of a people's culture, their art, dances, religions, history, geography, education, orature and literature, and the conscious elevation of the language of the colonizer. The domination of a peo-

ple's language by the languages of the colonizing nations was crucial to the domination of the mental universe of the colonized.

Take language as communication. Imposing a foreign language, and suppressing the native languages as spoken and written, were already breaking the harmony previously existing between the African child and the three aspects of language. Since the new language as a means of communication was a product of and was reflecting the "real language of life" elsewhere, it could never as spoken or written properly reflect or imitate the real life of that community. This may in part explain why technology always appears to us as slightly external, *their* product and not *ours*. The word "missile" used to hold an alien faraway sound until I recently learnt its equivalent in Gĩkũyũ, *ngurukuhĩ* and it made me apprehend it differently. Learning, for a colonial child, became a cerebral activity and not an emotionally felt experience.

But since the new, imposed languages could never completely break the native languages as spoken, their most effective area of domination was the third aspect of language as communication, the written. The language of an African child's formal education was foreign. The language of the books he read was foreign. The language of his conceptualization was foreign. Thought, in him, took the visible form of a foreign language. So the written language of a child's upbringing in the school (even his spoken language within the school compound) became divorced from his spoken language at home. There was often not the slightest relationship between the child's written world, which was also the language of his schooling, and the world of his immediate environment in the family and the community. For a colonial child, the harmony existing between the three aspects of language as communication was irrevocably broken. This resulted in the disassociation of the sensibility[11] of that child from his natural and social environment, what we might call colonial alienation. The alienation became reinforced in the teaching of history, geography, music, where bourgeois Europe was always the center of the universe.

The disassociation, divorce, or alienation from the immediate environment becomes clearer when you look at colonial language as a carrier of culture.

Since culture is a product of the history of a people which it in turn reflects, the child was now being exposed exclusively to a culture that was a product of a world external to himself. He was being made to stand outside himself to look at himself. *Catching Them Young* is the title of a book on racism, class, sex, and politics in children's literature by Bob Dixon.[12] "Catching them young" as an aim was even more true of a colonial child. The images of his world and his place in it implanted in a child take years to eradicate, if they ever can be.

Since culture does not just reflect the world in images but actually,   30

---

11. An echo of T. S. Eliot's famous term "dissociation of sensibility," a break from the past, when thought and feeling were unified.

12. Bob Dixon's *Catching Them Young* appeared in two volumes: *Sex, Race, and Class in Children's Fiction* and *Political Ideas in Children's Fiction*.

through those images, conditions a child to see that world a certain way, the colonial child was made to see the world and where he stands in it as seen and defined by or reflected in the culture of the language of imposition.

And since those images are mostly passed on through orature and litera-ture it meant the child would now only see the world as seen in the literature of his language of adoption. From the point of view of alienation, that is of seeing oneself from outside oneself as if one was another self, it does not mat-ter that the imported literature carried the great humanist tradition of the best Shakespeare, Goethe, Balzac, Tolstoy, Gorky, Brecht, Sholokhov,[13] Dickens. The location of this great mirror of imagination was necessarily Europe and its history and culture and the rest of the universe was seen from that center.

But obviously it was worse when the colonial child was exposed to images of his world as mirrored in the written languages of his colonizer. Where his own native languages were associated in his impressionable mind with low sta-tus, humiliation, corporal punishment, slow-footed intelligence and ability or downright stupidity, non-intelligibility and barbarism, this was reinforced by the world he met in the works of such geniuses of racism as a Rider Haggard or a Nicholas Monsarrat;[14] not to mention the pronouncement of some of the giants of western intellectual and political establishment, such as Hume (". . . The negro is naturally inferior to the whites . . ."), Thomas Jefferson (". . . The blacks . . . are inferior to the whites on the endowments of both body and mind . . ."), or Hegel[15] with his Africa comparable to a land of childhood still enveloped in the dark mantle of the night as far as the development of self-conscious history was concerned. Hegel's statement that there was noth-ing harmonious with humanity to be found in the African character is repre-sentative of the racist images of Africans and Africa such a colonial child was bound to encounter in the literature of the colonial languages. The results could be disastrous.

13. William Shakespeare (1564–1616), English playwright; Johann Wolfgang von Goethe (1749–1832), German novelist and playwright; Honoré de Balzac (1799–1850), French novelist; Leo (Count Lev Nikolayerich) Tolstoy (1828–1910), Russian novelist; Maxim Gorky (1868–1936), Russian dramatist; Bertolt Brecht (1898–1956), German dramatist; Mikhail Aleksandrovich Sholokhov (1905–1984), Russian novelist.

14. British novelist Nicholas Monsarrat's *The Tribe That Lost Its Head* (1956) was a satirical look at British colonialism and the African independence movement.

15. David Hume (1711–1776), Scottish philosopher; Jefferson (1743–1826), third U.S. president, 1801–9; Georg Wilhelm Friedrich Hegel (1770–1831), German philosopher.

QUESTIONS

1. The last paragraphs of Ngũgĩ's essay contain the names of many classic and contem-porary European writers. Why do you think he chose to include them? Can you relate their inclusion to the way Ngũgĩ chooses to present himself in this essay?

2. What literary writers did you read in secondary school? Was there any theme or purpose behind that selection? (You may find some help in Pollitt's essay on a literary canon, p. 1046.)

3. Write a paper characterizing the writers Ngũgĩ was assigned when he was at the British school. What do they have in common? Who is left out? Then speculate on why such writers were chosen.

ADRIENNE RICH   *When We Dead Awaken: Writing as Re-vision*

I BSEN'S[1] *When We Dead Awaken* is a play about the use that the male artist and thinker—in the process of creating culture as we know it—has made of women, in his life and in his work; and about a woman's slow struggling awakening to the use to which her life has been put. Bernard Shaw[2] wrote in 1900 of this play: "[Ibsen] shows us that no degradation ever devized or permitted is as disastrous as this degradation; that through it women can die into luxuries for men and yet can kill them; that men and women are becoming conscious of this: and that what remains to be seen as perhaps the most interesting of all imminent social developments is what will happen 'when we dead awaken.' "

It's exhilarating to be alive in a time of awakening consciousness; it can also be confusing, disorienting, and painful. This awakening of dead or sleeping consciousness has already affected the lives of millions of women, even those who don't know it yet. It is also affecting the lives of men, even those who deny its claims upon them. The argument will go on whether an oppressive economic class system is responsible for the oppressive nature of male/female relations, or whether, in fact, the sexual class system is the original model on which all the others are based. But in the last few years connections have been drawn between our sexual lives and our political institutions which are inescapable and illuminating. The sleepwalkers are coming awake, and for the first time this awakening has a collective reality; it is no longer such a lonely thing to open one's eyes.

Re-vision—the act of looking back, of seeing with fresh eyes, of entering an old text from a new critical direction—is for us more than a chapter in cultural history: it is an act of survival. Until we can understand the assumptions

Delivered as a public address in 1971 at a forum on "The Woman Writer in the Twentieth Century" and published in 1972 by College English, *a professional journal for English teachers. Reprinted in* On Lies, Secrets, and Silence: Selected Prose 1966–1978 *(1979).*

1. Henrik Ibsen (1828–1906), Norwegian dramatist.
2. George Bernard Shaw (1856–1950), Irish-born dramatist.

in which we are drenched we cannot know ourselves. And this drive to self-knowledge, for woman, is more than a search for identity: it is part of her refusal of the destructiveness of male-dominated society. A radical critique of literature, feminist in its impulse, would take the work first of all as a clue to how we live, how we have been living, how we have been led to imagine ourselves, how our language has trapped as well as liberated us; and how we can begin to see—and therefore live—afresh. A change in the concept of sexual identity is essential if we are not going to see the old political order reassert itself in every new revolution. We need to know the writing of the past, and know it differently than we have ever known it; not to pass on a tradition but to break its hold over us.

For writers, and at this moment for women writers in particular, there is the challenge and promise of a whole new psychic geography to be explored. But there is also a difficult and dangerous walking on the ice, as we try to find language and images for a consciousness we are just coming into, and with little in the past to support us. I want to talk about some aspects of this difficulty and this danger.

5   Jane Harrison, the great classical anthropologist, wrote in 1914 in a letter to her friend Gilbert Murray:[3] "By the by, about 'Women,' it has bothered me often—why do women never want to write poetry about Man as a sex—why is Woman a dream and a terror to man and not the other way around? . . . Is it mere convention and propriety, or something deeper?" I think Jane's question cuts deep into the myth-making tradition, the romantic tradition; deep into what women and men have been to each other; and deep into the psyche of the woman writer. Thinking about that question, I began thinking of the work of two twentieth-century women poets, Sylvia Plath and Diane Wakoski.[4] It strikes me that in the work of both Man appears as, if not a dream, a fascination, and a terror; and that the source of the fascination and the terror is, simply, Man's power—to dominate, tyrannize, choose or reject the woman. The charisma of Man seems to come purely from his power over her, and his control of the world by force; not from anything fertile or life-giving in him. And, in the work of both these poets, it is finally the woman's sense of *herself*—embattled, possessed—that gives the poetry its dynamic charge, its rhythms of struggle, need, will and female energy. Convention and propriety are perhaps not the right words, but until recently this female anger, this furious awareness of the Man's power over her, were not available materials to the female poet, who tended to write of Love as the source of her suffering, and to view that victimization by Love as an almost inevitable fate. Or, like Marianne Moore and Elizabeth Bishop,[5] she kept human sexual relationships at a measured and chiselled distance in her poems.

One answer to Jane Harrison's question has to be that historically men and women have played very different parts in each others' lives. Where woman has been a luxury for man, and has served as the painter's model and

3. Harrison (1850–1928); Murray (1866–1957), British classical scholar.
4. Plath (1932–1963) and Wakoski (b. 1937), American poets contemporary with Rich.
5. Moore (1882–1932) and Bishop (1911–1979), American poets.

the poet's muse, but also as comforter, nurse, cook, bearer of his seed, secretarial assistant, and copyist of manuscripts, man has played a quite different role for the female artist. Henry James repeats an incident which the writer Prosper Mérimée described, of how, while he was living with George Sand,[6]

> he once opened his eyes, in the raw winter dawn, to see his companion, in a dressing-gown, on her knees before the domestic hearth, a candle-stick beside her and a red *madras* round her head, making bravely, with her own hands, the fire that was to enable her to sit down betimes to urgent pen and paper. The story represents him as having felt that the spectacle chilled his ardor and tried his taste; her appearance was unfortunate, her occupation an inconsequence, and her industry a reproof—the result of all of which was a lively irritation and an early rupture.

I am suggesting that the specter of this kind of male judgment, along with the active discouragement and thwarting of her needs by a culture controlled by males, has created problems for the woman writer: problems of contact with herself, problems of language and style, problems of energy and survival.

In rereading Virginia Woolf's *A Room of One's Own* for the first time in some years, I was astonished at the sense of effort, of pains taken, of dogged tentativeness, in the tone of that essay. And I recognized that tone. I had heard it often enough, in myself and in other women. It is the tone of a woman almost in touch with her anger, who is determined not to appear angry, who is *willing* herself to be calm, detached, and even charming in a roomful of men where things have been said which are attacks on her very integrity. Virginia Woolf is addressing an audience of women, but she is acutely conscious—as she always was—of being overheard by men: by Morgan and Lytton and Maynard Keynes and for that matter by her father, Leslie Stephen.[7] She drew the language out into an exacerbated thread in her determination to have her own sensibility yet protect it from those masculine presences. Only at rare moments in that essay do you hear the passion in her voice; she was trying to sound as cool as Jane Austen, as Olympian as Shakespeare,[8] because that is the way the men of the culture thought a writer should sound.

No male writer has written primarily or even largely for women, or with the sense of women's criticism as a consideration when he chooses his materials, his theme, his language. But to a lesser or greater extent, every woman writer has written for men even when, like Virginia Woolf, she was supposed to be addressing women. If we have come to the point when this balance might begin to change, when women can stop being haunted, not only by

---

6. James (1843–1916), American novelist, expatriate; Mérimée (1803–1870), French novelist and historian; George Sand (1804–1876), pseudonym of Amandine Aurore Lucie Dupin, Baronne Dudevant, French novelist.

7. Edward Morgan Forster, novelist; Lytton Strachey, biographer; and John Maynard Keynes, economist—all members of the Bloomsbury group in London during the 1920s and 1930s; Sir Leslie Stephen (1832–1904), notable English man of letters.

8. Austen (1775–1817), English novelist; William Shakespeare (1564–1616), English dramatist.

"convention and propriety" but by internalized fears of being and saying themselves, then it is an extraordinary moment for the woman writer—and reader.

I have hesitated to do what I am going to do now, which is to use myself as an illustration. For one thing, it's a lot easier and less dangerous to talk about other women writers. But there is something else. Like Virginia Woolf, I am aware of the women who are not with us here because they are washing the dishes and looking after the children. Nearly fifty years after she spoke, that fact remains largely unchanged. And I am thinking also of women whom she left out of the picture altogether—women who are washing other people's dishes and caring for other people's children, not to mention women who went on the streets last night in order to feed their children. We seem to be special women here, we have liked to think of ourselves as special, and we have known that men would tolerate, even romanticize us as special, as long as our words and actions didn't threaten their privilege of tolerating or rejecting us according to *their* ideas of what a special woman ought to be. An important insight of the radical women's movement, for me, has been how divisive and how ultimately destructive is this myth of the special woman, who is also the token woman. Every one of us here in this room has had great luck; our own gifts could not have been enough, for we all know women whose gifts are buried or aborted. Our struggles can have meaning only if they can help to change the lives of women whose gifts—and whose very being—continue to be thwarted.

10   My own luck was being born white and middle-class into a house full of books, with a father who encouraged me to read and write. So for about twenty years I wrote for a particular man, who criticized and praised me and made me feel I was indeed "special." The obverse side of this, of course, was that I tried for a long time to please him, or rather, not to displease him. And then of course there were other men—writers, teachers—the Man, who was not a terror or a dream but a literary master and a master in other ways less easy to acknowledge. And there were all those poems about women, written by men: it seemed to be a given that men wrote poems and women frequently inhabited them. These women were almost always beautiful, but threatened with the loss of beauty, the loss of youth—the fate worse than death. Or, they were beautiful and died young, like Lucy and Lenore.[9] Or, the woman was like Maud Gonne,[10] cruel and disastrously mistaken, and the poem reproached her because she had refused to become a luxury for the poet.

A lot is being said today about the influence that the myths and images of women have on all of us who are products of culture. I think it has been a peculiar confusion to the girl or woman who tries to write, because she is peculiarly susceptible to language. She goes to poetry or fiction looking for *her* way of being in the world, since she too has been putting words and images together; she is looking eagerly for guides, maps, possibilities; and over and over in the "words' masculine persuasive force" of literature she comes up against something that negates everything she is about: she meets the image of Woman in

9. In poems by William Wordsworth and Edgar Allan Poe.
10. Irish revolutionary activist, subject of many love poems by William Butler Yeats.

books written by men. She finds a terror and a dream, she finds a beautiful pale face, she finds La Belle Dame Sans Merci, she finds Juliet or Tess or Salomé,[11] but precisely what she does not find is that absorbed, drudging, puzzled, sometimes inspired creature, herself, who sits at a desk trying to put words together.

So what does she do? What did I do? I read the older women poets with their peculiar keenness and ambivalence: Sappho, Christina Rossetti, Emily Dickinson, Elinor Wylie, Edna Millay, H.D. I discovered that the woman poet most admired at the time (by men) was Marianne Moore,[12] who was maidenly, elegant, intellectual, discreet. But even in reading these women I was looking in them for the same things I had found in the poetry of men, because I wanted women poets to be the equals of men, and to be equal was still confused with sounding the same.

I know that my style was formed first by male poets: by the men I was reading as an undergraduate—Frost, Dylan Thomas, Donne, Auden, MacNiece, Stevens, Yeats.[13] What I chiefly learned from them was craft. But poems are like dreams: in them you put what you don't know you know. Looking back at poems I wrote before I was twenty-one, I'm startled because beneath the conscious craft are glimpses of the split I even then experienced between the girl who wrote poems, who defined herself in writing poems, and the girl who was to define herself by her relationships with men. "Aunt Jennifer's Tigers," written while I was a student, looks with deliberate detachment at this split.

> Aunt Jennifer's tigers stride across a screen,
> Bright topaz denizens of a world of green.
> They do not fear the men beneath the tree,
> They pace in sleek chivalric certainty.
>
> Aunt Jennifer's fingers, fluttering through her wool,
> Find even the ivory needle hard to pull.
> The massive weight of Uncle's wedding-band
> Sits heavily upon Aunt Jennifer's hand.
>
> When Aunt is dead, her terrified hands will lie
> Still ringed with ordeals she was mastered by.
> The tigers in the panel that she made
> Will go on striding, proud and unafraid.

11. These female figures appear respectively in the poem "La Belle Dame sans Merci" by John Keats, Shakespeare's play *Romeo and Juliet*, Thomas Hardy's novel *Tess of the D'Urbervilles*, and Oscar Wilde's play *Salomé*.

12. Sappho (seventh century B.C.E.), Greek; Rossetti (1830–1894), English; Dickinson (1830–1886), Wylie (1885–1928), Millay (1892–1950), Hilda Doolittle (1886–1961), Marianne Moore (1887–1972), all American.

13. Robert Frost (1865–1963), American; Thomas (1914–1953), Welsh; John Donne (1572–1631), English; W. H. Auden (1907–1973), English-born, emigrated to the United States; Louis MacNiece (1907–1963), English; Wallace Stevens (1879–1955), American; William Butler Yeats (1865–1939), Irish.

In writing this poem, composed and apparently cool as it is, I thought I was creating a portrait of an imaginary woman. But this woman suffers from the opposition of her imagination, worked out in tapestry, and her life-style, "ringed with ordeals she was mastered by." It was important to me that Aunt Jennifer was a person as distinct from myself as possible—distanced by the formalism of the poem; by its objective, observant tone; even by putting the woman in a different generation.

In those years formalism was part of the strategy—like asbestos gloves, it allowed me to handle materials I couldn't pick up barehanded. (A later strategy was to use the persona of a man, as I did in "The Loser.")

A man thinks of the woman he once loved: first, after her wedding, and then nearly a decade later.

I

I kissed you, bride and lost, and went
home from that bourgeois sacrament,
your cheek still tasting cold upon
my lips that gave you benison
with all the swagger that they knew—
as losers somehow learn to do.

Your wedding made my eyes ache; soon
the world would be worse off for one
more golden apple dropped to ground
without the least protesting sound,
and you would windfall lie, and we
forget your shimmer on the tree.

Beauty is always wasted: if
not Mignon's song sung to the deaf,
at all events to the unmoved.
A face like yours cannot be loved
long or seriously enough.
Almost, we seem to hold it off.

II

Well, you are tougher than I thought.
Now when the wash with ice hangs taut
this morning of St. Valentine,
I see you strip the squeaking line,
your body weighed against the load,
and all my groans can do no good.

Because you still are beautiful,
though squared and stiffened by the pull
of what nine windy years have done.
You have three daughters, lost a son.
I see all your intelligence
flung into that unwearied stance.

My envy is of no avail.
I turn my head and wish him well
who chafed your beauty into use
and lives forever in a house
lit by the friction of your mind.
You stagger in against the wind.

1958

I finished college, published my first book by a fluke, as it seemed to me, and broke off a love-affair. I took a job, lived alone, went on writing, fell in love. I was young, full of energy, and the book seemed to mean that others agreed I was a poet. Because I was also determined to have a "full" woman's life, I plunged in my early twenties into marriage and had three children before I was thirty. There was nothing overt in the environment to warn me: these were the fifties, and in reaction to the earlier wave of feminism, middle-class women were making careers of domestic perfection, working to send their husbands through professional schools, then retiring to raise large families. People were moving out to the suburbs, technology was going to be the answer to everything, even sex; the family was in its glory. Life was extremely private; women were isolated from each other by the loyalties of marriage. I have a sense that women didn't talk to each other much in the fifties—not about their secret emptiness, their frustrations. I went on trying to write, my second book and first child appeared in the same month. But by the time that book came out I was already dissatisfied with those poems, which seemed to me mere exercises for poems I hadn't written. The book was praised, however, for its "graceful-ness"; I had a marriage and a child. If there were doubts, if there were periods of null depression or active despairing, these could only mean that I was un-grateful, insatiable, perhaps a monster.

About the time my third child was born, I felt that I had either to consider myself a failed woman and a failed poet, or try to find some synthesis by which to understand what was happening to me. What frightened me most was the sense of drift, of being pulled along on a current which called itself my destiny, but in which I seemed to be losing touch with whoever I had been, with the girl who had experienced her own will and energy almost ecstatically at times, walking around a city or riding a train at night or typing in a student room. In a poem about my grandmother, I wrote (of myself): "A young girl, thought sleeping, is certified dead." I was writing very little, partly from fatigue, that fe-male fatigue of suppressed anger and the loss of contact with her own being;

15

partly from the discontinuity of female life with its attention to small chores, errands, work that others constantly undo, small children's constant needs. What I did write was unconvincing to me; my anger and frustration were hard to acknowledge in or out of poem, because in fact I cared a great deal about my husband and my children. Trying to look back and understand that time I have tried to analyze the real nature of the conflict. Most, if not all, human lives are full of fantasy—passive daydreaming which need not be acted on. But to write poetry or fiction, or even to think well, is not to fantasize, or to put fantasies on paper. For a poem to coalesce, for a character or an action to take shape, there has to be an imaginative transformation of reality which is in no way passive. And a certain freedom of the mind is needed—freedom to press on, to enter the currents of your thought like a glider pilot, knowing that your motion can be sustained, that the buoyancy of your attention will not be suddenly snatched away. Moreover, if the imagination is to transcend and transform experience it has to question, to challenge, to conceive of alternatives, perhaps to the very life you are living at that moment. You have to be free to play around with the notion that day might be night, love might be hate; nothing can be too sacred for the imagination to turn into its opposite or to call experimentally by another name. For writing is re-naming. Now, to be maternally with small children all day in the old way, to be with a man in the old way of marriage, requires a holding-back, a putting-aside of that imaginative activity, and seems to demand instead a kind of conservatism. I want to make it clear that I am *not* saying that in order to write well, or think well, it is necessary to become unavailable to others, or to become a devouring ego. This has been the myth of the masculine artist and thinker; and I repeat, I do not accept it. But to be a female human being trying to fulfill traditional female functions in a traditional way *is* in direct conflict with the subversive function of the imagination. The word *traditional* is important here. There must be ways, and we will be finding out more and more about them, in which the energy of creation and the energy of relation can be united. But in those earlier years I always felt the conflict as a failure of love in myself. I had thought I was choosing a full life: the life available to most men, in which sexuality, work and parenthood could coexist. But I felt, at twenty-nine, guilt toward the people closest to me, and guilty toward my own being.

I wanted, then, more than anything, the one thing of which there was never enough: time to think, time to write. The fifties and early sixties were years of rapid revelations: the sit-ins and marches in the South, the Bay of Pigs,[14] the early anti-war movement raised large questions—questions for which the masculine world of the academy around me seemed to have expert and fluent answers. But I needed desperately to think for myself—about pacifism and dissent and violence, about poetry and society and about my own relationship to all these things. For about ten years I was reading in fierce snatches, scribbling in notebooks, writing poetry in fragments; I was looking

14. Site of a failed American invasion of Cuba, intended to overthrow the Castro regime.

desperately for clues, because if there were no clues then I thought I might be insane. I wrote in a notebook about this time: "Paralyzed by the sense that there exists a mesh of relationships—e.g. between my anger at the children, my sensual life, pacifism, sex (I mean sex in its broadest significance, not merely sexual desire)—an interconnectedness which, if I could see it, make it valid, would give me back myself, make it possible to function lucidly and passionately. Yet I grope in and out among these dark webs." I think I began at this point to feel that politics was not something "out there" but something "in here" and of the essence of my condition.

In the late fifties I was able to write, for the first time, directly about experiencing myself as a woman. The poem was jotted in fragments during children's naps, brief hours in a library, or at 3 A.M. after rising with a wakeful child. I despaired of doing any continuous work at this time. Yet I began to feel that my fragments and scraps had a common consciousness and a common theme, one which I would have been very unwilling to put on paper at an earlier time because I had been taught that poetry should be "universal," which meant, of course, non-female. Until then I had tried very much *not* to identify myself as a female poet. Over two years I wrote a ten-part poem called "Snapshots of A Daughter-in-Law," in a longer, looser mode than I've ever trusted myself with before. It was an extraordinary relief to write that poem. It strikes me now as too literary, too dependent on allusion; I hadn't found the courage yet to do without authorities, or even to use the pronoun *I*—the woman in the poem is always "she." One section of it, no. 2, concerns a woman who thinks she is going mad; she is haunted by voices telling her to resist and rebel, voices which she can hear but not obey.

2.

Banging the coffee-pot into the sink
she hears the angels chiding, and looks out
past the raked gardens to the sloppy sky.
Only a week since They said: *Have no patience.*

The next time it was: *Be insatiable.*
Then: *Save yourself; others you cannot save.*
Sometimes she's let the tapstream scald her arm,
a match burn to her thumbnail,

or held her hand above the kettle's spout
right in the woolly steam. They are probably angels,
since nothing hurts her any more, except
each morning's grit blowing into her eyes.

The poem "Orion," written five years later, is a poem of reconnection with a part of myself I had felt I was losing—the active principle, the energetic imagination, the "half-brother" whom I projected, as I had for many years, into the constellation Orion.

Far back when I went zig-zagging
through tamarack pastures
you were my genius, you
my cast-iron Viking, my helmed
lion-heart king in prison.
Years later now you're young

my fierce half-brother, staring
down from that simplified west
your breast open, your belt dragged down
by an oldfashioned thing, a sword
the last bravado you won't give over
though it weighs you down as you stride

and the stars in it are dim
and maybe have stopped burning.
But you burn, and I know it;
as I throw back my head to take you in
an old transfusion happens again:
divine astronomy is nothing to it.

Indoors I bruise and blunder,
break faith, leave ill enough
alone, a dead child born in the dark.
Night cracks up over the chimney,
pieces of time, frozen geodes
come showering down in the grate.

A man reaches behind my eyes
and finds them empty
a woman's head turns away
from my head in the mirror
children are dying my death
and eating crumbs of my life.

Pity is not your forte.
Calmly you ache up there
pinned aloft in your crow's nest,
my speechless pirate!
You take it all for granted
and when I look you back

it's with a starlike eye
shooting its cold and egotistical spear
where it can do least damage.
Breathe deep! No hurt, no pardon
out here in the cold with you
you with your back to the wall.

It's no accident that the words *cold and egotistical* appear in this poem,   20
and are applied to myself. The choice still seemed to be between "love"—womanly, maternal love, altruistic love—a love defined and ruled by the weight of
an entire culture—and egotism—a force directed by men into creation,
achievement, ambition, often at the expense of others, but justifiably so. For
weren't they men, and wasn't that their destiny as womanly love was ours? I
know now that the alternatives are false ones—that the word *love* is itself in
need of re-vision.

There is a companion poem to "Orion," written three years later, in which
at last the woman in the poem and the woman writing the poem become the
same person. It is called "Planetarium," and it was written after a visit to a real
planetarium, where I read an account of the work of Caroline Herschel, the
astronomer, who worked with her brother William, but whose name remained
obscure, as his did not.

> *(Thinking of Caroline*
> *Herschel, 1750–1848,*
> *astronomer, sister of*
> *William; and others)*

A woman in the shape of a monster
a monster in the shape of a woman
the skies are full of them

a woman   'in the snow
among the Clocks and instruments
or measuring the ground with poles'

in her 98 years to discover
8 comets

she whom the moon ruled
like us
levitating into the night sky
riding the polished lenses

Galaxies of women, there
doing penance for impetuousness
ribs chilled
in those spaces   of the mind

An eye,
        'virile, precise and absolutely certain'
        from the mad webs of Uranisborg
                        encountering the NOVA

every impulse of light exploding
from the core
as life flies out of us

Tycho[15] whispering at last
'Let me not seem to have lived in vain'

What we see, we see
and seeing is changing

the light that shrivels a mountain
and leaves a man alive

Heartbeat of the pulsar
heart sweating through my body

The radio impulse
pouring in from Taurus

    I am bombarded yet   I stand

I have been standing all my life in the
direct path of a battery of signals
the most accurately transmitted most
untranslatable language in the universe
I am a galactic cloud so deep   so invo-
luted that a light wave could take
years to travel through me   And has
taken   I am an instrument in the shape
of a woman trying to translate pulsations
into images   for the relief of the body
and the reconstruction of the mind.

In closing I want to tell you about a dream I had last summer. I dreamed I was asked to read my poetry at a mass women's meeting; but when I began to read, what came out were the lyrics of a blues song. I share this dream with you because it seemed to me to say a lot about the problems and the future of the woman writer, and probably of women in general. The awakening of consciousness is not like the crossing of a frontier—one step, and you are in another country. Much of women's poetry has been of the nature of the blues song: a cry of pain, of victimization, or a lyric of seduction. And today, much poetry by women—and prose for that matter—is charged with anger. I think we need to go through that anger, and we will betray our own reality if we try, as Virginia Woolf was trying, for an objectivity, a detachment; that would make us sound more like Jane Austen or Shakespeare. We know more than Jane Austen or Shakespeare knew: more than Jane Austen because our lives are more complex, more than Shakespeare because we know more about the lives of women, Jane Austen and Virginia Woolf included.

Both the victimization and the anger experienced by women are real, and have real sources, everywhere in the environment, built into society. They

---

15. Tycho Brahe (1546–1601), Danish astronomer.

must go on being tapped and explored by poets, among others. We can neither deny them, nor can we rest there. They are our birth-pains, and we are bearing ourselves. We would be failing each other as writers and as women, if we neglected or denied what is negative, regressive or Sisyphean[16] in our inwardness.

We all know that there is another story to be told. I am curious and expectant about the future of the masculine consciousness. I feel in the work of the men whose poetry I read today a deep pessimism and fatalistic grief; and I wonder if it isn't the masculine side of what women have experienced, the price of masculine dominance. One thing I am sure of: just as woman is becoming her own midwife, creating herself anew, so man will have to learn to gestate and give birth to his own subjectivity—something he has frequently wanted woman to do for him. We can go on trying to talk to each other, we can sometimes help each other, poetry and fiction can show us what the other is going through; but women can no longer be primarily mothers and muses for men: we have our own work cut out for us.

16. The reference is to the Greek myth of Sisyphus. He was condemned to roll a huge rock to the top of a hill, but the rock always rolled back down before it reached the top.

QUESTIONS

1. Rich describes herself as hesitant to use her own experience as evidence and illustration in this essay: it would be "a lot easier and less dangerous to talk about other women writers" (paragraph 9). The dangers are personal—i.e., self-exposure and violating the privacy of others—and rhetorical—i.e., relying on evidence that readers may find limited, unconvincing, and self-serving. Locate instances of the first. Consider the second. What do you think are the advantages and disadvantages of Rich's using her own experience?

2. How does Rich work her own experience into a larger argument about women writers—and all women—at a time when gender and gender roles were being called into question? Find particular instances for analysis.

3. How does Rich describe the experience of writing poetry? How does it follow that her life in the 1950s, as she describes it, was inimical to her writing?

4. Rich refers to "the influence that the myths and images of women have on all of us" (paragraph 11). There are also myths and images of men that influence us. Write an essay in which you consider one myth about either women or men, how it gets internalized, and how it affects the behavior of both women and men.

5. Write an essay on a larger issue in which you focus on your own experience as evidence and illustration.

VIRGINIA WOOLF   *In Search of a Room of One's Own*

I T WAS DISAPPOINTING not to have brought back in the evening some important statement, some authentic fact. Women are poorer than men because— this or that. Perhaps now it would be better to give up seeking for the truth, and receiving on one's head an avalanche of opinion hot as lava, discolored as dish-water. It would be better to draw the curtains; to shut out distractions; to light the lamp; to narrow the enquiry and to ask the historian, who records not opinions but facts, to describe under what conditions women lived, not throughout the ages, but in England, say in the time of Elizabeth.

For it is a perennial puzzle why no woman wrote a word of that extraordinary literature when every other man, it seemed, was capable of song or sonnet. What were the conditions in which women lived, I asked myself; for fiction, imaginative work that is, is not dropped like a pebble upon the ground, as science may be; fiction is like a spider's web, attached ever so lightly perhaps, but still attached to life at all four corners. Often the attachment is scarcely perceptible; Shakespeare's plays, for instance, seem to hang there complete by themselves. But when the web is pulled askew, hooked up at the edge, torn in the middle, one remembers that these webs are not spun in midair by incorporeal creatures, but are the work of suffering human beings, and are attached to grossly material things, like health and money and the houses we live in.

I went, therefore, to the shelf where the histories stand and took down one of the latest, Professor Trevelyan's *History of England*. Once more I looked up Women, found "position of," and turned to the pages indicated. "Wife-beating," I read, "was a recognised right of man, and was practised without shame by high as well as low. . . . Similarly," the historian goes on, "the daughter who refused to marry the gentleman of her parents' choice was liable to be locked up, beaten and flung about the room, without any shock being inflicted on public opinion. Marriage was not an affair of personal affection, but of family avarice, particularly in the 'chivalrous' upper classes. . . . Betrothal often took place while one or both of the parties was in the cradle, and marriage when they were scarcely out of the nurses' charge." That was about 1470, soon after Chaucer's time. The next reference to the position of women is some two hundred years later, in the time of the Stuarts. "It was still the exception for women of the upper and middle class to choose their own husbands, and when the husband had been assigned, he was lord and master, so far at least

From chapter 3 of Woolf's A Room of One's Own *(1929), a long essay that began as lectures given at Newnham College and Girton College, women's colleges at Cambridge University, in 1928. In chapter 1, Woolf advances the proposition that "a woman must have money and a room of her own if she is to write fiction." In chapter 2, she describes a day spent at the British Museum (now the British Library) looking for information about the lives of women.*

as law and custom could make him. Yet even so," Professor Trevelyan concludes, "neither Shakespeare's women nor those of authentic seventeenth-century memoirs, like the Verneys and the Hutchinsons, seem wanting in personality and character." Certainly, if we consider it, Cleopatra must have had a way with her; Lady Macbeth, one would suppose, had a will of her own; Rosalind, one might conclude, was an attractive girl. Professor Trevelyan is speaking no more than the truth when he remarks that Shakespeare's women do not seem wanting in personality and character. Not being a historian, one might go even further and say that women have burnt like beacons in all the works of all the poets from the beginning of time—Clytemnestra, Antigone, Cleopatra, Lady Macbeth, Phèdre, Cressida, Rosalind, Desdemona, the Duchess of Malfi, among the dramatists; then among the prose writers: Millamant, Clarissa, Becky Sharp, Anna Karenina, Emma Bovary, Madame de Guermantes—the names flock to mind, nor do they recall women "lacking in personality and character." Indeed, if woman had no existence save in the fiction written by men, one would imagine her a person of the utmost importance; very various; heroic and mean; splendid and sordid; infinitely beautiful and hideous in the extreme; as great as a man, some think even greater.[1] But this is woman in fiction. In fact, as Professor Trevelyan points out, she was locked up, beaten and flung about the room.

A very queer, composite being thus emerges. Imaginatively she is of the highest importance; practically she is completely insignificant. She pervades poetry from cover to cover; she is all but absent from history. She dominates the lives of kings and conquerors in fiction; in fact she was the slave of any boy whose parents forced a ring upon her finger. Some of the most inspired words, some of the most profound thoughts in literature fall from her lips; in real life she could hardly read, could scarcely spell, and was the property of her husband.

It was certainly an odd monster that one made up by reading the historians first and the poets afterwards—a worm winged like an eagle; the spirit of life and beauty in a kitchen chopping up suet. But these monsters, however amusing to the imagination, have no existence in fact. What one must do to bring her to life was to think poetically and prosaically at one and the same

5

---

1. "It remains a strange and almost inexplicable fact that in Athena's city, where women were kept in almost Oriental suppression as odalisques or drudges, the stage should yet have produced figures like Clytemnestra and Cassandra, Atossa and Antigone, Phèdre and Medea, and all the other heroines who dominate play after play of the 'misogynist' Euripides. But the paradox of this world where in real life a respectable woman could hardly show her face alone in the street, and yet on the stage woman equals or surpasses man, has never been satisfactorily explained. In modern tragedy the same predominance exists. At all events, a very cursory survey of Shakespeare's work (similarly with Webster, though not with Marlowe or Jonson) suffices to reveal how this dominance, this initiative of women, persists from Rosalind to Lady Macbeth. So too in Racine; six of his tragedies bear their heroines' names; and what male characters of his shall we set against Hermione and Andromaque, Bérénice and Roxane, Phèdre and Athalie? So again with Ibsen; what men shall we match with Solveig and Nora, Hedda and Hilda Wangel and Rebecca West?"—F. L. LUCAS, Tragedy, pp. 114–15 [Woolf's note].

moment, thus keeping in touch with fact—that she is Mrs. Martin, aged thirty-six, dressed in blue, wearing a black hat and brown shoes; but not losing sight of fiction either—that she is a vessel in which all sorts of spirits and forces are coursing and flashing perpetually. The moment, however, that one tries this method with the Elizabethan woman, one branch of illumination fails; one is held up by the scarcity of facts. One knows nothing detailed, nothing perfectly true and substantial about her. History scarcely mentions her. And I turned to Professor Trevelyan again to see what history meant to him. I found by looking at his chapter headings that it meant—

"The Manor Court and the Methods of Open-field Agriculture . . . The Cistercians and Sheep-farming . . . The Crusades . . . The University . . . The House of Commons . . . The Hundred Years' War . . . The Wars of the Roses . . . The Renaissance Scholars . . . The Dissolution of the Monasteries . . . Agrarian and Religious Strife . . . The Origin of English Seapower . . . The Armada . . ." and so on. Occasionally an individual woman is mentioned, an Elizabeth, or a Mary; a queen or a great lady. But by no possible means could middle-class women with nothing but brains and character at their command have taken part in any one of the great movements which, brought together, constitute the historian's view of the past. Nor shall we find her in any collection of anecdotes. Aubrey[2] hardly mentions her. She never writes her own life and scarcely keeps a diary; there are only a handful of her letters in existence. She left no plays or poems by which we can judge her. What one wants, I thought—and why does not some brilliant student at Newnham or Girton supply it?—is a mass of information; at what age did she marry; how many children had she as a rule; what was her house like; had she a room to herself; did she do the cooking; would she be likely to have a servant? All these facts lie somewhere, presumably, in parish registers and account books; the life of the average Elizabethan woman must be scattered about somewhere, could one collect it and make a book of it. It would be ambitious beyond my daring, I thought, looking about the shelves for books that were not there, to suggest to the students of those famous colleges that they should re-write history, though I own that it often seems a little queer as it is, unreal, lop-sided; but why should they not add a supplement to history? calling it, of course, by some inconspicuous name so that women might figure there without impropriety? For one often catches a glimpse of them in the lives of the great, whisking away into the background, concealing, I sometimes think, a wink, a laugh, perhaps a tear. And, after all, we have lives enough of Jane Austen; it scarcely seems necessary to consider again the influence of the tragedies of Joanna Baillie upon the poetry of Edgar Allan Poe; as for myself, I should not mind if the homes and haunts of Mary Russell Mitford[3] were closed to the

2. John Aubrey (1626–1697), whose biographical writings were published posthumously as *Brief Lives*.
3. Austen (1775–1817), English novelist; Baillie (1762–1851), Scottish dramatist and poet; Poe (1809–1849), American poet; Mitford (1787–1855), English novelist and essayist.

public for a century at least. But what I find deplorable, I continued, looking about the bookshelves again, is that nothing is known about women before the eighteenth century. I have no model in my mind to turn about this way and that. Here am I asking why women did not write poetry in the Elizabethan age, and I am not sure how they were educated; whether they were taught to write; whether they had sitting-rooms to themselves; how many women had children before they were twenty-one; what, in short, they did from eight in the morning till eight at night. They had no money evidently; according to Professor Trevelyan they were married whether they liked it or not before they were out of the nursery, at fifteen or sixteen very likely. It would have been extremely odd, even upon this showing, had one of them suddenly written the plays of Shakespeare, I concluded, and I thought of that old gentleman, who is dead now, but was a bishop, I think, who declared that it was impossible for any woman, past, present, or to come, to have the genius of Shakespeare. He wrote to the papers about it. He also told a lady who applied to him for information that cats do not as a matter of fact go to heaven, though they have, he added, souls of a sort. How much thinking those old gentlemen used to save one! How the borders of ignorance shrank back at their approach! Cats do not go to heaven. Women cannot write the plays of Shakespeare.

Be that as it may, I could not help thinking, as I looked at the works of Shakespeare on the shelf, that the bishop was right at least in this; it would have been impossible, completely and entirely, for any woman to have written the plays of Shakespeare in the age of Shakespeare. Let me imagine, since facts are so hard to come by, what would have happened had Shakespeare had a wonderfully gifted sister, called Judith, let us say. Shakespeare himself went, very probably—his mother was an heiress—to the grammar school, where he may have learnt Latin—Ovid, Virgil and Horace—and the elements of grammar and logic. He was, it is well known, a wild boy who poached rabbits, perhaps shot a deer, and had, rather sooner than he should have done, to marry a woman in the neighborhood, who bore him a child rather quicker than was right. That escapade sent him to seek his fortune in London. He had, it seemed, a taste for the theatre; he began by holding horses at the stage door. Very soon he got work in the theatre, became a successful actor, and lived at the hub of the universe, meeting everybody, knowing everybody, practicing his art on the boards, exercising his wits in the streets, and even getting access to the palace of the queen. Meanwhile his extraordinarily gifted sister, let us suppose, remained at home. She was as adventurous, as imaginative, as agog to see the world as he was. But she was not sent to school. She had no chance of learning grammar and logic, let alone of reading Horace and Virgil. She picked up a book now and then, one of her brother's perhaps, and read a few pages. But then her parents came in and told her to mend the stockings or mind the stew and not moon about with books and papers. They would have spoken sharply but kindly, for they were substantial people who knew the conditions of life for a woman and loved their daughter—indeed, more likely than not she was the apple of her father's eye. Perhaps she scribbled some pages up in an apple loft on the sly, but was careful to hide them or set fire to them. Soon, how-ever, before she was out of her teens, she was to be betrothed to the son of a neighboring wool-stapler. She cried out that marriage was hateful to her, and for that she was severely beaten by her father. Then he ceased to scold her. He begged her instead not to hurt him, not to shame him in this matter of her mar-riage. He would give her a chain of beads or a fine petticoat, he said; and there were tears in his eyes. How could she disobey him? How could she break his heart? The force of her own gift alone drove her to it. She made up a small par-cel of her belongings, let herself down by a rope one summer's night and took the road to London. She was not seventeen. The birds that sang in the hedge were not more musical than she was. She had the quickest fancy, a gift like her brother's, for the tune of words. Like him, she had a taste for the theatre. She stood at the stage door; she wanted to act, she said. Men laughed in her face. The manager—a fat, loose-lipped man—guffawed. He bellowed something about poodles dancing and women acting—no woman, he said, could possibly be an actress.[4] He hinted—you can imagine what. She could get no training in her craft. Could she even seek her dinner in a tavern or roam the streets at mid-night? Yet her genius was for fiction and lusted to feed abundantly upon the lives of men and women and the study of their ways. At last—for she was very young, oddly like Shakespeare the poet in her face, with the same grey eyes and rounded brows—at last Nick Greene the actor-manager took pity on her; she found herself with child by that gentleman and so—who shall measure the heat and violence of the poet's heart when caught and tangled in a woman's body?—killed herself one winter's night and lies buried at some cross-roads where the omnibuses now stop outside the Elephant and Castle.[5]

That, more or less, is how the story would run, I think, if a woman in Shakespeare's day had had Shakespeare's genius. But for my part, I agree with the deceased bishop, if such he was—it is unthinkable that any woman in Shakespeare's day should have had Shakespeare's genius. For genius like Shakespeare's is not born among laboring, uneducated, servile people. It was not born in England among the Saxons and the Britons. It is not born today among the working classes. How, then, could it have been born among women whose work began, according to Professor Trevelyan, almost before they were out of the nursery, who were forced to it by their parents and held to it by all the power of law and custom? Yet genius of a sort must have existed among women as it must have existed among the working classes. Now and again an Emily Brontë or a Robert Burns blazes out and proves its presence.[6] But cer-tainly it never got itself on to paper. When, however, one reads of a witch be-ing ducked, of a woman possessed by devils, of a wise woman selling herbs, or even of a very remarkable man who had a mother, then I think we are on the track of a lost novelist, a suppressed poet, of some mute and inglorious Jane

---

4. In the Elizabethan theater boys played women's parts.

5. A prominent landmark in London, south of the Thames.

6. Woolf's examples are Emily Brontë (1818–1848), the English novelist, and Robert Burns (1759–1796), the Scottish poet.

Austen,[7] some Emily Brontë who dashed her brains out on the moor or mopped and mowed about the highways crazed with the torture that her gift had put her to. Indeed, I would venture to guess that Anon, who wrote so many poems without signing them, was often a woman. It was a woman Edward Fitzgerald,[8] I think, suggested who made the ballads and the folk-songs, crooning them to her children, beguiling her spinning with them, or the length of the winter's night.

This may be true or it may be false—who can say?—but what is true in it, so it seemed to me, reviewing the story of Shakespeare's sister as I had made it, is that any woman born with a great gift in the sixteenth century would certainly have gone crazed, shot herself, or ended her days in some lonely cottage outside the village, half witch, half wizard, feared and mocked at. For it needs little skill in psychology to be sure that a highly gifted girl who had tried to use her gift for poetry would have been so thwarted and hindered by other people, so tortured and pulled asunder by her own contrary instincts, that she must have lost her health and sanity to a certainty. No girl could have walked to London and stood at a stage door and forced her way into the presence of actor-managers without doing herself a violence and suffering an anguish which may have been irrational—for chastity may be a fetish invented by certain societies for unknown reasons—but were none the less inevitable. Chastity had then, it has even now, a religious importance in a woman's life, and has so wrapped itself round with nerves and instincts that to cut it free and bring it to the light of day demands courage of the rarest. To have lived a free life in London in the sixteenth century would have meant for a woman who was poet and playwright a nervous stress and dilemma which might well have killed her. Had she survived, whatever she had written would have been twisted and deformed, issuing from a strained and morbid imagination. And undoubtedly, I thought, looking at the shelf where there are no plays by women, her work would have gone unsigned. That refuge she would have sought certainly. It was the relic of the sense of chastity that dictated anonymity to women even so late as the nineteenth century. Currer Bell, George Eliot, George Sand,[9] all the victims of inner strife as their writings prove, sought ineffectively to veil themselves by using the name of a man. Thus they did homage to the convention, which if not implanted by the other sex was liberally encouraged by them (the chief glory of a woman is not to be talked of, said Pericles,[10] himself a much-talked-of man), that publicity in women is detestable. Anonymity runs in their blood. The desire to be veiled

7. Woolf alludes to Thomas Gray's "Elegy Written in a Country Churchyard": "Some mute inglorious Milton here may rest."

8. Edward Fitzgerald (1809–1883), poet and translator of the *Rubáiyát of Omar Khayyám*.

9. The pseudonyms of Charlotte Brontë (1816–1855), English novelist; Mary Ann Evans (1819–1880), English novelist; and Amandine Aurore Lucie Dupin, Baronne Dudevant (1804–1876), French novelist.

10. Pericles (d. 429 B.C.E.), Athenian statesman.

still possesses them. They are not even now as concerned about the health of their fame as men are, and, speaking generally, will pass a tombstone or a sign-post without feeling an irresistible desire to cut their names on it, as Alf, Bert or Chas. must do in obedience to their instinct, which murmurs if it sees a fine woman go by, or even a dog, Ce chien est à moi.[11] And, of course, it may not be a dog, I thought, remembering Parliament Square, the Sieges Allee and other avenues; it may be a piece of land or a man with curly black hair. It is one of the great advantages of being a woman that one can pass even a very fine negress without wishing to make an Englishwoman of her.

10   That woman, then, who was born with a gift of poetry in the sixteenth century, was an unhappy woman, a woman at strife against herself. All the conditions of her life, all her own instincts, were hostile to the state of mind which is needed to set free whatever is in the brain. But what is the state of mind that is most propitious to the act of creation, I asked. Can one come by any notion of the state that furthers and makes possible that strange activity? Here I opened the volume containing the Tragedies of Shakespeare. What was Shakespeare's state of mind, for instance, when he wrote *Lear* and *Antony and Cleopatra*? It was certainly the state of mind most favorable to poetry that there has ever existed. But Shakespeare himself said nothing about it. We only know casually and by chance that he "never blotted a line."[12] Nothing indeed was ever said by the artist himself about his state of mind until the eighteenth century perhaps. Rousseau perhaps began it.[13] At any rate, by the nineteenth century self-consciousness had developed so far that it was the habit for men of letters to describe their minds in confessions and autobiographies. Their lives also were written, and their letters were printed after their deaths. Thus, though we do not know what Shakespeare went through when he wrote *Lear,* we do know what Carlyle went through when he wrote the *French Revolution;* what Flaubert went through when he wrote *Madame Bovary;* what Keats was going through when he tried to write poetry against the coming of death and the indifference of the world.

And one gathers from this enormous modern literature of confession and self-analysis that to write a work of genius is almost always a feat of prodigious difficulty. Everything is against the likelihood that it will come from the writer's mind whole and entire. Generally material circumstances are against it. Dogs will bark; people will interrupt; money must be made; health will break down. Further, accentuating all these difficulties and making them harder to bear is the world's notorious indifference. It does not ask people to write poems and novels and histories; it does not need them. It does not care whether Flaubert finds the right word or whether Carlyle scrupulously verifies this or that fact. Naturally, it will not pay for what it does not want. And so the

11. That dog is mine (French).

12. As recorded by his contemporary Ben Jonson in *Timber, or Discoveries Made upon Men and Matter.*

13. Jean-Jacques Rousseau (1712–1778), whose *Confessions* were published posthumously.

writer, Keats, Flaubert, Carlyle, suffers, especially in the creative years of youth, every form of distraction and discouragement. A curse, a cry of agony, rises from those books of analysis and confession. "Mighty poets in their misery dead"[14]—that is the burden of their song. If anything comes through in spite of all this, it is a miracle, and probably no book is born entire and uncrippled as it was conceived.

But for women, I thought, looking at the empty shelves, these difficulties were infinitely more formidable. In the first place, to have a room of her own, let alone a quiet room or a sound-proof room, was out of the question, unless her parents were exceptionally rich or very noble, even up to the beginning of the nineteenth century. Since her pin money, which depended on the good will of her father, was only enough to keep her clothed, she was debarred from such alleviations as came even to Keats or Tennyson or Carlyle,[15] all poor men, from a walking tour, a little journey to France, from the separate lodging which, even if it were miserable enough, sheltered them from the claims and tyrannies of their families. Such material difficulties were formidable; but much worse were the immaterial. The indifference of the world which Keats and Flaubert and other men of genius have found so hard to bear was in her case not indifference but hostility. The world did not say to her as it said to them, Write if you choose; it makes no difference to me. The world said with a guffaw, Write? What's the good of your writing? Here the psychologists of Newnham and Girton might come to our help, I thought, looking again at the blank spaces on the shelves. For surely it is time that the effect of discouragement upon the mind of the artist should be measured, as I have seen a dairy company measure the effect of ordinary milk and Grade A milk upon the body of the rat. They set two rats in cages side by side, and of the two one was furtive, timid and small, and the other was glossy, bold and big. Now what food do we feed women as artists upon? I asked, remembering, I suppose, that dinner of prunes and custard.[16] To answer that question I had only to open the evening paper and to read that Lord Birkenhead is of opinion—but really I am not going to trouble to copy out Lord Birkenhead's opinion upon the writing of women. What Dean Inge says I will leave in peace. The Harley Street specialist may be allowed to rouse the echoes of Harley Street with his vociferations without raising a hair on my head. I will quote, however, Mr. Oscar Browning,[17] because Mr. Oscar Browning was a great figure in Cambridge at one

14. From William Wordsworth's poem "Resolution and Independence."

15. John Keats (1795–1821) and Alfred, Lord Tennyson (1809–1892) were English poets; Thomas Carlyle (1795–1881) was a Scottish essayist.

16. In chapter 1, Woolf contrasts the lavish dinner—partridge and wine—she ate as a guest at a men's college at Cambridge University with the plain fare—prunes and custard—served at a women's college.

17. In chapter 2, Woolf lists the fruits of her day's research on the lives of women, which include Lord Birkenhead's, Dean Inge's, and Mr. Oscar Browning's opinions of women; she does not, however, quote them. Harley Street is where fashionable medical doctors in London have their offices.

time, and used to examine the students at Girton and Newnham. Mr. Oscar
Browning was wont to declare "that the impression left on his mind, after
looking over any set of examination papers, was that, irrespective of the marks
he might give, the best woman was intellectually the inferior of the worst
man." After saying that Mr. Browning went back to his rooms—and it is this
sequel that endears him and makes him a human figure of some bulk and
majesty—he went back to his rooms and found a stable-boy lying on the
sofa—"a mere skeleton, his cheeks were cavernous and sallow, his teeth were
black, and he did not appear to have the full use of his limbs. . . . 'That's
Arthur' [said Mr. Browning]. 'He's a dear boy really and most high-minded.' "
The two pictures always seem to me to complete each other. And happily in
this age of biography the two pictures often do complete each other, so that we
are able to interpret the opinions of great men not only by what they say, but
by what they do.

But though this is possible now, such opinions coming from the lips of important people must have been formidable enough even fifty years ago. Let us
suppose that a father from the highest motives did not wish his daughter to
leave home and become writer, painter or scholar. "See what Mr. Oscar Browning says," he would say; and there was not only Mr. Oscar Browning; there was
the *Saturday Review*; there was Mr. Greg[18]—the "essentials of a woman's being," said Mr. Greg emphatically, "are that *they are supported by, and they minister to, men*"—there was an enormous body of masculine opinion to the effect
that nothing could be expected of women intellectually. Even if her father did
not read out loud these opinions, any girl could read them for herself; and the
reading, even in the nineteenth century, must have lowered her vitality, and told
profoundly upon her work. There would always have been that assertion—you
cannot do this, you are incapable of doing that—to protest against, to overcome. Probably for a novelist this germ is no longer of much effect; for there
have been women novelists of merit. But for painters it must still have some
sting in it; and for musicians, I imagine, is even now active and poisonous in
the extreme. The women composer stands where the actress stood in the time
of Shakespeare. Nick Greene, I thought, remembering the story I had made
about Shakespeare's sister, said that a woman acting put him in mind of a dog
dancing. Johnson repeated the phrase two hundred years later of women
preaching.[19] And here, I said, opening a book about music, we have the very
words used again in this year of grace, 1928, of women who try to write music.
"Of Mlle. Germaine Tailleferre one can only repeat Dr. Johnson's dictum concerning a woman preacher, transposed into terms of music. 'Sir, a woman's
composing is like a dog's walking on his hind legs. It is not done well, but you
are surprised to find it done at all.' "[20] So accurately does history repeat itself.

18. Mr. Greg does not appear on Woolf's list (see preceding note).

19. Johnson's opinion is recorded in James Boswell's *The Life of Samuel Johnson,
L.L.D.* Woolf, in her tale of Judith Shakespeare, imagines the manager bellowing
"something about poodles dancing and women acting."

20. *A Survey of Contemporary Music*, Cecil Gray, p. 246 [Woolf's note].

Thus, I concluded, shutting Mr. Oscar Browning's life and pushing away the rest, it is fairly evident that even in the nineteenth century a woman was not encouraged to be an artist. On the contrary, she was snubbed, slapped, lectured and exhorted. Her mind must have been strained and her vitality lowered by the need of opposing this, of disproving that. For here again we come within range of that very interesting and obscure masculine complex which has had so much influence upon the woman's movement; that deep-seated desire, not so much that *she* shall be inferior as that *he* shall be superior, which plants him wherever one looks, not only in front of the arts, but barring the way to politics too, even when the risk to himself seems infinitesimal and the suppliant humble and devoted. Even Lady Bessborough, I remembered, with all her passion for politics, must humbly bow herself and write to Lord Granville Leveson-Gower[21]: " . . . notwithstanding all my violence in politics and talking so much on that subject, I perfectly agree with you that no woman has any business to meddle with that or any other serious business, farther than giving her opinion (if she is ask'd)." And so she goes on to spend her enthusiasm where it meets with no obstacle whatsoever upon that immensely important subject, Lord Granville's maiden speech in the House of Commons. The spectacle is certainly a strange one, I thought. The history of men's opposition to women's emancipation is more interesting perhaps than the story of that emancipation itself. An amusing book might be made of it if some young student at Girton or Newnham would collect examples and deduce a theory—but she would need thick gloves on her hands, and bars to protect her of solid gold.

But what is amusing now, I recollected, shutting Lady Bessborough, had to be taken in desperate earnest once. Opinions that one now pastes in a book labelled cock-a-doodle-dum and keeps for reading to select audiences on summer nights once drew tears, I can assure you. Among your grandmothers and great-grandmothers there were many that wept their eyes out. Florence Nightingale shrieked aloud in her agony.[22] Moreover, it is all very well for you, who have got yourselves to college and enjoy sitting-rooms—or is it only bedsitting-rooms?—of your own to say that genius should disregard such opinions; that genius should be above caring what is said of it. Unfortunately, it is precisely the men or women of genius who mind most what is said of them. Remember Keats. Remember the words he had cut on his tombstone. Think of Tennyson;[23] think—but I need hardly multiply instances of the undeniable, if very unfortunate, fact that it is the nature of the artist to mind excessively what is said about him. Literature is strewn with the wreckage of men who have minded beyond reason the opinions of others.

15

21. Henrietta, countess of Bessborough (1761–1821), and Lord Granville Leveson Gower, first Earl Granville (1773–1846). Their correspondence, edited by Castalia Countess Granville, was published as his *Private Correspondence, 1781 to 1821*, in 1916.

22. See *Cassandra,* by Florence Nightingale, printed in *The Cause,* by R. Strachey [Woolf's note]. Florence Nightingale (1820–1910), English nurse and philanthropist.

23. Keats's epitaph reads "Here lies one whose name was writ in water." Tennyson was notably sensitive to reviews of his poetry.

And this susceptibility of theirs is doubly unfortunate, I thought, returning again to my original enquiry into what state of mind is most propitious for
creative work, because the mind of an artist, in order to achieve the prodigious
effort of freeing whole and entire the work that is in him, must be incandescent, like Shakespeare's mind, I conjectured, looking at the book which lay
open at *Antony and Cleopatra*. There must be no obstacle in it, no foreign matter unconsumed.

For though we say that we know nothing about Shakespeare's state of
mind, even as we say that, we are saying something about Shakespeare's state
of mind. The reason perhaps why we know so little of Shakespeare—compared
with Donne or Ben Jonson or Milton[24]—is that his grudges and spites and antipathies are hidden from us. We are not held up by some "revelation" which reminds us of the writer. All desire to protest, to preach, to proclaim an injury, to
pay off a score, to make the world the witness of some hardship or grievance
was fired out of him and consumed. Therefore his poetry flows from him free
and unimpeded. If ever a human being got his work expressed completely, it
was Shakespeare. If ever a mind was incandescent, unimpeded, I thought,
turning again to the bookcase, it was Shakespeare's mind.

24. John Donne (1572–1631), Jonson (1572–1637), and John Milton (1608–1674)
were English poets and, in contrast to Shakespeare, all learned men.

QUESTIONS

1. At the beginning of her essay Woolf wonders about the conditions in which women
lived that made it difficult, if not impossible, for them to produce literature (paragraph
2). What does she reveal about those conditions in the course of her essay?

2. Throughout her essay Woolf supplies many examples of the obstacles faced by
women writers. Choose two or three that you found particularly effective and explain
why they are effective.

3. How does the phrase "A Room of One's Own" suggest a solution to the problems
Woolf has enumerated for women writers?

4. Has the woman writer of the twenty-first century overcome the obstacles Woolf describes as inhibiting the work of nineteenth-century women writers? Write an essay,
based on research and/or interviews, in which you argue yes or no.

JOHN UPDIKE   *Little Lightnings*

T HE BACKYARDS of my boyhood in summer were full of fireflies, but now I see them rarely. Is it that I have moved a few degrees north, or are the fireflies a quiet victim of the same environmental withering that has stolen the purple martins and the box turtles from our everyday lives? Or do I no longer look for them, with the delight depicted here?

Here, in eighteenth-century Japan, the young mother holds an exquisite little slatted box ready for their capture. In my Depression Pennsylvania, a pickle jar had to do, with holes punched in the lid and some grass lining the bottom, for the comfort of the captives. They were easy to catch, the obliging lightning bugs—soft-winged beetles that seldom rose higher than a child's hand could reach. In the palm, they lit up the creases with their cool yellow glow, whose rhythm seemed a kind of bleating.

Were they frightened? I imagined so, though the tempo of their bright pulse did not increase. If science can be believed, the signal is erotic, male to female and back again—like notes passed back and forth in class, like blushes or those dilations of the pupil that betray human arousal—and it is produced by an infusion of air through cells whose subtle load of luciferin becomes oxy-luciferin, the oxygen catalyzed by luciferase.

As my elders, not disapproving, sat back in the dark of the lawn, smoking their cigars and murmuring their gossip and making the wicker furniture squeak, I acted the wanton tyrant amid this docile glimmering race. The fire-flies in my imagination were afraid; their blinking constituted a plea to be set free, and usually they were, thankfully resuming their ornamental swim through the shadows of the trees, above the dew of the lawn. But once, with the clumsiness of a child, I knocked a firefly to the earth, or pinched it and let it fall, and in attempting to rescue it—to dig it up from between the blades of grass—I only poked it deeper. Horrified, I beheld its abdomen glimmering, fi-nally, out. This death, which I had both caused and witnessed, haunted me in giant proportions. I did not know, as the encyclopedia tells me now, that "adult fireflies of many species do not feed"; that they exist to mate, to engender lar-vae which feed on snails and earthworms, "injecting their prey with a paralyzing fluid"; that the firefly, in short, whose death I caused was already dying, enjoy-ing a mere momentary sexual dance between one generation of poisonous lar-vae and the next—already enjoying a kind of afterlife.

The boy and his mother seem to understand this, in this woodblock print   5
by Chōki.[1] They inhabit a kind of heaven, economical as a memory. Neither

Both this and "Moving Along" were originally written for the English version of the glossy French monthly Réalités; *they were reprinted in Updike's* Just Looking *(1981), a collec-tion of essays on art.*

1. Eishosai Chōki, Japanese printmaker, active c. 1789–95.

Снōкι
Catching Fireflies, mid-1790s
"Brocade" woodblock print on paper, 10 × 15″
The British Museum, Department of Oriental Antiquities, London

the running brook nor the listening iris protest their attempt to catch a few stars. Oddly, the one element of this print to show the effects of age is the age-less night itself—the purplish background of *sumi*[2] and mica, creased and scuffed as if with little lightnings.

2. Black ink in block form used especially by Chinese and Japanese artists for black-and-white paintings.

Moving Along

In dreams, one is frequently travelling, and the more hallucinatory moments of our waking life, many of them, are spent in cars, trains, and air-planes. For millennia, Man has walked or run to where he wanted to go; the first naked ape who had the mad idea of mounting a horse (or was it a *Camelops?*)[1] launched a series of subtle internal dislocations of which jet lag is a vivid modern form. When men come to fly through space at near the speed of light, they will return to earth a century later but only a few years older. Now, driving (say) from Boston to Pittsburgh in a day, we arrive feeling greatly aged by the engine's innumerable explosive heartbeats, by the monotony of the high-way surface and the constant windy press of unnatural speed. Beside the high-way, a clamorous parasitic life signals for attention and halt; localities where generations have lived, bred, labored, and died are flung through the wind-shield and out through the rearview mirror. Men on the move brutalize them-selves and render the world they arrow through phantasmal.

Our two artists, separated by two centuries, capture well the eeriness of travel. In the Punjab Hills painting, Baz Bahadur, prince of Malwa, has eloped with the lovely Rupmati;[2] in order to keep him faithful to her, the legend goes, she takes him riding by moonlight. The moon appears to exist not only in the sky but behind a grove of trees. Deer almost blend into the mauve-gray hills. A little citadel basks in starlight on a hilltop. In this soft night, nothing is brighter than the scarlet pasterns of the horses. Baz Bahadur's steed bears on his hide a paler version of the starry sky, and in his violet genitals carries a hint of this nocturnal ride's sexual undercurrent. To judge from the delicacy of their gestures and glances, the riders are being borne along as smoothly as on a merry-go-round. Though these lovers and their panoply are formalized to static perfection, if we cover them, a surprising depth appears in the top third of the painting, and carries the eye away.

The riders in Roy de Forest's[3] contemporary painting move through a for-

1. Extinct genus of camel.
2. Baz Bahadur and his beautiful wife Rani Rupmati ruled Malwa in India during the sixteenth century.
3. American artist (b. 1930).

Artist unknown
Baz Bahadur and Rupmati Riding by Moonlight, c. 1780
Pahari miniature in Kangra style, $8^{3}/_{4} \times 6^{1}/_{4}$ ″
The British Museum, Department of Oriental Antiquities, London

ROY DE FOREST
Canoe of Fate, 1974
Polymer on canvas, 66 ¾ × 90¼ ″
Philadelphia Museum of Art
The Adele Haas Turner and Beatrice Pastorius Turner Fund

est as crowded, garish, and menacing as the neon-lit main drag of a city. A throng of sinister bystanders, one built of brick and another with eyes that are paste gems, witness the passage of this *Canoe of Fate*, which with the coarseness of its stitching and the bulk of its passengers would make slow headway even on a less crowded canvas. Beyond the mountains, heavenly medallions and balloons of stippled color pre-empt space. Only the gesture of the black brave, echoing that of George Washington in another fabulous American crossing,[4] gives a sense of direction and promises to open a path. Two exotic birds, a slavering wolf, and what may be a fair captive (gazing backward toward settlements where other red-haired bluefaces mourn her) freight the canoe with a suggestion of allegory, of myths to which we have lost the key. The personnel of the aboriginal New World, at any rate, are here deep-dyed but not extinguished by the glitter and jazz of an urban-feeling wilderness.

In both representations, the movement is from right to left, like that of writing in the Semitic languages, like the motion of a mother when she instinctively shifts her baby to her left arm, to hold it closer to her heart. It feels natu-

---

4. A reference to Emanuel Leutze's famous 1851 painting, "Washington Crossing the Delaware." In Leutze's painting Washington is standing but not pointing; Updike may have misremembered the "gesture."

ral, this direction, and slightly uphill. We gaze at these dreamlike tapestries of travel confident that no progress will be made—we will awaken in our beds.

QUESTIONS

1. One reviewer of *Just Looking*, the book from which these short essays are taken, called Updike a dilettante about art; another said these pieces produced not criticism of art but "an enhanced understanding of the writer and his . . . preoccupations." Using both essays as examples, show how these critiques of Updike are or are not true.

2. On the basis of these two essays, what seem to be Updike's major interests when it comes to viewing pictures?

3. Compare the painting by Leutze (see www.metmuseum.org/explore/gw/el_gw.htm) to that of de Forest. What kinds of echoes does Updike seem most interested in bringing to our attention? Do you see any other connections?

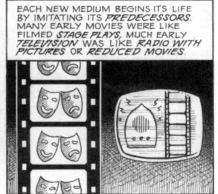

From Understanding Comics, *a graphic book published in 1994.*

WORDS AND PICTURES IN COMBINATION MAY NOT BE MY *DEFINITION* OF COMICS, BUT THE COMBINATION HAS HAD *TREMENDOUS INFLUENCE* ON ITS *GROWTH.*

com·ics (kom'iks) n. p... form, used with a singula... Juxtaposed pictori... ...er images in deliberat... ...ence, intended to conve... ...on and/or to prod... ...response in t... **2.** Superheroes... costumes; fighti... villains who want... ...ne words in violent s... ...use.

A HUGE RANGE OF HUMAN EXPERIENCES CAN BE *PORTRAYED* IN COMICS THROUGH EITHER WORDS OR PICTURES.

AS A RESULT--AND DESPITE ITS MANY *OTHER* POTENTIAL USES -- COMICS HAVE BECOME *FIRMLY IDENTIFIED* WITH THE ART OF *STORYTELLING.*

AND *INDEED,* WORDS AND PICTURES HAVE *GREAT* POWERS TO TELL STORIES WHEN CREATORS FULLY EXPLOIT THEM *BOTH.*

DADA
BIOGRAPHY HORROR
ROMANCE SURREALISM
BLANK VERSE HISTORICAL FICTION
EPIC POETRY FOLK TALES
SOCIAL ALLEGORY **SEQUENTIAL ART** EROTICA
ADAPTATIONS MYSTERY
RELIGIOUS TOPICS
STREAM OF CONSCIOUSNESS
SATIRE

AND SO FAR, WE'VE ONLY SEEN THE *TIP OF THE ICEBERG!*

AS CHILDREN, WE "SHOW AND TELL" *INTERCHANGEABLY,* WORDS AND IMAGES COMBINING TO TRANSMIT A *CONNECTED SERIES OF IDEAS.*

IT'S GOT ONE OF *THESE* THINGS.

THE DIFFERENT WAYS IN WHICH WORDS AND PICTURES CAN *COMBINE* IN COMICS IS VIRTUALLY *UNLIMITED.*

BUT LET'S TRY TO BREAK IT DOWN INTO SOME DISTINCT *CATEGORIES.*

PERHAPS THE MOST *COMMON* TYPE OF WORD/PICTURE COMBINATION IS THE *INTER-DEPENDENT*, WHERE WORDS AND PICTURES GO *HAND IN HAND* TO CONVEY AN IDEA THAT NEITHER COULD CONVEY *ALONE*.

MEANWHILE...

DID ANYONE *SEE* YOU?

THIS IS ALL I NEED TO *STOP* HIM!

I ASK YOU, DOES THIS GUY LOOK LIKE A *C.E.O.* TO *YOU*??

"AND JUST *GUESS* WHO DROVE UP IN BOB'S TRUCK AN HOUR LATER!"

HEY, MARGE!

OH, MY GOD!

"AFTER COLLEGE, I PURSUED A CAREER IN *HIGH FINANCE*."

HURRY UP, WILLYA?!

HE'S LYING.

UH-HUH.

INTERDEPENDENT COMBINATIONS AREN'T ALWAYS AN *EQUAL BALANCE* THOUGH AND MAY FALL *ANYWHERE* ON A SCALE BETWEEN TYPES ONE AND TWO.

GENERALLY SPEAKING, THE MORE IS SAID WITH *WORDS*, THE MORE THE PICTURES CAN BE FREED TO GO EXPLORING AND *VICE VERSA*.

$$\frac{P}{W}$$

$$\frac{W}{P}$$

IN COMICS AT ITS *BEST,* WORDS AND PICTURES ARE LIKE *PARTNERS* IN A *DANCE* AND EACH ONE TAKES TURNS *LEADING.*

WHEN *BOTH* PARTNERS TRY TO LEAD, THE COMPETITION CAN *SUBVERT* THE OVERALL GOALS...

YOW!

...THOUGH A LITTLE *PLAYFUL* *COMPETITION* CAN SOMETIMES PRODUCE *ENJOYABLE RESULTS.*

BUT WHEN THESE PARTNERS EACH *KNOW* THEIR ROLES--

--AND *SUPPORT* EACH OTHER'S *STRENGTHS--*

--COMICS CAN MATCH *ANY* OF THE ART FORMS IT DRAWS SO MUCH OF ITS STRENGTH FROM.

Questions

1. Scott McCloud announces in his title that he wants to help the reader "understand comics." What features of comics does McCloud explain? How do the features of the comic strip form itself aid in that explanation?

2. Choose a frame in which you think word and image work well together, and analyze why they do so. Use one or more of McCloud's categories of analysis.

3. Using the categories that McCloud introduces in the second half of this selection, analyze how a comic strip in your local newspaper works. If relevant, suggest how it might work even better.

Susan Sontag   *A Century of Cinema*

Cinema's hundred years appear to have the shape of a life cycle: an inevitable birth, the steady accumulation of glories, and the onset in the last decade of an ignominious, irreversible decline. This doesn't mean that there won't be any more new films one can admire. But such films will not simply be exceptions; that's true of great achievement in any art. They will have to be heroic violations of the norms and practices which now govern moviemaking everywhere in the capitalist and would-be capitalist world— which is to say, everywhere. And ordinary films, films made purely for entertainment (that is, commercial) purposes, will continue to be astonishingly witless; already the vast majority fail resoundingly to appeal to their cynically targeted audiences. While the point of a great film is now, more than ever, to be a one-of-a-kind achievement, the commercial cinema has settled for a policy of bloated, derivative filmmaking, a brazen combinatory or re-combinatory art, in the hope of reproducing past successes. Every film that hopes to reach the largest possible audience is designed as some kind of remake. Cinema, once heralded as *the* art of the twentieth century, seems now, as the century closes numerically, to be a decadent art.

Perhaps it is not cinema which has ended but only cinephilia—the name of the distinctive kind of love that cinema inspired. Each art breeds its fanatics. The love movies aroused was more imperial. It was born of the conviction that cinema was an art unlike any other: quintessentially modern; distinctively accessible; poetic and mysterious and erotic and moral—all at the same time. Cinema had apostles (it was like religion). Cinema was a crusade. Cinema was

Written in 1995 for the German newspaper Frankfurter Rundschau *and published in shortened form in the* New York Times Magazine *(February 25, 1996); later reprinted in a small circulation American journal* Parnassus *(1997) and, with editorial changes, in Sontag's collection of essays* Where the Stress Falls *(2001).*

a world view. Lovers of poetry or opera or dance don't think there is *only* poetry or opera or dance. But lovers of cinema could think there was only cinema. That the movies encapsulated everything—and they did. It was both the book of art and the book of life.

"The Arrival of a Train at La Ciotat Station," 1895.

As many have noted, the start of moviemaking a hundred years ago was, conveniently, a double start. In that first year, 1895, two kinds of films were made, proposing two modes of what cinema could be: cinema as the transcription of real, unstaged life (the Lumière brothers) and cinema as invention, artifice, illusion, fantasy (Méliès).[1] But this was never a true opposition. For those first audiences watching the Lumière brothers' *The Arrival of a Train at La Ciotat Station*, the camera's transmission of a banal sight was a fantastic experience. Cinema began in wonder, the wonder that reality can be transcribed with such magical immediacy. All of cinema is an attempt to perpetuate and to reinvent that sense of wonder.

Everything begins with that moment, one hundred years ago, when the train pulled into the station. People took movies into themselves, just as the public cried out with excitement, actually ducked, as the train seemed to move toward *them*. Until the advent of television emptied the movie theatres, it was from a weekly visit to the cinema that you learned (or tried to learn) how to strut, to smoke, to kiss, to fight, to grieve. Movies gave you tips about how to be attractive, such as . . . it looks good to wear a raincoat even when it isn't raining. But whatever you took home from the movies was only a part of the larger experience of losing yourself in faces, in lives that were *not* yours—which is the more inclusive form of desire embodied in the movie experience. The strongest experience was simply to surrender to, to be transported by, what was on the screen. You wanted to be kidnapped by the movie.

5   The prerequisite of being kidnapped was to be overwhelmed by the physical presence of the image. And the conditions of "going to the movies" secured that experience. To see a great film only on television isn't to have

1. Lumière brothers, Auguste (1864–1948) and Louis Jean (1862–1954), French inventors who in 1895 patented and demonstrated the Cinématographe, the first device for photographing, printing, and projecting films; Georges Méliès (1861–1938), early French experimenter with motion pictures, the first to film fictional narratives.

really seen that film. (This is
equally true of those made for
TV, like Fassbinder's *Berlin
Alexanderplatz* and the two
Heimat films of Edgar Reitz.)[2]
It's not only the difference of
dimensions: the superiority of
the larger-than-you image in
the theatre to the little image
on the box at home. The conditions of paying attention in a
domestic space are radically
disrespectful of film. Since film
no longer has a standard size,
home screens can be as big as
living room or bedroom walls.

"Nana," 1926.

But you are still in a living room or a bedroom, alone or with familiars. To be
kidnapped, you have to be in a movie theatre, seated in the dark among
anonymous strangers.

No amount of mourning will revive the vanished rituals—erotic, rumina-
tive—of the darkened theatre. The reduction of cinema to assaultive images, and
the unprincipled manipulation of images (faster and faster cutting) to be more
attention-grabbing, have produced a disincarnated, lightweight cinema that
doesn't demand anyone's full attention. Images now appear in any size and on a
variety of surfaces: on a screen in a theatre, on home screens as small as the
palm of your hand or as big as a wall, on disco walls and mega-screens hanging
above sports arenas and the outsides of tall public buildings. The sheer ubiquity
of moving images' has steadily undermined the standards people once had both
for cinema as art at its most serious and for cinema as popular entertainment.

In the first years there was, essentially, no difference between cinema as art
and cinema as entertainment. And *all* films of the silent era—from the masterpieces of Feuillade, D. W. Griffith, Dziga Vertov, Pabst, Murnau, King Vidor[3] to

2. Rainer Werner Fassbinder (1946–1982) and Reitz (b. 1932), both German film directors.

3. Feuillade (1873–1925), French film director who developed short adventure films
and screen serials in the period around World War I; David Wark Griffith (1875–1948),
American film director who innovated cross-cutting, close-ups, long shots, and flashbacks in such films as *The Birth of a Nation* (1915); Dziga Vertov (Denis Arkadyevich
Kaufman, 1896–1954), Soviet film director who developed the "film-eye" theory, which
made the camera operate as an instrument much like the human eye; Georg Wilhelm
Pabst (1885–1967), German film director who developed "montage" in such works as
The Joyless Street (1925) and *The Threepenny Opera* (1931); Friedrich Wilhelm Murnau
(1889–1931), German film director whose works include *Nosferatu* (1922), *The Last
Laugh* (1924), and *Sunrise* (1927); King Vidor (1894–1982), American film director who
created *The Crowd* (1928) and later *The Citadel* (1938), the black-and-white scenes of
The Wizard of Oz (1939), *The Fountainhead* (1949), and *War and Peace* (1956).

"Napoleon," 1927.

the most formula-ridden melodramas and comedies—look, are, better than most of what was to follow. With the coming of sound, the image-making lost much of its brilliance and poetry, and commercial standards tightened. This way of making movies—the Hollywood system—dominated filmmaking for about twenty-five years (roughly from 1930 to 1955). The most original directors, like Erich von Stroheim and Orson Welles,[4] were defeated by the system and eventually went into artistic exile in Europe—where more or less the same quality-defeating system was in place with lower budgets; only in France were a large number of superb films produced throughout this period. Then, in the mid-1950s, vanguard ideas took hold again, rooted in the idea of cinema as a craft pioneered by the Italian films of the early postwar era. A dazzling number of original, passionate films of the highest seriousness got made with new actors and tiny crews, went to film festivals (of which there were more and more), and from there, garlanded with festival prizes, into movie theatres around the world. This golden age actually lasted as long as twenty years.

It was at this specific moment in the hundred-year history of cinema that going to movies, thinking about movies, talking about movies became a passion among university students and other young people. You fell in love not just with actors but with cinema itself. Cinephilia had first become visible in the 1950s in France: its forum was the legendary film magazine *Cahiers du*

---

4. Erich von Stroheim (1885–1957), German filmmaker, most famous for *Greed* (1925); Orson Welles (1915–1985), American film director, most famous for *Citizen Kane* (1941).

"The 400 Blows," 1959.

Cinéma (followed by similarly fervent magazines in Germany, Italy, Great Britain, Sweden, the United States, Canada). Its temples, as it spread throughout Europe and the Americas, were the cinematheques and film clubs specializing in films from the past and directors' retrospectives. The 1960s and early 1970s were the age of feverish moviegoing, with the full-time cinephile always hoping to find a seat as close as possible to the big screen, ideally the third row center. "One can't live without Rossellini," declares a character in Bertolucci's *Before the Revolution* (1964)—and means it.

Cinephilia—a source of exultation in the films of Godard and Truffaut and the early Bertolucci and Syberberg;[5] a morose lament in the recent films of Nanni Moretti[6]—was mostly a Western European affair. The great directors of "the other Europe" (Zanussi in Poland, Angelopoulos in Greece, Tarkovsky and Sokurov in Russia, Jancsó and Tarr in Hungary) and the great Japanese directors (Ozu, Mizoguchi, Kurosawa, Naruse, Oshima, Imamura) have tended not to be cinephiles, perhaps because in Budapest or Moscow or Tokyo or Warsaw or Athens there wasn't a chance to get a cinematheque edu-

---

5. Jean-Luc Godard (b. 1930), French film director known for *Breathless* (1959), among others; François Truffaut (1932–1984), French director whose films include *The 400 Blows* (1959), *Day for Night* (1973), and *The Last Métro* (1980); Bernardo Bertolucci (b. 1940), Italian filmmaker whose work includes *Last Tango in Paris* (1973) and *The Last Emperor* (1987); Hans-Jurgen Syberberg (b. 1935), German director and critic, known for his *Parsifal* (1988) and his book *Hitler: A Film from Germany* (1982), for which Sontag wrote the English preface.

6. Italian filmmaker, best known for *Caro Diario* (Dear diary, 1993).

"Persona," 1967.

cation. The distinctive thing about cinephile taste was that it embraced both "art" films and popular films. Thus, European cinephilia had a romantic relation to the films of certain directors in Hollywood at the apogee of the studio system: Godard for Howard Hawks, Fassbinder for Douglas Sirk. Of course, this moment—when cinephilia emerged—was also the moment when the Hollywood studio system was breaking up. It seemed that moviemaking had re-won the right to experiment; cinephiles could *afford* to be passionate (or sentimental) about the old Hollywood genre films. A host of new people came into cinema, including a generation of young film critics from *Cahiers du Cinéma*; the towering figure of that generation, indeed of several decades of filmmaking anywhere, was Jean-Luc Godard. A few writers turned out to be wildly talented filmmakers: Alexander Kluge in Germany, Pier Paolo Pasolini in Italy. (The model for the writer who turns to filmmaking actually emerged earlier, in France, with Pagnol in the 1930s and Cocteau in the 1940s; but it was not until the 1960s that this seemed, at least in Europe, normal.) Cinema appeared to be reborn.

10   For some fifteen years there was a profusion of masterpieces, and one allowed oneself to imagine that this would go on forever. To be sure, there was always a conflict between cinema as an industry and cinema as an art, cinema as routine and cinema as experiment. But the conflict was not such as to make impossible the making of wonderful films, sometimes within and sometimes outside of mainstream cinema. Now the balance has tipped decisively in favor of cinema as an industry. The great cinema of the 1960s and 1970s has been thoroughly repudiated. Already in the 1970s Hollywood was plagiarizing and banalizing the innovations in narrative method and editing of successful new European and ever-marginal independent American films. Then came the catastrophic rise in production costs in the 1980s, which secured the worldwide reimposition of industry standards of making and distributing films on a far more coercive, this time truly global, scale. The result can be seen in the melancholy fate of some of the greatest directors of the last decades. What place is there today for a maverick like Hans Jurgen Syberberg, who has

"Breathless," 1959.

stopped making films altogether, or for the great Godard, who now makes films about the history of film on video? Consider some other cases. The internationalizing of financing and therefore of casts was a disaster for Andrei Tarkovsky[7] in the last two films of his stupendous, tragically abbreviated career. And these conditions for making films have proved to be as much an artistic disaster for two of the most valuable directors still working: Krzysztof Zanussi (*The Structure of Crystals, Illumination, Spiral, Contract*) and Theo Angelopoulos (*Reconstruction, Days of '36, The Travelling Players*). And what will happen now to Béla Tarr (*Damnation, Satantango*)? And how will Aleksandr Sokurov (*Save and Protect, Days of Eclipse, The Second Circle, Stone, Whispering Pages*) find the money to go on making films, his sublime films, under the rude conditions of Russian capitalism?[8]

Predictably, the love of cinema has waned. People still like going to the movies, and some people still care about and expect something special, necessary from a film. And wonderful films are still being made: Mike Leigh's *Naked*, Gianni Amelio's *Lamerica*, Hou Hsiao-hsien's *Goodbye South, Goodbye*, and Abbas Kiarostami's *Close-Up* and Koker trilogy. But one hardly finds

7. Soviet film director (1932–1986), whose work was censored at home but won acclaim in the West. His *Katok i skripka* (The steamroller and the violin, 1960) won a prize at the New York Film Festival, and his first full-length feature film, *Ivanovo detstvo* (Ivan's childhood, 1962), established his international reputation.

8. Zanussi (b. 1939), Polish film director; Angelopolous (b. 1935), Greek film director; Tarr (b. 1955), Hungarian filmmaker; Sokurov (b. 1951), Russian filmmaker who in 1997 produced the award-winning *Mat i syn* (Mother and son).

anymore, at least among the young, the distinctive cinephilic love of movies, which is not simply love of but a certain *taste* in films (grounded in a vast appetite for seeing and re-seeing as much as possible of cinema's glorious past). Cinephilia itself has come under attack, as something quaint, outmoded, snobbish. For cinephilia implies that films are unique, unrepeatable, magic experiences. Cinephilia tells us that the Hollywood remake of Godard's *Breathless* cannot be as good as the original. Cinephilia has no role in the era of hyperindustrial films. For by the very range and eclecticism of its passions, cinephilia cannot help but sponsor the idea of the film as, first of all, a poetic object; and cannot help but incite those outside the movie industry, like painters and writers, to want to make films, too. It is precisely this that must be defeated. That has been defeated.

If cinephilia is dead, then movies are dead . . . no matter how many movies, even very good ones, go on being made. If cinema can be resurrected, it will only be through the birth of a new kind of cine-love.

QUESTIONS

1. In her essay Sontag summarizes one hundred years of film history, from 1895 to 1995. Diagram her periodization of this history. Locate her moviegoing period (she was born in 1933) and yours on it. Which of the older films Sontag mentions have you seen? If you have seen other films made before you began going to the movies, name some of them. How did you see them—in a film-studies course, for example, or on your own?

2. What is Sontag's definition of a "cinephile"? Are you one? Is Susan Allen Toth one? See her "Going to the Movies" on the opposite page.

3. Sontag has harsh things to say about contemporary films: they are "astonishingly witless," "bloated, derivative," "a brazen combinatory or re-combinatory art" (paragraph 1), reduced to "assaultive images, and the unprincipled manipulation of images (faster and faster cutting) to be more attention-grabbing" and, at the same time, "disincarnated, lightweight," and they don't "demand anyone's full attention" (paragraph 6). Using at least three contemporary films that you have seen, write an essay in which you agree with, disagree with, or modify her charges.

4. Write an essay in which you compare what Sontag and Toth look for in film.

Susan Allen Toth *Going to the Movies*

AARON TAKES ME only to art films. That's what I call them, anyway: strange movies with vague poetic images I don't always understand, long dreamy movies about a distant Technicolor past, even longer black-and-white movies about the general meaninglessness of life. We do not go unless at least one reputable critic has found the cinematography superb. We went to *The Devil's Eye*,[1] and Aaron turned to me in the middle and said, "My God, this is *funny*." I do not think he was pleased.

When Aaron and I go to the movies, we drive our cars separately and meet by the box office. Inside the theater he sits tentatively in his seat, ready to move if he can't see well, poised to leave if the film is disappointing. He leans away from me, careful not to touch the bare flesh of his arm against the bare flesh of mine. Sometimes he leans so far I am afraid he may be touching the woman on his other side instead. If the movie is very good, he leans forward too, peering between the heads of the couple in front of us. The light from the screen bounces off his glasses; he gleams with intensity, sitting there on the edge of his seat, watching the screen. Once I tapped him on the arm so I could whisper a comment in his ear. He jumped.

After *Belle de Jour*[2] Aaron said he wanted to ask me if he could stay overnight. "But I can't," he shook his head mournfully before I had a chance to answer, "because I know I never sleep well in strange beds." Then he apologized for asking. "It's just that after a film like that," he said, "I feel the need to assert myself."

II

Bob takes me only to movies that he thinks have a redeeming social conscience. He doesn't call them films. They tend to be about poverty, war, injustice, political corruption, struggling unions in the 1930s, and the military-industrial complex. Bob doesn't like propaganda movies, though, and he doesn't like to be too depressed, either. We stayed away from *The Sorrow and the Pity*;[3] it would be, he said, just too much. Besides, he assured me, things are never that hopeless. So most of the movies we see are made in Hollywood. Because they are always very topical, these movies offer what Bob calls "food for

Originally published in Harper's Magazine *(May 1980) as "Cinematypes"; retitled and included in Toth's collection* How to Prepare for Your High School Reunion, and Other Essays *(1988).*

1. Swedish film (1960) about seduction, directed by Ingmar Bergman.
2. French film (1967) about erotic fantasies, directed by Luis Buñuel.
3. French documentary (1972) about the Nazi occupation of France.

thought." When we saw *Coming Home*,[4] Bob's jaw set so firmly with the first half hour that I knew we would end up at Poppin' Fresh Pies afterward.

5   When Bob and I go to the movies, we take turns driving so no one owes anyone else anything. We park far away from the theater so we don't have to pay for a space. If it's raining or snowing, Bob offers to let me off at the door, but I can tell he'll feel better if I go with him while he parks, so we share the walk too. Inside the theater Bob will hold my hand when I get scared if I ask him. He puts my hand firmly on his knee and covers it completely with his own hand. His knee never twitches. After a while, when the scary part is past, he loosens his hand slightly and I know that is a signal to take mine away. He sits companionably close, letting his jacket just touch my sweater, but he does not infringe. He thinks I ought to know he is there if I need him.

One night after *The China Syndrome*[5] I asked Bob if he wouldn't like to stay for a second drink, even though it was past midnight. He thought awhile about that, considering my offer from all possible angles, but finally he said no. Relationships today, he said, have a tendency to move too quickly.

III

Sam likes movies that are entertaining. By that he means movies that Will Jones in the *Minneapolis Tribune* loved and either *Time* or *Newsweek* rather liked; also movies that do not have sappy love stories, are not musicals, do not have subtitles, and will not force him to think. He does not go to movies to think. He liked *California Suite* and *The Seduction of Joe Tynan*,[6] though the plots, he said, could have been zippier. He saw it all coming too far in advance, and that took the fun out. He doesn't like to know what is going to happen. "I just want my brain to be tickled," he says. It is very hard for me to pick out movies for Sam.

When Sam takes me to the movies, he pays for everything. He thinks that's what a man ought to do. But I buy my own popcorn, because he doesn't approve of it; the grease might smear his flannel slacks. Inside the theater, Sam makes himself comfortable. He takes off his jacket, puts one arm around me, and all during the movie he plays with my hand, stroking my palm, beating a small tattoo on my wrist. Although he watches the movie intently, his body operates on instinct. Once I inclined my head and kissed him lightly just behind his ear. He beat a faster tattoo on my wrist, quick and musical, but he didn't look away from the screen.

When Sam takes me home from the movies, he stands outside my door and kisses me long and hard. He would like to come in, he says regretfully, but his steady girlfriend in Duluth wouldn't like it. When the *Tribune* gives a movie four stars, he has to save it to see with her. Otherwise her feelings might be hurt.

---

4. American film (1978) about a Vietnam veteran.
5. American film (1979) about a disaster in a nuclear power plant.
6. The first, American film (1978) with a script by Neil Simon; the second, American film (1979) about politics.

IV

I go to some movies by myself. On rainy Sunday afternoons I often sneak into   10
a revival house or a college auditorium for old Technicolor musicals, *Kiss Me
Kate, Seven Brides for Seven Brothers, Calamity Jane,* even, once, *The Sound of
Music.*[7] Wearing saggy jeans so I can prop my feet on the seat in front, I sit toward the rear where no one will see me. I eat large handfuls of popcorn with
double butter. Once the movie starts, I feel completely at home. Howard Keel
and I are old friends; I grin back at him on the screen, admiring all his teeth.
I know the sound tracks by heart. Sometimes when I get really carried away I
hum along with Kathryn Grayson, remembering how I once thought I would
fill out a formal like that. Skirts whirl, feet tap, acrobatic young men perform
impossible feats, and then the camera dissolves into a dream sequence I know
I can comfortably follow. It is not, thank God, Bergman.

    If I can't find an old musical, I settle for Hepburn and Tracy, vintage
Grant or Gable, on adventurous days Claudette Colbert or James Stewart. Before I buy my ticket I make sure it will all end happily. If necessary, I ask the
girl at the box office. I have never seen *Stella Dallas* or *Intermezzo.*[8] Over the
years I have developed other peccadilloes: I will, for example, see anything
that is redeemed by Thelma Ritter. At the end of *Daddy Long Legs*[9] I wait happily for the scene when Fred Clark, no longer angry, at last pours Thelma a
convivial drink. They smile at each other, I smile at them, I feel they are smiling at me. In the movies I go to by myself, the men and women always like
each other.

7. The first three were made in the 1950s, the fourth in the 1960s.
8. The first, American film (1937) about a mother's love for her daughter; the second,
American film (1939), a love story in which Ingrid Bergman made her American debut.
9. American film (1955) about a May–December romance.

QUESTIONS

1. Toth describes four kinds of movies by describing the men she sees them with:
Aaron, Bob, Sam, and finally no man. Make a list of the adjectives or descriptive
phrases she includes for each man. How do such descriptions convey, by implication,
her attitudes toward the movies?

2. Which kind of movie does Toth like best—or does she like them all equally? How do
you know?

3. Using Toth as a model, write an account of going to some event or participating in
some activity by describing the person(s) you go with. Like Toth, convey your response
to the event by means of your description of the person(s).

ANTHONY LANE   *The Sound of Music*

L ET'S START AT the very beginning. (It's a very good place to start.) Maria Augusta Kutschera was born in 1905. As a young woman, she became a postulant at the Nonnberg Abbey, in Salzburg, Austria, but suffered from ill health. It was deemed beneficial that she should venture outside and adopt the post of governess in the home of a naval captain. She married him in 1927, which put an end to any postulating. The captain already had seven children; Maria bore him three more and formed a family musical group, whose success was cut short when Hitler invaded his native land. Even now, no historian has been able to ascertain if this was a genuine bid for power or the only possible means whereby the Führer could eradicate the threat of close-harmony singing.

Maria and her family fled to Italy, England, and, finally, the United States. The captain died in 1947; two years later, Maria published *The Story of the Trapp Family Singers*. In 1956, the book was turned into a hit German movie; theatrical producers began to sniff around, and in November 1959, *The Sound of Music*, with original songs by Rodgers and Hammerstein, opened on Broadway. Twentieth Century Fox soon acquired the movie rights, but the film proved hard to bring to birth. After nearly five years of wrangles and pangs, *The Sound of Music*, directed by Robert Wise and starring Julie Andrews, had its New York premiere, on March 2, 1965. To date, the picture has earned 160 million dollars. It remains the most popular musical film in history. One woman in Wales has seen it almost a thousand times. In Hong Kong, it is entitled *Fairy Music Blow Fragrant Place, Place Hear*.

All of which is how I came to be standing on a sidewalk on a dark December evening, waving a foam nun.

The Prince Charles Cinema sits in central London, a hundred yards east of Piccadilly, between the Notre Dame dance hall and a row of Chinese restaurants. When it opened, in 1991, the idea was that you could catch new and recent pictures for less than two dollars—a fraction of what they cost around the corner, in the plush movie theatres of Leicester Square. Even now, the Prince Charles has nobly resisted the urge to smarten up; the furnishings are a touching tribute to wartime brown, and the stalls, flouting a rule of theatrical design which has obtained since the fifth century B.C., appear to slope downward toward the back, so that customers in the rear seats can enjoy an uncluttered view of their own knees. The cinema shows three or four films a day; come the weekend, everything explodes. Since August, every Friday evening and Sunday afternoon the program has been the same: "Singalong-a-Sound-of-Music."

5   The idea is simple. You watch the film—uncut, as nature intended, in a

Originally appeared in The New Yorker *(February 14, 2000), a magazine of literature, music, drama, and art; later included in a collection of Lane's reviews,* Nobody's Perfect *(2002).*

scuzzy print, with alarming color shifts as the reels change. The only differ-ence is the added subtitles, which come alive, like the hills, during every song. These enable viewers to join in, which they do with undisguised lustiness. The titling of *The Sound of Music* was prepared by Martin Wagner, for London's National Film Theatre, and it struck me as the one work of unquestionable ge-nius that I encountered last year. I tend to be embarrassed by subtitles; their audacious efforts to snatch at foreign vernaculars end up stressing, rather than allaying, the alien qualities of the setting. With *The Sound of Music*, however, they bring home just how tightly, even soothingly, we are wrapped in this unig-norable film. In a sense, Wagner had a head start; what was required was not translation from another tongue but the simple transcription, for karaoke pur-poses, of words that most of us know pretty well. (I was appalled to discover that, after a thirty-year break, I was close to word-perfect.) This, however, is where Wagner shows his hand; who else would have thought to include the *Latin chant* that rises from the abbey as we pan down from Julie Andrews on a hillside and get ready for "(How Do You Solve a Problem Like) Maria?" I had never noticed it before—no audience is meant to notice filler, the blah that keeps a soundtrack ticking along—but suddenly there it was at the bottom of the screen (*"In saecula saeculorum"*). Things get even better halfway through the picture, as the children gather at the foot of the stairs to bid the party guests good night. Friedrich sings, and the titles follow him closely.

> So long, farewell, auf Wiedersehen, adieu,
> Adieu, adieu, to yieu and yieu and yieu.

That was it for me. For thirty years, I have wondered about this torturing little rhyme. It should have been easy to avoid; if you want "Adieu" to chime with "you," don't pronounce it in French—simply opt for the Anglicized ver-sion, "Adyoo," and take it from there. But no: *The Sound of Music* made a tragic move to sound classy, and it paid the price. As for the yodelling in the puppet scene, it inspires Wagner to his finest work—a cluster bomb of mean-ingless vowels. For anyone who believes that *The Sound of Music* shows Holly-wood at its most hopelessly square, what could be more bracing than to see it reborn as a Dadaist art happening?

All nonsense is a pleasure, of course, from Lewis Carroll down to Alexan-der Haig, but what lends particular spice to *The Sound of Music* is that it is known nonsense, remembered and revered. And that is why the Prince Charles has become a place of pilgrimage. It occasionally screens *The Rocky Horror Picture Show*, too, to a gathering of addicts. But that film is already ar-mored by a sense of camp; nothing you can throw at it will dent its knowing-ness, whereas *The Sound of Music*, the most unwitting of cults, is blissfully up for grabs.

When I arrived on a Friday night, an hour before the start, the area around the cinema was packed. To be specific, it was packed with nuns. Many of them bore guitars. I was one of the few pathetic creatures who had not made the effort to come in costume. There were Nazis, naturally, as in every major city, plus a load of people who looked like giant parcels. I didn't get it. "Who are they?" I said to a nun who was having a quick cigarette before the film. She looked at me with celestial pity and blew smoke. "Brown Paper Packages Tied Up with Strings," she replied. I am relieved, on the whole, that I missed the rugby team who piled into one screening as Girls in White Dresses with Blue Satin Sashes; on the other hand, it is a source of infinite sadness to me that I wasn't at the Prince Charles when a guy turned up in a skintight, all-over body costume in bright yellow; asked which character he was intended to represent, he explained that he was Ray, a Drop of Golden Sun. I have hung around the entrance a couple of times as showtime approached, just in case this heroic gentleman returns as Warm Woollen Mittens—or, more challenging still, as Tea, a Drink with Jam and Bread—but no luck so far.

The impressive thing about all this is the apostolic level of dedication. I sat in a whole row of nuns—nurses from a private hospital, as it happened, having a cheap night out. (One had lovingly constructed her wimple from black cloth and a rolled-up pair of white knickers.) During the screening, they drank beer in almost Austrian quantities; one of them kept jumping up and hurrying to the exit; "What's the matter with that nun?" I asked the beefy sister beside me. "Pregnant," she said.

10   Nominally a reserved people, the British like to bottle up their exhibitionist tendencies and then, at opportune moments, let them flood out in a rush; this is the basis of pantomime, for instance, with its flagrant worship of cross-dressing. Even now, there is almost certainly a quiet soul who is preparing to attend The Sound of Music as Schnitzel with Noodles. To brush yourself with egg and roll around in bread crumbs for a while requires a nerveless ingenuity; but to walk to the nearest tube trailing ribbons of buttered pasta, and to sit on the train with a dignified expression, in the thick of the Friday rush hour, argues a fortitude bordering on the superhuman. I couldn't do it, but somebody will, and I think I know who that somebody will be. "Singalong-a-Sound-of-Music" is currently starting a British national tour, and then, in April, it will hit America, where bottling is less of an issue. Twentieth Century Fox will not yet name the lucky cinemas where it will screen, but I can safely reveal that New York and San Francisco, among others, should be girding their loins for Schnitzel Time.

It goes without saying that "Singalong-a-Sound-of-Music" is now a compulsory fixture on the gay calendar; it began life, indeed, as a one-off special for the London Lesbian and Gay Film Festival. Every screening gets its own emcee, who oversees a Best Costume competition during the intermission. (One week, just to confuse the issue, the winner was a real nun. What did she think the other nuns were?) At my screening, there was Rhona Cameron, a cheery Scottish lesbian who hosts a gay show on British TV. Rhona checked that there were no children in the audience, and then issued instructions: "Don't worry if you can't sing; the gay men in the audience will carry you." Fragrant music blow fairy place, place go wild.

I usually loathe any hint of live entertainment at the movies, preferring to hibernate in peace and quiet; but "Singalong-a-Sound-of-Music" launches so frontal an assault on reticence that everyone caves in. It is a stout rebuke to the couch culture of "home cinema"—a contradiction in terms, if ever I heard one. The bloodless interaction promised by DVD technology, for instance, in which the lone viewer can pause *The Matrix* to command a reverse view of Keanu Reeves's butt, cannot hold a candle to the sight of two hundred people whistling at Christopher Plummer when he enters with a riding crop, and waving their lighters above their heads, like a rock crowd, during his rendition of "Edelweiss." For an extra five dollars, ticket-holders at the Prince Charles can buy a helpful gift pack that includes a fake edelweiss, a packet of cough drops for sore throats, a head scarf, and, yes, a small foam-rubber nun, in which you are urged to "stick your fingers" and "sway along."

The repartee at "Singalong-a-Sound-of-Music" is of the very highest order. "Free the nuns!" was the cry as the sisters clustered behind an iron grille during Maria's wedding. Some of the backchat involves a dexterous cross-reference to other works; when Maria, having been ticked off by the Baroness (Eleanor Parker), packs her bag to leave, someone shouted, "Don't forget the hat stand!"—reminding us of a similar scene in *Mary Poppins*. And, as the Mother Abbess lingered in the shadows in preparation for "Climb Ev'ry Mountain," she was told in no uncertain terms, "Do not go into the light!"—the tag line from *Poltergeist*, if you please. The instructions issued to Rolf as he danced with Liesl in the gazebo came from somewhere behind my shoulder; they were explicit, and they were repeated with such urgency that, after a while, they acquired the pathos of a plea—as if it were in some way unsportsmanlike, even unromantic, for a seventeen-year-old Nazi not to deflower a motherless sixteen-year-old while he had the chance. "You need someone older and wiser telling you what to do," crooned Rolf, and we sniggered at his nerve.

The joke is, of course, that Charmian Carr, who plays Liesl, was already twenty-one when the film was made (she kept quiet at the audition), and thus in no need of tutelage from a mere boy; the deeper joke is that, in the history of blockbusting movies, nothing can touch *The Sound of Music* for sheer, blank indifference to the reproductive act. No wonder Heather Menzies, who played Louisa, answered the call to strip for *Playboy* in the 1970s; the pressure of untouchability must have felt like prison. Captain Von Trapp has seven children, but the enigma of his fertility remains as unplumbed as his willingness, as a serving naval officer, to play the guitar in public. The baroness, with her glinting coiffure and cinched suits, could be taken, in a certain light, for a woman of the world; yet the captain throws her over for the sake of a certifiable virgin with a boy's haircut. "For here you are, standing there, loving me," he and Maria sing to one another; love, in so immaculate a world, is pure abstraction, unruffled by the physical. In the intermission at the Prince Charles, Rhona Cameron asked one nun what she liked best about the film. Without hesitation, the nun replied, "The sex."

The Sound of Music is not a good film. It is blithe, efficient, and constructed   15
with care; the songs are carolled con brio; but it is not a good film. Famously, it received some of the most noxious notices of its era. Steeped in the flow of

the counterculture, American critics should have been ready for the sight of
small children dressed in flowery curtains, but somehow the psychedelic properties of the film eluded them. In the *Herald Tribune*, Judith Crist called it
"icky sticky," as if she'd needed to rinse her hands afterward. In *McCall's*,
Pauline Kael continued the candy motif, trashing the movie as a "sugar-coated
lie that people seem to want to eat"; her review so affronted readers that she
was fired from her post and landed shortly afterward at this magazine. Here
she reigned supreme for the next quarter of a century, thus proving that *The
Sound of Music* is so saintly that it confers a happy ending on all who touch its
hem, even those of little faith. The film did more than any other, perhaps, to
widen the split between critics and public from crack to chasm; it encouraged
producers, like political hopefuls, to reach out over the heads of professional
carpers and appeal directly to popular taste. (That it collared the Academy
Award for Best Picture in 1966 merely sealed the deal.) The way to solve a
problem like Maria is to love her for what she is, with or without wimple, and
the movie begs the same indulgence; by ignoring the mean of spirit, it wishes
them away.

To be fair, even some of his friends had trouble taking it in. When Burt
Lancaster ran into Lehman at the Fox commissary and learned what he was
working on, he said, "Jesus, you must need the money." That story comes from
Julia Antopol Hirsch's *The Sound of Music: The Making of America's Favorite
Movie*, a loving compendium of arcana. Here we learn, for instance, that both
Walter Matthau and Sean "Edelweish" Connery were considered for the role
of the captain. A more damning fact is that some of the Osmond boys turned
up to audition, thus demonstrating that, however much *The Sound of Music*
makes your flesh crawl, it could have been so much worse.

All of which serves only to confirm the Kael line, and to demonstrate that
you can fool all of the people all of the time. The lies perpetuated by Wise's
film range from the personal—the real Maria Von Trapp, for instance, looked
nothing like Julie Andrews and an awful not like Nice Guy Eddie from *Reservoir Dogs*—to the broadly historical. If the Nazis' worst crime had indeed been
to hang swastikas over people's doorways, the twentieth century would have
been somewhat easier to bear. I was a sucker for such untruths; my family
even travelled to Salzburg in order to haunt the byways where Julie Andrews
had made so ringingly clear what the first three notes just happened to be. Being below critical age, I did not yet grasp the criteria by which a film could be
adjudged good or bad, much less the procedures by which it arrived onscreen.
If you had explained that the screenplay for *The Sound of Music* came from
the pen of one Ernest Lehman, who had written *North by Northwest* and *Sweet
Smell of Success*, this bewildering detail would have been lost on me.

To be fair, even some of his friends had trouble taking it in. When Burt
Lancaster ran into Lehman at the Fox commissary and learned what he was
working on, he said, "Jesus, you must need the money." That story comes from
Julia Antopol Hirsch's *The Sound of Music: The Making of America's Favorite
Movie*, a loving compendium of arcana. Here we learn, for instance, that both
Walter Matthau and Sean "Edelweish" Connery were considered for the role
of the captain. A more damning fact is that some of the Osmond boys turned
up to audition, thus demonstrating that, however much *The Sound of Music*
makes your flesh crawl, it could have been so much worse.

You could argue that the triumphal saga of the Von Trapp family was so
sweetly outlandish that any dramatic representation of it was doomed to rot
the teeth. But consider another family, the Smiths of Missouri—equally close,
no less pure of heart, and, like the Von Trapps, given to bursting into song at
the slightest provocation. So why does *Meet Me in St. Louis* maintain the status of a nimble masterpiece, while *The Sound of Music* limps along behind?

Then again, how come Vincente Minnelli's picture of 1944 was reckoned merely a success, while Robert Wise's picture, made twenty years later, is a gold-plated phenomenon? The answer to both questions is the same: because Minnelli showed happiness to be the most fragile of possessions, whereas Wise backed it as a sure thing. For all the highs and lows of its melodrama, *The Sound of Music* never dreams that there is any way but up, whether you are ascending a scale or an alp; and that, today and forever, is what movie-goers want to hear. "From now on, our troubles will be out of sight," Judy Garland sings near the end of *Meet Me in St. Louis*, but the throb and catch in her voice give the lie to such game hope, and, by the penultimate line of the number, the message is decidedly mixed: "We'll have to muddle through somehow." Julie Andrews, by comparison, is a muddle-free zone: "I have confidence in confidence alone; Besides which, you see, I have confidence in me!"

Garland was singing during the Second World War, of course, when a certain lyrical worry was inevitable. Andrews hit her stride in the midst of the cold war; the whole of *The Sound of Music* can perhaps be read as the artistic equivalent of antifreeze. It offered one of the last breaths of innocence in American cinema—after all, the same year saw female nudity in *The Pawnbroker*, and *Bonnie and Clyde* was only two years away. That is why we go back to Wise's film; we all know better now, but most of us secretly wish that we didn't. The atmosphere at the Prince Charles, during "Singalong-a-Sound-of-Music," was strangely unmocking, even in its coarsest moments. We assume that deconstruction is a heartless business, in which the vengeful ironist strips the decorous past to its underclothes; but the hoarse crowd that streamed out into Leicester Square seemed to have drawn strength from a communal act of fond consolation. When they cried at "Edelweiss," it was not because the song is, in itself, anything more than slush; it was because they had cried at it in 1965.

Film, in other words, has revivified the Proustian principle that memory is not ours to command; that, for all our searchings and suppressings, the past comes unbidden or not at all. If, for millions of people, that past consists of a lonely goatherd on strings, so be it. Proust himself was more fortunate; for him, a typical throwback consisted of tripping over a paving stone and suddenly recalling a similar stumble in Venice. Few of us can rely on such tasteful apparitions. It is generally agreed, for example, that the last Golden Age of cinema occurred in the mid-seventies—the epoch of *The Godfather, Chinatown*, and *McCabe and Mrs. Miller*. I feel privileged to have been there; unfortunately, I spent my pocket money on tickets for *Zeppelin, Earthquake*, and *Rollercoaster* (in Sensurround). I now realize that *Chinatown* is a great picture and that *The Towering Inferno* is dreck; but the sight of a weary, begrimed Steve McQueen emerging from the tower is burned into my mind with a fierceness that Jack Nicholson, with his nicked nostril, can never match. I missed the Golden Age; catching up later was an education, but nothing I can do will bring it back.

What we feel about a movie—or, indeed, about any work of art, high or low—matters less than the rise and fall of our feelings over time. The *King*

Lear that we see as sons and daughters (of Cordelia's age, say) can never be the same play that we attend as parents; the sound of paternal fury, and of the mortal fears that echo beyond it, will knock ever more insistently at our hearts. Weekly critics cannot do justice to that process; when we are asked to nominate favorite films, all we can say is "Well, just now I quite like *Citizen Kane* or *Police Academy 4*, but ask me again next year." By then we will have grown, by a small but significant slippage, into someone else, and we have yet to know who that person will be, or what friable convictions he or she will hold. The revellers at the Prince Charles Cinema were all in their thirties and forties; no one younger than us would have had the remotest clue what we were doing there, or why we were having such fun. Even our younger selves, of ten years ago, would probably have been mystified, if not humiliated, by the air of semi-delirium that prevailed; how could consenting adults join forces to declare their love for a bad film? Time, as ever, has played its comic trick, and all I can do is adapt the words of Captain Von Trapp and his lovely governess: somewhere in our youth or childhood, we must have seen something good.

QUESTIONS

1. Anthony Lane describes his experience of seeing *The Sound of Music* in London at the Prince Charles Cinema, where it was playing as a cult film. What innovative features had been added to the film? What innovations did the audience bring to it? Why does Lane devote half of the essay (paragraphs 3–14) to this popular cult experience?

2. After describing an example of popular culture, Lane turns to an aesthetic judgment of *The Sound of Music*. What evidence does he give to support his assertion, "*The Sound of Music* is not a good film"? Is aesthetic judgment the primary goal of this essay?

3. In the final two paragraphs, Lane speculates about why some films grip our emotions, while others do not. What explanations does he suggest? What does he mean by "the Proustian principle"? What other explanations can you offer?

4. Analyze a film that has had an impact on you, trying to understand what in the film causes its effect but also what in your experience contributes to the experience.

TERRY TEACHOUT   *The Beatles Now*

THE BEATLES released *Let It Be*,[1] the last of their thirteen albums, 36 years ago.[2] Today there is no one musical group or soloist capable of commanding the attention paid to John Lennon, Paul McCartney, George Harrison, and Ringo Starr between 1964, when they first appeared on *The Ed Sullivan Show*,[3] and 1970, when McCartney announced that the group was disbanding. Just as there is no longer a common culture, so there is no longer a common style of music to which most English-speaking people listen. Yet the Beatles and their music continue to fascinate successive generations of music lovers, so much so that more than two dozen books have been published about them, the latest of which is a thousand-page biography by the journalist Bob Spitz.[4]

Written in a straightforwardly journalistic style, *The Beatles: The Biography* provides an exhaustive and generally reliable account of the bandmembers' lives and careers up to 1970, and is of no small value as a study in what might be called the sociology of celebrity. But like most pop-music biographies, it has little of interest to say about the Beatles' work; anyone in search of a thoughtful critical appraisal will find it unhelpful.[5]

Such an appraisal must begin by taking into account the fact that the Beatles were the first rock-and-roll musicians to be written about *as* musicians. Elvis Presley,[6] for instance, had attracted vast amounts of attention from the press, but for the most part he was treated as a mass-culture phe-

---

Published in Commentary *(February 2006), a magazine published by the American Jewish Committee that aspires to be "America's premier monthly magazine of opinion"; it covers politics, international affairs, societal issues, and religion, and includes regular features such as the music column written by Teachout.*

1. The Beatles' twelfth and last album, released in 1970.

2. The Beatles' commercial recordings have all been transferred to CD and remain in print. Readers unfamiliar with their music should listen first to *Rubber Soul* (Capitol 46440) and *Revolver* (46441). Also of interest is *The Beatles I* (29325), an anthology of 27 of the group's chart-topping singles. Except as indicated, all of the songs mentioned in this piece are included on these three CD's [Teachout's note].

3. John Lennon (1940–1980), Paul McCartney (b. 1940), George Harrison (1943–2001), Ringo Starr (b. 1940), the four members of the Beatles, appeared on a popular nighttime variety show that ran from 1940 until 1971, hosted by Ed Sullivan.

4. *The Beatles: The Biography*, Little, Brown, 983 pp., $29.95 [Teachout's note].

5. By far the best book published to date about the Beatles' music is Allan Kozinn's *The Beatles* (Phaidon, $24.95, paper), a brief life published as part of the "20th-Century Composers" series of classical-music monographs edited by Norman Lebrecht [Teachout's note].

6. Elvis Presley (1935–1977), American rock singer.

nomenon rather than as an artist, and so were the other rock musicians of the 50's and early 60's (and the swing-era bandleaders and vocalists who came before them). Not so the Beatles. Almost from the time they began making records in 1962, their music was taken seriously—and praised enthusiastically—by such noted classical composers as Leonard Bernstein, Aaron Copland, and Ned Rorem[7] and such distinguished critics and commentators as William Mann, Hans Keller, and Wilfrid Mellers.[8]

What was it that made these four musically untutored pop stars stand out in such high relief from their contemporaries? And has their music proved to be of lasting interest, as their admirers of four decades ago predicted it would?

5   In one sense, "the Beatles" can be understood as a shorthand term for the songs written by John Lennon and Paul McCartney, separately and together, between 1962 and 1970. (The two wrote some songs individually and some in collaboration, but all were credited as the joint work of "Lennon-McCartney.") Most of the Beatles' hit singles were Lennon-McCartney songs, many of which would later be performed and recorded by other artists. It was the best of these songs that initially won them the respect of musicians who had hitherto been indifferent or hostile to rock-and-roll.

Lennon and McCartney began to write together as teenagers. Their first hits—"Love Me Do," "She Loves You," and "I Want to Hold Your Hand"—were largely derivative of the lyrically naïve styles of the American pop stars of the 50's whom they most admired, including Elvis, Little Richard, and the Everly Brothers.[9] But even back then their music contained surprising glints of originality, in particular the modally colored tunes that would become one of their trademarks.[10] Within a brief time it became evident that, for all their lack of formal training, they were naturally gifted composers whose fast-growing musical sophistication was reminiscent of the similarly rapid stylistic evolution of another self-taught songwriter of genius, Irving Berlin.[11]

By 1964 the two were experimenting with the irregular phrase lengths and unexpectedly complex harmonies of such songs as "And I Love Her" (by Mc-

7. Leonard Bernstein (1918–1990), American conductor and composer; Aaron Copland (1900–1990), American composer; Ned Rorem (b. 1923), American composer and diarist.

8. William Mann, music critic at the New York Times; Hans Keller (1919–1985), American musician and author; Wilfrid Mellers (b. 1914), English music critic, composer, and musicologist.

9. Little Richard, born Richard Wayne Penniman (b. 1932), American singer, songwriter, and pioneer of rock-and-roll music; Isaac Donald Everly (b. 1937) and Philip Everly (b. 1939), brothers and influential rock-and-roll musicians.

10. Like most self-taught musicians who start out playing guitar rather than piano, both Lennon and McCartney were conditioned by the feel of the guitar fingerboard, whose stepwise layout facilitates the harmonization of the flattened-seventh, Mixolydian-mode melodies first heard in such early Beatles songs as "Can't Buy Me Love" and "A Hard Day's Night" [Teachout's note].

11. Russian-born, American-raised composer and lyricist (1888–1989).

Cartney) and "If I Fell" (by Lennon), whose stereotypical boy-meets-girl lyrics are far less interesting than the graceful, sinuous melodies to which they are set.[12] Indeed, it was for their music that Lennon and McCartney were first acclaimed, and it would not be until McCartney's "Yesterday" that they recorded a song whose lyrics were of correspondingly high quality.

Written in 1965, "Yesterday" is a perfectly balanced miniature whose long arches of melody arise organically out of the three-note cell ("*Yes*-ter-day") that constitutes the introductory phrase. The lyric is no less noteworthy for its unadorned directness: "Yesterday / All my troubles seemed so far away / Now it looks as though they're here to stay / Oh, I believe in yesterday." The result is a song reminiscent in its deceptive simplicity of classic Berlin ballads like "All Alone" and "Always," a fact that helps to explain why it was the first Beatles song to become a full-fledged pop standard. (It has been recorded by more than 2,000 other artists.)

Around the same time, Lennon began to listen closely to the music of Bob Dylan,[13] whose deliberately, even self-consciously poetic lyrics constituted a radical departure from the more conventional approach of his commercially-minded peers. Thanks in part to Dylan's influence, Lennon made his own, similar break with the clichés of the day, beginning to write allusive, increasingly cryptic lyrics that had little in common with the pop songs on which he had been raised: "He's a real nowhere man / Sitting in his nowhere land / Making all his nowhere plans for nobody / Doesn't have a point of view / Knows not where he's going to / Isn't he a bit like you and me?" ("Nowhere Man," 1965).

Unlike the professional-tradition songwriters of the pre-rock era, Lennon and McCartney lost interest in writing about romantic love, and from 1966 until the dissolution of the Beatles four years later they produced an amazingly varied portfolio of songs whose subject matter ranged from the wry domesticity of McCartney's "Lady Madonna" ("Lady Madonna / Children at your feet / Wonder how you manage to make ends meet") to the unsettling surrealism of Lennon's "She Said She Said" ("She said / I know what it's like to be dead / I know what it is to be sad / And she's making me feel like I've never been born"). These songs were as powerfully influential on the rock musicians of the 70's and 80's as the recordings of Louis Armstrong[14] were on the jazz soloists of the 30's and 40's, and their echo continues to be heard in the work of singer-songwriters not yet born in the days when the Beatles were still (in Lennon's much-quoted 1966 remark) "more popular than Jesus."

10

Yet for all the immense influence of the Lennon-McCartney songs, only "Yesterday" became a standard in the old-fashioned sense—that is, a song that continues to be regularly performed by large numbers of other singers. Indeed, not until the 90's did classic-style pop singers born in the 60's and 70's start to

12. Both songs are included on *A Hard Day's Night* (Capitol 46437) [Teachout's note].
13. American singer and songwriter (b. 1941).
14. American jazz musician (1901–1971).

reinterpret the songs of the Beatles in the same way that their predecessors had reinterpreted the classic songs of the pre-rock era.[15]

One reason for this is that the Beatles wrote most of their own material, recording only Beatles-written songs from 1966 on. Once this became common practice for most other rock groups, it was harder for "standards" to emerge from the vast body of new pop music. No less important, though, is the fact that the Beatles were among the first pop musicians to start thinking in terms of recordings, not songs or live performances, as the finished musical product that they would offer to the listening public.

Airchecks of their TV appearances indicate that while none of the four Beatles was an instrumental virtuoso, all of them were effective stage performers with an engaging, distinctive group style.[16] For the most part, their earliest recordings sought to reproduce this style, albeit in more polished form. But by 1965 the Beatles had become so popular—and their female fans so hysterically voluble—that they could barely hear themselves play over the screaming of the crowds that came to their concerts. This caused them to lose interest in live performance at more or less the same moment that George Martin,[17] the classically trained musician who produced their recordings, began to introduce them to the fast-growing range of techniques by which recorded sound could be manipulated and transformed in the studio.

It soon became clear to Lennon and McCartney that the sound of "the Beatles" on record need not be restricted to the simple guitar-bass-drums instrumentation of their live concerts. McCartney, for example, recorded "Yesterday" accompanied by his own acoustic guitar and a string quartet arranged by Martin. In 1965 the band released *Rubber Soul*, an album of extensively overdubbed studio performances in which Lennon, McCartney, and Harrison (as well as Martin) could also be heard playing piano, harmonium, sitar, bouzouki, and other instruments.[18] Not only was *Rubber Soul* too complex in texture to be reproduced in concert—at least not under the conditions prevailing in 1965—but it was meant to be experienced not as a collection of fourteen individual and free-standing songs but as something considerably more ambitious. "For the first time," Martin explained, "we began to think of albums as art on their own, as complete entities."

15   Needless to say, this approach to album-making did not begin with the Beatles. Other jazz and pop musicians had already experimented with thematically

15. See, for example, John Pizzarelli's 1999 album, *John Pizzarelli Meets the Beatles* (RCA 61432) [Teachout's note].

16. Some of these recordings have been collected on *Live at the BBC* (Capitol 31796, two CD's). In live performance, George Harrison played lead guitar, Lennon rhythm guitar, McCartney bass guitar, and Ringo Starr drums, with Lennon and McCartney splitting most of the lead vocals [Teachout's note].

17. Producer for the Beatles (b. 1926).

18. Harmonium: a kind of reed organ; sitar: a South Asian stringed instrument; bouzouki: a stringed instrument from the Greek tradition.

unified "concept albums," most notably Frank Sinatra[19] in *Only the Lonely* (which he recorded for Capitol, the Beatles' American label, in 1958). In addition, a number of classical performers and record producers, including Glenn Gould and John Culshaw,[20] had started to make studio recordings that were not meant to be literal "records" of live performances. As I have written elsewhere:

> Such famous albums as Glenn Gould's 1955 recording of the Bach Goldberg Variations, Frank Sinatra's *Only the Lonely*, Miles Davis's[21] *Kind of Blue*, or the Beatles' *Sgt. Pepper's Lonely Hearts Club Band* are not attempts to simulate live performances. They are, rather, unique experiences existing *only* on record, and the record itself, not the music or the performance, is the art object.[22]

After *Rubber Soul*, the Beatles stopped performing in public and thereafter devoted themselves exclusively to the making of just such recordings. The most artistically successful was *Revolver* (1966), in which the playing of the classical horn soloist Alan Civil and the string and brass sections heard on "Eleanor Rigby" and "Got to Get You Into My Life" are combined with a dazzlingly varied assortment of studio-crafted effects. *Sgt. Pepper's Lonely Hearts Club Band* (1967), *The Beatles* (1968, popularly known as the "white album"), and *Abbey Road* (1969) would make more extensive use of overdubbing and additional instruments, as did singles like "Penny Lane" and "All You Need Is Love" (both released in 1967). But it is on *Revolver*, the best of their thirteen albums, that the Beatles can be heard at their most disciplined and musically impressive.

It is, I suspect, no accident that after 1970, none of the four Beatles would write any songs or make any recordings comparable in quality to the ones they made as a group. Together, their musical limitations had been offset by the creative synergy of their collaboration (as well as by the discreet guidance of George Martin, their producer-mentor). When they began to work independently, the limitations overwhelmed them, and they spent the rest of their lives struggling in vain to rival the achievements of their youth.

The historical significance of these achievements, however, cannot be overstated. After the Beatles, rock-and-roll would never be the same. What started out as a stripped-down, popularized blending of country music and rhythm-and-blues intended for consumption by middle-class teenagers evolved into a new musical dialect in which it was possible to make state-

---

19. American singer and Academy Award-winning actor (1915–1998).

20. Glenn Gould (1932–1982), Canadian pianist; John Culshaw (1924–1980), English producer of classical records.

21. American jazz musician (1926–1991).

22. "Why Listening Will Never Be the Same" (*Commentary*, September 2002), reprinted in *A Terry Teachout Reader* (Yale, 2004) as part of the longer essay, "Life After Records" [Teachout's note].

ments complex and thoughtful enough to seize and hold the attention of adult listeners.

This is not to say that rock in general has always repaid such close attention. Unlike jazz, which developed with great speed from a purely functional accompaniment of social dancing into a full-fledged art music of the highest possible seriousness, most rock has remained as commercial as the simplest-minded pop music of the pre-rock era. But between the late 60's, when rock became the *lingua franca*[23] of the baby boomers, and the late 90's, when the disintegration of the common culture brought its stylistic hegemony to an end, the best rock groups had much to offer the serious music lover.

20   Without the Beatles, this might well not have been the case. Neither virtuoso instrumentalists nor pure songwriters, they instead explored the possibilities of the hybrid art of the record album as art object more successfully than any other popular musicians of their generation. For this—and for the beauty of their best music—they will be remembered.

23. Latin for "Frankish tongue," referring to a common language used by speakers of other languages.

QUESTIONS

1. Essayists often clear space for themselves by commenting on the limitations of the writing of others. Where does Teachout do so? What aspects of the Beatles does Teachout wish to discuss that other writers have not?

2. What, in Teachout's view, are the most important achievements of the Beatles *as rock-and-roll musicians*? How does the history of the group's development help the reader understand their achievement?

3. The Beatles stopped recording together in 1970. What explanation does Teachout give for this date and their dispersal as a group?

4. Choose a musician, artist, or actor/actress whose achievement you think is important. Analyze that achievement both by giving a history of his or her development and by pointing to the significant aspects of the achievement.

AARON COPLAND   *How We Listen*

W E ALL LISTEN to music according to our separate capacities. But, for the sake of analysis, the whole listening process may become clearer if we break it up into its component parts, so to speak. In a certain sense we all listen to music on three separate planes. For lack of a better terminology, one might name these: (1) the sensuous plane, (2) the expressive plane, (3) the sheerly musical plane. The only advantage to be gained from mechanically splitting up the listening process into these hypothetical planes is the clearer view to be had of the way in which we listen.

The simplest way of listening to music is to listen for the sheer pleasure of the musical sound itself. That is the sensuous plane. It is the plane on which we hear music without thinking, without considering it in any way. One turns on the radio while doing something else and absentmindedly bathes in the sound. A kind of brainless but attractive state of mind is engendered by the mere sound appeal of the music.

You may be sitting in a room reading this book. Imagine one note struck on the piano. Immediately that one note is enough to change the atmosphere of the room—proving that the sound element in music is a powerful and mysterious agent, which it would be foolish to deride or belittle.

The surprising thing is that many people who consider themselves qualified music lovers abuse that plane in listening. They go to concerts in order to lose themselves. They use music as a consolation or an escape. They enter an ideal world where one doesn't have to think of the realities of everyday life. Of course they aren't thinking about the music either. Music allows them to leave it, and they go off to a place to dream, dreaming because of and apropos of the music yet never quite listening to it.

Yes, the sound appeal of music is a potent and primitive force, but you 5 must not allow it to usurp a disproportionate share of your interest. The sensuous plane is an important one in music, a very important one, but it does not constitute the whole story.

There is no need to digress further on the sensuous plane. Its appeal to every normal human being is self-evident. There is, however, such a thing as becoming more sensitive to the different kinds of sound stuff as used by various composers. For all composers do not use that sound stuff in the same way. Don't get the idea that the value of music is commensurate with its sensuous appeal or that the loveliest sounding music is made by the greatest composer. If that were so, Ravel would be a greater creator than Beethoven.[1] The point is that the sound element varies with each composer, that his usage of sound

---

From Copland's classic guide, What to Listen for in Music *(1957).*

1. Maurice Ravel (1875–1937), French composer; Ludwig van Beethoven (1770–1827), German composer.

forms an integral part of his style and must be taken into account when listening. The reader can see, therefore, that a more conscious approach is valuable even on this primary plane of music listening.

The second plane on which music exists is what I have called the expressive one. Here, immediately, we tread on controversial ground. Composers have a way of shying away from any discussion of music's expressive side. Did not Stravinsky[2] himself proclaim that his music was an "object," a "thing," with a life of its own, and with no other meaning than its own purely musical existence? This intransigent attitude of Stravinsky's may be due to the fact that so many people have tried to read different meanings into so many pieces. Heaven knows it is difficult enough to say precisely what it is that a piece of music means, to say it definitely, to say it finally so that everyone is satisfied with your explanation. But that should not lead one to the other extreme of denying to music the right to be "expressive."

My own belief is that all music has an expressive power, some more and some less, but that all music has a certain meaning behind the notes and that that meaning behind the note constitutes, after all, what the piece is saying, what the piece is about. This whole problem can be stated quite simply by asking, "Is there a meaning to music?" My answer to that would be, "Yes." And "Can you state in so many words what the meaning is?" My answer to that would be, "No." Therein lies the difficulty.

Simple-minded souls will never be satisfied with the answer to the second of these questions. They always want music to have a meaning, and the more concrete it is the better they like it. The more the music reminds them of a train, a storm, a funeral, or any other familiar conception the more expressive it appears to be to them. This popular idea of music's meaning—stimulated and abetted by the usual run of musical commentator—should be discouraged wherever and whenever it is met. One timid lady once confessed to me that she suspected something seriously lacking in her appreciation of music because of her inability to connect it with anything definite. That is getting the whole thing backward, of course.

10   Still, the question remains, How close should the intelligent music lover wish to come to pinning a definite meaning to any particular work? No closer than a general concept, I should say. Music expresses, at different moments, serenity or exuberance, regret or triumph, fury or delight. It expresses each of these moods, and many others, in a numberless variety of subtle shadings and differences. It may even express a state of meaning for which there exists no adequate word in any language. In that case, musicians often like to say that it has only a purely musical meaning. They sometimes go farther and say that *all* music has only a purely musical meaning. What they really mean is that no appropriate word can be found to express the music's meaning and that, even if it could, they do not feel the need of finding it.

But whatever the professional musician may hold, most musical novices still search for specific words with which to pin down their musical reactions.

2. Igor Stravinsky (1882–1971), Russian-born American composer.

That is why they always find Tchaikovsky[3] easier to "understand" than Beethoven. In the first place, it is easier to pin a meaning-word on a Tchaikovsky piece than on a Beethoven one. Much easier. Moreover, with the Russian composer, every time you come back to a piece of his it almost always says the same thing to you, whereas with Beethoven it is often quite difficult to put your finger right on what he is saying. And any musician will tell you that that is why Beethoven is the greater composer. Because music which always says the same thing to you will necessarily soon become dull music, but music whose meaning is slightly different with each hearing has a greater chance of remaining alive.

Listen, if you can, to the forty-eight fugue themes of Bach's *Well Tempered Clavichord*.[4] Listen to each theme, one after another. You will soon realize that each theme mirrors a different world of feeling. You will also soon realize that the more beautiful a theme seems to you the harder it is to find any word that will describe it to your complete satisfaction. Yes, you will certainly know whether it is a gay theme or a sad one. You will be able, in other words, in your own mind, to draw a frame of emotional feeling around your theme. Now study the sad one a little closer. Try to pin down the exact quality of its sadness. Is it pessimistically sad or resignedly sad; is it fatefully sad or smilingly sad?

Let us suppose that you are fortunate and can describe to your own satisfaction in so many words the exact meaning of your chosen theme. There is still no guarantee that anyone else will be satisfied. Nor need they be. The important thing is that each one feel for himself the specific expressive quality of a theme or, similarly, an entire piece of music. And if it is a great work of art, don't expect it to mean exactly the same thing to you each time you return to it.

Themes or pieces need not express only one emotion, of course. Take such a theme as the first main one of the *Ninth Symphony*,[5] for example. It is clearly made up of different elements. It does not say only one thing. Yet anyone hearing it immediately gets a feeling of strength, a feeling of power. It isn't a power that comes simply because the theme is played loudly. It is a power inherent in the theme itself. The extraordinary strength and vigor of the theme results in the listener's receiving an impression that a forceful statement has been made. But one should never try to boil it down to "the fateful hammer of life," etc. That is where the trouble begins. The musician, in his exasperation, says it means nothing but the notes themselves, whereas the nonprofessional is only too anxious to hang on to any explanation that gives him the illusion of getting closer to the music's meaning.

Now, perhaps, the reader will know better what I mean when I say that   15
music does have an expressive meaning but that we cannot say in so many words what that meaning is.

3. Peter Ilich Tchaikovsky (1840–1893), Russian composer.

4. A work composed by Johann Sebastian Bach (1685–1750) in which forty-eight themes are presented by themselves and then elaborated in three voices.

5. Composed by Beethoven.

The third plane on which music exists is the sheerly musical plane. Besides the pleasurable sound of music and the expressive feeling that it gives off, music does exist in terms of the notes themselves and of their manipulation. Most listeners are not sufficiently conscious of this third plane. * * *

Professional musicians, on the other hand, are, if anything, too conscious of the mere notes themselves. They often fall into the error of becoming so engrossed with their arpeggios and staccatos that they forget the deeper aspects of the music they are performing. But from the layman's standpoint, it is not so much a matter of getting over bad habits on the sheerly musical plane as of increasing one's awareness of what is going on, in so far as the notes are concerned.

When the man in the street listens to the "notes themselves" with any degree of concentration, he is most likely to make some mention of the melody. Either he hears a pretty melody or he does not, and he generally lets it go at that. Rhythm is likely to gain his attention next, particularly if it seems exciting. But harmony and tone color are generally taken for granted, if they are thought of consciously at all. As for music's having a definite form of some kind, that idea seems never to have occurred to him.

It is very important for all of us to become more alive to music on its sheerly musical plane. After all, an actual musical material is being used. The intelligent listener must be prepared to increase his awareness of the musical material and what happens to it. He must hear the melodies, the rhythms, the harmonies, the tone colors in a more conscious fashion. But above all he must, in order to follow the line of the composer's thought, know something of the principles of musical form. Listening to all of these elements is listening on the sheerly musical plane.

20 Let me repeat that I have split up mechanically the three separate planes on which we listen merely for the sake of greater clarity. Actually, we never listen on one or the other of these planes. What we do is to correlate them—listening in all three ways at the same time. It takes no mental effort, for we do it instinctively.

Perhaps an analogy with what happens to us when we visit the theater will make this instinctive correlation clearer. In the theater, you are aware of the actors and actresses, costumes and sets, sounds and movements. All these give one the sense that the theater is a pleasant place to be in. They constitute the sensuous plane in our theatrical reactions.

The expressive plane in the theater would be derived from the feeling that you get from what is happening on the stage. You are moved to pity, excitement, or gayety. It is this general feeling, generated aside from the particular words being spoken, a certain emotional something which exists on the stage, that is analogous to the expressive quality in music.

The plot and plot development is equivalent to our sheerly musical plane. The playwright creates and develops a character in just the same way that a composer creates and develops a theme. According to the degree of your awareness of the way in which the artist in either field handles his material will you become a more intelligent listener.

It is easy enough to see that the theatergoer never is conscious of any of these elements separately. He is aware of them all at the same time. The same is true of music listening. We simultaneously and without thinking listen on all three planes.

In a sense, the ideal listener is both inside and outside the music at the   25 same moment, judging it and enjoying it, wishing it would go one way and watching it go another—almost like the composer at the moment he composes it; because in order to write his music, the composer must also be inside and outside his music, carried away by it and yet coldly critical of it. A subjective and objective attitude is implied in both creating and listening to music.

What the reader should strive for, then, is a more *active* kind of listening. Whether you listen to Mozart or Duke Ellington,[6] you can deepen your understanding of music only by being a more conscious and aware listener—not someone who is just listening, but someone who is listening *for* something.

6. Wolfgang Amadeus Mozart (1756–1791), Austrian composer; Edward Kennedy ("Duke") Ellington (1899–1974), American jazz composer and band leader.

QUESTIONS

1. List Copland's "three planes" of listening to music and explain what each entails. Are these three planes comprehensive? Is there another you would add?

2. In paragraphs 21–24, Copland uses the experience of going to the theater to illustrate his three planes of listening. Can you think of other artistic experiences that can be divided up into different "planes"? To what extent would the planes be the same as Copland's?

3. Copland uses classical music as examples in his explanation of the way humans listen to music. Write an essay about the ways you listen to another kind of music: folk, rap, jazz, hip-hop, pop, or rock.

PROSE FORMS: FABLES AND PARABLES

F̶ables and parables force us to think about our comfortable relationship to narratives. We are used to indirection in novels and short stories; we never demand a simple "point" or "moral" at the end. Not so with fables, which force moral readings upon us, not permitting us to escape their lessons easily. With fables and parables we leave the familiar world of classic fiction and enter a different one.

When we read a short story or novel, we become immersed in the lives of the characters and their desires, problems, and destinies. In Charles Dickens's Great Expectations, for example, the hero, Pip, undergoes many trials and triumphs as he moves from his rural village to London, from his work as a blacksmith's apprentice to his life as a gentleman. We may extract major ideas from Pip's life story—that he has expected the wrong things or the right things for the wrong reasons. Or we may find morals for our own lives and even write about them in a paper for a literature class—that the great values in life are not always to be found in what the world calls "success." But our primary interest in reading a novel like Great Expectations lies in the narrative itself, in the characters and fictional world that the novelist has created.

When ideas become as important as the story itself, perhaps even more important, we have moved to other forms of narrative: the fable, the allegory, the parable. When we read a fable, in contrast to a novel, we read with an eye to the lesson, the larger idea or moral that the story reveals. Fables—brief tales with animals as their primary characters—often state the moral explicitly at the end. Aesop's fable in this section concludes: "Let well enough alone!" Other fables produce equally useful (if also conventional) advice: Please all, and you will please none. Self-help is the best help. Injuries may be forgiven, but not forgotten. Honesty is the best policy.

Parables, like fables, tell stories that embed lessons, but often the moral is harder to extract or state in summary form. When Jesus told the parable of the ten virgins, his listeners could understand, as we do today, that he was advising them to prepare for the coming Kingdom of God and warning against unpreparedness. Indeed, the parable ends, "Watch therefore, for ye know neither the day nor the hour wherein the Son of man cometh." Yet certain aspects of the parable remain difficult to interpret: Why do half of the virgins prepare, while half do not? Why don't those who have prepared share their oil with the others? Why does the Lord refuse to acknowledge the foolish virgins at the day of his coming? The end of a parable may state a lesson, yet it also may express a paradox, some extra element of contradiction or complexity. Parables, like allegories, involve persons and objects that have equivalent meanings outside the story; sometimes the analogies are difficult to work out, often deliberately so, in order to make the reader think hard about the lesson.

When an essayist wishes both to express an idea and to exploit the appeal of a story, he or she often turns to a narrative form like the fable or the parable. In both, the idea is the heart of the composition; in both the idea assumes the form of a lesson about life, some moral truth of general consequence; and in both there are characters and actions. Ideas about life can be illustrated in life. Jesus often depended on parables in his teaching. Simple, economical, pointed, the parables developed a "story," but more important, they applied a moral truth to experience. Peter asked Jesus how often he must forgive the brother who sins against him, and Jesus answered with the parable of the king and his servants, one of whom asked and got forgiveness of the king for his debts but who would not in turn forgive a fellow servant his debt. The king, on hearing of this harshness, retracted his own benevolence and punished the unfeeling servant. Jesus concluded to Peter, "So likewise shall my heavenly Father do also unto you, if ye from your hearts forgive not every one his brother their trespasses." But before this direct drawing of the parallel, the lesson was clear in the outline of the narrative.

In writing a parable or fable, writers will verge continually on strict prose narrative, but through skill and tact they can preserve the essayist's essential commitment to the definition and development of ideas in relation to experience.

AESOP: *The Frogs Desiring a King*

The frogs always had lived a happy life in the marshes. They had jumped and splashed about with never a care in the world. Yet some of them were not satisfied with their easygoing life. They thought they should have a king to rule over them and to watch over their morals. So they decided to send a petition to Jupiter[1] asking him to appoint a king.

Jupiter was amused by the frogs' plea. Good-naturedly he threw down a log into the lake, which landed with such a splash that it sent all the frogs scampering for safety. But after a while, when one venturesome frog saw that the log lay still, he encouraged his friends to approach the fallen monster. In no time at all the frogs, growing bolder and bolder, swarmed over the log Jupiter had sent and treated it with the greatest contempt.

Dissatisfied with so tame a ruler, they petitioned Jupiter a second time, saying: "We want a real king, a king who will really rule over us." Jupiter, by this time, had lost some of his good nature and was tired of the frogs' complaining.

Aesop's fables were, according to the Greek historian Herodotus, composed by a slave on the island of Samos early in the sixth century B.C.E.

1. The king of the Roman gods.

So he sent them a stork, who proceeded to gobble up the frogs right and left. After a few days the survivors sent Mercury[2] with a private message to Jupiter, beseeching him to take pity on them once more.

"Tell them," said Jupiter coldly, "that this is their own doing. They wanted a king. Now they will have to make the best of what they asked for."

Moral: Let well enough alone!

2. The messenger of the gods.

PLATO: *The Allegory of the Cave*

And now, I said, let me show in a figure how far our nature is enlightened or unenlightened: Behold! human beings living in an underground den, which has a mouth open toward the light and reaching all along the den; here they have been from their childhood, and have their legs and necks chained so that they cannot move, and can only see before them, being prevented by the chains from turning round their heads. Above and behind them a fire is blazing at a distance, and between the fire and the prisoners there is a raised way; and you will see, if you look, a low wall built along the way, like the screen which marionette players have in front of them, over which they show the puppets.

I see.

And do you see, I said, men passing along the wall carrying all sorts of vessels, and statues and figures of animals made of wood and stone and various materials, which appear over the wall? Some of them are talking, others silent.

You have shown me a strange image, and they are strange prisoners.

5   Like ourselves, I replied; and they see only their own shadows, or the shadows of one another, which the fire throws on the opposite wall of the cave?

True, he said; how could they see anything but the shadows if they were never allowed to move their heads?

And of the objects which are being carried in like manner they would only see the shadows?

Yes, he said.

And if they were able to converse with one another, would they not suppose that they were naming what was actually before them?

10   Very true.

And suppose further that the prison had an echo which came from the other side, would they not be sure to fancy when one of the passers-by spoke that the voice which they heard came from the passing shadow?

No question, he replied.

From the Republic, *a dialogue in ten books written by Plato in the early years of his Academy, a school he founded (c. 380 B.C.E.) to give a philosophical education to men embarking on political careers. In this section Socrates questions Glaucon, a student.*

To them, I said, the truth would be literally nothing but the shadows of the images.

That is certain.

And now look again, and see what will naturally follow if the prisoners are 15 released and disabused of their error. At first, when any of them is liberated and compelled suddenly to stand up and turn his neck round and walk and look toward the light, he will suffer sharp pains; the glare will distress him and he will be unable to see the realities of which in his former state he had seen the shadows; and then conceive some one saying to him, that what he saw before was an illusion, but that now, when he is approaching nearer to being and his eye is turned toward more real existence, he has a clearer vision—what will be his reply? And you may further imagine that his instructor is pointing to the objects as they pass and requiring him to name them—will he not be perplexed? Will he not fancy that the shadows which he formerly saw are truer than the objects which are now shown to him?

Far truer.

And if he is compelled to look straight at the light, will he not have a pain in his eyes which will make him turn away to take refuge in the objects of vision which he can see, and which he will conceive to be in reality clearer than the things which are now being shown to him?

True, he said.

And suppose once more, that he is reluctantly dragged up a steep and rugged ascent, and held fast until he is forced into the presence of the sun himself, is he not likely to be pained and irritated? When he approaches the light his eyes will be dazzled and he will not be able to see anything at all of what are now called realities.

Not all in a moment, he said. 20

He will require to grow accustomed to the sight of the upper world. And first he will see the shadows best, next the reflections of men and other objects in the water, and then the objects themselves; then he will gaze upon the light of the moon and the stars and the spangled heaven; and he will see the sky and the stars by night better than the sun or the light of the sun by day?

Certainly.

Last of all he will be able to see the sun, and not mere reflections of him in the water, but he will see him in his own proper place, and not in another; and he will contemplate him as he is.

Certainly.

He will then proceed to argue that this is he who gives the season and the 25 years, and is the guardian of all that is in the visible world, and in a certain way the cause of all things which he and his fellows have been accustomed to behold?

Clearly, he said, he would first see the sun and then reason about him.

And when he remembered his old habitation, and the wisdom of the den and his fellow-prisoners, do you not suppose that he would felicitate himself on the change, and pity them?

Certainly, he would.

And if they were in the habit of conferring honors among themselves on those who were quickest to observe the passing shadows and to remark which of them went before, and which followed after, and which were together; and who were therefore best able to draw conclusions as to the future, do you think that he would care for such honors and glories, or envy the possessors of them? Would he not say with Homer,

> Better to be the poor servant of a poor master,

and to endure anything, rather than think as they do and live after their manner?

30   Yes, he said, I think that he would rather suffer anything than entertain these false notions and live in this miserable manner.

Imagine once more, I said, such an one coming suddenly out of the sun to be replaced in his old situation; would he not be certain to have his eyes full of darkness?

To be sure, he said.

And if there were a contest, and he had to compete in measuring the shadows with the prisoners who had never moved out of the den, while his sight was still weak, and before his eyes had become steady (and the time which would be needed to acquire this new habit of sight might be very considerable) would he not be ridiculous? Men would say of him that up he went and down he came without his eyes; and that it was better not even to think of ascending; and if any one tried to loose another and lead him up to the light, let them only catch the offender, and they would put him to death.

No question, he said.

35   This entire allegory, I said, you may now append, dear Glaucon, to the previous argument; the prison-house is the world of sight, the light of the fire is the sun, and you will not misapprehend me if you interpret the journey upwards to be the ascent of the soul into the intellectual world according to my poor belief, which, at your desire, I have expressed—whether rightly or wrongly God knows. But, whether true or false, my opinion is that in the world of knowledge the idea of good appears last of all, and is seen only with an effort; and, when seen, is also inferred to be the universal author of all things beautiful and right, parent of light and of the lord of light in this visible world, and the immediate source of reason and truth in the intellectual; and that this is the power upon which he who would act rationally either in public or private life must have his eye fixed.

I agree, he said, as far as I am able to understand you.

Moreover, I said, you must not wonder that those who attain to this beatific vision are unwilling to descend to human affairs; for their souls are ever hastening into the upper world where they desire to dwell; which desire of theirs is very natural, if our allegory may be trusted.

Yes, very natural.

And is there anything surprising in one who passes from divine contemplations to the evil state of man, misbehaving himself in a ridiculous manner; if, while his eyes are blinking and before he has become accustomed to the surrounding darkness, he is compelled to fight in courts of law, or in other places, about the images or the shadows of images of justice, and is endeavoring to meet the conceptions of those who have never yet seen absolute justice?

Anything but surprising, he replied. 40

Any one who has common sense will remember that the bewilderments of the eyes are of two kinds, and arise from two causes, either from coming out of the light or from going into the light, which is true of the mind's eye, quite as much as of the bodily eye; and he who remembers this when he sees any one whose vision is perplexed and weak, will not be too ready to laugh; he will first ask whether that soul of man has come out of the brighter life, and is unable to see because unaccustomed to the dark, or having turned from darkness to the day is dazzled by excess of light. And he will count the one happy in his condition and state of being, and he will pity the other; or, if he have a mind to laugh at the soul which comes from below into the light, there will be more reason in this than in the laugh which greets him who returns from above out of the light into the den.

That, he said, is a very just distinction.

JESUS: *Parables of the Kingdom*

THE TEN VIRGINS

Then shall the kingdom of heaven be likened unto ten virgins, which took their lamps, and went forth to meet the bridegroom.

And five of them were wise, and five were foolish.

They that were foolish took their lamps, and took no oil with them:

But the wise took oil in their vessels with their lamps.

While the bridegroom tarried, they all slumbered and slept. 5

And at midnight there was a cry made, Behold, the bridegroom cometh; go ye out to meet him.

Then all those virgins arose, and trimmed their lamps.

And the foolish said unto the wise, Give us of your oil; for our lamps are gone out.

But the wise answered, saying Not so; lest there be not enough for us and you: but go ye rather to them that sell, and buy for yourselves.

And while they went to buy, the bridgroom came; and they that were ready 10 went in with him to the marriage: and the door was shut.

Afterward came also the other virgins, saying, Lord, Lord, open to us.

But he answered and said, Verily I say unto you, I know you not.

Watch therefore, for ye know neither the day nor the hour wherein the Son of man cometh.

From Jesus' teachings, as written in Matthew 25 and Luke 15, King James Bible (1611).

THE TEN TALENTS

For the kingdom of heaven is as a man travelling into a far country, who called his own servants, and delivered unto them his goods.

And unto one he gave five talents,[1] to another two, and to another one; to every man according to his several ability; and straightway took his journey.

Then he that had received the five talents went and traded with the same, and made them other five talents.

And likewise he that had received two, he also gained other two.

5   But he that had received one went and digged in the earth, and hid his lord's money.

After a long time the lord of those servants cometh, and reckoneth with them.

And so he that had received five talents came and brought other five talents, saying, Lord, thou deliveredst unto me five talents: behold, I have gained beside them five talents more.

His lord said unto him, Well done, thou good and faithful servant: thou hast been faithful over a few things, I will make thee ruler over many things: enter thou into the joy of thy lord.

He also that had received two talents came and said, Lord, thou deliverdst unto me two talents: behold, I have gained two other talents beside them.

10   His lord said unto him, Well done, good and faithful servant; thou hast been faithful over a few things, I will make thee ruler over many things: enter thou into the joy of thy lord.

Then he which had received the one talent came and said, Lord, I knew thee that thou art an hard man, reaping where thou hast not sown, and gathering where thou hast not strawed:

And I was afraid, and went and hid thy talent in the earth: lo, there thou hast that is thine.

His lord answered and said unto him, Thou wicked and slothful servant, thou knewest that I reap where I sowed not, and gather where I have not strawed:

Thou oughtest therefore to have put my money to the exchanges, and then at my coming I should have received mine own with usury.

15   Take therefore the talent from him, and give it unto him which hath ten talents.

For unto every one that hath shall be given, and he shall have abundance: but from him that hath not shall be taken away even that which he hath.

And cast ye the unprofitable servant into outer darkness: there shall be weeping and gnashing of teeth.

When the Son of man shall come in his glory, and all the holy angels with him, then shall he sit upon the throne of his glory:

And before him shall be gathered all nations: and he shall separate them one from another, as a shepherd divideth his sheep from the goats:

20   And he shall set the sheep on his right hand, but the goats on the left.

---

1. A talent was a Middle Eastern coin.

Then shall the King say unto them on his right hand, Come, ye blessed of my Father, inherit the kingdom prepared for you from the foundation of the world:

For I was an hungred, and ye gave me meat: I was thirsty, and ye gave me drink: I was a stranger, and ye took me in:

Naked, and ye clothed me: I was sick, and ye visited me: I was in prison, and ye came unto me.

Then shall the righteous answer him, saying, Lord, when saw we thee an hungred, and fed thee? or thirsty, and gave thee drink?

When saw we thee a stranger, and took thee in? or naked, and clothed thee?   25

Or when saw we thee sick, or in prison, and came unto thee?

And the King shall answer and say unto them, Verily I say unto you, Inasmuch as ye have done it unto one of the least of these my brethren, ye have done it unto me.

Then shall he say also unto them on the left hand, Depart from me, ye cursed, into everlasting fire, prepared for the devil and his angels:

For I was an hungred, and ye gave me no meat: I was thirsty, and ye gave me no drink.

I was a stranger, and ye took me not in: naked, and ye clothed me not: 30 sick, and in prison, and ye visited me not.

Then shall they also answer him, saying, Lord, when saw we thee an hungred, or athirst, or a stranger, or naked, or sick, or in prison, and did not minister unto thee?

Then shall he answer them, saying, Verily I say unto you, Inasmuch as ye did it not to one of the least of these, ye did it not to me.

And these shall go away into everlasting punishment: but the righteous into life eternal.

THE PRODIGAL SON

And he said, A certain man had two sons;

And the younger of them said to his father, Father, give me the portion of goods that falleth to me. And he divided unto them his living.

And not many days after that, the younger son gathered all together, and took his journey into a far country, and there wasted his substance with riotous living.

And when he had spent all, there arose a mighty famine in that land; and he began to be in want.

And he went and joined himself to a citizen of that country; and he sent   5 him into his fields to feed swine.

And he would fain have filled his belly with the husks that the swine did eat; and no man gave unto him.

And when he came to himself, he said, How many of my father's hired servants have bread enough and to spare, and I perish with hunger!

I will arise and go to my father, and will say unto him, Father, I have sinned against heaven, and before thee,

And am no more worthy to be called thy son; make me as one of thy hired servants.

10   And he arose, and came to his father. But when he was yet a great way off, his father saw him, and had compassion, and ran, and fell on his neck, and kissed him.

And the son said unto him, Father, I have sinned against heaven, and in thy sight, and am no more worthy to be called thy son.

But the father said to his servants, Bring forth the best robe, and put it on him; and put a ring on his hand, and shoes on his feet.

And bring the fatted calf, and kill it; and let us eat, and be merry.

For this, my son, was dead, and is alive again; he was lost, and is found. And they began to be merry.

15   Now his elder son was in the field; and as he came and drew nigh to the house, he heard music and dancing.

And he called one of the servants, and asked what these things meant.

And he said unto him, Thy brother is come; and thy father hath killed the fatted calf, because he hath received him safe and sound.

And he was angry, and would not go in; therefore came his father out, and entreated him.

And he, answering, said to his father, Lo, these many years do I serve thee, neither transgressed I at any time thy commandment; and yet thou never gavest me a kid, that I might make merry with my friends.

20   But as soon as this, thy son, was come, who hath devoured thy living with harlots, thou hast killed for him the fatted calf.

And he said unto him, Son, thou art ever with me, and all that I have is thine.

It was meet that we should make merry, and be glad; for this, thy brother, was dead, and is alive again; and was lost, and is found.

Zen Parables

MUDDY ROAD

Tanzan and Ekido were once traveling together down a muddy road. A heavy rain was still falling.

Coming around a bend, they met a lovely girl in a silk kimono and sash, unable to cross the intersection.

"Come on, girl," said Tanzan at once. Lifting her in his arms, he carried her over the mud.

Ekido did not speak again until that night when they reached a lodging temple. Then he no longer could restrain himself. "We monks don't go near fe-

---

Zen Buddhists use parables, called koans, *as a means to enlightenment. These translations come from* Zen Flesh, Zen Bones *(1957).*

males," he told Tanzan, "especially not young and lovely ones. It is dangerous. Why did you do that?"

"I left the girl there," said Tanzan. "Are you still carrying her?"   5

A PARABLE

Buddha told a parable in a sutra:

A man traveling across a field encountered a tiger. He fled, the tiger after him. Coming to a precipice, he caught hold of the root of a wild vine and swung himself down over the edge. The tiger sniffed at him from above. Trembling, the man looked down to where, far below, another tiger was waiting to eat him. Only the vine sustained him.

Two mice, one white and one black, little by little started to gnaw away the vine. The man saw a luscious strawberry near him. Grasping the vine with one hand, he plucked the strawberry with the other. How sweet it tasted!

LEARNING TO BE SILENT

The pupils of the Tendai school used to study meditation before Zen entered Japan. Four of them who were intimate friends promised one another to observe seven days of silence.

On the first day all were silent. Their meditation had begun auspiciously, but when night came and the oil lamps were growing dim one of the pupils could not help exclaiming to a servant: "Fix those lamps."

The second pupil was surprised to hear the first one talk. "We are not supposed to say a word," he remarked.

"You two are stupid. Why did you talk?" asked the third.

"I am the only one who has not talked," concluded the fourth pupil.   5

MARK TWAIN: *The War Prayer*

It was a time of great and exalting excitement. The country was up in arms, the war was on, in every breast burned the holy fire of patriotism; the drums were beating, the bands playing, the toy pistols popping, the bunched firecrackers hissing and spluttering; on every hand and far down the receding and fading spread of roofs and balconies a fluttering wilderness of flags flashed in the sun; daily the young volunteers marched down the wide avenue gay and fine in their new uniforms, the proud fathers and mothers and sisters and sweethearts cheering them with voices choked with happy emotion as they swung by; nightly the packed mass meetings listened, panting, to patriot ora-

Dictated by Twain (a.k.a. Samuel Langhorne Clemens) in 1904 or 1905 in response to the Philippine-American War; submitted to Harper's Bazaar, *a women's magazine, but rejected; later published in* Harper's Monthly *during World War I (November 1916). This version comes from a collection of Twain's writings,* Europe and Elsewhere *(1923), compiled after his death.*

tory which stirred the deepest deeps of their hearts and which they interrupted at briefest intervals with cyclones of applause, the tears running down their cheeks the while; in the churches the pastors preached devotion to flag and country and invoked the God of Battles, beseeching His aid in our good cause in outpouring of fervid eloquence which moved every listener. It was indeed a glad and gracious time, and the half-dozen rash spirits that ventured to disapprove of the war and cast a doubt upon its righteousness straightway got such a stern and angry warning that for their personal safety's sake they quickly shrank out of sight and offended no more in that way.

Sunday morning came—next day the battalions would leave for the front; the church was filled; the volunteers were there, their young faces alight with martial dreams—visions of the stern advance, the gathering momentum, the rushing charge, the flashing sabers, the flight of the foe, the tumult, the enveloping smoke, the fierce pursuit, the surrender!—then home from the war, bronzed heroes, welcomed, adored, submerged in golden seas of glory! With the volunteers sat their dear ones, proud, happy, and envied by the neighbors and friends who had no sons and brothers to send forth to the field of honor, there to win for the flag or, failing die the noblest of noble deaths. The service proceeded; a war chapter from the Old Testament was read; the first prayer was said; it was followed by an organ burst that shook the building, and with one impulse the house rose, with glowing eyes and beating hearts, and poured out that tremendous invocation—

"God the all-terrible! Thou who ordainest,
Thunder thy clarion and lightning thy sword!"

Then came the "long" prayer. None could remember the like of it for passionate pleading and moving and beautiful language. The burden of its supplication was that an ever-merciful and benignant Father of us all would watch over our noble young soldiers and aid, comfort, and encourage them in their patriotic work; bless them, shield them in the day of battle and the hour of peril, bear them in His mighty hand, make them strong and confident, invincible in the bloody onset; help them to crush the foe, grant to them and to their flag and country imperishable honor and glory—

An aged stranger entered and moved with slow and noiseless step up the main aisle, his eyes fixed upon the minister, his long body clothed in a robe that reached to his feet, his head bare, his white hair descending in a frothy cataract to his shoulders, his seamy face unnaturally pale, pale even to ghastliness. With all eyes following him and wondering, he made his silent way; without pausing, he ascended to the preacher's side and stood there, waiting. With shut lids the preacher, unconscious of his presence, continued his moving prayer, and at last finished it with the words, uttered in fervent appeal, "Bless our arms, grant us the victory, O Lord our God, Father and Protector of our land and flag!"

The stranger touched his arm, motioned him to step aside—which the startled minister did—and took his place. During some moments he surveyed the spellbound audience with solemn eyes in which burned an uncanny light; then in a deep voice he said:

"I come from the Throne—bearing a message from Almighty God!" The words smote the house with a shock; if the stranger perceived it he gave no attention. "He has heard the prayer of His servant your shepherd and will grant it if such shall be your desire after I, His Messenger, shall have explained to you its import—that is to say, its full import. For it is like unto many of the prayers of men, in that it asks for more than he who utters it is aware of— except he pause and think.

"God's servant and yours has prayed his prayer. Has he paused and taken thought? Is it one prayer? No, it is two—one uttered, the other not. Both have reached the ear of Him Who heareth all supplications, the spoken and the unspoken. Ponder this—keep it in mind. If you would beseech a blessing upon yourself, beware! lest without intent you invoke a curse upon a neighbor at the same time. If you pray for the blessing of rain upon your crop which needs it, by that act you are possibly praying for a curse upon some neighbor's crop which may not need rain and can be injured by it.

"You have heard your servant's prayer—the uttered part of it. I am commissioned of God to put into words the other part of it—that part which the pastor, and also you in your hearts, fervently prayed silently. And ignorantly and unthinkingly? God grant that it was so! You heard these words: 'Grant us the victory, O Lord our God!' That is sufficient. The *whole* of the uttered prayer is compact into those pregnant words. Elaborations were not necessary. When you have prayed for victory you have prayed for many unmentioned results which follow victory—*must* follow it, cannot help but follow it. Upon the listening spirit of God the Father fell also the unspoken part of the prayer. He commandeth me to put it into words. Listen!

"O Lord our Father, our young patriots, idols of our hearts, go forth to battle—be Thou near them! With them, in spirit, we also go forth from the sweet peace of our beloved firesides to smite the foe. O Lord our God, help us to tear their soldiers to bloody shreds with our shells; help us to cover their smiling fields with the pale forms of their patriot dead; help us to drown the thunder of the guns with the shrieks of their wounded, writhing in pain; help us to lay waste their humble homes with a hurricane of fire; help us to wring the hearts of their unoffending widows with unavailing grief; help us to turn them out roofless with their little children to wander unfriended the wastes of their desolated land in rags and hunger and thirst, sports of the sun flames of summer and the icy winds of winter, broken in spirit, worn with travail, imploring Thee for the refuge of the grave and denied it—for our sakes who adore Thee, Lord, blast their hopes, blight their lives, protract their bitter pilgrimage, make heavy their steps, water their way with their tears, stain the white snow with the blood of their wounded feet! We ask it, in the spirit of love, of Him Who is the Source of Love, and Who is the ever-faithful refuge and friend of all that are sore beset and seek His aid with humble and contrite hearts. Amen.

(*After a pause*) "Ye have prayed it: if ye still desire it, speak! The messenger of the Most High waits."

10   It was believed afterward that the man was a lunatic, because there was no sense in what he said.

QUESTIONS ON FABLES AND PARABLES

1. Many parables end with a moral explicitly stated—as in the conclusion to Aesop's fable, "Let well enough alone!" Which parables in this section include such morals? Which do not? Why might some writers choose not to conclude with an explicit statement of the "moral"?

2. For those parables that do not include morals, write your own version of a moral or maxim that might be deduced from the narrative. Is it possible to deduce more than one moral?

3. Write a parable that, while using a narrative form, has a moral or maxim embedded within it.

PHILOSOPHY AND RELIGION

LANGSTON HUGHES *Salvation*

I WAS SAVED from sin when I was going on thirteen. But not really saved. It happened like this. There was a big revival at my Auntie Reed's church. Every night for weeks there had been much preaching, singing, praying, and shouting, and some very hardened sinners had been brought to Christ, and the membership of the church had grown by leaps and bounds. Then just before the revival ended, they held a special meeting for children, "to bring the young lambs to the fold." My aunt spoke of it for days ahead. That night I was escorted to the front row and placed on the mourners' bench[1] with all the other young sinners, who had not yet been brought to Jesus.

My aunt told me that when you were saved you saw a light, and something happened to you inside! And Jesus came into your life! And God was with you from then on! She said you could see and hear and feel Jesus in your soul. I believed her. I had heard a great many old people say the same thing and it seemed to me they ought to know. So I sat there calmly in the hot, crowded church, waiting for Jesus to come to me.

The preacher preached a wonderful rhythmical sermon, all moans and shouts and lonely cries and dire pictures of hell, and then he sang a song about the ninety and nine safe in the fold, but one little lamb was left out in the cold.[2] Then he said: "Won't you come? Won't you come to Jesus? Young lambs, won't you come?" And he held out his arms to all us young sinners there on the mourners' bench. And the little girls cried. And some of them jumped up and went to Jesus right away. But most of us just sat there.

A great many old people came and knelt around us and prayed, old women with jet-black faces and braided hair, old men with work-gnarled hands. And the church sang a song about the lower lights are burning, some poor sinners to be saved. And the whole building rocked with prayer and song.

From The Big Sea *(1940), Hughes's autobiography of his early life.*

1. A place in the front where potential converts sat during an evangelical service.
2. "The Ninety and Nine" and "Let the Lower Lights Be Burning," mentioned in the next paragraph, are the titles of famous evangelical hymns collected by Ira Sankey (1840–1908).

5   Still I kept waiting to *see* Jesus.

Finally all the young people had gone to the altar and were saved, but one boy and me. He was a rounder's[3] son named Westley. Westley and I were surrounded by sisters and deacons praying. It was very hot in the church, and getting late now. Finally Westley said to me in a whisper: "God damn! I'm tired o' sitting here. Let's get up and be saved." So he got up and was saved.

Then I was left all alone on the mourners' bench. My aunt came and knelt at my knees and cried, while prayers and songs swirled all around me in the little church. The whole congregation prayed for me alone, in a mightly wail of moans and voices. And I kept waiting serenely for Jesus, waiting, waiting—but he didn't come. I wanted to see him, but nothing happened to me. Nothing! I wanted something to happen to me, but nothing happened.

I heard the songs and the minister saying: "Why don't you come? My dear child, why don't you come to Jesus? Jesus is waiting for you. He wants you. Why don't you come? Sister Reed, what is this child's name?"

"Langston," my aunt sobbed.

10   "Langston, why don't you come? Why don't you come and be saved? Oh, Lamb of God! Why don't you come?"

Now it was really getting late. I began to be ashamed of myself, holding everything up so long. I began to wonder what God thought about Westley, who certainly hadn't seen Jesus either, but who was now sitting proudly on the platform, swinging his knickerbockered legs and grinning down at me, surrounded by deacons and old women on their knees praying. God had not struck Westley dead for taking his name in vain or for lying in the temple. So I decided that maybe to save further trouble, I'd better lie, too, and say that Jesus had come, and get up and be saved.

So I got up.

Suddenly the whole room broke into a sea of shouting, as they saw me rise. Waves of rejoicing swept the place. Women leaped in the air. My aunt threw her arms around me. The minister took me by the hand and led me to the platform.

When things quieted down, in a hushed silence, punctuated by a few ecstatic "Amens," all the new young lambs were blessed in the name of God. Then joyous singing filled the room.

15   That night, for the last time in my life but one—for I was a big boy twelve years old—I cried. I cried, in bed alone, and couldn't stop. I buried my head under the quilts, but my aunt heard me. She woke up and told my uncle I was crying because the Holy Ghost had come into my life, and because I had seen Jesus. But I was really crying because I couldn't bear to tell her that I had lied, that I had deceived everybody in the church, and I hadn't seen Jesus, and that now I didn't believe there was a Jesus any more, since he didn't come to help me.

---

3. A rounder was a loafer or wastrel.

QUESTIONS

1. Hughes describes how he lost his faith in Jesus at the age of twelve. How did the grown-ups in his life contribute to the experience?

2. Hughes expected to "see" Jesus. How did he understand the word "see"? How did he need to understand it?

3. Hughes was twelve ("going on thirteen") when the event he describes in first-person narration took place. How careful is he to restrict himself to the point of view of a twelve-year-old child? How does he insure that we, as readers, understand things that the narrator does not?

4. Write a first-person narrative in which you describe a failure—yours or someone else's—to live up to the expectations of parents or other authority figures.

ANDRÉ ACIMAN   *In a Double Exile*

THERE COMES the time at every Passover Seder when someone opens a door to let in the prophet Elijah. At that moment, something like a spell invariably descends over the celebrants, and everyone stares into the doorway, trying to make out the quiet movements of the prophet as he glides his way in and takes the empty seat among us.

But by then my mind has already drifted many, many times, and like all disbelievers who find themselves wondering why they are attending a Seder after last year's resolution, I begin to think of how little this ritual means to me—recalling the ten plagues, the crossing of the Red Sea, manna from heaven. All of it keenly arranged to let every kind of Jew find something to celebrate.

For the religious, Passover is the grateful remembrance of a homeward journey after years of suffering.

For those who believe in the spirit more than in the letter of the occasion, the holiday celebrates survival and deliverance from all forms of tyranny—survival after Auschwitz, freedom from anti-Semitism in Russia, Ethiopia, and Syria.

For yet others, Passover is an occasion to gather around a table and link arms with Jews from everywhere and all times.   5

I don't know Hebrew. Nor do I know any of the songs or prayers. I can't even tell when the Seder is officially over. Often I suspect the whole ceremony has petered out or has been cut short for my benefit—or been drawn out to

Included in Aciman's collection False Papers *(2000), a book of fourteen essays that explore the writer's experience of loss, from his forced departure from Alexandria as a teenager, through a period in Europe, to his making a home in New York City.*

prove a point. I always attend with misgivings, which I communicate to others at the table, and try to atone for by reading aloud when my turn comes, only to resent having been asked to read.

And as I sit and stew, feeling ever more trapped among the observant, I too begin to think of Egypt, of this Egypt everyone will invoke at sundown tomorrow night and which symbolizes suffering, exile, and captivity, and suddenly appears in our dining room like a mummy whose sleep has been disturbed: unreal, mythic, faraway Egypt, which everyone calls by its Hebrew name, *Mizrayim*; in Arabic, it is *Misr*. The same words, but eons apart.

Then, as happens every year, I begin to think of another Egypt, the one I was born in and knew and got to love and would never have left had a modern pharaoh by the name of President Nasser not forced me out for being Jewish. This was an Egypt many of us would have stayed in, even as the last Jews of the land, which we nearly were, even if we had had to beg to stay, which indeed we did.

Often in those years in Alexandria, when I was growing up, Passover coincided with Easter and Ramadan. During Ramadan, we would be let out of school at about noon every day, because Muslims, who fasted all day, needed to rest in the afternoon before breaking their fast at sunset.

10   To those of us who did not have to nap, these were the most magical hours of the year. The city was always quiet then, there was hardly any homework, and summer was only a few weeks away.

At the Seder, the men in my family would spar, my father begging my uncle to speed it up, my uncle deferring to tradition instead; everyone more or less giggling, including the one or two Christians visiting that evening who were hauled in to a dinner that reminded them so much of the Last Supper, they said, everyone garbling everything in a blithe chorus of *"Next year in Jerusalem,"* until we heard the cannon of Ramadan announce it was time for devout Muslims to eat.

It never occurred to us that a Seder in Egypt was a contradiction in terms.

Now, when everyone speaks of Pharaoh at Passover, I think back to my very last Seder in Egypt, on the eve of our departure for Italy in 1965—a long, mirthless, desultory affair, celebrated with weak lights and all the shutters drawn so that no one in the street might suspect what we were up to that night.

After almost three centuries of religious tolerance, we found ourselves celebrating Passover the way our Marrano ancestors had done under the Spanish Inquisition: in secret, verging on shame, without conviction, in great haste, and certainly without a clear notion of what we were celebrating. Was it the first exodus from Egypt? Or maybe the second from Spain? Or the third from Turkey? Or the fourth, when my family members fled Italy just before the Nazis took over? Or were we celebrating the many exoduses that went unrecorded but that every Jew knows he can remember if he tries hard enough, for each one of us is a dislodged citizen of a country that was never really his but that he has learned to long for and cannot forget. The fault lines of exile and diaspora always run deep, and we are always from elsewhere, and from elsewhere before that.

Everything in history happens twice, wrote Marx, the first time as tragedy, 15
the second as farce. He forgot to add that Jewish history is repetition, the history of repetition.

Caught in these loops and coils, my family forgot to remember the obvious—that Egypt was never our home, that we should never have come back after Moses, that we didn't even know where our home was, much less which language was ours. We had borrowed everyone else's. Some of us forgot we were Jews. Alexandria was our mirage—in the desert, we dreamed awhile longer.

In the end, Egyptian nationalism drove us all away. Today, religious intolerance wants to finish the job for everyone who remains, not just Jews. Copts—Christians who are thought to be among the most direct descendants of the ancient Egyptians—and Westernized Egyptians are watching the clouds darken around the country. Will Egypt drown again? In 1981, the assassination of President Anwar al-Sadat, in recent years the killings of tourists and Egyptian intellectuals, and in October 1995 the stabbing of the writer and Nobel laureate Naguib Mahfouz—are these the new plagues? Must I worry and remember for Egypt as well now?

Passover is the night for it. For on that night all Jews remember the night when Jewish memory began. That night each one of us thinks back to that private Egypt we each carry with us wherever we are. We may not always know what to remember, but we know we must remember.

In my case, I remember a city called Alexandria, a city as remote to me now as Egypt is to my American friends who will celebrate Passover, a city that was never mine, that no longer exists as I knew it, but that rushes into the room each time they open the door for Elijah to remind me that I will never say, Next year in Jerusalem, in Alexandria again.

QUESTIONS

1. Aciman writes of himself as an unbeliever participating in a religious ceremony. What are his motivations for participating? What do you think of his participation?

2. How does Aciman structure his essay? What devices or themes hold it together, since it's not a narrative with chronological order to give it shape?

3. Write of someone's ambivalence about a recurring ceremony that family members regard as important, for example, a religious ceremony, a birthday, a graduation, or some similar ceremony with cultural or family significance. What motivates the person who is ambivalent? How is his or her ambivalence dealt with by other family members?

RITA DOVE   *The Epistle of Paul the Apostle*
to the Ephesians

O N THE MYSTERIES of vision, H.D.[1] writes: "We begin
with sympathy of thought." One of the last great
modern mystics, H.D. scribbled her *Notes on
Thoughts and Vision* in a notebook marked "July,
Scilly Islands" in 1919, when she retreated to
these islands off the coast of Cornwall in order to re-
cuperate—from war, from illness and the breakup of her marriage, from the
death of her brother and the hazardous birth of her daughter Perdita. Sea air
and salt light to heal a wounded spirit: "The doctor prescribes rest."

I am reading H.D. on a grassy knoll overlooking the grounds of the Villa
Serbelloni, the "Study and Conference Center" of the Rockefeller Foundation
on Lake Como in northern Italy, trying to ignore a niggling restlessness I've had
ever since my arrival. Do I feel displaced in the serenity of this splendid retreat,
high above the tourist traffic of the village of Bellagio, here where terraced hills
plunge into clear waters and cypresses slope into the mists at evening? Five
weeks of hydrangeas and tiger lilies, white-coated butlers and silver candlesticks—what sumptuous reward for all the hours spent hunched in a sixty-watt
circle of light, smudging my way through a wilderness of words! At last no
meals to cook or phones to answer, little mail, no children; a room of one's
own, a study in the woods, and all around, beauty . . . but I'm not writing.

I've told myself it takes time to unwind, and I try to relax by reading afternoons when the *breva*[2] sweeps the fog from the lake, freshening the shore. I
read sprawled in a rattan chair set up outside, next to my study, hoping the sun
will burn off the stress and fill the emptiness with magic.

While browsing in the villa library this morning I talked with a poet from
Canada; he was convinced that the jewellike medieval painting of Saul on the
way to Damascus[3] that's mounted near the dictionaries is an unsigned Bono.
Unsure who Bono was but unwilling to show my ignorance, I scrutinized the
canvas for a signature—nothing in the tufted grass, the parched and rutted
road, no scrawls in the surreal blue heaven or bright curls of the seraphim—
and before I remembered to put on my museum demeanor I was captivated by
the wistful sincerity of the scene before me. Saul looked utterly terrified, his

Included in the collection Incarnation: Contemporary Writers on the New Testament
(1990), edited by the poet Alfred Corn.

1. Pen name of the American poet Hilda Doolittle (1886–1961).

2. A strong wind that blows across Lake Como in the afternoons and only starts to
weaken at sunset.

3. According to the New Testament (Acts 9:1–9), Saul of Tarsus was traveling on the
road to Damascus to destroy the Christian community there, when he was blinded by a
brilliant light and heard the voice of Jesus saying, "Saul, Saul, why persecutest thou
me?" This story recounts Saul's conversion to Christianity and his name change to Paul.

horse rearing and his fellow travelers baffled by such strange behavior on an ordinary day. How devastating an experience for a man so certain of his convictions! No wonder he spent three days in darkness afterward, emptied of himself, until Ananias came to claim him in the name of Christianity. No wonder his name changed, the same sound but a different beginning.

H.D.'s *Notes* drop to the grass. A few yards away, three goldfish hidden under the lily pads send up their perky semaphores: I hear this infinitesimal percolation even as wild birds overhead belt out Italian chorales and a speedboat growls across the lake. So that's what's been bothering me: the germ of a poem dealing with religion. But, as if I were a Jewish dyer trading in royal purple, I struggle against the notion of Christianity acquiring a poem from me—just as I struggle against the ideologue who has haunted me since adolescence, whose stony gaze I still feel whenever I rail against the strictures of institutional belief.

Life before Paul was milk and honey, grapes and warm bread, cardboard-and-glitter crèches. In those early Sunday-school years we were fed on floods and famines, raining roads and babies in baskets. Come twelve and the age of accountability, Christ appeared in the Temple and there followed a progression of sun-drenched miracles—Lazarus rising from his shroud, fish gleaming on proliferating hunks of bread. We loved the repetition of blessings, the palms fanning above the stolid head of a donkey, even the thirty pieces of silver. Blood and vinegar on the cross was swept over quickly, and Sunrise Services emphasized the rock rolled away, shining wings, astonishment, and His Glorious Resurrection. That was what a miracle was, after all: absence and light.

I was thirteen when the man who would introduce me to the apostle Paul walked into our senior Sunday-school class. He was tall, dark, and hellishly handsome, severely dressed in a matte-black narrow suit and black shirt from which rose a ring of shocking white, like a slipped halo. Never before had I seen a clerical collar (our minister wore standard suits with striped ties which peeked from his velvet-trimmed "preaching" robe); I thought the collar was his own invention, a kind of symbolic leash worn as a token of his service to God. He was the new assistant minister, straight out of theological school in the South (an exotic country to us in Akron, Ohio), and would take over the twelve-to-fifteen-year-olds, leaving our former teacher with the less unruly high schoolers.

Of course all the girls developed an immediate crush on him. We followed him breathlessly across the hall to a smaller, pale green classroom and without being asked formed a semicircle around the table he leaned against, like a male model from *Ebony* magazine, pinstriped trousers draping elegantly just above the buffed black wingtips. On his left hand glinted, to our disappointment, a large wedding band.

"What do you know of mortal sin?" he asked.

We goggled at him and tittered nervously. "Mortal" sounded all right to us. He frowned, straightening the crease in his pant leg, then patiently unveiled to us the concepts of irretrievable error and purgatory. Since we were past the age of twelve, he explained, we were accountable for our sins against the Ten Commandments, which were inviolable. And our transgressions against any of those laws—whether actual or commited *in thought only*—were unforgivable except through Jesus Christ.

We barely heard the Jesus Christ part. We were doomed, for we had just coveted another woman's husband; we had also disobeyed our parents, stolen, lied, cursed—and if one counted thinking (how can you control your thoughts?) as well, then we committed these transgressions all the time. In an instant, flirting had changed from harmless entertainment to hellfire.

Our church was A.M.E. Zion. The acronym stands for African Methodist Episcopal, an appellation that contains all the contradictions and acclimatizations black Americans have gone through to accommodate both the African memory and the American dream. Basically Methodist, our church believed in a moderate liturgy (responsive readings) but did not tolerate kneeling or chanting; the "Episcopal" distinguished us from the Baptists not only in decorum—we baptized with a few drops of water on a baby's forehead—but in class. Determinedly of the bourgeoisie ("boojy" we called our parents, among them dentists, general practitioners, dry-cleaning moguls), we did not approve of hee-hawing sermons, though the minister was permitted to shout out the last sixth of his text.

"African" meant many things. Sometimes it was the license to wear proud colors and hats piled high, as extravagant as platters—unlike the drab skirt-and-blouse attire of the white Lutherans one street over. "African" also referred to our intimate relationship with God and Christ, the permission to wipe Christ's sweat from our brows and talk to him like a brother, to identify our lot with that of the Israelites under Pharaoh. Martin Luther King, Jr. was our Moses, charged with delivering his people across the Selma bridge. "African" bore the very cadences of nostalgia for our lost homeland, wherever it may have been—though in those turbulent years of Miriam Makeba and Malcolm X there was an edge to that nostalgia as well, a defiant hope from those who wished for mercy but just might choose, if pressed, to prevail by whatever means necessary.

But "African" always meant righteous singing. I particularly loved the "old hundred" hymns, standard oldies sung during the formal catechism of the service, before the sermon, as well as the choral outbursts from the white-clad women in the front pew.

15   Ah, the deaconesses! Mostly widows with massive bosoms, all ancient, these women put on their blinding white shirtwaists, their chalky nylons, and Shinola-white shoes every Sunday. Some wore tiny starched bonnets, very much like nurses or pilgrims, and others preferred the pure ornament of a scrubbed dark face lifted to the Lord. They were the self-appointed brides of Christ and the acknowledged mothers of the church, the arbiters of the Holy Spirit, and they disapproved of flash and frivolity and black militancy. (Though they never complained about Afros, since several of them had let their hair "go back" to furry halos.) The deaconesses were already seated when the rest of the congregation trickled in. Usually they were bent in prayer, humming vigor-

ously to the mumbled supplications of a deacon, usually the oldest male, who by virtue of his sex and age was permitted to kneel on the first step leading to the altar.

The deaconesses were also intimate with what W. E. B. Du Bois[4] called the Sorrow Songs—older hymns, prehistoric canons that resembled nothing familiar or comforting. They had very few words and were frightening in their near-inarticulate misery. For at least a half hour before the processional signaled the official start of the service, the old women hummed, rocked, wailed these chants as parishioners arrived and drifted into the pews. Unlike gospel, "big with all the wrongs done done," these songs reeked with unappeasable loss and pain. They were the moans of slavery, the rhythms of an existence dulled by rote and brutality and hopelessness, an isolation so complete there could be no words.

The deaconesses led the congregation in that complex courtship between the Holy Spirit and mortal endeavor; the give and take, the surge and ebb between the minister's sermon and their shouted counterpoint was our clue to how well the minister was doing in bringing us closer to holiness, indeed, bringing us *in Christ*, in Paul's complex, mystical phrase, until heat and pinching waistbands dropped away and the message from the pulpit entered us directly, like an injection.

What is the mystery of grace? What does it mean to be *in Christ*? I watched the older women of the church "get happy"; I could see them gathering steam, pushing out the seams of their composure until it dropped down, the Holy Spirit, falling upon them like a hatchet from heaven. Instead of crumbling they rose up, incandescent, to perform amazing feats—they tightroped the backs of pews, skipped along the aisles, threw off ushers and a half-dozen able-bodied men with every shout. (Men rarely got happy; when they did theirs was a decorous performance, hardly an experience at all.) A woman "full of the Spirit" was indomitable; one could almost see sunbeams glancing off the breastplate of righteousness, the white wings twinkling on the sandals of faith. And when it was over, they were not diminished but serene, as if they'd been given a tonic.

Why couldn't I be filled, transfused with glory? The most I'd experienced was a "quickening"—a mini-transformation characterized by shortened breath and an intense longing for the indefinite . . . what? I was tongue-tied, hopelessly guilt-ridden and self-conscious to boot. The most I could do was get teary-eyed. In the face of those bolder ecstasies, I'd fall back into my own ashes, quenched.

Witnessing these transformations usually made me churlish for the rest of   20
the day. I decided God didn't like intelligence. And though we hadn't been meant to sample the Tree of Knowledge, surely we couldn't be blamed for the intelligence we'd been saddled with.

Sunday evenings after "60 Minutes" my father would push off his slippers and shrug into his overcoat, keys jangling. We knew the signal: another trip to

4. American civil rights leader, educator, historian, and author (1868–1963).

Grandma's on the East Side. It was a long way through town, along the gorge and then the slow climb up Market Street, past the defunct oats silos and the Fir Hill Conservatory of Music, then down Arlington and into the purgatorial Furnace Street, where the smoke and brimstone miraculously began, spewing from Plant One of the Goodyear Rubber Company and the smaller infernos of Mohawk and General Tire. This was the part of the journey I waited for. The backlit plumes of smoke and murky variations of exhaust and light were exciting, a negative snapshot of power and hope; the mere sight of a belching smokestack at night made me think of evening gowns and diamond lavaliers.

All across town the accompaniment was radio—the staid ministerial admonitions of a local Presbyterian congregation on the way, and afterward the surging gospels of Shiloh Baptist, my grandmother's own church, whose evening service she attended faithfully via the airwaves, rocking in her armchair in the back bedroom. I was awed by so much fervor: that one could go to church on Sunday morning and still have ardor left over to attend an evening service seemed strange, yet weirdly desirable. How simple life would be if one could believe that much! Later, in bed, I'd tuck my transistor radio under the pillow and tune into the Catholic broadcast at ten—after Shiloh Baptist's creaking ship of lamentations what a relief, a balm, *Hail Mary full of grace Blessed art thou among women and blessed is the fruit of thy womb Jesus* whispered over and over until I dozed off, safe for another night.

Into the intact world of childhood, Paul had introduced Doubt, and I resisted. As far as I was concerned, Saul/Paul was altogether too fervent—his persecution of the Christians too single-minded, his conversion too spectacular, his teachings too humorless. It wasn't the gaudiness of his martyr's life I distrusted (John's vision of the Apocalypse, in contrast, seemed absolute to me and vividly *correct*); rather, it was the contradiction between his life and his words. "Do as I say, not as I do"—we'd learned in Sunday school to nod, straight-faced, when reciting the commandments but to watch as scandals erupted in that orchestrated adult world: a senior usher ogling a pair of fine hips rolling under orange shantung, the occasional girl burgeoning under her choir robes. We waited for public recriminations, but all went on as before. We had a saying: Saints can backslide, but never trust a person who can't dance. Paul couldn't dance, but he shore could talk. Our assistant minister felt it his duty to initiate us into the world of words, the irretrievability of a vow.

I also distrusted the name change, from the Jew Saul to the astringent. New Age Paul. Paul—a name without history. Somehow I suspected him of abandoning with his born name the Old Testament, where Sauls and Jeremiahs flourished, and his desert treks and prison tenure had no aura. He was a traveling salesman, his epistles little more than shtick.

25   And Paul had no music; neither did he make a joyful noise before the Lord. He despised pageantry and silver ornament. His was a ministry of noon—no shadows or respite from the all-reaching rays of righteousness. I could not think of Paul without imagining parched mesas and the emblazoned killing ground of a Colosseum. Even the olives he preferred must have been sharp with rosemary, chewy and bitter.

But the god I knew understood the value of a wink. He was nothing like this Paul with his blind stare, his frozen faith burning in his eyes. Leave such clenched fervor to human beings; gods and angels are casual. No wonder he saw life in terms of architecture, and the body become church, a sacred building you entered silently and where you'd better not spit. And farther up the wine-dark aisle, the path of blood transfixed, this sacrificial artery leading to the plateau where no body lived but Thought reigned, gold and wax and velvet, paltry adornment designed to render palpable to the congregation the ineffable integrity of the spirit. This, then, was Christ presiding over the church, and Man presiding over Wife.

The mystery of Paul's ideology is revealed through his metaphors: comparing the church to a marriage. To be saved, to establish a mystical and *ongoing* spiritual strength, one does not try to become Christ or to identify with Christ; instead, one develops a *relationship to* him. This is a "primitive" concept: the ancient Greeks mingled freely with their gods and goddesses, with sometimes disastrous (poor Leda),[5] sometimes beneficent (Odysseus guided to Ithaca by Pallas Athene) results. African slaves in America transferred their attitudes toward divinities to the abstract figures of Christianity, telling Mary not to weep, exhorting Jonah not to despair, and rejoicing that Christ had personally reached down to lift them up. Black worshipers sat down to talk with God as with an old friend. When I was in my early teens, black disc jockeys favored a popular song that went: "I had a talk with my man last night; / He reassured me everything was all right." It was years before I heard the gospel song that had been its inspiration: "I had a talk with God last night." I was not as shocked by this discovery as perhaps I should have been; I was already on the way to secular humanism. After all, I had been talking to God for several years, bargaining and wheedling from the cave of my pillow, protesting my good intentions.

Human agency. I rolled the phrase around in my mouth as I perched on the curved lip of the pew, willing myself to remember the words through the sermon's climax and the preacher's ecstatic Call to Altar so that I might carry them home and find a use for them. *Human agency* was the key I'd been looking for in the rigid latticework the New Testament had raised around my daily living. Obedient though I was, I could not believe the thoughts that entered my daydreams so easily were forbidden. To hold the mind accountable—surely this wasn't what God had meant. Surely he did not want robots as children; surely a doll's house would be a bore for such a mighty spectator.

The world is protean. Every adolescent knows this, lives this . . . and is astonished at adults' ability to fasten onto the order of things with smug attentions. How can they skim the surface of such stormy oceans? Mother snapping her facial compact shut with a satisfied click, Father Turtle-waxing the Ford on Saturday afternoon: where is the pleasure to be located in these routines when the ultimate pleasure (as every adolescent discovers) is sexual—the disintegrating joy of a French kiss, the utterly selfish desire of the body to *know*

---

5. In Greek mythology, a mortal who was seduced by Zeus in the form of a swan and who gave birth to Helen of Troy.

more? Of course, we didn't understand the concept of guilt, major guilt—the kind that can't be erased from heart and mind, that distresses even ten, fifteen years later, whenever buried incidents float unbidden to the surface. How could we? We hadn't lived very much.

30   Saul watched as Stephen was stoned to death; Paul was celibate in order to serve his Christ more ardently. Aren't these flip sides of the same coin? And if not, where did Saul go? Who, if anyone, was in the body that sat three days in darkness in Damascus, who spoke before the crowds, who crouched in that dark prison cell and built up the body of Christian thought into a white and pillared building? Did he remember Saul at all—or had he, as Paul, burned away his past self so completely that with it fled the childhood words for stone and bread? What initially fills the void when the old self is struck down and out—what rushes in before the light, what rides the arrow tip of redemption into the benighted soul?

In the rattan chair beside the lily pond, far above the unspeakably blue waters of Lake Como, the poem for Paul takes shape:

On the Road to Damascus

They say I was struck down by the voice of an angel:
        flames poured through the radiant fabric of heaven
as I cried out and fell to my knees.

My first recollection was of Unbroken Blue,
        but two of the guards have already sworn by
the tip of my tongue set ablaze. As an official,

I recognize the lure of a good story:
        useless to suggest that my mount
had stumbled, that I was pitched into a clump

of wild chamomile, its familiar stink
        soothing even as my palms sprang blisters
under the nicked leaves. I heard shouts,

the horse pissing in terror—but my eyes
        had dropped to my knees, and I saw nothing.
I was a Roman and had my business

among the clouded towers of Damascus.
        I had not counted on earth rearing,
honey streaming down a parched sky,

a spear skewering me to the dust of the road
        on the way to the city I would never
enter now, her markets steaming with vendors

and compatriots in careless armor lifting a hand
        in greeting as they call out my name,
only to find no one home.

Paul's first visit to Ephesus lasted over two years, during which time he argued in the synagogue and converted "divers souls." Afterward he made for Jerusalem, sending back to Ephesus two disciples to keep the flame burning. In Paul's absence, the disciples met resistance from the silversmiths, who had a hefty business in shrines to the goddess Diana and naturally resented the loss in trade the new iconless religion would occasion. Led by the silversmith Demetrius, the people rose up in defense of their goddess; when the disciples tried to speak, the crowd outshouted them, for two hours chanting "Great is Diana of the Ephesians." Forced to retreat, the disciples were recalled by Paul, who "embraced them" and set out himself for Ephesus, where he gave the heretics "much exhortation" (Acts 20:1–2).

Did Paul's harsh words succeed at Ephesus, or did Diana prevail? The Bible is curiously silent on this point. In fact, the authorship of the Epistle to the Ephesians is heavily disputed among theological scholars—and it was almost certainly not written for the Ephesians, though of course we have other testimonies of his ministry there. It hardly matters whether Paul wrote this epistle or not—the spirit of his thought is still intact. We know from Acts that Paul appeared at Ephesus with a bag of tricks, handkerchiefs emerging from his sleeves to heal the sick and raise the dead . . . and yet the artisans with their silver statuettes of Diana were still able to rouse the people: We want Diana, thousand-breasted deity, they told Paul's disciples, who were forced to retreat. Was the light in Paul's eyes too empty? Or was it simply that two mysticisms—the matriarchal vision of fertility and wholeness, the patriarchal vision of order and clarity—were insisting on their separate paths to glory?

When I was a teenager Paul seemed to be a hard man with an unrealistically severe code of sacrifice, a fanatic who devised silly laws of diet, dress codes, and impossible rules of behavior; an ideologue who equated belief with ethics and transformation with institutional rhetoric. This was the world view our assistant minister promulgated; Paul was his boogeyman.

I see now that Paul's proclamations were demanded of him. At that time Christianity was still a heresy within a larger tradition; Saul's persecution of Christians, his conversion, and his consequent wrangles with the priests of the Temple—these events were all in the family, so to speak. At the time when the Pauline Epistles were written, the biggest question for the new religion was whether or not to accept Gentiles; once that quandary was settled, more mundane issues (Can they remain uncircumcised? Must they obey the Judaic rules of diet?) were the order of the day. The disciples attempted to thread a path through the existing Old Testament laws; they sought an extension, and fulfillment, of Judaism. Paul's public needed concrete rules, so he gave them restrictions to hold on to: Wife, obey your husband; husband, love your wife—just as you obey Christ and He loves you. Children, obey your parents. Servants (this is the tricky one), obey your masters—followed by a telling conditional: "according to the flesh, with fear and trembling, in singleness of your heart, as unto Christ" (Ephesians 6:5–6). And because pictures are worth a thousand words, he gave them metaphors: the Church as a bride, Christ as bride-groom, and martial imagery sure to delight a city devoted to the huntress Diana. Gird the loins with truth, slip the feet into the Gospel of peace, take up the breastplate of righteousness and the shield of faith! Blatant theatrics, but it worked.

35   Yet Paul *was* a mystic. Only a mystic would address the newly converted with "And you *hath he quickened*, who were dead in trespasses and sins." Or: "the fulness of him that filleth all in all." Devising a system for connecting and reflection, a guide for conducting a life of energized joy—this is Paul's abiding light.

Whenever I move to a new place, the first thing I usually do is "cozy up" my study; I throw down rugs, mount marionettes on the walls, place a crystal or a hand-carved elephant on a shelf where my fidgety gaze might fall for a moment and rest. This time, though, it was different. After leaving the Rocke-feller Study and Conference Center in Bellagio, I moved into what was easily the most nondescript room I have ever written poetry in—white brick, gray industrial-strength carpet—and yet, six months later I still could not bear to tack up so much as a single poster.

It was as if the photographs and paintings that used to provide companionship in my solitary hours of composition had ceased to serve as windows and begun to block the view. It seemed I required no distraction from the void. To put it less negatively: I no longer felt the need to focus in on an object in order to allow my thoughts free rein, unsupervised—a window had opened in me.

I was nearly finished writing "On the Road to Damascus" before I understood what about the gold-leaf-and-lapis universe in the painting the Canadian poet attributed to Bono had so moved me that morning in the Villa Serbelloni. Saul was terrified because the eyes that had studied the Law and looked calmly on at the slaying of another man had for the first time failed their owner. The Roman world, once as compact and manageable as the toylike apparition of the city of Damascus hovering on the horizon, had split apart, and he was falling into a mystery, bottomless and widening.

Paul's account of his conversion, on the other hand, is essentially the story of a seduction. He has been entered by Christ the Bridegroom and remade in the image of his Love. Then, as in any marriage, one must work at redemption; one must learn to forgive oneself.

40   H.D. writes: "We must be 'in love' before we can understand the mysteries of vision." This does not mean penetrating the mysterious, nor does it mean being taken by storm. Grace is a state of being, not an assault; and enlightenment, unlike epiphany, is neither brief nor particularly felicitous. The Saul in the painting knew better. Anyone who feels the need to connect the outside world with an interior presence must *absorb* the mysterious into the tangle of contradictions and longings that form each one of us. That's hard, ongoing work, and it never ends.

QUESTIONS

1. Reread Dove's last two sentences and see if they apply to her essay as a whole. What's hard about the work she describes?

2. How does Dove's framing her thoughts on Paul with scenes from her stay in Bellagio affect the presentations of her points? Could her points be made without this framing, or is it essential to her argument?

3. How seriously do Dove's twelve-to-fifteen-year-olds take the idea of mortal sin? Dove says they've all sinned, but do you believe her? To what extent have they sinned?

4. Write about learning some strong moral lesson in your own life, using Dove as your model.

DANIEL C. DENNETT *Common-Sense Religion*

CCORDING TO SURVEYS, most of the people in the world say that religion is very important in their lives. Many would say that without it, their lives would be meaningless. It's tempting just to take them at their word, to declare that nothing more is to be said—and to tiptoe away. Who would want to interfere with whatever it is that gives their lives meaning? But if we do that, we willfully ignore some serious questions. Can just any religion give lives meaning, in a way that we should honor and respect? What about people who fall into the clutches of cult leaders, or who are duped into giving their life savings to religious con artists? Do their lives still have meaning, even though their particular "religion" is a fraud?

In *Marjoe*, the 1972 documentary about the bogus evangelist Marjoe Gortner, we see poor people emptying their wallets and purses into the collection plate, their eyes glistening with tears of joy, thrilled to be getting "salvation" from the charismatic phony. The question that has been troubling me ever since I first saw the film is: Who is committing the more reprehensible act—Gortner, who lies to people to get their money, or the filmmakers who expose the lies (with Gortner's enthusiastic complicity), thereby robbing the good folk of the meaning they thought they had found for their lives? Consider what their lives may be like (I am imagining the details, which are not in the documentary): Sam is a high-school dropout, pumping gas at the station at the crossroads and hoping someday to buy a motorcycle; he is a Dallas Cowboys fan, and likes to have a few beers while watching the games on television. Lucille, who never married, is in charge of the night-shift shelf-stockers at the local supermarket and lives in the modest house she has always lived in, caring

Published in The Chronicle of Higher Education *on January 20, 2006, this essay is drawn from Dennett's book* Breaking the Spell: Religion as a Natural Phenomenon *(2006).*

for her aged mother. No adventurous opportunities beckon in the futures of Sam or Lucille, or for most of the others in the blissful congregation we see, but they have now been put in direct contact with Jesus and are saved for eternity, beloved members in good standing of the community of the born again. They have turned over a new leaf, in a most dramatic ceremony, and they face their otherwise uninspiring lives refreshed and uplifted. Their lives now tell a story, and it's a chapter of the Greatest Story Ever Told. Can you imagine anything else they could buy with those $20 bills they deposit in the collection plate that would be remotely as valuable to them?

Certainly, comes the reply. They could donate their money to a religion that was honest, and that actually used their sacrifices to help others who were still needier. Or they could join any secular organization that put their free-time, energy, and money to effective use ameliorating some of the world's ills. Perhaps the main reason that religions do most of the heavy lifting in large parts of America is that people really do want to help others—and secular organizations have failed to compete with religions for the allegiance of ordinary people. That's important, but it's the easy part of the answer, leaving untouched the hard part: What should we do about those whom we honestly think are being conned? Should we leave them to their comforting illusions or blow the whistle?

Dilemmas like that are all too familiar in somewhat different contexts, of course. Should the sweet old lady in the nursing home be told that her son has just been sent to prison? Should the awkward 12-year-old boy who wasn't cut from the baseball team be told about the arm-twisting that persuaded the coach to keep him on the squad? In spite of ferocious differences of opinion about other moral issues, there seems to be something approaching consensus that it is cruel and malicious to interfere with the life-enhancing illusions of others—unless those illusions are themselves the cause of even greater ills. The disagreements come over what those greater ills might be—and that leads to the breakdown of the whole rationale. Keeping secrets from people for their own good can often be wise, but it takes only one person to give away a secret, and since there are disagreements about which cases warrant discretion, the result is an unsavory miasma of hypocrisy, lies, and frantic, but fruitless, attempts at distraction.

5   What if Gortner were to con a cadre of sincere evangelical preachers into doing his dirty work? Would their innocence change the equation and give genuine meaning to the lives of those whose sacrifices they encouraged and collected? Or are all evangelical preachers just as false as Gortner? Certainly Muslims think so, even though they are generally too discreet to say it. And Roman Catholics think that Jews are just as deluded, and Protestants think that Catholics are wasting their time and energy on a largely false religion, and so forth. All Muslims? All Catholics? All Protestants? All Jews? Of course not. There are vocal minorities in every faith who blurt it out, like the Catholic movie star Mel Gibson, who was interviewed by Peter J. Boyer in a 2003 profile in *The New Yorker*. Boyer asked him if Protestants are denied eternal salvation.

"There is no salvation for those outside the Church," Gibson replied. "I believe it." He explained: "Put it this way. My wife is a saint. She's a much better person than I am. Honestly. She's, like, Episcopalian, Church of England. She prays, she believes in God, she knows Jesus, she believes in that stuff. And it's not fair if she doesn't make it, she's better than I am. But that is a pronouncement from the chair. I go with it."

Such remarks deeply embarrass two groups of Catholics: those who believe it but think it is best left unsaid, and those who don't believe it at all—no matter what "the chair" may pronounce. And which group of Catholics is larger, or more influential? That is utterly unknown and currently unknowable, a part of the unsavory miasma.

It is equally unknown how many Muslims truly believe that all infidels deserve death, which is what the Koran undeniably says. Most Muslims, I would guess, are sincere in their insistence that the injunction that apostates[1] be killed is to be disregarded, but it's disconcerting, to say the least, that fear of being regarded as an apostate is apparently a major motivation in the Islamic world. So it is not just we outsiders who are left guessing.

One reason, free-floating or not, for such systematically masked creeds is to avoid—or at least postpone—the collision between contradictory creeds that would otherwise oblige the devout to behave far more intolerantly than most people today want to behave. (It is always worth reminding ourselves that not so very long ago people were banished, tortured, and even executed for heresy and apostasy in the most "civilized" corners of Christian Europe.)

So what is the prevailing attitude today among those who call themselves religious but vigorously advocate tolerance? There are three main options: 10

- The disingenuous Machiavellian: As a matter of political strategy, the time is not ripe for candid declarations of religious superiority, so we should temporize and let sleeping dogs lie in hopes that those of other faiths can gently be brought around over the centuries.

- The truly tolerant: It really doesn't matter which religion you swear allegiance to, as long as you have some religion.

- The benign neglecters: Religion is just too dear to too many to think of discarding it, even though it really doesn't do any good and is simply an empty historical legacy we can afford to maintain until it quietly extinguishes itself sometime in the unforeseeable future.

It is no use asking people which they choose, since the extremes are so undiplomatic we can predict in advance that most people will go for some version of ecumenical tolerance, whether they believe it or not.

So we've got ourselves caught in a hypocrisy trap, and there is no clear path out. Are we like the families in which the adults go through all the motions of believing in Santa Claus for the sake of the kids, and the kids all pre-

---

1. Individuals who have renounced religion.

tend still to believe in Santa Claus so as not to spoil the adults' fun? If only our current predicament were as innocuous and even comical as that! In the adult world of religion, people are dying and killing, with the moderates cowed into silence by the intransigence of the radicals in their own faiths, and many adherents afraid to acknowledge what they actually believe for fear of breaking Granny's heart, or offending their neighbors to the point of getting run out of town, or worse.

If that is the precious meaning our lives are vouchsafed thanks to our allegiance to one religion or another, it is not such a bargain. Is that the best we can do? Is it not tragic that so many people around the world find themselves enlisted against their will in a conspiracy of silence?

What alternatives are there? There are moderates who revere the tradition they were raised in, simply because it is their tradition, and who are prepared to campaign, tentatively, for the details of their tradition, simply because, in the marketplace of ideas, somebody should stick up for each tradition until we can sort out the good from the better and settle for the best we can find, all things considered. That is like allegiance to a sports team, and it, too, can give meaning to a life—if not taken too seriously. I am a Red Sox fan, simply because I grew up in the Boston area and have happy memories of Ted Williams, Jimmy Piersall, Carl Yastrzemski, Pudge Fisk, and Wade Boggs, among others. My allegiance to the Red Sox is enthusiastic, but cheerfully arbitrary and undeluded. The Red Sox aren't my team because they are, in fact, the Best; they are the Best (in my eyes) because they are my team.

15   That is a kind of love, but not the rabid love that leads people to lie, and torture, and kill.

In order to adopt such a moderate position, however, you have to loosen your grip on the absolutes that are apparently one of the main attractions of many religious creeds. It isn't easy being moral, and it seems to be getting harder and harder these days. It used to be that most of the world's ills—disease, famine, war—were quite beyond the capacities of everyday people to ameliorate. There was nothing they could do about it, so people could ignore the catastrophes on the other side of the globe—if they even knew about them—with a clear conscience. Living by a few simple, locally applicable maxims could more or less guarantee that one lived about as good a life as was possible at the time. No longer.

Thanks to technology, what almost anybody can do has been multiplied a thousandfold, but our moral understanding about what we ought to do hasn't kept pace. You can have a test-tube baby or take a morning-after pill to keep from having a baby; you can satisfy your sexual urges in the privacy of your room by downloading Internet pornography, or you can copy your favorite music free instead of buying it; you can keep your money in secret offshore bank accounts or purchase stock in cigarette companies that are exploiting impoverished third-world countries; and you can lay minefields, smuggle nuclear weapons in suitcases, make nerve gas, and drop "smart bombs" with pinpoint accuracy. Also, you can arrange to have $100 a month automatically sent from your bank account to provide education for 10 girls in an Islamic country who otherwise would not learn to read and write, or to benefit 100 malnourished people, or provide medical care for AIDS sufferers in Africa. You can use the Internet to organize citizen monitoring of environmental hazards or to check the honesty and performance of government officials—or to spy on your neighbors. Now, what ought we to do?

In the face of such truly imponderable questions, it is entirely reasonable to look for a short set of simple answers. H. L. Mencken[2] cynically said, "For every complex problem, there is a simple answer . . . and it is wrong." But maybe he was wrong! Maybe one Golden Rule or the Ten Commandments or some other short list of absolutely nonnegotiable Dos and Don'ts resolves all the predicaments just fine, once you figure out how to apply them. Nobody would deny, however, that it is far from obvious how any of the favored rules or principles can be interpreted to fit all our quandaries. "Thou shalt not kill" is cited by religious opponents of the death penalty, and by proponents as well. The principle of the Sanctity of Human Life sounds bracingly clear and absolute: Every human life is equally sacred, equally inviolable; as with the king in chess, no price can be placed on it, since to lose it is lose everything. But in fact we all know that life isn't, and can't be, like chess. There are multitudes of interfering "games" going on at once. What are we to do when more than one human life is at stake? If each life is infinitely valuable and none more valuable than another, how are we to dole out the few transplantable kidneys that are available, for instance? Modern technology only exacerbates the issues, which are ancient. Solomon[3] faced tough choices with notable wisdom, and every mother who has ever had less than enough food for her own children (let alone her neighbor's children) has had to confront the impracticality of applying the principle of the Sanctity of Human Life.

Surely just about everybody has faced a moral dilemma and secretly wished, "If only somebody—somebody I trusted—could tell me what to do!" Wouldn't that be morally inauthentic? Aren't we responsible for making our own moral decisions? Yes, but the virtues of "do it yourself" moral reasoning have their limits, and if you decide, after conscientious consideration, that your moral decision is to delegate further moral decisions in your life to a trusted expert, then you have made your own moral decision. You have decided to take advantage of the division of labor that civilization makes possible and get the help of expert specialists.

We applaud the wisdom of that course in all other important areas of decision making (don't try to be your own doctor, the lawyer who represents himself has a fool for a client, and so forth). Even in the case of political decisions, like which way to vote, the policy of delegation can be defended. When my wife and I go to a town meeting, I know that she has studied the issues so much more assiduously than I that I routinely follow her lead, voting the way she tells me. Even if I'm not sure why, I have plenty of evidence for my conviction that, if we did take the time and energy to thrash it all out, she'd

20

2. Baltimore journalist, satirist, and social critic noted for his cynicism (1880–1956).
3. Biblical king of Israel famed for his wisdom.

persuade me that, all things considered, her opinion was correct. Is that a dereliction of my duties as a citizen? I don't think so, but it does depend on my having good grounds for trusting her judgment. Love is not enough.

That's why those who have an unquestioning faith in the correctness of the moral teachings of their religion are a problem: If they haven't conscientiously considered, on their own, whether their pastors or priests or rabbis or imams are worthy of such delegated authority over their lives, then they are taking a personally immoral stand.

That is perhaps the most shocking implication of my inquiry into the role religion plays in our lives, and I do not shrink from it, even though it may offend many who think of themselves as deeply moral. It is commonly supposed that it is entirely exemplary to adopt the moral teachings of one's own religion without question because—to put it simply—it is the word of God (as interpreted, always, by the specialists to whom one has delegated authority). I am urging, on the contrary, that anybody who professes that a particular point of moral conviction is not discussable, not debatable, not negotiable, simply because it is the word of God, or because the Bible says so, or because "that is what all Muslims (Hindus, Sikhs . . .) believe, and I am a Muslim (Hindu, Sikh . . .)" should be seen to be making it impossible for the rest of us to take their views seriously, excusing themselves from the moral conversation, inadvertently acknowledging that their own views are not conscientiously maintained and deserve no further hearing.

The argument is straightforward. Suppose I have a friend, Fred, who is (in my carefully considered opinion) always right. If I tell you I'm against stem-cell research because "my friend Fred says it's wrong, and that's all there is to it," you will just look at me as if I were missing the point of the discussion. I have not given you a reason that, in good faith, I could expect you to appreciate. Suppose you believe that stem-cell research is wrong because God has told you so. Even if you are right—that is, even if God does exist and has, personally, told you that stem-cell research is wrong—you cannot reasonably expect others who do not share your faith or experience to accept that as a reason. The fact that your faith is so strong that you cannot do otherwise just shows (if you really can't) that you are disabled for moral persuasion, a sort of robotic slave to a meme that you are unable to evaluate. And if you reply that you can, but you won't consider reasons for and against your conviction (because it is God's word, and it would be sacrilegious even to consider whether it might be in error), you avow your willful refusal to abide by the minimal conditions of rational discussion. Either way, your declarations of your deeply held views are posturings that are out of place, part of the problem, not part of the solution, and we others will just have to work around you as best we can.

Notice that my stand involves no disrespect and no prejudging of the possibility that God has told you. If God has told you, then part of your problem is convincing others, to whom God has not (yet) spoken. If you refuse or are unable to attempt that, you are actually letting your God down, in the guise of demonstrating your helpless love. You can withdraw from the discussion if you must—that is your right—but then don't blame us if we don't "get it."

Many deeply religious people have all along been eager to defend their   25
convictions in the court of reasonable inquiry and persuasion. They will have
no difficulty at all with my observations—aside from confronting the diplomatic decision of whether they will join me in trying to convince their less reasonable co-religionists that they are making matters worse for their religion by
their intransigence. That is one of the most intractable moral problems confronting the world today. Every religion—aside from a negligible scattering of
truly toxic cults—has a healthy population of ecumenical-minded people who
are eager to reach out to people of other faiths, or no faith at all, and consider
the moral quandaries of the world on a rational basis.

But such well-intentioned people are singularly ineffective in dealing with
the more radical members of their own faiths. In many instances they are,
rightly, terrified of them. Moderate Muslims have so far been utterly unable to
turn the tide of Islamic opinion against Wahhabists[4] and other extremists, but
moderate Christians and Jews and Hindus have been equally feckless in countering the outrageous demands and acts of their own radical elements.

It is time for the reasonable adherents of all faiths to find the courage and
stamina to reverse the tradition that honors helpless love of God—in any tradition. Far from being honorable, it is not even excusable. It is shameful. Here
is what we should say to people who follow such a tradition: There is only one
way to respect the substance of any purported God-given moral edict. Consider it conscientiously in the full light of reason, using all the evidence at our
command. No God pleased by displays of unreasoning love is worthy of worship.

4. Members of a particularly strict branch of Islam practiced most notably in Saudi
Arabia.

QUESTIONS

1. Evaluate the examples Dennett gives in support of his argument. Do they make
sense? Are they realistic? Do they all help clarify his argument?

2. What seems to be Dennett's ultimate test of religious truth? Can you conceive of
others? If so, how might you wish to modify Dennett's conclusion in paragraph 27?

3. Write about the variety of beliefs and practices that you have observed among adherents of a particular religious tradition, asking yourself whether Dennett's categories help
you understand the diversity you find and using them if they are helpful.

ROBERT GRAVES *Mythology*

YTHOLOGY IS THE STUDY of whatever religious or heroic legends are so foreign to a student's experience that he cannot believe them to be true. Hence the English adjective "mythical," meaning "incredible"; and hence the omission from standard European mythologies of all Biblical narratives even when closely paralleled by myths from Persia, Babylonia, Egypt, and Greece, and of all hagiological legends. * * *

Myth has two main functions. The first is to answer the sort of awkward questions that children ask, such as: "Who made the world? How will it end? Who was the first man? Where do souls go after death?" The answers, necessarily graphic and positive, confer enormous power on the various deities credited with the creation and care of souls—and incidentally on their priesthoods.

The second function of myth is to justify an existing social system and account for traditional rites and customs. The Erechtheid clan of Athens, who used a snake as an amulet, preserved myths of their descent from King Erichthonius, a man-serpent, son of the Smith-god Hephaestus and foster-son of the Goddess Athene. The Ioxids of Caria explained their veneration for rushes and wild asparagus by a story of their ancestress Perigune, whom Theseus the Erechtheid courted in a thicket of these plants; thus incidentally claiming cousinship with the Attic royal house. The real reason may have been that wild asparagus stalks and rushes were woven into sacred baskets, and therefore taboo.

Myths of origin and eventual extinction vary according to the climate. In the cold North, the first human beings were said to have sprung from the licking of frozen stones by a divine cow named Audumla; and the Northern afterworld was a bare, misty, featureless plain where ghosts wandered hungry and shivering. According to a myth from the kinder climate of Greece, a Titan named Prometheus, kneading mud on a flowery riverbank, made human statuettes which Athene—who was once the Libyan Moon-goddess Neith— brought to life, and Greek ghosts went to a sunless, flowerless underground cavern. These afterworlds were destined for serfs or commoners; deserving nobles could count on warm, celestial mead halls in the North, and Elysian Fields in Greece.

5 Primitive peoples remodel old myths to conform with changes produced by revolutions, or invasions and, as a rule, politely disguise their violence: thus a treacherous usurper will figure as a lost heir to the throne who killed a destructive dragon or other monster and, after marrying the king's daughter, duly succeeded him. Even myths of origin get altered or discarded. Prometheus' creation of men from clay superseded the hatching of all nature from a world-

Originally written as the introduction to the Larousse Encyclopedia of Mythology *(1959), a reference book on myths of the world.*

egg laid by the ancient Mediterranean Dove-goddess Eurynome—a myth common also in Polynesia, where the Goddess is called Tangaroa.

A typical case-history of how myths develop as culture spreads: Among the Akan of Ghana, the original social system was a number of queendoms, each containing three or more clans and ruled by a Queen-mother with her council of elder women, descent being reckoned in the female line, and each clan having its own animal deity. The Akan believed that the world was born from the all-powerful Moon-goddess Ngame, who gave human beings souls, as soon as born, by shooting lunar rays into them. At some time or other, perhaps in the early Middle Ages, patriarchal nomads from the Sudan forced the Akans to accept a male Creator, a Sky-god named Odomankoma, but failed to destroy Ngame's dispensation. A compromise myth was agreed upon: Odomankoma created the world with hammer and chisel from inert matter, after which Ngame brought it to life. These Sudanese invaders also worshipped the seven planetary powers ruling the week—a system originating in Babylonia. (It had spread to Northern Euope, bypassing Greece and Rome, which is why the names of pagan deities—Tuisto, Woden, Thor, and Frigg—are still attached to Tuesday, Wednesday, Thursday, and Friday.) This extra cult provided the Akan with seven new deities, and the compromise myth made both them and the clan gods bisexual. Towards the end of the fourteenth century A.D., a social revolution deposed Odomankoma in favor of a Universal Sun-god, and altered the myth accordingly. While Odomankoma ruled, a queendom was still a queendom, the king acting merely as a consort and male representative of the sovereign Queen-mother, and being styled "Son of the Moon": a yearly dying, yearly resurrected, fertility godling. But the gradual welding of small queendoms into city-states, and of city-states into a rich and populous nation, encouraged the High King—the king of the dominant city-state—to borrow a foreign custom. He styled himself "Son of the Sun," as well as "Son of the Moon," and claimed limitless authority. The Sun, which, according to the myth, had hitherto been reborn every morning from Ngame, was now worshipped as an eternal god altogether independent of the Moon's life-giving function. New myths appeared when the Akan accepted the patriarchal principle, which Sun-worship brought in; they began tracing succession through the father, and mothers ceased to be the spiritual heads of households.

This case-history throws light on the complex Egyptian corpus of myth. Egypt, it seems, developed from small matriarchal Moonqueendoms to Pharaonic patriarchal Sun-monarchy. Grotesque animal deities of leading clans in the Delta became city-gods, and the cities were federated under the sovereignty of a High King (once a "Son of the Moon"), who claimed to be the Son of Ra the Sun-god. Opposition by independent-minded city-rulers to the Pharaoh's autocratic sway appears in the undated myth of how Ra grew so old and feeble that he could not even control his spittle; the Moon-goddess Isis plotted against him and Ra retaliated by casting his baleful eye on mankind—they perished in their thousands. Ra nevertheless decided to quit the ungrateful land of Egypt, whereupon Hathor, a loyal Cow-goddess, flew him up to the vault of Heaven. The myth doubtless records a compromise that consigned the

High King's absolutist pretensions, supported by his wife, to the vague realm of philosophic theory. He kept the throne, but once more became, for all practical purposes, an incarnation of Osiris, consort of the Moon-goddess Isis—a yearly dying, yearly resurrected fertility godling.

Indian myth is highly complex, and swings from gross physical abandon to rigorous asceticism and fantastic visions of the spirit world. Yet it has much in common with European myth, since Aryan invasions in the second millennium B.C. changed the religious system of both continents. The invaders were nomad herdsmen, and the peoples on whom they imposed themselves as a military aristocracy were peasants. Hesiod, an early Greek poet, preserves a myth of pre-Aryan "Silver Age" heroes: "divinely created eaters of bread, utterly subject to their mothers however long they lived, who never sacrificed to the gods, but at least did not make war against one another." Hesiod put the case well: in primitive agricultural communities, recourse to war is rare, and goddessworship the rule. Herdsmen, on the contrary, tend to make fighting a profession and, perhaps because bulls dominate their herds, as rams do flocks, worship a male Sky-god typified by a bull or a ram. He sends down rain for the pastures, and they take omens from the entrails of the victims sacrificed to him.

When an invading Aryan chieftain, a tribal rainmaker, married the Moon-priestess and Queen of a conquered people, a new myth inevitably celebrated the marriage of the Sky-god and the Moon. But since the Moon-goddess was everywhere worshipped as a triad, in honor of the Moon's three phases—waxing, full, and waning—the god split up into a complementary triad. This accounts for three-bodied Geryon, the first king of Spain; threeheaded Cernunnos, the Gallic god; the Irish triad, Brian, Iuchar, and Iucharba, who married the three queenly owners of Ireland; and the invading Greek brothers Zeus, Poseidon, and Hades, who, despite great opposition, married the pre-Greek Moon-goddess in her three aspects, respectively as Queen of Heaven, Queen of the Sea, and Queen of the Underworld.

10　　The Queen-mother's decline in religious power, and the goddesses' continual struggle to preserve their royal prerogatives, appears in the Homeric myth of how Zeus ill-treated and bullied Hera, and how she continually plotted against him. Zeus remained a Thunder-god, because Greek national sentiment forbad his becoming a Sun-god in Oriental style. But his Irish counterpart, a thunder-god named The Dagda, grew senile at last and surrendered the throne to his son Bodb the Red, a war-god—in Ireland, the magic of rainmaking was not so important as in Greece.

One constant rule of mythology is that whatever happens among the gods above reflects events on earth. Thus a father-god named "The Ancient One of the Jade" (Yu-ti) ruled the pre-revolutionary Chinese Heaven: like Prometheus, he had created human beings from clay. His wife was the Queen-mother, and their court an exact replica of the old Imperial Court at Pekin, with precisely the same functionaries: ministers, soldiers, and a numerous family of the gods' sisters, daughters, and nephews. The two annual sacrifices paid by the Emperor to the August One of the Jade—at the winter solstice when the days first lengthen and at the Spring equinox when they become longer than the nights—

show him to have once been a solar god. And the theological value to the number 72 suggests that the cult started as a compromise between Moon-goddess worship and Sun-god worship. 72 means three-times-three, the Moon's mystical number, multipled by two-times-two-times-two, the Sun's mystical number, and occurs in solar-lunar divine unions throughout Europe, Asia, and Africa. Chinese conservatism, by the way, kept these gods dressed in ancient court-dress, making no concessions to the new fashions which the invading dynasty from Manchuria had introduced.

In West Africa, whenever the Queen-mother, or King, appointed a new functionary at Court, the same thing happened in Heaven, by royal decree. Presumably this was also the case in China; and if we apply the principle to Greek myth, it seems reasonably certain that the account of Tirynthian Heracles' marriage to Hera's daughter Hebe, and his appointment as Celestial Porter to Zeus, commemorates the appointment of a Tirynthian prince as vizier at the court of the Mycenaean High King, after marriage to a daughter of his Queen, the High Priestess of Argos. Probably the appointment of Ganymede, son of an early Trojan king, as cup-bearer to Zeus, had much the same significance: Zeus, in this context, would be more likely the Hittite king resident at Hattusas.

Myth, then, is a dramatic shorthand record of such matters as invasions, migrations, dynastic changes, admission of foreign cults, and social reforms. When bread was first introduced into Greece—where only beans, poppyseeds, acorns, and asphodel roots had hitherto been known—the myth of Demeter and Triptolemus sanctified its use; the same event in Wales produced a myth of "The Old White One," a Sow-goddess who went around the country with gifts of grain, bees, and her own young; for agriculture, pig breeding and bee-keeping were taught to the aborigines by the same wave of neolithic invaders. Other myths sanctified the invention of wine.

A proper study of myth demands a great store of abstruse geographical, historical, and anthropological knowledge, also familiarity with the properties of plants and trees, and the habits of wild birds and beasts. Thus a Central American stone sculpture, a Toad-god sitting beneath a mushroom, means little to mythologists who have not considered the worldwide association of toads with toxic mushrooms or heard of a Mexican Mushroom-god, patron of an oracular cult; for the toxic agent is a drug, similar to that secreted in the sweat glands of frightened toads, which provides magnificent hallucinations of a heavenly kingdom.

Myths are fascinating and easily misread. Readers may smile at the picture of Queen Maya and her prenatal dream of the Buddha descending upon her disguised as a charming white baby elephant—he looks as though he would crush her to pulp—when "at once all nature rejoiced, trees burst into bloom, and musical instruments played of their own accord." In English-speaking countries, "white elephant" denotes something not only useless and unwanted, but expensive to maintain; and the picture could be misread there as indicating the Queen's grave embarrassment at the prospect of bearing a child. In India, however, the elephant symbolizes royalty—the supreme God Indra rides one—

15

and white elephants (which are not albinos, but animals suffering from a vitilig-inous skin disease) are sacred to the Sun, as white horses were for the ancient Greeks, and white oxen for the British druids. The elephant, moreover, symbol-izes intelligence, and Indian writers traditionally acknowledge the Elephant-god Ganesa as their patron; he is supposed to have dictated the *Mahabharata*.[1]

Again, in English, a scallop shell is associated either with cookery or with medieval pilgrims returning from a visit to the Holy Sepulcher; but Aphrodite the Greek Love-goddess employed a scallop shell for her voyages across the sea, because its two parts were so tightly hinged together as to provide a sym-bol of passionate sexual love—the hinge of the scallop being a principal ingre-dient in ancient love-philters. The lotus-flower sacred to Buddha and Osiris has five petals, which symbolize the four limbs and the head; the five senses; the five digits; and, like the pyramid, the four points of the compass and the zenith. Other esoteric meanings abound, for myths are seldom simple, and never irresponsible.

1. A vast Indian epic of 200,000 lines, written before 500 C.E.

QUESTIONS

1. Graves begins by defining the term "mythology." How does (or doesn't) his definition fit with your previous understanding of the term? Why does he choose this particular definition?

2. What are the two functions of myths (paragraphs 2–3)? How does Graves illustrate and amplify these functions throughout the rest of his essay?

3. Can stories from a religious text—the Bible, the Koran, the sayings of Confucius—be treated as myths? Using a story from one of these sources, argue the case either for or against this view.

HENRY DAVID THOREAU *Where I Lived, and What I Lived For*

WHEN I FIRST took up my abode in the woods, that is, began to spend my nights as well as days there, which, by accident, was on Independence day, or the fourth of July, 1845, my house was not finished for winter, but was merely a defence against the rain, with-out plastering or chimney, the walls being of rough

From Thoreau's most famous book, Walden (1854), *an account of his life in a small cabin on Walden Pond, outside the village of Concord, Massachusetts; in* Walden *Thoreau not only describes his life in the woods but also develops a philosophy for living.*

weather-stained boards, with wide chinks, which made it cool at night. The upright white hewn studs and freshly planed door and window casings gave it a clean and airy look, especially in the morning, when its timbers were saturated with dew, so that I fancied that by noon some sweet gum would exude from them. To my imagination it retained throughout the day more or less of this auroral character, reminding me of a certain house on a mountain which I had visited the year before. This was an airy and unplastered cabin, fit to entertain a travelling god, and where a goddess might trail her garments. The winds which passed over my dwelling were such as sweep over the ridges of mountains, bearing the broken strains, or celestial parts only, of terrestrial music. The morning wind forever blows, the poem of creation is uninterrupted; but few are the ears that hear it. Olympus[1] is but the outside of the earth every where.

The only house I had been the owner of before, if I except a boat, was a tent, which I used occasionally when making excursions in the summer, and this is still rolled up in my garret; but the boat, after passing from hand to hand, has gone down the stream of time. With this more substantial shelter about me, I had made some progress toward settling in the world. This frame, so slightly clad, was a sort of crystallization around me, and reacted on the builder. It was suggestive somewhat as a picture in outlines. I did not need to go out doors to take the air, for the atmosphere within had lost none of its freshness. It was not so much within doors as behind a door where I sat, even in the rainiest weather. The Harivansa[2] says, "An abode without birds is like a meat without seasoning." Such was not my abode, for I found myself suddenly neighbor to the birds; not by having imprisoned one, but having caged myself near them. I was not only nearer to some of those which commonly frequent the garden and the orchard, but to those wilder and more thrilling songsters of the forest which never, or rarely, serenade a villager,—the wood-thrush, the veery, the scarlet tanager, the field-sparrow, the whippoorwill, and many others.

I was seated by the shore of a small pond, about a mile and a half south of the village of Concord and somewhat higher than it, in the midst of an extensive wood between that town and Lincoln, and about two miles south of that our only field known to fame, Concord Battle Ground;[3] but I was so low in the woods that the opposite shore, half a mile off, like the rest, covered with wood, was my most distant horizon. For the first week, whenever I looked out on the pond it impressed me like a tarn high up on the side of a mountain, its bottom far above the surface of other lakes, and, as the sun arose, I saw it throwing off its nightly clothing of mist, and here and there, by degrees, its soft ripples or its smooth reflecting surface was revealed, while the mists, like ghosts, were stealthily withdrawing in every direction into the woods, as at the breaking up

1. The mountain where the Greek gods dwell.
2. Fifth-century epic poem about the Hindu god Krishna.
3. Site of the famous Battle of Concord, April 19, 1775, considered the start of the American Revolution.

of some nocturnal conventicle. The very dew seemed to hang upon the trees later into the day than usual, as on the sides of mountains.

This small lake was of most value as a neighbor in the intervals of a gentle rain storm in August, when, both air and water being perfectly still, but the sky overcast, mid-afternoon had all the serenity of evening, and the wood-thrush sang around, and was heard from shore to shore. A lake like this is never smoother than at such a time; and the clear portion of the air above it being shallow and darkened by clouds, the water, full of light and reflections, becomes a lower heaven itself so much the more important. From a hill top near by, where the wood had been recently cut off, there was a pleasing vista southward across the pond, through a wide indentation in the hills which form the shore there, where their opposite sides sloping toward each other suggested a stream flowing out in that direction through a wooded valley, but stream there was none. That way I looked between and over the near green hills to some distant and higher ones in the horizon, tinged with blue. Indeed, by standing on tiptoe I could catch a glimpse of some of the peaks of the still bluer and more distant mountain ranges in the north-west, those true-blue coins from heaven's own mint, and also of some portion of the village. But in other directions, even from this point, I could not see over or beyond the woods which surrounded me. It is well to have some water in your neighborhood, to give buoyancy to and float the earth. One value even of the smallest well is, that when you look into it you see that earth is not continent but insular. This is as important as that it keeps butter cool. When I looked across the pond from this peak toward the Sudbury meadows, which in time of flood I distinguished elevated perhaps by a mirage in their seething valley, like a coin in a basin, all the earth beyond the pond appeared like a thin crust insulated and floated even by this small sheet of intervening water, and I was reminded that this on which I dwelt was but *dry land*.

5   Though the view from my door was still more contracted, I did not feel crowded or confined in the least. There was pasture enough for my imagination. The low shrub-oak plateau to which the opposite shore arose, stretched away toward the prairies of the West and the steppes of Tartary,[4] affording ample room for all the roving families of men. "There are none happy in the world but beings who enjoy freely a vast horizon,"—said Damodara,[5] when his herds required new and larger pastures.

Both place and time were changed, and I dwelt nearer to those parts of the universe and to those eras in history which had most attracted me. Where I lived was as far off as many a region viewed nightly by astronomers. We are wont to imagine rare and delectable places in some remote and more celestial corner of the system, behind the constellation of Cassiopeia's Chair, far from noise and disturbance. I discovered that my house actually had its site in such a withdrawn, but forever new and unprofaned, part of the universe. If it were worth the while to settle in those parts near to the Pleiades or the Hyades, to

4. A region that includes what is today northern Pakistan.
5. One of the many names of Krishna, the Hindu god.

Aldebaran or Altair,[6] then I was really there, or at an equal remoteness from the life which I had left behind, dwindled and twinkling with as fine a ray to my nearest neighbor, and to be seen only in moonless nights by him. Such was that part of creation where I had squatted;—

> "There was a shepherd that did live,
>   And held his thoughts as high
> As were the mounts whereon his flocks
>   Did hourly feed him by."[7]

What should we think of the shepherd's life if his flocks always wandered to higher pastures than his thoughts?

Every morning was a cheerful invitation to make my life of equal simplicity, and I may say innocence, with Nature herself. I have been as sincere a worshipper of Aurora[8] as the Greeks. I got up early and bathed in the pond; that was a religious exercise, and one of the best things which I did. They say that characters were engraven on the bathing tub of king Tching-thang[9] to this effect: "Renew thyself completely each day; do it again, and again, and forever again." I can understand that. Morning brings back the heroic ages. I was as much affected by the faint hum of a mosquito making its invisible and unimaginable tour through my apartment at earliest dawn, when I was sitting with door and windows open, as I could be by any trumpet that ever sang of fame. It was Homer's[10] requiem; itself an Iliad and Odyssey in the air, singing its own wrath and wanderings. There was something cosmical about it; a standing advertisement, till forbidden, of the everlasting vigor and fertility of the world. The morning, which is the most memorable season of the day, is the awakening hour. Then there is least somnolence in us; and for an hour, at least, some part of us awakes which slumbers all the rest of the day and night. Little is to be expected of that day, if it can be called a day, to which we are not awakened by our Genius, but by the mechanical nudgings of some servitor, are not awakened by our own newly-acquired force and aspirations from within, accompanied by the undulations of celestial music, instead of factory bells, and a fragrance filling the air—to a higher life than we fell asleep from; and thus the darkness bear its fruit, and prove itself to be good, no less than the light. That man who does not believe that each day contains an earlier, more sacred, and auroral hour than he has yet profaned, has despaired of life, and is pursuing a descending and darkening way. After a partial cessation of his sensuous life, the soul of man, or its organs rather, are reinvigorated each day, and

6. Cassiopeia's Chair, the Pleiades, and the Hyades are constellations; Aldebaran and Altair are stars.

7. Lines from "The Shepherd's Love for Philladay," from Thomas Evan's *Old Ballads* (1810).

8. Goddess of the dawn.

9. Confucius (551–479 B.C.E.), Chinese philosopher.

10. Greek epic poet (eighth century B.C.E.), author of the *Odyssey* and the *Iliad*.

his Genius tries again what noble life it can make. All memorable events, I should say, transpire in morning time and in a morning atmosphere. The Vedas[11] say, "All intelligences awake with the morning." Poetry and art, and the fairest and most memorable of the actions of men, date from such an hour. All poets and heroes, like Memnon,[12] are the children of Aurora, and emit their music at sunrise. To him whose elastic and vigorous thought keeps pace with the sun, the day is a perpetual morning. It matters not what the clocks say or the attitudes and labors of men. Morning is when I am awake and there is a dawn in me. Moral reform is the effort to throw off sleep. Why is it that men give so poor an account of their day if they have not been slumbering? They are not such poor calculators. If they had not been overcome with drowsiness they would have performed something. The millions are awake enough for physical labor; but only one in a million is awake enough for effective intellectual exertion, only one in a hundred millions to a poetic or divine life. To be awake is to be alive. I have never yet met a man who was quite awake. How could I have looked him in the face?

We must learn to reawaken and keep ourselves awake, not by mechanical aids, but by an infinite expectation of the dawn, which does not forsake us in our soundest sleep. I know of no more encouraging fact than the unquestionable ability of man to elevate his life by a conscious endeavor. It is something to be able to paint a particular picture, or to carve a statue, and so to make a few objects beautiful; but it is far more glorious to carve and paint the very atmosphere and medium through which we look, which morally we can do. To affect the quality of the day, that is the highest of arts. Every man is tasked to make his life, even in its details, worthy of the contemplation of his most elevated and critical hour. If we refused, or rather used up, such paltry information as we get, the oracles would distinctly inform us how this might be done.

I went to the woods because I wished to live deliberately, to front only the essential facts of life, and see if I could not learn what it had to teach, and not, when I came to die, discover that I had not lived. I did not wish to live what was not life, living is so dear, nor did I wish to practise resignation, unless it was quite necessary. I wanted to live deep and suck out all the marrow of life, to live so sturdily and Spartan-like as to put to rout all that was not life, to cut a broad swath and shave close, to drive life into a corner, and reduce it to its lowest terms, and, if it proved to be mean, why then to get the whole and genuine meanness of it, and publish its meanness to the world; or if it were sublime, to know it by experience, and be able to give a true account of it in my next excursion. For most men, it appears to me, are in a strange uncertainty about it, whether it is of the devil or of God, and have *somewhat hastily* concluded that it is the chief end of man here to "glorify God and enjoy him forever."

11. Sacred texts that contain hymns, incantations, and rituals from ancient India.

12. Son of Aurora, the goddess of dawn, and a mortal, Memnon was king of the Ethiopians; he was slain by Achilles while fighting the Greeks in Troy. When he died, his sad mother's tears formed the morning dew.

Still we live meanly, like ants; though the fable tells us that we were long   10
ago changed into men;[13] like pygmies we fight with cranes;[14] it is error upon
error, and clout upon clout, and our best virtue has for its occasion a superfluous and evitable wretchedness. Our life is frittered away by detail. An honest
man has hardly need to count more than his ten fingers, or in extreme cases
he may add his ten toes, and lump the rest. Simplicity, simplicity, simplicity! I
say, let your affairs be as two or three, and not a hundred or a thousand; instead of a million count half a dozen, and keep your accounts on your thumb
nail. In the midst of this chopping sea of civilized life, such are the clouds and
storms and quicksands and thousand-and-one items to be allowed for, that a
man has to live, if he would not founder and go to the bottom and not make
his port at all, by dead reckoning, and he must be a great calculator indeed
who succeeds. Simplify, simplify. Instead of three meals a day, if it be necessary eat but one; instead of a hundred dishes, five; and reduce other things in
proportion. Our life is like a German Confederacy, made up of petty states,
with its boundary forever fluctuating, so that even a German cannot tell you
how it is bounded at any moment. The nation itself, with all its so called internal improvements, which, by the way, are all external and superficial, is just
such an unwieldy and overgrown establishment, cluttered with furniture and
tripped up by its own traps, ruined by luxury and heedless expense, by want of
calculation and a worthy aim, as the million households in the land; and the
only cure for it as for them is in a rigid economy, a stern and more than Spartan simplicity of life and elevation of purpose. It lives too fast. Men think that
it is essential that the *Nation* have commerce, and export ice, and talk through
a telegraph, and ride thirty miles an hour, without a doubt, whether *they* do or
not; but whether we should live like baboons or like men, is a little uncertain.
If we do not get our sleepers, and forge rails, and devote days and nights to the
work, but go to tinkering upon our *lives* to improve *them*, who will build railroads? And if railroads are not built, how shall we get to heaven in season? But
if we stay at home and mind our business, who will want railroads? We do not
ride on the railroad; it rides upon us. Did you ever think what those sleepers
are that underlie the railroad? Each one is a man, an Irishman, or a Yankee
man. The rails are laid on them, and they are covered with sand, and the cars
run smoothly over them. They are sound sleepers, I assure you. And every few
years a new lot is laid down and run over; so that, if some have the pleasure of
riding on a rail, others have the misfortune to be ridden upon. And when they
run over a man that is walking in his sleep, a supernumerary sleeper in the
wrong position, and wake him up, they suddenly stop the cars, and make a hue
and cry about it, as if this were an exception. I am glad to know that it takes a
gang of men for every five miles to keep the sleepers down and level in their
beds as it is, for this is a sign that they may sometime get up again.

13. In a Greek fable Aeacus asks Zeus to increase a scanty population by turning ants
into men.
14. From the *Iliad*, Book III, lines 2–6, in which the Trojans are represented as the
cranes.

Why should we live with such hurry and waste of life? We are determined to be starved before we are hungry. Men say that a stitch in time saves nine, and so they take a thousand stitches to-day to save nine to-morrow. As for *work*, we haven't any of any consequence. We have the Saint Vitus' dance,[15] and cannot possibly keep our heads still. If I should only give a few pulls at the parish bell-rope, as for a fire, that is, without setting the bell, there is hardly a man on his farm in the outskirts of Concord, notwithstanding that press of engagements which was his excuse so many times this morning, nor a boy, nor a woman, I might almost say, but would forsake all and follow that sound, not mainly to save property from the flames, but, if we will confess the truth, much more to see it burn, since burn it must, and we, be it known, did not set it on fire,—or to see it put out, and have a hand in it, if that is done as handsomely; yes, even if it were the parish church itself. Hardly a man takes a half hour's nap after dinner, but when he wakes he holds up his head and asks, "What's the news?" as if the rest of mankind had stood his sentinels. Some give directions to be waked every half hour, doubtless for no other purpose; and then, to pay for it, they tell what they have dreamed. After a night's sleep the news is as indispensable as the breakfast. "Pray tell me any thing new that has happened to a man any where on this globe,"—and he reads it over his coffee and rolls, that a man has had his eyes gouged out this morning on the Wachito River;[16] never dreaming the while that he lives in the dark unfathomed mammoth cave of this world, and has but the rudiment of an eye himself.

For my part, I could easily do without the post-office. I think that there are very few important communications made through it. To speak critically, I never received more than one or two letters in my life—I wrote this some years ago—that were worth the postage. The penny-post is, commonly, an institution through which you seriously offer a man that penny for his thoughts which is so often safely offered in jest. And I am sure that I never read any memorable news in a newspaper. If we read of one man robbed, or murdered, or killed by accident, or one house burned, or one vessel wrecked, or one steamboat blown up, or one cow run over on the Western Railroad, or one mad dog killed, or one lot of grasshoppers in the winter,—we never need read of another. One is enough. If you are acquainted with the principle, what do you care for a myriad instances and applications? To a philosopher all *news*, as it is called, is gossip, and they who edit and read it are old women over their tea. Yet not a few are greedy after this gossip. There was such a rush, as I hear, the other day at one of the offices to learn the foreign news by the last arrival, that several large squares of plate glass belonging to the establishment were broken by the pressure,—news which I seriously think a ready wit might write a twelvemonth or twelve years beforehand with sufficient accuracy. As for Spain, for instance, if you know how to throw in Don Carlos and the Infanta, and Don Pedro and Seville and Granada, from time to time in the right pro-

15. A nervous disorder marked by jerky, spasmodic movements that occurs in cases of rheumatic fever involving the connective tissue of the brain.
16. In southern Arkansas.

portions,—they may have changed the names a little since I saw the papers,—
and serve up a bull-fight when other entertainments fail, it will be true to the
letter, and give us as good an idea of the exact state of ruin of things in Spain
as the most succinct and lucid reports under this head in the newspapers: and
as for England, almost the last significant scrap of news from that quarter was
the revolution of 1649;[17] and if you have learned the history of her crops for
an average year, you never need attend to that thing again, unless your speculations are of a merely pecuniary character. If one may judge who rarely looks
into the newspapers, nothing new does ever happen in foreign parts, a French
revolution not excepted.

What news! how much more important to know what that is which was
never old! "Kieou-he-yu (great dignitary of the state of Wei) sent a man to
Khoung-tseu to know his news. Khoung-tseu caused the messenger to be
seated near him, and questioned him in these terms: What is your master doing? The messenger answered with respect: My master desires to diminish the
number of his faults, but he cannot come to the end of them. The messenger
being gone, the philosopher remarked: What a worthy messenger! What a worthy messenger!" The preacher, instead of vexing the ears of drowsy farmers on
their day of rest at the end of the week,—for Sunday is the fit conclusion of an
ill-spent week, and not the fresh and brave beginning of a new one,—with this
one other draggle-tail of a sermon, should shout with thundering voice,—
"Pause! Avast! Why so seeming fast, but deadly slow?"

Shams and delusions are esteemed for soundest truths, while reality is
fabulous. If men would steadily observe realities only, and not allow themselves to be deluded, life, to compare it with such things as we know, would be
like a fairy tale and the Arabian Nights' Entertainments. If we respected only
what is inevitable and has a right to be, music and poetry would resound along
the streets. When we are unhurried and wise, we perceive that only great and
worthy things have any permanent and absolute existence,—that petty fears
and petty pleasures are but the shadow of the reality. This is always exhilarating and sublime. By closing the eyes and slumbering, and consenting to be deceived by shows, men establish and confirm their daily life of routine and
habit every where, which still is built on purely illusory foundations. Children,
who play life, discern its true law and relations more clearly than men, who
fail to live it worthily, but who think that they are wiser by experience, that is,
by failure. I have read in a Hindoo book, that "There was a king's son, who, being expelled in infancy from his native city, was brought up by a forester, and,
growing up to maturity in that state, imagined himself to belong to the barbarous race with which he lived. One of his father's ministers having discovered him, revealed to him what he was, and the misconception of his
character was removed, and he knew himself to be a prince. So soul," continues the Hindoo philosopher, "from the circumstances in which it is placed,

17. Sometimes called the Cromwellian Interlude, the period in British history between
1649 and 1660 in which the monarchy was replaced by the Commonwealth and Oliver
Cromwell became Lord Protector.

mistakes its own character, until the truth is revealed to it by some holy teacher, and then it knows itself to be *Brahme*."[18] I perceive that we inhabitants of New England live this mean life that we do because our vision does not penetrate the surface of things. We think that that *is* which *appears* to be. If a man should walk through this town and see only the reality, where, think you, would the "Mill-dam"[19] go to? If he should give us an account of the realities he beheld there, we should not recognize the place in his description. Look at a meeting-house, or a court-house, or a jail, or a shop, or a dwelling-house, and say what that thing really is before a true gaze, and they would all go to pieces in your account of them. Men esteem truth remote, in the outskirts of the system, behind the farthest star, before Adam and after the last man. In eternity there is indeed something true and sublime. But all these times and places and occasions are now and here. God himself culminates in the present moment, and will never be more divine in the lapse of all the ages. And we are enabled to apprehend at all what is sublime and noble only by the perpetual instilling and drenching of the reality that surrounds us. The universe constantly and obediently answers to our conceptions; whether we travel fast or slow, the track is laid for us. Let us spend our lives in conceiving then. The poet or the artist never yet had so fair and noble a design but some of his posterity at least could accomplish it.

15   Let us spend one day as deliberately as Nature, and not be thrown off the track by every nutshell and mosquito's wing that falls on the rails. Let us rise early and fast, or break fast, gently and without perturbation; let company come and let company go, let the bells ring and the children cry,—determined to make a day of it. Why should we knock under and go with the stream? Let us not be upset and overwhelmed in that terrible rapid and whirlpool called a dinner, situated in the meridian shallows. Weather this danger and you are safe, for the rest of the way is down hill. With unrelaxed nerves, with morning vigor, sail by it, looking another way, tied to the mast like Ulysses. If the engine whistles, let it whistle till it is hoarse for its pains. If the bell rings, why should we run? We will consider what kind of music they are like. Let us settle ourselves, and work and wedge our feet downward through the mud and slush of opinion, and prejudice, and tradition, and delusion, and appearance, that alluvion which covers the globe, through Paris and London, through New York and Boston and Concord, through church and state, through poetry and philosophy and religion, till we come to a hard bottom and rocks in place, which we can call *reality*, and say, This is, and no mistake; and then begin, having a *point d'appui*,[20] below freshet and frost and fire, a place where you might found a wall or a state, or set a lamp-post safely, or perhaps a gauge, not a Nilometer,[21] but a Realometer, that future ages might know how deep a

---

18. The supreme soul, the essence of all being, in Hinduism.

19. A dam built in 1635 in the town of Concord on the site of an Indian fishing weir. The places listed after are near it.

20. Reference point.

21. A gauge placed in the Nile River in ancient times to measure the rise of the water.

freshet of shams and appearances had gathered from time to time. If you stand right fronting and face to face to a fact, you will see the sun glimmer on both its surfaces, as if it were a cimeter,[22] and feel its sweet edge dividing you through the heart and marrow, and so you will happily conclude your mortal career. Be it life or death, we crave only reality. If we are really dying, let us hear the rattle in our throats and feel cold in the extremities; if we are alive, let us go about our business.

Time is but the stream I go a-fishing in. I drink at it; but while I drink I see the sandy bottom and detect how shallow it is. Its thin current slides away, but eternity remains. I would drink deeper; fish in the sky, whose bottom is pebbly with stars. I cannot count one. I know not the first letter of the alphabet. I have always been regretting that I was not as wise as the day I was born. The intellect is a cleaver; it discerns and rifts its way into the secret of things. I do not wish to be any more busy with my hands than is necessary. My head is hands and feet. I feel all my best faculties concentrated in it. My instinct tells me that my head is an organ for burrowing, as some creatures use their snout and forepaws, and with it I would mine and burrow my way through these hills. I think that the richest vein is somewhere hereabouts; so by the divining rod and thin rising vapors I judge; and here I will begin to mine.

22. A saber with a curved blade, usually spelled "scimitar."

QUESTIONS

1. Thoreau's title might be rephrased as two questions: "Where did I live?" and "What did I live for?" What answers does Thoreau give to each?

2. Throughout this essay Thoreau poses questions—for example, "Why is it that men give so poor an account of their day if they have not been slumbering?" (paragraph 7) or "Why should we live with such hurry and waste of life?" (paragraph 11). To what extent does he answer them? Why might he leave some unanswered or only partially answered?

3. Thoreau is known for his aphorisms (short, witty nuggets of wisdom). Find one you like and explain what it means.

4. If you have ever chosen to live unconventionally at some period of your life, even if only briefly, write about your decision, including the reasons and the consequences.

MARTHA NUSSBAUM *The Idea of World Citizenship in Greek and Roman Antiquity*

ASKED WHERE HE CAME FROM, the ancient Greek Cynic philosopher Diogenes replied, "I am a citizen of the world." He meant by this that he refused to be defined simply by his local origins and group memberships, associations central to the self-image of a conventional Greek male; he insisted on defining himself in terms of more universal aspirations and concerns.[1] The Stoics who followed his lead developed his image of the *kosmopolitēs*, or world citizen, more fully, arguing that each of us dwells, in effect, in two communities—the local community of our birth, and the community of human argument and aspiration that "is truly great and truly common." It is the latter community that is, most fundamentally, the source of our moral and social obligations. With respect to fundamental moral values such as justice, "we should regard all human beings as our fellow citizens and local residents."[2] This attitude deeply influenced the subsequent philosophical and political tradition, especially as mediated through the writings of Cicero,[3] who reworked it so as to allow a special degree of loyalty to one's own local region or group. Stoic ideas influenced the American republic through the writings of Thomas Paine, and also through Adam Smith and Immanuel Kant,[4] who themselves influenced the Founders.[5] Later on, Stoic thought was a major formative influence on both Emerson and Thoreau.[6]

From Cultivating Humanity: A Classical Defense of Reform in Liberal Education *(1997), a book-length argument for college courses that support (rather than hinder) critical thinking and intellectual freedom, and for a curricular diversity that supports the classic values of a liberal education, especially the goal of educating "world citizens."*

1. All judgments about the Cynics are tentative, given the thinness of our information. The central source is Diogenes Laertius' *Lives of the Philosophers*. See B. Branham and M.-O. Goulet-Cazé, eds., *The Cynics* (Berkeley: University of California Press, 1996) [Nussbaum's note].

2. Plutarch, *On the Fortunes of Alexander* 329AB = SVF 1.262; see also Seneca, *On Leisure* 4.1 [Nussbaum's note].

3. Roman orator and philosopher (106–43 B.C.E.).

4. Paine (1737–1809), American revolutionary patriot; Smith (1723–1790), Scottish economist; Kant (1724–1804), German philosopher.

5. For Paine, see *The Rights of Man*, pt. 2; for Smith, see "Of Universal Benevolence," in *The Theory of Moral Sentiments* (Indianapolis: Liberty Classica, 1982), vol. 6, pt. 2, p. 3, with special reference to Marcus Aurelius; for Kant, see *Perpetual Peace*, in *Kant's Political Writings*, ed. H. Reiss, trans. H. Nisbet, 2nd ed. (Cambridge: Cambridge University Press, 1991). For a discussion of Stoic ideas in Kant's political thought, see Martha C. Nussbaum, "Kant and Stoic Cosmopolitanism," *Journal of Political Philosophy* 5 (1997): 1–25 [Nussbaum's note].

6. Ralph Waldo Emerson (1803–1882) and Henry David Thoreau (1817–1862), American writers.

This form of cosmopolitanism is not peculiar to Western traditions. It is, for example, the view that animates the work of the influential, Indian philosopher, poet, and educational leader Rabindranath Tagore.[7] Tagore drew his own cosmopolitan views from older Bengali traditions although he self-consciously melded them with Western cosmopolitanism.[8] It is also the view recommended by Ghanaian philosopher Kwame Anthony Appiah, when he writes, concerning African identity: "We will only solve our problems if we see them as human problems arising out of a special situation, and we shall not solve them if we see them as African problems generated by our being somehow unlike others."[9] But for people who have grown up in the Western tradition it is useful to understand the roots of this cosmopolitanism in ancient Greek and Roman thought. These ideas are an essential resource for democratic citizenship. Like Socrates' ideal of critical inquiry, they should be at the core of today's higher education.

Contemporary debates about the curriculum frequently imply that the idea of a "multicultural" education is a new fad, with no antecedents in long-standing educational traditions. In fact, Socrates grew up in an Athens already influenced by such ideas in the fifth century B.C. Ethnographic writers such as the historian Herodotus[10] examined the customs of distant countries, both in order to understand their ways of life and in order to attain a critical perspective on their own society. Herodotus took seriously the possibility that Egypt and Persia might have something to teach Athens about social values. A cross-cultural inquiry, he realized, may reveal that what we take to be natural and normal is merely parochial and habitual. One cultural group thinks that corpses must be buried; another, that they must be burnt; another, that they must be left in the air to be plucked clean by the birds. Each is shocked by the practices of the other, and each, in the process, starts to realize that its habitual ways may not be the ways designed by nature for all times and persons.

Awareness of cultural difference gave rise to a rich and complex debate about whether our central moral and political values exist in the nature of things (by *phusis*), or merely by convention (*nomos*).[11] That Greek debate illustrates most of the positions now familiar in debates about cultural relativism and the source of moral norms. It also contains a crucial insight: if we should conclude that our norms are human and historical rather than immutable and

---

7. Tagore (1861–1941).

8. See Tagore, "Swadeshi Samaj," cited in Krishna Dutta and Andrew Robinson, *Rabindranath Tagore: The Myriad-Minded Man* (London: Bloomsbury, 1995) [Nussbaum's note].

9. Kwame Anthony Appiah, *In My Father's House: Africa in the Philosophy of Cultures* (New York: Oxford University Press, 1991) [Nussbaum's note].

10. Herodotus (c. 490–c. 425 B.C.E.), Greek historian.

11. See W. K. C. Guthrie, *History of Greek Philosophy*, vol. 3 (Cambridge: Cambridge University Press, 1969) [Nussbaum's note].

eternal, it does not follow that the search for a rational justification of moral norms is futile.

In the conventional culture of fifth-century B.C. Athens, recognition that Athenian customs were not universal became a crucial precondition of Socratic searching. So long as young men were educated in the manner of Aristophanes' Old Education,[12] an education stressing uncritical assimilation of traditional values, so long as they marched to school in rows and sang the old songs without discussion of alternatives, ethical questioning could not get going. Ethical inquiry requires a climate in which the young are encouraged to be critical of their habits and conventions; and such critical inquiry, in turn, requires awareness that life contains other possibilities.

Pursuing these comparisons, fifth-century Athenians were especially fascinated by the example of Sparta, Athens' primary rival, a hierarchical and nondemocratic culture that understood the goal of civic education in a very un-Athenian way. As the historian Thucydides1[13] depicts them, Spartan educators carried to an extreme the preference for uniformity and rule-following that characterized the Old Education of Athens in Aristophanes' nostalgic portrait. Conceiving the good citizen as an obedient follower of traditions, they preferred uncritical subservience to Athenian public argument and debate. Denying the importance of free speech and thought, they preferred authoritarian to democratic politics.

Athenians, looking at this example, saw new reasons to praise the freedom of inquiry and debate that by this time flourished in their political life. They saw Spartan citizens as people who did not choose to serve their city, and whose loyalty was therefore in a crucial way unreliable, since they had never really thought about what they were doing. They noted that once Spartans were abroad and free from the narrow constraint of law and rule, they often acted badly, since they had never learned to choose for themselves. The best education, they held, was one that equips a citizen for genuine choice of a way of life; this form of education requires active inquiry and the ability to contrast alternatives. Athenians denied the Spartan charge that their own concern with critical inquiry and free expression would give rise to decadence. "We cultivate the arts without extravagance," they proudly proclaimed, "and we devote ourselves to inquiry without becoming soft." Indeed, they insisted that Sparta's high reputation for courage was ill based: for citizens could not be truly courageous if they never chose from among alternatives. True courage, they held, requires freedom, and freedom is best cultivated by an education that awakens critical thinking. Crosscultural inquiry thus proved not only illuminating but also self-reinforcing to Athenians: by showing them regimes that did not practice such inquiry and what those regimes lacked in consequence, it gave Athenians reasons why they should continue to criticize and to compare cultures.

Plato, writing in the early to mid-fourth century B.C., alludes frequently to

12. Aristophanes (448?–385 B.C.E.), Greek comic dramatist, satirized this education in *The Clouds.*
13. Greek historian (460?–400 B.C.E.).

the study of other cultures, especially those of Sparta, Crete, and Egypt. In his *Republic,* which alludes often to Spartan practices, the plan for an ideal city is plainly influenced by reflection about customs elsewhere.[14] One particularly fascinating example of the way in which reflection about history and other cultures awakens critical reflection occurs in the fifth book of that work, where Plato's character Socrates produces the first serious argument known to us in the Western tradition for the equal education of women. Here Socrates begins by acknowledging that the idea of women's receiving both physical and intellectual education equal to that of men will strike most Athenians as very weird and laughable. (Athenians who were interested in cultural comparison would know, however, that such ideas were not peculiar in Sparta, where women, less confined than at Athens, did receive extensive athletic training.)[15] But he then reminds Glaucon that many good things once seemed weird in just this way. For example, the unclothed public exercise that Athenians now prize as a norm of manliness once seemed foreign, and the heavy clothing that they think barbaric once seemed natural. However, he continues, when the practice of stripping for athletic contests had been in effect for some time, its advantages were clearly seen—and then "the appearance of absurdity ebbed away under the influence of reason's judgment about the best." So it is with women's education, Socrates argues. Right now it seems absurd, but once we realize that our conventions don't by themselves supply reasons for what we ought to do, we will be forced to ask ourselves whether we really do have good reasons for denying women the chance to develop their intellectual and physical capacities. Socrates argues that we find no such good reasons, and many good reasons why those capacities should be developed. Therefore, a comparative cultural study, by removing the false air of naturalness and inevitability that surrounds our practices, can make our society a more truly reasonable one.

Cross-cultural inquiry up until this time had been relatively unsystematic, using examples that the philosopher or historian in question happened to know through personal travel or local familiarity. Later in the fourth century, however, the practice was rendered systematic and made a staple of the curriculum, as Aristotle apparently instructed his students to gather information about 153 forms of political organization, encompassing the entire known world, and to write up historical and constitutional descriptions of these regimes. The *Athenian Constitution,* which was written either by Aristotle or by one of his students, is our only surviving example of the project; it shows an intention to record everything relevant to critical reflection about that constitution and its suitability. When Aristotle himself writes political philosophy, his project is extensively cross-cultural. In his *Politics,* before describing his own

14. In the *Republic,* Plato uses dialogues between Socrates and other characters (Glaucon, Adeimantus, Cephalus, Polemarchus, and Thrasymachus) to explore the principles of an ideal city-state.

15. See Stephen Halliwell, *Plato: Republic V* (Warminster: Aris and Phillips, 1993) [Nussbaum's note].

views about the best form of government, he works through and criticizes many known historical examples, prominently including Crete and Sparta, and also a number of theoretical proposals, including those of Plato. As a result of this inquiry, Aristotle develops a model of good government that is in many respects critical of Athenian traditions, though he follows no single model.

By the beginning of the so-called Hellenistic era in Greek philosophy, then, cross-cultural inquiry was firmly established, both in Athenian public discourse and in the writings of the philosophers, as a necessary part of good deliberation about citizenship and political order.[16]

10   But it was neither Plato nor Aristotle who coined the term "citizen of the world." It was Diogenes the Cynic. Diogenes (404–323 B.C.) led a life stripped of the usual protections that habit and status supply. Choosing exile from his own native city, he defiantly refused protection from the rich and powerful for fear of losing his freedom, and lived in poverty, famously choosing a tub set up in the marketplace as his "home" in order to indicate his disdain for convention and comfort. He connected poverty with independence of mind and speech, calling freedom of speech "the finest thing in human life."[17] Once, they say, Plato saw him washing some lettuce and said, "If you had paid court to Dionysius, you would not be washing lettuce."[18] Diogenes replied, "If you had washed lettuce, you would not have paid court to Dionysius." This freedom from subservience, he held, was essential to a philosophical life. "When someone reproached him for being an exile, he said that it was on that account that he came to be a philosopher."

Diogenes left no written work behind, and it is difficult to know how to classify him. "A Socrates gone mad" was allegedly Plato's description—and a good one, it seems. For Diogenes clearly followed the lead of Socrates in disdaining external markers of status and focusing on the inner life of virtue and thought. His search for a genuinely honest and virtuous person, and his use of philosophical arguments to promote that search, are recognizably Socratic. What was "mad" about him was the public assault on convention that accompanied his quest. Socrates provoked people only by his questions. He lived a conventional life. But Diogenes provoked people by his behavior as well, spitting in a rich man's face, even masturbating in public. What was the meaning of this shocking behavior?

It appears likely that the point of his unseemly behavior was itself Socratic—to get people to question their prejudices by making them consider

---

16. The Hellenistic era is usually taken to begin at the death of Alexander the Great, 323 B.C.; Aristotle died in 322. Although Diogenes was a contemporary of Aristotle, his influence is felt in the later period. See A. A. Long, *Hellenistic Philosophy* (London: Duckworth, 1974) [Nussbaum's note].

17. The translation by R. D. Hicks in the Loeb Classical Library volume 2 of Diogenes Laertius is inadequate but gives the general idea. All citations here are from that *Life*, but the translations are mine [Nussbaum's note].

18. Dionysius was the one-man ruler of Syracuse in Sicily whom Plato attempted, without success, to turn into a "philosopher-king" [Nussbaum's note].

how difficult it is to give good reasons for many of our deeply held feelings. Feelings about the respect due to status and rank and feelings of shame associated with sexual practices are assailed by this behavior—as Herodotus' feelings about burial were assailed by his contact with Persian and Egyptian customs. The question is whether one can then go on to find a good argument for one's own conventions and against the behavior of the Cynic.

As readers of the *Life* of Diogenes, we ourselves quickly become aware of the cultural relativity of what is thought shocking. For one of the most shocking things about Diogenes, to his Athenian contemporaries, was his habit of eating in the public marketplace. It was this habit that gave him the name "dog," *kuōn*, from which our English label Cynic derives. Only dogs, in this culture, tore away at their food in the full view of all. Athenians evidently found this just about as outrageous as public masturbation; in fact his biographer joins the two offenses together, saying, "He used to do everything in public, both the deeds of Demeter and those of Aphrodite." Crowds, they say, gathered around to taunt him as he munched on his breakfast of beets, behaving in what the American reader feels to be an unremarkable fashion. On the other hand, there is no mention in the *Life* of shock occasioned by public urination or even defecation. The reason for this, it may be conjectured, is that Athenians, like people in many parts of the world today, did not in fact find public excretion shocking. We are amazed by a culture that condemns public snacking while permitting such practices. Diogenes asks us to look hard at the conventional origins of these judgments and to ask which ones can be connected by a sound argument to important moral goals. (So far as we can tell, Cynics supplied no answers to this question.)

Set in this context, the invitation to consider ourselves citizens of the world is the invitation to become, to a certain extent, philosophical exiles from our own ways of life, seeing them from the vantage point of the outsider and asking the questions an outsider is likely to ask about their meaning and function. Only this critical distance, Diogenes argued, makes one a philosopher. In other words, a stance of detachment from uncritical loyalty to one's own ways promotes the kind of evaluation that is truly reason based. When we see in how many different ways people can organize their lives we will recognize, he seems to think, what is deep and what is shallow in our own ways, and will consider that "the only real community is one that embraces the entire world." In other words, the true basis for human association is not the arbitrary or the merely habitual; it is that which we can defend as good for human beings—and Diogenes believes that these evaluations know no national boundaries.

The confrontational tactics Diogenes chose unsettle and awaken. They do not contain good argument, however, and they can even get in the way of thought. Diogenes' disdain for more low-key and academic methods of scrutinizing customs, for example the study of literature and history, seems most unwise. It is hard to know whether to grant Diogenes the title "philosopher" at all, given his apparent preference for a kind of street theater over Socratic questioning. But his example, flawed as it was, had importance for the Greek philosophical tradition. Behind the theater lay an important idea: that the life

15

of reason must take a hard look at local conventions and assumptions, in the light of more general human needs and aspirations.

The Stoic philosophers, over the next few centuries, made Diogenes' insight respectable and culturally fruitful.[19] They developed the idea of crosscultural study and world citizenship much further in their own morally and philosophically rigorous way, making the concept of the "world citizen," *kosmou politēs*, a centerpiece of their educational program.[20] As Seneca[21] writes, summarizing older Greek Stoic views, education should make us aware that each of us is a member of "two communities: one that is truly great and truly common . . . in which we look neither to this corner nor to that, but measure the boundaries of our nation by the sun; the other, the one to which we have been assigned by birth." The accident of where one is born is just that, an accident; any human being might have been born in any nation. Recognizing this, we should not allow differences of nationality or class or ethnic membership or even gender to erect barriers between us and our fellow human beings. We should recognize humanity—and its fundamental ingredients, reason and moral capacity—wherever it occurs, and give that community of humanity our first allegiance.

This does not mean that the Stoics proposed the abolition of local and national forms of political organization and the creation of a world state. The Greek Stoics did propose an ideal city, and the Roman Stoics did put ideas of world citizenship into practice in some ways in the governance of the empire. But the Stoics' basic point is more radical still: that we should give our first allegiance to *no* mere form of government, no temporal power, but to the moral community made up by the humanity of all human beings. The idea of the world citizen is in this way the ancestor and source of Kant's idea of the "kingdom of ends," and has a similar function in inspiring and regulating a certain mode of political and personal conduct. One should always behave so as to treat with respect the dignity of reason and moral choice in every human being, no matter where that person was born, no matter what that person's rank or gender or status may be. It is less a political idea than a moral idea that constrains and regulates political life.

The meaning of the idea for political life is made especially clear in Cicero's work *On Duties* (*De Officiis*), written in 44 B.C. and based in part on the writings of the slightly earlier Greek Stoic thinker Panaetius. Cicero argues that the duty to treat humanity with respect requires us to treat aliens on our soil with honor and hospitality. It requires us never to engage in wars of aggression, and to view wars based on group hatred and wars of extermination as especially pernicious. It requires us to behave honorably in the conduct of war, shunning treachery even toward the enemy. In general, it requires us to place

---

19. The Stoic school had an extraordinarily long life and a very broad influence, extending from the late fourth century B.C. to the second century A.D. in both Athens and Rome [Nussbaum's note].

20. Diogenes uses the single word *kosmopolitēs*, but Marcus Aurelius prefers the separated form [Nussbaum's note].

21. Roman philosopher and dramatist (4? B.C.E.–65 C.E.).

justice above political expediency, and to understand that we form part of a universal community of humanity whose ends are the moral ends of justice and human well-being. Cicero's book has been among the most influential in the entire Western philosophical tradition. In particular, it influenced the just-war doctrine of Grotius[22] and the political thought of Immanuel Kant; their views about world understanding and the containment of global aggression are crucial for the formation of modern international law.

Stoics hold, then, that the good citizen is a "citizen of the world." They hold that thinking about humanity as it is realized in the whole world is valuable for self-knowledge: we see ourselves and our customs more clearly when we see our own ways in relation to those of other reasonable people. They insist, furthermore, that we really will be better able to solve our problems if we face them in this broader context, our imaginations unconstrained by narrow partisanship. No theme is deeper in Stoicism than the damage done by faction and local allegiances to the political life of a group. Stoic texts show repeatedly how easy it is for local or national identities and their associated hatreds to be manipulated by self-seeking individuals for their own gain—whereas reason is hard to fake, and its language is open to the critical scrutiny of all. Roman political life in Seneca's day was dominated by divisions of many kinds, from those of class and rank and ethnic origin to the division between parties at the public games and gladiatorial shows. Part of the self-education of the Stoic Roman emperor Marcus Aurelius,[23] as he tells the reader of his *Meditations,* was "not to be a Green or Blue partisan at the races, or a supporter of the lightly armed or heavily armed gladiators at the Circus."[24] Politics is sabotaged again and again by these partisan loyalties, and by the search for honor and fame that accompanies them. Stoics argue that a style of citizenship that recognizes the moral/rational community as fundamental promises a more reasonable style of political deliberation and problem-solving.

But Stoics do not recommend world citizenship only for reasons of expediency. They insist that the stance of the *kosmou politēs* is intrinsically valuable: for it recognizes in people what is especially fundamental about them, most worthy of reverence and acknowledgment, namely their aspirations to justice and goodness and their capacities for reasoning in this connection. This essential aspect may be less colorful than local tradition and local identity, but it is, the Stoics argue, both lasting and deep.

To be a citizen of the world, one does not, the Stoics stress, need to give up local affiliations, which can frequently be a source of great richness in life. They suggest instead that we think of ourselves as surrounded by a series of concentric circles.[25] The first one is drawn around the self; the next takes in

20

22. Hugo Grotius (1583–1645), Dutch jurist and statesman.

23. Stoic philosopher (121–180) and emperor from 161 to 180.

24. See Marcus Aurelius, *Meditations,* trans. G. M. A. Grobe (Indianapolis: Hackett, 1983) [Nussbaum's note].

25. The image is suggested in Cicero and is explicit in Hierocles, a Stoic of the first–second centuries A.D. [Nussbaum's note].

one's immediate family; then follows the extended family; then, in order, one's neighbors or local group, one's fellow city-dwellers, one's fellow countrymen—and we can easily add to this list groups formed on the basis of ethnic, religious, linguistic, historical, professional, and gender identities. Beyond all these circles is the largest one, that of humanity as a whole. Our task as citizens of the world, and as educators who prepare people to be citizens of the world, will be to "draw the circles somehow toward the center," making all human beings like our fellow city-dwellers. In other words, we need not give up our special affections and identifications, whether national or ethnic or religious; but we should work to make all human beings part of our community of dialogue and concern, showing respect for the human wherever it occurs, and allowing that respect to constrain our national or local politics.

This Stoic attitude, then, does not require that we disregard the importance of local loves and loyalties or their salience in education. Adam Smith made a serious error when he objected to Stoicism on those grounds, and modern critics of related Kantian and Enlightenment conceptions make a similar error when they charge them with neglect of group differences. The Stoic, in fact, must be conversant with local differences, since knowledge of these is inextricably linked to our ability to discern and respect the dignity of humanity in each person. Stoics recognize love for what is near as a fundamental human trait, and a highly rational way to comport oneself as a citizen. If each parent has a special love for his or her own children, society will do better than if all parents try to have an equal love for all children. Much the same is true for citizenship of town or city or nation: each of us should take our stand where life has placed us, and devote to our immediate surroundings a special affection and attention. Stoics, then, do not want us to behave as if differences between male and female, or between African and Roman, are morally insignificant. These differences can and do enjoin special obligations that all of us should execute, since we should all do our duties in the life we happen to have, rather than imagining that we are beings without location or memory.

Stoics vary in the degree of concession they make to these special obligations. Cicero, for example, takes a wise course when he urges the Roman citizen to favor the near and dear on many occasions, though always in ways that manifest respect for human dignity. These special local obligations have educational consequences: the world citizen will legitimately spend a disproportionate amount of time learning about the history and problems of her or his own part of the world. But at the same time we recognize that there is something more fundamental about us than the place where we happen to find ourselves, and that this more fundamental basis of citizenship is shared across all divisions.

This general point emerges clearly if we consider the relationship each of us has to a native language. We each have a language (in some cases more than one) in which we are at home, which we have usually known from infancy. We naturally feel a special affection for this language. It defines our possibilities of communication and expression. The works of literature that move us most deeply are those that exploit well the resources of that language. On the other hand, we should not suppose—and most of us do not suppose— that English is best just because it is our own, that works of literature written in English are superior to those written in other languages, and so forth. We know that it is more or less by chance that we are English speakers rather than speakers of Chinese or German or Bengali. We know that any infant might have learned any language, because there is a fundamental language-learning capacity that is shared by all humans. Nothing in our innate equipment disposes us to speak Hindi rather than Norwegian.

In school, then, it will be proper for us to spend a disproportionate amount of time mastering our native language and its literature. A human being who tried to learn all the world's languages would master none, and it seems reasonable for children to focus on one, or in some cases two, languages when they are small. On the other hand, it is also very important for students to understand what it is like to see the world through the perspective of another language, an experience that quickly shows that human complexity and rationality are not the monopoly of a single linguistic community. 25

This same point can be made about other aspects of culture that should figure in a higher education. In ethics, in historical knowledge, in knowledge of politics, in literary, artistic, and musical learning, we are all inclined to be parochial, taking our own habits for that which defines humanity. In these areas as in the case of language, it is reasonable to immerse oneself in a single tradition at an early age. But even then it is well to become acquainted with the facts of cultural variety, and this can be done very easily, for example through myths and stories that invite identification with people whose form of life is different from one's own. As education progresses, a more sophisticated grasp of human variety can show students that what is theirs is not better simply because it is familiar.

The education of the *kosmou politēs* is thus closely connected to Socratic inquiry and the goal of an examined life. For attaining membership in the world community entails a willingness to doubt the goodness of one's own way and to enter into the give-and-take of critical argument about ethical and political choices. By an increasingly refined exchange of both experience and argument, participants in such arguments should gradually take on the ability to distinguish, within their own traditions, what is parochial from what may be commended as a norm for others, what is arbitrary and unjustified from that which may be justified by reasoned argument.

Since any living tradition is already a plurality and contains within itself aspects of resistance, criticism, and contestation, the appeal to reason frequently does not require us to take a stand outside the culture from which we begin. The Stoics are correct to find in all human beings the world over a capacity for critical searching and a love of truth. "Any soul is deprived of truth against its will," says Marcus Aurelius, quoting Plato. In this sense, any and every human tradition is a tradition of reason, and the transition from these more ordinary and intracultural exercises to a more global exercise of critical argument need not be an abrupt transition. Indeed, in the world today it is clear that internal critique very frequently takes the form of invoking what is found to be fine and just in other traditions.

People from diverse backgrounds sometimes have difficulty recognizing one another as fellow citizens in the community of reason. This is so, frequently, because actions and motives require, and do not always receive, a patient effort of interpretation. The task of world citizenship requires the would-be world citizen to become a sensitive and empathic interpreter. Education at all ages should cultivate the capacity for such interpreting. This aspect of the Stoic idea is developed most fully by Marcus Aurelius, who dealt with many different cultures in his role as emperor; he presents, in his *Meditations,* a poignantly personal account of his own efforts to be a good world citizen. "Accustom yourself not to be inattentive to what another person says, and as far as possible enter into his mind," he writes (6.53); and again, "When things are being said, one should follow every word, when things are being done, every impulse; in the latter case, to see straightway to what object the impulse is directed, in the former, to watch what meaning is expressed" (7.4). Given that Marcus routinely associated with people from every part of the Roman Empire, this idea imposes a daunting task of learning and understanding, which he confronts by reading a great deal of history and literature, and by studying closely the individual characters of those around him in the manner of a literary narrator. "Generally," he concludes, "one must first learn many things before one can judge another's action with understanding" (11.18).

30   Above all, Marcus finds that he has to struggle not to allow his privileged station (an obstacle to real thought, as he continually points out) to sever him, in thought, from his fellow human beings. "See to it that you do not become Caesarized," he tells himself, "or dyed with that coloring" (6.30). A favorite exercise toward keeping such accidents of station in their proper place is to imagine that all human beings are limbs of a single body, cooperating for the sake of common purposes. Referring to the fact that it takes only the change of a single letter in Greek to convert the word "limb" (*melos*) into the word "(detached) part" (*meros*), he concludes: "if, changing the word, you call yourself merely a (detached) part instead of a limb, you do not yet love your fellow men from the heart, nor derive complete joy from doing good; you will do it merely as a duty, not as doing good to yourself" (7.13). The organic imagery underscores the Stoic ideal of cooperation.

Can anyone really think like a world citizen in a life so full of factionalism and political conflict? Marcus gives himself the following syllogism: "Wherever it is possible to live, it is also possible to live a virtuous life; it is possible to live in a palace; therefore it is also possible to live a virtuous life in a palace" (5.16). And, recognizing that he himself has sometimes failed in citizenship because of impatience and the desire for solitude: "Let no one, not even yourself, any longer hear you placing the blame on palace life" (8.9). In fact, his account of his own difficulties being a world citizen in the turmoil of Roman politics yields some important advice for anyone who attempts to reconcile this high ideal with the realities of political involvement:

Say to yourself in the morning: I shall meet people who are interfering, ungracious, insolent, full of guile, deceitful and antisocial; they have all become like that because they have no understanding of good and evil. But I who have contemplated the essential beauty of good and the essential ugliness of evil, who know that the nature of the wrongdoer is of one kin with mine—not indeed of the same blood or seed but sharing the same kind, the same portion of the divine—I cannot be harmed by any one of them, and no one can involve me in shame. I cannot feel anger against him who is of my kin, nor hate him. We were born to labor together, like the feet, the hands, the eyes, and the rows of upper and lower teeth. To work against one another is therefore contrary to nature, and to be angry against a man or turn one's back on him is to work against him. (2.1)

One who becomes involved in politics in our time might find this paragraph comforting. It shows a way in which the attitude of world citizenship gets to the root of one of the deepest political problems in all times and places, the problem of anger. Marcus is inclined to intense anger at his political adversaries. Sometimes the anger is personal, and sometimes it is directed against a group. His claim, however, is that such anger can be mitigated, or even removed, by the attitude of empathy that the ideal of the *kosmou politēs* promotes. If one comes to see one's adversaries as not impossibly alien and other, but as sharing certain general human goals and purposes, if one understands that they are not monsters but people who share with us certain general goals and purposes, this understanding will lead toward a diminution of anger and the beginning of rational exchange.

World citizenship does not, and should not, require that we suspend criticism toward other individuals and cultures. Marcus continues to refer to his enemies as "deceitful and antisocial," expressing strong criticism of their conduct. The world citizen may be very critical of unjust actions or policies, and of the character of people who promote them. But at the same time Marcus refuses to think of the opponents as simply alien, as members of a different and inferior species. He refuses to criticize until he respects and understands. He carefully chooses images that reflect his desire to see them as close to him and similarly human. This careful scrutiny of the imagery and speech one uses when speaking about people who are different is one of the Stoics' central recommendations for the undoing of political hatred.

Stoics write extensively on the nature of anger and hatred. It is their well-supported view that these destructive emotions are not innate, but learned by children from their society. In part, they hold, people directly absorb negative evaluations of individuals and groups from their culture, in part they absorb excessively high evaluations of their own honor and status. These high evaluations give rise to hostility when another person or group appears to threaten their honor or status. Anger and hatred are not unreasoning instincts; they have to do with the way we think and imagine, the images we use, the language we find it habitual to employ. They can therefore be opposed by the patient critical scrutiny of the imagery and speech we employ when we confront those our tradition has depicted as unequal.

35   It is fashionable by now to be very skeptical of "political correctness," by which the critic usually means a careful attention to the speech we use in talking about minorities, or foreigners, or women. Such scrutiny might in some forms pose dangers to free speech, and of course these freedoms should be carefully defended. But the scrutiny of speech and imagery need not be inspired by totalitarian motives, and it need not lead to the creation of an anti-democratic "thought police." The Stoic demand for such scrutiny is based on the plausible view that hatred of individuals and groups is personally and politically pernicious, that it ought to be resisted by educators, and that the inner world of thought and speech is the place where, ultimately, hatred must be resisted. These ideas about the scrutiny of the inner world are familiar to Christians also, and the biblical injunction against sinning in one's heart has close historical links to Stoicism. All parents know that it is possible to shape a child's attitudes toward other races and nationalities by the selection of stories one tells and by the way one speaks about other people in the home. There are few parents who do not seek to influence their children's views in these ways. Stoics propose, however, that the process of coming to recognize the humanity of all people should be a lifelong process, encompassing all levels of education—especially since, in a culture suffused with group hatred, one cannot rely on parents to perform this task.

        What this means in higher education is that an attitude of mutual respect should be nourished both in the classroom itself and in its reading material. Although in America we should have no sympathy with the outright censoring of reading material, we also make many selections as educators, both in assigning material and in presenting it for our students. Few of us, for example, would present anti-Semitic propaganda in a university classroom in a way that conveyed sympathy with the point of view expressed. The Stoic proposal is that we should seek out curricula that foster respect and mutual solidarity and correct the ignorance that is often an essential prop of hatred. This effort is perfectly compatible with maintaining freedom of speech and the openness of a genuinely critical and deliberative culture.

        In our own time, few countries have been more rigidly divided, more corroded by group hatred, than South Africa. In spelling out its goals for society in its draft for the new Constitution, the African National Congress (ANC) recognized the need to address hatred through education, and specified the goal of education as the overcoming of these differences:

> Education shall be directed towards the development of the human personality and a sense of personal dignity, and shall aim at strengthening respect for human rights and fundamental freedoms and promoting understanding, tolerance and friendship amongst South Africans and between nations.[26]

26. This is material from a draft written by the ANC for the new constitution; it was presented by Albie Sachs to a meeting on human rights at Harvard University in October 1993 [Nussbaum's note].

Some of this language would have been new to Marcus Aurelius—and it would have been a good thing for Roman Stoics to have reflected more about the connections between the human dignity they prized and the political rights they frequently neglected. But the language of dignity, humanity, freedom, understanding, tolerance, and friendship would not have been strange to Marcus. (He speaks of his goal as "the idea of a Commonwealth with the same laws for all, governed on the basis of equality and free speech;" this goal is to be pursued with "beneficence, eager generosity, and optimism.") The ANC draft, like the Stoic norm of world citizenship, insists that understanding of various nations and groups is a goal for every citizen, not only for those who wish to affirm a minority identity. It insists that the goal of education should not be separation of one group from another, but respect, tolerance, and friendship—both within a nation and among nations. It insists that this goal should be fostered in a way that respects the dignity of humanity in each person and citizen.

Above all, education for world citizenship requires transcending the inclination of both students and educators to define themselves primarily in terms of local group loyalties and identities. World citizens will therefore not argue for the inclusion of cross-cultural study in a curriculum primarily on the grounds that it is a way in which members of minority groups can affirm such an identity. This approach, common though it is, is divisive and subversive of the aims of world community. This problem vexes many curricular debates. Frequently, groups who press for the recognition of their group think of their struggle as connected with goals of human respect and social justice. And yet their way of focusing their demands, because it neglects commonalities and portrays people as above all members of identity groups, tends to subvert the demand for equal respect and love, and even the demand for attention to diversity itself. As David Glidden, philosopher at the University of California at Riverside, expressed the point, "the ability to admire and love the diversity of human beings gets lost" when one bases the demand for inclusion on notions of local group identity. Why should one love or attend to a Hispanic fellow citizen, on this view, if one is oneself most fundamentally an Irish-American? Why should one care about India, if one defines oneself as above all an American? Only a human identity that transcends these divisions shows us why we should look at one another with respect across them.

QUESTIONS

1. What does Nussbaum mean by "world citizen" and "world citizenship"? How does she use the concepts of (or quotations from) other philosophers to work toward a definition? Where does she present her own definition?

2. Why does Diogenes the Cynic play such an important role in Nussbaum's exposition? What concepts or examples from his life contribute to her understanding of a "world citizen"?

3. Write an essay in which you answer the question posed in paragraph 31: "Can any-one really think like a world citizen in a life so full of factionalism and political con-flict?" Use examples not only from Nussbaum's essay but also from your own experience.

VIRGINIA WOOLF   *The Death of the Moth*

OTHS THAT FLY by day are not properly to be called moths; they do not excite that pleasant sense of dark autumn nights and ivy-blossom which the common-est yellow-underwing asleep in the shadow of the curtain never fails to rouse in us. They are hybrid creatures, neither gay like butterflies nor sombre like their own species. Nevertheless the present specimen, with his narrow hay-colored wings, fringed with a tassel of the same color, seemed to be con-tent with life. It was a pleasant morning, mid-September, mild, benignant, yet with a keener breath than that of the summer months. The plough was already scoring the field opposite the window, and where the share had been, the earth was pressed flat and gleamed with moisture. Such vigor came rolling in from the fields and the down beyond that it was difficult to keep the eyes strictly turned upon the book. The rooks too were keeping one of their annual festivi-ties; soaring round the tree tops until it looked as if a vast net with thousands of black knots in it had been cast up into the air; which, after a few moments sank slowly down upon the trees until every twig seemed to have a knot at the end of it. Then, suddenly, the net would be thrown into the air again in a wider circle this time, with the utmost clamor and vociferation, as though to be thrown into the air and settle slowly down upon the tree tops were a tremen-dously exciting experience.

The same energy which inspired the rooks, the ploughmen, the horses, and even, it seemed, the lean bare-backed downs, sent the moth fluttering from side to side of his square of the window-pane. One could not help watch-ing him. One was, indeed, conscious of a queer feeling of pity for him. The possibilities of pleasure seemed that morning so enormous and so various that to have only a moth's part in life, and a day moth's at that, appeared a hard fate, and his zest in enjoying his meagre opportunities to the full, pathetic. He flew vigorously to one corner of his compartment, and, after waiting there a second, flew across to the other. What remained for him but to fly to a third corner and then to a fourth? That was all he could do, in spite of the size of the downs, the width of the sky, the far-off smoke of houses, and the romantic voice, now and then, of a steamer out at sea. What he could do he did. Watch-

The title essay of Woolf's collection The Death of the Moth, and Other Essays *(1942), compiled after her death in 1941.*

ing him, it seemed as if a fiber, very thin but pure, of the enormous energy of the world had been thrust into his frail and diminutive body. As often as he crossed the pane, I could fancy that a thread of vital light became visible. He was little or nothing but life.

Yet, because he was so small, and so simple a form of the energy that was rolling in at the open window and driving its way through so many narrow and intricate corridors in my own brain and in those of other human beings, there was something marvellous as well as pathetic about him. It was as if someone had taken a tiny bead of pure life and decking it as lightly as possible with down and feathers, had set it dancing and zig-zagging to show us the true nature of life. Thus displayed one could not get over the strangeness of it. One is apt to forget all about life, seeing it humped and bossed and garnished and cumbered so that it has to move with the greatest circumspection and dignity. Again, the thought of all that life might have been had he been born in any other shape caused one to view his simple activities with a kind of pity.

After a time, tired by his dancing apparently, he settled on the window ledge in the sun, and, the queer spectacle being at an end, I forgot about him. Then, looking up, my eye was caught by him. He was trying to resume his dancing, but seemed either so stiff or so awkward that he could only flutter to the bottom of the window-pane; and when he tried to fly across it he failed. Being intent on other matters I watched these futile attempts for a time without thinking, un-consciously waiting for him to resume his flight, as one waits for a machine, that has stopped momentarily, to start again without considering the reason of its failure. After perhaps a seventh attempt he slipped from the wooden ledge and fell, fluttering his wings, on to his back on the window sill. The helpless-ness of his attitude roused me. It flashed upon me that he was in difficulties; he could no longer raise himself; his legs struggled vainly. But, as I stretched out a pencil, meaning to help him to right himself, it came over me that the failure and awkwardness were the approach of death. I laid the pencil down again.

The legs agitated themselves once more. I looked as if for the enemy against which he struggled. I looked out of doors. What had happened there? Presumably it was midday, and work in the fields had stopped. Stillness and quiet had replaced the previous animation. The birds had taken themselves off to feed in the brooks. The horses stood still. Yet the power was there all the same, massed outside indifferent, impersonal, not attending to anything in particular. Somehow it was opposed to the little hay-colored moth. It was use-less to try to do anything. One could only watch the extraordinary efforts made by those tiny legs against an oncoming doom which could, had it chosen, have submerged an entire city, not merely a city, but masses of human beings; noth-ing, I knew, had any chance against death. Nevertheless after a pause of ex-haustion the legs fluttered again. It was superb this last protest, and so frantic that he succeeded at last in righting himself. One's sympathies, of course, were all on the side of life. Also, when there was nobody to care or to know, this gigantic effort on the part of an insignificant little moth, against a power of such magnitude, to retain what no one else valued or desired to keep, moved one strangely. Again, somehow, one saw life, a pure bead. I lifted the

5

pencil again, useless though I knew it to be. But even as I did so, the unmistakable tokens of death showed themselves. The body relaxed, and instantly grew stiff. The struggle was over. The insignificant little creature now knew death. As I looked at the dead moth, this minute wayside triumph of so great a force over so mean an antagonist filled me with wonder. Just as life had been strange a few minutes before, so death was now as strange. The moth having righted himself now lay most decently and uncomplainingly composed. O yes, he seemed to say, death is stronger than I am.

QUESTIONS

1. Trace the sequence in which Woolf comes to identify with the moth. How does she make her identification explicit? How is it implicit in the language she uses to describe the moth?

2. Choose one of the descriptions of a small living creature or creatures in Annie Dillard's "Sight into Insight" below and compare it with Woolf's description of the moth. Does a similar identification take place in Dillard's essay? If so, how; if not, why not?

3. Henry David Thoreau, in "The Battle of the Ants" (p. 776), also humanizes small living creatures. How do his strategies differ from Woolf's?

4. Write two descriptions of the same living creature, one using Woolf's strategies, the other using Thoreau's. Or, alternatively, write an essay in which you analyze the differences between them.

ANNIE DILLARD   *Sight into Insight*

WHEN I WAS SIX or seven years old, growing up in Pittsburgh, I used to take a penny of my own and hide it for someone else to find. It was a curious compulsion; sadly, I've never been seized by it since. For some reason I always "hid" the penny along the same stretch of sidewalk up the street. I'd cradle it at the roots of a maple, say, or in a hole left by a chipped-off piece of sidewalk. Then I'd take a piece of chalk and, starting at either end of the block, draw huge arrows leading up to the penny from both directions. After I learned to write I labeled the arrows "SURPRISE AHEAD" or "MONEY THIS WAY." I was greatly excited, during all this arrowdrawing, at the thought of the first lucky passerby who would receive in this way, regardless of merit, a free gift from the universe. But

Originally published in Harper's Magazine *(February 1974), an American monthly that explores "the issues and ideas in politics, science, and the arts that drive our national conversation"; included in Dillard's Pulitzer Prize–winning book,* Pilgrim at Tinker Creek *(1974).*

I never lurked about. I'd go straight home and not give the matter another thought, until, some months later, I would be gripped by the impulse to hide another penny.

There are lots of things to see, unwrapped gifts and free surprises. The world is fairly studded and strewn with pennies cast broadside from a generous hand. But—and this is the point—who gets excited by a mere penny? If you follow one arrow, if you crouch motionless on a bank to watch a tremulous ripple thrill on the water, and are rewarded by the sight of a muskrat kit paddling from its den, will you count that sight a chip of copper only, and go your rueful way? It is very dire poverty indeed for a man to be so malnourished and fatigued that he won't stoop to pick up a penny. But if you cultivate a healthy poverty and simplicity, so that finding a penny will make your day, then, since the world is in fact planted in pennies, you have with your poverty bought a lifetime of days. What you see is what you get.

Unfortunately, nature is very much a now-you-see-it, now-you-don't affair. A fish flashes, then dissolves in the water before my eyes like so much salt. Deer apparently ascend bodily into heaven; the brightest oriole fades into leaves. These disappearances stun me into stillness and concentration; they say of nature that it conceals with a grand nonchalance, and they say of vision that it is a deliberate gift, the revelation of a dancer who for my eyes only flings away her seven veils.

For nature does reveal as well as conceal: now-you-don't-see-it, now-you-do. For a week this September migrating red-winged blackbirds were feeding heavily down by Tinker Creek at the back of the house. One day I went out to investigate the racket; I walked up to a tree, an Osage orange, and a hundred birds flew away. They simply materialized out of the tree. I saw a tree, then a whisk of color, then a tree again. I walked closer and another hundred blackbirds took flight. Not a branch, not a twig budged: the birds were apparently weightless as well as invisible. Or, it was as if the leaves of the Osage orange had been freed from a spell in the form of redwinged blackbirds; they flew from the tree, caught my eye in the sky, and vanished. When I looked again at the tree, the leaves had reassembled as if nothing had happened. Finally I walked directly to the trunk of the tree and a final hundred, the real diehards, appeared, spread, and vanished. How could so many hide in the tree without my seeing them? The Osage orange, unruffled, looked just as it had looked from the house, when three hundred red-winged blackbirds cried from its crown. I looked upstream where they flew, and they were gone. Searching, I couldn't spot one. I wandered upstream to force them to play their hand, but they'd crossed the creek and scattered. One show to a customer. These appearances catch at my throat; they are the free gifts, the bright coppers at the roots of trees.

It's all a matter of keeping my eyes open. Nature is like one of those line drawings that are puzzles for children: Can you find hidden in the tree a duck, a house, a boy, a bucket, a giraffe, and a boot? Specialists can find the most incredibly hidden things. A book I read when I was young recommended an easy

5

way to find caterpillars: you simply find some fresh caterpillar droppings, look up, and there's your caterpillar. More recently an author advised me to set my mind at ease about those piles of cut stems on the ground in grassy fields. Field mice make them; they cut the grass down by degrees to reach the seeds at the head. It seems that when the grass is tightly packed, as in a field of ripe grain, the blade won't topple at a single cut through the stem; instead, the cut stem simply drops vertically, held in the crush of grain. The mouse severs the bottom again and again, the stem keeps dropping an inch at a time, and finally the head is low enough for the mouse to reach the seeds. Meanwhile the mouse is positively littering the field with its little piles of cut stems into which, presumably, the author is constantly stumbling.

If I can't see these minutiae, I still try to keep my eyes open. I'm always on the lookout for ant lion traps in sandy soil, monarch pupae near milkweed, skipper larvae in locust leaves. These things are utterly common, and I've not seen one. I bang on hollow trees near water, but so far no flying squirrels have appeared. In flat country I watch every sunset in hopes of seeing the green ray. The green ray is a seldom-seen streak of light that rises from the sun like a spurting fountain at the moment of sunset; it throbs into the sky for two seconds and disappears. One more reason to keep my eyes open. A photography professor at the University of Florida just happened to see a bird die in midflight; it jerked, died, dropped, and smashed on the ground.

I squint at the wind because I read Stewart Edward White: "I have always maintained that if you looked closely enough you could *see* the wind—the dim, hardly-made-out, fine débris fleeing high in the air." White was an excellent observer, and devoted an entire chapter of *The Mountains* to the subject of seeing deer: "As soon as you can forget the naturally obvious and construct an artificial obvious, then you too will see deer."

But the artificial obvious is hard to see. My eyes account for less than 1 percent of the weight of my head; I'm bony and dense; I see what I expect. I once spent a full three minutes looking at a bullfrog that was so unexpectedly large I couldn't see it even though a dozen enthusiastic campers were shouting directions. Finally I asked, "What color am I looking for?" and a fellow said, "Green." When at last I picked out the frog, I saw what painters are up against: the thing wasn't green at all, but the color of wet hickory bark.

The lover can see, and the knowledgeable. I visited an aunt and uncle at a quarter-horse ranch in Cody, Wyoming. I couldn't do much of anything useful, but I could, I thought, draw. So, as we all sat around the kitchen table after supper, I produced a sheet of paper and drew a horse. "That's one lame horse," my aunt volunteered. The rest of the family joined in: "Only place to saddle that one is his neck"; "Looks like we better shoot the poor thing, on account of those terrible growths." Meekly, I slid the pencil and paper down the table. Everyone in that family, including my three young cousins, could draw a horse. Beautifully. When the paper came back it looked as though five shining, real quarter horses had been corraled by mistake with a papier-mâché moose; the real horses seemed to gaze at the monster with a steady, puzzled air. I stay away from horses now, but I can do a creditable goldfish. The point is that I just don't know what the lover knows; I just can't see the artificial obvious that those in the know construct. The herpetologist asks the native, "Are there snakes in that ravine?" "Nosir." And the herpetologist comes home with, yessir, three bags full. Are there butterflies on that mountain? Are the bluets in bloom, are there arrowheads here, or fossil shells in the shale?

Peeping through my keyhole I see within the range of only about 30 per-   10
cent of the light that comes from the sun; the rest is infrared and some little ultraviolet, perfectly apparent to many animals, but invisible to me. A night-mare network of ganglia, charged and firing without my knowledge, cuts and splices what I do see, editing it for my brain. Donald E. Carr points out that the sense impressions of one-celled animals are *not* edited for the brain: "This is philosophically interesting in a rather mournful way, since it means that only the simplest animals perceive the universe as it is."

A fog that won't burn away drifts and flows across my field of vision. When you see fog move against a backdrop of deep pines, you don't see the fog itself, but streaks of clearness floating across the air in dark shreds. So I see only tatters of clearness through a pervading obscurity. I can't distinguish the fog from the overcast sky; I can't be sure if the light is direct or reflected. Everywhere darkness and the presence of the unseen appalls. We estimate now that only one atom dances alone in every cubic meter of intergalactic space. I blink and squint. What planet or power yanks Halley's Comet out of orbit? We haven't seen it yet; it's a question of distance, density, and the pallor of reflected light. We rock, cradled in the swaddling band of darkness. Even the simple darkness of night whispers suggestions to the mind. This summer, in August, I stayed at the creek too late.

Where Tinker Creek flows under the sycamore log bridge to the tear-shaped island, it is slow and shallow, fringed thinly in cattail marsh. At this spot an astonishing bloom of life supports vast breeding populations of insects, fish, reptiles, birds, and mammals. On windless summer evenings I stalk along the creek bank or straddle the sycamore log in absolute stillness, watching for muskrats. The night I stayed too late I was hunched on the log staring spell-bound at spreading, reflected stains of lilac on the water. A cloud in the sky suddenly lighted as if turned on by a switch; its reflection just as suddenly ma-terialized on the water upstream, flat and floating, so that I couldn't see the creek bottom, or life in the water under the cloud. Downstream, away from the cloud on the water, water turtles smooth as beans were gliding down with the current in a series of easy, weightless push-offs, as men bound on the moon. I didn't know whether to trace the progress of one turtle I was sure of, risking sticking my face in one of the bridge's spider webs made invisible by the gathering dark, or take a chance on seeing the carp, or scan the mudbank in hope of seeing a muskrat, or follow the last of the swallows who caught at my heart and trailed it after them like streamers as they appeared from directly below, under the log, flying upstream with their tails forked, so fast.

But shadows spread and deepened and stayed. After thousands of years we're still strangers to darkness, fearful aliens in an enemy camp with our arms crossed over our chests. I stirred. A land turtle on the bank, startled, hissed the air from its lungs and withdrew to its shell. An uneasy pink here, an unfathomable blue there, gave great suggestion of lurking beings. Things were going on. I couldn't see whether that rustle I heard was a distant rattlesnake, slit-eyed, or a nearby sparrow kicking in the dry flood debris slung at the foot of a willow. Tremendous action roiled the water everywhere I looked, big action, inexplicable. A tremor welled up beside a gaping muskrat burrow in the bank and I caught my breath, but no muskrat appeared. The ripples continued to fan upstream with a steady, powerful thrust. Night was knitting an eyeless mask over my face, and I still sat transfixed. A distant airplane, a delta wing out of nightmare, made a gliding shadow on the creek's bottom that looked like a stingray cruising upstream. At once a black fin slit the pink cloud on the water, shearing it in two. The two halves merged together and seemed to dissolve before my eyes. Darkness pooled in the cleft of the creek and rose, as water collects in a well. Untamed, dreaming lights flickered over the sky. I saw hints of hulking underwater shadows, two pale splashes out of the water, and round ripples rolling close together from a blackened center.

At last I stared upstream where only the deepest violet remained of the cloud, a cloud so high its underbelly still glowed, its feeble color reflected from a hidden sky lighted in turn by a sun halfway to China. And out of that violet, a sudden enormous black body arced over the water. Head and tail, if there was a head and tail, were both submerged in cloud. I saw only one ebony fling, a headlong dive to darkness; then the waters closed, and the lights went out.

15   I walked home in a shivering daze, up hill and down. Later I lay open-mouthed in bed, my arms flung wide at my sides to steady the whirling darkness. At this latitude I'm spinning 836 miles an hour round the earth's axis; I feel my sweeping fall as a breakneck arc like the dive of dolphins, and the hollow rushing of wind raises the hairs on my neck and the side of my face. In orbit around the sun I'm moving 64,800 miles an hour. The solar system as a whole, like a merry-go-round unhinged, spins, bobs, and blinks at the speed of 43,200 miles an hour along a course set east of Hercules. Someone has piped, and we are dancing a tarantella until the sweat pours. I open my eyes and I see dark, muscled forms curl out of water, with flapping gills and flattened eyes. I close my eyes and I see stars, deep stars giving way to deeper stars, deeper stars bowing to deepest stars at the crown of an infinite cone.

"Still," wrote Van Gogh[1] in a letter, "a great deal of light falls on everything." If we are blinded by darkness, we are also blinded by light. Sometimes here in Virginia at sunset low clouds on the southern or northern horizon are completely invisible in the lighted sky. I only know one is there because I can see its reflection in still water. The first time I discovered this mystery I looked from cloud to no-cloud in bewilderment, checking my bearings over and over, thinking maybe the ark of the covenant[2] was just passing by south of Dead

1. Vincent van Gogh (1853–1890), Dutch Postimpressionist painter.
2. Repository for the stone tablets of the Ten Commandments, carried by the ancient Israelites during their desert wanderings.

Man Mountain. Only much later did I learn the explanation: polarized light from the sky is very much weakened by reflection, but the light in clouds isn't polarized. So invisible clouds pass among visible clouds, till all slide over the mountains; so a greater light extinguishes a lesser as though it didn't exist.

In the great meteor shower of August, the Perseid, I wail all day for the shooting stars I miss. They're out there showering down committing hara-kiri in a flame of fatal attraction, and hissing perhaps at last into the ocean. But at dawn what looks like a blue dome clamps down over me like a lid on a pot. The stars and planets could smash and I'd never know. Only a piece of ashen moon occasionally climbs up or down the inside of the dome, and our local star without surcease explodes on our heads. We have really only that one light, one source for all power, and yet we must turn away from it by universal decree. Nobody here on the planet seems aware of this strange, powerful taboo, that we all walk about carefully averting our faces, this way and that, lest our eyes be blasted forever.

Darkness appalls and light dazzles; the scrap of visible light that doesn't hurt my eyes hurts my brain. What I see sets me swaying. Size and distance and the sudden swelling of meanings confuse me, bowl me over. I straddle the sycamore log bridge over Tinker Creek in the summer. I look at the lighted creek bottom: snail tracks tunnel the mud in quavering curves. A crayfish jerks, but by the time I absorb what has happened, he's gone in a billowing smoke screen of silt. I look at the water; minnows and shiners. If I'm thinking minnows, a carp will fill my brain till I scream. I look at the water's surface: skaters, bubbles, and leaves sliding down. Suddenly, my own face, reflected, startles me witless. Those snails have been tracking my face! Finally, with a shuddering wrench of the will, I see clouds, cirrus clouds. I'm dizzy, I fall in.

This looking business is risky. Once I stood on a humped rock on nearby Purgatory Mountain, watching through binoculars the great autumn hawk migration below, until I discovered that I was in danger of joining the hawks on a vertical migration of my own. I was used to binoculars, but not, apparently, to balancing on humped rocks while looking through them. I reeled. Everything advanced and receded by turns; the world was full of unexplained foreshortenings and depths. A distant huge object, a hawk the size of an elephant, turned out to be the browned bough of a nearby loblolly pine. I followed a sharp-shinned hawk against a featureless sky, rotating my head unawares as it flew, and when I lowered the glass a glimpse of my own looming shoulder sent me staggering. What prevents the men at Palomar[3] from falling, voiceless and blinded, from their tiny, vaulted chairs?

I reel in confusion: I don't understand what I see. With the naked eye I   20
can see two million light-years to the Andromeda galaxy. Often I slop some creek water in a jar, and when I get home I dump it in a white china bowl. After the silt settles I return and see tracings of minute snails on the bottom, a planarian or two winding round the rim of water, roundworms shimmying, frantically, and finally, when my eyes have adjusted to these dimensions, amoe-

3. An astronomical observatory in California.

bae. At first the amoebae look like *muscae volitantes,* those curled moving spots you seem to see in your eyes when you stare at a distant wall. Then I see the amoebae as drops of water congealed, bluish, translucent, like chips of sky in the bowl. At length I choose one individual and give myself over to its idea of an evening. I see it dribble a grainy foot before it on its wet, unfathomable way. Do its unedited sense impressions include the fierce focus of my eyes? Shall I take it outside and show it Andromeda, and blow its little endoplasm? I stir the water with a finger, in case it's running out of oxygen. Maybe I should get a tropical aquarium with motorized bubblers and lights, and keep this one for a pet. Yes, it would tell its fissioned descendants, the universe is two feet by five, and if you listen closely you can hear the buzzing music of the spheres.

Oh, it's mysterious, lamplit evenings here in the galaxy, one after the other. It's one of those nights when I wander from window to window, looking for a sign. But I can't see. Terror and a beauty insoluble are a riband of blue woven into the fringe of garments of things both great and small. No culture explains, no bivouac offers real haven or rest. But it could be that we are not seeing something. Galileo[4] thought comets were an optical illusion. This is fertile ground: since we are certain that they're not, we can look at what our scientists have been saying with fresh hope. What if there are *really* gleaming, castellated cities hung up-side-down over the desert sand? What limpid lakes and cool date palms have our caravans always passed untried? Until, one by one, by the blindest of leaps, we light on the road to these places, we must stumble in darkness and hunger. I turn from the window. I'm blind as a bat, sensing only from every direction the echo of my own thin cries.

I chanced on a wonderful book called *Space and Sight,* by Marius Von Senden. When Western surgeons discovered how to perform safe cataract operations, they ranged across Europe and America operating on dozens of men and women of all ages who had been blinded by cataracts since birth. Von Senden collected accounts of such cases; the histories are fascinating. Many doctors had tested their patients' sense perceptions and ideas of space both before and after the operations. The vast majority of patients, of both sexes and all ages, had, in Von Senden's opinion, no idea of space whatsoever. Form, distance, and size were so many meaningless syllables. A patient "had no idea of depth, confusing it with roundness." Before the operation a doctor would give a blind patient a cube and a sphere; the patient would tongue it or feel it with his hands, and name it correctly. After the operation the doctor would show the same objects to the patient without letting him touch them; now he had no clue whatsoever to what he was seeing. One patient called lemonade "square" because it pricked on his tongue as a square shape pricked on the touch of his hands. Of another post-operative patient the doctor writes, "I have found in her no notion of size, for example, not even within the narrow limits which she might have encompassed with the aid of touch. Thus when I asked her to show me how big her mother was, she did not stretch out her hands, but set her two index fingers a few inches apart."

4. Italian astronomer (1564–1642).

For the newly sighted, vision is pure sensation unencumbered by meaning. When a newly sighted girl saw photographs and paintings, she asked, " 'Why do they put those dark marks all over them?' 'Those aren't dark marks,' her mother explained, 'those are shadows. That is one of the ways the eye knows that things have shape. If it were not for shadows, many things would look flat.' 'Well, that's how things do look,' Joan answered. 'Everything looks flat with dark patches.' "

In general the newly sighted see the world as a dazzle of "colorpatches." They are pleased by the sensation of color, and learn quickly to name the colors, but the rest of seeing is tormentingly difficult. Soon after his operation a patient "generally bumps into one of these color-patches and observes them to be substantial, since they resist him as tactual objects do. In walking about it also strikes him—or can if he pays attention—that he is continually passing in between the colors he sees, that he can go past a visual object, that a part of it then steadily disappears from view; and that in spite of this, however he twists and turns—whether entering the room from the door, for example, or returning back to it—he always has a visual space in front of him. Thus he gradually comes to realize that there is also a space behind him, which he does not see."

The mental effort involved in these reasonings proves overwhelming for   25
many patients. It oppresses them to realize that they have been visible to people all along, perhaps unattractively so, without their knowledge or consent. A disheartening number of them refuse to use their new vision, continuing to go over objects with their tongues, and lapsing into apathy and despair.

On the other hand, many newly sighted people speak well of the world, and teach us how dull our own vision is. To one patient, a human hand, unrecognized, is "something bright and then holes." Shown a bunch of grapes, a boy calls out, "It is dark, blue and shiny. . . . It isn't smooth, it has bumps and hollows." A little girl visits a garden. "She is greatly astonished, and can scarcely be persuaded to answer, stands speechless in front of the tree, which she only names on taking hold of it, and then as 'the tree with the lights in it.' " Another patient, a twenty-two-year-old girl, was dazzled by the world's brightness and kept her eyes shut for two weeks. When at the end of that time she opened her eyes again, she did not recognize any objects, but "the more she now directed her gaze upon everything about her, the more it could be seen how an expression of gratification and astonishment overspread her features; she repeatedly exclaimed: 'Oh God! How beautiful!' "

I saw color-patches for weeks after I read this wonderful book. It was summer; the peaches were ripe in the valley orchards. When I woke in the morning, color-patches wrapped round my eyes, intricately, leaving not one unfilled spot. All day long I walked among shifting color-patches that parted before me like the Red Sea and closed again in silence,[5] transfigured, wherever I looked back. Some patches swelled and loomed, while others vanished

5. According to the Bible, the Red Sea parted for the Israelites and closed over the Egyptians pursuing them (Exodus 15).

utterly, and dark marks flitted at random over the whole dazzling sweep. But I couldn't sustain the illusion of flatness. I've been around for too long. Form is condemned to an eternal danse macabre with meaning: I couldn't unpeach the peaches. Nor can I remember ever having seen without understanding; the color-patches of infancy are lost. My brain then must have been smooth as any balloon. I'm told I reached for the moon; many babies do. But the color-patches of infancy swelled as meaning filled them; they arrayed themselves in solemn ranks down distance which unrolled and stretched before me like a plain. The moon rocketed away. I live now in a world of shadows that shape and distance color, a world where space makes a kind of terrible sense. What Gnosticism[6] is this, and what physics? The fluttering patch I saw in my nursery window—silver and green and shape-shifting blue—is gone; a row of Lombardy poplars takes its place, mute, across the distant lawn. That humming oblong creature pale as light that stole along the walls of my room at night, stretching exhilaratingly around the corners, is gone, too, gone the night I ate of the bittersweet fruit, put two and two together and puckered forever my brain. Martin Buber[7] tells this tale: "Rabbi Mendel once boasted to his teacher Rabbi Elimelekh that evenings he saw the angel who rolls away the light before the darkness, and mornings the angel who rolls away the darkness before the light. 'Yes,' said Rabbi Elimelekh, 'in my youth I saw that too. Later on you don't see these things anymore.' "

Why didn't someone hand those newly sighted people paints and brushes from the start, when they still didn't know what anything was? Then maybe we all could see color-patches too, the world unraveled from reason, Eden before Adam gave names. The scales would drop from my eyes; I'd see trees like men walking; I'd run down the road against all orders, hallooing and leaping.

Seeing is of course very much a matter of verbalization. Unless I call my attention to what passes before my eyes, I simply won't see it. If Tinker Mountain erupted, I'd be likely to notice. But if I want to notice the lesser cataclysms of valley life, I have to maintain in my head a running description of the present. It's not that I'm observant; it's just that I talk too much. Otherwise, especially in a strange place, I'll never know what's happening. Like a blind man at the ball game, I need a radio.

30   When I see this way I analyze and pry. I hurl over logs and roll away stones; I study the bank a square foot at a time, probing and tilting my head. Some days when a mist covers the mountains, when the muskrats won't show and the microscope's mirror shatters, I want to climb up the blank blue dome as a man would storm the inside of a circus tent, wildly, dangling, and with a steel knife claw a rent in the top, peep, and, if I must, fall.

But there is another kind of seeing that involves a letting go. When I see this way I sway transfixed and emptied. The difference between the two ways of seeing is the difference between walking with and without a camera. When

6. Promise of secret knowledge of the divine.
7. Jewish religious philosopher (1878–1965).

I walk with a camera I walk from shot to shot, reading the light on a calibrated meter. When I walk without a camera, my own shutter opens, and the moment's light prints on my own silver gut. When I see this second way I am above all an unscrupulous observer.

It was sunny one evening last summer at Tinker Creek; the sun was low in the sky, upstream. I was sitting on the sycamore log bridge with the sunset at my back, watching the shiners the size of minnows who were feeding over the muddy sand in skittery schools. Again and again, one fish, then another, turned for a split second across the current and flash! the sun shot out from its silver side. I couldn't watch for it. It was always just happening somewhere else, and it drew my vision just as it disappeared: flash! like a sudden dazzle of the thinnest blade, a sparking over a dun and olive ground at chance intervals from every direction. Then I noticed white specks, some sort of pale petals, small, floating from under my feet on the creek's surface, very slow and steady. So I blurred my eyes and gazed toward the brim of my hat and saw a new world. I saw the pale white circles roll up, roll up, like the world's turning, mute and perfect, and I saw the linear flashes, gleaming silver, like stars being born at random down a rolling scroll of time. Something broke and something opened. I filled up like a new wineskin. I breathed an air like light; I saw a light like water. I was the lip of a fountain the creek filled forever; I was ether, the leaf in the zephyr; I was flesh-flake, feather, bone.

When I see this way I see truly. As Thoreau[8] says, I return to my senses. I am the man who watches the baseball game in silence in an empty stadium. I see the game purely; I'm abstracted and dazed. When it's all over and the white-suited players lope off the green field to their shadowed dugouts, I leap to my feet, I cheer and cheer.

But I can't go out and try to see this way. I'll fail, I'll go mad. All I can do is try to gag the commentator, to hush the noise of useless interior babble that keeps me from seeing just as surely as a newspaper dangled before my eyes. The effort is really a discipline requiring a lifetime of dedicated struggle; it marks the literature of saints and monks of every order east and west, under every rule and no rule, discalced[9] and shod. The world's spiritual geniuses seem to discover universally that the mind's muddy river, this ceaseless flow of trivia and trash, cannot be dammed, and that trying to dam it is a waste of effort that might lead to madness. Instead you must allow the muddy river to flow unheeded in the dim channels of consciousness; you raise your sights; you look along it, mildly, acknowledging its presence without interest and gazing beyond it into the realm of the real where subjects and objects act and rest purely, without utterance. "Launch into the deep," says Jacques Ellul,[10] "and you shall see."

8. Henry David Thoreau (1817–1862), American writer; see "Where I Lived, and What I Lived For" (p. 1164).
9. Shoeless, as the order of the Discalced Carmelites.
10. French Protestant theologian and critic of technology (1912–1994).

35   The secret of seeing, then, is the pearl of great price. If I thought he could teach me to find it and keep it forever I would stagger barefoot across a hundred deserts after any lunatic at all. But although the pearl may be found, it may not be sought. The literature of illumination reveals this above all: although it comes to those who wait for it, it is always, even to the most practiced and adept, a gift and a total surprise. I return from one walk knowing where the killdeer nests in the field by the creek and the hour the laurel blooms. I return from the same walk a day later scarcely knowing my own name. Litanies hum in my ears; my tongue flaps in my mouth, *Alim non,* alleluia![11] I cannot cause light; the most I can do is try to put myself in the path of its beam. It is possible, in deep space, to sail on solar wind. Light, be it particle or wave, has force: you rig a giant sail and go. The secret of seeing is to sail on solar wind. Hone and spread your spirit till you yourself are a sail, whetted, translucent, broadside to the merest puff.

When her doctor took her bandages off and led her into the garden, the girl who was no longer blind saw "the tree with the lights in it." It was for this tree I searched through the peach orchards of summer, in the forests of fall and down winter and spring for years. Then one day I was walking along Tinker Creek thinking of nothing at all and I saw the tree with the lights in it. I saw the backyard cedar where the mourning doves roost charged and transfigured, each cell buzzing with flame. I stood on the grass with the lights in it, grass that was wholly fire, utterly focused and utterly dreamed. It was less like seeing than like being for the first time seen, knocked breathless by a powerful glance. The flood of fire abated, but I'm still spending the power. Gradually the lights went out in the cedar, the colors died, the cells unflamed and disappeared. I was still ringing. I had been my whole life a bell, and never knew it until at that moment I was lifted and struck. I have since only very rarely seen the tree with the lights in it. The vision comes and goes, mostly goes, but I live for it, for the moment when the mountains open and a new light roars in spate through the crack, and the mountains slam.

11. To paraphrase, "A Muslim learned man no, praise ye Jehovah!"

QUESTIONS

1. Dillard works by accumulation: she heaps up examples. Sometimes, not always, they are accompanied by a terse, apothegmatic general statement, such as "nature is very much a now-you-see-it, now-you-don't affair" (paragraph 3). Locate other examples of these accumulations; mark the general statements that accompany them. What uses do these accumulations serve? In what kinds of writing are they appropriate, in what kinds inappropriate?

2. How does the kind of seeing Dillard describes at the end of her essay differ from the kind of seeing she describes at the beginning? How does the material that appears in the sections on sight help her describe insight?

3. Take one of Dillard's terse, apothegmatic general statements and write your own accumulation of examples for it.

4. Dillard says, "I see what I expect" (paragraph 8). Write a description of something familiar, paying attention to how you "edit" your seeing. Then write a parallel description of it as if you were seeing it "unedited," as Dillard tries to see "color-patches" like the newly sighted do (paragraph 27).

GILBERT HIGHET *The Mystery of Zen*

THE MIND NEED never stop growing. Indeed, one of the few experiences which never pall is the experience of watching one's own mind, and observing how it produces new interests, responds to new stimuli, and develops new thoughts, apparently without effort and almost independently of one's own conscious control. I have seen this happen to myself a hundred times; and every time it happens again, I am equally fascinated and astonished.

Some years ago a publisher sent me a little book for review. I read it, and decided it was too remote from my main interests and too highly specialized. It was a brief account of how a young German philosopher living in Japan had learned how to shoot with a bow and arrow, and how this training had made it possible for him to understand the esoteric doctrines of the Zen sect of Buddhism. Really, what could be more alien to my own life, and to that of everyone I knew, than Zen Buddhism and Japanese archery? So I thought, and put the book away.

Yet I did not forget it. It was well written, and translated into good English. It was delightfully short, and implied much more than it said. Although its theme was extremely odd, it was at least highly individual; I had never read anything like it before or since. It remained in my mind. Its name was *Zen in the Art of Archery*, its author Eugen Herrigel, its publisher Pantheon of New York. One day I took it off the shelf and read it again; this time it seemed even stranger than before and even more unforgettable. Now it began to cohere with other interests of mine. Something I had read of the Japanese art of flower arrangement seemed to connect with it; and then, when I wrote an essay on the peculiar Japanese poems called *haiku*, other links began to grow. Finally I had to read the book once more with care, and to go through some other works which illuminated the same subject. I am still grappling with the theme; I have not got anywhere near understanding it fully; but I have learned

From Talents and Geniuses: The Pleasures of Appreciation (1975), *a collection of essays on literature, philosophy, and the arts. Many of the essays originated in Tuesday evening broadcasts that Highet gave on the radio station WQXR in New York City, often about books that he was reading or writing.*

a good deal, and I am grateful to the little book which refused to be forgotten.

The author, a German philosopher, got a job teaching philosophy at the University of Tokyo (apparently between the wars), and he did what Germans in foreign countries do not usually do: he determined to adapt himself and to learn from his hosts. In particular, he had always been interested in mysticism—which, for every earnest philosopher, poses a problem that is all the more inescapable because it is virtually insoluble. Zen Buddhism is not the only mystical doctrine to be found in the East, but it is one of the most highly developed and certainly one of the most difficult to approach. Herrigel knew that there were scarcely any books which did more than skirt the edge of the subject, and that the best of all books on Zen (those by the philosopher D. T. Suzuki) constantly emphasize that Zen can never be learned from books, can never be studied as we can study other disciplines such as logic or mathematics. Therefore he began to look for a Japanese thinker who could teach him directly.

5   At once he met with embarrassed refusals. His Japanese friends explained that he would gain nothing from trying to discuss Zen as a philosopher, that its theories could not be spread out for analysis by a detached mind, and in fact that the normal relationship of teacher and pupil simply did not exist within the sect, because the Zen masters felt it useless to explain things stage by stage and to argue about the various possible interpretations of their doctrine. Herrigel had read enough to be prepared for this. He replied that he did not want to dissect the teachings of the school, because he knew that would be useless. He wanted to become a Zen mystic himself. (This was highly intelligent of him. No one could really penetrate into Christian mysticism without being a devout Christian; no one could appreciate Hindu mystical doctrine without accepting the Hindu view of the universe.) At this, Herrigel's Japanese friends were more forthcoming. They told him that the best way, indeed the only way, for a European to approach Zen mysticism was to learn one of the arts which exemplified it. He was a fairly good rifle shot, so he determined to learn archery; and his wife co-operated with him by taking lessons in painting and flower arrangement. How any philosopher could investigate a mystical doctrine by learning to shoot with a bow and arrow and watching his wife arrange flowers, Herrigel did not ask. He had good sense.

A Zen master who was a teacher of archery agreed to take him as a pupil. The lessons lasted six years, during which he practiced every single day. There are many difficult courses of instruction in the world: the Jesuits, violin virtuosi, Talmudic scholars, all have long and hard training, which in one sense never comes to an end; but Herrigel's training in archery equaled them all in intensity. If I were trying to learn archery, I should expect to begin by looking at a target and shooting arrows at it. He was not even allowed to aim at a target for the first four years. He had to begin by learning how to hold the bow and arrow, and then how to release the arrow; this took ages. The Japanese bow is not like our sporting bow, and the stance of the archer in Japan is different from ours. We hold the bow at shoulder level, stretch our left arm out ahead, pull the string and the nocked arrow to a point either below the chin or sometimes past the right ear, and then shoot. The Japanese hold the bow above the head, and then pull the hands apart to left and right until the left hand comes down to eye level and the right hand comes to rest above the right shoulder; then there is a pause, during which the bow is held at full stretch, with the tip of the three-foot arrow projecting only a few inches beyond the bow; after that, the arrow is loosed. When Herrigel tried this, even without aiming, he found it was almost impossible. His hands trembled. His legs stiffened and grew cramped. His breathing became labored. And of course he could not possibly aim. Week after week he practiced this, with the Master watching him carefully and correcting his strained attitude; week after week he made no progress whatever. Finally he gave up and told his teacher that he could not learn: it was absolutely impossible for him to draw the bow and loose the arrow.

To his astonishment, the Master agreed. He said, "Certainly you cannot. It is because you are not breathing correctly. You must learn to breathe in a steady rhythm, keeping your lungs full most of the time, and drawing in one rapid inspiration with each stage of the process, as you grasp the bow, fit the arrow, raise the bow, draw, pause, and loose the shot. If you do, you will both grow stronger and be able to relax." To prove this, he himself drew his massive bow and told his pupil to feel the muscles of his arms: they were perfectly relaxed, as though he were doing no work whatever.

Herrigel now started breathing exercises; after some time he combined the new rhythm of breathing with the actions of drawing and shooting; and, much to his astonishment, he found that the whole thing, after this complicated process, had become much easier. Or rather, not easier, but different. At times it became quite unconscious. He says himself that he felt he was not breathing, but being breathed; and in time he felt that the occasional shot was not being dispatched by him, but shooting itself. The bow and arrow were in charge; he had become merely a part of them.

All this time, of course, Herrigel did not even attempt to discuss Zen doctrine with his Master. No doubt he knew that he was approaching it, but he concentrated solely on learning how to shoot. Every stage which he surmounted appeared to lead to another stage even more difficult. It took him months to learn how to loosen the bowstring. The problem was this. If he gripped the string and arrowhead tightly, either he froze, so that his hands were slowly pulled together and the shot was wasted, or else he jerked, so that the arrow flew up into the air or down into the ground; and if he was relaxed, then the bowstring and arrow simply *leaked* out of his grasp before he could reach full stretch, and the arrow went nowhere. He explained this problem to the Master. The Master understood perfectly well. He replied, "You must hold the drawn bowstring like a child holding a grownup's finger. You know how firmly a child grips; and yet when it lets go, there is not the slightest jerk— because the child does not think of itself, it is not self-conscious, it does not say, 'I will now let go and do something else,' it merely acts instinctively. That is what you must learn to do. Practice, practice, and practice, and then the string will loose itself at the right moment. The shot will come as effortlessly as snow slipping from a leaf." Day after day, week after week, month after month, Herrigel practiced this; and then, after one shot, the Master suddenly bowed and broke off the lesson. He said "Just then *it* shot. Not you, but *it.*" And gradually thereafter more and more right shots achieved themselves; the young philosopher forgot himself, forgot that he was learning archery for some other purpose, forgot even that he was practicing archery, and became part of that unconsciously active complex, the bow, the string, the arrow, and the man.

10   Next came the target. After four years, Herrigel was allowed to shoot at the target. But he was strictly forbidden to aim at it. The Master explained that even he himself did not aim; and indeed, when he shot, he was so absorbed in the act, so selfless and unanxious, that his eyes were almost closed. It was difficult, almost impossible, for Herrigel to believe that such shooting could ever be effective; and he risked insulting the Master by suggesting that he ought to be able to hit the target blindfolded. But the Master accepted the challenge. That night, after a cup of tea and long meditation, he went into the archery hall, put on the lights at one end and left the target perfectly dark, with only a thin taper burning in front of it. Then, with habitual grace and precision, and with that strange, almost sleepwalking, selfless confidence that is the heart of Zen, he shot two arrows into the darkness. Herrigel went out to collect them. He found that the first had gone to the heart of the bull's eye, and that the second had actually hit the first arrow and splintered it. The Master showed no pride. He said, "Perhaps, with unconscious memory of the position of the target, *I* shot the first arrow; but the second arrow? *It* shot the second arrow, and *it* brought it to the center of the target."

At last Herrigel began to understand. His progress became faster and faster; easier, too. Perfect shots (perfect because perfectly unconscious) occurred at almost every lesson; and finally, after six years of incessant training, in a public display he was awarded the diploma. He needed no further instruction: he had himself become a Master. His wife meanwhile had become expert both in painting and in the arrangement of flowers—two of the finest of Japanese arts. (I wish she could be persuaded to write a companion volume, called *Zen in the Art of Flower Arrangement;* it would have a wider general appeal than her husband's work.) I gather also from a hint or two in his book that she had taken part in the archery lessons. During one of the most difficult periods in Herrigel's training, when his Master had practically refused to continue teaching him—because Herrigel had tried to cheat by *consciously* opening his hand at the moment of loosing the arrow—his wife had advised him against that solution, and sympathized with him when it was rejected. She in her own way had learned more quickly than he, and reached the final point together with him. All their effort had not been in vain: Herrigel and his wife had really acquired a new and valuable kind of wisdom. Only at this point, when he was about to abandon his lessons forever, did his Master treat him almost as an equal and hint at the innermost doctrines of Zen Buddhism. Only hints he gave; and yet, for the young philosopher who had now become a mystic, they were enough. Herrigel understood the doctrine, not with his logical mind, but with his entire being. He at any rate had solved the mystery of Zen.

Without going through a course of training as absorbing and as complete as Herrigel's, we can probably never penetrate the mystery. The doctrine of Zen cannot be analyzed from without: it must be lived.

But although it cannot be analyzed, it can be hinted at. All the hints that the adherents of this creed give us are interesting. Many are fantastic; some are practically incomprehensible, and yet unforgettable. Put together, they take us toward a way of life which is utterly impossible for westerners living in a western world, and nevertheless has a deep fascination and contains some values which we must respect.

The word Zen means "meditation." (It is the Japanese word, corresponding to the Chinese Ch'an and the Hindu Dhyana.) It is the central idea of a special sect of Buddhism which flourished in China during the Sung period (between A.D. 1000 and 1300) and entered Japan in the twelfth century. Without knowing much about it, we might be certain that the Zen sect was a worthy and noble one, because it produced a quantity of highly distinguished art, specifically painting. And if we knew anything about Buddhism itself, we might say that Zen goes closer than other sects to the heart of Buddha's teaching: because Buddha was trying to found, not a religion with temples and rituals, but a way of life based on meditation. However, there is something eccentric about the Zen life which is hard to trace in Buddha's teaching; there is an active energy which he did not admire, there is a rough grasp on reality which he himself eschewed, there is something like a sense of humor, which he rarely displayed. The gravity and serenity of the Indian preacher are transformed, in Zen, to the earthy liveliness of Chinese and Japanese sages. The lotus brooding calmly on the water has turned into a knotted tree covered with spring blossoms.

In this sense, "meditation" does not mean what we usually think of when   15
we say a philosopher meditates: analysis of reality, a long-sustained effort to solve problems of religion and ethics, the logical dissection of the universe. It means something not divisive, but whole; not schematic, but organic; not long-drawn-out, but immediate. It means something more like our words "intuition" and "realization." It means a way of life in which there is no division between thought and action; none of the painful gulf, so well known to all of us, between the unconscious and the conscious mind; and no absolute distinction between the self and the external world, even between the various parts of the external world and the whole.

When the German philosopher took six years of lessons in archery in order to approach the mystical significance of Zen, he was not given direct philosophical instruction. He was merely shown how to breathe, how to hold and loose the bowstring, and finally how to shoot in such a way that the bow and arrow used him as an instrument. There are many such stories about Zen teachers. The strangest I know is one about a fencing master who undertook to train a young man in the art of the sword. The relationship of teacher and pupil is very important, almost sacred, in the Far East; and the pupil hardly ever thinks of leaving a master or objecting to his methods, however extraordinary they may seem. Therefore this young fellow did not at first object when he was made to act as a servant, drawing water, sweeping floors, gathering wood for the fire, and cooking. But after some time he asked for more direct instruction. The master agreed to give it, but produced no swords. The routine went on just as before, except that every now and then the master would strike the young man with a stick. No matter what he was doing, sweeping the floor or weeding in the garden, a blow would descend on him apparently out of nowhere; he had always to be on the alert, and yet he was constantly receiving unexpected cracks on the head or shoulders. After some months of this, he saw his master stooping over a boiling pot full of vegetables; and he thought he would have his revenge. Silently he lifted a stick and brought it down; but without any effort, without even a glance in his direction, his master parried the blow with the lid of the cooking pot. At last, the pupil began to understand the instinctive alertness, the effortless perception and avoidance of danger, in which his master had been training him. As soon as he had achieved it, it was child's play for him to learn the management of the sword: he could parry every cut and turn every slash without anxiety, until his opponent, exhausted, left an opening for his counterattack. (The same principle was used by the elderly samurai for selecting his comrades in the Japanese motion picture *The Magnificent Seven.*[1])

These stories show that Zen meditation does not mean sitting and thinking. On the contrary, it means acting with as little thought as possible. The fencing master trained his pupil to guard against every attack with the same immediate, instinctive rapidity with which our eyelid closes over our eye when something threatens it. His work was aimed at breaking down the wall between thought and act, at completely fusing body and senses and mind so that they might all work together rapidly and effortlessly. When a Zen artist draws a picture, he does it in a rhythm almost the exact reverse of that which is followed by a Western artist. We begin by blocking out the design and then filling in the details, usually working more and more slowly as we approach the completion of the picture. The Zen artist sits down very calmly; examines his brush carefully; prepares his own ink; smooths out the paper on which he will work; falls into a profound silent ecstasy of contemplation—during which he does not think anxiously of various details, composition, brushwork, shades of tone, but rather attempts to become the vehicle through which the subject can express itself in painting; and then, very quickly and almost unconsciously, with sure effortless strokes, draws a picture containing the fewest and most effective lines. Most of the paper is left blank; only the essential is depicted, and that not completely. One long curving line will be enough to show a mountainside; seven streaks will become a group of bamboos bending in the wind; and yet, though technically incomplete, such pictures are unforgettably clear. They show the heart of reality.

All this we can sympathize with, because we can see the results. The young swordsman learns how to fence. The intuitional painter produces a fine

---

1. *The Seven Samurai* (1956), directed by Akira Kurosawa (1910–1998), is the Japanese film; *The Magnificent Seven* (1960) is an American remake of it as a Western.

picture. But the hardest thing for us to appreciate is that the Zen masters refuse to teach philosophy or religion directly, and deny logic. In fact, they despise logic as an artificial distortion of reality. Many philosophical teachers are difficult to understand because they analyze profound problems with subtle intricacy: such is Aristotle in his *Metaphysics*.[2] Many mystical writers are difficult to understand because, as they themselves admit, they are attempting to use words to describe experiences which are too abstruse for words, so that they have to fall back on imagery and analogy, which they themselves recognize to be poor media, far coarser than the realities with which they have been in contact. But the Zen teachers seem to deny the power of language and thought altogether. For example, if you ask a Zen master what is the ultimate reality, he will answer, without the slightest hesitation, "The bamboo grove at the foot of the hill" or "A branch of plum blossom." Apparently he means that these things, which we can see instantly without effort, or imagine in the flash of a second, are real with the ultimate reality; that nothing is more real than these; and that we ought to grasp ultimates as we grasp simple immediates. A Chinese master was once asked the central question, "What is the Buddha?" He said nothing whatever, but held out his index finger. What did he mean? It is hard to explain; but apparently he meant "Here. Now. Look and realize with the effortlessness of seeing. Do not try to use words. Do not think. Make no efforts toward withdrawal from the world. Expect no sublime ecstasies. Live. All *that* is the ultimate reality, and it can be understood from the motion of a finger as well as from the execution of any complex ritual, from any subtle argument, or from the circling of the starry universe."

In making that gesture, the master was copying the Buddha himself, who once delivered a sermon which is famous, but was hardly understood by his pupils at the time. Without saying a word, he held up a flower and showed it to the gathering. One man, one alone, knew what he meant. The gesture became renowned as the Flower Sermon.

In the annals of Zen there are many cryptic answers to the final question,   20
"What is the Buddha?"—which in our terms means "What is the meaning of life? What is truly real?" For example, one master, when asked "What is the Buddha?" replied, "Your name is Yecho." Another said, "Even the finest artist cannot paint him." Another said, "No nonsense here." And another answered, "The mouth is the gate of woe." My favorite story is about the monk who said to a Master, "Has a dog Buddha-nature too?" The Master replied, "Wu"—which is what the dog himself would have said.

Now, some critics might attack Zen by saying that this is the creed of a savage or an animal. The adherents of Zen would deny that—or more probably they would ignore the criticism, or make some cryptic remark which meant that it was pointless. Their position—if they could ever be persuaded to put in into words—would be this. An animal is instinctively in touch with reality, and

---

2. The *Metaphysics* of Aristotle (384–322 B.C.E.) is a compilation of Aristotle's philosophical treatises and lecture notes put together by Andronicus of Rhodes and called by him *Metaphysica* because in his edition they came "after the physics."

so far is living rightly, but it has never had a mind and so cannot perceive the Whole, only that part with which it is in touch. The philosopher sees both the Whole and the parts, and enjoys them all. As for the savage, he exists only through the group; he feels himself as part of a war party or a ceremonial dance team or a ploughing-and-sowing group or the Snake clan; he is not truly an individual at all, and therefore is less than fully human. Zen has at its heart an inner solitude; its aim is to teach us to live, as in the last resort we do all have to live, alone.

A more dangerous criticism of Zen would be that it is nihilism, that its purpose is to abolish thought altogether. (This criticism is handled, but not fully met, by the great Zen authority Suzuki in his *Introduction to Zen Buddhism*.) It can hardly be completely confuted, for after all the central doctrine of Buddhism is—Nothingness. And many of the sayings of Zen masters are truly nihilistic. The first patriarch of the sect in China was asked by the emperor what was the ultimate and holiest principle of Buddhism. He replied, "Vast emptiness, and nothing holy in it." Another who was asked the searching question "Where is the abiding-place for the mind?" answered, "Not in this dualism of good and evil, being and non-being, thought and matter." In fact, thought is an activity which divides. It analyzes, it makes distinctions, it criticizes, it judges, it breaks reality into groups and classes and individuals. The aim of Zen is to abolish that kind of thinking, and to substitute—not unconsciousness, which would be death, but a consciousness that does not analyze but experiences life directly. Although it has no prescribed prayers, no sacred scriptures, no ceremonial rites, no personal god, and no interest in the soul's future destination, Zen is a religion rather than a philosophy. Jung[3] points out that its aim is to produce a religious conversion, a "transformation": and he adds, "The transformation process is incommensurable with intellect." Thought is always interesting, but often painful; Zen is calm and painless. Thought is incomplete; Zen enlightenment brings a sense of completeness. Thought is a process; Zen illumination is a state. But it is a state which cannot be defined. In the Buddhist scriptures there is a dialogue between a master and a pupil in which the pupil tries to discover the exact meaning of such a state. The master says to him, "If a fire were blazing in front of you, would you know that it was blazing?"

"Yes, master."

"And would you know the reason for its blazing?"

25   "Yes, because it had a supply of grass and sticks."

"And would you know if it were to go out?"

"Yes, master."

"And on its going out, would you know where the fire had gone? To the east, to the west, to the north, or to the south?"

"The question does not apply, master. For the fire blazed because it had a supply of grass and sticks. When it had consumed this and had no other fuel, then it went out."

---

3. Carl Gustav Jung (1875–1961), Swiss psychologist, one of Freud's early followers, who explored symbolism and the unconscious.

"In the same way," replies the master, "no question will apply to the mean-   30
ing of Nirvana, and no statement will explain it."

Such, then, neither happy nor unhappy but beyond all divisive description, is the condition which students of Zen strive to attain. Small wonder that
they can scarcely explain it to us, the unilluminated.

Questions

1. In his essay Highet depends heavily on Eugen Herrigel's *Zen in the Art of Archery*.
What does Highet himself bring to the essay? Mark passages in which he makes important contributions and summarize them.

2. "Zen teachers," Highet observes, "seem to deny the power of language and thought
altogether" (paragraph 18). How, then, does Highet manage to write about Zen?

3. Highet says Zen is "a religion rather than a philosophy" (paragraph 22). How has he
led up to this conclusion? What definitions of religion and philosophy does it imply?

4. In his essay Highet addresses criticism of Zen only at the end, while Jean-Paul
Sartre, in "Existentialism" below, defends existentialism as he explains it. Consider the
differences these two approaches make in the content, organization, and tone of the
two essays. What might Highet's essay be like if he defended Zen throughout, Sartre's if
he addressed criticism of existentialism only at the end?

5. Write an essay in which you describe learning to perform a physical action. Pay particular attention to what you learned through language, what through action.

Jean-Paul Sartre *Existentialism*

MAN IS NOTHING ELSE but what he makes of himself.
Such is the first principle of existentialism. It is also
what is called subjectivity, the name we are labeled
with when charges are brought against us. But what
do we mean by this, if not that man has a greater
dignity than a stone or table? For we mean that
man first exists, that is, that man first of all is the being who hurls himself toward a future and who is conscious of imagining himself as being in the future. Man is at the start a plan which is aware of itself, rather than a patch of
moss, a piece of garbage, or a cauliflower; nothing exists prior to this plan;
there is nothing in heaven; man will be what he will have planned to be. Not
what he will want to be. Because by the word "will" we generally mean a con-

From Sartre's classic 1947 statement of his philosophy, L'existentialisme est un human-
isme (*translated variously as* Existentialism, Existentialism and Humanism, *or* Existentialism and Human Emotions). *The version printed here was translated by Bernard
Frechtman.*

scious decision, which is subsequent to what we have already made of ourselves. I may want to belong to a political party, write a book, get married; but all that is only a manifestation of an earlier, more spontaneous choice that is called "will." But if existence really does precede essence, man is responsible for what he is. Thus, existentialism's first move is to make every man aware of what he is and to make the full responsibility of his existence rest on him. And when we say that a man is responsible for himself, we do not only mean that he is responsible for his own individuality, but that he is responsible for all men.

The word "subjectivism" has two meanings, and our opponents play on the two. Subjectivism means, on the one hand, that an individual chooses and makes himself; and, on the other, that it is impossible for man to transcend human subjectivity. The second of these is the essential meaning of existentialism. When we say that man chooses his own self, we mean that every one of us does likewise; but we also mean by that that in making this choice he also chooses all men. In fact, in creating the man that we want to be, there is not a single one of our acts which does not at the same time create an image of man as we think he ought to be. To choose to be this or that is to affirm at the same time the value of what we choose, because we can never choose evil. We always choose the good, and nothing can be good for us without being good for all.

If, on the other hand, existence precedes essence, and if we grant that we exist and fashion our image at one and the same time, the image is valid for everybody and for our whole age. Thus, our responsibility is much greater than we might have supposed, because it involves all mankind. If I am a working-man and choose to join a Christian trade union rather than be a Communist, and if by being a member, I want to show that the best thing for man is resignation, that the kingdom of man is not of this world, I am not only involving my own case—I want to be resigned for everyone. As a result, my action has involved all humanity. To take a more individual matter, if I want to marry, to have children, even if this marriage depends solely on my own circumstances or passion or wish, I am involving all humanity in monogamy and not merely myself. Therefore, I am responsible for myself and for everyone else. I am creating a certain image of man of my own choosing. In choosing myself, I choose man.

This helps us understand what the actual content is of such rather grandiloquent words as anguish, forlornness, despair. As you will see, it's all quite simple.

First, what is meant by anguish? The existentialists say at once that man is anguish. What that means is this: the man who involves himself and who realizes that he is not only the person he chooses to be, but also a lawmaker who is, at the same time, choosing all mankind as well as himself, cannot help escape the feeling of his total and deep responsibility. Of course, there are many people who are not anxious; but we claim that they are hiding their anxiety, that they are fleeing from it. Certainly, many people believe that when they do something, they themselves are the only ones involved, and when someone says to them, "What if everyone acted that way?" they shrug their shoulders and answer, "Everyone doesn't act that way." But really, one should always ask himself, "What would happen if everybody looked at things that way?" There is no escaping this disturbing thought except by a kind of double-dealing. A man who lies and makes excuses for himself by saying "not everybody does that" is someone with an uneasy conscience, because the act of lying implies that a universal value is conferred upon the lie.

Anguish is evident even when it conceals itself. This is the anguish that Kierkegaard[1] called the anguish of Abraham. You know the story: an angel has ordered Abraham to sacrifice his son; if it really were an angel who has come and said, "You are Abraham, you shall sacrifice your son," everything would be all right. But everyone might first wonder, "Is it really an angel, and am I really Abraham? What proof do I have?"

There was a madwoman who had hallucinations; someone used to speak to her on the telephone and give her orders. Her doctor asked her, "Who is it who talks to you?" She answered, "He says it's God." What proof did she really have that it was God? If an angel comes to me, what proof is there that it's an angel? And if I hear voices, what proof is there that they come from heaven and not from hell, or from the subconscious, or a pathological condition? What proves that they are addressed to me? What proof is there that I have been appointed to impose my choice and my conception of man on humanity? I'll never find any proof or sign to convince me of that. If a voice addresses me, it is always for me to decide that this is the angel's voice; if I consider that such an act is a good one, it is I who will choose to say that it is good rather than bad.

Now, I'm not being singled out as an Abraham, and yet at every moment I'm obliged to perform exemplary acts. For every man, everything happens as if all mankind had its eyes fixed on him and were guiding itself by what he does. And every man ought to say to himself, "Am I really the kind of man who has the right to act in such a way that humanity might guide itself by my actions?" And if he does not say that to himself, he is masking his anguish.

There is no question here of the kind of anguish which would lead to quietism, to inaction. It is a matter of a simple sort of anguish that anybody who has had responsibilities is familiar with. For example, when a military officer takes the responsibility for an attack and sends a certain number of men to death, he chooses to do so, and in the main he alone makes the choice. Doubtless, orders come from above, but they are too broad; he interprets them, and on this interpretation depend the lives of ten or fourteen or twenty men. In making a decision he cannot help having a certain anguish. All leaders know this anguish. That doesn't keep them from acting; on the contrary, it is the very condition of their action. For it implies that they envisage a number of possibilities, and when they choose one, they realize that it has value only because it is chosen. We shall see that this kind of anguish, which is the kind that existentialism describes, is explained, in addition, by a direct responsibil-

1. Søren Kierkegaard (1813–1855), Danish religious philosopher.

ity to the other men whom it involves. It is not a curtain separating us from action, but is part of action itself.

10   When we speak of forlornness, a term Heidegger[2] was fond of, we mean only that God does not exist and that we have to face all the consequences of this. This existentialist is strongly opposed to a certain kind of secular ethics which would like to abolish God with the least possible expense. About 1880, some French teachers tried to set up a secular ethics which went something like this: God is a useless and costly hypothesis; we are discarding it; but, meanwhile, in order for there to be an ethics, a society, a civilization, it is essential that certain values be taken seriously and that they be considered as having an *a priori*[3] existence. It must be obligatory, *a priori*, to be honest, not to lie, not to beat your wife, to have children, etc., etc. So we're going to try a little device which will make it possible to show that values exist all the same, inscribed in a heaven of ideas, though otherwise God does not exist. In other words—and this, I believe, is the tendency of everything called reformism in France—nothing will be changed if God does not exist. We shall find ourselves with the same norms of honesty, progress, and humanism, and we shall have made of God an outdated hypothesis which will peacefully die off by itself.

The existentialist, on the contrary, thinks it very distressing that God does not exist, because all possibility of finding values in a heaven of ideas disappears along with Him; there can no longer be an *a priori* Good, since there is no infinite and perfect consciousness to think it. Nowhere is it written that the Good exists, that we must be honest, that we must not lie; because the fact is we are on a plane where there are only men. Dostoievsky[4] said, "If God didn't exist, everything would be possible." That is the very starting point of existentialism. Indeed, everything is permissible if God does not exist, and as a result man is forlorn, because neither within him nor without does he find anything to cling to. He can't start making excuses for himself.

If existence really does precede essence, there is no explaining things away by reference to a fixed and given human nature. In other words, there is no determinism, man is free, man is freedom. On the other hand, if God does not exist, we find no values or commands to turn to which legitimize our conduct. So, in the bright realm of values, we have no excuse behind us, nor justification before us. We are alone, with no excuses.

That is the idea I shall try to convey when I say that man is condemned to be free. Condemned, because he did not create himself, yet, in other respects is free; because, once thrown into the world, he is responsible for everything he does. The existentialist does not believe in the power of passion. He will never agree that a sweeping passion is a ravaging torrent which fatally leads a man to certain acts and is therefore an excuse. He thinks that man is responsible for his passion.

The existentialist does not think that man is going to help himself by find-

---

2. Martin Heidegger (1889–1976), German philosopher of existential phenomenology.
3. Without examination or analysis (Latin).
4. Fyodor Dostoyevsky (1821–1888), Russian novelist.

ing in the world some omen by which to orient himself. Because he thinks that man will interpret the omen to suit himself. Therefore, he thinks that man, with no support and no aid, is condemned every moment to invent man. Ponge,[5] in a very fine article, has said, "Man is the future of man." That's exactly it. But if it is taken to mean that this future is recorded in heaven, that God sees it, then it is false, because it would really no longer be a future. If it is taken to mean that, whatever a man may be, there is a future to be forged, a virgin future before him, then this remark is sound. But then we are forlorn.

To give you an example which will enable you to understand forlornness better, I shall cite the case of one of my students who came to see me under the following circumstances: his father was on bad terms with his mother, and, moreover, was inclined to be a collaborationist,[6] his older brother had been killed in the German offensive of 1940, and the young man, with somewhat immature but generous feelings, wanted to avenge him. His mother lived alone with him, very much upset by the half-treason of her husband and the death of her older son; the boy was her only consolation.

The boy was faced with the choice of leaving for England and joining the Free French forces—that is, leaving his mother behind—or remaining with his mother and helping her to carry on. He was fully aware that the woman lived only for him and that his going off—and perhaps his death—would plunge her into despair. He was also aware that every act that he did for his mother's sake was a sure thing, in the sense that it was helping her to carry on, whereas every effort he made toward going off and fighting was an uncertain move which might run aground and prove completely useless; for example, on his way to England he might, while passing through Spain, be detained indefinitely in a Spanish camp; he might reach England or Algiers and be stuck in an office at a desk job. As a result, he was faced with two very different kinds of action: one, concrete, immediate, but concerning only one individual; the other concerned an incomparably vaster group, a national collectivity, but for that very reason was dubious, and might be interrupted en route. And, at the same time, he was wavering between two kinds of ethics. On the one hand, an ethics of sympathy, of personal devotion; on the other, a broader ethics, but one whose efficacy was more dubious. He had to choose between the two.

Who could help him choose? Christian doctrine? No. Christian doctrine says, "Be charitable, love your neighbor, take the more rugged path, etc., etc." But which is the more rugged path? Whom should he love as a brother? The fighting man or his mother? Which does the greater good, the vague act of fighting in a group, or the concrete one of helping a particular human being to go on living? Who can decide *a priori?* Nobody. No book of ethics can tell him. The Kantian[7] ethics says, "Never treat any person as a means, but as an end."

---

5. François Ponge (1899–1988), French surrealist poet.

6. After the defeat of France by Germany in 1940, a French government headquartered in Vichy collaborated with the Germans; the French National Committee of Liberation (Free French), headquartered in London, fought with the Allies against them.

7. Immanuel Kant (1724–1804), German philosopher.

Very well, if I stay with my mother, I'll treat her as an end and not as a means; but by virtue of this very fact, I'm running the risk of treating the people around me who are fighting, as means; and, conversely, if I go to join those who are fighting, I'll be treating them as an end, and, by doing that, I run the risk of treating my mother as a means.

If values are vague, and if they are always too broad for the concrete and specific case that we are considering, the only thing left for us is to trust our instincts. That's what this young man tried to do; and when I saw him, he said, "In the end, feeling is what counts. I ought to choose whichever pushes me in one direction. If I feel that I love my mother enough to sacrifice everything else for her—my desire for vengeance, for action, for adventure—then I'll stay with her. If, on the contrary, I feel that my love for my mother isn't enough, I'll leave."

But how is the value of a feeling determined? What gives his feeling for his mother value? Precisely the fact that he remained with her. I may say that I like so-and-so well enough to sacrifice a certain amount of money for him, but I may say so only if I've done it. I may say "I love my mother well enough to remain with her" if I have remained with her. The only way to determine the value of this affection is, precisely, to perform an act which confirms and defines it. But, since I require this affection to justify my act, I find myself caught in a vicious circle.

20   On the other hand, Gide[8] has well said that a mock feeling and a true feeling are almost indistinguishable; to decide that I love my mother and will remain with her, or to remain with her by putting on an act, amount somewhat to the same thing. In other words, the feeling is formed by the acts one performs; so, I cannot refer to it in order to act upon it. Which means that I can neither seek within myself the true condition which will impel me to act, nor apply to a system of ethics for concepts which will permit me to act. You will say, "At least, he did go to a teacher for advice." But if you seek advice from a priest, for example, you have chosen this priest; you already knew, more or less, just about what advice he was going to give you. In other words, choosing your adviser is involving yourself. The proof of this is that if you are a Christian, you will say, "Consult a priest." But some priests are collaborating, some are just marking time, some are resisting. Which to choose? If the young man chooses a priest who is resisting or collaborating, he has already decided on the kind of advice he's going to get. Therefore, in coming to see me he knew the answer I was going to give him, and I had only one answer to give: "You're free, choose, that is, invent." No general ethics can show you what is to be done; there are no omens in the world. The Catholics will reply, "But there are." Granted—but, in any case, I myself choose the meaning they have.

When I was a prisoner,[9] I knew a rather remarkable young man who was a Jesuit. He had entered the Jesuit order in the following way: he had had a

8. André Gide (1864–1951), French novelist and dramatist.

9. Sartre, who served in the French army during World War II, was a prisoner of war from 1940 to 1941.

number of very bad breaks; in childhood, his father died, leaving him in poverty, and he was a scholarship student at a religious institution where he was constantly made to feel that he was being kept out of charity; then, he failed to get any of the honors and distinctions that children like; later on, at about eighteen, he bungled a love affair; finally, at twenty-two, he failed in military training, a childish enough matter, but it was the last straw.

This young fellow might well have felt that he had botched everything. It was a sign of something, but of what? He might have taken refuge in bitterness or despair. But he very wisely looked upon all this as a sign that he was not made for secular triumphs, and that only the triumphs of religion, holiness, and faith were open to him. He saw the hand of God in all this, and so he entered the order. Who can help seeing that he alone decided what the sign meant?

Some other interpretation might have been drawn from this series of setbacks; for example, that he might have done better to turn carpenter or revolutionist. Therefore, he is fully responsible for the interpretation. Forlornness implies that we ourselves choose our being. Forlornness and anguish go together.

As for despair, the term has a very simple meaning. It means that we shall confine ourselves to reckoning only with what depends upon our will, or on the ensemble of probabilities which make our action possible. When we want something, we always have to reckon with probabilities. I may be counting on the arrival of a friend. The friend is coming by rail or streetcar; this supposes that the train will arrive on schedule, or that the streetcar will not jump the track. I am left in the realm of possibility; but possibilities are to be reckoned with only to the point where my action comports with the ensemble of these possibilities, and no further. The moment the possibilities I am considering are not rigorously involved by my action, I ought to disengage myself from them, because no God, no scheme, can adapt the world and its possibilities to my will. When Descartes[10] said, "Conquer yourself rather than the world," he meant essentially the same thing.

The Marxists to whom I have spoken reply, "You can rely on the support of others in your action, which obviously has certain limits because you're not going to live forever. That means: rely on both what others are doing elsewhere to help you, in China, in Russia, and what they will do later on, after your death, to carry on the action and lead it to its fulfillment, which will be the revolution. You even *have* to rely upon that, otherwise you're immoral." I reply at once that I will always rely on fellow-fighters insofar as these comrades are involved with me in a common struggle, in the unity of a party or a group in which I can more or less make my weight felt; that is, one whose ranks I am in as a fighter and whose movements I am aware of at every moment. In such a situation, relying on the unity and will of the party is exactly like counting on the fact that the train will arrive on time or that the car won't jump the track. But, given that man is free and that there is no human nature for me to depend on, I cannot

25

10. René Descartes (1596–1650), French philosopher, scientist, and mathematician.

count on men whom I do not know by relying on human goodness or man's concern for the good of society. I don't know what will become of the Russian revolution; I may make an example of it to the extent that at the present time it is apparent that the proletariat plays a part in Russia that it plays in no other nation. But I can't swear that this will inevitably lead to a triumph of the proletariat. I've got to limit myself to what I see.

Given that men are free and that tomorrow they will freely decide what man will be, I cannot be sure that, after my death, fellow-fighters will carry on my work to bring it to its maximum perfection. Tomorrow, after my death, some men may decide to set up Fascism, and the others may be cowardly and muddled enough to let them do it. Fascism will then be the human reality, so much the worse for us.

Actually, things will be as man will have decided they are to be. Does that mean that I should abandon myself to quietism? No. First, I should involve myself; then, act on the old saw, "Nothing ventured, nothing gained." Nor does it mean that I shouldn't belong to a party, but rather that I shall have no illusions and shall do what I can. For example, suppose I ask myself, "Will socialization, as such, ever come about?" I know nothing about it. All I know is that I'm going to do everything in my power to bring it about. Beyond that, I can't count on anything. Quietism is the attitude of people who say, "Let others do what I can't do." The doctrine I am presenting is the very opposite of quietism, since it declares, "There is no reality except in action." Moreover, it goes further, since it adds, "Man is nothing else than his plan; he exists only to the extent that he fulfills himself; he is therefore nothing else than the ensemble of his acts, nothing else than his life."

According to this, we can understand why our doctrine horrifies certain people. Because often the only way they can bear their wretchedness is to think, "Circumstances have been against me. What I've been and done doesn't show my true worth. To be sure, I've had no great love, no great friendship, but that's because I haven't met a man or woman who was worthy. The books I've written haven't been very good because I haven't had the proper leisure. I haven't had children to devote myself to because I didn't find a man with whom I could have spent my life. So there remains within me, unused and quite viable, a host of propensities, inclinations, possibilities, that one wouldn't guess from the mere series of things I've done."

Now, for the existentialist there is really no love other than one which manifests itself in a person's being in love. There is no genius other than one which is expressed in works of art; the genius of Proust is the sum of Proust's works; the genius of Racine is his series of tragedies.[11] Outside of that, there is nothing. Why say that Racine could have written another tragedy, when he didn't write it? A man is involved in life, leaves his impress on it, and outside of that there is nothing. To be sure, this may seem a harsh thought to someone whose life hasn't been a success. But, on the other hand, it prompts people to

---

11. Marcel Proust (1871–1922), French novelist; Jean Baptiste Racine (1639–1699), French dramatist who wrote only tragedies.

understand that reality alone is what counts, that dreams, expectations, and hopes warrant no more than to define a man as a disappointed dream, as miscarried hopes, as vain expectations. In other words, to define him negatively and not positively. However, when we say, "You are nothing else than your life," that does not imply that the artist will be judged solely on the basis of his works of art; a thousand other things will contribute toward summing him up. What we mean is that a man is nothing else than a series of undertakings, that he is the sum, the organization, the ensemble of the relationships which make up these undertakings.

When all is said and done, what we are accused of, at bottom, is not our pessimism, but an optimistic toughness. If people throw up to us our works of fiction in which we write about people who are soft, weak, cowardly, and sometimes even downright bad, it's not because these people are soft, weak, cowardly, or bad; because if we were to say, as Zola did,[12] that they are that way because of heredity, the workings of environment, society, because of biological or psychological determinism, people would be reassured. They would say, "Well, that's what we're like, no one can do anything about it." But when the existentialist writes about a coward, he says that this coward is responsible for his cowardice. He's not like that because he has a cowardly heart or lung or brain; he's not like that on account of his physiological make-up; but he's like that because he has made himself a coward by his acts. There's no such thing as a cowardly constitution; there are nervous constitutions; there is poor blood, as the common people say, or strong constitutions. But the man whose blood is poor is not a coward on that account, for what makes cowardice is the act of renouncing or yielding. A constitution is not an act; the coward is defined on the basis of the acts he performs. People feel, in a vague sort of way, that this coward we're talking about is guilty of being a coward, and the thought frightens them. What people would like is that a coward or a hero be born that way.

From these few reflections it is evident that nothing is more unjust than the objections that have been raised against us. Existentialism is nothing else than an attempt to draw all the consequences of a coherent atheistic position. It isn't trying to plunge man into despair at all. But if one calls every attitude of unbelief despair, like the Christians, then the word is not being used in its original sense. Existentialism isn't so atheistic that it wears itself out showing that God doesn't exist. Rather, it declares that even if God did exist, that would change nothing. There you've got our point of view. Not that we believe that God exists, but we think that the problem of His existence is not the issue. In this sense existentialism is optimistic, a doctrine of action, and it is plain dishonesty for Christians to make no distinction between their own despair and ours and then to call us despairing.

12. Émile Zola (1840–1902), French writer whose novels about a single family, *Les Rougon-Macquart*, probed the influences of heredity and environment.

QUESTIONS

1. "Existence precedes essence": this concept is central to Sartre's existential philosophy. What does he mean by it?

2. Sartre develops his essay by definition: existentialism, he says, enables us to understand the "actual content" of three terms: "anguish," "forlornness," and "despair" (paragraph 4). What are Sartre's definitions of these three terms? How does he distinguish among them?

3. Throughout his essay Sartre defends existentialism against criticism as he explains it, in contrast, for example, to Gilbert Highet, who, in "The Mystery of Zen" (p. 1201), addresses criticism only at the end. Consider the differences these two approaches make in the content, organization, and tone of these two essays. What might Sartre's essay be like if he addressed criticism of existentialism only at the end, Highet's if he defended Zen throughout?

4. Sartre says, "when we say that a man is responsible for himself, we do not only mean that he is responsible for his own individuality, but that he is responsible for all men" (paragraph 1). Write an essay explaining how, in the framework of existentialist beliefs, this paradoxical statement is true.

AUTHORS

Edward Abbey (1927–1989)
American writer, essayist, and self-described "agrarian anarchist." Born in Pennsylvania, Abbey lived in the Southwest from 1948, when he arrived there to study at the University of New Mexico, until his death. A former ranger for the National Park Service, he took as his most pervasive theme the beauty of the Southwestern region and the ways it has been despoiled by government, business, and tourism. Abbey's books include the novels *Fire on the Mountain* (1963), *The Monkey Wrench Gang* (1975), and *Good News* (1980). He also published several collections of essays, among them *Desert Solitaire* (1968), *Abbey's Road* (1979), *Beyond the Wall: Essays from the Outside* (1984), and *One Life at a Time, Please* (1988).

André Aciman (b. 1951)
American essayist, memoirist, and scholar. Born in Alexandria, Egypt, to a Sephardic Jewish family of Turkish nationality, Aciman grew up among the various émigré communities of that city. Though French was spoken at home, Aciman attended English-language schools, first in Alexandria, and later, when his family moved to Italy in 1965, in Rome. In 1969, the family moved to the United States, where Aciman completed his B.A. at Lehman College and his Ph.D. in comparative literature at Harvard University. He is the author of *Out of Egypt* (1996), a memoir about his childhood as a secular Jew in Egypt in the 1950s and 1960s, for which he won the Whiting Award. He has also published *False Papers: Essays on Exile and Memory* (2001) and a novel, *Call Me by Your Name* (2007). In addition, he has coauthored and edited *Letters of Transit* (2000) and *The Proust Project* (2004). He currently teaches at the Graduate School and University Center of the City University of New York.

Aesop (c. 620–560 B.C.E.)
Legendary Greek storyteller. A collection of Greek fables, orally composed and transmitted, was ascribed to Aesop, a Phrygian slave, sometime in the third century C.E., but many are far older, having been found on Egyptian papyri of 800 to 1,000 years earlier. Preserved and copied during the Middle Ages, the fables probably made their way into English through the work of the Dutch scholar Erasmus (1466–1536), who translated them into Latin; Erasmus's Latin text was later rendered into English.

Marjorie Agosín (b. 1955)
Chilean American poet and activist. Born in Maryland, Agosín earned her B.A. at the University of Georgia and her M.A. and Ph.D. at Indiana University. Much of her work deals with her family's Jewish-Chilean history. Members of Agosín's family were killed in the Holocaust, and those who escaped emigrated to Chile, where Agosín lived from the age of three months to sixteen years. She is the author of numerous books of poetry and memoir, including *Dear Anne Frank* (1998), a collection of bilingual poems; *A Cross and a Star: Memories of a Jewish Girl in Chile* (1997), a book about her mother; and *Always from Somewhere Else* (2000), a book based on Agosín's memories of her father. Other work includes *Secrets in the Sand: The Young Women of Juarez* (2006) and *Writings Towards Hope* (2006). A committed human rights activist, Agosín was awarded the Gabriela Mistral Medal of Honor for Life Achievement in 2002 by the government of Chile. She is currently a professor of Spanish at Wellesley College.

Philip Alcabes (b. 1954)
American epidemiologist and essayist. Alcabes completed his B.S. at Union College, his M.A. at the University of California, Berkeley, his M.P.H. at Columbia University, and his Ph.D. at Johns Hopkins University. He is a professor at the City University of New York, Hunter College. He has published in scholarly journals such as *JAMA*, the *American Journal of Epidemiology*, and the *New England Journal of Medicine*. Known for his willingness to take on the

status quo on public health issues, Alcabes has written essays and Op-Eds for the *American Scholar*, *Newsday*, the *Chronicle of Higher Education*, and the *Washington Post*.

Maya Angelou (b. 1928)
African American writer, poet, playwright, actress, and singer. Born in St. Louis, Angelou attended public schools in Arkansas and California before studying music and dance. In a richly varied life, she has been a cook, streetcar conductor, singer, actress, dancer, teacher, and director, with her debut film *Down in the Delta* (1998). Author of several volumes of poetry and ten plays (stage, screen, and television), Angelou may be best known for her poem "On the Pulse of Morning," which she read at the inauguration of President William Jefferson Clinton in 1993. *I Know Why the Caged Bird Sings* (1970), the first volume of her autobiography, is one of the fullest accounts of the African American woman's experience in contemporary literature. Angelou published her sixth volume of autobiography, *A Song Flung Up to Heaven*, in 2002.

Gloria Anzaldúa (1942–2004)
Chicana American lesbian-feminist poet and writer. Born on a ranch in southern Texas, Anzaldúa worked as an agricultural laborer as an adolescent until she went to Pan American University, the first woman from her family to attend college. She received an M.A. in English from the University of Texas, Austin, and taught writing at several colleges, including San Francisco State University; the University of California, Santa Cruz; and Vermont College. She was also active in the migrant workers' rights movement. Her most ambitious work, *Borderlands/La Frontera* (1987), explores the situation of "border women" like herself who grew up neither within their Mexican Indian heritage nor within the Anglo-American society that considered them outsiders. Her other works include the American Book Award–winning anthology *This Bridge Called My Back* (1981), *Making Face, Making Soul/ Haciendo Caras* (1990), and the novel *La Prieta* (1997).

Hannah Arendt (1906–1975)
German American political scientist and philosopher. Born in Hanover, Germany, and educated at the University of Heidelberg, Arendt began her academic career in Germany, but was forced to leave when Hitler came to power. Arriving in the United States in 1940, she became chief editor for a major publisher and a frequent lecturer on college campuses. Arendt taught at a number of American colleges and universities, finishing her career at the New School for Social Research in New York City. She published over a dozen books, most notably *The Origins of Totalitarianism* (1951), which traces the roots of Nazism back to nineteenth-century imperialism and anti-Semitism; *Eichmann in Jerusalem: A Report on the Banality of Evil* (1963), which suggests that both the Nazis and those who passively stood by were responsible for the massive destruction of the Holocaust; and *On Revolution* (1965).

Isaac Asimov (1920–1992)
American biochemist, science writer, and novelist. Born in Russia, Asimov was educated in the United States and received a Ph.D. in biochemistry from Columbia University. In 1949 he became a member of the faculty at the School of Medicine, Boston University, where he taught biochemistry. An extraordinarily prolific author, Asimov published more than 250 books on topics as diverse as mathematics, astronomy, physics, chemistry, biology, mythology, Shakespeare, the Bible, and geography; his science fiction works include some of the most famous and influential in that genre. His books include *The Stars, Like Dust* (1951), *Science, Numbers and I* (1968), *ABC's of the Earth* (1971), *The Road to Infinity* (1979), *The Exploding Suns: The Secrets of Supernovas* (1985), and *The Tyrannosaurus Prescription* (1989).

Margaret Atwood (b. 1939)
Canadian novelist, poet, and literary critic. Born in Ontario, Atwood received degrees from the University of Toronto, Radcliffe College, and Harvard University. She began her career as a poet in the 1960s, and her later fiction builds on many of the feminist and survivalist themes she began exploring in her poetry. Well regarded by both critics and the general public, her novels include *The Edible Woman* (1969); *Surfacing* (1972); *Bodily Harm* (1982); *The Handmaid's Tale* (1986), which was made into a movie in 1990; *Cat's Eye* (1988); *The Robber Bride* (1993); *Alias Grace* (1996); *The Blind Assassin* (2000), winner of the Booker Prize; *Oryx and Crake* (2003); *The Penelopiad* (2005); and *The Tent* (2006).

Francis Bacon (1561–1626)

English civil servant, politician, statesman, and philosopher. Trained as a lawyer, Bacon served as a member of Parliament during the reign of Queen Elizabeth I. After her death, he found favor with King James I and advanced in government service to the position of lord chancellor. His career was cut short in 1621 when he was convicted of accepting bribes. Retired, he married and devoted the rest of his life to study and to writing philosophical works. Bacon's books include *The Advancement of Learning* (1605), *Novum Organum* (1620), and *Essays* (1597, rev. 1612 and 1625).

Matt Bai (b. 1968)

American journalist and author. Bai is a contributing writer for the *New York Times Magazine*, where he covered the 2004 presidential election. He has also written for *Newsday* and the *Boston Globe*. He is currently writing a book about "this moment in democratic politics and a group of people who are trying to rebuild a democratic movement."

James Baldwin (1924–1987)

African American essayist, novelist, and social activist. Baldwin was born in Harlem, became a minister at fourteen, and grew to maturity in an America disfigured by racism and prejudice. Only after moving to Paris in 1948 did he begin to write. Both his first novel, *Go Tell It on the Mountain* (1953), and his first play, *The Amen Corner* (1955), are autobiographical explorations. Although he would write other plays—*Blues for Mister Charlie* (1964) was one of his best—Baldwin concentrated his energies on essays and on novels such as *Giovanni's Room* (1956), *Another Country* (1962), and *If Beale Street Could Talk* (1974). His stories are collected in *Going to Meet the Man* (1965); his essay collections, including *Notes of a Native Son* (1955), *Nobody Knows My Name* (1961), and *The Fire Next Time* (1963), demonstrate Baldwin's skills as a social critic of insight and passion.

David Baltimore (b. 1938)

American biologist. Born in New York City, Baltimore attended Swarthmore College, where he earned his B.A., and Rockefeller University, where he earned his Ph.D. In 1975, he received the Nobel Prize for his discovery of reverse transcriptase, "a DNA polymerase enzyme that transcribes single-stranded RNA into double-stranded DNA." Reverse transcriptase is a key factor in the reproduction of HIV and other retroviruses. Baltimore is currently the Robert A. Millikan Professor of Biology at the California Institute of Technology. He is the president of the American Academy for the Advancement of Science and is an influential voice in national policy concerning recombinant DNA research and the AIDS epidemic.

Benjamin R. Barber (b. 1939)

American author and political theorist. Barber earned certificates from the London School of Economics and Albert Schweitzer College before receiving his B.A. from Grinnell College and his M.A. and Ph.D. from Harvard University. Barber is best known for *Jihad vs. McWorld* (1996), in which he argues that "neither global corporations nor traditional cultures are supportive of democracy." Other works include *Superman and Common Men: Freedom, Anarchy and the Revolution* (1971), *Strong Democracy: Participatory Politics for a New Age* (1984), *An Aristocracy of Everyone: The Politics of Education and the Future of America* (1992), *A Place for Us: How to Make Society Civil and Democracy Strong* (1998), *A Passion for Democracy: American Essays* (2000), *Fear's Empire: War, Terrorism, and Democracy in an Age of Interdependence* (2003), and *Consumed: How Markets Corrupt Children, Infantilize Adults, and Swallow Citizens Whole* (2007). He has advised numerous politicians, most notably Bill Clinton and Howard Dean. Barber teaches at the University of Maryland, College Park School of Public Policy.

Dennis Baron (b. 1944)

American scholar and author. Baron is Professor of English and Linguistics at the University of Illinois at Urbana-Champaign. His research interests include language legislation (policy and reform), technologies of communication, and issues in higher education and teaching. His books include *Grammar and Good Taste: Reforming the American Language* (1982), *Grammar and Gender* (1986), *Declining Grammar, and Other Essays on the English Vocabulary* (1988), *The English-Only Question: An Official Language for Americans?* (1990), and *Guide to Home Language Repair* (1994). He has published numerous essays and articles, both in academic journals and in popular newspapers such as the *New York Times*, the *Washington Post*, and the *Chicago Tribune*. He is currently working on *From Pencils to Pixels: Communicating in the Digital Age*, which he describes as "tracing the impact of technologies of communication on our reading and writing practices, and how the needs of readers and writers shape technological development, from the invention of writing to the digital age."

Andrea Barrett (b. 1954)
American novelist and short-story writer. Born in Boston, Massachusetts, Barrett earned a B.A. in biology from Union College in Schenectady, New York, before briefly attending a Ph.D. program in zoology. Barrett's background in science is reflected in her work, which is identified as "historical fiction." Many of the characters in her work are scientists, both historical and fictional. Barrett has taught in the Warren Wilson College M.F.A. Program and has been a visiting writer and lecturer at several institutions and writers' conferences, including the Breadloaf Writers' Conference in Vermont and the New York State Summer Writers' Institute at Skidmore College. She currently teaches at Williams College in Massachusetts. She has published six novels: *Lucid Stars* (1988), *The Forms of Water* (1988), *Secret Harmonies* (1989), *The Middle Kingdom* (1991), *The Voyage of the Narwhal* (1998), and *The Air We Breathe* (2007), and two collections of short stories: *Ship Fever* (1996), for which she won the National Book Award, and *Servants of the Map* (2002).

Roland Barthes (1915–1980)
French literary and cultural critic. A researcher at Paris's National Center for Scientific Research, the School for Advanced Study, and the Collège de France, Barthes wrote numerous essays—collected in books such as *Mythologies* (1957) and *S/Z* (1970)—that critique modern culture and expose hidden meanings behind everyday objects such as toys and cultural phenomena such as wrestling matches. His radical views on modern society and literature made his work controversial when it was published, but his methods have greatly informed those employed by contemporary cultural critics. Barthes's other works include *On Racine* (1963), *The Pleasure of the Text* (1973), and *Camera Lucida* (1980).

Daniel Bergner (b. 1960)
American journalist and writer. Bergner received his B.A. from Brown University and his M.F.A. from Columbia University's Fiction Writing Program. He has reported from many African countries, as well as from Afghanistan and Iraq. He is the author of *Moments of Favor* (1991), a novel that addresses the dangerous appeal of celebrity. His nonfiction works include *God of the Rodeo* (1999), which tells the stories of prisoners serving life sentences in Louisiana's Angola State Penitentiary and was named a *New York Times* Notable Book of the Year, and *In the Land of Magic Soldiers: A Story of White and Black in West Africa* (2003), a harrowing account of Sierra Leone, which won an Overseas Press Club Award and a Lettre-Ulysses Award and was named a *Los Angeles Times* Best Book of the Year. Bergner is a contributing writer for the *New York Times Magazine* and has written for *Harper's*, *Talk*, *Granta*, *Mother Jones*, and the *New York Times* Op-Ed page. His current book, about desire, will be published in September 2008.

Bruno Bettelheim (1903–1990)
Austrian American child psychologist, teacher, and writer. Born and educated in Vienna, Austria, Bettelheim came to the United States in 1939 and in 1944 joined the faculty of the University of Chicago, where he spent a long and distinguished teaching career, retiring in 1973. He wrote several dozen books, including *Love Is Not Enough: The Treatment of Emotionally Disturbed Children* (1950), *The Informed Heart: Autonomy in a Mass Age* (1960), *The Children of the Dream* (1969), *The Uses of Enchantment: The Meaning and Importance of Fairy Tales* (1976), and *A Good Enough Parent* (1987).

Ambrose Bierce (1842–1914?)
American journalist, poet, and writer. Bierce was born the tenth child of a poor Ohio family. After serving in the Civil War and working as a journalist in San Francisco, he went to England, where he wrote comic and satiric sketches for several publications. In 1876 he returned to San Francisco as a reporter for William Randolph Hearst's *Examiner*. The death of his two sons, along with a divorce, might well have led him to Mexico, where he reportedly rode with Pancho Villa's revolutionaries; he disappeared and is presumed to have died there. Bierce's

twelve-volume *Collected Works* (1909–12) include a generous sampling of his tales, essays, verses, and fables. Bierce may be best known for *The Devil's Dictionary* (1906), a collection of ironic definitions compiled while he was a Hearst correspondent in Washington, D.C.

Caroline Bird (b. 1915)
American journalist, public-relations specialist, and writer. Bird attended Vassar College, graduated from the University of Toledo, and received her master's from the University of Wisconsin (1939). She worked as a researcher at *Newsweek* and *Fortune* in the 1940s, then moved into public relations, which she left after twenty years to pursue writing full time. Bird is the author of a number of books focusing on feminist concerns: *Born Female: The High Cost of Keeping Women Down* (1968), *Everything a Woman Needs to Know to Get Paid What She's Worth* (1973), *The Case Against College* (1975), *The Good Years: Your Life in the Twenty-first Century* (1983), and *Lives of Our Own: Secrets of a Salty Old Woman* (1995).

William Blake (1757–1827)
English poet and artist. The son of a London haberdasher, Blake first studied drawing at age ten and became an engraver and illustrator by trade; he established a printing shop in London, where he engraved and printed his second volume of poems, *Songs of Innocence* (1789). Blake's poems and illuminations reflect an independent spirit seeking freedom from repression; they take their inspiration from nature and religion, both being transformed into a deeply personal and unorthodox vision. His major works include *The Marriage of Heaven and Hell* (1793), *Songs of Experience* (1794), *The Four Zoas* (1803), *Milton* (1804), and *Jerusalem* (1809).

Eavan Boland (b. 1944)
Irish poet. Boland was educated at Trinity College, Dublin, as well as in New York and London. She has published ten volumes of poetry, including *New Territory* (1967), *The War Horse* (1975), *In Her Own Image* (1980), *Night Feed* (1982), and *In a Time of Violence* (1994). *Against Love Poetry* (2001) was named a *New York Times* Notable Book of the Year. She has also written a prose memoir, *Object Lessons: The Life of the Woman and the Poet in Our Time* (1996). Her most recent book of poems is *Do-mestic Violence* (2007). She teaches at Stanford University.

Wayne C. Booth (1921–2005)
American writer, literary critic, and teacher. After receiving a Ph.D. from the University of Chicago in 1950, Booth began a teaching career that took him to Haverford College and Earlham College, then back to the University of Chicago. Among Booth's books are *The Rhetoric of Fiction* (1961), *A Rhetoric of Irony* (1974), *Modern Dogma and the Rhetoric of Assent* (1974), *Critical Understanding: The Powers and Limits of Pluralism* (1979), *The Vocation of a Teacher* (1988), *The Company We Keep: An Ethics of Fiction* (1988), *The Art of Growing Older* (1992), and *For the Love of It: Amateuring and Its Rivals* (1999).

Jennifer Britz (b. 1957)
American college admissions professional and writer. A native of Minnesota, Britz attended Carleton College and the University of Arizona, where she earned her B.A. and M.F.A. degrees. She has been the dean of admissions and financial aid at Kenyon College since July 2003. In 2005, she was named by the *Chronicle of Higher Education* as one of ten "New Thinkers." Britz garnered national attention in 2006, when she wrote an Op-Ed piece for the *New York Times* that addresses the decreasing number of male college applicants and the ways in which this disequilibrium is affecting the admissions process.

Jacob Bronowski (1908–1974)
English mathematician, scientist, and writer. Born in Poland and educated in England, where he received a Ph.D. in mathematics from Cambridge University in 1933, Bronowski served as a university lecturer before entering government service during World War II. From 1950 until 1963 he was head of research for Britain's National Coal Board; from 1964 until his death he was a resident fellow at the Salk Institute, La Jolla, California. The author of many books, among them *Science and Human Values* (1956; 1965), *Nature and Knowledge* (1969), and *Magic, Science, and Civilization* (1978), Bronowski is also known for the thirteen-part television series "The Ascent of Man" (1973–74).

David Brooks (b. 1961)
Canadian author and news commentator. Brooks is a columnist for the *New*

York Times and commentator on The News Hour with Jim Lehrer. He was previously the senior editor of the Weekly Standard and prior to that wrote and edited for the Wall Street Journal. He is the author of Bobos in Paradise: The New Upper Class and How They Got There (2000) and On Paradise Drive: How We Live Now (And Always Have) in the Future Tense (2004). His writing has been published in the New Yorker, the New York Times Magazine, Forbes, the Washington Post, TLS, Commentary, the Public Interest, and other magazines. Brooks was born in Toronto, grew up in New York City, and graduated from the University of Chicago in 1983 with a degree in history.

Kenneth A. Bruffee (b. 1934)
American teacher, scholar, and writer. Bruffee graduated from Wesleyan University and received his Ph.D. from Northwestern University. Professor of English and Director of the Scholars Program and the Honors Academy at Brooklyn College, City University of New York, he has also taught at Columbia University, Cooper Union, and the University of Pennsylvania. Bruffee is known for his work on composition, collaborative learning, peer tutoring, and liberal education. In addition to studies of Romantic poetry, he has published A Short Course in Writing (1993) and Collaborative Learning: Higher Education, Interdependence, and the Authority of Knowledge (1999).

Anthony Burgess (1917–1993)
John Anthony Burgess Wilson, English novelist, playwright, and editor. Born in Manchester, England, and a graduate of Manchester University, Burgess was a lecturer and teacher of English until 1954, when he became an education officer in the Colonial Service, stationed in Malaya. He began writing while there, but when told in 1959 that he had a year to live, Burgess returned to England and wrote five novels in one year. The diagnosis proved wrong, and Burgess lived to write several dozen more, including A Clockwork Orange (1962), which was made into a film by Stanley Kubrick; Enderby Outside (1968); Earthly Powers (1980); The End of the World News: An Entertainment (1984); Any Old Iron (1989); and A Dead Man in Deptford (1993). In addition, Burgess wrote critical studies, giving special attention to James Joyce and D. H. Lawrence.

Colby Buzzell (b. 1976)
American author, blogger, and former U.S. Army soldier. Born and raised in California, Buzzell joined the army at the age of 26. He went to Iraq in 2003 as a member of a Stryker Brigade Combat team. While in Iraq, Buzzell began writing a blog titled "CBFTW" in which he shared his war experiences. The blog became quite popular, as it provided an inside perspective on the war and on the daily experiences of a soldier that was otherwise unavailable. Buzzell went on to publish a book on his experiences, largely derived from and inspired by his blog, titled My War: Killing Time in Iraq (2005). In 2004, Buzzell was profiled by Esquire magazine in its "Best and Brightest" issue.

Rachel Carson (1907–1964)
American marine biologist and writer. Born in Springfield, Pennsylvania, Carson received a B.A. from Pennsylvania College for Women (now Chatham College) and an M.A. from the Johns Hopkins University. She joined the U.S. Fish and Wildlife Service in 1936, and her early works on sea life, Under the Sea Wind (1941), The Sea around Us (1951), and The Edge of the Sea (1954), were highly acclaimed. Her most influential book, Silent Spring (1962), exposed the dangers of the use of pesticides, particularly DDT. This work led to a presidential commission that later banned the use of DDT in American agriculture. Carson is often referred to as the founder of the modern environmental movement. She was posthumously awarded the Presidential Medal of Freedom.

David Chanoff (b. 1943)
American journalist. Chanoff received his B.A. from Johns Hopkins University and his Ph.D. in English and American literature from Brandeis University. He has written about literary history, education, foreign policy, and other subjects for the New York Times Magazine, the Washington Post, and the American Scholar. He has also published thirteen books. Among these are collaborations with key political figures, including former Chairman of the Joint Chiefs of Staff Admiral William Crowe Jr., former Surgeon General Joycelyn Elders, and Israeli prime minister Ariel Sharon, with whom Chanoff co-wrote Warrior: An Autobiography (1989).

Lord Chesterfield (1694–1773)

Philip Dormer Stanhope, fourth earl of Chesterfield, English statesman, diplomat, and writer. Although attracted to the literary world as a youth, Chesterfield entered diplomatic service and held important posts in Holland and Ireland. His literary reputation rests on his *Letters*. Addressed to his son Philip and written with near-daily frequency beginning in 1737, the letters became a handbook of gentlemanly conduct when they were published, in 1774. In a now-famous episode, Samuel Johnson sent the plan for his *Dictionary* to Chesterfield but received no response. Even though Chesterfield published two favorable reviews when the *Dictionary* was printed, Johnson, always sensitive to slights, wrote his "Letter to Lord Chesterfield," in which he scorns the nobleman's praise.

Judith Ortiz Cofer (b. 1952)

Puerto Rican American novelist, poet, and essayist. Born in Hormigueros, Puerto Rico, Cofer spent much of her childhood traveling between her Puerto Rican home and Paterson, New Jersey. Educated at Florida Atlantic University and Oxford University, Cofer is currently the Regents' and Franklin Professor of English and Creative Writing at the University of Georgia. *Silent Dancing* (1990) reflects her ongoing efforts to explore her bicultural and bilingual roots. Her other books include *The Latin Deli: Prose and Poetry* (1995), *Woman in Front of the Sun: On Becoming a Writer* (2000), *The Meaning of Consuelo* (2003), and the young adult novel *Call Me Maria* (2006).

Carl Cohen (b. 1931)

American philosopher and teacher. After taking a Ph.D. in philosophy at the University of California, Los Angeles (1955), Cohen became a member of the Department of Philosophy at the University of Michigan, Ann Arbor, where he has been a professor since 1960. With special interests in political philosophy, the philosophy of law, and medical ethics, Cohen has published widely in a number of journals. His books include *Civil Disobedience: Conscience, Tactics and the Law* (1971), *Democracy* (1973), *Introduction to Logic* (with Irving M. Copi, 2001, 2004), *The Animal Rights Debate* (with Tom Regan, 2001), and *Affirmative Action and Racial Preference* (2003), a point/counterpoint exchange with James Sterba.

Aaron Copland (1900–1990)

American composer, conductor, and writer. Born in New York City, Copland studied music theory and practice in Paris (1921–24), then returned to New York to compose, organize concert series, publish American scores, and further the cause of the American composer. After experimenting with the adaptation of jazz to classical composition, Copland developed a distinctly American style. He incorporated American folk songs and legends into many of his works, including three ballet scores: *Billy the Kid* (1938), *Rodeo* (1942), and *Appalachian Spring* (1944), which won the Pulitzer Prize. His other popular works include *Twelve Poems of Emily Dickinson*, songs for voice and piano (1950); *Lincoln Portrait* (1942), for narrator and orchestra; and *Fanfare for the Common Man* (1942). Copland also wrote music criticism and essays.

Sara Corbett (b. 1975)

American journalist. Corbett is a contributing writer to the *New York Times Magazine*. She has a particular interest in stories about environmental health and has also written extensively on women's sports, including a book about the 1996 U.S. women's Olympic basketball team, *Venus to the Hoop* (1998).

William Cronon (b. 1954)

American environmental historian. Born in Connecticut and raised in Wisconsin, Cronon was a double major in history and English at the University of Wisconsin. After winning a Rhodes scholarship and completing a degree at Oxford University, Cronon earned a Ph.D. from Yale University, where he taught for over a decade. He later returned to the University of Wisconsin, where he is the Frederick Jackson Turner Professor of History, Geography, and Environmental Studies. His books include *Nature's Metropolis* (1991), *Under an Open Sky* (1992), and *Uncommon Ground: Toward Reinventing Nature* (1995). His book *Changes in the Land*, first published in 1983, was reissued in 2003 with an updated afterword by the author and a revised preface by John Demos.

Amy Cunningham (b. 1955)

American journalist and essayist. Cunningham studied English at the University of Virginia and has been a freelance writer since she graduated in 1977. She has written articles on cultural and feminist topics for magazines such as *Glamour*, *Mademoiselle*, and the *Washington Post Magazine*, as well as several on-line journals.

Daniel Dennett (b. 1942)
American philosopher. Dennett was born in Boston, Massachusetts, and earned his B.A. in philosophy at Harvard University and his D.Phil. at Oxford University. He is University Professor and Austin B. Fletcher Professor of Philosophy and Co-Director of the Center for Cognitive Studies at Tufts University. Dennett's work examines free will, consciousness, and the evolutionary aspects of the conscious mind. His books include *Content and Consciousness* (1969), *Brainstorms* (1978), *The Intentional Stance* (1987), *Consciousness Explained* (1991), *Darwin's Dangerous Idea* (1995), *Freedom Evolves* (2003), and *Breaking the Spell* (2006).

Debra Dickerson (b. 1960)
African American lawyer and essayist. Raised in St. Louis, Missouri, Dickerson has been an officer in the U.S. Air Force, a senior editor at *US News and World Report*, and a lawyer for the NAACP Legal Defense Fund. She is a Senior Fellow at the New American Foundation in Washington, D.C. Her writing has appeared in the *New Republic*, the *New York Times*, and the *Nation*, among other periodicals. Her books include the memoir *An American Story* (2000) and *The End of Blackness* (2004).

Joan Didion (b. 1934)
American novelist, essayist, and screenwriter. A native Californian, Didion studied at the University of California at Berkeley. After winning *Vogue* magazine's Prix de Paris contest for excellence in writing, she began working for the magazine. Didion rose to associate feature editor before leaving *Vogue* in 1963, the year her first novel, *Run River*, was published. Since then, she has written five more novels, the most recent of which is *The Last Thing He Wanted* (1996). A frequent contributor to magazines and literary reviews, Didion has published her essays in collections that include *Slouching towards Bethlehem* (1969) and *The White Album* (1979). *Salvador*, a work of reportage based on her visit to El Salvador in 1983, marked Didion's growing concern with politics, as did *Miami* (1987), an attempt to come to terms with the complexities of an American

city, and her book *Political Fictions* (2001). Her recent works of nonfiction include *Fixed Ideas: America Since 9.11* (2003), and *The Year of Magical Thinking* (2005), a book-length essay that chronicles the year following her husband's death, a period in which Didion's daughter, Quintana (who has since passed away), was gravely ill. In November 2005, it won the National Book Award for nonfiction.

Annie Dillard (b. 1945)
American nature writer, poet, and novelist. Born in Pittsburgh, Pennsylvania, Dillard received her B.A. and M.A. from Hollins College. A keen observer, she has published a wide variety of books, from the poetry collections *Tickets for a Prayer Wheel* (1974) and *Mornings Like This: Found Poems* (1995) to the personal narratives/explorations *Holy the Firm* (1977) and *For the Time Being* (1999), the memoir *An American Childhood* (1987), the book of theory *Living by Fiction* (1982), the essay collection *Teaching a Stone to Talk* (1982), and the novel *The Living* (1992), about pioneers on Puget Sound. In her Pulitzer Prize–winning nonfiction narrative *Pilgrim at Tinker Creek* (1974) Dillard recounts years she spent living in seclusion in the natural world. In *The Writing Life* (1989) she tells personal stories about being a writer. Her most recent work is *The Maytrees: A Novel* (2007).

Kildare Dobbs (b. 1923)
Canadian poet and travel writer. Dobbs was born in India, raised in Ireland, and educated in Dublin, Cambridge, and London. His most recent book is a memoir, *Running the Rapids: A Writer's Life* (2005), which details his travels in various parts of the world. He served in the Royal Army before emigrating to Canada, where he co-founded *The Tamarack Review*. Some of his other works include *Running to Paradise* (1962), *Pride and Fall: A Novella and Six Stories* (1981), *Historic Canada* (1984), *Coastal Canada* (1985), and *The Eleventh Hour: Poems for the Third Millennium* (1997).

John Donne (1572–1631)
English poet, essayist, and cleric. Born into a Roman Catholic family at a time when Catholicism was barely tolerated in England, Donne attended Oxford and Cambridge Universities, but could not receive a degree because he was not a member of the Church of England.

Donne studied, although never practiced, law and, after quietly abandoning Catholicism sometime during the 1590s, entered government service. In 1615 he became an Anglican minister, and in 1621 he was named dean of St. Paul's Cathedral. Due in part to the enthusiasm and wit he had cultivated as a writer of love poems, he was considered one of the greatest religious orators of his age. Donne's literary reputation rests on his poetry as well as on his devotions and sermons.

Frederick Douglass (1818–1895)
African American abolitionist, orator, and writer. Born a slave in Maryland, Douglass learned at a young age how to read and write, an amazing feat since it was against the law to teach literacy to a slave. In 1836 he escaped from his master and fled to the North with Anna Murray, a free black woman, whom he later married. Douglass soon became an important orator in the abolitionist movement and, with the publication of his first autobiography, *Narrative of the Life of Frederick Douglass* (1845), an international spokesman for freedom. Douglass founded the antislavery newspaper the *North Star* in 1847 and actively recruited black soldiers to join the Union Army at the outbreak of the Civil War. He continued his autobiography in *My Bondage and My Freedom* (1855) and *The Life and Times of Frederick Douglass* (1881; rev. 1892).

Rita Dove (b. 1952)
American poet and author. Born in Akron, Ohio, Dove graduated *summa cum laude* from Miami University. After studying in Germany as a Fulbright scholar, she earned her M.F.A. at the University of Iowa. She has published numerous volumes of poetry, most recently *American Smooth* (2004). She has also published a book of short stories, *Fifth Sunday* (1985); a novel, *Through the Ivory Gate* (2004); a book of essays, *The Poet's World* (1995); and a play, *The Darker Face of the Earth* (1994). She received the Pulitzer Prize in Poetry in 1987 and served as the first African American Poet Laureate of the United States, from 1993 to 1995. She is currently Commonwealth Professor of English at the University of Virginia.

Lars Eighner (b. 1948)
American writer. Born in Corpus Christi, Texas, Eighner attended the University of Texas, in Austin, where he now lives. A self-described "skeptical Democrat," Eighner has worked in hospitals and drug-crisis programs. His book *Travels with Lizbeth* (1993), which describes his three years of surviving on the streets with his dog, was a best-seller. He has also published *Elements of Arousal* (1994), a how-to guide on writing gay erotica, and the comic novel *Pawn to Queen Four* (1995), about the gay subculture of a Texan town.

Loren Eiseley (1907–1977)
American anthropologist, sociologist, archaeologist, historian of science, and poet. Educated at the University of Nebraska and the University of Pennsylvania, Eiseley taught at the University of Kansas and Oberlin College before returning to the University of Pennsylvania, where he remained for thirty years. A humanist concerned with the whole spectrum of life on earth and our place in it, he established a national reputation with his writings. His books include *The Immense Journey* (1957), *Darwin's Century: Evolution and the Men Who Discovered It* (1958), *The Firmament of Time* (rev. ed., 1960), *The Mind as Nature* (1962), *The Night Country* (1971), and *The Unexpected Universe* (1972). A collection of Eiseley's poems, *Another Kind of Autumn*, was published posthumously in 1977.

Ralph Waldo Emerson (1803–1882)
American poet, philosopher, and essayist. Emerson entered Harvard University at fourteen. After graduation in 1821, he taught school for several years before beginning theological studies in 1825. In 1829 he was ordained a Unitarian minister. Although he enjoyed delivering sermons, his Christian faith began to waver under the influence of Romantic philosophers. In 1832 he resigned his pastorate and retired to Concord, Massachusetts, to a life of study and reflection. With the publication of his first book, *Nature* (1836), Emerson became an important figure in the development of American transcendentalism. Emerson's occasional lectures at Harvard and the publication of his *Essays* (1841) secured his reputation as a dominant force in American literature and one of the most influential American essayists.

Nora Ephron (b. 1941)
American journalist, director, and screenwriter. Born in New York City, Ephron

graduated from Wellesley College in 1962. She began her career as a journalist, writing for the *New York Post*, *Esquire* magazine, the *New York Times Magazine*, and *New York* magazine. Her books include the novel *Heartburn* (1996) and the essay collections *Wallflower at the Orgy* (1970), *Crazy Salad* (1975), *Scribble, Scribble* (1978), and *I Feel Bad About My Neck* (2006). Ephron left journalism to become a screenwriter and has since been nominated for three Academy Awards for best original screenplay, for *Silkwood* (1983), *When Harry Met Sally* (1989), and *Sleepless in Seattle* (1993). In the 1990s she began directing films, including *You've Got Mail* (1998), *Lucky Numbers* (2000), and *Bewitched* (2006).

Anne Fadiman (b. 1953)
American essayist and editor. Fadiman worked as an editor for *Life* and currently teaches creative writing at Yale University. She has contributed to numerous journals and magazines, including *Harper's* and the *New Yorker*, and she worked for three years as a columnist at the magazine *Civilization*, a publication of the Library of Congress. Her first book, *The Spirit Catches You and You Fall Down* (1997), about a family of Hmong refugees, won a National Book Critics Circle Award. Her second book, *Ex Libris: Confessions of a Common Reader* (1998), is a collection of essays about Fadiman's love of literature and language. Her most recent book is *At Large and At Small: Familiar Essays* (2007).

William Faulkner (1897–1962)
American novelist and short-story writer. Faulkner lived his whole life in his native Mississippi, apart from a short time in military service and a period spent writing screenplays in Hollywood. He attended the University of Mississippi, in the town of Oxford, and much of his writing depicts life in fictional Yoknapatawpha County, an imaginative reconstruction of the area near Oxford. With the help of the author Sherwood Anderson, Faulkner published his first novel, *Soldier's Pay*, in 1926. His major novels include *The Sound and the Fury* (1929), *As I Lay Dying* (1930), *Sanctuary* (1931), *Light in August* (1932), and *Absalom! Absalom!* (1936). His short stories are included in the collections *These Thirteen* (1931), *Go Down, Moses and Other Stories* (1942), and *The Collected Stories of William Faulkner* (1950). He received the Nobel Prize for literature in 1949.

Frances FitzGerald (b. 1940)
American journalist and writer. Coming from a family with a strong interest in politics and international affairs (her father was a deputy director of the CIA, her mother an ambassador to the United Nations), FitzGerald has worked as a freelance journalist since her graduation from Radcliffe College, in 1962. She went to Vietnam in 1966 and achieved critical success with her first book, *Fire in the Lake: The Vietnamese and Americans in Vietnam* (1972); it won four major awards, including a Pulitzer Prize and a National Book Award. Her other books include *America Revised: History Schoolbooks in the Twentieth Century* (1979), *Cities on a Hill: Journeys through American Cultures* (1986), and *Way Out There in the Blue: Reagan, Star Wars and the End of the Cold War* (2000). FitzGerald regularly contributes to several American periodicals, most notably the *New Yorker*.

Kitty Burns Florey (b. 1943)
American novelist, essayist, and editor. Florey was born in Syracuse, New York, and earned her B.A. and M.A. in English literature from Boston University and Syracuse University, respectively. She has written nine novels and numerous essays and short stories. Her most recent book is *Sister Bernadette's Barking Dog: The Quirky History and Lost Art of Diagramming Sentences* (2006), a nostalgic exploration of the history of sentence diagramming, which considers the possible reasons for the practice's decline and its revival in surprising places and ways.

Benjamin Franklin (1706–1790)
American statesman, inventor, writer, and diplomat. Apprenticed at twelve to his brother, a printer, Franklin learned all aspects of the trade, from setting type to writing editorials. At twenty-four, he was editor and publisher of the *Pennsylvania Gazette*. In 1733 he began writing *Poor Richard's Almanack*, a collection of aphorisms and advice. He retired from business at forty-two to devote himself to study and research, but soon found himself involved in colonial politics. From 1757 until 1763 he was diplomatic representative for the colonies in England. He served as a member of the committee appointed to draft the Declaration of Independence, and later was minister to France and delegate to the Paris peace conference that officially concluded the Revolutionary War.

H. Bruce Franklin (b. 1934)

American scholar and critic. Born in Brooklyn, New York, Franklin was educated at Amherst College and Stanford University. After a stint as a tugboat deckhand and several years in military service, Franklin returned to Stanford, as a scholar, critic, and social activist. He was the first tenured professor to be fired from Stanford after he urged his students to protest secret military testing on college campuses. Much of his popular writing explores the connections between modern war and the media. He also writes on science fiction and American literature. His books include *Victim as Criminal and Artist* (1978), *War Stars* (1988), *Prison Literature in America* (1989), *M.I.A., or Mythmaking in America* (1992), and *Prison Writing in 20th Century America* (1998). His essays have been published in *Science Fiction Studies*, the *Nation*, the *Progressive*, and the *Georgia Review*. Franklin is the John Cotton Dana Professor of English and American Studies at Rutgers University in Newark, New Jersey.

Northrop Frye (1912–1991)

Canadian literary critic and teacher. Educated at the University of Toronto and at Merton College, Oxford, Frye was a member of the faculty at Victoria College, University of Toronto, from 1939 until his death. Although he specialized in Renaissance and Romantic literature, Frye also wrote on Milton, the Bible, and Canadian literature. He published more than forty books, including *Fearful Symmetry: A Study of William Blake* (1947), *Anatomy of Criticism* (1957), *The Educated Imagination* (1964), *The Secular Scripture: A Study of the Structure of Romance* (1976), *The Great Code: The Bible and Literature* (1982), *A Natural Perspective: The Development of Shakespearean Comedy and Romance* (1988), *Double Vision* (1991), and *The Eternal Act of Creation* (1993).

Paul Fussell (b. 1924)

American writer and teacher. After distinguished military service in World War II, Fussell earned a Ph.D. at Harvard University and became an instructor of English at Connecticut College. In 1955 he was hired by the University of Pennsylvania, where he is a professor emeritus of English. Fussell's early books deal with poetic theory and eighteenth-century literature. With the publication of *The Great War and Modern Memory* (1975) and *Abroad: British Literary Traveling between the Wars* (1980), his attention shifted to the twentieth century. In 1983 he published *Class: A Guide through the American Status System*. Two of his essay collections are *The Boy Scout Handbook and Other Observations* (1982) and *Thank God for the Atom Bomb and Other Essays* (1988). Fussell has also edited *The Norton Book of Travel* (1987) and *The Norton Book of Modern War* (1990).

William Lloyd Garrison (1805–1879)

American journalist and antislavery activist. Garrison was one of the most influential members of the abolitionist movement preceding the Civil War. Born to a poor family in Newburyport, Massachusetts, he began an apprenticeship with a printer at thirteen. After working for various newspapers, he became coeditor of the *Genius of Universal Emancipation* in 1829. Two years later, finding that publication too moderate, Garrison founded the antislavery newspaper *The Liberator*, which became a crucial voice for the abolitionist movement in the North and South, spreading Garrison's cause through its own circulation as well as reaching other readers through reprints in major newspapers. In 1832 Garrison founded the New England Anti-Slavery Society, and the following year he helped create the American Anti-Slavery Society.

Henry Louis Gates Jr. (b. 1950)

African American scholar and literary critic. Born and raised in West Virginia, Gates was educated at Yale and Cambridge Universities. Now a professor at Harvard University, Gates balances his time between editing African American literature, writing literary criticism, and writing for general audiences. A proponent of multiculturalism and educational reform, Gates has been responsible for collecting thousands of short stories, poems, reviews, and other literary works written by and about African Americans in the nineteenth and early twentieth centuries. He created the television documentary "The Image of the Black in the Western Imagination," and his essays have appeared in the *New Yorker*, *Newsweek*, *Sports Illustrated*, and the *New York Times*. His books include *Figures in Black* (1987); *The Signifying Monkey* (1988); *Loose Canons* (1992); his autobiography, *Colored People* (1994); a collection of his *New Yorker* essays,

Thirteen Ways of Looking at a Black Man (1997); and *Wonders of the African World* (1999). He is the general coeditor of *The Norton Anthology of African American Literature* (2nd ed. 2004).

Malcolm Gladwell (b. 1963)
Canadian journalist and writer. Born in England and raised in Canada, Gladwell graduated from the University of Toronto and spent nine years as a writer for the *Washington Post*. As a staff writer for the *New Yorker*, he contributes articles on topics related to New York City as well as on health issues such as AIDS, plague anxiety, and health-care reform. His books include *The Tipping Point: How Little Things Can Make a Big Difference* (2000) and *Blink: The Power of Thinking Without Thinking* (2005).

William Golding (1911–1993)
English novelist. Educated at Marlborough Grammar School and Oxford University, Golding was a schoolmaster at Bishop Wordsworth's School, Salisbury, before becoming a novelist at forty-three. His novels are characterized by their darkly poetic tone, dense symbolism, and rejection of societal norms. His most famous work is *Lord of the Flies* (1954), a story of schoolboys marooned on an island, who revert to savagery. His other novels include *Pincher Martin* (1956), *The Spire* (1964), *The Pyramid* (1967), *Rites of Passage* (1980), *Close Quarters* (1987), and *Fire Down Below* (1989). In 1983 Golding received the Nobel Prize for literature.

Adam Goodheart (b. 1970)
American essayist and critic. Educated at Germantown Friends School and Harvard University, Goodheart has written reviews and articles on culture for the *Atlantic Monthly*, the *New York Times*, *Outside*, and *Salon.com*. He is a member of the editorial board of the *American Scholar*. In 2006, Washington College appointed Goodheart as the new director of the College's C. V. Starr Center for the Study of the American Experience.

Mary Gordon (b. 1949)
American novelist, literary critic, and memoirist. Gordon was born in Far Rockaway, New York. She received her B.A. from Barnard College in 1971 and her M.A. from Syracuse University in 1973. Her novels include *Final Payments* (1978), *The Company of Women* (1981), *Men and Angels* (1985), *The Other Side*

(1989), *Spending* (1998), and *Pearl* (2005). She is the author of three memoirs: *The Shadow Man: A Daughter's Search for Her Father* (1996), *Seeing Through Places: Reflections on Geography and Identity* (2000), and *Circling My Mother: A Memoir* (2007). She has also published a collection of essays, *Good Boys and Dead Girls* (1991), along with poems, short stories, and other works of nonfiction. She is currently Millicent C. McIntosh Professor of Writing at Barnard College.

Al Gore (b. 1948)
American politician, environmentalist, and author. Gore was born in Washington D.C. Like his father, Gore served as a U.S. Representative (1977–85) and Senator (1985–93). Gore was Vice President for the two-term Clinton administration (1993–2000). As Vice President he was an important advocate for the North American Free Trade Agreement (NAFTA), deficit reduction, and improvements in government efficiency. Gore was the Democratic nominee for president in 2000, and won the popular vote while losing the electoral vote in one of the closest and most controversial elections in U.S. history. Gore is president of the American television channel Current TV and chairman of Generation Investment Management. He lectures widely on the topic of global warming and starred in the 2006 Academy Award–winning climate change documentary, *An Inconvenient Truth*. In 2007 Gore and the U.N.'s Intergovernmental Panel on Climate Change won the Nobel Peace Prize. Gore is the author of three best-selling books: *Earth in the Balance* (1992), *An Inconvenient Truth* (2006), and *The Assault on Reason* (2007).

Stephen Jay Gould (1941–2002)
American paleontologist, essayist, and teacher. Raised in New York City, Gould graduated from Antioch College and received a Ph.D. from Columbia University in 1967. That same year he joined the faculty of Harvard University as a professor of geology and zoology and taught courses in paleontology, biology, and the history of science. Witty and fluent, Gould demystified science for lay readers in essays written for a regular column in *Natural History* magazine. Many of his essays have been collected in *Ever Since Darwin* (1977), *Hen's Teeth and Horse's Toes* (1983), and *Eight Little Piggies* (1993). Gould's *The Mismeasure of Man*

(1981), which questioned traditional ways of testing intelligence, won the National Book Critics Circle Award for essays and criticism. His last major study of Darwinian evolution, *The Structure of Evolutionary Theory,* appeared in 2002.

Philip Gourevitch (b. 1961)

American journalist. After covering the Rwandan civil war for the *New Yorker,* Gourevitch spent several years investigating the Hutus' attempted genocide of the Tutsis in Rwanda. He detailed his observations in his first book, *We Wish to Inform You That Tomorrow We Will Be Killed with Our Families: Stories from Rwanda* (1988), which won many awards, including the National Book Critics Circle Award for nonfiction. His most recent book, *A Cold Case* (2002), describes the investigation of an unsolved murder in New York City. He was named editor of *The Paris Review* in 2005.

Robert Graves (1895–1985)

English poet, novelist, and classical scholar. After a private education, distinguished service in World War I, and study at St. John's College, Oxford, Graves held a brief appointment at the University of Cairo before becoming a professional writer. In a long and prolific career, he published 130 works, ranging from poetry and novels to essays, lectures, and criticism. He is perhaps best known for his classic memoir, *Goodbye to All That* (1929); his historical novels, *I, Claudius* (1934) and *King Jesus* (1946); his work on writing, *The Reader over Your Shoulder* (1943); and his study of poetic myth, *The White Goddess* (1948). Graves's classical scholarship provided much of the material for his fiction and poetry.

Mark Greif (b. 1975)

American writer and literary critic. Greif is the co-founder and co-editor of the magazine *n + 1,* to which he contributes regularly. He also writes frequently for *American Prospect.* He earned his B.A. at Harvard University, where he studied history and literature. He attended Oxford University as a Marshall scholar, before undertaking graduate work in American Studies at Yale University. His writing addresses a wide variety of topics, including literature, pop culture, and conservative and leftist theory.

Lani Guinier (b. 1950)

African American law professor and writer. Born in Queens, New York, Guinier attended the Yale Law School with Bill and Hillary Clinton and now teaches at the University of Pennsylvania. President Clinton nominated her for assistant attorney general, but withdrew the nomination in response to protests over her alleged political views. Guinier has since written a book, *The Tyranny of the Majority* (1994), and numerous articles about the implications of this experience. Her other books include *Becoming Gentlemen* (1997), *Lift Every Voice* (1998), and *Who's Qualified?* (2001).

David Guterson (b. 1956)

American novelist and essayist. Born in Seattle, Washington, and educated at the University of Washington, Guterson taught high school for many years. Inspired by his own educational experience and that of his children, he has written numerous essays and a book, *Family Matters* (1993), in favor of homeschooling. He has also written a collection of stories, *The Country Ahead of Us, the Country Behind* (1989), and two novels, *Snow Falling on Cedars* (1994), which won the PEN/Faulkner Award in 1995, and *East of the Mountains* (1999). Guterson is a contributing editor to *Harper's Magazine* and has also published in the *New York Times Magazine* and the *Utne Reader.* Often writing about everyday subjects such as sports or shopping malls, Guterson says that he has an "ethical and moral duty . . . to tell stories that inspire readers to consider more deeply who they are." Guterson's 2003 novel, *Our Lady of the Forest,* is about a fictional Marian apparition witnessed by a teenage girl in Washington.

Nathaniel Hawthorne (1804–1864)

American novelist, short-story writer, and essayist. After graduating from Bowdoin College, Hawthorne returned to his home in Salem, Massachusetts, and devoted himself to writing fiction. In 1837 he published *Twice-Told Tales* and became a public literary figure. After his marriage in 1842, he and his wife moved to Concord, where they lived for three years. In 1846 Hawthorne was appointed surveyor of the Port of Salem, the first of a number of political positions that would culminate in his becoming American consul in Liverpool, England (1853). Although he may be best known for his fiction—the novels *The Scarlet Letter* (1850) and *The House of the Seven Gables* (1851) in particular—Hawthorne also wrote a series of valuable sketches for the *Atlantic Monthly*.

Ernest Hemingway (1899–1961)

American novelist and short-story writer. Hemingway began his professional writing career as a journalist, reporting for newspapers in Kansas City and Toronto. In the 1920s he lived in Paris as a part of the American expatriate community, known as "the Lost Generation," which included Gertrude Stein, F. Scott Fitzgerald, and Ezra Pound. Hemingway's literary reputation rests on his short stories, collected in *In Our Time* (1925) and *Men without Women* (1927), and his novels, including *The Sun Also Rises* (1926), *A Farewell to Arms* (1929), and *For Whom the Bell Tolls* (1940). *The Old Man and the Sea* (1952) was the last work published during his lifetime. Hemingway received the Nobel Prize for literature in 1954.

Gilbert Highet (1906–1978)

Scottish American scholar, poet, writer, and teacher. Born in Glasgow, Scotland, Highet was educated at the University of Glasgow and Oxford University. From 1932 until 1936 he taught at St. John's College, Oxford; he then accepted an appointment at Columbia University, where he taught Greek and Latin literature for thirty years. Considered a master teacher, Highet communicated his enthusiasm for classical literature not only in the classroom, but also in a number of books. Of the fourteen he wrote, perhaps the most famous are *The Classical Tradition* (1949), *The Art of Teaching* (1950), and *The Anatomy of Satire* (1962).

Jack Hitt (b. 1957)

American journalist. Hitt is a regular writer for the *New York Times Magazine*, a contributing editor for *GQ* and *Harper's*, and a contributing editor for the National Public Radio program *This American Life*. The author of *Off the Road: A Modern-Day Walk down the Pilgrim's Route into Spain* (1994), he has also edited *The Harper's Forum Book: What Are We Talking About?* (1991).

John Holt (1923–1985)

American teacher and theorist of education. Born in New York City, Holt taught for many years in high schools in Colorado and Massachusetts and then at Harvard University and the University of California at Berkeley. His numerous books, based on his teaching experiences

and centrally concerned with education, include *How Children Fail* (1964), *How Children Learn* (1967), *The Under-Achieving School* (1967), *Freedom and Beyond* (1972), and *Escape from Childhood* (1984).

Langston Hughes (1902–1967)

African American poet, playwright, and fiction writer. Hughes emerged as a key figure in the Harlem Renaissance of the 1920s and 1930s. Encouraged by his fellow artists, he published his first collection of poems, *The Weary Blues*, in 1926. Although critical response was mixed, the degree of public acceptance achieved by Hughes with this and subsequent works enabled him to become one of the few African American modernist writers to support himself from his writing and lecturing. He published in his lifetime seventeen volumes of poetry, two novels, seven collections of short stories, and twenty-six plays.

Zora Neale Hurston (1891–1960)

African American writer and folklorist. A central figure of the Harlem Renaissance of the 1920s and 1930s, Hurston was born in Eatonville, Florida, the daughter of a Baptist preacher and a seamstress. She attended Howard University and in 1928 received a B.A. from Barnard College, where she studied anthropology and developed an interest in black folk traditions and in oral history. Hurston's writing draws on her knowledge of folklore and uses a vigorous, rhythmical, direct prose style that influenced later American writers. Hurston's works include the play *Mule Bone: A Comedy of Negro Life in Three Acts* (1931), written with Langston Hughes, and the novels *Their Eyes Were Watching God* (1937), *Moses, Man of the Mountain* (1939), and *Seraph on the Suwanee* (1948).

Molly Ivins (1944–2007)

Mary Tyler Ivins, American columnist and writer. Born in California and raised in Houston, Texas, Ivins received a B.A. from Smith College and an M.A. in journalism from Columbia University. She worked on the staffs of the *Houston Chronicle*, the *Minneapolis Star Tribune*, the *Texas Observer*, and the *New York Times* and as a syndicated political columnist at the *Fort Worth Star-Telegram*. Ivins delighted in exposing politics at its worst and used humor to present serious issues such as gun control. Her articles appeared in *Mother Jones*, *Ms.*, the *Nation*, and the *Progressive*; collections include *Nothin' but Good Times Ahead* (1993) and *You Got to Dance with Them What Brung You* (1998). Her books included *Shrub: The Short but Happy Political Life of George W. Bush* (2000), *Bushwhacked: Life in George W. Bush's America* (2004), *Who Let the Dogs In?: Incredible Political Animals I Have Known* (2005), and, posthumously, *Bill of Wrongs: The Executive Branch's Assault on America's Fundamental Rights* (2007).

Thomas Jefferson (1743–1826)
American lawyer, architect, and writer; secretary of state to George Washington (1789–93), vice president to John Adams (1797–1801), and third president of the United States (1801–9). A learned man of significant accomplishments in many fields, Jefferson entered politics in his native Virginia, where he served in the House of Burgesses and eventually became governor (1779–81). In 1809 he founded the University of Virginia, designing both the buildings and the curriculum. A fluent stylist, Jefferson wrote books on science, religion, architecture, and even Anglo-Saxon grammar. He is probably best known for writing the Declaration of Independence; preliminary drafts were done by a committee, which relied on Jefferson for the drafts and the final revision.

Jesus (c. 4 B.C.E.–c. 30 C.E.)
Jesus of Nazareth, first-century religious teacher. Source of the Christian religion and Savior in the Christian faith, Jesus spent his short public career in Palestine, preaching a message of repentance and conversion. One of his favorite teaching devices was the parable, a literary form with a long history, used extensively in rabbinical tradition.

Samuel Johnson (1709–1784)
English lexicographer, critic, moralist, and essayist. In spite of childhood poverty, poor eyesight, and scant advanced education, Johnson achieved renown in his day as a wit, a conversationalist, and an astute observer of the human experience. In 1737, having failed as a schoolmaster, he sought his fortune in London, where he soon found work contributing essays and poems to the *Gentleman's Magazine*. Johnson's literary career prospered as he wrote and published poems, plays, and essays. In 1750 he founded the *Rambler*, a popular periodical containing essays, fables, and criticism. One of the greatest prose stylists of the English language, Johnson prepared the monumental *Dictionary of the English Language* (1755) and wrote *Rasselas* (1759), a didactic tale, and *The Lives of the Poets* (1779–81).

Ben Jonson (1572–1637)
English essayist, poet, and playwright. The publication of Jonson's *Works*, in 1616, completed his ascension to a position of renown as a professional author. His early life was riddled with controversy, including imprisonment for his contribution to the plays *The Isle of Dogs* and *Eastward Ho* and a Privy Council trial for allegations of "popery and treason" in his play *Sejanus*. By 1605, however, he had been commissioned by King James I to organize entertainment for the court; under the king's auspices, Jonson produced twenty-four masques that contributed to his growing popularity as a playwright. Jonson wrote a broad range of plays and poems, which, although diverse in style, all combined his deep classical learning, his hungry imagination, and his sharp capacity for human observation. *Timber, Or Discoveries Made upon Men and Matter* was published posthumously in his *Works* and is an important English commentary on poetics of the period.

Garrison Keillor (b. 1942)
American radio host, humorist, and writer. Born in Anoka, Minnesota, Keillor graduated from the University of Minnesota. He is the creator and host of the popular NPR radio program *A Prairie Home Companion*. He has won numerous awards, including a Grammy for best nonmusical recording (*Lake Wobegon Days*, 1987), and was inducted into the Music Broadcast Communications Radio Hall of Fame in 1994. He is the author of *Happy to Be Here* (1982), the bestselling *Lake Wobegon Days* (1985), *The Book of Guys* (1993), and the children's book *Cat, You Better Come Home* (1995). Recent books include *Wobegon Boy* (1997), *Minnesota Days: Our Heritage in Stories, Art, and Photos* (1999), and *Lake Wobegon Summer, 1956* (2001).

John Fitzgerald Kennedy (1917–1963)
American writer, orator, and thirty-fifth president of the United States. Born in Brookline, Massachusetts, Kennedy graduated *cum laude* from Harvard Uni-

versity. Before being elected to the House of Representatives at twenty-nine, he had received the Navy and Marine Corps Medal for his service in World War II and developed his senior thesis into a best-selling book, *Why England Slept* (1962). In 1952, after only six years in the House, Kennedy's family helped him campaign for the Massachusetts Senate election, which he narrowly won. The young senator's fame grew in the 1950s, and his eloquence and poise in televised debates against Richard Nixon helped Kennedy win the presidency in 1960. His inaugural address, calling for all citizens' participation in the affairs of their nation, is one of the best-known speeches in American history. On November 22, 1963, in Dallas, Texas, he was assassinated by Lee Harvey Oswald.

Jamaica Kincaid (b. 1949)
Caribbean American writer. Born in the West Indies, Kincaid moved to the United States when she was seventeen and worked as a domestic helper. Although she had barely the equivalent of a high school diploma, she took classes at the New School for Social Research and eventually became a staff writer for the *New Yorker*. Her books include *At the Bottom of the River* (1988), *A Small Place* (1988), *Lucy* (1990), *The Autobiography of My Mother* (1995), and *My Brother* (1997). Kincaid's interest in gardening has led to books on the subject, including *My Garden* (2001), a collection of essays. *Among Flowers: A Walk in the Himalayas* (2005) chronicles Kincaid's journey into the foothills of the Himalayas in search of rare plants to bring home to her Vermont garden.

Martin Luther King Jr. (1929–1968)
African American clergyman and Civil Rights leader. By the age of twenty-six, King had completed his undergraduate education, finished divinity school, and received a Ph.D. in religion from Boston University. The Montgomery, Alabama, bus boycott in 1956 marked his entry into public politics; blacks boycotted segregated buses, and King took a public stand in their support. Drawing on the New Testament teachings of Jesus and the principles of passive resistance of Mahatma Gandhi, King advocated nonviolent protest to effect significant social change. In the years following the boycott, he became a major figure in the Civil Rights movement. In 1963, Bir-

mingham, Alabama, perhaps the most segregated city in the South, became the focal point for violent confrontations between blacks and whites; 2,400 civil rights workers, King among them, were jailed. King then wrote his now-famous "Letter from Birmingham Jail." In 1964, at thirty-five, he became the youngest person ever to receive the Nobel Peace Prize. He was assassinated on April 14, 1968, in Memphis, Tennessee.

Maxine Hong Kingston (b. 1940)
Chinese American autobiographer and novelist. Born in California, the eldest of six children in a Chinese immigrant family, Kingston grew up in a culture in which English was a second language; friends and relatives regularly gathered at her family's laundry to tell stories in Chinese and reminisce about their native country. Graduating from the University of California at Berkeley, Kingston taught school in California and Hawaii and began publishing poetry, stories, and articles in a number of magazines, including the *New Yorker*, *New West*, the *New York Times Magazine*, *Ms.*, and the *Iowa Review*. Her acclaimed books of reminiscence, which both won National Book Critics Circle Awards, are *The Woman Warrior: Memoirs of a Girlhood among Ghosts* (1973) and *China Men* (1980). She has also published a novel, *Tripmaster Monkey: His Fake Book* (1989).

Melvin Konner (b. 1946)
American anthropologist, biologist, educator, and physician. Born in Brooklyn, New York, Konner graduated from Brooklyn College, City University of New York, and received his Ph.D. at Harvard University, where he began his teaching career as an anthropologist; he now holds a joint appointment in the departments of anthropology and medicine at Emory University. His writing focuses on the public debate over health care. His books include *The Tangled Wing* (1982), *Becoming a Doctor* (1988), *Why the Reckless Survive* (1990), *Dear America* (1993), and *Medicine at the Crossroads* (1993). He frequently contributes to the *New York Times* and *Newsweek*. In 2003 he published *Unsettled: An Anthropology of the Jews*.

Nicholas D. Kristof (b. 1959)
American journalist and political writer. Raised in Yamhill, Oregon, Kristof was educated at Harvard University and at

Magdalen College, Oxford, where he was a Rhodes scholar. He specializes in East Asia and has written several books in that area, including *China Wakes: The Struggle for the Soul of a Rising Power* (1994) and *Thunder from the East: Portrait of a Rising Asia* (2000), both coauthored with his wife, Sheryl WuDunn. In 1990, Kristof and WuDunn were awarded the Pulitzer Prize for International Reporting, in recognition of their coverage of the pro-democracy student movement in China and the Tiananmen square protests that accompanied it. Currently a columnist for the *New York Times*, Kristof has recently gained attention for his coverage of the crises in the Darfur region of the Sudan.

Joseph Wood Krutch (1893–1970)
American naturalist, journalist, and theater and literary critic. Born in Knoxville, Tennessee, Krutch studied science at the University of Tennessee before taking a Ph.D. in English at Columbia University; he later remarked that he knew "more about botany than any other New York critic, and more about the theater than any other botanist." A frequent contributor to such periodicals as the *Atlantic Monthly*, *Harper's Magazine*, *Saturday Review*, and *Natural History*, Krutch is best known for two widely read and influential books, *The Desert Year* (1952) and *The Modern Temper* (1956).

Elisabeth Kübler-Ross (1926–2004)
Swiss American psychologist. Born and educated in Switzerland, Kübler-Ross came to prominence in the United States, where she lived from 1958 until her death. Her work is largely a response to what she called "the horrifying experience of the [postwar European] concentration camps." She gave seminars and wrote about death and dying not only to better understand the process, but also to improve care for the terminally ill. Her books on the subject include the bestselling *On Death and Dying* (1969), *On Children and Death* (1983), *AIDS: The Ultimate Challenge* (1987), *The Wheel of Life: A Memoir of Living and Dying* (1997), and, with David Kessler, *Life Lessons: Two Experts on Death and Dying Teach Us about the Mysteries of Life and Living* (2000). *On Life after Death* (1995) retracts much of her earlier work.

Thomas S. Kuhn (1922–1996)
American philosopher and historian. Educated at Harvard University, where he

earned a Ph.D. in physics, Kuhn was a specialist in the history and philosophy of science. The author of *The Copernican Revolution* (1957) and *The Essential Tension: Selected Studies in Scientific Tradition and Change* (1977), he is perhaps best known for *The Structure of Scientific Revolutions* (1962; 1970; 1996). Before his death, Kuhn was Laurence S. Rockefeller Professor of Philosophy at the Massachusetts Institute of Technology.

Anthony Lane (b. 1962)
English book and film critic. Lane completed his undergraduate degree in English at Trinity College, Cambridge, where he also did graduate work on the poet T. S. Eliot. He worked as a freelancer and wrote book and film reviews for the *Independent* before joining the *New Yorker*, where he has been a film critic since 1993.

Chang-Rae Lee (b. 1965)
Korean American fiction writer. When he was three, Lee and his family emigrated from South Korea to the U.S., where they settled in Westchester, New York. He received his B.A. from Yale in 1987 and spent one year as an equities analyst before pursuing his M.F.A. at the University of Oregon. Lee has taught writing at the University of Oregon and Manhattan's Hunter College, and in 2002 he joined the faculty at Princeton University. Lee's first novel, *Native Speaker* (1995), examines a Korean American's search for identity; his *A Gesture Life* (1999) focuses on a former medic's memories of his experiences treating the "comfort women," Korean women forced to have sex with Japanese soldiers in World War II. Lee's 2004 novel, *Aloft*, is his first that does not feature an Asian protagonist. Instead, the main character is a white, wealthy, Long Island suburbanite, which allows Lee to come at the issues of race and "Americanness" from new angles. Lee has also published essays in newspapers and magazines such as the *New Yorker*, the *Village Voice*, and *Time*.

Aldo Leopold (1886–1948)
American essayist and environmentalist. Leopold graduated from Yale University's School of Forestry and worked as a forest ranger in the Arizona and New Mexico territories. A vocal member of the Forestry Service, he fought for legislation to protect ecosystems threatened by de-

velopment of the land. Leopold opposed purely economic views of land use and worked to protect America's wilderness from exploitation. His essays and lobbying fostered many of the environmental protection acts in place today, and his 1933 book, *Game Management*, advanced his "conservation ethic," which argued for the intrinsic value of nature. In 1949 a collection of essays about the Wisconsin farm where he lived in later life was published posthumously as *A Sand County Almanac, and Sketches Here and There*.

Michael Levin (b. 1943)
American philosopher and educator. Educated at Michigan State University and Columbia University, Levin was a member of the Department of Philosophy at Columbia from 1968 until 1980. He is currently professor of philosophy at City College of the City University of New York. His research interests include ethics, philosophy, and the mind. The author of a number of scholarly articles, Levin has published *Metaphysics and the Mind-Body Problem* (1979), *Feminism and Freedom* (1987), *Why Race Matters: Race Differences and What They Mean* (1997), and *Sexual Orientation and Human Rights* (1999).

Abraham Lincoln (1809–1865)
American lawyer and orator, and sixteenth president of the United States. Born in Kentucky, Lincoln was a self-made and self-taught man. In 1830 his family moved to Illinois, where Lincoln prepared himself for a career in law. In 1834 he was elected to the first of four terms in the Illinois state legislature; in 1847, to the U.S. Congress. Elected president in 1860, Lincoln sought to preserve the Union amid the strife of the Civil War while he worked for the passage of the Thirteenth Amendment, which would outlaw slavery "everywhere and forever" in the United States. During his first term, Lincoln delivered the "Gettysburg Address" (1863) at the site of one of the Civil War's bloodiest battles. Reelected in 1864, he gave his Second Inaugural Address, an eloquent appeal for reconciliation and peace, in 1865. Lincoln was assassinated by the actor John Wilkes Booth on April 15, 1865.

Barry Lopez (b. 1945)
American essayist, poet, and fiction writer. Born in Port Chester, New York, Lopez was raised in New York City and Southern California. He was educated at the University of Notre Dame and at the University of Oregon. His work is largely concerned with the relationship between human culture and the natural world, and Lopez is often compared to Henry David Thoreau. He has published numerous books, including *Arctic Dreams* (1986), for which he received the National Book Award, *Of Wolves and Men* (1978), and eight works of fiction, among them *Light Action in the Caribbean* (2000), *Field Notes* (1994), and *Resistance* (2004). He has also published two books of essays: *Crossing Open Ground* (1988) and *About This Life* (1998).

Ellen Lupton (b. 1963) and
J. Abbott Miller (b. 1963)
American graphic design scholars. Lupton is a curator of contemporary design at Cooper-Hewitt National Design Museum, and Miller was formerly vice president of the American Center for Design. They currently share a studio, Design/Writing/Research, a name reflecting their belief that design is a type of authorship. Both have published widely on the history of design and on issues in contemporary design, including their essay collection on modern design theory, *Design, Writing, Research: Writing on Graphic Design and Typography* (1996). Together they have curated museum exhibitions such as "The Process of Elimination: The Kitchen, the Bathroom, and the Aesthetics of Waste" and "The ABCs of [triangle, square, circle]: The Bauhaus and Design Theory from Pre-school to Post-modernism." In 1994 they received the first annual Chrysler Award for Innovation in Design, and in 1996 they won the *New York* Magazine Award, given to New Yorkers central to the development of the cultural life of the city.

Thomas Lynch (b. 1948)
American essayist, poet, and funeral director. Born in Detroit, Michigan, Lynch has been the head of a funeral home in Milford, Michigan, since 1974. In his memoir, *Booking Passage: We Irish and Americans* (2005), he traces his reconnection with his Irish heritage, beginning with his 1970 journey to Ireland, where he met family members and started to learn about his family's history. Lynch has published three collections of poetry: *Skating with Heather Grace* (1987), *Grimalkin & Other Poems* (1994), and *Still Life in Milford* (1998), and two collections of essays: *The Undertaking: Life*

Studies from the Dismal Trade (1997), which was a finalist for the National Book Award, and *Bodies in Motion and at Rest: On Metaphor and Mortality* (2001). His work has appeared in the *New Yorker*, the *Paris Review*, *Esquire*, and other periodicals.

Niccolò Machiavelli (1469–1527)
Florentine statesman and political philosopher. An aristocrat who held office while Florence was a republic, Machiavelli fell from favor when the Medicis returned to power in 1512. Briefly imprisoned, he was restored to an office of some influence, but he never regained his former importance. Machiavelli's most famous work, *The Prince* (1513), has exerted considerable literary and political influence within the Western tradition.

E. S. Maduro (pseudonym; DOB unknown)
American youth counselor and writer. E. S. Maduro is the pseudonym of the author of "Excuse Me While I Explode," one of twenty-six essays in *The Bitch in the House* (2003), a collection of pieces by women about their lives. The writer divides her time between New England and Central America.

Nancy Mairs (b. 1943)
American nonfiction writer and essayist. Married at nineteen, Mairs finished college, had a child, and earned an M.F.A. and a Ph.D. from the University of Arizona. The personal difficulties that inform her writing include six months spent in a state mental hospital, suffering from a near-suicidal mixture of agoraphobia and anorexia, and the later discovery that she suffered from multiple sclerosis. She found a dual salvation in writing and in Roman Catholicism, to which she converted in her thirties. Mairs's books include *Plain-text* (1986), *Carnal Acts* (1990), *Waist-High in the World: A Life among the Nondisabled* (1997), and *Troubled Guest: Life and Death Stories* (2001).

Scott McCloud (b. 1960)
American cartoonist and comics theorist. McCloud was born in Boston, Massachusetts. He is the creator of the science fiction/superhero comic book series *Zot!* His other print comics include *Destroy!!*, described as "a deliberately over-the-top, over-sized single-issue comic book, intended as a parody of formulaic superhero fights," and the graphic novel *The New Adventures of Abraham Lincoln*

(1998). In 1993, he published *Understanding Comics*, a scholarly work on the definition, history, and methodology of comics, done entirely in comics form. It is widely considered one of the definitive works on the subject. He followed this study with *Reinventing Comics* (2000) and *Making Comics* (2006).

Bill McKibben (b. 1960)
American environmentalist and writer. Born in Lexington, Massachusetts, McKibben attended Harvard University, where he was president of the *Harvard Crimson* newspaper. From 1982 to 1987 he worked as a staff writer at the *New Yorker*, where his first book, *The End of Nature* (1989), a study of climate change intended for a nonspecialist audience, was serialized before publication. The main topics of his writing are global warming, alternative energy, and human genetic engineering. In 2007, he spearheaded one of the biggest demonstrations against global warming in U.S. history. His most recent book is *Deep Economy* (2007), a work that McKibben describes as "challeng[ing] the prevailing view of our economy." His other books include *The Age of Missing Information* (1992), *Hope, Human and Wild: True Stories of Living Lightly on the Earth* (1995), *The Comforting Whirlwind: God, Job and the Scale of Creation* (2005), and *Wandering Home* (2005).

John McMurtry (b. 1939)
Canadian writer, teacher, and philosopher. Educated at the University of Toronto, McMurtry became a professional football player before earning his Ph.D. at the University of London. Now professor of philosophy at the University of Guelph, he has written several books, including *The Dimensions of English* (1970), *The Structure of Marx's World-View* (1978), *Understanding War* (1989), *Unequal Freedoms* (1998), *The Cancer Stage of Capitalism* (1999), and *Value Wars: Moral Philosophy and Humanity* (2002).

Jessica Mitford (1917–1996)
Anglo-American writer and social critic. Born into one of England's most famous aristocratic families, Mitford left for the United States shortly after completing her education in 1936. A naturalized American citizen (1944), she established herself as an investigative reporter with a talent for pungent social criticism. Her study of the American funeral industry, *The American Way of Death* (1963; 1998), was followed by *The Trial of Dr.*

Spock (1969) and *Kind and Unusual Punishment: The Prison Business* (1973). She also wrote *Faces of Philip: A Memoir of Philip Toynbee* (1984) and the biography *Grace Had an English Heart* (1989). Her last work echoes her earliest—*The American Way of Birth* (1992).

N. Scott Momaday (b. 1934)
Native American poet, writer, and artist. Momaday grew up on reservations in the Southwest, but he was strongly influenced by the example and traditions of the Kiowa people of his native Oklahoma. He studied at the University of New Mexico and Stanford University before beginning a teaching career. Currently, Momaday is Regents' Professor of the Humanities at the University of Arizona. He has published several volumes of poetry, including *Angle of Geese and Other Poems* (1973) and *The Gourd Dancer* (1976); a Pulitzer Prize–winning novel, *House Made of Dawn* (1968); an autobiography, *The Names: A Memoir* (1976); and a collection of Kiowa folktales, *The Way to Rainy Mountain* (1969). More recently, he has published *In the Presence of the Sun* (1992), a collection of stories and poems, and *The Man Made of Words: Essays, Stories, Passages* (1997).

Toni Morrison (b. 1931)
American writer and teacher. Born to working-class parents and raised in Lorain, Ohio, Morrison received her undergraduate education at Howard University before completing her master's degree at Cornell University. Her works, which center on the complexities of race and gender, have met with both critical and popular acclaim. By the time she won the Pulitzer Prize for *Beloved* in 1987, she had published four other novels: *The Bluest Eye* (1970), *Sula* (1973), *Song of Solomon* (1977), and *Tar Baby* (1981). After the publication of *Jazz* (1992) she received the Nobel Prize for literature in 1993. Morrison held teaching positions at Howard, Yale, and Rutgers Universities before moving to Princeton University, where she is currently a fellow in the Council of the Humanities. Her most recent novel, *Paradise*, was published in 1997. Her most recent novel is *Love* (2003).

John Muir (1838–1914)
American naturalist and writer. Muir's family emigrated from Scotland to the United States in 1849 and settled in Wisconsin. Muir was an avid student of nature and studied geology and botany at the University of Wisconsin, though he left without taking a degree. As a young man, Muir traveled widely in the western United States to study its flora and fauna. He became a vocal advocate for the preservation of forests, and his efforts in the last decade of the nineteenth century contributed to the creation of Yosemite National Park. His writings extol the natural beauty of the American West, and in his many magazine articles and popular books, such as *The Mountains of California* (1894) and *My First Summer in the Sierra* (1911), Muir shared his own fascination with the natural world with his readers.

Vladimir Nabokov (1899–1977)
Russian American fiction writer and educator. Born in Russia and educated at Trinity College, Cambridge, Nabokov came to the United States in 1940 to lecture at Stanford University and stayed for twenty years. While teaching at Wellesley College and Cornell University, he wrote dozens of novels and contributed essays, stories, and poems to several American magazines. Although he was well known in literary circles, Nabokov did not achieve fame until 1958, when his controversial novel *Lolita* was published. *Lolita* earned Nabokov enough money so that he could retire to Switzerland and pursue the writing of fiction. His subsequent novels include *Pale Fire* (1962), *Ada* (1969), and *Look at the Harlequins!* (1974).

Gloria Naylor (b. 1950)
African American fiction writer and essayist. Born in New York City to parents from southern sharecropping families, Naylor was a member of the Jehovah's Witnesses as a teenager and young adult. When she suffered a nervous breakdown in 1975 and left the church, Naylor began to read works by other African American women and returned to school, earning a B.A. from Brooklyn College and an M.A. in Afro-American studies from Yale University. She has been a writer in residence at George Washington University, the University of Pennsylvania, New York University, and Princeton University and is the author of *The Women of Brewster Place* (1982), which won the American Book Award for Best First Novel; *Linden Hills* (1985); *Mama Day* (1988); *Bailey's Cafe* (1992); and *The Men of Brewster Place* (1998).

Naylor's most recent work, *1996*, was published in 2005.

John Henry Newman (1801–1890)

English Roman Catholic prelate, poet, novelist, and theologian. Educated at Trinity College, Oxford, Newman became a priest in the Anglican Church. He was a major force in the Oxford movement, an effort to reestablish the authority and traditions of the Church of England. In 1845 Newman became a Roman Catholic; in 1846 he was ordained in Rome and returned to England. From 1852 on, he delivered not only sermons but also a number of influential lectures on education. The latter culminated in one of Newman's finest works, *The Idea of a University Defined and Illustrated* (1852), which ranks with his treatise *An Essay in Aid of a Grammar of Assent* (1870) as a classic statement of belief. Newman wrote two novels, *Loss and Gain* (1848) and *Callista* (1856); an explanation of his conversion, *Apologia Pro Vita Sua* (1864); and a visionary poem, "The Dream of Gerontius" (1865). In 1879 he became a cardinal in the Roman Catholic Church.

Ngũgĩ wa Thiong'o (b. 1938)

Kenyan novelist, playwright, and social critic. Born in British-controlled Kenya, Ngũgĩ wrote about the effects of British colonization on East Africans. In 1964 he published his first novel, *Weep Not, Child*, which, like his second, *A Grain of Wheat* (1967), depicts the Mau Mau rebellion against the British. From 1972 to 1977 Ngũgĩ taught literature at the University of Nairobi. In 1977 he wrote a controversial play, *Ngaahika Ndeenda* (translated as *I Will Marry When I Want*, 1982), in his native Gikuyu; threatened by its popularity with Gikuyu workers, the government banned the play and arrested Ngũgĩ, imprisoning him for a year. Since leaving Kenya in 1982, he has taught at a number of American universities, including New York University, where he joined the comparative literature department in 1992. In *Decolonising the Mind* (1986) Ngũgĩ argues for the use of native languages rather than English, believing that "when you destroy a people's language . . . you are in fact destroying that which helps them to define themselves." In 2006 he published his first new novel in nearly two decades, *Wizard of the Crow*, translated into English from Gĩkũyũ by the author.

Martha Nussbaum (b. 1947)

American professor of philosophy, classics, and law. Born in New York City, Nussbaum received her B.A. from New York University and her M.A. and Ph.D. from Harvard University. She has held positions as professor of philosophy or classics at Wellesley College, Brown University, and the University of Chicago, where she is currently a professor of law and ethics. She is the author and editor of several books, including *Poetic Justice: The Literary Imagination and Public Life* (1996), *Sex and Social Justice* (1999), *Upheavals of Thought: The Intelligence of Emotions* (2001), *Hiding from Humanity: Disgust, Shame and the Law* (2004), *Frontiers of Justice: Disability, Nationality, Species Membership* (2006), and *The Clash Within: Democracy, Religious Violence, and India's Future* (2007).

Mary Oliver (b. 1935)

American poet and essayist. Born in Cleveland, Ohio, Oliver briefly attended both Ohio State University and Vassar College, but did not receive a degree. During her teenage years, she lived for a short period in the home of the recently deceased Edna St. Vincent Millay, where she helped organize Millay's papers. Because of its detailed and appreciative attention to nature, Oliver's work is often compared to that of Walt Whitman and Henry David Thoreau. Much of her imagery is derived from her daily walks in Provincetown, Massachusetts, where she has lived for over forty years. She has received the National Book Award (1992), the Pulitzer Prize (1984), and a Guggenheim Foundation fellowship. The most recent of her many books is *Thirst: Poems* (2006). Other works include *Dreamwork* (1986), *Provincetown* (1987), *House of Light* (1990), *What Do We Know* (2002), *Owls and Other Fantasies: Poems and Essays* (2003), *Why I Wake Early: New Poems* (2004), and *Long Life: Essays and Other Writings* (2004).

George Orwell (1903–1950)

Pen name of Eric Blair, English journalist, essayist, novelist, and critic. Born in India and educated in England, Orwell was an officer in the Indian Imperial Police in Burma (1922–27), a part of his life that he later recounted in a novel, *Burmese Days* (1934). In 1927 he went to Europe to develop his writing talents. His first book, *Down and Out in Paris and London* (1933), depicts his years of poverty and struggle while working as a dishwasher and day laborer. Orwell's experiences fighting in the Spanish Civil War are the subject of his memoir, *Homage to Catalonia* (1938). Of his seven novels, *Animal Farm* (1945) and *Nineteen Eighty-Four* (1949), directed at totalitarian government, have become classics. Orwell published five collections of essays, including *Shooting an Elephant and Other Essays* (1950).

William G. Perry Jr. (1913–1998)
American educator. Born in Paris and educated at Harvard, Perry taught at Williams College from 1941 to 1945 before moving to Harvard University, where he was director of the Bureau of Study Counsel from 1948 and professor of education from 1964. With C. P. Whitelock, he wrote the *Harvard Reading Course* (1948). His *Forms of Intellectual and Ethical Development in the College Years: A Scheme* was published in 1968.

Alexander Petrunkevitch (1875–1964)
Russian-born zoologist and teacher. Petrunkevitch was educated in Russia and Germany before coming to the United States as a lecturer at Harvard University in 1904. In 1910 he joined the Department of Zoology at Yale University, where he became professor in 1917 and served until 1944. Petrunkevitch was an expert on the behavior of American spiders; his *Index Catalogue of Spiders of North, Central, and South America* (1911) and *An Inquiry into the Natural Classification of Spiders* (1933) are classic studies.

Jo-Ann Pilardi (b. 1941)
American philosopher. Pilardi earned her B.A. in English at Duquesne University, her M.A. in philosophy at Pennsylvania State University, and her Ph.D. in humanities at Johns Hopkins University. She was an activist in the women's liberation movement in Baltimore for many years. Her works include *Simone de Beauvoir Writing the Self: Philosophy Becomes Autobiography* (1999), and articles on feminism, abortion rights, and social and political philosophy. She recently published "From 'Alien' to 'Guest': A Philosophical Scrutiny of the Bush Administration's Guest Worker Initiative," a work of political philosophy that appeared in *Radical Philosophy Today: Philosophy against Empire*. She is Professor Emerita of Philosophy and Women's Studies at Towson University in Maryland.

Plato (c. 428–c. 348 B.C.E.)
Greek philosopher and teacher. When Socrates died in 399 B.C.E., his student Plato went into exile. Plato returned in the 380s and founded a school, the Academy. He adopted the Socratic method of teaching, a technique of asking rather than answering questions. Although most of Plato's writings take the form of dialogues, he occasionally uses parables and allegories.

Michael Pollan (b. 1955)
American environmentalist and author. Pollan is Professor of Journalism and Director of the Knight Program in Science and Environmental Journalism at the University of California, Berkeley. He was educated at Bennington College, where he received his B.A., at Mansfield College at Oxford University, and at Columbia University, where he earned his M.A. in English and was awarded a President's Fellowship as a Ph.D. student. Pollan is a contributing writer for the *New York Times Magazine*, a former executive editor of *Harper's*, and the author of four books: *The Omnivore's Dilemma: A Natural History of Four Meals* (2006), *The Botany of Desire: A Plant's-Eye View of the World* (2001), *A Place of My Own* (1997), and *Second Nature: A Gardener's Education* (1991). His recent work has focused on the U.S. meat industry.

Katha Pollitt (b. 1949)
American essayist, journalist, and poet. Born in New York City, Pollitt earned a B.A. from Harvard University and an M.F.A. from Columbia University. She has written for the *Nation* since 1982, initially as the literature editor and then as a contributing editor; since 1992 she has been an associate editor. Pollitt's *Antarctic Traveler* (1982) won the National Book Critics Circle Award for poetry. Her poems have appeared in the *New Yorker*, the *New Republic*, and *Poetry*, and she has collected her essays in *Reasonable Creatures: Essays on Women and Feminism* (1994). She has published two collections of columns: *Subject to Debate: Sense and Dissents on Women, Politics, and Culture* (2001), and *Virginity or Death!: And Other Social and Political Issues of Our Time* (2006). Her most recent book is *Learning to Drive: And Other Life Stories* (2007).

Neil Postman (1931–2003)
American critic and educator. Postman received his B.S. from the State Univer-

sity of New York at Fredonia and his M.A. and Ed.D. from Columbia University. He was Paulette Goddard Chair of Media Ecology at New York University and chair of the Department of Communications Culture. His pedagogical and scholarly interests included media and learning, as can be seen in many of his seventeen books, including *Amusing Ourselves to Death* (1985), *Conscientious Objections* (1988), *Technopoly: The Surrender of Culture to Technology* (1992), *The End of Education* (1995), and *Building a Bridge to the Eighteenth Century: How the Past Can Improve Our Future* (1999).

Anna Quindlen (b. 1953)
American journalist and novelist. Born in Philadelphia, Quindlen graduated from Barnard College and immediately began writing for the *New York Post*. Eventually she moved to the *New York Times*, where she was a regular columnist for over twenty years. Her columns allowed her to thrive by "taking things personally for a living," and they eventually earned her a Pulitzer Prize. They have been collected in *Living Out Loud* (1988) and *Thinking Out Loud: Thoughts on the Personal, the Political, the Public, and the Private* (1993). Quindlen resigned from the *New York Times* to spend more time writing fiction and has since published five novels: *Object Lessons* (1991); *One True Thing* (1994), which was made into a movie in 1998; *Black and Blue* (1998); *Blessings* (2002); and *Rise and Shine* (2006). *How Books Changed My Life* (1998) is her memoir about the importance of reading. She currently writes a bi-weekly column for *Newsweek*.

Jonathan Rauch (b. 1960)
American journalist. A contributing editor for the *National Journal* in Washington, D.C., Rauch writes about the contemporary American political scene. His books include *The Outnation: A Search for the Soul of Japan* (1992), *Kindly Inquisitors: The New Attacks on Free Thought* (1993), *Demosclerosis: The Silent Killer of the American Government* (1994), and *Government's End: Why Washington Stopped Working* (2000). His essays have appeared in the *New Republic*, the *Atlantic Monthly*, the *New York Times*, and the *Wall Street Journal*.

Tom Regan (b. 1938)
American philosopher and teacher. After receiving a Ph.D. in philosophy from the University of Virginia, Regan taught at Sweet Briar College before joining the Department of Philosophy and Religion at North Carolina State University. He does research in theoretical and applied ethics, and his writing reveals his particular interest in environmentalism and animal rights. His works include *All That Dwell Within* (1982), *The Case for Animal Rights* (1983), *The Thee Generation: Reflections on the Coming Revolution* (1991), and *Defending Animal Rights* (2001).

Adrienne Rich (b. 1929)
American poet and essayist. Rich's most recent books of poetry are *The School Among the Ruins: Poems 2000–2004*, and *Fox: Poems 1998–2000* (Norton). A selection of her essays, *Arts of the Possible: Essays and Conversations*, was published in 2001. A new edition of *What Is Found There: Notebooks on Poetry and Politics*, appeared in 2003. She is a recipient of the Lannan Foundation Lifetime Achievement Award, the Lambda Book Award, the Lenore Marshall/Nation Prize, the Wallace Stevens Award, the Bollingen Prize in Poetry, and the National Book Foundation's 2006 Medal for Distinguished Contribution to American Letters, among other honors. She lives in California.

Matt Ridley (b. 1958)
English science writer. Born at Newcastle upon Tyne, Ridley attended Oxford University, where he earned his B.A. and his D.Phil. in zoology. Ridley's work, accessible to a nonspecialist audience, explores ideas that have emerged from the gene revolution in biology. His books include *The Red Queen: Sex and the Evolution of Human Nature* (1993), *The Origins of Virtue: Human Instincts and the Evolution of Cooperation* (1996), *Genome: The Autobiography of a Species in 23 Chapters* (1999), *Nature via Nurture: Genes, Experience and What Makes Us Human* (2003), and *Francis Crick: Discoverer of the Genetic Code* (2006). He was the founding chairman for the International Centre for Life, a science park and educational project, from 1996 to 2003.

Alberto Alvaro Ríos (b. 1952)
American poet, fiction writer, and memoirist. Ríos was born in Nogales, Arizona, a town that straddles the U.S.-Mexican border, to an English mother and a Mexican father. His work reflects his

struggles to come to terms with his multicultural, bilingual identity. As a child Ríos spoke Spanish and English, but he was chastised by teachers for using Spanish and "forgot" the language until he encountered more encouraging mentors in high school. He earned a B.A. in literature from the University of Arizona in 1974 and another B.A. in psychology in 1975. Ríos briefly studied law before returning to the University of Arizona to earn an M.F.A. in 1979. He currently teaches creative writing at Arizona State University, where he holds the Katharine C. Turner Endowed Chair in English. Ríos is the author of nine books and chapbooks of poetry, most recently *The Theater of Night* (2006), along with three collections of short stories. His memoir *Capirotada* (1999) won the Latino Literary Hall of Fame Award.

Mary Roach (b. 1959)
American essayist and journalist. Born in Hanover, New Hampshire, Roach attended Wesleyan University. She has written articles, essays, and columns for *Salon.com*, *Wired*, *Outside*, *GQ*, *Discover*, *Vogue*, and the *New York Times Magazine*, and has published two books. The first, *Stiff: The Curious Lives of Human Cadavers* (2003), explores the postmortem fate of human bodies—from use in medical training, transportation safety research, and experiments by forensic scientists to cannibalism and various methods of burial or disposal. Her second book, *Spook: Science Tackles the Afterlife* (2005), explores efforts to find proof of a soul or afterlife. Roach maintains that she has "always gravitated toward the peculiar" in her writing.

Richard Rodriguez (b. 1944)
American essayist and teacher. The son of Mexican American immigrants, Rodriguez learned to speak English in a Catholic grammar school but later looked back with regret at the Spanish language he so willingly cast aside. He received a B.A. from Stanford University and an M.A. from Columbia University. Enrolled in the doctoral program in English literature at the University of California at Berkeley, Rodriguez won a Fulbright scholarship and attended the Warburg Institute in London (1972–73). He now works for the Pacific News Service and contributes commentaries to many journals and news programs. In *Hunger of Memory: The Education of Richard Rodriguez* (1982), he recounts

his assimilation into mainstream American society. His second book, *Days of Obligation: A Letter to My Mexican Father* (1992), describes his difficulties as a homosexual in America. His most recent books include *King's Highway* (1999), *Movements* (1999) and *Brown: The Last Discovery of America* (2002).

Betty Rollin (b. 1936)
American journalist, television reporter, and nonfiction writer. Rollin spent several years as a stage and television actress before beginning a career in journalism, first at *Vogue* (1964), then at *Look* (1965–71). Beginning in 1971, she worked as a network correspondent, chiefly for NBC. Rollin is the author of several books, including *First, You Cry* (1976), *Am I Getting Paid for This?: A Romance about Work* (1982), *Last Wish* (1985) and, with Jules Feiffer, *Here's the Bright Side: Of Failure, Fear, Cancer, Divorce, and other Bum Raps* (2007).

Eleanor Roosevelt (1884–1962)
American first lady, political activist. Roosevelt was born in New York City and educated by tutors until the age of fifteen. She was then sent to the Allenswood school for girls in England, where she remained until her return to the United States at eighteen. She married future U.S. president Franklin Delano Roosevelt, a distant cousin, and went on to become perhaps the most important and influential first lady in American history. Roosevelt was a strong supporter of her husband's New Deal legislation and of civil rights, and she continued to work actively for these and other causes after her husband's death in 1945. A devoted suffragist, she was committed to improving the status of working women, though she opposed the Equal Rights Amendment, which she felt would be detrimental to women. She was a leading supporter of the United Nations and chaired the committee that drafted and approved the Universal Declaration of Human Rights.

Scott Russell Sanders (b. 1945)
American writer and teacher. Born in Tennessee and educated at Brown and Cambridge Universities, Sanders has spent his entire teaching career in the Department of English at Indiana University at Bloomington, where he is now professor of English. He is best known

for his nature writing and his depictions of American places and people, including *Wilderness Plots: Tales about the Settlement of the American Land* (1983), *Audubon's Early Years* (1984), *In Limestone Country* (1985), *Staying Put: Making a Home in a Restless World* (1993), and *Writing from the Center* (1995). *The Paradise of Bombs* (1987) is a collection of essays on violence in the United States. He published his most recent book, *A Private History of Awe*, in 2006.

Jean-Paul Sartre (1905–1980)
French playwright, novelist, critic, philosopher, and political activist. After earning an advanced degree in philosophy, Sartre became a provincial schoolmaster, then a playwright and writer of philosophical essays. Described by the *New York Times* as "a rebel of a thousand causes, a modern Don Quixote," Sartre was a major force in the intellectual life of post–World War II France. His philosophy of existentialism influenced generations of artists and thinkers. Steadfastly independent, Sartre refused both the Nobel Prize for literature (1964) and the Legion of Honor. His major works include *The Flies* (1943), *Being and Nothingness* (1943), *No Exit* (1944), and *Life Situations* (1977).

Chief Seattle (c. 1786–1866)
Native American leader. A fierce young warrior, Seattle (also Seathl or Sealth) was chief of the Suquamish, Duwamish, and allied Salish-speaking tribes of the Northwest. In the 1830s he converted to Christianity and became an advocate of peace. Local settlers honored him and his work by naming their town Seattle. When the Port Elliott Treaty of 1855 established reservations for Native Americans, Seattle signed the treaty and lived the rest of his life at the Port Madison Reservation. Because of his example, his people did not become involved in the bloody warfare that marked the history of the territory from 1855 until 1870. His "Address" is a reply to a treaty proffered in 1854 by Governor Isaac Stevens, commissioner of Indian Affairs for the Washington Territory.

Richard Selzer (b. 1928)
American surgeon and essayist. Born in Troy, New York, Selzer earned his B.A. from Union College and his M.D. from Albany Medical College. He completed a surgical internship and residency at Yale University, where he remained as Assis-

tant Clinical Professor of Surgery until 1985. His writing is informed and inspired by his experiences as a doctor and often focuses on patients. In a review of *Rituals of Surgery* (1973), Selzer's first collection of short stories, in the *Village Voice*, Judith Ramsey praised Selzer for his "deftness of style, his imaginative use of medical and surgical materials, and his clear narrative talent." Selzer has received numerous honors, including an American Medical Writers Award and a Guggenheim Fellowship. His books include *Mortal Lessons: Notes on the Art of Surgery* (1976), *Confessions of a Knife* (1979), a collection of twenty-four essays, roughly half of which are surgical memoirs, *Letters to a Young Doctor* (1982), and *Down from Troy: A Doctor Comes of Age* (1992), his autobiography. *The Exact Location of the Soul: New and Selected Essays* (2001) is his most recent work.

Sonia Shah (b. 1969)
American essayist, journalist, and publisher. A member of the South End Press collective, Shah has edited *Dragon Ladies: Asian American Feminists Breathe Fire* (1997), a collection of essays about Asian American women and politics. She has written extensively about Asian American and feminist issues, and her work has appeared in *Ms.*, *Z Magazine*, *Onion*, *Salon*, and *The Nation*, as well as in anthologies such as *Listen Up!: Voices from the Next Feminist Generation* (1995). Recently she has published *Crude: The Story of Oil* (2004) and *The Body Hunters: Testing New Drugs on the World's Poorest Patients* (2006).

Lauren Slater (b. 1963)
American psychologist and author. Slater earned a B.A. in British and American literature from Brandeis, before completing her master's degree in psychology at Harvard University and her doctorate in psychology at Boston University. She is best known for *Opening Skinner's Box: Great Psychological Experiments of the Twentieth Century* (2004), a book in which she narrates psychology experiments as stories. Slater has written five other books: *Welcome to My Country* (1996), *Prozac Diary* (1998), *Lying: A Metaphorical Memoir* (2000), *Love Works Like This: Travels Through a Pregnant Year* (2003), and *Blue Beyond Blue: Extraordinary Tales for Ordinary Dilemmas* (2005).

Susan Sontag (1933–2004)

American writer, art critic, and filmmaker. Born in New York City, Sontag grew up in Tucson, Arizona, and Los Angeles. After graduating from high school at fifteen, she immediately started classes at the University of California at Berkeley, and later received degrees from the University of Chicago and Harvard University. Her collection of essays *Against Interpretation* (1966) established her reputation as a serious intellectual and critic, just as *Trip to Hanoi* (1968) established her reputation as a political and cultural critic. After a near-fatal bout with breast cancer, Sontag wrote *Illness as Metaphor* (1978), followed by *AIDS and Its Metaphors* (1988). She also wrote several films and plays and the novels *Volcano Lover* (1992) and *In America: A Novel* (2001). Her collection of essays, *Where the Stress Falls*, appeared in 2001.

Elizabeth Cady Stanton (1815–1902)

American feminist and women's rights activist. Born in Johnstown, New York, she married the prominent abolitionist Henry B. Stanton, and the two spent their honeymoon at the World's Antislavery Convention. Stanton joined Lucretia Mott and Susan B. Anthony to fight for women's rights. She cofounded the National Women Suffrage Association and was also one of the first women to try introducing legislation that would make divorce laws more sympathetic to women in abusive marriages. "The Declaration of Sentiments and Resolutions" grew out of the first American convention for women's rights, held in Seneca Falls, New York, in 1848.

Brent Staples (b. 1951)

African American journalist and writer. Born in Chester, Pennsylvania, Staples holds a Ph.D. in psychology from the University of Chicago. He is currently on the editorial board of the *New York Times*. His memoir, *Parallel Time: Growing Up in Black and White*, was published in 1994.

Wallace Stegner (1909–1993)

American essayist, novelist, and teacher. Influenced by Twain, Cather, and Conrad, Stegner wrote of the development of individuals within particular landscapes, most often those of the American West. In a long career, he wrote and edited more than forty books, among them the novels *Remembering Laughter* (1937), *The Big Rock Candy Mountain* (1943), and *Recapitulation* (1979), as well as historical narratives such as *Mormon Country* (1941) and *The Gathering of Zion: The Story of the Mormon Trail* (1964). Near the end of his life Stegner became a spokesman for environmental concerns. His last book was *Where the Bluebird Sings to the Lemonade Springs* (1992).

Gloria Steinem (b. 1934)

American essayist, journalist, and editor. After receiving a B.A. from Smith College, Steinem spent two years studying in India. On her return, she worked in publishing and as a writer for television, film, and political campaigns until 1968, when she and others founded *New York* magazine. Also a founding editor of *Ms.* magazine (1971), Steinem became an influential spokesperson for the women's movement. "The Good News Is: These Are Not the Best Years of Your Life" first appeared in *Ms.* with the title "Why Young Women Are More Conservative" (Sept. 1979). It was reprinted in *Outrageous Acts and Everyday Rebellions* (1983), a collection of Steinem's essays and articles. *Moving Beyond Words* (1995) is a later collection on women's issues. In 2002 Steinem won the PEN Center West Literary Award of Honor.

Sandra Steingraber (b. 1959)

American biologist, poet, and essayist. Diagnosed with bladder cancer when she was twenty, Steingraber has since devoted much of her time and energy to examining the impact of the environment on human health. Her 1997 *Living Downstream: An Ecologist Looks at Cancer and the Environment* examines the connection between environmental contaminants and the incidence of cancer; her epidemiological studies have suggested links between the chemicals used in industry and agriculture and increased risks of cancer in those exposed to these chemicals. Following the publication of *Living Downstream*, Steingraber was named "Woman of the Year" by *Ms. Magazine*. She now teaches at Cornell University in Ithaca, New York. Her new work, *Having Faith: An Ecologist's Journey to Motherhood* (2001), explores "the intimate ecology of motherhood."

Fred Strebeigh (b. 1951)

American nonfiction writer and teacher. Born in New York City and raised in Nonquitt, Massachusetts, Strebeigh attended Yale University, where he now teaches nonfiction writing jointly in the English department and the School of Forestry and Environmental Studies. His work has appeared in the *Atlantic Monthly*, *Audubon*, the *New Republic*, *Reader's Digest*, *Smithsonian*, the *New York Times Magazine*, and *Sierra Magazine*.

Andrew Sullivan (b. 1963)
American editor and journalist. Sullivan is a former model who became an openly gay media personality when he was named the editor of the *New Republic* at age twenty-eight. His most influential work, *Virtually Normal: An Argument about Homosexuality* (1995), argues in favor of same-sex marriages, asserting that "gay marriage is not a radical step; it is a profoundly humanizing, traditionalizing step." He has also edited *Same-Sex Marriages, Pros and Cons: A Reader* (1997) and is the author of *Love Undetectable: Notes on Friendship, Sex, and Survival* (1998). Sullivan currently blogs for *The Atlantic Online*, *The Atlantic Monthly's* online presence.

Jonathan Swift (1667–1745)
Anglo-Irish poet, satirist, and cleric. Born to English parents who resided in Ireland, Swift studied at Trinity College, Dublin, then departed for London (1689). There he became part of the literary and political worlds, beginning his career by writing political pamphlets in support of the Tory cause. Ordained in the Church of Ireland (1695), Swift was appointed dean of St. Patrick's Cathedral, Dublin, in 1713 and held the post until his death. One of the master satirists of the English language, he wrote several scathing attacks on extremism, including *The Tale of a Tub* (1704), *The Battle of the Books* (1704), and *A Modest Proposal* (1729), but he is probably best known for his novel *Gulliver's Travels* (1726).

Terry Teachout (b. 1956)
American critic and biographer. Born in Cape Girardeau, Missouri, Teachout received his B.S. in music journalism from William Jewell College in Liberty, Missouri. He is the drama critic at the *Wall Street Journal*, where he also writes a biweekly column on the arts in America called "Sightings." In addition, Teachout is the music critic at *Commentary*, keeps a blog called About Last Night (www.terry teachout.com), and has written about the arts for the *New York Times* and the

National Review. His books include *All in the Dances: A Brief Life of George Balanchine* (2004), *The Skeptic: A Life of H. L. Mencken* (2002), and *City Limits: Memories of a Small Town Boy* (1991). He is currently at work on a biography of Louis Armstrong.

Paul Theroux (b. 1941)
American novelist, essayist, and travel writer. Born in Medford, Massachusetts, Theroux took a B.A. at the University of Massachusetts and later taught in Africa and Asia. For some time he has lived in London, when he has not been traveling all over the world—by train whenever possible. Theroux's novels include *The Family Arsenal* (1976), *The Mosquito Coast* (1982), *O-Zone* (1986), *Kowloon Tong* (1997) and *Blinding Light* (2006). His best-known travel books are *The Great Railway Bazaar: By Train through Asia* (1975), *The Old Patagonian Express: By Train through the Americas* (1979), *The Happy Isles of Oceana* (1992), *Pillars of Hercules: A Grand Tour of the Mediterranean* (1995) and *Dark Star Safari* (2002). His essays are collected in *Sunrise with Seamonsters* (1985). His most recent book, *The Elephant Suite*, appeared in 2007.

Edward Thomas (1878–1917)
English poet and essayist. Born in London to a family of Welsh heritage, Thomas was educated at Lincoln College, Oxford. When World War I broke out, he joined the Artists' Rifles, a special forces regiment of the British Territorial Army. He was killed in action shortly after arriving in France. His poems are renowned for their detailed attention to the English countryside.

Lewis Thomas (1913–1993)
American physician, teacher, science writer, and humanist. Educated at Princeton University and Harvard Medical School, Thomas specialized in pediatrics, public health, and cancer research. From 1973 to 1980 he served as president of Memorial Sloan-Kettering Cancer Center in New York City. In 1970 Thomas began writing occasional essays for the *New England Journal of Medicine*. A number of these, gathered in *The Lives of a Cell* (1974), established Thomas's reputation as a science writer. Other collections are *The Medusa and the Snail* (1979), *The Youngest Science* (1983), *Late Night Thoughts on Listening to Mahler's Ninth*

Symphony (1983), *Et Cetera, Et Cetera* (1991), and *The Fragile Species* (1992).

Henry David Thoreau (1817–1862)
American philosopher, essayist, naturalist, and poet. A graduate of Harvard University, Thoreau worked at a number of jobs—schoolmaster, house painter, employee in his father's pencil factory—before becoming a writer and political activist. He became a friend of Emerson's and a member of the Transcendental Club, contributing frequently to its journal, the *Dial*. Drawn to the world of nature, he wrote his first book, *A Week on the Concord and Merrimac Rivers* (1849), about a canoe trip with his brother. Thoreau's strong stance against slavery led to his arrest for refusing to pay the Massachusetts poll tax (an act of protest against government sanction of the Mexican War, which he viewed as serving the interests of slaveholders). His eloquent essay defending this act, "Civil Disobedience" (1849); his probing meditation on the solitary life, *Walden* (1854); and his speech "A Plea for Captain John Brown" (1859) are classic literary documents in the history of American life and thought.

James Thurber (1894–1961)
American humorist, cartoonist, essayist, and fiction writer. Born in Columbus, Ohio, Thurber attended Ohio State University. He began his career as a professional writer working for the *Columbus Dispatch* (1920–24), then moved on to the *Chicago Tribune* and the *New York Evening Post*. In 1927, encouraged by E. B. White, he became managing editor of and staff writer for the *New Yorker*. Throughout his career he contributed stories, essays, and cartoons to the magazine. Thurber wrote more than thirty books, including *The Owl in the Attic and Other Perplexities* (1931), *The Beast in Me and Other Animals* (1948), and *The Secret Life of Walter Mitty* (1939).

Sallie Tisdale (b. 1957)
American nurse and essayist. A writer on a wide range of health and medical issues, Tisdale has contributed to the *Antioch Review*, *Esquire*, the *New York Times Magazine*, the *New Republic*, *Vogue*, and *Harper's Magazine*. She has written several books, including *The Sorcerer's Apprentice: Tales of the Modern Hospital* (1986), *Lot's Wife* (1988), *Talk Dirty to Me* (1994), *The Best Thing I Ever Tasted: The Secret of Food* (2000), and *Women of the Way: Discovering 2,500 Years of Buddhist Wisdom* (2006).

Susan Allen Toth (b. 1940)
American writer and educator. Born in Ames, Iowa, Toth was educated at Smith College, the University of California at Berkeley, and the University of Minnesota. She formerly taught English at Macalester College and is now a freelance writer. Although Toth did not begin writing fiction and essays until she was in her mid-thirties, she quickly published several books, including *Blooming* (1981), *Ivy Days* (1984), *Reading Rooms* (1991), *England as You Like It* (1995), and *Blooming: A Small-Town Girlhood* (1998).

Barbara Tuchman (1912–1989)
American historian. After graduating from Radcliffe College in 1933, Tuchman worked as a research assistant for the Institute of Pacific Relations, an experience that later found expression in *Stilwell and the American Experience in China* (1971), for which she won a Pulitzer Prize in 1971. During the 1930s and 1940s she wrote on politics for the *Nation*, covered the Spanish Civil War as a journalist in London, and after Pearl Harbor took a job with the Office of War Information in Washington, D.C. Critical and public acclaim followed the publication of *The Zimmerman Telegram* (1958) and *The Guns of August* (1962), both on the origins of World War I. Her other books include *The Proud Tower* (1966), *A Distant Mirror: The Calamitous Fourteenth Century* (1978), *The March of Folly* (1984), and *Practicing History* (1981), a collection of articles, reviews, and talks.

Mark Twain (1835–1910)
Pen name of Samuel L. Clemens, American novelist, journalist, and humorist. First apprenticed as a printer, Twain was by turns a riverboat pilot, a gold prospector, and a journalist. He achieved fame with his short story "The Celebrated Jumping Frog of Calaveras County," published in 1867. Twain subsequently wrote many articles, essays, and stories and lectured widely. Several of his novels, including *The Adventures of Tom Sawyer* (1876) and *The Adventures of Huckleberry Finn* (1885), are classics.

John Updike (b. 1932)
American fiction writer, poet, and critic. After graduating from Harvard University and attending the Ruskin School of Drawing and Fine Art at Oxford University, Updike joined the staff of the *New Yorker*, beginning an association that

continues today. The winner of two Pulitzer Prizes, he has described his subject as "the American Protestant small town middle class." Updike's more than forty books include collections of poetry, such as *The Carpentered Hen and Other Tame Creatures* (1958) and *Seventy Poems* (1972); collections of short stories, such as *The Music School* (1966) and *Trust Me* (1987); and novels, such as *Couples* (1968) and his quintet of "Rabbit" works, from the novel *Rabbit, Run* (1960) through the novella *Rabbit Remembered* (2000). His recent publications include the collections *More Matter: Essays and Criticism* (1999) and *Americana: And Other Poems* (2001) and the novels *Seek My Face* (2002), *Villages* (2004), and *Terrorist* (2006).

James Van Tholen (1964–2001)
American pastor. Van Tholen attended Calvin Theological Seminary before becoming the pastor of Rochester Christian Reformed Church in Rochester, New York. At thirty-three, he was diagnosed with a severe and fatal form of cancer. His struggle with the disease forced him to leave the church for seven months, but he returned to give the sermon "Surprised by Death," which was reprinted in *Best Christian Writing 2000* (2000) and *Best Spiritual Writing 2000* (2000). A collection of Van Tholen's sermons was published posthumously as *Where All Hope Lies: Sermons for the Liturgical Years* (2003).

Alice Walker (b. 1944)
African American poet, novelist, and essayist. Born and raised by sharecroppers in rural Georgia, Walker was educated at Spelman College and Sarah Lawrence College. Afterward she worked as an editor for *Ms.* magazine and became active in the Civil Rights movement. She received widespread fame for her Pulitzer Prize–winning novel, *The Color Purple* (1982) which has since been adapted for both film and Broadway. Her other novels include *Meridian* (1986), *The Temple of My Familiar* (1989), *Possessing the Secret of Joy* (1992), *By the Light of My Father's Smile* (1998), *The Way Forward Is with a Broken Heart* (2000), and *Now Is the Time to Open Your Heart* (2005). Walker has also published several volumes of poetry, collections of short stories, and nonfiction works, including *Sent by Earth: A Message from the Grandmother Spirit After the Bombing of the World Trade Center and Pentagon* (2001) and *We Are the Ones We Have Been Wait-*

ing For (2006). She lives in San Francisco and runs the publishing company Wild Tree Press.

Allison Wallace (b. 1960)
American scholar and author. Wallace was born in Louisiana and spent her childhood there and in coastal Texas and Mississippi. She attended the University of Mississippi, where she completed her B.A., and the University of North Carolina, where she earned her Ph.D. in American literature. Her publications include *A Keeper of Bees: Notes on Hive and Home* (2006) and *H. L. Mencken: A Research Guide* (1988), along with numerous articles.

David Foster Wallace (b. 1962)
American nonfiction writer. Born in Ithaca, New York, Wallace was educated at Amherst College, where he earned a B.A. in English and philosophy, and at the University of Arizona, where he completed an M.F.A. in creative writing. He began graduate work in philosophy at Harvard, but did not complete his degree. His first novel, *The Broom of the System*, was published in 1987. His second and most recent novel, *Infinite Jest*, was published in 1996. Wallace has also published essays, short stories, and magazine articles, including the short story collections *Girl with Curious Hair* (1989) and *Oblivion* (2004) and the essay collections *A Supposedly Fun Thing I'll Never Do Again* (1997), *Up Simba!* (2000), *Everything and More* (2003), and *Consider the Lobster* (2005). Wallace received a MacArthur Foundation Grant in 1997. He is the first Roy E. Disney Endowed Professor of Creative Writing and Professor of English at Pomona College.

Henry Wechsler (b. 1932)
American research psychologist and educator. Wechsler was born in Warsaw, Poland; his family immigrated to the United States during World War II. He received an A.B. from Washington and Jefferson College and an M.A. and a Ph.D. in social psychology from Harvard University. Wechsler has contributed to numerous books on medical and psychological topics and is currently a lecturer of social psychology at Harvard. Since 1988 he has been the director of Harvard's Youth Alcohol-Drug Program in the Department of Health and Social Behavior. Since 1990, Wechsler has studied binge drinking and its effects with a team of researchers at the Harvard School of Public Health, including Sonia Castillo,

Andrea Davenport, Charles Deutsch, George Dowdall, and Barbara Moeykens.

Eudora Welty (1909–2001)

American writer, critic, amateur painter, and photographer. Born and raised in Jackson, Mississippi, Welty retained her deep attachment to the people and places of the South. After graduating from the University of Wisconsin in 1929 and studying for a year at Columbia University's School of Business, she returned to Jackson and became a publicity agent for the Works Progress Administration, a New Deal social agency. With the help of Robert Penn Warren and Cleanth Brooks, she published several short stories that launched her literary career. Welty's work encompasses various collections of short stories, including *Collected Stories* (1980); novellas and novels, including *Delta Wedding* (1946), *Losing Battles* (1970), and *The Optimist's Daughter* (Pulitzer Prize, 1972); two volumes of photographs; and an acclaimed collection of critical essays, *The Eye of the Story* (1978). Three lectures delivered at Harvard University in April 1983 were published as *One Writer's Beginnings* (1984).

E. B. White (1899–1985)

American poet, journalist, editor, and essayist. After graduating from Cornell University in 1921, White became a reporter, then an advertising copywriter before beginning a sixty-year career on the staff of the *New Yorker*. With Harold Ross, the magazine's founding editor, and Katharine Angell, its literary editor, White made the *New Yorker* the most important publication of its kind in the United States. He wrote poems and articles for the magazine and served as a discreet and helpful editor. Among his many books, three written for children earned him lasting fame: *Stuart Little* (1945), *Charlotte's Web* (1952), and *The Trumpet of the Swan* (1970). White revised and edited William Strunk's text *The Elements of Style*, a classic guide to writing.

Walt Whitman (1819–1892)

American poet and writer. Born on Long Island and raised in Brooklyn, New York, Whitman received scant formal education before going to work at age eleven in a newspaper office. He taught school from 1835 to 1840 and worked at several government posts during his lifetime, but Whitman considered himself primarily a writer, publishing poetry, stories, and newspaper articles from the age of nineteen. In 1855 he published *Leaves of Grass*, a series of twelve poems that most scholars consider his finest work. As it evolved through a number of editions, *Leaves of Grass* came to include well over 100 poems, including "Song of Myself," "Crossing Brooklyn Ferry," and "Out of the Cradle Endlessly Rocking." In his poetry and prose, Whitman celebrates the landscape and people of the United States. Although he was an ardent Democrat, he supported Lincoln; indeed, Lincoln was the subject of Whitman's moving elegy "When Lilacs Last in the Dooryard Bloom'd" (1865).

Patricia Williams (b. 1951)

American legal scholar and critic. Williams received her B.A. from Wellesley College and her J.D. from Harvard Law School. She is currently the James L. Dohr Professor of Law at Columbia Law School. Williams writes a column for the *Nation* titled "Diary of a Mad Law Professor." Her books include *The Alchemy of Race and Rights: A Diary of a Law Professor* (1991), *The Rooster's Egg* (1995), *Seeing a Color-Blind Future: The Paradox of Race* (1997), and *Open House: Of Family, Friends, Food, Piano Lessons, and the Search for a Room of My Own* (2004). She has received a MacArthur Foundation Fellowship, along with numerous other honors.

Terry Tempest Williams (b. 1955)

American writer, naturalist, and environmental activist. Named by the *Utne Reader* as one of their "Utne 100 Visionaries," Williams grew up surrounded by the vast desert landscape of her native Utah. Her ideas, she says, "have been shaped by the Colorado Plateau and the Great Basin, . . . then sorted out through the prism of my culture—and my culture is Mormon." Her first book, *Pieces of White Shell: A Journey to Navajoland* (1984), is a personal exploration of Native American myths. "The Clan of One-Breasted Women" became the final section of one of her best-known books, *Refuge: An Unnatural History of Family and Place* (1991). She has since written *An Unspoken Hunger: Stories from the Field* (1994), *Desert Quartet: An Erotic Landscape* (1995), and *Leap* (2000). Her most recent books are *Red: Passion and Patience in the Desert* (2001), a collection of essays that chronicle her attachment to the deserts of Utah, and *The Open Space of Democracy* (2004), an argument for a democratic way of life that integrates social, ecological, and spiritual values.

E. O. Wilson (b. 1929)
American biologist, naturalist, and scholar. Wilson was born in Birmingham, Alabama. He earned his B.S. and M.S. degrees at the University of Alabama and his Ph.D. from Harvard University. He is a world-renowned scientist with particular expertise in the study of ants, the focus of his early career and work. He has also discovered hundreds of new species and established sociobiology, which he defines as "the systematic study of the biological basis of all social behavior," as a new science field. Wilson is considered by many to be "the father of biodiversity." Among his many books are *Sociobiology: The New Synthesis* (1975), *Genes, Mind and Culture: The Coevolutionary Process* (1981), *The Future of Life* (2002), and *The Creation: A Meeting of Science and Religion* (2006). Wilson has twice won the Pulitzer Prize, once for *On Human Nature* (1979) and again for *The Ants* (with Bert Holldobler) (1991). He is currently the Pellegrino Research Professor in Entomology for the Department of Organismic and Evolutionary Biology at Harvard University.

Tom Wolfe (b. 1931)
American journalist, essayist, novelist, and social commentator. After receiving a Ph.D. from Yale, Wolfe began a career in journalism that has taken him from newspapers such as the *Washington Post* and the *New York Herald Tribune* to magazines such as *New York*, *Esquire*, and *Vanity Fair*. Wolfe's books have established his reputation as a witty social critic and historian of popular culture. They include *The Kandy-Kolored Tangerine-Flake Streamline Baby* (1965), *Radical Chic and Mau-Mauing the Flak Catchers* (1970), *From Bauhaus to Our House* (1981), and the scathing satiric novels *Bonfire of the Vanities* (1987) and *A Man in Full* (1998). Wolfe's chronicle of the American space program, *The Right Stuff* (1979), was made into a successful film. His most recent collection of essays, *Hooking Up*, appeared in 2000. His most recent novel is *I Am Charlotte Simmons* (2005).

Mary Wollstonecraft (1759–1797)
English social critic, essayist, and novelist. Wollstonecraft was one of the first people to present a well-developed, radical argument against the inequality between women and men in eighteenth-century England. After a troubled early life, she left home and started a school, which soon closed. By 1787, the year she began channeling her ideas into writing, she had suffered the devastating losses of both her mother and her best friend. In the years that followed, Wollstonecraft published essays, translations, novels, an anthology, and a children's book. Her *Vindication of the Rights of Men* (1790), which supported the principles of the French Revolution, was an instant success and established her reputation in literary and political circles. Her *Vindication of the Rights of Women* (1792) is an important early feminist treatise.

Virginia Woolf (1882–1941)
English novelist, critic, and essayist. The daughter of respected philosopher and writer Sir Leslie Stephen, Woolf educated herself by unrestricted reading in her father's library. She lived at the center of the Bloomsbury group, a celebrated collection of artists, scholars, and writers. Woolf, together with her husband, socialist writer Leonard Woolf, founded the Hogarth Press. Her work, both nonfiction and fiction, is marked by a resonant autobiographical voice. *A Room of One's Own* (1929), a historical investigation of women and creativity; *Mrs. Dalloway* (1925), *To the Lighthouse* (1927), and *The Waves* (1931), novels about artistic consciousness and the development of personality; and *The Common Reader* (1925) and *The Second Common Reader* (1932), collections of essays on topics as diverse as literature and automobiles, all reveal penetrating intelligence as well as innovations in narrative technique.

William Zinsser (b. 1922)
American journalist, writer, editor, and educator. After graduating from Princeton University in 1944 and serving in the army for two years, Zinsser joined the staff of the *New York Herald Tribune*, first as a features editor, then as a drama editor and film critic, and finally as an editorial writer. In 1959 he became a freelance writer, and in 1971 he joined the English faculty at Yale University, where he taught until 1979. Zinsser is the author of more than a dozen books, among them the well-known *On Writing Well: An Informal Guide to Writing Non-Fiction* (1976; 1998).

PERMISSIONS ACKNOWLEDGMENTS

TEXT:

Abbey: "The Serpents of Paradise" from *Desert Solitaire* by Edward Abbey. Reprinted by permission of Don Congdon Associates, Inc. Copyright © 1968 by Edward Abbey, renewed © 1996 by Clarke Abbey.

Aciman: "In a Double Exile" from *False Papers: Essays on Exile and Memory* by André Aciman. Copyright © 2000 by André Aciman. Reprinted by permission of Farrar, Straus and Giroux, LLC.

Agosín: "Always Living in Spanish" by Marjorie Agosín, tr. by Celeste Kostopulos-Cooperman, first published in *Poets & Writers*, 1999, is reprinted by permission of Marjorie Agosín.

Alcabes: "The Bioterrorism Scare" from *The American Scholar* 73.2 (2004) is reprinted by permission of the author.

Angelou: Selection entitled "Graduation" (retitled) from *I Know Why the Caged Bird Sings* by Maya Angelou. Copyright © 1969 and renewed 1997 by Maya Angelou. Reprinted by permission of Random House, Inc.

Anzaldúa: "How to Tame a Wild Tongue" from *Borderlands/La Frontera: The New Mestiza.* Copyright © 1987, 1999 by Gloria Anzaldúa. Reprinted by permission of Aunt Lute Books.

Arendt: "Deportations from Western Europe" from *Eichmann in Jerusalem* by Hannah Arendt. Copyright © 1963, 1964 by Hannah Arendt. Used by permission of Viking Penguin, a division of Penguin Group (USA) Inc.

Asimov: "The Eureka Phenomenon" by Isaac Asimov. Copyright © 1971 by Mercury Press, Inc. Used by permission of the Estate of Isaac Asimov c/o Ralph M. Vincinanza Ltd.

Atwood: "True North" by Margaret Atwood from *Saturday Night* (Jan. 1987). Reprinted by permission of the author.

Bai: "World War II" originally published as "He Said No to Internment" in *The New York Times Magazine*, Dec. 25, 2005. Copyright © 2005 by The New York Times Co. Reprinted by permission.

Baldwin: "Stranger in the Village" from *Notes of a Native Son* by James Baldwin. Copyright © 1955, renewed © 1983, by James Baldwin. Reprinted by permission of Beacon Press, Boston.

Baltimore: "Limiting Science: A Biologist's Perspective" (1978), *Daedalus*, 134:4 (Fall 2005), p. 7–15. Copyright © 2005 by the American Academy of Arts and Sciences.

Barber: "America Skips School" by Benjamin R. Barber. Originally published in *Harper's Magazine*, Nov. 1993. Reprinted by permission of the author.

Baron: "When Professors Get A's and Machines Get F's" by Dennis Baron reprinted from *Chronicle of Higher Education*, Nov. 20, 1988. Reprinted by permission of the author.

Barrett: "A Hole in the Wall" is reprinted from *The American Scholar*, vol. 71, no. 1, Winter 2002. Copyright © 2002 by Andrea Barrett. By permission of The Wendy Well Agency, Inc.

Barthes: "Toys" from *Mythologies* by Roland Barthes, trans. by Annette Lavers. Translation copyright © 1972 by Jonathan Cape Ltd. Reprinted by permission of Hill and Wang, a division of Farrar, Straus and Giroux, LLC and Random House Group Ltd.

Bergner: "Chasing Evil" by Daniel Bergner originally published in *New York Times Magazine*, Dec. 25, 2005. Copyright © 2005 by The New York Times Co. Reprinted by permission.

Bettelheim: From *The Informed Heart* by Bruno Bettelheim. Copyright © 1960 by The Free Press, renewed © 1988 by Bruno Bettelheim. All rights reserved. Reprinted with permission of The Free Press, a Division of Simon & Schuster Adult Publishing Croup.

Bird: "College Is a Waste of Time and Money" from *The Case Against College* by Caroline Bird. Reprinted by permission of the author.

Boland: "The Woman, the Place, the Poet" from *Object Lessons: The Life of the Woman and The Poet in Our Time.* Copyright © 1995 by Eavan Boland. Used by permission of W.W. Norton & Company, Inc.

Booth: "Boring from Within: the Art of the Freshman Essay" from an address to the Illinois

Council of College Teachers in 1963. Copyright © Wayne C. Booth. Reprinted by permission of the author.

Britz: "The Dean's Daughter Gets Thin Envelope" by Jennifer Britz was originally published in *The New York Times*, March 23, 2006, as "All the Girls I've Rejected." Copyright © 2006 by The New York Times Co. Reprinted by permission.

Bronowski: "The Nature of Scientific Reasoning" from *Science and Human Values* by Jacob Bronowski. Copyright © 1956, 1965 by Jacob Bronowski. Copyright © renewed 1954, 1993 by Rita Bronowski. All rights reserved. Reprinted by permission of Scribner, a division of Simon & Schuster, Inc.

Brooks: "The Gender Gap at School" by David Brooks was originally published in *The New York Times*, June 11, 2006. Copyright © 2006 by The New York Times Co. Reprinted with permission.

Bruffee: From *Chronicle of Higher Education*, Feb. 9, 1999. Reprinted by permission of the author.

Burgess: "Is America Falling Apart?" from *The New York Times Magazine*, Nov. 7, 1971 is reprinted by permission. Copyright © The Estate of Anthony Burgess.

Buzzell: From *My War* by Colby Buzzell. Copyright © 2005 by Colby Buzzell. Used by permission of Penguin, a division of Penguin Group (USA) Inc.

Carson: From *Lost Woods: The Discovered Writing of Rachel Carson*. Copyright © 1998 by Roger Allen Christie. "The Moving Tides" from *The Sea Around Us*. Copyright © 1950 by Rachel L. Carson. Reprinted by permission of Frances Collin, Trustee.

Chanoff: "Education Is My Mother and My Father" by David Chanoff is reprinted from *The American Scholar*, vol. 74, no. 4, Autumn 2005. Copyright © 2005 by the author.

Cofer: "More Room" from *Silent Dancing: A Partial Remembrance of a Puerto Rican Childhood* by Judith Ortiz Cofer is reprinted with permission from the publisher. Copyright © 1990 by Arte Publico Press-University of Houston.

Cohen: "The Case for the Use of Animals in Biomedical Research" by Carl Cohen from the *New England Journal of Medicine*, Oct. 1986, vol. 315. Copyright © 1986 by Massachusetts Medical Society. All rights reserved.

Copland: "How We Listen" from *What to Listen for in Music* by Aaron Copland. Reprinted by permission of Aaron Copland Fund for Music, Inc., copyright owner.

Corbett: "Saved by Strangers" by Sara Corbett is reprinted by permission of International Creative Management. Copyright © 2005 by Sara Corbett. First appeared in *The New York Times Magazine*.

Cronon: "The Trouble with Wilderness; or, Getting Back to the Wrong Nature" by William Cronon from *Uncommon Ground*, ed. by William Cronon. Copyright © 1995 by William Cronon. Used by permission of W.W. Norton & Company, Inc.

Cunningham: "Why Women Smile" first appeared in *Lear's Magazine* 1993, reprinted with new material by permission of the author.

Dennett: "Common-Sense Religion" adaptation from *Breaking the Spell: Religion as Natural Phenomena* by Daniel C. Dennett. Copyright © 2006 by Daniel C. Dennett. Used by permission of Viking Penguin, a division of Penguin Group (USA) Inc.

Dickerson: "Who Shot Johnny?: A Day in the Life of Black America" by Debra Dickerson from the *New Republic*, Jan. 1, 1996. Reprinted by permission of the *New Republic*. Copyright © 1995 The New Republic, Inc.

Didion: "On Going Home" and "On Keeping a Notebook" from *Slouching Towards Bethlehem* by Joan Didion. Copyright © 1966, 1968, renewed 1996 by Joan Didion. Reprinted by permission of Farrar, Straus and Giroux, LLC.

Dillard: "Sight into Insight" by Annie Dillard from *Harper's Magazine*, Feb. 1974, is reprinted by permission of the author and Blanche C. Gregory, Inc. "An American Childhood" from *An American Childhood* by Annie Dillard, copyright © 1987 by Annie Dillard, is reprinted by permission of HarperCollins Publishers.

Dobbs: "The Shatterer of Worlds," first published in *Reading the Time* by Kildare Dobbs (Macmillan Canada, 1968), is reprinted by kind permission of the author, through the Jonathan Williams Literary Agency.

Dove: "The Epistle of Paul the Apostle to the Ephesians" from *Incarnation: Contemporary Writers on The New Testament*, Viking Press. Copyright © 1990 by Rita Dove. Reprinted by permission of the author.

Eighner: "On Dumpster Diving" from *Travels with Lisbeth: Three Years on the Road and On the Streets*. Copyright © 1993 by Lars Eighner. Reprinted by permission of St. Martin's Press.

Eiseley: "The Brown Wasps" from *The Night Country* by Loren Eiseley. Copyright © 1971 by

GENRES INDEX

Op-Eds

Parables

Profile of a Person, Mini-Biography

Profile of a Place

RHETORICAL INDEX

EXPOSITION

Analyzing Cause and Effect

THEMATIC INDEX

INDEX